CIVIL LIBERTIES
Cases, Materials, and Commentary

BAILEY, HARRIS & JONES

CIVIL LIBERTIES

CASES, MATERIALS, AND COMMENTARY

Sixth edition

S H BAILEY MA, LLB (Cantab)

Professor of Public Law
University of Nottingham

and

N TAYLOR M.PHIL (Hull), LLB (Leeds)

Senior Lecturer in Law
University of Leeds

Chapters 13 and 14 by

A McColgan LLM (Edin.) , MA (Cantab)

Professor of Human Rights Law
King's College London

OXFORD
UNIVERSITY PRESS

OXFORD
UNIVERSITY PRESS

Great Clarendon Street, Oxford OX2 6DP

Oxford University Press is a department of the University of Oxford.
It furthers the University's objective of excellence in research, scholarship,
and education by publishing worldwide in

Oxford New York

Auckland Cape Town Dar es Salaam Hong Kong Karachi
Kuala Lumpur Madrid Melbourne Mexico City Nairobi
New Delhi Shanghai Taipei Toronto

With offices in

Argentina Austria Brazil Chile Czech Republic France Greece
Guatemala Hungary Italy Japan Poland Portugal Singapore
South Korea Switzerland Thailand Turkey Ukraine Vietnam

Oxford is a registered trade mark of Oxford University Press
in the UK and in certain other countries

Published in the United States
by Oxford University Press Inc., New York

British Library Cataloguing in Publication Data

Data available

Library of Congress Cataloging in Publication Data

Data available

Typeset by Newgen Imaging Systems (P) Ltd., Chennai, India
Printed in Great Britain
on acid-free paper by
Ashford Colour Press Ltd, Gosport, Hampshire

ISBN 978-0-19-921855-4

1 3 5 7 9 10 8 6 4 2

PREFACE

There have been a number of changes in the course of the preparation of this new edition. First, there has been a change of publisher from Butterworths to Oxford University Press, a change that has proceeded very smoothly. Second, neither David Harris nor David Ormerod has been able to participate, in view of their other commitments. Stephen Bailey has been delighted to have been joined by Nick Taylor of the University of Leeds, as co-author, and Aileen McColgan of King's College London, who has contributed the chapters on discrimination law. Third, the book has been restructured into five Parts. After two introductory chapters in Part One, there are four Parts covering aspects of the substantive law of civil liberties: life, liberty and association; privacy; freedom of expression and discrimination. Each Part is introduced by a new, short, introductory chapter covering the ECHR framework that applies in that area, and which is now, following enactment of the Human Rights Act 1998, of fundamental importance. Fourth, the book has been reduced in size, which has meant amongst other things that there is now no room for the chapter on freedom of religion. Fifth, there has been a change in the title, better to reflect the fact that the book has always contained a large proportion of text and commentary.

The law in many areas covered by the book has been the subject of significant change in both case law and legislation. There has been a Labour government in power throughout the period since the last edition. Legislative changes have generally, but not invariably, been in the direction of restricting rather than enhancing civil liberties. It is difficult to discern a pattern in the case law. There have been some landmark judgments in which the judges have frustrated the wishes of the government, most notably in the field of terrorism; there have been others where decisions have been subsequently held by the European Court of Human Rights not to conform to the ECHR. There is perhaps greater clarity and consistency in the decisions on the Human Rights Act 1998, although outcomes are not always predictable. In preparing this book it is notable that significantly more relevant information is publicly available than was the case when even the last edition was written.

Stephen Bailey would like to thank Daniel Church for research assistance and Sue Chapman for typing new material for a number of chapters.

The manuscript was submitted in September 2008 and some subsequent developments have been noted in the text and below.

SHB
NWT
1.1.09

Addendum

The following are some recent developments that could not be incorporated into the text.

The National DNA Database

p. 239, note 9. In December 2008 in *S and Marper v United Kingdom* App. Nos 30562/04 and 30566/04, the European Court of Human Rights concluded that existing UK law on the retention of fingerprints, cellular samples and DNA profiles of persons suspected but not convicted of offences represented a disproportionate interference with the applicants' right to private life. In a decision that could have repercussions for the storage of personal information more widely, the European Court noted 'the mere storing of data relating to the private life of an individual amounts to an interference within the meaning of Article 8'. To determine whether any of the information stored engaged any private life aspects 'the Court will have due regard to the specific context in which the information at issue has been recorded and retained, the nature of the records, the way in which these records are used and processed and the results that may be obtained' (para 67). If private life is engaged by the relevant database then the law must be clear as to when personal information is to be stored, about whom, for what duration, and robust systems of security and challenge must be in place. The decision clearly does not reject the utility of a national DNA database, but requires reform to the existing legal regime.

Public order
p. 319. The House of Lords allowed an appeal in *Kay v Metropolitan Police Commissioner* [2008] UKHL 69, [2008] 1 WLR 2723, holding that a fixed and known route was not an essential characteristic of a procession commonly or customarily held.

p. 335. A public authority with powers to detain persons at a detention centre cannot claim under the Riot (Damages) Act 1886 in respect of a riot at the centre: *Yarl's Wood Immigration Ltd and others v Bedfordshire Police Authority* [2008] EWHC 2207 (Comm).

Terrorism
p. 431. Six defendants who knew or believed that one or more of the London bombers either intended to commit an act of terrorism or had so intended, and who gave assistance to them and failed to give information to the authorities were convicted for offences contrary to s. 38B and s. 4(1) of the Criminal Law Act 1967 (assisting an offender with intent to impede arrest or prosecution): *R v Sherif* [2008] EWCA Crim 2653.

p. 485. In *Secretary of State for the Home Department v AF* [2008] EWCA Civ 1148, the majority of the Court of Appeal dismissed an appeal in *AE*, while the appeals of the SSHD were allowed in the cases of *AN* and *AF*. Permission to appeal to the House of Lords was given in *AE, AF* and *AN* on all Art. 6-related issues. Silber J had adopted the correct approach in *AE*; Mitting J in *AN* had misdirected himself in concluding that there was an irreducible minimum of material which must be disclosed to the controlee as a matter of law; Stanley Burnton J had similarly misdirected himself in *AF*. Sedley LJ dissented, commenting at para. [119]:

As I understand it, *MB* decides (see especially 34, 43, 44, per Lord Bingham) that a complete withholding of the grounds for suspicion makes a fair hearing impossible. I regret that I am unable to follow the Master of the Rolls and the Vice-President (36ff) along their route…. It is not easy, and might even be thought hazardous given that the case is now almost certain to return to their Lordships' House, to spell out in unitary form (see 64) what has been differently—and not always compatibly—expressed in four distinct opinions. For myself, I am not at all sure that Baroness Hale's phrase (74) 'even though the whole evidential basis … is not disclosed' is intended to mean 'even though none of the evidential basis is disclosed'. As I understand her, she means 'even though not all of the evidential basis is disclosed'. In any event, Lord Carswell does not adopt such a formulation, and Lord Brown at 91 (subject to his mooted exception) rejects it. It should take a great deal more than this to call Lord Bingham's understanding of his Committee's collective view in question.

p. 493. The proposals concerning possible extensions of detention to 42 days were dropped from the Bill after a defeat by 191 votes in the House of Lords. The Home Secretary stated that it would be included in separate legislation if needed, and a provisional Bill was published by the Home Office. See *The Times*, 13 October 2008. The proposal to allow the Home Secretary to ban the public from a coroner's inquest in the interests of national security was also dropped, possibly to be included in separate legislation concerning coroners. The modified Bill received royal assent on 26 November.

p. 494. The Court of Appeal allowed an appeal in *A v HM Treasury* [2008] EWCA Civ 1187, the majority holding that the orders were valid, provided particular words were disregarded that extended the powers to situations where there was a reasonable suspicion that a person *may be* a person who commits terrorist acts.

p. 501. The inquest into the shooting by police of Jean Charles de Menezes returned an open verdict, after having been directed by the coroner, Sir Michael Wright, that they could not consider a verdict of unlawful killing. The jury did not accept some of the police version of events, finding that no warning had been shouted and that Mr de Menezes had not moved towards officers. See *The Times*, 12 December 2008.

Government secrecy

pp. 787–788. Prospects that the repeal of the 'catch-all' section 2 of the Official Secrets Act 1911 might be outflanked were raised by the decision of the Metropolitan Police to arrest Damian Green MP (a Conservative spokesman) on suspicion of conspiracy to commit misconduct in a public office, arising out of the leaking to him by a civil servant of information not covered by the Official Secrets Act 1989 but which was embarrassing to the government. The police searched his homes and his office in Parliament. At the time of writing (31 December 2008) there is speculation that the matter will be dropped by the police. It is clear that mere receipt of leaked information in these circumstances would not be an offence. It would be different if a leak were encouraged. The conduct of the police caused much concern across members of all political parties.

At about the same time, the prosecution of a local newspaper journalist, Sally Murrer, and a police source, former detective sergeant Mark Kearney, who leaked stories to her, collapsed after evidence derived from a Thames Valley police bugging operation was declared inadmissible. The judge ruled that the disclosures did not concern national security or serious crime and that the intrusive investigation violated the journalist's rights under Art. 10 ECHR. K had been charged with eight counts of misconduct in a public office and M on three counts of aiding and abetting. See *The Times*, 29 November 2008 and the *Guardian*, 28 November 2008. The juxtaposition of this ruling was particularly unfortunate for the police in the Green case.

ACKNOWLEDGEMENTS

Grateful acknowledgement is made to all the authors and publishers of copyright material which appears in this book, and in particular to the following for permission to reprint material from the sources indicated:

Parliamentary copyright material is reproduced with the permission of the Controller of Her Majesty's Stationery Office on behalf of Parliament. Crown copyright material is reproduced under Class Licence Number C2006010631 with the permission of the Controller of OPSI and the Queen's Printer for Scotland.

Extracts from the Judgments and Decisions of the European Court of Human Rights (ECHR) are published on the official site www.echr.coe.int/ECHR and the official reports are published by Carl Heymanns Verlag KG, Luxemburger Str. 449, D-50939 Cologne, Germany.

Cambridge University Press: extracts from G Wardlaw: *Political Terrorism* (2e, Cambridge University Press, 1989).

HarperCollins Publishers Ltd: extracts from J A G Griffiths: *The Politics of the Judiciary* (2e, Fontana, 1981)

Hodder Education: extract from C Wellman: 'A new conception of human rights' in E Kamenka and A E-S Tay (eds): *Human Rights* (Edward Arnold, 1978).

Incorporated Council of Law Reporting: extracts from the *Law Reports: Appeal Cases* (AC), *Industrial Case Reports* ICR), *King's Bench Division (KB), Queen's Bench Division* (QB), and *Weekly Law Reports* (WLR).

Liberty: extracts from Second Reading Briefing on the Criminal Justice and Immigration Bill in the House of Lords, January 2008.

Press Complaints Commission: extract from the UK newspaper and magazine industry's *Code of Practice*.

Reed Business Information: extracts from case report in *Estates Gazette*: *Burden v United Kingdom* (2008), copyright © Reed Business Information.

Reed Elsevier (UK) Ltd trading as LexisNexis: extracts from *All England Law Reports* (All ER), Butterworths Medico-Legal Reports (BMLR), and Justice of the Peace Reports (JP).

Sweet & Maxwell Ltd: extracts from *European Human Rights Reports* (EHRR), *Criminal Appeal Reports* (Cr App Rep]) and *Fleet Street Reports* (FSR).

Wiley-Blackwell Publishing Ltd and the author: extract from Daniel Moeckli: 'Stop and Search under the Terrorism Act 2000: A comment on *R (Gillan) v Commissioner of Police for the Metropolis*', 70 *Modern Law Review* 659:1 (2007).

Every effort has been made to trace and contact copyright holders prior to going to press but this has not been possible in every case. If notified, the publisher will undertake to rectify any errors or omissions at the earliest opportunity.

CONTENTS

Preface   v

Acknowledgements   ix

Table of Cases   xv

Table of Statutes   xxxix

PART ONE   INTRODUCTION

1   **CIVIL LIBERTIES AND HUMAN RIGHTS:**
   DEFINITIONS AND CONTEXT   1
   1. Introduction   1
   2. 'Civil liberties'   1
   3. Human rights   3
   4. 'Liberty' and 'right'   9

2   **PROTECTING CIVIL LIBERTIES AND**
   HUMAN RIGHTS IN ENGLISH LAW   11
   1. The former method   11
   2. The present method: The Human Rights Act 1998   16
   3. The future method of protecting rights: A domestic Bill of Rights?   65

PART TWO   LIFE, LIBERTY AND ASSOCIATION

3   **ECHR PROTECTION OF LIFE, LIBERTY AND**
   ASSOCIATION: ARTICLES 2, 3, 5 AND 11   69
   1. Article 2   69
   2. Article 3   81
   3. Article 5   84
   4. Article 11   86

4   **POLICING AND POLICE POWERS**   87
   Part One. Policing   87
   1. Introduction   87
   2. Accountable to law   88
   3. Police structure and organisation   91

4. Police accountability through auditing   97

5. Judicial scrutiny of policing   100

6. Self-policing: Accountability through internal monitoring
   of police conduct   107

7. Conclusion   114

Part Two. Police powers   115

1. Introduction and historical background   115

2. Assaults on and obstruction of the police   119

3. General aspects of police powers   134

4. Powers to stop and search   154

5. Entry, search and seizure   172

6. Arrest   197

7. Detention   209

8. Questioning and treatment of persons in custody   228

9. Admissibility of evidence   254

5 **PUBLIC ORDER**   275

1. Introduction   275

2. Demonstrations and riots   279

3. Developments in policing   283

4. Freedom of association   287

5. Public meetings and processions   291

6 **EMERGENCY POWERS; THE PROBLEM
   OF POLITICAL TERRORISM**   407

1. Introduction   407

2. Political terrorism   408

3. The Terrorism Act 2000   413

4. The Anti-terrorism, Crime and Security Act 2001   455

5. The Prevention of Terrorism Act 2005   475

6. The Terrorism Act 2006   485

7. The Counter-terrorism Bill 2007–08   492

8. The use of force   494

PART THREE   PRIVACY

7 **ECHR PROTECTION OF PRIVACY: ARTICLE 8**   503

8 THE PROTECTION OF PRIVACY 523

1. Introduction 523
2. A general right of privacy? 524
3. Indirect remedies in law for invasion of privacy 533
4. Privacy and media regulation 570
5. Surveillance 576
6. Personal data: Its electronic and manual storage and privacy 600

PART FOUR FREEDOM OF EXPRESSION

9 ECHR PROTECTION OF FREEDOM OF
EXPRESSION: ARTICLE 10 612

10 FREEDOM OF EXPRESSION: CENSORSHIP
AND OBSCENITY 630

1. Theatre censorship 630
2. Film censorship 631
3. Broadcasting 638
4. Obscenity and indecency 652

11 CONTEMPT OF COURT 684

1. Introduction 684
2. The Contempt of Court Act 1981 687
3. Publications prejudicial to a fair criminal trial 694
4. Publications prejudicial to civil proceedings 720
5. Publications interfering with the course of justice
as a continuing process 737
6. Contempt in the face of the court 745
7. Interference with the course of justice 761
8. Jurisdiction 762

12 GOVERNMENT SECRECY AND NATIONAL SECURITY 764

1. Introduction 764
2. The Official Secrets Acts 768
3. DA Notices 798
4. Breach of confidence 803
5. Security vetting 822

6. The security and intelligence services 831

7. Access to information 849

PART FIVE DISCRIMINATION

13 ECHR PROTECTION FROM DISCRIMINATION: ARTICLE 14 856

1. Introduction 856

2. Application of Art. 14 857

3. The protected grounds 859

4. Establishing 'discrimination' 861

5. Proving discrimination 866

6. Justifying differential treatment 872

7. Excusing sex discrimination? 878

14 STATUTORY DISCRIMINATION PROVISIONS 883

1. Introduction 883

2. Liability and duties of public authorities *qua* public authorities 887

3. Education 897

4. Goods, facilities and services 902

5. Housing/premises 911

6. Private clubs 914

7. Other miscellaneous statutory prohibitions on discrimination 918

8. General exceptions 920

9. Vicarious liability, enforcement and remedies 927

10. Protected grounds 930

11. 'Discrimination': The general part 942

12. Disability discrimination: Unique provisions 974

13. Miscellaneous criminal provisions 988

Index 993

TABLE OF CASES

*Page references in **bold** denote that a case judgment has been reproduced in part or in full*

A, Re [2006] EWCA Crim 04, [2006] 2 All ER 1 . . . 713

A v B [2008] EWHC 1512 (Admin) . . . 840

A v HM Treasury [2008] EWHC 869 (Admin) . . . 493

A v Hoare [2008] UKHL 6 [2008] 2 WLR 311 . . . 861

A v Secretary of State for the Home Department [2004] UKHL 56 . . . 34, 42, 57, 63, 412

A v Secretary of State to the Home Department (No. 2) [2004] EWCA Civ 1125 . . . 474–75

A v UK (1998) 27 EHRR 611 . . . 82

AE v Secretary of State for the Home Department [2008] EWHC 1743 . . . 482

A–G for England and Wales v Tomlinson [1999] 3 NZLR 722 . . . 790

A–G for New South Wales v John Fairfax & Sons Ltd [1980] 1 NSWLR 362, 368 (NSWCA) . . . 696

A–G for New South Wales v Mundey [1972] 2 NSWLR 887 at 910 . . . 742

A–G for State of Queensland v Colin Lovitt QC [2003] QSC 279 . . . 741

A–G for the United Kingdom v Heinemann Publishers Australia Pty Ltd (1987) 75 ALR 353 . . . 805

A–G for the United Kingdom v Heinemann Publishers Australia Pty Ltd (No. 2) (1988) 165 CLR 30, 78 ALR 449 . . . 805

A–G v Associated Newspapers Group plc [1989] 1 All ER 604, DC . . . 735

A–G v Associated Newspapers Ltd [1994] 2 AC 238 . . . 745

A–G v Associated Newspapers Ltd [1998] EMLR 711 . . . 703

A–G v BBC (1987) *Times*, 18 December . . . 800

A–G v BBC [1981] AC 303 . . . 706

A–G v BBC; A–G v Hat Trick Productions Ltd [1997] EMLR 76 . . . 703

A–G v Birmingham Post and Mail Ltd [1998] 4 All ER 49 . . . 703, 704

A–G v Blake (Jonathan Cape Ltd, third party) [2000] 4 All ER 385 . . . 821

A–G v Blake [2000] 4 All ER 385 . . . 820

A–G v British Broadcasting Corpn [2007] EWCA Civ 280 . . . 714

A–G v Butterworth [1962] 3 All ER 326 . . . 761

A–G v Butterworth [1963] 1 QB 696 . . . 753, 762

A–G v De Keyser's Royal Hotel Ltd [1920] AC 508 . . . 822

A–G v English [1983] 1 AC 116, [1982] 2 All ER 903, [1982] 3 WLR 278, House of Lords . . . 698–701, 735

A–G v Express Newspapers [2004] EWHC 2859 (Admin) . . . 703

A–G v Guardian Newspapers [1992] 3 All ER 38. . . . 703, 704, 705

A–G v Guardian Newspapers Ltd (No. 2) [1990] 1 AC 109 at 281, HL . . . 542, 544, 614, 661, 671, 684, 694, 800–01, 805, **806–813**, 816–17

A–G v Guardian Newspapers Ltd [1987] 3 All ER 316 . . . 804, 815

A–G v Hislop [1991] 1 QB 514 . . . 737

A–G v Independent Television News Ltd [1995] 2 All ER 370, DC . . . 703

A–G v Jackson [1994] COD 171, DC . . . 761

A–G v Jonathan Cape Ltd [1976] QB 752 . . . 817

A–G v Judd (1994) *Times*, 15 August . . . 761

A–G v Leveller Magazine Ltd [1979] 1 All ER 745, HL . . . 707, 709

A–G v Leveller Magazine Ltd [1979] AC 440 . . . 706, 709, 734

A–G v MGN Ltd [1997] 1 All ER 456 . . . 704

A–G v Mirror Group Newspapers Ltd [2002] EWHC 907 (Admin) . . . 703

A–G v Morgan; AG v News Group Newspapers Ltd [1998] EMLR 294 . . . 703

A–G v New Statesman [1981] QB 1 . . . 744

A–G v News Group Newspapers plc [1989] QB 110, [1988] 2 All ER 906, [1988] 3 WLR 163, 132 Sol Jo 934, 87 Cr App Rep 323, Queen's Bench Divisional Court . . . 716, 718–720

A–G v Newspaper 1990–11 April Publishing plc (1990) *Times*, 28 February . . . 805

A–G v Newspaper Publishing plc (1990) *Times*, 28 February . . . 733

A–G v Newspaper Publishing plc [1988] Ch 333 . . . 697, 804

A–G v Newspaper Publishing plc [1997] 3 All ER 159 . . . 734

A–G v Newspaper Publishing plc: [1989] FSR 457 . . . 805

A–G v Observer Newspapers Ltd (1986) *Times*, 26 July, [1986] NLJ Rep 799, [1989] 2 FSR 15 . . . 733, 804

A–G v Pelling [2005] EWHC 515, [2006] 1 FLR
93 . . . 711

A–G v Pelling [2006] 1 FLR 93 . . . 734

A–G v Scotcher [2004] UKHL 36, [2005] 3
All ER 1 . . . 745

A–G v Sport Newspapers Ltd [1992] 1 All
ER 503 . . . 716, 720

A–G v Sunday Business Newspapers Ltd
Unreported, 20 January 1998 . . . 704

A–G v Taylor [1975] 2 NZLR 675; A–G v Hancox
[1976] 1 NZLR 171 . . . 707, 708

A–G v Times Newspapers [2001] EWCA
Civ 97 . . . 791

A–G v Times Newspapers Ltd [1974] AC 273,
[1973] 3 All ER 54, [1973] 3 WLR 298, House of
Lords . . . 720, **721–26**, 762

A–G v Times Newspapers Ltd [1992] 1 AC
191 . . . 697–98, 718

A–G v TVS Television Ltd (1989) *Times*, 7 July,
DC . . . 704–05

A–G v Unger [1998] 1 Cr App Rep 308 . . .
70–04

AH (Sudan) v Secretary of State for the Home
Department [2007] UKHL 49, [2007] 3
WLR 832 . . . 473

AL v Secretary of State for the Home Department
[2007] EWHC 1970 (Admin) . . . 482

AS (Libya) v Secretary of State for the Home
Department [2008] EWCA Civ 289, [2008]
HRLR 28 . . . 473

AV v Secretary of State for the Home Department
[2008] EWHC 1895 (Admin) . . . 482

Abdulaziz v United Kingdom (1985) 7 EHRR
471 . . . **857–58**, 875, **878–80**, 882

Abu Rideh v Secretary of State for the Home
Department [2007] EWHC 2237 . . . 482

Adler v George [1964] 2 QB 7 . . . 781

Aerts v Belgium (1998) 29 EHRR 50 . . . 84

Ahmad v ILEA [1978] 1 All ER 574 . . . 51

Ahnee v DPP [1999] 2 AC 294 . . . 742–43

Al Fayed v Comr of Police for the Metropolis
[2004] EWCA Civ 1579 . . . 140, 149, 226

Alderson v Booth [1969] 2 QB 216, DC . . . 202

Aldred v Langmuir 1932 JC 22 . . . 299

Aldred v Miller [1925] JC 117 . . . 294, 299

Alexander v The Home Office [1988] IRLR
190 . . . 904

Alexandrou v Oxford [1993] 4 All ER 328 . . . 101

Allan v Ireland (1984) 79 Cr App R 206 . . . 336

Allan v United Kingdom (2002) 36 EHRR
143 . . . 268

Allonby v Accrington & Rossendale College
[2001] ICR 1189 . . . 968, 973

Amann v Switzerland, Judgment of 16 February
2000 . . . 768

Ambard v A–G for Trinidad and Tobago [1936]
AC 322, PC . . . 741

American Cyanamid Co v Ethicon Ltd [1975]
AC 396 . . . 814

Amin v Entry Clearance Officer, Bombay [1983] 2
AC 818 . . . 887, 890, 905

Anderson [2003] 1 AC 837 . . . 50

Anyanwu v South Bank Student Union [2001] 1
ICR 391 . . . 920

Applin v Race Relations Board [1975] AC 259,
291, HL . . . 905

Argyll v Argyll [1965] 1 All ER 611 . . . 541

Armstrong, Re (27 August 1992, unreported,
QBD . . . 317

Arrowsmith v Jenkins [1963] 2 QB 561 . . . 299

Ashdown v Telegraph Group Ltd [2001] 4 All ER
666 . . . 539

Ashworth Hospital Authority v MGN Ltd [2001] 1
All ER 991 . . . 760

Ashworth Hospital Authority v MGN Ltd
[2002] UKHL 29, [2002] 1 WLR 2033, House of
Lords . . . **754–58**

Assenov v Bulgaria (1998) 28 EHRR 652 . . . 85

Aston Cantlow and Wilmcote with Billesley
Parochial Church Council v Wallbank [2004]
UKHL 37 . . . 37

Atkin v DPP (1989) 89 Cr App R 199 . . . 341, 348

Atkins v DPP [2000] 2 All ER 425. DC . . . 680

Attorney General v Punch Ltd [2002] UKHL 50,
[2003] 1 AC 1046, House of Lords . . . **726–32**

Attorney General v Times Newspapers Ltd [1991]
2 All ER 398, [1992] 1 AC 191 . . . 733, 737

Attorney–General for Northern Ireland's
Reference (No. 1 of 1975) [1977] AC 105, [1976]
2 All ER 937, [1976] 3 WLR 235, House of Lords
(NI) . . . **494–95**

Attorney–General's Reference No. 4 of 2002
[2004] UKHL 43 . . . 425

Austin v Metropolitan Police Comr [2007] EWCA
Civ 989, [2008] 2 WLR 415 . . . 376, 391,
394–95

Australian Broadcasting Corpn v Lenah Game
Meats Pty Ltd . . . 558

Australian Capital Television Pty Ltd v The
Commonwealth (1992) 177 CLR 506 . . . 612

Averill v United Kingdom (2001) 31 EHRR
36 . . . 237

Aziz v Aziz [2007] EWCA liv 712 . . . 710

B v BAA plc [2005] IRLR 927 . . . 924–25

B v UK, P v UK (2002) EHRR 529 . . . 706

BBC v Sugar [2007] EWHC 905 (Admin), [2007] 4
All ER 518 . . . 849, 853

Badry v DPP of Mauritius [1983] 2 AC 297,
PC . . . 743

Bailey v Williamson (1873) LR 8 QB 118 . . . 300

Balfour v Foreign and Commonwealth Office [1994] 1 WLR 681 . . . 854

Balogh v St Albans Crown Court [1975] QB 73, [1974] 3 All ER 283, [1974] 3 WLR 314, Court of Appeal . . . 745–49, 752

Barclays Bank plc v Taylor [1989] 3 All ER 563 . . . 186

Barfod v Denmark (1989) 13 EHRR 493, ECtHR (Series A No. 149) . . . 743

Barker v DPP [2004] All ER (D) 339 (Oct) . . . 366

Baron Bernstein of Leigh v Skyviews and General Ltd [1978] QB 479 . . . 533

Baron v DPP (2000) 13 June, DC . . . 364

Barracks v Coles [2006] EWCA Civ 1041, [2007] IRLR 73 . . . 925

Barrett v Enfield London Borough Council [1999] 3 All ER 193 . . . 101

Barrymore v News Group Newspapers Ltd 1997] FSR 600, Ch D . . . 539, 541

Beard v Wood [1980] RR 454 . . . 171

Belfast City Council v Miss Behavin' Limited [2007] UKHL 19 . . . 654

Belgian Linguistic Case (No. 2) (1968) 1 EHRR 252 . . . 872, 874

Bellinger [2003] UKHL 21 . . . 50

Bentham v UK (1996) 22 EHRR 293 . . . 84

Bentley v Brudzinski (1982) 75 Cr App Rep 217 . . . 124–25

Bessell v Wilson (1853) 20 LTOS 233n . . . 208

Betts v Stevens [1910] 1 KB 1 . . . 134

Birch v DPP [2000] Crim LR 301 . . . 298

Birmingham Post and Mail Ltd v Birmingham City Council (1993) Times, 25 November . . . 709

Blackburn v BBC (1976) Times, 15 December . . . 697

Blackburn v Bowering [1994] 3 All ER 380 . . . 127

Blake v DPP [1993] Crim LR 586 . . . 329

Blake v UK, Judgment of 26 September 2006 . . . 822

Bloom v Illinois 391 US 194 (1968) . . . 686

Blum v DPP [2006] EWHC 3209 (Admin) . . . 304

Bodden v Metropolitan Police Comr [1990] 2 QB 397, CA . . . 750

Boddington v British Transport Police [1999] 2 AC 143 . . . 299

Bonnard v Perryman [1891] 2 Ch 269 at 284, CA . . . 537

Bonnard v Perryman [1891] 2 . . . 525, 725, 735

Borowski, Re (1971) 19 DLR (3d) 537 . . . 741

Borrie and Lowe . . . 726, 748

Bozano v France (1986) 9 EHRR 297 . . . 84

Bracegirdle v Oxley [1947] KB 349, DC . . . 354

Bradley v Chief Constable of the Royal Ulster Constabulary [1991] 2 NIJB 22, QBD (NI) 66) . . . 437

Brannigan and McBride v UK (1993) 17 EHRR 539 . . . 435

Brennan v United Kingdom (2002) 34 EHRR 18 . . . 237

Brickley and Kitson v Police Legal Action July 1988 . . . 318

Bridges v California; Times–Mirror Co v California 314 US 252 (1941) . . . 686, 742

Brighton Corpn v Packham (1908) 72 DP 318, Ch D . . . 299

Broadwith v Chief Constable of Thames Valley Police [2000] Crim LR 924 . . . 318

Brogan v UK (1988) 11 EHRR 117 . . . 85

Brogan v United Kingdom (1988) 11 EHRR 117 . . . 435–36

Brown v Stott [2001] 2 All ER 97, [2001] 2 WLR 817 . . . 36, 51, 56, 58

Brutus v Cozens [1973] AC 854 . . . 351–53

Bryan v Robinson [1960] 1 WLR 508 . . . 354

Bucher v DPP [2003] EWHC 580 (Admin) . . . 125

Buckley v DPP [2008] EWHC 136 (Admin) . . . 363

Buckley v United Kingdom (1994) 20 EHRR 277 . . . 517

Bucknell MB v DPP [2006] EWHC 1888 (Admin) . . . 397

Bugg v DPP [1993] 2 All ER 815, DC . . . 299

Bugg v DPP [1993] QB 473 . . . 376

Burden v United Kingdom [2008] 18 EG 126 (CS), (2008) Times, 7 May . . . 862–63

Burden v Rigler [1911] 1 KB 337, DC . . . 370

Burden v United Kingdom (2007) 44 EHRR 51 . . . 864

Burghartz v Switzerland . . . 506

Burmah Oil Co v Lord Advocate [1965] AC 75 . . . 822

Burris v Azadani [1995] 1 WLR 1372 . . . 359

Burris v Azadani [1995] 1 WLR 1372, CA . . . 536

C v CPS [2008] EWHC 148 (Admin) . . . 361

C v DPP [2003] All ER (D) 37 (Nov) . . . 125

CPS v Speede (1997) 17 December, DC . . . 399

Caballero v UK (2000) 30 EHRR 643 . . . 85

Calder (John) (Publications) Ltd v Powell [1965] 1 QB 509, DC at 515 . . . 663

Cambridgeshire and Isle of Ely County Council v Rust [1972] 2 QB 426, DC . . . 294

Camelot Group plc v Centaur Communications Ltd [1998] 1 All ER 251 . . . 759, 761

Camenzind v Switzerland (1997) 28 EHRR 458 . . . 184

Campbell and Cosans v UK (1982) 4 EHRR 293 ... 82

Campbell v Mirror Group Newspapers [2004] UKHL 22 ... 37, 39, **545–57**

Campbell v United Kingdom Application No. 13590/88; (1992) 15 EHRR 137 ... 519, 524, 542, 557–59

Capon v DPP (1998) *Independent*, 23 March, DC ... 374

Caraher v United Kingdom (Application No. 24520/94, 11 January 2000) ... 79

Carnduff v Chief Constable of West Midlands Police [2001] 1 WLR 1786 ... 101

Case 109/88 Handels–og Kontorfunktionaererernes Forbund I Danmark v Dansk Arbejdsgiverforenin g (acting for Danfoss) [1989] ECR 3199 ... 971

Case 13/94, P v S & Cornwall County Council [1996] ECR I–2143 ... 886

Case 170/84 Bilka–Kaufhaus GmbH v Weber von Hartz [1986] ECR 1607, European Court of Justice ... **970–74**

Case 171/88 Rinner–Kühn v FWW Spezial– Gebaudereinigung GmbH [1989] ECR 2743 ... 971

Case 187/00 Kutz–Bauer v Freie und Hansestadt Hamburg [2003] ECR I–02741 ... **971–74**

Case 226/98 Jørgensen v Foreningen af Speciallæger, Sygesikringens Forhandlingsudvalg [2000] ECR I–02447 ... 971

Case 303/06, Coleman v Attridge Law ... 885, 937, **947–48**

Case 77/02 Steinicke v Bundesanstalt für Arbeit [2003] ECR I–09027 ... 971

Case T–228/02 Organisation des Mojahedinas due peuple d'Iran v Council [2006] ECR II–4665 ... 426

Case T–229/02, Osman Oclan, on behalf of the Kurdistan Workers' Party (PKK) v Council 3 April 2008 ... 426

Cassell v Broome [1972] AC 1027, 1133, HL ... 13

Castells v Spain (1992) 14 EHRR 445 ... 620

Castorina v Chief Constable of Surrey (1988) NLJR 180, Lexis, Court of Appeal (Civil Division) ... **135–40**

Central Control Board (Liquor Traffic) v Cannon Brewery Co Ltd [1919] AC 744 ... 14

Central Television plc, Re [1991] 1 All ER 347 ... 713

Chahal v UK (1996) 23 EHRR 413 ... 84–5, 456

Chahal v United Kingdom Judgment of 15 November 1996 (1997) 23 EHRR 418 ... 767

Chambers and Edwards v DPP [1995] Crim LR 896 ... 347

Chandler v Director of Public Prosecutions [1964] AC 763, [1962] 3 All ER 142, [1962] 3 WLR 702, House of Lords ... 781, **783–86**

Chappell v DPP (1988) 89 Cr App Rep 82 ... 348

Chic Fashions (West Wales) Ltd v Jones (1968) 2 QB 299 ... 90, 188

Chief Constable of Humberside Police v McQuade [2001] EWCA Civ 1330 ... 395, 405

Chief Constable of Lancashire v Potter [2003] EWHC 2272 (Admin) ... 369

Chief Constable of Leicestershire Constabulary v Garavelli [1997] EMLR 543 ... 760

Chief Constable of Lincolnshire v Glowacki (1998) 18 June, CA (Cr D) ... 151

Chiron Corporation v Avery [2004] EWHC 493 ... 365

Christians against Racism and Fascism v United Kingdom (1980) 21 DR 148 ... 309, 317

Christie v Leachinsky [1947] AC 573, HL ... 192, 205, 436

Christie v United Kingdom App. No. 21482/93, 27 June 1994 ... 845

Citing Hoogendijk v Netherlands (App No. 58461/00) (admissibility decision, 6 January 2005) ... 869

Clark v TDG Ltd (t/a Novacold) [1999] ICR 951, Court of Appeal ... **975–77**

Clark v Chief Constable of Cleveland (1999) 7 May, CA (CivD) ... 100

Clarke v Chief Constable of North Wales (2000) 5 April, CA (Cr D), unreported ... 148, 226

Clarke v DPP (1997) 14 November, unreported ... 202

Clibbery v Allan [2002] Fam 261 ... 706

Clinton v Chief Constable of the Royal Ulster Constabulary [1991] 2 NIJB 53, QBD (NI) ... 437

Clymo v Wandsworth London Borough Council [1989] ICR 250 ... 968

Cobra Golf Ltd v Rata [1997] 2 All ER 150 ... 685

Coco v A N Clark (Engineers) Ltd [1969] RPC 41 ... 541, 558, 561

Coe v Central Television (1993) *Independent*, 11 August ... 714

Coffin v Smith (1980) 71 Cr App Rep 221 ... 120

Coles v Chief Constable of South Yorkshire (1998) CA (Cr D) ... 152

Collins v Royal National Theatre Board Ltd [2004] IRLR 395 ... 988

Collins v Wilcock [1984] 3 All ER 374 ... 119, 126

Commercial Bank of Australia Ltd v Preston [1981] 2 NSWLR 554, Sup Ct NSW ... 726

Commonwealth of Australia v John Fairfax & Sons Ltd (1980) 55 ALJR 45 ... 820

Condron v United Kingdom (2001) 31 EHRR 1 ... 237, 251

Conegate Ltd v Customs and Excise Comrs [1987] QB 254 ... 677

Constantine v Imperial Hotels Ltd [1944] 1 KB 693 ... 905

Conwell v Newham London Borough Council [2000] 1 All ER 696 ... 907

Copeland v Ministry of Defence 19 May 1999, unreported, QBD (NI) ... 499

Corelli v Wall (1906) 22 TLR 532, Chancery Division, Swinfen Eady J ... 536–37

Costello–Roberts v UK (1993) 19 EHRR 112 ... 82

Council of Civil Service Unions v Minister for the Civil Service [1985] AC 374, HL ... 63, 765, 830, 846

Couronne v Crawley Borough Council [2007] EWCA Civ 1086 ... 923

Court of Appeal v Collins [1982] 1 NSWLR 682, NSWCA ... 749

Cowan v Metropolitan Police Comr [2000] 1 WLR 254, CA (Civ D) ... 192

Cream Holdings v Banerjee [2004] UKHL 44 ... 364

Creation Records v News Group Newspapers [1997] EMLR 444 ... 542

Cremieux v France (1993) 16 EHRR 357 ... 184

Creswell v DPP [2006] EWHC 3379 (Admin), (2007) 171 JP 233 ... 329

Crook, Re(1989) 93 Cr App Rep 17 ... 707

Crozier v Cundey (1827) 6 B & C 232 ... 188

Cullen v Chief Constable of the RUC [2003] UKHL 39 ... 438

Cumming v Chief Constable of Northumbria Police [2003] EWCA Civ 1844 ... 148–49

Curlett v M'Kechnie (1938) JC 176 ... 130

Cyprus v Turkey (2001) 35 EHRR 30 ... 80

D, Re (1997) 45 BMLR 191 ... 709

D, Re (acquitted person: retrial) [2006] EWCA Crim 733, [2006] 1 WLR 1998 ... 711

D v L [2004] EMLR 1 ... 559

DD and AS v Secretary of State for the Home Department (27 April 2007) ... 473

DH v Czech Republic (2008) 47 EHRR 3, Grand Chamber ... 864, 868–75, 878

D H Edmonds Ltd v East Sussex Police Authority (1988) Times, 15 July ... 335

Daiichi UK Ltd v SHAC [2003] EWHC 2337 (QB) ... 362, 365

Dallison v Caffery [1965] 1 QB 348 ... 208, 395

Daly case ... 62

Dame Elizabeth Butler–Sloss in Re K (a child) [2001] 2 WLR 1141 at 1148, CA ... 63

Dame Elizabeth Butler–Sloss, in Re K (a child) (secure accommodation: right to liberty) [2001] 2 WLR 1144, CA ... 37

Darbo v DPP (1994) Times, 11 July ... 669

Davis v Bath and North East Somerset District Council Bristol CC, Claim No. 9324149 ... 889

Davis v Lisle [1936] 2 KB 434 ... 121, 195–196, 404

Dawes v DPP [1994] RTR 209, DC ... 206

Dawkins v Department of the Environment [1993] ICR 517 ... 933

De Court, Re (1997) Times, 27 November ... 761

De Morgan v Metropolitan Board of Works (1880) 5 QBD 155, DC ... 299

De Souza v Automobile Association [1986] ICR 514 ... 887

De Wilde, Ooms and Versyp v Belgium (the 'vagrancy' cases) (1971) 1 EHRR 373 ... 85

Dehal v Crown Prosecution Service [2005] EWHC 2154 (Admin) ... 351

Delbert–Evans v Davies and Watson [1945] 2 All ER 167, DC ... 716

Department for Work and Pensions v Thompson [2004] IRLR 248 ... 965

Department of Economics, Policy and Development of the City of Moscow v Bankers Trust Co [2004] EWCA Civ 314, [2005] QB 207 ... 707

Department of Trade v Williams (1995) 31 July, unreported ... 375

Department of Transport v Williams (1993) 138 SJLB 5 ... 292

Derbyshire County Council v Times Newspapers [1993] AC 534 ... 621

Despard v Wilcox (1910) 22 Cox CC 258, DC ... 302

Devine, Re [1999] NIJB 128 ... 431

Devlin v United Kingdom, Judgment of 30 October 2001 ... 767

Dhesi v Chief Constable of West Midlands Police (2000) Times 19 April, CA (Civ D) ... 206

Dibble v Ingleton [1972] 1 QB 480, DC ... 129

Dickson v United Kingdom [2006] ECHR 430 ... 516

Dillon v O'Brien and Davis (1887) 16 COX CC 245 ... 208

DPP v A and BC Chewing Gum Ltd [1968] 1 QB 159, DC ... 663

DPP v Bailie [1995] Crim LR 446 ... 318

DPP v Barnard (1999) Times, 9 November, DC ... 373

DPP v Bayer [2003] EWHC 2567 (Admin) ... 373

DPP v Billington [1988] 1 All ER 435 ... 234

DPP v Channel 4 Television Co Ltd [1993] 2 All ER 517 ... 761

DPP v Chapman (1988) 89 Cr App R 190 ... 121

DPP v Clarke (1992) 94 Cr App R 359, DC ... 348, 353, 355

DPP v Collins [2006] UKHL 40 ... 536

DPP v Cotcher and Cotcher [1993] COD 181 ... 337

DPP v Dunn [2001] 1 Cr App R 352 ... 362

DPP v Dziurzynski [2002] EWHC 1380 (Admin) ... 362

DPP v Godwin [1991] RTR 303, DC ... 171

DPP v Green [2004] EWHC 1225 (Admin) . . . 356

DPP v Hall [2005] EWHC 2612 (Admin), [2006] 1 WLR 1000 . . . 366

DPP v Haw [2007] EWHC 1931 (Admin), [2008] 1 WLR 379 . . . 304

DPP v Hawkins [1988] 3 All ER 673 . . . 121, 206

DPP v Jones [1999] 2 AC 240 . . . 292, 305, 319–25

DPP v Jones [2002] EWHC 110 (Admin) . . . 318

DPP v Jordan . . . 670

DPP v L [1999] Crim LR 752 . . . 127

DPP v M [2004] EWHC 1453 (Admin) . . . 356

DPP v McGladrigan [1991] RTR 297, DC . . . 171

DPP v Meadon [2004] 4 All ER 75 . . . 154, 189

DPP v Orum [1989] 1 WLR 88, DC . . . 347

DPP v Pal [2000] Crim LR . . . 356

DPP v Ping Lin [1976] AC 574, HL . . . 257

DPP v Ramos [2000] Crim LR 768 . . . 342

DPP v Smith [1990] 2 AC 783, HL . . . 299

DPP v Tilly [2001] EWHC Admin 821, (2001) 166 JP 22 . . . 373

DPP v Ward [1999] RTR 11, DC 9 . . . 234

DPP v Whyte [1972] AC 849, HL at 860 . . . 661–63

DPP v Williams (1998) 27 July, DC . . . 362

Dobson v Hastings [1992] . . . 762

Dockers' Labour Club and Institute Ltd v Race Relations Board [1976] AC 285 . . . 905

Dockers' Labour Club and Institute Ltd v Race Relations Board [1976] AC 285 . . . 915

Doherty v Ministry of Defence (1980, unreported, HL) . . . 499

Donnelly v Jackman [1970] 1 WLR 562 . . . 124–25

Donoghue v Poplar Housing and Regeneration Community Association [2001] EWCA Civ 595 . . . 37

Douglas v Hello! (No. 3) [2005] EWCA Civ 595 . . . 557, 561

Douglas v Hello! [2001] 2 All ER 289 . . . 16, 41

Douglas v Hello! [2001] QB 967 . . . 533, 542

Douglas v Hello! [2003] EWHC 786 . . . 510, 524, 527

Douiyeb v Netherlands (1999) 30 EHRR 790 . . . 206

Dove Group plc and Jaguar Cars Ltd v Hynes [1993] COD 174 . . . 726

Dr A S Rayan, Re (1983) 148 JP 569, DC . . . 753

Dudgeon v United Kingdom . . . 507

Duncan v Jones [1936] 1 KB 218, DC . . . 277, 392, 394, 404

Durant v Financial Services Authority [2003] EWCA Civ 1746 . . . 609

EB v France Application No. 43546/02, 22 January 2008 . . . 876–77

EDO MBM Technology Ltd v Axworthy [2005] EWHC 2490 (QB) . . . 364

EDO MBM Technology Ltd v Campaign to Smash EDO [2005] EWHC 837 (QB) . . . 365

EM (Lebanon) v Secretary of State for the Home Department [2006] EWCA Civ 1531 . . . 473

EOC v Birmingham City Council [1989] AC 1155 . . . 899

Edwards v UK (2002) 35 EHRR 487 . . . 80

Elias v Pasmore [1934] 2 KB 164 . . . 208

Elliott v Chief Constable of Wiltshire (1996) Times, 5 December . . . 100

Elsholz v Germany [2000] ECHR 25735/94, [2000] 2 FLR 486 . . . 875

Emerson Developments (Holdings) Ltd v Avery [2004] EWHC 194 . . . 365

Enfield London Borough Council v Mahoney [1983] 2 All ER 901, CA . . . 684

Engel v Netherlands (1976) 1 EHRR 647 . . . 84

Entick v Carrington (1765) 19 State Tr 1029, 2 Wils 275, 95 ER 807 . . . 88–90, 841

Equal Opportunities Commission for Northern Ireland's Application, Re [1989] IRLR 64 . . . 899

Equal Opportunities Commission v Director of Education [2001] 2 HKLRD 690 . . . 951

Equal Opportunities Commission v Secretary of State for Trade and Industry [2007] EWHC 483 (Admin) [2007] IRLR 327 . . . 962–64

Ergi v Turkey, Judgment of 28 July 1998 . . . 80

Eskester v UK (App. No. 18601/91, 2 April 1993) . . . 831, 845

Estes v Texas 381 US 532 (1965) . . . 715

Ettridge v Morrell (1986) 85 LGR 100 . . . 306

European Asian Bank AG v Wentworth (1986) 5 NSWLR 445 . . . 749

European Roma Rights Centre v Immigration Officer at Prague Airport [2005] 2 AC 1 . . . 868, 889–90, 950–53

Ezelin v France (1992) 14 EHRR 362 . . . 318

F, Re (a minor) (Publication of Information) [1977] Fam 58 . . . 711

Farah v Metropolitan Police Comr [1997] 2 WLR 824 . . . 104

Farrell v Secretary of State for Defence [1980] 1 All ER 1667 . . . 495, 497

Faulkner v Willetts [1982] RTR 159 Crim LR 543, DC . . . 197

Field v Metropolitan Police Receiver [1907] 2 KB 853 . . . 334

Finucane v UK (2003) 37 EHRR 29 . . . 81

Ford v Metropolitan Police District Receiver [1921] 2 KB 344 . . . 335

Foulkes v Chief Constable of the Merseyside Police [1998] 3 All ER 705 . . . 384, 395, 405

Fox, Campbell and Hartley v UK (1980) 13 EHRR 157 . . . 84–5, 135, 206, 436

Francis v United Kingdom (2007) App. No. 25624/02 . . . 56

Fredin v Sweden (1991) 13 EHRR 784 . . . 863

French v DPP [1997] COD 174, DC . . . 163

Fretté v France (2004) 38 EHRR 21 . . . 858, 875–77

Friedl v Austria (1995) 21 EHRR 83 . . . 287, 510

Friswell v Chief Constable of Essex Police [2004] EWHC 3009 (QB) . . . 405

Funke v France (1993) 16 EHRR 297 . . . 184, 246

Furniture, Timber and Allied Trades Union v Modgill; Pel Ltd v Modgill [1980] IRLR 142 . . . 900

G v Germany (1989) 60 DR 256 . . . 291

Gallagher v Durack (1983) 57 ALJR 191 . . . 741

Gaygasuz v Austria (1997) 23 EHRR 364 . . . 858, 875

General Medical Council v BBC [1998] 3 All ER 426 . . . 706

Gerald v Metropolitan Police Comr (1998) Times, 26 June, CA . . . 103

Ghaidan v Godin–Mendoza [2004] UKHL 30, [2004] 2 AC 557 . . . 37, 43, 50–51

Ghani v Jones [1970] 1 QB 693, CA . . . 183, 192

Gilham v Breidenbach [1982] RTR 328n . . . 197

Gill v El Vino Co Ltd [1983] QB 425 . . . 904

Gillow v United Kingdom (1986) 11 EHRR 335 . . . 877

Goodland v DPP [2000] 2 All ER 425 . . . 680

Goodwin v United Kingdom (2002) 35 EHRR 18 . . . 506

Gough v McFadyen 2 008 SCCR 20 . . . 749

Gouriet v Union of Post Office Workers [1978] AC 435 . . . 820

Govell v United Kingdom App. No. 27237/95 . . . 580

Green v DPP [1991] Crim LR 782 . . . 130

Green v United States 356 US 165 at 189 (1958) . . . 684

Greene v Associated Newspapers Ltd [2005] 1 All ER 30 . . . 537

Greene v Secretary of State for Home AB airs [1942] AC 284, HL . . . 103

Griggs v Duke Power Co (1971) 401 US 424 . . . 869, 965

Guardian Newspapers Ltd, ex p. [1999] 1 All ER 65, CA (Cr D) . . . 706

Guardian Newspapers, ex p. (1993) Times, 26 October . . . 713–14

Gudmundsson v Iceland . . . 877

Gunter v Metropolitan Police District Receiver (1888) 53 JP 249 . . . 335

HRH Prince of Wales v Mirror Group Newspapers Limited [2006] EWCA Civ 1776 . . . 558, 559

Halford v UK, App. No. 20605/92 . . . 580

Halford v United Kingdom (1997) 24 EHRR 523 . . . 515

Hall v Save New Church Guinea Pigs (Campaign) [2005] EWHC 372 (QB) . . . 365

Hall v Tanner (2000) 20 July, CA (CD) . . . 361

Hammond v DPP [2004] EWHC 69 (Admin) . . . 350

Hampson v Department of Education and Science [1989] ICR 179, Court of Appeal . . . 922, 968, 969

Handcock v Baker (1800) 2 Bos & P 260 . . . 405

Handyside v UK (1976) 1 EHRR 737 . . . 57, 614, 659

Hardial Singh, ex p. [1984] 1 WLR 704 . . . 456

Harman v Secretary of State for the Home Department [1983] 1 AC 280, HL . . . 685

Harndon v Rumsfeld (2006) 548 US 557 . . . 474

Hashman and Harrys v UK (2000) 30 EHRR 241 . . . 398–99

Hatton v United Kingdom (2003) 37 EHRR 611 . . . 518

Haw and Tucker v City of Westminster Magistrates' Court (2008) 172 JP 122 . . . 751

Heathrow Airport Ltd v Garman [2007] EWHC 1957 (QB) . . . 365–66

Hegarty, Doyle and Kelly v Ministry of Defence [1989] 9 NIJB 88 . . . 495

Heinz v Kenrick [2000] ICR 491 . . . 979

Hellewell v Chief Constable of Derbyshire [1995] 1 WLR 804 . . . 542

Hepburn v Chief Constable of Thames Valley [2002] EWCA Civ 1841 . . . 184, 189

Herbage v Pressdram [1984] 2 All ER 769, CA . . . 525

Herbecq v Belgium, App. No. 32200/96) . . . 578

Herrington v DPP 23 June 1992, unreported, DC . . . 354

Hewitt and Harman v United Kingdom (App. No. 20317/92, 1 September 1993) . . . 845

Hibberd v DPP (1996) 27 November . . . 372

Hickman v Maisey [1900] 1 QB 752 . . . 534

Hill v Anderton [1982] 2 All ER 963 . . . 207

Hill v Chief Constable of West Yorkshire [1989] 1 AC 53, HL . . . 101

Hillingdon London Borough Council v
   Commission for Racial Equality [1982] AC
   779 . . . 914

Hills v Ellis [1983] QB 680, [1983] 1 All ER
   667 . . . 134

Hipgrave v Jones [2004] EWHC 2901
   (QB) . . . 363, 365

Hirst v United Kingdom (2004) 38 EHRR 825 . . . 3

Hirst v United Kingdom (No. 2) (2005) 42 EHRR
   849 . . . 3

Hoare and Pierce [2004] 1 Cr App R 355 . . . 251

Hoare v United Kingdom App. No. 31211/96
   [1997] EHRLR 678 . . . 659

Hoffmann v Germany (App No. 34045/96) [2001]
   ECHR 34045/96 . . . 875

Holloway v DPP [2004] EWHC 2621
   (Admin) . . . 347

Homer v Cadman (1886) 16 Cox CC 51,
   DC . . . 294

Hooker, Re [1993] COD190 . . . 751

Hooper v UK, Judgment of 16 November
   2004 . . . 399

Hoser and Kotabi Pty Ltd v Thee Queen [2003]
   VSCA 194 . . . 741

Hough v Chief Constable of Staffordshire [2001]
   EWCA Civ 39 . . . 148

Howlett v Holding [2006] EWHC 41 (QB) . . . 361,
   364, 365

Huang v Secretary of State for the Home
   Department [2007] UKHL 11 . . . 36, 58

Hubbard v Pitt [1976] QB 142 . . . 293

Huber v Switzerland, Judgment of 23 October
   1990 . . . 85

Hudson v Chief Constable, Avon and Somerset
   Constabulary [1976] Crim LR 451 . . . 354

Hughes v Holley (1986) 86 Cr App R 130 . . . 400

Humphries v Connor (1864) 17 ICLR 1 . . . 390,
   392–94

Hunter v Canary Wharf [1997] 2 All ER
   426 . . . 293, 359, 535

Huntingdon Life Sciences Group plc v Stop
   Huntingdon Animal Cruelty 'SHAC' [2003]
   EWHC 1967 . . . 365

Huntingdon Life Sciences v Curtin (1997) 15
   October, CA . . . 362

Hussain v Lancaster City Council [2000] QB
   1 . . . 293

Hutchinson v Newbury Magistrates' Court (2000)
   122 ILR 499, DC . . . 329

I v DPP [2001] 2 WLR 765, HL . . . 337

IJL, GMR AKP v UK (2001) 33 EHRR 11 . . . 247

Ibrahim v R [1914] AC 599 at 609 . . . 257

Imbroscia v Switzerland (1993) 17 EHRR
   444 . . . 237

Imutran Ltd v Uncaged Campaigns Ltd [2001] 2
   All ER 385 at 391, Ch D . . . 41

Incal v Turkey (1998) 29 EHRR 449 . . . 620

Independent Publishing Co Ltd v A–G of Trinidad
   and Tobago [2005] 1 All ER 499 . . . 711, 761

Interfact Ltd v Liverpool City Council [2005] 1
   WLR 3118 . . . 635

Inze v Austria (1987) 10 EHRR 39 . . . 875

Ireland v UK (1978) 2 EHRR 25 . . . 81, 82

Irwin v Dowd 366 US 717 (1961) . . . 715

Isaac v Chief Constable for West Midlands Police
   [2001] All ER (D) 331 (Jul), CA (Civ D) . . . 103

JW Dwyer Ltd v Metropolitan Police District
   Receiver [1967] 2 QB 970 . . . 335

Jacobellis v Ohio (1964) 378 US 184 . . . 662

Jameel v Wall Street Journal Europe SPRL [2006]
   UKHL 44 . . . 621

James v Eastleigh Borough Council [1990] 2 AC
   751, House of Lords . . . 904, 948–50

James v Robinson (1963) 109 CLR 593 . . . 684, 715

Jelen v Katz (1989) 90 Cr App R 456 at 465,
   CA . . . 264

Jersild v Denmark (1994) 19 EHRR 1 . . . 621

Jerusalem v Austria, Judgment of 27 February
   2001 . . . 621

John Lewis & Co v Tims [1952] AC 676, HL . . . 208

John Reid Enterpris es Ltd v Pell . . . 761

John v Express Newspapers plc [2000] 3 All ER
   257 . . . 760

Johnson v Phillips [1975] 3 All ER 682 . . . 129

Johnston v RUC Case C–222/84 [1986] ECR
   01651 . . . 924

Jones v Tower Boot Co Ltd [1997] 2 All ER
   407 . . . 928

Jones v University of Manchester [1993] ICR
   474 . . . 968

Jordan v UK (2001) 37 EHRR 52 . . . 81, 869, 871

Karhuvaara and Iltalehti v Finland, Judgment of
   16 November 2004 . . . 620

Kaur & Shah v London Borough of Ealing . . . 893,
   895, 925

Kava v Turkey (1998) 28 EHRR 1 . . . 80

Kay v Lambeth LBC [2006] UKHL 10 . . . 559

Kay v London Borough of Lambeth; Leeds City
   Council v Price [2006] UKHL 10 . . . 35

Kay v Metropolitan Police Comr [2007] 4 All ER
   31 . . . 319

Kaya v Turkey (1998) 28 EHRR1 . . . 80

Kaye v Robertson [1991] FSR 62, Court of
   Appeal . . . 524–27, 534

Keegan v Chief Constable of Merseyside Police
   [2003] 1 WLR 2187 . . . 191

Keegan v United Kingdom [2006] ECHR 764 . . . 191

Kelly v Chief Constable of Hampshire (1993) *Independent*, 25 March . . . 395

Kelly v DPP [2002] EWHC 1428 (Admin) . . . 363

Kelly v UK, Judgment of 4 May 2001 . . . 81

Kelly v United Kingdom App. No. 17579/90 . . . 497

Kenlin v Gardner [1966] 3 All ER 931 . . . 121, 126, 206

Kent v Metropolitan Police Comr, *Times*, 15 May, 1981 . . . 316, 317

Kerr v DPP (1994) 158 JP 1048 . . . 125

Khan v UK [1997] AC 558 . . . 578, 580

Khan v UK [2000] Crim LR 684 . . . 578

Khan v United Kingdom (2001) 31 EHRR 45 . . . 108

Kidd v DRG [1985] ICR 405 . . . 968

King v DPP (2000) 20 June, DC . . . 361

King v Gardner (1979) 71 Cr App Rep 13, DC . . . 142

Kingsley International Pictures v Regents 360 US 684 (1959) . . . 614, 630

Kirkham v Chief Constable of Greater Manchester Police [1990] 2 QB 283, CA . . . 101

Klass v Germany (1979–80) 2 EHRR 214 . . . 522, 578, 768

Knuller (Publishing, Printing and Promotions Ltd) v DPP [1973] AC 435, HL. at 456 . . . 658–59, 662

Kopp v Switzerland (1998) 27 EHRR 91 . . . 578, 595

Kroon v Netherlands (1995) 19 EHRR 263 . . . 517

Kurt v Turkey (1998) 27 EHRR 91 . . . 80–81, 84

Kuru v State of New South Wales [2008] HCA 26 . . . 405

Kuruma v R [1955] AC 197 . . . 257

Kynaston v DPP (1987) 87 Cr App Rep 200, DC . . . 192

Kyprianou v Cyprus [2005] ECHR 73797/01 . . . 753

L, Re (a minor) (wardship: freedom of publication) [1988] 1 All ER 418 . . . 711

Lana v Positive Training in Housing (London) Ltd [2001] IRLR 501 . . . 928

Lancashire Council Council v Taylor [2005] 1 WLR 2668 . . . 37

Lange v Australian Broadcasting Corpn (1997) 189 CLR 520 . . . 612

Lansbury v Riley [1914] 3 KB 229, DC . . . 401

Laskey, Jaggard and Brown v United Kingdom (1997) 24 EHRR 39 . . . 507

Lau v DPP [2001] 1 FLR 799 . . . 363

Leach v Money (1765) 19 State Tr 1002 . . . 90

Leander v Sweden, Judgment of 25 Febuary 1997 (1987) 9 EHRR 433 . . . 767, 768, 855

Lehideux and Isorni v France (1998) 30 EHRR 665 . . . 621

Leigh v Cole (1853) 6 Cox CC 329 . . . 208

Levy v Victoria (1997) 189 CLR 579 . . . 612

Lewis v Chief Constable of Greater Manchester (1991) *The Independent* 24 October . . . 395

Lewis v Chief Constable of the South Wales Constabular [1991] 1 All ER 206 . . . 206

Lewis v Cox [1985] QB 509, [1984] 3 WLR 875, 148 JP 601 . . . 131–34

Lewis v DPP (1995) unreported DC . . . 349

Lewis, ex p. (1888) 21 QBD 191, DC . . . 300

Li Shu–Ling v R (1989) 1 AC 270 . . . 258

Lindsay v United Kingdom, App. No. 11089/84, (1987) 9 EHRR CD555 . . . 861

Lineham v DPP [2000] Crim LR 861 . . . 90, 121, 195

Lingens v Austria, Judgment of 8 July 1986, ECtHRR A103 (1986) 8 EHRR 407, European Court of Human Rights . . . 617–20

Linnett v Coles [1987] QB 555, CA . . . 694

Lippiatt v South Gloucestershire Council [2000] QB 51 . . . 293

Lister v Helsey Hall Ltd [2002] 1 AC 215 (HL) . . . 928

Lobban v R [1995] 1 WLR 877, PC . . . 257

Lodge v DPP (1988) *Times*, 26 October . . . 347

Lonrho plc, Re [1990] 2 AC 154 . . . 735

Lopez Ostra v Spain (1996) 23 EHRR 101 . . . 517

Lord Advocate v Scotsman Publications Ltd . . . 801, 817

Lord Saville of Newdigate v Harnden [2003] NICA 6 . . . 685

Lowdens v Keaveney [1903] 2 IR 82 . . . 293

Ludi v Switzerland (1993) 15 EHRR 173 . . . 273

Lynch v Ministry of Defence [1983] NI 216 . . . 495

Lynch, ex p. [1980] NI 126 . . . 436

Lyons v Chief Constable of West Yorkshire (1997) 24 April . . . 141

M, Re [1994] 1 AC 377, HL . . . 15

M v Secretary of State for the Home Department [2004] EWCA Civ 324, [2004] 2 All ER 863 (CA) . . . 471

M v Secretary of State for Work and Pensions [2006] 2 AC 91 . . . 558

MGN Pension Trustees Ltd v Bank of America National Trust and Savings Association [1995] 2 All ER 355 . . . 713

MM v The Netherlands (2004) 39 EHRR 19 . . . 594

MT (Algeria) v Secretary of State for the Home Department [2007] EWCA Civ 808, [2008] QB 534 . . . 474

McBean v Parker (1983) 147 JP 205 ... 395

McBride's Application for Judicial Review, Re [1999] NI 299 ... 498

McBride's Application, Re (No. 2) [2003] NI 319 ... 766

McCann v United Kingdom, ECtHRR A324, (1995) 21 EHRR 97 ... 69, 497

McCarrick v Oxford [1983] RTR 117 ... 208

McConnell v Chief Constable of the Greater Manchester Police [1990] 1 WLR 364 ... 395

Macdonald v Advocate General for Scotland [2003] UKHL ... 42

McGowan v Langmuir 1931 JC 10 ... 676

McGuigan v Ministry of Defence [1982] 19 NIJB, QBD (NI) ... 495, 499

McKee v Chief Constable of the RUC ... 437

McKennitt v Ash ... 557

McKeown v R (1971) 16 DLR (3d) 390 ... 749, 751

McKerr, Re [2004] UKHL 12, [2004] 1 WLR 807 ... 81

McKerry v Teesdale and Wear Valley Justices [2000] Crim LR 594 ... 711

McLaughlin v Ministry of Defence [1978] 7 NIJB, (NI CA) ... 495, 499

McLeod v MPC [1994] 4 All ER 553 ... 404–05

McLeod v St Aubyn [1899] AC 549, PC ... 740

McLorie v Oxford [1982] QB 1290, DC ... 90, 183, 208

Madarassy v Nomura International plc [2007] EWCA Civ 33 [2007] IRLR 246 ... 930

Magee v United Kingdom (2001) 31 EHRR 35 ... 237

Magill v Ministry of Defence [1987] NI 194 ... 495

Maharaj v A–G for Trinidad and Tobago (No. 2) [1979] AC 385, PC ... 751

Maile v McDowell [1980] Crim LR 586 ... 354

Majrowski v Guy's and St Thomas's NHS Trust [2006] UKHL 3436 ... 361

Makaratsis v Greece, Judgment of 20 December 2004 ... 80

Malone v Metropolitan Police Comr [1979] 1 ... 527, 541

Malone v United Kingdom (1984) ... 589

Manchester City Council v McCann [1999] 2 WLR 590 ... 705, 750

Manchester City Council v Romano (Disability Rights Commission intervening) [2005] 1 WLR 2775 ... 979

Mandla v Dowell Lee [1983] 2 AC 548 ... 899, 930, 933, 968

Marbury v Madison 5 US 1 (1 Cranch) 137 (1803) ... 64

Marcel v Metropolitan Police Comr [1992] Ch 225 ... 192

Margaret Murray v UK (1994) 19 EHRR 193 ... 84

Marsh v Arscott (1982) 75 Cr App Rep 211 ... 341, 346, 347

Martin v Metropolitan Police Comr (2001) 18 June, CA (Civ Div), unreported ... 206

Martin v Watson [1996] AC 74, HL ... 100

Martins v Choudhary [2007] EWCA Civ 1379 ... 364

Masterson v Holden [1986] 3 All ER 39 ... 354

Matto v Crown Court at Wolverhampton [1987] RTR 337 ... 267

Maxwell v Pressdram Ltd [1987] 1 All ER 656 ... 760

Mayor and Burgesses of the London Borough of Lewisham v Malcolm [2008] UKHL 43 ... 977–83, 985

Meechie v Multi–Media Market (Canterbury) Ltd (1995) 94 LGR 474 ... 635

Mella v Monahan [1961] Crim LR 175, DC ... 656

Mepstead v DPP [1996] Crim LR 111 ... 126, 203

Mersey Care NHS Trust v Ackroyd (No. 2) [2007] EWCA Civ 101, 94 BMLR 84 ... 758

Miailhe v France (1993) 16 EHRR 332 ... 184

Michael O'Mara Books Ltd v Express Newspapers ... 761

Mills v DPP (1998) 17 December DC ... 362

Ministry of Defence v Griffin [2008] UKHC 1542(QB) ... 822

Montgomery and Coulter v HM Advocate DRA Nos 1 and 2 of 2000 [2001] 2 WLR 779 ... 687

Montgomery v HM Advocate [2001] 2 WLR 779, PC ... 33

Montgomery v HM Advocate [2003] 1 AC 641 ... 714

Moore v Clerk of Assize, Bristol [1972] 1 All ER 58 ... 761

Morris v Beardmore [1981] AC 446 ... 90, 197

Morris v Crown Office [1970] 2 QB 114 ... 746, 749, 752

Morris v Knight (1998) 22 October (Bournemouth County Court). ... 361

Morrow v DPP [1993] Crim LR 58 (1991) 94 Cr App Rep 359 ... 349

Morrow, Beach and Thomas v DPP [1994] Crim LR 58 ... 349

Mortensen v Peters (1906) 8 F 93, Ct of Justiciary ... 14

Moscow Branch of the Salvation Army v Russia (2006) 44 EHRR 912 ... 942

Mosley v News Group Newspapers Ltd [2008] EWHC 1777, Queen's Bench ... 561–63

Müller v Switzerland (1988) 13 EHRR 212 ... 659

Munday v Metropolitan Police District Receiver [1949] 1 All ER 337 ... 335

Murgatroyd v Chief Constable of West Yorkshire Police (2000) 8 November, CA (CD) . . . 152

Murphy, Re [1991] 5 NIJB 72, QBD . . . 317

Murphy v Oxford (1988) 15 February 1988, DC . . . 141

Murray v Express Newspapers plc [2008] EWCA Civ 446, [2008] NLJR 706, (2008) *Times*, 12 May, [2008] All ER (D) 70, Court of Appeal . . . **559–61**

Murray v UK (1994) 19 EHRR 193 . . . 206

Murray v United Kingdom (1996) 22 EHRR 29 . . . 26, 34, 135, 237, 245–46

Myles v DPP [2004] 2 All ER 902 . . . 234

Nachova v Bulgaria (2005) 42 EHRR 43 . . . 80, **866–68**

Nagarajan v London Regional Transport [2000] 1 AC 501 . . . 958

National Union of Belgian Police v Belgium (1975) 1 EHRR 578 . . . 875

Nationwide News Pty. Ltd v Wills (1992) 177 CLR 1, HCA . . . 741–42

Nebraska Press Association v Stuart 427 US 539 (1976) . . . 715

Needham v DPP 11 March 1994, unreported . . . 302

Nelder v DPP (1998) *Times*, 11 June. DC . . . 372

New York Times v Sullivan (1964) 376 US 254 . . . 620

New York Times v United States 403 US 713 (1971) . . . 820

Newbury . . . 752

News Group Newspapers Ltd v Society of Graphical and Allied Trades '82 (No. 2) [1987] ICR 181 . . . 293

Niemietz v Germany App. No. 13710/88; (1992) 16 EHRR 97, European Court of Human Rights . . . 184, 504, 510

Norfolk CC v Webster [2007] 2 FLR 415 . . . 706

Norwich Pharmacal Co v Customs and Excise Comrs [1974] AC 133 . . . 759

Norwood v Director of Public Prosecutions [2002] EWHC 1564 (Admin) . . . 342–46

Nothman v London Borough of Barnet [1977] IRLR 489 . . . 945

Nottingham City Council v Z [2001] EWCA Civ 1248 . . . 293

Nye v United States 313 US 33 (1941) . . . 686

O, Re [1991] 2 QB 520, CA . . . 14

Oberschlick v Austria (1991) 19 EHRR 389 . . . 620

Observer and Guardian v 1991 UK (Series A No. 216) . . . 805, 816

O'Connor v Chief Constable of Norfolk (1997) 10 February, CA (Cr D) . . . 151

Odewale v DPP (2000) 28 November, DC . . . 192

Office of Government Commerce v Information Comr [2008] EWHC 774 (Admin) . . . 850–51, 853

O'Halloran v United Kingdom (2007) App. No. 15809/02 . . . 56

O'Hara v Chief Constable of the Royal Ulster Constabulary [1997] AC 286 . . . **143–47**

O'Hara v Chief Constable of the RUC (6 May 1994, unreported, CA (NI)) . . . 437

O'Hara v UK (2002) 34 EHRR 32 . . . 134, 148–49

O'Hara v United Kingdom, Judgment of 16 October 2001 . . . 435

O'Kelly v Harvey (1883) 14 LR Ir 105 . . . 384, 394

O'Loughlin v Chief Constable of Essex [1998] 3 WLR 374 . . . 90, 121, 154, 190, **193–96**

O'Moran v DPP, Whelan v DPP [1975] QB 864, DC . . . 288

Operation Dismantle [1985] 1 SCR 441 . . . 766

Oppenheimer v Cattermole [1976] AC 249, HL . . . 14

O'Reilly v Mackman [1983] 2 AC 237, HL . . . 11

Oscar v Chief Constable of the Royal Ulster Constabulary [1992] 9 NIJB 27 . . . 436–37

Osman v DPP (1999) 163 JP 725 . . . 121, 131, **164**

Osman v Ferguson [1993] 4 All ER 344, CA . . . 101

Osman v UK (1998) 29 EHRR 245 . . . 80, 83

Osman v United Kingdom (1998) 29 EHRR 245 . . . 101

Ostler v Elliott [1980] Crim LR 584, DC . . . 130

Othman (Jordan) v Secretary of State for the Home Department [2008] EWCA Civ 290 . . . 474

Ouellet, Re (1976) 67 DLR (3d) 73 . . . 741–42

PG and JH v UK [2002] Crim LR 308, ECtHR . . . 235, 593

Pakelli v FRG (1983) 6 EHRR 1 . . . 236

Pankhurst v Jarvis (1910) 22 Cox CC 228, DC . . . 302

Papworth v Coventry [1967] 1 WLR 663, DC . . . 302

Parkin v Norman [1983] QB 92 . . . 341

Parkin v Norman; Valentine v Lilley [1983] QB 92 . . . 353–54

Parry v DPP [2004] EWHC 3112 (Admin) . . . 356

Paul v National Probation Service [2004] IRLR 190 . . . 988

Paulik v Slovakia (2008) 46 EHRR 10 . . . 861, 864

Peach Grey & Co (a 1 rm) v Sommers [1995] 2 All ER 513 . . . 706

Peacock v London Weekend Television (1985) 150 JP 71, CA . . . 705, 762

Pearce v Governing Body of Mayfield School [2003] ICR 937 . . . 928, 930, 964–65

Peck v United Kingdom (2003) 36 EHRR 41 . . . 572, 578

Peck v United Kingdom, Application No. 44647/98; (2003) 36 EHRR 719 . . . 507–09, 578

Pedro v Diss [1981] 2 All ER 59, DC . . . 142

Peers v Greece (2002) 33 EHRR 51 . . . 81

Pendragon v UK [1999] EHRLR 223 . . . 291

Pennekamp v Florida 328 US 331 (1946) . . . 743

Percy v DPP [2001] EWHC Admin 1125 . . . 349

Percy v Hall [1997] QB 924 . . . 376

Perera v The Civil Service Commission [1983] ICR 428 . . . 968

Perharic v Hennessey [1997] CLY 4859 . . . 364

Perry v United Kingdom (2004) 39 EHRR 3 . . . 578, 593

Petrovic v Austria (1998) 33 EHRR 307 . . . 858, 875

Phytopharm plc v Avery [2004] EWHC 503 . . . 365

Pickering v Liverpool Daily Post and Echo Newspapers Ltd [1991] 2 AC 370 . . . 706, 711

Piddington v Bates [1961] 1 WLR 162 . . . 393–94

Plange v Chief Constable of South Humberside Police (1992) *Times*, 23 March, CA . . . 206

Poku v DPP [1993] Crim LR 705 . . . 349

Police v Reid [1987] Crim. L.R. 702 . . . 318

Pollard v Chief Constable of West Yorkshire (1998) 28 April, CA (Cr D) . . . 152

Pollard v Chief Constable of West Yorkshire [1999] PIQR 219 . . . 104

Pollard v Photographic Co (1889) 40 Ch D 345 . . . 568

Polly Peck International plc v Nadir (1991) *Times*,11 November . . . 706

Porter v Magill [2002] 2 AC 357 . . . 753

Porter v Metropolitan Police Comr (1999) 20 November, Court of Appeal . . . 121–23

Post Office v Jones [2001] ICR 805 (CA) . . . 983, 988

Pratt v DPP [2001] EWHC Admin 483 . . . 363

Pretty v UK (2002) 35 EHRR 1 . . . 80

Pretty v United Kingdom Application No. 2346/02 . . . 505–06

Price v Civil Service Commission [1978] ICR 27 . . . 968

Price v UK (2001) 34 EHRR 1285 . . . 81

Prince Albert v Strange (1849) 1 Mac and G 25, 1 H & TW 1, Court of Chancery . . . 539–541

Prouse v DPP (1999) All ER (D) 748 . . . 262

Pullar v United Kingdom (1996) 22 EHRR 391 . . . 687

Qadus v Henry Robinson (Ironfounders) Ltd . . . 900

Quinn v France (1995) 21 EHRR 529 . . . 84

Quinn v Williams Furniture Ltd [1981] ICR 328 . . . 904

R v A (No. 2) [2002] 1 AC 45 . . . 628

R v A [2001] UKHL 25 . . . 42, 50, 63

R v Absolam (1988) 88 CR App Rep 332, CA (Cr D) . . . 266–67

R v Abu Hamza [2006] EWCA Crim 2918 . . . 412, 714

R v Adams [1978] 5 NIJB . . . 423

R v Alladice (1988) 87 Cr App Rep 380, CA (Cr D) . . . 266

R v Almon (1765) Wilm 243 . . . 684

R v Anderson [1972] 1 QB 304, CA (Cr D) . . . 664–65, 676

R v Anderson [1993] Crim LR 447, CA (Cr D) . . . 266–67

R v Aquarius (1974) 59 Cr App Rep 165 . . . 749

R v Argent [1997] 2 Cr App R 27 . . . 248

R v Arnold [2008] EWCA Civ 705 . . . 356

R v Arundel Justices, ex p Westminster Press Ltd [1985] 2 All ER 390, DC . . . 709

R v Atkinson (1988) 10 Cr App Rep (S) 470, CA (Cr D) . . . 399

R v Atkinson [1976] Crim LR 307 . . . 191

R v Attorney–General of England and Wales [2003] UKPC 22 . . . 822

R v B [2006] EWCA Crim 2692 . . . 713

R v Badham [1997] Crim LR 202 (Wood Green Crown Court). . . . 195, 209

R v Bailey [1995] 2 Cr App R 262, CA . . . 262

R v Barber [2001] EWCA Crim 838 . . . 341

R v Barclay (Carole Andrea) (1997) 161 JP . . . 752

R v Barker (1996) 13 June, CA (Cr D), unreported . . . 190

R v Barot [2007] EWCA Crim 1119 . . . 412

R v Barton [1976] Crim LR 514 . . . 659

R v Beaconsfield Justices, ex p Westminster Press Ltd (1994) 158 JP 1055, QBD . . . 713

R v Beaverbrook Newspapers Ltd [1962] NI 15, QBD (NI) . . . 715

R v Bebbington [2005] EWCA Crim 2395 . . . 369

R v Beck, ex p Daily Telegraph plc [1993] 2 All ER 177 . . . 713

R v Bentley [1999] Crim LR 330, CA . . . 257

R v Betts and Hall [2001] 2 Cr App R 16 . . . 251

R v Beycan [1990] Crim LR 185, CA (Cr D) . . . 266

R v Billericay Justices and Dobbyn, ex p Frank Harris (Coaches) Ltd [1991] Crim LR 472. . . . 184

R v Bingham [1973] QB 870 . . . 781

R v Birmingham City Council, ex p Equal Opportunities Commission [1989] AC 1155 . . . 899, 950, 965

R v Blackford [2001] EWCA Civ 1479, CA (Cr D) . . . 240

R v Blackwood [2002] EWCA Crim 3102 . . . 336

R v Bolam, ex p Haigh (1949) 93 Sol Jo 220 . . . 697

R v Border Television Ltd, ex p A–G . . . 697

R v Bow St Metropolitan Stipendiary Magistrate, ex p Noncyp Ltd . . . 677

R v Bow Street Magistrates Court, ex p Proulx [2001] 1 All ER 57, DC . . . 274

R v Bow Street Magistrates' Court, ex p Mirror Group Newspapers Ltd [1992] COD 15 . . . 735

R v Bowden [1999] 2 Cr App R 176 . . . 246, 252

R v Bowden [2000] 2 All ER 418, CA (Cr D) . . . 680

R v Bowers (1997) 163 JP 33 . . . 248, 252

R v Braithwaite (1991) Times, 9 December, CA (Cr D) . . . 266

R v Brentwood Borough Council, ex p Peck [1998] EMLR 697 . . . 508

R v Bresa [2004] 1 All ER 1025 . . . 252

R v Bridger [2006] EWCA Crim 3169 . . . 357

R v Bristol [2007] All ER (D) 47 . . . 164

R v Broadcasting Complaints Commission, ex p Granada Television Ltd (1993) Times, 31 May, QBD . . . 575

R v Broadcasting Standards Commission, ex p BBC [2000] EMLR 587, CA . . . 575

R v Brogan [2004] NICC 27, Crown Court . . . 425

R v Bromell [1996] TLR 67 . . . 752

R v Brown (1976) 64 Cr App Rep 231 . . . 206

R v Brown [1996] 1 All ER 545 . . . 527

R v Bryce [1992] 4 All ER 567, CA (Cr D) . . . 267

R v Bulgin, ex p BBC (1977) Times, 14 July . . . 697

R v Butler (1992) 89 DLR 449 . . . 654

R v Butt [1999] Crim LR 414, CA (Cr D) . . . 238

R v Caird (1970) 54 Cr App Rep 499 . . . 276

R v Calder and Boyars Ltd [1969] 1 QB 151, CA (Cr D) . . . 662–63, 668, 670

R v Callinan (1973) Times, 20 January, C Cr Ct . . . 291

R v Canale [1990] 2 All ER 187, CA (Cr D) . . . 267

R v Cannings (2004) EWCA Crim 1 . . . 239

R v Central Criminal Court, ex p AJD Holdings Ltd [1992] Crim LR 669 . . . 186

R v Central Criminal Court, ex p Boulding [1984] 1 All ER 766 DC . . . 398

R v Central Criminal Court, ex p Bright [2001] 2 All ER 244 . . . 186

R v Central Criminal Court, ex p Brown (1992) Times, 7 September, DC . . . 185

R v Central Criminal Court, ex p Crook (1984) Times, 8 November, DC . . . 709

R v Central Criminal Court, ex p Rushbridger, Alton and Bright [2001] 2 All E R 244 . . . 792

R v Central Criminal Court, ex p W, B and C [2001] 1 Cr App Rep 7 . . . 711

R v Central Independent Television plc [1994] Fam 192 . . . 563, 568

R v Chalkey and Jeffries [1998] QB 848, CA . . . 205, 207, 257

R v Charnley (1937) 81 Sol Jo 108 . . . 288

R v Chee Kew Ong [2001] 1 Cr App R (S) 117 . . . 360

R v Chenia [2003] 2 Cr App R 83 . . . 248

R v Chief Constable of Devon and Cornwall, ex p CEGB [1982] QB 458 . . . 97

R v Chief Constable of Kent, ex p Kent Police Federation [2000] Crim LR 854 . . . 226

R v Chief Constable of Lancashire, ex p Parker [1993] QB 577 . . . 192

R v Chief Constable of South Yorkshire Police, ex p LS . . . 239

R v Chief Constable of South Yorkshire Police, ex p Marper [2004] UKHL 39 . . . 239

R v Chief Constable of Sussex, ex p Independent Traders Ferry Ltd [1998] 3 WLR 1260, HL . . . 99

R v Chief Constable of Warwickshire, ex p Fitzpatrick [1999] 1 All ER 65 . . . 192

R v Chief Immigration Officer, Heathrow Airport, ex p Salamat Bibi [1976] 1 WLR 979 . . . 36

R v Chief Registrar of Friendly Societies, ex p New Cross Building Society [1984] QB 227 . . . 706

R v Christou and Wright [1992] QB 979 . . . **269–71**

R v Chung (1990) 92 Cr App Rep 314, CA (Cr D) . . . 266

R v Clark (No. 2) [1964] 2 QB 315 . . . 293–94

R v Clarke, ex p Crippen (1910) 103 LT 636 . . . 705, 715

R v Clayton and Halsey [1963] 1 QB 163, CCA . . . 656

R v Clegg [2000] NI 305 . . . 498, 500

R v Clement (1821) 4 B & Ald 218 . . . 711

R v Clerkenwell Justices, ex p Trachtenberg [1993] COD 93 . . . 712

R v Clerkenwell Metropolitan Stipendiary Magistrate, ex p Hooper [1998] 1 WLR 800 . . . 399

R v Clerkenwell Metropolitan Stipendiary Magistrate, ex p Telegraph plc [1993] QB 462 . . . 712

R v Colahan [2001] EWCA Crim 1251 . . . 361, 364

R v Commission for Racial Equality, ex p Cottrell & Rothon [1980] IRLR 279 . . . 904

R v Comr of the Metropolitan Police, ex p Small, 27 August 1998 . . . 326

R v Comrs of English Heritage, ex p Chappell, 19 June 1986, unreported, CA . . . 305

R v Condron and Condron [1997] 1 Cr App R 185 . . . 248

R v Connor (2000) 13 March, CA (Cr D) . . . 337

R v Constanza [1997] 2 Cr App R 492 . . . 119

R v Conway [1994] Crim LR 838, CA (Cr D) . . . 262

R v Cox (1992) 96 CR App Rep 464, CA (Cr D) . . . 267

R v Crampton (1990) 92 Cr App Rep 369 at 372 . . . 261

R v Crown Court at Bristol, ex p Bristol Press and Picture Agency Ltd (1986) 85 Cr App Rep 190 . . . 186

R v Crown Court at CardiB , ex p Kellam (1993) 16 BMLR 76, DC . . . 187

R v Crown Court at Inner London Sessions, ex p Baines & Baines [1988] QB 579 . . . 186–87

R v Crown Court at Leicester, ex p DPP [1987] 1 WLR 1371 . . . 186

R v Crown Court at Manchester, ex p H [2000] 2 All ER 166 . . . 711

R v Crown Court at Manchester, ex p Taylor [1988] 1 WLR 705 . . . 186

R v Crown Court at Nottingham, ex p Brace (1989) 154 JP 161, CA . . . 399

R v Cullinane [2007] EWCA Crim 2682 . . . 751

R v Cunninghame Graham and Burns (1888) 16 Cox CC 420 . . . 300, 336

R v D [2000] Crim LR 178 . . . 252

R v Daily Herald, ex p Bishop of Norwich [1932] 2 KB 402 . . . 705

R v Daily Mail, ex p Farnsworth [1921] 2 KB 733 . . . 705

R v Daniel [1998] 2 Cr App R 373, CA . . . 249, 252

R v Davidson (1981, unreported) . . . 497

R v Davison [1992] Crim LR 31 . . . 337

R v DDP, ex p Kebilene [2000] 2 AC 326 at 373, HL . . . 50

R v Department of Health, ex p Source Informatics Ltd [2000] 1 All ER 786 at 790 CA . . . 544

R v Desmond [1998] Crim LR 659, CA . . . 252

R v Director of GCHQ, ex p Hodges (1988) Times, 26 July . . . 765, 830

R v Dixon [1993] Crim LR 579, CA (Cr D) . . . 337

R v Dodds [2002] EWCA Crim 1328 . . . 752

R v Doldur [2000] Crim LR 178, CA . . . 252

R v Doolan [1988] Crim LR 747, CA (Cr D) . . . 262

R v Dover Justices, ex p Dover District Council (1991) 156 JP 433 . . . 710

R v DPP [2001] EWHC Admin 1 . . . 363

R v DPP, ex p Duckenfield [2000] 1 WLR 55 . . . 105

R v DPP, ex p Kebilene [2000] 2 AC 326 at 367, HL . . . 51, 56

R v DPP, ex p Moseley (1999) 9 June, DC . . . 364

R v Duckenfield 24 July 2000 . . . 105

R v Duffy, ex p Nash [1960] 2 QB 188, DC . . . 716

R v Duffy; A–G v News Group Newspapers Ltd Unreported, 9 February 1996 . . . 716

R v Dunford (1990) 91 Cr App Rep 150, CA (Cr D) . . . 266

R v Dytham [1979] QB 722, CA (CrD) . . . 406

R v Ealing Justices, ex p Weafer (1982) 74 Cr App Rep 204, DC . . . 706

R v Edwards, ex p Welsh Church Temporalities Comrs (1933) 49 TLR 383 . . . 705

R v Emmerson (1990) 92 Cr App Rep 284, CA (Cr D) . . . 261

R v Evans [2004] EWCA Crim 3102, (2005) 169JP 129 . . . 366

R v Evening Standard Co Ltd [1954] 1 QB 578, [1954] 1 All ER 1026, 1954] 2 WLR 861, Queen's Bench Divisional Court . . . 695, 717

R v Evening Standard Co Ltd, ex p A–G (1976) Times, 3 November, DC . . . 697

R v Evening Standard, ex p DPP (1924) 40 TLR 833 . . . 697

R v Evesham Justices, ex p McDonagh (1987) 88 Cr App Rep 28, DC . . . 710

R v F [2007] EWCA Crim, [2007] QB 960 . . . 452

R v F [2007] EWCA Crim 243, [2007] QB 960 . . . 416

R v Felixstowe Justices, ex p Leigh [1987] QB 582 . . . 707

R v Fell [1974] Crim LR 673, CA (CrD) . . . 291

R v Fellows and Arnold [1997] 2 All ER 548 . . . 666, 680

R v Fiak [2005] EWCA Crim 2381 . . . 203

R v Fleming and Robinson (1989) 153 JP 517, CA (Cr D) . . . 336

R v Forbes and Webb (1865) 10 Cox CC 362 . . . 127

R v Francis [2006] EWCA Civ 3323, [2007] 1 W.L.R. 1021 . . . 342

R v Francom [2000] Crim LR 1018 . . . 257

R v Fulling [1987] QB 426 [1987] 2 All ER 65 . . . 258

R v G [2003] UKHL 50, [2004] 1 AC 1034 . . . 486

R v G [2008] EWCA Crim 922 the CA . . . 451

R v Gibson [1990] 2 QB 619 . . . 658

R v Gill [2001] 1 Cr App R 11 . . . 247

R v Giscombe (1985) 79 Cr App Rep 79, CA (Cr D) . . . 753

R v Glanzer (1963) 38 DLR (2d) 402 . . . 741

R v Glaves [1993] Crim LR 685, CA (Cr D) . . . 262

R v Goldenberg (1988) 88 Cr App R 285 . . . 262

R v Goring (Jonathan) [1999] Crim LR 670 . . . 665

R v Goult (1982) 76 Cr App Rep 140 . . . 761

R v Governor of Brixton Prison [1969] 2 QB 222, DC . . . 103

R v Graham–Kerr [1988] 1 WLR 1098 . . . 679

R v Grant [2005] EWCA Crim 1089 . . . 236

R v Gray [1900] 2 QB 36, 69 LJQB 502, 82 LT 534, 64 JP 484, Queen's Bench Divisional Court . . . 737–38, 740

R v Gri2 n (1989) 88 G App Rep 63 . . . 749

R v Griffin (1989) 88 G App Rep 63. . . . 751

R v Griffiths, ex p A–G [1957] 2 QB 192, DC . . . 717

R v Guardian Newspapers Ltd [2001] EWCA Crim 1351 . . . 712

R v Guildhall Magistrates' Court, ex p Primlaks Holdings Co (Panama) Inc. (1990) 1 QB 261 . . . 184, 187

R v H [2004] UKHL 3 . . . 148

R v Halliday [1917] AC 270, HL . . . 14

R v Hallstrom, ex p W [1986] QB 1090, QBD . . . 14

R v Ham (1995) 36 BMLR 169, CA . . . 262

R v Harris [2006] EWCA Crim 3303 . . . 367

R v Hasan (2005) 2 Cr App R 22 . . . 258

R v Havant Justices, ex p Palmer (1985) 149 JP 609 . . . 750

R v Hayter [2006] UKHL 6 . . . 258

R v Heaton [1993] Crim LR 593, CA (Cr D) . . . 261

R v Hebron and Spencer (1989) 11 Cr App Rep (S) 226 . . . 336

R v Hegarty [1986] NI 343 . . . 495

R v Henley [2000] Crim LR 582 . . . 363

R v Henn and Darby [1981] AC 850. [1980] 2 All ER 166 . . . 677

R v Hertfordshire County Council, ex p Green Environmental Industries Ltd [2000] 2 WLR 373 . . . 247

R v Heslop [1996] Crim LR 730 . . . 225

R v Hill [1986] Crim LR 457 . . . 752

R v Hill and Hall (1988) 89 Cr App R 74, CA . . . 329

R v Hills [2001] 1 FLR 580, CA (CrD) . . . 363

R v Historic Buildings and Ancient Monuments Commission for England (English Heritage), exp Firsoff 19 June 1991, unreported . . . 305

R v HM Coroner for Coventry, ex p Marshall [2001] EWHC Admin 804 . . . 106

R v Hogan [1997] 1 Cr App R 464 . . . 242

R v Holliday [2004] EWCA Crim 1847 . . . 360

R v Horseferry Road Metropolitan Stipendiary Magistrate, ex p Siadatan [1991] 1 QB 260 . . . 337–40

R v Horsham Justices, ex p Farquharson [1982] QB 762, CA . . . 711

R v Houghton and Francoisy (1978) 68 Cr App Rep 197 . . . 127

R v Hove Justices, ex p Gibbons (1981) *Times*, 19 June . . . 709

R v Howell [1982] QB 416 . . . 384, 395

R v Huggins [2007] EWCA Civ 732 . . . 751–52

R v Hughes [1988] Crim LR 519, CA . . . 268

R v Hughes [1995] Crim LR 957 . . . 152, 234, 261

R v Hundal; Rv Dhaliwal [2004] EWCA Crim 389 . . . 425

R v Hunt [1992] Crim LR 582, CA (Cr D) . . . 267

R v Hussain [1997] Crim LR 754, CA . . . 248

R v Ibrahim [2008] EWCA Crim 880 . . . 411

R v Ilminster Justices, ex p Hamilton (1983) *Times*, 23 June, DC . . . 397

R v Ingrams, ex p Goldsmith [1977] Crim LR 40, DC . . . 717

R v Inspectorate of Pollution, ex p Greenpeace (No. 2) [1994] 4 All ER 329, QBD . . . 39

R v IRC, ex p Rossminster Ltd [1980] 1002, HL . . . 103, 106

R v Ireland [1997] AC 148 . . . 342

R v Ireland [1998] AC 147 . . . 119

R v Ismail [1990] Crim LR 109, CA (Cr D) . . . 262

R v Jackson (Kenneth) [1984] Crim LR 674 . . . 127

R v Jales [2007] EWCA Crim 393 . . . 752

R v Jan [2006] EWCA Crim 2314 . . . 360

R v Johnson [1997] 1 WLR 367 . . . 360

R v Jones (Margaret) [2006] UKHL 16, [2007] 1 AC 136 . . . 329, 374

R v Jones [1974] ICR 310, CA (Cr D) . . . 336

R v Jones [2008] EWCA Civ 781 . . . 356

R v Jordan and Tyndall [1963] Crim LR 124, CCA . . . 290

R v K (1983) 78 G App Rep 82 . . . 751–52

R v K [2008] EWCA Crim 185 . . . 451

R v Kavanagh [2008] EWCA Crim 855 . . . 360

R v Keenan [1990] 2 QB 54, CA (Cr D) . . . 267

R v Kelly and Donnelly [2001] 2 Cr App R (S) 73 . . . 357

R v Kerawalla [1991] Crim LR 451, CA (CR D) . . . 154, 234

R v Khan [1997] AC 558, HL . . . 527

R v Kingston upon 2 ames Crown Court, ex p Guarino [1986] Crim LR 325 . . . 399

R v Kirk [2006] EWCA Crim 725 . . . 676

R v Kirkless Metropolitan Borough Council, ex p C [1993] 2 FLR 187, CA . . . 13

R v Kneafsey (1973) Times, 23 October . . . 291

R v Knight [2004] 1 WLR 340 . . . 252

R v Kopyto (1987) DLR 213 . . . 741

R v Kray (1969) 53 Cr App Rep 412, CA (Cr
    D) . . . 711

R v L [1994] Crim LR 839, CA (Cr D) . . . 261

R v Lambert [2001] 3 All ER 577 609, HL . . . 33,
    36, 42, 50

R v Land (Michael) [1998] QB 65 . . . 680

R v Latif and Shazad [1996] 2 Cr App Rep
    92 . . . 272

R v Lefroy (1873) 8 QB 134 . . . 750

R v Legal Aid Board, ex p Kaim Todner [1998] 3
    All ER 541 . . . 710

R v Lemsatef [1977] 1 WLR 812 . . . 127

R v Lichniak [2002] UKHL 47, [2003] 1 AC
    903 . . . 84

R v Liddle, R v Hayes [1998] 3 All ER 816 . . . 366

R v Lincoln Crown Court, ex p Jude[1998] 1 WLR
    24 . . . 399

R v Lincolnshire County Council, ex p Atkinson
    (1996) 8 Admin LR 529 . . . 327

R v Logan [1974] Crim LR 609 . . . 749

R v Loizou [2006] EWCA Crim 1719 . . . 251

R v Londonderry Justice (1891) 28 LR Ir
    440 . . . 398

R v Longman [1988] 1 WLR 619 . . . 191

R v Looseley [2001] UKHL 53, HL . . . 273

R v Loosely [2001] UKHL 53 . . . 274

R v Lord Saville of Newdigate, ex p A [1999] 4 All
    ER 860 . . . 62

R v Lord Saville of Newdigate, ex p B (No. 2)
    [1999] 4 All ER 860, CA . . . 499

R v Lorenc [1988] NI 96 . . . 451

R v M [2007] EWCA Crim 298 . . . 451

R v McGarry [1999] 1 Cr App R 377, CA . . . 252

R v McGovern (1990) 92 Cr App Rep 228, CA
    (Cr D) . . . 262

R v McLoughlin 8 October 1993, unreported, CA
    (Cr D) (NI) . . . 451

R v MacNaughton [1975] NI 203;R v Bohan [1979]
    5 NIJB, Belfast Crown Court . . . 495

R v Mahroof (1988) 88 Cr App Rep 317, CA (Cr
    D) . . . 336

R v Malik [1968] 1 All ER 582n . . . 697

R v Malvern Justices, ex p Evans [1988] QB 553,
    DC . . . 710

R v Manchester Crown Court, ex p R [1999] 1
    WLR 832, CA (Cr D) . . . 187

R v Marsden (1868) LR 1 CCR 131 . . . 405

R v Martin (1848) 5 Cox CC 356 . . . 761

R v Martin Secker Warburg [1954] 2 All ER
    683 . . . 656

R v Marylebone Magistrates' Court & MPC, ex p
    Amdrell Ltd trading as Get Stuffed (1998) 162
    JP 719, DC . . . 191

R v Mason [1988] 1 WLR 139 . . . 271

R v Matrix (Billy) [1997] Crim LR 901 . . . 680

R v Maxwell and Clanchy (1909) 2 Cr App R 26,
    CCA . . . 127

R v Menard [1995] 1 Cr App Rep 306, CA (Cr
    D) . . . 241

R v Metropolitan Police Commissioner, ex p
    Blackburn (No. 2) [1968] 2 QB 150, [1968]
    2 All ER 319, [1968] 2 WLR 1204, Court of
    Appeal . . . 738–40

R v Metropolitan Police Comr, ex p Blackburn
    (No. 3) [1973] QB 241 . . . 97, 657, 668

R v Metropolitan Police Comr, ex p Blackburn
    [1968] 2 QB 118 . . . 96

R v Miah [2001] EWCA Crim 228 . . . 361

R v Middlesex CC, ex p Khan (1997) 161 JP 240,
    DC . . . 399

R v Milford [2000] JPL 943, CA (Cr D) . . .
    248

R v Miller [1998] Crim LR 209, CA . . . 154, 267

R v Ministry of Defence, ex p Smith [1996] QB
    517 . . . 765

R v Mirza [2004] 1 AC 1118 . . . 745

R v Montague and Beckles [1999] Crim LR
    148 . . . 252

R v Moore (Peter Oliver Stace) (unreported, 12
    September 2000) . . . 752

R v Moran (1985) 81 G App Rep 51 . . . 752

R v Morpeth Ward Justices, ex p Ward). (1992) 95
    Cr App Rep 215, DC . . . 398

R v Morris [2005] EWCA Crim 609 . . . 336

R v Morrison [2008] EWCA Civ 22 . . . 367

R v Mould (David Frederick) (6 November 2000,
    unreported) . . . 680

R v Mountford [1999] Crim LR 575 . . . 252

R v Mulvaney [1982] Crim LR 462, DC . . . 761

R v Neil [1994] Crim LR 441, CA (Cr D) . . . 262

R v Nelson and Rose [1998] 2 Cr App R 399, CA
    (Cr D) . . . 262, 267

R v New Statesman Editor, ex p DPP (1928) 44
    TLR 301 . . . 740, 742

R v Newbury Justices, ex p Du Pont (1983) 148 JP
    248 . . . 752

R v Newcastle Chronicle and Journal Ltd, ex p
    A–G (1978) 68 Cr App Rep 375, DC . . . 697

R v News Group Newspapers Ltd (1999) Times, 21
    May . . . 713

R v Nickolson [1999] Crim LR 61 (CA) . . . 246

R v Nicol (1996) 160 JP 155 . . . 393

R v North West Lancashire Health Authority, ex p
    A [2000] 1 WLR 977 . . . 83

R v O'Loughlin and McLaughlin (1987) 85 Cr App Rep 157 at 163 . . . 268

R v O'Sullivan (1994) *Times*, 3 May . . . 662–63

R v Oakes [1959] 2 QB 350 . . . 781

R v Odham's Press Ltd, ex p A–G [1957] 1 QB 73 . . . 697, 717

R v Oliphant [1992] Crim LR 40, CA (Cr D) . . . 266

R v Owen [1976] 3 All ER 239 . . . 761

R v P [2001] 2 All ER 58 . . . 268

R v Palmer (1991) Legal Action, September, p. 21 . . . 263

R v Palmer [1992] 3 All ER 289, CA (Crim Div) . . . 694

R v Paris, Abdullahi and Miller (1992) 97 Cr App Rep 99 ('The Cardiff Three') . . . 261

R v Park (1994) 99 Cr App Rep 270, CA (Cr D) . . . 241

R v Parker [1995] Crim LR 233, CA . . . 261

R v Parris (1988) 89 Cr App Rep 68, CA (Cr D) . . . 266

R v Parrott (1913) 8 Cr App Rep 186, CCA . . . 781

R v Patel [2004] EWCA Crim 3284 . . . 363

R v Patrascu [2004] EWCA Crim 2417, [2004] 4 All ER 1066 . . . 762

R v Petkar [2004] 1 Cr App R 22 . . . 252

R v Phillips (1983) 78 Cr App Rep 88 . . . 752

R v Ponting . . . 628

R v Porter [2006] EWCA Crim 560. . . . 680

R v Poulson [1974] Crim LR 141 . . . 711

R v Powell (1993) 98 Cr App R 224 . . . 749

R v Prebble (1858) 1 F and F 325 . . . 120–21

R v Prime (1983) 5 Cr App Rep (S) 127 . . . 786

R v Prince [1981] Crim LR 638 Ware v Matthews (unreported) . . . 142

R v Quresh [2008] EWCA Crim 1054 . . . 451

R v R [1994] 1 WLR 758, CA (Cr D) . . . 187

R v RC [2005] SCC 61 . . . 239

R v Rahman; R v Mohammed [2008] EWCA Civ 1465 . . . 486

R v Rampling [1987] Crim LR 823 (CA) . . . 242

R v Reading Justices, Chief Constable of Avon and Somerset and Intervention Board for Agricultural Produce, ex p South West Meat Ltd [1992] Crim LR 672 . . . 191

R v Reigate Justices, ex p Argus Newspapers and Larcombe (1983) 147 JP 385, DC . . . 706

R v Rhuddlan Justices, ex p HTV Ltd [1986] Crim LR 329 . . . 712

R v Rimmington; R v Goldstein [2005] UKHL 63 . . . 360

R v Robinson [1984] 4 NIJB; R v Montgomery (1984, unreported) . . . 497

R v Robinson [1993] Crim LR 581, CA (Cr D) . . . 337

R v Roble [1997] Crim LR 449, CA . . . 248, 252

R v Rosenberg [2006] Crim LR 540 . . . 594

R v Rothwell and Barton [1993] Crim LR 662, CA (Cr D) . . . 336

R v Rowe [2007] EWCA Crim 635, [2007] QB 975 . . . 451

R v Roxburgh (1871) 12 Cox CC 8 . . . 120

R v Runting (1988) 89 Cr App Rep 243 . . . 761–62

R v S [1995] 2 Cr App Rep 347 . . . 712

R v S [2008] EWCA Crim 138 . . . 749

R v Samuel [1988] QB 615 . . . 208, 236–37, 264–66

R v Sanchez (1996) JP 321, [1996] Crim LR 572, CA . . . 337

R v Sanchez and Garcia, unreported, 5 July 1984 . . . 780

R v Sang [1980] AC 402 . . . 257

R v Saunders [2000] 1 Cr App R 458 . . . 357

R v Savundranayagan [1968] 3 All ER 439n . . . 715

R v Schot (Bonnie Belinda) . . . 752

R v Schulze and Schulze (1986) 8 Cr App Rep (S) 463 . . . 786

R v Secretary of State for Foreign and Commonwealth Affairs, ex p Everett [1989] QB 811, CA . . . 15

R v Secretary of State for the Environment, ex p Hammersmith and Fulham Borough Council [1990] 3 All ER 589, HL . . . 17

R v Secretary of State for the Home Department, ex p Bentley [1994] QB 349, CA . . . 15

R v Secretary of State for the Home Department, ex p Brind [1991] 2 WLR 588 . . . 646

R v Secretary of State for the Home Department, ex p Chahal [1995] 1 All ER 658 . . . 765

R v Secretary of State for the Home Department, ex p Fire Brigades Union [1995] 1 All ER 888, CA . . . 15

R v Secretary of State for The Home Department, ex p Manelfi 25 October 1996, unreported . . . 765

R v Secretary of State for the Home Department, ex p Muboyayi [1992] QB 244, CA . . . 12

R v Secretary of State for the Home Department, ex p Northumbria Police Authority [1989] QB 26 . . . 283, 407

R v Secretary of State for the Home Department, ex p Northumbria Police Authority [1988] 1 All ER 556 . . . 844

R v Secretary of State for the Home Department, ex p Ruddock [1987] 1 WLR 482 . . . 765, 831

R v Secretary of State for Transport, ex p de Rothschild [1989] 1 All ER 933, CA . . . 14

R v Security Service Tribunal, ex p Clarke Unreported, 20 May 1998 . . . 845

R v Security Service Tribunal, ex p Hewitt Unreported, 14 February 1992 . . . 844

R v Selby Justices, ex p Frame [1992] QB 72 . . . 751, 752

R v Sherwood, ex p Telegraph plc (2001) *Times*, 12 June . . . 713

R v Singleton [1995] 1 Cr App Rep 431, CA (Cr D) (dental records) . . . 186

R v Skirving [1985] QB 819, CA . . . 663

R v Smethurst (2002) 1 Cr Ap R 6 . . . 680

R v Smith, R v Jayson [2003] 1 Cr App Rep 212 . . . 680

R v Smith; R v Mercieca [2005] UKHL 12, [2005] 2 All ER 29 . . . 745

R v Smurthwaite and Gill [1994] 1 All ER 898 . . . 258, 274

R v Smurthwaite, R v Gill [1994] 1 All ER 898 . . . 271

R v Socialist Worker Printers and Publishers Ltd, ex p A–G [1975] QB 637, DC . . . 707, 709

R v Solicitor–General, ex p Taylor (1995) *Times*, 14 August . . . 714

R v South Molton Justices, ex p Ankerson (1989) 90 Cr App Rep 158 . . . 399

R v South Western Magistrates' Court, ex p Heslop 18 May 1994, unreported . . . 680

R v Stafforce Personnel Ltd (unreported, 24 November 2000) . . . 752

R v Stagg (1994) CCC, unreported, 14 September . . . 274

R v Stanley [1965] 1 All ER 1035 . . . 680

R v Stanley [1965] 2 QB 327, CCA . . . 676

R v Stone [2001] Crim LR 465 . . . 714

R v Surayzi [1998] EWCA Crim 3460 . . . 361

R v T (Child Pornography) (1999) 163 JP 349 . . . 680

R v Tamworth Justices, ex p Walsh (1994) *Times*, 3 March . . . 750

R v Taylor (Alan) (1994) *Times*, 4 February 1994, CA . . . 666, 709

R v Taylor and Taylor (1993) 98 Cr App R 361, CA (Cr D) . . . 714

R v Taylor, Ward and Hawthorne (1937) 81 Sol Jo 509 . . . 288

R v Thain [1985] NI 457 . . . 497

R v Thames Valley University Students Union Ex p Ogilvy [1997] CLJ. 2149 . . . 308

R v Thomson Newspapers, ex p A–G [1968] 1 All ER 268 . . . 697

R v Timmis [1976] Crim LR 129 . . . 105

R v Togher [2001] 3 All ER 463, CA . . . 64, 268

R v Tower Bridge Magistrates' Court, ex p Osborne . . . 710

R v Tsouli [2007] EWCA Crim 3300 . . . 412

R v Turner [2004] 1 All ER 1025 . . . 252

R v Tyler (1993) 96 Cr App Rep 332, CA (Cr D) . . . 334

R v Tyne Tees Television (1997) *Times*, 20 October, CA (Cr D) . . . 711

R v University College London, ex p Urtsula Rincker [1995] ELR 213 . . . 308

R v University of Liverpool, ex p Caesar–Gordon [1991] 1 QB 124 . . . 308

R v Uxbridge Justices, ex p David Webb [1994] CMLR 288 DC . . . 677

R v Va Kun Hau [1990] Crim LR 518, CA (Cr D) . . . 341

R v Video Appeals Committee of the British Board of Film Classification, ex p British Board of Film Classification [2000] COD 239 . . . 637

R v Vincent (1839) 9 C&P 91 . . . 336

R v Voisin [1918] 1 KB 531 . . . 263

R v Waddon (Graham Lester Ian) (unreported, 6 April 2000) . . . 666

R v Walker (1854) Dears CC 358 . . . 405

R v Walker [1998] Crim LR 211 . . . 262

R v Walsh (1989) 91 Cr App Rep 161 at 163, CA (Cr D) . . . 237, 266, 267

R v Ward (1994) 98 Cr App R 337, CA . . . 154

R v Warwickshall (1783) 1 Leach 263 . . . 263

R v Wass (2000) 11 May, CA (Cr D) . . . 363

R v Waterfield and Lynn [1964] 1 QB 164 . . . 121

R v Watford Magistrates' Court, ex p Lenman [1993] Crim LR 388 [1992] COD 474, DC . . . 709

R v Wealden District Council, ex p Wales . . . 327

R v Webber [2004] UKHL 1. . . . 248

R v Weekes (1992) 97 Cr App Rep 222, CA (Cr D) . . . 267

R v Westminster City Council, ex p Castelli (1995) 30 BMLR 123 . . . 710

R v White (Anthony) [2001] EWCA Crim 216 [2001] 1 WLR 1352 . . . 356

R v Wicks [1998] AC 92 . . . 299

R v Wishart [2005] 1 All ER 705 . . . 251

R v Wood (1937) 81 Sol Jo 108 . . . 288

R v Woods [2002] EWHC 85 (Admin) . . . 356

R v Worton (1989) 154 JP 201, CA (Cr D) . . . 336

R v Wright (1937) 81 Sol Jo 509 . . . 288

R v Wright [1994] Crim LR 55, CA (Cr D) . . . 195

R v Wyres (1956) 2 Russell on Crime (12th edn, 1964) 1397 . . . 568

R v Z [2005] UKHL 22, [2005] 2 AC 467 . . . 709

R v Z (Attorney General for Northern Ireland's Reference) [2005] UKHL 35 . . . 424

R v Zafar [2008] EWCA Crim 184 . . . 451

R (Al Rawi) v Secretary of State for Foreign and Commonwealth Affairs, R (E) v Governing Body of the Jews Free School and Couronnes v Crawley Borough Council [2006] EWCA Civ 1279, [2007] 2 WLR 1219 (CA); [2008] EWHC 1535 & 1536 (Admin), [2008] All ER (D) 54 (Jul) and [2007] EWCA Civ 1086, [2007] All ER (D) 50 (Nov) ... 891, 895, 923, 937–42, 957

R (Alconbury Developments Ltd) v Secretary of State for the Environment, Transport and the Regions [2001] 2 WLR 1389 at 1399, HL ... 35

R (Al–Skeini) v Ministry of Defence [2007] UKHL 26 ... 39

R (Al–Skeini) v Secretary of State for Defence [2007] UKHL 26, [2008] 1 AC 153 ... 35

R (a minor) (contempt: sentence), Re [1994] 2 All ER 144 ... 694

R (Baiai) v Secretary of State for the Home Department [2007] EWCA Civ 478 ... 42

R (Baker) v Secretary of State for Communities & Local Government [2008] EWCA Civ 141 ... 894, 896

R (BAPIO Action Ltd and Yousaf) v Secretary of State for the Home Department and Secretary of State for Health [2007] EWCA Civ 1139 ... 895

R (Begum) v Head Teacher and Governors of Denbeigh ... 899

R (Carson) v Secretary of State for Work and Pensions [2006] 1 AC 173 ... 973

R (Chavda) v Harrow LBC [2007] EWHC 3064 (Admin) ... 896

R (Cliff) v Secretary of State for the Home Department [2007] 1 AC 484 ... 859–60

R (Couronne) v Crawley Borough Council [2007] EWCA Civ 1086, [2007] All ER (D) 50 (Nov) ... 886

R (E) v JFS ... 902, 925, 933

R (Gillan) v Comr of Police for the Metropolis [2006] 2 AC 307 ... 952

R (Greenfield) v Secretary of State for the Home Department [2005] UKHL 14 ... 40

R (Heather) v Leonard Cheshire Foundation [2001] EWHC Admin. 429 ... 38

R (KB) v Mental Health Review Tribunal [2003] 2 All ER 209 ... 40

R (Mahmood) v Secretary of State for the Home Department [2001] 1 WLR 840 ... 58

R (Manning and Melbourne) v DPP [2000] EWHC Admin 342 ... 106

R (Mohammed) v Secretary of State for Defence [2007] All ER (D) 09 (CA) ... 891

R (Mohammed) v Secretary of State for Defence [2007] EWCA Civ 1023 ... 923

R (on application of Pelling) v Bow County Court [2001] UKHRR 165 ... 707

R (on the application of Abbasi) v Secretary of State for Foreign and Commonwealth Affairs [2002] EWCA Civ 15 ... 98, [2003] UKHRR 76 ... 474

R (on the application of Al Rawi) v Secretary of State for Foreign and Commonwealth Affairs [2006] EWCA Civ 1279, [2008] QB 289 ... 474

R (on the application of Amin) v Secretary of State for the Home Department [2003] UKHL 51, [2004] 1 AC 653 ... 81

R (on the application of Animal Defenders International) v Secretary of State For Culture, Media and Sport [2008] UKHL 15 ... 35

R (On The Application of Animal Defenders International) v Secretary of State For Culture, Media and Sport ... 645

R (on the application of Animal Defenders International) v Secretary of State for Culture, Media and Sport [2008] UKHL 15, [2008] 3 All ER 193, House of Lords ... 649–52

R (on the application of Bagdanavicius) v Secretary of State for the Home Department [2005] UKHL 38, [2005] 2 AC 668 ... 83

R (on the application of Brehony) v Chief Constable of Greater Manchester Police [2005] EWHC 640 ... 316, 318

R (on the application of Da Silva) v DPP [2006] EWHC 3204 (Admin) ... 501

R (on the application of Daltry) v Selby Magistrates' Court (2000) Times ... 751

R (on the application of Daly) v Secretary of State for the Home Department [2001] UKHL 26 ... 59

R (on the application of DPP) v Glendinning [2005] EWHC Admin 2333 ... 129

R (on the application of DPP) v Glendinning [2005] EWHC Admin 2333 ... 134

R (on the application of Elias) v Secretary of State for Defence [2005] EWHC (Admin) ... 891, 895

R (on the application of Fuller) v Chief Constable of Dorset Police [2001] EWHC Admin 1053 ... 326, 328

R (on the application of G) v Chief Constable of West Yorkshire Police [2008] EWCA Civ 28 ... 226

R (on the application of Gentle) v Prime Minister [2006] EWCA Civ 1689 ... 766

R (on the application of Giles) v Parole Board [2003] UKHL 42, [2004] 1 AC 1 ... 85

R (on the application of Gillan) v Metropolitan Police Comr [2006] 4 All ER 1041 ... 163

R (on the application of Gillan) v Comr of Police of the Metropolis [2006] UKHL 12 ... 440–50, 471

R (on the application of Green) v City of Westminster Magistrates' Court [2007] EWHC 2785 (Admin) ... 674

R (on the application of Harlow–Hayes) v Cambridge Crown Court [2008] EWHC 1023 (Admin) . . . 399

R (on the application of Haw) v Secretary of State for the Home Department [2006] EWCA Civ 532 . . . 304

R (on the application of Hurst) v Comr of Police for the Metropolis [2007] UKHL 13 . . . 81

R (on the application of International Transport Roth GmbH) v Secretary of State for the Home Department [2003] QB 728 . . . 58

R (on the application of Laporte) v Chief Constable of Gloucestershire [2007] 2 AC 105 . . . 330

R (on the application of Laporte) v Chief Constable of Gloucestershire [2006] UKHL 55, [2007] 2 AC 105 . . . 376

R (on the application of Limbuela) v Secretary of State for the Home Department [2005] UKHL 66, [2006] HRLR 4 . . . 83

R (on the application of Lonergan) v Lewes Crown Court [2005] EWHC 457 (Admin) . . . 368

R (on the application of Malik) v Manchester Crown Court [2008] EWHC 1362 (Admin) . . . 430

R (on the application of Malik v Central Criminal Court [2006] 4 All ER 1141 . . . 706

R (on the application of Malik) v Manchester Crown Court [2008] EWHC 1362 (Admin) . . . 429

R (on the application of Marchiori) v Environment Agency [2002] EWCA Civ 03 . . . 765

R (on the application of McCann) v Manchester Crown Court [2002] UKHL 39 . . . 369

R (on the application of Mersey Care Trust) v Mental Health Review Tribunal [2004] EWHC 1749 (Admin) . . . 706

R (on the application of Middleton) v West Somerset Coroner [2004] UKHL 10, [2004] 2 AC 182 . . . 81

R (on the application of Mohamed) v Secretary of State for Foreign and Commonwealth Affairs [2008] EWHC 2048 (Admin) . . . 475

R (on the application of O'Driscoll) v Secretary of State of the Home Department [2002] EWHC 2477 (Admin) . . . 429

R (on the application of Pretty) v Director of Public Prosecutions [2001] UKHL 61, [2002] 1 AC 800 . . . 83

R (on the application of Pro–Life Alliance) v BBC 2003] 2 All ER 977 . . . 645

R (on the application of R) v DPP [2006] EWHC 1375 (Admin), (2006) 170 JP 661 . . . 348

R (on the application of Razgar) [2004] UKHL 27, [2004] 2 AC 368 . . . 83

R (on the application of Roberts) v Parole Board [2005] UKHL 45, [2005] 2 AC 738 . . . 85

R (on the application of Saifi) v Governor of Brixton Prison [2001] 4 All ER 168, CA (Cr D) . . . 267

R (on the application of Singh) v Chief Constable of West Midlands Police [2006] EWCA Civ 1118 . . . 397

R (on the application of Smith) v Parole Board [2005] UKHL 1, [2005] 1 WLR 350 . . . 85

R (on the application of the Kurdistan Workers' Party) v Secretary of State for the Home Department [2002] EWHC Admin 644 . . . 424

R (on the application of Ullah) v Special Adjudicator [2004] UKHL 26 . . . 35

R (on the application of Ullah) v Special Adjudicator [2002] EWCA Civ 1856 . . . 83

R (on the application of Ullah) v Special Adjudicator [2004] UKHL 26, [2004] 2 AC 323 . . . 83, 473

R (on the application of W) v Acton Youth Court [2005] EWHC 954 (Admin) . . . 369

R (on the application of W) v Metropolitan Police Comr [2006] EWCA Civ 458, [2007] QB 399 . . . 397

R (on the application of Watts) v Bedford Primary Care Trust and the Secretary of State for Health [2003] EWHC 2228 . . . 83

R (Primrose) v Secretary of State for Justice [2008] All ER (D) 156 (Jul) . . . 886

R (Rusbridger) v Attorney General [2003] UKHL 38 . . . 37

R (Thompson) v Chief Constable of Northumbria [2001] EWCA Civ 321, CA (Civ D) . . . 235

R (Watkins– Singh) v Governing Body of Aberdare Girls' High School [2008] EWHC 1865 (Admin) . . . 896, 900

R(M) v MPC (2001) 13 July, CA (Cr D) . . . 235

RWE Npower plc v Carrol [2007] EWHC 947 (QB) . . . 365

Race Relations Board v Applin [1973] QB 815 . . . 945

Race Relations Board v Charter [1973] AC 868 . . . 905

Race Relations Board v Charter [1973] AC 868 . . . 915

Rai, Allmond and 'Negotiate Now' v UK 81–A D and R 146 (1995) . . . 300

Rance v Hastings Corpn (1913) 136 LT Jo 117 . . . 335

Rankin v Murray 2004 SCCR 422 . . . 426

Rasmussen v Denmark (1984) 7 EHRR 371 . . . 875

Raymond v Honey [1983] 1 AC 1, HL . . . 14, 762

Redbridge London Borough v Jacques [1970] 1 WLR 1604, DC . . . 294

Redgrave v United Kingdom (App. No.20271/92. 1 September 1993) . . . 845

Redmond–Bate v DPP (1999) 163 JP 789 . . . 202, 393–95

Rees v UK (1986) 9 EHRR 56 . . . 83

Reeves v Metropolitan Police Comr [1999] 3 All ER 897 . . . 101

Refah Partisi (The Welfare Party) v Turkey, Judgment of 13 February 2003 . . . 86

Regina (on the application of Laporte) v Chief Constable of Gloucestershire Constabulary [2006] UKHL 55 . . . 376–85

Reynolds v Metropolitan Police Comr [1984] 3 All ER 649 . . . 104

Reynolds v Secretary of State for Work and Pensions Laws LJ, in the Court of Appeal [2003] 3 All ER 577 . . . 858

Reynolds v Times Newspapers [2001] 2 AC 127 . . . 621

Rice v Connolly [1966] 2 QB 414 . . . 128–30

Ricketts v Cox (1981) 74 Cr App Rep 298, DC . . . 130

Robbins v Canadian Broadcasting Corpn (1958) 12 DLR (2d) 35, Quebec Sup Ct . . . 536

Roberts on v McFadyen; G ough v McFadyen 2008 SCCR 20 . . . 753

Robson v Hallett [1967] 2 QB 939 . . . 196, 404, 534

Roch LJ in Blackburn v Bowering [1994] 3 All ER 380 . . . 127

Roe v Wade 410 US 113 (1973) . . . 64

Rogers v DPP (unreported) 22 July 1999, DC . . . 348

Ropaigealach v Barclays Bank plc [2000] 1 QB 263 . . . 329

Ross v Ryanair January 2004, Central London County Court, unreported . . . 907 . . .

Rotaru v Romania, Judgment of 4 May 2000 . . . 768

Rowlands v Chief Constable of Merseyside Police [2006] EWCA Civ 1773 . . . 104

Rukwira v DPP (1993) 158 JP 65, DC . . . 342

Russell v Home Office [2001] All ER (D) 38 (Mar), CA (Civ D) . . . 103

Rutherford v Chief Constable of Kent (2001) 15 May . . . 103

Rutherford v Town Circle (No.2) [2006] UKHL 19 . . . 968

Rutherford v Towncircle Ltd ([2002] ICR 123 . . . 968

S v Van Niekerk [1970] 3 SA 655 (T) . . . 742

S (a child), Re [2004] UKHL 47, [2005] 1 AC 593, [2004] 3 WLR 1129, [2004] 4 All ER 83, [2005] EMLR 2, House of Lords . . . 564–68

S and G v United Kingdom App. No. 17634/91 . . . 659

S and Michael Marper v The United Kingdom (Nos 30562/04 and 30566/04) . . . 860

Sahin v Germany (2003) 36 EHRR 765 . . . 858

Salgueiro da Silva Mouta v Portugal . . . 875

Salman v Turkey (2000) 34 EHRR . . . 17

Samuels v Comr of Police for the Metropolis (1999) 3 March . . . 142

Santiago v R [2005] EWCA Crim 556 . . . 749, 753

Saunders, Re (1990) Times, 8 February . . . 712

Saunders v Punch Ltd [1998] 1 WLR 986 . . . 760

Saunders v UK (1997) 23 EHRR 313 . . . 238, 246, 253

Savjani v Inland Revenue Comrs [1981] QB 458 . . . 904

Scappaticci, Re [2003] NIQB 56 . . . 766

Scherer v Switzerland (1994) 18 EHRR 276 . . . 659

Schmidt v Austicks Bookshops [1978] ICR 85 . . . 965

Scott v Scott [1913] AC 417, HL . . . 706

Secretary of State for the Home Department v AE [2008] EWHC 585 (Admin) . . . 482, 485

Secretary of State for the Home Department v AH [2008] EWHC 1018 (Admin) . . . 482

Secretary of State for the Home Department v Alton [2008] EWCA Civ 443, (2008) Times, 13 May . . . 424

Secretary of State for the Home Department v AN [2008] EWHC 372 (Admin) . . . 484

Secretary of State for the Home Department v British Union for the Abolition of Vivisection [2008] EWHC 892 (QB) . . . 853

Secretary of State for the Home Department v Bullivant . . . 482

Secretary of State for the Home Department v E [2007] UKHL 47, [2008] 1 AC 499 . . . 482, 484

Secretary of State for the Home Department v Lord Alton of Liverpool [2008] EWCA Civ 443 . . . 422

Secretary of State for the Home Department v MB [2006] EWCA Civ 1140, [2006] HRLR 37 . . . 50, 483

Secretary of State for the Home Department v MB; Secretary of State for the Home Department v AF [2007] UKHL 46, [2008] 1 AC 440 . . . 482–84

Secretary of State for the Home Department v Rehman [2001] UKHL 47, [2003] 1 AC 153 . . . 471–72

Secretary of State for the Home Department v JJ and others [2007] UKHL 45 [2008] 1 AC 385 . . . 475–82

Segerstedt–Wiberg v Sweden, Judgment of 6 June 2006 . . . 768

Seide v Gillette [1980] IRLR 427 . . . 933

Sekfali, Banamira and Ouham v DPP [2006]
    EWHC Admin 894 . . . 129

Selmouni v France (2000) 29 EHRR 403 . . . 82

Shackell v United Kingdom 27 April 2000,
    Application No. 45851/99 . . . 861

Shamoon v Chief Constable of the Royal Ulster
    Constabulary (Northern Ireland) [2003] ICR
    337, House of Lords . . . 955–57

Shanaghan v United Kingdom, Judgment of 4 May
    2001 . . . 81

Sharpe v DPP [1993] RTR 392 . . . 267

Shaw v DPP [1962] AC 220. HL, at 268 . . . 658

Shaw v DPP [2005] EWHC 1215 (Admin) . . . 366

Shaw v Hamilton [1982] 2 All ER 718, DC . . . 398

Sheffield and Horsham v United Kingdom (1998)
    27 EHRR 163 . . . 58

Shelley Films v Rex Features Ltd [1994] EMLR
    134 . . . 542

Sheppard v Maxwell 384 US 333 (1966) . . . 715

Showboat Entertainment Centre v Owen [1984]
    ICR 65 . . . 945–46

Shuker's Application for Judicial Review, Re
    [2004] NIQB 20 . . . 766

Sidabras v Lithuania (2006) 42 EHRR 6 . . . 864,
    877

Sierny v DPP [2006] EWHC 716 (Admin) . . .
    397

Silver v United Kingdom (1983) 5 EHRR
    347 . . . 518

Slade v DPP (1996) 22 October, DC,
    unreported . . . 147

Slee v Meadows (1911) 75 JP 246, DC . . . 299

Smith and Grady v United Kingdom (1999) 29
    EHRR 493 . . . 62

Smith v Chief Constable of Sussex [1999] CLY
    4852 . . . 100

Smith v DPP (2001) 2 February, QBD, Admin
    Court . . . 153

Smith v Gardner Merchant Ltd [1999] ICR
    134 . . . 964

Smith v Reynolds [1986] Crim LR 559, DC . . . 326

Smith v Safeway plc [1995] ICR 868 . . . 965

Smithkline Beecham plc v Avery [2007] EWHC
    948 (QB) . . . 365

Snepp v United States 444 US 507 (1980) . . . 821

Snook v Mannion [1982] RTR 321 . . . 197

Socialist Party v Turkey (1998) 27 EHRR 51 . . . 86

Soering v UK (1989) 11 EHRR 439 . . . 83, 473

Solicitor General v Radio Avon Ltd [1978] 1 NZLR
    225, NZCA . . . 742

Sonia Raissi, Mohamed Raissi v The Comr
    of Police of the Metropolis [2007] EWHC
    2842 . . . 148

Southard v DPP[2006] EWHC 3449
    (Admin) . . . 348

Southeastern Promotions Ltd v Conrad 419 US
    892 (1975) . . . 614, 630

Special Hospital Services Authority v Hyde (1994)
    20 BMLR 75 . . . 760

Spencer v United Kingdom App. No. 28851/95;
    (1998) 25 EHRR CD 105 . . . 527

Stec v UK (2006) 20 BHRC 348 . . . 869, 878,
    880–82

Steel v Goacher [1983] RTR 98, DC . . . 171

Stephens v Avery [1988] 2 All ER 477 Ch . . . 541

Stewart v Cleveland Guest (Engineering) Ltd
    [1996] ICR 535 . . . 964

Stewart v United Kingdom Decn admiss of 10 July
    1984 . . . 497

Stokes v Brydges (1958) 5. S Ct Queensland . . . 535

Stoll v Switzerland Judgment of 10 December,
    2007 . . . 621, 629

Strathclyde Regional Council v Porcelli [1986]
    ICR 564 . . . 963, 965

Stubbings v United Kingdom (1996) 23 EHRR
    213 . . . 516, 861, 863, 875

Sunday Times v UK (No. 2) (Series A No.
    217) . . . 805, 816

Sunday Times v UK . . . 686

Sunday Times v United Kingdom, Judgment of 26
    April 1979, ECtHRR A30; (1979) 2 EHRR 245,
    European Court of Human Rights . . . 614–17

Sunderland City Council v Conn [2007] EWCA
    Div 1492 . . . 361

Sutcliffe v Chief Constable of West Yorkshire
    (1995) 159 JP 770, CA . . . 192

Swales v Cox [1981] QB 849, DC . . . 153

Swanston v DPP (1996) 161 JP 203, DC . . . 346

Swedish Engine Drivers' Union v Sweden (1976) 1
    EHRR 617 . . . 875

TD, DE and MF v UK Apps Nos 18600/91,
    18601/92 and 18602/91, 12 October 1992 . . . 831

Tameside case [1977] AC 1014, HL . . . 17

Tammer v Estonia (2003) 37 EHRR 43 . . . 620

Taylor v DPP [2006] EWHC 1202 (Admin) . . . 347

Taylor v Lancashire County Council [2005]
    EWCA Civ 284 . . . 39

Teixiera de Castro v Portugal (1998) 28 EHRR
    101 . . . 272–73

Tejani v The Superintendent Registrar for
    the District of Peterborough [1986] IRLR
    502 . . . 904

Telegraph plc, ex p. [1993] 2 All ER 971 . . . 713

Texeira de Castro v Portugal App. No.
    25829/94 . . . 596

The Church of Jesus Christ of Latter Day Saints v
    Price [2004] EWHC 3245 (QB) . . . 361

The Gypsy Council v UK App No. 66336/01, 14
    May 2002 . . . 31

Theospharious v Herald and Weekly Times Ltd
(1994) CLR 104 . . . 612

Thlimmenos v Greece (2001) 31 EHRR
15 . . . 864–66, 869, 878

Thomas v National Union of Mineworkers (South
Wales Area) [1985] 2 All ER 1 . . . 293

Thomas v News Group Newspapers Ltd [2001]
EWCA Civ 1233 . . . 361

Thomas v Sawkins [1935] 2 KB 249 . . . 196,
401–06

Thompson v Metropolitan Police Comr [1998] QB
498, Court of Appeal . . . 102–03

Thompson v R [1998] AC 811, PC . . . 258

Thomson v Times Newspapers Ltd [1969] 3 All ER
648 at 651, CA . . . 725

Thorgeir Thorgeirson v Iceland (1992) 14 EHRR
843 . . . 621

Times Newspapers Ltd, Re [2007] EWCA Crim
1925 . . . 709

Timishev v Russia (2007) 44 EHRR 37 . . . 875

Tinnelly and McEldu1 v United Kingdom
Judgment of 10 July 1998 (1998) 27 EHRR
249 . . . 767

Todd v DPP [1996] Crim LR 344 . . . 202, 372

Tolley v J S Fry & Sons Ltd [1931] AC 333,
HL . . . 537

Tolley v J S Fry & Sons Ltd . . . 524

Tolstoy Miloslavsky v UK (1995) 20 EHRR 442
and Rantzen v Mirror Group Newspapers
(1986) Ltd [1994] QB 670, CA . . . 36

Tolstoy Miloslavsky v UK (1995) 20 EHRR
442 . . . 621

Tomasi v France (1992) 15 EHRR 1 . . . 81

Tomlinson v Chief Constable of Hertfordshire
[2001] All ER (D) 109 (Mar), CA (Cr D) . . .
147

Triesman v Ali [2002] IRLR 489 . . . 917

Truth and Sportsman Ltd, ex p Bread
Manufacturers Ltd (1937) 37 SRNSW
242 . . . 720

Tucker v DPP [2007] All ER (D) 479 (Nov),
DC . . . 304

Tumelty v Ministry of Defence [1988] 3 NIJB
51 . . . 500

Turner , Re 174 NW (2d) 895 (1969) . . . 743

Tyrer v UK (1978) 2 EHRR 1 . . . 82

United Communist Party of Turkey v Turkey
(1998) 26 EHRR 121 . . . 86

University of Oxford v Broughton [2004] EWHC
2543 (QB) . . . 365

University of Oxford v Broughton [2006] EWCA
Civ 1305 . . . 365

University of Oxford v Broughton [2006] EWHC
1233 (QB) . . . 365

University of Oxford v Broughton [2008] EWHC
75 (QB) . . . 361

University of Oxford v Webb [2006] EWHC 2490
(QB) . . . 365

V v UK (1999) 30 EHRR 121 . . . 83

Valentine v DPP [1997] COD 339, DC . . . 342

Van Colle v Chief Constable of Hertfordshire
Police [2008] UKHL 50 . . . 101

Van Der Mussele v Belgium (1983) 6 EHRR
163 . . . 858, 861

Van Droogenbroek v Belgium (1982) 4 EHRR
443 . . . 84

Venables v News Group Newspapers [2001] 1 All
ER 908 . . . 543

Venables v News Group Newspapers [2001] Fam.
430 . . . 37, 38, 568

Verrall v Great Yarmouth Borough Council [1981]
QB 202, CA . . . 307

Vgt Verein Gegeng Tierfabriken v Switzerland
App. No. 24699/94; (2002) 34 EHRR 4 . . . 645,
652

Villiers v Villiers [1994] 2 All ER 149, CA . . . 694

Von Hannover v Germany, Application No.
59320/00; (2005) 40 EHRR 1 . . . **510–15**, 559,
576

W v Switzerland (1993) 17 EHRR 60 . . . 85

W v United Kingdom (1988) 10 EHRR 29 . . .
521

Waddington v Miah [1974] 1 WLR 683, HL . . . 14

Wainwright v Home Office [2003] UKHL 53,
[2004] 2 AC 406, [2003] 3 WLR 1137, [2003] 4
All ER 969, House of Lords . . . 224, **528–33**,
545, 557

Waitt, ex p. [1988] Crim LR 384 . . . 186

Waite v Taylor (1985) 149 JP 551 . . . 298

Wallersteiner v Moir [1974] 3 All ER 217 at 230,
CA . . . 725

Ward v Holman [1964] 2 QB 580 . . . 341

Ward v Police Service of Northern Ireland [2007]
UKHL 50 . . . 440

Wasson v Chief Constable of the Royal Ulster
Constabulary [1987] NI 420 . . . 500

Weathersfield Ltd t/a Van & Truck Rentals
v Sargent [1999] ICR 425, Court of
Appeal . . . 920, 945–46

Webb v Chief Constable of Merseyside [2000] 1
QB 427 . . . 192

Webb v EMO [1993] ICR 175 . . . 970

Webster v Newham London Borough Council
(1980) Times, 22 November, CA . . . 307

Webster v Southwark London Borough Council
[1983] QB 698, QBD . . . 306

Weeks v UK (1987) 10 EHRR 293 . . . 84–5

Wemho v Federal Republic of Germany (1968) 1 EHRR 55 . . . 85

Westminster City Council v Haw [2002] EWHC 2073 (QB) . . . 294–98

Weston v Central Criminal Court Courts' Administrator [1976] QB 32 . . . 753

White v Chief Constable of South Yorkshire [1991] 1 All ER 1 . . . 96, 104

Whitley v DPP (2004) 168 JP 350 . . . 234

Whitney v California 274 US 357 (1927) . . . 613

Wilkes v Lord Halifax (1769) 19 State Tr 1406 . . . 90

Wilkes v Wood (1763) 19 State Tr 1153 . . . 90

Wilkinson v Downton [1897] 2 QB 57, QBD . . . 533

Wilkinson v Downton' (1995) Anglo–American LR 299 . . . 359

Wilkinson v S [2003] EWCA Civ 95, [2003] 2 All ER 184 . . . 749, 753

Williams and O'Hare v DPP (1993) 98 Cr App Rep 209 . . . 271

Williams v Home Office (No. 2) [1981] 1 All ER 1211, QBD . . . 12

Williams v Settle [1960] 1 WLR 1072, [1960] 2 All ER 806, Court of Appeal . . . **538–39**

Wilson v Metropolitan Police Comr (2001) 6 July . . . 104

Winder v DPP (1996) 160 JP 713 . . . 373

Winter v Barlow [1980] RTR 209 at 213, DC . . . 171

Winterwerp v Netherlands (1979) 2 EHRR 387 . . . 84

Wise v Dunning [1902] 1 KB 167, DC . . . 277

Wiseman, Re [1969] NZLR 55 . . . 741

Witsch v Germany (Adm Dec 13 December 2005) . . . 621

Wood v Comr of Police for the Metropolis [2008] EWHC 1105 (Admin) . . . 594

Woolgar v Chief Constable of Sussex Police [1999] 3 All ER 604 . . . 101

Worm v Austria (1997) 25 EHRR 454 . . . 686

Wynne v UK (1994) 19 EHRR 333 . . . 85

X Ltd v Morgan–Grampian (Publishers) Ltd [1991] 1 AC 1 . . . 746, 754, 758, 760

X v UK (1981) 4 EHRR 188 . . . 85

X v United Kingdom (1981) EHRR 188 . . . 13

X v Y [1988] 2 All ER 648 . . . 544, 760

X, Y and Z v United Kingdom (1997) 24 EHRR 143 . . . 517

YL v Birmingham City Council [2007] UKHL 27 . . . 36, 38

Yasa v Turkey (1998) 28 EHRR 408 . . . 80

Youssef v Home O0 ce [2004] EWHC 1884 (QB) . . . 456

Zana v Turkey (1997) 27 EHRR 667 . . . 620

Zarb Adami v Malta (2006) 20 BHRC 703 . . . 869

Zarczynska v Levy [1979] ICR 184 . . . 945–46

TABLE OF STATUTES

*References in **bold** type indicate where the Act is set out in part or in full*

ACTS OF PARLIAMENT

Access to Health Records Act 1990 . . . 849
Access to Justice Act 1999
  s.78(2) . . . 301
  s.95(1) . . . 207
  s.97(4) . . . 207
  s.106 . . . 207
  Sch.11 . . . 301
  Sch.15 . . . 207
Access to Medical Reports Act 1988 . . . 849
Access to Personal Files Act 1987 . . . 849
Accessories and Abettors Act 1861
  s.8 . . . 334
Administration of Justice Act 1960
  s.11 . . . 717, 720
    (1) . . . 717
    (2) . . . 717
  s.12 . . . 708, 711
  s.13 . . . 763
Administration of Justice Act 1973
  Sch.5 . . . 398
Ancient Monuments and Archaeological Areas
  Act 1979 . . . 305
Animals (Scientific Procedures) Act 1986 . . . 852
  s.24 . . . 852
  s.75 . . . 852
Anti-social Behaviour Act 2003 . . . 277–78, 328
  Pt 7 . . . 278
  ss.1–11 . . . 369
  s.13 . . . 369
  s.30 . . . 396
    (6) . . . 397
  s.32 . . . 397
  ss.40–41 . . . 369
  ss.60–64 . . . 328
  s.57 . . . 314
  s.58 . . . 328
  s.59(1) . . . 371
    (2) . . . 371
  ss.85–86 . . . 368
  Sch.3 . . . 371
Anti-terrorism, Crime and Security Act
  2001 . . . 162, 238, 410, 429, 455, 475

  Pt 1 . . . 455
  Pt 2 . . . 455
  Pt 4 . . . 416, 455
  ss.1–3 . . . 455
  s.3 . . . 456
  ss.4–16 . . . 455
  ss.21–23 . . . 471
  ss.21–32 . . . 412, 455
  s.21(1) . . . 456
  s.23 . . . 42, 456
  s.25 . . . 456
  s.26 . . . 456
  s.29 . . . 471
  s.39 . . . 343, 355
    (1) . . . 367
    (5) . . . 367
    367
  s.116(1) . . . 837
  ss.117–120 . . . 455
  s.117(1) . . . 427
  s.118 . . . 440
  s.119 . . . 440
  s.122 . . . 455
  s.127(2) . . . 433
  Sch.1 . . . 455
  Sch.2 . . . 429, 431, 455
Armed Forces Act 2006 . . . 692
  Sch.16 . . . 692
Asylum and Immigration (Treatment of
  Claimants) Act 2004
  s.19(3) . . . 42
Atomic Energy Act 1946 . . . 780
  s.11 . . . 780
  s.13 . . . 780
Atomic Energy Authority Act 1954 . . . 821
  s.6(3) . . . 780
Bail Act 1976 . . . 228
Bill of Rights 1689 . . . 3, 12–13
British Nationality Act 1981
  s.40(2) . . . 472
Broadcasting Act 1990 . . . 638, 643
  s.10(3) . . . 645
  s.164(1)–(2) . . . 675
  Sch.20 . . . 688

Broadcasting Act 1996 . . . 643
Children Act 2004
s.58 . . . 83
Children and Young Persons Act 1933
s.39 . . . 564, 710–11
s.49 . . . 711
Cinemas Act 1985 . . . 631
Sch.2 . . . 682
Cinematography Films (Animals) Act
1937 . . . 633
City of London Police Act 1839
s.22 . . . 302
Civil Authorities (Special Powers) Act (NI)
1922 . . . 415
s.2 . . . 415
(4) . . . 415
Civil Aviation Act 1982
s.18 . . . 780
Communications Act 1985 . . . 845
Communications Act 2003 . . . 574, 638, 645
Pt 3 . . . 644
s.3 . . . 643
s.12(1) . . . 644
s.127 . . . 536
s.133 . . . 645
s.198 . . . **639**
s.319 . . . 574, **639–41**, 644
s.320 . . . **641**
s.321 . . . 42, **642–43**, 645
(2) . . . 649
s.336 . . . 645
s.406(1) . . . 592
Sch.17 . . . 592
Confiscation of Alcohol (Young Persons) Act
1997 . . . 369
Constables Protection Act 1750
s.6 . . . 104
Constitutional Reform Act 2005 . . . 18
Sch.9 . . . 691
Contempt of Court Act 1981 . . . 617, 685–687,
695, 720, 725, 735, 754, 762
s.1 . . . **688**, 694, 699, 720
ss.1–7 . . . 694
ss.2–7 . . . **688**
s.2 . . . 688, 694, 698
(1) . . . 698
(2) . . . 698, 701, 703–705, 725, 734–35
(3) . . . 716
(4) . . . 716
s.3 . . . **688**, 694, 716, 734
s.4 . . . **688**, 705, 711

(1) . . . 711–12, 720, 734
(2) . . . 711–713, 735
ss.5–8 . . . **689**
s.5 . . . 699, 702, 704–705, 720, 725, 734, 737
s.6(b) . . . 697, 712
s.7 . . . 762
s.8 . . . 744–45
ss.9–12 . . . **690**
s.9 . . . 751
(1) . . . 750
s.10 . . . 746, 759–61
s.11 . . . 709–710, 712
s.12 . . . 750
(1) . . . 750
(2) . . . 694, 750
(5) . . . 751
s.14 . . . **691**, 694
s.19 . . . **691**
s.53(2) . . . 763
Sch.1 . . . **692–94**, 716–17, 725, 734
Copyright Act 1956
s.17(3) . . . 539
Copyright, Designs and Patents Act 1988 . . . 539
s.11 . . . 539
s.85 . . . 539
s.87 . . . 539
s.97(2) . . . 539
Countryside and Rights of Way Act 2000 . . . 300
Pt I . . . 300
s.2(4) . . . 301
Sch.2 . . . 300
County Courts Act 1984
s.14(1) . . . 750
s.55(1) . . . 750
s.118 . . . 750
(1) . . . 750
County Courts (Penalties for Contempt) Act
1983 . . . 694
Courts Act 2003
s.109(1) . . . 667
Sch.3 . . . 710
Crime and Disorder Act 1998 . . . 277, 287, 355,
357, 368, 989, 990
s.1 . . . 369
(1) . . . 368
(6) . . . 368
s.1AA . . . 369
s.1AB . . . 369
s.1B . . . 369
s.1C . . . 369
s.1D . . . 369

s.1G... 369
s.1H... 369
s.28... 343, **355**, 989
s.29... 989
s.30... 989
s.31... 343, 355, 989
s.32... 367, 989
s.82... 357
Crime (International Co-operation) Act 2003
s.52... 453
Crimes Act 1914
s.79... 820
Criminal Appeal Act 1968...
s.2... 64
Criminal Damage Act 1971... 329
s.1(1)... 329
s.5(2)... 329
Criminal Evidence (Witness Anonymity) Act
2008... 710
Criminal Justice Act 1925
s.41... 751
Criminal Justice Act 1967
s.3... 711
Criminal Justice Act 1987
Pt I... 713
s.9(11)... 713
s.11... 710
s.11A... 710
Criminal Justice Act 1988... 188
s.93H... 791
s.134(1)... 501
s.139... 162
s.159... 707, 713, 763
s.160... 673, **679–80**
(2)... 680
s.162... 635
Sch.14... 238
Criminal Justice Act 1991
ss.76–79... 690
Sch.4... 694
Sch.11... 690
Criminal Justice Act 1993
Sch.3... 691
Criminal Justice Act 2003... 237, 262
s.4... 202
s.10... 238
s.41... 689
s.76... 711
s.82... 711
s.145... 357, 989
s.146... 989

s.322... 369
Sch.3... 689
Criminal Justice and Court Services Act 2000
s.41(1)... 678
s.74... 579
Sch.7... 579
Criminal Justice and Immigration Act
2008... 635, 989
s.28A... 989
s.28AB... 989
ss.28B–G... 989
s.29J... 989
s.29JA... 989
s.63... **672**
s.65... **673**
s.71... 655
s.119... 370
ss.123–124... 368
s.128(1)... 94
Sch.16... 278
Sch.20... 369
Criminal Justice and Police Act 2001... 93, 242,
252
Pt I... 277
Pt II... 228
ss.1–11... 370
ss.12–16... 369
ss.39–41... 762
s.42... 316, 367, 396
s.42A... 367, 396, 536
s.44... 363
(1)... 359
s.46... 683
s.47... 683
s.50... 187
s.51... 187
s.52... 187
s.53... 187
s.54... 187
s.73... 226
s.76... 242
s.78... 238
s.82... 238
Criminal Justice and Public Order Act
1994... 277, 315, 326, 370, 375
ss.34–39... 244
s.34... 245, 247–248
(2)... 252
(3)... 252
s.49... 711
s.51... 762

s.54 . . . 238
s.58 . . . 238
s.60 . . . **159**, 162, 164, 376
  (4A) . . . 162
s.60AA . . . **160**, 162
s.61 . . . 326–328
s.62 . . . 326, 327
ss.62A–62E . . . 328
ss.63–66 . . . 328
s.63 . . . 328
ss.68–69 . . . 375, 534
s.68 . . . **371–74**
  (2) . . . 374
  (3) . . . 372
s.69 . . . **371–72**, 374
  (3) . . . 372
s.72 . . . 329
s.73 . . . 330
ss.77–79 . . . 327
s.82 . . . 450
s.84 . . . 678
s.89 . . . 635
s.91 . . . 635
s.154 . . . 332, 337
Sch.10 . . . 314
Sch.11 . . . 678
Criminal Justice (Terrorism and Conspiracy) Act
1998 . . . 423
s.1 . . . 423
s.2 . . . 423
Criminal Law Act 1967
s.2(4) . . . 135
  (6) . . . 153
s.3 . . . **151–52**, 329, 349, 404
  (1) . . . 494, 496, 500
s.4(1) . . . 684
s.13(1) . . . 569
s.25 . . . 668
Criminal Law Act 1977 . . . 329
Pt I . . . 287
s.3 . . . 373
s.6 . . . 329, 375
s.7 . . . 330
s.8 . . . 330
s.9 . . . 330
s.53 . . . 655, 667, 669
  (5) . . . 667
  (6) . . . 669
  (7) . . . 669
s.62 . . . 234

Criminal Law and Procedure (Ireland) Act
1887 . . . 414
Criminal Law (NI) Act 1967
s.3(1) . . . 494, 496
Criminal Procedure and Investigations Act 1996
s.57(3) . . . 689
  (4) . . . 692
Crown Proceedings Act 1947
s.40(3) 71
Customs and Excise Management Act 1979
s.49 . . . 676
Customs Consolidation Act 1876 . . . 637
s.42 . . . **676**, 677
Data Protection Act 1984 . . . 609
Data Protection Act 1998 . . . 577–578, 602, 609,
610, 849, 852
s.1 . . . **602–04**
  (1) . . . 609
s.2 . . . **604**, 610
s.3 . . . **604**, 610
s.4 . . . **604**
s.7 . . . **604–06**, 610
s.10 . . . **606**, 610
s.13 . . . **607**, 610
s.14 . . . **607**
s.17 . . . 610
s.29 . . . 589
s.32 . . . **608**, 610
  (3) . . . 574
Sch.1 . . . **609–10**
Sch.6 . . . 853
Defamation Act 1996
Sch.2 . . . 689
Disability Discrimination Act 1995 . . . 883–886,
890, 893, 912, 937, 942, 944, 946, 961–963, 974,
977
Pt II . . . 919
Pt IV . . . 919
s.1 . . . **934**
s.2 . . . **934**
s.3 . . . 936
s.3A . . . **943**, 975, 985
  (2) . . . 985
  (3) . . . 983
s.3B . . . **961**
s.4A . . . 985
s.5(3) . . . 988
ss.15A–15C . . . 883
s.16B . . . 919
s.17A . . . 930
s.18 . . . 899

s.18B . . . 985
s.19 . . . 904, 906–907
  (2) . . . 907
  (3) . . . 904
  (4A) . . . 904, 906
  (5A) . . . 904
s.20 . . . **974–75, 984, 986**, 988
  (1) . . . 975
  (6) . . . 985
s.21 . . . 985
  (4) . . . 985
s.21ZA . . . 906, 987
s.21B . . . 892, 930
s.21D . . . 975, **984**, 987
  (4) . . . 988
  (5) . . . 988
s.21E . . . 985
s.21F . . . 915
s.21G . . . 975, 985, 988
s.22 . . . 912, 914
  (4) . . . 913
s.22A . . . 912
s.23 . . . 899, 913
ss.24–27 . . . 914
s.24 . . . 975, 985, 988
  (1) . . . 977
s.24A . . . 912
s.24C . . . 986
s.24D . . . 986
s.28A . . . 898
s.28B . . . 975, **983–85, 987**
  (3) . . . 985
  (7) . . . 988
s.28C . . . 986
s.28D . . . 898
s.28E . . . 898
s.28F . . . 898, 899
s.28G . . . 988
s.28Q . . . 988
s.28R . . . 898
  (3A) . . . 898
s.28S . . . 975, **983–85, 987**
  (5) . . . 988
s.28T(1) . . . 986
s.28U . . . 898
s.28UC . . . 919
s.28V . . . 930
s.31AB . . . 975, 985, 988
s.31AD . . . 983, 986
s.31ADA . . . 930
s.37 . . . 907

s.37A . . . 907
s.49A . . . 892, 896
s.49B(1) . . . 893
  893
s.49G . . . 912
s.59 . . . 921–922, 924
s.59A . . . 925
s.64A . . . 928
Sch.1 . . . **934–36**
Sch.4 . . . 898
Disability Discrimination Act 2005 . . . 885–86
Domestic Violence, Crime and Victims Act 2004
  s.60 . . . 366
Drugs Act 2005
  s.20 . . . 369
Drug Trafficking Offences Act 1994 . . . 188, 429
Education Act 1944
  s.30 . . . 51
Education Act 1980 . . . 922
Education (No.2) Act 1986
  s.43 . . . **307–08**
Employment Relations Act 1999
  ss.10–13 . . . 846
  s.15 . . . 846
  Sch.8 . . . 795–96, 846
Employment Rights Act 1996 . . . 795
  Pt IVA . . . 795, 846
  s.43B . . . 795
  s.47B . . . 795, 846
  s.111 . . . 795
  s.191 . . . 795
  s.193 . . . 795–96, 846
Employment Tribunals Act 1996
  s.10(1) . . . 795
    (2)–(9) . . . 796
    (5) . . . 795
Energy Act 2004
  s.57(1) . . . 433
    (2) . . . 433
  Sch.14 . . . 779
Environment and Safety Information Act 1990 . . . 849
Environmental Protection Act 1990
  s.71(2) . . . 247
Equal Pay Act 1970 . . . 883, 885, 957
Equality Act 2006 . . . 884–885, 890, 907, 912, 933, 944, 961, 965, 968, 972
  Pt I . . . 884
  s.6 . . . 921–922
  ss.22–24 . . . 884
  s.25 . . . 884

ss.28–30 ... 884

ss.31–32 ... 884

s.35 ... **937**

s.45 ... **901, 903, 943, 967**

(4) ... 968

s.46 ... 903, 916

s.47 ... 912

(3) ... 913

s.48 ... 913

(4) ... 890

s.49 ... **899–900**

s.50 ... 901–02

(2) ... 902

s.51 ... **901**

(3) ... 901

s.52 ... **889**, 892, 930

889–90

s.54 ... 919

s.57 ... **916**

(1)–(6) ... 917

s.58 ... **926–27**

s.59 ... 908

s.60 ... 927

s.61 ... 925

s.62 ... 907

s.63 ... 924

s.65 ... 930

s.66 ... 930

s.67 ... 930

s.68 ... 930

s.69 ... 930

s.71 ... 925

s.73 ... 919

s.74 ... 919

s.75 ... 928

Sch.1 ... 890

European Communities Act 1972 ... 11, 65, 886

s.3 ... 35

s.11(2) ... 780

Fair Employment (Northern Ireland) Act 1976

s.42 ... 767

Financial Services Act 1986

s.178 ... 760

Firearms Act 1968

s.47(3) ... 162–63

s.49(1) ... 162–63

(2) ... 162–63

Football (Disorder) Act 2000 ... 277

Football (Disorder) (Amendment) Act
2002 ... 277

Football (Disorder and Offences) Act 1989 ... 277

Football (Offences) Act 1991 ... 277, 989

s.3 ... 989

Freedom of Information Act 2000 ... 34, 764, 849

Pts 1–5 ... 849

Pt 2 ... 850

s.1(1) ... 852–53

s.2(1) ... 854

(3) ... 850

s.4 ... 849

s.5 ... 849

s.6 ... 849

s.7(1) ... 850

s.8 ... 849

s.9 ... 850

s.10 ... 850

ss.11–17 ... 852

s.12 ... 850

s.13 ... 850

s.14 ... 850

s.15 ... 854

s.16 ... 850

s.17 ... 850

s.19 ... 852

(3) ... 850

s.20 ... 852

s.21 ... 850, 853

s.22 ... 853

s.23 ... 850

s.24 ... 850

s.25(a) ... 850

s.28 ... 853

s.29 ... 851

s.30 ... 851

(1) ... 853

s.31 ... 851, 853

s.32 ... 850–51, 853

s.33 ... 851, 853

s.34 ... 850–51

s.35 ... 851, 853–54

s.36 ... 850–51, 853–54

s.37 ... 851

(1) ... 853

s.38 ... 851

s.39 ... 851

s.40 ... 850, 852

s.41 ... 850, 852

s.42 ... 852–53

s.43 ... 852–53

s.44 ... 950, 852

s.45 ... 852

s.46 ... 852

s.47 ... 852
s.48 ... 852
ss.50–52 ... 853
s.53 ... 853–54
s.54 ... 853
s.55 ... 853
s.56 ... 853
ss.57–59 ... 853
s.60 ... 853
s.61 ... 853
s.62 ... 853
s.63 ... 853
s.64 ... 853
s.66 ... 854
s.68(1) ... 602–604
   (2) ... 602–603
   (3) ... 604
s.69(1) ... 604
s.73 ... 605
Sch.1 ... 849
Sch.4 ... 773, 853
Sch.6 ... 605
Government of Wales Act 2006
s.92 ... 778
Sch.8 ... 778
Sch.10 ... 778
Sch.12 ... 778
Greater London Authority Act 1999
s.315 ... 96
ss.317–320 ... 96
Health and Safety at Work etc. Act 1974 ... 104
s.3 ... 104
   (1) ... 501
Health and Social Care Act 2008 ...
s.145 ... 38
Highways Act 1980
s.137 ... **294**, 298–99, 329
   (1) ... 298
Highways Act 1959
s.121 ... 294
Hotel Proprietors Act 1956
s.1(3) ... 904
Housing Act 1996
ss.153A–153E ... 369
Human Rights Act 1998 ... 1, 3, 5, 11, 13,
   15–16, **19–32**, 34, 62, 64, 66–67, 81, 104,
   118, 247, 268, 275, 327, 349, 355, 423, 471,
   497, 510, 522, 527, 539, 542, 558, 580,
   622, 694, 792, 892
s.1 ... 33
s.2 ... 33, 35

s.3 ... 13, 17, 33, 36–7, 43, 51–52, 63–65, 425,
   484, 745, 793
   (1) ... 50
   (2) ... 37, 51
s.4 ... 33, 37, 40, 64–65, 649
   (5) ... 63
   (6) ... 40, 63
s.6 ... 33, 36, 38, 472, 533
   (1) ... 37–40, 63
   (2) ... 37, 39, 63
   (3) ... 36
   (5) ... 40
s.7 ... 33, 37–8, 533
   (1) ... 39, 42
   (7) ... 39
s.8 ... 33
   (2) ... 40
   (3) ... 40
   (4) ... 40
s.9(1) ... 39
s.10 ... 33, 51, 64–65s
   (2) ... 40
s.11 ... 34
s.12 ... 41
   (3) ... 364
   (4) ... 41, 574
s.13 ... 41
s.14 ... 34
s.15(1) ... 33
s.19 ... 41
   (1) ... 652
   (2) ... 42
s.21(1) ... 37, 51
s.22(4) ... 42
Sch.1 ... 33
Sch.2 ... 41, 64
Sch.3 ... 33
Hunting Act 2004 ... 374–75
Immigration Act 1971
s.2A ... 472
s.3(5) ... 472
Immigration and Asylum Act 1999
Sch.14 ... 472
Immigration, Asylum and Nationality Act 2006
s.7 ... 472
s.56(1) ... 472
s.57(1) ... 472
Indecent Displays (Control) Act 1981 ... 657
s.1 ... **681–82**
s.2(2) ... 682
   (3) ... 682

s.3 ... 682

Intelligence Services Act 1994 ... 590, 796, 832, 842–43, 845–46
s.1 ... **834**
s.2 ... **834**
s.3 ... **834**
s.4 ... **835**
s.5 ... **835–36**, 843
s.6 ... **836**, 843
s.7 ... **837–39**, 846
s.10 ... **839**
Sch.3 ... 847
Sch.4 ... 773, 833

Interception of Communications Act 1985 ... 588, 590

Interpretation Act 1978
Sch.1 ... 362

Judicial Proceedings (Regulation of Reports) Act 1926 ... 711

Justices of the Peace Act 1361 ... 398, 299
s.1(7) ... 398

Knives Act 1977 ... 159

Landlord and Tenant Act 1927 ... 913

Legal Aid Act 1988
s.29 ... 751

Licensing Act 2003 ... 631–32
s.20 ... **631**
ss.150–171 ... 369
s.198(1) ... 656
Sch.6 ... 656

Local Government Act 1972
s.222 ... 292–93
s.235 ... 299

Local Government Act 1999 ... 94–5
Pt I ... 98
ss.21–29 ... 98

Local Government (Access to Information) Act 1985 ... 849

Magistrates' Courts Act 1980
s.1 ... **207**
(2) ... 207
(3) ... 207
(6) ... **207**
s.8 ... 711
s.8C ... 710
s.71 ... 710
s.97(4) ... 750
s.115 ... 398–99
s.125 ... 207

Magistrates' Courts (Appeals from Binding Over Orders) Act 1956 ... 398

Magna Carta 1215 ... 3

Malicious Communications Act 1988 ... 348, 397

Mental Health Act 1959 ... 85

Mental Health Act 1983 ... 85, 507
s.135 ... 225
s.136 ... 225

Metropolitan Police Act 1839
s.15(13) ... 340
s.18 ... 195
s.52 ... **301**
s.54(9) ... 301–02
(13) ... 354
s.66 ... 142, 162, 280

Metropolitan Police (Compensation) Act 1886 ... 335

Military Lands Act 1892
s.17(2) ... 299

Misuse of Drugs Act 1971 ... 163
s.23 ... 147, **163**, **188**

National Heritage Act 1983 ... 305

Nationality, Immigration and Asylum Act 2002
s.82(1) ... 472
472
s.84 ... 472
s.97 ... 472
s.97A ... 472

Northern Ireland Act 1998
s.90 ... 767

Northern Ireland (Emergency Provisions) Act 1973 ... 411, 415

Northern Ireland (Emergency Provisions) Act 1978
s.11 ... 436
s.22 ... 451

Northern Ireland (Emergency Provisions) Act 1991
s.32 ... 450
s.33 ... 450
s.34 ... 450

Northern Ireland (Emergency Provisions) Act 1996 ... 411, 413–14

Nuclear Installations Act 1965
Sch.1 ... 780

Obscene Publications Act 1959 ... 633, 635, 637, 656, 669, 673, 677
s.1 ... **660**, 663, **666**
(1) ... 658, 662, 664–65, 677
(2) ... 660
(3) ... 662
s.2 ... **655**, **659–60**, 664, 669, **671–72**
(3) ... 659
(4) ... 658
s.3 ... 661, **667**, 669, 679

(3) ... 668
(4) ... 668
s.4 ... 665, **669–70**
(1) ... 671
Obscene Publications Act 1964 ... 635, 656, 669, 677
s.1 ... **660**
(1) ... 655–56
(3) ... 662, **672**
(4) ... **667**
(5) ... 656
s.2(1) ... **660–61**
(2) ... 660
Offences Against the Person Act 1861
s.38 ... 119
s.42 ... 401
Official Secrets Act 1911 ... 790, 820
s.1 ... **768**, 779–80, 783, 785–86, 821
(2) ... 786
s.2 ... 764, 781, 786–788
(1) ... 820
(2) ... 787
s.3 ... 769, 780, 783
s.7 ... 769
s.8 ... 770
s.9 ... 781
(1) ... 779, 782, 792
s.12 ... **770**
Official Secrets Act 1920 ... 768, 820
s.1(1) ... 780
(2) ... 780
s.2 ... 780
s.3 ... 781
ss.4–5 ... 779–780
s.6 ... 780, 785
s.7 ... **770**, 781, 786
s.8(4) ... 708, 781
Official Secrets Act 1989 ... 569, 622, 732, 764, 781, 787–788, 791, 801–02, 820
ss.1–4 ... 622
s.1 ... **771**, 781, 793, 817
(1) ... 847
(3) ... 790
(4) ... 788
(5) ... 789
s.2 ... 772
(3) ... 789, 793
(4) ... 793
s.3 ... 772, 794
(4) ... 789
s.4 ... 773, 792

(4) ... 789
(5) ... 789
s.5 ... **774**, 789, 790
(2) ... 789
(3) ... 789
s.6 ... 775
(2) ... 789
(3) ... 789
s.7 ... 775
s.8 ... **776**
s.9 ... 777
s.10 ... 777
s.11 ... 777
s.12 ... 778
(3) ... 778
s.13 ... 779
s.15 ... 779
Open Spaces Act 1906
s.15 ... 299
Parks Regulation Act 1872 ... 300
s.1 ... 300
Peace Preservation (Ireland) Act 1881 ... 414
Persons and Property Act (Ireland) 1881 ... 414
Police Act 1964 ... 91, 95–6
s.41 ... 283
s.48 ... 96
s.51 ... 119
(1) ... 120, 126, 206
(3) ... 128–29, 131, 669
Police Act 1976 ... 108
Police Act 1996 ... 91, 95, 285
s.6(1) ... 92
s.6ZB ... 92
s.10(2) ... 93
s.11(2) ... 93
s.15(2) ... 93
s.22(1) ... 93
s.46 ... 94
s.47 ... 94
s.48 ... 94
s.50 ... 93, 94, 96
s.54 ... 94, 95
s.57 ... 94
s.63 ... 335
s.88 ... 96
s.89 ... **119**, 120, 127, 153, 329
(1) ... 127, 130
(2) ... 127, 130, 134
s.96(1) ... 91
s.103(1) ... 335
s.123 ... 93

s.124 ... 93
Police Act 1997 ... 578, 580, 590
   Pt III ... 578–580, 596
   s.92 ... 579
   s.93 ... **579**, 588
      (3) ... 578
   s.94 ... 579
   Sch.9 ... 778
Police and Criminal Evidence Act 1984 ...
   100, 115–16, 118–19, 127, 149, 150, 169,
   185, 227, 242–43, 257, 286, 429, 430,
   435, 658
   Pt II ... 183
   Pt IV ... 224
   Pt V ... 437
   Pt IX ... 108
   s.1 ... **154**, 162
      (8A) ... 162
   s.2 ... **156**, 163, 166
      (3) ... 164
   s.3 ... **157**
   s.4 ... 150, **158**
   s.7 ... 162
   ss.8–14 ... 184
   s.8 ... 90, 150, **172**, 186, 191–92
      (1B) ... 185
      (2) ... 191
   s.9 ... 173, 184, 186, 782
      (1) ... 185
      (2) ... 185
   s.10 ... **173**
   s.11 ... **174**
   s.12 ... 92, **174**, 187
   s.13 ... **174**
   s.14 ... **174**
   s.15 ... **175**, 184, 188–89, 192
   s.16 ... **176**, 184, 188–89
      (5) ... 191
   s.17 ... 90, 121, 154, **177**, 184, 189–90, 193, 196
      (1)(b) ... 192
      (5) ... 404
      (6) ... 404
   s.18 ... 90, 121, **178**, 184–85, 189–90
      (1) ... 190
      (2) ... 191
   s.19 ... **179**, 184–85, 191–92, 209
   s.20 ... 191
   s.22 ... **180**
   s.23 ... **181**, 192
      (3) ... 191
   s.24 ... **197**, 201

      (1) ... 202
      (3) ... 202
      (5) ... 202
   s.25 ... 201
   s.26 ... 395
   s.28 ... **198**, 206
      (1) ... 204
      (2) ... 204
      (3) ... 206
      (5) ... 204
   s.29 ... **198**, 209
   s.30 ... **198**
   s.30A–30D ... 202
   s.31 ... **200**, 208
   s.32 ... 185, 189–90, **200**, 209
   s.34 ... **209**
   s.36 ... **210**
   s.37 ... **211**, 226
      (7) ... 226
   s.37A ... **213**
      (3) ... 226
   s.37B ... **213**
   s.38 ... **214**
   s.39 ... **215**
   s.40 ... **216**, 226
   s.40A ... 226
   s.41 ... **218**, 224
   s.42 ... 150, **219**, 224
   s.43 ... 150, **221**, 224
   s.44 ... **223–24**
   s.45 ... 224
   s.45A ... 226
   s.46 ... **223–24**
   s.49 ... 224
   s.50 ... 224
   s.51 ... 224
      (1) ... 234
      (6) ... 234
   s.54 ... **228**
      (1) ... 234
      (3) ... 234
      (4) ... 234
   s.54A ... **229**
   s.55 ... **230**, 234
   ss.56–60 ... 257
   s.56 ... **231**, 234
      (2) ... 150
      (5) ... 235
   s.58 ... **232**, 234, 236, 264, 266
      (6) ... 150
      (8) ... 236

s.60A ... 242
s.61 ... 237
  (3) ... 237
  (7A) ... 238
s.61A ... 237
s.62 ... 237, 238
s.63 ... 237
s.64A ... 237, 238
s.67(8) ... 154
  (10) ... 100
ss.76–78 ... 257
s.76 ... 254, 262, 267
  (1) ... 258
  (2) ... 261–62
  (4) ... 263
  (8) ... 260–61
s.76A ... **255**, 262
s.77 ... 255, 262–63
s.78 ... 171, 237, 247, **256**, 258, 263–64, 267,
  268, 271–72, 274
s.82 ... **256**
  (1) ... 258
s.106(1) ... 91
s.117 ... **153**
Sch.1 ... **181–83**, 184–85, 189, 782
Police and Justice Act 2006 ... 94
  s.2 ... 92
  ss.23–27 ... 278
  s.26 ... 369
Police and Magistrates' Courts Act 1994
  s.37(a) ... 154
Police (Northern Ireland) Act 2000
  Sch.6 ... 778
Police Reform Act 2002 ... 95, 109, 277
  s.12 ... **109**
  s.14 ... **109**
  s.51 ... 113
    (6) ... 113
  ss.61–66 ... 277
  s.61(7) ... 368
  s.63 ... 369
  s.64 ... 369
  s.65 ... 369
Post Office Act 1953 ... 676
Postal Services Act 2000
  s.85 ... **675**
Powers of Criminal Courts (Sentencing) Act
2000
  ss.143–144 ... 187
  s.153 ... 357
Prevention of Corruption Act 1906 ... 760

Prevention of Crime Act 1953
  s.1 ... 329
Prevention of Crime (Ireland) Act 1882 ... 414
Prevention of Crimes Amendment Act 1885
  s.2 ... 195
Prevention of Terrorism Act 2005 ... 42, 410, 471,
475
  s.1(2) ... 475
  s.2 ... 475
  s.3(10) ... 50, 476
    (12) ... 482
  Sch. ... 483
Prevention of Terrorism (Additional Powers) Act
1996 ... 429
Prevention of Terrorism (Temporary Provisions)
Act 1974 ... 411, 414, 422
Prevention of Terrorism (Temporary Provisions)
Act 1976 ... 414
  s.12 ... 436
Prevention of Terrorism (Temporary Provisions)
Act 1984 ... 411, 414
  s.12 ... 435, 436
Prevention of Terrorism (Temporary Provisions)
Act 1989 ... 411, 413–14, 416, 422, 761
  s.3 ... 426
  s.14 ... 434–436
  s.16 ... 440
  s.16A ... 450
  s.16B ... 450
  s.20 ... 416
  s.30A ... 423
  s.30B ... 423
  Sch.3 ... 435–36
  Sch.5 ... 440
  Sch.7 ... 429, 761
Prevention of Violence (Temporary Provisions)
Act 1939 ... 414
Prison Act 1952 ... 63
Proceeds of Crime Act 2002 ... 188
Prosecution of Offences Act 1985 ... 118
  s.7(1) ... 334
  Sch.1 ... 692–93
Protection of Children Act 1978 ... 633, 666, 673,
679, 680
  s.1 ... **678**
    (1) ... 679–680
    (4) ... 680, 681
  s.1A ... 679
  s.2 ... **678**
    (3) ... 681
  s.4 ... 679
  s.5 ... 679

s.6 ... **678**
s.7(7) ... 681
Protection from Harassment Act 1997 ... 277,
   360, 361, 363–64, 366, 533
   s.1 ... **357**, 360, 364
      (1) ... 362, 364
      (2) ... 361
      (3) ... 364
   s.2 ... 358, 360–61, 363, 366–67
   s.3 ... 358, 360, 362–364, 535
   s.3A ... 362
   s.4 ... 358, 363, 366–67
   s.5 ... 366
      (5) ... 366
   s.7 ... **359**, 361
      (3) ... 362
      (5) ... 363
   ss.145–149 ... 278
Public Bodies Corrupt Practices Act 1889 ... 760
Public Health Act 1875
   s.164 ... 299
Public Health (Control of Disease) Act 1984
   s.37 ... 709
Public Interest Disclosure Act 1998 ... 795
   s.10 ... 795
Public Meetings Act 1908 ... 371
   s.1 ... **370**
Public Order Act 1936 ... 279, 318
   s.1 ... **287**, 289, 426
      (2) ... 288
   s.2 ... **290–91**
      (1) ... 290
      (5) ... 153
      (7) ... 370
   s.3 ... 309, 314
      (2) ... 307, 317
      (3) ... 316, 317
      (4) ... 317
   s.5 ... 333, 340–41, 346, 352, 354
   s.6 ... 370
   s.7 ... 288
      (1) ... 290
      (3) ... 288
   s.9 ... 288, 340
      (5) ... 316
   s.12 ... 318
   s.14 ... 318
      (1) ... 318
      (2) ... 318
Public Order Act 1986 ... 12, 130, 275, 277, 309,
   335, 362, 989

Pt I ... 333, 363
Pt II ... **309–14**
   ss.1–5 ... 334
   s.1 ... **330**
   s.2 ... **330**, 336
   s.3 ... 315, **331**
      (1) ... 337
      (3) ... 337
   s.4 ... 277, 289, **331**, 337, 340–42, 346, 347,
      354–55, 397
      (1) ... 338, 341
      (2) ... 341–42
   s.4A ... 277, **331**, 337, 342, 349, 351, 355
   s.5 ... 277, 289, 303, **332**, 337, 342, 345,
      347–350, 354, 355, 397
      (1) ... 342, 348
      (2) ... 348
      (3) ... 348–49
   s.6 ... **332**, 334, 349
      (3) ... 354
      (4) ... 354–55
      (5) ... 334
   s.7 ... **333**
   s.8 ... 333, 363, 396
   s.9 ... **333**
   s.10(1) ... 335
   ss.11–14 ... 303
   s.11 ... 318
      (1) ... 319, 396
      (3) ... 319
      (6) ... 319
      (7) ... 314
      (10) ... 314
   s.12 ... 315, 376
      (4) ... 314
      (5) ... 314
      (6) ... 314
      (8)–(10) ... 314
   s.13 ... 326, 376
      (1) ... 316
      (7) ... 314
      (8) ... 314
      (9) ... 314
      (11)–(13) ... 314
   s.14 ... 304
      (4) ... 314
      (5) ... 314
      (6) ... 314
      (8)–(10) ... 314
   s.14A ... 291–92, 319, 325
   s.14B ... 319

(1)–(3) ... 314
(5)–(7) ... 314
s.14C(3) ... 314
314
s.16 ... 318, 367
s.17 ... 989
ss.18–22 ... 989
s.20 ... **674–75**
s.23 ... 989
s.39 ... 326, 327
Public Services Ombudsman (Wales) Act 2000
Sch.1 ... 778
Race Relations Act 1968 ... 905
Race Relations Act 1976 ... 34, 883–886, 890, 893,
925, 944–45, 958, 961–963, 966, 970
Pts II–III ... 922
s.1 ... **943, 966**
(1) ... 950, 967–968, 970
(1A) ... 967–968, 972
(1B) ... 886, 996
s.1A ... 972
s.3 ... **931, 943**
s.3A ... **960–61**
s.11 ... 915
s.12 ... 915
s.13 ... 915
s.17 ... 898, 900, 938
(2) ... 898
s.18 ... 899
s.18A ... 899
s.18B ... 899
s.18D ... 899
s.19 ... 891, 904
s.19A ... 889
s.19B ... 472, **887**, 889–892, 905, 908, 923,
950–951, 957
(6) ... 890
s.19C ... **888**
s.19D ... **888**
(2) ... 889
s.19F ... **888**
s.20 ... 890, 903–905, 907–908, 913, 915, 917
(2) ... 905
s.21 ... 905, **911–12**, 913
(3) ... 912
(4) ... 913
s.21A ... 889
(9) ... 889
s.21B ... 889
s.22 ... **912–13**
s.23 ... 899

(1) ... 904
(2) ... 907–08
s.24 ... 913
s.25 ... **914–15**, 917
s.26 ... **915**
s.27 ... 907
s.28 ... 919
s.28F ... 899
s.29 ... **918–19**
(6) ... 919
s.30 ... **918–20**
s.31 ... **919–20**
s.32 ... **927**
(1) ... 928
(2) ... 908
s.33 ... **919**
s.34(1) ... 927
(2) ... 927
(2A) ... 927
(3A) ... 927
s.35 ... 900, **925–26**
s.36 ... 900
s.39 ... 908
s.41 ... 920, 922–923, 969
(1) ... 952
(1A) ... 922
(2) ... 922–23
s.42 ... 923, 924, 952
s.43(1) ... 927
s.44 ... **932–33**, 952
s.51 ... **920–21**
s.51A ... **921**
s.53 ... 930
s.57 ... 890, 930
s.57A ... 930
s.59 ... **921**
s.67A ... **924**
s.68 ... 930
s.71 ... **891–92**, 893–895, 897–898, 908, 925, 974
s.71A ... **892**
s.76A ... 928
s.76B ... 928
s.78(1) ... 913
Race Relations (Amendment) Act
2000 ... 885–886, 890, 951
Racial and Religious Hatred Act 2006 ... 278, 989
Regulation of Investigatory Powers Act
2000 ... 580, 589–90, 594
Pt I ... 580, 590
Pt II ... 580, 588, 590–591, 593, 596
Pt III ... 580, 596

Pt IV ... 580, 840
ss.1–9 ... 589
s.1 ... **580–82**, 588
  (3) ... 589–591
  (4) ... 589
  (5) ... 589
s.2 ... 582, 588
s.3 ... **582**
  (1) ... 588
  (2) ... 588
  (3) ... 588
s.4 ... **583**
s.5 ... **583–84**, 588
  (2) ... 588
  (3) ... 588
s.6 ... 588
s.8 ... **584–85**
  (1) ... 589
  (4) ... 589
s.9 ... **585–86**
  (6) ... 589
s.16 ... 589
s.17 ... 494, **586**, 589
s.18 ... 494, 589
  (4) ... 589
s.20 ... 589
ss.21–25 ... 589
s.21 ... **586**
s.22 ... **587**
  (2) ... 590
  (5) ... 590
s.23(8) ... 590
s.25 ... 590
s.26 ... **591–92**
  (2) ... 593
  (5) ... 594
  (7) ... 596
  (9) ... 594
s.27 ... **592**
s.30 ... 595
s.36(4) ... 595
ss.49–56 ... 600
s.49 ... **596–98**
  (2) ... 600
  (3) ... 600
s.50 ... **598–600**
s.52 ... 600
s.53(1) ... 600
s.57(1) ... 590
  (5) ... 590
s.58 ... 590

s.59 ... **840**
s.65 ... 590
ss.67(7)–(8) ... 590
  (8) ... 845
s.74 ... 835–36
s.75(1) ... 579
  (7) ... 579
s.81(3) ... 588
Sch.4 ... 833
Sch.5 ... 835, 838
Rent Act 1977 ... 43
Representation of the People Act 1949 ... 306
Representation of the People Act 1983 ... 370
  ss.95–96 ... 305
  s.95 ... 306
  s.97 ... 305, 370
  s.169 ... 370
  s.173 ... 370
  s.174 ... 370
Reserve Forces Act 1996
  Sch.10 ... 778
Riot (Damages) Act 1886 ... 335
  s.2(1) ... 104
Road Traffic Act 1998 ... 233
  s.8 ... 234
  s.159 ... 171
  s.163 ... 171
  (1) ... **171**
  (2) ... 171
  (3) ... 171
  s.172(2) ... 52
School Standards and Framework Act 1998
  s.99(2) ... 988
  (4) ... 988
Scotland Act 1998
  Sch.8 ... 778
Security Service Act 1989 ... 590, 789, 796, 831, 832, 843
  s.1 ... **832**
  (2) ... 843
  s.2 ... **833**
  s.3 ... 843
  s.5(4) ... 845
  Sch.1 ... 844
Security Service Act 1996 ... 841
  s.1(1) ... 833
  (2) ... 833
  s.2 ... 836
Serious Crime Act 2007 ... 159
  s.88 ... 593, 596
  Sch.12 ... 593, 596

Serious Organised Crime and Police Act
2005 ... 150, 161, 184–85, 201, 237–38, 285,
396
  Pt 4 ... 278
  s.3 ... 162
  s.4 ... 161–62
  s.5 ... 162
  s.55(1) ... 109
  s.59 ... 596
  s.121 ... 226
  ss.125–127 ... 367, 536
  s.125 ... 362
    (1) ... 357, 359
    (2) ... 357
    (7) ... 359
  s.126 ... 367
  s.127 ... 367, 396
  s.128 ... 328
  ss.132–138 ... 278, 303, 304
  s.132(1) ... 304
  s.134 ... 304
  s.135 ... 304
  s.136 ... 304
  ss.139–140 ... 368
  s.145 ... 367, 368
  s.146 ... 367
  s.149 ... 367
  Sch.4 ... 596, 778, 833
  Sch.7 ... 150
Sex Discrimination Act 1975 ... 34, 883–886,
889–890, 893, 907, 912, 924, 946, 966
  s.1 ... **943**
    (1) ... 967, 970
    (2) ... 967
    (3) ... 886, 966–67
  s.2A ... 950
  s.3 ... 950
  s.3A ... 957
  s.3B ... 957
  s.4A ... **960**
    (1) ... 961–62
    (3) ... 961
    (4) ... 962
  s.5 ... **943**
    (3) ... 956–57, 974
  s.18 ... 899
  s.21A ... 890, 892, 908, 930
  s.21B(7) ... 890
  s.22 ... **897–98**, 899
    (2) ... 898
  s.23 ... 899

  s.23A ... 899
  s.23B ... 899
  s.25A ... 899
  s.23D ... 899
  s.25 ... 899, 928
  ss.26–28 ... 900
  s.28 ... 919
  s.28F ... 899
  s.29 ... **902–05**, 908
    (1) ... 903–904
    (2) ... 903
    (3) ... 903
  s.30 ... 908, 912
  s.31 ... 913
  s.32 ... 908, 913
  s.33 ... 917
  s.34 ... 908
    (5) ... 908
  s.35 ... 897, **908–09**, 950
    (3) ... 904
  s.35ZA ... 903, 967
  s.36 ... 907
  ss.39–40 ... 919
  s.42A ... 917
  s.43 ... **926**
  s.44 ... 908
  s.45 ... **909**
  s.46 ... 897, 909
  s.51A ... 922
  s.52 ... **923**
  s.62 ... **928**, 930
  s.66 ... **928–30**
    (3) ... 930
  s.66A ... **929–30**
    (2) ... 930
  s.66B ... 925
  s.76 ... 930
  s.76A ... 892, 908
Sexual Offences Act 1985 ... 397
Sexual Offences Act 2003 ... 569, 679
  ss.67–68 ... **569**
  s.68(1) ... 569
  s.139 ... 678
Special Immigration Appeals Act 1997 ... 767
  s.2 ... 472
  s.6 ... 472
  s.7 ... 472
Special Education Needs and Disability Act
2001 ... 898
Telecommunications Act 1984
  s.43 ... 397

s.45 ... 589
Sch.4 ... 780
Terrorism Act 2000 ... 291, 411, 413, 416, 422
   Pt III ... 428, 429
   Pt VII ... 413–14
   s.1 ... 413
     (4) ... 416
   s.2 ... **413**
   s.3 ... **417**
     (1) ... 425
     (4) ... 422
     (5) ... 422
   s.4 ... **419**
   s.5 ... **419**
   s.7 ... 420
   s.9 ... **420**
   s.10 ... **420**
   s.11 ... **421**
     (1) ... 425, 488
     (2) ... 425
   s.12 ... 328, **421**, 426
   s.13 ... 426
   s.14 ... 428
   ss.15–28 ... 429
   s.15 ... 428
   s.16 ... 428–29
   s.17 ... 428
   s.18 ... 428
     (2) ... 429
   s.19 ... 428
     (3) ... 429
     (5) ... 428
     (6) ... 428
   s.20 ... 428
   s.21 ... 428
     (5) ... 429
   ss.21ZA–21ZC ... 428
   s.21A ... 429
   s.21B ... 429
   s.21D ... 429
   ss.21E–21H ... 429
   ss.24–31 ... 455
   s.32 ... **426**, 429
   ss.33–36 ... 429
   s.38B ... **426**
   s.39 ... **427**, 429
   s.40 ... **431**, 434
     (1) ... 435, 439
   s.41 ... **431**, 434–35, 438
   s.42 ... **432**
   s.43 ... **432**

   s.44 ... 417, **432**, 440, 448
   s.45 ... **433**, 440
   s.46 ... **434**
   s.47 ... **434**
   s.53 ... 440
   s.54 ... 450, 488
     (1) ... 487
     (6) ... 450
   s.55 ... 450
   ss.56–61 ... 453
   s.56 ... **448**, 450
     (2) ... 450
   s.57 ... **448**, 450, 451
     (4) ... 450
   s.58 ... **448**, 450–452
     (4) ... 450
   ss.59–61 ... 452
   s.59 ... **449**
   s.62 ... **449**
   s.63 ... **450**
   ss.63A–63E ... 453
   s.97 ... 440
   s.114 ... **453**
   s.115 ... 455
   s.116 ... **453**
   s.117 ... 455
   s.118 ... 429, 451, **453**, 455, 793
   s.119 ... 428
   s.121 ... **454**
   s.124 ... **454**
   s.126 ... 416
   Sch.2 ... 422
   Sch.3A ... 429
   Sch.5 ... 429, 430–31
   Sch.6 ... 430, 431
   Sch.6A ... 431
   Sch.7 ... 438, 440, 455
   Sch.8 ... 434, 438–440
   Sch.9 ... 766
   Sch.14 ... 455
Terrorism Act 2002 ... 952
Terrorism Act 2005 ... 412, 416
Terrorism Act 2006 ... 410, 416–17, 424, 485
   Pt 1 ... 486
   Pt 2 ... 486
   s.1 ... 486, **488–89**
   s.2 ... 486, **489–90**
     (2) ... 486
     (3) ... 487
     (4) ... 487
   s.3 ... 486–87

s.5 ... 487–88, **491**
s.6 ... 487–88
  (1) ... 487
ss.8–11 ... 488
s.8 ... 488
ss.9–11 ... 487
s.9 ... 487–88
s.10 ... 488
s.11 ... 488
s.17 ... 488
s.20 ... **491**
s.21 ... 418, 486
ss.22 ... 486
  (1)–(2) ... 419
  (3) ... 419
  (4) ... 419
  (5) ... 419
  (6) ... 419
  (9) ... 420
s.23 ... 439
s.24 ... 439, 486
s.26 ... 429, 486
s.28 ... 486
s.29 ... 440
s.30 ... 486
  (1) ... 433
  (2) ... 433
  (4) ... 433
s.31(1)–(4) ... 837
  (1) ... 839
  (8) ... 839
s.34(a) ... 413
s.37(1) ... 426
Sch.2 ... 486
Terrorism (Northern Ireland) Act 2006 ... 414
Theatres Act 1968 ... 630–31, 674
  s.1 ... **630**
  s.2(1) ... 674
  (4) ... **674**
Theft Act 1968
  s.26 ... **188**
Trade Union and Labour Relations
(Consolidation) Act 1992
  s.145A ... 795
  s.145B ... 795
  s.146 ... 795
  s.220 ... 303, 396
  s.241 ... 372
United Nations Act 1946 ... 493
  s.1 ... 493
Video Recordings Act 1984 ... 633–34, 636, 657

s.1 ... 635
s.2 ... 635
s.4(1) ... 635
s.4A ... 636
s.7 ... 635
ss.9–11 ... 635
s.9 ... 637
s.16A ... 635
Video Recordings Act 1993 ... 636
Violent Crime Reduction Act 2006
  s.27 ... 370
Wildlife and Countryside Act 1981
  s.19 ... 163
Youth Justice and Criminal Evidence Act 1999
  ss.44–52 ... 711
  s.59 ... 253
  Sch.2 ... 711
  Sch.3 ... 253

OTHER LEGISLATION

Convention on the Elimination of All Forms of
  Discrimination Against Women (1979) ... 14
Convention on the Elimination of All Forms of
  Racial Discrimination (1966) ... 14
Convention on the Rights of the Child
  (1989) ... 14
European Convention for the Prevention of
  Torture (1987) ... 14
European Convention for the Protection
  of Human Rights and Fundamental
  Freedoms ... 4–5, 17, **27–31**, 33, 51, 63, 67, 244,
  516
  Arts.2–12 ... 33
  Art.2 ... 69, 71, 79–81, 118, 405, 497, 498, 499,
    501, 766, 866, 871–72
    (1) ... 69, 80
    (2) ... 69, 80, 497
  Art.3 ... 81–83, 118, 261, 328, 412, 456,
    473–474, 497
  Art.5 ... 39, 63, 84, 118, 134, 208, 377, 391–92,
    397, 399, 412, 436, 476, 486
    (1) ... 84–5, 162, 317, 436–437, 456
    (2) ... **85**, 205, 206, 436
    (3) ... 34, 85, 435–36
    (4) ... 85, 767
    (5) ... 63, 435
  Art.6 ... 52, 63, 101, 162, 236, 247, 249, 253,
    268, 272, 328, 369, 397, 399, 430, 474, 483,
    485, 686, 706–07, 713, 751–52, 767
    (1) ... 50, 369, 438, 685–87, 753, 767–68,
    822

(3) ... 235, 438
Art.7 ... 452, 486
Art.8 ... 34–5, 59, 86, 118, 184, 235, 268, 287,
   328, 405–06, 503–507, 510, 515, 518, 522, 533,
   542, 558–560, 564, 568, 572, 578, 588, 590,
   610, 613, 767, 768, 831, 832, 845, 855
   (1) ... 503, 518, 831, 857, 875, 877
   s. ... 62, 405, 503, 509, 518, 522
Art.9 ... 41, 86, 350, 473, 486, 767, 900, 942
   62
Art.10 ... 35, 57, 86, 275, 291, 304–06, 317,
   349–351, 365, 374, 377, 391, 397, 486, 558,
   564, 568, 612–614, 616, 620–622, 629, 645,
   649, 660, 686, 694, 743, 753, 759, 767, 817
10(1) ... 855
10(2) ... 761
   s. ... 41, 62, 86, 564, 613, 616–617
Art.11 ... 34, 275, 291, 304, 306, 309, 317, 325,
   374, 375, 377, 391, 397, 767
   s. ... 86, 317
   s. ... 86, 304, 317
Art.13 ... 33, 62, 81, 108, 510, 767, 768, 832, 845
Art.14 ... 33, 34, 41, 43, 81, 118, 317, 325, 351,
   456, 471, **856**–58, 860–861, 863–866, 868,
   871–878, 883, 954, 958
Art.15 ... 34, 456, 472
   (1) ... 456, 471
Arts.16–18 ... 33
Art.17 ... 351
Art.27(2) ... 861
Art.34 ... 39
Art.35 ... 351
Art.41 ... 40
Art.53 ... 34
Protocol 1 ... 858, 861, 973
Protocol 2 ... 868
Protocol 12 ... **856**–857, 860, 878
European Social Charter (1961) ... 34
Genocide Convention (1948) ... 14
ILO Freedom of Association Convention
   (1987) ... 14
International Covenant on Civil and Political
   Rights (1966) ... 14
   Art.6 ... 118
   Art.7 ... 118
   Art.9 ... 118
   Art.17 ... 118
   Art.19 ... 275
      s. ... 612
   Art.21 ... 275

Art.26 ... 118
International Covenant on Economic, Social and
   Cultural Rights (1996) ... 34
UN Charter on the Rights of the Child ... 239
UN Convention Against Torture (1984) ... 14, 474
Universal Declaration of Human Rights (United
   Nations) (1948) ... 4, **5**–8, 14, 34

AUSTRALIA

Constitution ... 612

CANADA

Bill of Rights (1982) ... 13
Canada Act (1982)
   Sch.B ... 13
Charter of Rights and Freedoms ... 654
   s.2(b) ... 741
   s.7 ... 766
   s.33 ... 13
Criminal Code ... 654

FRANCE

Constitution ... 612
Declaration of the Rights of Man of the Citizen
   (1789) ... 3–4, 612

NEW ZEALAND

Bill of Rights (1990) ... 13

SWITZERLAND

Criminal Code ... 629

USA

Bill of Rights (1791) ... 3–4
Civil Rights Act 1964
   Title VII ... 965
Constitution ... 612–13
Intelligence Identities Protection Act
   (1982) ... 803

PART ONE: Introduction

1

CIVIL LIBERTIES AND HUMAN RIGHTS: DEFINITIONS AND CONTEXT

1. INTRODUCTION[1]

The purpose of this chapter is to say something of definitions of key concepts and of the context in which the law discussed in this book is to be found. As with many labels for areas of law, the term 'civil liberties' does not have a settled accepted meaning. Furthermore, given that a major vehicle for the protection of civil liberties has since 2 October 2008 been the Human Rights Act 1998, it is also necessary to consider the concept of 'human rights'. Within these expressions are the words 'liberty' and 'right', which also have their difficulty.

2. 'CIVIL LIBERTIES'

A starting point is the OED definition of 'civil liberty' as

> natural liberty[2] so far restricted by established law as is expedient or, necessary for the good of the community.

Writers cited include Milton:[3]

> When complaints are freely heard, deeply considered and speedily reformed, then is the utmost bound of civil liberty attained that wise men look for

and Austin:[4]

> Political or civil liberty is the liberty from legal obligation which is left or granted by a sovereign government to any of its subjects.

---

[1] See, generally, D. Feldman, *Civil Liberties and Human Rights in England and Wales* (OUP, Oxford, 2nd edn, 2002), Chap. 1; C. Gearty, *Civil Liberties* (OUP, Oxford, 2007).

[2] I.e. 'the state in which every one is free to act as he thinks fit, subject only to the laws of nature' (OED).

[3] *Areopagitica: A speech for the liberty of unlicensed printing to the Parliament of England* (1644).

[4] *Jurisprudence* (1879) I.vi.281.

This is useful but overbroad. 'Civil liberty' here is the residual freedom that is left after ration-ally devised laws have imposed restrictions for some publicly useful purpose. It seems that the law-makers are exhorted or expected to act rationally, but are not constrained by law to do so. There also seems to be no suggestion that some freedoms are more significant than others, with criteria put forward to explain why that should be so.

Modern usage tends to take that further step, identifying some liberties as deserving of particular attention, and indeed protection. At this point the exercise becomes analogous to that of identifying some 'rights' as fundamental and deserving of recognition as 'human rights', to which we return below.

For David Feldman,[5]

The notion that it is good for people to enjoy 'liberty', or freedom, is basic to political liberalism. In its sim-plest and most general sense, liberty entails non-interference by others with one's freedom of choice and action. It supports personal autonomy.

However, there is

no generally agreed way of separating civil liberties from other liberties.

Feldman's own approach is this:

Civil liberties are those which people enjoy by virtue of being citizens of a state, rather than by reason of being merely members of human society. To say that something is a civil liberty implies that (a) the liberty is particularly significant in allowing people to participate as a citizen in the functioning of the state, such as freedom of political expression, or (b) the liberty is particularly significant in defining the relationship between the state and its citizens, such as freedom from arbitrary or discriminatory treatment. In either case, describing something as a civil liberty indicates that one thinks that the state has a special obligation to protect one against interference with it, either as a matter of political morality or as a matter or law.

This takes matters further, but is not presented as a tight definition, given the obvious room for debate as to which liberties are 'particularly significant' for the stated purposes.

Conor Gearty in his book *Civil Liberties*[6] has recently articulated a distinctive character-isation of 'civil liberties':

...civil liberties is another name for the political freedoms that we must have available to us all if it is to be true to say of us that we live in a society that adheres to the principle of representative, or democratic, government. It follows that the subject is concerned with the right to vote, which...is the core civil liberty, and also with those other basic freedoms—life, liberty, thought, expression, assembly and association—that help give full meaning to that right. The prohibition on politically-motivated ill-treatment (at its most extreme, torture and other inhuman and degrading treatment) is also within this book's remit. These are the freedoms which are essential to the proper function of our contemporary political community.[7]

By way of shorthand,

it is about the law and practice of political freedom.[8]

---

[5] Op. cit., pp. 3–5.   [6] Op. cit.   [7] P. 3.   [8] Ibid.

This is a compelling analysis. However, our book continues to include materials on a broader basis than this, including police powers and the protection of privacy as core areas. The former area certainly bears directly on such matters as public order and terrorism, but are also more generally a key part of the whole criminal justice process and to that extent stray beyond Gearty's characterisation; the latter is further away still. Conversely, we have not included materials on the right to vote which is clearly at the core of political freedom, but which raises relatively few issues today in the UK,[9] where there has been general adult suffrage since 1948.[10] The result is that there are topics in the book which can be considered as human rights rather than civil liberties; the ultimate choice has been pragmatic rather than theoretically watertight.[11]

3. HUMAN RIGHTS

The concept of 'human rights' is broader than that of civil liberties. It has generated both a vast literature and a lack of consensus as to its historical evolution, contemporary foundations, status and content. One matter that is clear is that the need to promote and protect human rights is in practice recognised as a core feature of both international law and the national laws of most states in the world. It is also common to speak of a 'human rights movement' arguing for such developments. In the UK, overt effect to this has now been given by the enactment of the Human Rights Act 1998.

Issues that have generated particular debate include these. First, can the modern position of human rights be seen as the direct descendant of the rights and freedoms contained (for England) in Magna Carta (1215) and the Bill of Rights (1689), in the French Declaration of the Rights of Man and of the Citizen in 1789 and in the American Bill of Rights (the first 10 amendments to the US constitution, adopted in 1791)? The more persuasive view is that it cannot. None of these provided significant protection for ordinary citizens. Magna Carta and the English Bill of Rights were political settlements.[12]

The former, amongst many other, very specific provisions, did guarantee (by para. 29 of the 1297 version) the rights for a 'freeman' not to be 'taken or detained in prison, or be disseised of his freehold . . . but by lawful judgment of his peers, or by the law of the land'; but this was a right for property owning men.[13] Magna Carta was subsequently used by Sir Edmund Coke as a basis to develop arguments for the protection of property rights.[14] The 1689 Bill of Rights did guarantee free speech in Parliament, and provided that 'no excessive fine' be imposed 'nor cruel and unusual punishment inflicted,' but was essentially a settlement of the position of the new Protestant constitutional monarchy, and prohibited

---

9 See Gearty, op. cit., Chap. 4.

10 The main current controversy is the exclusion of prisoners from the right to vote, which has been held to be incompatible with First Protocol, Art. 3, ECHR: *Hirst v UK* (2004) 38 EHRR 825; *Hirst v UK (No. 2)* (2005) 42 EHRR 849; and the grudging steps of the UK Government to move towards compliance: see DCA, *Voting rights for convicted prisoners detained within the UK* (Consultation Paper CP29/06). As to issues concerning political advertising, see below, p. 649.

11 We accordingly do not repair the perceived failure of previous editions to provide theoretical insights marking out the territory of the subject of civil liberties: see the comments by K.D. Ewing and C. Gearty, *The Struggle for Civil Liberties* (OUP, Oxford, 2000).

12 A. Clapham, *Human Rights* (OUP, Oxford, 2007), p. 6.

13 Ibid. The 1297 version of Magna Carta is still on the statute book; almost all of its provisions have now been repealed.

14 Or 'misused': A. Woodiwiss, *Human Rights* (Routledge, Abingdon, 2005), p. 35, referring to Coke's *Institutes of the Laws of England* (1628–44).

for the future various actions that had been taken by the Catholic James II. The Declaration of the Rights of Man and of the Citizen did not involve respect for the rights of women[15] and did not prevent an era of state terror. The US Bill of Rights effectively was applied only to the (relatively insignificant) federal as opposed to state institutions until the twentieth century.[16]

As to foundations, views that justification for recognising the need for respect for human rights can be found in religion, or theories that people possess 'natural rights' are no longer widely held.[17] Gearty has developed an attractive argument that a basis can be found in the

evolutionary insight that to progress the human species needs kindliness, compassion and hospitality as well as the basic survival instincts of the (only ostensibly) fittest.[18]

Compassion here is more than 'mere kindness, pity and tolerance':

It is about enjoying and enabling the other to thrive rather than simply bearing with him or her. There is more here than forbearance from cruelty and humiliation…[T]his human rights language asserts that we are all equal in view of our humanity and that our dignity…demands that we each of us be given the chance to do the best we can to thrive, to flourish, to do something with ourselves.[19]

In terms of status, some take the view that 'rights' (and therefore 'human rights') are

a legally enforceable set of expectations as to how others, most obviously the state, should behave towards rights bearers.[20]

Others prefer a broader view that the concept stands also as a political and moral concept.

Finally, in terms of content there is much debate over the question which rights should receive the imprimatur of a label as 'human rights'.

One possible response to these difficulties is to see the 'human rights movement' simply as a modern political phenomenon, a reaction to the horrors of the Second World War, including genocide and torture. The key moment was the adoption in 1948 by the United Nations of the Universal Declaration of Human Rights.[21] This has led to the adoption through international and national political processes of statements of rights that are legally enforceable as a matter of international or national law. The Universal Declaration contains a long list of candidates for inclusion in such documents; it is then a matter for political debate as to which rights should be recognised in a particular statement; the wording that should be employed; and the extent to which and how they should be enforceable. This has led to a series of international covenants, conventions and treaties[22] and the recognition of fundamental rights in the constitutions of most states and under EU law.[23] Particularly significant for the UK has been accession to the European Convention on

---

[15] Ibid., p. 10.

[16] Woodiwiss, op. cit., pp. 40–41. See further K. Ewing and C. Gearty, *The Struggle for Civil Liberties* (OUP, Oxford, 2000), Chap. 1.

[17] See. C Gearty, *Can Human Rights Survive?* (CUP, Cambridge, 2006), Chap. 2.

[18] Ibid., p. 57.   [19] Ibid., p. 49.   [20] Woodiwiss, op.cit., p. xi.

[21] See generally J. Donnelly, *Universal Human Rights in Theory and Practice* (Cornell UP, New York, 2nd edn, 2003).

[22] See below p. 34; Feldman, op.cit., pp. 34–57.

[23] On the latter, see Feldman, op.cit., pp. 74–77.

Human Rights, and the measure of domestic incorporation effected by the Human Rights Act 1998.[24]

The Universal Declaration is of such fundamental significance that we set it out in full here.

- **Universal Declaration of Human Rights**

Preamble

Whereas recognition of the inherent dignity and of the equal and inalienable rights of all members of the human family is the foundation of freedom, justice and peace in the world,

Whereas disregard and contempt for human rights have resulted in barbarous acts which have outraged the conscience of mankind, and the advent of a world in which human beings shall enjoy freedom of speech and belief and freedom from fear and want has been proclaimed as the highest aspiration of the common people,

Whereas it is essential, if man is not to be compelled to have recourse, as a last resort, to rebellion against tyranny and oppression, that human rights should be protected by the rule of law,

Whereas it is essential to promote the development of friendly relations between nations,

Whereas the peoples of the United Nations have in the Charter reaffirmed their faith in fundamental human rights, in the dignity and worth of the human person and in the equal rights of men and women and have determined to promote social progress and better standards of life in larger freedom,

Whereas Member States have pledged themselves to achieve, in cooperation with the United Nations, the promotion of universal respect for and observance of human rights and fundamental freedoms,

Whereas a common understanding of these rights and freedoms is of the greatest importance for the full realization of this pledge,

Now, therefore,

The General Assembly,

Proclaims this Universal Declaration of Human Rights as a common standard of achievement for all peoples and all nations, to the end that every individual and every organ of society, keeping this Declaration constantly in mind, shall strive by teaching and education to promote respect for these rights and freedoms and by progressive measures, national and international, to secure their universal and effective recognition and observance, both among the peoples of Member States themselves and among the peoples of territories under their jurisdiction.

Article 1

All human beings are born free and equal in dignity and rights. They are endowed with reason and conscience and should act towards one another in a spirit of brotherhood.

Article 2

Everyone is entitled to all the rights and freedoms set forth in this Declaration, without distinction of any kind, such as race, colour, sex, language, religion, political or other opinion, national or social origin, property, birth or other status.

Furthermore, no distinction shall be made on the basis of the political, jurisdictional or international status of the country or territory to which a person belongs, whether it be independent, trust, non-self-governing or under any other limitation of sovereignty.

Article 3

Everyone has the right to life, liberty and security of person.

---

[24] See Chap. 2.

Article 4

No one shall be held in slavery or servitude; slavery and the slave trade shall be prohibited in all their forms.

Article 5

No one shall be subjected to torture or to cruel, inhuman or degrading treatment or punishment.

Article 6

Everyone has the right to recognition everywhere as a person before the law.

Article 7

All are equal before the law and are entitled without any discrimination to equal protection of the law. All are entitled to equal protection against any discrimination in violation of this Declaration and against any incitement to **such discrimination**.

Article 8

Everyone has the right to an effective remedy by the competent national tribunals for acts violating the fundamental rights granted him by the constitution or by law.

Article 9

No one shall be subjected to arbitrary arrest, detention or exile.

Article 10

Everyone is entitled in full equality to a fair and public hearing by an independent and impartial tribunal, in the determination of his rights and obligations and of any criminal charge against him.

Article 11

1. Everyone charged with a penal offence has the right to be presumed innocent until proved guilty according to law in a public trial at which he has had all the guarantees necessary for his defence.

2. No one shall be held guilty of any penal offence on account of any act or omission which did not constitute a penal offence, under national or international law, at the time when it was committed. Nor shall a heavier penalty be imposed than the one that was applicable at the time the penal offence was committed.

Article 12

No one shall be subjected to arbitrary interference with his privacy, family, home or correspondence, nor to attacks upon his honour and reputation. Everyone has the right to the protection of the law against such interference or attacks.

Article 13

1. Everyone has the right to freedom of movement and residence within the borders of each State.

2. Everyone has the right to leave any country, including his own, and to return to his country.

Article 14

1. Everyone has the right to seek and to enjoy in other countries asylum from persecution.

2. This right may not be invoked in the case of prosecutions genuinely arising from non-political crimes or from acts contrary to the purposes and principles of the United Nations.

Article 15

1. Everyone has the right to a nationality.

2. No one shall be arbitrarily deprived of his nationality nor denied the right to change his nationality.

Article 16

1. Men and women of full age, without any limitation due to race, nationality or religion, have the right to marry and to found a family. They are entitled to equal rights as to marriage, during marriage and at its dissolution.

2. Marriage shall be entered into only with the free and full consent of the intending spouses.

3. The family is the natural and fundamental group unit of society and is entitled to protection by society and the State.

Article 17

1. Everyone has the right to own property alone as well as in association with others.

2. No one shall be arbitrarily deprived of his property.

Article 18

Everyone has the right to freedom of thought, conscience and religion; this right includes freedom to change his religion or belief, and freedom, either alone or in community with others and in public or private, to manifest his religion or belief in teaching, practice, worship and observance.

Article 19

Everyone has the right to freedom of opinion and expression; this right includes freedom to hold opinions without interference and to seek, receive and impart information and ideas through any media and regardless of frontiers.

Article 20

1. Everyone has the right to freedom of peaceful assembly and association.

2. No one may be compelled to belong to an association.

Article 21

1. Everyone has the right to take part in the government of his country, directly or through freely chosen representatives.

2. Everyone has the right to equal access to public service in his country.

3. The will of the people shall be the basis of the authority of government; this will shall be expressed in periodic and genuine elections which shall be by universal and equal suffrage and shall be held by secret vote or by equivalent free voting procedures.

Article 22

Everyone, as a member of society, has the right to social security and is entitled to realization, through national effort and international co-operation and in accordance with the organization and resources of each State, of the economic, social and cultural rights indispensable for his dignity and the free development of his personality.

Article 23

1. Everyone has the right to work, to free choice of employment, to just and favourable conditions of work and to protection against unemployment.

2. Everyone, without any discrimination, has the right to equal pay for equal work.

3. Everyone who works has the right to just and favourable remuneration ensuring for himself and his family an existence worthy of human dignity, and supplemented, if necessary, by other means of social protection.

4. Everyone has the right to form and to join trade unions for the protection of his interests.

Article 24

Everyone has the right to rest and leisure, including reasonable limitation of working hours and periodic holidays with pay.

Article 25

1. Everyone has the right to a standard of living adequate for the health and well-being of himself and of his family, including food, clothing, housing and medical care and necessary social services, and the right to security in the event of unemployment, sickness, disability, widowhood, old age or other lack of livelihood in circumstances beyond his control.

2. Motherhood and childhood are entitled to special care and assistance. All children, whether born in or out of wedlock, shall enjoy the same social protection.

Article 26

1. Everyone has the right to education. Education shall be free, at least in the elementary and fundamental stages. Elementary education shall be compulsory. Technical and professional education shall be made generally available and higher education shall be equally accessible to all on the basis of merit.

2. Education shall be directed to the full development of the human personality and to the strengthening of respect for human rights and fundamental freedoms. It shall promote understanding, tolerance and friendship among all nations, racial or religious groups, and shall further the activities of the United Nations for the maintenance of peace.

3. Parents have a prior right to choose the kind of education that shall be given to their children.

Article 27

1. Everyone has the right freely to participate in the cultural life of the community, to enjoy the arts and to share in scientific advancement and its benefits.

2. Everyone has the right to the protection of the moral and material interests resulting from any scientific, literary or artistic production of which he is the author.

Article 28

Everyone is entitled to a social and international order in which the rights and freedoms set forth in this Declaration can be fully realized.

Article 29

1. Everyone has duties to the community in which alone the free and full development of his personality is possible.

2. In the exercise of his rights and freedoms, everyone shall be subject only to such limitations as are determined by law solely for the purpose of securing due recognition and respect for the rights and freedoms of others and of meeting the just requirements of morality, public order and the general welfare in a democratic society.

3. These rights and freedoms may in no case be exercised contrary to the purposes and principles of the United Nations.

Article 30

Nothing in this Declaration may be interpreted as implying for any State, group or person any right to engage in any activity or to perform any act aimed at the destruction of any of the rights and freedoms set forth herein.

It will be seen at once that civil liberties form a subset of the matters set out here, reflecting a broad distinction between political and civil rights on the one hand and economic and social rights on the other.

Finally, it must not be thought that the achievements of the 'human rights movement' have met universal acclaim. Recurrent criticisms include that the approach attaches too much significance to the rights of individuals at the expense of the interests of the less privileged, communities or societies;[25] that invocation of the need to protect human rights has been used as a rallying cry by states to justify their own widespread invasion of individual liberties;[26] and that reliance on the law rather than politics to provide significant protection for those most at risk is misplaced, not least because of all the costs and difficulties of access to legal systems. Two other major issues are first, the extent to which respect for human rights should go beyond the prevention of intrusion by the state to require the state to act positively to facilitate the exercise of freedoms;[27] and second, whether it is indeed desirable for there to be general declarations of rights in domestic law that can be used by the courts to strike down state action, including normally, but not in the UK, primary legislation.[28] There is always a risk that such declarations distract attention from the promotion of human rights interests through ordinary specific legislation. Conferral of a power to strike down primary legislation can also be a distraction, placing the judges in direct confrontation with politicians and legislatures, and 'downgrading the value of a political culture in which they play little or no part'.[29]

4. 'LIBERTY' AND 'RIGHT'

Finally, it should be noted that the terms 'liberty' and 'right' are often used loosely rather than precisely. Particularly helpful here is Hohfeld's identification of eight fundamental legal conceptions.[30] There are 'four conceptions of legal advantages and four of legal disadvantages'.[31] The former have been explained as follows:[32]

1 *A legal liberty.* One party *x* has a legal liberty in face of some second party *y* to perform some action *A* if and only if *x* has no legal duty to *y* to refrain from doing *A*. I have, for example, the legal liberty in face of Professor Tay to use her name in this example; I do not, however, have the legal liberty of referring to her in any libellous manner. Let us suppose that I have secretly, and profitably, contracted with Professor Kamenka to mention him rather than Professor Tay at this point. I would still have the legal liberty in face of Professor Tay to use her name here, for I have no legal duty to *her* to refrain from doing so. But I would not have the legal liberty vis-à-vis professor Kamenka to mention Professor Tay here, for under our contract I have a legal duty to him not to do so.

---

[25] Cf. Marx's critique: see Clapham, op.cit., pp.12–13.   [26] See pp. 409–410 below.

[27] See S. Fredman, *Human Rights Transformed: Positive Rights and Positive Duties* (OUP, Oxford, 2008).

[28] Compare the views of K.D. Ewing, 'The Futility of the Human Rights Act' [2004] PL 829 and C. Gearty, *Principles of Human Rights Adjudication* (OUP, Oxford, 2004), *Can Human Rights Survive?* (2006) and *Civil Liberties* (2007); Gearty endorses the approach of the HRA, but opposes any power to strike down primary legislation.

[29] Gearty, *Can Human Rights Survive?*, p. 72.

[30] W.N. Hohfeld, *Fundamental Legal Conceptions as Applied in Judicial Reasoning, and other legal essays* (edited by W.W. Cook, New Haven, 1919).

[31] C. Wellman, 'A new conception of human rights' in E. Kamenka and A.E.-S.Tay, *Human Rights* (Edward Arnold, London, 1978), p. 50.

[32] Ibid., pp. 50–51. This account uses different terminology from Hohfeld, who used 'privilege' for legal liberty and 'right' for legal claim.

2 *A legal claim*. One party *x* has a legal claim against some second party *y* that *y* do some action *A* if and only if *y* has a legal duty to *x* to do *A*. Thus, I have a legal claim against Jones, to whom I loaned ten dollars on the understanding that he repay me today, that he repay me today; similarly, I have a legal claim against Smith, whoever Smith may be, that he not strike me.

3 *A legal power*. One party *x* has a legal power over some second party *y* to bring about some specific legal consequence *C* for *y* if and only if some voluntary action of *x* would be legally recognized as having this consequence for *y*. For example, a policeman has the legal power over a fleeing suspect to place him under arrest, and the owner of a car has the legal power over someone offering to buy his car of making him the new owner of the car.

4 *A legal immunity*. One party *x* has a legal immunity against some second party *y* from some specified legal consequence *C* if and only if *y* lacks the legal power to do any action whatsoever that would be recognized by the law as having the consequence *C* for *x*. Thus, I have a legal immunity against my wife's renouncing my United States citizenship, but I lack a legal immunity against her spending the monies in our joint bank account. These, roughly indicated and briefly illustrated, are the four legal advantages Hohfeld takes to be fundamental in the law.[33] (The four corresponding legal disadvantages are a legal no-claim, a legal duty, a legal liability and a legal disability.)

Both the expressions 'civil liberties' and 'human rights' in practice may invoke any of these four conceptions. What is important is to understand which sense is employed in each particular context.

---

[33] Whether Hohfeld was correct to say that legal duties *always* have correlative rights need not concern us: see further J.W. Harris, *Legal Philosophies* (Butterworths, London, 1980), Chap. 7.

2

PROTECTING CIVIL LIBERTIES AND HUMAN RIGHTS IN ENGLISH LAW

1. THE FORMER METHOD

● Report of an Interdepartmental Working Group Concerning Legislation on Human Rights, with Particular Reference to the European Convention (1976–77) HL 81

Our arrangements for the protection of human rights are different from those of most other countries. The differences are related to differences in our constitutional traditions. Although our present constitution may be regarded as deriving in part from the revolution settlement of 1688–89, consolidated by the Union of 1707, we, unlike our European neighbours and many Commonwealth countries, do not owe our present system of government either to a revolution or to a struggle for independence. The United Kingdom—

(a) has an omnicompetent Parliament, with absolute power to enact any law and change any previous law; the courts in England and Wales have not, since the seventeenth century, recognised even in theory any higher legal order by reference to which Acts of Parliament could be held void;[1] in Scotland the courts, while reserving the right to treat an Act as void for breaching a fundamental term of the Treaty of Union [see *McCormick v Lord Advocate* 1953 SC 396], have made it clear that they foresee no likely circumstances in which they would do so;

(b) unlike other modern democracies, has no written constitution;

(c) unlike countries in civil law tradition, makes no fundamental distinction, as regards rights or remedies, between 'public law' governing the actions of the State and its agents, and 'private law' regulating the relationships of private citizens with one another; nor have we a coherent system of administrative law applied by specialised tribunals or courts and with its own appropriate remedies;[2]

(d) has not generally codified its law, and our courts adopt a relatively narrow and literal approach to the interpretation of statutes;

(e) unlike the majority of EEC countries and the United States, does not, by ratifying a treaty or convention, make it automatically part of the domestic law (nor do we normally give effect to such an international agreement by incorporating the agreement itself into our law).

---

[1] *Ed.* Following the European Communities Act 1972, the UK courts have recognised limitations upon parliamentary sovereignty that result from European Union law.

[2] *Ed.* This ceased to be wholly true with the introduction of the present Order 53 remedy for judicial review and the distinction between public and private law used in its application: see *O'Reilly v Mackman* [1983] 2 AC 237, HL.

In other countries the rights of the citizen are usually (thought not universally) to be found enunciated in general terms in a Bill of Rights or other constitutional document. The effectiveness of such instruments varies greatly. A Bill of Rights is not an automatic guarantee of liberty; its efficacy depends on the integrity of the institutions which apply it, and ultimately on the determination of the people that it should be maintained. The United Kingdom as such has no Bill of Rights of this kind. The Bill of Rights of 1688, though more concerned with the relationship between the English Parliament and the Crown, did contain some important safeguards for personal liberty—as did the Claim of Right of 1689, its Scottish equivalent. Among the provisions common to both the Bill of Rights and the Claim of Right are declarations that excessive bail is illegal and that it is the right of subjects to petition the Crown without incurring penalties. But the protection given by these instruments to the rights and liberties of the citizen is much narrower than the constitutional guarantees now afforded in many other democratic countries.[3]

The effect of the United Kingdom system of law is to provide, through the development of the common law and by express statutory enactment, a diversity of specific rights with their accompanying remedies. Thus, to secure the individual's right to freedom from unlawful or arbitrary detention, our law provides specific and detailed remedies such as habeas corpus[4] and the action for false imprisonment. The rights which have been afforded in this way are for the most part negative rights to be protected from interference from others, rather than positive rights to behave in a particular way. Those rights which have emerged in the common law can always be modified by Parliament. Parliament's role is all-pervasive—potentially, at least. It continually adapts existing rights and remedies and provides new ones, and no doubt this process would continue even if a comprehensive Bill of Rights were enacted.

The legal remedies provided for interference with the citizen's rights have in recent times been overlaid by procedures which are designed to afford not so much remedies in the strict sense of the term as facilities for obtaining independent and impartial scrutiny of action by public bodies about which an individual believes he has cause for complaint, even though the action may have been within the body's legal powers. For example, the actions of central government departments are open to scrutiny by the Parliamentary Commissioner for Administration; and complaints about the administration of the National Health Service are investigated by the Health Service Commissioners.

NOTES

1. As the penultimate paragraph of the above extract from the Report[5] indicates, before the Human Rights Act 1998 civil liberties were protected in the UK law by a mixture of legislation and common law. Dicey pointed out over a century ago[6] that when providing such protection Parliament and the courts did not usually make general positive statements of a right. There is, for example, no statute providing for a 'right to freedom of assembly'. Instead the technique was to legislate in detailed terms, making particular legislative provision, as in the Public Order Act 1986, from which the general right might be inferred. The courts were

---

[3] *Ed.* The Bill of Rights was relied upon (unsuccessfully) in *Williams v Home Office (No. 2)* [1981] 1 All ER 1211, QBD.

[4] *Ed.* Although habeas corpus is of value in some civil liberties contexts (e.g. obtaining the release of suspects being questioned by the police, and preventing deportation (*R v Secretary of State for the Home Department, ex p Muboyayi* [1992] QB 244, CA)), it has limitations in others (e.g. achieving the release of the mentally disordered: see *X v United Kingdom* (1981) EHRR 188). On habeas corpus, see R.J. Sharpe, *The Law of Habeas Corpus* (2nd edn, 1989) and A. Le Sueur [1992] PL 13.

[5] The Report was prepared in connection with the consideration of the question of a Bill of Rights by the House of Lords Select Committee on a Bill of Rights.

[6] *An Introduction to the Study of the Law of the Constitution* (10th edn by E.C.S. Wade, 1959), p. 197. First edition, 1885.

similarly restrained when developing the common law.[7] While sometimes making general statements,[8] they preferred to formulate particular rules, shaped by the facts of the cases before them. Moreover, the focus of judgments was often, as it was in legislation, upon matters, such as the need to ensure public order, other than the protection of the civil liberty concerned. Another characteristic of the common law approach was that the individual's civil liberties were treated truly as liberties, not as rights. It was a negative approach by which a court, when faced with a civil liberties issue, sought to discover whether there is a limitation in law upon the challenged action and, if there is not, to conclude that the action was lawful. A weakness of this approach was that it permitted interferences with civil liberties as well as protection of them.[9]

2. As the Report also states, nearly all countries protect civil liberties by means of a Bill of Rights.[10] Lord Lloyd[11] defines a Bill of Rights as a 'constitutional code of human rights' that is binding in law, is (inevitably) generally worded and has the following other key characteristics:

(a) The code should be given some sort of overriding authority over other laws.

(b) Power should be vested in the judiciary (whether generally or by way of a Constitutional or Supreme Court) to interpret the rights set forth in the Bill of Rights and to determine judicially their proper scope, extent and limits, and their relationship inter se.

(c) The judiciary will possess the power to declare legislation invalided which it holds to be repugnant to the rights guaranteed in the Bill of Rights.

3. The UK had, and still has,[12] no bill of rights in the above sense. A power of judicial review over legislation was claimed by Coke CJ in *Dr Bonham's Case*:[13] 'When an Act of Parliament is against common right and reason, or repugnant, or impossible to be performed, the common law will control it, and adjudge such Act to be void.' Had this claim been pressed and accepted, the resulting power could have been used to protect civil liberties in much the same way as a Bill of Rights does without any formal enactment. But it proved only to be rhetoric; no statute has ever been overturned on the basis of it. The position before the Human Rights Act 1998 was stated by Lord Reid in *British Railways Board v Pickin*:[14]

The idea that a court is entitled to disregard a provision in an Act of Parliament on any ground must seem strange and startling to anyone with any knowledge of the history and law of our constitution…In earlier

---

[7] See D.J. Harris, in F. Matscher (ed.), *The Implementation of Economic and Social Rights* (1991), p. 201.

[8] See, e.g., Lord Kilbrandon's reference in *Cassell v Broome* [1972] AC 1027 at 1133, HL, to a 'constitutional right to free speech'.

[9] See E.C.S. Wade and A.W. Bradley, *Constitutional and Administrative Law* (14th edn by A.W. Bradley and K.D. Ewing, 2007), Pt III. See also *R v Kirkless Metropolitan Borough Council, ex p C* [1993] 2 FLR 187, CA, in which counsel for a detained, mentally disordered person argued that there was no legal basis for the detention, and Stuart-Smith LJ stated that counsel had asked the wrong question: 'The real question is, on what basis can it be said that the council acted unlawfully', and there was none.

[10] Australia remains an exception. Canada and New Zealand adopted bills of rights in 1982 and 1990 respectively. The Canadian and New Zealand models were taken into account when the Human Rights Act 1998 was enacted. Although the 1998 Act differs significantly from both, it contains some echoes of the New Zealand Bill of Rights and the experience of the courts in implementing both systems was instructive.

[11] (1976) 39 MLR 121 at 122–123.

[12] The definition is one that fits the bills of rights in states such as the United States and Germany. The courts in Canada can overturn federal or provincial legislation unless the legislature concerned expressly provides that it may not do so: Canadian Charter of Rights and Freedoms, s. 33, which is enacted in Sch. B to the Canada Act 1982, Chap. 36. The courts in New Zealand have no power to overturn statutes; they apply a rule of interpretation similar to that in s. 3 of the Human Rights Act: see M. Taggart [1998] PL 266.

[13] (1610) 8 Co Rep 114a, 118.   [14] [1974] AC 765 at 765, 782, HL.

times many learned lawyers seem to have believed that an Act of Parliament could be disregarded in so far as it was contrary to the law of God or the law of nature or natural justice, but since the supremacy of Parliament was finally demonstrated by the Revolution of 1688 any such idea has become obsolete.

In *Oppenheimer v Cattermole*[15] the question was whether English courts should recognise a Nazi law that deprived German Jews resident abroad of their nationality and confiscated their property. A majority of the House of Lords took the view that the law was 'so grave an infringement of human rights that the courts of this country ought to refuse to recognise it as a law at all'.[16] Mann[17] refers to the case and notes that 'for more than 300 years England has been spared the necessity of facing' the question of the legality of such laws *within its own legal system*. He suggests that were it to arise 'English judges could no doubt find a legally convincing reason for reverting to the tradition of the fundamental law' and that the 'real question would be whether, in the condition which has been assumed, they would have the strength of character to search for it'.

4. Although subject to Parliament, the courts have always played an important role in the protection of civil liberties by the interpretation of statutes, the review of administrative action and the development of the common law. As far as the interpretation of statutes is concerned, the courts have developed certain presumptions that help. The presumption against the taking of property without compensation[18] is an example. So are the presumptions against the retrospective effect of legislation,[19] against denial of access to the courts,[20] against interference with the freedom from self-incrimination;[21] and against interference with the liberty of the subject.[22] The presumption that legislation complies with UK treaty obligations is important in that the UK is bound by a number of international human rights treaties, including the ECHR.[23] There is also a presumption that UK legislation complies with customary international law,[24] which contains a number of human rights guarantees (e.g. against torture).[25]

---

[15] [1976] AC 249, HL.   [16] Lord Cross at 278.

[17] (1978) 94 LQR 512, 513–514.

[18] *Central Control Board (Liquor Traffic) v Cannon Brewery Co. Ltd* [1919] AC 744 at 752, HL, per Lord Atkinson. See also *R v Secretary of State for Transport, ex p de Rothschild* [1989] 1 All ER 933, CA.

[19] *Waddington v Miah* [1974] 1 WLR 683, HL.

[20] *Raymond v Honey* [1983] 1 AC 1, HL.

[21] *Re O* [1991] 2 QB 520, CA.

[22] *R v Hallstrom, ex p W* [1986] QB 1090, QBD. This presumption does not apply in wartime: *R v Halliday* [1917] AC 270, HL.

[23] Other human rights treaties in force protecting civil and political rights to which the UK is a party include the Genocide Convention 1948, UKTS 58 (Cmnd 4421, 1970); the ILO Freedom of Association Convention (Cmnd 7638, ILO 87); the ILO Right to Organise Convention (Cmnd 7852, ILO 98); the International Covenant on Civil and Political Rights 1966, UKTS 6 (Cmnd 6702, 1977); the Convention on the Elimination of All Forms of Racial Discrimination 1966, UKTS 77 (Cmnd 4108, 1969); the Convention on the Elimination of All Forms of Discrimination against Women 1979, UKTS 2 (Cm 643, 1989); the UN Convention Against Torture 1984, UKTS 107 (Cm 1775, 1991); the European Convention for the Prevention of Torture 1987, UKTS 5 (Cm 1634, 1991); and the Convention on the Rights of the Child 1989, UKTS 44 (Cm 1976, 1992). The Universal Declaration of Human Rights 1948, GAOR, 3rd Sess., Part I, Resolutions, p. 71, is not a treaty and not in itself legally binding. However, it has come, at least in part, to be recognised as stating customary international law and British courts have made reference to it: see e.g. Lord Reid in *Waddington v Miah* [1974] 1 WLR 683 at 964, HL.

[24] *Mortensen v Peters* (1906) 8 F 93, Ct of Justiciary.

[25] See T. Meron, *Human Rights and Humanitarian Norms of Customary Law* (1989), Chap. 2.

5. The courts have a well-established power of judicial review of administrative action taken by national or local or other government authorities, including action bearing upon civil liberties. This had long been so where the action was based upon *statutory* powers but the exercise of *prerogative* powers may be subject to judicial review also, depending upon the subject matter of the power: *Council of Civil Service Unions v Minister of the Civil Service.*[26] The courts may quash or prevent executive decisions that are not authorised by law; that are not taken in accordance with the prescribed procedures; that are erroneous in law; that infringe the rules of natural justice; or that involve an exercise of discretion that is not proportionate in human rights cases.

6. The judges have a long and proud tradition of protecting civil liberties at common law against encroachment by the executive. *Entick v Carrington*[27] is a classic example. But although cases of this sort still occur,[28] some judges, before the Human Rights Act 1998, were less open to persuasion than others. It was a common complaint that the courts generally were not inclined to develop the law on a grand scale, at least in the field of civil liberties. Commenting upon the failure of the courts to develop a law of privacy in the way that the American courts have, Street[29] stated:

> But there is no spirit of adventure or progress, either in judges or counsel, in England today. Today's English judges are not the innovators that some of their distinguished predecessors were; in the hands of modern judges the common law has lost its capacity to expand. They have not been helped by counsel. Cases are argued and tried by a narrow circle of men who seldom look beyond the decided cases for guidance. The entire development of the American law of privacy can be traced to an article in a law periodical published by Harvard Law School.[30] It is inconceivable that the views of an academic journal would exercise similar influence in Britain. This inward- and backward-looking attitude of the English Bar serves only to increase the likelihood that the courts will fail to make the law fit the needs of the time.

Later in the same book he wrote:[31]

> Our judges may be relied on to defend strenuously some kinds of freedom. Their emotions will be aroused where personal freedom is menaced by some politically unimportant area of the executive: a case of unlawful arrest by a policeman, for example. Their integrity is, of course, beyond criticism. Yet there are obvious limitations to what they can be expected to do in moulding the law of civil liberties. Two factors stand in their way: their reluctance to have clashes with senior members of Government, their desire not to have a repetition of the nineteenth-century strife between Parliament and the courts; and secondly,

---

[26] [1985] AC 374, HL. In the *Council of Civil Service Unions* case, the prerogative power to determine conditions of employment in the civil service was considered 'justiciable' and hence subject to judicial review, but the powers to make treaties and to defend the realm were given (per Lord Roskill) as examples of powers that involved 'high policy' so that their exercise would not be subject to judicial review. In *R v Secretary of State for Foreign and Commonwealth Affairs, ex p Everett* [1989] QB 811, CA, the prerogative power to issue a British passport was held to be subject to judicial review. So is the prerogative of mercy: *R v Secretary of State for the Home Department, ex p Bentley* [1994] QB 349, CA.

[27] Below, Chap. 4.

[28] See the remarkable case of *Re M* [1994] 1 AC 377, HL, in which the Home Secretary was held in civil contempt of court for disobeying a court injunction not to deport a Zairean whose application for judicial review of the Home Office decision not to grant him asylum was under consideration by the courts. See also *R v Secretary of State for the Home Department, ex p Fire Brigades Union* [1995] 1 All ER 888, CA (Home Secretary could not introduce under the prerogative a criminal injuries scheme that was radically different from the statutory scheme).

[29] *Freedom, the Individual and the Law* (5th edn, 1982), p. 263.

[30] *Ed.* See below, Chap. 8.   [31] Op. cit., pp. 318–319.

their unwillingness to immerse themselves in problems of policy, which of course loom large in many of the issues examined here.

No doubt Street would have approved of the Court of Appeal's role in developing the law of privacy in *Douglas v Hello!*,[32] though the continued attachment to the law of confidence in many subsequent cases may illustrate that Street's arguments remain largely valid.

2. THE PRESENT METHOD: THE HUMAN RIGHTS ACT 1998

● **Rights Brought Home: The Human Rights Bill,** Cm 3782, pp. 4–7

THE EUROPEAN CONVENTION ON HUMAN RIGHTS

1.18 We…believe that the time has come to enable people to enforce their Convention rights against the State in the British courts, rather than having to incur the delays and expense which are involved in taking a case to the European Human Rights Commission and Court in Strasbourg and which may altogether deter some people from pursing their rights. Enabling courts in the United Kingdom to rule on the application of the Convention will also help to influence the development of case law on the Convention by the European Court of Human Rights on the basis of familiarity with our laws and customs and of sensitivity to practices and procedures in the United Kingdom. Our courts' decisions will provide the European Court with a useful source of information and reasoning for its own decisions. United Kingdom judges have a very high reputation internationally, but the fact that they do not deal in the same concepts as the European Court of Human Rights limits the extent to which their judgments can be drawn upon and followed. Enabling the Convention rights to be judged by British courts will also lead to closer scrutiny of the human rights implications of new legislation and new policies. If legislation is enacted which is incompatible with the Convention, a ruling by the domestic courts to that effect will be much more direct and immediate than a ruling from the European Court of Human Rights. The Government of the day, and Parliament, will want to minimise the risk of that happening.

1.19 Our aim is a straightforward one. It is to make more directly accessible the rights which the British people already enjoy under the Convention. In other words, to bring those rights home.

NOTES

1. The Human Rights Act 1998 had been preceded by a series of private members' bills during a period of 25 years or so proposing the introduction of a bill of rights.[33] Draft bills of rights had also been prepared by non-governmental organisations.[34] Parliamentary progress could not be made in the absence of support by the government of the day. The tide

---

[32] [2001] 2 All ER 289.

[33] For details of the private bills introduced by Lord Wade, Sir Edward Gardner, Mr Graham Allen and Lord Lester, see M. Zander, *A Bill of Rights* (4th edn, 1996), Chap. 1.

[34] See Institute for Public Policy Research, *A Written Constitution for the United Kingdom* (2nd revd edn, 1993), pp. 34ff and National Council for Civil Liberties, *A Peoples' Charter* (1991). Charter 88 also advocated a bill of rights: see *New Statesman*, 2 December 1988, p. 4 and N. Stranger, 8 *Index on Censorship* 14.

turned when the Labour Party decided to introduce a bill of rights[35] as party policy and later included it in its 1997 election manifesto.

2. One objection to a bill of rights is that it involves the courts in politics. Although the British courts have always had to rule on matters of political and social controversy,[36] a power of interpretation such as that in HRA, s. 3, based upon the standards of the ECHR, inevitably increases their participation in such matters. The question raised is whether unelected judges, who are necessarily difficult to dismiss, should be given a political and social role on this scale. The contrary argument is that persons taking decisions on human rights matters (which often concern minority groups and the unpopular) should be free from the 'tyranny of the majority'.[37]

3. Another concern has been that the judiciary is not a cross-section of society, as it should be to be properly qualified to take decisions that have great social impact. J.A.G. Griffiths states:[38]

Of 514 Circuit judges in post on 1 December 1994, 29 were women, and 4 were of ethnic minority origin. In 1996 there were 7 female judges on the High Court bench.

In summary, 80 per cent of the senior judiciary are products of public schools and of Oxford or Cambridge, with an average age of about sixty; 5.1 per cent are women; 100 per cent are white. Some explanation of the gross disproportions in gender and colour can no doubt be found in the structure of the legal profession, in the financial and other difficulties facing those wishing to qualify as barristers, and then needing to support themselves in the early years of practice. Another part of the explanation is sexual and racial discrimination within the profession.

4. Later in the same book, the same author, while recognising the independence of the judiciary, also expressed concern, as a commentator on the left, at entrusting judges with greater powers at the expense of Parliament because of their generally conservative (with a small 'c') philosophy:[39]

Judges in the United Kingdom are not beholden politically to the government of the day. And they have longer professional lives than most ministers. They, like civil servants, see governments come like water and go with the wind. They owe no loyalty to ministers, not even that temporary loyalty which civil servants owe. Coke said that Bracton said that the King ought to be under no man but under God and the law.[40] Judges are also lions under the throne but that seat is occupied in their eyes not by the Prime Minister but by the law and by their conception of the public interest. It is to that law and to that conception that they owe allegiance. In that lies their strength and their weakness, their value and their threat.

By allegiance to 'the law' judges mean the whole body of law, much of which has its origins in the judge-made common law. 'The law' also means the rule of law and here the allegiance is to the philosophical ideal that we should be ruled by laws and not by men. If that means that power should not be exercised arbitrarily or on the whim of rulers and their officials but should be dependent on and flow from properly constituted authority and from rules written down and approved by some form of representative assembly, it is an admirable and necessary, if partial, safeguard against tyranny. The proposition can hardly be taken

---

[35] See *A New Agenda for Democracy*, a party policy document adopted by the Party Conference in 1993.
[36] See, e.g., the *Tameside* case [1977] AC 1014, HL (comprehensive schooling) and *R v Secretary of State for the Environment, ex p Hammersmith and Fulham Borough Council* [1990] 3 All ER 589, HL (charge-capping).
[37] Further, see K. Ewing (2004) PL 829.   [38] *The Politics of the Judiciary* (5th edn, 1996), p. 21.
[39] Ibid., pp. 296, 326–327, 340–341. See also J.A.G. Griffiths (2000) 63 MLR 159.
[40] *Prohibitions del Roy* (1607) 12 Co Rep 63.

further because, in modern industrial society, it is impossible to avoid vesting considerable discretionary power in public officials if only because laws cannot be adequately framed to cover every eventuality.
...

When on 14 June 1995, it was put to the Lord Chief Justice that 'the very top judges' had in recent years been more 'robust' in standing up to the executive, Lord Taylor said, 'It is not that they have been more robust. We have developed judicial review. It did not exist as such before 1977.'

The reply was significant but evasive, suggesting that the judicial attitude to the executive had not changed, only that the means of review at the disposal of the judiciary had improved. Later, in his evidence to the Select Committee, Lord Taylor emphasized that the courts 'were very careful not to go too far' in overturning ministerial decisions and he cited challenges to Maastricht by Rees-Mogg, to the Anglo-Irish Agreement, and to the use of a statute brought in existence in 1939 for the national emergency. But these were surely examples of deliberate use of the courts for political propaganda. It was not surprising that the applications were dismissed.

However the question is answered, what is undeniable is that the courts have, during this decade, become more severe in their criticism and more strict in their scrutiny of the exercise of executive powers in some areas....

To some, the judicial view of the public interest appears merely as reactionary conservativism. It is not the politics of the extreme right. Its insensitivity is clearly rooted more in the unconscious assumptions than in a wish to oppress. But it is demonstrable that on ever major social issue which has come before the courts during the last thirty years—concerning industrial relations, political protest, race relations, governmental secrecy, police powers, moral behaviour—the judges have supported the conventional, established and settled interest. And they have reacted strongly against challenges to those interests. This conservatism does not necessarily follow the day-to-day political policies currently associated with the party of that name. But it is a political philosophy none the less.

Ewing and Gearty[41] reach a similar conclusion: 'The harsh reality is that we need to be protected by Parliament from the courts, as much as we need to be protected from the abuse of executive power.'

Lord Denning has expressed opposition to a US-style bill of rights on the different ground of the effect upon judicial independence and public confidence in the courts:[42]

...if judges were given power to overthrow sections or Acts of Parliament, they would become political, their appointments would be based on political grounds and the reputation of our Judiciary would suffer accordingly. One has only to see, in the great Constitutions of the United States of America and of India, the conflicts which arise from time to time between the judges and the Legislature. I hope we shall not have such conflicts in this country. The independence of our judges and their reputation for impartiality depend on their obeying the will of Parliament and on their being independent. The independence of the judges is the other pillar of our Constitution.

5. The Constitutional Reform Act 2005 established the new Judicial Appointments Commission[43] which seeks to provide for greater transparency in judicial appointments and encourage a wider range of applicants. In its first annual report[44] the Chair of the JAC noted, 'The overall number of applications received is encouraging and I am pleased that, in our first full year, many women and black and minority ethnic candidates successfully put their

---

[41] K. Ewing and C. Gearty, *Freedom Under Thatcher* (1990), pp. 270–271.
[42] 369 HL Deb, 25 March 1976, cols 797–798.
[43] See www.judicialappointments.gov.uk.
[44] Judicial Appointments Commission, *Annual Report 2006–7* (2007).

names forward.' However, more recently, the Justice Secretary stated that 'expectations that the new system of appointing judges would lead to a more diverse judiciary have so far not been fulfilled'.[45]

• Human Rights Act 1998

Introduction

1. The Convention rights

(1) In this Act 'the Convention rights' means the rights and fundamental freedoms set out in—

  (a) Articles 2 to 12 and 14 of the Convention,

  (b) Articles 1 to 3 of the First Protocol, and

  (c) Articles 1 and 2 of the Sixth Protocol,

  as read with Articles 16 to 18 of the Convention.

(2) Those Articles are to have effect for the purposes of this Act subject to any designated derogation or reservation (as to which see sections 14 and 15).

(3) The Articles are set out in Schedule 1.

(4) The Secretary of State may by order make such amendments to this Act as he considers appropriate to reflect the effect, in relation to the United Kingdom, of a protocol.

(5) In subsection (4) 'protocol' means a protocol to the Convention—

  (a) which the United Kingdom has ratified; or

  (b) which the United Kingdom has signed with a view to ratification.

(6) No amendment may be made by an order under subsection (4) so as to come into force before the protocol concerned in force in relation to the United Kingdom.

2. Interpretation of Convention rights

(1) A court or tribunal determining a question which has arisen in connection with a Convention right must take into account any—

  (a) judgment, decision, declaration or advisory opinion of the European Court of Human Rights,

  (b) opinion of the Commission given in a report adopted under Article 31 of the Convention,

  (c) decision of the Commission in connection with Article 26 or 27(2) of the Convention, or

  (d) decision of the Committee of Ministers taken under Article 46 of the Convention,

  whenever made or given, so far as, in the opinion of the court or tribunal, it is relevant to the proceedings in which that question has arisen.

(2) Evidence of any judgment, decision, declaration or opinion of which account may have to be taken under this section is to be given in proceedings before any court or tribunal in such manner as may be provided by rules.

(3) In this section 'rules' means rules of court or, in the case of proceedings before a tribunal, rules made for the purposes of this section—

  (a) by the Lord Chancellor or the Secretary of State, in relation to any proceedings outside Scotland;

---

[45] Joint Committee on Human Rights, *A Bill of Rights for the UK?*, 29th Report of Session 2007–8 HC 150 / HL 165, para. 248. The Constitutional Renewal Bill 2008 aims to remove the role of the Prime Minister entirely from the appointment of senior judges. See also, Ministry of Justice, *The Governance of Britain: Constitutional Renewal* (Cm 7342, 2008).

(*b*) by the Secretary of State, in relation to proceedings in Scotland; or

(*c*) by a Northern Ireland department, in relation to proceedings before a tribunal in Northern Ireland—

    (i) which deals with transferred matters; and

    (ii) for which no rules made under paragraph (a) are in force.

Legislation

3. Interpretation of legislation

(1) So far as it is possible to do so, primary legislation and subordinate legislation must be read and given effect in a way which is compatible with the Convention rights.

(2) This section—

(*a*) applies to primary legislation and subordinate legislation whenever enacted;

(*b*) does not affect the validity, continuing operation or enforcement of any incompatible primary legislation; and

(*c*) does not affect the validity, continuing operation or enforcement of any incompatible subordinate legislation if (disregarding any possibility of revocation) primary legislation prevents removal of the incompatibility.

4. Declaration of incompatibility

(1) Subsection (2) applies in any proceedings in which a court determines whether a provision of primary legislation is compatible with a Convention right.

(2) If the court is satisfied that the provision is incompatible with a Convention right, it may make a declaration of that incompatibility.

(3) Subsection (4) applies in any proceedings in which a court determines whether a provision of subordinate legislation, made in the exercise of a power conferred by primary legislation, is compatible with a Convention right.

(4) If the court is satisfied—

(*a*) that the provision is incompatible with a Convention right, and

(*b*) that (disregarding any possibility of revocation) the primary legislation concerned prevents removal of the incompatibility, it may make a declaration of that incompatibility.

(5) In this section 'court' means—

(*a*) the House of Lords;

(*b*) the Judicial Committee of the Privy Council;

(*c*) the Courts-Martial Appeal Court;

(*d*) in Scotland, the High Court of Justiciary sitting otherwise than as a trial court or the Court of Session;

(*e*) in England and Wales or Northern Ireland, the High Court or the Court of Appeal.

(6) A declaration under this section ('a declaration of incompatibility')—

(*a*) does not affect the validity, continuing operation or enforcement of the provision in respect of which it is given; and

(*b*) is not binding on the parties to the proceedings in which it is made.

5. Right of Crown to intervene

(1) Where a court is considering whether to make a declaration of incompatibility, the Crown is entitled to notice in accordance with rules of court.

(2) In any case to which subsection (1) applies—

    (*a*) a Minister of the Crown (or a person nominated by him),

    (*b*) a member of the Scottish Executive,

    (*c*) a Northern Ireland Minister,

    (*d*) a Northern Ireland department,

is entitled, on giving notice in accordance with rules of court, to be joined as a party to the proceedings.

(3) Notice under subsection (2) may be given at any time during the proceedings.

(4) A person who has been made a party to criminal proceedings (other then in Scotland) as the result of a notice under subsection (2) may, with leave, appeal to the House of Lords against any declaration of incompatibility made in the proceedings.

(5) In subsection (4)—

'criminal proceedings' includes all proceedings before the Courts-Martial Appeal Court; and

'leave' means leave granted by the court making the declaration of incompatibility or by the House of Lords.

Public authorities

6. Acts of public authorities

(1) It is unlawful for a public authority to act in a way which is incompatible with a Convention right.

(2) Subsection (1) does not apply to an act if—

    (*a*) as the result of one or more provisions of primary legislation, the authority could not have acted differently; or

    (*b*) in the case of one or more provisions of, or made under, primary legislation which cannot be read or given effect in a way which is compatible with the Convention rights, the authority was acting so as to give effect to or enforce those provisions.

(3) In this section 'public authority' includes—

    (*a*) a court or tribunal, and

    (*b*) any person certain of whose functions are functions of a public nature,

but does not include either House of Parliament or a person exercising functions in connection with proceedings in Parliament.

(4) In subsection (3) 'Parliament' does not include the House of Lords in its judicial capacity.

(5) In relation to a particular act, a person is not a public authority by virtue only of subsection (3)(b) if the nature of the act is private.

(6) 'An act' includes a failure to act but does not include a failure to—

    (*a*) introduce in, or lay before, Parliament a proposal for legislation; or

    (*b*) make any primary legislation or remedial order.

7. Proceedings

(1) A person who claims that a public authority has acted (or proposes to act) in a way which is made unlawful by section 6(1) may—

    (*a*) bring proceedings against the authority under this Act in the appropriate court or tribunal, or

    (*b*) rely on the Convention right or rights concerned in any legal proceedings,

but only if he is (or would be) a victim of the unlawful act.

(2) In subsection (1)(a) 'appropriate court or tribunal' means such court or tribunal as may be determined in accordance with rules; and proceedings against an authority include a counterclaim or similar proceeding.

(3) If the proceedings are brought on an application for judicial review, the applicant is to be taken to have a sufficient interest in relation to the unlawful act only if he is, or would be, a victim of that act.

(4) If the proceedings are made by way of a petition for judicial review in Scotland, the applicant shall be taken to have title and interest to sue in relation to the unlawful act only if he is, or would be, a victim of that act.

(5) Proceedings under subsection (1)(a) must be brought before the end of—

    (a) the period of one year beginning with the date on which the act complained of took place; or

    (b) such longer period as the court or tribunal considers equitable having regard to all the circumstances,

but that is subject to any rule imposing a stricter time limit in relation to the procedure in question.

(6) In subsection (1)(b) 'legal proceedings' includes—

    (a) proceedings brought by or at the instigation of a public authority; and

    (b) an appeal against the decision of a court or tribunal.

(7) For the purposes of this section, a person is a victim of an unlawful act only if he would be a victim for the purposes of Article 34 of the Convention if proceedings were brought in the European Court of Human Rights in respect of that act.

(8) Nothing in this Act creates a criminal offence.

(9) In this section 'rules' means—

    (a) in relation to proceedings before a court or tribunal outside Scotland, rules made by the Lord Chancellor or the Secretary of State for the purposes of this section or rules of court,

    (b) in relation to proceedings before a court or tribunal in Scotland, rules made by the Secretary of State for those purposes,

    (c) in relation to proceedings before a tribunal in Northern Ireland—

        (i) which deals with transferred matters; and

        (ii) for which no rules made under paragraph (a) are in force,

rules made by a Northern Ireland department for those purposes,

and includes provision made by order under section 1 of the Courts and Legal Services Act 1990.

(10) In making rules, regard must be had to section 9.

(11) The Minister who has power to make rules in relation to a particular tribunal may, to the extent he considers it necessary to ensure that the tribunal can provide an appropriate remedy in relation to an act (or proposed act) of a public authority which is (or would be) unlawful as a result of section 6(1), by order add to—

    (a) the relief or remedies which the tribunal may grant; or

    (b) the grounds on which it may grant any of them.

(12) An order made under subsection (11) may contain such incidental, supplemental, consequential or transitional provision as the Minister making it considers appropriate.

(13) 'The Minister' includes the Northern Ireland department concerned.

8. Judicial remedies

(1) In relation to ay act (or proposed act) of a public authority which the court finds is (or would be) unlawful, it may grant such relief or remedy, or make such order, within its powers as it considers just and appropriate.

(2) But damages may be awarded only by a court which has power to award damages, or to order the payment of compensation, in civil proceedings.

(3) No award of damages is to be made unless, taking account of all the circumstances of the case, including—

   (*a*) any other relief or remedy granted, or order made, in relation to the act in question (by that or any other court), and

   (*b*) the consequences of any decision (of that or any other court) in respect of that act, the court is satisfied that the award is necessary to afford just satisfaction to the person in whose favour it is made.

(4) In determining—

   (*a*) whether to award damages, or

   (*b*) the amount of an award,

   the court must take into account the principles applied by the European Court of Human Rights in relation to the award of compensation under Article 41 of the Convention.

(5) A public authority against which damages are awarded is to be treated—

   (*a*) in Scotland, for the purposes of section 3 of the Law Reform (Miscellaneous Provisions) (Scotland) Act 1940 as if the award were made in an action of damages in which the authority has been found liable in respect of loss or damage to the person to whom the award is made;

   (*b*) for the purposes of the Civil Liability (Contribution) Act 1978 as liable in respect of damage suffered by the person to whom the award is made.

(6) In this section—

   'court' includes a tribunal;

   'damages' means damages for an unlawful act of a public authority; and

   'unlawful' means unlawful under section 6(1).

9. Judicial acts

(1) Proceedings under section 7(1)(a) in respect of a judicial act may be brought only—

   (*a*) by exercising a right of appeal;

   (*b*) on an application (in Scotland a petition) for judicial review; or

   (*c*) in such other forum as may be prescribed by rules.

(2) That does not affect any rule of law which prevents a court from being the subject of judicial review.

(3) In proceedings under this Act in respect of a judicial act done in good faith, damages may not be awarded otherwise than to compensate a person to the extent required by Article 5(5) of the Convention.

(4) An award of damages permitted by subsection (3) is to be made against the Crown; but no award may be made unless the appropriate person, if not a party to the proceedings, is joined.

(5) In this section—

   'appropriate person' means the Minister responsible for the court concerned, or a person or government department nominated by him;

'court' includes a tribunal;

'judge' includes a member of a tribunal, a justice of the peace and a clerk or other officer entitled to exercise the jurisdiction of a court;

'judicial act' means a judicial act of a court and includes an act done on the instructions, or on behalf, of a judge; and

'rules' has the same meaning as in section 7(9).

Remedial action

10. Power to take remedial action

(1) This section applies if—

    (a) a provision of legislation has been declared under section 4 to be incompatible with a Convention right and, if an appeal lies—

        (i) all persons who may appeal have stated in writing that they do not intend to do so;

        (ii) the time for bringing an appeal has expired and no appeal has been brought within that time; or

        (iii) an appeal brought within that time has been determined or abandoned; or

    (b) it appears to a Minister of the Crown or Her Majesty in Council that, having regard to a finding of the European Court of Human Rights made after the coming into force of this section in proceedings against the United Kingdom, a provision of legislation is incompatible with an obligation of the United Kingdom arising from the Convention.

(2) If a Minister of the Crown considers that there are compelling reasons for proceeding under this section, he may by order make such amendments to the legislation as he considers necessary to remove the incompatibility.

(3) If, in the case of subordinate legislation, a Minister of the Crown considers—

    (a) that it is necessary to amend the primary legislation under which the subordinate legislation in question was made, in order to enable the incompatibility to be removed, and

    (b) that there are compelling reasons for proceeding under this section,

he may by order make such amendments to the primary legislation as he considers necessary.

(4) This section also applies where the provision in question is in subordinate legislation and has been quashed, or declared invalid, by reason of incompatibility with a Convention right and the Minister proposes to proceed under paragraph 2(b) of Schedule 2.

(5) If the legislation is an Order in Council, the power conferred by subsection (2) or (3) is exercisable by Her Majesty in Council.

(6) In this section 'legislation' does not include a Measure of the Church Assembly or of the General Synod of the Church of England.

(7) Schedule 2 makes further provision about remedial orders.

Other rights and proceedings

11. Safeguard for existing human rights

A person's reliance on a Convention right does not restrict—

    (a) any other right or freedom conferred on him by or under any law having effect in any part of the United Kingdom; or

    (b) his right to make any claim or bring any proceedings which he could make or bring apart from sections 7 to 9.

12. Freedom of expression

(1) This section applies if a court is considering whether to grant any relief which, if granted, might affect the exercise of the Convention right to freedom of expression.

(2) If the person against whom the application for relief is made ('the respondent') is neither present nor represented, no such relief is to be granted unless the court is satisfied—

(*a*) that the applicant has taken all practicable steps to notify the respondent; or

(*b*) that there are compelling reasons why the respondent should not be notified.

(3) No such relief is to be granted so as to restrain publication before trial unless the court is satisfied that the applicant is likely to establish that publication should not be allowed.

(4) The court must have particular regard to the importance of the Convention right to freedom of expression and, where the proceedings relate to material which the respondent claims, or which appears to the court, to be journalistic, literary or artistic material (or to conduct connected with such material), to—

(*a*) the extent to which—

(i) the material has, or is about to, become available to the public; or

(ii) it is, or would be, in the public interest for the material to be published;

(*b*) any relevant privacy code.

(5) In this section—

'court' includes a tribunal; and

'relief' includes any remedy or order (other than in criminal proceedings).

13. Freedom of thought, conscience and religion

(1) If a court's determination of any question arising under this Act might affect the exercise by a religious organisation (itself or its members collectively) of the Convention right to freedom of thought, conscience and religion, it must have particular regard to the importance of that right.

(2) In this section 'court' includes a tribunal.

Derogations and reservations

14. Derogations

(1) In this Act 'designated derogation' means—

any derogation by the United Kingdom from an Article of the Convention, or of any protocol to the Convention, which is designated for the purposes of this Act in an order made by the Secretary of State.

(2) …

(3) If a designated derogation is amended or replaced it ceases to be a designated derogation.

(4) But subsection (3) does not prevent the Secretary of State from exercising his power under subsection [(1)] … to make a fresh designation order in respect of the Article concerned.

(5) The Secretary of State must by order make such amendments to Schedule 3 as he considers appropriate to reflect—

(*a*) any designation order; or

(*b*) the effect of subsection (3).

(6) A designation order may be made in anticipation of the making by the United Kingdom of a proposed derogation.

15. Reservations

(1) In this Act 'designated reservation' means—

    (a) the United Kingdom's reservation to Article 2 of the First Protocol to the Convention; and

    (b) any other reservation by the United Kingdom to an Article of the Convention, or of any proto-col to the Convention, which is designated for the purposes of this Act in an order made by the Secretary of State.

(2) The text of the reservation referred to in subsection (1)(a) is set out in Part II of Schedule 3.

(3) If a designated reservation is withdrawn wholly or in part it ceases to be a designated reservation.

(4) But subsection (3) does not prevent the Secretary of State from exercising his power under sub-section (1)(b) to make a fresh designation order in respect of the Article concerned.

(5) The Secretary of state must by order make such amendments to this Act as he considers appropriate to reflect—

    (a) any designation order; or

    (b) the effect of subsection (3).

16. Period for which designated derogations have effect

(1) If it has not already been withdrawn by the United Kingdom, a designated derogation ceases to have effect for the purposes of this Act…at the end of the period of five years beginning with the date on which the order designating it was made.

(2) At any time before the period—

    (a) fixed by subsection (1)…, or

    (b) extended by an order under this subsection,

comes to an end, the Secretary of State may by order extend it by a further period of five years.

(3) An order under section 14(1)…ceases to have effect at the end of the period for consideration, unless a resolution has been passed by each House approving the order.

(4) Subsection (3) does not affect—

    (a) anything done in reliance on the order; or

    (b) the power to make a fresh order under section 14(1)…

(5) In subsection (3) 'period for consideration' means the period of forty days beginning with the day on which the order was made.

(6) In calculating the period for consideration, no account is to be taken of any time during which—

    (a) Parliament is dissolved or prorogued; or

    (b) both Houses are adjourned for more than four days.

(7) If a designated derogation is withdrawn by the United Kingdom, the Secretary of State must by order make such amendments to this Act as he considers are required to reflect that withdrawal.[46]

17. Periodic review of designated reservations

(1) The appropriate Minister must review the designated reservation referred to in section 15(l)(a)—

    (a) before the end of the period of five years beginning with the date on which section 1(2)came into force; and

---

[46] The words omitted were repealed by the Human Rights (Amendment) Order 2001, SI 2001/1216 (in force 1 April 2001). They provided for the UK derogation from its obligations under Art. 5(3) that was in issue in *Murray v UK* (1996) 22 EHRR 29. The derogation was withdrawn in 2001.

(b) if that designation is still in force, before the end of the period of five years beginning with the date on which the last report relating to it was laid under subsection (3).

(2) The appropriate Minister must review each of the other designated reservations (if any)—

(a) before the end of the period of five years beginning with the date on which the order designating the reservation first came into force; and

(b) if the designation is still in force, before the end of the period of five years beginning with the date on which the last report relating to it was laid under subsection (3).

(3) The Minister conducting a review under this section must prepare a report on the result of the review and lay a copy of it before each House of Parliament.

...

Parliamentary procedure

19. Statements of compatability

(1) A Minister of the Crown in charge of a Bill in either House of Parliament must, before Second Reading of the Bill—

(a) make a statement to the effect that in his view the provisions of the Bill are compatible with the Convention rights ('a statement of compatibility'); or

(b) make a statement to the effect that although he is unable to make a statement of compatibility the government nevertheless wishes the House to proceed with the Bill.

(2) The statement must be in writing and be published in such manner as the Minister making it considers appropriate.

...

SCHEDULES

Schedule 1

THE ARTICLES

PART I

THE CONVENTION RIGHTS AND FREEDOMS

ARTICLE 2
RIGHT TO LIFE

1. Everyone's right to life shall be protected by law. No one shall be deprived of his life intentionally save in the execution of a sentence of a court following his conviction of a crime for which this penalty is provided by law.

2. Deprivation of life shall not be regarded as inflicted in contravention of this Article when it results from the use of force which is no more than absolutely necessary:

   (a) in defence of any person from unlawful violence;

   (b) in order to effect a lawful arrest or to prevent the escape of a person lawfully detained;

   (c) in action lawfully taken for the purpose of quelling a riot or insurrection.

ARTICLE 3
PROHIBITION OF TORTURE

No one shall be subjected to torture or to inhuman or degrading treatment or punishment.

ARTICLE 4

PROHIBITON OF SLAVERY AND FORCED LABOUR

1. No one shall be held in slavery or servitude.

2. No one shall be required to perform forced or compulsory labour.

3. For the purpose of this Article the term 'forced or compulsory labour' shall not include:

    (a) any work required to be done in the ordinary course of detention imposed according to the provisions of Article 5 of this Convention or during conditional release from such detention;

    (b) any service of a military character or, in case of conscientious objectors in countries where they are recognised, service exacted instead of compulsory military service;

    (c) any service exacted in case of an emergency or calamity threatening the life or well-being of the community;

    (d) any work or service which forms part of normal civic obligations.

ARTICLE 5

RIGHT TO LIBERTY AND SECURITY

1. Everyone has the right to liberty and security of person. No one shall be deprived of his liberty save in the following cases and in accordance with a procedure prescribed by law:

    (a) the lawful detention of a person after conviction by a competent court;

    (b) the lawful arrest or detention of a person for non-compliance with the lawful order of a court or in order to secure the fulfilment of any obligation prescribed by law;

    (c) the lawful arrest or detention of a person effected for the purpose of bringing him before the competent legal authority on reasonable suspicion of having committed an offence or when it is reasonably considered necessary to prevent his committing an offence or fleeing after having done so;

    (d) the detention of a minor by lawful order for the purpose of educational supervision or his lawful detention for the purpose of bringing him before the competent legal authority;

    (e) the lawful detention of persons for the prevention of the spreading of infectious diseases, of persons of unsound mind, alcoholics or drug addicts or vagrants;

    (f) the lawful arrest or detention of a person to prevent his effecting an unauthorised entry into the country or of a person against whom action is being taken with a view to deportation or extradition.

2. Everyone who is arrested shall be informed promptly, in a language which he understands, of the reasons for his arrest and of any charge against him.

3. Everyone arrested or detained in accordance with the provisions of paragraph 1(c) of this Article shall be brought promptly before a judge or other officer authorised by law to exercise judicial power and shall be entitled to trial within a reasonable time or to release pending trial. Release may be conditioned by guarantees to appear for trial.

4. Everyone who is deprived of his liberty by arrest or detention shall be entitled to take proceedings by which the lawfulness of his detention shall be decided speedily by a court and his release ordered if the detention is not lawful.

5. Everyone who has been the victim of arrest or detention in contravention of the provisions of this Article shall have an enforceable right to compensation.

ARTICLE 6
RIGHT TO A FAIR TRIAL

1. In the determination of his civil rights and obligations or of any criminal charge against him, every-one is entitled to a fair and public hearing within a reasonable time by an independent and impartial tribunal established by law. Judgment shall be pronounced publicly but the press and public may be excluded from all or part of the trial in the interest of morals, public order or national security in a democratic society, where the interests of juveniles or the protection of the private life of the parties so require, or to the extent strictly necessary in the opinion of the court in special circumstances where publicity would prejudice the interests of justice.

2. Everyone charged with a criminal offence shall be presumed innocent until proved guilty according to law.

3. Everyone charged with a criminal offence has the following minimum rights:

    (a) to be informed promptly, in a language which he understands and in detail, of the nature and cause of the accusation against him;

    (b) to have adequate time and facilities for the preparation of his defence;

    (c) to defend himself in person or through legal assistance of his own choosing or, if he has not sufficient means to pay for legal assistance, to be given it free when the interests of justice so require;

    (d) to examine or have examined witnesses against him and to obtain the attendance and examin-ation of witnesses on his behalf under the same conditions as witnesses against him;

    (e) to have the free assistance of an interpreter if he cannot understand or speak the language used in court.

ARTICLE 7
NO PUNISHMENT WITHOUT LAW

1. No one shall be held guilty of any criminal offence on account of any act or omission which did not constitute a criminal offence under national or international law at the time when it was committed. Nor shall a heavier penalty be imposed than the one that was applicable at the time the criminal offence was committed.

2. This Article shall not prejudice the trial and punishment of any person for any act or omission which, at the time when it was committed, was criminal according to the general principles of law recognised by civilised nations.

ARTICLE 8
RIGHT TO RESPECT FOR PRIVATE AND FAMILY LIFE

1. Everyone has the right to respect for his private and family life, his home and his correspondence.

2. There shall be no interference by a public authority with the exercise of this right except such as is in accordance with the law and is necessary in a democratic society in the interests of national security, public safety or the economic well-being of the country, for the prevention of disorder or crime, for the protection of health or morals, or for the protection of the rights and freedoms of others.

ARTICLE 9
FREEDOM OF THOUGHT, CONSCIENCE AND RELIGION

1. Everyone has the right to freedom of thought, conscience and religion; this right includes freedom to change his religion or belief and freedom, either alone or in community with others and in public or private, to manifest his religion or belief, in worship, teaching, practice and observance.

2. Freedom to manifest one's religion or beliefs shall be subject only to such limitations as are pre-
    scribed by law and are necessary in a democratic society in the interests of public safety, for the
    protection of public order, health or morals, or for the protection of the rights and freedoms of
    others.

ARTICLE 10
FREEDOM OF EXPRESSION

1. Everyone has the right to freedom of expression. This right shall include freedom to hold opinions and
    to receive and impart information and ideas without interference by public authority and regardless
    of frontiers. This Article shall not prevent States from requiring the licensing of broadcasting, televi-
    sion or cinema enterprises.

2. The exercise of these freedoms, since it carries with it duties and responsibilities, may be subject to
    such formalities, conditions, restrictions or penalties as are prescribed by law and are necessary in
    a democratic society, in the interests of national security, territorial integrity or public safety, for the
    prevention of disorder or crime, for the protection of health or morals, for the protection of the repu-
    tation or rights of others, for preventing the disclosure of information received in confidence, or for
    maintaining the authority and impartiality of the judiciary.

ARTICLE 11
FREEDOM OF ASSEMBLY AND ASSOCIATION

1. Everyone has the right to freedom of peaceful assembly and to freedom of association with others, includ-
    ing the right to form and to join trade unions for the protection of his interests.

2. No restrictions shall be placed on the exercise of these rights other than such as are prescribed by
    law and are necessary in a democratic society in the interests of national security or public safety, for
    the prevention of disorder or crime, for the protection of health or morals or for the protection of the
    rights and freedoms of others. This Article shall not prevent the imposition of lawful restrictions on
    the exercise of these rights by members of the armed forces, of the police or of the administration of
    the State.

ARTICLE 12
RIGHT TO MARRY

Men and women of marriageable age have the right to marry and to found a family, according to the
national laws governing the exercise of this right.

ARTICLE 14
PROHIBITON OF DISCRIMINATION

The enjoyment of the rights and freedoms set forth in this Convention shall be secured without discrimination on any ground such as sex, race, colour, language, religion, political or other opinion, national or
social origin, association with a national minority, property, birth or other status.

ARTICLE 16
RESTRICTIONS ON POLITICAL ACTIVITY OF ALIENS

Nothing in Articles 10, 11 and 14 shall be regarded as preventing the High Contracting Parties from
imposing restrictions on the political activity of aliens.

ARTICLE 17
PROHIBITION OF ABUSE OF RIGHTS

Nothing in this Convention may be interpreted as implying for any State, group or person any right to
engage in any activity or perform any act aimed at the destruction of any of the rights and freedoms set
forth herein or at their limitation to a greater extent than is provided for in the Convention.

ARTICLE 18

LIMITATION ON USE OF RESTRICTIONS ON RIGHTS

The restrictions permitted under this Convention to the said rights and freedoms shall not be applied for any purpose other than those for which they have been prescribed.

PART II

THE FIRST PROTOCOL

ARTICLE 1

PROTECTION OF PROPERTY

Every natural or legal person is entitled to the peaceful enjoyment of his possessions. No one shall be deprived of his possessions except in the public interest and subject to the conditions provided for by law and by the general principles of international law.

The preceding provisions shall not, however, in any way impair the right of a State to enforce such laws as it deems necessary to control the use of property in accordance with the general interest or to secure the payment of taxes or other contributions or penalties.

ARTICLE 2

RIGHT TO EDUCATION

No person shall be denied the right to education. In the exercise of any functions which it assumes in relation to education and to teaching, the State shall respect the right of parents to ensure such education and teaching in conformity with their own religious and philosophical convictions.

ARTICLE 3

RIGHT TO FREE ELECTIONS

The High Contracting Parties undertake to hold free elections at reasonable intervals by secret ballot, under conditions which will ensure the free expression of the opinion of the people in the choice of the legislature.

PART III

THE SIXTH PROTOCOL

ARTICLE 1

ABOLITION OF THE DEATH PENALTY

The death penalty shall be abolished. No one shall be condemned to such penalty or executed.

ARTICLE 2

DEATH PENALTY IN TIME OF WAR

A State may make provision in its law for the death penalty in respect of acts committed in time of war or of imminent threat of war; such penalty shall be applied only in the instances laid down in the law and in accordance with its provisions. The State shall communicate to the Secretary General of the Council of Europe the relevant provisions of that law.

Schedule 2

REMEDIAL ORDERS

Orders

1. (1) A remedial order may—

    (a) contain such incidental, supplemental, consequential or transitional provisions as the person making it considers appropriate;

    (b) be made so as to have effect from a date earlier than that on which it is made;

(c)   make provision for the delegation of specific functions;

(d)   make different provision for different cases.

(2) The power conferred by sub-paragraph (1)(a) includes—

(a)   power to amend primary legislation (including primary legislation other than that which contains the incompatible provision); and

(b)   power to amend or revoke subordinate legislation (including subordinate legislation other than that which contains the incompatible provision).

(3) A remedial order may be made so as to have the same extent as the legislation which it affects.

(4) No person is to be guilty of an offence solely as a result of the retrospective effect of a remedial order.

Procedure

2. No remedial order may be made unless—

(a)   a draft of the order has been approved by a resolution of each House of Parliament made after the end of the period of 60 days beginning with the day on which the draft was laid; or

(b)   it is declared in the order that it appears to the person making it that, because of the urgency of the matter, it is necessary to make the order without a draft being so approved.

Orders laid in draft

3. (1) No draft may be laid under paragraph 2(a) unless—

(a)   the person proposing to make the order has laid before Parliament a document which contains a draft of the proposed order and the required information; and

(b)   the period of 60 days, beginning with the day on which the document required by this sub-paragraph was laid, has ended.

(2) If representations have been made during that period, the draft laid under paragraph 2(a) must be accompanied by a statement containing—

(a)   a summary of the representations; and

(b)   if, as a result of the representations, the proposed order has been changed, details of the changes.

Urgent cases

4. (1) If a remedial order ('the original order') is made without being approved in draft, the person making it must lay it before Parliament, accompanied by the required information, after it is made.

(2) If representations have been made during the period of 60 days beginning with the day on which the original order was made, the person making it must (after the end of that period) lay before Parliament a statement containing—

(a)   a summary of the representations; and

(b)   if, as a result of the representations, he considers it appropriate to make changes to the original order, details of the changes.

(3) If sub-paragraph (2)(b) applies, the person making the statement must—

(a)   make a further remedial order replacing the original order; and

(b)   lay the replacement order before Parliament.

(4) If, at the end of the period of 120 days beginning with the day on which the original order was made, a resolution has not been passed by each House approving the original or replacement order, the order ceases to have effect (but without that affecting anything previously done under either order or the power to make a fresh remedial order).

...

NOTES

1. *The Scheme of the Human Rights Act.*[47] This is both complicated and unique. The HRA provides for the indirect incorporation of the rights in the European Convention on Human Rights into UK law as 'the Convention rights' (s. 1). This has two main consequences. First, in all cases coming before them, the UK courts must interpret primary legislation compatibly with Convention rights so far as is possible (s. 3), taking into account the interpretation that has been given to them at Strasbourg (s. 2). If, despite all efforts, primary legislation cannot be interpreted compatibly with Convention rights, the courts may make a 'declaration of incompatibility' (s. 4). This does not affect the validity, continuing operation or enforcement of the legislation concerned. Instead, the legislation continues to apply, but a Minister may decide to legislate to remove the incompatibility, with the possibility of using a 'fast track' legislative procedure to do so (s. 10). Subordinate legislation that is incompatible with Convention rights is, in most cases, invalid (s. 3).

Second, 'public authorities' must act in accordance with Convention rights, unless incompatible primary or subordinate legislation leaves them no choice (s. 6). If they do not do so, a 'victim' of the resulting breach of the HRA has a public law right of action against the public authority concerned, or may rely on the Convention right in other legal proceedings (s. 7).[48] A court may award damages or grant other relief to the victim (s. 8).

There are also consequences for the common law, which must be applied and developed by the courts, as 'public authorities', in accordance with Convention rights.

2. *Section 1: The Convention rights.* The HRA applies to the Convention rights listed in s. 1. These are the rights in Arts 2–12, 14 and 16–18 of the ECHR, Arts 1–3 of the First Protocol to the ECHR[49] and Art. 1 of the 13th Protocol.[50] The HRA thus extends to almost all of the rights in the ECHR and its Protocols. The missing rights are the right to an effective remedy in national law guaranteed by Art. 13 of the ECHR,[51] and the rights in the 4th, 6th, 7th and 9th Protocols, which the UK has not ratified.[52] The Convention rights have to be read with Arts 16–18, which permit restrictions on the political activities of aliens (Art. 16); prohibit the use of Convention rights so as to subvert other rights (Art. 17);[53] and prohibit the use of a permitted restriction for an improper purpose (Art. 18).

---

[47] On the HRA, see R. Clayton and H. Tomlinson, *The Law of Human Rights* (2nd edn, 2006); J. Wadham and H. Mountfield, *The Human Rights Act 1998* (4th edn, 2007); M. Amos, *Human Rights Law* (2006); H. Fenwick, G. Phillipson and R. Masterman, *Judicial Reasoning Under the HRA* (2007); S. Grosz, J. Beatson and P. Duffy, *Human Rights: The 1998 Act and the European Convention* (2000); Lord Lester and D. Pannick, *Human Rights Law and Practice* (2nd edn, 2004); C. Gearty, *Principles of Human Rights Adjudication* (2004).

[48] E.g. criminal proceedings against the victim.

[49] The inclusion of the right to education in Art. 2, First Protocol is subject to the reservation to that article made by the UK upon ratification of the ECHR: see s. 15(1)(a) HRA. For the text of the reservation, see Sch. 3, Pt II HRA.

[50] For the text see HRA, Sch. 1.

[51] Lord Irvine LC explained the omission of Art. 13 as follows: 'The courts would be bound to ask what was intended beyond the existing scheme of remedies set out in the Act. It might lead them to fashion remedies other than clause [now section] 8 remedies, which we regard as sufficient and clear. We believe that clause 8 provides effective remedies before our courts... I cannot conceive of any state of affairs in which an English court, having held an act to be unlawful because of its infringement of a Convention right, would under clause 8(1) be disabled from giving an effective remedy': 583 HL Deb, 18 November 1997, cols 475, 479. Cf. Lord Hope in *Montgomery v HM Advocate* [2001] 2 WLR 779 at 794, PC. However, Lord Irvine LC noted that although Art. 13 was not included as a Convention right, the courts may none the less 'have regard to Article 13' when applying the HRA: ibid., col. 477. See the reliance upon it by Lord Hope in *R v Lambert* [2001] 3 All ER 577 at 609, HL.

[52] The 4th Protocol has been signed but not ratified.

[53] E.g. by relying upon freedom of expression or association to replace a democratic society by one that does not protect Convention rights generally.

The HRA does not apply to a Convention right to the extent of any derogation from it that the UK has made under Art. 15 of the ECHR and that has been 'designated' for this purpose under the HRA.[54] There is no such 'designated derogation' at present.[55]

3. The HRA does not extend to all human rights. A small number of civil and political rights are omitted. In addition to the ECHR rights that are not incorporated (see preceding note), a few other civil and political rights that are not included in the ECHR are absent. For example, there is no guarantee of freedom of information, the right to recognition as a person in law, or the right of a detained person to be treated with humanity and dignity.[56]

Human rights include economic, social and cultural rights as well as civil and political rights.[57] The former are not protected by the ECHR[58] and hence the HRA. Instead, within the Council of Europe, economic, social and cultural rights are guaranteed by the European Social Charter 1961,[59] which is enforceable through the assessment of national reports by the European Committee of Social Rights in Strasbourg and a right of collective (but not individual) complaint.[60] The Charter has not been incorporated into UK law.[61]

4. Of course, UK law may protect these missing human rights, or may protect Convention rights more extensively than the ECHR requires, outside of the regime of the HRA.[62] In such situations, the advantages of the HRA are not available, including its rules of interpretation and remedies. Instead, the rules of interpretation that were developed by the UK courts in human rights cases before the HRA continue to apply, as do the familiar, non-HRA judicial remedies in national law.

5. *Section 2: Reliance upon Strasbourg jurisprudence in the interpretation of Convention rights.* This section requires a court (or tribunal) to 'take into account' the interpretation given to the ECHR by the European Court of Human Rights and other specified Strasbourg

---

[54] HRA, s. 14.

[55] Originally, s. 14(1)(a) expressly designated the derogation from ECHR, Art. 5(3) that was in issue in *Murray v UK* (1999) 22 EHRR 29. However, in 2001 the UK withdrew this derogation and the HRA was amended accordingly, with s. 14(1)(a) being repealed: see SI 2001/1216. A further derogation issued after the terrorist attacks in New York in 2001 relating to detention without trial was withdrawn following the House of Lords decision in *A v Secretary of State for the Home Department* [2004] UKHL 56: see, Human Rights Act 1998 (Amendment) Order 2005, SI 2005/1071.

[56] See also the criticism of the underlying ECHR ideology (individualistic, not socialist) in K. Ewing and C. Gearty [1997] EHRLR 146.

[57] See the Universal Declaration of Human Rights 1948, which extends to all five categories of rights.

[58] But see the guarantees of the right to respect for family life (Art. 8 ECHR), the right to freedom of association (Art. 11 ECHR), the right to property (Art. 1, First Protocol) and the right to education (Art. 2, First Protocol), which, to some extent concern economic, social or cultural rights. On inadequacies of social rights protection in the UK, see K. Ewing [1999] PL 104.

[59] UKTS 38 (Cmnd 2643, 1965); 529 UNTS 89; ETS 35. In force 1965. The Charter was replaced for the parties thereto by the Revised European Social Charter 1996, ETS 163. See D. Harris, *The European Social Charter* (2nd edn, 2001, by D. Harris and J. Darcy). See also www.coe.int.

[60] See the 1995 Collective Complaints Protocol to the 1961 Charter, ETS 158. In force 1998. The UK has not yet accepted to be bound by the procedure.

[61] Nor has its UN counterpart, the International Covenant of Economic, Social and Cultural Rights 1996. The UK is a party to the Covenant.

[62] This is recognised by s. 11 HRA. See also Art. 53 ECHR. See, e.g., the Sex Discrimination Act 1975, the Race Relations Act 1976, and the Freedom of Information Act 2000. Nearly all of the prohibitions of discrimination in the first two of these fall outside Art. 14 ECHR. Some of them (concerning *private* discrimination in employment, etc.) are not directly covered by the 12th ECHR Protocol either, although that Protocol is likely to be interpreted as imposing positive obligations on states to control private conduct.

bodies. Strasbourg jurisprudence is thus persuasive but not legally binding.[63] In *R (Alconbury Developments Ltd) v Secretary of State for the Environment, Transport and the Regions*,[64] Lord Slynn stated:

Although the Human Rights Act 1998 does not provide that a national court is bound by these decisions (of the European Court of Human Rights) it is obliged to take account of them so far as they are relevant. In the absence of some special circumstances it seems to me that the court should follow any clear and constant jurisprudence of the European Court of Human Rights. If it does not do so there is at least the possibility that the case will go to that court which is likely in the ordinary case to follow its own constant jurisprudence.

As the above indicates, if the UK courts adopt an interpretation that is less favourable to a litigant relying upon the ECHR than that adopted previously at Strasbourg, there is always the possibility of a successful challenge at Strasbourg. This may also be the case where the interpretation goes to the balance between two Convention rights. If, for example, a UK court were to interpret the right to respect for privacy (Art. 8 ECHR) more extensively than the European Court of Human Rights and at the expense of the right to freedom of expression (Art. 10), a newspaper might be able to bring a successful Strasbourg claim under Art. 10.

In *R (on the application of Ullah) v Special Adjudicator*[65] Lord Bingham stated:

...a national court subject to a duty such as that imposed by section 2 should not without strong reason dilute or weaken the effect of the Strasbourg case law. It is indeed unlawful under section 6 of the 1998 Act for a public authority, including a court, to act in a way which is incompatible with a Convention right. It is of course open to member states to provide for rights more generous than those guaranteed by the Convention, but such provision should not be the product of interpretation of the Convention by national courts, since the meaning of the Convention should be uniform throughout the states party to it. The duty of national courts is to keep pace with the Strasbourg jurisprudence as it evolves over time: no more, but certainly no less.[66]

The jurisprudence of the UK courts indicates a clear intent to follow the interpretation of the ECHR at Strasbourg. However, the House of Lords have made clear that domestic rules of precedent still apply and thus lower courts must still follow higher courts even when the latter decision may conflict with a clear Strasbourg authority (unless it was a pre HRA decision).[67] Is this consistent with Lord Bingham's comment (above) that national courts must keep pace with Strasbourg jurisprudence? Was it Parliament's intention that the courts mirror Strasbourg jurisprudence or that domestic courts should develop a human rights jurisprudence of their own?[68] Section 2 requires only that domestic courts 'take into account' Strasbourg jurisprudence. However, if the ECHR provides a level below which domestic rights must not fall, but UK courts should not imply more than that, does

---

[63] The jurisprudence of the European Court of Justice is legally binding: see European Communities Act 1972, s. 3.

[64] [2001] 2 WLR 1389 at 1399, HL.

[65] [2004] UKHL 26 at para. 20. See also, *R (on the application of Marper) v Chief Constable of South Yorkshire* [2004] 1 WLR 2196.

[66] See also, *R (Al-Skeini) v Secretary of State for Defence* [2007] UKHL 26, [2008] 1 AC 153, para. 106; *R (on the application of Animal Defenders International) v Secretary of State for Culture, Media and Sport* [2008] UKHL 15 para. 53.

[67] *Kay v London Borough of Lambeth; Leeds City Council v Price* [2006] UKHL 10.

[68] See J. Lewis [2007] PL 720; See also, Joint Committee on Human Rights, *A Bill of Rights for the UK?*, 29th Report of Session 2007–8 HC 150/HL 165, p. 21; see also, R. Clayton [2007] EHRLR 11.

this effectively meaning that Strasbourg jurisprudence is binding?[69] In the recent case of *Huang v Secretary of State for the Home Department*,[70] the Lords were clear in stating that Strasbourg jurisprudence is not binding. It appears that the exceptions to being bound by Strasbourg are when (a) the Strasbourg interpretation is not clear because some aspect of English law has been misinterpreted, or (b) when there are 'special circumstances' such as that a conclusion fundamentally at odds with the British constitution would result. Rarely have these exceptions been invoked leading Lewis to comment: 'It follows that the mirror principle is practically inescapable.'[71] Does the reference to taking account of Strasbourg 'jurisprudence' rather than 'decisions' suggest that it is the broader principles in the cases that are to be followed rather than seeking to discover binding precedent?[72]

6. *Section 3: Interpretation of legislation compatibly with Convention rights.* On the approach to be followed by a court (or tribunal) when applying the 'so far as it is possible' rule in s. 3 HRA to decide whether legislation is compatible with the Convention rights: see *Ghaidan v Godin-Mendoza* below and the notes thereto. Although they do not apply a 'margin of appreciation' doctrine when deciding whether legislation is compatible with Convention rights, the courts have accepted that they should in appropriate cases defer to Parliament's legislative judgment as to whether a particular limitation upon a Convention right in a Westminster statute is compatible with it: see *Brown v Stott* below and the notes thereto.

The rule of interpretation in s. 3 HRA extends only to the compatibility of legislation[73] with Convention rights. As far as its compatibility with the UK's other human rights treaty obligations is concerned, the position was explained by Lord Denning in *R v Chief Immigration Officer, Heathrow Airport, ex p Salamat Bibi*:[74]

The position as I understand it is that if there is any ambiguity in our statutes, or uncertainty in our law, then these courts can look to the Convention as an aid to clear up the ambiguity and uncertainty...but I would dispute altogether that the Convention is part of our law. Treaties and declarations do not become part of our law until they are made law by Parliament.

This statement concerning the (then) unincorporated ECHR must apply to other human rights treaties also.

7. *The HRA and the common law.* By virtue of s. 6 HRA, the courts, as public authorities,[75] must not act incompatibly with Convention rights. As far as their application of the common law is concerned, this means that the courts must not act inconsistently with Convention rights procedurally[76] or in the provision of remedies.[77] It also means that any existing substantive rule of common law that is incompatible with Convention rights must give way to them, with a court being obliged to ignore otherwise binding precedent to the contrary. Moreover, the substantive common law cannot be developed incompatibly with Convention rights.[78] More positively, Convention rights may be used by the courts as a basis for their

---

[69] R. Masterman [2004] PL 725.   [70] [2007] UKHL 11.

[71] Lewis, op. cit., p. 731.   [72] Ibid., p. 747.

[73] This includes the HRA itself: *R v Lambert* [2001] 3 All ER 577 at 612, per Lord Hope.

[74] [1976] 1 WLR 979 at 984.

[75] See s. 6(3) HRA. On the meaning of 'public authority' see, *YL v Birmingham City Council* [2007] UKHL 27.

[76] E.g. in criminal proceedings in the application of common law rules of evidence.

[77] E.g. the level of damages must comply with Convention rights: see *Tolstoy Miloslavsky v United Kingdom* (1995) 20 EHRR 442 and *Rantzen v Mirror Group Newspapers (1986) Ltd* [1994] QB 670, CA.

[78] See Lord Irvine LC, 583 HL Debs, 24 November 1997, col. 783: 'We also believe that it is right as a matter of principle for the courts to have the duty of acting compatibly with the Convention not only in cases involving other public authorities but also in developing the common law in deciding cases between individuals.'

taking the initiative to develop common law rules or causes of action that further those rights, as in *Campbell v Mirror Group Newspapers*.[79] However, s. 6 does not mean that the courts, as 'public authorities', must allow one private person to sue another for a breach of a Convention right.[80]

8. *Section 4: Declarations of incompatibility.* Primary legislation[81] that, despite the application of the rule of interpretation in s. 3, is incompatible with Convention rights is not thereby rendered invalid, inoperative or unenforceable.[82] Instead, a court may make a 'declaration of incompatibility'. In *Ghaidan v Godin-Mendoza* (see below) the House rejected the notion that s. 4 should be used in preference to s. 3. The purpose of a declaration of incompatibility is to give notice of the incompatibility to the government, so that it may initiate remedial action, not to provide a remedy for any victim. In contrast, incompatible subordinate legislation is invalid, inoperative and unenforceable unless the incompatibility flows unavoidably from the enabling primary legislation,[83] in which latter case a declaration of incompatibility may be made. Note that s. 4 provides a *discretion* to grant a declaration. It is suggested that such a declaration may be granted in favour of someone not a 'victim' as such but this is likely to be a scenario in which the discretion will not be exercised.[84]

9. *Section 6: Acts of public authorities.* Section 6(1) HRA makes it unlawful for a 'public authority' to act incompatibly with a Convention right. However, an act, which includes a failure to act, is not unlawful if the authority has no choice but to act in this way because of incompatible primary legislation.[85] In such a case, no claim may be brought by the victim of the act against the authority under s. 7 HRA; the only remedy is a declaration of incompatibility. For example, a court will not commit an unlawful act if it is required to take a decision or give judgment in a certain way by incompatible primary legislation.

There has been a good deal of case law on the meaning of 'public authority' with a distinction being drawn between core public authorities, whose activities fall within s. 6, and hybrid public authorities whose functions may be of a public or private nature.[86] In relation to the latter, the central debate has surrounded whether the body in question has the organisational characteristics of a public body or whether the task it is performing is akin to that of a public body. The Court of Appeal has stated that the definition of who is a public authority and what is a public function should be given a 'generous interpretation',[87] but

---

79   For *Campbell v Mirror Group Newspapers* see Chap. 8.

80   See, e.g., *Venables v News Group Newspapers* [2001] Fam 430 below. Contrast the position under s. 7 HRA, by which a private individual has a *statutory* cause of action against a *public authority* (but not a private individual) for conduct incompatible with a Convention right.

81   For the meaning of primary legislation, see s. 21(1) HRA. see P. Billings and B. Pontin [2001] PL 21.

82   HRA, s. 3(2)(b).

83   HRA, s. 3(2)(c). Incompatible subordinate legislation does not in itself render its enabling legislation incompatible: per Dame Elizabeth Butler-Sloss, in *Re K (a child) (secure accommodation: right to liberty)* [2001] 2 WLR 1144 at 1155, CA. For the meaning of subordinate legislation, see s. 21(1) HRA.

84   See, e.g., *R (Rusbridger) v Attorney General* [2003] UKHL 38; *Lancashire Council Council v Taylor* [2005] 1 WLR 2668.

85   HRA, s. 6(2). However, in the case of executive acts, there will usually be some discretion which can be exercised consistently with Convention rights. As to the courts, they must apply the common law and, so far as possible, interpret legislation in accordance with Convention rights.

86   *Aston Cantlow and Wilmcote with Billesley Parochial Church Council v Wallbank* [2004] UKHL 37.

87   *Donoghue v Poplar Housing and Regeneration Community Association* [2001] EWCA Civ 595, para. [58], per Lord Woolf CJ.

this approach has not been consistently followed.[88] The Parliamentary Joint Committee on Human Rights[89] has commented:

> We consider that the Government's campaign to educate public authorities in their responsibilities under the HRA will be of limited value if it can only direct its efforts towards 'pure' public authorities. We consider that the current approach of the courts to the meaning of public authority will inhibit the development of a positive human rights culture in the United Kingdom. In so far as it prevents the direct application of the HRA to significant numbers of vulnerable people, such as the residents of privately-run care homes, this approach helps to perpetuate the myth that the HRA creates no real benefits for 'ordinary people' in their day to day lives.

The decision of the House of Lords in *YL v Birmingham City Council*[90] confirmed the courts' narrow approach to the definition, basing the interpretation upon the nature of the task performed. In that case, a private nursing home which cared for residents under a contract with the local authority was not deemed to be a public authority for the purposes of the HRA. The care home existed and was run in order to make profits in a competitive market and entered private contractual agreements to take in residents. Section 145 of the Health and Social Care Act 2008 has reversed this finding and care homes are now public authorities for the purposes of the HRA.[91] Whether this will provide the impetus for a broader approach to the interpretation of s. 6, HRA remains to be seen.

10. *Acts of private persons.*[92] The Act creates the right to bring a claim for a breach of Convention rights only against a public authority (vertical effect).[93] However, the Act also makes it unlawful for a public authority (including a court) to act in a way that is incompatible with a Convention right. Therefore, to what extent is a court obliged to reach a solution that is compatible with Convention rights in a dispute between two private parties? On the one hand the structure of the Act would suggest that this was not the intention and Convention rights are rights against the state. On the other hand, it is unlikely that the intention behind the Act was that it would have no effect at all on relations between private parties. The position endorsed thus far appears to be neither full horizontal effect nor no effect at all but a middle position, as espoused by Baroness Hale in *Venables v News Group Newspapers* in stating that s. 6(1):[94]

> does not seem to me to encompass the creation of a free-standing cause of action based directly upon the articles of the convention,

---

[88] See, e.g., *R (Heather) v Leonard Cheshire Foundation* [2001] EWHC 429 (Admin), where the court held that a charitable foundation which ran a care home, the majority of whose residents were funded by their local authority or health authority, was not exercising a public function. See also, M. Sunkin [2004] PL 643; cf. D. Oliver [2002] PL 476 and [2004] PL 329 suggesting that a broad approach is not necessarily desirable. Further, see P. Craig [2002] LQR 551; C.M. Donnelly [2005] PL 785.

[89] Joint Committee on Human Rights 9th Report of Session 2006–7, *The Meaning of Public Authority Under the Human Rights Act* (2007) HL 77/HC 410, para. 30; see also, Eighth Report of Session 2007–08, *Legislative Scrutiny: Health and Social Care Bill*, HL 46/HC 303, paras 1.8–1.10 and 1.14.

[90] [2007] UKHL 27.

[91] A private members' bill brought forward in 2007 sought to redefine 'public authority'. See the Human Rights Act 1998 (Meaning of Public Authorities) Bill 2006–7. See also, Joint Committee on Human Rights, *A Bill of Rights for the UK?*, 29th Report of Session 2007–8 HC 150 /HL 165, p. 6.

[92] There has been much academic discussion on this subject, see, e.g., M. Hunt [1998] PL 423; Sir Richard Buxton (2000) 116 LQR 48; G. Phillipson (1999) 62 MLR 824; I. Leigh (1999) 48 ICLQ 57.

[93] Ss. 6, 7.   [94] [2001] Fam 430 at para. 27.

but does require the court,

to act compatibly with Convention rights in adjudicating upon existing common law causes of action, and that includes a positive as well as a negative obligation....[95]

11. *Section 7: Claims by victims.* Section 7(1) allows a victim to claim in court that a public authority has acted unlawfully contrary to s. 6(1). A claim may be brought or made in one of two ways. First under s. 7(1)(a) a claim may be brought against a public authority before the appropriate court or tribunal.[96] The HRA thus introduces a public law right of action for the breach of a Convention right by a public authority. This cause of action applies only to acts by public authorities; as noted above, it does not extend to acts by private persons. Moreover, a public authority is not liable where it cannot act otherwise because of the constraints of incompatible primary legislation.[97] Nor does s. 7(1) apply to judicial acts by courts or tribunals: instead a claim of incompatibility must be made on appeal to a higher court or tribunal or in judicial review proceedings.[98]

Second, a victim may raise an issue of incompatibility in legal proceedings that have been commenced on some other basis,[99] for example, criminal proceedings in which the victim is a defendant, a civil claim in contract or tort to which the victim is a party, or judicial review proceedings brought on other established judicial review grounds.

Claims under s. 7 may only be made by a 'victim' of the act. 'Victim' has the same meaning as it has in Art. 34 ECHR, which contains the locus standi requirement for bringing a Strasbourg application.[100] This requirement means essentially that the applicant must be directly or indirectly affected by the act of the public authority.[101] This is a more restrictive rule than that in judicial review proceedings under UK law, which allows non-governmental organisations to bring proceedings about a matter of general concern in respect of which they have a 'sufficient interest'.[102] The reason for limiting claims under s. 7 in this way was explained in Parliament as follows:[103]

As a government, our aim is to grant access to victims. It is not to create opportunities to allow interest groups from SPUC to Liberty...to venture into frolics of their own in the courts. The aim is to confer access to rights, not to license interest groups to clog up the courts with test cases.

If a UK public authority has jurisdiction overseas a victim could bring action under the HRA if the authority acts incompatibly with Convention rights.[104]

12. *Section 8: Damages or other relief.* Where a claim succeeds under s. 7, the court or tribunal may award damages or grant such other remedy or relief as it considers 'just and appropriate'. Damages,[105] like other remedies or relief, are discretionary and may only be awarded

---

[95] See also *Campbell v Mirror Group Newspapers* [2004] UKHL 22 at para. 132 per Baroness Hale.

[96] Such claims are heard in the ordinary courts.

[97] HRA, s. 6(2). Where s. 6(2) applies, the remedy is a declaration of incompatibility under s. 4, not a claim under s. 7.

[98] HRA, s. 9(1).   [99] HRA, s. 7(1)(b).

[100] HRA, s. 7(7). On Art. 34 (formerly Art. 25), see D. Harris, M. O'Boyle and C. Warbrick, *The Law of the European Convention on Human Rights* (1995), pp. 630–638.

[101] See *Taylor v Lancashire County Council* [2005] EWCA Civ 284.

[102] See, e.g., *R v Inspectorate of Pollution, ex p Greenpeace (No. 2)* [1994] 4 All ER 329, QBD.

[103] Mr O'Brien, Under Secretary of State, Home Office, 314 HC Deb, 24 June 1998, col. 1086.

[104] *R (Al-Skeini) v Ministry of Defence* [2007] UKHL 26.

[105] In accordance with the usual rule of judicial immunity, damages may not be awarded in respect of a judicial act done in good faith, except as compensation for detention contrary to Art. 5 ECHR: s. 9(3) HRA.

by a court or tribunal with the power to award damages or compensation in civil proceedings.[106] Damages may not be awarded unless the court is satisfied that this is necessary to afford 'just satisfaction',[107] which is the criterion for the award of damages by the European Court of Human Rights.[108] When deciding whether to award damages, and the amount of any award, a court must 'take into account' the principles applied at Strasbourg.[109] Though there are examples of courts awarding damages analogous to those in tort[110] the House of Lords have suggested that the ECtHR principles ought to be the guide. Lord Bingham, rejecting a domestic scale of damages, stated:[111]

> ...there are in my opinion broader reasons why this approach should not be followed. First, the 1998 Act is not a tort statute. Its objects are different and broader. Even in a case where a finding of violation is not judged to afford the applicant just satisfaction, such a finding will be an important part of his remedy and an important vindication of the right he has asserted. Damages need not ordinarily be awarded to encourage high standards of compliance by member states, since they are already bound in international law to perform their duties under the Convention in good faith, although it may be different if there is felt to be a need to encourage compliance by individual officials or classes of official. Secondly, the purpose of incorporating the Convention in domestic law through the 1998 Act was not to give victims better remedies at home than they could recover in Strasbourg but to give them the same remedies without the delay and expense of resort to Strasbourg. This intention was clearly expressed in the White Paper 'Rights Brought Home: The Human Rights Bill' (Cm 3782, 1 October 1997), para 2.6:
>
>> 'The Bill provides that, in considering an award of damages on Convention grounds, the courts are to take into account the principles applied by the European Court of Human Rights in awarding compensation, so that people will be able to receive compensation from a domestic court equivalent to what they would have received in Strasbourg.'
>
> Thirdly, section 8(4) requires a domestic court to take into account the principles applied by the European Court under article 41 not only in determining whether to award damages but also in determining the amount of an award. There could be no clearer indication that courts in this country should look to Strasbourg and not to domestic precedents. The appellant contended that the levels of Strasbourg awards are not 'principles' applied by the Court, but this is a legalistic distinction which is contradicted by the White Paper and the language of section 8 and has no place in a decision on the quantum of an award, to which principle has little application. The Court routinely describes its awards as equitable, which I take to mean that they are not precisely calculated but are judged by the Court to be fair in the individual case. Judges in England and Wales must also make a similar judgment in the case before them. They are not inflexibly bound by Strasbourg awards in what may be different cases. But they should not aim to be significantly more or less generous than the Court might be expected to be, in a case where it was willing to make an award at all.

13. *Section 10: Remedial action: legislation to remove an incompatibility.* A declaration of incompatibility that is made by a court under s. 4 HRA does not render the legislation invalid, inoperative or ineffective.[112] Instead, the provision for 'remedial action' in s. 10 applies. By s. 10(2), after any appeal proceedings in the case have been completed, a Minister 'may'[113] proceed by 'remedial order' to amend the offending legislation to eliminate

---

[106] HRA, s. 8(2). Criminal courts are excluded.

[107] HRA, s. 8(3).   [108] Art. 41 ECHR.

[109] HRA, s. 8(4). For the Strasbourg practice, see A. Mowbray [1997] PL 647. See also Sir Robert Carnwath (2000) 49 ICLQ 517.

[110] E.g., see *R (KB) v Mental Health Review Tribunal* [2003] 2 All ER 209.

[111] *R (Greenfield) v Secretary of State for the Home Department* [2005] UKHL 14, para. 19.

[112] HRA, s. 4(6)(a). Nor is the declaration binding on the parties to the case: s. 4(6)(b) HRA.

[113] The Minister thus has a power, not a duty, to initiate legislative change. Failure to make a remedial order is not a breach of s. 6(1): s. 6(5) HRA.

the incompatibility. The order may be given retrospective effect.[114] Section 10(3) gives a similar power to correct primary legislation that prevents the alteration of incompatible subordinate legislation. A remedial order may be adopted by the use of a 'fast track' procedure, involving an affirmative resolution of each of the two Houses of Parliament.[115] However, a Minister may act by way of remedial order only if he considers that there are 'compelling reasons' for doing so; otherwise, a statute will be needed.[116] Lord Hoffmann has stated: 'If the courts make a declaration of incompatibility, the political pressure upon the government to bring the law into line will be hard to resist.'[117] Would this be true in all cases? What about a case involving a legal point that would not attract much public interest?

The power to make a 'remedial order' is also available to a Minister where the European Court of Human Rights has given a judgment, whether against the UK or another state, which suggests that UK legislation is contrary to the ECHR.[118]

14. *Section 12: Freedom of expression.* Section 12 of the HRA was introduced because of concerns that the HRA might serve as a vehicle for the introduction of a right to privacy at the expense of the right to freedom of expression on the part of the media. However, the direction to 'have particular regard to the importance of the Convention right to freedom of expression' in the introductory wording of s. 12(4) has not had the desired effect. Instead, it was used to further the common law protection of privacy at the expense of the press in *Douglas v Hello! (No. 1)*,[119] the Court of Appeal taking account of (a) the fact that the reference in s. 12(4) is to the 'Convention right' to freedom of expression, which includes the permissibility in Art. 10(2) of restrictions to protect the 'rights of others' (including the right to privacy), and (b) the reference to 'any relevant privacy code' in s. 12(4), which includes the Press Complaints Commission Code.

15. *Section 13: Freedom of religion.* Section 13 requires courts to have 'particular regard to the importance of' the right to freedom of religion in Art. 9 ECHR. It was introduced by the Government in place of amendments that had been successfully promoted by the churches in the House of Lords who feared that their activities might be affected by the HRA by the guarantee of freedom of 'thought, conscience and religion' in Art. 9 and the prohibition on discrimination in Art. 14 ECHR.[120]

16. *Section 19: Parliamentary statements of compatibility.* Section 19 requires that when a Bill is introduced into Parliament, a Minister make a statement before the second reading on its compatibility with Convention rights. The Bill may proceed even though the statement is

---

[114] Sch. 2, para. 1(1)(b) HRA. A person cannot be convicted of a criminal offence by the retrospective application of a remedial order: para. 1(3).

[115] For the details of the procedure see Sch. 2, HRA. The remedial order must be laid before both Houses of Parliament for 60 days: para. 2(a). The 60-day period may be dispensed with in urgent cases: para. 2(b).

[116] The 'compelling reasons' limitation was inserted because Parliament was concerned about giving Ministers too wide a power to bypass ordinary legislative procedures. Lord Simon expressed concern about the use of Henry VIII clauses: 583 HL Deb, 27 November 1997, col. 1141. A decision on the existence of 'compelling reasons' may be subject to judicial review: see K. Ewing (1999) 62 MLR 70 at 93.

[117] (1999) 62 MLR 159 at 160.   [118] HRA, s. 10(1)(b).

[119] [2001] QB 967. Section 12(4) does not 'require the court to treat freedom of speech as paramount' or 'direct the court to place even greater weight on the importance of freedom of expression than it does already'; instead, 'the requirement "to pay particular regard" contemplates specific and separate consideration being given to this factor': per Sir Andrew Morritt V-C, in *Imutran Ltd v Uncaged Campaigns Ltd* [2001] 2 All ER 385 at 391, Ch D. See also *Ashdown v Telegraph Group Ltd* [2001] EWCA Civ 1142, [2001] 2 All ER 370, Ch D, in which s. 12(4) did not prevent a successful breach of copyright claim for the unauthorised publication of a minute of a private meeting.

[120] For these concerns and generally on s. 13, see P. Cumper [2000] PL 154.

not able to confirm compatibility.[121] No such obligation exists in respect of any amendments introduced during the passage of the Bill. Section 19 statements are not binding on the courts and do not have persuasive authority.[122] In 2007 the Constitution Committee of the House of Lords stated:

Notwithstanding ministerial statements under section 19, there have been cases in which it is clear that ministers have initially adopted a far too optimistic view about the compatibility of provisions in a bill. Although few statutory provisions enacted since the HRA came into force have been subject to declarations of incompatibility by the courts, on a number of occasions the Government has had to make or accept major amendments to bills to bring them into line with Convention rights (as Parliament views them).[123]

Declarations of incompatibility relating to post HRA-legislation have been made in *A v Secretary of State for the Home Department*[124] in relation to s. 23 of the Anti-terrorism, Crime and Security Act 2001 permitting detention without trial (subsequently repealed by the Prevention of Terrorism Act 2005) and *R (Baiai) v Secretary of State for the Home Department*[125] in relation to s. 19(3) of the Asylum and Immigration (Treatment of Claimants) Act 2004 dealing with immigration procedures where sham marriages are suspected. Details of pre-HRA legislation found to be incompatible can be found in the 2007 House of Lords Select Committee Report of the Constitution.[126]

17. *Section 22: Retrospective effect.* Section 22(4) means that a victim cannot bring proceedings under s. 7(1)(a) in respect of acts by public authorities that occurred before the HRA entered into force on 2 October 2000. The HRA does not apply to an appeal against a conviction by a court made before that date.[127] What was a contentious issue initially is waning in importance as time passes.

18. *The Parliamentary Joint Committee on Human Rights.* The Joint Committee on Human Rights is a Select Committee of the two Houses of Parliament. Its work can be separated into three areas: (1) legislative scrutiny, to consider compliance with human rights;[128] (2) thematic inquiries into issues relating to human rights; and (3) scrutiny of Government responses to adverse judgments from the European Court in Strasbourg and declarations of incompatibility made under s. 4 by domestic courts. The JCHR has suggested that it does not always have sufficient time to carry out its scrutiny role effectively:

...we regret that the rapid progress of the Bill through Parliament has made it impossible for us to scrutinise the Bill comprehensively for human rights compatibility in time to inform debate in Parliament.[129]

---

[121] HRA, s. 19(2). See Communications Act 2003, s. 321 where no statement of compatibility was made.

[122] Per Lord Hope in *R v A* [2001] UKHL 25 at para. 69.

[123] Select Committee on the Constitution, *Relations between the Executive, Judiciary and Parliament*, 6th Report of Session 2006–7 (2007) HL Paper 151.

[124] See Chap. 6.   [125] [2007] EWCA Civ 478.

[126] (2007) HL Paper 151 above, Appendix 6.

[127] *R v Lambert* [2001] 3 All ER 577, HL. See also *Macdonald v Advocate General for Scotland* [2003] UKHL 30, in which the possibility of retrospective effect in civil proceedings was rejected.

[128] D.J. Feldman [2002] PL 323.

[129] Joint Committee on Human Rights, Tenth Report of Session 2004–05, Prevention of Terrorism Bill, HL 68/HC 334, p. 3.

From 2007 the Committee produces an annual report on its work.[130] In a 2004 report[131] the Joint Committee made out a case for a human rights commission which would help to develop and foster a culture of human rights. The Government responded with plans for an all-encompassing human rights and equality body. The Equality and Human Rights Commission began work in October 2007. For details, see Chapter 14.

- **Ghaidan v Godin-Mendoza** [2004] UKHL 30, [2004] 2 AC 557, [2004] 3 All ER 411, [2004] 3 WLR 113, House of Lords

The respondent had lived in a stable homosexual relationship with the deceased. The Rent Act 1977 provided only for rights of succession for a person living with the tenant 'as his or her wife or husband'. The respondent claimed that this unfairly discriminated against him and was thus a breach of Art. 14. The House of Lords, under s. 3 of the HRA, reinterpreted the Rent Act to allow succession to any couple who had been living together in a stable relationship.

Lord Nicholls of Birkenhead:

4. I must first set out the relevant statutory provisions and then explain how the Human Rights Act 1998 comes to be relevant in this case. Paragraphs 2 and 3 of Schedule 1 to the Rent Act 1977 provide:

'2(1) The surviving spouse (if any) of the original tenant, if residing in the dwelling-house immediately before the death of the original tenant, shall after the death be the statutory tenant if and so long as he or she occupies the dwelling-house as his or her residence.

(2) For the purposes of this paragraph, a person who was living with the original tenant as his or her wife or husband shall be treated as the spouse of the original tenant.

3(1) Where paragraph 2 above does not apply, but a person who was a member of the original tenant's family was residing with him in the dwelling-house at the time of and for the period of 2 years immediately before his death then, after his death, that person or if there is more than one such person such one of them as may be decided by agreement, or in default of agreement by the county court, shall be entitled to an assured tenancy of the dwelling-house by succession.'

5. On an ordinary reading of this language paragraph 2(2) draws a distinction between the position of a heterosexual couple living together in a house as husband and wife and a homosexual couple living together in a house. The survivor of a heterosexual couple may become a statutory tenant by succession, the survivor of a homosexual couple cannot. That was decided in *Fitzpatrick's* case. The survivor of a homosexual couple may, in competition with other members of the original tenant's 'family', become entitled to an assured tenancy under paragraph 3. But even if he does, as in the present case, this is less advantageous. Notably, so far as the present case is concerned, the rent payable under an assured tenancy is the contractual or market rent, which may be more than the fair rent payable under a statutory tenancy, and an assured tenant may be evicted for non-payment of rent without the court needing to be satisfied, as is essential in the case of a statutory tenancy, that it is reasonable to make a possession order. In these and some other respects the succession rights granted by the statute to the survivor of a homosexual couple in respect of the house where he or she is living are less favourable than the succession rights granted to the survivor of a heterosexual couple.

---

[130] Joint Committee on Human Rights Sixth Report, Session 2007–8, *The Work of the Committee in 2007 and the State of Human Rights in the UK*, HL 38/HC 270.

[131] Joint Committee on Human Rights Sixth Report, Session 2002–3, *The Case for a Human Rights Commission*, HL 67/HC 489.

6. Mr Godin-Mendoza's claim is that this difference in treatment infringes article 14 of the European Convention on Human Rights read in conjunction with article 8. Article 8 does not require the state to provide security of tenure for members of a deceased tenant's family. Article 8 does not in terms give a right to be provided with a home: *Chapman v United Kingdom* (2001) 33 EHRR 399, 427, para 99. It does not 'guarantee the right to have one's housing problem solved by the authorities': *Marzari v Italy* (1999) 28 EHRR CD 175, 179. But if the state makes legislative provision it must not be discriminatory. The provision must not draw a distinction on grounds such as sex or sexual orientation without good reason. Unless justified, a distinction founded on such grounds infringes the Convention right embodied in article 14, as read with article 8. Mr Godin-Mendoza submits that the distinction drawn by paragraph 2 of Schedule 1 to the Rent Act 1977 is drawn on the grounds of sexual orientation and that this difference in treatment lacks justification.

7. That is the first step in Mr Godin-Mendoza's claim. That step would not, of itself, improve Mr Godin-Mendoza's status in his flat. The second step in his claim is to pray in aid the court's duty under section 3 of the Human Rights Act 1998 to read and give effect to legislation in a way which is compliant with the Convention rights. Here, it is said, section 3 requires the court to read paragraph 2 so that it embraces couples living together in a close and stable homosexual relationship as much as couples living together in a close and stable heterosexual relationship. So read, paragraph 2 covers Mr Godin-Mendoza's position. Hence he is entitled to a declaration that on the death of Mr Wallwyn-James he succeeded to a statutory tenancy.

8. The first of the two steps in Mr Godin-Mendoza's argument requires him to make good the proposition that, as interpreted in *Fitzpatrick's* case, paragraph 2 of Schedule 1 to the Rent Act 1977 infringes his Convention right under article 14 read in conjunction with article 8. Article 8 guarantees, among other matters, the right to respect for a person's home. Article 14 guarantees that the rights set out in the Convention shall be secured 'without discrimination' on any grounds such as those stated in the non-exhaustive list in that article....

13. In the present case paragraph 2 of Schedule 1 to the Rent Act 1977 draws a dividing line between married couples and cohabiting heterosexual couples on the one hand and other members of the original tenant's family on the other hand. What is the rationale for this distinction? The rationale seems to be that, for the purposes of security of tenure, the survivor of such couples should be regarded as having a special claim to be treated in much the same way as the original tenant. The two of them made their home together in the house in question, and their security of tenure in the house should not depend upon which of them dies first.

14. The history of the Rent Act legislation is consistent with this appraisal. A widow, living with her husband, was accorded a privileged succession position in 1920. In 1980 a widower was accorded the like protection. In 1988 paragraph 2(2) was added, by which the survivor of a cohabiting heterosexual couple was treated in the same way as a spouse of the original tenant.

15. Miss Carss-Frisk QC submitted there is a relevant distinction between heterosexual partnerships and same sex partnerships. The aim of the legislation is to provide protection for the traditional family. Same sex partnerships cannot be equated with family in the traditional sense. Same sex partners are unable to have children with each other, and there is a reduced likelihood of children being a part of such a household.

16. My difficulty with this submission is that there is no reason for believing these factual differences between heterosexual and homosexual couples have any bearing on why succession rights have been conferred on heterosexual couples but not homosexual couples. Protection of the traditional family unit may well be an important and legitimate aim in certain contexts. In certain contexts this may be a cogent reason justifying differential treatment: see *Karner v Austria* (2003) 2 FLR 623, 630, para 40. But it is important to identify the element of the 'traditional family' which paragraph 2, as it now stands, is seeking to protect. Marriage is not now a prerequisite to protection

under paragraph 2. The line drawn by Parliament is no longer drawn by reference to the status of marriage. Nor is parenthood, or the presence of children in the home, a precondition of security of tenure for the survivor of the original tenant. Nor is procreative potential a prerequisite. The survivor is protected even if, by reasons of age or otherwise, there was never any prospect of either member of the couple having a natural child.

20. In the present case the only suggested ground for according different treatment to the survivor of same sex couples and opposite sex couples cannot withstand scrutiny. Rather, the present state of the law as set out in paragraph 2 of Schedule 1 of the Rent Act 1977 may properly be described as continuing adherence to the traditional regard for the position of surviving spouses, adapted in 1988 to take account of the widespread contemporary trend for men and women to cohabit outside marriage but not adapted to recognise the comparable position of cohabiting same sex couples. I appreciate that the primary object of introducing the regime of assured tenancies and assured shorthold tenancies in 1988 was to increase the number of properties available for renting in the private sector. But this policy objective of the Housing Act 1988 can afford no justification for amending paragraph 2 so as to include cohabiting heterosexual partners but not cohabiting homosexual partners. This policy objective of the Act provides no reason for, on the one hand, extending to unmarried cohabiting heterosexual partners the right to succeed to a statutory tenancy but, on the other hand, withholding that right from cohabiting homosexual partners. Paragraph 2 fails to attach sufficient importance to the Convention rights of cohabiting homosexual couples.

24. In my view, therefore, Mr Godin-Mendoza makes good the first step in his argument: paragraph 2 of Schedule 1 to the Rent Act 1977, construed without reference to section 3 of the Human Rights Act, violates his Convention right under article 14 taken together with article 8.

SECTION 3 OF THE HUMAN RIGHTS ACT 1998

25. I turn next to the question whether section 3 of the Human Rights Act 1998 requires the court to depart from the interpretation of paragraph 2 enunciated in *Fitzpatrick's* case.

26. Section 3 is a key section in the Human Rights Act 1998. It is one of the primary means by which Convention rights are brought into the law of this country. Parliament has decreed that all legislation, existing and future, shall be interpreted in a particular way. All legislation must be read and given effect to in a way which is compatible with the Convention rights 'so far as it is possible to do so'. This is the intention of Parliament, expressed in section 3, and the courts must give effect to this intention.

27. Unfortunately, in making this provision for the interpretation of legislation, section 3 itself is not free from ambiguity. Section 3 is open to more than one interpretation. The difficulty lies in the word 'possible'. Section 3(1), read in conjunction with section 3(2) and section 4, makes one matter clear: Parliament expressly envisaged that not all legislation would be capable of being made Convention-compliant by application of section 3. Sometimes it would be possible, sometimes not. What is not clear is the test to be applied in separating the sheep from the goats. What is the standard, or the criterion, by which 'possibility' is to be judged? A comprehensive answer to this question is proving elusive. The courts, including your Lordships' House, are still cautiously feeling their way forward as experience in the application of section 3 gradually accumulates.

28. One tenable interpretation of the word 'possible' would be that section 3 is confined to requiring courts to resolve ambiguities. Where the words under consideration fairly admit of more than one meaning the Convention-compliant meaning is to prevail. Words should be given the meaning which best accords with the Convention rights.

29. This interpretation of section 3 would give the section a comparatively narrow scope. This is not the view which has prevailed. It is now generally accepted that the application of section 3 does not depend upon the presence of ambiguity in the legislation being interpreted. Even if, construed according to the ordinary principles of interpretation, the meaning of the legislation admits of no doubt, section 3 may

nonetheless require the legislation to be given a different meaning. The decision of your Lordships' House in *R v A (No 2)* [2002] 1 AC 45 is an instance of this. The House read words into section 41 of the Youth Justice and Criminal Evidence Act 1999 so as to make that section compliant with an accused's right to a fair trial under article 6. The House did so even though the statutory language was not ambiguous.

30. From this it follows that the interpretative obligation decreed by section 3 is of an unusual and far-reaching character. Section 3 may require a court to depart from the unambiguous meaning the legislation would otherwise bear. In the ordinary course the interpretation of legislation involves seeking the intention reasonably to be attributed to Parliament in using the language in question. Section 3 may require the court to depart from this legislative intention, that is, depart from the intention of the Parliament which enacted the legislation. The question of difficulty is how far, and in what circumstances, section 3 requires a court to depart from the intention of the enacting Parliament. The answer to this question depends upon the intention reasonably to be attributed to Parliament in enacting section 3.

31. On this the first point to be considered is how far, when enacting section 3, Parliament intended that the actual language of a statute, as distinct from the concept expressed in that language, should be determinative. Since section 3 relates to the 'interpretation' of legislation, it is natural to focus attention initially on the language used in the legislative provision being considered. But once it is accepted that section 3 may require legislation to bear a meaning which departs from the unambiguous meaning the legislation would otherwise bear, it becomes impossible to suppose Parliament intended that the operation of section 3 should depend critically upon the particular form of words adopted by the parliamentary draftsman in the statutory provision under consideration. That would make the application of section 3 something of a semantic lottery. If the draftsman chose to express the concept being enacted in one form of words, section 3 would be available to achieve Convention-compliance. If he chose a different form of words, section 3 would be impotent.

32. From this the conclusion which seems inescapable is that the mere fact the language under consideration is inconsistent with a Convention-compliant meaning does not of itself make a Convention-compliant interpretation under section 3 impossible. Section 3 enables language to be interpreted restrictively or expansively. But section 3 goes further than this. It is also apt to require a court to read in words which change the meaning of the enacted legislation, so as to make it Convention-compliant. In other words, the intention of Parliament in enacting section 3 was that, to an extent bounded only by what is 'possible', a court can modify the meaning, and hence the effect, of primary and secondary legislation.

33. Parliament, however, cannot have intended that in the discharge of this extended interpretative function the courts should adopt a meaning inconsistent with a fundamental feature of legislation. That would be to cross the constitutional boundary section 3 seeks to demarcate and preserve. Parliament has retained the right to enact legislation in terms which are not Convention-compliant. The meaning imported by application of section 3 must be compatible with the underlying thrust of the legislation being construed. Words implied must, in the phrase of my noble and learned friend Lord Rodger of Earlsferry, 'go with the grain of the legislation'. Nor can Parliament have intended that section 3 should require courts to make decisions for which they are not equipped. There may be several ways of making a provision Convention-compliant, and the choice may involve issues calling for legislative deliberation.

34. Both these features were present in *In re S (Minors) (Care Order: Implementation of Care Plan)* [2002] 2 AC 291. There the proposed 'starring system' was inconsistent in an important respect with the scheme of the Children Act 1989, and the proposed system had far-reaching practical ramifications for local authorities. Again, in *R (Anderson) v Secretary of State for the Home Department* [2003] 1 AC 837 section 29 of the Crime (Sentences) Act 1997 could not be read in a Convention-compliant way without giving the section a meaning inconsistent with an important feature expressed clearly in the legislation. In *Bellinger v Bellinger* [2003] 2 AC 467 recognition of Mrs Bellinger as female for the purposes of section 11(c) of the Matrimonial Causes Act 1973 would have had exceedingly wide ramifications, raising issues ill-suited for determination by the courts or court procedures.

35. In some cases difficult problems may arise. No difficulty arises in the present case. Paragraph 2 of Schedule 1 to the Rent Act 1977 is unambiguous. But the social policy underlying the 1988 extension of security of tenure under paragraph 2 to the survivor of couples living together as husband and wife is equally applicable to the survivor of homosexual couples living together in a close and stable relationship. In this circumstance I see no reason to doubt that application of section 3 to paragraph 2 has the effect that paragraph 2 should be read and given effect to as though the survivor of such a homosexual couple were the surviving spouse of the original tenant. Reading paragraph 2 in this way would have the result that cohabiting heterosexual couples and cohabiting heterosexual couples would be treated alike for the purposes of succession as a statutory tenant. This would eliminate the discriminatory effect of paragraph 2 and would do so consistently with the social policy underlying paragraph 2. The precise form of words read in for this purpose is of no significance. It is their substantive effect which matters.

36. For these reasons I agree with the decision of the Court of Appeal. I would dismiss this appeal.

Lord Steyn:

37. In my view the Court of Appeal came to the correct conclusion. I agree with the conclusions and reasons of my noble and learned friends Lord Nicholls of Birkenhead, Lord Rodger of Earlsferry and Baroness Hale of Richmond. In the light of those opinions, I will not comment on the case generally.

38. I confine my remarks to the question whether it is possible under section 3(1) of the Human Rights Act 1998 to read and give effect to paragraph 2(2) of Schedule 1 to the Rent Act 1977 in a way which is compatible with the European Convention on Human Rights. In my view the interpretation adopted by the Court of Appeal under section 3(1) was a classic illustration of the permissible use of this provision. But it became clear during oral argument, and from a subsequent study of the case law and academic discussion on the correct interpretation of section 3(1), that the role of that provision in the remedial scheme of the 1998 Act is not always correctly understood. I would therefore wish to examine the position in a general way.

40. My impression is that two factors are contributing to a misunderstanding of the remedial scheme of the 1998 Act. First, there is the constant refrain that a judicial reading down, or reading in, under section 3 would flout the will of Parliament as expressed in the statute under examination. This question cannot sensibly be considered without giving full weight to the countervailing will of Parliament as expressed in the 1998 Act.

41. The second factor may be an excessive concentration on linguistic features of the particular statute. Nowhere in our legal system is a literalistic approach more inappropriate than when considering whether a breach of a Convention right may be removed by interpretation under section 3. Section 3 requires a broad approach concentrating, amongst other things, in a purposive way on the importance of the fundamental right involved.

42. In enacting the 1998 Act Parliament legislated 'to bring rights home' from the European Court of Human Rights to be determined in the courts of the United Kingdom. That is what the White Paper said: see Rights Brought Home: The Human Rights Bill (1997) (cm 3782), para 2.7. That is what Parliament was told. The mischief to be addressed was the fact that Convention rights as set out in the ECHR, which Britain ratified in 1951, could not be vindicated in our courts. Critical to this purpose was the enactment of effective remedial provisions.

44. It is necessary to state what section 3(1), and in particular the word 'possible', does not mean. First, section 3(1) applies even if there is no ambiguity in the language in the sense of it being capable of bearing two *possible* meanings. The word 'possible' in section 3(1) is used in a different and much stronger sense. Secondly, section 3(1) imposes a stronger and more radical obligation than to adopt a purposive interpretation in the light of the ECHR. Thirdly, the draftsman of the Act had before him the model of the New Zealand Bill of Rights Act which imposes a requirement that the interpretation to be

adopted must be reasonable. Parliament specifically rejected the legislative model of requiring a reasonable interpretation.

45. Instead the draftsman had resort to the analogy of the obligation under the EEC Treaty on national courts, as far as possible, to interpret national legislation in the light of the wording and purpose of directives. In *Marleasing SA v La Comercial Internacional de Alimentación SA* (Case C-106/89) [1990] ECR I-4135, 4159 the European Court of Justice defined this obligation as follows:

> 'It follows that, in applying national law, whether the provisions in questions were adopted before or after the directive, the national court called upon to interpret it is required to do so, as far as possible, in light of the wording and the purpose of the directive in order to achieve the result pursued by the latter and thereby comply with the third paragraph of Article 189 of the Treaty'

Given the undoubted strength of this interpretative obligation under EEC law, this is a significant signpost to the meaning of section 3(1) in the 1998 Act.

46. Parliament had before it the mischief and objective sought to be addressed, viz the need 'to bring rights home'. The linch-pin of the legislative scheme to achieve this purpose was section 3(1). Rights could only be effectively brought home if section 3(1) was the prime remedial measure, and section 4 a measure of last resort. How the system modelled on the EEC interpretative obligation would work was graphically illustrated for Parliament during the progress of the Bill through both Houses. The Lord Chancellor observed that 'in 99% of the cases that will arise, there will be no need for judicial declarations of incompatibility' and the Home Secretary said 'We expect that, in almost all cases, the courts will be able to interpret the legislation compatibly with the Convention': Hansard (HL Debates,) 5 February 1998, col 840 (3rd reading) and Hansard (HC Debates,) 16 February 1998, col 778 (2nd reading). It was envisaged that the duty of the court would be to strive to find (if possible) a meaning which would best accord with Convention rights. This is the remedial scheme which Parliament adopted.

47. Three decisions of the House can be cited to illustrate the strength of the interpretative obligation under section 3(1). The first is *R v A (No. 2)* [2002] 1 AC 45 which concerned the so-called rape shield legislation. The problem was the blanket exclusion of prior sexual history between the complainant and an accused in section 41(1) of the Youth Justice and Criminal Evidence Act 1999, subject to narrow specific categories in the remainder of section 41. In subsequent decisions, and in academic literature, there has been discussion about differences of emphasis in the various opinions in *A*. What has been largely overlooked is the unanimous conclusion of the House. The House unanimously agreed on an interpretation under section 3 which would ensure that section 41 would be compatible with the ECHR. The formulation was by agreement set out in paragraph 46 of my opinion in that case as follows:

> 'The effect of the decision today is that under section 41(3)(c) of the 1999 Act, construed where necessary by applying the interpretive obligation under section 3 of the Human Rights Act 1998, and due regard always being paid to the importance of seeking to protect the complainant from indignity and from humiliating questions, the test of admissibility is whether the evidence (and questioning in relation to it) is nevertheless so relevant to the issue of consent that to exclude it would endanger the fairness of the trial under article 6 of the Convention. If this test is satisfied the evidence should not be excluded.'

This formulation was endorsed by Lord Slynn of Hadley at p 56, para 13 of his opinion in identical wording. The other Law Lords sitting in the case expressly approved the formulation set out in para 46 of my opinion: Lord Hope of Craighead, at pp 87–88, para 110, Lord Clyde, at p 98, para 140; and Lord Hutton, at p 106, para 163. In so ruling the House rejected linguistic arguments in favour of a broader approach. In the subsequent decisions of the House in *In re S (Minors) (Care Order: Implementation of Case Plan)* [2002] 2 AC 291 and *Bellinger v Bellinger* [2003] 2 AC 467, which touched on the remedial structure of the 1998 Act, *the decision* of the House in the case of *A* was not questioned. And in the present case nobody suggested that *A* involved a heterodox exercise of the power under section 3.

48. The second and third decisions of the House are *Pickstone v Freemans plc* [1989] AC 66 and *Litster v Forth Dry Dock & Engineering Co Ltd* [1990] 1 AC 546 which involve the interpretative obligation under EEC law. *Pickstone* concerned section 1(2) of the Equal Pay Act 1970, (as amended by section 8 of the Sex Discrimination Act 1975 and regulation 2 of the Equal Pay (Amendment) Regulations 1983 (SI 1983/1794) which implied into any contract without an equality clause one that modifies any term in a woman's contract which is less favourable than a term of a similar kind in the contract of a man:

'(a) where the woman is employed on like work with a man in the same employment…

(b) where the woman is employed on work rated as equivalent with that of a man in the same employment…

(c) where a woman is employed on work which, not being work in relation to which paragraph (a) or (b) above applies, is, in terms of the demands made on her (for instance under such headings as effort, skill and decision), of equal value to that of a man in the same employment'.

Lord Templeman observed (at pp. 120–121):

'In my opinion there must be implied in paragraph (c) after the word 'applies' the words 'as between the woman and the man with whom she claims equality.' This construction is consistent with Community law. The employers' construction is inconsistent with Community law and creates a permitted form of discrimination without rhyme or reason.'

That was the ratio *decidendi* of the decision. *Litster* concerned regulations intended to implement an EC Directive, the purpose of which was to protect the workers in an undertaking when its ownership was transferred. However, the regulations only protected those who were employed 'immediately before' the transfer. Having enquired into the purpose of the Directive, the House of Lords interpreted the Regulations by reading in additional words to protect workers not only if they were employed 'immediately before' the time of transfer, but also when they would have been so employed if they had not been unfairly dismissed by reason of the transfer: see Lord Keith of Kinkel, at 554. In both cases the House eschewed linguistic arguments in favour of a broad approach. *Picksone* and *Litster* involved national legislation which implemented EC Directives. *Marleasing* extended the scope of the interpretative obligation to unimplemented Directives. *Pickstone* and *Litster* reinforce the approach to section 3(1) which prevailed in the House in the rape shield case.

49. A study of the case law listed in the Appendix to this judgment reveals that there has sometimes been a tendency to approach the interpretative task under section 3(1) in too literal and technical a way. In practice there has been too much emphasis on linguistic features. If the core remedial purpose of section 3(1) is not to be undermined a broader approach is required. That is, of course, not to gainsay the obvious proposition that inherent in the use of the word 'possible' in section 3(1) is the idea that there is a Rubicon which courts may not cross. If it is not possible, within the meaning of section 3, to read or give effect to legislation in a way which is compatible with Convention rights, the only alternative is to exercise, where appropriate, the power to make a declaration of incompatibility. Usually, such cases should not be too difficult to identify. An obvious example is *R (Anderson) v Secretary of State for the Home Department* [2003] 1 AC 837. The House held that the Home Secretary was not competent under article 6 of the ECHR to decide on the tariff to be served by mandatory life sentence prisoners. The House found a section 3(1) interpretation not 'possible' and made a declaration under section 4. Interpretation could not provide a substitute scheme. *Bellinger* is another obvious example. As Lord Rodger of Earlsferry observed '…in relation to the validity of marriage, Parliament regards gender as fixed and immutable': [2003] 2 WLR 1174, 1195, para 83. Section 3(1) of the 1998 Act could not be used.

50. Having had the opportunity to reconsider the matter in some depth, I am not disposed to try to formulate precise rules about where section 3 may not be used. Like the proverbial elephant such a case ought generally to be easily identifiable. What is necessary, however, is to emphasise that interpretation

under section 3(1) is the prime remedial remedy and that resort to section 4 must always be an exceptional course. In practical effect there is a strong rebuttable presumption in favour of an interpretation consistent with Convention rights. Perhaps the opinions delivered in the House today will serve to ensure a balanced approach along such lines.

51. I now return to the circumstances of the case before the House. Applying section 3 the Court of Appeal interpreted 'as his or her wife or husband' in the statute to mean *'as if they were* his wife or husband'. While there has been some controversy about aspects of the reasoning of the Court of Appeal, I would endorse the reasoning of the Court of Appeal on the use of section 3(1) in this case. It was well within the power under this provision.

Appeal dismissed.

Lord Rodger and **Baroness Hale** concurred. **Lord Millett** dissented.

NOTES

1. In this case, the House of Lords considered the approach to the interpretation of legislation to be taken by the courts when applying the requirement in s. 3(1) HRA that '[s]o far as it is possible to do so, primary legislation and subordinate legislation must be read and given effect in a way which is compatible with the Convention rights'. There has been considerable debate on the scope of s. 3 ranging from a broad construction in *R v A*[132] to a narrower interpretation in *Anderson*[133] and *Bellinger*.[134] The above case appears to have settled the issue in favour of a broad construction.

2. As *Ghaidan* shows, a lot may be done in the application of s. 3 to temper legislation to achieve Convention compliance and so avoid the need for a declaration of incompatibility and new legislation. Section 3 takes matters much further than the longstanding rule of statutory interpretation by which any ambiguity in a statute must be resolved consistently with UK treaty obligations. The rule in s. 3 also differs fundamentally from those which generally apply in the interpretation of statutes. In *R v A*[135] Lord Steyn stated that:

Under ordinary methods of interpretation a court may depart from the language of the statute to avoid absurd consequences: section 3 goes much further. Undoubtedly, a court must always look for a contextual and purposive interpretation: section 3 is more radical in its effect…In accordance with the will of Parliament as reflected in section 3 it will sometimes be necessary to adopt an interpretation which linguistically may appear strange. The techniques to be used will not only involve the reading down of express language in a statute but also the implication of provisions. A declaration of incompatibility is a measure of last resort.

Note in connection the application of s. 3 the use by judges of the terms 'reading in' and 'reading down'.[136] 'Reading in' means reading words into a statute that will cause it not to be incompatible with Convention rights. 'Reading down' means reading wording that might lead to incompatibility in a limited way so as to prevent this. However, as Lord Nicholls states above, the interpretation must not be inconsistent with a fundamental feature of legislation.

---

[132] [2002] 1 AC 45.   [133] [2003] 1 AC 837.   [134] [2003] UKHL 21.

[135] [2002] 1 AC 45, at paras 43–45.

[136] See, e.g., Lord Hope in *R v Lambert* [2001] 3 All ER 577 at 604, HL; and Lord Cooke in *R v DDP, ex p Kebilene* [2000] 2 AC 326 at 373, HL. E.g., *Secretary of State for the Home Department v MB* [2006] EWCA Civ 1140, [2006] HRLR 37 where the procedural requirements of s. 3(10) of the Prevention of Terrorism Act 2005 were 'read down' to secure compliance with Art. 6(1).

3. In *Ghaidan*, Lord Millett dissented, suggesting that the use of s. 3 would result in the thrust of the legislation being defeated:

It is obvious that, if paragraph 2(2) of Schedule 1 to the Rent Act 1977 as amended had referred expressly to 'a person of the opposite sex' who was living with the original tenant as his or her husband or wife, it would not be possible to bring the paragraph into conformity with the Convention by resort to section 3. The question is whether the words 'of the opposite sex' are implicit; for if they are, then same result must follow. Reading the paragraph as referring to persons whether of the same or opposite sex would equally contradict the legislative intent in either case. I agree that the operation of section 3 does not depend critically upon the form of words found in the statute; the court is not engaged in a parlour game. But it does depend upon identifying the essential features of the legislative scheme; and these must be gathered in part at least from the words that Parliament has chosen to use. Drawing the line between the express and the implicit would be to engage in precisely that form of semantic lottery to which the majority rightly object. [para. 77]

4. How close to the line between interpretation and legislation does the House of Lords decision in *Ghaidan* come? Does it overstep that line? Is the role of the courts under s. 3 to read into a statutory provision, if necessary, wording that makes it compatible with Convention rights so long as the statute does not contain express and clear wording to the contrary?[137] In Parliament, Lord Irvine suggested that, in view of s. 3, 'in 99 per cent of the cases that will arise, there will be no need for judicial declarations of incompatibility'.[138]

5. The fact that a court is not able to interpret primary legislation as being compatible with Convention rights does not affect its 'validity, continuing operation or enforcement'.[139] Instead, the court must apply it in the case before the court and in subsequent cases, unless and until the competent Minister has taken remedial action under s. 10 HRA.[140] However, subordinate legislation[141] that is incompatible with a Convention right is invalid, etc., unless the 'primary legislation prevents the removal of the incompatibility'.[142] Subject to this exception, incompatible subordinate legislation is invalid whenever it is made and even though the statute authorising it post-dates the HRA.

6. There is an inevitable tension between s. 3 and s. 4 as only the former can guarantee a remedy to the claimant.

- **Brown v Stott** [2001] 2 All ER 97, [2001] 2 WLR 817, Privy Council

The defendant was suspected of stealing a bottle of gin from a superstore in the early hours. When asked by the police, who suspected she had been drinking alcohol, how she had

---

[137] In *Ahmad v ILEA* [1978] 1 All ER 574 Lord Denning read into s. 30 of the Education Act 1944, the words 'if the timetable so permits'. If that were done to achieve compatibility with a Convention right (the reverse was true in that case), would that be in accord with the *Ghaidan* approach to s. 3? For more detail on the approach to s. 3 see H. Fenwick, G. Phillipson and R. Masterman (eds), *Judicial Reasoning under the Human Rights Act* (2007), Chap. 5; J. van Zyl Smit [2007] MLR 294; A. Kavanagh (2006) OJLS 179; A. Kavanagh [2005] EHRLR 259; A. Kavanagh [2004] PL 537; F. Klug [2003] EHRLR 125; G. Marshall [2003] PL 236; D. Nicol [2004] PL 273.

[138] 585 HL Debs, 5 February 1998, col. 840.

[139] HRA, s. 3(2)(b). The normal rule of implied repeal of statutes by later inconsistent statutes does not apply to a pre-HRA statute that is contrary to the HRA.

[140] Per Lord Steyn, in *R v DPP, ex p Kebilene* [2000] 2 AC 326 at 367, HL.

[141] Mainly regulations, statutory orders in council, devolved legislation in Scotland, Northern Ireland and Wales. See s. 21(1) HRA.

[142] HRA, s. 3(2)(c).

reached the superstore, the defendant pointed to a car, which she said was hers. She was charged with theft and taken to the police station. There, under s. 172(2)(a) of the Road Traffic Act 1988, the defendant was required to indicate who had been driving the car when she travelled to the superstore, and admitted that it was her. After a positive breath test, the defendant was charged with driving while her breath alcohol level was above the legal limit. In the Scottish High Court of Judiciary, it was held that the evidence compulsorily obtained from her under s. 172(2)(a) could not be led by the procurator fiscal because s. 172(2)(a) infringed the defendant's Convention right to a fair trial in Art. 6 ECHR, particularly the implied right to freedom from self-incrimination that had been read into Art. 6(1) by the European Court of Human Rights. The procurator fiscal and the Advocate General appealed. The Privy Council first held that the case raised a devolution issue so that the question of the compatibility of s. 172(2)(a) with Convention rights could be raised. It then unanimously upheld an appeal from the decision of the High Court of Justiciary on the ground that, as read in accordance with s. 3 HRA, s. 172(2)(a) was not incompatible with Art. 6 ECHR.

Lord Steyn:

In the first real test of the Human Rights Act 1998 it is opportune to stand back and consider what the basic aims of the Convention are. One finds the explanation in the very words of the preambles of the Convention. There were two principal objectives. The first was to maintain and further realise human rights and fundamental freedoms. The framers of the Convention recognised that it was not only morally right to promote the observance of human rights but that it was also the best way of achieving pluralistic and just societies in which all can peaceably go about their lives. The second aim was to foster effective political democracy. This aim necessarily involves the creation of conditions of stability and order under the rule of law, not for its own sake, but as the best way to ensuring the well being of the inhabitants of the European countries. After all, democratic government has only one raison d'etre, namely to serve the interests of all the people. The inspirers of the European Convention, among whom Winston Churchill played an important role, and the framers of the European Convention, ably assisted by English draftsmen, realised that from time to time the fundamental right of one individual may conflict with the human right of another. Thus the principles of free speech and privacy may collide. They also realised only too well that a single-minded concentration on the pursuit of fundamental rights of individuals to the exclusion of the interests of the wider public might be subversive of the ideal of tolerant European liberal democracies. The fundamental rights of individuals are of supreme importance but those rights are not unlimited: we live in communities of individuals who also have rights. The direct lineage of this ancient idea is clear: the European Convention (1950) is the descendant of the Universal Declaration of Human Rights (1948) which in article 29 expressly recognised the duties of everyone to the community and the limitation on rights in order to secure and protect respect for the rights of others. It is also noteworthy that article 17 of the European Convention prohibits, among others, individuals from abusing their rights to the detriment of others. Thus, notwithstanding the danger of intolerance towards ideas, the Convention system draws a line which does not accord the protection of free speech to those who propagate racial hatred against minorities: article 10; *Jersild v Denmark* (1994) 19 EHRR 1, 26, para 31. This is to be contrasted with the categorical language of the First Amendment to the United States Constitution which provides that 'Congress shall make no law...abridging the freedom of speech.' The European Convention requires that where difficult questions arise a balance must be struck. Subject to a limited number of absolute guarantees, the scheme and structure of the Convention reflects this balanced approach. It differs in material respects from other constitutional systems but as a European nation it represents our Bill of Rights. We must be guided by it. And it is a basic premise of the Convention system that only an entirely neutral, impartial, and independent judiciary can carry out the primary task of securing and enforcing Convention rights. This contextual scene is not only directly relevant to the issues arising on the present appeal but may be a matrix in which many challenges under the Human Rights Act 1998 should be considered....

The present case is concerned with article 6 of the Convention which guarantees to every individual a fair trial in civil and criminal cases....

It is well settled, although not expressed in the Convention, that there is an implied privilege against self-incrimination under article 6. Moreover, section 172(2) undoubtedly makes an inroad on this privilege. On the other hand, it is also clear that the privilege against self-incrimination is not an absolute right. While there is no decision of the European Court of Human Rights directly in point, it is noteworthy that closely related rights have been held not to be absolute. It is significant that the basic right of access to the courts has been held to be not absolute: *Colder v United Kingdom* 1 EHRR 524. The principle that everyone charged with a criminal offence shall be presumed innocent until proved guilty according to law is connected with the privilege against self-incrimination. Yet the former has been held not to be absolute: *Salabiaku v France* 13 EHRR 379. The European Court has also had occasion to emphasise the close link between the right of silence and the privilege against self-incrimination: *Murray v United Kingdom* 22 EHRR 29. In *Murray* the European Court held that the right of silence is not absolute.

In these circumstances it would be strange if a right not expressed in the Convention or any of its Protocols, but implied into article 6 of the Convention, had an absolute character. In my view the right in question is plainly not absolute. From this premise it follows that an interference with the right may be justified if the particular legislative provision was enacted in pursuance of a legitimate aim and if the scope of the legislative provision is necessary and proportionate to the achievement of the aim....

In considering whether an inroad on the privilege against self-discrimination can be justified, it is necessary to concentrate on the particular context. An intense focus on section 172(2) is required. It reads:

> 'Where the driver of a vehicle is alleged to be guilty of an offence to which this section applies—(a) the person keeping the vehicle shall give such information as to the identity of the driver as he may be required to give by or on behalf of a chief officer of police, and (b) any other person shall if required as stated above give any information which it is in his power to give and may lead to identification of the driver.'

The penalty for failing to comply with section 172(2) is a fine of not more than £1,000. In addition an individual may be disqualified from driving and endorsement of the driver's licence is mandatory. It is well established that an oral admission made by a driver under section 172(2) is admissible in evidence: *Foster v Farrell* 1963 JC 46.

The subject of section 172(2) is the driving of vehicles. It is a notorious fact that vehicles are potentially instruments of death and injury. The statistics placed before the Board show a high rate of fatal and other serious accidents involving vehicles in Great Britain. The relevant statistics are as follows:

	1996	1997	1998
Fatal and serious accidents	40,601	39,628	37,770

The effective prosecution of drivers causing serious offences is a matter of public interest. But such prosecutions are often hampered by the difficulty of identifying the drivers of the vehicles at the time of, say, an accident causing loss of life or serious injury or potential danger to others. The tackling of this social problem seems in principle a legitimate aim for a legislature to pursue.

The real question is whether the legislative remedy in fact adopted is necessary and proportionate to the aim sought to be achieved. There were legislative choices to be made. The legislature could have decided to do no more than to exhort the police and prosecuting authorities to redouble their efforts. It may, however, be that such a policy would have been regarded as inadequate. Secondly, the legislature could have introduced a reverse burden of proof clause which placed the burden on the registered owner to prove that he was not the driver of the vehicle at a given time when it is alleged that an offence was committed. Thirdly, and this was the course actually adopted, there was the possibility of requiring information about the identity of the driver to be revealed by the registered owner and others. As between the second and third techniques it may be said that the latter involves the securing of an admission of a constituent element of the offence. On the other hand, such an admission, if wrongly made, is not conclusive. And it must be measured against the alternative of a reverse burden clause which could without further investigation of the identity of the driver lead to a prosecution. In their impact on the citizen the two techniques are not widely different. And it is rightly conceded that a properly drafted reverse burden of proof provision would have been lawful.

It is also important to keep in mind the narrowness of the interference. Section 172(2) is directed at obtaining information in one category, namely the identity of the driver at the time when an offence was allegedly committed. The most important part of section 172(2) is paragraph (a) since the relevant information is usually peculiarly within the knowledge of the owner. But there may be scope for using (b) in a limited category of cases, e g when only the identity of a passenger in the car is known. Section 172(2) does not authorise general questioning by the police to secure a confession of an offence. On the other hand, section 172(2) does, depending on the circumstances, in effect authorise the police officer to invite the owner to make an admission of one element in a driving offence. It would, however, be an abuse of the power under section 172(2) for the police officer to employ improper or overbearing methods of obtaining the information. He may go no further than to ask who the driver was at the given time. If the police officer strays beyond his power under section 172(2) a judge will have ample power at trial to exclude the evidence. It is therefore a relatively narrow interference with the privilege in one area which poses widespread and serious law enforcement problems. . . .

Under the Convention system the primary duty is placed on domestic courts to secure and protect Convention rights. The function of the European Court of Human Rights is essential but supervisory. In that capacity it accords to domestic courts a margin of appreciation, which recognises that national institutions are in principle better placed than an international court to evaluate local needs and conditions. That principle is logically not applicable to domestic courts. On the other hand, national courts may accord to the decisions of national legislatures some deference *where the context justifies* it: see *R v Director of Public Prosecutions, Ex p Kebilene* [2000] 2 AC 326, 380–381 per Lord Hope of Craighead; see also: Singh, Hunt and Demetriou, 'Is there a Role for the "Margin of Appreciation" in National Law after the Human Rights Act?' [1999] EHRLR 15. This point is well explained in *Lester & Pannick, Human Rights Law and Practice* (1999), p 74:

> 'Just as there are circumstances in which an international court will recognise that national institutions are better placed to assess the needs of society, and to make difficult choices between competing considerations, so national courts will accept that there are some circumstances in which the legislature and the executive are better placed to perform those functions.'

In my view this factor is of some relevance in the present case. Here section 172(2) addresses a pressing social problem, namely the difficulty of law enforcement in the face of statistics revealing a high accident rate resulting in death and serious injuries. The legislature was entitled to regard the figures of serious accidents as unacceptably high. It would also have been entitled to take into account that it was necessary to protect other Convention rights, viz the right to life of members of the public exposed to the danger of accidents: see article 2(1). On this aspect the legislature was in as good a position as a court to assess the gravity of the problem and the public interest in addressing it. It really then boils down to the question whether in adopting the procedure enshrined in section 172(2), rather than a reverse burden technique, it took more drastic action than was justified. While this is ultimately a question for the court, it is not unreasonable to regard both techniques as permissible in the field of the driving of vehicles. After all, the subject invites special regulation; objectively the interference is narrowly circumscribed; and it is qualitatively not very different from requiring, for example, a breath specimen from a driver. Moreover, it is less invasive than an essential modern tool of crime detection such as the taking of samples from a suspect for DNA profiling. If the matter was not covered by authority, I would have concluded that section 172(2) is compatible with article 6....

The decision of the European Court in *Saunders v United Kingdom* 23 EHRR 313 gave some support to the view of the High Court of Justiciary. With due respect I have to say that the reasoning in *Saunders* is unsatisfactory and less than clear: see the critique in Andrews, 'Hiding Behind the Veil: Financial Delinquency and the Law' (1997) 22 ELR 369; Eriksen and Thorkildsen, 'Self-Incrimination, The Ban on Self-Incrimination after the Saunders Judgment' (1997) 5 JFC 182; Davies, 'Do polluters have the right not to incriminate themselves?' (1999) 143 SJ 924. The European Court did not rule that the privilege against self-incrimination is absolute. Surprisingly in view of its decision in *Murray* 22 EHRR 29 that the linked right of silence is not absolute it left the point open in respect of the privilege against self-incrimination: 23 EHRR 313, 339–340, para 74. On the other hand, the substance of its reasoning treats both privileges are not absolute. The court observed, at p 337, para 68:

'The court recalls that, although not specifically mentioned in article 6 of the Convention, the right to silence and the right not to incriminate oneself, are generally recognised international standards which lie at the heart of the notion of a fair procedure under article 6. Their rationale lies, inter alia, in the protection of the accused against improper compulsion by the authorities thereby contributing to the avoidance of miscarriages of justice and to the fulfilment of the aims of article 6.'

The court emphasised the rationale of improper compulsion. It does not hold that *anything* said under compulsion of law is inadmissible. Admittedly, the court also observed, at para 68:

'The right not to incriminate oneself, in particular, presupposes that the prosecution in a criminal case seek to prove their case against the accused without resort to evidence obtained through methods of coercion or oppression in defiance of the will of the accused. In this sense the right is closely linked to the presumption of innocence contained in article 6(2) of the Convention.'

Again one finds the link with the non-absolute right of silence. In any event 'methods of coercion or oppression in defiance of the will of the accused' is probably another way of referring to improper compulsion. This is consistent with the following passage, at p 338, para 69:

'In the present case the court is only called upon to decide whether the use made by the prosecution of the statements obtained from the applicant by the inspectors amounted to an unjustifiable infringement of the right. This question must be examined by the court in the light of all the circumstances of the case. In particular, it must be determined whether the applicant has been subject to compulsion to give evidence and whether the use made of the resulting testimony at his trial offended the basic principles of a fair procedure inherent in article 6(1) of which the right not to incriminate oneself is a constituent element.'

The expression 'unjustifiable infringement of the right' implies that some infringements may be justified. In my view the observations in *Saunders* do not support an absolutist view of the privilege against self-incrimination. It may be that the observations in *Saunders* will have to be clarified in a further case by the European Court. As things stand, however, I consider that the High Court of Justiciary put too great weight on these observations. In my view they were never intended to apply to a case such as the present....

That brings me back to the decision of the High Court of Justiciary. It treated the privilege against self-incrimination as virtually absolute. That conclusion fits uneasily into the balanced. Convention system, and cannot be reconciled with article 6 in all its constituent parts and the spectrum of jurisprudence of the European Court on the various facets of article 6.

I would hold that the decision of the High Court of Justiciary on the merits was wrong. The procurator fiscal is entitled to lead the evidence of Miss Brown's admission under section 172(2)....

I am in complete agreement with Lord Hope of Craighead that a devolution issue has been raised and I would respectfully endorse his reasons.

For these reasons, as well as the reasons given by Lord Bingham of Cornhill, I would allow the appeal and quash the declaration made by the High Court.

Appeal allowed.

Lord Bingham, Lord Hope, Lord Clyde and **the Right Honourable Ian Kirkwood** also delivered judgments allowing the appeal.[143]

NOTES

1. *Deference to Parliament.* Lord Steyn's judgment in *Brown v Stott* articulates the 'deference to Parliament' principle that the courts apply when deciding whether Westminster legislation is incompatible with Convention rights. Lord Bingham spoke in *Brown v Stott*[144] in similar terms:

While a national court does not accord the margin of appreciation recognised by the European Court as a supra-national court, it will give weight to the decisions of a representative legislature and a democratic government within the discretionary area of judgment accorded to these bodies: see Lester and Pannick, *Human Rights Law and Practice* (1999), pp. 73–76.

Earlier, Lord Hope had taken the same position in *R v DPP, ex p Kebilene:*[145]

The doctrine of the 'margin of appreciation' is a familiar part of the jurisprudence of the European Court of Human Rights. The European Court has acknowledged that, by reason of their direct and continuous contact with the vital forces of their countries, the national authorities are in principle better placed to evaluate local needs and conditions than an international court: *Buckley v United Kingdom* (1996) 23 EHRR 101, 129, paras. 74–75. Although this means that, as the European Court explained in *Handyside v United Kingdom* (1976) 1 EHRR 737, 753, para. 48, 'the machinery of protection established by the Convention is subsidiary to the national systems safeguarding human rights,' it goes hand in hand with a European supervision. The extent of this supervision will vary according to such factors as the nature of the Convention right in issue, the importance of that right for the individual and the nature of the activities involved in the case.

This doctrine is an integral part of the supervisory jurisdiction which is exercised over state conduct by the international court. By conceding a margin of appreciation to each national system, the court has recognised that the Convention, as a living system, does not need to be applied uniformly by all states but may vary in its application according to local needs and conditions. This technique is not available to the national courts when they are considering Convention issues arising within their own countries. But in the hands of the national courts also the Convention should be seen as an expression of fundamental principles rather than as a set of mere rules. The questions which the courts will have to decide in the application of these principles will involve questions of balance between competing interests and issues of proportionality.

---

[143] The decision has subsequently been confirmed by the Strasbourg Court in *O'Halloran v UK* (2007) App. No. 15809/02; *Francis v United Kingdom* (2007) App. No. 25624/02.

[144] [2001] 2 WLR 817 at 835, HL.   [145] [2000] 2 AC 326 at 380, HL.

In this area difficult choices may have to be made by the executive or the legislature between the rights of the individual and the needs of society. In some circumstances it will be appropriate for the courts to recognise that there is an area of judgment within which the judiciary will defer, on democratic grounds, to the considered opinion of the elected body or person whose act or decision is said to be incompatible with the Convention. This point is well made at p. 74, para. 3.21 of *Human Rights Law and Practice* (1999), of which Lord Lester of Herne Hill and Mr. Pannick are the general editors, where the area in which these choices may arise is conveniently and appropriately described as the 'discretionary area of judgment'. It will be easier for such an area of judgment to be recognised where the Convention itself requires a balance to be struck, much less so where the right is stated in terms which are unqualified. It will be easier for it to be recognised where the issues involve questions of social or economic policy, much less so where the rights are of high constitutional importance or are of a kind where the courts are especially well placed to assess the need for protection. But even where the right is stated in terms which are unqualified the courts will need to bear in mind the jurisprudence of the European Court which recognises that due account should be taken of the special nature of terrorist crime and the threat which it poses to a democratic society: *Murray v United Kingdom* (1994) 19 EHRR 193, 222, para. 47.

More recently, in *A v Secretary of State for the Home Department*[146] Lord Nicholls discussed deference in the context of terrorism legislation:

80 …In enacting legislation and reaching decisions Parliament and ministers must give due weight to fundamental rights and freedoms. For their part, when carrying out their assigned task the courts will accord to Parliament and ministers, as the primary decision-makers, an appropriate degree of latitude. The latitude will vary according to the subject matter under consideration, the importance of the human right in question, and the extent of the encroachment upon that right. The courts will intervene only when it is apparent that, in balancing the various considerations involved, the primary decision-maker must have given insufficient weight to the human rights factor.

81. In the present case I see no escape from the conclusion that Parliament must be regarded as having attached insufficient weight to the human rights of non-nationals. The subject matter of the legislation is the needs of national security. This subject matter dictates that, in the ordinary course, substantial latitude should be accorded to the legislature. But the human right in question, the right to individual liberty, is one of the most fundamental of human rights.

Therefore, even in areas in which the judiciary sees a clear need for deference this does not extend to the decision in its entirety.

2. The 'margin of appreciation' doctrine to which their Lordships refer is well established in the jurisprudence of the European Court of Human Rights. It was formulated most famously in *Handyside v United Kingdom* in the context of limitations on freedom of expression (Art. 10 ECHR):[147]

By reason of their direct and continuous contact with the vital forces of their countries, state authorities are in principle in a better position than the international judge to give an opinion on the exact content of those requirements [of morals] as well as on the 'necessity' of a 'restriction' or 'penalty' intended to meet them…

Nevertheless, Article 10(2) does not give the contracting states an unlimited power of appreciation. The Court, which, with the Commission, is responsible for ensuring the observance of those states' engagements, is empowered to give the final ruling on whether a 'restriction' or 'penalty' is reconcilable with freedom of expression as protected by Article 10. The domestic margin of appreciation thus goes hand in hand with a European supervision.

---

[146] [2004] UKHL 56.   [147] [1976] 1 EHRR 737.

By means of the doctrine, the European Court of Human Rights allows states, whether acting through their legislature, executive or judiciary, a certain degree of latitude in borderline cases in deciding whether a limitation upon a Convention right is justifiable by the public interest. It does so because of the local knowledge of state institutions. There is, as it were, a presumption in favour of their assessment of the facts and of what is called for in the light of them. It is also used as a basis for not pressing a state on a matter of social policy where European values are in flux.[148] As Lord Steyn states, the margin of appreciation doctrine, or principle, is not 'logically applicable' in the different context of national courts assessing the compatibility of national legislation with Convention rights. However, the 'deference to Parliament' principle, while having a different justification, ie recognition of the special position of a democratically elected legislature 'where the context justifies it',[149] may lead to the same result on the facts of a particular case.

3. In *R (on the application of International Transport Roth GmbH) v Secretary of State for the Home Department*[150] Laws LJ formulated four principles stating how UK courts should approach the issue of deference. These are that: (1) 'greater deference is to be paid to an Act of Parliament than a decision of the Executive or subordinate measure'; (2) there is more scope for deference 'where the Convention itself requires a balance to be struck much less where the right is stated in terms which are unqualified'; (3) 'greater deference will be due to the democratic powers where the subject-matter in hand is peculiarly within their constitutional responsibility and less when it lies more particularly within the constitutional responsibility of the courts'; and (4) 'greater or lesser deference will be due according to whether the subject-matter lies more readily within the actual or potential expertise of the democratic powers or the courts'.

4. In *Huang v Secretary of State for the Home Department*[151] the House of Lords recognised the difficulty in the term 'deference' and confirmed that it is not a doctrine that can prevent a court from holding that a particular decision is a disproportionate interference with a Convention right.[152]

5. When reviewing decisions where the decision-maker is required to comply with the Convention as a matter of law the approach to be adopted was summarised by Lord Phillips MR in *R (Mahmood) v Secretary of State for the Home Department*.[153] First, even where human rights are at stake, the role of the court was supervisory; it did not substitute its own decision for that of the executive and there would often be an area of discretion permitted to the executive before a response could be demonstrated to infringe the Convention (see above). Secondly, in conducting a review of a decision affecting human rights, the court should subject it to 'the most anxious scrutiny'. Thirdly, instead of merely applying the tests of *Wednesbury* unreasonableness, the court should 'ask the question, applying an objective test, whether the decision-maker could reasonably have concluded that the interference was necessary to achieve one or more of the legitimate aims recognised by the Convention'. The third of these propositions was subject to modification by the House of Lords in the following case.

---

148 E.g. the legal status of transsexuals: see *Sheffield and Horsham v UK* (1998) 27 EHRR 163.
149 Per Lord Steyn, extract from *Brown v Stott* above.   150 [2003] QB 728, paras [83]–[87].
151 [2007] UKHL 11.
152 See also, Lord Steyn [2005] PL 346; R. Clayton [2004] PL 33; J. Rivers [2006] CLJ 174; F. Klug [2003] EHRLR 125; T. Hickman [2005] PL 306; C. O'Cinneide (2004) 57 CLP; J. Jowell [2004] PL 592; T.R.S. Allen [2006] CLJ 671.
153 [2001] 1 WLR 840 at paras [37]–[40].

- **R (on the application of Daly) v Secretary of State for the Home Department**
  [2001] UKHL 26, [2001] 2 WLR 1622, House of Lords

Home Office policy on the searching of prisoners' cells in closed prisons was set out in a 1995 Security Manual. This provided that prisoners were not to be present when searches took place. This restriction was justified on the grounds that prison officers might be intimidated by prisoners who were present and that it was necessary to keep searching methods secret. Under the policy, officers could, *inter alia,* examine prisoners' correspondence with their legal advisers to check that it was bona fide legal correspondence and that it did not conceal anything else. However, they could not read it unless there was reasonable cause to suspect that its contents endangered prison security, or the safety of others, or was otherwise of a criminal nature.

In this case, the applicant applied for judicial review of the policy in so far as it concerned legal correspondence that he kept in his cell. The House of Lords upheld his appeal against a Court of Appeal decision dismissing his application for judicial review. It did so on the basis that the policy infringed the common law right of a prisoner to legal professional privilege in his communications with his legal adviser. This was because the possibility that a prison officer might, improperly, read the correspondence and this would have a chilling effect on freedom of communication. Although the general wording of the Prison Rules might justify some limitation on the common law right to professional legal privilege, they could not justify a policy that extended to all prisoners, whether or not there was reason to believe that they might be abusing their freedom of correspondence.

The House of Lords also held that the executive decision underlying the policy was an interference with a Convention right, viz. the right to respect for correspondence in Art. 8 ECHR. The following extract from Lord Steyn's judgment addresses the ECHR issue only. In particular, it indicates the judicial review criterion to be followed by the courts when considering whether an executive decision complies with the ECHR. The other members of the House of Lords concurred in his judgment on this point. The extracts from Lord Bingham's and Lord Cooke's judgment consider the overlap between the position at common law and under the HRA.

Lord Bingham:

23. I have reached the conclusions so far expressed on an orthodox application of common law principles derived from the authorities and an orthodox domestic approach to judicial review. But the same result is achieved by reliance on the European Convention. Article 8(1) gives Mr Daly a right to respect for his correspondence. While interference with that right by a public authority may be permitted if in accordance with the law and necessary in a democratic society in the interests of national security, public safety, the prevention of disorder or crime or for protection of the rights and freedoms of others, the policy interferes with Mr Daly's exercise of his right under article 8(1) to an extent much greater than necessity requires. In this instance, therefore, the common law and the Convention yield the same result. But this need not always be so. In *Smith and Grady v United Kingdom* (1999) 29 EHRR 493, the European Court held that the orthodox domestic approach of the English courts had not given the applicants an effective remedy for the breach of their rights under article 8 of the Convention because the threshold of review had been set too high. Now, following the incorporation of the Convention by the Human Rights Act 1998 and the bringing of that Act fully into force, domestic courts must themselves form a judgment whether a Convention right has been breached (conducting such inquiry as is necessary to form that judgment) and, so far as permissible under the Act, grant an effective remedy. On this aspect of the case, I agree with and adopt the observations of my noble and learned friend Lord Steyn which I have had the opportunity of reading in draft.

Lord Steyn:

24. My Lords, I am in complete agreement with the reasons given by Lord Bingham of Cornhill in his speech. For the reasons he gives I would also allow the appeal. Except on one narrow but important point I have nothing to add.

25. There was written and oral argument on the question whether certain observations of Lord Phillips of Worth Matravers MR in *R (Mahmood) v Secretary of State for the Home Department* [2001] 1 WLR 840 were correct. The context was an immigration case involving a decision of the Secretary of State made before the Human Rights Act 1998 came into effect. The Master of the Rolls nevertheless approached the case as if the Act had been in force when the Secretary of State reached his decision. He explained the new approach to be adopted. The Master of the Rolls concluded, at p 857, para 40:

> 'When anxiously scrutinising an executive decision that interferes with human rights, the court will ask the question, applying an objective test, whether the decision-maker could reasonably have concluded that the interference was necessary to achieve one or more of the legitimate aims recognised by the Convention. When considering the test of necessity in the relevant context, the court must take into account the European jurisprudence in accordance with section 2 of the 1998 Act.'

These observations have been followed by the Court of Appeal in *R (Isiko) v Secretary of State for the Home Department* The Times, 20 February 2001; Court of Appeal (Civil Division) Transcript No 2272 of 2000 and by Thomas J in *R (Samaroo) v Secretary of State for the Home Department* (unreported) 20 December 2000.

26. The explanation of the Master of the Rolls in the first sentence of the cited passage requires clarification. It is couched in language reminiscent of the traditional *Wednesbury* ground of review (*Associated Provincial Picture Houses Ltd v Wednesbury Corpn* [1948] 1 KB 223), and in particular the adaptation of that test in terms of heightened scrutiny in cases involving fundamental rights as formulated in *R v Ministry of Defence, Ex p Smith* [1996] QB 517, 554E–G per Sir Thomas Bingham MR. There is a material difference between the *Wednesbury* and *Smith* grounds of review and the approach of proportionality applicable in respect of review where Convention rights are at stake.

27. The contours of the principle of proportionality are familiar. In *de Freitas v Permanent Secretary of Ministry of Agriculture, Fisheries, Lands and Housing* [1999] 1 AC 69 the Privy Council adopted a three-stage test. Lord Clyde observed, at p 80, that in determining whether a limitation (by an act, rule or decision) is arbitrary or excessive the court should ask itself:

> 'whether: (i) the legislative objective is sufficiently important to justify limiting a fundamental right; (ii) the measures designed to meet the legislative objective are rationally connected to it; and (iii) the means used to impair the right or freedom are no more than is necessary to accomplish the objective.'

Clearly, these criteria are more precise and more sophisticated than the traditional grounds of review. What is the difference for the disposal of concrete cases? Academic public lawyers have in remarkably similar terms elucidated the difference between the traditional grounds of review and the proportionality approach: see Professor Jeffrey Jowell QC, 'Beyond the Rule of Law: Towards Constitutional Judicial Review' [2000] PL 671; *Craig, Administrative Law,* 4th ed (1999), pp 561–563; Professor David Feldman, 'Proportionality and the Human Rights Act 1998', essay in *The Principle of Proportionality in the Laws of Europe* edited by Evelyn Ellis (1999), pp 117, 127 et seq. The starting point is that there is an overlap between the traditional grounds of review and the approach of proportionality. Most cases would be decided in the same way whichever approach is adopted. But the intensity of review is somewhat greater under the proportionality approach. Making due allowance for important structural differences between various convention rights, which I do not propose to discuss, a few generalisations are perhaps permissible. I would mention three concrete differences without suggesting that my statement is exhaustive. First, the doctrine of proportionality may require the reviewing court to assess the balance which the decision maker has struck, not merely whether it is within the range of rational or reasonable decisions. Secondly, the proportionality test may go further than the traditional grounds of review inasmuch as it may require attention to be directed to the relative weight accorded to interests and considerations. Thirdly, even the heightened scrutiny test developed in *R v Ministry of Defence, ex p Smith* [1996] QB 517, 554 is not necessarily appropriate to the protection of human rights. It will be recalled that in Smith the Court of Appeal reluctantly felt compelled to reject a limitation on homosexuals in the army. The challenge based on article 8 of the Convention for the Protection of Human Rights and Fundamental Freedoms (the right to respect for private and family life) foundered on the threshold required even by the anxious scrutiny test. The European Court of Human Rights came to the opposite conclusion: *Smith and Grady v United Kingdom* (1999) 29 EHRR 493. The court concluded, at p 543, para 138:

> 'the threshold at which the High Court and the Court of Appeal could find the Ministry of Defence policy irrational was placed so high that it effectively excluded any consideration by the domestic courts of the question of whether the interference with the applicants' rights answered a pressing social need or was proportionate to the national security and public order aims pursued, principles which lie at the heart of the court's analysis of complaints under article 8 of the Convention.'

In other words, the intensity of the review, in similar cases, is guaranteed by the twin requirements that the limitation of the right was necessary in a democratic society, in the sense of meeting a pressing social need, and the question whether the interference was really proportionate to the legitimate aim being pursued.

28. The differences in approach between the traditional grounds of review and the proportionality approach may therefore sometimes yield different results. It is therefore important that cases involving Convention rights must be analysed in the correct way. This does not mean that there has been a shift to merits review. On the contrary, as Professor Jowell [2000] PL 671, 681 has pointed out the respective roles of judges and administrators are fundamentally distinct and will remain so. To this extent the general tenor of the observations in *Mahmood* [2001] 1 WLR 840 are correct. And Laws LJ rightly emphasised in *Mahmood,* at p 847, para 18, 'that the intensity of review in a public law case will depend on the subject matter in hand'. That is so even in cases involving Convention rights. In law context is everything.

Lord Cooke of Thorndon:

29. My Lords, having had the advantage of reading in draft the speeches of my noble and learned friends, Lord Bingham of Cornhill and Lord Steyn, I am in full agreement with them. I add some brief observations on two matters, less to supplement what they have said than to underline its importance.

30. First, while this case has arisen in a jurisdiction where the European Convention for the Protection of Human Rights and Fundamental Freedoms applies, and while the case is one in which the Convention and the common law produce the same result, it is of great importance, in my opinion, that the common law by itself is being recognised as a sufficient source of the fundamental right to confidential communication with a legal adviser for the purpose of obtaining legal advice. Thus the decision may prove to be in point in common law jurisdictions not affected by the Convention. Rights similar to those in the Convention are of course to be found in constitutional documents and other formal affirmations of rights elsewhere. The truth is, I think, that some rights are inherent and fundamental to democratic civilised society. Conventions, constitutions, bills of rights and the like respond by recognising rather than creating them.

31. To essay any list of these fundamental, perhaps ultimately universal, rights is far beyond anything required for the purpose of deciding the present case. It is enough to take the three identified by Lord Bingham: in his words, access to a court; access to legal advice; and the right to communicate confidentially with a legal adviser under the seal of legal professional privilege. As he says authoritatively from the

woolsack, such rights may be curtailed only by clear and express words, and then only to the extent rea-sonably necessary to meet the ends which justify the curtailment. The point that I am emphasising is that the common law goes so deep.

32. The other matter concerns degrees of judicial review. Lord Steyn illuminates the distinctions between 'traditional' (that is to say in terms of English case law, *Wednesbury*) standards of judicial review and higher standards under the European Convention or the common law of human rights. As he indi-cates, often the results are the same. But the view that the standards are substantially the same appears to have received its quietus in *Smith and Grady v United Kingdom* (1999) 29 EHRR 493 and *Lustig-Prean and Beckett v United Kingdom* (1999) 29 EHRR 548. And I think that the day will come when it will be more widely recognised that *Associated Provincial Picture Houses Ltd v Wednesbury Corpn* [1948] 1 KB 223 was an unfortunately retrogressive decision in English administrative law, in so far as it suggested that there are degrees of unreasonableness and that only a very extreme degree can bring an administrative decision within the legitimate scope of judicial invalidation. The depth of judicial review and the defer-ence due to administrative discretion vary with the subject matter. It may well be, however, that the law can never be satisfied in any administrative field merely by a finding that the decision under review is not capricious or absurd.

33. I, too, would therefore allow the present appeal.

Appeal allowed.

Lord Hutton and **Lord Scott** concurred.

NOTES

1. As Lord Steyn indicates in his judgment in the *Daly* case, in a passage that was accepted by the other four judges, the test to be used when deciding for the purposes of the HRA whether executive decisions are compatible with Convention rights is whether they are a proportionate response to a pressing social need (para. 27). This test is one that has been developed by the European Court of Human Rights when deciding whether a limitation on a Convention right is acceptable under Arts 8(2), 9(2) and 10(2) ECHR, and one that it has required national courts to use when deciding whether a limitation on a Convention right is a breach of the ECHR. If they do not, they are not providing an effective remedy for the purposes of Art. 13 ECHR. As Lord Steyn states, the Strasbourg Court has made it clear in a number of British cases that the much more relaxed *Wednesbury* criterion for judicial review (see next note) is not rigorous enough for this purpose. Moreover, the stricter ver-sion of it in the *Smith* case was not good enough when that case went to Strasbourg as *Smith and Grady v United Kingdom.*[154] It was in this context that the proportionality test was introduced in the *Daly* case. Note that no 'margin of appreciation' language is used by Lord Steyn, and it is clear that no such margin applies. At the same time, as Lord Steyn indicates, the proportionality test does not mean substituting a judge's decision on the merits for one by a member of the executive. The court's power is still one of review, not of decision, and involves only deciding whether what has been done is one of possibly a number of propor-tionate responses.

---

[154] (1999) 29 EHRR 493. In *Smith*, the Court of Appeal had reluctantly held that it could not overturn the executive prohibition on homosexuals in the armed forces. At Strasbourg, the Court found a breach of Art. 8 ECHR: on the facts, even allowing for a margin of appreciation, the action, taken against the particular appli-cants had been disproportionate. Note that the 'heightened scrutiny' test did provide a remedy in *R v Lord Saville of Newdigate, ex p A* [1999] 4 All ER 860, CA (decision of the Bloody Sunday Tribunal of Inquiry not to allow soldiers to give evidence anonymously quashed as unreasonable).

2. The *Wednesbury* test to which Lords Steyn and Cooke refer is one of 'unreasonableness', or, in Lord Diplock's term, 'irrationality'. It was expounded by Lord Diplock in the following classic passage:[155]

By 'irrationality' I mean what can by now be succinctly referred to as '*Wednesbury* unreasonableness' (*Associated Provincial Picture Houses Ltd. v. Wednesbury Corporation* [1948] 1 KB 223). It applies to a decision which is so outrageous in its defiance of logic or of accepted moral standards that no sensible person who had applied his mind to the question to be decided could have arrived at it.

3. The *Daly* case is an example of the role of the courts in ensuring that acts of the executive are not incompatible with Convention rights. In that case, it would not have been difficult for Home Office policy on cell searching to have conformed with Convention rights within the limits of the enabling primary legislation, i.e. the Prison Act 1952. Generally, it will be very unusual for the powers given to the executive by primary legislation to be so tightly drawn that a Minister or other executive member will have no choice but to act incompatibly with Convention rights, particularly in view of the rule of interpretation in s. 3 HRA.[156] As a result, executive action incompatible with Convention rights will almost always be invalid, rather than lead to a declaration of incompatibility.

In relation to the declaration of incompatibility the reader should cross reference to the case of *A v Secretary of State for the Home Department* reported fully below in Chapter 6.

4. A declaration of incompatibility may only be made at the level of court indicated in s. 4(5), viz. in England and Wales, the High Court and above. A magistrates' court, Crown Court, county court or tribunal may not make such a declaration; instead, the point must be taken on appeal.

5. As a declaration of incompatibility, like the initial judicial determination of incompatibility, does not affect the legal validity, operation or enforcement of the legislative provision concerned,[157] the curious result is that a litigant who successfully raises an issue of incompatibility may well not benefit.[158] For example, a person who successfully claimed that he was detained under legislation that was incompatible with the Convention right to freedom of the person in Art. 5 ECHR would none the less have no right to release; an order for his detention could be renewed under the incompatible law despite a declaration of incompatibility concerning it.[159] In such a case, it is much better for an alleged victim of a violation of a Convention right if the court, applying s. 3 HRA, manages to stretch the meaning of a statute in the victim's favour, rather than find an incompatibility. However, there is an important exception to the rule that a finding of incompatibility cannot work to the advantage of the individual victim in the instant case. This concerns criminal convictions where the defendant has been denied a fair trial contrary to the Convention right in Art. 6 ECHR. In such cases, the conviction would almost certainly be set aside as 'unsafe', as provided in

---

155 *Council of Civil Service Unions v Minister for the Civil Service* [1985] AC 374 at 408, HL.

156 Cf. K. Ewing (1999) 62 MLR 79 at 87.　　157 HRA, s. 4(6).

158 Damages or other relief would not be available under s. 3 because the act of the public authority would, if a case where a declaration of incompatibility is available, not be unlawful for the purposes of s. 6(1): s. 6(2) HRA.

159 Per Dame Elizabeth Butler-Sloss in *Re K (a child)* [2001] 2 WLR 1141 at 1148, CA (legislation authorising the detention of children in secure units; in fact held not contrary to Art. 5 ECHR). Moreover, the detainee would not have the Art. 5(5) ECHR right to compensation: ibid.

s. 2 of the Criminal Appeal Act 1968.[160] In other, non-criminal cases, the only possibility is that any remedial action taken by the government following the declaration of incompatibility is given retroactive application, which the HRA allows.[161] Otherwise, in non-criminal cases the remedy for the litigant, as it was before the HRA was enacted, is to take the case on the long road to Strasbourg, armed with a declaration of incompatibility, which will be a powerful weapon before the European Court. Although these considerations suggest that in some cases there may be insufficient incentive under the HRA for an individual[162] to raise a question of incompatibility, note that a 'compatibility' argument may be added to other arguments in criminal, civil or judicial review proceedings brought on some other legal basis without much trouble. A litigant who presents such an argument may be rewarded with a s. 3 reading of a statute that makes it compatible with Convention rights from which he or she can profit in the instant case.[163]

The device of the 'declaration of incompatibility' is ingenious and not found in any other legal system. It was prompted by a wish to respect the principle of parliamentary sovereignty.[164] Lord Irvine LC stated in Parliament:[165]

The design of the Bill is to give the courts as much space as possible to protect human rights, short of a power to set aside or ignore Acts of Parliament. In the very rare cases where the higher courts will find it impossible to read and give effect to any statute in a way which is compatible with convention rights, they will be able to make a declaration of incompatibility. Then it is for Parliament to decide whether there should be remedial legislation. Parliament may, not must, and generally will, legislate. If a Minister's prior assessment of compatibility (under Clause 19) is subsequently found by declaration of incompatibility by the courts to have been mistaken, it is hard to see how a Minister could withhold remedial action. There is a fast-track route for Ministers to take remedial action by order. But the remedial action will not retrospectively make unlawful an act which was a lawful act—lawful since sanctioned by statute. This is the logic of the design of the Bill. It maximises the protection of human rights without trespassing on parliamentary sovereignty.

The power given to the UK courts by ss. 3 and 4 HRA falls far short of the power of judicial review of legislation of certain other national courts such as the US Supreme Court.[166] For example, in the famous case of *Roe v Wade*,[167] state criminal abortion statutes that interfered with a woman's constitutional right to privacy were struck down by the US Supreme Court, so that they did not apply to the petitioners' cases and had no further legal effect. Does the absence of such a power on the part of UK courts mean that the HRA is not a 'bill of rights'?

---

[160] *R v Togher* [2001] 3 All ER 463, CA. See N. Taylor and D. Ormerod [2004] Crim LR 266; I. Dennis (2003) CLP 211.

[161] See s. 10 and Sch. 2, para. 1(1)(b) HRA. The remedial order may also make 'different provision for different cases': para. 1(1)(d).

[162] A court, which must apply Convention rights, may raise a compatibility issue on its own initiative.

[163] See *R v A* [2001] UKHL 25, where evidence that might contribute to an acquittal was admissible.

[164] Whether the motivation for doing so was a genuine respect for that principle or the need to ease the passage of the HRA through a Parliament that might not be sympathetic to a surrender of its powers, or a mixture of the two, is not clear. On parliamentary sovereignty and the HRA, see N. Bamforth [1998] PL 572; M. Elliott (1999) 115 LQR 119; K. Ewing (1999) 62 MLR 79 at 91; S. Freeman (1998) 114 LQR 538.

[165] 582 HL Debs, 3 November 1997, cols 1228–1229.

[166] Remarkably, the Supreme Court's power is an implied one, read into the US constitution by the Supreme Court itself: *Marbury v Madison* 5 US 1 (1 Cranch) 137 (1803).

[167] 410 US 113 (1973).

Nonetheless, although the courts are not be empowered to strike down primary legislation, might not the combined effect of ss. 3, 4 and 10 HRA result over time in a considerable erosion in practice of the sovereignty of Parliament and an important constitutional shift in the balance of power between Parliament and the courts?[168]

3. THE FUTURE METHOD OF PROTECTING RIGHTS: A DOMESTIC BILL OF RIGHTS?

The HRA will always stir debate about whether it ought to be applied cautiously or otherwise.[169] Undoubtedly the HRA has been dogged by misinterpretation and myth as reflected in several reports. The Joint Committee on Human Rights reported:

3. The Human Rights Act reached the statute book ten years ago, with the support of all the main political parties. Today it is under threat. It is frequently and inaccurately derided in the tabloid press as a charter for terrorists, criminals and illegal immigrants. The Leader of the Opposition has even called on a number of occasions for the Act to be repealed. Calls from a high level for the Human Rights Act to be repealed or substantially modified first gained momentum in the wake of the infamous Anthony Rice case, in which the Government followed the media in asserting that the Human Rights Act had been responsible for the tragic death of Naomi Bryant because it had required her killer to be released. We inquired carefully into the matter to ascertain if this was true and established that there was no evidence that Naomi Bryant had been killed as a result of officials misinterpreting the Human Rights Act. Despite our clear finding, however, both the Government and the media have continued to repeat the unfounded assertion that the Human Rights Act caused the death of an innocent woman. Similarly, before that, the Human Rights Act had not been responsible for the provision of a takeaway meal to a prisoner making a rooftop protest or the provision of pornography to a serial killer in prison (an application which, in any case, failed): unfortunately the catalogue of mythology continues to grow.[170]

The current Government has accepted that there is no case for repealing the Act and is committed to developing human rights legislation. In 2007 a Green Paper[171] was published providing for a bill of rights and responsibilities.

A Bill of Rights and Duties could provide explicit recognition that human rights come with responsibilities and must be exercised in a way that respects the human rights of others. It would build on the basic principles of the Human Rights Act, but make explicit the way in which a democratic society's rights have to be balanced by obligations...However, a framework of civic responsibilities—were it to be given legislative force—would need to avoid encroaching upon personal freedoms and civil liberties which have been hard won over centuries of our history.[172]

---

[168] Cf. the consequences of the European Communities Act 1972, which also, technically, can be explained consistently with classical parliamentary sovereignty.

[169] Joint Committee on Human Rights 32nd Report, Session 2005–06, *The Human Rights Act: the DCA and Home Office Reviews*, HL 278, HC 1716; Government Responses to the 32nd Report, Cm 7011, 2007. See also, C. Gearty, *Can Human Rights Survive?* (2006); K. Ewing [2004] PL 829; S. Harris-Short (2005) 17 CFLQ 329.

[170] Joint Committee, Sixth Report, op. cit., at para. 3; see also, Department for Constitutional Affairs, *Review of the Implementation of the Human Rights Act* (2006), p. 29.

[171] The Governance of Britain Green Paper, Research Paper 07/72 (2007).

[172] Ministry of Justice, *The Governance of Britain* (Cm 7170, 2007), paras 209–210.

Both the Conservative and Liberal Democrat parties are also committed to developing a domestic Bill of Rights.[173] In 2008 the JCHR determined that there was a case for a Bill of Rights and Freedoms[174] which would encompass a wider range of rights than under the HRA.

We recommend for inclusion, amongst others, the right to trial by jury, the right to administrative justice and international human rights as yet not incorporated into UK law. We believe that there is a strong case for a Bill of Rights and Freedoms having detailed rights for children, and we recommend that the public should be consulted about including specific rights for other vulnerable groups. In addition, we argue that there is a strong case for including the right to a healthy and sustainable environment in a Bill of Rights and Freedoms. One of the biggest controversies in the debate on the Bill of Rights is whether it should include social and economic rights. We believe that there is strong public support for including rights to health, housing and education.[175]

The Labour Government's motivation for a Bill of Rights includes:[176]

i) To provide a means of balancing rights with responsibilities;

ii) To provide a framework for our shared national values as part of the Prime Minister's 'Britishness' agenda;

iii) To educate the public, by providing greater clarity for people about their rights and responsibilities;

iv) To provide greater ownership of the protected rights than is the case with the HRA;

v) To include some recognition of the importance of social and economic rights such as health and education; and

vi) To protect the weak and vulnerable against the strong and powerful.

In addition, the JCHR found other arguments in favour of a Bill of Rights to include:[177]

• would provide ownership and promote citizenship;

• would 'help form a common bond across our increasingly mobile and diverse nation because it can help emphasise our togetherness and jointly shared political values';

• would 'reinvigorate our democracy' and 'ingrain fundamental principles that otherwise might remain implied or implicit';

• would 'renew […] and strengthen […] democracy in 21st century Britain, and empower […] the individuals and communities in its embrace';

• would be a 'defence against incursions by transnational jurisdictions' and strengthen the position of the UK before international courts;

• would protect people from state power and commercial bodies and strengthen the means of remedying individual grievances against such bodies;

• would have a 'symbolic' or 'iconic' role

• would set out 'the long-term values and commitments of society at large, around which it agrees to be ordered for the foreseeable future';

---

[173] See, e.g., speech by David Cameron to the Centre for Policy Studies, 'Balancing freedom and security—A modern British Bill of Rights', 26 June 2006; Liberal Democrat Policy Paper 83, *For the People, by the People*, August 2007.

[174] Joint Committee on Human Rights, *A Bill of Rights for the UK?*, 29th Report of Session 2007–8 HC 150/ HL 165.

[175] Ibid., p. 5.   [176] Ibid., p. 16.   [177] Ibid., p. 17.

- would 'provide human rights with superiority over all ordinary law';
- would provide a 'unifying force in a diverse society';
- could 'restore the checks and balances that have been eroded by the torrent of counter-terrorism laws and practices...[and] confer positive rights on all communities';
- would protect the right to privacy and other traditional civil liberties;
- would provide 'constitutional stability'; and
- could remedy the problems caused by the HRA.

NOTES

1. Despite the implementation of the HRA there have been a number of areas in which civil liberties have been eroded, including the legislation to introduce identity cards; broad legislation directed towards the prevention of terrorism; and vastly increased powers of surveillance and data collection. Is the HRA inadequate in this respect or is it inevitable that the Government of the day will ensure considerable flexibility to legislate under any rights instrument? Would a stronger Bill of Rights necessitate a move away from the current parliamentary model of rights protection to one where the courts were able to strike down legislation?

2. The HRA has often received a negative press and public reaction.[178] Is the demand for a domestic Bill of Rights based on a misunderstanding of the current scope and powers available under the HRA or the result of a genuine demand for a domestic rights instrument?

3. Given that the UK is a signatory to the ECHR it is likely that new proposals will have to operate alongside the existing rights framework rather than replace it altogether. It should also be noted that the ECHR is a guarantor of a minimum level of rights and therefore in this sense any new document ought to add to, rather than take away from current rights.

4. There will inevitably be considerable debate as to what the Bill of Rights ought to include, such as social and economic rights, but there is also a wider question of whether such a Bill should contain rights that are real and effective or whether it should also have an aspirational dimension. Evidence gathered by the JCHR appeared to find public support for the inclusion of social and economic rights.

---

150. In the most recent Joseph Rowntree State of the Nation poll, in October 2006, 88% of people questioned thought that the right to hospital treatment on the NHS within a reasonable time should be included in a Bill of Rights. This was only 1% less than the 89% who thought that the right to a fair trial before a jury should be included. 65% thought that the right of the homeless to be housed should also be included.

151. Opinion polls conducted on behalf of the Northern Ireland Human Rights Commission as part of the consultation process leading towards the adoption of a Northern Ireland Bill of Rights convey the same message. The Commission found a high level of support in Northern Ireland for economic and social rights. 87% of Protestants and 91% of Catholics supported including the rights to health care and an adequate standard of living in a Bill of Rights.

---

[178] Joint Committee, Sixth Report, op. cit., at para. 3; see also, Department for Constitutional Affairs, *Review of the Implementation of the Human Rights Act* (2006) p. 29.

152. It seems that the rights which have been gradually conferred over the last 60 years or so by the welfare state, such as the right to health, housing and education, are now seen in the popular imagination as being just as fundamental as what are perceived to be the ancient rights in Magna Carta.

The most frequently heard argument against the adoption of economic and social rights is that decisions about the allocation of scarce resources would be taken away from elected representatives and given to an unelected judiciary. Are the courts already engaged in such activity through their powers of judicial review?

5. The JCHR also discusses the relevance of 'third generation' rights to a domestic Bill of Rights. Such rights fall outside the scope of the traditional civil and political and social and economic classification. Most pertinently in the modern age is a debate as to whether environmental rights ought to be given consideration.

6. A new Bill of Rights will involve attention to a number of major constitutional questions such as the relationship between the judiciary and the executive; possible entrenchment of rights; the ability of Parliament to override the Bill; and what powers should be available in times of national emergency. Such controversial questions will inevitably provide a fertile ground for debate in the coming years.

PART TWO: Life, liberty and association

3

ECHR PROTECTION OF LIFE, LIBERTY AND ASSOCIATION: ARTICLES 2, 3, 5 AND 11

The purpose of this chapter is to provide a brief overview of the main ECHR articles that protect life, liberty and association.[1]

1. ARTICLE 2

This provides generally that 'everyone's right to life shall be protected by law'. More specifically, 'no one shall be deprived of his life intentionally' save in the execution of a sentence of a court following his conviction of a crime for which this penalty is provided by law'.[2] Furthermore, deprivation of life is not to be regarded as a contravention of Art. 2, 'when it results from the use of force which is no more than absolutely necessary a in defence of any person from unlawful violence; b in order to effect a lawful arrest or to prevent the escape of a person lawfully detained; c in action lawfully taken for the purpose of quelling a riot or insurrection'.[3]

This ranks as one of the most fundamental provisions in the Convention and is non-derogable in peacetime. Its parameters are considered in the leading case, *McCann v United Kingdom* (below).

- **McCann v United Kingdom, ECtHRR A324** (1995) 21 EHRR 97, European Court of Human Rights

The facts of those cases as found by the court were as follows. Prior to March 1988, the UK, Spanish and Gibraltar authorities became aware that the Provisional IRA were planning a terrorist attack in Gibraltar. It appeared that the target would be a changing of the guard ceremony carried out every Tuesday in an assembly area. The Gibraltar Commissioner of

---

[1] For full accounts, see A.R. Mowbray, *Cases and Materials on the European Convention on Human Rights* (OUP, 2nd edn, 2007); M. Janis and A.W. Bradley, *European Human Rights Law* (OUP, 3rd edn, 2008), Chaps 4–6. Some passages are based on material in S.H. Bailey, J.P.L. Ching and N.W. Taylor, *Smith, Bailey and Gunn: The Modern English Legal System* (Sweet & Maxwell, London, 5th edn, 2007), Chap. 8.

[2] Art. 2(1).   [3] Art. 2(2).

Police was advised by a group that included a senior military advisor (an SAS officer, soldier F), an SAS attack commander (Soldier E) and a bomb-disposal adviser (Soldier G). The Ministry of Defence issued Soldier F with Rules of Engagement under which military forces were to assist the Gibraltar police to arrest the IRA active service unit involved. The Rules provided 'inter alia':

USE OF FORCE

4. You and your men will not use force unless requested to do so by the senior police officer(s) designated by the Gibraltar Police Commissioner; or unless it is necessary to do so in order to protect life. You and your men are not then to use more force than is necessary in order to protect life . . .

OPENING FIRE

5. You and your men may only open fire against a person if you or they have reasonable grounds for believing that he/she is currently committing, or is about to commit, an action which is likely to endanger your or their lives, or the life of any other person, and if there is no other way to prevent this.

FIRING WITHOUT WARNING

6. You and your men may fire without warning if the giving of a warning or any delay in firing could lead to death or injury to you or them or any other person, or if the giving of a warning is clearly impracticable.

WARNING BEFORE FIRING

7. If the circumstances in paragraph 6 do not apply, a warning is necessary before firing. The warning is to be as clear as possible and is to include a direction to surrender and a clear warning that fire will be opened if the direction is not obeyed.

There was a reported sighting of the active service unit (ASU) on 4 March in Malaga in Spain. An operational briefing took place on 5/6 March. The Security Service assessment stated that the IRA intended to attack the parade on 8 March; that an ASU of three (Daniel McCann, Sean Savage (an 'expert' bomb-maker) and a third member, later identified as Mairead Farrell) would carry out the attack; that they were believed to be dangerous terrorists who would almost certainly be armed and who, if confronted by security forces, would be likely to use their weapons; that the attack would be by way of a car bomb; that it was possible, but unlikely, that a 'blocking car' would be parked earlier to save a space later to be used by a second car with the bomb. It was thought that the use of a remote-control device to detonate the bomb was more likely that a timer device or control wire. The military witnesses present were convinced it would be a remote-control device and that it was likely that if confronted the person with the device would seek to detonate it. Arrangements were made for surveillance at the border and a plan formulated for the arrest of the ASU members on foot in the assembly area after parking a car which the intended to leave. In the afternoon of 6 March, Savage was identified as a man who had earlier parked a car in the assembly area. At about the same time, there was a possible sighting of McCann and Farrell crossing the frontier on foot into Gibraltar. It was then reported that the three had met and were looking at a car in the assembly area. They then moved off. The identification was confirmed. Soldier G inspected the car, noted that it had a rusty aerial out of place with the car's age and reported that it was a 'suspect car bomb'. This information was passed on but understood by Soldiers A, B, C and D from Soldier E to be confirmation that there was a car bomb that could be detonated by one of the three suspects. It was subsequently established that Solder G was neither a radio-communicator nor explosives expert.

The Commissioner requested the military to arrest the suspects. Soldiers A and B and C and D, operating in pairs, were so instructed. Soldiers A and B approached McCann and

Farrell. According to their evidence at the inquest, McCann and Farrell made movements which were interpreted as going for the button to detonate the bomb. Both were shot a number of times by each solder. The soldiers subsequently denied the allegations of some witnesses that McCann and Farrell had been shot while attempting to surrender and had then been shot while lying on the ground. Soldiers C and D followed Savage. They gave evidence that they heard gunfire. C shouted 'Stop', Savage spun round, his arm went down towards his right-hand hip area and they shot him, believing he was going for a detonator. They denied the allegation of a witness that they shot him while on the ground.

When the bodies of McCann, Farrell and Savage were searched no weapons or detonating devices were found. Car keys were found in Farrell's handbag. The relevant car was subsequently found in La Linea; inside this car were the keys to another car in Marbella which was found to contain an explosive device with a timer set to explode at the time of the parade on 8 March. This second car had been rented by 'Katherine Smith', the name on the passport in Farrell's handbag.

An inquest was held in September. The jury returned verdicts of lawful killing by nine to two. Actions for damages were commenced in the High Court in Northern Ireland on behalf of the estates of the deceased against the MoD; these were blocked by certificates of the Secretary of State for Foreign and Commonwealth Affairs issued under the s. 40(3) Crown Proceedings Act 1947 which stated conclusively that any alleged liability of the Crown arose neither in respect of HM Government in the UK or in Northern Ireland.

Evidence was subsequently made available that the UK police had briefed the Spanish police that McCann, Farrell and Savage were possible ASU members; the Spanish police had observed them arrive at Malaga Airport on 4 March. It was alleged that the car had been under surveillance by the Spanish authorities and that it would have been impossible for the three suspects to have detonated the bomb in the assembly area from the places where they were shot.

The applicants complained that the killings violated Art. 2 ECHR. The Commission found by 11 to 6 that there had been no violation.

JUDGMENT OF THE COURT

AS TO THE LAW

I. ALLEGED VIOLATION OF ARTICLE 2 (ART. 2) OF THE CONVENTION...

A. INTERPRETATION OF ARTICLE 2 (ART. 2)

1. General approach

146. The Court's approach to the interpretation of Article 2 (art. 2) must be guided by the fact that the object and purpose of the Convention as an instrument for the protection of individual human beings requires that its provisions be interpreted and applied so as to make its safeguards practical and effective (see, inter alia, the *Soering v. the United Kingdom* judgment of 7 July 1989, Series A no. 161, p. 34, para. 87, and the *Loizidou v. Turkey* (Preliminary Objections) judgment of 23 March 1995, Series A no. 310, p. 27, para. 72).

147. It must also be borne in mind that, as a provision (art. 2) which not only safeguards the right to life but sets out the circumstances when the deprivation of life may be justified, Article 2 (art. 2) ranks as one of the most fundamental provisions in the Convention—indeed one which, in peacetime, admits of no derogation under Article 15 (art. 15). Together with Article 3 (art. 15+3) of the Convention, it also enshrines one of the basic values of the democratic societies making up the Council of Europe (see the above-mentioned Soering judgment, p. 34, para. 88). As such, its provisions must be strictly construed.

148. The Court considers that the exceptions delineated in paragraph 2 (art. 2-2) indicate that this provision (art. 2-2) extends to, but is not concerned exclusively with, intentional killing. As the Commission has pointed out, the text of Article 2 (art. 2), read as a whole, demonstrates that paragraph 2 (art. 2-2) does not primarily define instances where it is permitted intentionally to kill an individual, but describes the situations where it is permitted to 'use force' which may result, as an unintended outcome, in the deprivation of life. The use of force, however, must be no more than 'absolutely necessary' for the achievement of one of the purposes set out in sub-paragraphs (a), (b) or (c) (art. 2-2-a, art. 2-2-b, art. 2-2-c) (see application no. 10044/82, *Stewart v. the United Kingdom*, 10 July 1984, Decisions and Reports 39, pp. 169–71).

149. In this respect the use of the term 'absolutely necessary' in Article 2 para. 2 (art. 2-2) indicates that a stricter and more compelling test of necessity must be employed from that normally applicable when determining whether State action is 'necessary in a democratic society' under paragraph 2 of Articles 8 to 11 (art. 8-2, art. 9-2, art. 10-2, art. 11-2) of the Convention. In particular, the force used must be strictly proportionate to the achievement of the aims set out in sub-paragraphs 2 (a), (b) and (c) of Article 2 (art. 2-2-a-b-c).

150. In keeping with the importance of this provision (art. 2) in a democratic society, the Court must, in making its assessment, subject deprivations of life to the most careful scrutiny, particularly where deliberate lethal force is used, taking into consideration not only the actions of the agents of the State who actually administer the force but also all the surrounding circumstances including such matters as the planning and control of the actions under examination.

2. The obligation to protect life in Article 2 para. 1 (art. 2-1)

[The Court found that there was no breach of Art. 2(1). The difference between Art. 2, ECHR and Art. 2 of the Gibraltar Constitution (which provided for a 'reasonably justifiable' standard rather than 'absolutely necessary' was) was 'not sufficiently great that a violation of Art. 2(1) could be found on this ground alone' (para. 155). The alleged shortcomings in the inquest proceedings had not 'subsequently hampered the carrying out of a thorough, impartial and careful examination of the circumstances surrounding the killings'(para. 163).]

B. APPLICATION OF ARTICLE 2 (ART. 2) TO THE FACTS OF THE CASE

1. General approach to the evaluation of the evidence

[The Court concluded that the Commission's establishment of the facts could be taken as 'an accurate and reliable account' (para. 169), but that it was for the Court to assess whether they disclosed a violation of Art. 2 ECHR (para. 171).]

2. Applicants' allegation that the killings were premeditated…

178. The Commission concluded that there was no evidence to support the applicants' claim of a premeditated plot to kill the suspects.

179. The Court observes that it would need to have convincing evidence before it could conclude that there was a premeditated plan, in the sense developed by the applicants.

180. In the light of its own examination of the material before it, the Court does not find it established that there was an execution plot at the highest level of command in the Ministry of Defence or in the Government, or that Soldiers A, B, C and D had been so encouraged or instructed by the superior officers who had briefed them prior to the operation, or indeed that they had decided on their own initiative to kill the suspects irrespective of the existence of any justification for the use of lethal force and in disobedience to the arrest instructions they had received. Nor is there evidence that there was an implicit encouragement by the authorities or hints and innuendoes to execute the three suspects.

181. The factors relied on by the applicants amount to a series of conjectures that the authorities must have known that there was no bomb in the car. However, having regard to the intelligence information

that they had received, to the known profiles of the three terrorists, all of whom had a background in explosives, and the fact that Mr Savage was seen to 'fiddle' with something before leaving the car (see paragraph 38 above), the belief that the car contained a bomb cannot be described as either implausible or wholly lacking in foundation.

182. In particular, the decision to admit them to Gibraltar, however open to criticism given the risks that it entailed, was in accordance with the arrest policy formulated by the Advisory Group that no effort should be made to apprehend them until all three were present in Gibraltar and there was sufficient evidence of a bombing mission to secure their convictions (see paragraph 37 above).

183. Nor can the Court accept the applicants' contention that the use of the SAS, in itself, amounted to evidence that the killing of the suspects was intended. In this respect it notes that the SAS is a special unit which has received specialist training in combating terrorism. It was only natural, therefore, that in light of the advance warning that the authorities received of an impending terrorist attack they would resort to the skill and experience of the SAS in order to deal with the threat in the safest and most informed manner possible.

184. The Court therefore rejects as unsubstantiated the applicants' allegations that the killing of the three suspects was premeditated or the product of a tacit agreement amongst those involved in the operation.

3. Conduct and planning of the operation...

(b) The Court's assessment

(1) Preliminary considerations

192. In carrying out its examination under Article 2 (art. 2) of the Convention, the Court must bear in mind that the information that the United Kingdom authorities received that there would be a terrorist attack in Gibraltar presented them with a fundamental dilemma. On the one hand, they were required to have regard to their duty to protect the lives of the people in Gibraltar including their own military personnel and, on the other, to have minimum resort to the use of lethal force against those suspected of posing this threat in the light of the obligations flowing from both domestic and international law.

193. Several other factors must also be taken into consideration. In the first place, the authorities were confronted by an active service unit of the IRA composed of persons who had been convicted of bombing offences and a known explosives expert. The IRA, judged by its actions in the past, had demonstrated a disregard for human life, including that of its own members. Secondly, the authorities had had prior warning of the impending terrorist action and thus had ample opportunity to plan their reaction and, in co-ordination with the local Gibraltar authorities, to take measures to foil the attack and arrest the suspects. Inevitably, however, the security authorities could not have been in possession of the full facts and were obliged to formulate their policies on the basis of incomplete hypotheses.

194. Against this background, in determining whether the force used was compatible with Article 2 (art. 2), the Court must carefully scrutinise, as noted above, not only whether the force used by the soldiers was strictly proportionate to the aim of protecting persons against unlawful violence but also whether the anti-terrorist operation was planned and controlled by the authorities so as to minimise, to the greatest extent possible, recourse to lethal force. The Court will consider each of these points in turn.

(2) Actions of the soldiers...

199. All four soldiers admitted that they shot to kill. They considered that it was necessary to continue to fire at the suspects until they were rendered physically incapable of detonating a device.... According to the pathologists' evidence Ms Farrell was hit by eight bullets, Mr McCann by five and Mr Savage by sixteen....

200. The Court accepts that the soldiers honestly believed, in the light of the information that they had been given, as set out above, that it was necessary to shoot the suspects in order to prevent them from detonating a bomb and causing serious loss of life (see paragraph 195 above). The actions which they took, in obedience to superior orders, were thus perceived by them as absolutely necessary in order to safeguard innocent lives.

It considers that the use of force by agents of the State in pursuit of one of the aims delineated in paragraph 2 of Article 2 (art. 2–2) of the Convention may be justified under this provision (art. 2-2) where it is based on an honest belief which is perceived, for good reasons, to be valid at the time but which subsequently turns out to be mistaken. To hold otherwise would be to impose an unrealistic burden on the State and its law-enforcement personnel in the execution of their duty, perhaps to the detriment of their lives and those of others.

It follows that, having regard to the dilemma confronting the authorities in the circumstances of the case, the actions of the soldiers do not, in themselves, give rise to a violation of this provision (art. 2-2).

201. The question arises, however, whether the anti-terrorist operation as a whole was controlled and organised in a manner which respected the requirements of Article 2 (art. 2) and whether the information and instructions given to the soldiers which, in effect, rendered inevitable the use of lethal force, took adequately into consideration the right to life of the three suspects.

(3) Control and organisation of the operation

202. The Court first observes that, as appears from the operational order of the Commissioner, it had been the intention of the authorities to arrest the suspects at an appropriate stage. Indeed, evidence was given at the inquest that arrest procedures had been practised by the soldiers before 6 March and that efforts had been made to find a suitable place in Gibraltar to detain the suspects after their arrest....

203. It may be questioned why the three suspects were not arrested at the border immediately on their arrival in Gibraltar and why, as emerged from the evidence given by Inspector Ullger, the decision was taken not to prevent them from entering Gibraltar if they were believed to be on a bombing mission. Having had advance warning of the terrorists' intentions it would certainly have been possible for the authorities to have mounted an arrest operation. Although surprised at the early arrival of the three suspects, they had a surveillance team at the border and an arrest group nearby.... In addition, the Security Services and the Spanish authorities had photographs of the three suspects, knew their names as well as their aliases and would have known what passports to look for....

204. On this issue, the Government submitted that at that moment there might not have been sufficient evidence to warrant the detention and trial of the suspects. Moreover, to release them, having alerted them to the authorities' state of awareness but leaving them or others free to try again, would obviously increase the risks. Nor could the authorities be sure that those three were the only terrorists they had to deal with or of the manner in which it was proposed to carry out the bombing.

205. The Court confines itself to observing in this respect that the danger to the population of Gibraltar—which is at the heart of the Government's submissions in this case—in not preventing their entry must be considered to outweigh the possible consequences of having insufficient evidence to warrant their detention and trial. In its view, either the authorities knew that there was no bomb in the car—which the Court has already discounted (see paragraph 181 above)—or there was a serious miscalculation by those responsible for controlling the operation. As a result, the scene was set in which the fatal shooting, given the intelligence assessments which had been made, was a foreseeable possibility if not a likelihood.

The decision not to stop the three terrorists from entering Gibraltar is thus a relevant factor to take into account under this head.

206. The Court notes that at the briefing on 5 March attended by Soldiers A, B, C, and D it was considered likely that the attack would be by way of a large car bomb. A number of key assessments were made. In particular, it was thought that the terrorists would not use a blocking car; that the bomb would be detonated by a radio-control device; that the detonation could be effected by the pressing of a button; that it was likely that the suspects would detonate the bomb if challenged; that they would be armed and would be likely to use their arms if confronted....

207. In the event, all of these crucial assumptions, apart from the terrorists' intentions to carry out an attack, turned out to be erroneous. Nevertheless, as has been demonstrated by the Government, on

the basis of their experience in dealing with the IRA, they were all possible hypotheses in a situation where the true facts were unknown and where the authorities operated on the basis of limited intelligence information.

208. In fact, insufficient allowances appear to have been made for other assumptions. For example, since the bombing was not expected until 8 March when the changing of the guard ceremony was to take place, there was equally the possibility that the three terrorists were on a reconnaissance mission. While this was a factor which was briefly considered, it does not appear to have been regarded as a serious possibility....

In addition, at the briefings or after the suspects had been spotted, it might have been thought unlikely that they would have been prepared to explode the bomb, thereby killing many civilians, as Mr McCann and Ms Farrell strolled towards the border area since this would have increased the risk of detection and capture.... It might also have been thought improbable that at that point they would have set up the trans-mitter in anticipation to enable them to detonate the supposed bomb immediately if confronted....

Moreover, even if allowances are made for the technological skills of the IRA, the description of the detonation device as a 'button job' without the qualifications subsequently described by the experts at the inquest..., of which the competent authorities must have been aware, over-simplifies the true nature of these devices.

209. It is further disquieting in this context that the assessment made by Soldier G, after a cursory exter-nal examination of the car, that there was a 'suspect car bomb' was conveyed to the soldiers, according to their own testimony, as a definite identification that there was such a bomb.... It is recalled that while Soldier G had experience in car bombs, it transpired that he was not an expert in radio communications or explosives; and that his assessment that there was a suspect car bomb, based on his observation that the car aerial was out of place, was more in the nature of a report that a bomb could not be ruled out....

210. In the absence of sufficient allowances being made for alternative possibilities, and the definite reporting of the existence of a car bomb which, according to the assessments that had been made, could be detonated at the press of a button, a series of working hypotheses were conveyed to Soldiers A, B, C and D as certainties, thereby making the use of lethal force almost unavoidable.

211. However, the failure to make provision for a margin of error must also be considered in combin-ation with the training of the soldiers to continue shooting once they opened fire until the suspect was dead. As noted by the Coroner in his summing-up to the jury at the inquest, all four soldiers shot to kill the suspects.... Soldier E testified that it had been discussed with the soldiers that there was an increased chance that they would have to shoot to kill since there would be less time where there was a 'button' device.... Against this background, the authorities were bound by their obligation to respect the right to life of the suspects to exercise the greatest of care in evaluating the information at their disposal before transmitting it to soldiers whose use of firearms automatically involved shooting to kill.

212. Although detailed investigation at the inquest into the training received by the soldiers was pre-vented by the public interest certificates which had been issued..., it is not clear whether they had been trained or instructed to assess whether the use of firearms to wound their targets may have been war-ranted by the specific circumstances that confronted them at the moment of arrest.

Their reflex action in this vital respect lacks the degree of caution in the use of firearms to be expected from law enforcement personnel in a democratic society, even when dealing with dangerous terrorist suspects, and stands in marked contrast to the standard of care reflected in the instructions in the use of firearms by the police which had been drawn to their attention and which emphasised the legal responsibilities of the individual officer in the light of conditions prevailing at the moment of engagement....

This failure by the authorities also suggests a lack of appropriate care in the control and organisation of the arrest operation.

213. In sum, having regard to the decision not to prevent the suspects from travelling into Gibraltar, to the failure of the authorities to make sufficient allowances for the possibility that their intelligence assessments might, in some respects at least, be erroneous and to the automatic recourse to lethal force when the soldiers opened fire, the Court is not persuaded that the killing of the three terrorists constituted the use of force which was no more than absolutely necessary in defence of persons from unlawful violence within the meaning of Article 2 para. 2 (a) (art. 2-2-a) of the Convention.

214. Accordingly, the Court finds that there has been a breach of Article 2 (art. 2) of the Convention.

FOR THESE REASONS, THE COURT

1. Holds by ten votes to nine that there has been a violation of Article 2 (art. 2) of the Convention;

2. Holds unanimously that the United Kingdom is to pay to the applicants, within three months, £38,700 (thirty-eight thousand seven hundred) for costs and expenses incurred in the Strasbourg proceedings, less 37,731 (thirty-seven thousand seven hundred and thirty-one) French francs to be converted into pounds sterling at the rate of exchange applicable on the date of delivery of the present judgment;

3. Dismisses unanimously the applicants' claim for damages;

4. Dismisses unanimously the applicants' claim for costs and expenses incurred in the Gibraltar inquest;

5. Dismisses unanimously the remainder of the claims for just satisfaction.

JOINT DISSENTING OPINION OF JUDGES RYSSDAL, BERNHARDT, THÓR VILHJÁLMSSON, GÖLCÜKLÜ, PALM, PEKKANEN, SIR JOHN FREELAND, BAKA AND JAMBREK

8. Before turning to the various aspects of the operation which are criticised in the judgment, we would underline three points of a general nature.

First, in undertaking any evaluation of the way in which the operation was organised and controlled, the Court should studiously resist the temptations offered by the benefit of hindsight. The authorities had at the time to plan and make decisions on the basis of incomplete information. Only the suspects knew at all precisely what they intended; and it was part of their purpose, as it had no doubt been part of their training, to ensure that as little as possible of their intentions was revealed. It would be wrong to conclude in retrospect that a particular course would, as things later transpired, have been better than one adopted at the time under the pressures of an ongoing anti-terrorist operation and that the latter course must therefore be regarded as culpably mistaken. It should not be so regarded unless it is established that in the circumstances as they were known at the time another course should have been preferred.

9. Secondly, the need for the authorities to act within the constraints of the law, while the suspects were operating in a state of mind in which members of the security forces were regarded as legitimate targets and incidental death or injury to civilians as of little consequence, would inevitably give the suspects a tactical advantage which should not be allowed to prevail. The consequences of the explosion of a large bomb in the centre of Gibraltar might well be so devastating that the authorities could not responsibly risk giving the suspects the opportunity to set in train the detonation of such a bomb. Of course the obligation of the United Kingdom under Article 2 para. 1 (art. 2-1) of the Convention extended to the lives of the suspects as well as to the lives of all the many others, civilian and military, who were present in Gibraltar at the time. But, quite unlike those others, the purpose of the presence of the suspects in Gibraltar was the furtherance of a criminal enterprise which could be expected to have resulted in the loss of many innocent lives if it had been successful. They had chosen to place themselves in a situation where there was a grave danger that an irreconcilable conflict between the two duties might arise.

10. Thirdly, the Court's evaluation of the conduct of the authorities should throughout take full account of (a) the information which had been received earlier about IRA intentions to mount a major terrorist attack in Gibraltar by an active service unit of three individuals; and (b) the discovery which...had been

made in Brussels on 21 January 1988 of a car containing a large amount of Semtex explosive and four detonators, with a radio-controlled system—equipment which, taken together, constituted a device familiar in Northern Ireland.

[In the light of (a), the decision that members of the SAS should be sent to take part in the operation in response to the request of the Gibraltar Commissioner of Police for military assistance was wholly justifiable; the detailed operational briefing on 5 March 1988 showed the reasonableness, in the circumstances as known at the time, of the assessments then made; the operational order of the Gibraltar Commissioner of Police, expressly proscribed the use of more force than necessary and required any recourse to firearms to be had with care for the safety of persons in the vicinity. All of this was indicative of appropriate care on the part of the authorities. So, too, was the cautious approach to the eventual passing of control to the military on 6 March 1988.]

11. As regards the particular criticisms of the conduct of the operation which are made in the judgment, foremost among them is the questioning (in paragraphs 203–05) of the decision not to prevent the three suspects from entering Gibraltar. It is pointed out in paragraph 203 that, with the advance information which the authorities possessed and with the resources of personnel at their disposal, it would have been possible for them 'to have mounted an arrest operation' at the border.

The judgment does not, however, go on to say that it would have been practicable for the authorities to have arrested and detained the suspects at that stage. Rightly so, in our view, because at that stage there might not be sufficient evidence to warrant their detention and trial. To release them, after having alerted them to the state of readiness of the authorities, would be to increase the risk that they or other IRA members could successfully mount a renewed terrorist attack on Gibraltar. In the circumstances as then known, it was accordingly not 'a serious miscalculation' for the authorities to defer the arrest rather than merely stop the suspects at the border and turn them back into Spain.

12. Paragraph 206 of the judgment then lists certain 'key assessments' made by the authorities which, in paragraph 207, are said to have turned out, in the event, to be erroneous, although they are accepted as all being possible hypotheses in a situation where the true facts were unknown and where the authorities were operating on the basis of limited intelligence information. Paragraph 208 goes on to make the criticism that 'insufficient allowances appear to have been made for other assumptions'.

13. As a first example to substantiate this criticism, the paragraph then states that since the bombing was not expected until 8 March 'there was equally the possibility that the...terrorists were on a reconnaissance mission'.

There was, however, nothing unreasonable in the assessment at the operational briefing on 5 March that the car which would be brought into Gibraltar was unlikely, on the grounds then stated, to be a 'blocking' car.... So, when the car had been parked in the assembly area by one of the suspects and all three had been found to be present in Gibraltar, the authorities could quite properly operate on the working assumption that it contained a bomb and that, as the suspects were unlikely to risk two visits, it was not 'equally' possible that they were on a reconnaissance mission.

In addition, Soldier F, the senior military adviser to the Gibraltar Commissioner of Police, gave evidence to the inquest that, according to intelligence information, reconnaissance missions had been undertaken many times before: reconnaissance was, he had been told, complete and the operation was ready to be run. In these circumstances, for the authorities to have proceeded otherwise than on the basis of a worst-case scenario that the car contained a bomb which was capable of being detonated by the suspects during their presence in the territory would have been to show a reckless failure of concern for public safety.

14. Secondly, it is suggested in the second sub-paragraph of paragraph 208 that, at the briefings or after the suspects had been spotted, 'it might have been thought unlikely that they would have been prepared to explode the bomb, thereby killing many civilians, as Mr McCann and Ms Farrell strolled towards the border area since this would have increased the risk of detection and capture'.

Surely, however, the question is rather whether the authorities could safely have operated on the assumption that the suspects would be unlikely to be prepared to explode the bomb when, even if for the time being moving in the direction of the border, they became aware that they had been detected and were faced with the prospect of arrest. In our view, the answer is clear: certainly, previous experience of IRA activities would have afforded no reliable basis for concluding that the killing of many civilians would itself be a sufficient deterrent or that the suspects, when confronted, would have preferred no explosion at all to an explosion causing civilian casualties....

15. [As to the second sentence of the second sub-paragraph of para. 208:] Here, the question ought, we consider, to be whether the authorities could prudently have proceeded otherwise than on the footing that there was at the very least a possibility that, if not before the suspects became aware of detection then immediately afterwards, the transmitter would be in a state of readiness to detonate the bomb.

16. [As to the third sub-paragraph of para. 208:] The exact purport of this criticism is perhaps open to some doubt. What is fully clear, however, is that, as the applicants' own expert witness accepted at the inquest, a transmitter of the kind which was thought likely to be used in the present case could be set up so as to enable detonation to be caused by pressing a single button; and in the light of past experience it would have been most unwise to discount the possibility of technological advance in this field by the IRA.

17. Paragraph 209 of the judgment expresses disquiet that the assessment made by Soldier G that there was a 'suspect car bomb' was conveyed to the soldiers on the ground in such a way as to give them the impression that the presence of a bomb had been definitely identified. But, given the assessments which had been made of the likelihood of a remote control being used, and given the various indicators that the car should indeed be suspected of containing a bomb, the actions which the soldiers must be expected to have taken would be the same whether their understanding of the message was as it apparently was or whether it was in the sense which Soldier G apparently intended. In either case, the existence of the risk to the people of Gibraltar would have been enough, given the nature of that risk, justifiably to prompt the response which followed.

18. Paragraph 209, in referring to the assessment made by Soldier G, also recalls that while he had experience with car bombs, he was not an expert in radio communications or explosives. In considering that assessment, it would, however, be fair to add that, although his inspection of the car was of brief duration, it was enough to enable him to conclude, particularly in view of the unusual appearance of its aerial in relation to the age of the car and the knowledge that the IRA had in the past used cars with aerials specially fitted, that it was to be regarded as a suspect car bomb.

The authorities were, in any event, not acting solely on the basis of Soldier G's assessment. There had also been the earlier assessment...that a 'blocking' car was unlikely to be used. In addition, the car had been seen to be parked by Savage, who was known to be an expert bomb-maker and who had taken some time (two to three minutes, according to one witness) to get out of the car, after fiddling with something between the seats.

19. [As to the para. 210:] We further question the conclusion that the use of lethal force was made 'almost unavoidable' by failings of the authorities in these respects. Quite apart from any other consideration, this conclusion takes insufficient account of the part played by chance in the eventual outcome. Had it not been for the movements which were made by McCann and Farrell as Soldiers A and B closed on them and which may have been prompted by the completely coincidental sounding of a police car siren, there is every possibility that they would have been seized and arrested without a shot being fired; and had it not been for Savage's actions as Soldiers C and D closed on him, which may have been prompted by the sound of gunfire from the McCann and Farrell incident, there is every possibility that he, too, would have been seized and arrested without resort to shooting.

20. The implication at the end of paragraph 211 that the authorities did not exercise sufficient care in evaluating the information at their disposal before transmitting it to soldiers 'whose use of firearms

automatically involved shooting to kill' appears to be based on no more than 'the failure to make provision for a margin of error' to which the beginning of the paragraph refers. We have dealt already with the 'insufficient allowances for alternative possibilities' point (see, again, paragraphs 13–16 above), which we take to be the same as the alleged failure to provide for a margin of error which is referred to here. Any assessment of the evaluation by the authorities of the information at their disposal should, in any event, take due account of their need to reckon throughout with the incompleteness of that information…; and there are no cogent grounds for any suggestion that there was information which they ought reasonably to have known but did not.

22. [As to para. 212:] As regards any suggestion that, if an assessment on the issue had been required by their training or instruction to be carried out by the soldiers, shooting to wound might have been considered by them to have been warranted by the circumstances at the time, it must be recalled that those circumstances included a genuine belief on their part that the suspects might be about to detonate a bomb by pressing a button. In that situation, to shoot merely to wound would have been a highly dangerous course: wounding alone might well not have immobilised a suspect and might have left him or her capable of pressing a button if determined to do so….

24. We are far from persuaded that the Court has any sufficient basis for concluding, in the face of the evidence at the inquest and the extent of experience in dealing with terrorist activities which the relevant training reflects, that some different and preferable form of training should have been given and that the action of the soldiers in this case 'lacks the degree of caution in the use of firearms to be expected of law-enforcement personnel in a democratic society'. (We also question, in the light of the evidence, the fairness of the reference to 'reflex action in this vital respect'—underlining supplied. To be trained to react rapidly and to do so, when the needs of the situation require, is not to take reflex action.)

Accordingly, we consider the concluding stricture, that there was some failure by the authorities in this regard suggesting a lack of appropriate care in the control and organisation of the arrest operation, to be unjustified.

25. The accusation of a breach by a State of its obligation under Article 2 (art. 2) of the Convention to protect the right to life is of the utmost seriousness. For the reasons given above, the evaluation in paragraphs 203 to 213 of the judgment seems to us to fall well short of substantiating the finding that there has been a breach of the Article (art. 2) in this case. We would ourselves follow the reasoning and conclusion of the Commission in its comprehensive, painstaking and notably realistic report. Like the Commission, we are satisfied that no failings have been shown in the organisation and control of the operation by the authorities which could justify a conclusion that force was used against the suspects disproportionately to the purpose of defending innocent persons from unlawful violence. We consider that the use of lethal force in this case, however regrettable the need to resort to such force may be, did not exceed what was, in the circumstances as known at the time, 'absolutely necessary' for that purpose and did not amount to a breach by the United Kingdom of its obligations under the Convention.

NOTES[4]

1. This was the first leading case on Art. 2 ECHR. The decision was described as the court's 'most politically controversial decision for a decade'. It was strongly criticised by the Conservative Government and by Unionists, although not by the Labour opposition.[5] However, the judgment 'accepted almost all of the arguments put forward by the

---

[4] See F. Ni Aoláin, *The Politics of Force* (2000), pp. 198–205; S. Joseph, 'Denouement of the Deaths on the Rock: the Right of Life of Terrorists' (1996) 14 NQHR 5; J. Merrills (1996) 67 BYBIL 609; P. Cumper (1995) Nott LJ 207. Cf. the decision in *Caraher v UK*, App. No. 24520/94, 11 January 2000.

[5] P. Cumper, op. cit., pp. 207–208.

Government and placed the finding of a violation on the narrowest possible ground'.[6] Subsequent European Court of Human Rights cases have developed the points that states must 'take all feasible precautions in the choice of means and methods of a security operation mounted against an opposing group with a view to avoiding and, in any event, to minimising, incidental loss of civilian life[7] and must conduct effective investigations into unlawful killings, whether or not by state agents.[8]

The Court accepted the Government's claim that the domestic standard of 'reasonable justification' was interpreted and applied in such a way as to negate any difference in protection from Art. 2 ECHR. It has been argued that such claims should be the subject of substantive examination.[9] Note Joseph's argument[10] that the finding of a violation by implication indicates that the *Kelly* case[11] was wrongly decided. The increase of risk to the ASU's lives that arose from the failure to arrest them at the border could not on the facts be justified by the argument that had they been arrested they would have had to be released for lack of evidence and that this would increase the risk that they or other IRA members could mount a renewed terrorist attack on Gibraltar.

2. In exceptional circumstances, there may be liability under Art. 2 in respect of a disproportionate use of force that does not result in death.[12]

3. No right to die, whether at the hands of a third person or with the assistance of a public authority, can be derived from Art. 2.[13]

4. Art. 2(2)(b) cannot be relied upon where it is known that the person to be arrested poses no threat to life and limb and is not suspected of committing a violent offence.[14]

5. The general obligation under Art. 2(1) requires each state not only to have appropriate provisions of substantive criminal law, but also in appropriate circumstances, to take positive operational measures to protect individuals at risk.[15]

6. A further implied requirement is that states must undertake effective investigations into all killings (whether or not by stage agents), involving 'some form of independence and public scrutiny capable of leading to a determination of whether the force used was or was not justified'.[16] The European Court of Human Rights declared admissible a series of applications raising issues under Art. 2 arising out of deaths in Northern Ireland. The cases raised issues as to the proportionality of the use of force and the thoroughness of the investigation

---

[6] J. Merrills, op. cit., p. 612.   [7] *Ergi v Turkey*, Judgment of 28 July 1998, para. 79.

[8] *Kaya v Turkey* (1998) 28 EHRR 1; *Kurt v Turkey* (1998) 27 EHRR 91; *Yasa v Turkey* (1998) 28 EHRR 408; *Cyprus v Turkey* (2001) 35 EHRR 30 (duty to investigate may arise where people have disappeared in life-threatening circumstances).

[9] F. Ní Aoláin, op. cit., p. 200.   [10] Op. cit., p. 17.

[11] Below, p. 497.

[12] *Makaratsis v Greece*, Judgment of 20 December 2004 (repeated use of revolvers, pistols and sub-machine guns against driver who drove through red traffic lights).

[13] *Pretty v UK* (2002) 35 EHRR 1, para. 39.

[14] *Nachova v Bulgaria* (2005) 42 EHRR 43. See also reliance on Art. 2(2)(c) in *Stewart v UK*, below, p. 497.

[15] *Osman v UK* (1998) 29 EHRR 245 (no violation of Art. 2(1) on the facts where police failed to arrest person who subsequently murdered Mr Osman and seriously injured his son; it must be established 'that the authorities knew or ought to have known at the time of the existence of a real and immediate risk to the life of an identified individual or individuals from the criminal act of a third party and that they failed to take measures within the scope of their powers which, judged reasonably, might have been expected to avoid the risk' (para. 120). Cf. *Kaya v Turkey*, Judgment of 28 March 2000 (violation established); *Edwards v UK* (2002) 35 EHRR 487 (violation found in respect of killing of prisoner by cellmate); cf. *Van Colle v Chief Constable of Hertfordshire* [2008] UKHL 50 (no breach found where police failed to prevent murder of prosecution witness).

[16] *Kava v Turkey* (1998) 28 EHRR 1.

following death (Art. 2), the discriminatory use of force (Art. 14) and the lack of an effective remedy, including criticisms of arrangements for inquests (Art. 13). The Northern Ireland Human Rights Commission submitted to the court that the UK was 'failing to protect the rights to life by failing to ensure that its mechanisms of accountability are open, accountable, prompt and facilitating punitive sanctions when death has been caused by an agent of the state'.[17] The Court subsequently found the UK to have breached Art. 2, in respect of the inadequacies of the investigations.[18] Investigations must be (1) independent from those implicated; (2) effective in the sense that it is capable of leading to a determination of whether the force used was or was not justified in the circumstances; (3) prompt and reasonably expeditious; (4) subject to a sufficient element of public scrutiny; and (5) the next of kin must be involved to an appropriate extent.[19]

7. So far as claims under the Human Rights Act 1998 are concerned, the House of Lords in *Re McKerr*[20] held that the Act does not apply in respect of pre-commencement deaths. This has been criticised on the basis that procedural right is 'associated not with an individual violation (to the immediate victim of which it would be of no use) but with the state's obligation to maintain an effective system to protect life'.[21] This also means that Art. 2 complaints in respect of such deaths will continue to be taken to Strasbourg.

2. ARTICLE 3

This provides that 'no one shall be subjected to torture or to inhuman or degrading treatment or punishment'. It is the subject of no exceptions and cannot be the subject of a derogation. 'Inhuman treatment' has been held to include such matters as the adoption of a practice of violence by police officers leading to intense suffering and physical injury[22] and the causing of severe mental distress and anguish;[23] 'degrading treatment' to include actions 'such as to arouse in their victims feelings of fear, anguish and inferiority capable of humiliating and debasing them and possibly breaking their physical or moral resistance';[24] and 'degrading

---

[17] *Submission to the European Court of Human Rights,* 23 March 2000 (published on the NICHR website).

[18] E.g. *Jordan v UK* (2001) 37 EHRR 52 (arising out of the shooting of Pearse Jordan by RUC officers in 1992); *Kelly v UK ,* Judgment of 4 May 2001 (arising out of the deaths of nine men killed by the security forces in an operation at Loughgall in 1987); *Shanaghan v UK,* Judgment of 4 May 2001 (arising out of the shooting of Patrick Shanaghan, for which responsibility was claimed by the UFF; RUC collusion was alleged); *McKerr v UK* (2002) 34 EHRR 20 (arising out of the shooting of Gervaise McKerr, Eugen Toman and Sean Burns by an RUC Home Support Unit in 1982; John Stalker regarded the investigation of the matter as slipshod and in some aspects woefully inadequate: *Stalker* (1988), pp. 40–43); *Finucane v UK* (2003) 37 EHRR 29; cf. *R (on the application of Amin) v Secretary of State for the Home Department* [2003] UKHL 51, [2004] 1 AC 653; *R (on the application of Middleton) v West Somerset Coroner* [2004] UKHL 10, [2004] 2 AC 182 (inquest procedure not sufficient to meet Art. 2 requirements).

[19] *Kelly v UK,* paras 95–98.

[20] [2004] UKHL 12, [2004] 1 WLR 807. See also *R (on the application of Hurst) v Comr of Police for the Metropolis* [2007] UKHL 13 (modification of Coroners Rules necessary to secure compliance with Art. 2 not applicable in respect of pre-commencement deaths).

[21] Janis et al., op. cit., p. 153.

[22] *Ireland v UK* (1978) 2 EHRR 25, para. 174 (interrogation techniques used in Northern Ireland in 1971); *Tomasi v France* (1992) 15 EHRR 1 (large number of blows inflicted on terrorist suspect).

[23] *Kurt v Turkey* (1998) 27 EHRR 91.

[24] *Ireland v UK,* above, para. 167. The Court has to have regard to whether the objective of the treatment is to humiliate and debase the person concerned, but the absence of such an intention does not conclusively rule out a violation of Art. 3: *Peers v Greece* (2002) 33 EHRR 51, para. 74; *Price v UK* (2001) 34 EHRR 1285 (conditions of detention in prison of severely disabled person held to constitute degrading treatment, where she was

punishment' to include judicial corporal punishment.[25] The assessment of whether the level reaches the minimum necessary for a finding that Art. 3 has been violated depends on all the circumstances of the case, such as the nature and content of the treatment, its duration, its physical and mental aspects and, in some circumstances, the sex, age and state of health of the victim.[26]

The distinction between 'torture' and the other conduct prohibited by Art. 3, was considered by the ECtHR in *Ireland v United Kingdom*, which arose out of the adoption of five coercive interrogation techniques[27] by the authorities in Northern Ireland. The UK Government did not contest that they amounted to ill-treatment under Art. 3. The Court held by 13 to 4 that they did not constitute torture. The Court stated:

167. The five techniques were applied in combination, with premeditation and for hours at a stretch; they caused, if not actual bodily injury, at least intense physical and mental suffering to the persons subjected thereto and also led to acute psychiatric disturbances during interrogation. They accordingly fell into the category of inhuman treatment within the meaning of Article 3. The techniques were also degrading since they were such as to arouse in their victims feelings of fear, anguish and inferiority capable of humiliating and debasing them and possibly breaking their physical or moral resistance....

In order to determine whether the five techniques should also be qualified as torture, the Court must have regard to the distinction, embodied in Article 3, between this notion and that of inhuman or degrading treatment.

In the court's view, this distinction derives principally from a difference in the intensity of the suffering inflicted.

The court considers in fact that, whilst there exists on the one hand violence which is to be condemned both on moral grounds and also in most cases under the domestic law of the Contracting States but which does not fall within Article 3 of the Convention, it appears on the other hand that it was the intention that the Convention, with its distinction between 'torture' and 'inhuman or degrading treatment', should by the first of these terms attach a special stigma to deliberate inhuman treatment causing very serious and cruel suffering.

Moreover, this seems to be the thinking lying behind Article 1 in fine of Resolution 3452 (XXX) adopted by the General Assembly of the United Nations on 9 December 1975, which declares: 'Torture constitutes an aggravated and deliberate form of cruel, inhuman or degrading treatment or punishment'.

Although the five techniques, as applied in combination, undoubtedly amounted to inhuman and degrading treatment, although their object was the extraction of confessions, the naming of others and/or information and although they were used systematically, they did not occasion suffering of the particular intensity and cruelty implied by the word torture as so understood.

The ECtHR is, however, imposing increasingly high standards.[28]

Apart from liability based on the actions of state officials themselves, the state is obliged by Art. 3 to undertake an effective official investigation where an individual raises an arguable claim that he or she has been seriously ill-treated by state officials in breach

---

dangerously cold, risked developing sores and was unable to go to the toilet or keep clean without the greatest of difficulty).

[25] *Tyrer v UK* (1978) 2 EHRR 1; cf. *Campbell and Cosans v UK* (1982) 4 EHRR 293 (no breach of Art. 3 arising from risk of corporal punishment in state school); *Costello-Roberts v UK* (1993) 19 EHRR 112 (no breach of Art. 3 arising from case of corporal punishment in non-state funded school).

[26] *A v UK* (1998) 27 EHRR 611 at para. 20.

[27] Wall-standing, hooding, subjection to noise, deprivation of sleep, deprivation of food and drink.

[28] *Selmouni v France* (2000) 29 EHRR 403, para. 101 (torture found in respect of assaults and other serious mistreatment of suspect during police questioning, including one officer urinating on him).

of that article.[29] Furthermore, the state must take positive steps, including the enactment of appropriate criminal offences, to protect persons from being subject to Art. 3 mistreatment by other private persons,[30] although there is a wide margin of appreciation.[31]

It is a breach of the Art. 3 to take action in relation to someone within the jurisdiction which carries the real risk that it will expose that person to infringement of his or her Art. 3 rights outside the jurisdiction.[32] Where the risk arises from the actions of non-state actors it must also be shown that the state has failed to provide reasonable protection.[33] Furthermore, the principle may apply where the risk is of a flagrant infringement of other articles.[34]

In *Z v United Kingdom*[35] the Court held that the failure of a local authority to take steps to protect four children in its area from severe neglect, deprivation and abuse at the hands of their parents constituted a breach of Art. 3; the authorities had been aware of the serious ill-treatment and neglect suffered by the children for over four years. The Government did not contest the Commission's findings of a breach of Art. 3. On the other hand, the refusal by the Director of Public Prosecutions of proleptic immunity from prosecution to a husband whose wife was suffering from a progressive degenerative illness and who wished to assist her suicide has been held not to fall within Art. 3. It did not constitute proscribed 'treatment' and the state was not under a positive obligation to ensure that a competent, terminally ill person who wished but was unable to take her own life should be entitled to seek assistance of another without that person being exposed to the risk of prosecution.[36] Furthermore, the determination of priorities in the provision of healthcare[37] and delays in receiving medical treatment have been held not to give rise to a remedy under Art. 3.[38]

---

[29] *Assenov v Bulgaria* (1998) 28 EHRR 652; *Salman v Turkey* (2000) 34 EHRR 17 (inadequate investigation of death in police custody; obligation to investigate not confined to cases where it is apparent that the killing was caused by an agent of the state); *MC v Bulgaria* (2003) 40 EHRR 20 (obligation extends to require investigation of ill treatment by private individuals (alleged rapes)).

[30] *A v UK* (1998) 27 EHRR 611 (caning of child by stepfather sufficiently serious to engage Art. 3; criminal law that provided defence of reasonable chastisement to be disproved beyond reasonable doubt held to be inadequate protection). The law was changed by the removal of the defence of reasonable chastisement for assaults causing actual bodily harm or worse by the Children Act 2004, s. 58. See H. Keating (2006) 29 LS 394.

[31] Cf. *Osman v UK* (1998) 29 EHRR 245, paras. 115–116 (Art. 2); *Rees v UK* (1986) 9 EHRR 56, para. 37 (Art. 8), cited by Lord Bingham in *R (on the application of Pretty) v Director of Public Prosecutions* [2001] UKHL 61, [2002] 1 AC 800, para. [15].

[32] *Soering v UK* (1989) 11 EHRR 439 (extradition to a country where there was a real risk that the person concerned would face a real risk of being subjected to torture or to inhuman or degrading treatment or punishment); *R (on the application of Ullah) v Special Adjudicator* [2002] EWCA Civ 1856, per Lord Phillips of Worth Matravers at para. [29].

[33] *R (on the application of Bagdanavicius) v Secretary of State for the Home Department* [2005] UKHL 38, [2005] 2 AC 668.

[34] *R (on the application of Ullah) v Special Adjudicator* [2004] UKHL 26, [2004] 2 AC 323; *R (on the application of Razgar)* [2004] UKHL 27, [2004] 2 AC 368.

[35] Judgment of 10 May 2001. Cf. *V v UK* (1999) 30 EHRR 121, where the court held that the trial and sentence of two 11-year-old boys for the murder of a two-year-old (when they were 10) did not violate Art. 3; *R (on the application of Limbuela) v Secretary of State for the Home Department* [2005] UKHL 66, [2006] HRLR 4 (application of Art. 3 threshold to asylum seeker refused support).

[36] *R (on the application of Pretty) v Director of Public Prosecutions* [2001] UKHL 61, [2002] 1 AC 800.

[37] *R v North West Lancashire Health Authority, ex p A* [2000] 1 WLR 977 (decision not to fund gender reassignment surgery other than in exceptional circumstances; per Auld LJ at 996: 'It is plain, in my view, that Art. 3 was not designed for circumstances of this sort of case where the challenge is as to a health authority's allocation of finite funds between competing demands').

[38] *R (on the application of Watts) v Bedford Primary Care Trust and the Secretary of State for Health* [2003] EWHC 2228 (Admin) (*ex p A*, followed; in addition nothing the claimant had to endure was so severe or so humiliating as to engage Art. 3).

3. ARTICLE 5

Article 5 provides safeguards against arbitrary detention. For it to apply there must be a 'deprivation' of physical liberty, and not merely a restriction on freedom of movement. The distinction is one of degree, and turns on such matters as the type, duration, effects and manner of implementation of the measure in question.[39] To be lawful, the deprivation must fall within one or more of the prescribed situations, which are to be narrowly interpreted, and be in accordance with a procedure prescribed by law. There are implied obligations that when the state detains a person, the authorities must 'account for his or her whereabouts', and that the authorities 'must take effective measures to safeguard against the risk of disappearance and to conduct a prompt effective investigation into an arguable claim that a person has been taken into custody and has not been seen since'.[40]

For lawful detention after conviction under Art. 5(1)(a) the punishment must not be arbitrary and disproportionate[41] and there has to be a sufficient connection between the order of the court following conviction and the detention in question.[42] This has been held to cover the exercise by the Home Secretary of power to recall a life sentence prisoner who committed further offences after his release.[43] Article 5(1)(b), *inter alia*, authorises detention in accordance with a court order, and is not violated merely because the order is set aside on appeal.[44] Article 5(1)(c) authorises the lawful exercise of police powers of arrest[45] provided there is on the facts 'reasonable suspicion' or arrest or detention is 'reasonably considered necessary' as the case may be. Where challenged, the Government must 'furnish at least some facts or information capable of satisfying the Court that the arrested person was reasonably suspected of having committee the alleged offence'.[46]

For a person to be detained as a person of 'unsound mind' under Art. 5(1)(e), he or she must be 'reliably shown to be of "unsound mind"', the mental disorder 'must be of a kind or degree warranting compulsory confinement' and the 'validity of continued confinement depends upon the persistence of such a disorder'.[47] Such a person must be detained in a hospital, clinic or other appropriate institution.[48]

Detention for the purposes of deportation or extradition under Art. 5(1)(f) will not be justified where it exceeds a reasonable time[49] or where, in the absence of a power to extradite, a person is deported in circumstances that amount to disguised extradition.[50]

---

[39] *Engel v Netherlands* (1976) 1 EHRR 647 (detention of soldier in locked cell fell within Art. 5; confinement during off duty hours in an unlocked building in barracks did not); *R (on the application of Gillan) v Comr of Police of the Metropolis*, below, p. 440; cases on control orders, below pp. 475–485. (Restrictions on freedom of movement are covered by the Fourth Protocol, Art. 2, which has not been ratified by the UK.)

[40] *Kurt v Turkey* (1998) 27 EHRR 91, para. 124.

[41] *Engel* at para. 58; *R v Lichniak* [2002] UKHL 47, [2003] 1 AC 903 (mandatory life sentence not arbitrary and disproportionate).

[42] *Van Droogenbroek v Belgium* (1982) 4 EHRR 443, para. 39.

[43] *Weeks v UK* (1987) 10 EHRR 293.   [44] *Bentham v UK* (1996) 22 EHRR 293.

[45] See Chap. 4.

[46] *Fox, Campbell and Hartley v UK* (1980) 13 EHRR 157, para. 34; the fact that F and C had previous convictions for terrorist acts connected with the IRA was insufficient on its own to constitute reasonable suspicion of the commission of terrorist offences seven years later. Cf. *Margaret Murray v UK* (1994) 19 EHRR 193.

[47] *Winterwerp v Netherlands* (1979) 2 EHRR 387, para. 39.

[48] *Aerts v Belgium* (1998) 29 EHRR 50.

[49] *Quinn v France* (1995) 21 EHRR 529; cf. *Chahal v UK* (1996) 23 EHRR 413 (C had been detained for a considerable time but the authorities had acted with due diligence).

[50] *Bozano v France* (1986) 9 EHRR 297.

By virtue of Art. 5(2)

any person arrested must be told, in simple, non technical language that he can understand, the essential legal and factual grounds for his arrest, so as to be able, if he sees fit, to apply to a court to challenge its lawfulness in accordance with paragraph 4....[51]

The information must be conveyed promptly, although not necessarily at the very moment of arrest. This echoes the requirement of the common law as to the exercise of arrest powers.[52]

Those arrested under Art. 5(1)(c) must be brought before a judicial officer promptly (Art. 5(3)). Review by a public prosecutor is likely to be insufficient.[53] Exercises of power to keep terrorist suspects in custody for up to five days without review by a judge have been held to violate this requirement.[54] Where persons arrested under Art. 5(1)(c) are to be tried, they are also entitled to trial within a reasonable time or to release pending trial, the time requirement here being less onerous than the requirement of 'promptness' as regards the review of detention. Neither the proceedings themselves nor the provisional detention of accused persons may be prolonged beyond a reasonable time, the former covering the whole period to the end of the trial.[55] What is reasonable naturally depends on the circumstances.[56] A provision automatically denying bail in specified circumstances is likely to be held to violate this requirement.[57]

Where a person is detained by a person or body which is not itself a 'court', such as the police, he or she must be entitled to take proceedings by which the lawfulness of the detention is decided speedily by a court (Art. 5(4)). To be a court, a body must be independent of the executive and the parties, be able to consider all aspects of the justification for detention and able to make a binding decision.[58] Where a person is detained indefinitely,[59] reviews must normally be available at reasonable intervals.[60]

---

[51] *Fox, Campbell and Hartley v UK* (1990) 13 EHRR 157, para. 40.

[52] See below, p. 205.

[53] *Huber v Switzerland*, Judgment of 23 October 1990; *Assenov v Bulgaria* (1998) 28 EHRR 652.

[54] *Brogan v UK* (1988) 11 EHRR 117. See further below, p. 435.

[55] *Wemhoff v Federal Republic of Germany* (1968) 1 EHRR 55, paras 4–9.

[56] *Wemhoff*, paras 10–17 (W's detention between 1961 and his conviction in 1965 in exceptionally complicated fraud case held to be reasonable); *W v Switzerland* (1993) 17 EHRR 60.

[57] *Caballero v UK* (2000) 30 EHRR 643.

[58] *De Wilde, Ooms and Versyp v Belgium* (the 'vagrancy' cases) (1971) 1 EHRR 373; *Chahal v UK* (1996) 23 EHRR 413 (judicial review and advisory panel ('Three Advisers') system insufficient for compliance in respect of detention in the context of deportation on national security grounds; see below, p. 767); *R (on the application of Smith) v Parole Board* [2005] UKHL 1, [2005] 1 WLR 350 and *R (on the application of Roberts) v Parole Board* [2005] UKHL 45, [2005] 2 AC 738 (Parole Board proceedings must be procedurally fair for there to be compliance with Art. 5(4)).

[59] Not where the sentence of a court is determinate: see *R (on the application of Giles) v Parole Board* [2003] UKHL 42, [2004] 1 AC 1 (imposition by judge of extended sentence to protect the public from serious harm under s. 2(2)(b) of the Criminal Justice Act 1991 did not attract requirement of further reviews).

[60] *Winterwerp*, para. 55; *X v UK* (1981) 4 EHRR 188 (review by habeas corpus proceedings of detention under Mental Health Act 1959, following recall, insufficient for compliance with Art. 5(4) as habeas corpus proceedings dealt only with the lawfulness of detention under domestic law; reviews by Mental Health Review Tribunals were also insufficient as their functions were advisory only, the position on this point subsequently being changed to secure compliance by the Mental Health Act 1983); *Weeks v UK* (1987) 10 EHRR 293 (role of Parole Board and judicial review in considering recall of discretionary life sentence prisoner and periodic examination of detention insufficient for compliance with Art. 5(4)); cf. *Wynne v UK* (1994) 19 EHRR 333 (no requirement for a continuing remedy in respect of mandatory life sentence prisoners).

4. ARTICLE 11

Article 11(1) states that 'Everyone has the right to freedom and peaceful assembly and to freedom of association with others.' This includes 'a right to form and join trade unions for the protection of his interests'. By Art. 11(2), 'no restrictions may be imposed other than such are prescribed by law and necessary in a democratic society in the interests of national security or public safety, for the prevention of disorder or crime, for the protection of health or morals or for the protection of the rights and freedoms of others'. This repeats many of the elements of Art. 10(2).[61] Article 11 'shall not prevent the imposition of lawful restrictions on the exercise of these rights by members of the armed forces, of the police or of the administration of the State'.[62]

Violations have been found where a state dissolved a political party.[63] In applying the exceptions, the same general approach is followed as under Arts 8, 9 and 10, and there is a particularly close relationship with Art. 10.[64] Issues have arisen in a variety of contexts dealt with in Part Two of this book, including limitations on public assembly and the banning of quasi-military and terrorist organisations[65] and in the banning of trade unions at GCHQ.[66]

---

[61] See below, Chap. 9.

[62] This, e.g., enables states to prohibit such persons from joining a union.

[63] *United Communist Party of Turkey v Turkey* (1998) 26 EHRR 121; *Socialist Party v Turkey* (1998) 27 EHRR 51. Cf. *Refah Partisi (The Welfare Party) v Turkey*, Judgment of 13 February 2003 (no breach in respect of dissolution of party whose programme furthering fundamentalist Islamic views including the introduction of Sharia law was regarded as threatening Convention rights and freedoms).

[64] See Chaps 7 and 9.   [65] See pp. 287, 304, 317, 322 and 417.

[66] See p. 846.

4

POLICING AND
POLICE POWERS

PART ONE. POLICING

1. INTRODUCTION

Many organisations and state bodies serve to protect civil liberties and also have the potential to infringe them. The most conspicuous group is the police.[1] Part One seeks to provide an understanding of the structure and organisation of the police so as to appreciate the impact they have on some citizens' most basic rights: liberty, protest and expression, privacy, etc.

An immediate problem in exploring the role of the police is that it is almost impossible to provide a comprehensive definition or explanation of their function in modern society. As Morgan and Newburn observe:

> Most realistic discussion of police work suggests that at the very least the police role includes: order maintenance; crime control; environmental and traffic functions; assistance in times of emergency; crime prevention; and conciliation in conflict resolution.[2]

How can an organisation playing such a diverse role in society be effectively monitored and assessed to ensure that it remains subject to the rule of law?

The central theme running throughout Part One of this chapter will be to consider the ways in which the police are accountable for their actions.[3] The task of balancing efficiency and effectiveness whilst protecting rights is increasingly complex and it is vital that the police remain answerable for their actions. Accountability arises through central government's imposition of organisational structure, through its requirement of consultation and local policing policies, and through financial control. The police must also remain accountable in law through the 'ordinary law of the land', i.e. paying damages when torts are committed, being prosecuted when crimes are committed. Finally, the police must provide a degree of self-regulation—as with other major organisations and professions. Part One concludes with a consideration of the problems associated with complaints and discipline within the police.

---

[1] For general information see www.police.uk/.

[2] R. Morgan and T. Newburn, *The Future of Policing* (1997), p. 74. See further the articles collected in R. Reiner, *Policing I* (1996), Part II, 'The Role of the Police in Practice'; R. Reiner, *The Future of Policing* (2000). For an illustration of the diversity see Home Office, *Diary of a Police Officer* (2001).

[3] See also Council of Europe 12th Proceedings, *Police Powers and Accountability in a Democratic Society* (1999); see also J. Cheung (2005) PJ 78(3).

2.   ACCOUNTABLE TO LAW

The following case was a landmark in requiring clear legal authority to be shown to justify invasions of the rights of others:

- **Entick v Carrington** (1765) 19 State Tr 1029, 2 Wils 275, 95 ER 807,
  Court of Common Pleas, Lord Camden CJ

On 6 November 1762, the Earl of Halifax, one of the principal Secretaries of State, issued a warrant to four King's messengers (Nathan Carrington, James Watson, Thomas Ardran and Robert Blackmore) 'to make strict and diligent search for John Entick, the author of, or one concerned in writing, several weekly very seditious papers, intitled the Monitor, or British Freeholder...; and him, having found you are to seize and apprehend, and to bring, together with his books and papers, in safe custody before me to be examined...' The messengers entered E's house, the outer door being open, apprehended him, and searched for his books and papers in rooms and in one bureau, one writing desk and several drawers. Where necessary these were broken open. They seized some books and papers and read others, remaining for about four hours. They then took E and the items seized to Lovel Stanhope, law-clerk to the Secretaries of State. E was released on 17 November. He subsequently brought an action in trespass against the messengers. The jury gave a special verdict and assessed the damages at £300. The defendants argued that their acts were done in obedience to a lawful warrant.

Lord Camden CJ: ... [I]f this point should be determined in favour of the jurisdiction, the secret cabinets and bureaus of every subject in this kingdom will be thrown open to the search and inspection of a messenger, whenever the secretary of state shall think fit to charge, or even to suspect, a person to be the author or, printer, or publisher of a seditious libel.

This power so assumed by the secretary of state is an execution upon all the party's papers, in the first instance. His house is rifled; his most valuable secrets are taken out of his possession, before the paper for which he is charged is found to be criminal by any competent jurisdiction, and before he is convicted either of writing, publishing, or being concerned in the paper. This power, so claimed by the secretary of state, is not supported by one single citation from any law book extant....

The arguments, which the defendants' counsel have thought fit to urge in support of this practice, are of this kind.

That such warrants have issued frequently since the Revolution, which practice has been found by the special verdict; ...

That the case of the warrants bears a resemblance to the-case of search for stolen goods.

They say too, that they have been executed without resistance upon many printers, booksellers, and authors who have quietly submitted to the authority; that no action hath hitherto been brought to try the right; and that although they have been often read upon the returns of Habeas Corpus, yet no court of justice has ever declared them illegal.

And it is further insisted, that this power is essential to government, and the only means of quieting clamours and sedition....

If it is law, it will be found in our books. If it is not to be found there, it is not law.

The great end, for which men entered into society, was to secure their property. That right is preserved sacred and incommunicable in all instances, where it has not been taken away or abridged by some public law for the good of the whole. The cases where this right of property is set aside by positive law, are various. Distresses, executions, forfeitures, taxes, &c. are all of this description; wherein every man by every common consent gives up that right, for the sake of justice and the general good. By the laws of England, every invasion of private property, be it ever so minute, is a trespass. No man can set his foot upon my ground without my licence, but he is liable to an action, though the damage be nothing; which is proved by every declaration in trespass, where the defendant is called upon to answer for bruising the grass and even treading upon the soil. If he admits the fact, he is bound to show by way of justification, that some positive law has empowered or excused him. The justification is submitted to the judges, who are to look into the books; and see if such a justification can be maintained by the text of the statute law, or by the principles of common law. If no such excuse can be found or produced, the silence of the books is an authority against the defendant, and the plaintiff must have judgment.

Where is the written law that gives any magistrate such a power? I can safely answer, there is none, and therefore it is too much for us without such authority to pronounce a practice legal, which would be subversive of all the comforts of society.

But though it cannot be maintained by any direct law, yet it bears a resemblance, as was urged, to the known case of search and seizure for stolen goods.

I answer, that the difference is apparent. In the one, I am permitted to seize my own goods, which are placed in the hands of a public officer, till the felon's conviction shall intitle me to restitution. In the other, the party's own property is seized before and without conviction, and he has no power to reclaim his goods, even after his innocence is cleared by acquittal.

The case of searching for stolen goods crept into the law by imperceptible practice. It is the only case of the kind that is to be met with. No less a person than my lord Coke (4 Inst. 176,) denied its legality; and therefore if the two cases resembled each other more than they do, we have no right, without an act of parliament, to adopt a new practice in the criminal law, which was never yet allowed from all antiquity.

Observe too the caution with which die law proceeds in this singular case....

I come now to the practice since the Revolution, which has been strongly urged, with this emphatical addition, that an usage tolerated from the era of liberty and continued downwards to this time through the ages of constitution, must necessarily have a legal commencement....

With respect to the practice itself; if it goes no higher, every lawyer will tell you, it is much too modern to be evidence of the common law; and if it should be added, that these warrants ought to acquire some strength by the silence of those Courts, which have heard them read so often upon return without censure or animadversion. I am able to borrow my answer to that pretence from the Court of King's-bench, which lately declared with great unanimity in the Case of General Warrants, that as no objection was taken to them upon the returns, and the matter passed *sub silentio*, the precedents were of no weight. I most heartily concur in that opinion;...

But still it is insisted, that there has been a general submission, and no action brought to try the right.

I answer, there has been a submission of guilt and poverty to power and the terror of punishment. But it would be strange doctrine to assert that all the people of this land are bound to acknowledge that to be universal law, which a few criminal booksellers have been afraid to dispute....

It is then said, that it is necessary for the ends of government to lodge such a power with a state officer; and that it is better to prevent the publication before than to punish the offender afterwards. I answer, if the legislature be of that opinion, they will revive the Licensing Act. But if they have not done that I conceive they are not of that opinion. And with respect to the argument of state necessity, or a distinction that has been aimed at between state offences and others, the common law does not understand that kind of reasoning, nor do our books take notice of any such distinction.

Serjeant Ashley was committed to the Tower in the 3d of Charles 1st, by the House of Lords only for asserting in argument, that there was a 'law of state' different from the common law; and the ShipMoney judges were impeached for holding, first that state-necessity would justify the raising money without consent of parliament; and secondly, that the king was judge of that necessity.

If the king himself has no power to declare when the law ought to be violated for reason of state, I am sure we his judges have no such prerogative...

[U]pon the whole we are all of opinion, that the warrant to seize and carry away the party's papers in the case of a seditious libel, is illegal and void....

NOTES

1. *Entick v Carrington* was one of four leading cases which followed the publication of No. 45 of the *North Briton*[4]—a weekly paper, of which John Wilkes was joint editor and a leading contributor. Its main purpose was to abuse and ridicule the recently appointed administration of the Earl of Bute. After No. 45 was published, the two Secretaries of State, Lords Egremont and Halifax, issued a general warrant for the arrest of its 'authors, printers and publishers'. Over 45 people were arrested under this warrant, including Wilkes. The warrant was held to be illegal, and damages were awarded for trespass.[5]

2. This case is a classic illustration of the principle that any public officer must be able to point to lawful authority for actions of his which infringe the rights of others, and not merely some general conception of state necessity. This is an important aspect of the rule of law. It also reflects an unwillingness to 'invent' or 'discover' lawful authority, which has not been shared by some judges in some more recent cases. For example, in *Chic Fashions (West Wales) Ltd v Jones*[6] the Court of Appeal held, contrary to previous authority,[7] that:

> when a constable enters a house by virtue of a search warrant for stolen goods, he may seize not only the goods which he reasonably believes to be covered by the warrant, but also any other goods which he believes on reasonable grounds to have been stolen and to be material evidence on a charge of stealing or receiving against the person in possession of them or anyone associated with him.[8]

Lord Denning MR noted, *inter alia*, there was 'ever-increasing wickedness...about' and that if a constable who came across stolen goods not mentioned in the warrant was forced to leave in order to obtain such a warrant 'in nine cases out of ten, by the time he came back...these other goods would have disappeared'.[9] These appear to be the kinds of arguments disapproved of in *Entick v Carrington*. More recently, reforms to PACE, s 8 provide for warrants to search unspecified premises. Does this erode the principle in *Entick v Carrrington*?

3. By contrast, the spirit of *Entick v Carrington* can be seen in the decisions of the House of Lords in *Morris v Beardmore*[10] and of the Divisional Court in *McLorie v Oxford*[11] (where *Ghani v Jones* was held not to have created a new right to *enter* premises as distinct from a right to *seize* goods). Moreover, a series of cases show that any unlawful act (subject to the *de minimis* principle) by a police officer will take him outside the execution of his duty.[12] In yet more recent cases, the courts have recognised the need for officers to explain more fully their reasons for entry to search to effect an arrest (PACE, s. 17), and to search after an arrest (s. 18).[13]

---

[4] See Sir William Holdsworth, *A History of English Law* (1938), Vol. X, pp. 659–672; G. Rudé, *Wilkes and Liberty* (1962), Chap. II; A. Williamson, *Wilkes, A Friend to Liberty* (1974), Chap. IV.

[5] See *Wilkes v Wood* (1763) 19 State Tr 1153; *Leach v Money* (1765) 19 State Tr 1002; and *Wilkes v Lord Halifax* (1769) 19 State Tr 1406.

[6] [1968] 2 QB 299.

[7] See L.H. Leigh, *Police Powers in England and Wales* (1975), pp. 189–190.

[8] Per Lord Denning MR at 313.

[9] Ibid.   [10] [1981] AC 446.

[11] [1982] QB 1290.   [12] See Part Two below.

[13] See *O'Loughlin v Chief Constable of Essex* [1998] 3 WLR 374; *Lineham v DPP* [2000] Crim LR 861 and commentary, both discussed in Part Two below.

3. POLICE STRUCTURE AND ORGANISATION[14]

The effectiveness of the control of the police can only be properly examined with an understanding of its structure and organisation. Similarly, the changes in the law relating to police powers discussed in Part Two must be seen against the background of substantial and significant developments in policing in the last 30 years.[15] As the diversity and potential intrusiveness of police activity increases, the organisational structure of the police has come under close scrutiny and been the subject of much debate. However, the comparative de-politicisation of the structure of governance has led to a period of relative calm in the last decade.

The current basic tripartite structure of police governance was established by the Police Act 1964, but this was subject to modification by the Police Act 1996. The 1964 Act established 43 police forces which remains the current model. The relationship between chief constables, local police authorities and the Home Secretary in the tripartite structure has been contested for many years and in general terms there has been a continuing drift towards increasing centralisation of power.

The Police Act 1996, s. 96(1), replacing the Police and Criminal Evidence Act 1984, s. 106(1), provides that:

Arrangements shall be made in each police area for obtaining the views of people in that area about matters concerning the policing of the area and for obtaining their co-operation with the police in preventing crime and anti social behaviour in the area.

In all areas, the police authority facilitates this co-operation after consultation with the chief constable.

(A) POLICE AUTHORITIES[16]

The major reforms effected by the Conservative Government in the Police and Magistrates' Courts Act 1994 took matters in a new direction, with a change from elected (or partly elected) police authorities to smaller, appointed police authorities.[17]

The police authority normally comprises 17 members.[18] Nine of these are to be members of a relevant council, and they are involved in the selection of the remaining eight independent members. Three of the selection panel members are appointed by the police authority and one is appointed by the Home Secretary. The fifth member, or independent assessor, is appointed by the other four members from a list compiled by the Home Secretary. One of

---

[14] See T. Jones, 'The governance and accountability of policing' in T. Newburn (ed.), *The Handbook of Policing* (2003). See also J. Cheung (2005) PJ 78(3).

[15] On the historical context see: C. Emsley, *The English Police: A Political and Social History* (2nd edn, 1996); R. Morgan and T. Newburn, *The Future of Policing* (1997), Chap. 1.

[16] See the Association of Police Authorities at www.apa.police.uk/apa.

[17] R. Morgan and T. Newburn, *The Future of Policing* (1997), Chap. 4; R. Sullivan, 'The Politics of British Policing in the Thatcher/Major State' (1998) 37 Howard Journal 300; E. McLaughlin, *The New Policing* (2007), Chap. 7.

[18] See Police Authority Regulations 2008.

the selected independent members must be a lay justice.[19] The chairman of the authority is appointed from among its members.[20]

It is the duty of every police authority 'to secure the maintenance of an efficient and effective police force for its area'[21] and 'hold the chief officer of police of that force to account for the exercise of his functions and those of persons under his direction and control'.[22] In discharging its functions, the authority must have regard to any strategic priorities determined by the Secretary of State and any plans or performance targets established by the authority.[23]

NOTES

1. At the outset of each financial year every police authority must issue a policing plan[24] setting out its policing objectives for the area during that year and proposed arrangements for a period of three years. The chief officer, when exercising independent direction and control of the force, must have regard to the policing plan. The Policing Plan Regulations 2008 state that the plan must include:

a) The police authority's expectations for the local police force: what it is expected to deliver in the three years covered by the plan in terms of both national and local policing priorities, the resources expected to be available, any planned increases in efficiency and productivity and how the force's performance will be measured and judged.

b) Any action taken or action that it plans to take to address the findings from audit and inspection reports, or following directions from the Home Secretary.

c) How they are exercising their duties as responsible authorities under the Crime and Disorder Act 1998 to consider the priorities agreed by local Crime and Disorder Reduction Partnerships (Community Safety Partnerships in Wales) in determining the policing contribution to be made to the three year CDRP plans and, in England only, Local Area Agreements. The regulations do not detract from the duty on police authorities to contribute to the development Crime and Disorder Plans.

d) Information on planned increases in efficiency and productivity and how the force proposes to meet any target set for increased efficiency and productivity

e) Information on collaborative working between the local police force and other forces, and any proposals to consider collaborative working arrangements between forces, should be included.

f) Any planned improvements in the delivery of protective services, and how those improvements will be delivered

g) Out-turn information for Statutory Performance Indicators (SPIs) in their policing plans. This will be in the abridged Best Value Performance Plan 2008/09...

Given that the authority must have regard to centrally determined performance targets, to what extent is the police authority independent of central government? Does the authority provide any more than a veneer of local accountability?

[19] Police Authority Regulations 2008, reg. 11.   [20] Ibid., reg. 12.

[21] Police Act 1996, s. 6(1).

[22] Ibid., inserted by the Police and Justice Act 2006, s. 2. See also Home Office, *Guidance on the handling of complaints relating to the direction and control of a police force by a Chief officer*, HO Circular 19/2005 (2005).

[23] The Police Authority must set local policing objectives under the Policing Plan Regulations 2008.

[24] Police Act 1996, s. 6ZB, inserted by the Police and Justice Act 2006, s. 2.

2. Police authorities are responsible for a police force's finance and therefore set the budget, in conjunction with the local authority, for that force.

3. The 2003 Home Office Report, *Policing: Building Safer Communities Together*, found that 9.2 per cent of police authority members, and 21.5 per cent of independent members, are now drawn from minority ethnic communities. Almost one-third of police authority members are women.[25]

(B) THE CHIEF CONSTABLE[26]

Section 10(1) of the Police Act 1996 provides that:

a police force maintained under section 2…shall be under the direction and control of the Chief Constable….

In discharging his or her functions, every chief constable shall have regard to the local policing plan.[27] The chief constable must submit an annual report on policing in that area to the police authority for which his force is maintained.[28] The chief constable is appointed by the police authority, but subject to the approval of the Secretary of State and such regulations as may be made under Police Act 1996, s. 50. The authority, also with the approval of the Secretary of State, may call upon the chief constable to retire 'in the interests of efficiency or effectiveness'.[29] Civilian employees of the authority are normally under the direction and control of the chief constable.[30]

The Criminal Justice and Police Act 2001 requires every police force to appoint a deputy chief constable, and provides for the appropriate powers for the deputy to exercise functions of the chief constable.[31] Performance monitoring and evaluation against national and local performance indicators are the responsibility of chief officers.

NOTES

1. Jones and Newburn suggest that the operational independence of the chief constable, which was threatened by the local authorities in the 1980s, has now come to be threatened by central government.[32] Given the policing objectives specified above, is it realistic to expect chief constables to have significantly different approaches to policing? To what extent can an individual chief constable's approach to policing still make a difference to the way his force operates? (Consider, for example, the policy of zero-tolerance policing in Cleveland, or the policing of Greater Manchester under James Anderton.) Does diversity diminish accountability?

2. Following criticism of the Humberside police in the Bichard Inquiry[33] for failing to pass on details of the Soham murderer, Ian Huntley, to the Cambridgeshire police that may have

---

25 Home Office, *Policing: Building Safer Communities Together* (2003), para. 5.42.

26 See D. Wall, *The Chief Constables in England and Wales* (1998); R. Reiner, *The Chief Constable* (1991).

27 Police Act 1996, s. 10(2).   28 Police Act 1996, s. 22(1).

29 Police Act 1996, s. 11(2). See the resignation in 1998 of Ian Oliver, the Chief Constable of Grampian, after criticism of the force for its conduct of a murder investigation. See also the resignation of P. Whitehouse from Sussex Police, June 2001; and the resignation of Terry Grange from Dyfed-Powys in November 2007.

30 Police Act 1996, s. 15(2).   31 Police Act 1996, ss. 123 and 124.

32 *Policing After the Act* (above), p. 6.

33 The Bichard Inquiry, *An independent inquiry arising from the Soham murders* (2004).

prevented him gaining employment in the victims' school, the Home Secretary requested that the local police authority suspend the chief constable. Following their refusal to do so the Home Secretary threatened legal action under the Police Reform Act 2002. Any ensuing case would have provided a clear answer as to the extent of the police authority's diminishing powers in the face of the increasingly powerful Home Secretary. However, a compromise was reached which allowed the chief constable to remain in post albeit with an earlier retirement date. Does this episode reflect the police authority's diminishing power or does it suggest that the tripartite structure is robust and operating effectively?

3. The Association of Chief Police Officers (ACPO), which has the status of a private company, claims to be 'an independent, professionally led strategic body. In the public interest and, in equal and active partnership with Government and the Association of Police Authorities, ACPO leads and coordinates the direction and development of the police service in England, Wales and Northern Ireland.'[34] Its members are police officers who hold the rank of chief constable, deputy chief constable or assistant chief constable and it wields a considerable degree of influence. ACPO sits outside of the tripartite structure but given its coordination in 'direction and development' does this undermine the system of accountability?

(C) THE SECRETARY OF STATE

In addition to the numerous powers already mentioned, the Secretary of State has power to determine the annual aggregate of grants and the amount of the grant to be made to each authority;[35] make regulations for police forces;[36] appoint inspectors of constabulary;[37] provide and maintain or contribute to the provision or maintenance of common organisations, facilities or services (e.g. training and hardware).[38]

The Secretary of State's position in the tripartite arrangements has, over the years, become increasingly significant. Key policing priorities and how they are to be measured are outlined in the Home Secretary's National Policing Plan, which clearly has enormous impact across the force. Apart from formal legal powers, significant influence is maintained through Home Office circulars and arrangements for inspection by HM Inspectors of Constabulary, central assistance for police authorities in satisfying policing priorities through the National Policing Improvement Agency,[39] and indirectly by its influence with ACPO. The Local Government Act 1999 gives the Secretary of State additional powers to order inspection of a police authority regarding its 'Best Value'—i.e. its efficient supply of services. This further control is another example of managerialism in policing control which has become a common theme. Is the *financial* accountability of the police a primary concern?

Despite the Home Secretary's very wide and diverse powers, it is nevertheless important to note that the Secretary of State (like police authorities) has only limited powers to give directions, and these do not extend to *operational* matters.

---

[34] www.acpo.police.uk.
[35] Police Act 1996, ss. 46, 47, 48. Annual funding figures for police forces are available from the Home Office. See www.homeoffice.gov.uk/ppd/pru/pgranta.htm/.
[36] Police Act 1996, s. 50.   [37] Police Act 1996, s. 54.
[38] Police Act 1996, s. 57, amended by the Criminal Justice and Immigration Act 2008, s. 128(1).
[39] Established under the Police and Justice Act 2006. See www.npia.police.uk.

(D) HER MAJESTY'S INSPECTORATE
OF CONSTABULARY

Another mechanism for internal review and accountability of the police exists in the shape of Her Majesty's Inspectorate of Constabulary. HMIC was established 150 years ago, and it now derives its powers from the Police Act 1996, s. 54. It is responsible for examining the efficiency and effectiveness of the police service. It is independent of the tripartite structure. The role of the Inspectorate is defined in the Police Acts (1994 and 1996) and the Local Government Act 1999, relating to 'Best Value', and further powers of inspection and report are contained in the Police Reform Act 2002.

HMIC plays an important role in ensuring police accountability. It describes its function as:

(a) The formal inspection and assessment of the 43 police forces in England and Wales; the Police Service of Northern Ireland (supporting the Chief Inspector of Criminal Justice in Northern Ireland); ... and the Serious Organised Crime Agency. Thematic inspections are also undertaken, some in conjunction with other bodies, especially the other Criminal Justice System Inspectorates.

(b) HMIC plays a key advisory role within the tripartite system (Home Office, chief officer and police authority/Northern Ireland Policing Board), where its independence and professional expertise are recognised by all parties. HMIs also provide a crucial link between forces and the Home Office, and, as the Home Secretary's principal professional police adviser, HMCIC links directly with the Home Office Crime Reduction and Community Safety Group.

(c) HMIC advises the Home Secretary on senior appointments in the Police Service, via the Senior Appointments Panel which HMCIC chairs.[40]

NOTE

1. In 2005 HMIC[41] recommended that the existing structure of 43 police forces be reformed and reduced.

... when viewed from the context of the range of challenges and future threats now facing the service and the communities it polices, the 43 force structure is no longer fit for purpose. In the interests of the efficiency and effectiveness of policing it should change. Whilst some smaller forces do very well, and some larger forces less so, our conclusion is that below a certain size there simply is not a sufficient critical mass to provide the necessary sustainable level of protective services that the 21st century increasingly demands.[42]

Proposals for such changes were included in the Police and Justice Bill 2005 but met with considerable opposition from both police forces and police authorities. Despite financial incentives to put forward business cases for police area mergers, no police authority did so. In 2006 the proposals were withdrawn. Clearly such mergers would impact on local accountability and though the retention of 43 areas might be seen as a victory for local accountability the trend towards centralisation and accountability through auditing continues.

---

[40] HMIC, *The Role of Her Majesty's Inspectorate of Constabulary* (2008), available at: http://inspectorates. homeoffice.gov.uk/hmic/.

[41] HMIC, *Closing the Gap: A Review of the Fitness for Purpose of the Current Structure of Policing in England & Wales* (2005).

[42] Ibid., para. 1.60.

(E) CONSTABULARY INDEPENDENCE

Despite the increasing statutory obligations of consultation and greater direction in broader areas from central government, much is still made of the so-called doctrine of 'constabulary independence' articulated most forcefully by Lord Denning MR in *R v Metropolitan Police Comr, ex p Blackburn*:[43]

> I have no hesitation in holding that, like every constable in the land, he should be, and is, independent of the executive. He is not subject to the orders of the Secretary of State, save that under the Police Act 1964, the Secretary of State can call upon him to give a report, or to retire in the interests of efficiency. I hold it to be the duty of the Commissioner of Police of the Metropolis, as it is of every Chief Constable, to enforce the law of the land. He must take steps so to post his men that crimes may be detected; and that honest citizens may go about their affairs in peace. He must decide whether or not suspected persons are to be prosecuted: and if need be, bring the prosecution or see that it is brought. But in all these things he is not the servant of anyone, save of the law itself. No Minister of the Crown can tell him that he must, or must not, keep observation on this place or that; or that he must, or must not, prosecute this man or that one. Nor can any police authority tell him so. The responsibility for law enforcement lies on him. He is answerable to the law and to the law alone. That appears sufficiently from *Fisher v Oldham Corporation* [1930] 2 KB 364, and *Attorney-General for New South Wales v Perpetual Trustee* Co *Ltd* [1955] AC 457, PC.

Lustgarten[44] commented that 'seldom have so many errors of law and logic been compressed into one paragraph'. Among these are the points that the Commissioner of Police of the Metropolis was not a constable, was not subject to the Police Act 1964 powers and has been given orders by the Secretary of State.[45] Moreover, the cases cited merely stood for the proposition (in effect bypassed by s. 48 of the Police Act 1964) that there is no master and servant relationship between a police officer and the police authority.[46] Nevertheless:

> the reality is that *Blackburn No. 1* has over nearly two decades embedded itself in the lore and learning of both judges and police, and it is inconceivable that, without parliamentary intervention, the courts would resile from the position they have reached.[47]

Note that it is a perfectly respectable principle of administrative law that, where a discretion is conferred on a particular official or body, he or it may not act under the dictation of a third party and may not fetter the exercise of that discretion by self-created rules of policy.[48] This applies as much to insulate police constables in the exercise of their powers 'from dictation by superiors as it does to insulate chief constables from dictation by the executive'. Is this the true essence of constabulary independence?[49] In *Ex p Blackburn*, Lord Denning MR indicated that, in extreme cases, such as a directive from a chief constable 'that no person should be prosecuted for stealing any goods less than £100 in value',

---

[43] [1968] 2 QB 118 at 135–136.   [44] *The Governance of Police* (1986), pp. 64–67.

[45] See now Police Act 1996, s. 50 and the Greater London Authority Act 1999, ss. 315, 317–320. All Commissioners are now police officers.

[46] In *White v Chief Constable of South Yorkshire* [1999] 1 All ER 1, HL it was accepted that police officers are not servants of the chief constable (see Lord Steyn at 36). The tortious liability is discussed below; note that the chief constable is liable for the torts of his officers: Police Act 1996, s. 88.

[47] Lustgarten, op. cit., p. 67.

[48] See, generally, Sir William Wade and C. Forsyth, *Administrative Law* (9th edn, 2004).

[49] Cf. Lustgarten, op. cit., pp. 13–15.

the courts might interfere.[50] In the case itself, the Commissioner's decision not to enforce certain gaming laws had already been rescinded, and no order of mandamus (an order compelling action from the Commissioner) was granted. In subsequent cases, the courts have declined to intervene.[51] Decisions to prosecute may be subject to judicial review but the courts are similarly reluctant to interfere.

4. POLICE ACCOUNTABILITY THROUGH AUDITING

(A) 'MANAGERIAL' AND 'CONSUMERIST' POLICING

The preceding paragraphs have noted changes in police accountability tending towards managerialist and consumerist models. The changes outlined have seen police authorities becoming free-standing organisations, separated from the local authority, with the responsibility of drawing up local policing plans, setting objectives and targets, and establishing the budget. The chief constable is consulted in the drawing up of the police plan and has a degree of autonomy as to how to allocate his budget. The Home Secretary continues to measure police performance in terms of efficiency through HMIC and standardises performance and best practice through the NPIA and the issuance of Codes of Practice and Home Office Circulars. The question that follows is whether such performance management leads the police to concentrate on activities which have measurable results at the expense of other forms of policing, or whether such evaluation leads to a greater need to explain and justify performance and therefore enhanced accountability.

Whilst initially continuing the trend towards centralisation the Labour Government has, more recently, viewed police management from the centre as potentially counter productive. It has viewed crime prevention as needing greater involvement from local communities.[52] In 2003 the Government's new focus was outlined in *Policing: Building Safer Communities Together*.

> 5.12 We want to explore greater, effective delegation to police leaders at the BCU [Basic Command Unit] level—in terms of deploying resources and taking operational decisions for example—so that they can be more responsive to local needs.
>
> 5.13 BCU commanders and their staff could consider ways of ensuring better local engagement in discussing local priorities through visible and genuinely inclusive arrangements. We are aware that there are good examples now of community consultation and engagement carried out by BCU commanders. But we want this to develop into a process which genuinely helps shape local policing decisions—and a practice which is embedded in police forces across England and Wales
>
> 5.15 In terms of officers ultimately in charge of their police forces, the Government is clear that in wanting to clarify and strengthen accountability arrangements, it is not seeking to interfere in operational decisions which are the right and duty of chief officers to take—a position which is enshrined in law.

---

[50] Ibid., p. 136.

[51] *R v Metropolitan Police Comr, ex p Blackburn (No. 3)* [1973] QB 241; *R v Chief Constable of Devon and Cornwall, ex p CEGB* [1982] QB 458.

[52] See M. Docking, *Public perceptions of police accountability and decision making*, Home Office Online Report 38/03 (2003).

Police forces are under the 'direction and control' of their chief officer—not politicians. The political impartiality of the police is absolutely vital for public confidence.

5.16 But the Government is similarly clear that chief officers and their forces are accountable to the communities they serve…we believe that the often-used term 'operational independence' is in fact a stumbling block in talking about accountability of the police service. We believe that instead we should begin focusing on the *operational responsibility* of chief officers—because to say 'independence' suggests a lack of accountability. Chief officers are in charge of, and have responsibility for, day to day operational decisions. The police exercise important powers and must be capable of being held to account for the way in which they are used. But more than this, chief officers should be accountable, and be seen to be accountable, for reform of the police service, the positive development of policing in general and working with police authorities in terms of the performance of their particular force. This is what we mean by *operational responsibility*.

5.30 We are committed to strengthening the existing accountability arrangements for policing; to building a more 'bottom up' approach—in which the public can engage and hold to account those responsible for community safety. This is vital for community confidence.

5.35 Community safety is not just a matter for the police. Other bodies, such as local authorities and the emergency services, have an important role too. Effective partnership working between all the relevant bodies, with strong accountability mechanisms, are key to lasting, sustainable community safety.

5.37 Partnerships are crucial to the success of our overall policing agenda—they are key in terms of helping to hold the police to account, on behalf of communities. But they are also important in supporting the police and helping them do their job more effectively.

NOTES

1. Basic Command Units are now at the forefront of community and neighbourhood policing. There are now over 300 BCUs in England and Wales varying in size from over 1000 officers to fewer than 100. In order to more effectively fulfill their role the chief constable has devolved greater decision-making powers to BCU commanders.

2. Neighbourhood Policing Teams[53] are now commonplace and include uniformed police, community support officers, special constables, other neighbourhood wardens, and other authority figures such as security guards. The aim of such teams is to provide increased police visibility on the streets.[54] Morgan and Newburn have confirmed earlier research findings that people continue to press for more visible police foot patrols:[55] 'presented with a choice, [the public] would choose problem-solving over crime fighting as the approach the police should adopt'.[56] Is the 'customer' always right? Do such reform measures reflect a move towards greater 'localisation' of policing or is this simply a way of masking increased centralisation of power?

3. The local policing plan produced by the police authority must give details of the proposals for compliance with the 'best value' requirements of the Local Government Act 1999, Pt I.[57] The Act places a responsibility on all police authorities to ensure best value in all local policing services, i.e. that all local services are continually under review for improvement having regard to economy, efficiency and effectiveness.[58] In addition, all the accounts

---

[53] Home Office, *Neighbourhood policing your police; your community; our commitment* (2005).

[54] B. Loveday and A. Reid, *Going Local: Who should run Britain's police?* (2003).

[55] Op. cit., p. 102.   [56] Op. cit., p. 102.   [57] Ss. 21–29.

[58] On 'Best Value', see Home Office, *Best Value—The Police Authority Role* (1999): 'A key principle of best value is that local people should be the judge of the services they receive' (p. 3). Section 6 of the Local

of the police authority are subject to audit in accordance with the Audit Commission Act 1998.[59] Best Value adds to the other statutory obligations of consultation by requiring police authorities to consult with service users (local businesses, other criminal justice agencies, etc.). The courts have also acknowledged that the *efficient use* of resources is a proper matter for the police to consider when deploying its officers: *R v Chief Constable of Sussex, ex p Independent Traders Ferry Ltd.*[60] This empowers chief constables considerably.

4. In 2004[61] the Home Office reiterated its consumerist approach:

1.4 The main thrust of our reforms is to pass power from the political centre to local citizens and communities, to create new democratic accountabilities and scrutiny, and to reinforce the role of elected councillors in local policing…

1.32 The Government will seek to improve markedly the responsiveness and customer service culture of the police.

A fundamental question underpinning this consumerist and community policing drive is whether the Government's aim is to provide local communities with the policing policies they desire, or merely to alter the public's perception of policing policy. Reiner argues that:

In the past thirty years the process of growing acceptance of the police in Britain has been reversed. A number of changes have plunged them into acute controversy and conflict: corruption and miscarriage of justice scandals; accusations of race and sex discrimination; increasing public disorder and the militarization of police tactics; rising crime and an apparently declining police ability to deal with it; decreasing public accountability as forces have grown larger, more centralised and more reliant on technology. In recent years the leadership of police forces has recognised this problem and tried to introduce reforms to deal with it. They have sought to professionalise management standards, improve training, streamline working procedures, and become more open to the public through consultation of various kinds. They have tried to re-orient the culture of policing around an explicit mission of service and an ethos of consumerism.[62]

To what extent can the assessments of efficiency provide a valid indicator of the success of the police from the perspective of civil liberties? This forms part of a much broader question about the production of policing plans. Fielding observes that:

Because the resolution of conflict is central to the community police mission, and conflict is unpredictable, police initiated activity is hard to plan. It is therefore difficult to define a set of concrete tasks for community police.[63]

It is questionable whether it is possible, useful, or even appropriate to provide performance indicators for policing. 'If policing consists of a large number of diverse tasks then

Government Act requires the authority to publish an annual 'Best Value Performance Plan' covering a five-year period. The Act also empowers HMIC to inspect a police authority regarding its Best Value plan.

[59] See *Best Value—The Police Authority Role* (1999); A. Leigh, G. Mundy and R. Tuffin, *Best Value Policing: Making Preparations* (1999).

[60] [1998] 3 WLR 1260, HL.

[61] Home Office, *Building Communities, Beating Crime: A better police service for the 21st century* (Cm 6360, 2004).

[62] R. Reiner, 'Policing and the Police' in M. Maguire, R. Morgan and R. Reiner (eds), *Oxford Handbook of Criminology* (2nd edn, 1997), p. 1036 (references omitted).

[63] *Community Policing* (1995), p. 45.

clearly there can be no single or overall measure of police performance.'[64] In addition, there remains the underlying question: to what extent is an economically efficient police force a 'better' police force?

5. JUDICIAL SCRUTINY OF POLICING

Issues as to the *legality* (as distinct from the propriety) of police action may arise in a number of contexts. We give here some examples of the situations that are most likely to occur—actions in tort, criminal prosecutions and through judicial review. Note that breach of PACE Codes of Practice (discussed in Part Two) will not of itself give rise to liability in crime or tort: s. 67(10).

Bringing the police 'to book' through the courts is a very clear demonstration that they are subject to the rule of law, but are the obstacles inherent in the process of litigation too oner-ous for it to be an effective mechanism for securing accountability? It is important to note that few tort claims ever go to court.

(A) ACTIONS IN TORT

A citizen may sue a police officer for trespass to the person (assault; false imprisonment), trespass to goods or trespass to land, and the officer may seek to establish the defence that he had lawful authority for this action. Conversely, a police officer may wish to sue a citizen for assaulting him.

(I) MALICE?

There are a number of tortious actions that may be brought provided the claimant establishes malice, with the most obvious being a claim for malicious prosecution against a police offi-cer. The claimant must show that the criminal process was set in motion against him without reasonable and probable cause, that it was done maliciously (i.e. with spite or ill will against the claimant, or a motive other than bringing someone to justice), and that he suffered dam-age as a result.[65] Obviously, the criminal proceedings must have terminated in favour of the claimant.[66]

An officer might also be liable for the tort of misfeasance in public office as in *Elliott v Chief Constable of Wiltshire*,[67] where an officer disclosed a person's convictions for an improper purpose and with intent to injure. See also the (discontinued) prosecution of a senior police officer for misfeasance where he used police vehicles to taxi his family to school, shops, etc.[68]

---

[64] C. Horton and D. Smith, *Evaluating Police Work* (1988), p. 21. See also K. Thompson, 'Examining the prop-osition that police efficiency and legal and community accountability are inextricably interdependent' (1996) 69(2) Pol J 131.

[65] On non-police witnesses who lie being sued for malicious prosecution, see *Martin v Watson* [1996] AC 74, HL.

[66] See *Smith v Chief Constable of Sussex* [1999] CLY 4852, where police were held to have had no honest suspicion for arrest during which they assaulted C. See also the damages of £2,000 for malicious prosecu-tion of D, not affected by his conduct on arrest: *Clark v Chief Constable of Cleveland* (1999) 7 May, CA (Civ D).

[67] (1996) Times, 5 December.

[68] (2001) JPN 500.

(II) NEGLIGENCE

The police have always been subject to proceedings in negligence for activities they undertake other than the investigation of crime *per se*, as for example in failing to take reasonable care of prisoners or for negligence in driving. As in any negligence claim, the claimant would have to establish a duty of care, breach of that duty and a resultant loss to a recognised interest. The House of Lords in *Hill v Chief Constable of West Yorkshire*[69] established a 'blanket immunity' for negligence in police action regarding the job of fighting crime. In *Hill*, the plaintiff was the mother of a victim of the serial-killer Peter Sutcliffe, the 'Yorkshire Ripper'. She claimed that the police had been negligent in failing to apprehend him after his earlier killings, as a result of which her daughter, one of his later victims, was murdered. The House of Lords, heavily influenced by considerations of policy, held that police forces owe no general duty of care to the general public to identify or apprehend an unknown criminal. This was applied in cases such as *Alexandrou v Oxford*[70] (no claim where police fail to attend and deal with burglar alarm).

The *Hill* immunity came under attack from the European Court of Human Rights.[71] In the bizarre case of *Osman v Ferguson*,[72] the offender had formed an obsessive attachment to a former pupil (the claimant) and had become violent towards the claimant and his family and their property. The police were alerted to this but did not detain the offender until he had shot and killed the father of the claimant. A civil claim against the police was struck out by the Court of Appeal, holding that although there was a 'very close degree of proximity amounting to a special relationship',[73] nevertheless, 'the House of Lords decision on public policy in *Hill*'s case dooms this action to failure'.[74] The English Court of Appeal had treated *Hill v Chief Constable of Yorkshire* as granting blanket immunity to the police. The case was taken to the European Court of Human Rights,[75] where it was held, unanimously, that there was a denial of the right to a fair trial under Art. 6.[76] The blanket immunity was an 'unjustified restriction on an applicant's right to have a determination on the merits of his or her claim against the police in deserving cases'. This decision was the subject of considerable criticism.[77]

(III) DAMAGES

Police forces paid out more than £44 million in compensation and damages in the period 2002–07.[78] Clayton et al.[79] list many cases of damages awards against the police. For earlier

---

[69] [1989] 1 AC 53, HL.   [70] [1993] 4 All ER 328.

[71] *Osman v UK* (1998) 29 EHRR 245.

[72] [1993] 4 All ER 344, CA.   [73] Per McCowan LJ at 350.

[74] Ibid., at p. 354.

[75] See comments on the case: R. Bernstein, 'Police Immunity Undermined' (1999) 143 SJ 10; E. Morgan, 'Police Immunity, Public Policy and Proportionality' (1999) 149 NLJ 13.

[76] The Court also considered, but rejected, a claim under Art. 2—protecting the right to life.

[77] See, e.g., T. Weir [1999] 58 CLJ 4; the speech of Lord Browne-Wilkinson in *Barrett v Enfield London Borough Council* [1999] 3 All ER 193 at 198; see also L. Hoyano (1999) MLR 912. On the police duty of care to witnesses, see *Van Colle v Chief Constable of Hertfordshire* Police [2008] UKHL 50. See also *Woolgar v Chief Constable of Sussex Police* [1999] 3 All ER 604; *Carnduff v Chief Constable of West Midlands Police* [2001] 1 WLR 1786; *Reeves v Metropolitan Police Comr* [1999] 3 All ER 897; *Kirkham v Chief Constable of Greater Manchester Police* [1990] 2 QB 283, CA.

[78] (2007) Times, 3 December.

[79] R. Clayton, H. Tomlinson, E. Bucket and A. Davies, *Civil Actions against the Police* (3rd edn, 2005). See also A. Sanders and R. Young, *Criminal Justice* (3rd edn, 2007), Chap. 12.

examples, see the 4th edition of this work. These cases all turn on their own facts, and what is more significant is that the Court of Appeal has laid down guidelines governing directions to juries on the appropriate levels of damages to be awarded.

- **Thompson v Metropolitan Police Comr** [1998] QB 498, Court of Appeal[80]

The case involved two co-joined appeals relating to damages awards against the Metropolitan Police Commissioner. In the case involving Mr Hsu, three officers assaulted Mr Hsu when he attempted to prevent them entering his house. His arms were twisted behind his back, he was placed in a headlock, he was punched in the face, struck across the face with a set of keys and kicked in the back (he later passed blood in his urine). He was also racially abused. His neighbours, a former lodger, and her father observed part of this conduct. He had a most uncomfortable journey to the police station, where he was placed in a cell for about one and a quarter hours. He was refused police transport home, although he had nothing on his feet. A friend took him home only to find that, in his absence, his house had been entered and, in addition to the belongings of the lodger being removed, some of his own property was missing. Mr Hsu sustained cuts, bruises and a stiff neck. He had a predisposition to depression and was socially and culturally isolated and, three years after the incident, he was still suffering some symptoms of a post-traumatic stress disorder which would be alleviated by the disposal of this litigation. His award was reduced from £220,000 to £35,000.

Miss Thompson was lawfully arrested for a drink and driving offence to which she later pleaded guilty. 'Considerable and unnecessary' force was used to place Miss T in a cell with four or five officers involved. In the course of this, hair was pulled out and, in Miss Thompson's own words, 'it was like I was being abused physically and sexually by all of them'. As a result of this assault, in addition to the loss of hair, Miss Thompson was bruised and had pain in the back and hands. Her award of £45,000 was upheld.

> **Lord Woolf MR:** This is the judgment of the court.
> [After reviewing the circumstances in which the Court of Appeal can interfere with the jury's assessment of damages, and drawing comparisons with the Court of Appeal's preparedness to intervene in defamation awards.]
>
> While there is no formula which is appropriate for all cases and the precise form of a summing-up is very much a matter within the discretion of the Trial Judge, it is suggested that in many cases it will be convenient to include in a summing-up on the issue of damages additional directions on the following lines. As we mention later in this judgment we think it may often be wise to take the jury's verdict on liability before they receive directions as to quantum.
>
> ...
>
> In a straightforward case of wrongful arrest and imprisonment the starting point is likely to be about £500 for the first hour during which the plaintiff has been deprived of his or her liberty. After the first hour an additional sum is to be awarded, but that sum should be on a reducing scale so as to keep the damages proportionate with those payable in personal injury cases and because the plaintiff is entitled to have a higher rate of compensation for the initial shock of being arrested. As a guideline we consider, for example, that a plaintiff who has been wrongly kept in custody for twenty-four hours should for this alone normally be regarded as entitled to an award of about £3,000. For subsequent days the daily rate will be on a progressively reducing scale. [These figures are lower than those mentioned by the Court of Appeal of Northern Ireland in *Oscar v Chief Constable of The Royal Ulster Constabulary* (1993) unreported, where a figure of about £600 per hour was thought to be appropriate for the first 12 hours. *That case, however*

---

[80] See G. Smith (1997) 147 NLJ 287, 319.

only involved unlawful detention for two periods of 30 minutes in respect of which the Court of Appeal of Northern Ireland awarded £300 for the first period and £200 for the second period. On the other hand, the approach is substantially more generous than that adopted by this court in the unusual case of *Cumber v Hoddinott* [(1995) 23 January (unreported) in which this court awarded £350 global damages where the jury had awarded no compensatory damages and £50 exemplary damages.]

...

Where exemplary damages are appropriate they are unlikely to be less than £5,000. Otherwise the case is probably not one which justifies an award of exemplary damages at all. In this class of action the conduct must be particularly deserving of condemnation for an award of as much as £25,000 to be justified and the figure of £50,000 should be regarded as the absolute maximum, involving directly officers of at least the rank of superintendent.

...

The figures given will of course require adjusting in the future for inflation. We appreciate that the guideline figures depart from the figures frequently awarded by juries at the present time. However they are designed to establish some relationship between the figures awarded in this area and those awarded for personal injuries. In giving guidance for aggravated damages we have attached importance to the fact that they are intended to be compensatory and not punitive although the same circumstances may justify punishment.

NOTES

1. Are the sums awarded to the claimants in this case adequate? Would higher awards deter the police from unlawful activity? In *Gerald v Metropolitan Police Comr*[81] the Court of Appeal held that the *Thompson* guidelines as to amount are not a rigid code and are not to be applied in a mechanistic manner, they do no more than provide for jury directions as to normal brackets for basic damages and maxima for aggravated and exemplary damages. See also the £50,000 out of court settlement in *Rutherford v Chief Constable of Kent*,[82] where the officers had falsified records and assaulted R. Is it better to spend such sums on rectifying the wrongdoings of forces or to invest it in improving future policing?[83]

2. Where claimants had been assaulted in the course of their attempted escape from prison, they were entitled to aggravated but not exemplary damages: *Russell v Home Office*.[84] In *Isaac v Chief Constable for West Midlands Police*[85] the court held that there was nothing in *Thompson* that suggested that where an award of exemplary damages was made, it followed that an award of aggravated damages was also to be made.

3. In civil actions for damages, once the claimant has proved the wrong it is for the defendant to establish any justification in law.[86] However, if the defendant establishes the statutory conditions for the exercise of power which would justify the trespass, and the essence of the claimant's complaint is that there has been an *ultra vires* abuse of discretion, the onus lies on the claimant to establish the relevant facts.[87] Most of the cases in this

---

[81] (1998) Times, 26 June, CA.   [82] (2001) Times 15 May.

[83] On compensation arrangements following miscarriages of justice, see N. Taylor, *Victims of Miscarriages of Justice* (with J. Wood) in C. Walker and K. Starmer, *Miscarriages of Justice: A Review of Justice in Error* (1999); N. Taylor [2003] JCL 220.

[84] [2001] All ER (D) 38 (Mar), CA (Civ D).   [85] [2001] All ER (D) 331 (Jul), CA (Civ D).

[86] *R v IRC, ex p Rossminster Ltd* [1980] 1002 at 1011, HL, per Lord Diplock.

[87] *Greene v Secretary of State for Home Affairs* [1942] AC 284, HL, as explained in *R v Governor of Brixton Prison* [1969] 2 QB 222, DC. See, generally, Sir William Wade and C. Forsyth, *Administrative Law* (9th edn, 2004), Chap. 12.

area have issues as to whether the relevant statutory conditions have been fulfilled—commonly, whether an officer is able to satisfy the court that he has had 'reasonable cause' for his actions. An example is the successful appeal by the Chief Constable of West Yorkshire against the award of damages to P, who was bitten by a police dog during arrest. The Court of Appeal held that the use of a properly trained dog was not unreasonable force to effect an arrest of youths who had been smashing streetlights.[88] Following the HRA the police (as a public authority) are required to act in compliance with the ECHR, and they will need to be able to show that the uses of their powers which infringe human rights are 'proportionate' to the aim pursued.

4. The Police Authority is also liable to pay compensation where damage or loss occurs as a result of 'civil commotion': see the Riot (Damages) Act 1886, s. 2(1).

5. The Police Act 1996 s. 88 provides that a chief constable is vicariously liable in respect of torts committed by constables under his direction and control in the performance or purported performance of their functions. This is the equivalent of an employer's liability for employees' torts, but no relationship of employer/employee, or principal and agent is created by the Act.[89] The ability to sue the chief constable is also important where the individual officer is not identifiable. See, for example, the claim for personal injuries sustained by a football supporter hit by a police truncheon without cause. The officer was recorded on CCTV hitting W: *Wilson v Metropolitan Police Comr.*[90] An award of exemplary damages may be made against a chief officer found liable under s. 88.[91]

6. Under s. 6 of the Constables Protection Act 1750, a police officer has a good defence to an action brought against him in respect of 'any thing done in obedience to any action brought under the hand or seal of any justice of the peace ... notwithstanding any defect of jurisdiction in such justice'. The protection extends to 'any person or persons acting by his order and in his aid'. The defence is, however, only available if the limits of the warrant have been strictly observed. If this defence is available, the possible cause of action will be for malicious prosecution.[92]

7. Following the fatal shooting of Jean Charles de Menezes at Stockwell tube station in July 2005 the Metropolitan Police were prosecuted under the Health and Safety at Work etc. Act 1974.[93] Section 3 states: 'It shall be the duty of every employer to conduct his undertaking in such a way as to ensure, so far as is reasonably practicable, that persons not in his employment who may be affected thereby are not thereby exposed to risks to their health or safety.' The Metropolitan Police were fined £175,000.

(B) STATISTICS ON CIVIL ACTIONS

Remarkably there are no figures available for the whole of England and Wales in relation to civil actions against the police. The Metropolitan Police Service provided the following statistics in its 2007–08 *Annual Report*:[94]

---

[88] *Pollard v Chief Constable of West Yorkshire* [1999] PIQR 219.

[89] *Farah v Metropolitan Police Comr* [1997] 2 WLR 824; *White v Chief Constable of South Yorkshire* [1991] 1 All ER 1.

[90] (2001) 6 July.   [91] *Rowlands v Chief Constable of Merseyside Police* [2006] EWCA Civ 1773.

[92] See *Reynolds v Metropolitan Police Comr* [1984] 3 All ER 649.

[93] IPCC, *Stockwell One: Investigation into the shooting of Jean Charles de Menezes at Stockwell Underground Station on July 22nd 2005* (2007), p. 6.

[94] Metropolitan Police Service, *Policing London Annual Report 2007/08* (2008).

THREATENED/CIVIL ACTIONS AND DAMAGE PAID

	2005–06	2006–07	2007–08
Actions received			
Civil actions	50	78	108
Threatened actions	433	446	400
Number of threatened &			
civil action cases settled			
Settled civil actions	40	48	57
Settled threatened actions	82	85	83
Court awards	4	5	4
Settlement amount			
Settled civil actions	£1,149,992	£1,057,828	£508,299
Settled threatened actions	£760,015	£274,603	£392,376
Court awards	£24,370	£62,500	£16,000

To what extent are tort claims, which are primarily concerned with securing compensation for claimants, an effective mechanism for ensuring police accountability?

(C) CRIMINAL PROSECUTIONS

A citizen who resists police action may find himself prosecuted for assault on or obstruction of the police in the execution of their duty[95] or the common law offence of escaping from lawful custody: *R v Timmis*.[96] He may wish to establish that the police action was unlawful and that the resistance or escape was, as a consequence, lawful. Conversely, a prosecution may be brought against the police officer for assault or false imprisonment or other offences committed. There is always the possibility of a private prosecution, as in *R v Duckenfield*.[97] That case resulted in an acquittal for one of the officers involved in the policing at Hillsborough Stadium in 1989 when 96 football fans died.

In many cases the police officer has been subject to internal discipline, but it has been claimed that there are too few prosecutions of those officers against whom disciplinary procedures have been brought.[98] The Butler Report, *Inquiry into Crown Prosecution Service Decision Making in Relation to Deaths in Custody and Related Matters* (1999), considered several high-profile cases in which no prosecution was brought following a death in custody. The application of the standard CPS procedure for determining whether to prosecute (asking whether there was a reasonable prospect of conviction and whether it was in the public interest to prosecute) came under close scrutiny:

…It is almost inconceivable that the public interest test will not be satisfied in the case of a death in custody. The system employed by Central Casework to arrive at a decision as to whether or not to prosecute is 'inefficient and fundamentally unsound'. The vice of the system is clearly demonstrated by the cases of Mr. Lapite and Mr. O'Brien [two high-profile deaths in custody]…A decision not to prosecute,

---

[95] See Part Two below.   [96] [1976] Crim LR 129. See further, *Archbold* (2007), para. 28–191.
[97] See news reports for 24 July 2000 and see *R v DPP, ex p Duckenfield* [2000] 1 WLR 55. See also P. Scratton, 'Policing with Contempt: the degrading truth and denial of justice in the aftermath of the Hillsborough disaster' (1999) 26(7) J Law and Soc 273.
[98] See B. Hilliard, 'No Action is Being Taken' (1996) 146 NLJ 1092.

if erroneously made, can have even more undesirable consequences for the public interest than an erroneous decision to prosecute … The advice of Counsel must be sought more often than it has in the past. … The
judicial review proceedings in the cases of Mr. Lapite and Mr. O'Brien were dealt with in an unsatisfactory
manner by the CPS. But there was no dishonest or deceitful conduct. There are no guidelines in existence
setting out the procedure to be followed when the CPS are made respondents to judicial reviews that raise
matters of sensitivity, importance or complexity. In none of the cases … considered, including those of Mr.
Lapite and Mr. O'Brien, [was there] unfair bias. The overall standard of the review notes was adequate.
This was found not to be so, however, in the case of *R v DPP, ex parte Treadaway*.[99]

Judge Butler's recommendations included that all cases of death in custody, whether of
the police or prison service, should be dealt with at CPS Central Casework, and that *every*
case of a death in custody should be sent for decision as to whether or not to prosecute to
the Assistant Chief Crown Prosecutor, who must consider *the whole of the relevant* documentation and prepare a report. If it decided not to prosecute, Senior Treasury Counsel
should review that decision. If counsel advises that there should be a prosecution, the
matter has to be reconsidered by the ACCP.[100]

Following *R (Manning and Melbourne) v DPP*[101] where an inquest returns a verdict of
unlawful killing, if the CPS still decides not to prosecute the person who is identifiable
(though not yet named), they must give a detailed reason for the decision.

It is not just in cases of deaths in custody that prosecutions are controversial. Following
the shooting of Jean Charles de Menezes at Stockwell tube station, no individual officer faced
charges.[102] In one of the most infamous cases, in 1983, two police officers who shot Stephen
Waldorf in the mistaken belief that he was a dangerous escaped prisoner, David Martin, were
tried for attempted murder and wounding with intent to cause grievous bodily harm; one
of the officers who pistol-whipped him after he had been shot was charged in addition with
causing grievous bodily harm with intent: the officers were acquitted.[103]

Given the close relationship between the CPS and the police can decisions as to whether to
prosecute be seen as independent?

(D) APPLICATIONS FOR JUDICIAL REVIEW

A citizen may challenge executive action on the ground that it is *ultra vires* (and on certain
other grounds) by making an 'application for judicial review' to the Administrative Court
under CPR 54. A variety of remedies may be sought including an order, for example, to
quash a warrant (see *R v IRC, ex p Rossminster Ltd*),[104] or a declaration (i.e. that a seizure
of property is unlawful).[105] Note, however, that the House of Lords held that if there is a
substantial conflict of evidence the matter is not suitable for resolution on an application
for judicial review, where evidence is normally only received in affidavit form: the matter
should instead be determined by a civil action for trespass. Proceedings for habeas corpus
may be brought under CPR 54 to challenge the legality of personal detention.

---

[99] References omitted. See also *R v HM Coroner for Coventry, ex p Marshall* [2001] EWHC 804 (Admin).
[100] See G. Smith (1999) 149 NLJ 20; M. Burton [2001] Crim LR 371.
[101] [2000] EWHC 342 (Admin).
[102] *The Times*, 25 July 2006.
[103] *The Times*, 13–20 October 1983. It was reported that he subsequently received £120,000 damages plus legal
expenses from the police in an out of court settlement (*The Times*, 8 March 1984).
[104] [1980] AC 952, HL.   [105] Ibid.

6. SELF-POLICING: ACCOUNTABILITY THROUGH INTERNAL MONITORING OF POLICE CONDUCT

(A) THE POLICE DISCIPLINARY PROCEDURE

In the last two decades police (mis)conduct has come under increasing scrutiny from the media and researchers. The RCCP and the RCCJ each commissioned research projects and the Metropolitan Police Service suffered damning criticism in the Macpherson Report on the investigation of the murder of Stephen Lawrence.[106] In response to some of the recommendations in that report, the Home Office published a Code of Conduct for Police Officers. In 2005 the Taylor Report[107] recommended a number of further changes to the police disciplinary system.

It is important in understanding police conduct to recognise that the number of public complaints and internal disciplinary matters are very small when measured against the myriad of public contacts and extensive range of police service activity. However, policing can be intrusive and coercive and such is its importance to social cohesion that the conduct of those entrusted with the role merits close control, accountability and scrutiny.

The Police (Conduct) Regulations 2008 take into account the recommendations of the Taylor Report in implementing a reformed disciplinary procedure. The procedure applies to all ranks and concerns allegations against an officer that may amount to misconduct or gross misconduct. An officer has a right to be legally represented at the misconduct hearing. Whilst the case is being investigated the officer concerned may be redeployed or suspended with pay. The Taylor Report hoped that the new regulations would provide:

A new single code (incorporating ethics and conduct) ... to be a touchstone for individual behaviour and a clear indication of organisational and peer expectations.

NOTES

1. There is an expectation in the Conduct Regulations that officers report improper behaviour of colleagues. Kleinig[108] observes that 'the primary loyalty of police officers often seems to be the horizontal loyalty of peers'.[109] Will the publication of a code of conduct affect that? Is it ever likely to be possible to overcome the closing of ranks?

2. The standard of proof for disciplinary charges is no longer the criminal standard. It is more likely that disciplinary charges will follow a successful civil claim now that both are determined on a balance of probabilities.

---

[106] *The Stephen Lawrence Inquiry* (Cm 4262, 1999).
[107] The Taylor Report, *Review of Police Disciplinary Arrangements* (2005).
[108] *The Ethics of Policing* (1996).   [109] Ibid., p. 70.

(B) POLICE COMPLAINTS

Arrangements for police discipline and the handling of complaints against the police overlap but are not coterminous. Disciplinary proceedings may be instituted as the result of a complaint from a member of the public; more commonly, the force itself instigates them internally. Major reforms since 1964 first saw the establishment, by the Police Act 1976, of a Police Complaints Board with power to recommend, and in the last resort to direct, the institution of disciplinary proceedings in a particular case. The Board was replaced by the Police Complaints Authority (PCA), established by Pt IX of the PACE Act 1984.[110] The independence of the body was regularly called into question. In *Khan v United Kingdom*[111] the European Court found that the lack of independence in the investigation of complaints meant that the PCA could not provide an adequate remedy for the purposes of Art. 13. The Court stated:

45. As regards the various other avenues open to the applicant in respect of the Article 8 complaint, the Court observes, again with the Commission in the Govell case, that complaints only have to be referred to the Police Complaints Authority in circumstances where they contain allegations that the relevant conduct resulted in death or serious injury or where the complaint is of a type specified by the Secretary of State. In other circumstances the Chief Constable of the area will decide whether or not he is the appropriate authority to decide the case. If he concludes that he is the correct authority, then the standard procedure is to appoint a member of his own force to carry out the investigation. Although the Police Complaints Authority can require a complaint to be submitted to it for consideration under section 87 of PACE, the extent to which the Police Complaints Authority oversees the decision-making process undertaken by the Chief Constable in determining if he is the appropriate authority is unclear (see paragraph 68 of the Commission's report in the Govell case cited above).

46. The Court also notes the important role played by the Secretary of State in appointing, remunerating and, in certain circumstances, dismissing members of the Police Complaints Authority. In particular, the Court observes that under section 105(4) of the Act the Police Complaints Authority is to have regard to any guidance given to it by the Secretary of State with respect to the withdrawal or preferring of disciplinary charges and criminal proceedings (ibid., § 69).

47. Accordingly, the Court finds that the system of investigation of complaints does not meet the requisite standards of independence needed to constitute sufficient protection against the abuse of authority and thus provide an effective remedy within the meaning of Article 13. There has therefore been a violation of Article 13 of the Convention.

The Home Affairs Committee[112] therefore recommended changes to the discipline process. Pressure for an independent system increased following the Macpherson Report, particularly Recommendation 58:

That the Home Secretary, taking into account the strong expression of public perception in this regard, considers what steps can and should be taken to ensure that serious complaints against police officers are independently investigated. Investigation of police officers by their own or another Police Service is widely regarded as unjust, and does not inspire public confidence.[113]

---

[110] For further discussion of the system, see the fourth Report of the Home Affairs Committee, 1991–92 HC 179, *Police Complaints Procedures* and Government Reply (Cm 1996, 1992); M. Maguire and C. Corbett, *A Study of the Police Complaints System* (1991); Home Office, *Guidance on Police Unsatisfactory Performance, Complaints and Misconduct Procedures* (2000); A. Goldsmith and C. Lewis, *Civilian Oversight of Policing* (2000).

[111] (2001) 31 EHRR 45.

[112] First Report, *Police Disciplinary and Complaints Procedure* HC 258 (1998).

[113] Op. cit.

Under the Police Reform Act 2002[114] the new Independent Police Complaints Commission (IPCC) was established and it became operational in 2004.[115] Its Chair (currently Nick Hardwick) is appointed by the Crown and there are to be no fewer than 10 other members of the Commission (there are currently 13). An Annual Report must be presented to the Secretary of State.

● Police Reform Act 2002

12 Complaints, matters and persons to which Part 2 applies[116]

(1) In this Part references to a complaint are references (subject to the following provisions of this section) to any complaint about the conduct of a person serving with the police which is made (whether in writing or otherwise) by—

(a) a member of the public who claims to be the person in relation to whom the conduct took place;

(b) a member of the public not falling within paragraph (a) who claims to have been adversely affected by the conduct;

(c) a member of the public who claims to have witnessed the conduct;

(d) a person acting on behalf of a person falling within any of paragraphs (a) to (c).

(2) In this Part 'conduct matter' means (subject to the following provisions of this section, paragraph 2(4) of Schedule 3 and any regulations made by virtue of section 23(2)(d)) any matter which is not and has not been the subject of a complaint but in the case of which there is an indication (whether from the circumstances or otherwise) that a person serving with the police may have—

(a) committed a criminal offence; or

(b) behaved in a manner which would justify the bringing of disciplinary proceedings.

[(2A) In this Part 'death or serious injury matter' (or 'DSI matter' for short) means any circumstances (other than those which are or have been the subject of a complaint or which amount to a conduct matter)—

(a) in or in consequence of which a person has died or has sustained serious injury; and

(b) in relation to which the requirements of either subsection (2B) or subsection (2C) are satisfied.

(2B) The requirements of this subsection are that at the time of the death or serious injury the person—

(a) had been arrested by a person serving with the police and had not been released from that arrest; or

(b) was otherwise detained in the custody of a person serving with the police.

(2C) The requirements of this subsection are that—

(a) at or before the time of the death or serious injury the person had contact (of whatever kind, and whether direct or indirect) with a person serving with the police who was acting in the execution of his duties; and

(b) here is an indication that the contact may have caused (whether directly or indirectly) or contributed to the death or serious injury.

---

114 See also Home Office, *Complaints Against the Police: Framework for a New System* (2000).
115 G. Smith (2004) 44 Brit Jo Criminol 28.
116 All changes in square brackets were made by Serious Organised Crime and Police Act 2005, s. 55(1).

(2D) In subsection (2A) the reference to a person includes a person serving with the police, but in relation to such a person 'contact' in subsection (2C) does not include contact that he has whilst acting in the execution of his duties.]

(3) The complaints that are complaints for the purposes of this Part by virtue of subsection (1)(b) do not, except in a case falling within subsection (4), include any made by or on behalf of a person who claims to have been adversely affected as a consequence only of having seen or heard the conduct, or any of the alleged effects of the conduct.

(4) A case falls within this subsection if—

(a) it was only because the person in question was physically present, or sufficiently nearby, when the conduct took place or the effects occurred that he was able to see or hear the conduct or its effects; or

(b) the adverse effect is attributable to, or was aggravated by, the fact that the person in relation to whom the conduct took place was already known to the person claiming to have suffered the adverse effect.

(5) For the purposes of this section a person shall be taken to have witnessed conduct if, and only if—

(a) he acquired his knowledge of that conduct in a manner which would make him a competent witness capable of giving admissible evidence of that conduct in criminal proceedings; or

(b) he has in his possession or under his control anything which would in any such proceedings constitute admissible evidence of that conduct.

(6) For the purposes of this Part a person falling within subsection 1(a) to (c) to shall not be taken to have authorised another person to act on his behalf unless—

(a) that other person is for the time being designated for the purposes of this Part by the Commission as a person through whom complaints may be made, or he is of a description of persons so designated; or

(b) the other person has been given, and is able to produce, the written consent to his so acting of the person on whose behalf he acts.

(7) For the purposes of this Part, a person is serving with the police if—

(a) he is a member of a police force;

(b) he is an employee of a police authority who is under the direction and control of a chief officer; or

(c) he is a special constable who is under the direction and control of a chief officer.

14 Direction and control matters

(1) Nothing in Schedule 3 shall have effect with respect to so much of any complaint as relates to the direction and control of a police force by—

(a) he chief officer of police of that force; or

(b) a person for the time being carrying out the functions of the chief officer of police of that force.

(2) The Secretary of State may issue guidance to chief officers and to police authorities about the handling of so much of any complaint as relates to the direction and control of a police force by such a person as is mentioned in subsection (1).

(3) It shall be the duty of a chief officer and of a police authority when handling any complaint relating to such a matter to have regard to any guidance issued under subsection (2).

NOTES

1. The IPCC can only deal with complaints about the behaviour of police officers and staff and does not consider complaints relating to operational decisions, police policies and procedures. Such complaints should be made to the chief constable or the local police authority.[117]

2. If a complaint is made to the police or the IPCC then in most cases the complaint must initially be sent to the Professional Standards Department of the relevant police force (provided that the complainant consents). If the complaint is not recorded by the Professional Standards Department that decision may be the subject of an appeal to the IPCC. If it is recorded then a decision must then be made as to how it can most appropriately be resolved. A complaint may be dealt with by 'local resolution' if the complainant agrees.[118] If so, the process will be agreed between the complainant and the police. Whilst being a flexible and simple way to resolve a complaint, this process cannot lead to disciplinary proceedings against an individual police officer. If the complainant does not agree to local resolution or the IPCC feel that the case is not suitable for local resolution then an officer will be appointed to investigate the complaint. The outcome of the investigation is also subject to an appeal to the IPCC. A 2007 report into the handling of complaints locally:

found that the Local Resolution process has real potential for dealing with low-level complaints, but that it is not always used to its full potential. In particular, it noted that neither officers nor complainants are well informed at the outset about the process. The process for communicating the conclusion of the resolution has also been poor.[119]

3. If a complaint is deemed to be serious then the Professional Standards Department may refer it to the IPCC. Certain allegations must be sent directly to the IPCC such as: incidents where someone has died or been seriously injured following direct or indirect contact with the police; serious assault by a member of the police service; serious sexual assault by a member of the police service; serious corruption or a criminal offence or behaviour aggravated by discriminatory behaviour. In these circumstances the IPCC may decide to conduct a supervised, managed or independent investigation. A supervised investigation is conducted by, and under the direction and control of, the police, but supervised by the IPCC. Supervised investigations are carried out when the IPCC decides that a complaint is of considerable significance and probable public concern. There is a right to appeal to the IPCC. A managed investigation is conducted by the police but under the direction and control of the IPCC because the allegations are of such significance and public concern that an independent element is required. An independent investigation will be conducted by IPCC staff when the incident is deemed to have the greatest level of public concern, and could have the greatest potential to impact on communities or have serious implications for the reputation of the police service. The IPCC only investigates the most serious complaints and therefore the police continue to investigate themselves in the majority of cases. Is this satisfactory? In practical terms, who is capable of policing the police?

---

[117] Home Office, *Guidance on the handling of complaints relating to the direction and control of a police force by a Chief officer*, HO Circular 19/2005 (2005).

[118] See H. Warburton, T. May and M. Hough, *Opposite side of the same coin: Police perspectives on informally resolved complaints* (2003).

[119] IPCC, *Annual Report 2007–08* (2008) HC 898, p. 26.

4. The outcome of a complaint may be that the police have to revise their procedures or an individual officer may be disciplined. Part 3 of the Act deals with removal, suspension and discipline. If there is sufficient evidence that an offence has been committed then the case may be forwarded to the Crown Prosecution Service. In cases that have been the subject of local resolution the outcome might be an apology or an explanation to clear up a misunderstanding.

5. In 2007 the IPCC conducted research into public confidence in the complaints system.[120] This report followed a similar one conducted months after the IPCC was set up in 2004. The 2007 survey found 'that there has been a slight improvement overall in 2007'.[121] Of those surveyed it was found that complaints were most likely to follow incidences of physical assault (88 per cent) or the use of racist or insulting language (85 per cent).[122] Many agreed with the statement that a complaint would make no difference (37 per cent).[123] Of those surveyed 32 per cent did not know how to make a complaint as compared to 28 per cent in 2004.[124] Just over one quarter (26 per cent) of the sample thought that the IPCC was linked to the police,[125] but 67 per cent were confident or fairly confident that complaints would be handled impartially.[126] Whilst the IPCC considers that this still leaves a gap to close, they are 'encouraging results'.[127] The IPCC recognised that there was still some way to go in improving public confidence:

> The new complaints system has seen an 83 per cent increase in recorded complaints—from 15,885 in 2003/04 to 28,998 in 2006/07. This is a dramatic rise, and we expect a further increase in 2007/08. But people's actual experience of the system does not appear to match their expectations. Most complaints are dealt with by the police themselves, not the IPCC. The 2005/06 British Crime Survey found that only 24 per cent of people who had made a complaint were satisfied with the way the police had handled it.[128]

For 2008/9 the IPCC stated that four aims would help to secure increased public confidence in the system. These are: (a) *Engagement*: increase awareness, accessibility and engagement in the complaints system; (b) *Learning*: enable police to learn from complaints and enhance professional standards; (c) *Proportionality*: improve the proportionality of the resolution of complaints and conduct issues; and (d) *Accountability*: improve the transparency and accountability of the complaints system.[129]

6. In 2005–6 a total of 26,268 complaint cases were recorded. This represented a 15 per cent rise in complaints on the previous year, but IPCC Chair, Nick Hardwick, said:

> Nobody should be critical of the rise in complaints. The increase in the number of complaints shows that people have greater confidence that it is worth complaining. It also shows that the Commission and the police service have made the system more accessible and usable. More and more people recognise that if you have a grievance the police service will take it seriously.

In 2005/6 38,199 individual allegations were completed of which 46 per cent were dealt with by local resolution; 28 per cent by an investigation; and 14 per cent were dispensed with from

---

[120] IPCC, *Confidence in the Police Complaints System: a second survey of the general population* (2007).
[121] Ibid., p. 4.   [122] Ibid., p. 10.   [123] Ibid., p. 12.
[124] Ibid., p. 13.   [125] Ibid., p. 20.   [126] Ibid., p. 21.
[127] IPCC, *Annual Report 2007–08* (2008) HC 898, p. 2.
[128] Ibid., p. 3.   [129] Ibid., p. 62.

the requirement to be investigated; and 12 per cent were withdrawn by the complainant. 12 per cent of allegations were substantiated.[130]

(C) INDEPENDENT CUSTODY VISITORS

Yet another method of monitoring police action at the ground level is the custody visitors scheme operated by the Independent Custody Visiting Association. Independent custody visitors are local community members who check on the welfare of people in police custody, by visiting police stations unannounced. This scheme was placed on a statutory footing by the Police Reform Act 2002, s. 51. Under s. 51(6) the Secretary of State issued a code of practice which took effect in 2003. Police authorities and independent custody visitors must have regard to this code in carrying out their relevant functions. As to working arrangments, the Code states:

35. Visits should normally be undertaken by pairs of independent custody visitors working together. Visits should only be undertaken by a single independent custody visitor working alone where the police authority has carried out a thorough and robust assessment of the risks that presents and has concluded that it is, in all the circumstances, the best option.

36. Independent custody visitors must be admitted to the custody area immediately. Delay is only permitted when immediate access may place the visitors in danger. A full explanation must be given to the visitors as to why access is being delayed and that explanation must be recorded by the visitors in their report.

37. Independent custody visitors must have access to all parts of the custody area and to associated facilities such as food preparation areas and medical rooms. However, it is not part of their role to attend police interviews with detainees.

39. The custody officer or a member of custody staff must accompany independent custody visitors during visits. (See paragraph 46).

40. Subject to the exceptions referred to in paragraph 43, independent custody visitors must be allowed access to any person detained at the police station. However, detainees may only be spoken to with their consent and the escorting officer is responsible for establishing whether they wish to speak to the independent custody visitors.

43. The police may limit or deny independent custody visitors' access to a specific detainee if an officer of or above the rank of inspector reasonably believes that to be necessary for the visitors' safety. Such an officer may also deny or restrict access where they reasonably believe that such access could interfere with process of justice.

46. Discussions between detainees and independent custody visitors must normally take place in sight but out of hearing of the escorting officer where that is practical.

47. Discussions must focus on checking whether detainees have been offered their rights and entitlements under PACE and confirming whether the conditions of detention are adequate.

48. Independent custody visitors must remain impartial and must not seek to involve themselves in any way in the process of investigation. If a detainee seeks to make admissions or otherwise discuss an alleged offence, the visitor must tell them that the relevant contents of the visit may be disclosed in legal proceedings.

DEALING WITH ISSUES AND COMPLAINTS

55. Where a detainee makes a complaint or raises an issue about their general treatment or conditions, independent custody visitors must (subject to the detainee's consent) take this up as soon as possible

---

[130] IPCC, *Police Complaints: Statistics for England and Wales 2005/06* (2006).

with police staff in order to seek a resolution. The same applies to similar issues identified by visitors in the course of their attendance.

56. If a detainee makes a complaint of misconduct by a specific police officer, they must be advised to address it to the duty officer in charge of the police station.

REPORTING ON A VISIT

58. At the end of each visit, and while they are still at the police station, independent custody visitors must complete a report of their findings in a standard format. One copy of the report must remain at the station for the attention of the officer in charge. Copies must go to the co-ordinator of the local independent custody visiting group.

NOTES

1. The ICVA receives £291,000 from a range of sources including £188,000 from the Home Office and £29,000 from Police Authority subscriptions. The Home Office does not play a part in the governance of the ICVA. It was 'established to promote the efficient and effective provision of custody visiting in the United Kingdom and elsewhere to raise public awareness about matters and issues concerning the rights and entitlements of people held in police custody'.[131]

2. A review of the operation of the ICVA presented mixed results. 'The governance of the Association was described to us as being slow, bureaucratic and of unclear accountability and transparency.' Furthermore, 'From those surveyed there is perceived to be little activity in awareness-raising and promotion to the public to date and there are mixed views about the extent to which ICVA should raise awareness to public.' However, 'the role that ICVA has played in raising the awareness of custody visiting and making it a statutory duty is valued and recognised; and there is a perception that ICVA has a strong influencing role with regard to policy'.[132]

3. The Office for Public Management has recommended that the ICVA becomes part of a broader body, a new National Independent CJS Visitors and Monitors Council, funded by the Home Office and the Association of Police Authorities which encompasses the voices of all those who volunteer to visit people held in various forms of custody.[133]

7. CONCLUSION

Morgan and Newburn have claimed that there is 'little evidence that anything the police do has much more than a very marginal impact on crime levels'.[134] If this is the case, it raises fundamental questions about the role of the police and the public perceptions of policing. It is clear that policing will continue to change at a rapid pace. The material discussed in Part One demonstrates that policing develops as a result of (sometimes unpredictable) political, economic and social factors. Ongoing developments have also given rise to concern. These include: increasing centralization and moves towards a national police force; increased militarisation of the police force; increased use of invasive surveillance techniques and data

---

[131] Office of Public Management, *Independent Custody Visiting Association: Review of governance and capacity* (2007), p. 2.

[132] Ibid., p.3.   [133] Ibid., p. 4.   [134] *The Future of Policing*, op. cit., p. 9.

gathering and sharing; and the continued rise of the private security sector.[135] These issues raise both important questions of accountability and the extent of police powers, the latter of which is the focus of Part Two.

What are the most important changes that should be made to police structure and accountability: from the point of view of (a) the police (b) the citizen? To what extent are they irreconcilable aims?

PART TWO. POLICE POWERS[136]

1. INTRODUCTION AND HISTORICAL BACKGROUND

The materials in Part Two illustrate the powers and duties of the police in the enforcement of the criminal law.[137] The powers have undergone radical change in the last 30 years, and there is continuous expansion in this area. The position was transformed by the Police and Criminal Evidence Act 1984. In the first edition of this book, we described the previous law as follows:[138]

> The present law satisfies nobody. It is far too complex, contained in a miscellany of, often archaic, statutes and cases. Problems which are difficult enough as examination questions are trickier still for the 'policeman on the beat' who will often have to act without prolonged deliberation. If the rules are known their precise meaning may be uncertain. And when their meaning is clear their content is often unsatisfactory. Many powers of the police are of unduly wide scope and yet, at the same time, the police do not possess certain powers which many would regard as necessary to the performance of their tasks. And when the law is reasonably clear and its content reasonably satisfactory there may be difficulties in ensuring compliance with those rules. Police officers perform their duties subject to the possibilities of prosecution, civil claim and internal disciplinary action if they exceed their powers. Yet for most of those with whom they deal the opportunity to prosecute or sue (notwithstanding possible punitive damages—see *Cassell & Co Ltd v Broome* [1972] AC 1027, HL) may be of little practical value, and, despite new arrangements, there still exists a division of opinion as to the way in which complaints against the police are handled. Moreover, with the exception of the rules about confessions, the judges have declined to use the rules about admissibility of evidence as a method of 'policing' the police.
>
> In the past a large amount of police work has relied on the co-operation and consent of citizens together with a certain amount of 'bluff' as to the extent of police powers. With cooperation and consent

---

135 M. Button, *Private Policing* (2002).

136 Where sections of PACE are reproduced in this chapter subsequent amendments and substitutions are of course noted, but for reasons of space the very many pieces of amending legislation are not noted.

137 See, generally, on police powers R. Clayton, H. Tomlinson, E. Buckett and A. Davies, *Civil Actions Against the Police* (3rd edn, rev. 2005); D. Clark, *Bevan and Lidstone's Investigation of Crime: A Guide to Police Powers* (3rd edn, 2004); D. Feldman, *Civil Liberties and Human Rights in England and Wales* (2002), Chaps 6, 10; M. Zander, *The Police and Criminal Evidence Act 1984* (6th edn, 2008); Symposia [1985] PL 388ff; [1985] Crim LR 535ff; [1990] Crim LR 452ff; A. Ashworth and M. Redmayne, *The Criminal Process* (3rd edn, 2005); A. Sander and R. Young, *Criminal Justice* (3rd edn, 2007); see also the annual volumes of *Blackstones Criminal Practice* and *Archbold*.

138 At p. 33.

apparently diminishing and a greater awareness of people as to their 'rights', the need grows for a thorough review and reform of the law of police powers.

These matters were considered by the Royal Commission on Criminal Procedure (RCCP) that reported in 1981.[139] In a summary of the report, the RCCP outlined its task:

● **Royal Commission on Criminal Procedure; The Balance of Criminal Justice: Summary of the Report** (HMSO, 1981)

The Royal Commission on Criminal Procedure began work in February 1978. Its terms of reference were:

To examine, having regard both to the interests of the community in bringing offenders to justice and to the rights and liberties of persons suspected or accused of crime, and taking into account also the need for the efficient and economical use of resources, whether changes are needed in England and Wales in

i. the powers and duties of the police in respect of the investigation of criminal offences and the rights and duties of suspect and accused persons, including the means by which these are secured;

ii. the process of and responsibility for the prosecution of criminal offences; and

iii. such other features of criminal procedure and evidence as relate to the above; and to make recommendations.

Matter of fact though these subjects may appear, they form one of the central threads in the history of liberty in Britain. Criminal justice has provided for centuries a natural arena in which the struggle to establish the rights of the individual citizen in relation to the security of society and the power of the state has been waged.

The Commission's task was to try to achieve a balance between a host of competing rights and objectives, a task made the more difficult by the lack of consensus about the content or even the existence of some of the rights. On the one hand there were those who saw the fight to bring criminals to justice as being paramount. They tended to see the police as struggling against increasing crime, shackled by laws and procedures which, during their investigations, their questioning of suspects, and finally at the trial, favour the criminal. On the other side are those who believed that the cards were in practice stacked against suspects and defendants, that the individual had insufficient legal protection against police power, and that the safeguards against abuse and oppression were inadequate. The majority of public and professional opinion was (and remains) inevitably between the two. But where can a balance be found which will secure the confidence of the public?

In its review of investigation and prosecution, the Commission applies throughout three standards for judging both the existing system and its own recommendations. Are the arrangements, actual or proposed, fair and clear? Are they open, that is, not secret, and is there accountability? Are they workable and efficient?

The Commission recommended that police powers should be extended in a number of significant respects, but that this should be balanced by the improvement of safeguards against abuse and the extension of safeguards across the whole field of police powers. The Government accepted many (although not all) of the recommendations concerning police powers and implemented them in the Police and Criminal Evidence Act 1984

---

[139] *RCCP Report* (Cmnd 8092, 1981); *Law and Procedure* volume (Cmnd 8092–1, 1981).

(PACE), which received Royal Assent on 31 October 1984 and generally took effect on 1 January 1986.[140]

A common theme running through many of the commentaries on the RCCP Report was that police powers were to be extended but that the proposed safeguards which required that a subject of the exercise of a power be informed of the reasons for it; that the reasons be recorded contemporaneously; periodic review by senior police officers or magistrates of exercises of power; improvement in complaints procedures; reliance on codes of conduct, breach of which by a police officer would constitute a disciplinary offence, were not as strong as at first sight might appear. McConville and Baldwin[141] argued (inter alia) that while the RCCP commissioned an extensive body of research, the results of that research were used selectively: for example, 'No evidence is adduced to demonstrate a need for the increased powers of stop and search, to arrest, to fingerprint, or to search property and seize goods and articles which are proposed'.[142]

Moreover,

No research was conducted into the efficacy of police disciplinary procedures or of civil actions, either as means of inducing police compliance with the rules or as remedies to citizens in the event of breach. No research was conducted to test whether the Commission's confidence that requiring police officers to record in writing their reasons, say, for arrest, for prolonged interrogation of suspects, or for refusing access to a solicitor, would provide adequate opportunity for subsequent review was well-founded or not.[143]

As was only to be expected, some took a more favourable view than others. Leigh[144] noted that the RCCP Report 'engendered strong reactions, some almost Pavlovian in character': in his view, the report, with some exceptions 'on balance would improve the present system and ought to be implemented'.

The role and powers of the police again came under a measure of scrutiny by the Royal Commission on Criminal Justice (RCCJ), chaired by Lord Runciman, which reported in 1993.[145] Its terms of reference were:

to examine the effectiveness of the criminal justice system in England and Wales in securing the conviction of those guilty of criminal offences and the acquittal of those who are innocent, having regard to the efficient use of resources.[146]

Furthermore, it was 'in particular to consider what changes are needed in eight specific areas of the criminal justice process'. The first of these was:

the conduct of police investigations and their supervision by senior police officers, and in particular the degree of control that is exercised by those officers over the conduct of the investigation and the gathering and preparation of evidence.

---

140 On the Report of the Royal Commission see the symposium in the Criminal Law Review: [1981] Crim LR 445ff; L.H. Leigh (1981) 44 MLR 296; B. Smythe [1981] PL 184, 481; M. McConville and J. Baldwin 10 Int J Sociology of Law 287. On the Police and Criminal Evidence Bill, see the *Police and Criminal Bill Briefing Guide* (Home Office, 1984); L. Bridges and T. Bunyan (1983) 10 JLS 85; L. Christian, *Policing By Coercion* (GLC Police Committee Support Unit, 1983).
141 Op. cit., n. 141.   142 Ibid., p. 299.
143 M. McConville and J. Baldwin, 'The Research Programme' (1981) 131 NLJ 1117, 1118.
144 (1981) 44 MLR 296, 307–308.
145 Cm 2263.   146 Ibid., p. i.

The background to the appointment of the RCCJ was the spate of high-profile cases, many involving convictions for terrorist offences, in which the Court of Appeal had found there to have been a miscarriage of justice.[147] Police malpractice, in the form of the suppression or falsification of evidence, was a significant factor in several of these cases. By 1993, the emphasis of the Government's concerns had shifted from the problem of miscarriages of justice to a perceived lack of effectiveness of the criminal justice system in controlling crime. The RCCJ made 352 recommendations. Commentators (other than the police) were largely hostile, noting that the recommendations seemed directed more to promoting the efficiency of the system in obtaining convictions than to the prevention or remedying of miscarriages of justice.[148] This persistent drive for efficiency in the criminal justice system echoes the changes in policing considered in Part One of this chapter.

In the area of policing, Reiner[149] noted that the RCCJ appeared to have taken the view that the Report of the Philips Royal Commission, largely incorporated in PACE and the Prosecution of Offences Act 1985:

laid down a framework which is broadly on the right lines. In this sense, the policing proposals of the Runciman Commission can largely be seen as a set of footnotes to Philips rather than a new departure.

In addition to reforms flowing from these reports police powers in England and Wales have been influenced by relevant international standards. These include the protection of the right to life (Art. 2 ECHR; Art. 6 ICCPR); the prohibition of torture or inhuman or degrading treatment or punishment (Art. 3 ECHR; Art. 7 ICCPR (which also outlaws 'cruel' treatment or punishment); the right to liberty and security of person (Art. 5 ECHR; Art. 9 ICCPR); the right to respect for private life (Art. 8 ECHR; Art. 17 ICCPR); and the enjoyment of the protected rights and freedoms without discrimination (Art. 14 ECHR, cf. Art. 26 ICCPR (general entitlement without any discrimination to the equal protection of the law)).[150] The implementation of the Human Rights Act 1998 has inevitably resulted in a much more direct influence of the ECHR jurisprudence on police powers, and its impact is considered throughout the chapter. Nevertheless, the trend of diluting safeguards for the suspect originally introduced in PACE 1984 continues with the expansion of, for example, increased powers of search, wider powers of arrest, broader powers to take samples and retain them, and to invite juries to draw inferences from the suspect's behaviour during the investigation. In 2004 the Government stated:

1.3 The provisions of PACE reflect the principles of fairness, openness and workability representing a clear statement of the rights of the individual and the powers of the police. The PACE codes of practice interpret the provisions of the Act into operational application.

---

[147] On these cases see J. Rozenberg, 'Miscarriages of Justice' in E. Stockdale and S. Casale (eds), *Criminal Justice Under Stress* (1992); C. Walker, 'Introduction' in C. Walker and K. Starmer (eds), *Justice in Error* (1993). See also the writings of the victims of these miscarriages: P. Hill and R. Burnett, *Stolen Years* (1990); G. Conlon, *Proved Innocent* (1990).

[148] See generally, M. McConville and L. Bridges, *Criminal Justice in Crisis* (1994); S. Field and P. Thomas (eds), 'Justice and Efficiency? The Royal Commission on Criminal Justice' (1994) 12 JLS 1–164 (special issue); Symposium [1993] Crim LR 808, 926; L. Bridges and M. McConville (1994) 57 MLR 75; M. Zander, ibid., p. 264, reply by Bridges and McConville, ibid., p. 267.

[149] [1993] Crim LR 808, 810.

[150] See above, Chap. 1. The application of international standards to police powers is considered by R. Reiner and L. Leigh, 'Police Powers' in G. Chambers and C. McCrudden (eds), *Individual Rights and the Law* in *Britain* (1993) and S.H. Bailey, 'Rights in the Administration of Justice' in D.J. Harris and S. Joseph (eds), *The ICCPR and United Kingdom Law* (1995).

1.4 In 2002, the Home Secretary announced a fundamental review of PACE and the codes. That was carried out jointly by Home Office and Cabinet Office and involved consultation with stakeholders. The Review reported in November 2002.

1.5 The Review concluded that PACE is viewed positively by police, the courts and the legal profession as having standardised and professionalised police work and the investigative process. However, it does require updating and should more accurately reflect the changes in society over the last 20 years.[151]

The most recent review of PACE in 2008 has made further recommendations for change in areas such as stop and search, arrest, the provision of warrants and detention.[152]

2. ASSAULTS ON AND OBSTRUCTION OF THE POLICE

Before examining the powers available to the police in terms of search, arrest, detention etc., it is worth considering the offences most often used to prosecute those who do not comply with police actions. Many of the cases in which the courts are called upon to determine the lawfulness of police action involve prosecutions under s. 89 of the Police Act 1996.[153]

(A) THE OFFENCES

- **Police Act 1996, s. 89**

(1) Any person who assaults a constable in the execution of his duty, or a person assisting a constable in the execution of his duty, shall be guilty of an offence and liable on summary conviction to imprisonment for a term not exceeding six months or to a fine not exceeding level 5 on the standard scale, or to both.

(2) Any person who resists or wilfully obstructs a constable in the execution of his duty, or a person assisting a constable in the execution of his duty, shall be guilty of an offence and liable on summary conviction to imprisonment for a term not exceeding one month or to a fine not exceeding level 3 on the standard scale, or to both.

(I) 'ASSAULT'

This includes both a technical assault and a battery (the two are often misleadingly used interchangeably). Thus, an assault is committed where the defendant, D, intentionally or recklessly causes another person to apprehend immediate[154] and unlawful personal violence, as where D waves a weapon at V, or makes oral threats in such a way that V apprehends immediate violence.[155] A battery is committed when D intentionally or recklessly inflicts

---

[151] Home Office, *Modernising Police Powers to Meet Community Needs* (2004).

[152] Home Office, *PACE Review: Government proposals in response to the Review of the Police and Criminal Evidence Act 1984* (2008); see also Home Office, *Review of the Police and Criminal Evidence Act 1984* (2007).

[153] This replaced the offences in Police Act 1964, s. 51; see also the offence of assault with intent to resist or prevent arrest contrary to s. 38 of the Offences Against the Person Act 1861.

[154] *R v Constanza* [1997] 2 Cr App R 492.

[155] See *R v Ireland* [1998] AC 147, per Lord Steyn especially at 161. See also *Collins v Wilcock* [1984] 3 All ER 374.

unlawful force on V. This is satisfied by the slightest touch, and there is no need to prove any injury. The offence under s. 89 requires proof of either an assault or a battery in the sense described here.

(II) IN THE EXECUTION OF HIS DUTY

- **Coffin v Smith** (1980) 71 Cr App Rep 221, Queen's Bench Divisional Court

Police officers were summoned to a boys' club by the youth leader there to ensure that various people left before a disco started. S and H assaulted the officers. The magistrates dismissed charges under the Police Act 1964, s. 51(1) on the ground that the officers were not acting in the execution of their duty as they were doing something that they were not compelled by law to do.[156] The Divisional Court allowed the prosecutors' appeal.

Donaldson LJ: The modern law on the subject is, I think, to be found in two different cases. The first is a decision of the Court of Criminal Appeal, *Waterfield and Lynn* (1963) 48 Cr App Rep 42, [1964] 1 QB 164, where Ashworth J delivering the judgment of the Court, at p. 47 and 170 respectively, said: 'In the judgment of this court it would be difficult, and in the present case it is unnecessary, to reduce within specific limits the general terms in which the duties of police constables have been expressed. In most cases it is probably more convenient to consider what the police constable was actually doing and in particular whether such conduct was prima facie an unlawful interference with a person's liberty or property. If so, it is then relevant to consider whether (a) such conduct falls within the general scope of any duty imposed by statute or recognised at common law and (b) whether such conduct, albeit within the general scope of such a duty, involved an unjustifiable use of powers associated with the duty.'

Applying that basis, it is quite clear that these constables were on duty, they were in uniform, and they were not doing anything that was prima facie any unlawful interference with a person's liberty or property.

Further guidance on the scope of the police officer's duty in this context is I think to be derived from the judgment of Lord Parker CJ in *Rice v Connolly* [1966] 2 QB 414, and the passage to which I would like to refer is at p. 419 'It is also in my judgment clear that it is part of the obligations and duties of a police constable to take all steps which appear to him necessary for keeping the peace, for preventing crime or for protecting property from criminal injury. There is no exhaustive definition of the powers and obligations of the police, but they are at least those, and they would further include the duty to detect crime and to bring an offender to justice.'

In a word, a police officer's duty is to be a keeper of the peace and to take all necessary steps with that in view. These officers, just like the ordinary officer on the beat, were attending a place where they thought that their presence would assist in the keeping of the peace. I know that Mr Staddon says 'Oh no, this is all part and parcel of the assistance which they gave to the youth leader in ejecting these people'. Even if that was so, they would have been doing no more than a police officer's duty in all the circumstances. In fact it is clear that there was a break. Both the respondents went away and came back. The officers were in effect simply standing there on their beat in the execution of their duty when they were assaulted. This is a very clear case indeed.

Bristow J agreed.

Appeal allowed.

NOTES

1. The term 'duty' is ambiguous. It could mean: (a) a function which in a general sense can be termed part of a police officer's job but without necessarily any element of obligation;

---

[156] As earlier cases had required: *R v Prebble* (1858) 1 F and F 325; *R v Roxburgh* (1871) 12 Cox CC 8.

(b) the same as (a) but with the qualification that the officer be in the exercise of some specific legal power or performance of some specific legal duty; (c) a function which an officer is specifically required by his superiors or police regulations to perform; (d) a function which a police officer is obliged by law to perform in the sense that failure to do so constitutes a crime or tort. *Coffin v Smith* appears to reject meanings (c) and (d).

2. If a constable is acting in the purported exercise of specific legal powers or duties he must remain within the limits set by law to those powers or duties.[157] For example, a constable has been held to have exceeded his powers and thus acted outside the execution of his duty where he has trespassed on private land: *Davis v Lisle;*[158] or assaulted someone: *Kenlin v Gardner.*[159] Thus, a police officer is not acting in the execution of his duty if he restrains someone in the mistaken belief that another officer has already arrested that person.[160] If a police officer makes an unlawful arrest, he is not in the execution of his duty,[161] but where the arrest is lawful but it is impracticable for the officer to inform the suspect of the grounds for arrest he is still in the execution of his duty.[162] An officer is not in the execution of his duty where he searches a suspect without supplying his name and station,[163] nor where he searches premises under s. 17 or 18 of PACE without informing the occupier of the reasons for entry.[164] The prosecution must prove that the officer was acting in the execution of his duty.[165] The failure of the court in *Coffin v Smith* to provide precise guidance has led to further judicial disagreement, as seen in *Porter v Metropolitan Police Comr*.

(i) Police duty as 'keeping the peace'?

- **Porter v Metropolitan Police Comr** (1999) 20 November, Court of Appeal, Civil Division, unreported

P was annoyed when the electricity board had failed to keep an appointment at her flat. She went to the electricity board shop to complain. She became very angry at her treatment and refused to leave until the board arranged for a visit to her flat. Police officers were called and forcibly removed her from the premises at the request of the staff. P bit one of the officers, but charges of assaulting an officer in the execution of his duty were dropped and she brought a civil action against the MPC claiming false imprisonment. The court discussed the question of whether the police officers were acting in the execution of their duty.

Judge LJ: Mr Blaxland [counsel for the claimant] suggested that although the police officers who attended the LEB showroom were on duty and in uniform, they were not present nor acting as police officers in the execution of their duty. They arrived to deal with the civil wrong of trespass. In that capacity they enjoyed no powers greater than those which could be exercised in ordinary circumstances by members of the LEB staff themselves, or if the LEB had arranged to use them, guards or attendants employed by 'civilian security' organisations. As a matter of public policy, so Mr Blaxland argued, it is undesirable for police officers to act at the behest of private individuals engaged in a private dispute, unless there is something to suggest an actual or pending breach of the peace. If they do, they are likely to be perceived by one side or the other to be taking sides. As the only report received by the police was that the plaintiff was refusing to leave the showroom and she was not causing any trouble beyond that, there was nothing requiring their attendance.

---

[157] *R v Waterfield and Lynn* [1964] 1 QB 164.   [158] [1936] 2 KB 434.
[159] [1966] 3 All ER 931.   [160] *Kerr v DPP* [1995] Crim LR 394.
[161] *DPP v Chapman* (1989) 89 Cr App R 190.   [162] *DPP v Hawkins* [1988] 3 All ER 673.
[163] *Osman v DPP* (1999) 163 JP 725.
[164] *Lineham v DPP* [2000] Crim LR 861; *O'Loughlin v Chief Constable of Essex* [1998] 3 WLR 374.
[165] *DPP v Chapman* (1988) 89 Cr App R 190.

In my judgment the obvious organisation to be contacted for assistance in a troublesome situation like the ejection of a trespasser is the police. Indeed if the police response were to the effect that 'this is not police business', some might sensibly ask, 'Why ever not?' A good example of the consequences of police inertia is provided by the tendency in earlier days to regard threatened or actual violence between spouses, or partners, as 'only domestic'. With a more positive police response a number of unpleasant incidents of violence might have been discouraged, if not altogether avoided. Mr Blaxland's proposal, said to be based on public policy, would create an environment in which the police would avoid, and be expected to keep clear of any involvement 'only civil', in an area of modern life affecting the community peace.

On analysis it is not strictly necessary to decide whether the police officers were acting in the execution of their duty when they first laid hands on the plaintiff, nor whether *Coffin v Smith* (1980) 72 Cr App R 221 correctly overruled *R v Prebble & Others* [1858] 1 F & F 325 and *R v Roxburgh* [1871] 12 Cox CC8. In my judgment the critical question in this case is not whether they were acting in the execution of their duty, but rather whether they were acting lawfully when they seized the plaintiff physically in order to remove her from the premises.

On the question of the lawfulness of the police behaviour, whether or not *R v Roxburgh* was rightly or wrongly decided in relation to the execution of a police officer's duty, Cockburn CJ observed that

> 'Although, no doubt, the prosecutor might not have been acting strictly speaking in the execution of his duty as a police officer, since he was not actually obliged to assist in ejecting the prisoner, yet he was acting quite lawfully in doing so; for the landlord had a right to eject the prisoner under the circumstances, and the prosecutor might lawfully assist him in so doing.'

(For more recent examples of the practical application of this reasoning, see *Glasbrook v Glamorgan County Council* [1925] AC 270: *R v Chief Constable of Devon and Cornwall, ex p CEGB* [1982] 1QB 458, particularly per Templeman LJ at 479–480). The present case provides another example of the same principle in operation.

The officers were not only acting lawfully when they arrived at and eventually began to remove the plaintiff from the showroom, but while so acting, even if not strictly in the execution of their duty, they were also entitled to arrest any individual responsible for or threatening or likely to cause a breach of the peace.

> 'Every citizen in whose presence a breach of the peace is being, or reasonably appears to be about to be, committed has the right to take reasonable steps to make the person who is breaking or threatening to break the peace refrain from doing so; and those reasonable steps in appropriate cases will include detaining him against his will. At common law this is not only the right of every citizen, it is also his duty, although, except in the case of the citizen who is a constable, it is a duty of imperfect obligation.' (Per Lord Diplock in *Albert v Lavin* [1982] AC 546 at 565.)

In my judgment this is a straightforward case. The first police officers to attend the showroom did so in direct response to a request for assistance made to their police station by a member of the public. They were at work as police officers, on duty, in uniform, when the call was received, and when they arrived. The woman police officers responded to a request for assistance from their male colleagues. They too were at work, on duty, and in uniform. These police officers were present to sort out a problem between members of the public in which there was an inherent risk of trouble, and by their presence, as well as by their efforts at persuasion, were seeking to ensure so far as they could, that the peace was maintained. If the plaintiff persisted in her refusal to leave voluntarily they were ultimately entitled to lay hands on her and physically remove her from the showroom against her wishes, again, a situation fraught with potential difficulty. This, in the end, is what they did. For the reasons already given their actions were lawful.

As I understood it, Mr Blaxland's argument seemed to predicate that until grounds for arrest existed, the execution of the police officers' duty was somehow postponed or deferred. I do not accept that a police officer on duty, offering practical assistance to a member of the public enforcing his civil rights, is not acting in the execution of his duty as a police officer until grounds for arrest have arisen. Police officers on duty are required to maintain and preserve the peace, if possible, before it is broken, as well as to restore it after things have gone wrong.

As to authority, this view is supported by the decision in *Coffin v Smith* (above) where the argument that a police officer cannot be held to be acting in the execution of his duty unless he is doing something that he is 'compelled by law to do', was emphatically rejected.

Sedley LJ: I agree with Lord Justice Judge that London Electricity were entitled to call the police and that the police were right to respond to the call. But it is important to be clear why this was so.

There is long-established authority that a constable may lawfully assist others in self-help, but acting as an individual and not as a constable: *R v Prebble* (1858) 1 F & F 325, *R v Roxburgh* (1871) 12 Cox CC 8. Equally, it is clear that everyone, whether a constable or not, has both a power and a duty to detain persons committing or provoking a breach of the peace, in order to abate or prevent it: *Albert v Lavin* [1982] AC 546. But neither of these powers is a power of arrest. The power of arrest, the purpose of which is to bring a person before a court, will arise if a person creates or threatens to create a fracas in the course of being lawfully removed, whether the police are assisting in the removal or (as they may be wiser sometimes to do) are standing by to keep the peace while the occupier removes the trespasser.

But it is argued by Mr McLeod for the Commissioner that a constable who assists in an eviction, provided he is present in performance of his general peacekeeping function, is acting in the execution of his duty even if no crime or breach of the peace has been committed and no power of arrest has arisen. If then, he argues, the trespasser fails to co-operate and compels the officers to use force, she has caused a breach of the peace. It is on this basis that he defends the judge's ruling, relying on the decision of a divisional court (Donaldson and Bristow JJ) in *Coffin v Smith* (1980) 72 Cr App R 221.

If it were necessary to analyse the reasoning in *Coffin v Smith*, I would have difficulty in accepting it as wholly correct, even though I have no doubt about the correctness of the conclusion. But as Lord Justice Judge has pointed out, the present case does not turn on whether the constables who removed Mrs Porter were acting in the execution of their duty: it turns on whether they were acting lawfully. In my judgment they were. By assisting London Electricity's staff to evict Mrs Porter they were acting as lawfully as the staff themselves would have been had they evicted her. This is established by the decisions in *Prebble* and *Roxburgh*, which I consider still to be good law. It was not necessary for the Divisional Court to overrule them in *Coffin v Smith* because there the constables were acting in the execution of their duty in standing by to keep the peace, not in taking any active part in the eviction of the youths.

In the present case, by contrast, a trespasser was being removed by police constables acting as voluntary agents for the occupiers of the premises. This they were free to do. If in the course of the eviction whoever was carrying it out a breach of the peace occurred or became imminent, their continuing duty as constables required them to intervene by detention or arrest. Such a breach of the peace 'is committed only when an individual causes harm, or appears likely to cause harm, to persons or property, or acts in a manner the natural consequence of which would be to provoke violence in others'

Appeal dismissed.

May LJ also delivered a judgment dismissing the appeal.

NOTES

1. See the discussion of the breach of the peace power, below, Chapter 5.

2. When the police are called to a civil dispute of this nature, it is likely that they will choose to exercise a power of arrest for breach of the peace. Is that not very likely to provoke anger from one of the parties and lead to an obstruction charge out of what was a mere civil dispute? The arrest power for breach of the peace should be used exceptionally only.

(ii) Physical contact in the course of 'exercising' duty

The question whether an officer has exceeded his powers when making 'trivial' contact with another has come under close scrutiny in a series of cases beginning with *Donnelly v Jackman*[166] which was later interpreted as having created only a very limited exception: *Bentley v Brudzinski*.

- **Bentley v Brudzinski** (1982) 75 Cr App 217, Queen's Bench Divisional Court

At about 3.30 a.m. PC Phillips was looking for a vehicle reported to have been taken without consent. He saw the defendant and his brother running barefoot along certain streets. They broadly fitted the description of the two men said to have taken the vehicle. The constable questioned them. They denied, truthfully, any involvement with the vehicle and after various interchanges moved off. PC Butler, who had just arrived on the scene, said 'Just a minute' then, not in any hostile way, but merely to attract attention he placed his right hand on [the defendant's] left shoulder. The defendant punched PC Butler in the face. The magistrates held there was no case to answer on a charge under s. 51(1) on the ground that PC Butler was not acting in the execution of his duty. The prosecutor's appeal to the Divisional Court was dismissed.

McCullough J: *Donnelly v Jackman* (1970) 54 Cr App Rep 229, [1970] 1 WLR 562 was in some ways similar case to the present on its facts. Mr Donnelly was charged with the same offence as here, assaulting a police constable in the execution of his duty. A Police Constable Grimmett had wanted to ask him certain questions. He had asked him to stop and tapped him on the shoulder. Mr Donnelly then tapped the officer's shoulder and said 'Now we are even, copper.' The police constable tapped Mr Donnelly on the shoulder a second time. It was found by the justices that his intention in so doing was to stop him and ask him further questions. Mr Donnelly's reaction was to strike the officer with some force. He was convicted, and appealed unsuccessfully by way of case stated to this Court.

In giving the first judgment, with which Ashworth J and Lord Parker CJ both agreed, Talbot J said at p. 232 and p. 565 of the respective reports:

'Turning to the facts of this matter, it is not very clear what precisely the justices meant or found when they said the officer touched the defendant on the shoulder, but whatever it was they really did mean, it seems clear to me that they must have felt it was a minimal matter by the way they treated this matter and the result of the case. When one considers the problem: was this officer acting in the course of his duty, one ought to bear in mind that it is not every trivial interference with a citizen's liberty that amounts to a course of conduct sufficient to take the officer out of the course of his duties. The facts that the magistrates found in this case do not justify the view that the police officer was not acting in the execution of his duty when he went up to the defendant and wanted to speak to him. Therefore the assault was rightly found to be an assault upon this officer whilst acting in the execution of his duty and I would dismiss this appeal.'

I observe that in that paragraph Talbot J simply referred 'to the officer going up to the defendant, wanting to speak to him and tapping him on the shoulder. He does not specifically advert in that paragraph, or anywhere in his judgment, to the justices' finding that the defendant was being stopped by the police officer.

I, for my part, think that in cases of this kind a great deal will inevitably turn on the impression that the witnesses have given to the justices. In *Donnelly's* case (supra) this Court was plainly of the view that what had happened was trivial and was not enough to take the officer out of the ordinary scope of his duties. The fact that that was the decision in *Donnelly v Jackman* (supra) does not of course necessarily mean that the decision will be the same in every case in which an officer goes up to a person in the street to ask him questions.

---

[166] [1970] 1 WLR 562.

In the next case, *Ludlow v Burgess* (1971) 25 Cr App Rep 227, which also is in many ways rather similar to the present case, the decision went the other way. It is only reported shortly in [1971] Crim LR 238. Again it is a decision of this Court with Lord Parker CJ presiding. What had happened was this. While a constable was getting on a bus he was kicked by a youth. The constable thought it was a deliberate kick but the defendant said it was accidental. The constable, who did not have his warrant card with him, told him not to use foul language and said that he was a police officer, whereupon the defendant began to walk away. The constable put a hand on his shoulder, not with the intention of arresting him, but to detain him for further conversation and inquiries. Then the defendant struggled and kicked the constable. Others joined in. In due course the defendant was charged with the same offence as here. He was convicted. His appeal was allowed by this Court, which said that 'the detention of a man against his will without arresting him was an unlawful act and a serious interference with the citizen's liberty. Since it was an unlawful act, it was not an act done in the execution of the constable's duty.

Although the precise circumstances of the touching are not apparent from the very short report, *Ludlow v Burgess* (supra) when compared with *Donnelly v Jackman* (supra) demonstrates that the decision in any individual case will turn on the particular circumstances in which the police officer and the citizen come into, if I may use a neutral word, engagement with one another. I have no doubt, looking at the circumstances as a whole, that both constables were trying to stop the defendant and his brother from going home in order to detain them and to question them further.

We have to ask ourselves whether the justices arrived at a decision which no bench could reasonably have reached. I can well understand, why they reached the decision they did. I would have reached the same decision myself.

Donaldson LJ: ... I entirely agree with McCullough J's conclusion and the reasons which led him to that conclusion.

NOTES

1. Bailey and Birch commented:[167]

The facts of *Donnelly v Jackman* and *Bentley v Brudzinski* are, however difficult to reconcile. It is possible that the tap on the shoulder *(Donnelly)* was genuinely more 'trivial' than the hand *(Bentley)*. This would be a very fine distinction, and one arguably untenable as the intentions of the officers in the two cases seem the same, i.e. to stop for questioning. Perhaps the real explanation is that the facts of the two cases are essentially the same, that the two benches of magistrates took divergent views, and the Divisional Court was not in a position to say that either was so unreasonable or perverse as to enable it to impose a different view.[168]

2. In *Kerr v DPP*,[169] K struck an officer who took hold of her arm in order to detain her, and began to caution her, in the mistaken belief that she had already been placed under arrest by another officer. The Divisional Court set aside her conviction for assaulting the officer in the execution of his duty. The officer's conduct was not so trivial as to fall within *Donnelly v Jackman*, he was clearly exceeding his powers and his mistaken (albeit honest and reasonable) belief was insufficient to cause him to be acting in the execution of his duty.

---

[167] [1982] Crim LR at 481–482.

[168] For further recent examples of the difficulty of drawing the boundaries of conduct which is within the exercise of the constable's duty see *Bucher v DPP* [2003] EWHC 580 (Admin) *and C v DPP* [2003] All ER (D) 37 (Nov).

[169] (1994) 158 JP 1048.

3. Is it possible to lay down cast-iron rules on the degree of interference that will be necessary to take an officer outside the execution of his duty? Note the court's desire to maintain consistency between this offence and the mainstream offences of assault. A further example of the problem was provided in *Mepstead v DPP*[170] in which police officers gave M a parking ticket having warned him about his parking. When M became abusive, one officer, L, took hold of M's arm and said 'Don't be silly, calm down, it's only a ticket'. The magistrates found that L was not seeking to arrest or detain M but held him solely in order to draw his attention to the content of what was being said to him and in attempt to calm the situation down. M assaulted L. Balcombe LJ stated:

Having already read the facts in detail it seems to me that the answer to the question can only be one, that is, yes, the police officer who takes a man's arm, not intending to detain or arrest him, but in order to draw his attention to the content of what was being said to him can be seen as acting within the execution of his duty. It is, of course, for the tribunal of fact to decide whether the physical contact goes beyond what is acceptable by the ordinary standards of everyday life and, as I said a little earlier in this judgment, if the period of contact had gone on for any length of time it might well be said to be a finding of fact, to which no reasonable court would come, to say that there was not an intention to detain.

Commenting on the case Birch[171] observed that '*Collins v Wilcock*' opens the door to the explicit argument that society should be more tolerant of direct and perhaps even slightly rough contact between a police officer and a citizen who is drunk or angry or otherwise behaving unreasonably'. Is that tolerance desirable?

(iii) There is no common law power to detain for questioning

● **Kenlin v Gardiner** [1967] 2 QB 510, [1987] 2 WLR 129, [1966] 3 All ER 931, 131 JP 191, 110 Sol Jo 848, Queen's Bench Divisional Court

Two boys were visiting homes of members of their school rugby team to remind them of a forthcoming match. Two plain-clothed police officers became suspicious of the boys' behaviour. One approached the boys and asked them what they were doing. He stated that he was a policeman and showed his warrant card but this information did not register in the minds of the boys. One boy tried to run away but was restrained by the officer. The boy, not realising the restrainer was a police officer, struck the officer and escaped. Further struggle ensued. The boys were charged under s. 51(1) of the Police Act 1964. They appealed against conviction.

Winn LJ: [W]as this officer entitled in law to take hold of the first boy by the arm? I feel myself compelled to say that the answer to that question must be in the negative. This officer might or might not in the particular circumstances have possessed a power to arrest these boys. I leave that question open, saying no more than that I feel some doubt whether he would have had a power of arrest: but on the assumption that he had a power of arrest, it is to my mind perfectly plain that neither of these officers purported to arrest either of these boys. What was done was not done as an integral step in the process of arresting, but was done in order to secure an opportunity, by detaining the boys from escape, to put to them or to either of them the question which was regarded as the test question to satisfy the officers whether or not it would be right in the circumstances, and having regard to the answer obtained from that question, if any, to arrest them.

I regret to say that I think there was a technical assault by the police officer.

Widgery J and **Lord Parker CJ** agreed.
Appeal allowed.

---

[170] [1996] Crim LR 111, 160 JP 475.   [171] [1996] Crim LR 612.

NOTES

1. For further judicial denials of the existence of any power at common law to detain for questioning see *R v Lemsatef*[172] and *R v Houghton and Francoisy*.[173]

2. In *DPP v L*,[174] because L had not been informed that she was under arrest, despite it being practicable for an officer to do so, her arrest was unlawful. However, that did not prevent her being convicted of assaulting a police officer in the execution of his duty, when the officer she assaulted was not the arrester but the custody officer at the station: the custody officer was in the execution of *his* duty. The Divisional Court held that a custody officer was entitled to assume that there had been a lawful arrest (see below).

3. PACE Code of Practice A governing stop and search (the latest draft of which came into effect in February 2008 and which is discussed in full below) confirms that the Code does not 'affect the ability of an officer to speak to or question a person in the ordinary course of the officer's duties without detaining him or exercising any element of compulsion'.[175]

(B) ASSAULT ON A POLICE OFFICER

There will usually be little doubt that the defendant has assaulted the officer, but questions as to whether the officer was in the execution of his duty and of the defendant's mistaken beliefs frequently arise. As for mistakes about the status of the officer, a person may be guilty under s. 89 even if he is unaware (whether reasonably or unreasonably) that the person he is assaulting is a constable.[176] In practice it will be much easier to establish a defence of self-defence founded on a mistake of fact where the defendant is unaware that the person assaulting or restraining him is a police officer, or honestly disbelieves the claim of, for example, a scruffy-looking individual to be a constable. If the defendant, not knowing his victim is a police officer, applies force to the officer believing that he is under attack, and that force would be reasonable if the victim had not been a police officer the defendant does not commit an offence under s. 89(1). The reason is that the defendant lacks the mens rea required for the assault since he does not intend to apply unlawful force to his victim and he is not reckless as to the risk of such force being applied.[177] A mistake of *law* as to the extent of a police officer's duty cannot be a defence. The defence of self-defence may, however, be established where there is a mistake of fact as to whether a constable is acting in the execution of his duty.[178]

(C) OBSTRUCTION OF A POLICE OFFICER

The offence under s. 89(2) is broader in its scope than that under s. 89(1). There is no need for proof of any physical contact, nor even an assault. The main cause for concern is whether it has been extended too far towards a position where simple disobedience to police instructions or even a lack of co-operation may constitute the offence.

---

[172] [1977] 1 WLR 812, per Lawton LJ at 816.

[173] (1978) 68 Cr App 197, per Lawton LJ at 205–206.

[174] [1999] Crim LR 752. [175] PACE Code A, para. 1, Note 1B.

[176] *R v Forbes and Webb* (1865) 10 Cox CC 362; *R v Maxwell and Clanchy* (1909) 2 Cr App R 26, CCA; see further, D. Ormerod, *Smith and Hogan on Criminal Law* (11th edn, 2005), p. 544.

[177] *Blackburn v Bowering* [1994] 3 All ER 380. See also *R v Jackson (Kenneth)* [1984] Crim LR 674.

[178] See Roch LJ in *Blackburn v Bowering* [1994] 3 All ER 380 at 389.

(I) REFUSING TO ANSWER QUESTIONS DOES NOT
CONSTITUTE OBSTRUCTION

- **Rice v Connolly** [1966] 2 QB 414, [1966] 2 All ER 649, [1966] 3 WLR 17, 130 JP 322, Queen's Bench Divisional Court

Police officers, patrolling late at night in an area where a number of break-in offences had just been committed, observed Rice loitering about the streets. The officers asked him where he was going to, where he had come from and for his name and address. Rice gave only his surname and the name of the street on which he said he lived. The officers asked Rice to accompany them to a nearby police-box so that this information could be checked. Rice refused to move unless arrested. The officers obliged. Rice appealed against conviction under s. 51(3) of the Police Act 1964.

Lord Parker CJ: What the prosecution have to prove is that there was an obstructing of a constable; that the constable was at the time acting in the execution of his duty and that the person obstructing did so wilfully. To carry the matter a little further, it is in my view clear that 'obstruct' under section 51(3) of the Police Act 1964, is the doing of any act which makes it more difficult for the police to carry out their duty. That description of obstructing I take from *Hinchliffe v Sheldon* [1955] 1 WLR 1207. It is also in my judgment clear that it is part of the obligations and duties of a police constable to take all steps which appear to him necessary for keeping the peace, for preventing crime or for protecting property from criminal injury. There is no exhaustive definition of the powers and obligations of the police, but they are at least those, and they would further include the duty to detect crime and to bring an offender to justice.

Pausing there, it seems to me quite clear that the defendant was making it more difficult for the police to carry out their duties, and that the police at the time and throughout were acting in accordance with their duties. The only remaining ingredient, and the one upon which in my judgment this case revolves, is whether the obstructing of which the defendant was guilty was a wilful obstruction. 'Wilful' in this context not only in my judgment means 'intentional' but something which is done without lawful excuse, and that indeed is conceded by Mr Skinner, who appears for the prosecution in this case. Accordingly, the sole question here is whether the defendant had a lawful excuse for refusing to answer the questions put to him. In my judgment he had. It seems to me quite clear that though every citizen has a moral duty or, if you like, a social duty to assist the police, there is no legal duty to that effect, and indeed the whole basis of common law is the right of the individual to refuse to answer questions put to him by persons in authority, and to refuse to accompany those in authority to any particular place; short, of course, of arrest.

In my judgment there is all the difference in the world between deliberately telling a false story—something which in no view a citizen has a right to do and preserving silence or refusing to answer something which he has every right to do.

Marshall J: I agree. In order to uphold this conviction it appears to me that one has to assent to the proposition that where a citizen is acting merely within his legal rights, he is thereby committing a criminal offence. Nor can I see that the manner in which he does it can make any difference whatsoever, and for me reasons given by my Lord I agree that this appeal should be allowed.

James J: Also for the reasons given by my Lord Chief Justice, I agree that this appeal should be allowed. For my own part, I would only add this, that I would not go so far as to say that there may not be circumstances in which the manner of a person together with his silence could amount to an obstruction within the section; whether it does remains to be decided in any case that happens hereafter, not in this case, in which it has not been argued.

Appeal allowed.

NOTES

1. The decision has been criticised on the ground that a sensible result was achieved by the doubtful mechanism of holding that the word 'wilfully' incorporated the concept of 'without lawful excuse'.

2. *Rice v Connolly* requires the courts to draw a distinction between certain acts of obstruction which s. 89(2) prohibits and other acts of obstruction which remain lawful notwithstanding the apparent terms of the subsection.

In accomplishing this task the courts have sometimes distinguished between active and passive obstruction. In *Dibble v Ingleton*,[179] in order to frustrate the administration of a breathalyser test, the defendant drank from a bottle of whisky. He was convicted under s. 51(3) of the Police Act 1964 and appealed. Giving the judgment of the Divisional Court, Bridge J said (at 488):

I would draw a clear distinction between a refusal to act, on the one hand, and the doing of some positive act on the other. In a case, as in *Rice v Connolly* [1966] 2 QB 414 where the obstruction alleged consists of a refusal by the defendant to do the act which the police constable had asked him to do to give information, it might be, or to give assistance to the police constable can see readily the soundness of the principle that such a refusal to act cannot amount to a wilful obstruction under section 51 unless the law imposes upon the person concerned some obligation in the circumstances to act in the manner requested by the police officer.

On the other hand, I can see no basis in principle or in any authority which has been cited for saying that where the obstruction consists of a positive act, it must be unlawful independently of its operation as an obstruction of a police constable under section 51. If the act relied upon as an obstruction had to be shown to be an offence independently of its effect as an obstruction it is difficult to see what use there would be in the provision of section 51 of the Police Act 1964.

In my judgment the act of the defendant in drinking whisky when he did with the object and effect of frustrating the procedure under sections 2 and 3 of the Road Safety Act 1967 was a wilful obstruction of Police Constable Tully.

Similarly, in *Sekfali, Banamira and Ouham v DPP*[180] three youths were approached by plain clothes officers on the street who wished to question them in relation to a recently reported occurrence of shoplifting. When the officers produced their warrant cards the youths ran away but were chased and caught. They were charged under s. 89(2) and the Divisional Court upheld their convictions for obstruction. The Court held that the youths were entitled to refuse to answer questions but by running away and impeding the asking of questions the youths were guilty of obstruction. However, although obstructive inaction is more likely to be excused by the courts than obstructive action, this is not always so. For example, in *Johnson v Phillips*,[181] in order to allow the passage of an ambulance, a police officer ordered the defendant to reverse the 'wrong way' down a one-way street. The defendant's refusal to do so was held to constitute an obstruction of the officer. The court asserted that a constable in purported exercise of his power to control traffic on a public road has the right to disobey a traffic regulation provided that he was acting to protect life and property and such a course of action was reasonably necessary: 'if he himself has that right then it follows that he can oblige

---

[179] [1972] 1 QB 480, DC.
[180] [2006] EWHC 894 (Admin); see also *R (on the application of DPP) v Glendinning* [2005] EWHC 2333 (Admin).
[181] [1975] 3 All ER 682.

others to comply with his instructions to disobey such a regulation'.[182] However, in *Green v DPP*,[183] the Divisional Court confirmed that it was not obstruction to advise a third party of his right not to answer questions. The fact that G did so in abusive terms and also told the police to 'fuck off' did not make any difference; the justices' finding that G's behaviour made it impossible for the officers to confirm or allay their suspicions of the third party meant no more than that they were unable to obtain answers.

3. The decision in *Ricketts v Cox*[184] has been widely criticised. Here the justices found that two police officers approached Ricketts and another man, named Blake, explained that a serious assault had taken place and that it was believed that 'coloured' youths were responsible, and asked 'would you care to tell me where you have been?' R and B 'were abusive, uncooperative and positively hostile to the officers from the outset. They used obscene language calculated to provoke and antagonise the officers and ultimately made to walk away from the officers before the completion of their inquiries'. The justices held that the totality of this behaviour amounted to obstruction. R was convicted of this offence. (B was charged only with assault on the police officer in the execution of his duty, but was acquitted as the blow was in response to the unlawful act of one of the constables taking hold of his arm.) The Divisional Court merely asserted that the justices were entitled to reach this conclusion and that the case was of the kind envisaged by James J in *Rice v Connolly* (above). On this basis the decision is highly doubtful.[185] If a refusal to answer questions is lawful it is difficult to see that accompanying it by abuse makes any difference. Ormrod LJ stated that the defendant had used threats,[186] although no weight was attached by either the justices or the court to the threats in isolation. In fact the stated case reveals that only B had appeared to use threats: 'You only think you're fucking big because you've got that uniform on man. I'll take you white blokes on any time.'[187] This could not be relevant to R's liability. Would it have justified the conviction of B for obstruction? Glanville Williams argues not: whatever was threatened, 'the police could not reasonably have believed that they were in danger of being assaulted, because they knew that all they had to do in order to close the incident was to cease pestering him with unwelcome questions'.[188]

However, the police are just as entitled to ask questions (provided they do not attempt to detain for questioning) as citizens are entitled to refuse to answer them (and, it appears, to tell the police to 'fuck off' or 'get stuffed' or whatever). Is it realistic to say that a threat to thump a police officer if he does not stop asking questions should not constitute an obstruction under s. 89(2)? Note that it is the threats in isolation that would constitute the obstruction, not the threats in conjunction with other lawful acts. Threats may constitute an offence of assault, or an offence under the Public Order Act.

4. In Scotland 'obstruct' has been limited to situations of physical interference however small.[189] Do you think this is a more satisfactory approach?

5. The requirement of 'wilfulness' (which does not appear in s. 89(1)) is taken as requiring that the defendant know or at least be reckless as to whether the person he is obstructing is a police officer: *Ostler v Elliott*.[190] Here, the defendant had taken a prostitute by car to a secluded place. Three 'informally dressed' young officers opened the passenger door. One

---

[182] Ibid., at 685. Note the criticisms of this case by U. Ross [1977] Crim LR 187.

[183] [1991] Crim LR 782.   [184] (1981) 74 Cr App Rep 298, DC.

[185] See G. Williams, *Textbook of Criminal Law* (2nd edn, 1983), p. 204; D. Ormerod, *Smith and Hogan Criminal Law* (11th edn, 2005), p. 549; K. Lidstone [1983] Crim LR 29, 33–35.

[186] (1981) 74 Cr App R 298 at 300.   [187] Ibid., at 299.

[188] G. Williams (1983) op. cit., p. 204.   [189] *Curlett v M'Kechnie* (1938) JC 176.

[190] [1980] Crim LR 584, DC.

said that they were police officers and asked the prostitute to get out (their intention was to arrest her for soliciting); but no identification was shown. The defendant drove off and let her out of the car. The court held that he was rightly acquitted of a charge under s. 51(3). He had reasonably supposed that the officers were accomplices of the prostitute who intended to rob him. Note that in *Osman v DPP*[191] the Divisional Court held that the officer's failure to provide his name and station meant that he was not in the execution of his duty when searching the suspect.

(II) THE SIGNIFICANCE OF THE PURPOSE OF INTERFERENCE WITH POLICE AUTHORITY

- **Lewis v Cox** [1985] QB 509, [1984] 3 WLR 875, 148 JP 601, Queen's Bench Divisional Court

A drunk was arrested and placed in the back of a police van. C opened the rear door to ask him where he was being taken. PC Lewis, the driver, closed the door, warned C that if he opened it again he would be arrested for obstruction. C did it again, and L arrested him. The justices acquitted C on a charge under s. 51 (3) of the Police Act 1964, holding that his conduct was not aimed at the police and that he did not intend to obstruct the police. The Divisional Court allowed the prosecutor's appeal.

Webster J: [T]here is a line of authority that the word 'wilfully' in the context of section 51(3) of the Police Act, 1964 connotes an element of mens rea. I find it necessary to consider this line of authority, although not every case in it, in some detail because it cannot, in my view, confidently be asserted that the test, whether the actions of the defendant are aimed at the Police', is the definitive and authoritative test.

It can, however, in my view be confidently stated, as I have already mentioned, that the word 'wilfully' imports an element of mens rea. In *Betts v Stevens* [1910] 1 KB I, a case arising out of the warnings given at the time by AA patrol men to those who were exceeding the speed limit of the existence of a nearby police trap, Darling J, dealing with the question of intention, said at page 8: 'The gist of the offence to my mind lies in the intention with which the thing is done'.

In *Willmott v Atack* [1977] QB 498, [1976] 3 All ER 794, the defendant had intervened and obstructed a Police Officer while the Officer was attempting to restrain a man under arrest and take him to a police car. The Justices convicted him of an offence under section 51(3) of the Police Act, 1964. Although they found that the defendant had intervened in the belief that he could resolve the situation better than the Police, they concluded that his deliberate conduct had obstructed the Police, and that he was therefore guilty of wilful obstruction. This Court allowed him appeal against that conviction. Before this Court, Counsel for the defendant contended (see page 500), that: 'The proper interpretation of "wilfully obstructs" within section 51(3) of the Police Act 1964 is that there should not merely be an intention on the part of the defendant to do something which happens to result in an obstruction of a Police Officer in the execution of his duty, but that there should also be an element of hostility and criminal intent towards the Police Officer.'

Croom-Johnson J, who gave the first judgment, said at pages 504–5: 'When one looks at the whole context of section 51, dealing as it does with assaults upon Constables in subsection (1) and concluding in sub-section (3) with resistance and wilful obstruction in the execution of the duty, I am of the view that the interpretation of this sub-section for which the defendant contends is the right one. It fits the words 'wilfully obstructs' in the context of the sub-section, and in my view there must be something in the nature

[191] (1999) 163 JP 725.

of a criminal intent of the kind which means that it is done with the idea of some form of hostility to the Police with the intention of seeing that what is done is to obstruct, and that it is not enough merely to show that he intended to do what he did and that it did in fact have the result of the Police being obstructed'.

May J (as he then was) agreed. He observed that the word 'wilfully' had been inconsistently interpreted in various statutes which defined criminal offences, and continued: I agree with Croom-Johnson J that when one looks at the judgment of Darling J in *Betts v Stevens* [1910] 1 KB I (supra) it is clear that 'wilfully' in this particular statute does import a requirement of mens rea'.

Lord Widgery, in a very short judgment at page 505, agreed that the question posed should be answered in the negative, that question being (see page 502): 'whether upon a charge of wilfully obstructing a Police Officer in the execution of his duty it is sufficient for the prosecution to prove that the defendant wilfully did an act which obstructed the Police Officer in the execution of his duty, or must the prosecution further prove that the defendant intended to obstruct the Police Officer'.

In *Moore v Green* [1983] 1 All ER 663, DC, the facts of which are immaterial for present purposes, McCullough J, at page 665, having cited the passage from the judgment of Croom-Johnson J in *Willmott v Alatk* [1977] QB 498, DC (which I have just cited) said: 'I do not understand the reference to "hostility" to indicate a separate element of the offence. I understand the word to bear the same meaning as the phrase which Croom-Johnson J used immediately afterwards, namely 'the intention of seeing that what is done is to obstruct'...

Griffiths LJ agreed with the judgment of McCullough J. Finally, on this aspect of the matter, I return to *Hills v Ellis* [1983] QB 680, [1983] 1 All ER 667. In that case the appellant, while leaving a football match, saw two men fighting and formed the view that one of them was the innocent party in the fight. He then saw a Police Officer arresting the man he thought was innocent. He approached them with the intention of intervening on the part of the arrested man and, being unable to make his voice heard above the noise of the crowd, he grabbed the Police Officer's elbow to draw the Officer's attention to the fact that he was arresting the wrong man.

Another Police Officer warned the appellant that if he did not desist, he might himself be arrested for obstructing the Police. The appellant persisted in trying to stop the arrest, and was charged with wilful obstruction of a Police Officer in the execution of his duty. The Magistrates convicted him.

On his appeal he contended, inter alia, that, since his motive was to correct the Police Officer's error in arresting the wrong person, he had not acted with hostility towards the Police Officer. It was conceded that the Officer was lawfully arresting that man.

Griffiths LJ at page 670 cited the same passage from the judgment of Croom-Johnson J in *Willmott v Atack*...and continued: 'The appellant's Counsel argues from that passage that, as the motive here was merely to correct the policeman's error, it cannot be said that he, the appellant, was acting with hostility towards the Police. But in my view the phrase hostility towards the Police in that passage means no more than that the actions of the defendant are aimed at the Police. There can be no doubt here that his action in grabbing a policeman's arm was aimed at that policeman. It was an attempt to get that policeman to desist from the arrest that he was making. In my view, this is as clear a case as we can have of obstructing a Police Officer in the course of his duty, and the Justices came to the right decision.'

McCullough J agreed with the judgment of Griffiths LJ, and added, at page 671: 'I am uncertain what Croom-Johnson J had in mind when he used the word "hostility". Hostility suggests emotion and motive, but motive and emotion are alike irrelevant in criminal law. What matters is intention that is what state of affairs the defendant intended to bring about. What motive he had while so intending is irrelevant. What is meant by "an intention to obstruct"? I would construe "wilfully obstructs" as doing deliberate acts with the intention of bringing about a state of affairs which, objectively regarded, amount to an obstruction as that phrase was explained by Lord Parker in *Rice v Connolly* [1966] 2 QB 414, [1966] 2 All ER 649 at 651, i.e. making it more difficult for the Police to carry out their duty. The fact that the defendant might not himself have called that state of affairs an obstruction is, to my mind, immaterial. That is not to say that it is enough to do deliberate actions which, in fact, obstruct; there must be an intention that those actions should result in the further state of affairs to which I have been referring'.

Lord Parker CJ, on the same page of his judgment in *Rice v Connolly* [1966] 2 QB 414 at page 419 said that 'wilful' in the context of this section 'not only in my judgment means "intentional" but something which is done without lawful excuse'; and Lord Parker's explanation of 'wilfully obstructs' as being something which makes it more difficult for the Police to carry out their duties was taken by him from the judgment of Lord Goddard CJ in *Hinchliffe v Sheldon* [1955] 3 All ER 406, [1955] 1 WLR 1207, where Lord Goddard said: 'Obstructing, for the present purpose, means making it more difficult for the Police to carry out their duties'.

For my part I conclude that, although it may not be unhelpful in certain cases to consider whether the actions of a defendant were aimed at the Police, the simple facts which the Court has to find are whether the defendant's conduct in fact prevented the Police from carrying out their duty, or made it more difficult for them to do so, and whether the defendant intended that conduct to prevent the Police from carrying out their duty or to make it more difficult to do so.

In the present case the test which the Justices applied was whether the defendant had deliberately done some act which was aimed at the Police, they found that his actions were not aimed at the Police and they accordingly dismissed the charge. In my view, for the reasons which I have given, the justices did not ask themselves the right question for the purposes of the present case, or the whole of the right question.

[His Lordship examined the facts. He noted, *inter alia*, that C must have known that the police van could not be driven away with the door open, and, before he opened the door the second time, that L was about to drive the van away. It was not suggested that C had a lawful excuse for his conduct.]

In my view, therefore, if the Justices had also asked themselves whether the respondent had, by opening the door, intended to make it more difficult for the Police to perform their duties in order to carry out his intention of asking where Marsh was to be taken they must, on the evidence, have been satisfied so as to feel sure that he had such an intention.

Although the question whether a defendant's conduct is aimed at the Police may not be an unhelpful question in certain circumstances, where, as here: a defendant intended to do one thing in order to carry out his intention of doing another, that test, which might be appropriate if the Court had to find what was the defendant's predominant intention, can, in my view, mislead the Court if it is not necessary to do that. For my part I conclude, therefore, that if the Justices had directed themselves properly in the way in which I have set out they must, on the evidence, have decided that the respondent, when he opened the door on the second occasion, intended to make it more difficult for the Police to carry out their duties, even though that was not his predominant intention, and they ought, therefore, to have convicted him of the charge against him.

Kerr LJ: I agree with Webster J's analysis of the authorities. The actus reus is the doing of an act which has the effect of making it impossible or more difficult for members of the Police to carry out their duty. The word 'wilfully' clearly imports an additional requirement of mens rea. The act must not only have been done deliberately, but with the knowledge and intention that it will have this obstructive effect. But in the absence of a lawful excuse, the defendant's purpose or reason for doing the act is irrelevant, whether this be directly hostile to, or 'aimed at', the Police, or whether he has some other purpose or reason. Indeed, in the majority of cases the intention to obstruct the Police will not be simply 'anti-Police', but will stem from some underlying reason or objective of the defendant which he can only achieve by an act of intentional obstruction. This may be to assist an offender, which could be termed 'hostile' to the Police. Equally, the motivation could be public-spirited, for instance, by intervening on behalf of someone whom the defendant believes to be innocent, as in *Hills v Ellis* [1983] QB 680, [1983] 1 All ER 667, DC. Or it may be for some neutral reason for instance because the defendant consider that something else should have a higher priority than the duty on which the Police Officer is immediately engaged. In all such cases, if the defendant intentionally does an act which he realises will, in fact, have the effect of obstructing the Police in we sense defined above, he will in my view be guilty of having done so 'wilfully', with the necessary mens rea. In the absence of a lawful excuse, the defendant's underlying intention, reason or purpose for intentionally obstructing the Police is irrelevant, because the intention to obstruct is present at the same time. *Willmott v Atack* [1977] QB 498, [1976] 3 All ER 794 only went the other way because the defendant's intention was in fact to assist the police.

Appeal allowed. Case remitted with a direction to convict.

NOTES

1. Some of the cases discussed raise the problem of defendants with mixed purposes. A person may: (1)(a) intend to obstruct a policeman in the performance of one task, (b) with the further intention of aiding him in the performance of another task;[192] or (2)(a) intend to obstruct a policeman in the performance of a task, (b) with the further intention of pursuing some private purpose of his own (e.g. *Lewis v Cox*). The law could say either (1) that the presence of an intention to obstruct is sufficient for liability, irrespective of any other purpose, or (2) that the presence of an intention to help is sufficient for an acquittal or (3) that the answer should depend upon which motive was dominant. *Hills v Ellis* seems to adopt the first of these approaches; *Willmott v Atack* the second. It is difficult to see that the conduct in *Willmott v Atack* is distinguishable from that in *Hills v Ellis* and one of the cases is accordingly wrongly decided. Which do you prefer? *Lewis v Cox* is rightly decided on either approach as the defendant clearly is not entitled to set his own private purposes above those of the officer.

2. Some of the cases also illustrate the point that no physical obstruction is necessary. For example, the offence under s. 89(2) may be committed where a warning is given in order that the commission of a crime may be suspended whilst there is a danger of detection, for example, a warning to motorists who are speeding that a police speed trap is ahead: *Betts v Stevens*;[193] a warning to a licensee suspected of serving drinks after hours that the police are outside (so that it could not then be proved that an offence had been committed).

3. GENERAL ASPECTS OF POLICE POWERS

(A) THE CONCEPT OF 'REASONABLE SUSPICION'

Most of the coercive powers of the police are conditioned on the presence of reasonable 'suspicion', 'cause' or 'belief' in the existence of a state of affairs—commonly that the object of the power is involved, actually or potentially, in a particular criminal offence. The significance of this trigger should not be underestimated, especially since it forms the basis of one of the grounds upon which detention can occur within Art. 5 of the European Convention. In *O'Hara v United Kingdom*[194] the European Court commented that 'reasonable suspicion presupposes the existence of facts or information which would satisfy an objective observer

---

[192] E.g. *Hills v Ellis* [1983] QB 680, [1983] 1 All ER 667.

[193] [1910] 1 KB 1. See also *R (on the application of DPP) v Glendinning* [2005] EWHC 2333 (Admin).

[194] (2002) 34 EHRR 32.

that the person concerned may have committed a criminal offence'.[195] What may be regarded as 'reasonable' will however depend on all the circumstances.[196]

PACE Code of Practice G which governs the power of arrest provides little guidance on what amounts to 'reasonable suspicion'. Some judicial guidance was provided in the following case.

● **Castorina v Chief Constable of Surrey** (1988) NLJR 180, Lexis,
   Court of Appeal (Civil Division)

Detectives reasonably concluded that the burglary of a company's premises was an 'inside job'. The managing director, Mrs Wilton, told them that she had recently dismissed someone (the plaintiff) although she did not think it would have been her, and that the documents taken would be useful to someone with a grudge. The detectives interviewed the plaintiff having found out that she had no criminal record, and arrested her under the Criminal Law Act 1967, s. 2(4). She was detained for three and three-quarter hours at the police station and interrogated, and then released without charge. She claimed damages for wrongful arrest and detention. Judge Lermon QC held that the officers had a prima facie case for suspicion but the arrest was premature; he applied as a definition of reasonable cause 'honest belief founded on reasonable suspicion leading an ordinary cautious man to the conclusion that the person arrested was guilty of the offence', and stated that an ordinary man would have sought more information from the suspect, including an explanation for any grudge on her part. A jury awarded £4,500. The Court of Appeal (Purchas and Woolf LJJ, and Sir Frederick Lawton) allowed an appeal by the chief constable.

Purchas LJ: The powers under which the police officers acted are contained in section 2(4) of the Criminal Law Act 1967. This section provides:

'2(4) Where a constable, with reasonable cause, suspects that an arrestable offence has been committed, he may arrest without warrant anyone whom he, with reasonable cause, suspects to be guilty of the offence.'

No question arises on the first part of this section, namely the commission of an arrestable offence. The debate centres solely around the words 'whom he, with reasonable cause, suspects to be guilty of the offence'. These powers have now been replaced by section 24(6) of the Police and Criminal Evidence Act 1984 which, however, repeats in substance the same phrase 'he may arrest without a warrant anyone whom he has reasonable grounds for suspecting to be guilty of the offence'. The exercise, therefore, is to consider the information available to the arresting officer at the time when he makes his decision to arrest in order to see whether that information is sufficient to form 'reasonable' cause for the officer's suspicion.

Mr Wilson, who appeared for the appellant, submitted that the judge directed himself incorrectly on this aspect of the law...He submitted that the judge's definition extended the strictness of the requirements imposed upon the arresting officer beyond those imposed in the section in the respect that the honest belief must lead an ordinary cautious man to the conclusion that the person was guilty of the offence. Mr Wilson illustrated the distinction by reference to a police officer investigating a crime which could only have been committed by one individual but where there were two or more candidates in respect of whom

---

[195] Ibid., paras 34, 36.
[196] See *Fox, Campbell and Hartley v UK* (1990) 13 EHRR 157, para. 32. The European Court of Human Rights has also held that the level of suspicion need not be as high as that required to prefer charges: *Murray v UK* (1995) 19 EHRR 193, para. 55.

it was perfectly possible to hold a reasonable suspicion that one or other was guilty, whilst it would be impossible to have reason to believe in the conclusion that more than one was guilty. A similar analogy, Mr Wilson submitted, was to be found in the case of a person charged who was found in the possession of stolen goods but who might, as a result of the doctrine of recent possession, be guilty of the theft rather than handling the goods...

I turn first, however, to the judgment of Peter Pain J [in *Holtham v Metropolitan Police Comr* (1987) Times, 8 January] which, subsequently to the judgment of Judge Lermon QC, was reversed in the Court of Appeal on 25 November 1987 [(1987) Times, 28 November]. Mr Wilson referred to an extract from the judgment of Peter Pain J which was cited by the Master of the Rolls in the *Holtham* case. This passage was part of the transcript which was before the trial judge:

> 'the police do not have to have good evidence which would establish a prima facie case before they arrest. All they have to have is reasonable grounds for suspicion, which may be a good deal less. It may even involve matters which would not be admissible in evidence in court. But the statute requires them to have reasonable grounds for suspicion, and that, in my view, is something a good deal more than suspicion. ...'

The Master of the Rolls criticised this passage in the following terms:

> 'With all respect to the learned judge, I do not think that this is a correct statement of the law. As it was put by Lord Devlin in *Hussien v Chong Fook Kam* [1970] AC 942 at 948, "Suspicion in its ordinary meaning is a state of conjecture or surmise where proof is lacking: I suspect but I cannot prove". Suspicion may or may not be based upon reasonable grounds, but it still remains suspicion and nothing more. By applying a test of something which was not suspicion but was "something a good deal more than suspicion", I think that the learned judge erred and that this error was fundamental to his conclusion.'

Mr Wilson submitted that, following the approach of Peter Pain J, the judge in this case had relied upon a definition which required a state of mind higher than suspicion, namely a state of mind which concluded that the person arrested was in fact guilty of the offence.

It is clear from the notes made by the judge at the end of the evidence that the passage from the judgment of Lord Devlin in *Hussien v Chong Fook Kam* [1970] AC 942 was to the mind of the judge. It is helpful to read a little more of the context in which the passage cited by the Master of the Rolls is to be found. *Hussien's* case concerned sections of the criminal code in Malaysia but the equivalent sections dealing with malicious prosecution, on the one hand, and false imprisonment, on the other, carried similar distinctions to those present in the law of this country. Citing from the judgment of Lord Devlin at [1970] AC page 947H:

> 'Mr Gratiaen has criticised the test adopted in the Federal Court. Suffian FJ, who delivered the judgment of the court, said that the information available to the police was insufficient to prove prima facie a case against the plaintiffs under section 304A of the Penal Code or under section 34A of the Road Traffic Ordinance. Mr Gratiaen submits that this is the test appropriate in actions for malicious prosecution and not in actions for false imprisonment.
>
> Whether or not this is so—and their Lordships do not wish to add any further formulae to those already devised for the action for false imprisonment—it would appear to be a much stiffer test than the reasonable suspicion, which is the foundation of the power given in section 23(i)(a) of the Criminal Procedure Code. Suspicion in its ordinary meaning is a state of conjecture or surmise where proof is lacking: "I suspect but I cannot prove." Suspicion arises at or near the starting-point of an investigation of which the obtaining of prima facie proof is the end. When such proof has been obtained, the police case is complete; it is ready for trial and passes on to its next stage. It is indeed desirable as a general rule that an arrest should not be made until the case is complete. But if arrest before that were forbidden, it could seriously hamper the police. To give power to arrest on reasonable suspicion does not mean that it is always or even ordinarily to be exercised. It means that there is an executive discretion on the exercise of it many factors have to

be considered besides the strength of the case. The possibility of escape, the prevention of further crime and the obstruction of police inquiries are examples of those factors which all judges who have had to grant or refuse bail are familiar. There is no serious danger in a large measure of executive discretion in the first instance because in countries where common law principles prevail the discretion is subject indirectly to judicial control.'

There are two quite distinct considerations apparent in this passage, namely what is sufficient in order to establish the right in the arresting officer to make the arrest, namely suspicion on reasonable grounds, and the second stage, namely whether in all the circumstances the officer has in making his executive decision acted within his discretion or whether he is subject to criticism under the *Wednesbury* principle (See *Associated Provincial Picture Houses v Wednesbury Corpn* [1948] 1 KB 223, [1947] 2 All ER 680) for wrongful exercise of an executive discretion. In this appeal we are concerned solely with the first of these two aspects.

I now turn to *Dumbell v Roberts* [1944] 1 All ER 326 which was the third authority listed by the judge. It is to be remembered that this case concerned special powers of arrest contained in section 513, in association with section 507 of the Liverpool Corporation Act 1921. The effect of these sections is to give a power of arrest where a person was found in possession of, in that case, an excessive quantity of soap flakes for the possession of which he was unable to give a reasonable explanation. The passages upon which the judge appears to have relied in the judgment of Scott LJ are:

> 'The police are not called on before acting to have anything like a prima facie case for conviction; but the duty of making such inquiry as the circumstances of the case ought to indicate to a sensible man is, without difficulty, presently practicable, does rest on them; for to shut your eyes to the obvious is not to act reasonably.
>
> They may have to act on the spur of the moment and have no time to reflect and be bound, therefore, to arrest, to prevent escape; but where there is no danger of the person who has ex hypothesi aroused their suspicion, that he is probably an "offender" attempting to escape, they should make all the presently practicable enquiries from persons present or immediately accessible who are likely to be able to answer their enquiries forthwith. I am not suggesting a duty on the police to try to prove innocence; that is not their function; but they should act on the assumption that their prima facie suspicion may be ill founded. That duty attaches particularly where slight delay does not matter because there is no probability, in the circumstances of the arrest or intended arrest, of the suspected person running away.'

Basing himself upon this passage from the judgment of Scott LJ, the learned judge formed his conclusion that the arrest was premature....

In the judgment of Goddard LJ, with whom Luxmoore LJ agreed, in *Dumbell's* case it is made clear that the majority of the court dealt with the case as one arising particularly under the provisions of the Liverpool Corporation Act in which section 513 gave a power to arrest 'when the common law grounds are absent'. The remarks of Scott LJ did not, therefore, form part of the *ratio decidendi* of the majority of the court.

Mr Wilson also attacked the reference to 'honest belief' in the legal definition of reasonable cause. The test provided by the section requires that the suspicion must arise from reasonable cause. Reasonable cause, it is not disputed, is to be determined as an objective matter from the information available to the arresting officer and cannot have anything to do with the subjective state of the officer's mind. This may well be relevant in the offence of malicious prosecution. With all respect to the learned judge it appears that he has confused belief, which plays no part in the power of arrest under the section, and suspicion, based upon reasonable grounds which does. Honest belief, therefore, cannot be relevant. To the extent that the judge has specifically found honest belief and stated it in his judgment this is an indication that he has misdirected himself....

With respect to the judge I agree with Mr Wilson's submissions that, in concentration on what the officers might or might not have done by way of further inquiry before arrest, the judge's attention was deflected from the critical question, namely when they arrested her did they have reasonable cause for suspecting that the respondent was guilty of the offence? (See *Holgate-Mohammed v Duke* [1984] AC 437, [1984] 1 All ER 1054). In that case the trial judge had found that the detective constable had had reasonable cause to suspect the plaintiff of having committed an arrestable offence but, because the constable had decided not to interview her under caution but to subject her to the greater pressure of arrest and detention so as to induce a confession, there had been a wrongful exercise of the power of arrest. From the speech of Lord Diplock, who delivered the leading speech, it is clear that the failure to interrogate before arrest did not impair the lawfulness of the arrest in the first instance under the powers of section 2(4) but that the exercise of those powers before interrogation in order to enhance the chances of obtaining a confession had to be tested against the principles laid down in *Associated Provincial Picture Houses Ltd v Wednesbury Corpn* [1948] 1 KB 223, [1947] 2 All ER 680. Their Lordships decided that in the circumstances of that case there had been no such breach of the *Wednesbury* principle.

There is ample authority for the proposition that courses of inquiry which may or may not be taken by an investigating police officer before arrest are not relevant to the consideration whether, on the information available to him at the time of the arrest, he had reasonable cause for suspicion. Of course, failure to follow an obvious course in exceptional circumstances may well be grounds for attacking the executive exercise of that power under the *Wednesbury* principle. The position is very starkly pointed out in a passage from the judgment of Sir John Arnold P in *Mohammed-Holgate's* case in the Court of Appeal [1984] 1 QB 209, [1983] 3 All ER 526 at page 216C of the former report:

'As to the proposition that there were other things which he might have done, no doubt there were other things which he might have done first. He might have obtained a statement from her otherwise than under arrest to see how far he could get. He might have obtained a specimen of her handwriting and sent that off for forensic examination against a specimen of the writing of the person who had obtained the money by selling the stolen jewellery, which happened to exist in the case. All those things he might have done. He might have carried out fingerprint investigations if he had first obtained a print from the plaintiff: but the fact that there were other things which he might have done does not, in my judgment, make that which he did do into an unreasonable exercise of the power of arrest if what he did do, namely to arrest, was within the range of reasonable choices available to him.'

At an earlier stage of the hearing in dealing with an argument as to a preliminary point, Sir John Arnold referred to the judgment of Scott LJ in *Dumbell's* case confirming that the passage upon which the judge had relied went not to the question of suspicion on reasonable grounds but to the executive exercise of a discretionary power—see [1983] 3 All ER 526 at page 530F:

'The real reason why this line of argument fails is simply that the whole of what Scott LJ says is plainly directed in the context in which it was said not to the question of whether the police arrested with reasonable cause a person whom they suspected of having committed the crime, but whether it was reasonable to carry out the arrest even if the power were available, in other words the very point which was decided by the judge against the police and on which the main appeal is founded.'

This court has recently commented upon this part of the judgment of Scott LJ in the case of *Ward v Chief Constable of Avon and Somerset Constabulary* (unreported) Court of Appeal transcript for 25th June 1986. After pointing out that the arrest in *Dumbell's* case was under the special powers of the Liverpool Corporation Act Croom-Johnson LJ said this:

'After saying the plaintiff's appeal would be allowed, and a new trial ordered, Lord Justice Scott made some general observations which were obiter, about what might amount to reasonable suspicion of guilt justifying an arrest. The passage relied on (p. 329G) stressed the need for the police to 'make all presently practicable enquiries from persons present or immediately accessible who are likely to be able to answer their enquiries forthwith. Thus is it said here that Det Sgt Edwards' enquiries were not detailed enough.

But it is necessary for the police to probe every explanation. Section 2(4) of the Criminal Law Act 1967 requires the constable to have 'reasonable cause' for suspicion before he arrests.'

With respect, I adopt the approach of Croom-Johnson LJ in this case. The strictures made by Judge Lermon about the failure of the arresting police officers to inquire of the respondent whether she did or did not actually have a grudge against her erstwhile employers fall within the criticism made more than once in this court of the approach based on the judgment of Scott LJ. It can be tested by asking whether the investigation would have been advanced if the police officers had pursued the point and were met with a flat denial. In my judgment, the judge was wrong to rely on the judgment of Scott LJ and this led him erroneously to conclude that the arrest was premature and, therefore, unlawful. I have, therefore, come to the conclusion that Mr Wilson's submissions on this aspect of the case are made out and that the learned judge misdirected himself in applying the provisions of section 2(4) of the Act.

[Purchas LJ then rejected the plaintiff's argument that the court should order a retrial before a jury; the primary facts were not in dispute, and it was 'open to the court to draw the necessary inferences of secondary fact in order to determine whether the arresting officers had reasonable cause to suspect'. On this question, he continued:]

Mr Scrivener urged upon us that there was a duty upon the police officers to have made these inquiries, in other words that the judge was right in holding that the arrest was premature. He also submitted that there had been no lie or inconsistency in the responses given by the respondent prior to arrest, or indeed subsequent thereto. His submissions were based on an assertion that at the time of arrest, without an inquiry as to whether or not the respondent held a grudge, there was insufficient information upon which the officers could have had reasonable cause to suspect that she had committed the offence. But, with respect to Mr Scrivener, this approach discloses the fallacy of looking at what the officers might have done by way of inquiry rather than looking at the information they had gained in order to apply the test required by section 2(4). Of course, if it was relevant to consider what inquiries the officers might have made, then it would be equally relevant to consider what the result of those inquiries might have been. The evidence led before the learned judge of the inquiries made by the police officers after receiving the respondent's emphatic denial that she had a grudge, disclosed further grounds for suspicion. The note of the evidence of DC Thorne reads:

'Further enquiries. 'Phoned Mrs Wilson [*sic. Ed.*] to learn more about ill feeling by the Plaintiff. Mrs Wilson told me that the Plaintiff had made false statements to other people about the Company. Specifically had told others within the Company that the Company was heading for financial ruin. That is the Plaintiff was running the Company down in a malicious way.'

The names of other people were obtained from Mrs Wilton but inquiries of these people did not prove fruitful. Mrs Wilton's evidence as noted by the judge was:

'Two days after the Plaintiff left I had telephone calls, one from our Manchester supervisor, Mrs Templeton. She said that the Plaintiff had told her that she had left the Company which was in financial difficulties and that it was unlikely that her interviewers would get paid for the work. Also two other telephone calls, one of a similar nature from another supervisor and one from the field director of NOP who had also been told that we were in financial difficulties. I understood then that rumours were going about the Company which concerned me. Prior to the burglary I had contacted my solicitor as a result of the 'phone calls. She suggested writing a letter threatening litigation. She drafted a letter which was sent to the Plaintiff together with her salary cheque "unless she stopped slandering the Company we would take further proceedings".'

Had the police officers pressed their inquiries further she may well have told them all of this. This evidence demonstrates the difficult and unsatisfactory waters into which the inquiry drifts if the approach advocated by the judge had been adopted. For the reasons already given in this judgment, however, I consider that the failure to carry out this line of inquiry is not relevant to considering the objective question of reasonable cause within the meaning of section 2(4). I, therefore, find myself unable to accede to Mr Scrivener's submissions in support of the judgment based on premature arrest.

This leaves the final inquiry to be made by this court as to whether or not as an objective criterion there was sufficient information available to the arresting officers to give them 'reasonable cause to suspect that the respondent was guilty of the burglary'. I have already outlined the unusual features of the burglary which became apparent to the arresting officers on their visit to the Company's premises on the morning of 23rd June. These features need not be repeated here. They do indicate a very specific and particular character which could safely be attributed to the burglar in a number of different respects, i.e. experience, motive and inside knowledge of affairs within the Company's premises. In addition to this the information also given to the arresting officers by Mrs Wilton at the first stage of their inquiries identified the respondent as the only person who possessed these particular qualities. In the circumstances of this case, and I emphasise that every case has to be determined upon its particular facts, I am satisfied that the arresting officers had reasonable cause to suspect that the respondent was guilty of this unusual burglary.

For these reasons, therefore, I would allow this appeal and set aside the award of damages made by the jury enshrined in the judge's order.

Woolf LJ and **Sir Frederick Lawton** delivered concurring judgments.

Appeal allowed.

NOTES

1. In his judgment, Woolf LJ stated that, in a case where it is alleged that there has been an unlawful arrest, there are three questions to be answered:

1. Did the arresting officer suspect that the person who was arrested was guilty of the offence? The answer to this question depends entirely on the findings of fact as to the officer's state of mind.

2. Assuming the officer had the necessary suspicion, was there reasonable cause for that suspicion? This is a purely objective requirement to be determined by the judge, if necessary on facts found by a jury.

3. If the answer to the two previous questions is in the affirmative, then the officer has a discretion which entitles him to make an arrest and in relation to that discretion the question arises as to whether the discretion has been exercised in accordance with the principles laid down by Lord Greene MR in *Associated Provincial Picture Houses Ltd v Wednesbury Corpn* [1948] 1 KB 223, [1947] 2 All ER 680.

This three question test was reaffirmed by Auld LJ in *Al Fayed v Comr of Police for the Metropolis*.[197]

Clayton and Tomlinson[198] argue that *Castorina* was incorrect in holding that the possibility of 'further inquiries' cannot be relevant to the question whether there are reasonable grounds for an arrest:

It is clear law that reasonable cause will only be present if a reasonable man, in the position of the officer at the time of arrest, would have thought that the plaintiff was probably guilty of the offence: see *Dallison v Caffery* [1965] 1 QB 348, 371 and *Wiltshire v Barrett* [1966] 1 QB 312, 322.

---

[197] [2004] EWCA Civ 1579, at para. 83.
[198] 'Arrest and reasonable grounds for suspicion' (1988) 85 LS Gaz, 7 September, p. 22.

Thus, whether or not there is 'reasonable cause to suspect' depends on an overall assessment of the reliability of the evidence incriminating the suspect. [I]t is submitted that a reasonable man would, before thinking that a person was probably guilty of an offence, probe the evidence available to him by making any obvious and simply available inquiries.[199]

They further submitted that *Castorina* was inconsistent with one of the justifications for the requirement that an officer give reasons for an arrest,[200] namely that the person arrested 'may be able to give more than a bare and unconvincing denial if he is in fact innocent' (per Sir John Donaldson in *Murphy v Oxford*):[201]

If an arresting officer is obliged to give reasons on arrest he must be under a correlative obligation to consider any answers given by the suspect and, if appropriate, to investigate them. Otherwise, the giving of reasons would simply be an empty formality.[202]

Finally, the authors regard the conclusion that there was 'reasonable cause' on the facts as 'remarkable':

If the police are justified in arresting a middle aged women of good character on such flimsy grounds, without even questioning her as to her alibi or possible motives, then the law provides very scant protection for those suspected of crime.[203]

(I) APPLYING CASTORINA

Inevitably the application of the reasonable suspicion test will involve difficult borderline cases. In *Lyons v Chief Constable of West Yorkshire*[204] the Court of Appeal (Civil Division) held that the judge was right to accept that reasonable suspicion can be formed despite information from a third party claiming that the suspect had an alibi, but wrong to conclude that those comments were relevant to the decision to exercise the power of arrest. A relative of the suspect had told the police, before they had spoken to the suspect, that he had an alibi for the whole day in question. Hutchison LJ (with whom Hobhouse and Evans LJJ agreed) said:

The officers had a number of grounds for regarding an arrest as desirable in the interests of furthering their inquiries and this new factor, insufficient as it was to undermine their belief, was in my view not material (save in the most general sense of being part of the overall picture) to the exercise of discretion. It is easy to envisage circumstances which may militate against exercising a power to arrest a person suspected on reasonable grounds to have committed on offence. Ordinarily those circumstances will be extraneous to the question of reasonable suspicion; for example that the suspect has the sole care of young children. I would not go so far as to say that the strength or weakness of the evidence justifying the reasonable suspicion can never be a material factor at this stage; but in most cases it will not be so, and will be material only to the question whether the conditions precedent to the exercise of the discretion existed.

The danger of abuse of the discretion within the reasonable suspicion test and of the difficulty for the courts to monitor the use of the discretion are obvious. The objective element—that the grounds be reasonable—plays a vital role. There are numerous cases considering

---

[199] Ibid., at p. 25. [200] Op. cit., pp. 109–111.
[201] (1988) 15 February 1988, DC, unreported. [202] (1988) 85 LS Gaz., op. cit., at p. 26.
[203] Ibid., at p. 26. [204] (1997) 24 April, unreported.

this element. In *King v Gardner*[205] officers received a radio message describing suspects loitering about, and Gardner, who fitted the description (blue jeans and long hair) was arrested after refusing to show them what was in a large canvas bag he was carrying when challenged. He was prosecuted for assaulting one of the officers. The sender of the message was not called to give evidence as to the identity of the defendant or as to acts which could be said to have given rise to reasonable suspicion. No evidence was called relating to the personal description given in the radio message, apart from PC Parker's bare assertion that Gardner fitted the description of the man in the area. The Divisional Court held that the Metropolitan Stipendiary Magistrate had been entitled to conclude that there was no satis-factory evidence that would constitute reasonable suspicion under s. 66 of the Metropolitan Police Act 1839. His decision was essentially one of fact that could only be upset if it was perverse.[206]

In *Samuels v Comr of Police for the Metropolis*[207] S was stopped when walking home along a London street in the middle of the morning, carrying no bags or other articles and in everyday casual clothes. The officer said that S looked suspicious because S was not 'walking purposefully', because he turned to look at the officer and when asked 'Why are you walk-ing?' had replied, 'Am I not allowed to walk? I thought it was a free country'. The officer said he wanted to search S's pockets on suspicion of burglary. S told him he was not a burglar and that he lived in this area. He then took his keys out of his pocket and stepped into his front garden. The policeman grabbed hold of his arm and twisted it round his back. PC Senior later explained that he thought the claimant could possibly have had a screwdriver on him. The judge concluded that there were reasonable grounds to justify the officer in reaching the conclusion that he should stop and search S.

Brooke LJ: The only matter on which the judge appears to have relied in his ruling is the fact that when the officer asked the plaintiff if he minded telling him if he was going anywhere in particular the plaintiff said, 'It's a free country. I can go where I want' and moved away. The judge was rightly not willing to attach much significance to the fact that the plaintiff looked back, or that he was walking at a fairly leisurely pace, although these were matters to which the officer had referred when he was justifying the action he took. Indeed, the officer told the plaintiff that he wanted to search the plaintiff before ever he came up to talk to him.

Mr Buckett seeks to support the judge's ruling by relying also on other matters that were in evidence. First, that the area was known as a high risk burglary area by the police, and statistics were read to the jury which illustrated this fact. Next, that PC Senior told the plaintiff that it was a high risk burglary area, and made clear his wish to know what the plaintiff was doing. Thirdly, that the officer told the jury that he wanted to search the plaintiff in case he was carrying something with him to use in connection with burglary.

As I have made clear, in my judgment the judge was right to attach little significance to the evidence that the plaintiff looked round in the manner described, or that he was ambling along in a leisurely manner on this very hot day, as amounting to a reasonable ground for suspecting that he was going equipped for burg-lary. The fact that the police officer knew that this was a high risk area for burglary and told the plaintiff this fact cannot in my judgment in itself add anything. Everything turns on the behaviour of the plaintiff when he was stopped, since, in my judgement, the fact that the plaintiff, like many young men, had his hands in his pockets (if he did) cannot add anything.

---

[205] (1979) 71 Cr App R 13, DC.

[206] See also *R v Prince* [1981] Crim LR 638; *Ware v Matthews* (unreported); and *Pedro v Diss* [1981] 2 All ER 59, DC, discussed by S.H. Bailey and D.J. Birch [1982] Crim LR at pp. 476–477.

[207] (1999) 3 March, transcript from Lexis.

[Brooke LJ referred to *Rice v Connolly* and the well-established principle that a citizen is not obliged to answer police questions.]

It is unfortunate that the plaintiff gave the police officer unhelpful answers. In this, as Mr Buckett accepted, he would have been reacting in a manner no different to that of many young black men and indeed many young white men in London today when they feel that the police are picking on them. In my judgment, however, if the officer did not have reasonable grounds for suspecting that the plaintiff had a prohibited article on him before he came up to him, the fact that the plaintiff walked away after giving him a truthful answer that this was a free country could not turn what was an unreasonable suspicion into a reasonable suspicion that he was going equipped for burglary and does not add anything in the context of the present case.

Appeal allowed with costs.

What were the matters relied on by the officer as forming his reasonable suspicion? S had his hands in his pockets, was not walking purposefully, and was in an area of high crime? Would that *ever* be sufficient to amount to reasonable suspicion? Samuels was Black. Phillips and Brown, found that the standard of reasonable suspicion to arrest a Black or Asian person was lower than that required to arrest a White, and 'this was not explained by differences in the kinds of offence for which ethnic minority and white suspects were arrested'.[208]

(II) REASONABLE SUSPICION AS AN OPERATIONAL QUESTION

- **O'Hara v Chief Constable of the Royal Ulster Constabulary**
  [1997] AC 286, [1997] 1 All ER 129, [1997] 2 WLR 1

O's house was searched early one morning by the RUC, and he was detained for questioning on suspicion of terrorist offences. He was released without charge. He sued the RUC for, *inter alia*, false imprisonment. At trial the judge found that the officers' arrest had been lawful, being based on a reasonable suspicion. The Court of Appeal upheld that decision.

Lord Steyn: So far as it is material section 12(1) [of the Prevention of Terrorism (Temporary Provisions) Act 1984] reads as follows:

'... a constable may arrest without warrant a person whom he has reasonable grounds for suspecting to be...

(b) a person who is or has been concerned in the commission, preparation or instigation of acts of terrorism to which this Part of this Act applies;...'

The constable made the arrest in connection with a murder which was undoubtedly an act of terrorism within the meaning of section 12(1) of the 1984 Act. It was common ground that subjectively the constable had the necessary suspicion. The question was whether the constable objectively had reasonable grounds for suspecting that the appellant was concerned in the murder. The constable said in evidence that his reasonable grounds for suspecting the appellant were based on a briefing by a superior officer. He was told that the appellant had been involved in the murder. The constable said that the superior officer ordered him to arrest the appellant. He did so. Counsel for the appellant took the tactical decision not to cross-examine the constable about the details of the briefing. The trial judge described the evidence as scanty. But he inferred that the briefing afforded reasonable grounds for the necessary suspicion. In other words

---

[208] HORS No. 49, *Entry into the Criminal Justice System: a survey of arrests and their outcomes* (1998), p. 45.

the judge inferred that some further details must have been given in the briefing. The legal burden was on the respondent to prove the existence of reasonable grounds for suspicion. Nevertheless I am persuaded that the judge was entitled on the sparse materials before him to infer the existence of reasonable grounds for suspicion. On this basis the Court of Appeal was entitled to dismiss the appeal. That means that the appeal before your Lordships House must also fail on narrow and purely factual grounds.

[T]he decision of the House of Lords in *Mohammed-Holgate v Duke* [1984] AC 437 is of assistance. The House had to consider the issue whether an arrest was lawful in the context of a statutory provision which authorised arrest when a constable suspected on reasonable grounds that an arrestable offence had been committed. Lord Diplock made the following general observations, at p. 445B–E:

'My Lords, there is inevitably the potentiality of conflict between the public interest in preserving the liberty of the individual and the public interest in the detection of crime and the bringing to justice of those who commit it. The members of the organised police forces of the country have, since the mid-19th century, been charged with the duty of taking the first steps to promote the latter public interest by inquiring into suspected offences with a view to identifying the perpetrators of them and of obtaining sufficient evidence admissible in a court of law against the persons they suspect of being the perpetrators as would justify charging them with the relevant offence before a magistrates' court with a view to their committal for trial for it.

The compromise which English common and statutory law has evolved for the accommodation of the two rival public interests while these first steps are being taken by the police is two-fold:

(1) no person may be arrested without warrant (i.e. without the intervention of a judicial process) unless the constable arresting him has reasonable cause to suspect him to be guilty of an arrestable offence…

(2) a suspect so arrested and detained in custody must be brought before a magistrates' court as soon as practicable….'

Lord Diplock made those observations in the context of statutes containing provisions such as section 12(1). He said that the arrest can only be justified if the constable arresting the alleged suspect has reasonable grounds to suspect him to be guilty of an arrestable offence. The arresting officer is held accountable. That is the compromise between the values of individual liberty and public order.

Section 12(1) authorises an arrest without warrant only where the constable 'has reasonable grounds for' suspicion. An arrest is therefore not lawful if the arresting officer honestly but erroneously believes that he has reasonable grounds for arrest but there are unknown to him in fact in existence reasonable grounds for the necessary suspicion, e.g. because another officer has information pointing to the guilt of the suspect. It would be difficult without doing violence to the wording of the statute to read it in any other way.

A strong argument can be made that in arresting a suspect without warrant a constable ought to be able to rely on information in the possession of another officer and not communicated to him: Feldman, *The Law Relating to Entry, Search & Seizure* (1986), pp. 204–205. Arguably that ought as a matter of policy to provide him with a defence to a claim for wrongful arrest. Such considerations may possibly explain why Art. 5(1) of the European Convention for the Protection of Human Rights and Freedoms 1950 contains a more flexible provision. It reads as follows:

'Everyone has the right to liberty and security of person. No one shall be deprived of his liberty save in the following cases and in accordance with a procedure prescribed by law:…

c. the lawful arrest or detention of a person effected for the purpose of bringing him before the competent legal authority on reasonable suspicion of having committed an offence or when it is reasonably considered necessary to prevent his committing an offence or fleeing after having done so; …'

It is clear from the drafting technique employed in Art. 5(1)*c*, and in particular the use of the passive tense, that it contemplates a broader test of whether a reasonable suspicion exists and does not confine it to matters present in the mind of the arresting officer. That is also the effect of the judgment of the European Court of Human Rights in *Fox v United Kingdom* (1990) 13 EHRR 157, 167–169, paras. 33–35. But section 12(1), and similar provisions, cannot be approached in this way: they categorise as reasonable grounds for suspicion only matters present in the mind of the constable. In *Civil Liberties & Human Rights in England and Wales* (1993), Professor Feldman lucidly explained the difference between two classes of statutes, at p. 199:

> 'Where reasonable grounds for suspicion are required in order to justify the arrest of someone who turns out to be innocent, the [Police and Criminal Evidence Act 1984] requires that the constable personally has reasonable grounds for the suspicion, and it would seem to follow that he is not protected if, knowing nothing of the case, he acts on orders from another officer who, perhaps, does have such grounds. On the other hand, under statutes which require only the objective existence of reasonable grounds for suspicion, it is possible that the officer need neither have the reasonable grounds nor himself suspect anything; he can simply follow orders.'

Section 12(1) is undeniably a statutory provision in the first category. The rationale for the principle in such cases is that in framing such statutory provisions Parliament has proceeded on the longstanding constitutional theory of the independence and accountability of the individual constable: Marshall and Loveday, *The Police Independence and Accountability in The Changing Constitution*, (3rd edn, ed. by Jowell and Oliver, 295 et seq); Christopher L. Ryan and Katherine S. Williams, 'Police Discretion', [1986] Public Law 285, at 305. This case must therefore be approached on the basis that under section 12(1) the only relevant matters are those present in the mind of the arresting officer.

Certain general propositions about the powers of constables under a section such as section 12(1) can now be summarised. (1) In order to have a reasonable suspicion the constable need not have evidence amounting to a prima facie case. Ex hypothesi one is considering a preliminary stage of the investigation and information from an informer or a tip-off from a member of the public may be enough: *Hussien v Chong Fook Kam* [1970] AC 942, 949. (2) Hearsay information may therefore afford a constable a reasonable grounds to arrest. Such information may come from other officers: *Hussien's* case, ibid. (3) The information which causes the constable to be suspicious of the individual must be in existence to the knowledge of the police officer at the time he makes the arrest. (4) The executive 'discretion' to arrest or not as Lord Diplock described it in *Mohammed-Holgate v Duke* [1984] AC 437, 446, vests in the constable, who is engaged on the decision to arrest or not, and not in his superior officers.

Given the independent responsibility and accountability of a constable under a provision such as section 12(1) of the Act of 1984 it seems to follow that the mere fact that an arresting officer has been instructed by a superior officer to effect the arrest is not capable of amounting to reasonable grounds for the necessary suspicion within the meaning of section 12(1). It is accepted, and rightly accepted, that a mere request to arrest without any further information by an equal ranking officer, or a junior officer, is incapable of amounting to reasonable grounds for the necessary suspicion. How can the badge of the superior officer, and the fact that he gave an order, make a difference? In respect of a statute vesting an independent discretion in the particular constable, and requiring him personally to have reasonable grounds for suspicion, it would be surprising if seniority made a difference. It would be contrary to the principle underlying section 12(1) which makes a constable individually responsible for the arrest and accountable in law. In *R v Chief Constable of Devon and Cornwall, ex p Central Electricity Generating Board* [1982] QB 458, 474 Lawton LJ touched on this point. He observed:

> '[Chief constables] cannot give an officer under command an order to do acts which can only lawfully be done if the officer himself with reasonable cause suspects that a breach of the peace has occurred or is imminently likely to occur or an arrestable offence has been committed.'

Such an order to arrest cannot without some further information being given to the constable be suffi-cient to afford the constable reasonable grounds for the necessary suspicion. That seems to me to be the legal position in respect of a provision such as section 12(1). For these reasons I regard the submission of counsel for the respondent as unsound in law. In practice it follows that a constable must be given some basis for a request to arrest somebody under a provision such as section 12(1), e.g. a report from an informer.

Subject to these observations, I agree that the appeal ought to be dismissed.

Lord Hope of Craighead: My Lords, the test which section 12(1) of the Act of 1984 has laid down is a simple but practical one. It relates entirely to what is in the mind of the arresting officer when the power is exercised. In part it is a subjective test, because he must have formed a genuine suspicion in his own mind that the person has been concerned in acts of terrorism. In part also it is an objective one, because there must also be reasonable grounds for the suspicion which he has formed. But the application of the objective test does not require the court to look beyond what was in the mind of the arresting officer. It is the grounds which were in his mind at the time which must be found to be reasonable grounds for the suspicion which he has formed. All that the objective test requires is that these grounds be examined objectively and that they be judged at the time when the power was exercised.

This means that the point does not depend on whether the arresting officer himself thought at that time that they were reasonable. The question is whether a reasonable man would be of that opinion, having regard to the information which was in the mind of the arresting officer. It is the arresting officer's own account of the information which he had which matters, not what was observed by or known to anyone else. The information acted on by the arresting officer need not be based on his own observations, as he is entitled to form a suspicion based on what he has been told. His reasonable suspicion may be based on information which has been given to him anonymously or it may be based on information, perhaps in the course of an emergency, which turns out later to be wrong. As it is the information which is in his mind alone which is relevant however, it is not necessary to go on to prove what was known to his informant or that any facts on which he based his suspicion were in fact true. The question whether it provided reason-able grounds for the suspicion depends on the source of his information and its context, seen in the light of the whole surrounding circumstances.

This approach to the wording of section 12(1) of the Act of 1984 is consistent with authority. In *Dallison v Caffery* [1965] 1 QB 348, which preceded the enactment of section 2(4) of the Criminal Law Act 1967, the arrest had been effected in the exercise of the common law power. Diplock LJ's descrip-tion, at p. 354, of the test to be applied does however provide a useful starting point for the examination of the power which has been given by the statute. What he said was:

> 'The test whether there was reasonable and probable cause for the arrest or prosecution is an objective one, namely, whether a reasonable man, assumed to know the law and possessed of the information which in fact was possessed by the defendant, would believe that there was reasonable and probable cause.'

Many other examples may be cited of cases where the action of the constable who exercises a statutory power of arrest or of search is a member of a team of police officers, or where his action is the culmin-ation of various steps taken by other police officers, perhaps over a long period and perhaps also involving officers from other police forces. For obvious practical reasons police officers must be able to rely upon each other in taking decisions as to whom to arrest or where to search and in what circumstances. The statutory power does not require that the constable who exercises the power must be in possession of all the information which has led to a decision, perhaps taken by others, that the time has come for it to be exercised. What it does require is that the constable who exercises the power must first have equipped himself with sufficient information so that he has reasonable cause to suspect before the power is exercised.

My Lords, in this case the evidence about the matters which were disclosed at the briefing session to the arresting officer was indeed scanty. But, as Mr. Coghlin pointed out, the trial judge was entitled to weigh up that evidence in the light of the surrounding circumstances and, having regard to the source of that information, to draw inferences as to what a reasonable man, in the position of the independent observer, would make of it. I do not think that either the trial judge or the Court of Appeal misdirected themselves as to the test to be applied. I would dismiss this appeal.

Lords Hoffmann, Mustill and **Goff** concurred.[209]

NOTES

1. Hunt suggests that the case is a 'valiant attempt to reconcile the demands of operational context with traditional constitutional principle'.[210] Do you agree?

2. Research into stop and search distinguishes 'high' and 'low' exercises of discretion. A high discretion stop would be where an officer stops an unknown person late at night in a high-crime area. A low discretion stop would be where the officer targeted a named individual on the basis of an instruction from fellow officers or the public. Phillips and Brown[211] found that 28 per cent of all arrests based on reasonable suspicion came from an instruction from the control room.[212] Fewer than 25 per cent of all arrests were from proactive policing.

3. How realistic is Lord Steyn's opinion that 'a mere request to arrest without any further information by an equal ranking officer, or a junior officer, is incapable of amounting to reasonable grounds for the necessary suspicion'? How likely is a junior officer to ignore such an instruction and go off in search of his own grounds for suspicion? Does the constitutional principle of constabulary independence really reflect the way that modern policing is conducted?

4. Research by Phillips and Brown found that of the 4,250 arrests they examined, in 71 per cent of cases the arresting officer claimed that the basis of his reasonable suspicion was from only one source of evidence. In 21 per cent of cases there were two sources and in 8 per cent of cases three of more. In 40 per cent of all cases the main ground for the suspicion derived from 'a police observation of the offence'.[213] Even such observation can lack objective bases: in *Slade v DPP*[214] the court upheld the trial judge's finding that reasonable grounds for suspicion to search under s. 23 of the Misuse of Drugs Act 1971 existed where an officer saw S in the vicinity of a house known for drug dealing, with his hand in his pocket and a 'smug' smile on his face. Can this ever be more than at best a hunch and at worst prejudice?

In deciding whether a reasonable suspicion exists, it is not legitimate for the court to consider evidence of subsequent conduct alleged to constitute a course of harassment by the officers: *Tomlinson v Chief Constable of Hertfordshire*.[215]

---

[209] See also *O'Hara v UK* (2002) 34 EHRR 32.
[210] A. Hunt (1997) 113 LQR 548, 550.
[211] HORS No. 49, *Entry into the Criminal Justice System: a survey of arrests and their outcomes* (1998).
[212] Ibid., p. 34.   [213] Ibid., p. 41.
[214] (1996) 22 October, DC, unreported.
[215] [2001] All ER (D) 109 (Mar), CA (Cr D).

5. In *Clarke v Chief Constable of North Wales*[216] it was held that it was not really necessary for each officer to 'satisfy himself that the information conveyed by other officers comes from a reliable source'. Sedley LJ observed that:

> Of course if the briefing makes it apparent that the sources are unreliable or non-existent, the arresting constable's suspicion will not be reasonable in the absence of other grounds for it. And if the briefing officer has told the arresting officer that there is reliable information when there is not, the chief constable may become vicariously liable for a wrongful arrest but on behalf of the briefing officer not of the arresting officer. These, it seems to me are the protections the law affords against arrest on unjustified suspicion. They do not extend, and do not need to extend, to requiring each constable involved in an arrest and search operation to make an independent evaluation of the grounds for suspicion. Nothing in *O'Hara* suggests otherwise.

Is this what you understand *O'Hara* to require?

6. In *Hough v Chief Constable of Staffordshire*[217] the court held that the reasonable suspicion could arise from reliance on a Police National Computer (PNC) check for a vehicle—in that case it was an erroneous entry and H, who was completely innocent, was arrested by an armed police unit. Simon Brown LJ emphasised that, except in emergencies, the police ought to make checks beyond the PNC to found a reasonable suspicion.

7. In *Sonia Raissi, Mohamed Raissi v Comr of Police of the Metropolis*[218] the court held that 'if information given to an arresting officer at a briefing by a superior is insufficient to supply to the arresting reasonable grounds for suspicion of the arrested person, it will, in my judgment, avail the arresting officer nothing to say, "Well, I thought that my superior probably did have other information justifying the arrest but he did not tell me what it was".'

8. How are officers supposed to demonstrate reasonable suspicion when the basis for that suspicion comes from an informer? In *O'Hara v United Kingdom* the European Court stated:

> Terrorist crime poses particular problems, as the police may be called upon, in the interests of public safety, to arrest a suspected terrorist on the basis of information which is reliable but which cannot be disclosed to the suspect or produced in court, without jeopardising the informant. However, though Contracting States cannot be required to establish the reasonableness of the suspicion grounding the arrest of a suspected terrorist by disclosing confidential sources of information, the Court has held that the exigencies of dealing with terrorist crime cannot justify stretching the notion of 'reasonableness' to the point where the safeguard secured by Article 5(1)(c) is impaired. Even in those circumstances, the respondent Government has to furnish at least some facts or information capable of satisfying the Court that the arrested person was reasonably suspected of having committed the alleged offence.[219]

9. In *Cumming v Chief Constable of Northumbria Police*[220] five claimants worked for the local authority monitoring the recordings of the CCTV cameras. There was evidence that some tapes showing the commission of an offence had been tampered with. The five were all of good character and had no links with the alleged offender caught on the recordings. They argued that merely because they had all had the opportunity to tamper with

---

[216] (2000) 5 April, CA (Cr D), unreported.
[217] [2001] EWCA Civ 39.   [218] [2007] EWHC 2842.
[219] (2002) 34 EHRR 32, para. 35. On the correct approach see *R v H* [2004] UKHL 3, para. 41.
[220] [2003] EWCA Civ 1844.

the tapes that could not amount to reasonable suspicion. The Court of Appeal disagreed, stating that in the absence of evidence excluding them the opportunity to commit the offence was in principle enough to establish reasonable grounds. It was noted earlier that in *O'Hara v United Kingdom*[221] the European Court commented that reasonable suspicion presupposes the existence of facts or information which would satisfy an objective observer that *the person concerned* may have committed a criminal offence. Is *Cumming* consistent with this idea?[222]

(III) REASONABLE SUSPICION: AN UNDEFINABLE CONCEPT?

A question that has been debated since before the enactment of PACE is whether a definition of reasonable suspicion can ever be satisfactorily provided. It must be sufficiently flexible to allow the police to operate effectively, but it is important to ensure the protection of civil liberties that there are sufficient safeguards against its abuse. The Royal Commission on Criminal Procedure (RCCP) concluded that the requirements of notifying reasons, making records and the monitoring of such records by superior officers would be the most effective way of reducing the risk of random action.

Home Office research into stop and search has confirmed that officers' suspicions are aroused as a result of appearance, includeing: youth; type of vehicle; incongruence; 'in some cases' ethnicity; being known to the police; and fitting the suspect description.[223] Can officers be expected not to base suspicion on hunches?

(IV) REASONABLE SUSPICION AND STEREOTYPES

One of the most controversial areas in which the reasonable suspicion question arises is in relation to stop and search. PACE Code A sets out guidance on the question of reasonable suspicion. The most recent version of Code A came into force on 1 February 2008.

2.2 Reasonable grounds for suspicion depend on the circumstances in each case. There must be an objective basis for that suspicion based on facts, information, and/or intelligence which are relevant to the likelihood of finding an article of a certain kind or, in the case of searches under section 43 of the Terrorism Act 2000, to the likelihood that the person is a terrorist. Reasonable suspicion can never be supported on the basis of personal factors alone without reliable supporting intelligence or information or some specific behaviour by the person concerned. For example, a person's race, age, appearance, or the fact that the person is known to have a previous conviction, cannot be used alone or in combination with each other as the reason for searching that person. Reasonable suspicion cannot be based on generalisations or stereotypical images of certain groups or categories of people as more likely to be involved in criminal activity. A person's religion cannot be considered as reasonable grounds for suspicion and should never be considered as a reason to stop or stop and search an individual.

2.3 Reasonable suspicion can sometimes exist without specific information or intelligence and on the basis of some level of generalisation stemming from the behaviour of a person. For example, if an officer encounters someone on the street at night who is obviously trying to hide something, the officer may (depending on the other surrounding circumstances) base such suspicion on the fact that this kind of

---

[221] (2002) 34 EHRR 32.

[222] See also *Al Fayed v Metropolitan Police Comr* [2004] EWCA Civ 1579.

[223] See P. Quinton, N. Bland and J. Miller, *Police Stops, Decision-making in Practice* (2000) (HORS Paper No. 130).

behaviour is often linked to stolen or prohibited articles being carried. Similarly, for the purposes of section 43 of the Terrorism Act 2000, suspicion that a person is a terrorist may arise from the person's behaviour at or near a location which has been identified as a potential target for terrorists.

2.4 However, reasonable suspicion should normally be linked to accurate and current intelligence or information, such as information describing an article being carried, a suspected offender, or a person who has been seen carrying a type of article known to have been stolen recently from premises in the area. Searches based on accurate and current intelligence or information are more likely to be effective. Targeting searches in a particular area at specified crime problems increases their effectiveness and minimises inconvenience to law-abiding members of the public. It also helps in justifying the use of searches both to those who are searched and to the public. This does not however prevent stop and search powers being exercised in other locations where such powers may be exercised and reasonable suspicion exists.

2.5 Searches are more likely to be effective, legitimate, and secure public confidence when reasonable suspicion is based on a range of factors. The overall use of these powers is more likely to be effective when up to date and accurate intelligence or information is communicated to officers and they are well-informed about local crime patterns.

2.6 Where there is reliable information or intelligence that members of a group or gang habitually carry knives unlawfully or weapons or controlled drugs, and wear a distinctive item of clothing or other means of identification to indicate their membership of the group or gang, that distinctive item of clothing or other means of identification may provide reasonable grounds to stop and search a person.

NOTES

1. Does this provide officers with an opportunity to harass certain groups within society because of the way they dress?

2. Waddington comments that 'if the police can use their extensive discretion to define crime, they can use that same discretion to concentrate attention on vulnerable sections of the population and cast them in the role of criminals'.[224] To what extent do powers triggered by a flexible standard like 'reasonable suspicion' allow the police to determine *what* is criminal? Does a requirement of accurate record keeping and monitoring of the use of the police powers provide adequate protection against abuse?

(B) POWERS RESTRICTED TO 'SERIOUS' OFFENCES

The RCCP recommended that certain of the powers of the police should be available only in respect of 'grave offences'. The 1984 Act used instead the concept of 'serious arrestable offence' in relation to the powers given by ss. 4 (road checks), 8 (search warrants), 42 and 43 (continued detention), 56(2) (delay in informing a friend or relative that a person has been arrested), and 58(6) (delayed access to legal advice). In the Serious Organised Crime and Police Act 2005 the concept of the serious arrestable offence was abolished and replaced throughout PACE by the term 'indictable offence' which includes a much broader range of circumstances.[225] 'Indictable' offence is a term which covers both offences triable only on indictment and those triable either way (i.e. in the magistrates' court or the Crown Court).

---

[224] *Policing Citizens* (1999), Chap. 2, p. 35. See also comments in J. Kleinig, *The Ethics of Policing* (1996), p. 86; Fielding, *Community Policing* (1995).

[225] Serious Organised Crime and Police Act 2005, Sch. 7, para. 43.

(C) THE USE OF FORCE

- **Criminal Law Act 1967**

3. Use of force in making arrest, etc

(1) A person may use such force as is reasonable in the circumstances in the prevention of crime, or in effecting or assisting in the lawful arrest of offenders or suspected offenders or of persons unlawfully at large.

(2) Subsection (1) above shall replace the rules of the common law on the question when force used for a purpose mentioned in the subsection is justified by that purpose.

NOTES

1. This section authorises the use of reasonable force in the making of an arrest.[226] It also authorises the use of reasonable force to resist an unlawful arrest, such force constituting force used in 'the prevention of crime'. In a civil case the question of reasonable force is entirely objective. In a criminal case the reasonableness of the force the defendant used will be judged—by the jury (objectively) on the facts as the accused (subjectively) believed them to exist (however unreasonable the belief).

2. 'Reasonable force' presumably will not exceed the minimum necessary to make or resist an arrest. However, it may well be that the minimum force necessary to make or resist arrest will exceed what is reasonable. For example, a person unlawfully arrested (e.g. because no power of arrest exists in connection with the offence for which the arrest was made) might be regarded by a court as using unreasonable force in using even a small amount of force in trying to escape if in the circumstances it was likely that the mistake could be pointed out to superior officers and the arrested person be released within a brief period.

3. In *O'Connor v Chief Constable of Norfolk*,[227] the court held that a male officer, accompanied by another, had gone beyond what was reasonable when applying the 'Koti Hinari' grip to arrest a suspected woman drink driver whom he thought might try to escape even though she was out of her car and in the presence of two officers. The grip fractured her wrist. See also the decision in *Chief Constable of Lincolnshire v Glowacki*,[228] where an off-duty officer had used an unapproved method to restrain G, causing two fractures.

4. In 2004 the Home Secretary allowed chief officers of all forces to make the taser gun available to all firearms officers. In September 2007 10 police forces were chosen for further trials of the taser gun to specially trained non-firearms officers.[229] In a 2004 survey[230] only 36 per cent of the public thought they knew what a taser was, yet 81 per cent thought its use should be extended for police protection and the prevention of violent crime. Only 1 per cent of respondents thought that no officers should be armed compared to 38 per cent who suggested that all officers should be armed. Between April 2004 and February 2008 tasers had been deployed on 2,056 occasions,[231] and discharged 685 times.

---

[226] See J.C. Smith, 'Using Force in Self-Defence and the Prevention of Crime' (1994) 47 CLP 101.

[227] (1997) 10 February, CA (Cr D).   [228] (1998) 18 June, CA (Cr D).

[229] See Association of Chief Police Officers, *Extended Operational Deployment of Taser for Specially Trained Units* (2007).

[230] PriceWaterhouseCoopers, *Evaluation of Taser—Digest of Public Opinion Survey* (2004) available at www. westmercia.police.uk.

[231] HOSDB, *Reported and Recorded Uses of Taser* (2008).

5. The attenuating energy projectile (AEP) was introduced into operational service in June 2005. It is the successor to the baton round and is used to deal with people who are posing an immediate threat to life, during circumstances in which use of a firearm would otherwise be necessary.[232] The discriminating irritant projectile (DIP) delivers a localised cloud or burst of sensory irritant in the immediate proximity of an individual aggressor with the aim of neutralising the immediate threat.[233]

6. The use of force under s. 3 is justified not only on what the person believed was being done to him, but what he feared was about to be done to him: *R v Hughes*[234]—a raised truncheon caused H to struggle with an officer and resist what H thought was going to be a battering.

7. Kleinig[235] asserts that 'To grant that police should have the authority to use force is only the first step in any justification of their use of that force.'[236] Does English law require sufficient justification of the use of force by police officers?

8. On the use of police dogs to effect arrest compare *Coles v Chief Constable of South Yorkshire*[237] and *Pollard v Chief Constable of West Yorkshire*.[238] The question is one of fact as Swinton Thomas LJ stated in *Coles*:

once the concept of reasonableness is introduced [in s. 3] then whether it is reasonable to instruct the dog to bite a human being must depend on the circumstances. Police officers are accustomed to exercising their judgement, and for my own part, I doubt very much whether many cases will arise in which it is possible for a plaintiff to establish that that judgement has been exercised wrongly.

In *Murgatroyd v Chief Constable of West Yorkshire Police*[239] the court held that the use of a police dog to disable a suicidal occupant of a house that the police had forcibly entered was unreasonable. The dog was used to protect the police from harm rather than to prevent the occupier self-harming, but the police were already adequately protected against a 'puny' man.

9. *Using lethal force.* Guidance as to discharge of firearms is provided by the Association of Chief Police Officers' *Manual of Guidance on the Police Use of Firearms* (2003). Chapter 5 of the guidelines states that firearms are to be fired by AFOs (authorised firearms officers) in the course of duty, only when 'absolutely necessary' after conventional methods have been tried and failed or must, from the nature of the circumstances, be unlikely to succeed if tried. Warning shots are strongly discouraged since they might escalate the situation, and cause the suspect to begin firing. Oral warnings should be given that armed police are present unless it would endanger an officer or would be pointless. Officers are advised to target the central body mass rather than shooting to injure.

10. Following the investigation into the shooting of Jean Charles de Menzes in Stockwell tube station in July 2005 the IPCC made 16 recommendations for change to the police use of firearms; surveillance operations; post-incident management; the communications infrastructure; training and exercises; and community reassurance. Instructions in respect of the

---

232 See Association of Chief Police Officers, *Attenuating Energy Projectile (AEP) Guidance* (2005) available at www.westmercia.police.uk.

233 On the use of CS spray, see the Police Complaints Authority, *CS Spray: Increasing Public Safety* (2000). See also ACPO, *Guidance on the Use of Incapacitant Spray* (2006).

234 [1995] Crim LR 957.   235 *The Ethics of Policing* (1996).

236 Ibid., at p. 98.   237 (1998) CA (Cr D).

238 (1998) 28 April, CA (Cr D). No evidence that handler had intended or foresaw that dog might react otherwise than in accordance with training.

239 (2000) 8 November, CA (CD).

issue of firearms are produced by the Home Office (in association with Centrex—now part of the National Policing Improvement Agency) in its Code of Practice on *Police Use of Firearms and Less Lethal Weapons* (2003).[240] When the police are confronted with a suspected suicide bomber is there an alternative to a shoot to kill policy?

11. The statistics for April 2006 to March 2007 show that the number of police operations in which firearms were authorised was 18,053. The police discharged a conventional firearm in three incidents. Recent figures are as follows: 2001/2 – 13,991; 2002/3 – 14,827; 2003/4 – 16,657; 2004/5 – 15,981; 2005/6 – 18,891.[241]

- **Police and Criminal Evidence Act 1984**

117. Power of constable to use reasonable force

Where any provision of this Act—

(*a*) confers a power on a constable; and

(*b*) does not provide that the power may only be exercised with the consent of some person, other than a police officer, the officer may use reasonable force, if necessary, in the exercise of the power.

NOTE

1. Some specific police powers expressly authorise the use of force if the need arises.[242] In *Swales v Cox*,[243] the court held that the power to enter premises, 'if need be by force', to effect an arrest, conferred by the Criminal Law Act 1967, s. 2(6), was intended to be a 'comprehensive code' on the right to enter for this purpose. The right to use force was qualified only by the requirement that it be necessary. The court defined 'force' as the application of any energy to an obstacle, such as turning a door handle or the opening of a door or a window. There was no longer any *legal* requirement that there be a prior request before force might be used, but any person who sought to enter by force without a prior request would have a 'very severe burden to displace' in establishing 'necessity'.[244] An example of a case where this might be justified would be where it was essential for an officer's protection that he give no warning of his approach to a house where a very dangerous man was to be found.[245] What if the protection is for the occupant? In *Smith v DPP*[246] S was charged with an offence under s. 89 of the Police Act 1996 after police had been called to the house following an abandoned 999 call (i.e. one where the caller hung up). As Brooke LJ explained:

The officers arrive wishing to enter the premises for the purposes of their duty to save life and limb. Secondly, PC Atkins was aware that Mr Smith lived at the premises. Thirdly, Mr Smith was shouting and banging at the door. Fourthly, Mr Smith was not impeding the officers from gaining access to the house, but he refused to move away from it, stating incorrectly that it was nothing to do with them. Fifthly, the

---

[240] See www.npia.police.uk. The most recent version, 2004, is currently under review.

[241] Home Office, *Statistics on the Police Use of Firearms 2006–7* (2007). See also Independent Police Complaints Commission, *Shootings by Police Officers in England and Wales since 1985* (2008) available at www.ipcc.gov.uk.

[242] E.g. Public Order Act 1936, s. 2(5).   [243] [1981] QB 849, DC.

[244] See Donaldson LJ at 1119.

[245] See S.H. Bailey and D.J. Birch [1982] Crim LR 475, 478–480.

[246] (2001) 2 February, QBD, Admin Court.

stipendiary magistrate made a finding of fact as to PC Atkins state of mind when he found that he took Mr Smith by the arm because he wished to lead him away so that the police officers could deal with the abandoned 999 call without interference. Sixthly, that he was entitled to use reasonable force as a matter of law in the execution of his duty to enter the house and save life and limb. Seventhly, the stipendiary magistrate made a finding of fact that it was perfectly reasonable for the officer to require Mr Smith to move away to allow the police to execute their duty and investigate the call without his interference.

In *O'Loughlin v Chief Constable of Essex*[247] it was held that 'unless circumstances made it impossible impracticable or undesirable, a police officer exercising powers of entry by force pursuant to s. 17 of PACE should first give the occupier the true reason for seeking to enter'. (See below for discussion in context of search.) The reasonableness should be determined in the context of the purpose for which the force was used: *DPP v Meadon*.[248]

(D) CODES OF PRACTICE

There are at present eight codes of practice issued in accordance with PACE s. 66: Code A deals with the Exercise by Police Officers of Statutory Powers of Stop and Search; Code B: Searching of Premises by Police Officers and the Seizure of Property found by Police Officers on Persons or Premises; Code C: Detention, Treatment and Questioning of Persons by Police Officers; Code D: Code of Practice for the Identification of Persons by Police Officers; Code E deals with Audio Recording of Interviews with Suspects; Code F deals with with the visual recording with sound of interviews with suspects; Code G deals with powers of arrest; and Code H sets out the requirements for the detention, treatment and questioning of suspects related to terrorism in police custody. There have been a number of revisions to the codes and the latest set of codes came into effect in 2008 (for Codes A–E), January 2006 for F–G, and Code H in July 2006. It is vital to rely on the correct code of practice (see *R v Miller*[249] in which the trial judge had relied on the out of date version of Code C and failed to recognise breaches of the new code). Similarly, the court should be sure to use the Queen's Printers copy rather than rely on those reproduced in the textbooks: *R v Keriwala*.[250] A court should refer to a current code when considering events prior to the implementation of that code if it is necessary to do justice: *R v Ward*.[251]

By virtue of the Police and Magistrates' Courts Act 1994, s. 37(a), repealing PACE, s. 67(8), breach of one of the codes is not automatically a disciplinary office.

4. POWERS TO STOP AND SEARCH

- **Police and Criminal Evidence Act 1984**

PART 1

POWERS TO STOP AND SEARCH

1.— Power of constable to stop and search persons, vehicles etc.

(1) A constable may exercise any power conferred by this section—

    (a) in any place to which at the time when he proposes to exercise the power the public or any section of the public has access, on payment or otherwise, as of right or by virtue of express or implied permission; or

---

[247] [1998] 1 WLR 374.   [248] [2004] 4 All ER 75.   [249] [1998] Crim LR 209, CA.
[250] (1991) Times, 4 January, CA.   [251] (1994) 98 Cr App R 337, CA.

(b) in any other place to which people have ready access at the time when he proposes to exercise the power but which is not a dwelling.

(2) Subject to subsection (3) to (5) below, a constable—

    (a) may search—

        (i) any person or vehicle;

        (ii) anything which is in or on a vehicle,

        for stolen or prohibited articles, any article to which subsection (8A) below applies or any firework to which subsection (8B) below applies; and

    (b) may detain a person or vehicle for the purpose of such a search.

(3) This section does not give a constable power to search a person or vehicle or anything in or on a vehicle unless he has reasonable grounds for suspecting that he will find stolen or prohibited articles or, any article to which subsection (8A) below applies or any firework to which subsection (8B) below applies.

(4) If a person is in a garden or yard occupied with and used for the purposes of a dwelling or on other land so occupied and used, a constable may not search him in the exercise of the power conferred by this section unless the constable has reasonable grounds for believing—

    (a) that he does not reside in the dwelling; and

    (b) that he is not in the place in question with the express or implied permission of a person who resides in the dwelling.

(5) If a vehicle is in a garden or yard occupied with and used for the purposes of a dwelling or on other land so occupied and used, a constable may not search the vehicle or anything in or on it in the exercise of the power conferred by this section unless he has reasonable grounds for believing—

    (a) that the person in charge of the vehicle does not reside in the dwelling; and

    (b) that the vehicle is not in the place in question with the express or implied permission of a person who resides in the dwelling.

(6) If in the course of such a search a constable discovers an article which he has reasonable grounds for suspecting to be a stolen or prohibited article, an article to which subsection (8A) below applies or a firework to which subsection (8B) below applies, he may seize it.

(7) An article is prohibited for the purposes of this Part of this Act if it is—

    (a) an offensive weapon; or

    (b) an article—

        (i) made or adapted for use in the course of or in connection with an offence to which this subparagraph applies; or

        (ii) intended by the person having it with him for such use by him or by some other person.

(8) The offences to which subsection (7)(b)(i) above applies are—

    (a) burglary;

    (b) theft;

    (c) offences under section 12 of the Theft Act 1968 (taking motor vehicle or other conveyance without authority);

    (d) fraud (contrary to section 1 of the Fraud Act 2006)

    (e) offences under section 1 of the Criminal Damage Act 1971 (destroying or damaging property).

(8A) This subsection applies to any article in relation to which a person has committed, or is committing or is going to commit an offence under section 139 of the Criminal Justice Act 1988.

(8B) This subsection applies to any firework which a person possesses in contravention of a prohibition imposed by fireworks regulations.

...

2. Provisions relating to search under section 1 and other powers.

(1) A constable who detains a person or vehicle in the exercise—

    (a) of the power conferred by section 1 above; or

    (b) of any other power—

        (i) to search a person without first arresting him; or

        (ii) to search a vehicle without making an arrest,

    need not conduct a search if it appears to him subsequently—

        (i) that no search is required; or

        (ii) that a search is impracticable.

(2) If a constable contemplates a search, other than a search of an unattended vehicle, in the exercise—

    (a) of the power conferred by section 1 above; or

    (b) of any other power, except the power conferred by section 6 below and the power conferred by section 27(2) of the Aviation Security Act 1982—

        (i) to search a person without first arresting him; or

        (ii) to search a vehicle without making an arrest,

    it shall be his duty, subject to subsection (4) below, to take reasonable steps before he commences the search to bring to the attention of the appropriate person—

        (i) if the constable is not in uniform, documentary evidence that he is a constable; and

        (ii) whether he is in uniform or not, the matters specified in subsection (3) below;

    and the constable shall not commence the search until he has performed that duty.

(3) The matters referred to in subsection (2)(ii) above are—

    (a) the constable's name and the name of the police station to which he is attached;

    (b) the object of the proposed search;

    (c) the constable's grounds for proposing to make it; and

    (d) the effect of section 3(7) or (8) below, as may be appropriate.

(4) A constable need not bring the effect of section 3(7) or (8) below to the attention of the appropriate person if it appears to the constable that it will not be practicable to make the record in section 3(1) below.

(5) In this section 'the appropriate person' means —

    (a) if the constable proposes to search a person, that person; and

    (b) if he proposes to search a vehicle, or anything in or on a vehicle, the person in charge of the vehicle.

(6) On completing a search of an unattended vehicle or anything in or on such a vehicle in the exercise of any such power as is mentioned in subsection (2) above a constable shall leave a notice—

    (a) stating that he has searched it;

    (b) giving the name of the police station to which he is attached;

    (c) stating that an application for compensation for any damage caused by the search may be made to that police station; and

    (d) stating the effect of section 3(8) below.

(7) The constable shall leave the notice inside the vehicle unless it is not reasonably practicable to do so without damaging the vehicle.

(8) The time for which a person or vehicle may be detained for the purposes of such a search is such time as is reasonably required to permit a search to be carried out either at the place where the person or vehicle was first detained or nearby.

(9) Neither the power conferred by section 1 above nor any other power to detain and search a person without first arresting him or to detain and search a vehicle without making an arrest is to be construed—

    (a) as authorising a constable to require a person to remove any of his clothing in public other than an outer coat, jacket or gloves; or

    (b) as authorising a constable not in uniform to stop a vehicle.

(10) This section and section 1 above apply to vessels, aircraft and hovercraft as they apply to vehicles.

3. Duty to make records concerning searches.

(1) Where a constable has carried out a search in the exercise of any such power as is mentioned in section 2(1) above, other than a search—

    (a) under section 6 below; or

    (b) under section 27(2) of the Aviation Security Act 1982,

he shall make a record of it in writing unless it is not practicable to do so.

(2) If—

    (a) a constable is required by subsection (1) above to make a record of a search; but

    (b) it is not practicable to make the record on the spot,

he shall make it as soon as practicable after the completion of the search.

(3) The record of a search of a person shall include a note of his name, if the constable knows it, but a constable may not detain a person to find out his name.

(4) If a constable does not know the name of a person whom he has searched, the record of the search shall include a note otherwise describing that person.

(5) The record of a search of a vehicle shall include a note describing the vehicle.

(6) The record of a search of a person or a vehicle—

    (a) shall state—

        (i) the object of the search;

        (ii) the grounds for making it;

        (iii) the date and time when it was made;

        (iv) the place where it was made;

        (v) whether anything, and if so what, was found;

        (vi) whether any, and if so what, injury to a person or damage to property appears to the constable to have resulted from the search; and

    (b) shall identify the constable making it.

(7) If a constable who conducted a search of a person made a record of it, the person who was searched shall be entitled to a copy of the record if he asks for one before the end of the period specified in subsection (9) below.

(8) If—

(a) the owner of a vehicle which has been searched or the person who was in charge of the vehicle at the time when it was searched asks for a copy of the record of the search before the end of the period specified in subsection (9) below; and

(b) the constable who conducted the search made a record of it,

the person who made the request shall be entitled to a copy.

(9) The period mentioned in subsections (7) and (8) above is the period of 12 months beginning with the date on which the search was made.

(10) The requirements imposed by this section with regard to records of searches of vehicles shall apply also to records of searches of vessels, aircraft and hovercraft.

4.— Road checks.

(1) This section shall have effect in relation to the conduct of road checks by police officers for the purpose of ascertaining whether a vehicle is carrying—

(a) a person who has committed an offence other than a road traffic offence or a vehicle excise offence;

(b) a person who is a witness to such an offence;

(c) a person intending to commit such an offence; or

(d) a person who is unlawfully at large.

(2) For the purposes of this section a road check consists of the exercise in a locality of the power conferred by section 163 of the Road Traffic Act 1988 in such a way as to stop during the period for which its exercise in that way in that locality continues all vehicles or vehicles selected by any criterion.

(3) Subject to subsection (5) below, there may only be such a road check if a police officer of the rank of superintendent or above authorises it in writing.

(4) An officer may only authorise a road check under subsection (3) above—

(a) for the purpose specified in subsection (1)(a) above, if he has reasonable grounds—

(i) for believing that the offence is an indictable offence; and

(ii) for suspecting that the person is, or is about to be, in the locality in which vehicles would be stopped if the road check were authorised;

(b) for the purpose specified in subsection (1)(b) above, if he has reasonable grounds for believing that the offence is an indictable offence;

(c) for the purpose specified in subsection (1)(c) above, if he has reasonable grounds—

(i) for believing that the offence would be an indictable offence; and

(ii) for suspecting that the person is, or is about to be, in the locality in which vehicles would be stopped if the road check were authorised;

(d) for the purpose specified in subsection (1)(d) above, if he has reasonable grounds for suspecting that the person is, or is about to be, in that locality.

(5) An officer below the rank of superintendent may authorise such a road check if it appears to him that it is required as a matter of urgency for one of the purposes specified in subsection (1) above.

(6) If an authorisation is given under subsection (5) above, it shall be the duty of the officer who gives it—

(a) to make a written record of the time at which he gives it; and

(b) to cause an officer of the rank of superintendent or above to be informed that it has been given.

(7) The duties imposed by subsection (6) above shall be performed as soon as it is practicable to do so.

(8) An officer to whom a report is made under subsection (6) above may, in writing, authorise the road check to continue.

(9) If such an officer considers that the road check should not continue, he shall record in writing—

(a) the fact that it took place; and

(b) the purpose for which it took place.

(10) An officer giving an authorisation under this section shall specify the locality in which vehicles are to be stopped.

(11) An officer giving an authorisation under this section, other than an authorisation under subsection (5) above—

(a) shall specify a period, not exceeding seven days, during which the road check may continue; and

(b) may direct that the road check—

(i) shall be continuous; or

(ii) shall be conducted at specified times, during that period.

(12) If it appears to an officer of the rank of superintendent or above that a road check ought to continue beyond the period for which it has been authorised he may, from time to time, in writing specify a further period, not exceeding seven days, during which it may continue.

(13) Every written authorisation shall specify—

(a) the name of the officer giving it;

(b) the purpose of the road check; and

(c) the locality in which vehicles are to be stopped.

(14) The duties to specify the purposes of a road check imposed by subsections (9) and (13) above include duties to specify any relevant [indictable offence].

(15) Where a vehicle is stopped in a road check, the person in charge of the vehicle at the time when it is stopped shall be entitled to obtain a written statement of the purpose of the road check if he applies for such a statement not later than the end of the period of twelve months from the day on which the vehicle was stopped.

(16) Nothing in this section affects the exercise by police officers of any power to stop vehicles for purposes other than those specified in subsection (1) above.

• Criminal Justice and Public Order Act 1994

60 Powers to stop and search in anticipation of [, or after,] violence[252]

[(1) If a police officer of or above the rank of inspector reasonably believes—

(a) that incidents involving serious violence may take place in any locality in his police area, and that it is expedient to give an authorisation under this section to prevent their occurrence,

---

252 This section has been the subject of virtually annual amendments and substitutions too numerous to reference here, ranging from the Knives Act 1997 to the Serious Crime Act 2007.

[(aa) that—

   (i) an incident involving serious violence has taken place in England and Wales in his police area;

   (ii) a dangerous instrument or offensive weapon used in the incident is being carried in any locality in his police area by a person; and

   (iii) it is expedient to give an authorisation under this section to find the instrument or weapon;] or

(b) that persons are carrying dangerous instruments or offensive weapons in any locality in his police area without good reason,

he may give an authorisation that the powers conferred by this section are to be exercisable at any place within that locality for a specified period not exceeding 24 hours.]

(2) …

(3) If it appears to [an officer of or above the rank of] superintendent that it is expedient to do so, having regard to offences which have, or are reasonably suspected to have, been committed in connection with any [activity] falling within the authorisation, he may direct that the authorisation shall continue in being for a further [24] hours.

[(3A) If an inspector gives an authorisation under subsection (1) he must, as soon as it is practicable to do so, cause an officer of or above the rank of superintendent to be informed.]

(4) This section confers on any constable in uniform power—

(a) to stop any pedestrian and search him or anything carried by him for offensive weapons or dangerous instruments;

(b) to stop any vehicle and search the vehicle, its driver and any passenger for offensive weapons or dangerous instruments.

[(4A)…]

(5) A constable may, in the exercise of [the powers conferred by subsection (4) above], stop any person or vehicle and make any search he thinks fit whether or not he has any grounds for suspecting that the person or vehicle is carrying weapons or articles of that kind.

(6) If in the course of a search under this section a constable discovers a dangerous instrument or an article which he has reasonable grounds for suspecting to be an offensive weapon, he may seize it.

(7) This section applies (with the necessary modifications) to ships, aircraft and hovercraft as it applies to vehicles.

(8) A person who fails

[(a) to stop, or to stop a vehicle; or

(b) …]

when required to do so by a constable in the exercise of his powers under this section shall be liable on summary conviction to imprisonment for a term not exceeding [51 weeks] or to a fine not exceeding level 3 on the standard scale or both.

…

60AA. Powers to require removal of disguises

(1) Where—

(a) an authorisation under section 60 is for the time being in force in relation to any locality for any period, or

(b) an authorisation under subsection (3) that the powers conferred by subsection (2) shall be exercisable at any place in a locality is in force for any period,

those powers shall be exercisable at any place in that locality at any time in that period.

(2) This subsection confers power on any constable in uniform—

(a) to require any person to remove any item which the constable reasonably believes that person is wearing wholly or mainly for the purpose of concealing his identity;

(b) to seize any item which the constable reasonably believes any person intends to wear wholly or mainly for that purpose.

(3) If a police officer of or above the rank of inspector reasonably believes—

(a) that activities may take place in any locality in his police area that are likely (if they take place) to involve the commission of offences, and

(b) that it is expedient, in order to prevent or control the activities, to give an authorisation under this subsection,

he may give an authorisation that the powers conferred by this section shall be exercisable at any place within that locality for a specified period not exceeding twenty-four hours.

(4) If it appears to an officer of or above the rank of superintendent that it is expedient to do so, having regard to offences which—

(a) have been committed in connection with the activities in respect of which the authorisation was given, or

(b) are reasonably suspected to have been so committed,

he may direct that the authorisation shall continue in force for a further twenty-four hours.

(5) If an inspector gives an authorisation under subsection , he must, as soon as it is practicable to do so, cause an officer of or above the rank of superintendent to be informed.

(6) Any authorisation under this section—

(a) shall be in writing and signed by the officer giving it; and

(b) shall specify—

(i) the grounds on which it is given;

(ii) the locality in which the powers conferred by this section are exercisable;

(iii) the period during which those powers are exercisable;

and a direction under subsection (4) shall also be given in writing or, where that is not practicable, recorded in writing as soon as it is practicable to do so.

(7) A person who fails to remove an item worn by him when required to do so by a constable in the exercise of his power under this section shall be liable, on summary conviction, to imprisonment for a term not exceeding one month or to a fine not exceeding level 3 on the standard scale or both.

…

NOTES

1. The Serious Organised Crime and Police Act 2005 substituted the word 'indictable' for 'serious arrestable offence' in s. 4 thus broadening its scope considerably from what previously would have been viewed as an exceptional power.

2. Section 5 requires the annual reports of chief officers of police to include information about the number of searches and road checks carried out under ss. 3 and 4. This should facilitate independent scrutiny by police authorities and Inspectors of Constabulary to ensure that the powers are not used randomly.

3. In PACE, s. 1(8A) the offence referred to under s. 139 of the Criminal Justice Act 1988 is the offence of having an article with a point or blade in a public place unless the person in possession can establish a defence that, for example, the blade was used for work purposes. It has been established that this reverse burden does not breach Art. 6 of the European Convention: *L v DPP*.[253]

4. *Stop and search.* Section 1 of PACE extended the powers of the police to stop and search without warrant in a number of important respects. First, it gave power to search for any offensive weapon: previously, there was only a power to search for firearms.[254] Secondly, the power to search for stolen goods, previously available in the metropolitan area,[255] and in a number of other locations in the country (enshrined in local legislation) was extended throughout England and Wales, the earlier legislation being repealed.[256] Thirdly, there was a new power to stop and search for equipment used in offences such as burglary (e.g. jemmies or picklocks).

5. The power conferred by s. 60 of the CJPO Act 1994 does not depend on any 'reasonable suspicion' held by the officer conducting the stop-search. The Minister of State at the Home Office, David Maclean MP, stated[257] that the Government was:

persuaded that the need to meet the tests of reasonable suspicion seriously inhibits effective preventive action by the police when they believe that violence is likely to break out.

The power would, for example, enable the police to search a group of people where there are grounds to believe that some although not all are carrying a weapon. The power in s. 60(4A) relating to the removal of face masks gives two powers—one to remove and one to seize items. These were explained as being targeted at 'youths with balaclavas covering their faces who hijack cars and drive them at high speed around housing estates'.[258] Could such people not have been arrested and searched under the general PACE powers or those in the Road Traffic Acts? In *DPP v Avery*,[259] the Court held that the officer exercising powers under s. 60(4A) was not required to give his name, station or reasons for his action, as his actions would be self-explanatory. Section 60(AA) was inserted by the Anti-terrorism Crime and Security Act 2001. In practical terms does it provide a power to stop and search any individual wearing or carrying a face-covering within a particular locality?

6. Article 5 of the ECHR does not expressly authorise stops and searches. The ECHR powers are drafted in terms of 'deprivation of liberty' and 'detention'. Although most of the powers in England and Wales are exercisable only on proof of an officer's reasonable suspicion, some, such as s. 60 above, do not contain this requirement. The Convention provides that a deprivation of liberty on reasonable suspicion is legitimate provided, under Art. 5(1)(c), that the detention relates to the commission of an offence *and* is

---

[253] [2002] 2 All ER 854.
[254] Firearms Act 1968, ss. 47(3), 49(1) and (2): these powers continued to be available after the 1984 Act.
[255] Metropolitan Police Act 1839, s. 66.
[256] PACE, s. 7.   [257] 241 HC Deb, 12 April 1994, col. 69.
[258] M. O'Brien, Under Secretary of State for the Home Office, Commons Standing Committee B, 9 June 1998, col. 804.
[259] [2003] 1 Cr App R 31.

with the purpose of bringing the suspect to court. See *R (on the application of Gillan) v Metropolitan Police Comr*[260] detailed in Chapter 5.

7. Another important general stop and search power is contained in the Misuse of Drugs Act 1971:

23(2).—If a constable has reasonable grounds to suspect that any person is in possession of a controlled drug in contravention of this Act of any regulations made there under, the constable may—

(*a*) search that person, and detain him for the purpose of searching him;

(*b*) search any vehicle or vessel in which the constable suspects that the drug may be found, and for that purpose require the person in control of the vehicle or vessel to stop it;

(*c*) seize and detain, for the purposes of proceedings under this Act, anything found in the course of the search which appears to the constable to be evidence of an offence under this Act.

In this subsection 'vessel' includes a hovercraft within the meaning of the Hovercraft Act 1968; and nothing in this subsection shall prejudice any power of search or any power to seize or detain property which is exercisable by a constable apart from this subsection.

This power, and certain other stop and search powers[261] survived the 1984 Act, but are subject to the safeguards set out in s. 2. Note that the requirements of s. 2 operate in respect of *searches* and therefore not where a *stop* does not lead to a search. In *French v DPP*[262] F successfully appealed against his conviction for obstructing an officer in the execution of his duty. The officer had strip searched F at the police station after a different officer had detained F following his being stopped and searched under s. 23 by two further officers. Since the officer exercising the stop and search under s. 23 had not given evidence, it was not possible to conclude that the strip search was lawful.

(A) REASONABLE SUSPICION AND DISCRETION IN STOP AND SEARCH

'Stop and search epitomises the exercise of police discretion and the issues associated with it.'[263] It is important to consider to what extent the discretion is necessary for the power to be workable. With the maximum discretion given to the officer on the beat (at the lowest point in the organisational structure) is he or she capable of being monitored and supervised effectively?

Quinton, Bland and Miller[264] concluded that their research demonstrated that:

in practice, generalisations of various kinds play an important role in how officers form suspicion and decide to carry out stops and searches. However, we have observed that this involves a clear tension between:

– the need to draw on generalisations for effective targeting of police activity; and

– the alienation that generalisations, potentially, and negative stereotypes, in particular, cause.

---

[260] [2006] 4 All ER 1041.

[261] E.g. the Wildlife and Countryside Act 1981, s. 19; the Firearms Act 1968, ss. 47(3), 49(1), (2).

[262] [1997] COD 174, DC.   [263] P.A.J. Waddington, *Policing Citizens* (1999), p. 50.

[264] *Police Stops, Decision-making and Practice* (2000) Police Research Series Paper No. 130.

For example, generalisations which link crime with age, appearance, time and place, and behaviour can sometimes provide a useful basis for the effective targeting of stops and searches. However, these generalisations (which in some sense might seem reasonable) will mean that people will be identified by the police as suspicious when they do not warrant police attention. This can be a cause of public resentment.

Secondly, we noted how the poor handling of stop or search encounters can impact negatively on public confidence. Research has shown that public satisfaction with encounters is dependent on the politeness of the officer, whether the person was given an acceptable reason for the stop and whether they were searched. As such, improving public confidence can be achieved in part by better handling of stops and searches…

Legality. We have seen that the notion of PACE reasonable suspicion in relation to searches, in practice, operates more along a continuum than as a simple dichotomy. The working practices of officers reveal that suspicion is based on a range of different factors in which a person might appear more or less suspicious to police officers. Furthermore, the research clearly showed differences in the level of suspicion required by different officers to do stops and searches. This is likely to be reflected across the police service. As such, the discretion that officers exercise in this respect can potentially be a risk to legality. Specifically, the report points out the following concerns.

First, the variation between officers in their decisions to carry out stops and searches raises questions about the rule of law and the extent to which police interventions are evenly applied. Secondly, it is clear that reasonable suspicion for searches is not, in some cases, being achieved. The levels of evidence recorded in grounds are also low: in both the lack of specific detail and a failure to refer to all the available direct and indirect evidence. This points to guidance both in the operational use of reasonable suspicion and in its written articulation for search records.

Effectiveness. Effectiveness is likely to be strongest when suspicion is well-informed, and decisions are based on direct and accurate information—maximising encounters with active offenders and minimising them with the general public.

Direct evidence, that is evidence pointing to specific individuals, is less ambiguous—there is a greater certainty about the person the police intend to stop. As such, the risks to effectiveness are lower when suspicion relies on direct evidence. Regardless of whether evidence is direct or indirect, the reliability of suspicion will be affected by the accuracy of the information and intelligence available to officers. The generalisations about current high-crime areas, for example, will be more reliable when based on up-to-date intelligence.

To reduce the risks to effectiveness and, in turn, public confidence, it is important that suspicions are, as far as possible, well-informed, reliable and based good quality information.[265]

[The authors provided a series of Recommendations for the Home Office, National Police Training (NPT) and the Association of Chief Police Officers (ACPO).]

(B) ADEQUATE RECORDING AND MONITORING?

In *Osman v DPP*[266] it was held that a stop and search was rendered unlawful where the officers had failed to identify themselves in accordance with s. 2(3)(a). The search was conducted under s. 60 of the 1994 Act.

- **Osman v DPP (1999) 163 JP 725, Divisional Court**

Sedley LJ: [W]hat the officers are required by law to do is to take 'reasonable steps' before beginning the search to bring the prescribed data to the attention of the members of the public whom they are proposing

---

265 Pp. 64–67.   266 (1999) 163 JP 725, DC; see also, *R v Bristol* [2007] All ER (D) 47.

to search. On the evidence set out in the Crown Court's findings, no step whatever was taken in this direction. It is impossible, therefore, to begin to attach the epithet 'reasonable' to what was done.

It seems to me, having heard Mr Boothby's submission, that while there is an element of formality and, perhaps, of excessive use of time in having to recite the constable's name and station to every person searched, it is nevertheless Parliament's view that such formality is of great importance in relation to civil liberties. There would be nothing, I would have thought, to prevent uniformed officers, who are sent out to make searches of this kind from carrying in their pocket slips of paper giving their name and station, so that the person searched not only is told what these are but can carry the information away with him or her, and the officer is saved the trouble of going through an oral rigmarole. That, however, is beside the present point. This search was unlawful for the reasons given.

This being so, the appellant's conduct in presenting himself as if he were consenting to the search—assuming that that was a legitimate finding—was nothing to the point. That he may have consented to being searched would not make the search that was being inaugurated and attempted by the officers a lawful one. What is more, I have the gravest doubts about whether the officers were entitled to infer from the conduct described that there was consent to the search, much less to infer from the appellant's resistance to being searched anywhere but at a police station that he might well be carrying a weapon. Nothing in the Crown Court's conclusions or in Mr Boothby's submissions is predicated upon any suggestion that some independent ground for search, based on reasonable suspicion, had arisen in the course of the confrontation—rightly so, in my judgment, because the questions posed to do not touch on the point.

It follows that I would answer the second question in the affirmative; that is to say, I would hold that the failure of the officers to supply details of their names and station rendered the search unlawful. The availability of information on the officer's lapels is in law neither here nor there; and in any case nothing that we know of suggests that these officers, uniquely, were carrying details of their names and station on their lapels. In the ordinary way, one would expect their numbers but no more to be visible there, and there is no different finding in this case.

This being so, I would, if necessary, answer the first pair of questions in the negative. I do not think that the appellant's conduct amounted to consent; nor, if it did amount to consent, would it have entitled the officers, without more, to commit what technically, on any view, would have been an assault on the appellant. The question, however, for the reasons I have given, is not a necessary question. The case is concluded in the appellant's favour by the answer to the second of the questions posed.

Accordingly, I would allow this appeal and quash both convictions.

Collins J: This is, no doubt, because Parliament has recognised that a search of a person is a serious interference with his liberty, and all proper safeguards must be followed. The facts found show that there was no reason why the officers could not have given the necessary information. It is not for the court to disapply the duties set out in the Act, but only to decide whether, in a given set of circumstances, the officers have taken all reasonable steps to do what Parliament has required them to do. I emphasise that we are not concerned with the admissibility of evidence found as a result of a search, but whether the search itself was lawful, so that the officers were acting in the execution of their duty when carrying it out.

The first question asked by the Crown Court concerns consent. Consent is not relevant. If the officer fails to comply with section 2, there can be no proper consent. The ordinary lawabiding citizen no doubt usually accepts the constable's word that he has the powers he asserts and, if he has nothing to hide, will accept that he can be searched. But that apparent consent cannot mean that the officer is acting in the execution of his duty in carrying out the search. In any event, I cannot see how the Crown Court could reasonably have found that the officers could have assumed consent. The respondent's reaction, when the officer took hold of him in order to search him, made it as clear as it could be that he was not consenting. He said, 'You cannot fucking search me here, take me to a fucking police station.'

NOTES

1. Is it realistic to expect officers to comply with this approach? The need to comply with the terms of s. 2 applies even where a police officer has reason to believe that a suspect is about to swallow or otherwise dispose of drugs (or other items). In *Bristol*[267] the Court of Appeal suggested that the requirements of s. 2 can be complied with very quickly: for example, by saying 'Mansson; Charing Cross; Drugs search. Spit it out'. If the terms of s. 2 are not complied with then a defendant who struggles when searched cannot be guilty of obstruction or assault as the officer will be acting unlawfully.

2. An officer who has carried out a power to search must make a record of this as soon as practicable and give a copy to the person searched. In addition, following recommendations in the McPherson Report[268] persons stopped and asked to account for themselves should also be provided with a record of the encounter.[269] Code A states that, 'When an officer requests a person in a public place to account for themselves, i.e. their actions, behaviour, presence in an area or possession of anything, a record of the encounter must be completed at the time and a copy given to the person who has been questioned. The record must identify the name of the officer who has made the stop and conducted the encounter.'[270] These records are provided not only for the person stopped but allow for supervising officers to monitor the use of stop and search powers and guard against, for example, inappropriate generalisations being made.[271]

3. The *Flanagan Report*[272] has recommended further changes to the recording of 'stop and account':

5.57 What has evolved is a manually recorded system of Stop and Account which takes on average 7 minutes per individual encounter and which, as I witnessed, however careful an officer is in explaining the purpose of the process, usually leads to suspicion on the part of the member of the public involved. In London alone, it has been estimated that Stop and Account consumes over 48,000 hours annually of officers' time. This does not include the time taken to log each form once it is returned to the station, or the time supervisors spend checking and countersigning each form.

5.58 I do not believe that what we have developed as the Stop and Account process is fulfilling the need identified by the *Stephen Lawrence Inquiry*. The process has become bureaucratic rather than focusing on what I believe is most important in the one to one interactions between the police and members of the public—courtesy, respect and accountability. I do, however, remain convinced that there is a need for officers to demonstrate accountability to individual members of the public. This purpose could be best be served through an overhaul of the current Stop and Account process.

5.61 I believe this is best served not by filling in a lengthy form to be used for statistical analysis, but by ensuring our officers are aware of the responsibility they must exercise when they ask someone to account for themselves. I have explored with 'Airwave' the practicality of an officer digitally recording the details of the encounter verbally rather than manually in writing.

---

[267] [2007] EWCA Crim 3214.

[268] *The Stephen Lawrence Inquiry: Report of an Inquiry by Sir William MacPherson of Cluny* (Cm 4262, 1999).

[269] See P. Quinton and N. Bland, *Modernising the Tactic: Improving the Use of Stop and Search* (1999).

[270] Code A para. 4.12.   [271] Code A para. 5.1.

[272] *The Review of Policing Final Report* (The Flanagan Report) (2008). The Government Response to the PACE Review (2008) suggests that disproportionality and bureaucracy are two most significant concerns surrounding stop and search, and similarly suggest a more streamlined recording procedure: see paras 6.1–6.6.

4. To what extent have the rights to be free from police interference in everyday life been substituted for a right to have a written (or, in future, digital) record of its occurrence?

(C) PUBLIC PERCEPTIONS OF STOP AND SEARCH

Although complaints about stop and search have declined over the years,[273] this may be a reflection of the 'acceptance among young people that being stopped is a fact of life'.[274] Is being stopped and searched in the street a fact of life? Should it be?

Stone and Pettigrew[275] explored public experiences of stop and search, particularly in light of the Stephen Lawrence Inquiry and perceptions of discrimination in police practice. The main conclusions were:

There is general support for stops and searches amongst all ethnic groups but only if there are fundamental changes in the way they are used by the police. Whilst the Inquiry's recommendations were perceived by the public as potentially enhancing accountability, it was important for the police to ensure that records are made by officers and effective monitoring occurs. Public confidence in police use of stops and searches is primarily based on being treated fairly and with respect, and being given a satisfactory reason for the stop or search.

Public views on the use of stops and searches

There was a very strong perception that the way in which stops and searches are currently handled causes more distrust, antagonism, and resentment than any of the positive effects they can have. Despite this, respondents from all ethnic groups felt that if there were fundamental changes in the ways they are used, who they are targeted at, attitudes of the police, and reasons given, then there was a role for stops and searches. The following were felt to be the two most important factors that should change:

1. There were very strong views that there needed to be considerable changes in attitudes of the police during stops and searches.

2. Respondents believed that stops and searches should be carried out for legitimate reasons and that a person should be given a valid genuine and credible reason at all times whenever he/she is stopped or searched.[276]

(D) INTELLIGENCE GATHERING AND STOP AND SEARCH

In what sense are powers of stop and search or stop and account 'important' when arrests rates following from them are as low as 12 per cent?[277] To what extent is it legitimate for stop and search powers to be used primarily as an intelligence-gathering tool? Quinton and Bland[278] found that some forces used the power to stop the same individuals repeatedly as

---

[273] See M. Fitzgerald, MPS Report, *Searches in London* (1999).

[274] Peter Moorhouse, Chairman of the Police Complaints Authority, commenting on the release of M. Fitzgerald's report, press release of the PCA, 15 December 1999.

[275] *The Views of the Public on Stops and Searches* (2000), Police Research Series Paper No. 129.

[276] Ibid., pp. 52–54.

[277] The use of stop and search has increased, but the hit rate has gradually declined: see D. Brown, *PACE Ten Years On: A Review of Research* (1997) HORSD No. 49. See also *Arrests for Recorded Crime and the Operation of Certain Police Powers Under PACE: England and Wales 2005–06* (2007).

[278] *Modernising the Tactic* (1999).

a means of monitoring the whereabouts of 'known criminals'. This was recognised as an effective use of the power.

Operational effectiveness One of the key concerns of forces is to maximise the impact searches have on people actively involved in crime and to minimise their use on law-abiding members of the public…We suggested that improved targeting of searches can help increase the arrest rate from searches. One useful way in which this might be achieved is by ensuring that individual searches are linked to intelligence-led patrols, as well as reliable and accurate information…These might be based on effective structures for the sharing and dissemination of up-to-date and accurate intelligence, and specific intelligence-led patrol tasks. There might also be a role for linking searches with strategic and planned police operations, whereby individual searches are based on strong intelligence and observation with the consent of local communities. It is clear that efforts which emphasise the need to increase effectiveness need also to act against the potential development of perverse incentives and competition by, again, having an effective system for recording-keeping and supervision. The working practices of officers themselves can also be a useful avenue for identifying good practice. This might provide a good source of information for developing specific training packages which respond to local needs. However, as with all these interventions, forces need to ensure that interventions are implemented fully and their progress monitored.[279]

Can civil liberties concerns be met by managerial monitoring? Is the Flanagan Report's recommendation for digital recording of stops more appropriate? Quinton, Bland and Miller, *Police Stops, Decision-making and Practice*[280] concluded:

The research has emphasised the need for stops and searches to be based on good quality information and intelligence that is up-to-date, detailed, accurate and reflects the needs of operational officers. For example, as officers will, in practice, make common sense generalisations about high-crime areas as a basis for suspicions, it is important that the information on which generalisations are based is current and specific. Rather than just knowing the broad high-crime areas, officers will need to know—where the current problems are in a high-crime area;

– the exact nature of the problem;

– when it occurs; and

– who the current active offenders are.

It is clear that though this does occur, it does not do so routinely and consistently across the police service. Forces should ensure that the systems they have in place provide officers with such information. A review of information and intelligence systems will need to examine the collection and storage process, and whether the information is disseminated and acted upon quickly and effectively.

The reliability of suspect descriptions is a key factor in suspicion. In order to improve, forces will need to clarify in more detail the central, necessary elements of a description to be usable by officers. This will also have training implications for call-handling staff, and more widely, for improving the way in which interactions with victims and witnesses are handled to maximise the quality and quantity of information about suspects.

Forces need to ensure that reasonable suspicion for searches has been fulfilled for each search and that the recorded grounds accurately reflect all the available direct and indirect factors in detail (e.g. recording the nature of a person's behaviour not just 'suspicious behaviour'). Bland, et al. (above) examine in greater detail how this might be achieved through management interventions, looking in part at the role

---

[279] Ibid., p. 73.   [280] (2000) Police Research Series Paper No. 130.

of the supervisor. Shift supervisors might provide, for example, a safeguard against unfair use of negative stereotypes by challenging broad generalisations made by officers and the information which they are based on. Forces could usefully produce guidance on the standards expected from officers and supervisors in this respect.

(E) STATISTICS ON STOP AND SEARCH

Statistics on stop and search have been produced by a number of bodies. The Home Office Research, Development and Statistics Directorate publishes annual reports on the operation of 'certain police powers under PACE'.[281]

Searches of persons or vehicles under PACE, s. 1: 2000/1 – 714,000; 2001/2 – 741,000; 2002/3 – 895,300; 2003/4 – 749,400; 2004/5 – 851,200; 2005-/6 – 888,700. In 2004/5 11% of searched led to an arrest, increasing to 12 per cent in 2005/6. The most recent figures show that most stops and searches are made for drugs (43%) followed by stolen property (23%).[282]

Other search statistics:

Section 60 CJPOA stops and searches have increased considerably in recent years: 2000/1 – 11,330; 2001/2 – 18,900; 2002/3 – 44,400; 2003/4 – 40,400; 2004/5 – 41,600; 2005/6 – 36,300. In the latest statistics only 5 per cent of such stops and searches led to arrests.[283]

Section 44 Terrorism Act 2000. Figures for stops and searches of pedestrians and vehicles to prevent acts of terrorism: 2000/1 – 6,400; 2001/2 – 10,200; 2002/3 – 32,100; 2003/4 – 33,800; 2004/5 – 37,000; 2005/6 – 50,000.[284]

(F) WHO GETS STOPPED?

Figures for 2004/5[285] reflect a fairly constant trend through the previous 20 years such that young men aged 16–24 remain statistically the group most likely to be stopped. Of all those stopped, 3 per cent are stopped on foot and 10 per cent in a vehicle. Nine per cent of adults stopped in a vehicle are White, compared to 13 per cent who are Asian and 15 per cent who are Black.

(G) ETHNICITY AND STOPS AND SEARCHES

Much has been written on the disproportionate number of stops and searches of ethnic minority groups.[286] Statistics on this issue should be treated with caution, since there is a

---

281 *Arrests for Recorded Crime and the Operation of Certain Police Powers under PACE: England and Wales 2005–06* (2007).

282 Ibid., para. 19.   283 Ibid., p. 13.

284 Ibid., p. 14.

285 *Policing and the Criminal Justice System—public confidence and perceptions: finding from the 2004/5 British Crime Survey*, Home Office Online report 07/06 (2006).

286 See Fitzgerald, Chap. 3; A. Marlow and J. Maddock (1998) 71 Pol J 317; Home Office, *Race and the Criminal Justice System* (1999), Chaps 1 and 2; B. Bowling and C. Phillips, *Racism, Crime and Justice* (2002); M. Feilzer and R. Hood, *Differences or Discrimination—Minority Ethnic Young People in the Youth Justice System* (2004); K. Jansson, *Ethnicity and victimisation; findings from the 2004/05 British Crime Survey* (Home Office, 2006).

greater likelihood that a stop of a Black person will lead to a search and therefore a greater likelihood that it will be recorded. Miller[287] looked at the ethnicity of those stopped and searched and exposed the complexity behind the statistics:

the resident population is not a reliable measure of the available population. However, the question remains as to whether police officers are more likely to stop or search those from minority ethnic backgrounds among those they actually encounter in the available population. This issue was investigated in depth in this study. Overall, across the five sites, the findings of this research did not suggest any general pattern of bias against those from minority ethnic backgrounds. This was true for minority ethnic groups as whole, as well as any particular minority ethnic group. Asian people tended to be under-represented in those stopped or searched, compared to their numbers in the available population, with some notable exceptions. The general picture for black people was mixed. Perhaps surprisingly, the most consistent finding across sites was that white people tended to be stopped and searched at a higher rate than their numbers in the available population would predict.[288]

The conclusions were that a disproportionate number of searches could be due to: ethnic bias in officers; a larger proportion of ethnic groups in the population available to be stopped and searched; and a higher concentration of minority groups in the areas targeted. But this raises the question why those areas are targeted:

While the overall picture does not, on the face of it, suggest a general pattern of discrimination against those from minority ethnic groups, it is important to flag-up certain caveats. First, the findings do indicate there are some situations where ethnic bias does occur. While it should not be assumed that discrimination underlies such biases, it does remind us that we should not be complacent in assuming there is no problem.

In many respects, the findings of this research are a problem for the police. Most significantly, they suggest that disproportionality is, to some extent, a product of structural factors beyond the control of the police. Therefore, they may lack the power to eliminate disproportionality, based upon residential population measures, by changing their practices. So, despite the best efforts of police forces, those from minority ethnic backgrounds may continue to be stopped and searched more often than white people.[289]

In 2005/6 the number of stops and searches increased and this was due in the main to an increase in stops and searches of Black people (increase of 11.8 per cent) and Asian people (14 per cent) and other minority ethnic groups (16 per cent). The rise in the stops and searched of White people was 0.2 per cent. This is partly explained by increased use of such powers after the London bombings in July 2005. Black people are now statistically seven times more likely to be searched than White people.[290] Can ethnic profiling be an appropriate justification for stop and search?[291]

(H) EFFECTIVENESS

The arrest rate from stops and searches is consistently found to be below 15 per cent. Should there be a stricter application of the reasonable suspicion test so that 'hit rates' would be

---

[287] *Profiling Populations Available for Stops and Searches* (2000), Police Research Series Paper No. 131. See also Home Office, *Crime Policing and Justice, the experience of ethnic minorities*.

[288] P. 84.

[289] P. 87. See also P. Waddington, K. Stenson and D. Don, 'In Proportion: Race and Police Stop and Search' (2004) 44 Brit Jo Criminol 889.

[290] Ministry of Justice, *Statistics on Race and the Criminal Justice System 2006* (2007), Chap. 4.

[291] See J. English and R. Card, *Police Law* (9th edn, 2005), p. 45.

much higher? What would you consider to be an appropriate 'hit rate'? It has been shown that stops and searches do have some effect on the crime rate in an area. Fitzgerald, found that there was a statistically significant rise in crime in 1999 corresponding to the decrease in stops and searches that year.

Miller, Bland and Quinton found there to be a 'substantial variation between forces in the extent to which searches are used'.[292] Most strikingly it was found that 'searches appear to have a minor role in detecting offenders for the range of all crimes that they address, and a relatively small role in detecting offenders for such crimes that come to the attention of the police'.[293] Despite this some officers interviewed claimed that they would be powerless without the stop and search and that 'crime would go through the roof'.[294] Searches were found to have 'only a limited direct disruptive impact on crime by intercepting those going out to commit offences'[295] and it was estimated that only 0.2 per cent of disruptable crimes were affected in 1997. Contrary to popular belief, and that of some officers interviewed, 'it is unlikely that searches make a substantial contribution to undermining drug-markets or drug related crime'.[296] In sum, 'there is little evidence' that searches have any 'marginal deterrent effect on offending'.[297]

(I) ROAD CHECKS

Section 163 (1) of the Road Traffic Act 1988 provides that:

> A person driving a mechanically propelled vehicle on a road must stop the vehicle on being required to do so by a constable in uniform.

Section 163(2) makes similar provision for a person riding a cycle and s. 163(3) makes failure to comply an offence. It has been held that it is not necessary for a constable acting under this section to be 'acting in the execution of his duty under some common law powers. It would seem on the face of it that the constable derives his duty as well as his power from the terms of s. 159 [now s. 163] itself'.[298] Accordingly, a constable may stop a vehicle to check whether the driver has valid documents, even though he has no reasonable grounds to suspect that he does not.[299] However, a constable may not act 'in bad faith' or 'capriciously':[300] the section does not give a constable 'a power willy-nilly to stop a motor vehicle'.[301] The result is that a motorist may be stopped more or less at random, provided that it is done for some purpose related to police duties. If the constable reasonably suspects the driver has been drinking the breathalyser legislation will become applicable. Although random *tests* are not permitted, (more or less) random stops are.[302] The reasonable suspicion may be based on such factors as the manner of driving, the smell of alcohol on the driver's breath or the admission by the driver that he has been drinking.[303] In the absence of reasonable cause, evidence subsequently obtained may be excluded under s. 78 of PACE.[304]

---

[292] *The Impact of Stops and Searches on Crime and the Community* (2000) HOR No. 127, p. 12.

[293] Ibid., p. 27.   [294] Ibid., p. 16.   [295] Ibid., p. 45.

[296] Ibid., p. 45.   [297] Ibid., p. 33.

[298] *Beard v Wood* [1980] RR 454 at 457–458, DC, per Wien J.

[299] Ibid.   [300] [1980] RTR 454 at 457–459.

[301] *Winter v Barlow* [1980] RTR 209 at 213, DC, per Eveleigh LT. See also *Steel v Goacher* [1983] RTR 98, DC; Commentary by D.J. Birch [1982] Crim LR 689 and D.P.J. Walsh [1994] Crim LR 187.

[302] D.J. Birch [1982] Crim LR 689.   [303] *DPP v McGladrigan* [1991] RTR 297, DC.

[304] *DPP v Godwin* [1991] RTR 303, DC.

Road checks under s. 4, number of vehicles stopped: 2000/1 – 17,900; 2001/2 – 14,800; 2002/3 – 32,000; 2003/4 – 7,500; 2004/5 – 12,500; 2005/6 – 11,300.[305]

The Terrorism Act 2000, s. 44(1) empowers the police to stop and search vehicles and their occupants and this power has been used with increasing frequency (see (G) above).

5. ENTRY, SEARCH AND SEIZURE

● **Police and Criminal Evidence Act 1984**

PART II

Powers of Entry, Search and Seizure

8 Power of justice of the peace to authorise entry and search of premises

(1) If on an application made by a constable a justice of the peace is satisfied that there are reasonable grounds for believing—

(a) that [an indictable offence] has been committed; and

(b) that there is material on premises [mentioned in subsection (1A) below] which is likely to be of substantial value (whether by itself or together with other material) to the investigation of the offence; and

(c) that the material is likely to be relevant evidence; and

(d) that it does not consist of or include items subject to legal privilege, excluded material or special procedure material; and

(e) that any of the conditions specified in subsection (3) below applies [in relation to each set of premises specified in the application],

he may issue a warrant authorising a constable to enter and search the premises.

[(1A) The premises referred to in subsection (1)(b) above are—

(a) one or more sets of premises specified in the application (in which case the application is for a 'specific premises warrant'); or

(b) any premises occupied or controlled by a person specified in the application, including such sets of premises as are so specified (in which case the application is for an 'all premises warrant').

(1B) If the application is for an all premises warrant, the justice of the peace must also be satisfied—

(a) that because of the particulars of the offence referred to in paragraph (a) of subsection (1) above, there are reasonable grounds for believing that it is necessary to search premises occupied or controlled by the person in question which are not specified in the application in order to find the material referred to in paragraph (b) of that subsection; and

(b) that it is not reasonably practicable to specify in the application all the premises which he occupies or controls and which might need to be searched.]

[(1C) The warrant may authorise entry to and search of premises on more than one occasion if, on the application, the justice of the peace is satisfied that it is necessary to authorise multiple entries in order to achieve the purpose for which he issues the warrant.

---

[305] *Arrests for Recorded Crime and the Operation of Certain Police Powers Under PACE: England and Wales 2005–06* (2007), p. 15.

(1D) If it authorises multiple entries, the number of entries authorised may be unlimited, or limited to a maximum.]

(2) A constable may seize and retain anything for which a search has been authorised under subsection (1) above.

(3) The conditions mentioned in subsection (1)(e) above are—

(a) that it is not practicable to communicate with any person entitled to grant entry to the premises;

(b) that it is practicable to communicate with a person entitled to grant entry to the premises but it is not practicable to communicate with any person entitled to grant access to the evidence;

(c) that entry to the premises will not be granted unless a warrant is produced;

(d) hat the purpose of a search may be frustrated or seriously prejudiced unless a constable arriving at the premises can secure immediate entry to them.

(4) In this Act 'relevant evidence', in relation to an offence, means anything that would be admissible in evidence at a trial for the offence.

...

9 Special provisions as to access

(1) A constable may obtain access to excluded material or special procedure material for the purposes of a criminal investigation by making an application under Schedule 1 below and in accordance with that Schedule.

(2) Any Act (including a local Act) passed before this Act under which a search of premises for the purposes of a criminal investigation could be authorised by the issue of a warrant to a constable shall cease to have effect so far as it relates to the authorisation of searches—

(a) for items subject to legal privilege; or

(b) for excluded material; or

(c) for special procedure material consisting of documents or records other than documents.

...

10 Meaning of 'items subject to legal privilege'

(1) Subject to subsection (2) below, in this Act 'items subject to legal privilege' means—

(a) communications between a professional legal adviser and his client or any person representing his client made in connection with the giving of legal advice to the client;

(b) communications between a professional legal adviser and his client or any person representing his client or between such an adviser or his client or any such representative and any other person made in connection with or in contemplation of legal proceedings and for the purposes of such proceedings; and

(c) items enclosed with or referred to in such communications and made—

(i) in connection with the giving of legal advice; or

(ii) in connection with or in contemplation of legal proceedings and for the purposes of such proceedings,

when they are in the possession of a person who is entitled to possession of them.

(2) Items held with the intention of furthering a criminal purpose are not items subject to legal privilege.

11 Meaning of 'excluded material'

(1) Subject to the following provisions of this section, in this Act 'excluded material' means—

 (a) personal records which a person has acquired or created in the course of any trade, business, profession or other occupation or for the purposes of any paid or unpaid office and which he holds in confidence;

 (b) human tissue or tissue fluid which has been taken for the purposes of diagnosis or medical treatment and which a person holds in confidence;

 (c) journalistic material which a person holds in confidence and which consists—

  (i) of documents; or

  (ii) of records other than documents.

(2) A person holds material other than journalistic material in confidence for the purposes of this section if he holds it subject—

 (a) to an express or implied undertaking to hold it in confidence; or

 (b) to a restriction on disclosure or an obligation of secrecy contained in any enactment, including an enactment contained in an Act passed after this Act.

(3) A person holds journalistic material in confidence for the purposes of this section if—

 (a) he holds it subject to such an undertaking, restriction or obligation; and

 (b) it has been continuously held (by one or more persons) subject to such an undertaking, restriction or obligation since it was first acquired or created for the purposes of journalism.

12 Meaning of 'personal records'

In this Part of this Act 'personal records' means documentary and other records concerning an individual (whether living or dead) who can be identified from them and relating—

 (a) to his physical or mental health;

 (b) to spiritual counselling or assistance given or to be given to him; or

 (c) to counselling or assistance given or to be given to him, for the purposes of his personal welfare, by any voluntary organisation or by any individual who—

  (i) by reason of his office or occupation has responsibilities for his personal welfare; or

  (ii) by reason of an order of a court has responsibilities for his supervision.

13 Meaning of 'journalistic material'

(1) Subject to subsection (2) below, in this Act 'journalistic material' means material acquired or created for the purposes of journalism.

(2) Material is only journalistic material for the purposes of this Act if it is in the possession of a person who acquired or created it for the purposes of journalism.

(3) A person who receives material from someone who intends that the recipient shall use it for the purposes of journalism is to be taken to have acquired it for those purposes.

14 Meaning of 'special procedure material'

(1) In this Act 'special procedure material' means—

 (a) material to which subsection (2) below applies; and

 (b) journalistic material, other than excluded material.

(2) Subject to the following provisions of this section, this subsection applies to material, other than items subject to legal privilege and excluded material, in the possession of a person who—

(a) acquired or created it in the course of any trade, business, profession or other occupation or for the purpose of any paid or unpaid office; and

(b) holds it subject—

   (i) to an express or implied undertaking to hold it in confidence; or

   (ii) to a restriction or obligation such as is mentioned in section 11(2)(b) above.

(3) Where material is acquired—

(a) by an employee from his employer and in the course of his employment; or

(b) by a company from an associated company,

it is only special procedure material if it was special procedure material immediately before the acquisition.

(4) Where material is created by an employee in the course of his employment, it is only special procedure material if it would have been special procedure material had his employer created it.

...

15 Search warrants—safeguards

(1) This section and section 16 below have effect in relation to the issue to constables under any enactment, including an enactment contained in an Act passed after this Act, of warrants to enter and search premises; and an entry on or search of premises under a warrant is unlawful unless it complies with this section and section 16 below.

(2) Where a constable applies for any such warrant, it shall be his duty—

(a) to state—

   (i) the ground on which he makes the application; ...

   (ii) the enactment under which the warrant would be issued; [and]

   [(iii) if the application is for a warrant authorising entry and search on more than one occasion, the ground on which he applies for such a warrant, and whether he seeks a warrant authorising an unlimited number of entries, or (if not) the maximum number of entries desired;]

[(b) to specify the matters set out in subsection (2A) below; and]

(c) to identify, so far as is practicable, the articles or persons to be sought.

[(2A) The matters which must be specified pursuant to subsection (2)(b) above are—

[(a) if the application relates to one or more sets of premises specified in the application, each set of premises which it is desired to enter and search;]

(b) [if the application relates to any premises occupied or controlled by a person specified in the application—]

   (i) as many sets of premises which it is desired to enter and search as it is reasonably practicable to specify;

   (ii) the person who is in occupation or control of those premises and any others which it is desired to enter and search;

   (iii) why it is necessary to search more premises than those specified under sub-paragraph (i); and

   (iv) why it is not reasonably practicable to specify all the premises which it is desired to enter and search.]

(3) An application for such a warrant shall be made ex parte and supported by an information in writing.

(4) The constable shall answer on oath any question that the justice of the peace or judge hearing the application asks him.

(5) A warrant shall authorise an entry on one occasion only [unless it specifies that it authorises multiple entries].

[(5A) If it specifies that it authorises multiple entries, it must also specify whether the number of entries authorised is unlimited, or limited to a specified maximum.]

(6) A warrant—

   (a) shall specify—

      (i) the name of the person who applies for it;

      (ii) the date on which it is issued;

      (iii) the enactment under which it is issued; and

      [(iv) each set of premises to be searched, or (in the case of an all premises warrant) the person who is in occupation or control of premises to be searched, together with any premises under his occupation or control which can be specified and which are to be searched; and]

   (b) shall identify, so far as is practicable, the articles or persons to be sought.

[(7) Two copies shall be made of a [warrant] (see section 8(1A)(a) above) which specifies only one set of premises and does not authorise multiple entries; and as many copies as are reasonably required may be made of any other kind of warrant.]

(8) The copies shall be clearly certified as copies.

16 Execution of warrants

(1) A warrant to enter and search premises may be executed by any constable.

(2) Such a warrant may authorise persons to accompany any constable who is executing it.

[(2A) A person so authorised has the same powers as the constable whom he accompanies in respect of—

   (a) the execution of the warrant, and

   (b) the seizure of anything to which the warrant relates.

(2B) But he may exercise those powers only in the company, and under the supervision, of a constable.]

(3) Entry and search under a warrant must be within [three months] from the date of its issue.

[(3A) If the warrant is an all premises warrant, no premises which are not specified in it may be entered or searched unless a police officer of at least the rank of inspector has in writing authorised them to be entered.]

[(3B) No premises may be entered or searched for the second or any subsequent time under a warrant which authorises multiple entries unless a police officer of at least the rank of inspector has in writing authorised that entry to those premises.]

(4) Entry and search under a warrant must be at a reasonable hour unless it appears to the constable executing it that the purpose of a search may be frustrated on an entry at a reasonable hour.

(5) Where the occupier of premises which are to be entered and searched is present at the time when a constable seeks to execute a warrant to enter and search them, the constable—

   (a) shall identify himself to the occupier and, if not in uniform, shall produce to him documentary evidence that he is a constable;

   (b) shall produce the warrant to him; and

   (c) shall supply him with a copy of it.

(6) Where—

    (a) the occupier of such premises is not present at the time when a constable seeks to execute such a warrant; but

    (b) some other person who appears to the constable to be in charge of the premises is present,

subsection (5) above shall have effect as if any reference to the occupier were a reference to that other person.

(7) If there is no person present who appears to the constable to be in charge of the premises, he shall leave a copy of the warrant in a prominent place on the premises.

(8) A search under a warrant may only be a search to the extent required for the purpose for which the warrant was issued.

(9) A constable executing a warrant shall make an endorsement on it stating—

    (a) whether the articles or persons sought were found; and

    (b) whether any articles were seized, other than articles which were sought [and,

unless the warrant is a ... warrant specifying one set of premises only, he shall do so separately in respect of each set of premises entered and searched, which he shall in each case state in the endorsement].

[(10) A warrant shall be returned to the appropriate person mentioned in subsection (10A) below—

    (a) when it has been executed; or

    (b) in the case of a specific premises warrant which has not been executed, or an all premises warrant, or any warrant authorising multiple entries, upon the expiry of the period of three months referred to in subsection (3) above or sooner.

(10A) The appropriate person is—

    (a) if the warrant was issued by a justice of the peace, the designated officer for the local justice area in which the justice was acting when he issued the warrant;

    (b) if it was issued by a judge, the appropriate officer of the court from which he issued it.]

(11) A warrant which is returned under subsection (10) above shall be retained for 12 months from its return—

    (a) by the [designated officer for the local justice area], if it was returned under paragraph (i) of that subsection; and

    (b) by the appropriate officer, if it was returned under paragraph (ii).

(12) If during the period for which a warrant is to be retained the occupier of [premises] to which it relates asks to inspect it, he shall be allowed to do so.

17 Entry for purpose of arrest etc

(1) Subject to the following provisions of this section, and without prejudice to any other enactment, a constable may enter and search any premises for the purpose—

    (a) of executing—

        (i) a warrant of arrest issued in connection with or arising out of criminal proceedings; or

        (ii) a warrant of commitment issued under section 76 of the Magistrates' Courts Act 1980;

    (b) of arresting a person for an [indictable] offence;

    (c) of arresting a person for an offence under—

        (i) section 1 (prohibition of uniforms in connection with political objects) ... of the Public Order Act 1936;

    (ii)   any enactment contained in sections 6 to 8 or 10 of the Criminal Law Act 1977 (offences relating to entering and remaining on property);

   [(iii)   section 4 of the Public Order Act 1986 (fear or provocation of violence);]

  [(iiia)   section 4 (driving etc when under influence of drink or drugs) or 163 (failure to stop when required to do so by constable in uniform) of the Road Traffic Act 1988;

  (iiib)   section 27 of the Transport and Works Act 1992 (which relates to offences involving drink or drugs);]

   [(iv)   section 76 of the Criminal Justice and Public Order Act 1994 (failure to comply with interim possession order);]

    [(v)   any of sections 4, 5, 6(1) and (2), 7 and 8(1) and (2) of the Animal Welfare Act 2006 (offences relating to the prevention of harm to animals);]

[(ca)   of arresting, in pursuance of section 32(1A) of the Children and Young Persons Act 1969, any child or young person who has been remanded or committed to local authority accommodation under section 23(1) of that Act;

[(caa)   of arresting a person for an offence to which section 61 of the Animal Health Act 1981 applies;]

 (cb)   of recapturing any person who is, or is deemed for any purpose to be, unlawfully at large while liable to be detained—

    (i)   in a prison, remand centre, young offender institution or secure training centre, or

   (ii)   in pursuance of [section 92 of the Powers of Criminal Courts (Sentencing) Act 2000] (dealing with children and young persons guilty of grave crimes), in any other place;]

  (d)   of recapturing [any person whatever] who is unlawfully at large and whom he is pursuing; or

  (e)   of saving life or limb or preventing serious damage to property.

(2) Except for the purpose specified in paragraph (e) of subsection (1) above, the powers of entry and search conferred by this section—

  (a)   are only exercisable if the constable has reasonable grounds for believing that the person whom he is seeking is on the premises; and

  (b)   are limited, in relation to premises consisting of two or more separate dwellings, to powers to enter and search—

    (i)   any parts of the premises which the occupiers of any dwelling comprised in the premises use in common with the occupiers of any other such dwelling; and

   (ii)   any such dwelling in which the constable has reasonable grounds for believing that the person whom he is seeking may be.

(3) The powers of entry and search conferred by this section are only exercisable for the purposes specified in subsection (1)(c)(ii) [or (iv)] above by a constable in uniform.

(4) The power of search conferred by this section is only a power to search to the extent that is reasonably required for the purpose for which the power of entry is exercised.

(5) Subject to subsection (6) below, all the rules of common law under which a constable has power to enter premises without a warrant are hereby abolished.

(6) Nothing in subsection (5) above affects any power of entry to deal with or prevent a breach of the peace.

18 Entry and search after arrest

(1) Subject to the following provisions of this section, a constable may enter and search any premises occupied or controlled by a person who is under arrest for an [indictable] offence, if he has

reasonable grounds for suspecting that there is on the premises evidence, other than items subject to legal privilege, that relates—

(a) to that offence; or

(b) to some other [indictable] offence which is connected with or similar to that offence.

(2) A constable may seize and retain anything for which he may search under subsection (1) above.

(3) The power to search conferred by subsection (1) above is only a power to search to the extent that is reasonably required for the purpose of discovering such evidence.

(4) Subject to subsection (5) below, the powers conferred by this section may not be exercised unless an officer of the rank of inspector or above has authorised them in writing.

[(5) A constable may conduct a search under subsection (1)—

(a) before the person is taken to a police station or released on bail under section 30A, and

(b) without obtaining an authorisation under subsection (4),

if the condition in subsection (5A) is satisfied.

(5A) The condition is that the presence of the person at a place (other than a police station) is necessary for the effective investigation of the offence.]

(6) If a constable conducts a search by virtue of subsection (5) above, he shall inform an officer of the rank of inspector or above that he has made the search as soon as practicable after he has made it.

(7) An officer who—

(a) authorises a search; or

(b) is informed of a search under subsection (6) above, shall make a record in writing—

(i) of the grounds for the search; and

(ii) of the nature of the evidence that was sought.

(8) If the person who was in occupation or control of the premises at the time of the search is in police detention at the time the record is to be made, the officer shall make the record as part of his custody record.

19 General power of seizure etc

(1) The powers conferred by subsections (2), (3) and (4) below are exercisable by a constable who is lawfully on any premises.

(2) The constable may seize anything which is on the premises if he has reasonable grounds for believing—

(a) that it has been obtained in consequence of the commission of an offence; and

(b) that it is necessary to seize it in order to prevent it being concealed, lost, damaged, altered or destroyed.

(3) The constable may seize anything which is on the premises if he has reasonable grounds for believing—

(a) that it is evidence in relation to an offence which he is investigating or any other offence; and

(b) that it is necessary to seize it in order to prevent the evidence being concealed, lost, altered or destroyed.

(4) The constable may require any information which is [stored in any electronic form] and is accessible from the premises to be produced in a form in which it can be taken away and in which it is visible and

legible [or from which it can readily be produced in a visible and legible form] if he has reasonable grounds for believing—

(a) that—

    (i) it is evidence in relation to an offence which he is investigating or any other offence; or

    (ii) it has been obtained in consequence of the commission of an offence; and

(b) that it is necessary to do so in order to prevent it being concealed, lost, tampered with or destroyed.

(5) The powers conferred by this section are in addition to any power otherwise conferred.

(6) No power of seizure conferred on a constable under any enactment (including an enactment contained in an Act passed after this Act) is to be taken to authorise the seizure of an item which the constable exercising the power has reasonable grounds for believing to be subject to legal privilege.

20 Extension of powers of seizure to computerised information

(1) Every power of seizure which is conferred by an enactment to which this section applies on a constable who has entered premises in the exercise of a power conferred by an enactment shall be construed as including a power to require any information [stored in any electronic form] and accessible from the premises to be produced in a form in which it can be taken away and in which it is visible and legible [or from which it can readily be produced in a visible and legible form].

...

22 Retention

(1) Subject to subsection (4) below, anything which has been seized by a constable or taken away by a constable following a requirement made by virtue of section 19 or 20 above may be retained so long as is necessary in all the circumstances.

(2) Without prejudice to the generality of subsection (1) above—

(a) anything seized for the purposes of a criminal investigation may be retained, except as provided by subsection (4) below,—

    (i) for use as evidence at a trial for an offence; or

    (ii) for forensic examination or for investigation in connection with an offence; and

(b) anything may be retained in order to establish its lawful owner, where there are reasonable grounds for believing that it has been obtained in consequence of the commission of an offence.

(3) Nothing seized on the ground that it may be used—

(a) to cause physical injury to any person;

(b) to damage property;

(c) to interfere with evidence; or

(d) to assist in escape from police detention or lawful custody,

may be retained when the person from whom it was seized is no longer in police detention or the custody of a court or is in the custody of a court but has been released on bail.

(4) Nothing may be retained for either of the purposes mentioned in subsection (2)(*a*) above if a photograph or copy would be sufficient for that purpose.

...

23 Meaning of 'premises' etc

In this Act—

'premises' includes any place and, in particular, includes—

(a) any vehicle, vessel, aircraft or hovercraft;

(b) any offshore installation;

[(ba) any renewable energy installation;]

(c) any tent or movable structure; …

…

SCHEDULE 1

Special Procedure

Making of orders by circuit judge

1 If on an application made by a constable a *circuit judge* [judge] is satisfied that one or other of the sets of access conditions is fulfilled, he may make an order under paragraph 4 below.

2 The first set of access conditions is fulfilled if—

(a) there are reasonable grounds for believing—

(i) that [an indictable offence] has been committed;

(ii) that there is material which consists of special procedure material or also includes special procedure material and does not also include excluded material on premises specified in the application [, or on premises occupied or controlled by a person specified in the application (including all such premises on which there are reasonable grounds for believing that there is such material as it is reasonably practicable so to specify)];

(iii) that the material is likely to be of substantial value (whether by itself or together with other material) to the investigation in connection with which the application is made; and

(iv) that the material is likely to be relevant evidence;

(b) other methods of obtaining the material—

(i) have been tried without success; or

(ii) have not been tried because it appeared that they were bound to fail; and

(c) it is in the public interest, having regard—

(i) to the benefit likely to accrue to the investigation if the material is obtained; and

(ii) to the circumstances under which the person in possession of the material holds it,

that the material should be produced or that access to it should be given.

3 The second set of access conditions is fulfilled if—

(a) there are reasonable grounds for believing that there is material which consists of or includes excluded material or special procedure material on premises specified in the application[, or on premises occupied or controlled by a person specified in the application (including all such premises on which there are reasonable grounds for believing that there is such material as it is reasonably practicable so to specify)];

(b) but for section 9(2) above a search of [such premises] for that material could have been authorised by the issue of a warrant to a constable under an enactment other than this Schedule; and

(c) the issue of such a warrant would have been appropriate.

4 An order under this paragraph is an order that the person who appears to the [judge] to be in possession of the material to which the application relates shall—

    (a) produce it to a constable for him to take away; or

    (b) give a constable access to it,

not later than the end of the period of seven days from the date of the order or the end of such longer period as the order may specify.

5 Where the material consists of information [stored in any electronic form]—

    (a) an order under paragraph 4(a) above shall have effect as an order to produce the material in a form in which it can be taken away and in which it is visible and legible [or from which it can readily be produced in a visible and legible form]; and

    (b) an order under paragraph 4(b) above shall have effect as an order to give a constable access to the material in a form in which it is visible and legible.

6 For the purposes of sections 21 and 22 above material produced in pursuance of an order under paragraph 4(a) above shall be treated as if it were material seized by a constable.

Notices of applications for orders

7 An application for an order under paragraph 4 above shall be made inter partes.

8 Notice of an application for such an order may be served on a person either by delivering it to him or by leaving it at his proper address or by sending it by post to him in a registered letter or by the recorded delivery service.

…

11 Where notice of an application for an order under paragraph 4 above has been served on a person, he shall not conceal, destroy, alter or dispose of the material to which the application relates except—

    (a) with the leave of a judge; or

    (b) with the written permission of a constable,

until—

      (i) the application is dismissed or abandoned; or

      (ii) he has complied with an order under paragraph 4 above made on the application.

Issue of warrants by circuit judge

12 If on an application made by a constable a *circuit judge* [judge]—

    (a) is satisfied—

      (i) that either set of access conditions is fulfilled; and

      (ii) that any of the further conditions set out in paragraph 14 below is also fulfilled [in relation to each set of premises specified in the application]; or

    (b) is satisfied—

      (i) that the second set of access conditions is fulfilled; and

      (ii) that an order under paragraph 4 above relating to the material has not been complied with,

he may issue a warrant authorising a constable to enter and search the premises [or (as the case may be) all premises occupied or controlled by the person referred to in paragraph 2(a)(ii) or 3(a), including such sets of premises as are specified in the application (an 'all premises warrant')].

[12A The judge may not issue an all premises warrant unless he is satisfied—

(a) that there are reasonable grounds for believing that it is necessary to search premises occupied or controlled by the person in question which are not specified in the application, as well as those which are, in order to find the material in question; and

(b) that it is not reasonably practicable to specify all the premises which he occupies or controls which might need to be searched.]

13 A constable may seize and retain anything for which a search has been authorised under paragraph 12 above.

14 The further conditions mentioned in paragraph 12(a)(ii) above are—

(a) that it is not practicable to communicate with any person entitled to grant entry to the premises…;

(b) that it is practicable to communicate with a person entitled to grant entry to the premises but it is not practicable to communicate with any person entitled to grant access to the material;

(c) that the material contains information which—

(i) is subject to a restriction or obligation such as is mentioned in section 11(2)(b) above; and

(ii) is likely to be disclosed in breach of it if a warrant is not issued;

(d) that service of notice of an application for an order under paragraph 4 above may seriously prejudice the investigation.

15 (1) If a person fails to comply with an order under paragraph 4 above, a [judge] may deal with him as if he had committed a contempt of the Crown Court.

(2) Any enactment relating to contempt of the Crown Court shall have effect in relation to such a failure as if it were such a contempt.

16 …

17 In this Schedule 'judge' means [a judge of the High Court, a Circuit judge, a Recorder] or a District Judge (Magistrates' Courts).][306]

NOTES[307]

1. *The common law background.* Part II of PACE extended police powers in a number of significant respects. At common law there was no general power to enter premises to search for evidence, and there was no general power to obtain warrants to authorise such searches, although there were some specific powers. Lord Denning MR noted in *Ghani v Jones*[308] that there was no power to search premises for evidence of murder. There was a power to search the premises of a person arrested there (perhaps only in his immediate vicinity) but it had to be exercised contemporaneously with the arrest.[309] If the police were lawfully on premises, whether by consent or in the execution of a warrant or a power to enter premises without a warrant, the decision in *Ghani v Jones* authorised the seizure of a wide range of material, the ambit of the power to seize being wider than the powers of entry and search. The RCCP supported the extension of powers along the lines of Part II although they would have applied

---

[306] Not in force at time of publication.

[307] For a detailed consideration, see: R. Stone, *Entry, Search and Seizure* (4th edn, 2005).

[308] [1970] 1 QB 693, CA.   [309] *McLorie v Oxford* [1982] QB 1290, DC.

the special procedure involving a circuit judge to all warrants to search for evidence, and confined the power to 'grave offences'.

2. *The main features of Part II of PACE*: (1) new general powers to search for evidence (ss. 8–14 and Sch. 1); (2) provisions applying generally to search warrants (ss. 15, 16); (3) general powers of entry (s. 17); (4) a power to enter and search after arrest (s. 18); and (5) general powers of seizure (s. 19).

3. *The human rights context*: Powers of entry and search will inevitably engage the right to respect for private life. As such, in order to be compatible with the ECHR action taken by the state must be 'in accordance with law', in pursuit of a legitimate objective (usually satisfied in this context by the prevention of disorder or crime), and 'necessary in a democratic society'. 'The exercise of powers to interfere with home and private life must be confined within reasonable bounds to minimise the impact of such measures on the personal sphere of the individual guaranteed under Article 8 which is pertinent to security and well-being.'[310] On the ECHR and search and seizure, see *Miailhe v France*,[311] where the indiscriminate seizure of 15,000 documents without a warrant was in breach of Art. 8. The Court stressed that the derogations in Art. 8(2) are to be narrowly construed (see also *Cremieux v France*).[312] It is vital that there are adequate safeguards against abuse, notwithstanding the margin of appreciation: see *Niemitz v Germany*.[313] Warrants must be sufficiently clearly prescribed *Funke v France*.[314]

4. PACE, s. 8 provides for the police to seek a warrant to enter and search premises. The warrant must be authorised by a justice of the peace. It must be established that there are reasonable grounds to believe that an indictable offence has been committed. Again, the term 'indictable offence' was inserted by the Serious Organised Crime and Police Act 2005 (SOCPA) replacing 'serious arrestable offence'. This represents a broader range of circumstances as to when a search warrant might be obtained and therefore the courts will have to scrutinize warrants closely to ensure their proportionality to what on occasion might be relatively minor offences. The warrant must be authorised to enable a search for material which is likely to be of substantial value to the investigation of the offence and which will be admissible at trial. There must also be reasonable grounds to believe that the material does not consist of or include items subject to legal privilege, excluded material or special procedure material.[315] These 'protected categories' are considered below. A warrant to enter and search premises does not confer a power to search persons in those premises: *Hepburn v Chief Constable of Thames Valley*.[316] Unlike the position under s. 9, below, it is not a condition precedent to the granting of a warrant that other methods had been tried without success or would be bound to fail.[317] Is the authorisation process therefore merely a rubber stamping exercise? In *R v Guildhall Magistrates' Court, ex p Primlaks Holdings Co (Panama) Inc*,[318] Parker LJ emphasised the importance of the magistrate's role.

I find it necessary to make certain observations with regard to applications under section 8 of the Act. It confers a draconian power and it is of vital importance that it should be clearly understood by all concerned that it is for the justice to satisfy himself that there are reasonable grounds for believing the

---

[310] *Keegan v UK* (2006) App. No. 28867/03.   [311] (1993) 16 EHRR 332.

[312] (1993) 16 EHRR 357.   [313] (1992) 16 EHRR 97.

[314] (1993) 16 EHRR 297, para. 56; see also, *Camenzind v Switzerland* (1997) 28 EHRR 458 on other procedural safeguards regarding search warrants.

[315] See *R v Chesterfield Justices, ex p Bramley* [2000] 1 All ER 411, DC.

[316] *Hepburn v Chief Constable of Thames Valley* [2002] EWCA Civ 1841.

[317] *R v Billericay Justices and Dobbyn, ex p Frank Harris (Coaches) Ltd* [1991] Crim LR 472.

[318] *R v Guildhall Magistrates' Court, ex p Primlaks Holdings Co (Panama) Inc* [1990] 1 QB 261.

various matters set out. The fact that a police officer, who has been investigating the matter, states in the information that he considers that there are reasonable grounds is not enough. The justice must himself be satisfied.[319]

5. The 'all premises' warrant. In its 2004 Consultation Paper, *Modernising Police Powers to Meet Community Needs*, the Government stated that:

3.2 Crime and technology have both moved on significantly since the introduction of PACE. Evidence and the proceeds of crime can be moved very quickly between locations to thwart investigations.

3.3 Applying repeatedly for warrants for different premises owned by the same individual can cause delay and impede investigations. Complex cases, for example those involving financial and IT crime, can require extended police presence on premises. This can mean officers remaining on premises for long periods to gather evidence rather than breach the conditions of the warrant on single access.

3.6 To ease the burden on police officers in seeking out material which is moved around between locations, PACE (and other relevant legislation) could be amended to enable a search warrant to authorise access to any premises occupied or controlled by or accessible by a specified person, where there are reasonable grounds to believe that person to be in control of the material identified in the warrant. That person would not necessarily have to be a suspect.

3.7 Such a system would better reflect the reality of finding specific material, where the identifiable link is often to an individual rather than to premises. However, scope for the traditional premises-based warrant would have to be preserved.

3.8 A 'super warrant' as suggested here would undoubtedly raise issues about interference with the basic right to privacy. However, officers would still need to have justification for entry onto specific premises. The advantage would be in removing the need for them to obtain a new warrant merely because the key individual who was the effective target of the search had moved location or made use of alternative premises.

As a result the new 'all premises' warrant was introduced through amendments made to s. 8 by SOCPA 2005. The changes allow for a warrant which permits multiple entries to one set of premises or a warrant in relation to multiple premises. For the all premises warrant the justice of the peace must be satisfied that there are reasonable grounds to believe that the warrant is 'necessary' (s. 8(1B)(a)).

6. *General powers to obtain evidence.* Generally speaking, the police do not have direct access to items subject to legal privilege (s. 9(2)(a)). Access to excluded or special procedure material can only be authorised under s. 9(1) and Sch. 1. Of these two classes, excluded material is regarded as more sensitive, and may only be the subject of an order or warrant under Sch. 1 if, but for s. 9(2), a warrant could have been used under a pre-existing power.[320] This restriction does not apply to special procedure material, and orders or warrants for the production of such material are much more common.

Excluded or special procedure material can be seized during the course of a search under post-arrest powers (ss. 18, 32), or under any other warranted search and whenever a constable is lawfully on premises and comes across such material (s. 19): Excluded material can

---

[319] Ibid., at p. 272.

[320] *See R v Central Criminal Court, ex p Brown* (1992) Times, 7 September, DC, where it was held that no production order could be made in respect of a medical report from a hospital administration for a murder investigation as no warrant could have been issued for its seizure prior to PACE.

also be disclosed voluntarily by the maker or holder independently of s. 9(1) and Sch. 1: *R v Singleton.*[321]

7. The powers to grant warrants to search for evidence under ss. 8 and 9 of PACE (and associated provisions) have given rise to a series of cases raising both procedural and substantive issues. Thus, it has been held that the material in question must be specified, either in the notice of application or otherwise: *R v Crown Court at Manchester, ex p Taylor;*[322] but the evidence on which the application is based need not: *R v Crown Court at Inner London Sessions, ex p Baines & Baines.*[323] The suspect need not be notified by the applicant if he is not the holder of the material: *R v Crown Court at Leicester, ex p DPP,*[324] and a bank is not impliedly under a contractual duty to notify its client or to contest the application: *Barclays Bank plc v Taylor.*[325] This position is strongly criticised by A.A.S. Zuckerman,[326] on the ground that the person most affected by the order is not given the opportunity to challenge it, and that if there is a risk that that person would impede or frustrate the order if he were given notice, the warrant procedure is available under Sch. 1, paras 12–14.

As to substantive matters arising under Sch. 1, in *R v Crown Court at Bristol, ex p Bristol Press and Picture Agency Ltd,*[327] the Divisional Court upheld the decision of Stuart-Smith J to order the applicant to produce press photographs taken during the 1986 riots in the St Pauls area of Bristol. This was special procedure material and the first set of access conditions in Sch. 1 were applied. The court held that the judge had been entitled to conclude that there were reasonable grounds to believe that the material was 'likely to be of substantial value…to the investigation in connection with which the application was made' and 'likely to be relevant evidence',[328] notwithstanding that it could not identify any particular photograph as relating to any particular incident of violence or other criminal offence; it was likely that the press would attempt to photograph 'newsworthy' incidents, some at least relating to the actions of those engaged in violence. Within Sch. 1 the judge must also be satisfied that the production of, or access to the material is in the public interest under para. 2(c). In this case the Divisional Court determined that the judge was entitled to conclude that the public interest in the conviction of those guilty of serious crimes here required an access order to be made.

Less protection is afforded to special procedure material and journalists' material than legally privileged material, but the courts claim that they will still require strong evidence before issuing an order.[329]

In *Ex p Waitt,*[330] Macpherson J stated that Sch. 1 constitutes;

a serious inroad upon the liberty of the subject. The responsibility for ensuring that the procedure is not abused lies with circuit judges. It is of cardinal importance that circuit judges should be scrupulous in discharging that responsibility.

Costigan, argues that the judiciary have failed to provide adequate protection for journalist material, particularly film footage. The 'pragmatic judiciary has exploited the vague

---

[321] [1995] 1 Cr App R 431, CA (Cr D) (dental records).
[322] [1988] 1 WLR 705.
[323] [1988] QB 579; cf. *R v Central Criminal Court, ex p AJD Holdings Ltd* [1992] Crim LR 669.
[324] [1987] 1 WLR 1371.   [325] [1989] 3 All ER 563.   [326] [1990] Crim LR 472.
[327] (1986) 85 Cr App R 190.   [328] Para. 2(a)(iii), (iv).
[329] See *R v Central Criminal Court, ex p Bright* [2001] 2 All ER 244.
[330] [1988] Crim LR 384.

formulation of the special procedure in PACE...to drive a coach and horses through the intended safeguards for journalists' material in pursuit of crime control'.[331]

8. Hospital records of patients' admission to and discharge from a mental hospital are 'personal records' within PACE, s. 12, as they are records 'relating to' their mental health: *R v Crown Court at Cardiff, ex p Kellam*.[332]

9. An item is covered by legal professional privilege if it is a communication made in connection with the giving of advice; records of conveyancing transactions are themselves, accordingly, not privileged, although correspondence containing advice relating to such transactions would be: *R v Crown Court at Inner London Sessions, ex p Baines & Baines*.[333] In *R v R*,[334] it was held that a blood sample provided by the defendant to his doctor at the request of his solicitors for the purposes of his defence was an item subject to legal privilege. In *R v Manchester Crown Court, ex p R*,[335] the police were granted an order to recover appointment records from a solicitor's office when investing a claim that a murder suspect, R, had visited the offices after the stabbing had taken place. The Divisional Court held that legal professional privilege only applies to communications made for the purpose of seeking and receiving legal advice. This purpose was to be determined by consideration of the function and nature of the documents in question. A record of the time of an appointment or fee record was not a communication concerned with obtaining legal advice.

A practical problem was that no power to seize legally privileged material exists though it might on occasion be difficult when on the premises to make a determination as to whether something is legally privileged, or whether there is material that cannot practicably be separated from legally privileged material. The Criminal Justice and Police Act 2001 sought to respond to this problem by providing the power to remove material to be examined elsewhere, and by allowing for the removal of intrinsically linked material (e.g. on a computer hard disk) some of which may be legally privileged. Under s. 52, there is a requirement to give the occupier and/or some other person or persons from whom material has been seized under the powers in s. 50 (property) or s. 51 (personal search) a notice specifying what has been seized and the grounds on which it has been seized. The information must include the notification of a right to apply to a judge for the return of seized material and an explanation of how to apply to be present at any examination of the material seized. Section 53 prescribes how the examination of the property seized under ss. 50 and 51 should take place and what material can be retained. Subsection (4) gives the occupier or some other person with an interest in the property an opportunity to be present at the examination. Under s. 54 specific protection is provided to legally privileged material which, under ss. 50 and 51 can be seized. Officers are obliged to return such material if seized, but sub-ss. (2) and (3) provide that legally privileged material can be retained if it is inextricably linked to other seizable material.

10. *Other statutory seizure powers.* Many such powers exist, for example ss. 143 and 144 of the Powers of Criminal Courts (Sentencing) Act 2000 to confiscate property lawfully seized or in the offender's possession when he was apprehended which was used for the purpose of committing, or facilitating the commission of, any offence or was intended to be used for that purpose; or the offence, or an offence which the court has taken into consideration in determining his sentence, consists of unlawful possession of property which has been lawfully seized from him or was in his possession when he was apprehended. Powers under

---

[331] [1996] Crim LR 231.   [332] (1993) 16 BMLR 76, DC.

[333] [1988] QB 579. See also *R v Guildhall Magistrates' Court, ex p Primlaks Holdings Co (Panama) Inc* [1990] 1 QB 261.

[334] [1994] 1 WLR 758, CA (Cr D).   [335] [1999] 1 WLR 832, CA (Cr D).

the Drug Trafficking Act 1994 and the Criminal Justice Act 1988 have been replaced by the Proceeds of Crime Act 2002. This Act provides for the recovery of assets from a defendant who has benefited from a criminal lifestyle and the recovery of property obtained through unlawful conduct. Controversially, the latter power can follow even where there is no criminal conviction. Does such a power infringe the individual's presumption of innocence?

11. *Specific powers to obtain search warrants.*[336] There are many specific powers whereby a court, judge or magistrate may issue a search warrant in respect of an offence. They have different limitations as to the geographical area for which a warrant may be granted, the persons who may execute the warrant, and the items which may be seized. The safeguards and other provisions relating to execution contained in ss. 15 and 16 are applicable to all these powers, thus removing some of these variations.[337] Examples include the following:

- **Theft Act 1968**

> 26. (1) If it is made to appear by information on oath before a justice of the peace that there is reasonable cause to believe that any person has in his custody or possession or on his premises any stolen goods, the justice may grant a warrant to search for and seize the same; but no warrant to search for stolen goods shall be addressed to a person other than a constable except under the authority of an enactment expressly so providing...
>
> (3) Where under this section a person is authorised to search premises for stolen goods, he may enter and search the premises accordingly, and may seize any goods he believes to be stolen goods.

It is not clear whether sub-s. (3) is an exhaustive statement of the items that may be seized under a warrant in addition to those specified in it. At common law a constable executing a warrant to search for stolen goods[338] could seize items 'likely to furnish evidence of the identity of the specified stolen goods as well as goods 'reasonably believed' to be those specified in the warrant.[339]

- **Misuse of Drugs Act 1971**

> 23. Powers to search and obtain evidence
>
> (1) A constable or other person authorised in that behalf by a general or special order of the Secretary of State... shall, for the purposes of the execution of this Act, have power to enter the premises of a person carrying on business as a producer or supplier of controlled drugs and to demand the production of, and to inspect, any books or documents relating to dealings in any such drugs and to inspect any stocks of any such drugs.
>
> (2) [Given above at p. 163]
>
> (3) If a justice of the peace... is satisfied by information on oath that there is reasonable ground for suspecting—
>
> (a) that any controlled drugs are, in contravention of this Act or of any regulations made there under, in the possession of a person on any premises; or

---

[336] The Government Response to the PACE Review (2008) recommends that the plethora of search warrants should be rationalised into a single statutory framework under PACE. See paras 9.1–9.5.

[337] See generally, R.T.H. Stone, *Entry, Search and Seizure* (4th edn, 2005).

[338] *Crozier v Cundey* (1827) 6 B & C 232.

[339] *Chic Fashions (West Wales) Ltd v Jones* [1968] 2 QB 321.

(b) that a document directly or indirectly relating to, or connected with, a transaction or dealing which was, or an intended transaction or dealing which would if carried out be, an offence under this Act, or in the case of a transaction or dealing carried out or intended to be carried out in a place outside the United Kingdom, an offence against the provision of a corresponding law in force in that place, is in the possession of a person on any premises.

he may grant a warrant authorising any constable acting for the police area in which the premises are situated at anytime or times within one month from the date of the warrant, to enter, if need be by force, the premises named in the warrant, and to search the premises and any persons found therein and, if there is reasonable ground for suspecting that an offence under this Act has been committed in relation to any controlled drugs found on the premises or in the possession of any such person, or that a document so found is such a document as is mentioned in paragraph (b) above, to seize and detain those drugs on that document, as the case may be…

Note that sub-s. (3) expressly empowers a justice to issue a warrant authorising the search of *persons* found on the premises specified.[340] In *Hepburn v Chief Constable of Thames Valley Police*[341] the court confirmed that a warrant to search premises for drugs does not include a power to search persons therein unless the grounds set out in sub-s. (3) can be satisfied. Is it proper to assume that the different formulations as to whether persons can be searched have been adopted deliberately by Parliament, so as to deny the police power to search persons under a warrant unless both the relevant statutory provisions and the warrant expressly authorise such search?

12. *The execution of warrants: PACE Code requirements.* The Code applies to (a) searches of premises for the purposes of a criminal investigation, with the occupier's consent, other than routine scenes of crime searches and searches following the activation of fire or burglar alarms or calls to a fire or a burglary made on behalf of an occupier or bomb threat calls or searches under B. 5.4 (below); (b) searches under ss. 17, 18 and 32 of PACE; searches of premises by virtue of a warrant issued under s. 15 and s. 16 of PACE .

Code B supplements the requirements of PACE in a number of respects. Before applying for a warrant or production order, the officer must take reasonable steps to check his information is accurate, recent and has not been provided maliciously or irresponsibly; and an application may not be made on the basis of information from an anonymous source where corroboration has not been sought; he must ascertain as specifically as is possible in the circumstances the nature and location of the articles concerned; he must make reasonable inquiries about the likely occupier of the premises, and their nature, and whether they have been previously searched; no application for a search warrant may be made without the authority of an officer of at least the rank of inspector (or, in cases of urgency where no inspector is readily available, the senior officer on duty), or, in the case of a production order or warrant under Sch. 1 to PACE, an officer of at least the rank of superintendent; and, except in cases of urgency, the local police/community liaison officer must be consulted before a search if there is reason to believe that it might have an adverse effect on police/community relations. If an application is refused, no further application may be made unless supported by additional grounds.[342]

If it is proposed to search premises with consent, that consent must be given in writing before the search takes place; then the officer must make inquiries to satisfy himself that the

---

[340] See also *DPP v Meadon* [2004] 4 All ER 75.
[341] *Hepburn v Chief Constable of Thames Valley Police* [2002] EWCA Civ 1841.
[342] Code B.3.1–3.8.

person is in a position to give that consent; and, before seeking that consent, the officer in charge of the search must state its purpose, and inform the person concerned that he is not obliged to consent, that anything seized may be produced in evidence and, if it is so, that he is not suspected of an offence.[343] In *R v Barker*,[344] the court held that acquiescence by an occupier to a search which was in breach of Code B.5.2 should be sufficient to render the evidence discovered admissible. The court was persuaded that there was nothing to show that the occupier would have refused if B.5.2 had been complied with. An officer cannot enter and search, or continue to search premises by consent if the consent is given under duress or is withdrawn before the search is completed.[345] Consent need not be sought if this would cause disproportionate inconvenience to the person concerned (e.g. a brief check of gardens along the route of a pursuit).[346]

Where an entry is made without consent, the officer must first attempt to communicate with the occupier, or any other person entitled to grant access, unless (i) the premises are known to be unoccupied, (ii) the occupier etc. is known to be absent, or (iii) there are reasonable grounds for believing that to alert him would frustrate the object of the search or endanger the officers concerned or other people. Where the premises are occupied, before the search begins the officer must identify himself, if not in uniform show his warrant card, and state the purpose of the search and the grounds for undertaking it (unless (iii) above applies).[347] See *O' Loughlin v Chief Constable of Essex*[348] discussed below.

The officer must, unless it is impracticable, provide the occupier with a 'notice of powers and rights', (i) specifying whether the search is made under a warrant, or with consent or under s. 17, 18 or 32 of PACE; (ii) summarising the extent of the powers of search and seizure under the Act; (iii) explaining the rights of the occupier and the owner of property seized; (iv) explaining that compensation maybe payable for damage; (v) stating that a copy of the Code is available at any police station. If the occupier is present, copies of the notice and the warrant (if any) should if practicable be given to him before the search starts, unless the officer in charge reasonably believes that this would frustrate the object of the search or endanger the officers concerned or other people. If he is not present, copies of the notice and warrant (where appropriate) should be left in a prominent place on the premises and endorsed with the name of the officer in charge, his police station and the date and time of the search.[349]

As to the conduct of searches, premises may be searched only to the extent necessary to achieve the object of the search, having regard to the size and nature of whatever is sought; a search under warrant may not continue under the authority of the warrant once all the things specified in it have been found, or the officer in charge is satisfied they are not there.[350] Searches must be conducted with due consideration for the occupier's property and privacy, and with no more disturbance than necessary.[351] If the occupier wishes to ask a friend, neighbour or other person to witness the search he must be allowed to do, unless the officer in charge has reasonable grounds for believing that this would seriously hinder the investigation; a search need not be unreasonably delayed for this purpose. Premises entered by force must be left secure.[352]

A full record must be kept of searches[353] and a search register must be maintained at each sub-divisional police station with copies of all records required by Code B.[354]

Under s. 18(1) the premises must be controlled by a person under arrest. There is no clear judicial guidance as to what degree of control is necessary.

---

343 Code B.5.1–5.2.   344 (1996) 13 June, CA (Cr D), unreported.   345 Code B.5.3.
346 Code B.5.4. and 5C.   347 Code B.6.4–6.5.   348 [1998] 1 WLR 374.
349 Code B.6.7–6.8.   350 Code B.6.9A–6.9B.   351 Code B.6.10.
352 Code B.6.11–6.13.   353 Code B.8.   354 Code B.9.1.

13. In *R v Longman*[355] the Court of Appeal held that s. 16(5) was not to be interpreted as requiring the preliminaries set out in paras (a)–(c) to be observed before *entry* to the premises; it was sufficient that this be done before the *search* begins, as set out in Code B. 5. 5. The case concerned the execution of a warrant to enter and search L's premises for drugs. It was not the first time that the premises had been the subject of such a search and the police knew that there would almost certainly be great difficulty in effecting an entry. On this occasion, warnings were shouted as soon as the police entered. The court noted that a requirement that the preliminaries be observed before entry would stultify 'the whole object of the more important type of search operation', particularly in drugs cases 'because unless the officers move very quickly indeed, by the time they have reached the back of the premises the offending drugs will be flushed down the lavatory pan…'[356] Other points made by the court were (a) that the police were entitled to subterfuge as an alternative to force (here, a police woman in plain clothes pretending to be delivering flowers from Interflora); and (b) that for a warrant to be 'produced' in accordance with s. 16(5)(b), it must be made available for inspection by and not merely shown to the occupier.

The execution of search warrants cannot lawfully be delegated to other persons: see *R v Reading Justices, Chief Constable of Avon and Somerset and Intervention Board for Agricultural Produce, ex p South West Meat Ltd*,[357] where the Divisional Court granted declarations and awarded £25,000 damages in respect of a search under a warrant issued under PACE, s. 8, that was, *inter alia*, too general in its terms, where the search was conducted by board officials rather than the police; and the material was then retained unlawfully by the board, the statutory power of retention being with the police. The presence of a film crew when a search warrant was being exercised was deplored but did not invalidate the warrant in *R v Marylebone Magistrates' Court & MPC, ex p Amdrell Ltd trading as Get Stuffed*.[358]

14. In *R v Atkinson*,[359] the Court of Appeal held that a warrant obtained under s. 23(3) for the search of 'Flat 45' in certain premises could not justify the search of Flat 30, even though the police bona fide believed that A's flat was Flat 45. However, misspellings or trivial errors in the description of premises would not necessarily invalidate a warrant. In *Keegan v United Kingdom*[360] the police searched a house having secured a warrant on the genuine belief that the suspect was residing there. In fact the house was occupied by another family who had indeed been there for some six months. Despite the genuineness of the officers' belief the European Court found that basic steps to verify the connection between the address and the offence under investigation had not been effectively carried out and the resulting police action was thus disproportionate and a breach of Art. 8. That the police were not malicious in their actions was not decisive as the Convention provided protection against abuse of power however caused.

15. *Seizure.* The RCCP recommended that the ambit of the power of seizure under a warrant should extend to items which could be the subject of a warrant: i.e. on their recommendation, goods whose possession is an offence and material relating to 'grave offences'. The Act is wider in this respect (see ss. 19, 20). Sections 8(2) and 18(2), however, authorise the seizure of goods 'reasonably believed' to be the goods specified in the warrant. Should the courts permit a similar extension here, or should any seizure not justified by s. 8(2) or 18(2) have to

355 [1988] 1 WLR 619.   356 P. 153.   357 [1992] Crim LR 672.
358 (1998) 162 JP 719, DC.   359 [1976] Crim LR 307.
360 *Keegan v UK* [2006] ECHR 764; *Keegan v Chief Constable of Merseyside Police* [2003] 1 WLR 2187.

be justified under s. 19? Material unlawfully seized may not be retained under s. 22: *R v Chief Constable of Lancashire, ex p Parker.*[361]

Police owe a duty to the owner of seized property to take reasonable care to prevent damage during its retention: *Sutcliffe v Chief Constable of West Yorkshire.*[362]

It has been held that the police have powers under ss. 18 and 19 to seize the premises themselves where they are mobile. In *Cowan v Metropolitan Police Comr,*[363] a search of the suspect's premises was undertaken in respect of allegations of serious sexual abuse of children. It was believed that the suspect's car might yield vital forensic evidence. The police seized the vehicle. Under s. 23 of PACE, a vehicle is defined as being premises. The court held that the power to seize 'anything' which is on the premises included a power to seize the premises where movable. See also the statements of Lord Denning MR in *Ghani v Jones,*[364] recognising such a right at common law. Consider the implications for caravan dwellers and New Age travellers.

In *R v Chief Constable of Warwickshire, ex p Fitzpatrick,*[365] it was confirmed that the warrant under ss. 8 and 15 must be drafted in terms of the premises not the material belonging to a named person.

16. *Retention.* In *Marcel v Metropolitan Police Comr,*[366] discussing the constraints placed on prosecuting authorities as to their use of material seized. Dillon LJ[367] stated that:

> Parliament should not be taken to have authorised use of seized documents for any purpose the police think fit.... Police are authorised to seize, retain and use documents only for public purposes related to the investigation and prosecution of crime and the return of stolen property to the true owner.

In *Webb v Chief Constable of Merseyside*[368] the Court of Appeal held that the police were not entitled to retain monies that they had seized from W when they were arresting him on drugs charges (of which he was later acquitted). The police power to seize the moneys was beyond question, but once the police power to hold them for the purposes of the trial had come to an end, W had a better claim than the police.

17. *Entry.* For entry to premises to be justified by reference to s. 17(1)(b), the police officer entering must have reasonable grounds to suspect the person sought to be guilty of the offence in question; the provision cannot justify entry to effect an unlawful arrest: *Kynaston v DPP.*[369] Here, the justices were held to be entitled to infer that the officers had the necessary reasonable suspicion. The officers knew a robbery had taken place; they desired to arrest one Doyle for it; they had reasonable grounds for believing he was in the premises; they stated when they entered that they wished to arrest him for robbery. 'If that does not raise an inference that they had reasonable grounds for suspecting him of the robbery, I am bound to say I do not know what else it would amount to... That is an inference which could have been rebutted but was not.'[370] Whether there was a lawful arrest triggering the s. 18 power will often be critical to the case: see, for example, *Odewale v DPP*[371] comparing *Kynaston* and *Riley* (inference of lawful arrest not permissible).

Should police officers seeking to exercise a right of entry be required to give reasons, by analogy with *Christie v Leachinsky?*[372]

---

[361] [1993] QB 577. [362] (1995) 159 JP 770, CA. [363] [2000] 1 WLR 254, CA (Civ D).
[364] [1970] 1 QB 693. [365] [1999] 1 All ER 65. [366] [1992] Ch 225.
[367] Ibid., at 234. [368] [2000] 1 QB 427.
[369] (1987) 87 Cr App R 200, DC. [370] Per Parker LJ at 206.
[371] (2000) 28 November, DC. [372] [1947] AC 573, HL.

- **O'Loughlin v Chief Constable of Essex** [1998] 1 WLR 374, Court of Appeal

Police attended O's house following a complaint from neighbours that Mrs O had smashed a car windscreen with a cricket bat. The police found O and Mrs O barricading themselves in behind the front door. The officers used force to gain entry and arrest O. The judge ruled that 'unless circumstances made it impossible, impracticable or undesirable, a police officer exercising powers of entry by force, pursuant to section 17 of PACE should first give the occupier the true reason for seeking to enter'. As police had not done so, O's claim for trespass succeeded.

The Court of Appeal (Thorpe LJ dissenting) agreed.

Buxton LJ: [His lordship referred to *Swales v Cox.*] Donaldson LJ did not refer to any authority in formulating the approach that the Divisional Court adopted in *Swales v Cox,* but in my view that approach is fully in line with the general law of police powers. As was made clear in *Christie v Leachinsky* the obligation to inform a citizen why his liberty is being interfered with is not absolute: circumstances may make communication impossible or unnecessary. Subject to that, however, it is a strong obligation, and one that Parliament must be taken to have had in mind when conferring the power on the police that it created in section 2 of the 1967 Act and continued in PACE. The very strong distinction between powers of arrest and powers of questioning recognised in *Rice v Connolly* must also have been in Parliament's mind when creating these powers of entry to effect *arrest.* It is wholly unlikely that Parliament would have thought that those powers could be exercised because of, or be adequately explained to the subject in terms of, a wish to investigate.

The position is no different under PACE. We were shown various sections of the Act where there is an ex press obligation to communicate, but those tend either to address limited situations, such as the use of search warrants, or to deal with *ex post facto* giving or recording of information, such as recording of reasons for delay in taking a person to the police station, or informing a detained person of the reasons for his detention. It is wholly unlikely that the presence of these sections in PACE indicates any intention on the part of Parliament to alter the implications for forcible entry to arrest contained in section 2 of the 1967 Act when that provision was replaced in substantially the same terms by sections 17 and 117 of PACE.

That is the effect of sections 17 and 117 of PACE is further reinforced by the terms of paragraph 5.4 of the *Code of Practice for Searching of Premises by Police Officers* formulated under PACE, paragraph 5.4 of which states, subject to certain exceptions not at present relevant, that the officer in charge shall first attempt to communicate with the occupier or any other person entitled to grant access to the premises by explaining the authority under which he seeks entry to the premises and ask the occupier to allow him in.

This paragraph strictly speaking did not apply in the present case, because no search was contemplated. It is, however, a strong indication of the importance and relevance of the officer who seeks entry explaining his authority, and certainly explaining the reason why he seeks entry.

I therefore respectfully agree with the burden of Donaldson LJ's judgment that a very important factor in deciding whether the police have proved that use of force to enter was necessary, as section 117 requires, is whether before using force the police have explained the (proper) reason why they require entry, and nonetheless had been refused.

[The Chief Constable sought to resist that construction of PACE by relying on the unreported Divisional Court case of *Lunt v DPP* (1993). His lordship referred to that case.]

If *Lunt v DPP* addressed the issue now before this court I do not need to say that I would be strongly disposed to follow it, even though it is not, strictly speaking, binding on us. But since the Divisional Court in that case was deprived of considering these issues because of the way in which the argument was presented to them, I cannot find the case of any assistance.

Lunt v DPP was the subject of an abbreviated report at [1993] Crim LR 534, where it attracted the considerable benefit of a note by Professor Sir John Smith. We were not shown that note, but it is of interest to see that in it Professor Smith, without suggesting that the point arose in *Lunt's case* itself, asks should it not be necessary, by analogy with the common law rule regarding arrest laid down in *Christie v Leachinsky* [1947] A.C. 573, for the officer to give reasons? Freedom of the home from invasion is an interest of comparable importance to freedom from arrest and is deserving of a comparable degree of protection.

I respectfully agree. But I go further, by saying that I consider that that important rule of the common law, applying not only to arrest but, as in *Brazil,* to other interferences with liberty, does indeed apply to the exercise of powers under sections 17 and 117 of PACE.

Roch LJ [agreed with Buxton LJ.]

Thorpe LJ: In my judgment, the trial in the court below was most unsatisfactory and resulted in a quite unjust conclusion. The facts of the case were exceptional and neither authority nor evidence compelled the defendant's case on liability to be determined by the judge without the involvement of the jury.

Section 17(1)(b) of the Police and Criminal Evidence Act 1984 allows entry and search. Section 117 permits the officer to use reasonable force, if necessary, in the exercise of the power conferred by section 117. The judgment of Donaldson LJ in the Divisional Court in 1980 suggests that where the issue in any case is 'was the force necessary' the burden of proof is on the officer who resorted to force and that is a very heavy burden: *Swales v Cox* [1981] Q.B. 849 at 855 B–D. Whilst that judgment is upon similar sections of the Criminal Law Act 1967, it obviously commands great respect. Nevertheless, I would not wish to see the severity of the burden exaggerated. It is essentially a burden to prove on the balance of probabilities that the use of force was indeed necessary. Applying the objective test, would the reasonable police constable standing in the defendant's shoes have concluded that the use of force was reasonably necessary? That the test is an objective test is clearly stated in the judgment of Diplock LJ in this court in the case of *Dallison v Caffery* [1965] 1 Q.B. 348 at 371 E–F. Although that statement is upon the exercise of the common law power of arrest, it seems to me equally applicable to the exercise of the statutory power under section 17.

On the question that diverted the judge's attention, namely as to whether the use of force must be preceded by a statement of the reason for requiring entry, I conclude that none of the authorities is directly in point.

Thus I am of the firm opinion that in determining any question as to whether or not the use of force was necessary the court should throughout restrict itself to that issue having established through the medium of the jury the relevant facts and circumstances to enable the issue to be approached and decided. Of course in many cases, the communication between the officer and the householder prior to the use of force will be a highly relevant factor. But in my judgment, it should never be elevated to the extent that it predetermines the essential issue. Even if an explanation was plainly required, in the absence of concession it is always for the jury to determine whether it was given. If the jury determines that it was not then the way is clear for the judge to decide that without it the use of force had not been proved to be necessary.

The relevance of Code 'B' made under the Police and Criminal Evidence Act 1984 was considerably debated in the court below. Section 67(11) of the Police and Criminal Evidence Act 1984 is generously drawn: [his Lordship referred to that section]

NOTES

1. Buxton LJ was unimpressed by the argument that although the police had not announced that they wished to enter to arrest her, the wish to talk to a suspect could 'be elided into a wish to arrest her'.

2. The need to give reasons for entry also applies under s. 18: see *Lineham v DPP*.[373]

3. The requirement that entry under s. 18 be authorised in writing is not satisfied by a note in an officer's notebook recording an oral authorisation: an independent document is required: *R v Badham*.[374] A failure to make a record in the custody record will not necessarily lead to the exclusion of evidence from the search: *R v Wright*.[375]

4. *Consensual searches.* Apart from any right to enter premises conferred by law, a police officer may enter premises with the express or implied permission (or 'licence') of the owner. This point was raised in the following case.

- **Davis v Lisle** [1936] 2 KB 434, [1936] 2 All ER 213, 105 LLKB 593, 155 LT 23, 52 TLR 475, 34 LGR 253, Cox CC, King's Bench Divisional Court

Sidney Davis was a member of a firm which occupied a railway arch as a garage. Two police officers entered the garage to make inquiries as to the person responsible for obstructing the highway with a lorry, which had subsequently been moved into the garage. D, using abusive and obscene language, told them to get out. L was in the act of producing his warrant card when D struck him in the chest and stomach with his fist, damaging his tunic. D was convicted by the justices of (1) assaulting a police officer in the execution of his duty contrary to the Metropolitan Police Act 1839, s. 18; (2) obstructing an officer in the execution of his duty contrary to the Prevention of Crimes Amendment Act 1885, s. 2; and (3) maliciously damaging a serge tunic (by tearing it), to the amount of 7s 6d. D appealed unsuccessfully to quarter sessions, and then appealed to the Divisional Court by way of case stated.

Lord Hewart CJ: The point which is raised here with regard to the appellant's first two convictions is whether the officers were at the material time acting in the execution of their duty. In my opinion they were not, and there are no grounds on which they can be held to have been so acting. The only ground which is put forward in support of the contention that they were so acting seems to me to be quite beside the point. I feel a difficulty in envisaging the legal proposition that because the police officers had witnessed an offence being committed on the highway they were acting in the execution of their duty in entering and remaining on private premises because the offenders then were on those premises. Admittedly, the officers were at liberty to enter his garage to make an inquiry, but quite a different thing to say that they were entitled to remain when, not without emphasis, the appellant had said: 'Get outside. You cannot come here without a search warrant.' From that moment on, while the officers remained where they were, it seems to me that they were trespassers and it is quite clear that the act which the respondent was doing immediately before the assault complained of was tantamount to putting forward a claim as of right to remain where he was. The respondent was in the act of producing his warrant card. That was after the emphatic order to 'get out' had been made. Mr Raphael, with his usual candour, has admitted that, if the finding in the case that the respondent was in the act of producing his warrant card is fairly to be construed as meaning that he was asserting his right to remain on the premises, it is not possible to contend that at that moment the respondent was acting in the execution of his duty. I think it is quite clear that the act of producing his warrant card constituted the making of such a claim, I cannot think that there is any ambiguity about it…

In my opinion, it is not possible to maintain the conclusion that at the material time the respondent was acting in the execution of his duty as a constable. But that conclusion by no means disposes of everything contained in this case. It does not dispose of the question whether the assault which was in fact committed was justified. We have not the materials before us which would enable us to determine that question.

---

[373] [2000] Crim LR 861.   [374] [1997] Crim LR 202 (Wood Green Crown Court).
[375] [1994] Crim LR 55, CA (Cr D).

Nor was the appellant prosecuted for assault. He was prosecuted for assaulting and obstructing a police officer in the execution of his duty. Furthermore, the conclusion to which I have come does not affect the third conviction—that of damaging a tunic by 'wilfully and maliciously tearing' it. On that part of the case no question arises whether at that moment the officer was acting in the execution of his duty and I see no reason why we should interfere with that conviction...

Du Parq and **Goddard JJ** delivered concurring judgments.

Appeal allowed as to first two convictions.

NOTES

1. The officers in this case were not entering in order to prevent crime, but to investigate.[376]

2. In this case, the officers asserted a right to remain. Otherwise, persons requested to leave must be given reasonable time to depart. In *Robson v Hallett*,[377] a police sergeant was told to leave a private house where he was making inquiries. He at once turned and walked towards the front door but was then jumped on. Two constables went to his aid from the front path. The Divisional Court held that the sergeant had not become a trespasser the instant he was told to depart. Lord Parker CH stated:[378]

When a licence is revoked as a result of which something has to be done by the licensee, a reasonable time must be implied in which he can do so, in this case to get off the premises; no doubt it will be a very short time, but he was doing here his best to leave the premises.

The constables were lawfully in the front garden, as they, like any other members of the public, had implied leave and licence to walk up to the front door, and that implied licence had never been revoked. They were acting in the execution of their duty in assisting the sergeant and avoiding any further breach of the peace. Lord Parker stated[379] that 'even if they had been outside the gate, it seems to me that they would have abundant right to come onto private property in those circumstances'. Diplock LJ said of the constables[380] that:

once a breach of the peace was taking place under their eyes, they had not only an independent right but a duty to go and stop it, and it matters not from that moment onwards whether they started off on their journey to stop it from outside the premises...or...inside...

3. In *R v Thornley*,[381] the Court of Appeal held that a licence to enter premises given by a wife in the course of a domestic dispute could not be revoked by the husband who had been the subject of a complaint to the police. It was accepted that the judge had been right to direct the jury that when the officers entered the house they were not trespassers because they had been invited to enter by the wife 'who was co-occupier'.

4. In *Riley v DPP*,[382] the Divisional Court held that police officers were lawfully on premises, when permitted to enter by the owner's son, and subsequently met by the owner, who raised no objection to their presence. Moreover, s. 17 of PACE did not set out a complete code for entry by police officers, it only applied where entry was without the occupier's consent.[383]

---

[376] Cf. *Thomas v Sawkins* [1935] 2 KB 249.   [377] [1967] 2 QB 939.
[378] Ibid., at 952–953.   [379] *Obiter* at 953.
[380] Ibid., at 954.   [381] (1980) 72 Cr App R 302, [1981] Crim LR 637.
[382] (1989) 91 Cr App R 14.   [383] See *O'Loughlin v Chief Constable of Essex* [1998] 1 WLR 374.

5. A trespassing officer may not validly require a person to take a breath test: *Morris v Beardmore*.[384] Accordingly a number of cases have turned on whether the officer was a trespasser. It has been held that whether the words 'fuck off' used by the owner of the house constitute revocation of the implied licence to be in the driveway or mere vulgar abuse is a question of fact for the justices: *Snook v Mannion*,[385] *Gilham v Breidenbach*[386] (both cases decided adversely to the defendant). In *Faulkner v Willetts*,[387] D's wife opened the front door to a constable. He explained that he wished to interview D in connection with a road accident. She walked back into the house giving him the impression that it was an implied invitation to enter. No indication was subsequently given refusing him entry or requiring him to leave; indeed he was offered a cup of coffee. The court held the justices were entitled to conclude that this constituted implied permission to enter.

6. ARREST

- **Police and Criminal Evidence Act 1984**

PART III

ARREST

24 Arrest without warrant: constables

[(1) A constable may arrest without a warrant—

(a) anyone who is about to commit an offence;

(b) anyone who is in the act of committing an offence;

(c) anyone whom he has reasonable grounds for suspecting to be about to commit an offence;

(d) anyone whom he has reasonable grounds for suspecting to be committing an offence.

(2) If a constable has reasonable grounds for suspecting that an offence has been committed, he may arrest without a warrant anyone whom he has reasonable grounds to suspect of being guilty of it.

(3) If an offence has been committed, a constable may arrest without a warrant—

(a) anyone who is guilty of the offence;

(b) anyone whom he has reasonable grounds for suspecting to be guilty of it.

(4) But the power of summary arrest conferred by subsection (1), (2) or (3) is exercisable only if the constable has reasonable grounds for believing that for any of the reasons mentioned in subsection (5) it is necessary to arrest the person in question.

(5) The reasons are—

(a) to enable the name of the person in question to be ascertained (in the case where the constable does not know, and cannot readily ascertain, the person's name, or has reasonable grounds for doubting whether a name given by the person as his name is his real name);

(b) correspondingly as regards the person's address;

(c) to prevent the person in question—

(i) causing physical injury to himself or any other person;

(ii) suffering physical injury;

---

[384] [1981] AC 446.   [385] [1982] RTR 321.   [386] [1982] RTR 328n.
[387] [1982] RTR 159, [1982] Crim LR 543, DC.

      (iii) causing loss of or damage to property;

      (iv) committing an offence against public decency (subject to subsection (6)); or

      (v) causing an unlawful obstruction of the highway;

  (d) to protect a child or other vulnerable person from the person in question;

  (e) to allow the prompt and effective investigation of the offence or of the conduct of the person in question;

  (f) to prevent any prosecution for the offence from being hindered by the disappearance of the person in question.

(6) Subsection (5)(c)(iv) applies only where members of the public going about their normal business cannot reasonably be expected to avoid the person in question.]

...

28 Information to be given on arrest

(1) Subject to subsection (5) below, where a person is arrested, otherwise than by being informed that he is under arrest, the arrest is not lawful unless the person arrested is informed that he is under arrest as soon as is practicable after his arrest.

(2) Where a person is arrested by a constable, subsection (1) above applies regardless of whether the fact of the arrest is obvious.

(3) Subject to subsection (5) below, no arrest is lawful unless the person arrested is informed of the ground for the arrest at the time of, or as soon as is practicable after, the arrest.

(4) Where a person is arrested by a constable, subsection (3) above applies regardless of whether the ground for the arrest is obvious.

(5) Nothing in this section is to be taken to require a person to be informed—

  (a) that he is under arrest; or

  (b) of the ground for the arrest,

if it was not reasonably practicable for him to be so informed by reason of his having escaped from arrest before the information could be given.

29 Voluntary attendance at police station etc

Where for the purpose of assisting with an investigation a person attends voluntarily at a police station or at any other place where a constable is present or accompanies a constable to a police station or any such other place without having been arrested—

  (a) he shall be entitled to leave at will unless he is placed under arrest;

  (b) he shall be informed at once that he is under arrest if a decision is taken by a constable to prevent him from leaving at will.

30 Arrest elsewhere than at police station

[(1) Subsection (1A) applies where a person is, at any place other than a police station—

  (a) arrested by a constable for an offence, or

  (b) taken into custody by a constable after being arrested for an offence by a person other than a constable.

(1A) The person must be taken by a constable to a police station as soon as practicable after the arrest.

(1B) Subsection (1A) has effect subject to section 30A (release on bail) and subsection (7) (release without bail).]

(2) Subject to subsections (3) and (5) below, the police station to which an arrested person is taken under [subsection (1A)] above shall be a designated police station.

(3) A constable to whom this subsection applies may take an arrested person to any police station unless it appears to the constable that it may be necessary to keep the arrested person in police detention for more than six hours.

(4) Subsection (3) above applies—

(a) to a constable who is working in a locality covered by a police station which is not a designated police station; and

(b) to a constable belonging to a body of constables maintained by an authority other than a police authority.

(5) Any constable may take an arrested person to any police station if—

(a) either of the following conditions is satisfied—

(i) the constable has arrested him without the assistance of any other constable and no other constable is available to assist him;

(ii) the constable has taken him into custody from a person other than a constable without the assistance of any other constable and no other constable is available to assist him; and

(b) it appears to the constable that he will be unable to take the arrested person to a designated police station without the arrested person injuring himself, the constable or some other person.

(6) If the first police station to which an arrested person is taken after his arrest is not a designated police station, he shall be taken to a designated police station not more than six hours after his arrival at the first police station unless he is released previously.

[(7) A person arrested by a constable at any place other than a police station must be released without bail if the condition in subsection (7A) is satisfied.

(7A) The condition is that, at any time before the person arrested reaches a police station, a constable is satisfied that there are no grounds for keeping him under arrest or releasing him on bail under section 30A.]

(8) A constable who releases a person under subsection (7) above shall record the fact that he has done so.

(9) The constable shall make the record as soon as is practicable after the release.

[(10) Nothing in subsection (1A) or in section 30A prevents a constable delaying taking a person to a police station or releasing him on bail if the condition in subsection (10A) is satisfied.

(10A) The condition is that the presence of the person at a place (other than a police station) is necessary in order to carry out such investigations as it is reasonable to carry out immediately.

(11) Where there is any such delay the reasons for the delay must be recorded when the person first arrives at the police station or (as the case may be) is released on bail.]

(12) Nothing in [subsection (1A) or section 30A] above shall be taken to affect—

(a) paragraphs 16(3) or 18(1) of Schedule 2 to the Immigration Act 1971;

(b) section 34(1) of the Criminal Justice Act 1972; or

[(c) any provision of the Terrorism Act 2000.]

(13) Nothing in subsection (10) above shall be taken to affect paragraph 18(3) of Schedule 2 to the Immigration Act 1971.

...

31 Arrest for further offence

Where—

   (a) a person—

      (i) has been arrested for an offence; and

      (ii) is at a police station in consequence of that arrest; and

   (b) it appears to a constable that, if he were released from that arrest, he would be liable to arrest for some other offence,

he shall be arrested for that other offence.

32 Search upon arrest

(1) A constable may search an arrested person, in any case where the person to be searched has been arrested at a place other than a police station, if the constable has reasonable grounds for believing that the arrested person may present a danger to himself or others.

(2) Subject to subsections (3) to (5) below, a constable shall also have power in any such case—

   (a) to search the arrested person for anything—

      (i) which he might use to assist him to escape from lawful custody; or

      (ii) which might be evidence relating to an offence; and

   [(b) if the offence for which he has been arrested is an indictable offence, to enter and search any premises in which he was when arrested or immediately before he was arrested for evidence relating to the offence].

(3) The power to search conferred by subsection (2) above is only a power to search to the extent that is reasonably required for the purpose of discovering any such thing or any such evidence.

(4) The powers conferred by this section to search a person are not to be construed as authorising a constable to require a person to remove any of his clothing in public other than an outer coat, jacket or gloves [but they do authorise a search of a person's mouth].

(5) A constable may not search a person in the exercise of the power conferred by subsection (2)(a) above unless he has reasonable grounds for believing that the person to be searched may have concealed on him anything for which a search is permitted under that paragraph.

(6) A constable may not search premises in the exercise of the power conferred by subsection (2)(b) above unless he has reasonable grounds for believing that there is evidence for which a search is permitted under that paragraph on the premises.

(7) In so far as the power of search conferred by subsection (2)(b) above relates to premises consisting of two or more separate dwellings, it is limited to a power to search—

   (a) any dwelling in which the arrest took place or in which the person arrested was immediately before his arrest; and

   (b) any parts of the premises which the occupier of any such dwelling uses in common with the occupiers of any other dwellings comprised in the premises.

(8) A constable searching a person in the exercise of the power conferred by subsection (1) above may seize and retain anything he finds, if he has reasonable grounds for believing that the person searched might use it to cause physical injury to himself or to any other person.

(9) A constable searching a person in the exercise of the power conferred by subsection (2)(a) above may seize and retain anything he finds, other than an item subject to legal privilege, if he has reasonable grounds for believing—

(a) that he might use it to assist him to escape from lawful custody; or

(b) that it is evidence of an offence or has been obtained in consequence of the commission of an offence.

(10) Nothing in this section shall be taken to affect the power conferred by [section 43 of the Terrorism Act 2000].

NOTES

1. The Serious Organised Crime and Police Act 2005 made significant changes to the powers of arrest. Previously, PACE, s. 24 provided a power of arrest for certain 'arrestable' offences (offences carrying a sentence of five years or more in addition to others listed in a schedule) and under s. 25 any offence was arrestable if certain conditions were met. In 2004 the Government published its paper *Modernising Police Powers to Meet Community Needs*,[388] in which it sought to justify changes to the powers of arrest. It stated:

2.1 Arrest is a powerful weapon in the police armoury for tackling crime. PACE did much to clarify powers of arrest by establishing a systematic structure based on clear principles of necessity and seriousness.

2.2 It has achieved some success but the basis of arrest remains diverse—it is not always straightforward or clear to police officers or members of the public when and if the power of arrest exists for offences at the lower end of seriousness. As indicated by the Association of Chief Police Officers in responding to the Joint Review of PACE, there is a 'myriad of different qualifiers' to effect arrest.

2.3 There is a common perception that a constable has the power of arrest provided he has reasonable grounds to suspect an offence has been committed. In fact, there is a complex and often bewildering array of powers and procedures. The current focus is on seriousness—any offence attracting a sentence of five years or more is considered sufficiently serious to attract the power of arrest. But added to this are:

• the general arrest conditions for all offences where there is doubt about the identity or address of the suspect or concern over safety or further offending;

• an extensive list of individual offences deemed by Parliament to require a power of arrest;

• preserved powers of arrest under PACE;

• arrest warrants on application to a court;

• common law powers of arrest for breach of the peace.

2.4 PACE also provides for the category of 'serious arrestable offence'. This offers a threshold for a range of powers and procedures including extended detention, being held incommunicado and delaying access to legal advice.

2.5 Whilst the existing PACE provisions are generally adequate to cover the large majority of situations, there is a confusing range of approaches to exercising this fundamental and potent power. The present structure is based on the concept of seriousness of the offence and not the complexity of the investigation. We should be building on the accrued benefits of PACE and moving towards a straightforward, universal framework which focusses on the nature of an offence in relation to the circumstances of the victim, the offender and the needs of the investigation.

2.6 Removing the gateway of seriousness would enable all offences to be subject to the power of arrest. A constable would still be required to have reasonable grounds to believe that a person is committing, has committed or is about to commit an offence AND importantly, that an arrest is necessary...

These recommendations have been put into effect. PACE, s. 24 now permits arrest for any offence provided that it is 'necessary'.

---

[388] Home Office, *Modernising Police Powers to Meet Community Needs* (2004).

2. *Requisites of a valid arrest.* There are a number of elements which must be present for an arrest to be valid:

(a)   There must either be an arrest warrant or a legal power to arrest without warrant.

(b)   The factual requirements of the relevant powers must be fulfilled: commonly the requirement of 'reasonable suspicion'. If the arresting officer has made a reasonable but erroneous interpretation of the law, he will not have a reasonable suspicion and the arrest will be unlawful: *Todd v DPP*.[389] The reasonableness of the officer's decision is to be based on the information available to him at that time: *Redmond-Bate v DPP*.[390] The Divisional Court in *Clarke v DPP*,[391] described it as a 'golden rule' that the prosecution should ask the arresting officer when he is giving evidence at trial what he had in mind when arresting the suspect. PACE, s. 24(1)(a) and (b) and s. 24(3)(a) permit arrest without reasonable suspicion provided that it transpires that the suspect was about to commit, was in the course of committing, or had committed an offence. Might this encourage the arrest of the 'usual suspects' on the grounds that the police are likely to find something that would justify an arrest?

(c)   The arrest must be 'necessary'. PACE Code G states:

> 1.3 The use of the power must be fully justified and officers exercising the power should consider if the necessary objectives can be met by other, less intrusive means. Arrest must never be used simply because it can be used. Absence of justification for exercising the powers of arrest may lead to challenges should the case proceed to court. When the power of arrest is exercised it is essential that it is exercised in a non-discriminatory and proportionate manner.

If the officer has reasonable grounds to suspect but does not believe that an arrest is necessary there are various other options to consider, such as the issuing of a fixed penalty notice, a report for summons or granting street bail.[392] For an arrest to be necessary it must be for one of the grounds stipulated in s. 24(5). These grounds are broad and include, for example, that an arrest is necessary 'to enable the name of the person in question to be ascertained (in the case where the constable does not know, and cannot readily ascertain, the person's name, or has reasonable grounds for doubting whether a name given by the person as his name is his real name)'. Does this make it more likely that 'Joe Bloggs' or 'John Bull' will be liable to be arrested having committed minor offences? A further ground allows for arrest 'to allow the prompt and effective investigation of the offence or of the conduct of the person in question'. Does this provide a sufficient limit the power of arrest?

(d)   At common law it was necessary for the arrestor to make it clear that the arrestee was under compulsion either (i) by physical means (such as taking him by the arm) or (ii) by notifying him of the fact of compulsion by word of mouth. There was a danger where the arrestor relied on words alone that the words might not sufficiently indicate compulsion. For example, in *Alderson v Booth*[393] following a positive breathalyser test a constable said to the defendant 'I shall have to ask you to come to the police station for further tests'. D accompanied the constable to the police station. At his trial the defendant defended charges of driving with an excess of alcohol in his blood by claiming that he had not been arrested by the constable (a lawful arrest having being made being a condition precedent to conviction

---

[389]   [1996] Crim LR 344.   [390]   [1999] Crim LR 998.

[391]   (1997) 14 November, unreported.

[392]   Criminal Justice Act 2003, s. 4 which amends ss. 30A–30D of PACE. This came into force in January 2004. See also Home Office, *Criminal Justice Act 2003: Bail Elsewhere than at a Police Station* (2003) Circular 61/2003 Part C.

[393]   [1969] 2 QB 216, DC.

under the drink and drive legislation). He was acquitted and the prosecution's appeal was dismissed. Lord Parker CJ (with whom Blain and Donaldson JJ agreed) said:

...the narrow point here was whether the justices were right in holding, as they did, that there never had been an arrest.

In their opinion, which is clearly partly opinion and partly finding of fact, they say:

'We were of the opinion that when the respondent accompanied the constable to the police station it was not made clear to him either physically or by word of mouth that he was under compulsion. We consider that compulsion is a necessary element of arrest, and we therefore did not regard the respondent as a person who had been arrested.'

...I for my part have little doubt that, just looking at the words used here, 'I shall have to ask you to come to the police station for further tests,' that they were in their context words of command which one would think would bring home to a defendant that he was under compulsion. But the justices here had the evidence not only of the police constable but of the defendant, and they were not satisfied, having heard him, that it had been brought home unequivocally to him that he was under compulsion. I confess it surprised me that he was believed but believed he was when he said or conveyed that he was not going to the police station because he thought he was under compulsion, but was going purely voluntarily. It seems to me that this is so much a question of fact for the justices that, surprising as this decision is, I feel that this court cannot interfere.

I would only say this, if what I have said is correct in law, it is advisable that police officers should use some very clear words to bring home to a person that he is under compulsion. It certainly must not be left in the state that a defendant can go into the witness-box and merely say 'I did not think I was under compulsion.' If difficulties for the future are to be avoided, it seems to me that by far and away the simplest thing is for a police officer to say 'I arrest you.' If the defendant goes to the police station after hearing those words, it seems to me that he simply could not be believed if he thereafter said 'I did not think there was any compulsion, I was only going voluntarily.

See *Mepstead v DPP*[394] holding that for an officer to touch the arm of another is not an arrest nor actionable in trespass *per se*. In *R v Fiak*[395] the appellant was suspected of being in charge of a vehicle when he had consumed excess alcohol. Two officers witnessed him leaning out of his vehicle and vomiting. When he got out of the car his breath smelled of alcohol and he was unsteady on his feet. He claimed he had had an argument with his wife and was sat in his car to get some fresh air, but he had not driven the car. The officers approached his house to question his wife to see if she would support the story. The appellant was told to wait where he was but he continued to try to make his way into the house. He claimed that the officers could not prevent him entering his house. One officer told him 'You are being detained in order for us to establish whether an offence has been committed. Now stay where you are.' The appellant's wife could not corroborate his story and a scuffle ensued between one officer and the appellant. He was then told that he was being arrested for being in charge of a motor vehicle and for assaulting a police officer with intent to resist arrest. Having been convicted at first instance, the Court of Appeal dismissed the appeal.

Judge LJ: We shall begin with count two, the assault on PC Smith. Mr Belger suggested that the only power to arrest his client arose under s 4(6) of the Road Traffic Act 1988 , which provides, 'any constable may arrest anyone he has reasonable cause to suspect of having committed the offence of... being in

[394] [1996] Crim LR 111.   [395] [2005] EWCA Crim 2381.

charge of a vehicle when under the influence of drink or drugs.' He suggested that until the appellant was lawfully arrested he was at liberty to resist any unlawful attempt to restrain him. He submitted that even if, which his client denied, he had hurt PC Smith in the way she alleged, he had not assaulted her to avoid or prevent his own lawful arrest. That arrest did not take place until after he was fully under the physical control of the police and he was told expressly why he had been arrested. Mr Belger drew our attention to *Collins v Wilcock* [1984] 1WLR 1172 , in support of the proposition that a police officer has no greater rights than the ordinary citizen to restrain another, except when lawfully exercising his powers of arrest. If a police officer is not exercising the power of arrest, but seeks to reinforce a request to someone he has asked to wait by using force or the threat of force, then his purported detention of the other person is unlawful. Our analysis is simple. Mr Belger's submission depends on the proposition that until PC Smith used the actual word 'arrest', explaining the reasons for the physical restraint of the appellant, her actions, and those of PC Short were unlawful. However Mr Belger accepted that when PC Smith told the appellant that he was being detained and that he should stay where he was, she already had ample grounds to justify his arrest under the relevant Road Traffic Act provisions. Indeed he made clear that if she had used the word 'arrest' at that earlier stage, there would have been no argument. An arrest takes place when an individual is taken into custody and words or actions restrain him from moving anywhere beyond the control of the person affecting the arrest. (*Holgate-Mohammed v Duke* [1984] AC 437). As the judge said to the jury, 'Whether a person has been arrested depends not on the legality of his arrest but on whether he has been deprived of his liberty to go where he pleases.' (*Lewis v Chief Constable of South Wales Constabulary* [1991] 1 AER 206, citing *Spicer v Holt* [1977] AC 987 at 1000, per Viscount Dilhorne.) Although the point was not addressed before us, it is arguable that the appellant was arrested when PC Smith told him in unequivocal terms that he was being detained and that he should stay where he was, and physically sought to prevent him from going into his home. At that time he knew precisely why she had given him that instruction, but she was willing to check his story that he had been in his home all evening, and as he asserted, neither driving nor in charge of his vehicle. If it was true, that would be the end of the incident. There would be no need to remove the appellant from his street, and take him down to the police station, with the appropriate statutory procedure to follow. He could simply return to his home, without any inconvenience to anyone, including most particularly, the appellant himself. If on the other hand it was untrue, then the implementation of the statutory procedure would continue to its proper conclusion. In short, and dealing with the point as it was argued before us, rather than act officiously and in complete disregard of what she was told by an apparently respectable, even if intoxicated citizen, PC Smith sensibly elected to postpone the formal completion of the arrest until the facts were more fully investigated. In our judgment this was all part of a single process, not to be artificially compartmentalised, or fragmented into a series of individual processes. In these circumstances, her conduct was not rendered unlawful because she did not formally use the word 'arrest' until her brief investigation into the appellant's story was completed. By the time the exchange between the appellant and his wife finished PC Smith had very good reason to complete the arrest, and indeed it became obvious to her that help would be needed to affect it. Given that she knew that the appellant knew precisely why he had been detained, and that he had demonstrated a fixed determination to get back into his house where he seems to have believed that he would be immune from arrest, and given finally the scene she observed when she left the appellant's home, her express communication of the reasons for the appellant's arrest took place as soon as reasonably practicable.

On these facts do you think the police had done enough to make the appellant aware that he was under arrest? When did the arrest take place?

(e) There is a requirement that in *all* cases the arrestee must be informed of the *fact* of arrest, except where the arrest is made by a private citizen and the fact of arrest is obvious: s. 28(1), (2) and (5).

(f) The arrestee must be informed of the ground for arrest as soon as is practicable except where the arrest is by a private citizen and the ground of arrest is obvious. This was an important common law requirement (although the exception where the ground was 'obvious' applied to police arrests as well as citizen arrests): *Christie v Leachinsky.*[396] The reasons for the rule were stated as follows by Viscount Simon:[397]

> [T]his is for the obvious purpose of securing that a citizen who is prima facie entitled to personal freedom should know why for the time being his personal freedom is interfered with. Scott LJ argued that if the law circumscribed the issue of warrants for arrest in this way it would hardly be that a policeman acting without a warrant was entitled to make an arrest without stating the charge on which the arrest was made...No one, I think, would approve a situation in which when the person arrested asked for the reason, the policeman replied 'that has nothing to do with you: come along with me.'...
>
> ...And there are practical considerations, as well as theory, to support the view I take. If the charge on suspicion of which the man is arrested is then and there made known to him, he has the opportunity of giving an explanation of any misunderstanding or of calling attention to other persons for whom he may have been mistaken, with the result that further inquiries may save him from the consequences of false accusation...

His Lordship also stated that this 'does not mean that technical or precise language need be used'. Lord Simonds put the point like this (at 593):

> [I]t is not an essential condition of lawful arrest that the constable should at the time of arrest formulate any charge at all, much less the charge which may ultimately be found in the indictment. But this, and this only, is the qualification which I would impose upon the general proposition. It leaves untouched the principle, which lies at the heart of the matter, that the arrested man is entitled to be told what is the act for which he is arrested. The 'charge' ultimately made will depend upon the view taken by the law of his act. In ninety-nine cases out of a hundred the same words may be used to define the charge or describe the act, nor is any technical precision necessary: for instance, if the act constituting the crime is the killing of another man, it will be immaterial that the arrest is for murder and at a later hour the charge of manslaughter is substituted. The arrested man is left in no doubt that the arrest is for that killing. This is I think, the fundamental principle, viz.., that a man is entitled to know what...are 'the facts which are said to constitute a crime on his part'...

Note 3 to PACE Code G also now states:

> An arrested person must be given sufficient information to enable them to understand they have been deprived of their liberty and the reason they have been arrested, e.g. when a person is arrested on suspicion of committing an offence they must be informed of the suspected offence's nature, when and where it was committed. The suspect must also be informed of the reason or reasons why arrest is considered necessary. Vague or technical language should be avoided.

Explaining true grounds for arrest. In *R v Chalkey and Jeffries,*[398] the Court of Appeal considered that it was sufficient for a suspect to be told of the ground for his arrest even if there was an ulterior motive (to investigate his involvement in other serious crimes) that was not disclosed to him. Is it legitimate to inform a suspect of the valid reason for arrest even if it is not the true reason for the arrest? Note that under Art. 5(2) a suspect must be informed

---

[396] [1947] AC 573, HL.   [397] Ibid., at 585, 588.   [398] [1998] QB 848, CA.

properly in a language he understands of the reason for his arrest: see also *Murray v United Kingdom*.[399]

Will a suspect's awareness of the true nature of the investigation render more reliable his answers in interview? Will the investigation be fairer? If an arresting officer is satisfied that the arrest conditions are met, his private views as to the likelihood of a charge resulting from that arrest are not relevant provided he is not acting mala fides or in the knowledge that no charge would result: *Martin v Metropolitan Police Comr*.[400]

As to the requirement that suspects are informed of their arrest under Art. 5(2) of the ECHR, in *Fox, Campbell and Hartley v United Kingdom*[401] the ECHR held that an arrestee must be told in simple, non-technical language that he can understand, the essential legal and factual grounds for his arrest, so as to be able, if he sees fit, to challenge its lawfulness. Technical errors are unlikely to invalidate an arrest under the Convention: see *Douiyeb v Netherlands*.[402]

An arrest is unlawful if the person arrested is not told the ground of arrest in compliance with s. 28(3); however, the arrest becomes lawful once the ground is given: *Lewis v Chief Constable of the South Wales Constabular*.[403] Moreover, if it is not practicable for the ground of arrest to be given at the time of arrest the arrest is not rendered unlawful retrospectively when the ground is not supplied when this does become practicable thereafter: *DPP v Hawkins*[404] (conviction for assault on a police officer under s. 51(1) of the Police Act 1964 upheld). Failure to inform of the ground of arrest at the time does not taint all further police action. If a suspect is arrested by one officer and informed of the ground of arrest by another, s. 28 is satisfied.[405]

In *Dawes v DPP*,[406] D took a car without authority; the vehicle had been prepared by the police so that when the door was opened, they were automatically informed, and after the car had been driven a few yards, the engine cut out and D was trapped inside. The police arrived on the scene within minutes and informed D that he was arrested and of the reason. The court held that D had been arrested when the doors locked on him, and that he had been given the reason as soon as practicable. Kennedy LJ did, however, say that if the police were slow to respond, a court might find that he was not informed as soon as practicable:

> It may, therefore, be prudent for police forces who wish to use this type of device to consider whether it would be practicable to put in the car something which would advise the person detained that they are under arrest and the reason why they are under arrest, but that is a matter for them.[407]

(A sealed envelope marked 'For the attention of any car thief'?)

(g) The arrestor must regard his action as an arrest in the sense of a possible first step in the criminal process. For example, if he simply detains someone to question him without any thought of arrest the action will be unlawful (see *Kenlin v Gardiner*[408] and *R v Brown*).[409]

(h) The exercise of discretion must not be an *ultra vires* abuse of power: *Plange v Chief Constable of South Humberside Police*[410] (arrest where officer knew that there was no possibility of a charge would be unlawful as the officer had acted on some irrelevant consideration

---

399 (1994) 19 EHRR 193.   400 (2001) 18 June, CA (Civ D), unreported.
401 (1990) 13 EHRR 157, para. 19.   402 (1999) 30 EHRR 790.
403 [1991] 1 All ER 206.   404 [1988] 1 WLR 1166.
405 *Dhesi v Chief Constable of West Midlands Police* (2000) Times, 19 April, CA (Civ D).
406 [1994] RTR 209, DC.   407 P. 125.
408 [1966] 3 All ER 931.   409 (1976) 64 Cr App R 231.
410 (1992) Times, 23 March, CA.

or for an improper purpose). See the *dicta* in *R v Chalkey and Jeffries*[411] regarding the legitimacy of a properly executed arrest for one offence with the real purpose being to investigate others:

> we acknowledge the importance of the liberty of the subject. It is a fundamental right of which he may only be deprived by the due process of law, which process includes an entitlement to be told why he is being deprived of it. However, a collateral motive for an arrest on otherwise good and stated grounds does not necessarily make it unlawful. It depends on the motive. That is clear from the materially different facts of *Christie v Leachnisky* and the qualified manner in which the Members of the Judicial Committee expressed the important principle for which the case is famous. [His lordship referred to the judgments in *Christie*). The reasoning for that well-known and respectable aid to justice 'a holding charge', seems to us equally appropriate to circumstances where, as here, the police have, and have so informed the subjects when arresting them, reasonable grounds for doing so, but were motivated by a desire to investigate and put a stop to further, far more serious, crime.[412]

In Phillips and Brown's Home Office Study (above), 11 per cent of people were arrested for two offences and 2 per cent for three or more.[413]

3. Under s. 1 of the Magistrates' Courts Act 1980:

> Upon an information being laid before a justice of the peace...that any person has, or is suspected of having, committed an offence.

the justice may either (a) issue a summons requiring that person to appear before a magistrates' court or (b) issue a warrant to arrest that person and bring him before a magistrates' court. There are geographical limitations to the justice's power (s. 1(2)) and the information must be in writing and substantiated on oath (s. 1(3)). Where the offence charged is an indictable offence, a warrant may be issued at any time notwithstanding that a summons has previously been issued (s. 1(6)). A decision to issue a warrant or summons is a 'judicial act' and cannot be delegated by a justice without express authority.[414]

Section 125 of the Magistrates' Courts Act 1980, as amended by the 1984 Act, provides:

> (1) A warrant of arrest issued by a justice of the peace shall remain in force until it is executed or withdrawn or it ceases to have effect in accordance with the rules.
>
> (2) A warrant of arrest, warrant of commitment, warrant of detention, warrant of distress or search warrant issued by a justice of peace may be executed anywhere in England and Wales by any person to whom it is directed or by any constable acting within his police area...
>
> This subsection does not apply to a warrant of commitment, [warrant of detention[415]] or a warrant of distress issued under Part VI of the General Rate Act 1967.
>
> [(3) A warrant to [which this subsection applies] may be executed by a constable notwithstanding that it is not in his possession at the time; but the warrant shall, on the demand of the person arrested, be shown to him as soon as practicable...[416]]

---

[411] [1998] QB 848, CA.   [412] Per Auld LJ.
[413] Home Office Research and Statistics Paper 185 (1998) at p. 27.
[414] Per Lord Roskill, *obiter,* in *Hill v Anderton* [1982] 2 All ER 963 at 971–972, HL.
[415] Inserted by the Access to Justice Act 1999, ss. 95(1), 97(4), 106, Sch. 15, Part V(8).
[416] Prospectively repealed by the Access to Justice Act 1999, Sch. 15.

Subsection (4) lists the warrants to which sub-s. (3) applies, and includes arrest warrants and various other warrants under the 1980 Act and other Acts.

4. *Disposition after arrest.* A person arrested by or handed over to a constable must be taken to a police station as soon as 'practicable', unless his presence elsewhere 'is necessary in order to carry out such investigations as it is reasonable to carry out immediately'.[417] This appears to put into statutory form the *dicta* of Lord Denning MR in *Dallison v Caffery*.[418] Here, a suspect had been taken to check out an alibi instead of direct to the police station: however, as it had been done with his consent, he could not complain of it anyway. It does not appear that the suspect can require a constable to make a detour to check out an explanation of his conduct that would clear him: *McCarrick v Oxford*.[419]

More recent amendments to PACE also provide for 'street bail'. Therefore, a suspect need not be taken to a station as soon as practicable in every case. A person may be released on bail by a constable at any time before he arrives at a police station and must be required to attend a police station. No other requirement may be imposed on the person as a condition of bail.

If a private person makes an arrest he 'must, as soon as he reasonably can, hand the man over to a constable or take him to the police station or take him before a magistrate'.[420] However, there is no requirement that this be done immediately: *John Lewis & Co v Tims*.[421] Here, Mrs Tims and her daughter were arrested for shoplifting by store detectives employed by the appellant firm. After being arrested they were taken to the office of the chief store detective. They were detained there until the chief detective and a manager arrived to give instructions whether to bring proceedings. They were handed into police custody within an hour of arrest. Mrs Tims claimed damages for false imprisonment. She alleged that the detectives were obliged to give her into the custody of the police immediately upon arrest. The House of Lords held that the delay was reasonable in the circumstances: 'there are advantages in refusing to give private detectives a free hand and leaving the determination of whether to prosecute or not to a superior official'.[422]

Under s. 31, a second arrest may be delayed until shortly before release from the first arrest is about to occur: *R v Samuel*.[423] Phillips and Brown,[424] found that 8 per cent of suspects were re-arrested while in custody for offences additional to those for which they had been originally detained.[425]

5. *Search on arrest.* The provisions of s. 32 are similar to the powers at common law,[426] but with some significant modifications.[427] Note there is no *automatic* right to search in every case. The search may extend to premises where the suspect had been 'immediately' before arrest; at common law it was apparently only possible to search premises where the arrestee was at the time of arrest (and possibly only in the 'immediate vicinity' of arrestee): see *McLorie v Oxford*;[428] cf. *Dillon v O'Brien and Davis*,[429] *Elias v Pasmore*.[430] If this is not done

---

[417] S. 30(1), (10).   [418] [1965] 1 QB 348 at 366–367, CA.

[419] [1983] RTR 117, Commentary by D.J. Birch [1982] Crim LR 751. See also the discussion of Art. 5 of the ECHR in Chap. 1 above.

[420] Per Lord Denning MR in *Dallison v Caffery* at 366–367.

[421] [1952] AC 676, HL.   [422] Per Lord Porter at 691.

[423] [1988] QB 615. See also Code C 10.3–10.4.

[424] HORS Paper No. 185 (1998).   [425] Op. cit., p. 52.

[426] See *Dillon v O'Brien and Davis* (1887) 16 Cox CC 245; *Bessell v Wilson* (1853) 20 LTOS 233n; *Leigh v Cole* (1853) 6 Cox CC 329 at 332.

[427] For searches *at* police stations see below, ss. 54, 55.

[428] [1982] QB 1290.   [429] (1887) 16 Cox CC 245.

[430] [1934] 2 KB 164, Horridge J.

'immediately' entry and search must be based instead on s. 18: *R v Badham*[431] (is s. 32 *clearly* so limited?).

If the police can properly undertake a s. 32 search, is it necessarily wrong for them to have in mind the point that, once lawfully on the premises, s. 19 of PACE confers very broad powers of seizure? If it is wrong, are the police nevertheless protected provided they 'genuinely' intend to act under s. 32; or is the exercise of power unlawful because a legally irrelevant consideration has been taken into account?

6. Section 29 makes it clear that a person at a police station 'helping police with their inquiries' is not under arrest unless he is told to the contrary. This reflects the present position although many may not realise it. The question of 'voluntary attendance' is considered by McKenzie, Morgan and Reiner.[432] They argue that any encounter between the police and a suspect (as distinct from a witness) is inherently coercive and that all 'voluntary attendees' who are suspects should be told that they are free to leave at any time, are under obligation to answer questions, and are entitled to have someone told of their whereabouts and to consult a solicitor in private. They also commend a formal recording procedure adopted by one force for voluntary attendees.

7. *Statistics on arrest.* In 2005/6 there were a total of 1,429,800 arrests for recorded crime. 1,182,100 arrestees were male (83 per cent); 332,800 were juveniles (under 17). The number of arrests represented a 6 per cent rise on 2004/5. There was a 13 per cent rise in arrests for violence against the person compared with a rise in such crimes of just 1 per cent. A survey by Man *et al*[433] illustrates that alcohol can play a part in an arrest in up to one-third of cases.

7. DETENTION

- **Police and Criminal Evidence Act 1984**

PART IV[434]

Detention—conditions and duration

34 Limitations on police detention

(1) A person arrested for an offence shall not be kept in police detention except in accordance with the provisions of this Part of this Act.

(2) Subject to subsection (3) below, if at any time a custody officer—

   (a) becomes aware, in relation to any person in police detention, that the grounds for the detention of that person have ceased to apply; and

   (b) is not aware of any other grounds on which the continued detention of that person could be justified under the provisions of this Part of this Act,

   it shall be the duty of the custody officer, subject to subsection (4) below, to order his immediate release from custody.

(3) No person in police detention shall be released except on the authority of a custody officer at the police station where his detention was authorised or, if it was authorised at more than one station, a custody officer at the station where it was last authorised.

---

[431] [1987] Crim LR 202, Wood Green Crown Court.   [432] [1990] Crim LR 22 at 27–33.

[433] L. Man, D. Best, J. Marshall, C. Godfrey and T. Budd, *Dealing with Alcohol Related Detainees in the Custody Suite* (2002), Home Office Findings 178.

[434] Underlined sections in this Part were not in force at the time of publication.

(4) A person who appears to the custody officer to have been unlawfully at large when he was arrested is not to be released under subsection (2) above.

(5) A person whose release is ordered under subsection (2) above shall be released without bail unless it appears to the custody officer—

    (a) that there is need for further investigation of any matter in connection with which he was detained at any time during the period of his detention; or

    [(b) that, in respect of any such matter, proceedings may be taken against him or he may be reprimanded or warned under section 65 of the Crime and Disorder Act 1998,]

    and, if it so appears, he shall be released on bail.

(6) For the purposes of this Part of this Act a person arrested under [section 6D of the Road Traffic Act 1988] [or section 30(2) of the Transport and Works Act 1992 (c 42)] is arrested for an offence.

[(7) For the purposes of this Part a person who—

    (a) attends a police station to answer to bail granted under section 30A,

    (b) returns to a police station to answer to bail granted under this Part, or

    (c) is arrested under section 30D or 46A,

    is to be treated as arrested for an offence and that offence is the offence in connection with which he was granted bail.]

[(8) Subsection (7) does not apply in relation to a person who is granted bail subject to the duty mentioned in section 47(3)(b) and who either—

    (a) attends a police station to answer to such bail, or

    (b) is arrested under section 46A for failing to do so,

    (provision as to the treatment of such persons for the purposes of this Part being made by section 46ZA).]

36 Custody officers at police stations

(1) One or more custody officers shall be appointed for each designated police station.

(2) A custody officer for [a police station designated under section 35(1) above] shall be appointed—

    (a) by the chief officer of police for the area in which the designated police station is situated; or

    (b) by such other police officer as the chief officer of police for that area may direct.

[(2A) A custody officer for a police station designated under section 35(2A) above shall be appointed—

    (a) by the Chief Constable of the British Transport Police Force; or

    (b) by such other member of that Force as that Chief Constable may direct.]

(3) *No officer may be appointed a custody officer unless he is at least the rank of sergeant.*

[(3) No person may be appointed a custody officer unless—

    (a) he is a police officer of at least the rank of sergeant; or

    (b) he is a staff custody officer.]

(4) An officer of any rank may perform the functions of a custody officer at a designated police station if a custody officer is not readily available to perform them.

(5) Subject to the following provisions of this section and to section 39(2) below, none of the functions of a custody officer in relation to a person shall be performed by [an individual] who at the time when the function falls to be performed is involved in the investigation of an offence for which that person is in police detention at that time.

(6) Nothing in subsection (5) above is to be taken to prevent a custody officer—

    (a) performing any function assigned to custody officers—

        (i) by this Act; or

        (ii) by a code of practice issued under this Act;

    (b) carrying out the duty imposed on custody officers by section 39 below;

    (c) doing anything in connection with the identification of a suspect; or

    (d) doing anything under [sections 7 and 8 of the Road Traffic Act 1988].

(7) Where an arrested person is taken to a police station which is not a designated police station, the functions in relation to him which at a designated police station would be the functions of a custody officer shall be performed—

    (a) by an officer [or a staff custody officer] who is not involved in the investigation of an offence for which he is in police detention, if [such a person] is readily available; and

    (b) if no [such person] is readily available, by the officer who took him to the station or any other officer.

[(7A) Subject to subsection (7B), subsection (7) applies where a person attends a police station which is not a designated station to answer to bail granted under section 30A as it applies where a person is taken to such a station.

(7B) Where subsection (7) applies because of subsection (7A), the reference in subsection (7)(b) to the officer who took him to the station is to be read as a reference to the officer who granted him bail.]

(8) References to a custody officer in [section 34 above or in] the following provisions of this Act include references to [a person] other than a custody officer who is performing the functions of a custody officer by virtue of subsection (4) or (7) above.

(9) Where by virtue of subsection (7) above an officer of a force maintained by a police authority who took an arrested person to a police station is to perform the functions of a custody officer in relation to him, the officer shall inform an officer who—

    (a) is attached to a designated police station; and

    (b) is of at least the rank of inspector,

that he is to do so.

(10) The duty imposed by subsection (9) above shall be performed as soon as it is practicable to perform it.

[(11) In this section, 'staff custody officer' means a person who has been designated as such under section 38 of the Police Reform Act 2002.]

37 Duties of custody officer before charge

(1) Where—

    (a) a person is arrested for an offence—

        (i) without a warrant; or

        (ii) under a warrant not endorsed for bail,...

    (b) ...

the custody officer at each police station where he is detained after his arrest shall determine whether he has before him sufficient evidence to charge that person with the offence for which he was arrested and may detain him at the police station for such period as is necessary to enable him to do so.

(2) If the custody officer determines that he does not have such evidence before him, the person arrested shall be released either on bail or without bail, unless the custody officer has reasonable grounds for believing that his detention without being charged is necessary to secure or preserve evidence relating to an offence for which he is under arrest or to obtain such evidence by questioning him.

(3) If the custody officer has reasonable grounds for so believing, he may authorise the person arrested to be kept in police detention.

(4) Where a custody officer authorises a person who has not been charged to be kept in police detention, he shall, as soon as is practicable, make a written record of the grounds for the detention.

(5) Subject to subsection (6) below, the written record shall be made in the presence of the person arrested who shall at that time be informed by the custody officer of the grounds for his detention.

(6) Subsection (5) above shall not apply where the person arrested is, at the time when the written record is made—

(a) incapable of understanding what is said to him;

(b) violent or likely to become violent; or

(c) in urgent need of medical attention.

(7) Subject to section 41(7) below, if the custody officer determines that he has before him sufficient evidence to charge the person arrested with the offence for which he was arrested, the person arrested—

[(a) [shall be—

(i) released without charge and on bail, or

(ii) kept in police detention,

for the purpose] of enabling the Director of Public Prosecutions to make a decision under section 37B below,

(b) shall be released without charge and on bail but not for that purpose,

(c) shall be released without charge and without bail, or

(d) shall be charged].

[(7A) The decision as to how a person is to be dealt with under subsection (7) above shall be that of the custody officer.

(7B) Where a person is [dealt with under subsection (7)(a)] above, it shall be the duty of the custody officer to inform him that he is being released[, or (as the case may be) detained,] to enable the Director of Public Prosecutions to make a decision under section 37B below.]

(8) Where—

(a) a person is released under subsection (7)(b) [or (c)] above; and

(b) at the time of his release a decision whether he should be prosecuted for the offence for which he was arrested has not been taken,

it shall be the duty of the custody officer so to inform him.

[(8A) Subsection (8B) applies if the offence for which the person is arrested is one in relation to which a sample could be taken under section 63B below and the custody officer—

(a) is required in pursuance of subsection (2) above to release the person arrested and decides to release him on bail, or

(b) decides in pursuance of subsection (7)(a) or (b) above to release the person without charge and on bail.

(8B) The detention of the person may be continued to enable a sample to be taken under section 63B, but this subsection does not permit a person to be detained for a period of more than 24 hours after the relevant time.]

(9) If the person arrested is not in a fit state to be dealt with under subsection (7) above, he may be kept in police detention until he is.

(10) The duty imposed on the custody officer under subsection (1) above shall be carried out by him as soon as practicable after the person arrested arrives at the police station or, in the case of a person arrested at the police station, as soon as practicable after the arrest.

...

(15) In this Part of this Act—

'arrested juvenile' means a person arrested with or without a warrant who appears to be under the age of 17...;

'endorsed for bail' means endorsed with a direction for bail in accordance with section 117(2) of the Magistrates' Courts Act 1980.

[37A Guidance]
[(1) The Director of Public Prosecutions may issue guidance—

(a) for the purpose of enabling custody officers to decide how persons should be dealt with under section 37(7) above or 37C(2) [or 37CA(2)] below, and

(b) as to the information to be sent to the Director of Public Prosecutions under section 37B(1) below.

(2) The Director of Public Prosecutions may from time to time revise guidance issued under this section.

(3) Custody officers are to have regard to guidance under this section in deciding how persons should be dealt with under section 37(7) above or 37C(2) [or 37CA(2)] below.

(4) A report under section 9 of the Prosecution of Offences Act 1985 (report by DPP to Attorney General) must set out the provisions of any guidance issued, and any revisions to guidance made, in the year to which the report relates.

(5) The Director of Public Prosecutions must publish in such manner as he thinks fit—

(a) any guidance issued under this section, and

(b) any revisions made to such guidance.

(6) Guidance under this section may make different provision for different cases, circumstances or areas.]

[37B Consultation with the Director of Public Prosecutions]
[(1) Where a person is [dealt with under section 37(7)(a)] above, an officer involved in the investigation of the offence shall, as soon as is practicable, send to the Director of Public Prosecutions such information as may be specified in guidance under section 37A above.

(2) The Director of Public Prosecutions shall decide whether there is sufficient evidence to charge the person with an offence.

(3) If he decides that there is sufficient evidence to charge the person with an offence, he shall decide—

(a) whether or not the person should be charged and, if so, the offence with which he should be charged, and

(b) whether or not the person should be given a caution and, if so, the offence in respect of which he should be given a caution.

(4) The Director of Public Prosecutions [shall give notice] of his decision to an officer involved in the investigation of the offence.

[(4A) Notice under subsection (4) above shall be in writing, but in the case of a person kept in police detention under section 37(7)(a) above it may be given orally in the first instance and confirmed in writing subsequently.]

(5) If his decision is—

   (a) that there is not sufficient evidence to charge the person with an offence, or

   (b) that there is sufficient evidence to charge the person with an offence but that the person should not be charged with an offence or given a caution in respect of an offence,

a custody officer shall give the person notice in writing that he is not to be prosecuted.

(6) If the decision of the Director of Public Prosecutions is that the person should be charged with an offence, or given a caution in respect of an offence, the person shall be charged or cautioned accordingly.

(7) But if his decision is that the person should be given a caution in respect of the offence and it proves not to be possible to give the person such a caution, he shall instead be charged with the offence.

(8) For the purposes of this section, a person is to be charged with an offence either—

   [(a) when he is in police detention at a police station (whether because he has returned to answer bail, because he is detained under section 37(7)(a) above or for some other reason), or]

   (b) in accordance with section 29 of the Criminal Justice Act 2003.

(9) In this section 'caution' includes—

   (a) a conditional caution within the meaning of Part 3 of the Criminal Justice Act 2003, and

   (b) a warning or reprimand under section 65 of the Crime and Disorder Act 1998.]

...

38 Duties of custody officer after charge

(1) Where a person arrested for an offence otherwise than under a warrant endorsed for bail is charged with an offence, the custody officer shall[, subject to section 25 of the Criminal Justice and Public Order Act 1994,] order his release from police detention, either on bail or without bail, unless—

   (a) if the person arrested is not an arrested juvenile—

      (i) his name or address cannot be ascertained or the custody officer has reasonable grounds for doubting whether a name or address furnished by him as his name or address is his real name or address;

      [(ii) the custody officer has reasonable grounds for believing that the person arrested will fail to appear in court to answer to bail;

      (iii) in the case of a person arrested for an imprisonable offence, the custody officer has reasonable grounds for believing that the detention of the person arrested is necessary to prevent him from committing an offence;

      [(iiia) in a case where a sample may be taken from the person under section 63B below, the custody officer has reasonable grounds for believing that the detention of the person is necessary to enable the sample to be taken from him;]

      (iv) in the case of a person arrested for an offence which is not an imprisonable offence, the custody officer has reasonable grounds for believing that the detention of the person arrested is necessary to prevent him from causing physical injury to any other person or from causing loss of or damage to property;

(v) the custody officer has reasonable grounds for believing that the detention of the person arrested is necessary to prevent him from interfering with the administration of justice or with the investigation of offences or of a particular offence; or

(vi) the custody officer has reasonable grounds for believing that the detention of the person arrested is necessary for his own protection;]

(b) if he is an arrested juvenile—

(i) any of the requirements of paragraph (a) above is satisfied [(but, in the case of paragraph (a)(iiia) above, only if the arrested juvenile has attained the minimum age)]; or

(ii) the custody officer has reasonable grounds for believing that he ought to be detained in his own interests.

(2) If the release of a person arrested is not required by subsection (1) above, the custody officer may authorise him to be kept in police detention [but may not authorise a person to be kept in police detention by virtue of subsection (1)(a)(iiia) after the end of the period of six hours beginning when he was charged with the offence].

[(2A) The custody officer, in taking the decisions required by subsection (1)(a) and (b) above (except (a)(i) and (vi) and (b)(ii)), shall have regard to the same considerations as those which a court is required to have regard to in taking the corresponding decisions under paragraph [2(1)] of Part I of Schedule I to the Bail Act 1976 [(disregarding paragraph 2(2) of that Part)].]

(3) Where a custody officer authorises a person who has been charged to be kept in police detention, he shall, as soon as practicable, make a written record of the grounds for the detention.

(4) Subject to subsection (5) below, the written record shall be made in the presence of the person charged who shall at that time be informed by the custody officer of the grounds for his detention.

(5) Subsection (4) above shall not apply where the person charged is, at the time when the written record is made—

(a) incapable of understanding what is said to him;

(b) violent or likely to become violent; or

(c) in urgent need of medical attention.

[[(6) Where a custody officer authorises an arrested juvenile to be kept in police detention under subsection (1) above, the custody officer shall, unless he certifies—

(a) that, by reason of such circumstances as are specified in the certificate, it is impracticable for him to do so; or

(b) in the case of an arrested juvenile who has attained the [age of 12 years], that no secure accommodation is available and that keeping him in other local authority accommodation would not be adequate to protect the public from serious harm from him,

secure that the arrested juvenile is moved to local authority accommodation.

...

39 Responsibilities in relation to persons detained

(1) Subject to subsections (2) and (4) below, it shall be the duty of the custody officer at a police station to ensure—

(a) that all persons in police detention at that station are treated in accordance with this Act and any code of practice issued under it and relating to the treatment of persons in police detention; and

(b) that all matters relating to such persons which are required by this Act or by such codes of practice to be recorded are recorded in the custody records relating to such persons.

(2) If the custody officer, in accordance with any code of practice issued under this Act, transfers or
permits the transfer of a person in police detention—

(a) to the custody of a police officer investigating an offence for which that person is in police detention; or

(b) to the custody of an officer who has charge of that person outside the police station,

the custody officer shall cease in relation to that person to be subject to the duty imposed on him by
subsection (1)(a) above; and it shall be the duty of the officer to whom the transfer is made to ensure
that he is treated in accordance with the provisions of this Act and of any such codes of practice as
are mentioned in subsection (1) above.

(3) If the person detained is subsequently returned to the custody of the custody officer, it shall be
the duty of the officer investigating the offence to report to the custody officer as to the manner in
which this section and the codes of practice have been complied with while that person was in his
custody.

(4) If an arrested juvenile is [moved to local authority accommodation] under section 38(6) above, the
custody officer shall cease in relation to that person to be subject to the duty imposed on him by
subsection (1) above.

(5) …

(6) Where—

(a) an officer of higher rank than the custody officer [(or, if the custody officer is a staff custody
officer, any police officer or any police employee)] gives directions relating to a person in police
detention; and

(b) the directions are at variance—

(i)   with any decision made or action taken by the custody officer in the performance of a duty
imposed on him under this Part of this Act; or

(ii)   with any decision or action which would but for the directions have been made or taken by
him in the performance of such a duty,

the custody officer shall refer the matter at once to an officer of the rank of superintendent or above
who is responsible for the police station for which the custody officer is acting as custody officer.

…

40 Review of police detention

(1) Reviews of the detention of each person in police detention in connection with the investigation
of an offence shall be carried out periodically in accordance with the following provisions of this
section—

(a) in the case of a person who has been arrested and charged, by the custody officer; and

(b) in the case of a person who has been arrested but not charged, by an officer of at least the rank
of inspector who has not been directly involved in the investigation.

(2) The officer to whom it falls to carry out a review is referred to in this section as a 'review officer'.

(3) Subject to subsection (4) below—

(a) the first review shall be not later than six hours after the detention was first authorised;

(b) the second review shall be not later than nine hours after the first;

(c) subsequent reviews shall be at intervals of not more than nine hours.

(4) A review may be postponed—

(a) if, having regard to all the circumstances prevailing at the latest time for it specified in subsection (3) above, it is not practicable to carry out the review at that time;

(b) without prejudice to the generality of paragraph (a) above—

(i) if at that time the person in detention is being questioned by a police officer and the review officer is satisfied that an interruption of the questioning for the purpose of carrying out the review would prejudice the investigation in connection with which he is being questioned; or

(ii) if at that time no review officer is readily available.

(5) If a review is postponed under subsection (4) above it shall be carried out as soon as practicable after the latest time specified for it in subsection (3) above.

(6) If a review is carried out after postponement under subsection (4) above, the fact that it was so carried out shall not affect any requirement of this section as to the time at which any subsequent review is to be carried out.

(7) The review officer shall record the reasons for any postponement of a review in the custody record.

(8) Subject to subsection (9) below, where the person whose detention is under review has not been charged before the time of the review, section 37(1) to (6) above shall have effect in relation to him, but with [the modifications specified in subsection (8A).]

[(8A) The modifications are—

(a) the substitution of references to the person whose detention is under review for references to the person arrested;

(b) the substitution of references to the review officer for references to the custody officer; and

(c) in subsection (6), the insertion of the following paragraph after paragraph (a)—

'(aa) asleep;'.]

(9) Where a person has been kept in police detention by virtue of section 37(9) [or 37D(5)] above, section 37(1) to (6) shall not have effect in relation to him but it shall be the duty of the review officer to determine whether he is yet in a fit state.

(10) Where the person whose detention is under review has been charged before the time of the review, section 38(1) to [(6B)] above shall have effect in relation to him, with [the modifications specified in subsection (10A)].

…

(11) Where—

(a) an officer of higher rank than the review officer gives directions relating to a person in police detention; and

(b) the directions are at variance—

(i) with any decision made or action taken by the review officer in the performance of a duty imposed on him under this Part of this Act; or

(ii) with any decision or action which would but for the directions have been made or taken by him in the performance of such a duty, the review officer shall refer the matter at once to an officer of the rank of superintendent or above who is responsible for the police station for which the review officer is acting as review officer in connection with the detention.

(12) Before determining whether to authorise a person's continued detention the review officer shall give—

(a) that person (unless he is asleep); or

(b) any solicitor representing him who is available at the time of the review,

an opportunity to make representations to him about the detention.

(13) Subject to subsection (14) below, the person whose detention is under review or his solicitor may make representations under subsection (12) above either orally or in writing.

(14) The review officer may refuse to hear oral representations from the person whose detention is under review if he considers that he is unfit to make such representations by reason of his condition or behaviour.

...

41 Limits on period of detention without charge

(1) Subject to the following provisions of this section and to sections 42 and 43 below, a person shall not be kept in police detention for more than 24 hours without being charged.

(2) The time from which the period of detention of a person is to be calculated (in this Act referred to as 'the relevant time')—

(a) in the case of a person to whom this paragraph applies, shall be—

(i) the time at which that person arrives at the relevant police station; or

(ii) the time 24 hours after the time of that person's arrest,

whichever is the earlier;

(b) in the case of a person arrested outside England and Wales, shall be—

(i) the time at which that person arrives at the first police station to which he is taken in the police area in England or Wales in which the offence for which he was arrested is being investigated; or

(ii) the time 24 hours after the time of that person's entry into England and Wales,

whichever is the earlier;

(c) in the case of a person who—

(i) attends voluntarily at a police station; or

(ii) accompanies a constable to a police station without having been arrested,

and is arrested at the police station, the time of his arrest;

[(ca) in the case of a person who attends a police station to answer to bail granted under section 30A, the time when he arrives at the police station;]

(d) in any other case, except where subsection (5) below applies, shall be the time at which the person arrested arrives at the first police station to which he is taken after his arrest.

(3) Subsection (2)(a) above applies to a person if—

(a) his arrest is sought in one police area in England and Wales;

(b) he is arrested in another police area; and

(c) he is not questioned in the area in which he is arrested in order to obtain evidence in relation to an offence for which he is arrested;

and in sub-paragraph (i) of that paragraph 'the relevant police station' means the first police station to which he is taken in the police area in which his arrest was sought.

(4) Subsection (2) above shall have effect in relation to a person arrested under section 31 above as if every reference in it to his arrest or his being arrested were a reference to his arrest or his being arrested for the offence for which he was originally arrested.

(5) If—

(a) a person is in police detention in a police area in England and Wales ('the first area'); and

(b) his arrest for an offence is sought in some other police area in England and Wales ('the second area'); and

(c) he is taken to the second area for the purposes of investigating that offence, without being questioned in the first area in order to obtain evidence in relation to it,

the relevant time shall be—

(i) the time 24 hours after he leaves the place where he is detained in the first area; or

(ii) the time at which he arrives at the first police station to which he is taken in the second area,

whichever is the earlier.

(6) When a person who is in police detention is removed to hospital because he is in need of medical treatment, any time during which he is being questioned in hospital or on the way there or back by a police officer for the purpose of obtaining evidence relating to an offence shall be included in any period which falls to be calculated for the purposes of this Part of this Act, but any other time while he is in hospital or on his way there or back shall not be so included.

(7) Subject to subsection (8) below, a person who at the expiry of 24 hours after the relevant time is in police detention and has not been charged shall be released at that time either on bail or without bail.

(8) Subsection (7) above does not apply to a person whose detention for more than 24 hours after the relevant time has been authorised or is otherwise permitted in accordance with section 42 or 43 below.

(9) A person released under subsection (7) above shall not be re-arrested without a warrant for the offence for which he was previously arrested unless new evidence justifying a further arrest has come to light since his release[; but this subsection does not prevent an arrest under section 46A below].

42 Authorisation of continued detention

(1) Where a police officer of the rank of superintendent or above who is responsible for the police station at which a person is detained has reasonable grounds for believing that—

(a) the detention of that person without charge is necessary to secure or preserve evidence relating to an offence for which he is under arrest or to obtain such evidence by questioning him;

[(b) an offence for which he is under arrest is an [indictable] offence; and]

(c) the investigation is being conducted diligently and expeditiously,

he may authorise the keeping of that person in police detention for a period expiring at or before 36 hours after the relevant time.

(2) Where an officer such as is mentioned in subsection (1) above has authorised the keeping of a person in police detention for a period expiring less than 36 hours after the relevant time, such an officer may authorise the keeping of that person in police detention for a further period expiring not more than 36 hours after that time if the conditions specified in subsection (1) above are still satisfied when he gives the authorisation.

(3) If it is proposed to transfer a person in police detention to another police area, the officer determining whether or not to authorise keeping him in detention under subsection (1) above shall have regard to the distance and the time the journey would take.

(4) No authorisation under subsection (1) above shall be given in respect of any person—

  (a) more than 24 hours after the relevant time; or

  (b) before the second review of his detention under section 40 above has been carried out.

(5) Where an officer authorises the keeping of a person in police detention under subsection (1) above, it shall be his duty—

  (a) to inform that person of the grounds for his continued detention; and

  (b) to record the grounds in that person's custody record.

(6) Before determining whether to authorise the keeping of a person in detention under subsection (1) or (2) above, an officer shall give—

  (a) that person; or

  (b) any solicitor representing him who is available at the time when it falls to the officer to determine whether to give the authorisation,

an opportunity to make representations to him about the detention.

(7) Subject to subsection (8) below, the person in detention or his solicitor may make representations under subsection (6) above either orally or in writing.

(8) The officer to whom it falls to determine whether to give the authorisation may refuse to hear oral representations from the person in detention if he considers that he is unfit to make such representations by reason of his condition or behaviour.

(9) Where—

  (a) an officer authorises the keeping of a person in detention under subsection (1) above; and

  (b) at the time of the authorisation he has not yet exercised a right conferred on him by section 56 or 58 below,

  the officer—

    (i) shall inform him of that right;

    (ii) shall decide whether he should be permitted to exercise it;

    (iii) shall record the decision in his custody record; and

    (iv) if the decision is to refuse to permit the exercise of the right, shall also record the grounds for the decision in that record.

(10) Where an officer has authorised the keeping of a person who has not been charged in detention under subsection (1) or (2) above, he shall be released from detention, either on bail or without bail, not later than 36 hours after the relevant time, unless—

  (a) he has been charged with an offence; or

  (b) his continued detention is authorised or otherwise permitted in accordance with section 43 below.

(11) A person released under subsection (10) above shall not be re-arrested without a warrant for the offence for which he was previously arrested unless new evidence justifying a further arrest has come to light since his release[; but this subsection does not prevent an arrest under section 46A below].

43 Warrants of further detention

(1) Where, on an application on oath made by a constable and supported by an information, a magistrates' court is satisfied that there are reasonable grounds for believing that the further detention of the person to whom the application relates is justified, it may issue a warrant of further detention authorising the keeping of that person in police detention.

(2) A court may not hear an application for a warrant of further detention unless the person to whom the application relates—

(a) has been furnished with a copy of the information; and

(b) has been brought before the court for the hearing.

(3) The person to whom the application relates shall be entitled to be legally represented at the hearing and, if he is not so represented but wishes to be so represented—

(a) the court shall adjourn the hearing to enable him to obtain representation; and

(b) he may be kept in police detention during the adjournment.

(4) A person's further detention is only justified for the purposes of this section or section 44 below if—

(a) his detention without charge is necessary to secure or preserve evidence relating to an offence for which he is under arrest or to obtain such evidence by questioning him;

(b) an offence for which he is under arrest is [an indictable offence]; and

(c) the investigation is being conducted diligently and expeditiously.

(5) Subject to subsection (7) below, an application for a warrant of further detention may be made—

(a) at any time before the expiry of 36 hours after the relevant time; or

(b) in a case where—

(i) it is not practicable for the magistrates' court to which the application will be made to sit at the expiry of 36 hours after the relevant time; but

(ii) the court will sit during the 6 hours following the end of that period,

at any time before the expiry of the said 6 hours.

(6) In a case to which subsection (5)(b) above applies—

(a) the person to whom the application relates may be kept in police detention until the application is heard; and

(b) the custody officer shall make a note in that person's custody record—

(i) of the fact that he was kept in police detention for more than 36 hours after the relevant time; and

(ii) of the reason why he was so kept.

(7) If—

(a) an application for a warrant of further detention is made after the expiry of 36 hours after the relevant time; and

(b) it appears to the magistrates' court that it would have been reasonable for the police to make it before the expiry of that period,

the court shall dismiss the application.

(8) Where on an application such as is mentioned in subsection (1) above a magistrates' court is not satisfied that there are reasonable grounds for believing that the further detention of the person to whom the application relates is justified, it shall be its duty—

    (a) to refuse the application; or

    (b) to adjourn the hearing of it until a time not later than 36 hours after the relevant time.

(9) The person to whom the application relates may be kept in police detention during the adjournment.

(10) A warrant of further detention shall—

    (a) state the time at which it is issued;

    (b) authorise the keeping in police detention of the person to whom it relates for the period stated in it.

(11) Subject to subsection (12) below, the period stated in a warrant of further detention shall be such period as the magistrates' court thinks fit, having regard to the evidence before it.

(12) The period shall not be longer than 36 hours.

(13) If it is proposed to transfer a person in police detention to a police area other than that in which he is detained when the application for a warrant of further detention is made, the court hearing the application shall have regard to the distance and the time the journey would take.

(14) Any information submitted in support of an application under this section shall state—

    (a) the nature of the offence for which the person to whom the application relates has been arrested;

    (b) the general nature of the evidence on which that person was arrested;

    (c) what inquiries relating to the offence have been made by the police and what further inquiries are proposed by them;

    (d) the reasons for believing the continued detention of that person to be necessary for the purposes of such further inquiries.

(15) Where an application under this section is refused, the person to whom the application relates shall forthwith be charged or, subject to subsection (16) below, released, either on bail or without bail.

(16) A person need not be released under subsection (15) above—

    (a) before the expiry of 24 hours after the relevant time; or

    (b) before the expiry of any longer period for which his continued detention is or has been authorised under section 42 above.

(17) Where an application under this section is refused, no further application shall be made under this section in respect of the person to whom the refusal relates, unless supported by evidence which has come to light since the refusal.

(18) Where a warrant of further detention is issued, the person to whom it relates shall be released from police detention, either on bail or without bail, upon or before the expiry of the warrant unless he is charged.

(19) A person released under subsection (18) above shall not be re-arrested without a warrant for the offence for which he was previously arrested unless new evidence justifying a further arrest has come to light since his release[; but this subsection does not prevent an arrest under section 46A below.]

44 Extension of warrants of further detention

(1) On an application on oath made by a constable and supported by an information a magistrates' court may extend a warrant of further detention issued under section 43 above if it is satisfied that there are reasonable grounds for believing that the further detention of the person to whom the application relates is justified.

(2) Subject to subsection (3) below, the period for which a warrant of further detention may be extended shall be such period as the court thinks fit, having regard to the evidence before it.

(3) The period shall not—

(a) be longer than 36 hours; or

(b) end later than 96 hours after the relevant time.

(4) Where a warrant of further detention has been extended under subsection (1) above, or further extended under this subsection, for a period ending before 96 hours after the relevant time, on an application such as is mentioned in that subsection a magistrates' court may further extend the warrant if it is satisfied as there mentioned; and subsections (2) and (3) above apply to such further extensions as they apply to extensions under subsection (1) above.

(5) A warrant of further detention shall, if extended or further extended under this section, be endorsed with a note of the period of the extension.

(6) Subsections (2), (3), and (14) of section 43 above shall apply to an application made under this section as they apply to an application made under that section.

(7) Where an application under this section is refused, the person to whom the application relates shall forthwith be charged or, subject to subsection (8) below, released, either on bail or without bail.

(8) A person need not be released under subsection (7) above before the expiry of any period for which a warrant of further detention issued in relation to him has been extended or further extended on an earlier application made under this section.

46 Detention after charge

(1) Where a person—

(a) is charged with an offence; and

(b) after being charged—

(i) is kept in police detention; or

(ii) is detained by a local authority in pursuance of arrangements made under section 38(6) above,

he shall be brought before a magistrates' court in accordance with the provisions of this section.

(2) If he is to be brought before a magistrates' court [in the local justice] area in which the police station at which he was charged is situated, he shall be brought before such a court as soon as is practicable and in any event not later than the first sitting after he is charged with the offence.

(3) If no magistrates' court [in that area] is due to sit either on the day on which he is charged or on the next day, the custody officer for the police station at which he was charged shall inform the [designated officer] for the area that there is a person in the area to whom subsection (2) above applies.

(4) If the person charged is to be brought before a magistrates' court [in a local justice] area other than that in which the police station at which he was charged is situated, he shall be removed to that area as soon as is practicable and brought before such a court as soon as is practicable after his arrival in the area and in any event not later than the first sitting of a magistrates' court [in that area] after his arrival in the area.

(5) If no magistrates' court [in that area] is due to sit either on the day on which he arrives in the area or on the next day—

(a) he shall be taken to a police station in the area; and

(b) the custody officer at that station shall inform the [designated officer] for the area that there is a person in the area to whom subsection (4) applies.

(6) Subject to subsection (8) below, where [the designated officer for a local justice] area has been informed—

(a) under subsection (3) above that there is a person in the area to whom subsection (2) above applies; or

(b) under subsection (5) above that there is a person in the area to whom subsection (4) above applies,

[the designated officer] shall arrange for a magistrates' court to sit not later than the day next following the relevant day.

(7) In this section 'the relevant day'—

(a) in relation to a person who is to be brought before a magistrates' court [in the local justice] area in which the police station at which he was charged is situated, means the day on which he was charged; and

(b) in relation to a person who is to be brought before a magistrates' court [in any other local justice] area, means the day on which he arrives in the area.

(8) Where the day next following the relevant day is Christmas Day, Good Friday or a Sunday, the duty of the [designated officer] under subsection (6) above is a duty to arrange for a magistrates' court to sit not later than the first day after the relevant day which is not one of those days.

(9) Nothing in this section requires a person who is in hospital to be brought before a court if he is not well enough.

NOTES

1. Part IV established a new system for police detention. It created a division of functions (wherever possible) between the officers conducting an investigation and a 'custody officer' responsible for supervision of each suspect's detention, provided for written records to be kept and provided for periodic reviews of the need for the continued detention of the suspect. It does not affect 'any right of a person in detention to apply for habeas corpus or other prerogative remedy' (s. 51(d)). Statistics of detention must be kept and published in the annual reports of chief officers of police (s. 50). Periods in police detention count towards custodial sentences (s. 49).

2. The basic period of permitted detention without charge is limited to 24 hours from the 'relevant time': (s. 41), usually the first time at which the arrestee arrives at the first police station to which he is taken after the arrest. In the case of an indictable offence an officer of the rank of superintendent or above may authorise detention up to 36 hours from the 'relevant time' (s. 42); a magistrates' court may issue a warrant of further detention for a period up to a further 36 hours (s. 43); and a magistrates' court may extend the warrant for a still further period up to 36 hours, provided that the total time does not exceed 96 hours from the 'relevant time' (s. 44). Times are to be treated as 'approximate only' (s. 45). A person must normally be brought before a magistrates' court as soon as it is practicable and in any event not later than the first sitting after he is charged with the offence (s. 46).

3. The provisions of the Act are supplemented by the *Code of Practice for the Detention, Treatment and Questioning of Persons by Police Officers,*[435] which applies to persons who are in custody at police stations whether or not they have been arrested for an offence; and to those who have been removed to a police station as a place of safety under ss. 135 and 136 of the Mental Health Act 1983.[436] Phillips and Brown found that around 1 per cent of suspects were believed to be suffering from a mental disorder on arrival at the station.[437] In total, 2 per cent of arrestees were treated as mentally disordered.[438] The notes for guidance state that those at a police station voluntarily to assist with an investigation should be treated with no less consideration than those in custody, and enjoy an absolute right to obtain legal advice or to communicate with anyone outside the station.[439]

4. A custody record must be opened as soon as it is practicable for each person who is brought to a police station under arrest or is arrested at the police station having attended there voluntarily.[440] The custody officer is responsible for the accuracy and completeness of the custody record and for ensuring that it accompanies the detained person on any transfer to another station.[441] Phillips and Brown found that 4 per cent of arrestees were too drunk to be dealt with on arrival, 1 per cent were violent and 1 per cent were totally unco-operative with the custody officer.[442] In 2002 Man et al.[443] found that of the custody records sampled, one-third of the arrests were alcohol related, and such alcohol-related detainees spent significantly longer in custody than other detainees. They were also found to be more likely to be noisy, disruptive and violent.

Where the person leaves police detention, or is taken before a court, he, his legal representative or his appropriate adult is entitled, on request, to be given a copy of the record and, on giving reasonable notice, to inspect the original.[444] The custody record will prove crucial if a challenge is made to the detention of the suspect in an attempt to have evidence excluded. In *R v Heslop,*[445] the Court of Appeal dismissed H's appeal where his admission to murder was recorded in the officer's notebook and signed by H. H had claimed that it should also have been recorded in the custody record. The court denied any such statutory requirement. The revised 2008 Code C.11.13 now requires that 'a written record shall be made of any comments made by a suspect, including unsolicited comments, which are outside the context of an interview but which might be relevant to the offence. Any such record must be timed and signed by the maker. When practicable the suspect shall be given the opportunity to read that record and to sign it as correct or to indicate how they consider it inaccurate.'

5. Section 15 of Code C covers reviews and extensions of detentions. Points additional to the provisions of PACE include the following. On a review of detention, persons other than a solicitor or appropriate adult who have an interest in the person's welfare may make representations;[446] before conducting a review, the review officer must ensure that the detained person is reminded of his entitlement to free legal advice.[447] The notes for guidance state that if the detained person is likely to be asleep at the latest time when a review of detention or an authorisation of continued detention may take place, then it should be brought

---

[435] PACE Code C, Revised Edition, 2008.   [436] Code C.1.10.

[437] Op. cit., p. 281, p. 51.   [438] Op. cit., p. 24.   [439] Code C.1A.

[440] Code C.2.1.   [441] Code C.2.3.

[442] Op. cit., p. 51. see also HORS Paper No. 183, *Drugs and Crime: The Results of Research on Drug Testing and Interviewing Arrestees.* See also A. Sondhi et al., *Statistics from the arrest referral monitoring programme* (Home Office , 2001).

[443] L. Man, D. Best, J. Marshall, C. Godfrey and T. Budd, *Dealing with Alcohol Related Detainees in the Custody Suite* (2002), Home Office Findings 178.

[444] Code C.2.4, C.2.4A, C.2.5.   [445] [1996] Crim LR 730.   [446] Code C.15.3(a).

[447] Code C.15.4.

forward so that the detained person can make representations without being woken up.[448] An application for a warrant of further detention or an extension should be made between 10 a.m. and 9 p.m. and if possible during normal court hours.[449]

6. In *R v Chief Constable of Kent, ex p Kent Police Federation*[450] it was held that the review under s. 40 could not occur by video-link. Although the primary purpose of the review is to assess the validity of the continued detention, the review officer also has a responsibility to monitor the welfare of the suspect. The Criminal Justice and Police Act 2001 (s. 73 inserting ss. 40A and 45A) reversed the decision, allowing for reviews to be conducted by telephone or by video-link where necessary.[451] Does a video-link provide an adequate guarantee of the welfare of the detainee? Does it render the system more efficient?

7. Ayres and Murray report that the number of warrants for detention in recent years has been as follows: 2000/1 – 326 applications (7 refused); 2001/2 – 325 (8 refused); 2002/3 – 302 (8 refused); 2003/4 – 304 (0 refused); 2004/5 – 423 (8 refused).[452]

8. The role of the custody officer was designed as a key element in the protection of the rights of the detainee. In *Clarke v Chief Constable of North Wales*,[453] the court held that the custody officer is entitled to assume, in the absence of any evidence to the contrary, that the arrest is lawful. Should the custody officer not make sure for himself in order to better protect the suspect? In *Al Fayed v Metropolitan Police Comr*[454] the court suggested that PACE would become unworkable if the custody officer had to ask for full details and evidence about a case before he could make a decision as to detention.

The custody officer determines whether there is sufficient evidence to charge the person (s. 37). In recent years there have been significant changes to custody officers' role in charging. Since the policy was laid out in *Justice for All*[455] and enacted in the Criminal Justice Act 2003, the custody officer retains the decision as to whether there is sufficient evidence to charge, but the decision to actually charge in all but routine cases (e.g. those under the Road Traffic Acts not involving dangerous driving, etc.) will be on the advice of the Crown Prosecutor. The decision as to whether the suspect should be released or charged, with or without bail, is that of the custody officer (subject to s. 41(7) which states that the suspect must be released with or without bail at the expiration of the detention limit) but in making that decision he must have regard to the DPP's *Guidance on Charging* (s. 37A(3)). Under s. 37(7)(a) the custody officer may keep the suspect in police detention for the purpose of enabling the DPP (Crown Prosecutor in practice) to make a decision about whether there is sufficient evidence to charge and what those charges ought to be.[456] As soon as is practicable the officer involved in the investigation must provide the Crown Prosecutor with as much information as is specified in the DPP's *Guidance on Charging*. Where the Crown Prosecutor is unable to make the charging decision on the information available at that time, the detainee may be released without charge and on bail.

9. A custody officer must be at least the rank of sergeant, though under SOCPA 2005, s. 121 the police are able to appoint civilian custody officers, who are able to perform certain of the functions of the police custody officer. Such appointments are open to the criticism that civilians will not be sufficiently able to uphold suspects' rights in the face of pressure from

---

[448] Code C.15C.   [449] Code C.15D.   [450] [2000] Crim LR 854.

[451] Code C.15(9)–15(11).

[452] *Arrests for Recorded Crime and the Operation of Powers Under PACE 2004–2005* HORSD 21/05 (2005).

[453] (2000) 22 May, CA (Civ D), unreported.

[454] *Al Fayed v Metropolitan Police Comr* [2004] EWCA Civ 1579.

[455] Justice for All (Cm 5563, 2002).

[456] See *R (on the application of G) v Chief Constable of West Yorkshire Police* [2008] EWCA Civ 28.

investigating officers. In view of the importance of the role of the custody officer, ought the function to be performed by officers of an independent body?

Custody officers were described by McConville, Sanders and Leng, as 'complicitous in the creation of an off-the-record interview by permitting the case officer to visit the suspect in the cells or by authorising his release to the interview room without recording it'.[457] Can the problem of bias or perceived bias towards the investigating officers be avoided if the custody officer is a non-police role?

10. Statistics on detention times have been controversial since the original studies conducted for the RCCP. The RCCP found that about 75 per cent of suspects were dealt with within six hours and about 95 per cent within 24 hours. A survey conducted by the Metropolitan Police for three months in 1979 showed that only 0.4 per cent of 48,343 persons had been held for over 72 hours without charge or release.[458] A study by Brown[459] of 10 forces found considerable variations from station to station in the length of detention without charge, this being strongly linked with the seriousness of the crime in question, but also perhaps with differences in the custody officer's approach to PACE. The RCCJ did not think any changes in detention limits was necessary although further national statistics should be maintained.[460]

11. *Further statistics on detention.*[461] The number of people detained for more than 24 hours before being released without charge was: 505 in 2000/1; 505 in 2001/2; 633 in 2002/3; 621 in 2003/4; 1132 in 2004/5.

Phillips and Brown (above) found that the average time spent without charge was six hours 40 minutes. The average time for those who sought legal advice was just over nine hours while for those who did not it was five and a half hours. Other commentators have noted dramatic falls in the levels of complaints about treatment by the police in the charge room or cells[462] and improvements in arrangements for the welfare of suspects.[463] On the other hand the initial authorisation of detention by the custody officer is in practice a formality.[464] Phillips and Brown found it to be exceptional for the custody officer to refuse detention. Of the 4,250 cases examined, only one case was refused.[465] Brown[466] stated that 'custody officers show considerable independence in the way they carry out their job although practical constraints limit their examination of the evidence against a suspect when considering whether to authorise detention'.[467]

Philips and Brown examined the outcomes of arrests and report that 52 per cent of those arrested in their survey were charged, 17 per cent cautioned, and in 20 per cent of cases there was no further action. Around 17 per cent of suspects were initially bailed for further inquiries, but 44 per cent of these led to no further action. Black and Asian suspects were more likely to be bailed than White suspects.[468]

---

457 *The Case for the Prosecution* (1991), p. 58.   458 RCCP Report, para. 3.96.
459 *Detention at the Police Station under the Police and Criminal Evidence Act 1984* (1989), Home Office Research Study 104.
460 Cm 2263, 1993, p. 30.
461 Taken from *Arrests for Recorded Crime and the Operation of Certain Police Powers Under PACE 2004–2005* HORSD 21/05 (2005). Not all forces statistics were included across all years.
462 M. Maguire (1988) 28 Br J Crim 19, 41.
463 Ibid.; B.L. Irving and I.K. McKenzie, *Police Interrogation: the effects of the Police and Criminal Evidence Act 1984* (1989), pp. 196–198 (replicating the RCCP Research Study No. 2, 1980).
464 I. McKenzie, R. Morgan and R. Reiner [1990] Crim LR 22, 22–27.
465 Ibid., p. 49.
466 D. Brown, *PACE Ten Years On: A Review of Research* (1997) HORSD No. 49.
467 Ibid., p. 2.   468 Op. cit., p. 82.

12. Release on police bail is governed by provisions of the Bail Act 1976, as amended by Part II of the Criminal Justice and Public Order Act 1994.

8. QUESTIONING AND TREATMENT OF PERSONS IN CUSTODY

- Police and Criminal Evidence Act 1984

PART V

54 Searches of detained persons

(1) The custody officer at a police station shall ascertain . . . everything which a person has with him when he is—

  (a) brought to the station after being arrested elsewhere or after being committed to custody by an order or sentence of a court; or

  [(b) arrested at the station or detained there[, as a person falling within section 34(7), under section 37 above] [or as a person to whom section 46ZA(4) or (5) applies]].

[(2) The custody officer may record or cause to be recorded all or any of the things which he ascertains under subsection (1).

(2A) In the case of an arrested person, any such record may be made as part of his custody record.]

(3) Subject to subsection (4) below, a custody officer may seize and retain any such thing or cause any such thing to be seized and retained.

(4) Clothes and personal effects may only be seized if the custody officer—

  (a) believes that the person from whom they are seized may use them—

    (i) to cause physical injury to himself or any other person;

    (ii) to damage property;

    (iii) to interfere with evidence; or

    (iv) to assist him to escape; or

  (b) has reasonable grounds for believing that they may be evidence relating to an offence.

(5) Where anything is seized, the person from whom it is seized shall be told the reason for the seizure unless he is —

  (a) violent or likely to become violent; or

  (b) incapable of understanding what is said to him.

(6) Subject to subsection (7) below, a person may be searched if the custody officer considers it necessary to enable him to carry out his duty under subsection (1) above and to the extent that the custody officer considers necessary for that purpose.

[(6A) A person who is in custody at a police station or is in police detention otherwise than at a police station may at any time be searched in order to ascertain whether he has with him anything which he could use for any of the purposes specified in subsection (4)(a) above.

(6B) Subject to subsection (6C) below, a constable may seize and retain, or cause to be seized and retained, anything found on such a search.

(6C) A constable may only seize clothes and personal effects in the circumstances specified in subsection (4) above.]

(7) An intimate search may not be conducted under this section.

(8) A search under this section shall be carried out by a constable.

(9) The constable carrying out a search shall be of the same sex as the person searched.

[54A Searches and examination to ascertain identity]
[(1) If an officer of at least the rank of inspector authorises it, a person who is detained in a police station
     may be searched or examined, or both—

   (a) for the purpose of ascertaining whether he has any mark that would tend to identify him as a
        person involved in the commission of an offence; or

   (b) for the purpose of facilitating the ascertainment of his identity.

(2) An officer may only give an authorisation under subsection (1) for the purpose mentioned in para-
    graph (a) of that subsection if—

   (a) the appropriate consent to a search or examination that would reveal whether the mark in ques-
        tion exists has been withheld; or

   (b) it is not practicable to obtain such consent.

(3) An officer may only give an authorisation under subsection (1) in a case in which subsection (2) does
    not apply if—

   (a) the person in question has refused to identify himself; or

   (b) the officer has reasonable grounds for suspecting that that person is not who he claims to be.

(4) An officer may give an authorisation under subsection (1) orally or in writing but, if he gives it orally,
    he shall confirm it in writing as soon as is practicable.

(5) Any identifying mark found on a search or examination under this section may be
    photographed—

   (a) with the appropriate consent; or

   (b) if the appropriate consent is withheld or it is not practicable to obtain it, without it.

(6) Where a search or examination may be carried out under this section, or a photograph may be taken
    under this section, the only persons entitled to carry out the search or examination, or to take the
    photograph, are [constables].

(7) A person may not under this section carry out a search or examination of a person of the opposite sex
    or take a photograph of any part of the body of a person of the opposite sex.

(8) An intimate search may not be carried out under this section.

(9) A photograph taken under this section—

   (a) may be used by, or disclosed to, any person for any purpose related to the prevention or detec-
        tion of crime, the investigation of an offence or the conduct of a prosecution; and

   (b) after being so used or disclosed, may be retained but may not be used or disclosed except for a
        purpose so related.
...

(11) In this section—

   (a) references to ascertaining a person's identity include references to showing that he is not a par-
        ticular person; and]

   [(b) references to taking a photograph include references to using any process by means of which
        a visual image may be produced, and references to photographing a person shall be construed
        accordingly.

(12) In this section 'mark' includes features and injuries; and a mark is an identifying mark for the purposes of this section if its existence in any person's case facilitates the ascertainment of his identity or his identification as a person involved in the commission of an offence.

[(13) Nothing in this section applies to a person arrested under an extradition arrest power.]]

55 Intimate searches

(1) Subject to the following provisions of this section, if an officer of at least the rank of [inspector] has reasonable grounds for believing—

(a) that a person who has been arrested and is in police detention may have concealed on him anything which—

(i) he could use to cause physical injury to himself or others; and

(ii) he might so use while he is in police detention or in the custody of a court; or

(b) that such a person—

(i) may have a Class A drug concealed on him; and

(ii) was in possession of it with the appropriate criminal intent before his arrest,

he may authorise [an intimate search] of that person.

(2) An officer may not authorise an intimate search of a person for anything unless he has reasonable grounds for believing that it cannot be found without his being intimately searched.

(3) An officer may give an authorisation under subsection (1) above orally or in writing but, if he gives it orally, he shall confirm it in writing as soon as is practicable.

[(3A) A drug offence search shall not be carried out unless the appropriate consent has been given in writing.

(3B) Where it is proposed that a drug offence search be carried out, an appropriate officer shall inform the person who is to be subject to it—

(a) of the giving of the authorisation for it; and

(b) of the grounds for giving the authorisation.]

(4) An intimate search which is only a drug offence search shall be by way of examination by a suitably qualified person.

(5) Except as provided by subsection (4) above, an intimate search shall be by way of examination by a suitably qualified person unless an officer of at least the rank of [inspector] considers that this is not practicable.

(6) An intimate search which is not carried out as mentioned in subsection (5) above shall be carried out by a constable.

(7) A constable may not carry out an intimate search of a person of the opposite sex.

(8) No intimate search may be carried out except—

(a) at a police station;

(b) at a hospital;

(c) at a registered medical practitioner's surgery; or

(d) at some other place used for medical purposes.

(9) An intimate search which is only a drug offence search may not be carried out at a police station.

(10) If an intimate search of a person is carried out, the custody record relating to him shall state—

(a) which parts of his body were searched; and

(b) why they were searched.

[(10A) If the intimate search is a drug offence search, the custody record relating to that person shall also state—

(a) the authorisation by virtue of which the search was carried out;

(b) the grounds for giving the authorisation; and

(c) the fact that the appropriate consent was given.]

(11) The information required to be recorded by [subsections (10) and (10A)] above shall be recorded as soon as practicable after the completion of the search.

(12) The custody officer at a police station may seize and retain anything which is found on an intimate search of a person, or cause any such thing to be seized and retained—

(a) if he believes that the person from whom it is seized may use it—

(i) to cause physical injury to himself or any other person;

(ii) to damage property;

(iii) to interfere with evidence; or

(iv) to assist him to escape; or

(b) if he has reasonable grounds for believing that it may be evidence relating to an offence.

(13) Where anything is seized under this section, the person from whom it is seized shall be told the reason for the seizure unless he is—

(a) violent or likely to become violent; or

(b) incapable of understanding what is said to him.

[(13A) Where the appropriate consent to a drug offence search of any person was refused without good cause, in any proceedings against that person for an offence—

(a) the court, in determining whether there is a case to answer;

(b) a judge, in deciding whether to grant an application made by the accused under paragraph 2 of Schedule 3 to the Crime and Disorder Act 1998 (applications for dismissal); and

(c) the court or jury, in determining whether that person is guilty of the offence charged,

may draw such inferences from the refusal as appear proper.]

...

56 Right to have someone informed when arrested

(1) Where a person has been arrested and is being held in custody in a police station or other premises, he shall be entitled, if he so requests, to have one friend or relative or other person who is known to him or who is likely to take an interest in his welfare told, as soon as is practicable except to the extent that delay is permitted by this section, that he has been arrested and is being detained there.

(2) Delay is only permitted—

(a) in the case of a person who is in police detention for [an indictable offence]; and

(b) if an officer of at least the rank of [inspector] authorises it.

(3) In any case the person in custody must be permitted to exercise the right conferred by subsection (1) above within 36 hours from the relevant time, as defined in section 41(2) above.

(4) An officer may give an authorisation under subsection (2) above orally or in writing but, if he gives it orally, he shall confirm it in writing as soon as is practicable.

(5) [Subject to subsection (5A) below] an officer may only authorise delay where he has reasonable grounds for believing that telling the named person of the arrest—

    (a) will lead to interference with or harm to evidence connected with [an indictable offence] or interference with or physical injury to other persons; or

    (b) will lead to the alerting of other persons suspected of having committed such an offence but not yet arrested for it; or

    (c) will hinder the recovery of any property obtained as a result of such an offence.

[(5A) An officer may also authorise delay where he has reasonable grounds for believing that—

    (a) the person detained for [the indictable offence] has benefited from his criminal conduct, and

    (b) the recovery of the value of the property constituting the benefit will be hindered by telling the named person of the arrest.

(5B) For the purposes of subsection (5A) above the question whether a person has benefited from his criminal conduct is to be decided in accordance with Part 2 of the Proceeds of Crime Act 2002.]

(6) If a delay is authorised—

    (a) the detained person shall be told the reason for it; and

    (b) the reason shall be noted on his custody record.

(7) The duties imposed by subsection (6) above shall be performed as soon as is practicable.

(8) The rights conferred by this section on a person detained at a police station or other premises are exercisable whenever he is transferred from one place to another; and this section applies to each subsequent occasion on which they are exercisable as it applies to the first such occasion.

(9) There may be no further delay in permitting the exercise of the right conferred by subsection (1) above once the reason for authorising delay ceases to subsist.

[(10) Nothing in this section applies to a person arrested or detained under the terrorism provisions.]

58 Access to legal advice

(1) A person arrested and held in custody in a police station or other premises shall be entitled, if he so requests, to consult a solicitor privately at any time.

(2) Subject to subsection (3) below, a request under subsection (1) above and the time at which it was made shall be recorded in the custody record.

(3) Such a request need not be recorded in the custody record of a person who makes it at a time while he is at a court after being charged with an offence.

(4) If a person makes such a request, he must be permitted to consult a solicitor as soon as is practicable except to the extent that delay is permitted by this section.

(5) In any case he must be permitted to consult a solicitor within 36 hours from the relevant time, as defined in section 41(2) above.

(6) Delay in compliance with a request is only permitted—

    (a) in the case of a person who is in police detention for [an indictable offence]; and

    (b) if an officer of at least the rank of superintendent authorises it.

(7) An officer may give an authorisation under subsection (6) above orally or in writing but, if he gives it orally, he shall confirm it in writing as soon as is practicable.

(8) [Subject to subsection (8A) below] an officer may only authorise delay where he has reasonable grounds for believing that the exercise of the right conferred by subsection (1) above at the time when the person detained desires to exercise it—

(a) will lead to interference with or harm to evidence connected with [an indictable offence] or interference with or physical injury to other persons; or

(b) will lead to the alerting of other persons suspected of having committed such an offence but not yet arrested for it; or

(c) will hinder the recovery of any property obtained as a result of such an offence.

[(8A) An officer may also authorise delay where he has reasonable grounds for believing that—

(a) the person detained for [the indictable offence] has benefited from his criminal conduct, and

(b) the recovery of the value of the property constituting the benefit will be hindered by the exercise of the right conferred by subsection (1) above.

(8B) For the purposes of subsection (8A) above the question whether a person has benefited from his criminal conduct is to be decided in accordance with Part 2 of the Proceeds of Crime Act 2002.]

(9) If delay is authorised—

(a) the detained person shall be told the reason for it; and

(b) the reason shall be noted on his custody record.

(10) The duties imposed by subsection (9) above shall be performed as soon as is practicable.

(11) There may be no further delay in permitting the exercise of the right conferred by subsection (1) above once the reason for authorising delay ceases to subsist.

[(12) Nothing in this section applies to a person arrested or detained under the terrorism provisions.]

NOTES

1. Under Code C, where a person arrives at a police station under arrest, or is arrested there, the custody officer must tell him clearly of (1) his right to have someone informed of the arrest, (2) his right to consult privately with a solicitor, and the fact that independent legal advice is available free of charge, and (3) his right to consult the codes of practice. He must be given (1) a written notice setting out these rights, his right to a copy of the custody record, the terms of the caution (see below), and the arrangements for obtaining legal advice; and (2) an additional notice setting out his entitlements while in custody.[469] Special arrangements apply where the person appears to be deaf, or there is doubt about his hearing, or is juvenile, or is mentally handicapped or suffering from a mental disorder, or is blind or seriously visually handicapped or unable to read.[470] These normally require the involvement of an independent third party such as an interpreter, an approved social worker or an 'approved adult' as the case may be.

A person who attends a police station voluntarily may leave at will unless arrested. If it is decided that he should not be allowed to leave, then he must at once be arrested and brought before the custody officer. If a person is not arrested, but is cautioned, the officer who cautions him must also inform him that he is not under arrest, that he is not obliged to remain at the police station, but that if he remains he may obtain free and independent legal advice.[471]

The notes for guidance state that the right to consult the codes of practice does not entitle the person concerned to delay unreasonably any necessary investigative or administrative action while he does so; procedures requiring the provision of breath, blood or urine specimens under the Road Traffic Act 1998, or the taking of fingerprints, footwear impressions or

---

[469] Code C.3.1–3.2.   [470] Code C.3.12–C.3.20.   [471] Code C.3.21.

non-intimate samples need not be delayed.[472] Detailed rules govern the conditions of detention: for example, cells must be adequately heated, cleaned, ventilated and lit; bedding must
be of a reasonable standard and in a clean and sanitary condition; access to toilet and wash-
ing facilities must be provided; at least two light meals and one main meal must be offered in
any period of 24 hours; brief outdoor exercise must be offered daily if practicable;[473] detainees
should be visited every hour (every half hour if drunk).[474] Any complaints must be reported
to an officer of the rank of inspector or above not connected with the investigation.[475] There
are detailed provisions governing the medical treatment of person in custody.[476]

2. *Searches of detained persons.* A search may be carried out in any case where the custody
officer considers it necessary to enable him to perform his duty to ascertain everything the
arrestee has with him: s. 51(1), (6). Anything may be seized except that limiting conditions
attach to clothes and personal effects: s. 54(3), (4).

The custody officer is responsible for ascertaining and safeguarding a detained person's
property.[477] It is for the custody officer to determine whether a record should be made of the
property. Personal effects are defined as items which a person may lawfully need or use or
refer to while in detention, but not cash and other items of value.[478] The notes of guidance
state that s. 54(1) of PACE does not require *every* detained person to be searched, but requires
a search 'where it is clear that the custody officer will have continuing duties in relation to
that person or where that person's behaviour or offence made an inventory appropriate'.[479]
Does it?

Intimate and strip searches must be conducted in accordance with Annex A to Code C.
A strip search is a search involving the removal of more than outer clothing, and may take
place only if the custody officer considers it to be necessary to remove an article which the
detained person would not be allowed to keep.[480] Statistics must be kept of intimate searches
under s. 55 and published in the annual reports of chief officers of police (s. 55(15)).

3. *Statistics on intimate searches.*[481] In 1999/2000 there were 170 intimate searches, 2000/1 –
131; 2001/2 – 102; 2002/3 – 172; 2003/4 – 81; 2004/5 – 93. In 2004/5 of the 93 searches, 13
were carried out by a police officer, 12 in the presence of a suitably qualified person, and
68 by the suitably qualified person.[482] Strip searches are conducted in around 3 per cent of
cases.[483]

The Court of Appeal held that an intimate search required physical intrusion into the
orifice rather than visual inspection.[484] Do you agree?

4. *Right to have someone informed when arrested.* Such a right was first created by the
Criminal Law Act 1977, s. 62. On the meaning of 'held in custody' in ss. 56 and 58, see
R v Kerawalla[485] where it was held that this meant where an appropriate authority has

---

[472] Code C.3D, confirming *DPP v Billington* [1988] 1 All ER 435, criticised by D. Tucker [1990] Crim LR 177.
See also *DPP v Ward* [1999] RTR 11, DC 9: failure to supply a specimen under s. 8 of the Road Traffic Act cannot
be justified on the basis of a suspect request to take time reading Codes of Practice. See also *Whitley v DPP* (2004)
168 JP 350; and *Myles v DPP* [2004] 2 All ER 902.

[473] Code C.8.   [474] Code C9.3.   [475] Code C.9.2.
[476] Code C.9.5–9.14.   [477] Code C.4.4.   [478] Code C.4.3.
[479] Code C.4A.   [480] C, Annex A.10.

[481] *Arrests for Recorded Crime and the Operation of Certain Police Powers under PACE* (2005), op. cit., p. 16.

[482] Some data on those conducting searches was not available for 1999/2000. For a discussion of the ethical
issues for medical practitioners who perform intimate searches see J. Marston (1999) 163 JP 646.

[483] T. Bucke and D. Brown, *In police custody: police powers and suspects' rights under the revised PACE codes
of practice* (1997), p. 48.

[484] *R v Hughes* [1995] Crim LR 407.

[485] [1991] Crim LR 451, CA (Cr D).

authorised detention in custody in a police station. One-fifth of suspects exercise the right.[486]

Under Code C, if the friend etc., chosen cannot be contacted, the person who made the request may choose up to two alternatives; attempts beyond these may be allowed as a matter of discretion.[487] The person in custody may receive visits at the custody officer's discretion.[488] If a friend etc. makes inquiries about his whereabouts, the information must be given if he agrees and unless the right not to be held incommunicado can properly be delayed.[489] The person in custody should be supplied with writing materials on request, and allowed to speak on the telephone for a reasonable time to one person; a letter or call can be denied or delayed by an officer of the rank of inspector or above if he considers that they may result in either of the conditions in s. 56(5)(a) or (b).[490] The person must be informed that the letter, call or message (other than to a solicitor) may be read or listened to as appropriate and may be given in evidence; a telephone call may be terminated if abused; the costs can be at public expense at the discretion of the custody officer.[491]

5. *Right of access to legal advice.* Code C provides that all people in police detention must be informed that they may at any time consult and communicate privately, whether in person, in writing or on the telephone, with a solicitor and that independent legal advice is available free of charge from the duty solicitor.[492] The term 'solicitor' includes a solicitor with a current practising certificate or an accredited or probationary representative included in the list of representatives by the Legal Services Commission. A poster advertising the right to legal advice must be prominently displayed in the charging area of every police station.[493]

Where a person is permitted to consult a solicitor, who is available when the interview begins or is in progress, the solicitor must be allowed to be present at the interview.[494] The solicitor may only be required to leave if his conduct is such that the investigating officer is unable properly to put questions, and on the authority of an officer not below the rank of superintendent (if readily available), and otherwise an officer not below the rank of inspector who is not connected with the investigation.[495] A non-accredited or probationary representative is to be admitted to the police station to provide advice on behalf of a solicitor unless an officer of the rank of inspector or above considers that such a visit will hinder the investigation of crime and directs otherwise; that officer should consider whether the non-accredited or probationary representative's identity and status have been satisfactorily established, whether he is of suitable character to provide legal advice, and any other matters in any letter of authorisation sent by the solicitor, the solicitor and the detained person must be informed if access is refused.[496]

Note that it is not appropriate or lawful for a chief constable to place a blanket ban on a particular solicitor's representative from entering police stations to advise detainees. The chief constable is entitled to publish guidelines for officers to follow on such matters: *R (Thompson) v Chief Constable of Northumbria*.[497] The representative in question was a former police officer who had been dismissed following allegations of sexual misconduct.

---

[486] D. Brown, *PACE Ten Years On* (above), p. 3.   [487] Code C.5.1.
[488] Code C.5.4.   [489] Code C.5.5.   [490] Code C.5.6.
[491] Code C.5.7. See now *R(M) v MPC* (2001) 13 July, CA (Cr D) holding that failure to provide the accused with a room for private consultation did not breach Art. 6(3). Note also *PG and JH v UK* [2002] Crim LR 308, ECtHR finding a breach of Art. 8 where police cells were bugged.
[492] Code C.6.1.   [493] Code C.6.3.   [494] Code C.6.8.
[495] Code C.6.9, C.6.10.   [496] Code C.6.12A–6.14.
[497] [2001] EWCA Civ 321, CA (Civ D).

The notes for guidance state that the solicitor may seek to intervene in order to seek clarification or to challenge an improper question to his client or the manner in which it is put, or advise his client not to reply to particular questions, or if he wishes to give his client further legal advice. Paragraph C.6.9 only applies if the solicitor's approach or conduct prevents or unreasonably obstructs proper questions being put to the suspect or his response being recorded.[498]

On police eavesdropping see *R v Grant*,[499] where the police interfered with legally privileged conversations by conducting covert surveillance of the suspect's communications with his solicitor. The court held that this so seriously undermined the rule of law that the prosecution was stayed on grounds of abuse of process, even though there appeared to be no prejudicial material obtained as a result.

6. *Delaying legal advice.* This right can only be delayed in accordance with s. 58(8), and provided that the suspect 'has not yet been charged with an offence'[500] ('an' here means 'any' *R v Samuel*).[501] On the very strict interpretation of s. 58, see *R v Samuel*[502] in which it was noted that instances in which an officer could 'genuinely' believe that a solicitor *will*, if allowed to consult with a suspect, commit an offence will be rare. Inadvertent or unwitting conduct apart, the police officer must believe that a solicitor *would,* if allowed to consult the person in police detention, commit a criminal offence. The grounds put forward would have to be by reference to a specific solicitor.[503] Phillips and Brown[504] found no instance of this in their survey of 4,250 cases. No police officer must at any time do or say anything with the intention of dissuading a person in detention from obtaining legal advice.

The delay in providing legal advice is a very rare occurrence. In one research study, there was no such finding in a sample of 12,500 cases, and previous research has found the percentage of cases to be less than 1 per cent.[505] On ECHR guarantees of free legal representation, see Art. 6 and *Pakelli v FRG*.[506]

7. *Use of legal advice.* Phillips and Brown confirmed earlier research finding that those who might benefit most from legal advice 'often did not request it because they were anxious not to delay their time in custody or because they were told that they probably would not be charged'.[507] Requests for legal advice varied depending on the offence, and the station at which the suspect was held. In addition, 'significant predictors of demand for legal advice [included] ethnic[ity], employment status; previous convictions; condition on arrival at the station; and whether answering police bail'.[508] The use of unqualified legal advisers continues to present concern. Thirty-five per cent of cases where the suspect had requested his own solicitor involved unqualified advisers (prior to the Law Society's accreditation scheme). Are suspects now guaranteed prompt access to effective legal advice?

On occasion the advice received from the legal adviser has been so poor that the court has excluded evidence obtained from the suspect despite the legal advice. The advice must be so poor as to be tantamount to a denial of access to a lawyer: see, for example, a murder case which collapsed because of the poor legal advice, discussed in *Matter of a Solicitor and in the*

---

[498] Code C.6D.   [499] *R v Grant* [2005] EWCA Crim 1089.
[500] Code C, Annex B.A. (1).   [501] [1988] QB 615.   [502] Ibid.
[503] *R v Silcott, Braithwaite and Raghip* (1991) Times, 9 December, CA.
[504] Op. cit.   [505] T. Bucke and D. Brown, p. 23.
[506] (1983) 6 EHRR 1.
[507] Home Office Research and Statistics Paper 185 (1998), p. 59.
[508] Ibid, p. 62.

Matter of the Solicitors' Act 1974.[509] The ECtHR has emphasised the importance of prompt access to legal advice: *Imbroscia v Switzerland,*[510] *Murray v United Kingdom.*[511]

The right of access to a solicitor is backed by a statutory 24-hour duty solicitor scheme. Research on the operation of this arrangement indicated that there was a significant increase in the number of suspects seeking legal advice, although they still only constituted a minority; that a variety of ploys were used by the police to discourage exercise of the right; that only a small proportion of suspects had a lawyer with them during police interrogation; and that there might have been a rise in the number of suspects who refused to make admissions.[512] The report by Sanders et al. was critical of the quality of service provided by duty solicitors, with a high proportion relying on telephoned advice rather than attendance in person. Phillips and Brown confirm that telephone advice was still much more likely from a duty solicitor than a suspect's own.[513]

The improper denial of the right to legal advice is likely to lead to exclusion of a confession under s. 78: see *R v Samuel.*[514] The courts have not taken a particularly strict line on the exclusion of evidence for refusal or delay regarding legal advice. In *R v Walsh*[515] Saville J. said:

The main object of section 58 of the Act and indeed the Codes of Practice is to achieve fairness to an accused or suspected person so as, among other things, to preserve and protect his legal rights; but also fairness for the Crown and its officers so that again, among other things, there might be reduced the incidence or effectiveness of unfounded allegations of malpractice.[516]

The right is recognised as important under the Convention, but is not absolute. It is of 'paramount importance' when inferences from silence are in issue: *Murray v United Kingdom.*[517] See also *Condron v United Kingdom;*[518] *Magee v United Kingdom;*[519] *Averill v United Kingdom;*[520] *Brennan v United Kingdom.*[521]

8. *Fingerprints, photographs and body samples.*[522] PACE made separate provision for the taking of fingerprints (s. 61); impressions of footwear (s. 61A); intimate samples (s. 62); non-intimate samples (s. 63); and photographs (s. 64A). In recent years, the circumstances have grown considerably in which a person's *fingerprints* may be taken without consent. Previously this required the authorisation of an inspector but this was removed by the Criminal Justice Act 2003. Section 61(3) provides that the fingerprints of a person detained at a police station may be taken without consent if (a) he is detained in consequence of his arrest for a recordable offence (one carrying a penalty of imprisonment) and (b) he has not had his fingerprints taken in the course of the investigation of the offence by the police. SOCPA 2005 seeks to broaden the circumstances still further by providing that a constable may take fingerprints

---

[509] (1999) DC, unreported.   [510] (1993) 17 EHRR 444.   [511] (1996) 22 EHRR 29.

[512] See A. Sanders and R. Young, *Criminal Justice* (3rd edn, 2007), pp. 454–460 and for earlier accounts see S.H. Bailey and M. Gunn, *Smith and Bailey on the Modern English Legal System* (3rd edn, 1995), pp. 503–507, citing D. Brown, *Detention at the Police Station under the Police and Criminal Evidence Act 1984* (HORS 104, 1989), Chap. 3 and HORPU Bulletin 26:26; A. Sanders et al., *Advice and Assistance at Police Stations and the 24 Hour Duty Solicitor Scheme* (LCD, 1989) and A. Sanders and L. Bridges [1990] Crim LR 494; B.L. Irving and I.K. McKenzie, *Police Interrogation* (1989), pp. 53–59, 113–115, 157–164, 199–200.

[513] Home Office Research and Statistics Paper 185 (1998), p. 66.

[514] (1988) 87 Cr App R 232; see discussion of case under 'exclusion of evidence' below.

[515] (1990) 91 Cr App R 161, CA.   [516] Ibid., p. 163.

[517] (1996) 22 EHRR 29 at 67.   [518] (2001) 31 EHRR 1.   [519] (2001) 31 EHRR 35.

[520] (2001) 31 EHRR 36.   [521] (2002) 34 EHRR 18.

[522] PACE Code D Revised 2008. See Home Office, *Proposals for Revising Legislative Measures on Fingerprints, Footprints and DNA Samples* (1999); see also Parliamentary Joint Committee on Human Rights, First Report, Session 2000–01 HC 427, Part IV.

without consent if he reasonably suspects that the person is committing or attempting to commit an offence, or has committed or attempted to commit an offence; and (a) the name of the person is unknown to, and cannot be readily ascertained by, the constable or; (b) the constable has reasonable grounds for doubting whether the name provided is his real name.[523] Section 78(8) CJPA 2001 extended the definition of fingerprints to 'a record of the skin pattern and other physical characteristics or features of the fingers or palms', and s. 78(7) allowed for electronic fingerprinting. Section 78 also authorised fingerprints to be retaken from a person detained in consequence of his arrest for a recordable offence if the quality was poor or the originals are unusable etc. SOCPA also stipulates that before a person's fingerprints are taken he must be informed that they may be the subject of a speculative search against the police database.[524] Section 82 of CJPA 2001 removed the obligation to destroy fingerprints when the individual is found not guilty for the offence for which they were taken, or a decision is made not to prosecute. Fingerprints are now taken as a matter of routine. Should this be the case? The Anti-terrorism Crime and Security Act 2001 further amended PACE (s. 64A) to provide powers to photograph detainees without consent.

Non-intimate samples, which include (s. 65) samples of hair (other than pubic hair), nails, swabs from any part of the body including the mouth (but not body orifices), saliva, and impressions from the body (e.g. footprints) can be taken. The restrictions in PACE have been relaxed and, following the Criminal Justice Act 2003, s. 10, non-intimate samples can now be taken without consent from anyone arrested for a recordable offence. The authorisation of an inspector or above is required and force may be used. The definition of an 'intimate sample' was changed by the CJPOA 1994, s. 58. By comparison with the old definition, the reference to a dental impression was added, but mouth swabs switched to the non-intimate category,[525] thus potentially adding greater numbers to the DNA database.

Intimate samples may be taken if there is (a) the authority of an inspector (or above) *and* (b) there is consent in writing. Authorisation need not precede consent: *R v Butt*.[526] The authorising officer will often be of lower rank than the requesting officer. Does this compromise their independence? Under PACE, the authorising officer had to have reasonable grounds to suspect involvement in a serious arrestable offence; this was broadened significantly to *any* recordable offence by the Criminal Justice and Public Order Act 1994, s. 54 amending s. 62.

Suspects' consent cannot be overridden but they should be cautioned in accordance with Code D Note for Guidance 6D: 'You do not have to provide this sample/allow this swab or impression to be taken, but I must warn you that if you refuse without good cause, your refusal may harm your case if it comes to trial.'

An intimate sample other than a sample of urine may only be taken by a registered medical practitioner or health care professional. Home Office researchers found that intimate samples are taken 'very rarely'[527] with blood being the most common form of sample.

The use of intimate samples will not constitute a breach of any privilege against self-incrimination. As the ECtHR noted in *Saunders v United Kingdom*,[528] the right not to incriminate oneself does not extend to the use in criminal proceedings of material 'which may be obtained from the accused through the use of compulsory powers but which has an existence independent of the will of the suspect such as, *inter alia*, documents acquired

---

[523] As of September 2007 this section had not been brought into force.

[524] PACE, s. 61(7A)(a).

[525] The latter change was effected in Northern Ireland by the Criminal Justice Act 1988, Sch. 14; for criticism see M. Gelowitz [1989] Crim LR 198 and C. Walker and I. Cram [1990] Crim LR 479.

[526] [1999] Crim LR 414, CA (Cr D).   [527] T. Bucke and D. Brown, p. 46.

[528] (1997) 23 EHRR 313.

pursuant to a warrant, breath, blood and urine samples, and bodily tissues for the purpose of DNA testing'.[529] Might circumstances arise, however, where the taking of samples (particularly non-intimate) amounts to a disproportionate interference with the right to respect for private life?

9. *The National DNA Database.* The increasing range of circumstances in which information can be collected relating to intimate and non intimate samples and fingerprints has been the cause of some debate.[530] A result of this availability of information is that the UK has the largest DNA database in the world (per head of population).[531] DNA analysis is undoubtedly a powerful investigative tool. It can lead to the exoneration of the innocent and can provide probative evidence to ensure the guilty are convicted. The proposition of a National DNA Database might be seen as an attractive one. Its value in detecting and preventing serious crime helps to secure greater freedom for all. However, the very fact personal information can be taken and placed on a database where it might remain in perpetuity has a capacity to undermine individual freedoms. Firstly, one must question the over-representation of certain ethnic groups on the database. What circumstances should lead to someone appearing on the database? Should it be those convicted of serious offences? Any offences? Those merely suspected of offences? Secondly, there are a large number of children on the database which is potentially in breach of Art. 40 of the UN Charter on the Rights of the Child which requires that children be afforded special treatment in the legal system to protect them from stigma.[532] Should all children be placed on the database to ultimately bring about a comprehensive national database? Thirdly, there remain serious questions as to reliability and the manner in which scientific evidence is presented in court.[533] Inevitably, the procedural scheme that is adopted for the purposes of establishing a DNA database will be both over- or under-inclusive. It will be over-inclusive in the sense that it will result in the storage of DNA samples etc. taken from people who will never, or are unlikely to commit the type of offence in respect of which DNA analysis might be utilised; and it will be under-inclusive in that there may be offenders who will commit such offences, or are likely to do so, but who have not been required to provide a DNA sample under the scheme.[534] Was it the intention of Parliament that the DNA profiles of those who 'were free of any taint of suspicion' be *routinely* added to the database?

10. *The interrogation process.* Code C lays down detailed rules governing the conduct of interviews.[535] There are special requirements where an interpreter is needed (Code C.13). Phillips and Brown[536] found that an interpreter was required in 2 per cent of cases.[537] Particular difficulty has been caused by the issue of what constitutes an 'interview' for the purpose of determining whether the requirements of Code C apply.[538] The term was

---

[529] (1997) 23 EHRR 313 at para. 69.

[530] See, e.g., Science & Technology Committee, Seventh Report of Session 2004–05, *Forensic Science on Trial*, HC 96-I.

[531] The National DNA Database currently comprises over four million profiles: See Nuffield Council on Bioethics, *The Forensic Use of Bioinformation: ethical issues* (2007), para. 1.22.

[532] Further, see *R v RC* [2005] SCC 61.

[533] E.g., *R v Cannings* (2004) EWCA Crim 1. For a consideration of some of these issues see: *R v Chief Constable of South Yorkshire Police, ex p LS*; *R v Chief Constable of South Yorkshire Police, ex p Marper* [2004] UKHL 39, [2004] 4 All ER 193; C. McCartney, *Forensic Identification and Criminal Justice* (2006); A. Roberts and N. Taylor [2003] EHRLR 86.

[534] Even a comprehensive database, i.e. consisting of the entire population, might be under-inclusive. It would not, for example, contain the DNA profiles of those not domiciled in the UK but who might commit serious crime while residing temporarily.

[535] Code C.11, above, pp. 317–319, and C.12.

[536] Op. cit.   [537] Ibid., p. 56.

[538] See H. Fenwick [1993] Crim LR 174 and S. Field (1993) 13 LS 254.

not defined in the first version of Code C but a definition is now found in Code C.11.1A. The matter is of importance because the close regulation of the conduct of interviews in the police station, including tape-recording, provide an incentive to the police to seek to obtain admissions on the way to the station, perhaps by the use of inducements or threats, or to invent confessions. The RCCJ found it 'impossible to estimate the frequency of such practices'.[539] Research studies showed that questioning outside the police station still occurred in a significant proportion of cases (10 per cent in one study, 8 per cent in another). The RCCJ did not wish to rule out carefully researched and monitored progress towards the 'greater use of tape-recorders outside the police station'. Furthermore, on the RCCJ's recommendation, Code C has been amended to require at the beginning of an interview carried out at the police station 'significant statements or silence' which occurred before the interview to be put to the suspect.[540] Brown[541] concluded that 'little supervision or monitoring of interviews occurs . . . [and] some unregulated interviewing continues to occur outside the interview room'.

What may begin as a general inquiry may become an 'interview' (to which Code C applies) where answers to questions give rise to a suspicion that an offence has been committed. In *R v Blackford*,[542] the court noted that what amounts to grounds to suspect:

has troubled this Court on a number of previous occasions. It has been described as a singularly imprecise concept. (See *R v James* 8 March (1996) per Simon Brown LJ at transcript p. 18.) It may range from the country house murder as recorded in fiction where all twelve occupants have had opportunity and motive to the case where the suspect is caught knife in hand standing over the prostrate body of his victim. So it is not surprising that some attempt has been made to give it shape. In *R v Shah* (1994) CLR 125 Jowitt J giving the judgment of the court stated at p. 4E:

'First, it is to be seen that paragraph 10.1 sets out an objective test. There must be grounds of suspicion. Secondly it is not enough that the questioner is suspicious. He must have grounds for that suspicion. Grounds, obviously may fall well short of evidence which would support a prima facie case of guilt. Nonetheless, they must exist. A mere hunch or a sixth sense that something is not as it should be is not, in the view of this Court such as to provide the grounds for bringing the case within paragraph 10.1 of Code C. Moreover the grounds have to be such as to lead to suspicion, not simply that an offence has been committed, but committed by the person who is being questioned. It seems to this Court that, in any event, it was perfectly proper for Mr Campbell to ask the questions he did, and to which objection was taken, about the ownership of the briefcase. In our judgment, at that time when he asked those questions, Mr Campbell had no grounds for suspicion. Mr Campbell had no grounds to suspect that an offence had been committed by the appellant. Accordingly, there was no need for a caution and we agree with the learned judges ruling that the evidence should be admitted.'

James is binding upon this court. And, though he might not have known of it, it was also binding upon the trial judge. So it was legitimate for him to put the rhetorical question to the jury which he presumably put to himself. We paraphrase; without more would the grounds of suspicion in this case have justified the police officers in arresting the appellant and if not how can it be said that they were such as to bring C.10.1 into play?

It cannot be said, therefore, that the trial judge misdirected himself as to the proper approach. He reminded himself of the provisions of C10.1 and in particular of the need for the grounds of suspicion to have related to the appellant. He heard evidence. He reached certain findings of fact. Should this Court interfere? Although in James the matter was treated as one of discretion under section 78 of the 1984 Act

---

539 Ibid., pp. 27–28.   540 Code C.11.4.
541 *PACE Ten Years On* (1997), p. 30.   542 [2001] EWCA Civ 1479, CA (Cr D).

whereas we are considering a prior determination of fact, it seems to us that the same principles apply. This court should be slow to interfere with the findings of the tribunal of fact reached after hearing evidence and on consideration of the relevant principles of law. It should only do so if the conclusions reached are unreasonable. As much is implicit in the judgment of this court in *R v Nelson & Rose* (1998) 2 Cr App R 399, where the court felt able to make its own finding in a case where the trial judge had failed to reach one of his own.

In this situation, the Court of Appeal has suggested that a record should be made of the earlier questions and answers as soon as practicable, the reason for the absence of a contemporaneous note should be recorded and the suspect given the opportunity to check the record: *R v Park*.[543] The volunteering of information other than in response to questions is not an 'interview': *R v Menard*.[544] See also cases where confessions outside the police station have been excluded for breach of PACE requirements.[545]

Code C.12 applies to interviews in police stations. The custody officer is responsible for deciding whether to deliver a detained person into the custody of an interviewing officer. In any period of 24 hours, a detained person must normally be allowed eight hours rest free from questioning, travel or interruption arising out of the investigation. No person unfit through drink or drugs to the extent that he is unable to appreciate the significance of questions put to him and his answers may be questioned except in accordance with Annex G.[546] Note that Phillips and Brown[547] found that 10 per cent of suspects were suffering some degree of intoxication from alcohol; 4 per cent were too drunk to be dealt with on arrival at the station and 2 per cent were under the influence of drugs. Interview rooms must as far as practicable be adequately heated, lit and ventilated. Interviewing officers should identify themselves and other officers present. Provision is made for meal and refreshment breaks, complaints of breaches of the Code and documentation.[548]

Where an officer considers that there is sufficient evidence to produce a realistic prospect of conviction and that the person has said all he wished to say about the offence, he must without delay bring him before the custody officer, who is then responsible for considering whether he should be charged.[549] If he is detained in respect of more than one offence, it is permissible to delay until the conditions are satisfied in respect of all the offences.[550] When a detained person is charged with or informed that he may be prosecuted for an offence, he must be cautioned and, if charged, given a written notice with the particulars of the offence and other specified information.[551] Questions relating to an offence may not be put to a person after he has been charged with, or informed that he may be prosecuted for that offence:

- unless they are necessary for the purpose of preventing or minimising harm or loss to some other person or to the public or;
- for clearing up an ambiguity in a previous answer; or
- where it is in the interests of justice that the person should have put to him and have an opportunity to comment on information concerning the offence which has come to light since that time.[552]

The RCCJ recommended that questioning be permitted after charge provided the suspect is cautioned and has access to a solicitor.[553]

[543] (1994) 99 Cr App R 270, CA (Cr D). [544] [1995] 1 Cr App R 306, CA (Cr D).
[545] See the section on exclusion of evidence below. [546] C.12.1–C12.3.
[547] Op. cit., p. 51. [548] C.12.4–12.14. [549] Code C.16.1.
[550] Subject to Code C.11.6. [551] Code C.16.3. [552] Code C.16.5.
[553] Cm 2263, pp. 16–17.

Around 90 per cent of suspects are questioned only once.[554] Research studies since the introduction of PACE have consistently recorded that confession rates are around 55–60 per cent. Of those who confess, women are more likely (65 per cent) than men (55 per cent) and juveniles more likely (65 per cent) than adults (55 per cent) to do so. Of those who receive legal advice, 47 per cent make a confession compared to 66 per cent of those who do not receive legal advice.[555]

Rejecting the idea that verballing is perpetrated by rogue officers only McConville, Sanders and Leng claim[556] that 'police work is systematically geared to the construction of evidence: the creation of evidence in one way or another is not a deviant police act but a standard form of production'.

11. *Recording interviews.* All interviews by police officers at police stations with persons suspected of an indictable offence must be tape-recorded in accordance with the provisions of PACE Code E.[557] As a result, disputes over the contents of interviews at police stations should be rare.[558] The RCCJ unreservedly welcome[d] this advance'.[559] The main practical difficulties have arisen in respect of the preparation by the police of summaries (a 'written record of the interview'), originally required by PACE (Code E.5.3). The exercise is very time-consuming for the police; at the same time, research by John Baldwin found that in fewer than a third of the cases examined could the summaries be said to provide an accurate and succinct record of the interview.[560]

The Criminal Justice and Police Act 2001 made provision for the video-taping of interviews (s. 76, inserting s. 60A into PACE), and these are now governed by PACE Code F under regulations very similar to those governing tape-recordings. The RCCJ noted Baldwin's finding[561] that there were additional benefits to video over audio-taping in some 20 per cent of the cases studied, although showing such recordings to jurors and magistrates might have some prejudicial effect; for example symptoms of nervousness might be mistaken for symptoms of guilt; a powerful visual impact might distract from what was said. The video can only record what occurs in the room and when it is switched on. Are there advantages in being able to see the suspect give his account? Should interviews with key witnesses also be recorded?

12. *The use of interrogations.* The interrogation of persons in custody was originally discouraged by the judges, but came to be 'the principal interrogation strategy employed by the police'.[562] Confessions and incriminating statements have been found in some 60 per cent of cases where there is an interrogation and around 80 per cent of guilty pleas.[563] At the same time, the importance of confessions was probably overstated.[564] More recently, there has been growing recognition of the risk of false confessions.[565] Unreliable confessions, as a result of police pressure, mental instability or a combination of both, have been at the heart

---

554 T. Bucke and D. Brown, op. cit., p. 31.   555 Ibid., pp. 33–34.

556 *The Case for the Prosecution* (1991), pp. 83–87.

557 PACE Code E, Revised 2008.

558 On the use to be made of tapes at trial and by the jury on retirement see *R v Rampling* [1987] Crim LR 823 (CA) and *R v Hogan* [1997] 1 Cr App R 464.

559 Cm 2263, p. 39.

560 *Preparing the Record of Taped Interview*, RCCJ Study No. 2 (HMSO, 1992).

561 See RCCJ, Cm 2263, pp. 39–40; J. Baldwin, *Video Taping Police Interviews with Suspects: A National Evaluation*, Police Research Series Paper No. 1 (Home Office, 1992); HO Circular 6/93.

562 M. McConville et al., *The Case for the Prosecution* (1991), p. 56.

563 A. Sanders and R. Young, *Criminal Justice* (2007), p. 219.

564 See M. McConville and J. Baldwin, *Courts, Prosecution and Conviction* (1981), Chaps 7, 8.

565 See G. Gudjonsson, *The Psychology of Interrogations, Confessions and Testimony* (1992).

of many of the high profile miscarriage of justice cases.[566] Access to taped records of inter-views has demonstrated the very poor quality of much of the interviewing conducted by police officers.[567] In response:

the police service, on an official level at least, has been stressing of late that questioning a suspect is only part of the process of investigation—and a decreasingly important part.[568]

Home Office Circular 22/1992 laid down Principles for Investigative Interviewing, empha-sising, *inter alia,* the points that the role of interviewing should be to obtain accurate and reliable information in order to discover the truth about matters under police investigation, that interviewing should be approached with an open mind, that when questioning anyone a police officer must act fairly and that vulnerable people must be treated with particular consideration at all times. Home Office Circular 7/1993 announced the availability of a new national training package for basic interviewing skills. These developments were welcomed by the RCCJ.[569]

Notwithstanding the many concerns, the RCCJ (by majority) did not recommend intro-duction of a requirement that confessions be corroborated, but unanimously recommended that the judge should give a strong warning that great care is needed before convicting on the basis of a confession alone.[570]

13. *The 'right to silence'.* Code C provides that a person whom there are grounds to sus-pect of an offence must be cautioned before questions about it are put to him regarding his involvement or suspected involvement in that offence if his answers or silence may be given in evidence to a court in a prosecution (and not, for example, to establish his identity or his ownership of a vehicle or to search him in the exercise of a power of stop and search).[571] A person must be cautioned upon arrest for an offence unless it is practicable by reason of his condition or behaviour or he has already been cautioned under para. C.10.1.[572]

The caution was originally in the terms:

You do not have to say anything unless you wish to do so, but what you say might be given in evidence.

The 1984 Act did not seek to attenuate the accused's 'right to silence'. Proposals to this effect were made by the Criminal Law Revision Committee in its Eleventh Report,[573] but received much adverse criticism and were not implemented.[574] The RCCP noted that the right was not a right which the generality of suspects chose to exercise and recommended, by a majority, that the present law on the right of silence should not be altered.[575] In 1988, the Home Secretary announced (after a period of public debate in which widely divergent

---

[566] Walker in C. Walker and K. Starmer (eds), *Justice in Error* (1993), p. 14, citing the *Guildford Four, Birmingham Six, Judith Ward, Tottenham Three* and *Cardiff Three* cases; see also I. Dennis [1993] PL 291.

[567] See J. Baldwin, 'Police Interview Techniques' (1993) 33 Brit J Crim 325.

[568] Baldwin, op. cit., pp. 325–326.

[569] Cm 2263, pp. 11–14 (see T. Williamson, 'Reflections on Current Police Practice' in D. Morgan and G.M. Stephenson (eds), *Suspicion and Silence* (1994), Chap. 7, noting (at p. 111) that the principles of investi-gative interviewing were not yet widely understood).

[570] Cm 2263, pp. 63–68. See further R. Pattenden (1991) 107 LQR 317.

[571] Code C.10.1.   [572] Code C.10.3.

[573] *Evidence (General)* (Cmnd 4991, 1972).

[574] See e.g. M. Zander in P. Glazebrook (ed.), *Reshaping the Criminal Law* (1978), pp. 349–354.

[575] Report, pp. 80–91.

views were expressed) that the case for change was strong; he commissioned a report by a Working Group on the precise form the change should take. The Working Group reported in 1989 that the recommendations in the Eleventh Report should be implemented, with modifications.[576] The change was, however, postponed.[577] The position was changed in Northern Ireland in 1989. The RCCJ majority[578] expressed the view that adverse inferences should not be drawn from silence at the police station because of the risk that this might result in more convictions of the innocent: however, once the prosecution case was fully disclosed, defendants should be required to offer an answer to the charges made against them at the risk of adverse comment at trial on any new defence then disclosed or any departure from the defence which they previously disclosed. Apart from the latter change, the position as to silence at trial should continue.

The position was controversially rejected by the Government, and the Criminal Justice and Public Order Act 1994, ss. 34–39 extended the rules applying in Northern Ireland (with some modifications) to England and Wales. 'Such inferences as appear proper' may be drawn at various stages of the trial process by a court or jury (and in some circumstances, a judge) or a magistrates' court inquiring into the offence as examining justices in four situations. By s. 34(1), the first is:

where, in any proceedings against a person for an offence, evidence is given that the accused—

(*a*) at any time before he was charged with the offence, on being questioned under caution by a constable trying to discover whether or by whom the offence had been committed, failed to mention any fact relied on in his defence in those proceedings; or

(*b*) on being charged with the offence or officially informed that he might be prosecuted for it, failed to mention any such fact, being a fact which in the circumstances existing at the time the accused could reasonably have been expected to mention when so questioned, charged or informed, as the case may be.

The second is where a person arrested by a constable fails or refuses to account on request for objects, substances or marks on his person, in or on his clothing or footwear, or otherwise in his possession, or in any place in which he is at the time of his arrest; the arresting or investigating officer must reasonably believe that the object etc. may be attributable to the suspect's participation in the commission of an offence specified by the officer who must inform the suspect that he so believes (s. 36(1)). This applies to the condition of clothing or footwear as it applies to a substance or mark thereon (s. 36(3)). The constable must inform the suspect in ordinary language of the effect of the section should he fail or refuse to comply with the request (s. 35(4)). Similar provisions apply to an accused's failure or refusal to account for his presence at a place at or about the time the offence for which he was arrested is alleged to have been committed (s. 37). Finally, inferences may be drawn from the accused's failure to give evidence at trial on his refusal, without good cause, to answer any question (s. 35). These provisions were amended to ensure compliance with the ECHR.

[576] *Report of the Working Group on the Right of Silence* (Home Office, 1989).

[577] For powerful adverse criticism of the proposals, see A.A.S. Zuckerman [1989] Crim LR 855; J. Wood and A. Crawford, *The Right of Silence: The Case for Retention* (1989); S. Greer (1990) 53 MLR 709; and B. Irving and I. McKenzie (1990) 1 J Forensic Psychiatry 167. for arguments in favour of change, see G. Williams, 'The Right of Silence and the Mental Element' [1988] Crim LR 97.

[578] Cm 2263, pp. 49–56.

34 [(2A) where the accused was at an authorised place of detention at the time of the failure, subsections (1) and (2) above do not apply if he had not been allowed an opportunity to consult a solicitor prior to being questioned, charged, or informed as mentioned in subsection (1) above.]

36 [(4A) where the accused was at an authorised place of detention at the time of the failure or refusal, subsections (1) and (2) above do not apply if he had not been allowed an opportunity to consult a solicitor prior to the request being made.]

37 [(3A) where the accused was at an authorised place of detention at the time of the failure or refusal, subsections (1) and (2) above do not apply if he had not been allowed an opportunity to consult a solicitor prior to the request being made.]

38 [(2A) in each of the sections 34(2A), 36(4A) and 37(4A) 'authorised place of detention' means (a) a police station; or (b) any other place prescribed for the purposes by order made by the Secretary of State.]

In each of the sections, if the accused was at an authorised place of detention (i.e. police station or other designated place), the drawing of inferences is prohibited unless he has been allowed the opportunity to consult a legal adviser prior to the questioning/request for material.[579]

(I) THE CAUTION

Note that s. 34 only applies where a person is 'questioned under caution' or charged. Note also that 'interviews outside the police station are not normally permitted, to that extent restricting the operation of s. 34(1)(a) to interviews at the police station. Such interviews should be properly recorded; moreover, by that time the suspect should have had the opportunity to take legal advice.

The standard caution is: 'You do not have to say anything. But it may harm your defence if you do not mention when questioned something which you later rely on in court. Anything you do say may be given in evidence.'[580] Research suggests that the police and legal advisers doubt whether the majority of suspects understand the caution.[581] In fact, there is some suggestion that the caution is used as an intimidatory tactic by investigating officers, who repeat the terms of the caution to put pressure on suspects to speak.[582]

14. *Who stays silent.* Bucke et al.[583] found that since the Act, there was no significant rise in the proportion of suspects requesting legal advice. The figure remained stable at around 40 per cent.[584] The percentage of suspects exercising their right to silence has not altered dramatically since the Act. Before the Act, 10 per cent of suspects refused to answer all questions, 13 per cent refused to answer some, and 77 per cent answered all. Under the Act, 6 per cent refused to answer all questions, 10 per cent refused to answer some, and 84 per cent answered all.[585] Those who obtained legal advice were 'far more likely to refuse' all questions than those who had not.[586] More serious allegations were more likely to lead to silence as was a suspect having a previous record (13 per cent as opposed to 5 per cent). Of

---

[579] This is a response to the judgment in *Murray v UK* (below).

[580] Code C.10.5.

[581] T. Bucke, R. Street and B. Brown, *The Right to Silence: The Impact of the Criminal Justice and Public Order Act 1994* (2000), Chap. 1. See also T. Bucke and D. Brown, *In police custody: police powers and suspects' rights under the revised PACE codes of practice* (1997), Chap. 4.

[582] Ibid., p. 29.　　[583] Op. cit.　　[584] Op. cit., p. 21.　　[585] Op. cit., p. 31.

[586] Op. cit., p. 78.

those who received legal advice before the Act, 20 per cent refused to answer all questions, 19 per cent refused to answer some, and 61 per cent answered all. After the Act those figures are 13 per cent, 9 per cent and 78 per cent. For those who did not receive legal advice, the figures before the 1994 Act were: 3 per cent refused to answer all: 9 per cent refused to answer some; and 88 per cent answered all questions. After the Act, the figures are 2 per cent, 6 per cent, and 92 per cent.[587] The Act seems to have had the greatest impact on Black suspects far fewer of who now refuse to answer questions.

In view of the fact that the Act was aimed at preventing 'hardened' or professional criminals playing the system, there is some suggestion that it has been successful in meeting that aim. It is impossible to monitor whether the provisions have had an impact on case outcomes, since these depend on an infinite number of variables of the suspects' motivations and the many possible reasons for decisions by the trier of fact are not disclosed. Assumptions based on only those cases which are reported are unlikely to be reliable since such cases represent only the appeals on difficult points.

(II) SECTIONS 34–37 GENERALLY[588]

The provisions are to be read strictly as they restrict a right which is recognised to protect against injustice: see Lord Bingham CJ in *R v Bowden*,[589] and Maurice Kay J in *R v Nickolson*.[590]

The ECtHR has delivered a number of important judgments on the silence of the suspect. In *Funke v France*,[591] which involved the legitimacy of the French tax authorities' investigative powers, the Court, recognised:

the right of anyone charged with a criminal offence, within the autonomous meaning of the expression in Article 6, to remain silent and not to contribute to incriminating himself.

In construing the Northern Irish legislation on which the current English provisions are constructed, the ECHR held in *Murray v United Kingdom*[592] that drawing inferences:

is a matter to be determined in the light of all the circumstances of the case, having particular regard to the situations where inferences may be drawn, the weight to be attached to them by the national courts and their assessment of the evidence and the degree of compulsion inherent.[593]

In *Saunders v United Kingdom*,[594] the defendant had been convicted of offences in relation to the Guinness-Distillers takeover. His conviction rested in part on the answers he provided to questions under compulsion—i.e. where the failure to answer is itself an offence.

---

[587] Op. cit., p. 33.

[588] For academic comment on the implementation and operation of the sections, see P. Mirfield, *Silence Confessions and Improperly Obtained Evidence* (1998). See also I. Dennis (1995) 54 CLJ 342, [1995] Crim LR 4; S. Easton [1998] 2 Int J E & P; J. Jackson [1993] 44 NILQ 103; R. Pattenden [1995] Crim LR 602; R. Pattenden [1998] 2 Int J of E & P 141; D. Birch [1999] Crim LR 769. For a summary of the debate preceding enactment, see the Home Office Research Study, T. Bucke, R. Street and B. Brown, *The Right to Silence: The Impact of the Criminal Justice and Public Order Act 1994* (2000), Chap. 1.

[589] [1999] 2 Cr App R 176.   [590] [1999] Crim LR 61, CA.

[591] (1993) 16 EHRR 297.   [592] [1996] 22 EHRR 29.

[593] Para. 61. See above for the legislative changes resulting from the decision.

[594] (1997) 23 EHRR 313.

The European Court held that this constituted an infringement of the privilege against self-incrimination. The majority stated:

> the right not to incriminate oneself, in particular, presupposes that the prosecution in a criminal case seek to prove their case against the accused without resort to evidence obtained through means of coercion or oppression in defiance of the will of the accused. In this sense the right is closely linked to the presumption of innocence contained in article 6(2).

Once again, English law responded by introducing legislative amendments to the 1994 Act. However, in *IJL, GMR AKP v United Kingdom*,[595] the European Court refused to accept the argument that 'a legal requirement for an individual to give information demanded by an administrative body necessarily infringes Article 6 of the Convention'. The Court restricted the scope of the protection of the privilege against self-incrimination to cases where the inquiry is a criminal one by a prosecutorial body. This has been influential in the House of Lords' consideration of cases arising under the Human Rights Act 1998. In *R v Hertfordshire County Council, ex p Green Environmental Industries Ltd*[596] it was held that a notice to supply information under the Environmental Protection Act 1990, s. 71(2), was not a breach of Art. 6. This was an 'extra-judicial' inquiry, and s. 78 of PACE gave a discretion to exclude evidence which would therefore have ensured a fair trial.

(III) SECTION 34

The section applies to any suspect who has been cautioned, irrespective of whether an arrest has been made. The Court of Appeal provided guidance on the use of s. 34 in the case of *R v Argent*:[597]

> **Lord Bingham CJ:** What then are the formal conditions to be met before the jury may draw such an inference? In our judgment there are six such conditions. The first is that there must be proceedings against a person for an offence; that condition must necessarily be satisfied before section 34(2)(d) can bite. The second condition is that the alleged failure must occur before a defendant is charged. The third condition is that the alleged failure must occur during questioning under caution by a constable. The requirement that the questioning should be by a constable is not strictly a condition, as is evident from section 34(4). The fourth condition is that the constable's questioning must be directed to trying to discover whether or by whom the alleged offence had been committed. The fifth condition is that the alleged failure by the defendant must be to mention any fact relied on in his defence in those proceedings. That raises two questions of fact: first, is there some fact which the defendant has relied on in his defence; and second, did the defendant fail to mention it to the constable when he was being questioned in accordance with the section? Being questions of fact these questions are for the jury as the tribunal of fact to resolve. The sixth condition is that the appellant failed to mention a fact which in the circumstances existing at the time the accused could reasonably have been expected to mention when so questioned. The time referred to is the time of questioning, and account must be taken of all the relevant circumstances existing at that time. The courts should not construe the expression 'in the circumstances' restrictively: matters such as time of day, the defendant's age, experience, mental capacity, state of health, sobriety, tiredness, knowledge, personality and legal advice are all part of the relevant circumstances; and those are only examples of

---

[595] (2001) 33 EHRR 11, [2001] Crim LR 133.   [596] [2000] 2 WLR 373.

[597] [1997] 2 Cr App R 27. A failure to give an adequate warning could result in a conviction being quashed: *R v Gill* [2001] 1 Cr App R 11.

things which may be relevant. When reference is made to 'the accused' attention is directed not to some hypothetical, reasonable accused of ordinary phlegm and fortitude but to the actual accused with such qualities, apprehensions, knowledge and advice as he is shown to have had at the time. It is for the jury to decide whether the fact (or facts) which the defendant has relied on in his defence in the criminal trial, but which he had not mentioned when questioned under caution before charge by the constable investigating the alleged offence for which the defendant is being tried, is (or are) a fact (or facts) which in the circumstances as they actually existed the actual defendant could reasonably have been expected to mention.

The crucial questions are whether there is a 'fact' that is being relied on by the defence, and whether there are reasonable grounds for the silence. Lord Taylor CJ, in the debates in the House of Lords on the Criminal Justice and Public Order Bill 1994 stated that:

if a defendant maintains his silence from the first to last, and does not rely on any particular fact by way of defence but simply puts the prosecution to proof, then [s. 34] would not bite at all.[598]

In determining whether something relied on is a 'fact' for these purposes, the court applies a dictionary definition and this is not limited to events and acts: *R v Milford*.[599] More recently, in *R v Webber*,[600] Lord Bingham stated:

Since the object of s 34 is to bring the law back into line with common sense, we think it clear that 'fact' should be given a broad and not a narrow or pedantic meaning. The word covers any alleged fact which is in issue and is put forward as part of the defence case: if the defendant advances at trial any pure fact or exculpatory explanation or account which, if it were true, he could reasonably have been expected to advance earlier, s 34 is potentially applicable.

Defendants are not obliged to disclose responses to allegations until they have had adequate knowledge of the allegations. If the police do not put the allegations to the suspect in specific enough terms, his silence cannot found an inference under s. 34: *R v Bowers*;[601] cf. *R v Hussain*[602] (police do not have to disclose case prior to the interview). Similarly, it may be reasonable to fail to comment at the time of the interview if the case is a very complex one or the events occurred a long time ago: *R v Roble*.[603] Other factors that might provide a reasonable basis for a suspect's silence were referred to by Lord Bingham CJ in *R v Argent*.[604] These include the defendant's age and experience, his state of health and sobriety or tiredness, his personality and the legal advice he had been given and the wide range of circumstances existing at the time. Bucke et al. report that there is no reported 'miscarriage of justice' resulting from a vulnerable suspect losing his right to silence.[605]

The Court of Appeal held that if a legal adviser recommends silence, this does not in itself prevent an adverse inference from being drawn. Otherwise, the section could be very easily circumvented: *R v Condron and Condron*.[606] In that case the suspect was convicted of heroin dealing, and claimed that her silence during questioning was on the advice of her solicitor who believed her to be unfit owing to the heroin withdrawal symptoms. The Court of

---

[598] HL Debs, Vol. 55, col. 519.

[599] [2000] JPL 943, CA (Cr D). See also *R v Chenia* [2003] 2 Cr App R 83.

[600] [2004] UKHL 1.   [601] (1997) 163 JP 33.

[602] [1997] Crim LR 754, CA.   [603] [1997] Crim LR 449, CA.

[604] [1997] 2 Cr App R 27.   [605] *The Right to Silence—The Impact of the CJPOA (1994)* (2000).

[606] [1997] 1 Cr App R 185.

Appeal felt that the conviction was not unsafe given the amount of other evidence, and the fact that a medical examiner had declared her fit for interview. Stuart-Smith LJ suggested, *obiter,* that the jury could be directed to draw adverse inferences where they concluded that the failure was attributable to the suspect having later fabricated the evidence.[607] When the case was taken to Strasbourg, the ECtHR ruled that this was a breach of Art. 6 and that the applicant had been denied a fair trial:

The Court recalls that in its *John Murray* judgment it proceeded on the basis that the question whether the right to silence is an absolute right must be answered in the negative (pp. 49–50, § 47). It noted in that case that whether the drawing of adverse inferences from an accused's silence infringes Article 6 is a matter to be determined in the light of all the circumstances of the case, having regard to the situations where inferences may be drawn, the weight attached to them by the national courts in their assessment of the evidence and the degree of compulsion inherent in the situation (ibid. § 47). The Court stressed in the same judgment that since the right to silence, like the privilege against self-incrimination, lay at the heart of the notion of a fair procedure under Article 6, particular caution was required before a domestic court could invoke an accused's silence against him. Thus it observed that it would be incompatible with the right to silence to base a conviction solely or mainly on the accused's silence or on a refusal to answer questions or to give evidence himself. Nevertheless, the Court found that it is obvious that the right cannot and should not prevent that the accused's silence, in situations which clearly call for an explanation from him, be taken into account in assessing the persuasiveness of the evidence adduced by the prosecution (ibid. § 47).

58. The Court notes that the domestic law and practice of the respondent State attempts to strike an appropriate balance between the exercise by an accused of his right to silence during police interview and the drawing of an adverse inference from that fact at a jury trial.

59. It observes, in line with the Government' submissions, that the applicants were under no legal compulsion to co-operate with the police and could not be exposed to any penal sanction for their failure to do so. The police were required under domestic law to administer a clear warning to the applicants about the possible implications of withholding information which they might later rely on at their trial. The Court does not accept the applicants' argument that the caution was ambiguous or unclear as to the consequences of their refusal to answer police questions. Furthermore, the question whether the applicants were sufficiently lucid at the material time to comprehend the consequences of their silence, as opposed to their fitness for interview, is a separate consideration which must be examined from the standpoint of the trial judge's direction on this matter.

60. It must also be observed that the applicants' solicitor was present throughout the whole of their interviews and was able to advise them not to volunteer any answers to the questions put to them. The fact that an accused person who is questioned under caution is assured access to legal advice, and in the applicants' case the physical presence of a solicitor during police interview, must be considered a particularly important safeguard for dispelling any compulsion to speak which may be inherent in the terms of the caution. For the Court, particular caution is required when a domestic court seeks to attach weight to the fact that a person who is arrested in connection with a criminal offence and who has not been given access to a lawyer does not provide detailed responses when confronted with questions the answers to which may be incriminating (see the above-mentioned *John Murray* judgment,[608] p. 55, § 66). At the same time, the very fact that an accused is advised by his lawyer to maintain his silence must also be given appropriate weight by the domestic court. There may be good reason why such advice may be given.

---

[607] This was applied in *R v Daniel* [1998] 2 Cr App R 373, CA, to drawing an adverse inference where silence was attributable to an unwillingness to be subjected to additional questioning while in a vulnerable position.

[608] [2000] 31 EHRR 1, [2000] Crim LR 679.

The applicants in the instant case state that they held their silence on the strength of their solicitor's advice that they were unfit to answer questions. Their solicitor testified before the domestic court that his advice was motivated by his concern about their capacity to follow questions put to them during interview (see paragraph 18 above).

As with the issue of the applicants' lucidity at the time of interview, the question whether the trial judge gave sufficient weight to the applicants' reliance on legal advice to explain their silence at interview must equally be examined from the standpoint of his directions on this matter. The Court would observe at this juncture that the fact that the applicants were subjected to cross-examination on the content of their solicitor's advice cannot be said to raise an issue of fairness under Article 6 of the Convention. They were under no compulsion to disclose the advice given, other than the indirect compulsion to avoid the reason for their silence remaining at the level of a bare explanation. The applicants chose to make the content of their solicitor's advice a live issue as part of their defence. For that reason they cannot complain that the scheme of section 34 of the 1994 Act is such as to override the confidentiality of their discussions with their solicitor.

61. It is to be noted that the trial judge directed the jury on the issue of the applicants' silence in accordance with the terms of the relevant specimen direction at the time (see paragraph 32 above). The Court notes, however, that the formula employed by the trial judge cannot be said to reflect the balance which the Court in its *John Murray* judgment sought to strike between the right to silence and the circumstances in which an adverse inference may be drawn from silence, including by a jury. It reiterates that the Court stressed in that judgment that, provided appropriate safeguards were in place, an accused's silence, in situations which clearly call for an explanation, could be taken into account in assessing the persuasiveness of the evidence adduced by the prosecution against him (see paragraph 56 above). The Court further noted, with reference to Articles 4 and 6 of the Criminal Evidence (Northern Ireland) Order 1988, that those provisions only permitted a judge to draw common-sense inferences which he considered proper in the light of the evidence against the accused (ibid., p. 50, § 51). However, in the instant case the applicants put forward an explanation for their failure to mention during the police interview why certain items were exchanged between them and their co-accused, Mr Curtis (see paragraph 19 above). They testified that they acted on the strength of the advice of their solicitor who had grave doubts about their fitness to cope with police questioning (see paragraph 21 above). Their solicitor confirmed this in his testimony in the voir dire proceedings (see paragraph 18 above). Admittedly the trial judge drew the jury's attention to this explanation. However he did so in terms which left the jury at liberty to draw an adverse inference notwithstanding that it may have been satisfied as to the plausibility of the explanation. It is to be observed that the Court of Appeal found the terms of the trial judge's direction deficient in this respect (see paragraph 27 above). In the Court's opinion, as a matter of fairness, the jury should have been directed that it could only draw an adverse inference if satisfied that the applicants' silence at the police interview could only sensibly be attributed to their having no answer or none that would stand up to cross-examination.

62. Unlike the Court of Appeal, the Court considers that a direction to that effect was more than merely 'desirable' (see paragraph 27 above). It notes that the responsibility for deciding whether or not to draw such an inference rested with the jury. As the applicants have pointed out, it is impossible to ascertain what weight, if any, was given to the applicants' silence. In its *John Murray* judgment the Court noted that the trier of fact in that case was an experienced judge who was obliged to explain the reasons for his decision to draw inferences and the weight attached to them. Moreover, the exercise of the judge's discretion to do so was subject to review by the appellate courts (ibid., p. 51, § 51). However, these safeguards were absent in the instant case. It was thus even more compelling to ensure that the jury was properly advised on how to address the issue of the applicants' silence. It is true that the judge was under no obligation to leave the jury with the option of drawing an adverse inference from their silence and, left with that option, the jury had a discretion whether or not to do so. It is equally true that the burden of proof lay with

the prosecution to prove the applicants' guilt beyond reasonable doubt and the jury was informed that the applicants' silence could not 'on its own prove guilt' (see paragraph 22 above). However, notwithstanding the presence of these safeguards, the Court considers that the trial judge's omission to restrict even further the jury's discretion must be seen as incompatible with the exercise by the applicants of their right to silence at the police station.[609]

Prior to the ruling of the ECtHR in *Condron*, the recommended direction to a jury where a defendant relies on his legal adviser's recommendation for silence, was:

You should consider whether or not he is able to decide for himself what he should do or having asked for a solicitor to advise him he would not challenge that advice.[610]

In *R v Betts and Hall*[611] the Court of Appeal returned to the issue of silence following advice and determined that genuineness of the decision was the key. No adverse inference should be drawn if it was a plausible explanation that the reason for not mentioning facts when interviewed was that the defendant had acted on his solicitor's advice and not because he had had no satisfactory answer to give. *Hoare and Pierce*[612] provided a further twist, however. Here the defendant relied on legal advice to remain silent though he claimed he had wanted to explain himself. What was crucial to the court was not simply whether the suspect's reliance was genuine, but whether it was reasonable. This ambiguity in the authorities was addressed in *R v Beckles*,[613] wherein the Court of Appeal stated:

...in a case where a solicitor's advice is relied upon by the defendant, the ultimate question for the jury remains under s 34 whether the facts relied on at the trial were facts which the defendant could reasonably have been expected to mention at interview. If they were not, that is the end of the matter. If the jury consider that the defendant genuinely relied on the advice, that is not necessarily the end of the matter. It may still not have been reasonable for him to rely on the advice, or the advice may not have been the true explanation for his silence. In *R v Betts* [2001] 2 Cr App R 257 at [54], Kay LJ was particularly concerned with 'whether or not the advice was truly the reason for not mentioning the facts'. In the same paragraph he also says:

'A person, who is anxious not to answer questions because he has no or no adequate explanation to offer, gains no protection from his lawyer's advice because that advice is no more than a convenient way of disguising his true motivation for not mentioning facts.'

If, in the last situation, it is possible to say that the defendant genuinely acted upon the advice, the fact that he did so because it suited his purpose may mean he was not acting reasonably in not mentioning the facts. His reasonableness in not mentioning the facts remains to be determined by the jury. If they conclude he was acting unreasonably they can draw an adverse inference from the failure to mention the facts.

In order to establish genuineness and reasonableness the defendant may wish to give an explanation as to why his legal adviser advised silence (e.g., the police have not disclosed the case yet etc.). In doing so, this may be treated as waiving privilege if he goes beyond a simple explanation that he refused to answer on legal advice (*R v Wishart*),[614] and seeks to provide

---

609 *Condron v UK*, paras 56–62.
610 Per Lord Bingham in *Argent*, above, at 34.
611 [2001] 2 Cr App R 16.   612 [2004] 1 Cr App R 355.   613 [2005] 1 All ER 705.
614 [2005] EWCA Crim 1337; see also *R v Loizou* [2006] EWCA Crim 1719.

details of the advice (*R v Bowden*),[615] and there is unlikely to be a problem of inadmissibility of that as evidence on the grounds of hearsay: *R v Desmond;*[616] *R v Roble.*[617] Is it legitimate to hold the suspect's silence against him when he has acted in accordance with the advice of his legal representative? Is it desirable that solicitors should have to give evidence to explain why they made professional decisions?

Where a defendant produces a prepared statement in the interview but refuses to answer questions, the judge should compare the statement with the evidence that the defendant has given at trial to see if there is any fact relied upon that he did not mentioned in his prepared statement. If the statement and the evidence are wholly consistent then adverse inferences should not be drawn.[618]

Research has shown that one impact of the provisions has been to encourage legal advisers to ask for more information at the time of the interviews.[619] This leads to greater pressure on the investigator—the reverse of the intended impact of the provisions. However, this has also made the legal advisers task more difficult, since 'wrong' advice on silence could lead to serious consequences at trial. A number of legal advisers have raised concerns at the implications for lawyer/client privilege.[620]

The Criminal Justice and Public Order Act 1994 has placed more pressure on legal advisers and suspects in the already strained environment of the police station. It leads to more tactical games being played at the police station.

15. *What inferences can be drawn?* At trial the court is entitled to draw inferences from silence in deciding whether there is a case to answer (s. 34(2)(c)) but this may not be the sole basis for a finding of a case to answer (s. 38(3)): *R v D.*[621] In practice s. 34 will usually only bite once the defendant provides a defence at trial—i.e. after submissions of no case have been rejected. There is no rule that the inferences cannot be drawn where a defendant does not testify at trial, provided he has relied on a 'fact' etc.: *R v Bowers.*[622] The jury do not need to be told that there is a case to answer before they rely on the silence: *R v Doldur.*[623] The inferences can be drawn even where the facts relied on by the defence were raised before the trial proper: *R v Daniel;*[624] *R v Montague and Beckles.*[625] Research suggests that there is often reluctance in the legal profession when prosecuting to rely on the provisions at trial out of a sense of 'fairness to the accused', and a fear of creating sympathy with the jury.[626] The Court of Appeal has provided guidance[627] on the use of the adverse inferences at trial and approved a Judicial Studies Board specimen direction.[628]

A direction may be unnecessary where the fact relied on by the defendant is so crucial that, if it is rejected, there is no question but that he will be found guilty: *R v Mountford*[629] (defendant did not mention until trial that his companion was the drug dealer, not he). If no adverse inferences can be drawn the judge must direct the jury of that: *R v McGarry,*[630] otherwise they are left without guidance, and, as before the Act they were instructed against drawing such inferences, that should continue to be the case where the statute does

---

[615] [1999] 2 Cr App R 176.   [616] [1998] Crim LR 659, CA.   [617] [1997] Crim LR 449.
[618] *R v Knight* [2004] 1 WLR 340; see also *R v Turner* [2004] 1 All ER 1025.
[619] Bucke et al., p. 23.   [620] See Bucke et al., p. 51.   [621] [2000] Crim LR 178.
[622] (1999) 163 JP 33.   [623] [2000] Crim LR 178, CA.   [624] [1998] 2 Cr App R 73.
[625] [1999] Crim LR 148.   [626] T. Bucke et al., p. 48.
[627] *R v Petkar* [2004] 1 Cr App R 22; see also *R v Bresa* [2004] 1 All ER 1025.
[628] www.jsboard.co.uk.   [629] [1999] Crim LR 575.
[630] [1999] 1 Cr App R 377, CA.

not apply.[631] A misdirection in these circumstances does not necessarily lead to a conviction being unsafe: *R v Francom*.[632]

16. *The effectiveness of the provisions.* 'There are strong grounds for arguing that the provisions have led to greater efficiency in the investigative and prosecution process.'[633] In particular, the legal adviser is better able to advise his client because the police will have been compelled to disclose more of their case at an earlier stage. This leads to a more efficient decision-making process regarding charging. A benefit to the suspect is also that in more cases than before, the police are compelled to investigate the story provided by the suspect. This leads to the weeding out of weaker cases and encourages investigation of all lines of inquiry relating to the crime rather than the suspect *per se*. In addition, the provisions lead to greater certainty of conviction in cases where the evidence is already strong.[634] Bucke et al. conclude that: 'whatever philosophical standpoint is adopted, it seems clear that the change in the law has not led to undue practical disadvantages to the defendant'.[635] However, Birch has argued that the sections are too costly in terms of the number of appeals that they generate and the collateral issues they produce at trial.[636] If there are efficiency gains in the pre-trial procedure that affect thousands, is this worth the additional expense incurred in appellate court time for a few dozen cases? To what extent is the restriction of the right to silence about increasing efficiency in the criminal justice system?[637]

17. *Compulsory questions.* In *Saunders v United Kingdom*[638] the ECtHR ruled that incriminating answers obtained under compulsory questioning (i.e. where a failure to answer is itself an offence) should not be admissible. The Attorney-General subsequently published guidelines preventing the use of answers obtained in such circumstances being used at trial unless the defendant himself introduced the answers or the prosecution was for an offence of refusing to answer etc. These were placed on a statutory footing in the Youth Justice and Criminal Evidence Act 1999. Section 59 of and Sch. 3 to the 1999 Act apply these rules to those statutes in which compulsory questioning is provided for.[639] The supply of documents to the receiver (under compulsion) does not amount to self-incrimination contrary to Art. 6: *Attorney-General's Reference (No. 7 of 2000)*.[640] The courts will still have to deal with cases in which the compulsory questions give rise to other evidence of an incriminating nature. The use of evidence which is uncovered as a result of compulsory questioning is particularly difficult. If inferences from the failure to answer the compulsory questions are forbidden, and the answers made in the absence of adequate legal advice etc are to be excluded, can use be made of the material uncovered? Does it depend on whether the evidence existed prior to the interview? Is the reliability of the evidence the key issue?

(IV) SECTIONS 36 AND 37

These sections have attracted far less attention. The special warning that must be given under Code C: 10.10 is given in 39 per cent of cases in which a suspect has remained silent.[641] The warning must explain the offence that is being investigated, what the suspect is to account

---

[631] [1999] 1 Cr App R 377, CA.   [632] [2000] Crim LR 1018.   [633] T. Bucke et al., p. 70.

[634] See T. Bucke et al., pp. 70–73.   [635] Ibid., p. 73.   [636] [1999] Crim LR 769.

[637] The number of appeals in the first few years of the statute's life is likely to be higher.

[638] (1995) 23 EHRR 313.

[639] On *Saunders,* see S. Nash and M. Furse [1995] Crim LR 854. On the ECHR, implications for the 1994 provisions, see R. Munday [1996] Crim LR 370 and A. Ashworth [1999] Crim LR 261.

[640] [2001] Crim LR 736 and commentary.   [641] T. Bucke et al., p. 39.

for, the officer's belief that the fact may be due to the suspect's involvement in the offence, that a court may draw an inference from a refusal to account for the fact and that a record of the interview will be available as evidence. Research suggests that the warning is often not understood by the suspects.[642]

9. ADMISSIBILITY OF EVIDENCE

- Police and Criminal Evidence Act 1984

76. Confessions

(1) In any proceedings a confession made by an accused person may be given in evidence against him in so far as it is relevant to any matter in issue in the proceedings and is not excluded by the court in pursuance of this section.

(2) If, in any proceedings where the prosecution proposes to give in evidence a confession made by an accused person, it is represented to the court that the confession was or may have been obtained—

   (a) by oppression of the person who made it; or

   (b) in consequence of anything said or done which was likely, in the circumstances existing at the time, to render unreliable any confession which might be made by him in consequence thereof,

the court shall not allow the confession to be given in evidence against him except in so far as the prosecution proves to the court beyond reasonable doubt that the confession (notwithstanding that it may be true) was not obtained as aforesaid.

(3) In any proceedings where the prosecution proposes to give in evidence a confession made by an accused person, the court may of its own motion require the prosecution, as a condition of allowing it to do so, to prove that the confession was not obtained as mentioned in subsection (2) above.

(4) The fact that a confession is wholly or partly excluded in pursuance of this section shall not affect the admissibility in evidence—

   (a) of any facts discovered as a result of the confession; or

   (b) where the confession is relevant as showing that the accused speaks, writes or expresses himself in a particular way, of so much of the confession as is necessary to show that he does so.

(5) Evidence that a fact to which this subsection applies was discovered as a result of a statement made by an accused person shall not be admissible unless evidence of how it was discovered is given by him or on his behalf.

(6) Subsection (5) above applies—

   (a) to any fact discovered as a result of a confession which is wholly excluded in pursuance of this section; and

   (b) to any fact discovered as a result of a confession which is partly so excluded, if the fact is discovered as a result of the excluded part of the confession.

(7) Nothing in Part VII of this Act shall prejudice the admissibility of a confession made by an accused person.

(8) In this section 'oppression' includes torture, inhuman or degrading treatment, and the use or threat of violence (whether or not amounting to torture).

---

[642] Ibid., pp. 39–40.

(9) Where the proceedings mentioned in subsection (1) above are proceedings before a magistrates' court inquiring into an offence as examining justices this section shall have effect with the omission of—

    (a) in subsection (1) the words 'and is not excluded by the court in pursuance of this section', and

    (b) subsections (2) to (6) and (8).

76A. Confessions may be given in evidence for co-accused

(1) In any proceedings a confession made by an accused person may be given in evidence for another person charged in the same proceedings (a co-accused) in so far as it is relevant to any matter in issue in the proceedings and is not excluded by the court in pursuance of this section.

(2) If, in any proceedings where a co-accused proposes to give in evidence a confession made by an accused person, it is represented to the court that the confession was or may have been obtained—

    (a) by oppression of the person who made it; or

    (b) in consequence of anything said or done which was likely, in the circumstances existing at the time, to render unreliable any confession which might be made by him in consequence thereof,

the court shall not allow the confession to be given in evidence for the co-accused except in so far as it is proved to the court on the balance of probabilities that the confession (notwithstanding that it may be true) was not so obtained.

(3) Before allowing a confession made by an accused person to be given in evidence for a co-accused in any proceedings, the court may of its own motion require the fact that the confession was not obtained as mentioned in subsection (2) above to be proved in the proceedings on the balance of probabilities.

77. Confessions by mentally handicapped persons

(1) Without prejudice to the general duty of the court at a trial on indictment with a jury to direct the jury on any matter on which it appears to the court appropriate to do so, where at such a trial—

    (a) the case against the accused depends wholly or substantially on a confession by him; and

    (b) the court is satisfied—

        (i) that he is mentally handicapped; and

        (ii) that the confession was not made in the presence of an independent person,

the court shall warn the jury that there is special need for caution before convicting the accused in reliance on the confession, and shall explain that the need arises because of the circumstances mentioned in paragraphs (a) and (b) above.

(2) In any case where at the summary trial of a person for an offence it appears to the court that a warning under subsection (1) above would be required if the trial were on indictment with a jury, the court shall treat the case as one in which there is a special need for caution before convicting the accused on his confession.

(2A) In any case where at the trial on indictment without a jury of a person for an offence it appears to the court that a warning under subsection (1) above would be required if the trial were with a jury, the court shall treat the case as one in which there is a special need for caution before convicting the accused on his confession.

(3) In this section—

    'independent person' does not include a police officer or a person employed for, or engaged on, police purposes;

'mentally handicapped,' in relation to a person, means that he is in a state of arrested or incomplete development of mind which includes significant impairment of intelligence and social functioning; and

'police purposes' has the meaning assigned to it by section 101(2) of the Police Act 1996.

78. Exclusion of unfair evidence

(1) In any proceedings the court may refuse to allow evidence on which the prosecution proposes to rely to be given if it appears to the court that, having regard to all the circumstances, including the circumstances in which the evidence was obtained, the admission of the evidence would have such an adverse effect on the fairness of the proceedings that the court ought not to admit it.

(2) Nothing in this section shall prejudice any rule of law requiring a court to exclude evidence.

(3) This section shall not apply in the case of proceedings before a magistrates' court inquiring into an offence as examining justices.

82. Part VIII—Interpretation

(1) In this Part of this Act—

'confession' includes any statement wholly or partly adverse to the person who made it, whether to a person in authority or not and whether made in words or otherwise;...

(2) Nothing in this Part of this Act shall prejudice any power of a court to exclude evidence (whether by preventing questions from being put or otherwise) at its discretion.

NOTES

1. *Principles underlying the exclusion of admissible evidence.* Commentators have identified a number of principles that might underlie the existence of a discretion, exercisable by the judge at a criminal trial, to exclude evidence that would otherwise, according to the law of evidence, be admissible. To an extent some of these principles overlap.

Such a discretion might exist:

(a) to ensure that evidence that is unreliable, although technically admissible, is not placed before a jury: the 'reliability' principle;

(b) to deter the police or other law enforcement agencies from obtaining evidence by illegal or improper means or to 'punish' them for so acting: the 'disciplinary' principle;

(c) to protect the rights of citizens to be treated in accordance with the standards prescribed by law for the conduct of criminal investigations: the 'protective' principle.[643] This can be seen as a corollary of (b);

(d) to protect an accused person from being compelled to incriminate himself: the 'privilege against self-incrimination' principle (this can be regarded as an example of (c));

(e) to uphold the right of a person to be treated fairly: the 'fairness' principle, which may simply be a general principle underlying (*inter alia*) principles (a), (c) and (d) or may operate more narrowly to ensure simply that the trial proceedings are conducted 'fairly'.

(f) to preserve the moral authority of the verdict.[644]

---

[643] See A. Ashworth [1977] Crim LR 723.
[644] See I. Dennis (1989) CLP 21 and see I. Dennis, *The Law of Evidence* (1999).

English common law has tended to confine the discretion so as to reflect only the reliability principle and the need to protect the right against self-incrimination, although there have been some statements that support the 'fairness' principle. There are many judicial statements to the effect that the court should not exclude evidence under PACE as a mark of disapproval for the way in which it was obtained.[645]

2. *Admissibility of physical evidence at common law.* In *Kuruma v R*[646] the Privy Council held that relevant evidence was admissible however it was obtained except that in a criminal trial the judge had a discretion to disallow evidence if the strict rules of admissibility:

would operate unfairly against an accused...If, for instance, some...piece of evidence, e.g. a document, had been obtained from a defendant by a trick, no doubt the judge might properly rule it out.[647]

In *R v Sang*[648] the House of Lords took a restrictive view of this discretion. The House held unanimously that there was no discretion to exclude evidence merely on the basis that it was given by an *agent provacateur*. Indeed, Lord Diplock and Viscount Dilhorne indicated that apart from the well-established discretion to exclude evidence on the ground that its prejudicial effect outweighs its probative value, a discretion existed only 'with regard to admissions and confessions and generally with regard to evidence obtained from the accused after commission of the offence'.[649] The essential purpose underlying the discretion was to ensure that an accused was not induced to incriminate himself by deception.[650]

The common law discretion to exclude extends only to prosecution evidence: *Lobban v R.*[651]

3. *Admissibility of confessions at common law.* At common law a person's confession was admissible provided the prosecution showed to the satisfaction of the judge that it had 'not been obtained from him either by fear of prejudice or hope of advantage exercised or held out by a person in authority'.[652] The decision in *DPP v Ping Lin*[653] made it clear that there had to be a casual link between the 'fear' or 'hope' and the confession for the confession to be excluded, and that the whole issue of 'voluntariness' was essentially one of fact that was not to be treated 'legalistically'.

At the same time, there were frequent assertions by judges of a residual *discretion* to exclude confessions. There was, however, much confusion over the permissible grounds for such exclusion, the cases referring to such matters as oppression (which in truth was not a matter of discretion at all), the use of a trick, unfairness or just breaches of the Judge's Rules.[654] Where the case is before the court although the events occurred before PACE was in force, as with appeals referred by the Criminal Case Review Commission, the court can have regard to the provisions of PACE: *R v Bentley.*[655]

4. *Confessions under PACE.* The interrogation process is now regulated by ss. 56–60 and 76–78 of the 1984 Act and PACE Code C. The admissibility of the other evidence obtained

---

[645] See, e.g., *R v Chalkey and Jeffries* [1998] QB 848.

[646] [1955] AC 197.   [647] Per Lord Goddard CJ at 204.

[648] [1980] AC 402.   [649] [1980] AC at 437 at 442.   [650] See Lord Diplock at 436.

[651] [1995] 1 WLR 877, PC (no discretion to exclude parts of confession as one co-accused which he relies on although they incriminate a co-accused).

[652] Per Lord Sumner in *Ibrahim v R* [1914] AC 599 at 609.

[653] [1976] AC 574, HL.

[654] On the admissibility of confessions at common law see R. Pattenden, op. cit., pp. 274–281; C.R. Williams, 'Judicial discretion in relation to confessions' (1983) 3 OJLS 222.

[655] [1999] Crim LR 330, CA.

improperly is governed by s. 78, though confession evidence can also be excluded under s.78 (and indeed this is more often the case). In the interpretation of these sections it must be remembered that PACE is a codifying Act and the proper course is to look to the words of the statute and not how the law previously stood: *R v Fulling* (see below); *R v Smurthwaite and Gill*.[656] See also *Thompson v R*[657] on the relationship between the common law power to include confessions and that contained in PACE.

5. Section 82(1) states that a 'confession' includes any statement wholly or partly adverse to the person who made it. In *R v Hasan*[658] *sub nom R v Z* the House of Lords held that this would not include a wholly exculpatory statement. However, a non-verbal action, such as a nod of the head, can amount to a confession, as can a re-enactment: *Li Shu-Ling v R*.[659]

6. Section 76(1) states that a confession made by an accused person may be given in evidence 'against him'. In *R v Hayter*,[660] A, through a middleman B, took out a contract with C to murder his (A's) wife. The prosecution evidence against C consisted of statements of admission made to his girlfriend which also implicated both A and B. The middleman, B, was charged with murder but the case against him depended upon it being established that A was the contractor and C the killer. The trial judge rightly directed the jury that C's confession could not be used in evidence against B. However, the judge further stated that if the jury found C guilty on the basis of his admissions then they could consider the guilt of C in determining the guilt of B. The House of Lords, by a 3 to 2 majority, agreed. The majority held that there was a difference between using the confession against B and using it as a fact in building up the case against him. Do you agree? Is this decision compatible with the wording of s. 76(1)?

7. *Grounds for exclusion.*

- **R v Fulling** [1987] QB 426, [1987] 2 All ER 65, [1987] 2 WLR 923 (pet dis), [1987] 1 WLR 1196, HL, Court of Appeal (Criminal Division)

F claimed over £5,000 from an insurance company in respect of a burglary at her flat. An informant subsequently told the police that the burglary was bogus, and had been instigated by one Drewery, with whom F had been living and with whom she was infatuated. F was arrested and interviewed. She initially said nothing, but eventually confessed. At her trial for obtaining property by deception, she argued that the confession was or might have been obtained by oppression. She claimed that during a break in an interview, one of the police officers told her that Drewery, her lover, had for the last three years or so been having an affair with a Christine Judge, who had also been arrested in the light of the informant's disclosures and was occupying the next cell. This so distressed her that 'she just couldn't stand being in the cells any longer', and so she agreed to make a statement. The trial judge assumed, without deciding, that her claims were true, but ruled that the confession was admissible. The Court of Appeal dismissed her appeal.

Lord Lane CJ delivered the judgment of the court (*Lord Lane CJ, Taylor* and *Henry JJ*): The material part of the [trial judge's] ruling runs:

'Bearing in mind that whatever happens to a person who is arrested and questioned is by its very nature oppressive, I am quite satisfied that in section 76(2)(*a*) of the Police and Criminal Evidence Act, the word

---

[656] [1994] 1 All ER 898.   [657] [1998] AC 811, PC.
[658] (2005) 2 Cr App R 22.   [659] (1989) 1 AC 270.
[660] [2006] UKHL 6.

oppression means something above and beyond that which in inherently oppressive in police custody and must import some impropriety, some oppression actively applied in an improper manner by police. I do not find that what was done in this case can be so defined and, in those circumstances, I am satisfied that oppression cannot be made out on the evidence I have head in the context required by the statutory provision. I go on to add simply this, that I have not addressed my mind as to whether or not I believe the police or the defendant on this issue because my ruling is based exclusively upon the basis that, even if I wholly believed the defendant, I do not regard oppression as having been made out. In those circumstances, her confession—if that is the proper term for it—the interview in which she confessed, I rule to be admissible.'

Mr. Davey has drawn our attention to a number of authorities on the meaning of 'oppression'. Sachs L.J. in *R v Priestly (Note)* (1965) 51 Cr App R 1 said, at pp. 1, 2–3:

'to my mind [oppression] in the context of the principles under consideration imports something which tends to sap, and has sapped, that free will which must exist before a confession is voluntary…the courts are not concerned with ascertaining the precise motive of a particular statement. The question before them is whether the prosecution have shown the statement to be voluntary, whatever the motive may be, and that is always the point to which all arguments must return. To solve it, the court has to look to the questions which I have already mentioned. First, was there in fact something which could properly by styled or might well be oppression? Secondly, did whatever happened in the way of oppression or likely oppression induce the statement in question?'

R v Prager [1972] 1 WLR 260, was another decision on note (*e*) to the Judges' Rules 1964, which required that a statement by the defendant before being admitted in evidence must be proved to be 'voluntary' in the sense that it has not been obtained by fear or prejudice or hope of advantage or being oppressed. Edmund Davies LJ, who delivered the judgment of the court, said, at p. 266:

'As we have already indicated, the criticism directed in the present case against the police is that their interrogation constituted "oppression". This word appeared for the first time in the Judge's Rules 1964, and it closely followed the observation of Lord Parker CJ in *Callis v Gunn* [1964] 1 QB 495, 501, condemning confessions obtained in an oppressive manner.'

In an address to the Bentham Club in 1968, Lord MacDermott described 'oppressive questioning' as 'questioning which by its nature, duration, or other attendant circumstances (including the fact of custody) excites hopes (such as the hope of release) or fears, or so affects the mind of the subject that his will crumbles and he speaks when otherwise he would have stayed silent'. We adopt these definitions or descriptions…

DPP v Ping Lin [1976] AC 574, was again a case in which the question was whether a statement by the defendant was shown to be voluntary. It was held that a trial judge faced by the problem should approach the task in a common sense way and should ask himself whether the prosecution had proved that the contested statement was voluntary in the sense that it was not obtained by fear of prejudice or hope of advantage excited or held out by a person in authority. Lord Wilberforce, Lord Morris or Borth-y-Gest and Lord Hailsham of St. Marylebone expressed the opinion that

'it is not necessary, before a statement is held to be inadmissible because not shown to have been voluntary, that it should be thought or held that there was impropriety in the conduct of the person to whom the statement was made.'

What has to be considered is whether a statement is shown to have been voluntarily rather than one brought about in one of the ways referred to.

Finally Mr. Davey referred us to a judgment of this court in *R v Rennie* [1982] 1 WLR 64. Mr Davey submits to us that on the strength of those decisions the basis of the judge's ruling was wrong, in particular when he held that the word 'oppression' means something above and beyond that which is inherently oppressive in police custody and must import some impropriety, some oppression actively applied in an improper manner by the police. It is submitted that that flies in the face of the opinions of their Lordships in *DPP v Ping Ling* [1976] AC 574.

The point is one of statutory construction. The wording of the Act of 1984 does not follow the wording of earlier rules or decisions, nor is it expressed to be a consolidating Act, nor yet to be declaratory of the common law ...

It is a codifying Act, and there the principles set out in *Bank of England v Vagliano Bros* [1891] AC 107, 144 apply. Lord Herschell, having pointed out that the Bills of Exchange Act 1882 which was under consideration was intended to be a codifying Act, said, at pp. 144–145:

'I don't think the proper cause is in the first instance to examine the language of the statute and to ask what is its natural meaning, uninfluenced by any considerations derived from the previous state of the law, and not to start with inquiring how the law previously stood, and then, assuming that it was probably intended to leave it unaltered, to see if the words of the enactment will bear an interpretation in conformity with this view. If a statute, intended to embody in a code a particular branch of the law, is to be treated in this fashion, it appears tome that its utility will be almost entirely destroyed, and the very object with which it was enacted will be frustrated. The purpose of such a statute surely was that on any point specifically dealt with by it, the law should be ascertained by interpreting the language used instead of, as before, by roaming over a vast number of authorities in order to discover what the law was, extracting it by a minute critical examination of the prior decisions, dependant upon a knowledge of the exact effect even of an obsolete proceeding such as a demurrer to evidence' ...

Section 76(2) of the Act of 1984 distinguishes between two different ways in which a confession may be rendered inadmissible: (a) where it has been obtained by oppression; (b) where it has been made in consequence of anything said or done which was likely in the circumstances to render unreliable any confession which might be made by the defendant in consequence thereof. Paragraph (b) is wider than the old formulation, namely that the confession must be shown to be voluntary in the sense that it was not obtained by fear of prejudice or hope of advantage, executed or held out by a person in authority. It is wide enough to cover some of the circumstances which under the earlier rule were embraced by what seems to us to be the artificially wide definition of oppression approved in *R v Prager* [1972] 1 WLR 360.

This in turn leads us to believe that 'oppression' in section 76(2)(*a*) should be given its ordinary dictionary meaning. The *Oxford English Dictionary* as its third definition of the word runs as follows; 'Exercise of authority of power in a burdensome, harsh, or wrongful manner; unjust or cruel treatment of subjects, inferiors, etc.; the imposition of unreasonable or unjust burdens.' One of the questions given under that paragraph runs as follows: 'there is not a word in our language which expresses more detestable wickedness than oppression.'

We find it hard to envisage any circumstances in which such oppression would not entail some impropriety on the part of the interrogator. We do not think that the judge was wrong in using that test. What, however, is abundantly clear is that a confession may be invalidated under section 76(2)(*b*) where there is no suspicion of impropriety. No reliance was placed on the words of section 76(2)(*b*) either before the judge at trial or before this court. Even if there had been such reliance, we do not consider that the policeman's remark was likely to make unreliable any confession of the appellant's own criminal activities, and she expressly exonerated—or tried to exonerate—her unfaithful lover.

In those circumstances, in the judgment of this court, the judge was correct to reject the submission made to him under section 76 of the Act of 1984. The appeal is accordingly denied.

Appeal dismissed.

NOTES

1. The partial definition in s. 76(8) was not mentioned. Might that have made a difference? To date, there are very few decisions in which a confession has been excluded on this ground.

Breaches of the law or codes will not necessarily constitute oppression: *R v Parker*.[661] In *R v Hughes*,[662] through a misunderstanding, D did not see the duty solicitor; it was held that in the absence of police misconduct, there was no oppression. In *R v Emmerson*,[663] it was held that the use by a police officer of a raised voice and bad language, expressing impatience and irritation, for a short time during an otherwise low-key interview, did not amount to oppression.[664] Note that it is for the prosecution to prove that the confession was not obtained by oppression or in circumstances of unreliability. The standard of proof is beyond reasonable doubt.

The most notorious case where oppression has been found is *R v Paris, Abdullahi and Miller*,[665] where the Court of Appeal (Criminal Division) quashed the convictions of the three appellants for murder. M was interviewed for some 13 hours. Having denied involvement well over 300 times, he was finally persuaded to make admissions. Lord Taylor CJ stated[666] that each member of the court had been 'horrified' by what they had heard in the tape-recording of one interview.

Miller was bullied and hectored. The officers...were not questioning him so much as shouting at him what they wanted him to say. Short of physical violence, it is hard to conceive of a more hostile and intimidating approach by officers to a suspect.

Moreover, M's solicitor:

appears to have been gravely at fault for sitting passively through this travesty of an interview.[667]

The court concluded that the tenor and length of all the interviews would have been oppressive and the confessions obtained unreliable even with a suspect of normal mental capacity; in fact there was evidence that M was on the border of mental handicap. The convictions of P and A were quashed as the jury might have been prejudiced by the evidence of M's interviews.

It was stressed in *Paris*[668] that 'it is perfectly legitimate for officers to pursue their interrogation of a suspect with a view to eliciting his account or gaining admissions. They are not required to give up after the first denial or even after a number of denials'. The distinction between oppressive and non-oppressive conduct is a matter of degree.[669] Article 3 of the European Convention prohibits the use of torture and inhuman or degrading treatment or punishment. Clearly this overlaps with s. 76(8) and therefore s. 76(2)(a).

2. The 'unreliability' hurdle has been invoked more frequently than the 'oppression' hurdle. 'The word "unreliable"...means "cannot be relied upon as being the truth".'[670] Moreover, the question is whether *any* confession which the accused might make in consequence of anything said or done was likely to be rendered unreliable, not whether the confession

---

[661] [1995] Crim LR 233, CA.   [662] [1988] Crim LR 545, CA (Cr D).

[663] (1990) 92 Cr App R 284, CA (Cr D).

[664] See also *R v Heaton* [1993] Crim LR 593, CA (Cr D) and *R v L* [1994] Crim LR 839, CA (Cr D) (pressure applied in interview did not cross the threshold of what was acceptable); *R v Paris* (below) distinguished.

[665] (1992) 97 Cr App R 99 (The 'Cardiff Three').

[666] At 103.   [667] P. 104.   [668] Per Lord Taylor CJ at 104.

[669] Cf. *R v Emmerson* and *R v Heaton*, above.

[670] Per Stuart-Smith LJ in *R v Crampton* (1990) 92 Cr App R 369 at 372.

made was unreliable.[671] The thing 'said or done' must be by someone other than the accused himself.[672]

In *R v Walker*,[673] W claimed to have been under the influence of crack cocaine at the time of the interview, having smuggled it into the station to take. Psychiatric evidence demonstrated that she suffered from a personality disorder that could render her admissions unreliable, and that this was exacerbated by her drug-taking. The judge rejected the evidence of the psychiatrist and of her having taken drugs. The Court of Appeal held that the conviction should be quashed: the judge had failed to recognise that the 'anything said or done' need not be done or said by the police. The drug taking was a relevant consideration. Cf. *R v Goldenberg*.[674]

3. Breaches of Code C may make it more likely that a confession may be excluded under s. 76(2)(b): see, for example, *R v Doolan*.[675]

4. Where an interview is improperly conducted this may lead to the exclusion as 'tainted' of subsequent interviews even though they are conducted according to the rules: see, for example, *R v Ismail*;[676] *R v McGovern*;[677] *R v Glaves*;[678] *R v Neil*;[679] *R v Conway*.[680] This is a question of fact and degree: *R v Neil*.[681] The extent to which the factors which led to the exclusion of the first interview impact on the others will be a crucial factor, as will the extent to which the suspect had an opportunity to exercise informed and independent choice regarding the subsequent interview: *R v Nelson and Rose*.[682] The opportunity to seek legal advice before the subsequent interview is also very important: see *Prouse v DPP*.[683]

5. *Use of confession by co-accused.* As stated above, a confession by A cannot be used in evidence against B. However, B will be able to use a confession by A in his own defence if the confession has been admitted in evidence against A. Where the confession evidence was not adduced in the case of A this presented problems for an accused in B's position. The Criminal Justice Act 2003 sought to resolve the issue by inserting s. 76A into PACE. This section virtually replicates s. 76 save that when the co-accused seeks to adduce the evidence in court he must prove the necessary conditions (that s. 76(2) (a) and (b) do not apply) to the civil standard (balance of probabilities) whereas the prosecution must satisfy the criminal standard (beyond reasonable doubt). This might lead to a scenario where A's confession cannot be used by the prosecution but could be used by B in his defence.

6. *Protection for vulnerable suspects.* The interests of mentally handicapped defendants are also subject to the limited protection afforded by s. 77 of PACE,[684] which requires a warning to the jury of the need for caution in the circumstances set out in the section. A suspect's mental handicap is to be proved by medical expertise not by a police officer testifying: *R v Ham*.[685] In *R v Bailey*,[686] s. 77 was applied where a suspect had confessed to a member of

---

[671] Ibid.

[672] *R v Goldenberg* (1988) 88 Cr App R 285, CA (Cr D); *R v Crampton*, above (doubtful whether merely holding an interview with a suspect undergoing withdrawal symptoms is something 'done' within the meaning of s. 76(2)).

[673] [1998] Crim LR 211.   [674] (1988) 88 Cr App R 285.

[675] [1988] Crim LR 747, CA (Cr D).   [676] [1990] Crim LR 109, CA (Cr D).

[677] (1990) 92 Cr App R 228, CA (Cr D).   [678] [1993] Crim LR 685, CA (Cr D).

[679] [1994] Crim LR 441, CA (Cr D).   [680] [1994] Crim LR 838, CA (Cr D).

[681] [1994] Crim LR 441, CA (Cr D).   [682] [1998] 2 Cr App R 399, CA (Cr D).

[683] (1999) All ER (D) 748. See further P. Mirfield, *Silence, Confessions and Improperly Obtained Evidence* (1998).

[684] Above, p. 255.   [685] (1995) 36 BMLR 169, CA.   [686] [1995] 2 Cr App R 262, CA.

the public, but without an appropriate adult present. Is this what s. 77 was intended to guard against?

Note that this section does not extend to the mentally ill. The RCCJ recommended that this point should be reconsidered, as it is inconsistent with other provisions in PACE and the PACE Codes.[687] Brown,[688] found that 2 per cent of detainees are mentally handicapped/disordered, with 33 per cent being detained as a safety measure rather than for commission of an offence. There have been numerous calls for review of the procedures by which vulnerable suspects are identified as such.

Under PACE, an appropriate adult must be provided for juveniles and mentally disordered and mentally handicapped suspects.[689] The person should be an adult, i.e. over 18: *R v Palmer.*[690] Research found that in the majority of cases, the appropriate adult for juveniles was a parent or guardian (59 per cent). Social workers were used in 23 per cent of cases.[691] In the case of mentally disordered detainees, 60 per cent of appropriate adults were social workers. However, in only 66 per cent of cases did appropriate adults attend the station in the case of mentally disordered suspects.[692] There is very strong evidence that adults (other than social workers) who were acting as appropriate adults were often unaware of the role they should fulfil, and in many cases they behave inappropriately—for example, being threatening towards or even assaulting the child for whom they are the appropriate adult.[693] Brown concluded that 'there is a particular risk of interviews with mentally handicapped suspects producing unreliable evidence and the passivity of appropriate adults during interviews suggests that they do not provide an adequate safeguard against this danger'.[694]

7. *Excluding material obtained from an inadmissible confession.* Section 76(4)(a) allows for the admissibility of material discovered as a result of inadmissible confessions—for example, where a confession has been excluded on grounds of oppression, but the confession revealed the whereabouts of the weapon involved in the crime, the weapon can be admitted but no reference can be made by the prosecution as to the inadmissible confession. This follows the common law: *R v Warwickshall.*[695] Section 76(4)(b) also follows the common law by allowing the prosecution to adduce evidence of the manner in which a suspect expresses himself even if the confession in which that is revealed is inadmissible (e.g. suspect's unusual spelling ('Blady Belgiam') identical to that used by the offender: *R v Voisin*).[696]

Admissibility of unfair or illegal evidence under PACE. Section 78 applies to any evidence on which the prosecution proposes to rely and thus can also apply to confession evidence. A vast body of case law has considered the application of s. 78 and the courts have been considerably more active than was anticipated. The circumstances of each case are almost always different and the judges may well take different views in the proper exercise of their discretion even when the circumstances are similar. This is not an apt field for hard case law and well-founded distinctions between cases, per Auld LJ in

---

[687] Cm 2263, p. 59.   [688] *PACE Ten Years On* (above).

[689] On vulnerable groups in detention see T. Bucke and D. Brown, *In police custody: police powers and suspects' rights under the revised PACE codes of practice* (1997), Chap. 2.

[690] (1991) Legal Action, September, p. 21.   [691] T. Bucke and D. Brown, Chap. 2.

[692] Ibid., p. 8.

[693] Ibid., Chap. 2. The Home Office does provide guidance on the role of an appropriate adult. See: http://police.homeoffice.gov.uk.

[694] Ibid., p. 3. See also the danger of authority figures as appropriate adults for those with disability: J. Williams [2000] Crim LR 910.

[695] (1783) 1 Leach 263.   [696] [1918] 1 KB 531.

Jelen v Katz.[697] The largest number of cases in which a confession has been excluded involve exclusion under s. 78.

- **R v Samuel** [1988] QB 615, [1988] 2 WLR 920, [1988] 2 All ER 135,
  (1988) 87 Cr App R 232, Court of Appeal (Criminal Division)

S was arrested for armed robbery of a building society and after being questioned asked to see a solicitor. His request was refused under s. 58 by Superintendent Cresswell, who certified, *inter alia,* that there was a 'likelihood of other suspects to be arrested being inadvertently warned'. S had two further interviews, at the second of which he confessed to two burglaries, while denying the robbery. After he was charged with the burglaries his solicitor telephoned, but was refused access. Shortly afterwards S confessed to the robbery at a third interview, and was subsequently convicted of that offence.

The Court of Appeal quashed the conviction.

The judgment of the court (**Glidewell LJ, Hodgson** and **Rougier JJ**) was given by **Hodgson J** [who stated the facts and held (1) that the superintendent was entitled to conclude that the robbery had been a serious arrestable offence given the use of a shotgun and hand gun and the intention to cause serious financial loss to the society; (2) that the right to delay access to a lawyer could not be denied once S had been charged with the burglaries in view of para. 1 of Annex B(A)(a) of Code C, which provided that the right could only be delayed, *inter alia,* if the suspect 'has not yet been charged with an offence'. His Lordship continued:]

Mr. Escott Cox's second point raises, in the judgment of this Court, more fundamental and important issues. He challenged on the voire dire and challenged before us the correctness of both Mr. Cresswell's first decision to delay access and, even more emphatically, the decision to refuse access to Mr. Warner at 4.45 p.m. on 7 August.

Perhaps the most important right given (or rather renewed) to a person detained by the police is his right to obtain legal advice. That right is given in section 58 of the Act, subsection (1) of which is precise and unambiguous.

[His Lordship read s. 58:]

The words of the section clearly imply that the officer does so believe. Therefore a court which has to decide whether denial of access to a solicitor was lawful has to ask itself two questions: 'did the officer believe?', a subjective test, 'were there reasonable grounds for that belief?,' an objective test.

What it is the officer must satisfy the court that he believed is this: (1) that delaying consultation with a solicitor (2) will (3) lead to or hinder one or more of the things set out in (8)(*a*) to (*c*). The use of the word 'will' is clearly of great importance. There were available to the draftsman many words or phrases by which he could have described differing nuances as to the officer's state of mind, for example 'might', 'could', 'there was a risk', 'there was a substantial risk', etc. The choice of 'will' must have been deliberately restrictive.

Of course, anyone who says that he believes that something will happen, unless he is speaking of one of the immutable laws of nature, accepts the possibility that it will not happen, but the use of the word 'will' in conjunction with belief implies in the believer a belief that it will very probably happen.

What is it that the officer has to satisfy the court he believed? The right denied is a right 'to consult a solicitor privately'. The person denied that right is in police detention. In practice, the only way that the person can make any of (a) to (c) happening he will, almost inevitably, commit a serious criminal offence. Therefore, inadvertent or unwitting conduct apart, the officer must believe that a solicitor will, if allowed

---

697   (1989) 90 Cr App R 456 at 465, CA.

to consult with a detained person, thereafter commit a criminal office. Solicitors are officers of the court. We think that the number of times that a police officer could genuinely be in that state of belief will be rare. Moreover it is our view that, to sustain such a basis for refusal, the ground put forward would have to have reference to a specific solicitor. We do not think they could ever be successfully advanced in relation to solicitors generally.

However, the experience of some members of this court and, so he tells us, of Mr. Escott Cox, is that the practice adopted in this case is becoming more and more usual. An officer's 'reasonable belief is more and more being based upon the 'inadvertent' or 'unwitting' conduct of a solicitor.

At first sight the wording of the subsection does not seem apt to cover inadvertent or unwitting conduct by a solicitor. But what is said is that the detained person will be able to bring about one or more of the happenings (a) to (c) by causing the solicitor to pass on unwittingly some form of coded message. Whether there is any evidence that this has or may have happened in the past we have no way of knowing. Solicitors are intelligent professional people; persons detained by the police are frequently not very clever and the expectation that one of (a) to (c) will be brought about in this way seems to contemplate a degree of intelligence and sophistication in persons detained, and perhaps a naivete and lack of common sense in solicitors, which we doubt often occurs. When and if it does, we think it would have to have reference to the specific person detained. The archetype would, we imagine, be the sophisticated criminal who is known or suspected of being a member of a gang of criminals.

The task of satisfying a court that reasonable grounds existed at the time the decision was made, either in respect of intentional or inadvertent conduct will, we think, prove even more formidable. Any officer attempting to justify his decision to delay the exercise of this fundamental right of a citizen will, in our judgment, be unable to do so save by reference to specific circumstances including evidence as to the person detained or the actual solicitor sought to be consulted.

In this connection it is relevant to note that at many police stations a duty solicitor scheme is in operation…

Duty solicitors will be well known to the police, and we think it will therefore be very difficult to justify consultation with the duty solicitor being delayed. If the duty solicitor has the reputation, deserved or not, for advising persons detained to refuse to answer questions that would, of course, be no reason for delaying consultation.

[On the facts, His Lordship concluded that whoever had decided to refuse access before the third interview could not have had reasonable grounds for the belief required by s. 58(8): by this time 'the police knew the identity of the solicitor, a highly respected and very experienced professional lawyer, unlikely to be hoodwinked by a 24-year old'. That person was 'very probably motivated by a desire to have one last chance of interviewing the appellant in the absence of a solicitor'.]

Having ruled against the defence submissions on both the construction point and the more fundamental submission on the exercise of the power under section 58(8), the trial judge briefly considered his discretion. He said:

'However, had I decided that an offence meant any offence I would, in the exercise of the discretion which I undoubtedly have, have exercised it on the basis of justice, fairness and common sense and would in any event have allowed the evidence to be given to the jury.'

It is to be noted that he there makes no reference to his decision on the second ground. Mr. Escott Cox submits that it is clear that the judge did not consider how he would have exercised his discretion if he had applied his mind to the situation at 4.45 p.m. and still held that the refusal at that time was proper. Secondly, he submits that, having found wrongly on both submissions, it was really impossible for him properly to consider how he would have exercised his discretion.

Mr. Warner gave evidence. He said it was not his policy always to advice a client not to answer questions put to him by the police. In his view, in many cases, it was of advantage to someone in detention to answer proper questions put to him. However on this occasion, knowing that his client had already been interviewed on four occasions and at each had strenuously denied complicity in the robbery and had already been charged with two serious offences, he would probably, after consultation, have advised his client, for the time being at any rate, to refuse to answer further questioning. The probable result of allowing the appellant to exercise his right would therefore, in all probability, have been that, had a further interview taken place (and we think it improbable that the police would, in those circumstances, have thought it worth their while to interview him further) no incriminating replies would have been given.

Mr. Esscot Cox further submits that he was handicapped in his conduct of the appellant's defence by the judge's ruling on the construction of the Annex. That was a ruling on a point of law and therefore prevented him cross-examining the police on the propriety of the refusal of access on that ground.

It is undesirable to attempt any general guidance as to the way in which a judge's decision under section 78 or his inherent powers should be exercised. Circumstances vary infinitely. Mr. Jones has made the extreme submission that, in the absence of impropriety, the discretion should never be exercised to exclude admissible evidence. We have no hesitation in rejecting that submission, although the propriety or otherwise of the way in which the evidence was obtained is something which a court is, in terms, enjoined by the section 58(8) point, the judge failed properly to address his mind to the point in time which was most material and did not in terms give consideration to what his decision would have been had he ruled in favour of the defence on this more fundamental issue before him.

In this case this appellant was denied improperly one of the most important and fundamental rights of a citizen. The trial judge fell into error in not so holding. If he had arrived at correct decisions on the two points argued before him he might well have concluded that the refusal of access and consequent unlawful interview compelled him to find that the admission of evidence as to the final interview would have 'such an adverse effect on the fairness of the proceedings' that he ought not to admit it. Such a decision would, of course, have very significantly weakened the prosecution case (the failure to charge earlier ineluctably shows this), in those circumstances this court feels that it has no alternative but to quash the appellant's conviction on count 1 in the indictment, the charge of robbery.

Appeal allowed. Conviction quashed.

NOTES

1. Further examples include the following situations:

(a) Where the police have denied access to a solicitor in breach of s. 58: *R v Parris*[698] (superintendent's order that D to be kept incommunicado under s. 56 wrongly assumed to exclude access to a solicitor under s. 58); *R v Walsh*;[699] *R v Chung*;[700] *R v Braithwaite*.[701] Exclusion is not, however, automatic, and may not follow where D is aware of his rights: *R v Alladice*[702] (D admitted he was well able to cope with the interviews, that he understood the caution and was aware of his rights); *R v Dunford*[703] (D had a record and was aware of his right not to answer questions); *R v Oliphant*[704] (presence of a solicitor would have added nothing to what 0 knew of his legal rights); *R v Anderson*[705] (even if a solicitor had been present and advised silence, A would not have acted on such advice).

(b) Where D has not been advised of the right to legal advice: *R v Absolam*;[706] *R v Beycan*.[707]

---

[698] (1988) 89 Cr App R 68, CA (Cr D).   [699] (1989) 91 Cr App R 161, CA (Cr D).
[700] (1990) 92 Cr App R 314, CA (Cr D).   [701] (1991) Times, 9 December, CA (Cr D).
[702] (1988) 87 Cr App R 380, CA (Cr D).   [703] (1990) 91 Cr App R 150, CA (Cr D).
[704] [1992] Crim LR 40, CA (Cr D).   [705] [1993] Crim LR 447, CA (Cr D).
[706] (1988) 88 CR App R 332, CA (Cr D).   [707] [1990] Crim LR 185, CA (Cr D).

(c) Where a proper record of the interview was not made: *R v Abolsam*[708] (no caution before questioning; no proper record); *R v Keenan*[709] (officers unaware of Code C); *R v Walsh*;[710] *R v Canale*[711] (where the breaches were described as 'flagrant', 'deliberate' and 'cynical'); *R v Bryce*[712] (interview after tape-recorder switched off at B's request; no fresh caution and no contemporaneous record); *R v Cox*[713] (questioning before arrival at police station held to be 'interview' to which Code C.11 requirements applied); admissible as D's solicitor's clerk was present at the interview and so able to protect his interests.

(d) Where there is a breach of a requirement to caution: *R v Absolam*;[714] *R v Hunt*[715] (H seen by a police officer to have a flick knife and asked what it was for; it was held that there was ample evidence to suspect commission of an offence and he should have been cautioned): *R v Bryce*.[716] The correct time to caution is when there are grounds for suspicion (objectively assessed) but insufficient evidence to support a prima facie case of guilt: *R v Nelson and Rose*;[717] *R v Blackford*;[718] a second caution may be necessary on arrival at the station if conversations with the suspect then occur: *R v Miller*.[719]

(e) Where a juvenile is interviewed in the absence of an appropriate adult: *R v Weekes*.[720]

2. The Court of Appeal has emphasised that 'not every breach or combination of breaches of the codes will justify the exclusion of interview evidence under section 76 or section 78...they must be significant and substantial' (per Hodgson J in *R v Keenan*).[721]

Furthermore, exclusion will not follow automatically even where there is a 'significant or substantial breach':

The task of the court is not merely to consider whether there would be an adverse effect on the fairness of the proceedings, but such an adverse effect that justice requires the evidence to be excluded.[722]

3. The 'burden of proof' under s. 78 is unclear, in contrast to the position under s. 76.[723] There is no academic consensus as to where the burden of proof lies in s. 78. In *R (on the application of Saifi) v Governor of Brixton Prison*[724] the Court of Appeal doubted whether there was truly a 'burden of proof issue'. Is there a burden of proving the facts on which the judge must exercise the discretion?

4. The courts have rarely used s. 78 to exclude real evidence on the ground that it has been obtained illegally or otherwise improperly. One relevant factor is whether police officers have acted in bad faith,[725] though this does not automatically lead to exclusion.[726] On the other hand, subsequent cases have confirmed that evidence may be excluded under s. 78 even where it is not established that the police have acted in bad faith.

In *Khan*[727] the House of Lords held that the police recording of conversations made by K incriminating him in drug dealing were admissible even though they had been obtained by

---

708 Above.   709 [1990] 2 QB 54, CA (Cr D).   710 Above.
711 [1990] 2 All ER 187, CA (Cr D).   712 [1992] 4 All ER 567, CA (Cr D).
713 (1992) 96 CR App R 464, CA (Cr D).   714 (1988) 88 Cr App R 332, CA (Cr D).
715 [1992] Crim LR 582, CA (Cr D).   716 [1992] 4 All ER 567, CA (Cr D).
717 [1998] 2 Cr App R 399, CA (Cr D).   718 Above, p. 240.
719 [1998] Crim LR 209, CA (Cr D).   720 (1992) 97 Cr App R 222, CA (Cr D).
721 [1990] 2 QB 54 at 69.
722 Per Saville J, in *R v Walsh* (1989) 91 Cr App R 161 at 163, CA (Cr D).
723 See *R v Anderson* [1993] Crim LR 447.   724 [2001] 4 All ER 168, CA (Cr D).
725 *Matto v Crown Court at Wolverhampton* [1987] RTR 337.
726 Per Buckley J in *Sharpe v DPP* [1993] RTR 392 at 398–399, DC.
727 [1997] AC 558, HL.

the police fixing a secret listening device to the private property of K's associate. The House recognised that the action was probably in breach of Art. 8 of the ECHR, but, although that was a relevant matter, the evidence was still correctly admitted by the trial judge. The ECtHR ruled, unanimously, that there had been a breach of Art. 8 in that K's right to respect for his private and family life had been violated. There was no statutory regime governing the English police use of such equipment at the time, and therefore the Court was not prepared to accept that the interference was 'in accordance with the law'. The Court held that there was no breach of Art. 6, since the s. 78 discretion meant that the proceedings were not wholly unfair. Moreover, it was not the task of the ECtHR to rule on admissibility in domestic proceedings. The House of Lords have confirmed that the s. 78 discretion adequately safeguards the fairness of the trial: *R v P*.[728] In *Button*,[729] following an argument that the court should rule as admissible evidence gathered in breach of Art. 8, as otherwise would involve the court breaching Art. 8, the court stated:

Persuasively though they were put we do not accept these submissions. We come back to what we said in para 9 that the breach of art 8 is the interference with or intrusion upon private life which is involved in covert surveillance. The court has played no part in this. Its function is to determine whether the evidence obtained in this way is admissible. In performing this task it must act fairly and art 6 and s 78 of PACE set the standards by which it must proceed. If it decides to admit the evidence it is not itself acting in breach of art 8. The intrusion or interference has already occurred, the evidence obtained is admissible under English law and so the court's obligation is confined to deciding whether or not, having regard to the way in which the evidence was obtained, it would be fair to admit it.

The far reaching consequences of Mr Webster's submissions also support the view that they cannot be correct. What he is saying is that the court is bound to exclude any evidence obtained in breach of art 8 because otherwise it would be acting unlawfully. This is a startling proposition and one which we are pleased and relieved to be able to reject.

Khan was distinguished in *Allan v United Kingdom*.[730] A had been arrested for murder but, on advice, consistently refused to answer police questions. An experienced informer was fitted with a listening device and placed in the same cell as A for the purpose of questioning him regarding the murder. The Court of Appeal overturned his conviction[731] and held that statements made by A to the informer were not spontaneous but were effectively in response to questioning which sidestepped the safeguards of a formal interview.

5. 'Fairness' in s. 78 comprises both fairness to the accused and fairness to the prosecution; *R v O'Loughlin and McLaughlin*;[732] *R v Hughes*.[733] Is it any fairer to admit illegally obtained evidence of a murder than of shoplifting? Should s. 78 be restructured so that courts were able to take account of broader issues of fairness?[734]

For a discussion of the relationship between abuse of process and s. 78, see Choo and Nash,[735] arguing that courts should adopt an approach more akin to that when considering abuse of process—with the focus on the pre-trial conduct of the police rather than the resulting evidence, and that s. 78 requires consideration of the fairness of the whole proceedings, not just the trial. The HRA has forced the Court of Appeal to address the relationship between fairness, safety and abuse of process doctrines.[736]

---

[728] [2001] 2 All ER 58.   [729] [2005] EWCA Crim 516.   [730] (2002) 36 EHRR 143.

[731] [2004] EWCA Crim 2236.   [732] (1987) 85 Cr App R 157 at 163.

[733] [1988] Crim LR 519, CA; See also K. Grevling (1997) 113 LQR 667.

[734] Grevling, p. 685.   [735] A. Choo and S. Nash [1999] Crim LR 929.

[736] See *R v Togher* [2001] Crim LR 140; N. Taylor and D. Ormerod [2004] Crim LR 266; I. Dennis (2003) CLP 211.

(I) ADMISSIBILITY OF EVIDENCE DERIVED FROM POLICE DECEPTION

- **R v Christou and Wright** [1992] QB 979, [1992] 3 WLR 228,
  [1992] 4 All ER 559, Court of Appeal (Criminal Division)

In 1990, in order to combat a high rate of burglary and robbery in North London, police set up an undercover operation. A shop ('Stardust Jewellers') was established in Tottenham, run by two undercover officers ('Gary' and 'Aggi') who purported to be shady jewellers willing to buy in stolen property. Over three months, a series of transactions was recorded by cameras and sound recording equipment. The conversations included questions that would be asked by shady jewellers, such as the area of London in which it would be unwise to resell the goods. The officers also required the vendors to sign receipts recording the money paid and the specific goods. This was something which shady jewellers would be likely to do, but also had the effect of obtaining fingerprints. In the event the fingerprints were not used. C and W were vendors of stolen property charged in respect of a number of transactions. At their trial for handling stolen goods, the judge ruled that the evidence from the operation was admissible, and they accordingly pleaded guilty. Their appeal to the Court of Appeal was dismissed.

> The judgment of the court (Lord Taylor of Gosforth CJ, Boreham and Auld JJ) was delivered by **Lord Taylor of Gosforth CJ**:
>
> [His Lordship referred to *dicta* in *R v Sang* (above, pp. 351–352) and continued:]
>
> In view of the terms of those dicta, the paucity of cases in which the discretion had been exercised so as to exclude legally admissible evidence is not surprising. In the present case the judge decided that, since the evidence from Stardust Jewellers had admittedly been obtained from the appellants by a trick and after the offences charged had been committed, he had a discretion to exclude the evidence if its admission would prejudice a fair trial. He also considered the alternative submission that, pursuant to section 78 of the Act of 1984, he ought to exclude the evidence...
>
> The judge held that the discretion under section 78 may be wider than the common law discretion identified in *R v Sang* [1980] AC 402, the latter relating solely to evidence obtained from the defendant after the offence is complete, the statutory discretion not being so restricted. However, he held that the criteria of unfairness are the same whether the trial judge is exercising his discretion at common law or under the statute. We agree. What is unfair cannot sensibly be subject to different standards depending on the source of the discretion to exclude it.
>
> In the result the judge concluded that to admit the challenged evidence would not have an adverse effect on the fairness of the trial. He said:
>
>> 'Nobody was forcing the defendants to do what they did. They were not persuaded or encouraged to do what they did. They were doing in that shop exactly what they intended to do and in all probability, what they intended to do from the moment they got up that morning. They were dishonestly disposing of dishonest goods. If the police had never set up the jewellers shop, they would, in my judgment, have been doing the same thing, though of course they would not have been doing it in that shop, at that time. They were not tricked into doing what they would not otherwise have done, they were tricked into doing what they wanted to do in that place and before witnesses and devices who can now speak of what happened. I do not think that is unfair or leads to an unfairness in the trial.'
>
> Putting it in different words, the trick was not applied to the appellants; they voluntarily applied themselves to the trick. It is not every trick producing evidence against an accused which results in unfairness. There are, in criminal investigations, a number of situations in which the police adopt ruses or tricks in the public interest to obtain evidence. For example, to trap a blackmailer, the victim may be used as an agent of the police to arrange an appointment and false or marked money may be laid as bait to catch the offender.

A trick, certainly; in a sense too, a trick which results in a form of self-incriminations; but not one which could reasonably be thought to involve fairness. Cases such as *R v Payne* [1963] 1 WLR 637 and *R v Mason (Carl)* [1988] 1 WLR 139 are very different from the present case or the blackmail example. In *R v Mason* as in *R v Payne* [1963] 1 WLR 637, the defendant was in police custody at a police station. Officers lied to both the defendant and his solicitor. Having no evidence against the defendant, they falsely asserted that his fingerprints had been found in an incriminating place in order to elicit admissions from him. After advice from his solicitor, the defendant made admissions. This court quashed his conviction.

In the present case the argument was at one stage canvassed that requesting the receipt with the consequence obtaining of fingerprints, should be regarded separately from the main issue, that it amounted to a separate trick within a trick. However, Mr. Thornton made clear that in his submission requesting the receipt was merely an incident in the operation of the shop. The whole operation was a single trick, all the fruits of which should be excluded. We agree that the operation should be considered as a whole. In the end, the judge treated the receipts as 'part of the general deceit concerning the dishonest jewellers, the general pretence by them that it was a proper jeweller's shop'. It was not unfair. He gave, as a further reason, that had no request been made for a receipt, fingerprints could easily have been obtained in other ways, e.g. by dusting the counter. For this he relied upon *R v Apicella* (1985) 82 Cr App Rep R 295 and *Director of Public Prosecutions v Marshall* [1988] 3 All ER 683.

The judge's exercise of his discretion could only be impugned if it was unreasonably according to *Wednesbury* principles (*Associated Provincial Picture Houses Ltd v Wednesbury Corporation* [1948] 1 KB 223): see *R v O'Leary* (1988) 87 Cr App R 387, 391. In our judgment, not only can the judge's conclusion on this issue not be so stigmatised, we think he was right.

[The other ground of appeal turns on para. 10.1 of Code C of the PACE Codes, above.]

It is submitted that the first sentence of that paragraph applied to the conversations in the shop. Accordingly, a caution should have been given. It is obvious that if this submission is correct, setting up Stardust Jewellers would have been pointless. Mr. Thornton and Mr. Taylor grasped that nettle. They say that the operation should not have been undertaken. If a caution was required, it cannot be dispensed with simply to facilitate the operation. It is accepted that Gary and Aggi had grounds to suspect each of the appellants of an offence. The issue is whether the Code applied to this situation at all. The judge concluded it did not…

In our view, although the Code extends beyond the treatment of those in detention, what is clear is that it was intended to protect suspects who are vulnerable to abuse or pressure from police officers or who may believe themselves to be so. Frequently, the suspect will be a detainee. But the Code will also apply where a suspect, not in detention, is being questioned about an offence by a police officer acting as a police officer for the purpose of obtaining evidence. In that situation, the officer and the suspect are not on equal terms. The officer is perceived to be in a position of authority; the suspect may be intimidated or undermined.

The situation at Stardust Jewellers was quite difficult. The appellants were being questioned by police officers acting as such. Conversation was on equal terms. There could be no question of pressure or intimidation by Gary or Aggi as persons actually in authority or believed to be so. We agree with the judge that the Code simply was not intended to apply in such a context.

In reaching that conclusion, we should ourselves administer a caution. It would be wrong for police officers to adopt or use an undercover pose or disguise to enable themselves to ask questions about an offence uninhibited by the requirements of the Code and with the effect of circumventing it.

Were they to do so, it would be open to the judge to exclude the questions and answers under section 78 of the Act of 1984. It is therefore necessary here to see whether the questioning by Gary and Aggi was such as to require the judge in his discretion to exclude the conversation. The judge carefully reviewed the evidence on this issue. He concluded that the questions and comments from Gary and

Aggi were for the most part simply those necessary to conduct the bartering and maintain their cover. They were not 'about the offence'. The only exception was the questioning about which area should be avoided in reselling the goods. However, even that was partly to maintain cover since it was the sort of questioning to be expected from a shady jeweller.

We are of the view that the judge's approach to the aspect of the case concerned with the Code cannot be faulted...

Appeals dismissed.

NOTES

1. *Christou and Wright* deals with two distinct, but related issues: (a) the discretion to exclude evidence obtained by a trick; and (b) the question of 'entrapment'. The evidence obtained may in either event be confession or real evidence. To what extent is it fair to say that the defendants in *Christou* applied the trick to themselves?

2. *Tricks.* In *R v Mason*,[737] mentioned by Lord Taylor CJ in *R v Christou and Wright*, Watkins LJ described the conduct of the police as 'most reprehensible'. The trial judge in exercising his discretion under s. 78 had failed to take any account of the deceit practised upon M's solicitor. If he had done so, he would clearly have ruled the confession inadmissible. The court stated that 'this was not the place to discipline the police' but they hoped 'never again to hear of deceit such as this being practised upon an accused person, and more particularly possibly on a solicitor, whose duty it is to advise him unfettered by false information from the police'.[738] The court also confirmed that s. 78 could be used to exclude evidence of confessions and admissions.

3. Lord Taylor in *Christou and Wright* emphasised that undercover operations must not be employed to enable police officers to ask questions about an offence uninhibited by the requirements of Code C. That line was crossed in *R v Bryce*,[739] where an undercover police officer posed as a potential buyer and agreed by telephone to buy a stolen car (actually worth £23,000) from B for £2,800. When they met, the officer asked B (*inter alia*) how long the car had been stolen, and was told two or three days. Lord Taylor noted that: 'Those questions went to the heart of the vital issue of dishonesty. They were not even necessary to the undercover operation.'[740] They were also hotly disputed, and there was no contemporary record (unlike the position in *Christou and Wright* where the conversations were recorded). The court held that the answers should have been excluded.

In *Williams and O'Hare v DPP*,[741] the Divisional Court upheld the admissibility of evidence of interfering with a vehicle with intent to commit theft, where the police left a van unattended, with what seemed to be a valuable load of cigarettes, and W and O'H succumbed to the temptation. Have the police incited theft? Does this render the situation different from *Christou* in which the police had no intention to encourage the crime?[742]

Entrapment and agents provocateurs. In *R v Smurthwaite, R v Gill*[743] the Court of Appeal confirmed that s. 78 had not altered the common law rule laid down in *Sang* that entrapment or the use of an agent provocateur does not *per se* afford a defence in law to a criminal charge. However, if the judge considered that in all the circumstances the obtaining of the evidence

---

[737] [1988] 1 WLR 139. [738] At 144.
[739] [1992] 4 All ER 567, CA (Cr D). [740] At pp. 571–572.
[741] (1993) 98 Cr App R 209. [742] See also D. Birch [1994] 47 CLP 73.
[743] [1994] 1 All ER 898.

in that way had such an adverse affect on the fairness of the proceedings that the court ought
not to admit it, it could be excluded under s. 78.[744]

His Lordship continued:[745]

In exercising his discretion whether to admit the evidence of an undercover officer, some, but not an
exhaustive list, of the factors that the judge may take into account are as follows. Was the officer acting as
an agent provocateur in the sense that he was enticing the defendant to commit an offence he would not
otherwise have committed? What was the nature of any entrapment? Does the evidence consist of admissions to a completed offence, or does it consist of the actual commission of an offence? How active or passive was the officer's role in obtaining the evidence? Is there an unassailable record of what occurred, or is
it strongly corroborated? In R v Christou [1992] 4 All ER 559, [1992] QB 979 this court held that discussions
between suspects and undercover officers, not overtly acting as police officers, were not within the ambit
of the codes under the 1984 Act. However, officers should not use their undercover pose to question suspects so as to the circumvent the code. In R v Bryce [1992] 4 All ER 567 the court held that the undercover
officer had done just that. Accordingly, a further consideration for the judge in deciding whether to admit
an undercover officer's evidence is whether he has abused his role to ask questions which ought properly
to have been asked as a police officer and in accordance with the codes.

Here, police officers in two separate cases posed as contract killers, and were solicited
by S and G to kill their respective spouses. On the facts in each case, tape-recorded conversations 'showed no sign of an unwilling defendant being persuaded or cajoled into
an agreement to a murder she [or he] would not otherwise have entered'.[746] In S's case,
all the conversations were recorded; in G's case an unrecorded conversation given in
evidence by the officer was corroborated by later recorded conversations and held to be
admissible.

Although the matter was considered by the House of Lords in *Sang,* the House again
addressed it in *R v Latif and Shazad.*[747] The defendants had been involved in a conspiracy
to import heroin, and the British Customs and US Drug Enforcement Agency had partici-
pated. One of the officers had actually imported the drugs without a licence (the House of
Lords was prepared to assume that he was guilty of an offence although that had not been
argued at trial). The House held that the trial judge had exercised the discretion whether
to stay the proceedings for abuse and had conducted the correct balancing of the interests
involved, including the need for the law enforcement agencies to fight serious crime. The
same balance needed to be struck with s. 78 and the trial judge was right not to exclude the
evidence.

Commenting on *Latif* [748] Sir John Smith stated that 'the graver the offence to be prevented, the more the law enforcement authorities can get away with. It is a question of
expediency'.[749] Is it? Should it be?

As the pressure to combat crime, and particularly those types of crime in which detection
is very difficult—drug dealing being a prime example—the use of entrapment techniques
has increased in recent years. The leading decision of the European Court of Human Rights
is that in *Teixiera de Castro v Portugal,*[750] in which there was found to be a breach of Art. 6
where the undercover officers incited the offender to commit an offence which he would
not otherwise have committed. The police had relied on T's predisposition to commit other
offences:

---

[744] Lord Taylor CJ at 902.   [745] At 903.   [746] Lord Taylor CJ at 909.
[747] [1996] 2 Cr App R 92.   [748] [1996] Crim LR 446.   [749] Ibid.
[750] (1998) 28 EHRR 101.

the use of undercover agents must be restricted and safeguards put in place even in cases concerning the fight against drug trafficking. While the rise in organised crime undoubtedly requires that appropriate measures be taken, the right to a fair administration of justice nevertheless holds such a paramount place that it cannot be sacrificed for the sake of expedience. The general requirements of fairness embodied in Article 6 apply to proceedings concerning all types of criminal offence, from the most straightforward to the most complex. The public interest cannot justify the use of evidence obtained as a result of police incitement.

The ECtHR distinguished the earlier case of *Ludi v Switzerland*,[751] where the undercover police officer had actively been involved in buying drugs from someone who was already dealing drugs, and this case, in which the police had initiated the deal with someone who was not engaged in drug dealing. The European approach focuses on whether the suspect is 'predisposed' to commit the crime. Does this mean: (a) has a general disposition towards crime; (b) has a disposition towards this type of crime; (c) has a disposition to commit this specific crime on this occasion?[752] What are the implications for those with a criminal record?

Ashworth has examined the many arguments that can be advanced for and against deceptive police practices.[753] These include arguments that: criminals deserve reduced rights only, so no harm is done to them by police deception; the criminal relies on deception, so it is not unfair for him to be treated in similar fashion; entrapment and deception might be wrong in general, but in the specific context they will benefit the community. On the other hand, by deceiving suspects, the police infringe the integrity principle, they abuse the power of the state, and reduce confidence in the criminal justice system. There are arguments that deceptive practices ought to be used only exceptionally (Who decides? Is it fair to treat some crimes differently in terms of investigations? Which crimes and why?).

The House of Lords has again considered entrapment issues in *R v Looseley*.[754] The House held that English law was not in conflict with the ECtHR approach in *Teixeira*. The Lords held that the officers in *Looseley* had not overstepped the mark since they had made one approach to a person who was suspected of drug dealing and had bought drugs on their first request. In *A-G's Reference (No. 3 of 2000)*,[755] the officers had overstepped the mark when they had pressurised the suspect over a period of time and offered inducements.

It was held that it would be unfair (and should lead to an abuse of process) for an undercover officer to incite or instigate an offence that the suspect would not otherwise have committed. If the officer merely provides an unexceptional opportunity for the suspect to take advantage there would be no unfairness in admitting the evidence at trial and no stay of proceedings. The House of Lords also emphasised that the previous record of the accused is not determinative, but that a reasonable suspicion of offending or willingness to offend is important. The House of Lords emphasised that in *Teixeira* the officers had been acting without judicial supervision and had no reasonable grounds to suspect T of drug dealing.

The Court of Appeal followed *Looseley* in *Jones*[756] where the police became aware that someone was leaving graffiti messages on trains, seeking to entice children for sexual purposes. Both a journalist and later a police officer responded to the messages, a meeting was

---

751 (1993) 15 EHRR 173.   752 See A. Ashworth [1999] 10 Arch News p. 5.
753 See (1998) 114 LQR 108.   754 [2001] UKHL 53, HL.   755 [2001] UKHL 53.
756 [2007] EWCA Crim 1118.

arranged and the appellant was arrested when he turned up at the meeting place. Thomas LJ said:

> It is clear, in our view, from the appellant's conduct in relation to the journalist, that he was looking for opportunities to incite a child to penetrative sexual activity; the incitement in those communications went beyond what was stated in the graffiti and included a specific incitement to penetrative sexual activity. The police officer's conduct in relation to the appellant followed on from those events. Far from instigating the offence, the police officer's conduct provided only the opportunity for the appellant to attempt to commit a similar offence and provide the evidence necessary for a conviction. The police officer's response to the invitation in the graffiti by pretending to be a child was a necessary pretence to that end; the pretence did not go beyond providing the necessary opportunity for the appellant to attempt to commit the offence by inciting a person whom he believed to be under the age of 13 to engage in penetrative sex. The police officer's replies thereafter to the text messages were entirely acceptable in a covert operation of this kind, as otherwise the nature of her actions would have increased the suspicions of the appellant. It was the appellant who, after he had been told of the person's age, continued and went on to incite penetrative sexual activity on more than one occasion on the days that followed.[757]

Should evidence from entrapment be received because it is reliable? Should it be excluded by way of disciplining the police for engaging in deceit? Does the deceit involved render a conviction morally flawed?

The courts take a much stricter approach to officers targeting an individual not to incite him to commit an offence, but to question him about an offence that has already occurred. In such cases, the statutory procedures for questioning must be complied with. See *R v Stagg*,[758] and *R v Bow Street Magistrates Court, ex p Proulx*.[759]

English law has rejected the possibility of a defence of entrapment in the criminal law. See *R v Sang* and the statements of Lord Taylor in *R v Smurthwaite*: 's. 78 has not altered the substantive law, that entrapment or the use of an agent provocateur does not *per se* afford a defence to a criminal charge'.[760] Should there be a defence of entrapment in the substantive criminal law rather than a series of ill-defined discretions to exclude evidence?

NOTES

1. Can the end justify the means?

2. As in other areas of police powers the regulation of police conduct is increasingly governed by codes of conduct rather than primary statutory material. Can the courts ensure the same accountability of the police?

---

[757] Ibid., para. 23.

[758] (1994) CCC, unreported, 14 September. See D. Ormerod [1996] Crim LR 863.

[759] [2001] 1 All ER 57, DC, [2000] Crim LR 997 and commentary.

[760] [1994] 1 All ER 898 confirmed by the House of Lords in *R v Loosely* [2001] UKHL 53.

5

PUBLIC ORDER

1. INTRODUCTION[1]

The liberty of the people to assemble in public in order to express their views on political matters is generally regarded as an essential element in a free and open society. It is recognised in such international standards as Arts 10 and 11 ECHR[2] and Arts 19 and 21 ICCPR. It forms an important part of the subject of civil liberties, which are (or at least include) those freedoms that are essential to the proper functioning of our contemporary political community.[3] The introduction of the Human Rights Act 1998 has certainly had an impact on the way cases in this area are argued. Public order law tends to impact on both freedom of expression and of association, and restrictions may be challenged *inter alia* on the ground that they are disproportionate. How far this has led to differences in outcome is debatable, but there have been some decisions that have seem to have shifted the balance in favour of protest.[4]

Ewing and Gearty distinguish between primary civil liberties—those which deal with the right of the individual to participate directly in the process of government—and secondary liberties—those which deal with the right to influence the government, including such matters as freedom of expression and assembly.[5] Public order law often involves both types of liberty. The extent to which they may be exercised in this country depends partly on the existing state of the law, and partly on the way in which the law is enforced by police, prosecutors and courts. As this chapter shows, there are many ways in which public meetings or processions may fall foul of the law, both civil and criminal. Just as important is what is likely to happen in practice. On this latter point it is extremely difficult to generalise. Much (many would say too much) depends on 'the policeman on the spot'.[6] Moreover, the attitude of the authorities seems to vary according to current political circumstances. The more stable the political system, the greater is the toleration of political protest. As the effectiveness, or likely or even feared effectiveness, of protest increases, so toleration is reduced: the law is enforced more rigorously, and may be strengthened. In addition to being concerned

---

[1] The main works cited in this chapter are: *Williams*: D.G.T. Williams, *Keeping the Peace* (1967); *Brownlie*: M. Supperstone, *Brownlie's Law of Public Order and National Security* (2nd edn, 1981); *Smith and Hogan*: D. Ormerod, *Smith and Hogan Criminal Law* (12th edn, 2008); *Ewing and Gearty*: K.D. Ewing and C.A. Gearty, *The Struggle for Civil Liberties* (2000); *Smith*: A.T.H. Smith, *Offences against Public Order* (1987). On the 1986 Act, see D. Bonner and R. Stone [1987] PL 449; Symposium [1987] Crim LR 153ff; See also P.A.J. Waddington, *Policing Citizens: Authority and Rights* (1999), Chap. 3 and N. Whitty, T. Murphy and S. Livingstone, *Civil Liberties Law: The Human Rights Era* (2001). For a discussion of the theoretical issues relating to civil disobedience, rights of free speech and constitutional principle, see T.R.S. Allan [1996] CLJ 89.

[2] Above, Chaps 2, 3.   [3] Above, p. 86 and below, Chap. 9.

[4] See e.g. *Westminster City Council v Haw*, below, p. 294 and *Laporte*, below, p. 376.

[5] *Ewing and Gearty*, p. 18.

[6] See *Williams*, Chap. 5, and see the articles in R. Reiner, *Policing*, Vol. II (1996) Part I on police discretion.

with the mechanics of protest (How many protestors? Where are they? Are they disorderly? Are they violent?), the authorities may be more inclined to focus their attention on the content of the protest (Is it seditious? Does it incite to disaffection?). A further point to be borne in mind when considering the issues in this chapter is the argument that

> the main purpose of civil liberties is to promote political participation and that as such it is a discipline which encourages the development of an active political culture: it is about freedom *to* rather than freedom *from*.[7]

Consider throughout the chapter the extent to which the courts and the vastly increased body of public order legislation go beyond the restriction of these liberties positively to facilitate their exercise. It will come as no surprise that the balance is much towards the former.

At present, most of the law in the context of political protest relates to its 'public order' aspect. A major theme is the control of the advocacy or use of violence as a means of obtaining political change (at its minimum the prevention of breaches of the peace).[8] Another theme is the protection of other legitimate interests of citizens (e.g. the right to use the highway; the right not to have an unwanted crowd gathering in one's own front garden).

This concentration on the 'public order' aspect has three consequences. First, the control of political assemblies is seen as part of the general police function of keeping the peace. The problems posed by disorderly political demonstrators have been regarded as analogous to those posed by vandals, quarrelling neighbours, 'mods' and 'rockers', 'football hooligans' and drunks. The laws applicable are the same for all. It is open to argument whether the law should operate in the same way in relation to all the categories mentioned, although this is a point on which a very firm view was expressed in *R v Caird* that it should.[9]

Secondly, by checking violent protest, it is possible that the law checks the very kind of protest which is most likely to obtain fundamental change. The justifications advanced are that any violence in society is unacceptable, and that violence in this context distorts the 'proper' democratic political process for obtaining reform.

> protesters who meekly assemble to hear speeches protesting at some grievance are not only acting lawfully, they are acting virtuously for they are actively engaged in the political process–the right peacefully to protest or mobilise political opinion is the quintessence of citizenship.... [but it is that political dimension] that makes public disorder ambiguous: any crowd activity could be an assertion of political rectitude, an understandable albeit mistaken response to provocation, or an orgy of mindless violence, depending on which interpretation ultimately prevails.[10]

Thirdly, laws which seek to maintain public order are easier to justify than those which impinge directly on freedom of expression. Indeed, free expression is essential to the operation of those democratic processes which the maintenance of order is supposed to facilitate. However, laws preserving public order may have significant effects on freedom of expression (a) if they are enforced discriminatorily according to the nature of the political opinions held by particular individuals;[11] (b) if they interfere with the *effective*

---

[7] Ewing and Gearty, p. 33.   [8] See pp. 330–357 and 376–397.

[9] (1970) 54 Cr App R 499 (below, p. 336).

[10] P.A.J. Waddington, *Policing Citizens: Authority and Rights* (1999), pp. 66–67.

[11] As has frequently been alleged: see R. Kidd, *British Liberty in Danger* (1940), Chap. 5; B. Cox, *Civil Liberties in Britain* (1975), Chap. 1 and see, generally, *Ewing and Gearty*.

communication of views;[12] and (c) in so far as the use of particular words, such as those which incite or provoke violence, is proscribed.[13]

The law relating to public order was modified and extended by the Public Order Act 1986[14] and by a steady stream of legislation through the 1990s and beyond. There has been a whole series of Acts, with provisions directed at particular forms of protest and more generally, at a multitude of perceived forms of anti-social behaviour. Recurring themes have been: the expansion of the range of criminal offences; the expansion of police powers of arrest;[15] the extension of unstructured discretionary powers conferred on the police in dealing with particular situations, with penalties for non-compliance with police instructions; an increasing emphasis on administrative enforcement measures (particularly fixed penalty notices); and the absence of any serious attempt to facilitate the exercise of recognised liberties. The following are the major landmarks.

There has been a series of Acts directed at football hooliganism.[16] The menace of 'stalking' was tackled by the Protection from Harassment Act 1997, although its broad provisions impact on protesters. The Criminal Justice and Public Order Act 1994 significantly extended the ambit of the criminal law in seeking to control, *inter alia*, acts of trespass and acts that disrupt lawful activities. The 1994 Act was particularly controversial, attracting opposition from such diverse quarters as members of the House of Lords, 'clergy, lawyers, police, MPs, civil rights groups, ecology groups and the disaffected young'.[17] Mike Bennett, chairman of the Metropolitan Police Federation, described the public order provisions as unworkable, being 'legislation directed against a certain section of the population...people whose lifestyle, culture and attitude to life differs from other people'. On the day it was passed, 'other campaigners started a series of rolling protests across the country... with "mass trespass"—a new offence created under the Act—at road construction sites'.[18] The Crime and Disorder Act 1998 introduced novel powers for courts to make anti-social behaviour orders in an effort to combat repeated acts of harassment and disorder on housing estates,[19] and created a series of racially aggravated offences where assaults, public order offences or damage are caused with racial hostility.

Part 1 of the Criminal Justice and Police Act 2001 introduced a new fixed penalty notice scheme, which empowers an officer to issue a fixed penalty notice (i.e. fixed fine) to any person he has reasonable grounds to believe to be committing a specified offence (including being drunk in a public place and causing harassment, alarm and distress contrary to s. 5 of the Public Order Act 1986). This again has significant implications for protesters. The fixed penalty notice is not a criminal sanction and no criminal record results from paying it—merely 'an opportunity to discharge liability' (What liability? Is there a crime or tort

---

[12] See, e.g., *Duncan v Jones* [1936] 1 KB 218, DC, below, p. 392, and cf. *Laporte*, below, p. 376.

[13] See, e.g., *Wise v Dunning* [1902] 1 KB 167, DC, below, p. 385; Public Order Act 1986, ss. 4, 4A, 5, below, pp. 337–355; the law of sedition and incitement to disaffection.

[14] This was preceded by the *Review of the Public Order Act 1936 and related legislation* (Green Paper, Cmnd 7891, 1980); the Fifth Report from the Home Affairs Committee, Session 1979–80, *The Law Relating to Public Order* (1979–80 HC 756: the Committee had a Conservative majority and divided on party lines on many issues); the Law Commission's Report, *Criminal Law: Offences Relating to Public Order* (Law Com No. 123, 1983) and the White Paper, *Review of Public Order Law* (Cmnd 9510, 1985). Hereafter these are cited as *Green Paper, HAC Report, Law Com No. 123* and *White Paper*.

[15] Through expansion of their general powers (see Chap. 4) and the increased number of offences.

[16] Football Offences Act 1991, Football (Disorder and Offences) Act 1999, Football (Disorder) Act 2000, Football (Disorder) (Amendment) Act 2002.

[17] *Independent*, 4 November 1994.   [18] Ibid.

[19] These powers were subsequently extended by the Police Reform Act 2002, ss. 61–66 and the Anti-social Behaviour Act 2003.

proved against D?). The recipient may contest the notice and demand a trial, in which case the full penalty for the offence is available on conviction. Failure to pay the fine may lead to the imposition of a fine of 1.5 times the penalty.

The Anti-social Behaviour Act 2003[20] introduced a formidable battery of provisions designed to deal with such matters as the closure of premises where drugs are used unlawfully; the anti-social behaviour of tenants; parenting contracts and orders in respect of criminal and anti-social behaviour of children and young persons; and the dispersal of groups of young people. Part 7 of the Act expanded powers to deal with public assemblies, raves and trespass. Part 4 of the Serious Organised Crime and Police Act 2005 broadened the Protection from Harassment Act 1997, created a new offence of trespassing on a designated site, introduced new controls on demonstrations in the vicinity of Parliament and further amended the law governing ASBOs. Sections 145 to 149 introduced new protections for animal research organisations and their employees. The Racial and Religious Hatred Act 2006 created offences involving stirring up hatred against persons on religious grounds. Schedule 16 to the Criminal Justice and Immigration Act 2008 introduced an offence of stirring up hatred on the ground of sexual orientation. Unusually, in a rare move to relax restrictions, the Draft Constitutions Renewal Bill[21] does include the repeal of ss. 132–138 of SOCPA 2005 concerning demonstrations in the vicinity of Parliament.

The fundamental principles that should apply in the policing of public protest were stated in the following extract by Lord Scarman in his Report on the Red Lion Square Disorders.

- **The Red Lion Square Disorders of 15 June 1974: Report of Inquiry by the Rt. Hon. Lord Scarman OBE** (Cmnd 5919, 1975)

FIRST PRINCIPLES

5. Amongst our fundamental human rights there are, without doubt, the rights of peaceful assembly and public protest and the right to public order and tranquillity. Civilised living collapses—it is obvious—if public protest becomes violent protest or public order degenerates into the quietism imposed by successful oppression. But the problem is more complex than a choice between two extremes—one, a right to protest whenever and wherever you will and the other, a right to continuous calm upon our streets unruffled by the noise and obstructive pressure of the protesting procession. A balance has to be struck, a compromise found that will accommodate the exercise of the right to protest within a framework of public order which enables ordinary citizens, who are not protesting, to go about their business and pleasure without obstruction or inconvenience. The fact that those who at any one time are concerned to secure the tranquillity of the streets are likely to be the majority must not lead us to deny the protesters their opportunity to march: the fact that the protesters are desperately sincere and are exercising a fundamental human right must not lead us to overlook the rights of the majority.

6. This Inquiry has been concerned to discover where the balance should be struck, and the role of the police in maintaining it. Indiscipline amongst demonstrators, heavy-handed police reaction to disorder are equally mischievous: for each can upset the balance. Violent demonstrators by creating public disorder infringe a fundamental human right which belongs to the rest of us: excessively violent police reaction to public disorder infringes the rights of the protesters. The one and the other are an affront to civilised living.

---

[20] Amended by ss. 23–27 of the Police and Justice Act 2006 (parenting contracts and orders; anti-social behaviour injunctions).

[21] Cm 7342–II, March 2008.

THE ROLE OF THE POLICE

7. The police are not to be required in any circumstances to exercise political judgment. Their role is the maintenance of public order—no more, and no less. When the National Front marches, the police have no concern with their political message; they will intervene only if the circumstances are such that a breach of the peace is reasonably apprehended. Even if the message be 'racist', it is not for the police to 'ban the march' or compel it to disperse unless public order is threatened....

2. DEMONSTRATIONS AND RIOTS

Developments in public order law need to be seen in the context of the recent history of demonstrations , riots and other forms of public protest. In general, contrary to the popular image, in the period 1900 to 1975 there was a marked and generally downward trend in the number of violent disorders, from a high point in the first two decades of the century.[22] The same point has been made in respect of industrial disputes.[23]

(I) FROM RED LION SQUARE TO THE MINERS' STRIKE

In 1974, a serious public order incident at Red Lion Square led to an inquiry chaired by Lord Scarman. This was a serious disturbance that arose out of a clash between a National Front[24] march and a counter-demonstration involving a range of left-wing groups. A Warwick University student, Kevin Gately, was killed during the disturbance.

Prior to the Red Lion Square disorder there had been only 54 incidents of protest giving rise to disorder (with a total of 623 arrests) in the previous three years. The MPC Report[25] attributed such low rates of disorder, arrest and injury to the 'unique relationship' between police and protestors who rely on mutual goodwill. Political demonstrations 'seem to give satisfaction in the main to those taking part'. The right to hold them was 'much valued and jealously preserved'. The public tended only to be interested if there was violence, leading to speculation as to whether the police should have prohibited or regulated a particular political demonstration. However, no useful purpose was achieved 'by prohibitions or regulations incapable of enforcement, or in respect of which judicial penalties are likely to be slight'. Demonstrators who could rely on massive support, were unlikely to be deterred by such restrictions and political extremists were likely to welcome them. Disregard or defiance was sure to achieve maximum publicity at very little cost. Accordingly, the metropolitan police had always been disinclined to seek an order under the Public Order Act 1936 prohibiting political processions for a specified period[26] 'on the grounds that this encourages extremist minority groups to threaten violence with the object of achieving the suppression of opposition opinion'.

Since the Red Lion Square disorder there have been numerous other serious incidents— some localised to riots on housing estates, some national trade union disputes (e.g. the

---

[22] See E. Dunning et al., 'Violent disorders in twentieth-century Britain' in G. Gaskell and R. Benewick (eds), *The Crowd in Contemporary Britain* (1987). For information on earlier struggles, see *Ewing and Gearty* and the references given in the 5th edition of this work at p. 393, n. 2.

[23] R. Geary, *Policing Industrial Disputes* (1985).

[24] A right-wing organisation widely regarded as neo-fascist and racist.

[25] See Sir Robert Mark CPM, 'The Metropolitan Police and political demonstrations' (Appendix 8 to the Report of the Commissioner of Police of the Metropolis for the year 1974).

[26] See p. 314.

miners' strike), Of particular note in 1979 was serious disorder in Southall[27] and arising out of meetings held during the General Election by the National Front in Leicester, West Bromwich and Bradford.[28] On 2 April 1980, there was serious disorder in the St Paul's district of Bristol.[29] In 1981 there were what were described as the most serious outbreak of public disorder in England and Wales since 1945, in Brixton,[30] Toxteth in Liverpool (where the use of CS was authorised for the first time on the British mainland to control public disorder) and Moss Side in Liverpool, and elsewhere in the country.[31]

The next major influence on public order legislation and policing was the miners' strike, which was to alter radically policing practices and public perceptions of policing.

- **Report of Her Majesty's Chief Inspector of Constabulary for 1984** (1984–85 HC 469)

PUBLIC ORDER

GENERAL

8.1 ...the NUM dispute dominated public order policing in 1984, and was the greatest challenge to the police capacity to deal with disorder since the civil disturbances in 1981. In some ways its presented a more gruelling test of determination and stamina as the months continued and the overall levels of disorder did not significantly decrease. The largest concentration of demonstrators was at Mansfield on 14 May when 12,000 attended an NUM rally. In the disorder that followed, several hundred of those who had attended threw bricks and bottles at the police and attacked others as well, including an ITV crew who were filming the incident. More than 1,000 officers, some mounted officers among them, were deployed to deal with the disorder: 87 arrests were made and 88 officers were injured. On 29 and 30 May and 1 June thousands of pickets gathered at the Orgreave coking plant to try to prevent convoys of coke-carrying lorries from leaving the works. The attempts were unsuccessful but, over the 3 days, there was considerable violence as bricks and petrol bombs were thrown at the police. In all there were more than 100 arrests and more than 50 police injuries. On 18 June 10,000 pickets demonstrated at Orgreave and again the ensuing violence was such that mounted officers with shields and helmets had to be deployed to disperse the crowds. The incident caused 28 police injuries and led to 93 arrests.

8.2 In addition to these instances of particularly serious disorders, there were many occasions on which large numbers of pickets congregated outside collieries and elsewhere, and the tactics adopted included not just missile-throwing but the building of barricades, the spilling of oil and nails on the roads and the placing of tripwires. In the first stages of the dispute such picketing was largely in Nottinghamshire as, for example, when on 9 April 2,000 pickets demonstrated at Babbington colliery, but as the return to work spread more widely, other police force areas also faced disorder. On 2 November, for example,

---

[27] See *Southall 23 April 1979: The Report of the Unofficial Committee of Enquiry* (NCCL, 1980); *The Death of Blair Peach: The Supplementary Report of the Unofficial Committee of Inquiry* (NCCL, 1980); C. Harlow [1980] PL 241.

[28] See the *Report of HM Chief Inspector of Constabulary for 1979* (1979–80 HC 725), p. 50.

[29] See 983 HC Deb, 28 April 1980, cols 971–981; M. Kettle and L. Hodges, *Uprising!* (1982), Chap. 1.

[30] See the Report by Lord Scarman, *The Brixton Disorders 10–12 April 1981* (Cmnd 8427, 1981). Lord Scarman found that they were largely caused by the hostility between Black youths and the police as a result of a breakdown of communication with the community and a loss of confidence in the police; this included an operation in which over a hundred officers were deployed in Lambeth to detect and arrest burglars and robbers, relying on powers to stop and search for unlawfully obtained property under s. 66 of the Metropolitan Police Act 1839, done without any warning to community leaders or local police officers. For references on the 1981 riots see the 5th edition of this book at p. 396, n. 10.

[31] See *Report of HM Chief Inspector of Constabulary for 1981* (1981–82 HC 463), paras 8.1–8.4.

3 police force areas had sites which were the targets for more than 1,000 demonstrators—Arkwright in Derbyshire, Woolley in West Yorkshire and Steetlcy Quarry in Durham. On other occasions pickets tried to block major routes such as the AI/M by moving slowly in convoys of large numbers. The continuing scenes of public disorder, of which the above are just a few examples, took place against a background of individual acts of criminal damage, assault and intimidation in connection with the dispute, and were on. such a scale that on some days more than 8,000 officers were deployed on mutual aid. Every police force in England and Wales either provided or received mutual aid,...

8.3 By comparison, the anti-nuclear demonstrations were significantly smaller in scale....

8.4 Despite the different tactics and approaches adopted in the various forms of demonstration and picketing described above, the police forces continued to rely on the traditional methods of public order policing in this country, using the minimum of force to deal with violent disorder, and seeking to maintain order by co-operation and agreement whenever possible. For the most part demonstrations and pickets were policed using officers wearing ordinary uniform and in close contact with the demonstrators. Protective equipment such as overalls, shields and helmets were used where necessary, and the horses of the mounted branches again proved their worth in dispersing crowds of disorderly demonstrators. Ironically for an operation which involved such large-scale mutual aid, the policing of the NUM dispute also demonstrated chief officers' awareness of the importance of policing communities by local officers as far as possible.

- **Report of Her Majesty's Chief Inspector of Constabulary for 1985** (1985–86 HC 437)

NUM DISPUTE

8.2 The decision in March by the National Union of Mineworkers to return to work ended one of the longest and most bitter industrial disputes ever seen in this country.... In the final phase, as miners began to return to work at collieries which had been strike-bound, bitterness between working and striking miners intensified. There were more instances of attempted intimidation involving, in some cases, personal assaults and attacks on homes. The main centres of violence were in Yorkshire, Northumberland and Durham and, to a lesser extent, in South Wales. The role of the police throughout the dispute remained constant: to maintain public order, to enforce the criminal law and to ensure that those who wished to work or otherwise to go about their lawful business could do so. Despite physical discomfort and inevitable domestic upheaval, the police sought throughout to maintain the rule of law. I was heartened by the overall level of professionalism which was displayed.

8.3 The success of the police in meeting the formidable challenges of the dispute undoubtedly owes much to the effectiveness of the mutual aid arrangements which enabled over 7,000 officers to be deployed for sustained periods on such duties. Despite misunderstanding and misrepresentation of its roles, the National Reporting Centre efficiently fulfilled its function of co-ordinating requests from Chief Officers for mutual aid. The more professional arrangements for public order training and tactics, which had followed the inner-city riots of 1981, meant that the police were much better able to handle the disorder. Protective equipment again proved its worth. It was notable that, despite the severity of the disorders, the police were able to cope without resort to the use of CS smoke, water cannon and similar equipment. It is unlikely that other police forces in Europe would have been able to cope with such disorder without the use of much more aggressive measures. I have mentioned elsewhere, however, that if the scale of violence increases in these situations the use of this type of equipment may be inevitable....

8.5 The dispute also took its toll on ordinary policing throughout the country but it is not possible to say what effect, if any, the dispute had on national crime figures. The financial and resource consequences were severe, despite the scale of central assistance, and there were increased stress and welfare implications for those officers left in forces due to additional workloads and extended hours of duty.

Peter Wallington's 'overview' was as follows:[32]

The policing of the dispute has attracted strong comments, many almost as partisan as the positions of the protagonists to the dispute itself. The police deserve much of the praise they received for undertaking a task of such daunting magnitude and complexity. Many of the criticisms of their behaviour, unfortunately, are also deserved, and the police are not well served by the crude loyalty of some of their supporters. But the real issue for those concerned with the lessons of the policing of the dispute was whether the police role was a proper one. Effectively they filled the vacuum created by the failure of the N.C.B. and others to use the civil law; effectively they became, wittingly or otherwise, the agency by which the strike was contained and eventually broken. How far this was an inexorable product of the circumstances, and in particular the strike leaders' own tactical choices, will continue to be a matter of controversy.

The police were given whatever resources they needed to preserve law and order and access to the pits. This enabled them to make the choice to preserve order by containment or prevention of picketing. With fewer resources it might in some cases have been necessary, and would certainly have been lawful, to preserve the peace by preventing individual returning miners from attempting to pass through picket lines. Resources enabled a choice to be made as to whose activities were to be curtailed, even (certainly in the case of the operation of a blanket turn-back policy) whose lawful activities were to be curtailed. Those critics of the police who argue that they took a partisan position can at least point to legal authority that would have justified a different approach. It is scarcely conceivable in the political climate of the time that the alternative would have been adopted as a matter of policy, but that it was avoided at the cost of serious reductions in the level of policing in much of the country suggests a conscious choice.

In England and Wales, 9,808 people were arrested, of whom 7,917 (81 per cent) were charged with over 10,000 offences, including conduct likely to cause a breach of the peace (4,107); obstructing a constable (1,682); criminal damage (1,019); obstructing the highway (640); unlawful assembly (509); actual bodily harm (429); assaulting police (360); theft (352); watching and besetting/intimidation (275); breach of the peace (207) and riot (137). All the riot charges failed or were dropped. The overall acquittal rate was estimated at about 25 per cent. Conspiracy charges were 'conspicuous by their absence'.[33]

(II) THE CHANGING FACE OF PROTEST

Other major instances of public disorder in the last 25 years have included: anti-nuclear demonstrations at Greenham Common and other RAF bases (1984); 'Stop the City' demonstrations (1984); serious riots at Handsworth, Brixton and Broadwater Farm, Tottenham, in which four people died (a press photographer in Brixton, two shopkeepers in a sub-post office in Handsworth and PC Keith Blakelock at Tottenham) (1985); the 'Peace Convoy' in

---

[32] 'Policing the Miners' Strike' (1985) 14 ILJ 145, 1591. For other appraisals, from varying standpoints, of the policing of the miners' strike, see B. Fine and R. Millar (eds), *Policing the Miners' Strike* (1985); P. Scraton and P. Thomas (eds), *The State v The People: Lessons from the Coal Dispute* (1985) 12 JLS, Winter issue; S. McCabe and P. Wallington, *The Police, Public Order and Civil Liberties: Legacies of the Miners' Strike* (1988).

[33] P. Wallington (1985) 14 ILJ 145, 150.

the vicinity of Stonehenge (1986, 1988);[34] the News International dispute at Wapping (1986); the poll tax riot in central London on 31 March 1990;[35] and an increasing number of 'free festivals' attracting 'New Age travellers' (e.g. Castlemorton in May 1992).[36] Others include mass public protests at GM crops and road development, anti-globalisation and anti-capitalism protests, demonstrations against paedophile residents on housing estates, transportation of live animals and petrol prices and in respect of climate change. In 2004 a pro-hunting countryside alliance demonstration near Parliament became violent.

There has been a fundamental shift in the types of public disorder occurring. There have been relatively few disturbances arising out of clashes between far left and far right groups and no major industrial disputes anywhere near the significance of the miners' strike. There has been a dramatic increase in the number of environmental campaign groups in the 1990s and liaison among campaign groups has led to much larger and targeted protests. The use of e-mail and the widespread ownership of mobile phones has revolutionised the way in which protests are organised, advertised and executed. In addition, the targets of the protests have shifted. The focus tends to be on individual companies or development sites rather than 'state' or 'establishment' institutions. The impact this has had on policing is considerable. The leaders and organisers are less readily identifiable, there is less information available to the police and greater unpredictability as to the size and location of the protests. Any symbol of capitalism (e.g. McDonald's) may be the target and the protest arranged exclusively by e-mail contact within a few minutes.

3. DEVELOPMENTS IN POLICING

Since Red Lion Square there have been a number of developments in the policing of disturbances.

(I) POLICE EQUIPMENT

First, there have been changes in equipment. Better protective headgear and flame resistant clothing have been supplied and widely used. Protective shields were first used in disturbances arising out of a National Front march in Lewisham in 1977, and were used again at the Notting Hill carnival in the same year. New forms of baton have been introduced.[37]

More controversial has been the provision and use of baton rounds and CS gas, spray or smoke. The first point to note here is that police authorities do not have the power to prevent chief officers obtaining such equipment. In *R v Secretary of State for the Home Department, ex p Northumbria Police Authority*[38] the Court of Appeal held that the Home Secretary had power by a circular to authorise the Home Office to supply CS gas and plastic baton rounds to a chief constable for operational use by the police, even though the local police authority declined to approve the supply of such equipment. The power was available either under s. 41 of the Police Act 1964 or under the royal prerogative to keep the peace.

Secondly, there have been persisting, serious concerns abut the use of 'rubber bullets' or projectiles fired from a baton gun (baton rounds). These were originally solid polyurethane.

---

[34] See p. 326.   [35] See D. Burns, *Poll Tax Rebellion* (1992), Chaps 4, 5.

[36] See J. Baxter, 'Castlemorton and beyond' (1992) 8 Policing 222.

[37] See PCA Report, *The Police Use of New Batons* (1998).

[38] [1989] QB 26. See A.W. Bradley [1988] PL 298.

There were a number of deaths in Northern Ireland caused by their use.[39] In 1998, the UN Committee on Torture recommended their use be discontinued.[40] In 2001, a 'less lethal' impact round, the L21A1, was introduced.[41] It was more accurate, with an optical sight, and there was an independent medical assessment that the probability of it causing serious injury had been reduced. ACPO considered that this made it 'suitable for use in dealing with people who are posing an immediate threat to life in circumstances in which use of a firearm would otherwise be necessary'. This was in addition to its use in situations of public disorder. However, there would also be a research programme to see whether there was an 'acceptable, effective and less potential lethal alternative to the plastic baton round'. This has been one of the strands of work arising out of the Patten Report on *Policing in Northern Ireland*.[42] A UK-wide Steering Group has produced five reports.[43] There was also a *Review of the Discharge of Baton Rounds by Police in England and Wales 2002–2004*,[44] which concluded that in at least seven of the 37 incidents reviewed it was probable that conventional firearms would have been used with fatal consequences. There had been no life-threatening injuries in any incident. *Revised guidelines on the use of baton rounds in situations of serious public disorder* were issued on 8 December 2003.[45] The L21A1 has been replaced by a further device: the Attenuating Energy Projectile has been introduced from 21 June 2005. This is less rigid and carries a lower risk. It is not authorised for use in public order/crowd control situations,[46] although it has been used against violent individuals during serious disorder.[47]

The Joint Committee on Human Rights has accepted that this can be justified in human rights terms as a proportionate response to serious violence which threatens the lives of police or the public, but that their use should continue to be subject to close scrutiny.[48] ACPO has issued extensive guidance,[49] which (*inter alia*) refers to relevant international standards and domestic legislation and states that AEP may be deployed in a variety of operational situations, but is designed to be fired at individual aggressors. Nevertheless,

Officers trained in the use of the AEP system may also be deployed in situations of serious public disorder where their use is judged to be necessary to reduce a serious risk of:

(i)   loss of life or serious injury, or;

(ii) substantial and serious damage to property where there is, or is judged to be, a sufficiently serious risk of loss of life or serious injury to justify their use.[50]

A yet further device that has been introduced more recently is the M26 and X26 Taser® which can be used by authorised firearms officers as a less lethal alternative where a

---

[39] Statewatch Bulletin, Vol. 8 No. 5, 1998, col. 68W; http://news.bbc.co.uk/1/hi/northern_ireland/1460116.stm. This form was available but not used operationally in England and Wales.

[40] Concluding observations on the UK's Third Periodic Report, 17 November 1998, A/54/44.

[41] Jack Straw MP, *Hansard*, HC, 2 April 2001, col. 68W.

[42] September 1999, Recommendations 69 and 70 relating to public order equipment.

[43] www.nio.uk. These provide an extensive source of information. They include an evaluation of scientific and legal aspects of their use. It is now the Steering Group on Alternative Policing Approaches to the Management of Conflict, and its work continues.

[44] ACPO/HO, 12/06. The first use of the L21A1 was in February 2002 in North Wales.

[45] Steering Group Report No. 4 (2004), p. 113.

[46] Steering Group Report No. 5 (2006); *Hansard*, HL, 8 March 2007, col. WS 31.

[47] Steering Group Report No. 5, p. 40.   [48] 19th Report 2005–06, pp. 57–59.

[49] ACPO Attenuating Energy Projectile (AEP) Guidance Amended 16 May 2008: see http://police.homeoffice.gov.uk/operational-policing/firearms/aep-dip/.

[50] Para. 1.15.

firearms authority has been granted. This is battery-operated and generates a high voltage electrical current.[51]

A different kind of device that has been used in riot control is CS gas[52] ('tear gas') or smoke. Early versions were used in riots in Northern Ireland,[53] and then in Toxteth, Liverpool, in 1981. CS smoke is significantly more indiscriminate in its effects to be suitable for use in public disorder situations (as distinct from sieges).[54] Indeed it has not been used in such situations in Great Britain or Northern Ireland since the introduction of baton rounds.

The use of CS smoke from canisters fired into crowds of protestors is to be distinguished from what is now the routine equipping of individual uniformed police patrol officers with CS sprays.[55] There is ACPO Guidance.[56] The PCA concluded that CS spray

does not appear to present a serious risk to the public . . . [and it] has made a real impact in making life safer for police officers.[57]

Finally, water cannon have been used in Northern Ireland.[58]

The research and monitoring of information the use of these various devices available publicly today is commendable, but there remain concerns that the risks to health are understated.[59]

(II) MUTUAL ASSISTANCE

The second major development in the last 20 years concerns the mutual aid arrangements under which one chief officer of police provides assistance to another whose force-is under pressure. The co-operation between forces is sanctioned by the Police Act 1996.[60] The development of NCIS and NCS, and now SOCA, have also played a significant part in the ability to police public order incidents, through the availability of national intelligence and specialist registers such as those for animal rights protestors.[61] Particular emphasis is now placed on intelligence-led policing.[62]

(III) TRAINING AND MILITARISATION

The third development has been in the training of police officers in public order policing. Police Support Units were established in all forces, each typically comprising an inspector, two sergeants and 20 constables, trained to work as a group. Some forces have established elite groups under various names (e.g. the Territorial Support Group in

---

[51] See ibid., pp. 40–45; http://police.homeoffice.gov.uk/operational-policing/firearms/taser/.

[52] 2-chlorobenzalmalononitrile.

[53] Which gave rise to the report of the Himsworth Inquiry in 1971 (Cmnd 4775) into the medical and toxicological aspects of CS.

[54] L. Jason-Lloyd (1991) 141 NLJ 1043.

[55] CS spray was introduced in 1997 in England and Wales and 2003 in Northern Ireland. A second incapacitant spray, PAVA, is also now in use. See Steering Group, 5th Report, pp. 46–49. See PCA Report, CS Spray: Increasing Public Safety (2000).

[56] Guidance on the use of Incapacitant Spray (September 2006): www.acpo.police.uk.

[57] CS Spray: Increasing Public Safety (2000), p. 27.

[58] Steering Group 4th Report, pp. 51–60; 5th Report, pp. 49–50.

[59] See B. Rappert (2002) BJ Crim 689, Non-Lethal Weapons as Legitimizing Forces?: Technology, Politics and the Management of Conflict (Frank Cass, London, 2003).

[60] S. 23.   [61] See p. 367.

[62] HMIC Thematic Report, Keeping the Peace (1999).

the Metropolitan Police). These have been associated with a more aggressive approach to disturbances—

and represent a significant move away from the traditional approach to public order policing which was based on containment and the use of minimum force.[63]

New techniques, involving special formations of officers and the use of police horses, were incorporated in the revised *Public Order Manual of Tactical Options and Related Matters* prepared by the Association of Chief Police Officers.[64] The Government has formally rejected the option of establishing a 'third force' to deal specifically with public disorder, modelled on forces in European countries, such as the French CSU.[65] The arguments against a 'third force' were summarised by the Chief Inspector of Constabulary in his Report for 1984:[66] mutual aid arrangements were effective in practice; we could not afford to have a large body of law enforcement officers kept in reserve for public order situations; and such a force would come under centralised control and consequently be more readily susceptible to political influence. The various developments outlined above seem to be steps towards at least the de facto establishment of the equivalent of a 'third force'.[67] It has, however, also been argued that paramilitary policing is the most effective way of maintaining impartial and consensual public order policing.[68]

(IV) EVIDENCE GATHERING

The investigation of offences arising out of major disorder is difficult in practice, despite the advances in policing with advanced equipment and mutual assistance between the forces.

Frankly, the police record for successfully prosecuting those who engage in serious public disorder is dismal. Currently, where a senior investigating officer (SIO) is appointed after the event, suspects who plead 'not guilty' stand only a one in five chance of being convicted.[69]

However, modern practice includes the use of police officers and civilian photographers as 'evidence gatherers', the use of static video cameras, the power to seek a production order for press material under PACE, the organisation of hospital welfare teams to question casualties (police and public) and the establishment of charge centres.[70] Use of CCTV cameras has become more prevalent, and evidence from such cameras/recordings is routinely admitted as evidence in criminal trials, even in relation to disputed identification.[71]

---

[63] K.D. Ewing and C.D. Gearty, *Freedom under Thatcher* (1990), p. 105. See also T. Jefferson, *The Case Against Paramilitary Policing* (1990), Chap. 1.

[64] K.D. Ewing and C.D. Gearty, op. cit., pp. 105–106; G. Northam, *Shooting in the Dark: Riot Police in Britain* (1988).

[65] T. Jefferson, op. cit., p. 2, referring to a Home Office Working Party between 1961 and 1971.

[66] 1984–85 HC 469, pp. 4–5.

[67] For criticism, see T. Jefferson, *The Case Against Paramilitary Policing* (1990).

[68] P.A.J. Waddington, 'Towards paramilitarism? Dilemmas in policing civil disorder' (1987) 27 B J Criminol 37. See also P. Waddington, *The Strong Arm of the Law* (1991); K. Bryett, 'Who Polices Violence' (1991) 1 Policing & Society 285.

[69] Det. Supt. E. Williams, 'Investigating major disorder' (1994) 10 Policing 134. On police tactics see M. King and M. Brearley (eds), *Public Order Policing* (1996).

[70] Ibid.

[71] See M. Gill and A. Spriggs, *Assessing the impact of CCTV* (HORS 292, 2005). On the use of CCTV and even airship surveillance in combating public disorder, see HMIC *Keeping the Peace* (1999), p. 55.

The Crime and Disorder Act 1998 assists policing major disorder of this type by empowering officers to require a person to remove a face mask or covering (see below). In *Friedl v Austria*[72] the Court of Human Rights considered the practice of the Austrian police in video-recording and taking still photographs of the protestors at a homelessness demonstration. These images were used in the subsequent prosecution of the demonstrators for breaches of the relevant criminal offences relating to unauthorised demonstrations. The Commission found that there had been no breach of Art. 8.

4. FREEDOM OF ASSOCIATION

The ECHR guarantees a right of assembly. Article 11 provides:

> Everyone has the right to freedom of peaceful assembly and to freedom of association with others, including the right to form and to join trade unions for the protection of his interests.

As far as English law is concerned, there are few express legal limits on the freedom of people to associate together for political purposes. The criminal law of conspiracy only applies to agreements to commit a crime, to defraud or to do an act which tends to corrupt public morals or outrage public decency.[73] Accordingly, the fact that people associate to perform certain acts will not render them criminally liable unless those acts would be illegal if performed by an individual, subject to the two limited exceptions stated. The tort of conspiracy is committed where two or more people agree to do an unlawful act, or to do a lawful act by unlawful means, or to perform acts other than for their own legitimate benefit, with the object of inflicting damage on a third party.[74] The tort of conspiracy is thus now appreciably wider in scope than the crime, although it is necessary in tort for the claimant to prove that he has suffered damage.

The following section illustrates some statutory limitations on freedom of association in the public order context.

- **Public Order Act 1936**

> *An Act to prohibit the wearing of uniforms in connection with political objects and the maintenance by private persons of associations of military or similar character; and to make further provision for the preservation of public order on the occasion of public processions and meetings and in public places.*

> **1. Prohibition of uniforms in connection with political objects**
>
> (1) Subject as hereinafter provided, any person who in any public place or at any public meeting wears uniform signifying his association with any political organisation or with the promotion of any political object shall be guilty of an offence:
>
> Provided that, if the chief officer of police is satisfied that the wearing of any such uniform as aforesaid on any ceremonial, anniversary, or other special occasion will not be likely to involve risk of public disorder, he may, with the consent of a Secretary of State, by order permit the wearing of such uniform on that occasion either absolutely or subject to such conditions as may be specified in the order....

---

[72] (1995) 21 EHRR 83.   [73] Criminal Law Act 1977, Part I; *Smith and Hogan*, pp. 399–401.

[74] A.M. Dugdale and M.A. Jones (eds), *Clerk and Lindsell on Torts* (19th edn), paras 25.116–25.137; *Lonrho Ltd v Shell Petroleum Co Ltd (No. 2)* [1982] AC 173; *Lonrho plc v Fayed* [1992] 1 AC 448; *Revenue and Customs Comrs v Total Network SL* [2008] UKHL 19, [2008] 2 All ER 413.

9. Interpretation, etc

(1) In this Act the following expressions have the meanings hereby respectively assigned to them, that is to say—

'Meeting' means a meeting held for the purpose of the discussion of matters of public interest or for the purpose of the expression of views on such matters;

'Private premises' means premises to which the public have access (whether on payment or otherwise) only by permission of the owner, occupier, or lessee of the premises;

'Public meeting' includes any meeting in a public place and any meeting which the public or any section thereof are permitted to attend, whether on payment or otherwise;

['Public place' includes any highway and any other premises or place to which at the material time the public have or are permitted to have access, whether on payment or otherwise;] ...

NOTES

1. The maximum penalty under s. 1 is currently three months' imprisonment, a fine not exceeding level 4 on the standard scale or both.[75] The consent of the Attorney-General is required for a prosecution: s. 1(2). Section 7(3) gives a power of arrest.

2. Section 1 was introduced in response to the increasing use of uniforms by political groups, notably the Fascists.[76] 'In the year following enactment of the POA 1936, there were no fewer than 12,011 meeting in the Metropolitan Police district alone, 3,094 of them fascist, 4,364 of them anti-fascist with a further 4,553 connected with neither political position.'[77] The first prosecutions were of Blackshirts: *R v Wood*[78] (D sold Fascist newspapers while wearing a black peak cap with two emblems, black shirt, tie and leather motoring coat, dark trousers and dark footwear: fined £2); *R v Charnley*[79] (at public meetings D wore black trousers, dark navy blue pullover and red brassard on his left arm: convicted and bound over).[80] Thus the wearing of a complete outfit is not necessary for a conviction. The section has also been used against members of the Ku Klux Klan[81] and supporters of the Irish republican movement.[82]

In *O'Moran,* members of a funeral party accompanying the body of Michael Gaughan, a self-confessed IRA member who died on a hunger strike while in Parkhurst prison, wore black or dark blue berets, dark glasses and dark clothing. They were not identically dressed. An oration beside the coffin referred to the Irish republican movement, and an Irish tricolour flag was placed on the coffin. In *Whelan,* the defendants assembled with others at Speakers' Corner in order to march as a protest on the first anniversary of internment in Northern Ireland. The march was organised by Provisional Sinn Fein and other groups. The leaders all wore black berets and some also wore dark clothing, dark glasses and carried Irish flags and banners. The Divisional Court upheld convictions under s. 1(1). Per Lord Widgery CJ:[83]

---

[75] Act, s. 7, as amended.   [76] See *Williams,* pp. 216–220; *Ewing and Gearty,* pp. 300–320.
[77] *Ewing and Gearty,* p. 325.   [78] (1937) 81 Sol Jo 108.   [79] (1937) 81 Sol Jo 108.
[80] See also *R v Wright* (1937) 81 Sol Jo 509; E.R. Ivamy [1949] CLP 184–187; cf. *R v Taylor, Ward and Hawthorne* (1937) 81 Sol Jo 509: Social Credit Party members in green shirts, ties and armlets found not guilty.
[81] *The Times,* 8 October 1965.   [82] *O'Moran v DPP, Whelan v DPP* [1975] QB 864, DC.
[83] At pp. 873–874.

'Wearing' in my judgment implies some article of wearing apparel. I agree with the submission made in argument that one would not describe a badge pinned to the lapel as being a uniform worn for present purposes. In the present instance however the various items relied on, such as the beret, dark glasses, the pullovers and the other dark clothing, were clearly worn and therefore satisfy the first requirement of the section.

The next requirement is that that which was worn was a uniform,…the policeman or the soldier is accepted as wearing uniform without more ado, but the isolated man wearing a black beret is not to be regarded as wearing a uniform unless it is proved that the beret in its association has been recognised and is known as the uniform of some particular organisation, proof of which would have to be provided by evidence in the usual way.

In this case [O'Moran] the eight men in question were together. They were not seen in isolation. Where an article such as a beret is used in order to indicate that a group of men are together and in association, it seems to me that that article can be regarded as uniform without any proof that it has been previously used as such. The simple fact that a number of men deliberately adopt an identical article of attire justifies in my judgment the view that that article is uniform if it is adopted in such a way as to show that its adoption is for the purposes of showing association between the men in question. Subject always to the de minimis rule, I see no reason why the article or articles should cover the whole of the body or a major part of the body, as was argued at one point, or indeed should go beyond the existence of the beret by itself. In this case the articles did go beyond the beret. They extended to the pullover, the dark glasses and the dark clothing, and I have no doubt at all in my own mind that those men wearing those clothes on that occasion were wearing uniform within the meaning of the Act.

Evidence has been called in this case from a police sergeant to the effect that the black beret was commonly used, or had been frequently used, by members of the IRA, and I recognise that it is possible to prove that an article constitutes uniform by that means as well.

The next point, and perhaps the most difficult problem of all, is the requirement of the section that the uniform so worn shall signify the wearer's association with any political organisation. This can be done in my judgment in two ways. The first I have already referred to. It is open to the prosecution, if they have the evidence and wish to call it, to show that the particular article relied upon as uniform has been used in the past as the uniform of a recognised association, and they can by that means, if the evidence is strong enough, and the court accepts it, prove that the black beret, or whatever it may be, is associated with a particular organisation. In my judgment it is not necessary for them to specify the particular organisation because in many instances the name of the organisation will be unknown or may have been recently changed. But if they can prove that the article in question has been associated with a political organisation capable of identification in some manner, then that would suffice for the purposes of the section.

Alternatively, in my judgment the significance of the uniform and its power to show the association of the wearer with a political organisation can be judged from the events to be seen on the occasion when the alleged uniform was worn. In other words, it can be judged and proved without necessarily referring to the past history at all, because if a group of persons assemble together and wear a piece of uniform such as a black beret to indicate their association one with the other, and furthermore by their conduct indicate that that beret associates them with other activity of a political character, that is enough for the purposes of the section.

Could the wearing of any clothing or badge constitute an offence under s. 4 or 5 of the Public Order Act 1986 (causing harassment, alarm or distress)? Could the offence under s. 1 of the Public Order Act 1936 be committed by wearing animal masks at an anti-vivisectionist protest?

● Public Order Act 1936

2. Prohibition of quasi-military organisations

(1) If the members or adherents of any association of persons, whether incorporated or not, are—

    (a) organised or trained or equipped for the purpose of enabling them to be employed in usurping the functions of the police or of the armed forces of the Crown; or

    (b) organised and trained or organised and equipped either for the purpose of enabling them to be employed for the use or display of physical force in promoting any political object, or in such manner as to arouse reasonable apprehension that they are organised and either trained or equipped for that purpose;

then any person who takes part in the control or management of the association, or in so organising or training are aforesaid any members or adherents thereof, shall be guilty of an offence under this section:

Provided that in any proceedings against a person charged with the offence of taking part in the control or management of such an association as aforesaid it shall be a defence to that charge to prove that he neither consented to nor connived at the organisation, training, or equipment of members or adherents of the association in contravention of the provisions of this section.

(2) No prosecution shall be instituted under this section without the consent of the Attorney-General.

(3) [This authorises the forfeiture of the property of an association which is unlawful under this section]…

(5) [This authorises a High Court judge to grant a search warrant if there is reasonable ground for suspecting an offence under s. 2]

(6) Nothing in this section shall be construed as prohibiting the employment of a reasonable number of persons as stewards to assist in the preservation of order at any public meeting held upon private premises, or the making of arrangements for that purpose or the instruction of the persons to be so employed in their lawful duties as such stewards, or their being furnished with badges or other distinguishing signs.

NOTES

1. The maximum penalties under this section are six months' imprisonment, a £5,000 fine or both on summary conviction, and two years, a fine of any amount or both on conviction on indictment.[84]

2. This section was passed to meet the growth of private armies, in particular fascist groups, between 1933 and 1936.[85]

3. Note that there is no reference to the promotion of a political object in s. 2(1)(a). Vigilante groups might accordingly offend against this provision.

4. The first prosecution under s. 2(1)(b) was *R v Jordan and Tyndall*.[86] J and T took part in the organisation of 'Spearhead', part first of the British National Party and later of the National Socialist Movement. At various times in 1961 and 1962 uniformed members of Spearhead

---

[84] Public Order Act 1936, s. 7(1) as amended.

[85] *Williams*, pp. 220–221; R. Benewick, 'The Threshold of Violence' in Benewick and Smith (eds), *Direct Action and Democratic Politics* (1972); *Ewing and Gearty*, Chap. 6.

[86] [1963] Crim LR 124, CCA; *Williams* pp. 222–223.

were seen practising foot drill, carrying out attack and defence exercises at a tower building and exchanging Nazi salutes. At a camp near Cheltenham, the Horst Wessel song was sung and cries of 'Sieg Heil' were heard. The police searched the Movement's headquarters under a warrant issued under s. 2, and found documents referring to the former German National Socialist Storm Troopers and containing phrases such as 'Task Force', 'Front Line Fighters' and 'Fighting Efficiency'. They also found tins of sodium chlorate (weed killer) which could be used in making bombs. On one tin, the words 'Jew Killer' had been written. J and T were convicted of organising Spearhead members in such a way as to arouse reasonable apprehension that they were organised to be employed for the use or display of physical force promoting a political object. The Court of Criminal Appeal approved the trial judge's direction that: 'reasonable apprehension means an apprehension or fear which is based not upon undue timidity or excessive suspicion or still less prejudice but one which is founded on grounds which to you appear to be reasonable. Moreover the apprehension or fear must be reasonably held by a person who is aware of all the facts.....' J was sentenced to nine, and T to six months' imprisonment, the Court of Criminal Appeal regarding it as an appropriate occasion for the imposition of deterrent sentences.[87] The section has also been employed in respect of the organisers of IRA units.[88]

5. On the proscription of organisations under the Terrorism Act 2000, see below. In the *Review of the Public Order Act 1936 and related legislation*[89] the Government rejected an argument that since much recent disorder had resulted from confrontations between the supporters of the National Front and others, including members of the Socialist Workers Party, there were grounds for banning one or both of these organisations. Proscription had been confined to organisations openly and avowedly dedicated to violent terrorist acts and to the overthrow of the civil authorities.[90]

5. PUBLIC MEETINGS AND PROCESSIONS

In this country there are no unfettered legal rights to hold public meetings or processions. The law regulates (a) the location and (b) the conduct of public assemblies. Issues may arise under Arts 10[91] and 11 ECHR. The latter applies in a diverse range of circumstances including where the assembly is alleged to be illegal,[92] and applies to both public and private assemblies. Challenges may include other 'rights' such as those involving freedom of religion. In *Pendragon v United Kingdom*[93] the application of Arthur U. Pendragon, a druid, challenging the banning order under s. 14A POA 1986 (below) relating to Stonehenge, was declared inadmissible. P was arrested at a 'service' he was conducting for druids, and he claimed that his right to religion under Art. 9 was infringed, along with his rights under Arts 10, 11 and 14. The Commission found that the order under s. 14A complied with a sufficiently clear procedure, was limited and could be challenged before the courts.

---

87 See further M. Walker, *The National Front* (1977), pp. 39–42, 44–45.

88 *R v Callinan* (1973) Times, 20 January, C Cr Ct; *R v Kneafsey* (1973) Times, 23 October; *R v Fell* [1974] Crim LR 673, CA (Cr D). On the prosecution under s. 2 of members of the 'Free Wales Army' see D.G.T. Williams [1970] CLJ 103.

89 Cmnd 7891, 1980, p. 11.

90 Compare *Ewing and Gearty*, Chaps 3 and 6, discussing the difficulties in policing the Communist Party and Fascist supporters in the 1920s and 1930s.

91 See *Steel v UK*, below, p. 399 and generally Chap. 9.

92 *G v Germany* (1989) 60 DR 256.   93 [1999] EHRLR 223.

(A) THE LOCATION OF MEETINGS AND PROCESSIONS

All land is vested in some person or institution. People may be permitted to assemble at the landowner's discretion. Assembling without permission is a trespass, although proceedings may well not be taken.[94] Meetings and processions must also conform to the common law of nuisance and to any specific statutory restrictions as to location. The residual freedom or 'liberty' to assemble must be exercised without infringement of the rights of others, and with due regard for their liberties. It is an important question whether English law gives sufficient weight to freedom of assembly. It is also open to argument whether judges have attached sufficient importance to this interest where the law only proscribes conduct that is 'unreasonable', and the conflicting interests of different people have accordingly to be balanced. The materials considered here illustrate the courts' reliance on property law rather than constitutional principles to resolve public order disputes and the limits of freedom to assemble although the latter have carried greater weight in more recent decisions.

(I) THE HIGHWAY

1. Tort

A highway is, in general terms any way over which all members of the public have the right to pass and repass. The use of the highway for meetings and processions is restricted by both the law of tort and the criminal law. Aspects of the law of tort which are theoretically relevant include trespass, public nuisance and private nuisance, and now the law of harassment.[95]

Trespass   If the highway is used in a manner that falls outside the parameters of the public right of way, that conduct will constitute a trespass as against the owner of the land over which the right of way exists.[96] It is crucial therefore to identify those parameters. The House of Lords confirmed in *DPP v Jones*[97] that a peaceful non-obstructive demonstration on a road is not a trespassory assembly for the purposes of s. 14A of the Public Order Act 1986.[98] The majority held that there was no limitation that the use of the highway had to be restricted to passage and repassage or to uses incidental or ancillary thereto. It is a question of fact and degree for the magistrates in each case whether a particular use is reasonable. Lords Irvine and Hutton acknowledged a right of peaceful assembly, provided that it does not obstruct the public right of passage. Lord Clyde, the other member of the majority found that there was no trespass on the facts.

Where a highway is maintainable at the public expense, as is usually the case with made up roads, it vests in the highway authority.[99] There is in fact no reported case of such an authority suing demonstrators or the participants in a meeting for trespass.

Public nuisance as a tort   Unreasonable interference with a public right such as a public right of way constitutes the common law criminal offence of *public nuisance*.[100] The Attorney-General or a local authority (acting under s. 222 of the Local Government

---

[94] But see *Department of Transport v Williams* (1993) 138 SJLB 5, where the Court of Appeal upheld the grant of interlocutory injunctions against persons demonstrating against the motorway constructions at Twyford Down to restrain trespasses and, in one case, interference with business.

[95] See below, pp. 357–367.   [96] See p. 319.   [97] [1999] 2 AC 240.

[98] See below, p. 312.   [99] Highways Act 1980, ss. 1, 263, 265–267.

[100] See below p. 294.

Act 1972)[101] may seek an injunction to restrain a threatened offence. A public nuisance is actionable in tort at the suit of any person who suffers some particular or special loss over and above the inconvenience suffered by the public at large (special damage).[102] Accordingly, to constitute public nuisance, the misuse of a highway must amount to 'unreasonable user'.[103] In *Hubbard v Pitt*[104] Forbes J assumed that 'unreasonableness' was established if it could be shown that passage was obstructed. That assumption has been criticised.[105] Wallington argues:

> The test is...not whether a demonstration is something reasonably incidental to passage, but whether it is reasonable in the context of rights of highway users generally. If passers-by must make a detour, their inconvenience must be balanced against the interest in allowing the demonstration; it will be relevant to consider the degree of obstruction and whether the demonstration could conveniently have been held at a less obstructive venue or off the highway.[106]

Private nuisance   Private nuisance is described in *Winfield and Jolowicz on Tort*[107] as 'unlawful interference with a person's use or enjoyment of land, or some right over, or in connection with it'. This includes infringement of a servitude.[108] Only those who have a right to exclusive possession of the land can sue in nuisance.[109] The blocking of access to private premises is an example of private nuisance.[110] The Court of Appeal has held that D can only be liable in private nuisance where the unreasonable interference with C's land arises from the use by D of his or her own land.[111] This formed one ground for holding that the council was not liable for the serious harassment of the claimants by tenants of a council estate who congregated outside their shop on the estate. This has been doubted;[112] and the cases is better regarded as resting on a second ground, which is that a landlord is in any event only liable for a nuisance created by a tenant in very limited circumstances which did not apply here.[113] In other cases, it has been held that unreasonable picketing may constitute private nuisance.[114]

---

[101] See, e.g., *Nottingham City Council v Z* [2001] EWCA Civ 1248, [2002] 1 WLR 607 (injunction to restrain drug dealing).

[102] W.V.H. Rogers, *Winfield and Jolowicz on Tort* (Sweet & Maxwell, London, 17th edn, 2006), pp. 644–646.

[103] *Lowdens v Keaveney* [1903] 2 IR 82; *R v Clark (No. 2)* [1964] 2 QB 315, CCA; *News Group Newspapers Ltd v Society of Graphical and Allied Trades '82 (No. 2)* [1987] ICR 181 (daily mass picketing and demonstrations at NGN's Wapping plant constituted unreasonable use of the highway and public and private nuisance).

[104] [1976] QB 142. Here, the defendants picketed a firm of estate agents as part of a campaign against property developers. The estate agents brought an action alleging nuisance, libel and conspiracy, and were granted an interlocutory injunction by the Court of Appeal (affirming Forbes J, although not necessarily agreeing with all aspects of his judgment).

[105] See P. Wallington [1976] CLJ 82, 101–106. Cf. the debate in *DPP v Jones*.

[106] Ibid., p. 104.   [107] 17th edn, 2006, p. 646.

[108] Ibid., pp. 664–666.   [109] *Hunter v Canary Wharf Ltd* [1997] 2 All ER 426; see below, p. 535.

[110] *Winfield*, pp. 686–687.   [111] *Hussain v Lancaster City Council* [2000] QB 1.

[112] *Lippiatt v South Gloucestershire Council* [2000] QB 51 (licensor of land could be liable in nuisance where licensees (here, travellers) were alleged to have used the land as a base for trespassing on neighbouring land and doing a series of acts there including dumping rubbish, causing damage, and threatening and assaulting neighbours and their employees).

[113] See *Winfield*, pp. 674–677.

[114] *Thomas v National Union of Mineworkers (South Wales Area)* [1985] 2 All ER 1 (regular picketing of the home of a working miner, regardless of the number of people involved and regardless of the peaceful nature of their conduct, would constitute a common law nuisance; mass picketing would also constitute common law nuisance); *News Group Newspapers Ltd v Society of Graphical and Allied Trades '82 (No. 2)* [1987] ICR 181, above.

2. Crime

Obstruction of the highway may constitute the crime of *public nuisance*.[115] In *R v Clark (No. 2)*,[116] C, the field secretary of the Campaign for Nuclear Disarmament, led a crowd through various streets in London in the course of a Committee of 100 demonstration during the visit of the King and Queen of Greece. Several streets were partially or completely blocked. C was convicted on a charge of inciting persons to commit a public nuisance by obstructing the highway and sentenced to 18 months' imprisonment. His conviction was quashed as the deputy chairman at the London Sessions had failed to direct the jury on the question whether, granted obstruction, there was an unreasonable user of the highway. He had merely directed that if there was a physical obstruction, that constituted nuisance, and that C, if he incited it, was guilty. Much more commonly, criminal proceedings for *obstruction of the highway* are brought under the following provision.

● Highways Act 1980

137. Penalty for wilful obstruction

(1) If a person, without lawful authority or excuse, in any way wilfully obstructs the free passage along a highway he shall be guilty of an offence and shall be liable in respect thereof to a fine not exceeding level 3 on the standard scale.

NOTES

1. This section was formerly s. 121 of the Highways Act 1959. It is much used in respect of demonstrations—particularly where people sit down in the street.

2. It is not open to the local authority to authorise an obstruction of the highway so as to afford a defence to criminal proceedings: *Redbridge London Borough v Jacques*;[117] *Cambridgeshire and Isle of Ely County Council v Rust*.[118]

3. Cases under s. 137 and analogous statutory provisions have consistently taken the line that the obstruction of any part of the highway constitutes obstruction for these purposes, notwithstanding that there is room for persons to pass by, or that delay is minimal. [119]

4. Reasonable user of the highway will constitute 'lawful excuse' under s. 137. The scope of this defence has been expanded in recent years, as shown in the following case.

● **Westminster City Council v Haw** [2002] EWHC 2073 (QB),
    Gray J (Official transcript from Westlaw)

From 2001, Brian Haw had been conducting a protest in Parliament Square. The local authority sought an injunction to restrain him on the ground that his conduct constituted an offence against s. 137 of the Highways Act 1980.

Gray J:
This application raises questions as to the interaction between the right and the duty of a local authority to remove obstructions from its highways, on the one hand, and the right of the individual citizen to use those highways to exercise his or her right to freedom of expression, on the other hand. It is an

---

[115] See p. 360.   [116] [1964] 2 QB 315.   [117] [1970] 1 WLR 1604, DC.
[118] [1972] 2 QB 426, DC. See A.J. Ashworth [1974] Crim LR 652; A.T.H. Smith (1985) 14 Anglo-Am LR 3.
[119] *Homer v Cadman* (1886) 16 Cox CC 51, DC. Cf. *Aldred v Miller* [1925] JC 117 (High Court of Justiciary).

application by Westminster City Council, which is the local authority responsible for the highways, including the pavements, in Parliament Square in London, to restrain Mr Brian Haw from obstructing the pavement opposite the House of Commons by displaying there a considerable number of placards supporting his protest against the policies of the Government in relation to Iraq.

2. What is sought is a final injunction that the defendant cease the obstruction in Parliament Square and elsewhere in Westminster, and that he remove the placards and other paraphernalia....

5. On behalf of the defendant, it is accepted that he has been conducting a protest from the pavement in Parliament Square ever since June 2001. He has been doing so, so he says, on a 24-hour a day basis, every day, since then. According to his witness statement, Mr Haw sleeps and eats there, and he has from time to time been fasting. He, too, exhibits to his witness statement numerous photographs of the placards and posters which have, from time to time, been on display. It is not necessary for me to go into detail; it suffices to say that the placards and posters criticise in trenchant terms the policy adopted by the Government towards the regime in Iraq and the effect of that policy on Iraqi citizens.

6. The case for the defendant is, in essence, that he is not obstructing the highway but rather is using it in a lawful and reasonable manner to exercise his rights of freedom of expression and assembly contained respectively in Articles 10 and 11 of the European Convention on Human Rights, and now incorporated as part of English domestic law by the Human Rights Act.

7. It is stating the obvious to say that Mr Haw feels passionately about the policy currently being adopted towards Iraq and the effect it is having, but no-one has doubted his sincerity....

13. It is accepted on behalf of the defendant that the rights arising under Articles 10 and 11 are not unqualified, but it is contended on his behalf that there is no pressing social need to restrict his rights and that the action being taken against him by the Council is in any event disproportionate.

14. Since the relief being sought by the Council is a final injunction, the Council must establish affirmatively its entitlement to that relief. I accept, for what it is worth, that the standard of proof is somewhat higher than the usual balance of probability, since it is a criminal offence which the Council is alleging. I also bear in mind in this connection that I am enjoined by section 12.4 of the Human Rights Act to have 'particular regard' to the Convention right to freedom of expression.

15. What is it necessary for the Council to prove in order to establish a breach of section 137 of the Highways Act which I have quoted earlier? There must first be established the fact of physical obstruction. As I have said, there is an abundance of photographic evidence. Neither the number nor the position of the placards remains static. Some of the placards are, according to the photographs, positioned on the grass in Parliament Square, which comes under the jurisdiction of the Greater London Authority and not that of Westminster City Council. I am concerned only with the obstruction of the pavement.

16. It has been agreed between the parties that Mr Schwartz, of the defendant's solicitors, accurately describes the extent of the physical obstruction and encroachment on the pavement when he says that the placards encroach on the pavement, which is 11 feet wide, by some 1½ feet, and that the bed on which the defendant sleeps on the pavement encroaches to the extent of about 2 feet. Miss Favata suggests that obstruction of the pavement of that kind and magnitude is *de minimis* and therefore can be disregarded. I do not agree. The authorities to which I have been referred indicate that the degree of obstruction would indeed have to be trifling in order for the Court to ignore it. I think the fact of physical obstruction is established. I also accept that the obstruction is 'wilful' in the sense that it is, and has been, deliberate.

17. But it also seems clear from the authorities that the mere fact of wilful obstruction is not of itself sufficient to give rise to an offence under section 137 and highways can, according to the authorities, be lawfully used for purposes other than 'passage and repassage.' *Nagy v Weston* [1965] 1 All ER 78, a case concerning a hot dog van in Oxford, Lord Parker CJ said at page 80:

> 'Counsel for the appellant concedes, as indeed he is bound to concede, that any occupation of part of a road, thus interfering with people having the use of the whole of the road, is an obstruction. He also concedes that wilful obstruction is when the obstruction is caused purposely or deliberately.'

He goes on, however, to say that:

'Before anyone can be convicted of this offence, two further elements must be proved: first, that the defendant had no lawful authority or excuse; and secondly, that the user to which he was putting the highway was an unreasonable user. For my part, I think that excuse and reasonableness are really the same ground, but it is quite true that it has to be proved that there was no lawful authority. It is really difficult to think of any argument that can be used in the present case to the effect that the appellant had lawful authority to obstruct the highway if what happened was an obstruction. It is undoubtedly true, counsel for the appellant is quite right, that there must be proof that the user in question was an unreasonable user. Whether or not the user amounting to an obstruction is or is not an unreasonable use of the highway is a question of fact but it depends on all the circumstances, including the length of time the obstruction continues, the place where it occurs, the purpose for which it is done and, of course, whether it does in fact cause an actual obstruction as opposed to a potential obstruction.'

That passage was quoted with approval by Glidewell LJ in *Hirst and Agu v Chief Constable of West Yorkshire* (1987) 85 Cr App R 143.... Glidewell LJ continued at page 150 as follows:

'As counsel pointed out to us in argument, if that is not right there are a variety of activities which quite commonly go on in the street which may well be the subject of prosecution under section 137. For instance, what is now relatively commonplace, at least in London and large cities, distributing advertising material or free periodicals outside stations when people are arriving in the morning. Clearly that is an obstruction. Clearly it is not incidental to passage up and down the street because the distributors are virtually stationary. The question must be: is it a reasonable use of the highway or not? In my judgment, that is a question that arises. It may be decided that if the activity grows to an extent that is unreasonable by reason of the space occupied or the duration of time for which it goes on, that an offence would be committed, but it is a matter on the facts for the magistrates, in my view.'

Later on he added:

'I emphasise that for there to be a lawful excuse for what would otherwise be an obstruction of the highway, the activity in which the person causing the obstruction is engaged must itself be inherently lawful. If it is not, the question of whether it is reasonable does not arise so an obstruction of the highway caused by unlawful picketing in pursuance of a trade dispute cannot be said to be an activity for which there is a lawful excuse, but in this case it is not suggested that the activity itself—distributing pamphlets and displaying banners in opposition to the wearing of animal furs as garments—was itself unlawful.'

I suggest that the correct approach for justices who are dealing with the issues which arose and arise in the present case is as follows. First, they should consider: is there an obstruction? Unless the obstruction is so small that one can consider it comes within the rule of *de minimis*, any stopping on the highway, whether it be on the carriageway or on the footway is *prima facie* an obstruction. To quote Lord Parker: 'Any occupation of part of a road thus interfering with people having the use of the whole of the road, is an obstruction.' The second question then will arise: was it wilful; that is to say, deliberate? Clearly in many cases a pedestrian or a motorist has to stop because the traffic lights are against the motorist. Were there other people in the way, not because he wishes to do so, such stopping is not wilful but if stopping is deliberate then there is wilful obstruction. Then there arises the third question: have the prosecution proved that the obstruction was without lawful authority or excuse? Lawful authority includes permits and licences granted under statutory provision, as I have already said, such as for markets and street traders and no doubt for those collecting for charitable causes on Saturday mornings. 'Lawful excuse' embraces activities otherwise lawful in themselves which may, or may not, be reasonable in all the circumstances mentioned by Lord Parker in *Nagy v Weston*.'

18. Next, and finally, in *DPP v Jones* [1999] 2 WLR 625, a case concerning alleged trespassory assembly Lord Irvine said this:

'I conclude therefore the law to be that the public highway is a public place which the public may enjoy for any reasonable purpose, provided the activity in question does not amount to a public or private nuisance and does not obstruct the highway by unreasonably impeding the primary right of the public to pass and re-pass. Within these qualifications there is a public right of peaceful assembly on the highway.'

In his speech, Lord Irvine was seeking to accommodate the requirements imposed by Article 11, that the same reasoning must apply in the case of Article 10.

[His Lordship then rejected an argument that the placards constituted advertisements the display of which would be unlawful under the Town and Country Planning Act 1990, and therefore unreasonable.]

20. ... As has been seen, the factors which come into play when judging reasonableness include the length of time for which the obstruction continues, the place where it occurs, its purpose and whether actual obstruction occurs.

21. It is an important feature of this case that the obstruction has been continuing for some 15 months, albeit in circumstances where the subject matter of the placards has remained topical throughout that period. The duration of the obstruction is an indication of unreasonableness. Against that, the point is fairly made for the defendant that, given that his objective is to influence Parliament in relation to policy towards Iraq, the location opposite the Houses of Parliament is a suitable one. The defendant assets an entitlement to continue to protest for so long as it is necessary for him to achieve, if he can, the change in policy which he is advocating. As to the extent of the interference with the right of passage and re-passage, according to the unchallenged evidence, the pavement which surrounds the grassed area in Parliament Square is not easily reached by pedestrians. There are no designated pedestrian crossings, and access to pedestrians is, according to the evidence, if anything, discouraged. In stark contrast to the pavement on the other side of the roads around Parliament Square, relatively few pedestrians use the inner pavements. The evidence of observations carried out by the street enforcement officers of the Council is that less than 30 pedestrians per hour use those inner pavements. There is no evidence of any actual obstruction of any pedestrian seeking to walk along the pavement. In all the time that the defendant has been present, the police have not once considered it necessary to take action against Mr Haw or even to warn him of any possible future action. There is no suggestion of any violence or disorder or breach of the peace arising out of the presence of Mr Haw in Parliament Square. The unchallenged evidence is that the defendant goes to great pains to ensure that the area is kept clean and tidy.

22. Apart from these considerations, which all bear on the question of reasonableness, there is another, to my mind, significant, consideration which I should also take into account. It is the fact that the defendant is exercising his right to freedom of expression, and doing so on a political issue. (Miss Favata relied also on Article 11 but I do not think that the right of assembly is engaged in the present case.)

23. The importance to be accorded to the right of freedom of expression, especially in the context of political discussion or debate, is emphasised in numerous domestic and Strasburg authorities, some of which I have mentioned earlier in this judgment. [His Lordship referred to Lord Steyn in *Ex p Simms* [2000] 2 AC 115, 126(e) and Laws LJ in *R (on the application of ProLife Alliance) v BBC* [2002] EWCA Civ 297 para [32].]

24. Mr Powell rightly points out that the right to freedom of expression is not unqualified by Article 10.2. Interference with the right is permissible where it is necessary—that is, where there is a pressing social need—to do so in order to protect the rights of others. Mr Powell submits that there is such a need to protect the right of pedestrians to pass and re-pass along the pavement in Parliament Square. He also mentioned the right of other protestors to protest from the pavement. I certainly do not accept that Article 10 is a trump card entitling any political protestor to circumvent regulations relating to planning and the use of highways and the like, but in my judgment the existence of the right to freedom of expression conferred by Article 10 is a significant consideration when assessing the reasonableness of any obstruction to which the protest gives rise. I am not satisfied in the circumstances of this case that there

is any pressing social need to interfere with the display of placards so as to protect the right of others to pass and re-pass. Objection may be taken to the defendant's activities on the ground that they constitute an eyesore, but that is a different matter. Moreover, as already mentioned, there is a requirement in section 12(4) of the Human Rights Act that on an application of the present kind, I should pay particular attention to the right of freedom of expression.

25. Looking at the issue of reasonableness in the round, and taking account of the duration, place, purpose and effect of the obstruction, as well as the fact that the defendant is exercising his Convention right, I have come to the conclusion that the obstruction for which the defendant is responsible is not unreasonable. Accordingly, I decline to grant the injunction sought.

NOTES

1. This is a very significant case that demonstrates that the scope of the s. 137 offence has been narrowed to take proper account of freedom of expression. *Hirst and Agu* had previously taken a step in that direction in rejecting the narrow view expressed in *Waite v Taylor*[120] handing out leaflets and holding banners was not incidental to the lawful use of the highway to pass and repass and, therefore, that the reasonableness of the activity was not relevant.

2. The Government's determination to stop Mr Haw's protest led to ill-judged legislation to introduce new controls. See below.[121]

3. In *Birch v DPP*[122] B had sat down in the road outside the premises being targeted as part of a demonstration and was arrested for obstruction. He sought to challenge the arrests under s. 137(1) by adducing evidence of the unlawful activities occurring within the premises. The magistrates declined to allow the evidence and the Divisional Court approved this decision. The case was distinguishable from *Hirst* (above) where the activity (handing out leaflets) was lawful in itself; lying down in the road on its face was not, Rose LJ said:

Whether or not preventing crime affords a defence to a particular charge must depend on the circumstances.

There may be circumstances in which preventing an actual, or imminently apprehended, breach of the peace or other serious offence, on or near the highway, will afford a lawful excuse for obstructing the passage along the highway of one or more vehicles.

But that is not the present case. An honest and reasonable belief that the progress of a vehicle may contribute to criminal activity not amounting to an imminent breach of the peace or other serious offence is not, in my judgment, capable of affording lawful excuse for obstructing the passage along the highway of that vehicle, still less of other vehicles unconnected with it.

A demonstration involving lying down in the road, as it seems to me, may possibly draw attention to crime but it cannot, in my judgment, give rise to the prevention of crime within either the [common law] principle…or section 3 of the [Criminal Law Act 1967] As Mr Perry points out, there was, at the time of this lying down, no crime occurring in the road. There was an obstruction not only of a vehicle destined for SARP's premises but a considerable number of other vehicles which were entitled to pass and repass on the highway.

Smith J also noted that before there can be a conviction under s.137 the prosecution must show that the defendant had no lawful excuse for obstructing the highway, although there will be an evidential burden on the defendant to show the circumstances relied upon.

---

[120] (1985) 149 JP 551.   [121] P. 303.   [122] [2000] Crim LR 301.

4. As to mens rea, it has been held that 'if anybody, by an exercise of free will, does something which causes an obstruction, then an offence is committed'; there is no additional requirement to show that D 'knowingly does a wrongful act'[123] In this case, Pat Arrowsmith was the main speaker at a meeting in Nelson Street, Bootle. For five minutes, both carriageway and pavements were obstructed by a crowd, and a passageway for vehicles was then cleared by the police, with A's help, and a fire engine and other vehicles were guided through the crowd. The carriageway was partially obstructed for a further 15 minutes. A's conviction under the forerunner of s. 137 was upheld by the Divisional Court.

A.T.H. Smith comments[124] that:

Although it could undoubtedly be said that she intended to cause an obstruction in the sense that she intended that the crowd should gather around her, it may be doubted whether in the circumstances her conduct in causing the obstruction was properly described as 'wilful'...[W]here no contemporaneous objection is taken by those whose official function it is to preserve the way free from obstruction, it is unduly restrictive of freedom of speech for the courts to hold that the obstruction is wilful when the speaker acts in reliance on that official, and perfectly proper, connivance.

(II) OPEN SPACES

Open spaces, parks, recreation grounds and the like are usually vested in the Crown, or in a local authority. They may be subject to regulations or byelaws made under a variety of statutory powers.[125] The Local Government Act 1972, s. 235 empowers district and London borough councils to make byelaws for the 'good rule and government' of the whole or any part of their area, 'and for the prevention and suppression of nuisances therein'. These commonly cover such topics as the use in public of musical instruments, amplifiers or indecent language.

The general public may not acquire a private law right to hold meetings on land.[126] 'No such right...is known to the law.'[127]

It is possible for a defendant in a criminal trial to challenge, on any ground, the validity of a byelaw, subject to the statute precluding such challenge.[128] The defence will always bear the burden of proving such invalidity. However, challenges to byelaws which prohibit the holding of meetings at particular places or without prior consent have generally been unsuccessful.[129] Conversely, byelaws restricting access to RAF Greenham Common, made under the Military Lands Act 1892, s. 17(2), were held to be *ultra vires* in *DPP v Hutchinson; DPP v Smith*.[130] The byelaws on their face prejudicially affected rights of common, and this was specifically prohibited by the enabling Acts. The appellants, who did not assert any right of common, were nevertheless entitled to argue in their defence that the byelaws were *ultra vires*.[131]

---

[123] *Arrowsmith v Jenkins* [1963] 2 QB 561.   [124] *Smith*, pp. 204–205.

[125] See *Brownlie*, pp. 35–38; Public Health Act 1875, s. 164; Open Spaces Act 1906, s. 15.

[126] *De Morgan v Metropolitan Board of Works* (1880) 5 QBD 155, DC and *Brighton Corpn v Packham* (1908) 72 DP 318, Ch D.

[127] Per Lush J in *De Morgan* at 157.

[128] *Boddington v British Transport Police* [1999] 2 AC 143; *R v Wicks* [1998] AC 92.

[129] *De Morgan*, above; *Slee v Meadows* (1911) 75 JP 246, DC; *Aldred v Miller* 1925 JC 21; *Aldred v Langmuir* 1932 JC 22.

[130] [1990] 2 AC 783, HL.

[131] See A.W. Bradley [1989] PL 1 and [1990] PL 193. Cf. *Bugg v DPP* [1993] 2 All ER 815, DC.

Bailey v Williamson[132] concerned the validity of regulations under the Parks Regulation Act 1872 which (*inter alia*) prohibited public addresses in Hyde Park except at certain places. Section 1 of the Act provided that nothing in the Act authorised 'any interference with any right whatever to which any person or persons may be by law entitled'. The Court of Queen's Bench held that there was no 'right' to hold public meetings in the Park. Cockburn CJ said:[133] '... whatever enjoyment the public have been allowed to have of these parks and royal possessions for any purpose has been an enjoyment which the public have had by the gracious concession of the Crown'. The use of Hyde Park is now regulated by the Royal and Other Open Spaces Regulations 1997.[134]

Two cases in 1888 confirmed that there was no 'right' of public meeting in Trafalgar Square.[135] Conduct in Trafalgar Square and Parliament Square Garden is now regulated by byelaws made by the Mayor of London, the Trafalgar Square and Parliament Square Garden Byelaws.[136] The byelaws prohibit a number of acts, including polluting water in any fountain, failing to keep an animal under control, feeding the birds, using a kite, or failing to comply with a reasonable direction given by an authorised person to leave the squares. There are then a number of acts for which written permission is required. In *Rai, Allmond and 'Negotiate Now' v United Kingdom*[137] a challenge to the Trafalgar Square statutory instrument on grounds that the discretion conferred was not adequately clearly prescribed by law was rejected by the European Commission. The apparently general and unlimited terms of the Statutory Instrument had been adequately explained by statements to the House of Commons. This is yet an example of the Strasbourg jurisprudence taking a generous view of whether English law adequately defines its proscribed activities in public order contexts. The Commission also rejected a challenge to the Government's refusal to make an exception to its general policy not to permit rallies or meetings in Trafalgar Square concerning Northern Ireland. Other venues were available (including Hyde Park); there was no blanket prohibition; and the judgment that the proposed rally was not 'controversial' fell within the margin of appreciation. Accordingly, the restriction was proportionate.

The Countryside and Rights of Way Act 2000 introduces a statutory right of access to open land (as defined in Part I of the Act), and provides for landowners to exclude or restrict access for any reason for up to 28 days per year, and to impose other specific restrictions relating to dogs on specified land at certain times of the year. Landowners may gain permission from the Countryside Agency to exclude the public for other reasons.[138] The public's right of access to land is for the purposes of 'open air recreation' and on condition that they enter without damaging any wall, fence or gate and that they comply with the restrictions in Sch. 2 (e.g. committing criminal offences; doing anything intended to intimidate persons engaged in lawful activity on that or adjoining land so as to deter them from engaging in it or to obstruct or disrupt that activity; without reasonable excuse, doing anything which disturbs, annoys or obstructs any persons engaged in a lawful activity on

---

132 (1873) LR 8 QB 118.   133 At 125.   134 SI 1997/1639, as amended by SI 2004/1308.

135 *R v Cunninghame Graham and Burns* (1888) 16 Cox CC 420; *Ex p Lewis* (1888) 21 QBD 191, DC (holding that Trafalgar Square was regulated entirely by Act of Parliament, and the right of public meeting was not found in the legislation).

136 As amended. See http://www.london.gov.uk/trafalgarsquare/manage/byelaws.jsp. Trafalgar Square was previously regulated by the Trafalgar Square Regulations 1952, SI 1952/776 and then the Royal Parks and Open Spaces Regulations 1997, SI 1997/1639. It was taken out of the scope of the 1999 Regulations by SI 2004/1308. Management of the Square was formerly vested in the Ministry of Works and then the Secretary of State, but has passed to the Greater London Authority.

137 81-A D and R 146 (1995). For the history of Trafalgar Square, see R. Mace, *Trafalgar Square* (1976).

138 See S.H. Bailey, *Cross on Local Government Law*, paras 23.21–23.35.

the land). Breach of a restriction will lead to the loss of a right of access for 72 hours, and to the wrongdoer being treated as a trespasser (s. 2(4)).

(III) NEAR PARLIAMENT

In addition to the legislative provisions mentioned below, from at least 1713 both Houses of Parliament at the commencement of each session directed the Metropolitan Police Commissioner to keep the streets leading to Parliament open and ordered that the access to Parliament of Lords and members was not to be obstructed. The power to give such sessional orders derives from parliamentary privilege.[139] The Commissioner enforced these orders by giving directions under s. 52 of the Metropolitan Police Act 1839.[140]

- **Sessional Order of the House of Commons**[141]

METROPOLITAN POLICE

MOTION MADE, AND QUESTION PROPOSED

That the Commissioner of the Police of the Metropolis do take care that during the Session of Parliament the passages through the streets leading to this House be kept free and open, and that no obstruction be permitted to hinder the passage of Members to and from this House, and that no disorder be allowed in Westminster Hall, or in the passages leading to this House, during the Sitting of Parliament, and that there be no annoyance therein or thereabouts; and that the Serjeant at Arms attending this House do communicate this Order to the Commissioner aforesaid.

- **Metropolitan Police Act 1839**

52. Commissioners may make regulations for the route of carriages, and persons,
and for preventing obstruction of the streets during public processions, etc.,
or in the neighbourhood of public buildings, etc.

...It shall be lawful for the commissioners of police from time to time, and as occasion shall require, to make regulations for the route to be observed by all carts, carriages, horses, and persons, and for preventing obstruction of the streets and thoroughfares within the metropolitan police district, in all times of public processions, public rejoicings, or illuminations, and also to give directions to the constables for keeping order and for preventing any obstruction of the thoroughfares in the immediate neighbourhood of her Majesty's palaces and the public offices, the High Court of Parliament, the courts of law and equity, the [magistrates' courts][142] the theatres, and other places of public resort, and in any case when the streets or thoroughfares may be thronged or may be liable to be obstructed.

NOTES

1. By s. 54(9) of this Act, 'every person' commits an offence 'who, after being made acquainted with the regulations or directions' made under s. 52, 'shall wilfully disregard or not conform himself thereunto'. The maximum penalty is a fine not exceeding level 2 on the standard scale.

---

[139] See D. Limon and W. McKay (eds), *Erskine May, Parliamentary Practice* (22nd edn, 1997), p. 180.
[140] Below.
[141] Last adopted by the HC in 2005: HC Deb, 17 May 2005, col. 28. A similar order is still made by the House of Lords: HL Deb, 6 November 2007. See *Erskine May*, op. cit., p. 180, and further below.
[142] As substituted by the Access to Justice Act 1999, s. 78(2), Sch. 11, paras 1, 2.

2. In *Papworth v Coventry*,[143] the Commissioner had directed that all assemblies or processions in a specified area 'shall be dispersed and shall not be in or proceed' in that area on any day on which while Parliament was sitting. P and others took part in a 'vigil' in Whitehall (within the area) on both sides of Downing Street to call attention to the situation in Vietnam. They were spaced apart and stationary, and were not disorderly. They refused to move when requested and prosecuted under s. 54(9). The court held: (a) that the sessional order itself could have no effect outside the walls and precincts of the Houses of Parliament; and (b) that the direction was to be construed as if it referred only to such assemblies or processions of persons as are capable of causing consequential obstruction to the free passage of members to and from the Houses of Parliament or their departure therefrom, or disorder in the neighbourhood or annoyance thereabouts. Any wider sense would have been *ultra vires* the Commissioner. The case was remitted to the stipendiary magistrate to determine whether the conduct 'constituted an assembly which was capable of giving rise consequentially either to obstruction of streets and thoroughfares in the immediate neighbourhood of the Houses of Parliament, or to disorder, annoyance of the kind itself likely to lead to a breach of the peace'. Papworth was subsequently acquitted.[144]

In *Needham v DPP*[145] the Divisional Court held that it was sufficient to 'acquaint' someone of a direction to summarise it (and it would be insufficient merely to state its existence). However, N's conviction under s. 54(9) in respect of her participation in a sit-down protest in the roadway in Parliament Square was quashed as the Commissioner's direction in force on that day enabled the police to stop or divert 'pedestrian traffic' but did not apply to persons sitting down on the thoroughfare.

3. The power to give directions was relied on as the basis of the use of roadblocks in the Wapping area during the News International dispute. These had a significant effect on the freedom of movement of residents.[146] The directions were not published and copies were not given to residents. The analogous power in the City of London Police Act 1839, s. 22, was used to combat 'Stop the City' demonstrations in the City.[147]

4. The enforcement of sessional orders has also been secured by the prosecution of persons for wilfully obstructing the police in the execution of their duty. See *Pankhurst v Jarvis*[148] and *Despard v Wilcox*,[149] cases concerning suffragettes.

5. Processions were stopped at the boundary of the 'Sessional Area' and marchers allowed to proceed independently to Parliament to lobby MPs.[150]

6. Disorder within the precincts of Parliament is dealt with by police under the direction of the Serjeant at Arms, as in 1966, where some members of the Committee of 100 attempted to make speeches in the House of Commons, and others sat down in Old Palace Yard.[151] The police on duty in the House are technically under the direction of the Serjeant at Arms. Both Houses have power to imprison any person offending the privileges of the House concerned or anyone in contempt of the House. The power has not been exercised since 1880.[152] On September 2004, eight protesters against the Hunting Bill entered the Palace of Westminster and five of them the Commons chamber. They were arrested for

---

143 [1967] 1 WLR 663, DC   144 *Brownlie*, p. 60.   145 11 March 1994, unreported.

146 See NCCL, *No Way in Wapping* (1986).   147 *New Statesman,* 11 May 1984, p. 5.

148 (1910) 22 Cox CC 228, DC.   149 (1910) 22 Cox CC 258, DC.

150 See P.A.J. Waddington, *Liberty and Order* (1994), pp.66–68.

151 *Report of the Comr of Police of the Metropolis for 1966,* Cmnd 3315, p. 13.

152 On the Serjeant at Arms' power to take into custody any person misconducting himself in the public gallery, see HC Standing Orders (Public Business) 2007/161, and the similar powers of the Gentleman of the Black Rod. See HL Standing Orders (Public Business) (2007) No. 13.

various offences including uttering a forged instrument (a letter purporting to invite them to a meeting), burglary with intent to commit criminal damage, and violent disorder.[153] They were convicted of offences of disorderly conduct under s. 5 of the Public Order Act 1986.[154]

7. The Sessional Order arrangements were reviewed by the House of Commons Select Committee on Procedure,[155] which recommended that the Government should introduce legislation to prohibit long-term demonstrations and to ensure that the laws about access are adequate and enforceable. Legislation was needed; without it the Sessional Order was misleading and, with it, it would be unnecessary. In the meantime, revised wording was proposed. A number of MPs had complained about the ongoing protest on the pavement in Parliament Square (conducted by Brian Haw); the Sub-Dean of Westminster Abbey had written that the long-term display of placards 'reduced one of the most important squares in London to an eyesore'.[156] The Government promised to consult developing legislation and agreed that the Sessional Order should be abandoned.[157]

In the event, the Government secured the passage of ss. 132–138 of the Serious Organised Crime and Police Act 2005, which appear under the heading 'Demonstrations in the vicinity of Parliament'. This provides that any person who organises or takes part in or carries on by himself a demonstration in a public place[158] in the designated area[159] is guilty of an offence if, when the demonstration starts, authorisation for the demonstration has not been given under s. 134(2).[160] It is a defence for a person to show that he or she reasonably believed that authorisation had been given.[161] This does not apply to a public procession of which notice is required to be given under s. 11(1) of the Public Order Act 1986[162] or a public procession for the purposes of s. 12 or 13 of that Act.[163] Section 14 of the 1986 Act[164] does not apply in relation to a public assembly which is also a demonstration in a public place in the designated area. A person seeking authorisation for a demonstration in the area must give prior notice.[165] If this is received within the specified time limits, the Metropolitan Police Commissioner must give authorisation, but may attach such conditions relating to the demonstration as in his 'reasonable opinion' are necessary for the purpose of preventing hindrance to any person wishing to enter or leave the Palace of Westminster, or to the proper operation of Parliament, serious public disorder or damage to property, disruption to the life of the community, a security risk in any part of the designated area, or a risk to safety of members of the public (including demonstrators). Non-compliance by an organiser or demonstrator with conditions is an offence, except where that arises from circumstances beyond his or her control, or something done with the agreement, or by the direction of a police officer.[166] The senior police officer at the scene may impose additional conditions or vary conditions on the same

---

[153] *The Guardian*, 16 September 2004.   [154] *The Times*, 26 May 2005.

[155] Third Report, 2002–03 HC 855, *Sessional Orders and Resolutions*.

[156] Ibid., p. 9

[157] HC Procedure Committee, Third Special Report 2003–04 HC 613, *The Government's Response to the Committee's Third Report of Session 2002–03*.

[158] Defined in s. 132(7)(b).

[159] The area must be within 1km of Parliament Square and is specified by the Secretary of State under s. 138; see Serious Organised Crime and Police Act 2005 (Designated Area) Order 2005, SI 2055/1537.

[160] 2005 Act, s. 132(1).   [161] 2005 Act, s. 132(2).   [162] See p. 301.

[163] 2005 Act, s. 132(3). Or to conduct lawful under s. 220 of the Trade Union and Labour Relations (Consolidation) Act 1992: s. 132(4).

[164] See p. 311.

[165] Six days, if reasonably practicable; otherwise, as soon as it is and in any event at least 24 hours before the time the demonstration is to start: s. 133.

[166] 2005 Act, s. 134.

basis.[167] With certain exceptions (including an emergency), loudspeakers may not be operated in any street in the designated area.[168]

This legislation is to be repealed by the Constitutional Renewal Bill 2008. In the meantime it has generated some interesting case law, mostly centred on the ongoing demonstration against Iraq by Brian Haw. The main milestones were first, the refusal of an injunction to Westminster City Council to stop Mr Haw's use of the pavement for his static demonstration, which began in 2001.[169] Secondly, the Court of Appeal held[170] (reversing the Divisional Court)[171] that the provisions were applicable to a demonstration that had started before commencement (1 August 2005), being deemed for the purposes of the Act to have commenced on that date. Otherwise the repeal of s. 14 of the 1986 Act in respect of the designated area would have left a gap in the powers of control in respect of preexisting demonstrations. The order specifying the designated area came into force on 1 July 2005. The Commissioner delegated his powers under s. 134 to an officer of the rank of superintendent or above. Superintendent Terry gave Mr Haw an authorisation subject to conditions, including that the site not exceed 3m in width, 3m in height and 1m in depth, that H supervise the site with diligence and care to ensure that nothing could be added to it without his knowledge, that he must not use articles that would allow others to conceal items within them, and that he maintain the site in a manner that allowed any person present to tell at a glance whether suspicious items were present thereon. H was prosecuted for breech of these conditions, in that the area behind the display was covered in disused placards, boxes and sheeting. The district judge held that there was no power to delegate the s. 134 duty and that the opinion of police officers of the meaning of the conditions that they were of insufficient clarity to be 'prescribed by law' for the purposes of Art. 11 ECHR. The Divisional Court[172] held that delegation was not precluded. Furthermore, the police were entitled to impose the conditions, given their purpose was not to impede the demonstration but to ensure that others would not use the demonstration as cover for terrorist activities. However, there was no basis to interfere with the district judge's conclusion on the uncertainty point.

It was conceded in *Blum v DPP*[173] that s. 132(1)(a) and (b) were not themselves incompatible with Arts 10, 11 ECHR. A number of prosecutions for holding demonstrations without prior authorisation were held on the facts to be compatible. The court rejected an argument that it was necessary for it to be established that the arrest, decision to prosecute and conviction were justifiable by reference to Art. 11(2) in the light of D's conduct during the demonstration. This argument was based on *Percy, Hammond* and *Dehal;*[174] the court held that these decisions were distinguishable as they all concerned charges where there was a defence that the conduct was reasonable, there being no such defence under ss. 132–138. Accordingly, as the requirement of authorisation was itself proportionate, 'Parliament must be entitled to impose sanctions where authorisation has not been obtained, otherwise the finding that the sections are compatible is illusory'.[175] (Does this follow?)

---

[167] 2005 Act, s. 135.   [168] 2005 Act, s. 136.   [169] See p. 294.

[170] *R (on the application of Haw) v Secretary of State for the Home Department* [2006] EWCA Civ 532, [2006] QB 780. See I. Loveland (2007) 3 EHRL Rev 251.

[171] [2006] QB 359.

[172] *DPP v Haw* [2007] EWHC 1931 (Admin), [2008] 1 WLR 379.

[173] [2006] EWHC 3209 (Admin). The concession was held to be rightly made in *Tucker v DPP* [2007] All ER (D) 479 (Nov), DC.

[174] See above, pp. 342–351.   [175] Per Waller LJ (V-P) at para. [29].

(IV) PUBLICLY OWNED PREMISES

As the holding of street meetings may be unlawful,[176] and therefore dependent in practice upon the goodwill of the police, it becomes even more crucial to those that wish to organise meetings that premises be available. Political meetings today seem to arouse such little public enthusiasm that finding premises is less of a problem than filling them. Extremist groups which are likely to arouse opposition naturally have most difficulty. One of the contributory factors in the decline of Mosley's British Union of Fascists after 1936 was the difficulty in hiring halls for their rallies.[177] Prior to the Olympia meeting in June 1934,[178] the police prevented a BUF rally at White City by persuading the chairman of the White City Board to demand so high a bond upon the safety of the hall that Mosley had to decline the booking.

The traditional importance of meetings during elections is recognised by ss. 95 and 96 of the Representation of the People Act 1983,[179] which entitle candidates during election campaigns (including European Parliamentary Elections) to the use of a suitable school room or meeting room (maintained at public expense) for the purpose of holding public meetings. Expenses are payable and damage must be paid for but the use is otherwise free of charge. In addition the discretionary powers of management of public premises must be exercised within the constraints of the *ultra vires* doctrine. Accordingly, a fixed policy to refuse the use of premises to particular groups or for particular purposes may fall foul of the rule that requires individual exercises of discretion, and decisions based on improper considerations may also be challenged.[180] Section 97 of the Representation of the People Act 1983 provides that acting or inciting others to act in a disorderly manner for the purposes of preventing such a meeting is an illegal practice.

In *R v Historic Buildings and Ancient Monuments Commission for England (English Heritage), ex p Firsoff*[181] the Court of Appeal dismissed a renewed application for leave to apply for judicial review of English Heritage's decision to close Stonehenge over the night of the summer solstice on 21–22 June 1991. EH's decision was taken on the advice of the police in view of disorder attending this occasion in previous years.[182] Under the Ancient Monuments and Archaeological Areas Act 1979, as amended by the National Heritage Act 1983, the public had access to Stonehenge, but EH had statutory power, if it considered it necessary or expedient to do so in the interest of safety or for the maintenance or preservation of the monument, to exclude the public from access for such period as it thought fit. The court held that there was no arguable case on any of the judicial review grounds.[183]

Finally, it should be noted that the ECtHR has stated that Art 10,

notwithstanding the acknowledged importance of freedom of expression, does not bestow any freedom of forum for the exercise of that right. While it is true that demographic, social, economic and

176 See above, pp. 292–299.

177 J. Stevenson and C. Cook, *Britain in the Depression* (1994), p. 233. See also K.D. Ewing and C.A. Gearty, op. cit., Chap. 6.

178 See below, p. 406.

179 As amended by the Representation of the People Act 1995, Sch. 4, para. 28 and the Greater London Authority Act 1999, s. 17.

180 H. Woolf, J. Jowell and A. Le Sueur, *De Smith's Judicial Review*, Chap. 5.

181 19 June 1991, unreported. See generally P. English, 'Disputing Stonehenge' [2002] 1 Ent Law 1.

182 See *DPP v Jones*, p. 319.

183 See also *R v Comrs of English Heritage, ex p Chappell*, 19 June 1986, unreported, CA, referred to in the 1991 case.

technological developments are changing the ways in which people move around and come into contact with each other, the Court is not persuaded that this requires the automatic creation of rights of entry to private property, or even, necessarily, to all publicly owned property (government offices and ministries, for instance). Where, however, the bar on access to property has the effect of preventing any effective exercise of freedom of expression or it can be said that the essence of the right has been destroyed, the Court would not exclude that a positive obligation could arise for the State to protect the enjoyment of the Convention rights by regulating property rights. A corporate town where the entire municipality is controlled by a private body might be an example.

Accordingly, there was no breach of Art. 10 or 11 where the applicants were prohibited from protesting (against a proposed development) in a privately-owned city centre (the 'Galleries' in Washington, Tyne and Wear). There were many other places where they could protest, including, with the shop's permission, inside any of the shops in the centre. This has been described as a 'very poor decision'.[184]

NOTES

1. Local councils with a general policy of refusing to allow their premises to be used for National Front meetings have been compelled to accede to requests to hold election meetings where the Front have had candidates in parliamentary elections.[185] In *Webster v Southwark London Borough Council*[186] Forbes J granted a declaration that a National Front candidate at a parliamentary by-election was entitled to use a room in accordance with the equivalent provision in the Representation of the People Act 1949.[187] In the light of continued refusal to make a room available leave was given for the issue of a writ of sequestration, although disobedience to a declaration, as a non-coercive order, did not amount to contempt of court. In *Ettridge v Morrell*,[188] the Court of Appeal held that the right of a local election candidate to have a suitable school room made available was a private right enforceable by an action in the Queen's Bench Division and not a public law right to be protected by an application for judicial review. The court permitted the meeting to take place.[189]

What is the position if the organisers of a National Front meeting, purportedly held under s. 95 of the Representation of the People Act 1983, only allow Front members or ticket holders into the meeting? What if the decision is taken by police outside in order to preserve the peace? Would the police be entitled to be present in the meeting in case of a breach of the peace?[190] Clayton[191] argues that the expression 'public meeting', which is not defined, should be construed as 'a meeting to which the public have access' rather than 'a meeting which a section of the public is permitted to attend, whether on payment or otherwise':

it would seem proper to construe the words narrowly so that section 95 is not construed as giving a candidate a right to use a room, on payment of bare expenses only, for the purpose of addressing the party faithful.

---

[184] E. Barendt, *Freedom of Speech* (2nd edn, 2005), p. 288 'the shopping centre occupied a huge area and had been partly financed with public money'.

[185] E.g. Manchester City Council: *The Times*, 20 April 1978.

[186] [1983] QB 698, QBD.   [187] S. 82.   [188] (1986) 85 LGR 100.

[189] P. Thornton, *Public Order Law* (1987), p. 162.   [190] See *McLeod*, below, p. 404.

[191] R. J. Clayton, *Parker's Conduct of Parliamentary Elections* (1983), pp. 101–102. See also P. Thornton, op. cit., pp. 162–163.

2. In October 1979, the Court of Appeal held that the Labour-controlled Great Yarmouth Council could not veto a booking for the annual conference of the National Front which had been accepted by the council when the Conservatives had been in power. The NF had paid over £6,000 for the booking fee and insurance to cover the risk of damage to council property. Lord Denning MR stated that the conference should go ahead in the interests of freedom of speech and assembly and of the importance of upholding a contract: *Verrall v Great Yarmouth Borough Council*.[192] Note again the reliance on private law (contract) to substantiate an important issue of constitutional principle.

3. See the *Green Paper*;[193] *HAC Report*;[194] *White Paper*.[195] The *HAC* proposed a procedure similar to s. 3(2) of the Public Order Act 1936[196] to enable the Home Secretary to require a candidate to hold his meeting elsewhere in the constituency or electoral area.[197] This was rejected by the Government on the ground that it would 'encroach upon the right of the candidate to convey his message to the electorate in the area of his choice; and it would involve the police and the public authorities in decisions bearing upon the political fortunes of particular candidates.'

4. Concerns regarding the freedom of expression in universities resulted in legislation.

- **Education (No. 2) Act 1986**

43. **Freedom of speech in universities, polytechnics and colleges**

(1) Every individual and body of persons concerned in the government of any establishment to which this section applies shall take such steps as are reasonably practicable to ensure that freedom of speech within the law is secured for members, students and employees of the establishment and for visiting speakers.

(2) The duty imposed by subsection (1) above includes (in particular) the duty to ensure, so far as is reasonably practicable, that the use of any premises of the establishment is not denied to any individual or body of persons on any ground connected with—

(a) the beliefs or views of that individual or of any member of that body; or

(b) the policy or objectives of that body.

(3) The governing body of every such establishment shall, with a view to facilitating the discharge of the duty imposed by subsection (1) above in relation to that establishment, issue and keep up to date a code of practice setting out—

(a) the procedures to be followed by members, students and employees of the establishment in connection with the organisation—

(i) of meetings which are to be held on premises of the establishment and which fall within any class of meeting specified in the code; and

(ii) of other activities which are to take place on those premises and which fall within any class of activity so specified; and

(b) the conduct required of such persons in connection with any such meeting or activity; and dealing with such other matters as the governing body consider appropriate.

(4) Every individual and body of persons concerned in the government of any such establishment shall take such steps as are reasonably practicable (including where appropriate the initiation of

[192] [1981] QB 202, CA. Cf. *Webster v Newham London Borough Council* (1980) Times, 22 November, CA.
[193] Pp. 24–26.   [194] Pp. xxv–xxvii.   [195] Pp. 36–37.
[196] Below, p. 314.   [197] P. xxvi.

disciplinary measures) to secure that the requirements of the code of practice for that establishment, issued under subsection (3) above, are complied with....

(6) In this section—

'governing body', in relation to any university, means the executive governing body which has responsibility for the management and administration of its revenue and property and the conduct of its affairs (that is to say the body commonly called the council of the university);

'university' includes a university college and any college, or institution in the nature of a college, in a university....

(8) Where a students' union occupies premises which are not premises of the establishment in connection with which the union is constituted, any reference in this section to the premises of the establishment shall be taken to include a reference to the premises occupied by the students' union.

NOTES

1. By sub-s. (5), as amended, the section applies to any university, any institution other than a university within the higher education sector; any establishment of higher or further education maintained by a local education authority; and any institution within the further education sector. An LEA maintaining an institution is taken to be concerned in its government.

2. For comments on this section, see Barendt,[198] who notes that this section—

will principally benefit controversial politicians and students disposed to listen to them. There is therefore little case in principle for imposing these unusual duties to secure free speech on university premises, when the law otherwise almost always treats freedom of speech as a mere liberty and is unwilling to recognise rights of access.[199]

3. In *R v University of Liverpool, ex p Caesar-Gordon*,[200] the university authorities granted permission to the student Conservative Association to hold a meeting subject to conditions that information about the meeting be treated as confidential until 9 a.m. on the day of the meeting; that the meeting be open only to those producing a valid staff or student card; and that the university reserved the right to charge the Association with the cost of security. Permission was subsequently withdrawn on the ground that it was likely that good order would not be maintained. The Divisional Court granted a declaration that the university was not entitled to take account of the risk of disorder other than on the university's premises, and there occasioned by members of the public over whom the university had no control. (The university had taken account of the serious concern expressed by the police at the risk of disorder in nearby Toxteth.) However, the court held that the conditions were *intra vires*.

4. Members of staff and students at a university may in an appropriate case rely on s. 43. See *R v University College London, ex p Urtsula Rincker*,[201] where Sedley J held that a contractual

---

[198] E. Barendt, 'Free Speech in the Universities' [1987] PL 344.

[199] Ibid., pp. 349–350.   [200] [1991] 1 QB 124.

[201] [1995] ELR 213. See also *R v Thames Valley University Students Union, ex p Ogilvy* [1997] CLJ 2149 (decision to exclude student from student union premises as a result of his verbally abusive behaviour not an infringement of freedom of speech and so not amenable to judicial review).

condition excluding R from involvement in matters concerning the running of, or entering, the language centre, did not interfere with freedom of speech and so did not give rise to a public law matter amenable to judicial review.

5. Copies of relevant codes of practice should be available from the university or college authorities and may be set out in the institution's Calendar or Regulations.

(V) POWERS TO BAN OR CONTROL PROCESSIONS AND ASSEMBLIES

There are no general powers whereby public bodies or officials may prohibit in advance the holding of a *meeting,* although there are such powers in relation to land whose management or control is vested in the state.[202] General statutory powers to ban or control *processions* were provided in s. 3 of the Public Order Act 1936. The 1986 Act remodelled and extended those powers and introduced new powers to control (although not ban) meetings and static demonstrations. Moreover, any meeting or procession which constitutes an unlawful assembly may be dispersed, and it may be lawful to disperse a lawful assembly where necessary to prevent a breach of the peace.[203]

The European Commission of Human Rights has recognised the compatibility with Art. 11 of prior notice requirements, and, in some circumstances, a ban for a procession:

a general ban on demonstrations can only be justified if there is a real danger of their resulting in disorder which cannot be prevented by other less stringent measures. In this connection, the authority must also take into account the effect of a ban on procedures which do not themselves constitute a danger for public order. Only if the disadvantage of such processions being caught by the ban is clearly outweighed by the security consideration justifies the issue of the ban, and if there is no possibility of avoiding such undesirable side-effects of the ban by a narrow circumspection of its scope in terms of its territorial application and duration, can the ban be regarded as necessary [under Art. 11(2)].[204]

- **Public Order Act 1986**

PART II[205]

PROCESSIONS AND ASSEMBLIES

11. Advance notice of public processions

(1) Written notice shall be given in accordance with this section of any proposal to hold a public procession intended—

    (*a*) to demonstrate support for or opposition to the views or actions of any person or body of persons,

    (*b*) to publicise a cause or campaign, or

    (*c*) to mark or commemorate an event,

unless it is not reasonably practicable to give any advance notice of the procession.

(2) Subsection (1) does not apply where the procession is one commonly or customarily held in the police area (or areas) in which it is proposed to be held or is a funeral procession organised by a funeral director acting in the normal course of his business.

---

[202] See, e.g., pp. 305–309.   [203] See pp. 376–397.

[204] *Christians against Racism and Fascism v UK* (1980) 21 DR 148, para. 5.

[205] See generally D.G.T. Williams [1987] Crim LR 167.

(3) The notice must specify the date when it is intended to hold the procession, the time when it is intended to start it, its proposed route, and the name and address of the person (or of one of the persons) proposing to organise it.

(4) Notice must be delivered to a police station—

    (a) in the police area in which it is proposed the procession will start, or

    (b) where it is proposed the procession will start in Scotland and cross into England, in the first police area in England on the proposed route.

(5) If delivered not less than 6 clear days before the date when the procession is intended to be held, the notice may be delivered by post by the recorded delivery service; but section 7 of the Interpretation Act 1978 (under which a document sent by post is deemed to have been served when posted and to have been delivered in the ordinary course of post) does not apply.

(6) If not delivered in accordance with subsection (5), the notice must be delivered by hand not less than 6 clear days before the date when the procession is intended to be held or, if that is not reasonably practicable, as soon as delivery is reasonably practicable.

(7) Where a public procession is held, each of the persons organising it is guilty of an offence if—

    (a) the requirements of this section as to notice have not been satisfied, or

    (b) the date when it is held, the time when it starts, or its route, differs from the date, time or route specified in the notice.

(8) It is a defence for the accused to prove that he did not know of, and neither suspected nor had reason to suspect, the failure to satisfy the requirements or (as the case may be) the difference of date, time or route.

(9) To the extent that an alleged offence turns on a difference of date, time or route, it is a defence for the accused to prove that the difference arose from circumstances beyond his control or from something done with the agreement of a police officer or by his direction....

12. Imposing conditions on public processions

(1) If the senior police officer, having regard to the time or place at which and the circumstances in which any public procession is being held or is intended to be held and to its route or proposed route, reasonably believes that—

    (a) it may result in serious public disorder, serious damage to property or serious disruption to the life of the community, or

    (b) the purpose of the persons organising it is the intimidation of others with a view to compelling them not to do an act they have a right to do, or to do an act they have a right not to do,

he may give directions imposing on the persons organising or taking part in the procession such conditions as appear to him necessary to prevent such disorder, damage, disruption or intimidation, including conditions as to the route of the procession or prohibiting it from entering any public place specified in the directions.

(2) In subsection (1) 'the senior police officer' means—

    (a) in relation to a process being held, or to a procession intended to be held in a case where persons are assembling with a view to taking part in it, the most senior in rank of the police officers present at the scene, and

    (b) in relation to a procession intended to be held in a case where paragraph (a) does not apply, the chief officer of police.

(3) A direction given by a chief officer of police by virtue of subsection (2)(*b*) shall be given in writing.

(4) A person who organises a public procession and knowingly fails to comply with a condition imposed under this section is guilty of an offence, but it is a defence for him to prove that the failure arose from circumstances beyond his control.

(5) A person who takes part in a public procession and knowingly fails to comply with a condition imposed under this section is guilty of an offence, but it is a defence for him to prove that the failure arose from circumstances beyond his control.

(6) A person who incites another to commit an offence under subsection (5) is guilty of an offence....

13. Prohibiting public processions

(1) If at any time the chief officer of police reasonably believes that, because of particular circumstances existing in any district or part of a district, the powers under section 12 will not be sufficient to prevent the holding of public processions in that district or part from resulting in serious public disorder, he shall apply to the council of the district for an order prohibiting for such period not exceeding 3 months as may be specified in the application the holding of all public processions (or of any class of public procession so specified) in the district or part concerned.

(2) On receiving such an application, a council may with the consent of the Secretary of State make an order either in the terms of the application or with such modifications as may be approved by the Secretary of State.

(3) Subsection (1) does not apply in the City of London or the metropolitan police district.

(4) If at any time the Commissioner of Police for the City of London or the Commissioner of Police of the Metropolis reasonably believes that, because of particular circumstances existing in his police area or part of it, the powers under section 12 will not be sufficient to prevent the holding of public processions in that area or part from resulting in serious public disorder, he may with the consent of the Secretary of State make an order prohibiting for such period not exceeding 3 months as may be specified in the order the holding of all public processions (or of any class of public procession so specified) in the area or part concerned.

(5) An order made under this section may be revoked or varied by a subsequent order made in the same way, that is, in accordance with subsections (1) and (2) or subsection (4), as the case may be.

(6) Any order under this section shall, if not made in writing, be recorded in writing as soon as practicable after being made.

(7) A person who organises a public procession the holding of which he knows is prohibited by virtue of an order under this section is guilty of an offence.

(8) A person who takes part in a public procession the holding of which he knows is prohibited by virtue of an order under this section is guilty of an offence.

(9) A person who incites another to commit an offence under subsection (8) is guilty of an offence....

14. Imposing conditions on public assemblies

(1) If the senior police officer, having regard to the time or place at which and the circumstances in which any public assembly is being held or is intended to be held, reasonably believes that—

    (*a*) it may result in serious public disorder, serious damage to property or serious disruption to the life of the community, or

    (*b*) the purpose of the persons organising it is the intimidation of others with a view to compelling them not to do an act they have a right to do, or to do an act they have a right not to do, he may give directions imposing on the persons organising or taking part in the assembly such conditions as to the place at which the assembly may be (or continue to be) held, its maximum duration, or the maximum number of persons who may constitute it, as appear to him necessary to prevent such disorder, damage, disruption or intimidation.

(2) In subsection (1) 'the senior police officer' means—

(a) in relation to an assembly being held, the most senior in rank of the police officers present at the scene, and

(b) in relation to an assembly intended to be held, the chief officer of police.

(3) A direction given by a chief officer of police by virtue of subsection (2)(b) shall be given in writing.

(4) A person who organises a public assembly and knowingly fails to comply with a condition imposed under this section is guilty of an offence, but it is a defence for him to prove that the failure arose from circumstances beyond his control.

(5) A person who takes part in a public assembly and knowingly fails to comply with a condition imposed under this section is guilty of an offence, but it is a defence for him to prove that the failure arose from circumstances beyond his control.

(6) A person who incites another to commit an offence under subsection (5) is guilty of an offence....

[14A. Prohibiting trespassory assemblies

(1) If at any time the chief officer of police reasonably believes that an assembly is intended to be held in any district at a place on land to which the public has no right of access or only a limited right of access and that the assembly—

(a) is likely to be held without the permission of the occupier of the land or to conduct itself in such a way as to exceed the limits of any permission of his or the limits of the public's right of access, and

(b) may result—

(i) in serious disruption to the life of the community, or

(ii) where the land, or a building or monument on it, is of historical, architectural, archaeological or scientific importance, in significant damage to the land, building or monument,

he may apply to the council of the district for an order prohibiting for a specified period the holding of all trespassory assemblies in the district or a part of it, as specified.

(2) On receiving such an application, a council may—

(a) in England and Wales, with the consent of the Secretary of State make an order either in the terms of the application or with such modifications as may be approved by the Secretary of State;...

(3) Subsection (1) does not apply in the City of London or the metropolitan police district.

(4) [This gives the same power to the Commissioner of Police for the City of London or the Commissioner of Police of the Metropolis, with the consent of the Secretary of State.]

(5) An order prohibiting the holding of trespassory assemblies operates to prohibit any assembly which—

(a) is held on land to which the public has no right of access or only a limited right of access, and

(b) takes place in the prohibited circumstances, that is to say, without the permission of the occupier of the land or so as to exceed the limits of any permission of his or the limits of the public's right of access.

(6) No order under this section shall prohibit the holding of assemblies for a period exceeding 4 days or in an area exceeding an area represented by a circle with a radius of 5 miles from a specified centre.

(7) An order made under this section may be revoked or varied by a subsequent order made in the same way, that is, in accordance with subsection (1) and (2) or subsection (4), as the case may be.

(8) Any order under this section shall, if not made in writing, be recorded in writing as soon as practicable after being made.

(9) In this section and sections 14B and 14C—

'assembly' means an assembly of 20 or more persons;

'land' means land in the open air;

'limited', in relation to a right of access by the public to land, means that their use of it is restricted to use for a particular purpose (as in the case of a highway or road) or is subject to other restrictions;

'occupier' means—

(a) in England and Wales, the person entitled to possession of the land by virtue of an estate or interest held by him;…

and in subsections (1) and (4) includes the person reasonably believed by the authority applying for or making the order to be the occupier;

'public' includes a section of the public; and

'specified' means specified in an order under this section.…

(11) In relation to Wales, the references in subsection (1) above to a district and to the council of the district shall be construed, as respects applications on and after 1 April 1996, as references to a county or county borough and to the council for that county or county borough.

14B. Offences in connection with trespassory assemblies and arrest therefor

(1) A person who organises an assembly the holding of which he knows is prohibited by an order under section 14A is guilty of an offence.

(2) A person who takes part in an assembly which he knows is prohibited by an order under section 14A is guilty of an offence.

(3) In England and Wales, a person who incites another to commit an offence under subsection (2) is guilty of an offence.…][206]

[14C. Stopping persons from proceeding to trespassory assemblies

(1) If a constable in uniform reasonably believes that a person is on his way to an assembly within the area to which an order under section 14A applies which the constable reasonably believes is likely to be an assembly which is prohibited by that order, he may, subject to subsection (2) below—

(a) stop that person, and

(b) direct him not to proceed in the direction of the assembly.

(2) The power conferred by subsection (1) may only be exercised within the area to which the order applies.

(3) A person who fails to comply with a direction under subsection (1) which he knows has been given to him is guilty of an offence.…][207]

---

[206] Inserted by the Criminal Justice and Public Order Act 1994, s. 70.
[207] Inserted by 1994 Act, s. 71.

15. Delegation

(1) The chief officer of police may delegate, to such extent and subject to such conditions as he may specify, any of his functions under sections 12 to [14A][208] to a deputy or assistant chief constable; and references in those sections to the person delegating shall be construed accordingly.

(2) Subsection (1) shall have effect in the City of London and the metropolitan police district as if 'an assistant chief constable' read 'an assistant commissioner of police'.

16. Interpretation

In this Part—

'the City of London' means the City as defined for the purposes of the Acts relating to the City of London police;

'the metropolitan police district' means that district as defined in section 76 of the London Government Act 1963;

'public assembly' means an assembly of [2][209] or more persons in a public place which is wholly or partly open to the air;

'public place' means—

(a) any highway,..., and

(b) any place to which at the material time the public or any section of the public has access, on payment or otherwise, as of right or by virtue of express or implied permission;

'public procession' means a procession in a public place....

NOTES

1. *Penalties and police powers.* A person guilty of an offence under ss. 11(7), 12(5), 13(8), 14(5), 14B(2), 14C(3) is liable on summary conviction to a fine not exceeding level 3 on the standard scale; and under ss. 12(4), (6), 13(7), (9), 14(4), (6), 14B(1), (3) on summary conviction to a fine not exceeding level 4 on the standard scale, or three months' imprisonment, or both.[210] The Crime and Disorder Act 1998 created new powers relating to stop and search.[211] These include the power for a constable to require a person to remove a face mask or other covering which he believes is worn to conceal the person's identity.

2. *Banning orders.* Section 3 of the Public Order Act 1936 gave powers to a chief officer of police to give directions to those organising or taking part in a procession if he had reasonable grounds to apprehend that it might occasion serious public disorder. If he was 'of opinion' that this would not be sufficient, he could apply for an order to ban all or any class of public processions in the area for a specified period. These powers were introduced in response, *inter alia*, to disturbances arising from the activities of the British Union of Fascists in the 1930s.[212]

The main changes effected by Part II of the 1986 Act were (a) the introduction of advance notice requirements for *processions;*[213] (b) the extension of the circumstances in

---

[208] Substituted by 1994 Act, Sch. 10, para. 60.

[209] Substituted for '20' by the Anti-social Behaviour Act 2003, s. 57.

[210] 1986 Act, ss. 11(10), 12(8)–(10), 13(11)–(13), 14(8)–(10), 14B(5)–(7), 14C(5).   [211] See above.

[212] See J. Stevenson and C. Cook, *Britain in the Depression: Society and Politics, 1929–1939* (2nd edn, 1994), Chaps 11, 12; R. Thurlow, *The Secret State* (1994), Chap. 5; and see the comprehensive discussion by *Ewing and Gearty,* especially Chap. 6.

[213] S. 11: see below, p. 318.

which conditions may be imposed on *processions*;[214] and (c) a new power to impose conditions on (but not to ban) public *assemblies*.[215] A power to ban 'trespassory assemblies' was added by the Criminal Justice and Public Order Act 1994.

The provisions governing banning orders[216] are very similar to the old s. 3. The Government considered but rejected adding further grounds for banning orders,[217] e.g. (a) 'that the views to be expressed would be seriously offensive: this would place an impossible task upon the police and be an unacceptable infringement of freedom of speech'; (b) a test of disruption: 'too restrictive'; (c) disproportionate cost: 'this would be haphazard in its effect and tend to concentrate major marches in the areas with larger forces'; (d) the procession 'would incite racial hatred': this 'would present insuperable problems of enforcement and could easily backfire by creating martyrs for free speech out of groups' whose policies had been decisively rejected by the electorate.

The power to impose conditions now extends to (a) 'serious damage to property'; (b) 'serious disruption to the life of the community' and (c) 'intimidation'. Ground (b) enables the police to impose conditions 'to re-route a procession in order to limit traffic congestion, or to prevent a bridge from being blocked, or to reduce the severe disruptions sometimes suffered by pedestrians, business and commerce'.[218] Examples include the policy of the Metropolitan Police to discourage demonstrators from using Oxford Street during business hours. Ground (c) enables conditions to be imposed 'to prevent the coercion of individuals', for example, where a march is organised to 'stop' or 'smash' opponents; where the National Front organise a march through Asian districts, and the response of the local community is to board up their shops and businesses and to stay at home; where animal rights protesters march on furriers' shops or food factories with the intention of preventing the employees from working; or where a very large crowd marches on the home of an individual councillor or inquiry inspector.[219] How these powers are used in practice is obviously of great importance. A.T.H. Smith commented on their introduction:[220]

There is a danger that, if the powers are used too freely, the symbolic significance of a demonstration may be lost. For example, if the proposed route of the march takes the participants past an embassy or a particular factory against whose occupants the organisers wish to protest, the prescription of a different route or terminus may obviate the whole point of the demonstration, and amount to in effect a disguised ban.

The new power to impose conditions on static demonstrations and meetings was justified in the *White Paper*[221] on the ground that they:

may just as frequently be the occasion of public disorder as marches.... Since 1980 some of the most serious public order problems have been associated with static demonstrations—at Greenham Common, the picketing at Warrington, and of the course the mass pickets during the miners' dispute.

The Government did not then propose a power to ban, noting that:

Meetings and assemblies are a more important means of exercising freedom of speech than are marches.[222]

---

[214] S. 12.   [215] S. 14.   [216] S. 13.
[217] *White Paper*, Chap. 4.   [218] *White Paper*, p. 27.   [219] *White Paper*, p. 28.
[220] *Public Order Offences* (1987), p. 134.   [221] P. 31.
[222] *White Paper*, pp. 31–32.

Nevertheless, the power to ban *trespassory assemblies* was added in 1994, prompted particularly by concern over the disruption caused by 'free festivals'.[223]

Waddington refers to the growth in police negotiation pre-protest, and how this gives the activity an air of respectability and renders it institutionalised. By compelling the protesters to take part in such democratic negotiations, the police control 'ordinary decent protestors' and will guarantee their protection—even where the protest is one challenging lawful activity and/or 'fundamental state interests'.[224]

3. May a specified procession be banned under s. 13(1)? If it is known that only one group is planning a march on a particular day, would it be lawful to ban 'all marches' on that day? The *White Paper*[225] proposed that the law be amended to allow a single march to be banned; this change did not appear in the Act on the ground that 'it would place the police in a situation where they would be subject to allegations of political motivation and partiality whenever they exercised the power to seek a ban on a particular march'.[226]

4. Directions and orders under these sections are potentially reviewable in the courts under the *ultra vires* doctrine. A challenge might be made directly, on an application for judicial review under CPR 54, or collaterally, as a defence to a prosecution. There is, however, no challenge on the merits.[227] It will, however, be difficult in practice to establish that a ban or other order is *ultra vires*. In *Kent v Metropolitan Police Comr,*[228] a ban was made under s. 3(3) of the Public Order Act 1936 in the aftermath of the Brixton (and other) disorders, prohibiting all processions within the Metropolitan Police District (786 square miles) 'except those traditionally held on May 1 to celebrate May Day and those of a religious character customarily held'. This had the incidental effect of preventing a planned CND procession. CND sought a declaration that the ban was *ultra vires* on the ground that in imposing such a wide ban the Commissioner had not directed himself properly as to the matters to be considered. The Court of Appeal rejected the claim: he had considered the relevant matters, the court could not substitute its judgment for his and CND could apply under s. 9(3)[229] for the order to be relaxed. The Commissioner was entitled to conclude that there was a risk that either the march or the police escorting the march would be attacked by hooligans. Moreover he was entitled to ban a 'class' of marches by exclusion. By virtue of the HRA, directions and orders, as restrictions on freedom of assembly and of expression may also now be challenged on the ground of lack of proportionality, although this is also difficult to establish.[230]

---

[223] See above, p. 283, and below, p. 326.

[224] Op. cit., p. 73. Note also the power to direct protesters away from a dwelling under s. 42 of the Criminal Justice and Police Act 2001.

[225] P. 25.

[226] *Smith,* pp. 136–137, citing the Minister of State at the Home Office.

[227] Cf. *The Times,* 21 April 1980, p. 2.   [228] *The Times,* 15 May, 1981.

[229] See now s. 13(5), 1986 Act.

[230] *R (on the application of Brehony) v Chief Constable of Greater Manchester Police* [2005] EWHC 640 (chief constable entitled to impose conditions requiring long standing demonstration against Marks and Spencer's support for the Government of Israel (and a counter-demonstration) to be moved to a location half a mile away during the Christmas period when the number of visitors to the city was expected to treble; his 'legitimate aim of preventing serious disruption and disorder in the pedestrian area of Manchester City Centre on the busiest shopping days of the year could not be achieved by means which interfered less with the Claimant's Convention rights' (Bean J at para. [25]).

It will similarly be difficult to establish on judicial review that a refusal to ban or impose conditions is *ultra vires*.[231] It is doubtful whether the police can rely on the powers in ss. 11 to 14 of the 1986 Act unless they expressly have them in mind.[232]

5. In *Application No. 8440/78 Christians against Racism and Fascism v United Kingdom*[233] the Commission held inadmissible a claim that a ban under s. 3(3) of the Public Order Act 1936 in February 1978 was contrary to ECHR Arts 5(1), 10, 11 and 14, on the ground that the claim was manifestly ill-founded. On Art. 11 the Commission noted that the right of peaceable assembly guaranteed by Art. 11(1) could not as such be taken away simply by the prospect of violent counter-demonstrations. However, the ban was justified under Art. 11(2) as it complied with the principle that:

a general ban on demonstrations can only be justified if there is real danger of their resulting in disorder that cannot be prevented by other less stringent measures.[234]

6. In *Flockhart v Robinson*[235] F was prosecuted under s. 3 of the Public Order Act 1936. The Metropolitan Police Commissioner on 3 October 1949 banned all public processions of a political character within the Metropolitan Police District. On 15 October, F organised a procession of members of a political group, the Union Movement, which procession lawfully dispersed on reaching Temple Bar. Later that day he met about 150 members at Hyde Park Corner who followed him in loose formation when he moved along Piccadilly, and then closed ranks. He gave signals to guide them through the traffic and direction signals. Members other than F sang the Horst Wessel and shouted political slogans. F led them round Piccadilly Circus and into Coventry Street, where they were broken up by the police. F's conviction for 'organising' a procession contrary to s. 3(4) was upheld by the Divisional Court.[236] Lord Goddard CJ stated:[237] 'A procession is not a mere body of persons: it is a body of persons moving along a route. Therefore the person who organises the route is the person who organises the procession.' In *Kent v MPC*[238] Lord Denning adopted a dictionary definition of procession:

A public procession is the act of a body of persons marching along in orderly succession—see the *Oxford English Dictionary*. All kinds of processions take place every day up and down the country—carnivals, weddings, funerals, processions to the Houses of Parliament, marches to Trafalgar Square and so forth.

7. Before 1981 bans under s. 3(2) and (3) of the 1936 Act were uncommon. However, in that year 39 banning orders were made in England and Wales. 'Many of the orders were in response to tension following the civil disturbances'.[239] The figure fell to 13 in 1982, 9 in 1983 and 11 in 1984. The commonest wording of a ban was 'all public processions except those of a religious, educational, festive or ceremonial character customarily held'. The Metropolitan Police have on occasion resisted pressure to seek bans, claiming that the requirements were

231 See the discussion of two cases under analogous legislation in Northern Ireland, the Public Order (N.I.) Order 1987, SI 1987/463 (*Re Murphy* [1991] 5 NIJB 72, QBD (NI), and 88, CA(NI); *Re Armstrong* (27 August 1992, unreported, QBD(NI)) by B. Hadfield in 'Public Order Police Powers and Judicial Review' [1993] Crim LR 915).

232 See discussion in *Austin v Comr of Police of the Metropolis* [2007] EWCA Civ 989, [2008] QB 660 at paras 74–83, doubting the contrary view of the trial judge on this point, but leaving it open.

233 (1981) 21 DR 148.   234 P. 198. See also *Pendragon v UK* (above, p. 291).

235 [1950] 2 KB 498, DC.   236 Lord Goddard CJ and Morris J, Finnemore J dissenting.

237 [1950] 2 KB 498 at 502.   238 Above.

239 *Report of HM Chief Inspector of Constabulary for 1981* (1981–82 HC 463), para. 8.6.

'so onerous that it was a practical impossibility' and that enforcement was 'more trouble than it was worth'.[240]

8. *Conditions on processions and assemblies.* In practice, the power to impose conditions under the 1936 Act was rarely used, the police preferring to discuss the plans for a march with the organisers and to negotiate an informal agreement about the route and other matters.[241] Compare the power to impose conditions under ss. 12 and 14 with the common law powers of the police to preserve the peace.[242] The s. 14 power has been significantly extended by the change of the definition of 'public assembly' to one involving two rather than 20 people.[243] A condition under s. 14 may be unlawful if the conduct in question falls short of intimidation on the facts,[244] or if it is not known where the assembly will take place.[245] A s. 14(2)(b) direction must identify which limb of s. 14(1) is being relied on, (a) or (b). If it is under s. 14(1)(a), it must identify whether the reasonable belief is that the assembly may result in serious public disorder, or serious damage to property, or serious disruption to the life of the community (or all three or only two of them), and sufficient reasons given to enable the demonstrators to understand why directions are being given, and to enable a court (if the matter goes to court) to assess, once the judge is presented with evidence as to the facts, whether the belief was reasonable or not.[246]

The power to impose conditions as to the place where an assembly can be held does not confer power to provide disembarkation and embarkation points away from the assembly area.[247] Sufficient steps must be taken to bring notice of a condition to the attention of persons for him to be knowingly in breach.[248] A condition has been held applicable to a person who came with others intending to demonstrate and then deliberately walked away from the main group and sought to enter a road closed off by the police.[249]

9. *Advance notice.* Section 11 of the 1986 Act introduced a general requirement of advance notice of public processions. This replaced notice requirements (in varying terms) in many local Acts. Lord Scarman, in his report on the Red Lion Square disorders,[250] had rejected suggestions for notice requirements on the ground that the need for them had not been established.[251] In 1981, he took a different view.[252] Section 11 is incapable of dealing with spontaneous protests of the type which are becoming increasingly common. There is no opportunity for advance notice. The section leaves the scope of the exemption for processions 'commonly or customarily' held ambiguous.[253]

---

[240] P.A.J. Waddington, *Liberty and Order* (1994), pp. 58–61.

[241] *White Paper*, pp. 26–27.   [242] Below, pp. 376–397.

[243] Anti-social Behaviour Act 2003, s. 57, amending the 1986 Act, s. 16.

[244] *Police v Reid* [1987] Crim LR 702 (demonstration outside South African embassy where R and about 20 others shouted slogans ('apartheid murderers get out of Britain'), raised their arms and waved their fingers at guests arriving for a reception).

[245] *DPP v Bailie* [1995] Crim LR 446 (a free festival to which B was giving directions by phone).

[246] *R (on the application of Brehony) v Chief Constable of Greater Manchester Police* [2005] EWHC 640 (sufficient reasons given on the facts).

[247] *DPP v Jones* [2002] EWHC 110 (Admin).

[248] *Brickley and Kitson v Police Legal Action* July 1988, p. 211 (Knightsbridge Crown Court) (not established on the facts where police had addressed demonstrators through a megaphone).

[249] *Broadwith v Chief Constable of Thames Valley Police* [2000] Crim LR 924; cf. *Ezelin v France* (1992) 14 EHRR 362.

[250] Cmnd 5919, 1975.   [251] Paras 128, 129.

[252] *The Brixton Disorders* (Cmnd 8427, p. 124) as did the Home Affairs Committee (*HAC*, pp. xii–xv) and the *White Paper*, pp. 21–22. On the process of negotiation between the Metropolitan police and the organisers of demonstrations, see P.A.J. Waddington, *Liberty and Order*, Chap. 4.

[253] See further R. Card, *Public Order Law*, Chap. 6. Presumably religious festivals are the principal category.

In *Kay v Metropolitan Police Comr*[254] the Court of Appeal[255] held that a mass cycle ride (Critical Mass)[256] held at a set time on the last Friday of each month, and starting near the National Film Theatre, was not a procession commonly or customarily held. This was because it had no common route or end point, the cyclists in front on each occasion deciding what direction to take. The Divisional Court[257] had previously rejected arguments that the event had no organiser or alternatively no route which was capable of being notified under s. 11(3). Furthermore, it had held that the s. 11(6) exemption was designed to accommodate demonstrations occurring in reaction to sudden events, and that it would be open to a court to conclude that there was a collective intention under s. 11(1) to support the cause of self-propelled mobility in cities dominated by cars and lorries, to campaign to make the streets safer for cyclists, and to demonstrate opposition to the motor vehicle lobby. No appeal was taken on these points. In the Court of Appeal, Leveson LJ also commented[258] that there might be 'commonly held processions' that start at the same point at the same time and end up at the same place albeit by different routes; or which are held at different times or dates but follow the same route. In each case it is a question of fact and degree. The House of Lords allowed an appeal (see Preface).

10. *Prohibition of trespassory assemblies.* The House of Lords considered the interpretation of ss. 14A and 14B in the following case.

- **DPP v Jones** [1999] 2 AC 240, House of Lords

On 1 June 1995, at about 6.40 p.m. Police Inspector Mackie counted 21 people on the roadside verge of the southern side of the A344, adjacent to the perimeter fence of the monument at Stonehenge. Some were bearing banners with the legends, 'Never Again', 'Stonehenge Campaign 10 years of Criminal Injustice' and 'Free Stonehenge'. He concluded that they constituted a 'trespassory assembly' and told them so. When asked to move off, many did, but some, including the appellants, Mr Lloyd and Dr Jones, were determined to remain and put their rights to the test. They were arrested for taking part in a 'trespassory assembly' and convicted by the Salisbury Justices on 3 October 1995. Their appeals to the Salisbury Crown Court, however, succeeded. The court held that neither of the appellants, nor any member of their group, was 'being destructive, violent, disorderly, threatening a breach of the peace or, on the evidence, doing anything other than reasonably using the highway'. About an hour before, a different group of people had scaled the fence of the monument and entered it. They had been successfully escorted away by police officers without any violence or arrests; but there were no grounds for apprehension that any of the group of which Mr Lloyd and Dr Jones were members proposed an incursion into the area of the monument.

Their convictions were overturned by the Crown Court, restored by the Divisional Court and finally, by a bare majority, quashed by the House of Lords.

Lord Irvine of Lairg LC: My Lords, this appeal raises an issue of fundamental constitutional importance: what are the limits of the public's rights of access to the public highway? Are these rights so restricted that they preclude in all circumstances any right of peaceful assembly on the public highway?

...[In the Divisional Court] it was assumed for the purposes of that appeal...that: (a) the grass verge constituted part of the public highway; and (b) the group was peaceful, did not create an obstruction and did not constitute or cause a public nuisance....The central issue in the case thus turns on two

---

[254] [2007] 4 All ER 31. [255] Sir Mark Potter P and Leveson LJ, Wall LJ dissenting.
[256] See http://critical-mass.info/; http://www.criticalmasslondon.org.uk/main.html.
[257] [2006] EWHC 1536 (Admin), [2006] RTR 469. [258] At para. [32].

interrelated questions: (i) what are the 'limits' of the public's right of access to the public highway at common law? and (ii) what is the 'particular purpose' for which the public has a right to use the public highway?...[I]n broad terms the basis of the Divisional Court's decision is the proposition that the public's right of access to the public highway is limited to the right to pass and repass, and to do anything incidental or ancillary to that right. Peaceful assembly is not incidental to the right to pass and repass. Thus peaceful assembly exceeds the limits of the public's right of access and so is conduct which fulfils the actus reus of the offence of 'trespassory assembly'.

THE POSITION AT COMMON LAW

The Divisional Court's decision is founded principally on three authorities. In *Ex parte Lewis* (1888) 21 Q.B.D. 191 the Divisional Court held obiter that there was no public right to occupy Trafalgar Square for the purpose of holding public meetings. However, Wills J, giving the judgment of the court, had in mind, at p. 197, an assembly '... to the detriment of others having equal rights... in its nature irreconcilable with the right of free passage'. Such an assembly would probably also amount to a public nuisance, and, today, involve the commission of the offence of obstruction of the public highway contrary to section 137(1) of the Highways Act 1980 ('the 1980 Act'). Such an assembly would probably also amount to unreasonable user of the highway. It by no means follows that this same reasoning should apply to a peaceful assembly which causes no obstruction nor any public nuisance.

In *Harrison v. Duke of Rutland* [1893] 1 Q.B. 142 the plaintiff had used the public highway, which crossed the defendant's land, for the sole and deliberate purpose of disrupting grouse-shooting upon the defendant's land, and was forcibly restrained by the defendant's servants from doing so. The plaintiff sued the defendant for assault: and the defendant pleaded justification on the basis that the plaintiff had been trespassing upon the highway. Lord Esher M.R. held, at p. 146:

'... on the ground that the plaintiff was on the highway, the soil of which belonged to the Duke of Rutland, not for the purpose of using it in order to pass and repass, *or for any reasonable or usual mode of using the highway as a highway,* I think he was a trespasser.' (Emphasis added.)

Plainly Lord Esher M.R. contemplated that there may be 'reasonable or usual' uses of the highway beyond passing and repassing. He continued, at pp. 146–147:

'Highways are, no doubt, dedicated prima facie for the purpose of passage; but things are done upon them by everybody which are recognised as being rightly done, and as constituting a reasonable and usual mode of using a highway as such. If a person on a highway does not transgress such reasonable and usual mode of using it, I do not think that he will be a trespasser.'

Lopes LJ, by contrast, stated the law in more rigid terms, at p. 154:

'... if a person uses the soil of the highway for any purpose other than that in respect of which the dedication was made and the easement acquired, he is a trespasser. The easement acquired by the public is a right to pass and repass at their pleasure for the purpose of legitimate travel, and the use of the soil for any other purpose, whether lawful or unlawful, is an infringement of the rights of the owner of the soil...'

Similarly, Kay L.J. stated, at p. 158:

'... the right of the public upon a highway is that of passing and repassing over land the soil of which may be owned by a private person. Using that soil for any other purpose lawful or unlawful is a trespass.'

The rigid approach of Lopes L.J. and Kay L.J. would have some surprising consequences. It would entail that two friends who meet in the street and stop to talk are committing a trespass; so too a group of children playing on the pavement outside their homes; so too charity workers collecting donations; or political activists handing out leaflets; and so too a group of members of the Salvation Army singing hymns and addressing those who gather to listen.

The question to which this appeal gives rise is whether the law today should recognise that the public highway is a public place, on which all manner of reasonable activities may go on. For the reasons I set out below in my judgment it should. Provided these activities are reasonable, do not involve the commission of a public or private nuisance, and do not amount to an obstruction of the highway unreasonably impeding the primary right of the general public to pass and repass, they should not constitute a trespass. Subject to these qualifications, therefore, there would be a public right of peaceful assembly on the public highway.

The third authority relied upon by the Divisional Court is the decision of the Court of Appeal in *Hickman v Maisey* [1900] 1 Q.B. 752. In that case, the defendant, a racing tout, had used a public highway crossing the plaintiff's property for the purpose of observing racehorses being trained on the plaintiff's land. A. L. Smith L.J. expressly followed the approach of Lord Esher M.R. in *Harrison*. Applying that reasoning, he accepted, at p. 756, that a man resting at the side of the road, or taking a sketch from the highway, would not be a trespasser. The defendant's activities, however, fell outside 'an ordinary and reasonable user of the highway' and so amounted to a trespass. Collins L.J. similarly approved Lord Esher M.R.'s approach, noting, at pp. 757–758, that:

'… in modern times a reasonable extension has been given to the use of the highway as such… The right of the public to pass and repass on a highway is subject to all those reasonable extensions which may from time to time be recognised as necessary to its exercise in accordance with the enlarged notions of people in a country becoming more populous and highly civilised, but they must be such as are not inconsistent with the maintenance of the paramount idea that the right of the public is that of passage.'

Romer L.J. was to similar effect, at p. 759.

I do not, therefore, accept that, to be lawful, activities on the highway must fall within a rubric incidental or ancillary to the exercise of the right of passage. The meaning of Lord Esher's judgment in *Harrison*, at pp. 146–147 is clear: it is not that a person may use the highway only for passage and repassage and acts incidental or ancillary thereto; it is that any 'reasonable and usual' mode of using the highway is lawful, provided it is not inconsistent with the general public's right of passage. I understand Collins L. J.'s acceptance in *Hickman,* at pp. 757–758, of Lord Esher's judgment in *Harrison* in that sense.

To commence from a premise, that the right of passage is the only right which members of the public are entitled to exercise on a highway, is circular: the very question in this appeal is whether the public's right is confined to the right of passage. I conclude that the judgments of Lord Esher M.R. and Collins L.J. are authority for the proposition that the public have the right to use the public highway for such reasonable and usual activities as are consistent with the general public's primary right to use the highway for purposes of passage and repassage.

Nor can I attribute any hard core of meaning to a test which would limit lawful use of the highway to what is incidental or ancillary to the right of passage. In truth very little activity could accurately be described as 'ancillary' to passing along the highway; perhaps stopping to tie one's shoe lace, consulting a street-map, or pausing to catch one's breath. But I do not think that such ordinary and usual activities as making a sketch, taking a photograph, handing out leaflets, collecting money for charity, singing carols, playing in a Salvation Army band, children playing a game on the pavement, having a picnic, or reading a book, would qualify. These examples illustrate that to limit lawful use of the highway to that which is literally 'incidental or ancillary' to the right of passage would be to place an unrealistic and unwarranted restriction on commonplace day-to-day activities. The law should not make unlawful what is commonplace and well accepted.

Nor do I accept that the broader modern test which I favour materially realigns the interests of the general public and landowners. It is no more than an exposition of the test Lord Esher proposed in 1892. It would not permit unreasonable use of the highway, nor use which was obstructive. It would not, therefore, afford carte blanche to squatters or other uninvited visitors. Their activities would almost certainly be unreasonable or obstructive or both. Moreover the test of reasonableness would be strictly applied where narrow highways across private land are concerned, for example, narrow footpaths or bridle-paths, where even a small gathering would be likely to create an obstruction or a nuisance.

Nor do I accept that the 'reasonable user' test is tantamount to the assertion of a right to remain, which right can be acquired by express grant, but not by user or dedication. That recognition, however, is in no way inconsistent with the 'reasonable user' test. If the right to use the highway extends to reasonable user not inconsistent with the public's right of passage, then the law does recognise, (and has at least since Lord Esher's judgment in *Harrison* recognised), that the right to use the highway goes beyond the minimal right to pass and repass. That user may in fact extend, to a limited extent, to roaming about on the highway, or remaining on the highway. But that is not of the essence of the right. That is no more than the scope which the right might in certain circumstances have, but always depending on the facts of the particular case. On a narrow footpath, for example, the right to use the highway would be highly unlikely to extend to a right to remain, since that would almost inevitably be inconsistent with the public's primary right to pass and repass.

...I conclude therefore the law to be that the public highway is a public place which the public may enjoy for any reasonable purpose, provided the activity in question does not amount to a public or private nuisance and does not obstruct the highway by unreasonably impeding the primary right of the public to pass and repass: within these qualifications there is a public right of peaceful assembly on the highway.

Since the law confers this public right, I deprecate any attempt artificially to restrict its scope. It must be for the magistrates in every case to decide whether the user of the highway under consideration is both reasonable in the sense defined and not inconsistent with the primary right of the public to pass and repass. In particular, there can be no principled basis for limiting the scope of the right by reference to the subjective intentions of the persons assembling. Once the right to assemble within the limitations I have defined is accepted, it is self-evident that it cannot be excluded by an intention to exercise it. Provided an assembly is reasonable and non- obstructive, taking into account its size, duration and the nature of the highway on which it takes place, it is irrelevant whether it is premeditated or spontaneous: what matters is its objective nature. To draw a distinction on the basis of anterior intention is in substance to reintroduce an incidentality requirement. For the reasons I have given, that requirement, properly applied, would make unlawful commonplace activities which are well accepted. Equally, to stipulate in the abstract any maximum size or duration for a lawful assembly would be an unwarranted restriction on the right defined. These judgments are ever ones of fact and degree for the court of trial.

Further, there can be no basis for distinguishing highways on publicly owned land and privately owned land. The nature of the public's right of use of the highway cannot depend upon whether the owner of the sub-soil is a private landowner or a public authority. Any fear, however, that the rights of private landowners might be prejudiced by the right as defined are unfounded. The law of trespass will continue to protect private landowners against unreasonably large, unreasonably prolonged or unreasonably obstructive assemblies upon these highways.

Finally, I regard the conclusion at which I have arrived as desirable, because it promotes the harmonious development of two separate but related chapters in the common law. It is neither desirable in theory nor acceptable in practice for commonplace activities on the public highway not to count as breaches of the criminal law of wilful obstruction of the highway, yet to count as trespasses (even if intrinsically unlikely to be acted against in the civil law), and therefore form the basis for a finding of trespassory assembly for the purposes of the Public Order Act. A system of law sanctioning these discordant outcomes would not command respect.

ARTICLE 11 OF THE EUROPEAN CONVENTION ON HUMAN RIGHTS

...Unless the common law recognises that assembly on the public highway *may* be lawful, the right contained in Article 11(1) of the Convention is denied. Of course the right may be subject to restrictions (for example, the requirements that user of the highway for purposes of assembly must be reasonable and non-obstructive, and must not contravene the criminal law of wilful obstruction of the highway). But in my judgment our law will not comply with the Convention unless its *starting-point* is that assembly on the highway will not necessarily be unlawful. I reject an approach which entails that such an assembly will always be tortious and therefore unlawful. The fact that the letter of the law may not in practice always be invoked is irrelevant: mere toleration does not secure a fundamental right. Thus, if necessary, I would invoke Article 11 to clarify or develop the common law in the terms which I have held it to be; but for the reasons I have given I do not find it necessary to do so. I would therefore allow the appeal.

Lord Clyde [having referred to earlier cases]: In the generality there is no doubt but that there is a public right of assembly. But there are restrictions on the exercise of that right in the public interest. There are limitations at common law and there are express limitations laid down in Article 11 of the Convention on Human Rights. I would not be prepared to affirm as a matter of generality that there is a right of assembly on any place on a highway at any time and in any event I am not persuaded that the present case has to be decided by reference to public rights of assembly. If a group of people stand in the street to sing hymns or Christmas carols they are in my view using the street within the legitimate scope of the public right of access to it, provided of course that they do so for a reasonable period and without any unreasonable obstruction to traffic. If there are shops in the street and people gather to stand and view a shop window, or form a queue to enter the shop, that is within the normal and reasonable use which is matter of public right. A road may properly be used for the purposes of a procession. It would still be a perfectly proper use of the road if the procession was intended to serve some particular purpose, such as commemorating some particular event or achievement. And if an individual may properly stop at a point on the road for any lawful purpose, so too should a group of people be entitled to do so. All such activities seem to me to be subsidiary to the use for passage. So I have no difficulty in holding that in principle a gathering of people at the side of a highway within the limits of the restraints which I have noted may be within the scope of the public's right of access to the highway.

In my view the argument for the appellants, and indeed the reasoning of the Crown Court, went further than it needed to go in suggesting that any reasonable use of the highway, provided that it was peaceful and not obstructive, was lawful, and so a matter of public right. Such an approach opens a door of uncertain dimensions into an ill-defined area of uses which might erode the basic predominance of the essential use of a highway as a highway. I do not consider that by using the language which it used Parliament intended to include some distinct right in addition to the right to use the road for the purpose of passage.

I am not persuaded that in any case where there is a peaceful non-obstructive assembly it will necessarily exceed the public's right of access to the highway. The question then is, as in this kind of case it may often turn out to be, whether on the facts here the limit was passed and the exceeding of it established. The test then is not one which can be defined in general terms but has to depend upon the circumstances as a matter of degree. It requires a careful assessment of the nature and extent of the activity in question. If the purpose of the activity becomes the predominant purpose of the occupation of the highway, or if the occupation becomes more than reasonably transitional in terms of either time or space, then it may come to exceed the right to use the highway.

The only point which has caused me some hesitation in the circumstances of the present case is the evident determination by the two appellants to remain where they were. That does seem to look as if they were intending to go beyond their right and to stay longer than would constitute a reasonable period. But I find it far from clear that there was an assembly of twenty or more persons who were so determined and in light of the fluidity in the composition of the grouping and in the consistency of its component individuals I consider that the Crown Court reached the correct conclusion.

I do not find it possible to return any general answer to the certified question. The matter is essentially one to be judged in light of the particular facts of the case. But I am prepared to hold that a peaceful assembly which does not obstruct the highway does not necessarily constitute a trespassory assembly so as to constitute the circumstances for an offence where an order under section 14A(2) is in force. I would allow the appeal.

Lord Hutton:

…[His Lordship referred to *Harrison v. Duke of Rutland* and other cases]…[T]he issue which arises in the present appeal is whether the right of the public to use the highway, as stated by Lopes L.J. in *Harrison v. Duke of Rutland,* should be extended and should include the right to hold a peaceful public assembly on a highway, such as the A344, which causes no obstruction to persons passing along the highway and which the Crown Court found to be a reasonable user of the highway.

In my opinion your Lordships' House should so hold for three main reasons which are as follows. First, the common law recognises that there is a right for members of the public to assemble together to express views on matters of public concern and I consider that the common law should now recognise that this right, which is one of the fundamental rights of citizens in a democracy, is unduly restricted unless it can be exercised in some circumstances on the public highway. Secondly, the law as to trespass on the highway should be in conformity with the law relating to proceedings for wilful obstruction of the highway under section 137 of the Highways Act 1980 that a peaceful assembly on the highway may be a reasonable use of the highway. Thirdly, there is a recognition in the authorities that it may be appropriate that the public's right to use the highway should be extended, in the words of Collins L.J. in *Hickman v. Maisey* at p. 758:

> 'in accordance with the enlarged notions of people in a country becoming more populous and highly civilised, but they must be such as are not inconsistent with the maintenance of the paramount idea that the right of the public is that of passage.'

…I would not hold that a peaceful and non-obstructive public assembly on a highway is always a reasonable user and is therefore not a trespass.

It is for the tribunal of fact to decide whether the user was reasonable. In *Hirst and Agu* at p. 150 Glidewell L.J. makes it clear that a reasonable activity in the street may become unreasonable by reason of the space occupied or the duration of time for which it goes on, 'but it is a matter on the facts for the magistrates, in my view'.

If members of the public took part in an assembly on a highway but the highway was, for example, a small, quiet country road or was a bridleway or a footpath, and the assembly interfered with the landowner's enjoyment of the land across which the highway ran or which it bordered, I think it would be open to the Justices to hold that, notwithstanding the importance of the democratic right to hold a public assembly, nevertheless in the particular circumstances of the case the assembly was an unreasonable user of the highway and therefore constituted a trespass.

…I consider that there is an argument of some force that a reasonable user of the highway by an assembly may become an unreasonable user so that the non-trespassory assembly becomes a trespassory assembly if it appears that members of the assembly are about to commit unlawful acts. However, this point did not arise in the questions stated for the opinion of the Divisional Court and was not argued before the Divisional Court, and the point does not arise on the question stated for the opinion of your Lordships' House. Therefore it would not be right to decide the appeal on this point. Accordingly I express no concluded opinion on the point or on the circumstances in which a non-trespassory assembly may become a trespassory assembly.

NOTES

1. Lord Slynn, dissenting, held that:

The fact that the purpose of the demonstration or assembly is one which most or many people would approve does not change what is otherwise a trespass into a legal right. Nor does the fact that an assembly is peaceful or unlikely to result in violence, or that is not causing an obstruction at the particular time when the police intervene, in itself change what is otherwise a trespass into a legal right of access.

It is objected that very often people on the highway singly or in groups take part in activities which go beyond passage and repassage and are not stopped. That is no doubt so, but reasonable tolerance does not create a new right to use the highway and indeed may make it unnecessary to create such a right which in its wider definition goes far beyond what is justified or needed.

Lord Hope, dissenting, held that:

The proposition that the public are entitled to do anything on the highway which amounts in itself to a reasonable user may seem at first sight to be an attractive one. But it seems to me to be tantamount to saying that members of the public are entitled to assemble, occupy and remain anywhere upon a highway in whatever numbers as long as they wish for any reasonable purpose so long as they do not obstruct it. I do not think that there is any basis in the authorities for such a fundamental rearrangement of the respective rights of the public and of those of public and private landowners.

2. The case is not one in which there is a simple division with a bare majority; there is a spectrum of opinion from Lord Irvine's very broad approach to Lord Slynn's very narrow one. Even within the majority, it is not straightforward to discern the ratio. Lord Clyde does not go as far as Lords Irvine and Hutton, in that, in his view, there is an additional limitation that the purpose of the activity must not become the predominant purpose of the occupation of the highway. Subject to this, in general terms, the majority required the use of the highway to be reasonable and usual, while the minority focused on whether the use was associated with the passage. On the latter view, what sorts of activities would be sufficiently connected with passage and re-passage on the highway? Is there a clear majority agreeing that there is a right to assemble in English law, and as to the extent of that right? The majority accept that an activity may be non-obstructive, but still unreasonable. Can you think of any examples?

3. Clayton[259] describes the case as 'an endorsement of the right to peaceful assembly...and an important vindication of a fundamental civil liberty'. Do you share this enthusiasm? Is the decision an invitation for hot-dog stand owners to set up shop anywhere they fancy? Is the case decided on principles of land law or principles of constitutional law? Does the case provide clear guidance to the average protester of his rights?

4. There is surprisingly little discussion of the ECHR from the Law Lords. Writing before the case, Fitzpatrick and Taylor questioned whether 'section 14A could indeed be the object of a successful challenge under the European Convention'.[260] To what extent has the decision in *Jones* assuaged those fears?

5. In *The Gypsy Council v United Kingdom*,[261] the ECtHR rejected claims that an order under s. 14A prohibiting the holding of Hosmorden Horse Fair violated Arts 11 and 14. The fair had been held annually for at least 50 and possibly 300 years, but there had been a range of incidents in previous years. The court found it to be proportionate, noting that a site was made available 20 miles away and a limited procession was permitted in Hosmorden on the day in question.

---

[259] G. Clayton, (2000) MLR 252. See also I. Hare [1999] CLJ 265; H. Fenwick and G. Phillipson [2000] PL 627.

[260] [1998] EHRLR 292 at 297.

[261] App No. 66336/01, 14 May 2002.

(VI) POWERS TO DIRECT TRESPASSERS TO LEAVE LAND

It is increasingly common for legislation to provide police with specific powers to direct the conduct of meetings and processions. Section 39 of the Public Order Act 1986 enabled a senior police officer to direct trespassers to leave land. The officer had reasonably to believe that two or more persons had entered land as trespassers and were present there with the common purpose of residing there for any period; that reasonable steps had been taken by or on behalf of the occupier to ask them to leave; and that any of those persons had caused damage to property on the land or used threatening, abusive or insulting words or behaviour towards the occupier, a member of his family or an employee or agent of his, or that those persons had between them brought 12 or more vehicles on to the land. It was an offence to fail to leave the land as soon as reasonably practicable or, having left, to return as a trespasser within three months. This provision was designed as a response to large incidents of mass trespass involving such groups as Hell's Angels and hippies. In particular, in 1986, a 'Peace Convoy' of hippies attempting a pilgrimage to Stonehenge, trespassed on a farm owned by a Mr Attwell with over 100 buses, trucks, caravans and other assorted vehicles. They stayed for seven days, and left peacefully when a High Court eviction order was granted.[262] It was doubted whether the creation of this offence was necessary,[263] given the existence of recently streamlined civil remedies, the very wide criminal damage offence and the powers of the police to deal with breaches of the peace. Section 39 was used by the police in subsequent years to discourage mass trespass and other disorderly activity by the Peace Convoy and others in the period leading up to the summer solstice.[264] In 1989, processions and marches within a four-mile radius of Stonehenge were banned over a short period around the summer solstice under s. 13 of the Public Order Act 1986.[265]

Disturbances in the early 1990s involving new age travellers (in particular, the encampment at Castlemorton, Worcestershire, with 20,000 people attending a free festival) provoked widespread concern.[266] Section 39 was replaced by much more draconian powers under the Criminal Justice and Public Order Act 1994. Section 61 is similar to the old s. 39, except that the officer must reasonably believe that two or more persons 'are trespassing'; the presence of six vehicles rather than 12 is sufficient to trigger the power; there is express power to direct the removal of vehicles or other property; there is express provision in respect of common land; the term 'vehicle' includes any vehicle whether or not in a fit state for use on roads and any chassis or body, with or without wheels, appearing to have formed part of such a vehicle, and any load carried by, and anything attached to, such a vehicle; and there is a power for a constable to seize and remove any vehicle not removed in accordance with a direction, or taken with a person subject to a direction re-entering within three months.[267]

The 1994 Act provisions were the subject of a detailed Home Office Research Study.[268] This concluded that the Act did not make any difference to the type of public order situation

---

[262] See P. Vincent-Jones, 'Private Property and Public Order: The Hippy Convoy and Criminal Trespass' (1986) 13 JLS 343; NCCL, *Stonehenge* (1986); K.D. Ewing and C.D. Gearty, *Freedom under Thatcher* (1990), pp. 125–128. For charges under s. 51(3) of the Police Act 1964, now s. 89 of the Police Act 1996, arising out of the Peace Convoy, see *Smith v Reynolds* [1986] Crim LR 559, DC.

[263] *Smith* (1st edn), pp. 259–260.

[264] *Reports of the Chief Inspector of Constabulary for 1987* (1987–88 HC 521), pp. 57–58; *1988* (1988–89 HC 449), p. 66.

[265] *Report of the Chief Inspector of Constabulary for 1989* (1989–90 HC524), p. 67.

[266] J. Baxter (1992) Policing 222; *Hansard* HL, 25 April 1994, col. 584.   [267] S. 62.

[268] T. Bucke and Z. James, *Trespass and Protest: policing under the Criminal Justice and Public Order Act 1994* (HORS 190, 1998).

with which the police sought to deal, but placed officers in a stronger legal position when dealing with these incidents.[269] The successful application of directions meant that there were relatively few prosecutions,[270] which were much less common than those under the old s. 39 powers.[271] The power to issue a three month ban under s.61 was used very rarely, since it was almost impossible to prove an individual's identity in such cases because no record of identity is kept at the time of the initial expulsion.[272] Police forces expressed reservations concerning the use of the seizure powers in s. 62, claiming that they are administratively complicated and expensive.[273] The provisions were heavily criticised by others for criminalising 'lifestyles' (gypsies and new age travellers).[274]

The Home Office issued guidelines emphasising the importance of making adequate inquiry into the welfare of trespassers before the exercise of the power.[275] These issues involve the presence of the elderly, invalids, pregnant women and children. Section 61 imports a *discretion* to direct the trespassers to leave—whether the police decide to order them to leave is an operational decision. The factors the police take into account should include considerations of 'common humanity' such as those listed in the circular.

Since 1994 there has been a significant shift in Government policy towards gypsies and travellers, with their recognition by Government as excluded populations and with increasing recognition by public services that their needs should be addressed. Associated with this has been the requirement that the police, like other public services, should 'engage with gypsies and travellers beyond the enforcement requirements of the CJPOA'.[276] The major responsibilities for dealing with gypsy and traveller issues fall to local authorities, with whom the police are required to work in partnership.[277]

Exercise of the legal powers have also been transformed through the impact of the Human Rights Act 1998. The courts have confirmed that the police must have regard to consideration of common humanity,[278] although they do not themselves have to carry out full welfare inquiries and are entitled to assume that a local authority seeking their assistance is not acting in breach of human rights.[279] Furthermore, it is recognised that all evictions have to be justifiable as proportionate.[280] Early use of s.61 should always be considered where it is likely to be a proportionate response, and especially where there is evidence of individual criminal activity, significant disruption to the life of the surrounding community or serious beaches

---

[269] P. 63.   [270] P. 57.   [271] P. 17.   [272] P. 11.   [273] P. 12.

[274] See Liberty, *Criminalising Diversity, Criminalising Dissent: a report on the use of the public order provisions of the Criminal Justice and Public Order Act 1994* (1995). See also R. Geary and C. O'Shea (1995) 17 JSW and Fam Law 67; S. Campbell [1995] Crim LR 28.

[275] Home Office Circular 45/1994.

[276] Z. James, 'Policing marginal spaces: controlling gypsies and travellers' (2007) 7 Criminology and Criminal Justice 367, 369. James notes examples of good practice but also questions the degree to which this can be achieved.

[277] ODPM/Home Office, *Guidance on Managing Unauthorised Camping* (2004) (www.communities.gov.uk).

[278] *R v Comr of the Metropolitan Police, ex p Small*, 27 August 1998, Collins J, unreported. Leave application cited by C. Johnson, A. Murdoch and M Willers, *The Law Relating to Gypsies and Travellers* (www.gypsy-traveller.org/pdfs/The_law_relating_to.pdf) at para. 2.3. This case is quoted in ACPO Guidance on s. 61 and in *Managing Unauthorised Camping*, para. 6.9.

[279] *R (on the application of Fuller) v Chief Constable of Dorset Police* [2001] EWHC 1053 (Admin); [2002] 3 All ER 57 at paras [67]–[69].

[280] *Managing Unauthorised Camping*, para. 5.8. Detailed guidance is given on welfare enquiries that must be made. Local authorities have separate powers to direct unauthorised campers to leave land and to seek a court order: 1994 Act, ss. 77–79. See *R v Wealden District Council, ex p Wales*; *R v Lincolnshire County Council, ex p Atkinson* (1996) 8 Admin LR 529, where orders were quashed as the council had failed to take account of welfare considerations set out in DoE Circular 18/94. See further *Cross on Local Government Law*, para. 19.185.

of the peace or disorder caused by the encampment.[281] This would seem to confine reliance on s. 61 to exceptional circumstances.

It has been held that as s. 61 creates a criminal offence (indeed a draconian procedure) it is to be construed narrowly.[282] Accordingly, (a) a direction under s. 61 can only lawfully be given after the trespassers have failed to comply with the occupier's request for them to leave; and (b) a direction cannot be given to leave at a future time. However, s. 61 is not incompatible with the ECHR.[283]

Parallel with these developments has been the creation by the Anti-social Behaviour Act 2003[284] of an alternative regime for the police to follow. This enables a senior police officer to direct the removal of a person and one or more others who are trespassing on land with the common purpose of residing there for any period and with at least one vehicle. If it appears to the officer that the person has one or more caravans in his possession or under his control on the land, there must be a suitable pitch on a relevant caravan site in the local authority's area for each of them. Non compliance with a direction without reasonable excuse is an offence. There is a power of seizure.

(VII) TRESPASS ON A DESIGNATED SITE

Trespass to land is not normally a criminal offence. An exception is provided by s. 128 of the Serious Organised Crime and Police Act 2005,[285] in respect of nuclear sites and other sites designated by the Secretary of State.[286] The latter must be on Crown land or it must appear to the Secretary of State that it is appropriate to designate the site in the interests of national security. It is a defence for a person charged to prove that he or she did not know, and had no reasonable cause to suspect, that the site in question was designated. The Attorney-General must consent to any prosecution.

(VIII) RAVES

Sections 63–66 of the 1994 Act confer relatively narrow powers to stop the holding of a 'rave', and to stop people proceeding to one. This is a gathering on land in the open air of 100 or more persons (whether or not trespassers) at which amplified music is played during the night, and as such is, by reason of its loudness and duration and the time at which it is played, likely to cause serious distress to the inhabitants of the locality. Vehicles and equipment can be seized and sound equipment forfeited. By the time the Act was in force 'illegal raves had become a rare phenomenon compared with the late 1980s'.[287] The powers are relatively infrequently used.[288] They were extended by the Anti-social Behaviour Act 2003[289] to reduce the number of persons to 20, and to apply in addition to indoor trespassing raves.

---

[281] Ibid., para. 6.8.

[282] Stanley Burnton J in *R (on the application of Fuller) v Chief Constable of Dorset Police* [2001] EWHC 1057 (Admin), [2002] 3 All ER 567 at para. [42].

[283] Ibid., Stanley Burnton J, considering Arts 3, 6 and 8.

[284] Ss. 60–64, inserting ss. 62A–62E in the 1994 Act. Further guidance has been given: ODPM, *Supplement to 'Managing Unauthorised Camping: A Good Practice Guide* (2005) (www.communities.gov.uk).

[285] As amended by the Terrorism Act 2006, s. 12. See Home Office Circular, 017/2007.

[286] See SIs 2005/3447, 2007/930, 2007/1387, designating the Palace of Westminster and Portcullis House and a range of government buildings, royal residences and naval and RAF bases.

[287] T. Bucke and Z. James, op. cit., p. 25.

[288] Ibid., p. 30. See further the 5th edition of this book at pp. 457–459.

[289] Section 58, amending s. 63 of the 1994 Act.

(B) THE CONDUCT OF PROCESSIONS AND ASSEMBLIES

(I) INTRODUCTION

There are many criminal offences which may be committed by those who take part in or disrupt meetings, processions and other activities. Some have already been mentioned, including the Police Act 1996, s. 89[290] and the Highways Act 1980, s. 137.[291] The Criminal Damage Act 1971 makes it an offence to destroy or damage property belonging to another without lawful excuse.[292] This is a broad offence and has been used in numerous prosecutions of protesters.[293] It is no defence that the defendant believes that he has the consent of God (to writing a Biblical quotation on a concrete pillar at the perimeter of the Houses of Parliament in protest at the Gulf War.[294] In *R v Hill and Hall*[295] CND protesters were caught in possession of wire cutters. They intended to cut through the perimeter fence of a USAF base, believing that if the base closed there would be less likelihood of a Soviet nuclear attack directed at the area and that therefore their houses would be safe. The defence in s. 5(2)(b) of the Criminal Damage Act 1971 that the houses were in need of protection from immediate danger failed:

In our view that must mean evidence that the [accused] believed that immediate action had to be taken to do something which would otherwise be a crime in order to prevent the immediate risk of something worse happening.[296]

This defence was also not available in respect of the destruction of badger traps by protesters as badgers were not 'property belonging to another'.[297] It is no defence to a prosecution for criminal damage at an airbase to argue that the activities there constitute the crime of aggression under customary international law; s. 3 of the Criminal Law Act 1967[298] can only be relied on to prevent a 'crime' in domestic law, and aggression is not such a crime.[299]

It is an offence for a person to have with him in any public place an offensive weapon without lawful authority or reasonable excuse (Prevention of Crime Act 1953, s. 1).[300]

The Criminal Law Act 1977 made it an offence for any person other than the displaced residential occupier or a protected intending occupier to use or threaten violence to secure entry to premises;[301] to occupy premises as a trespasser and fail to leave on being required

---

[290] Above, p. 119.   [291] Above, p. 294.   [292] S. 1(1).

[293] On the acquittal of GM crop destroyers (Lord Melchett and members of Greenpeace) charged under the Criminal Damage Act 1971, see news reports for 21 September 2000.

[294] *Blake v DPP* [1993] Crim LR 586.   [295] (1988) 89 Cr App R 74, CA.

[296] Per Lane LCJ at 80.   [297] *Creswell v DPP* [2006] EWHC 3379 (Admin), (2007) 171 JP 233.

[298] See p. 151.

[299] *R v Jones (Margaret)* [2006] UKHL 16, [2007] 1 AC 136. Cf. *Hutchinson v Newbury Magistrates' Court* (2000) 122 ILR 499, DC (no defence based claim that storage of atomic warheads at Aldermarston was contrary to international law).

[300] See *Smith and Hogan*, pp. 661–668.

[301] S. 6, as amended by the Criminal Justice and Public Order Act 1994, s. 72 (s. 6 is very wide since no actual entry is required and a threat of violence will suffice; the offence clearly covers the threat of a demonstration or 'sit in'; s. 7 provides an immediate remedy to deal with squatters). See further, E. Griew, *The Criminal Law Act 1977* (1977); A. Prichard, *Squatting* (1980). See also *Ropaigealach v Barclays Bank plc* [2000] 1 QB 263 on the protection of s. 6.

to do so by a displaced residential occupier or a protected intending occupier;[302] to trespass with a weapon of offence;[303] to trespass upon consular or diplomatic premises;[304] and to obstruct court officers executing process for possession against unauthorised occupiers.

Offences unlikely now to be charged (at least outside wartime) are treason, treason felony, sedition (inciting violence for the purpose of disturbing constitutional authority) and incitement to mutiny or disaffection among the armed forces or police.[305]

Finally, any person has power to prevent breaches of the peace. The parameters of this power were restated in R (on the application of Laporte) v Chief Constable of Gloucestershire,[306] which is considered below.[307]

We deal in more detail here with the main offences under the Public Order Act 1986; harassment; anti-social behaviour orders; and the disruption of lawful meetings and other activities.

(II) PART I OF THE PUBLIC ORDER ACT 1986

- **Public Order Act 1986**

PART I

NEW OFFENCES

1. Riot

(1) Where 12 or more persons who are present together use or threaten unlawful violence for a common purpose and the conduct of them (taken together) is such as would cause a person of reasonable firmness present at the scene to fear for his personal safety, each of the persons using unlawful violence for the common purpose is guilty of riot.

(2) It is immaterial whether or not the 12 or more use or threaten unlawful violence simultaneously.

(3) The common purpose may be inferred from conduct.

(4) No person of reasonable firmness need actually be, or be likely to be, present at the scene.

(5) Riot may be committed in private as well as in public places.

(6) A person guilty of riot is liable on conviction on indictment to imprisonment for a term not exceeding ten years or a fine or both.

2. Violent disorder

(1) Where 3 or more persons who are present together use or threaten unlawful violence and the conduct of them (taken together) is such as would cause a person of reasonable firmness present at the scene to fear for his personal safety, each of the persons using or threatening unlawful violence is guilty of violent disorder.

(2) It is immaterial whether or not the 3 or more use or threaten unlawful violence simultaneously.

(3) No person of reasonable firmness need actually be, or be likely to be, present at the scene.

(4) Violent disorder may be committed in private as well as in public places.

(5) A person guilty of violent disorder is liable on conviction on indictment to imprisonment for a term not exceeding 5 years or a fine of both, or on summary conviction to imprisonment for a term not exceeding 6 months or a fine not exceeding the statutory maximum or both.

---

[302] S. 7, as substituted by the 1994 Act, s. 73.   [303] S. 8.   [304] S. 9.
[305] See G. Robertson and A. Nicol, *Media Law* (5th edn, 2007), pp. 671–675.
[306] [2007] 2 AC 105.   [307] pp. 376–397.

3. Affray

(1) A person is guilty of affray if he uses or threatens unlawful violence towards another and his conduct is such as would cause a person of reasonable firmness present at the scene to fear for his personal safety.

(2) Where 2 or more persons use or threaten the unlawful violence, it is the conduct of them taken together that must be considered for the purposes of subsection (1).

(3) For the purposes of this section a threat cannot be made by the use of words alone.

(4) No person of reasonable firmness need actually be, or be likely to be, present at the scene.

(5) Affray may be committed in private as well as in public places......

(7) A person guilty of affray is liable on conviction on indictment to imprisonment for a term not exceeding 3 years or a fine or both, or on summary conviction to imprisonment for a term not exceeding 6 months or a fine not exceeding the statutory maximum or both.

4. Fear or provocation of violence

(1) A person is guilty of an offence if he—

(a) uses towards another person threatening, abusive or insulting words or behaviour, or

(b) distributes or displays to another person any writing, sign or other visible representation which is threatening, abusive or insulting,

with intent to cause that person to believe that immediate unlawful violence will be used against him or another by any person, or to provoke the immediate use of unlawful violence by that person or another, or whereby that person is likely to believe that such violence will be used or it is likely that such violence will be provoked.

(2) An offence under this section may be committed in a public or a private place, except that no offence is committed where the words or behaviour are used, or the writing, sign or other visible representation is distributed or displayed, by a person inside a dwelling and the other person is also inside that or another dwelling....

(4) A person guilty of an offence under this section is liable on summary conviction to imprisonment for a term not exceeding 6 months or a fine not exceeding level 5 on the standard scale or both.

[4A. Intentional harassment, alarm or distress

(1) A person is guilty of an offence if, with intent to cause a person harassment, alarm or distress, he—

(a) uses threatening, abusive or insulting words or behaviour, or disorderly behaviour, or

(b) displays any writing, sign or other visible representation which is threatening, abusive or insulting,

thereby causing that or another person harassment, alarm or distress.

(2) An offence under this section may be committed in a public or a private place, except that no offence is committed where the words or behaviour are used, or the writing, sign or other visible representation is displayed, by a person inside a dwelling and the person who is harassed, alarmed or distressed is also inside that or another dwelling.

(3) It is a defence for the accused to prove—

(a) that he was inside a dwelling and had no reason to believe that the words or behaviour used, or the writing, sign or other visible representation displayed, would be heard or seen by a person outside that or any other dwelling, or

(b) that his conduct was reasonable.

(5) A person guilty of an offence under this section is liable on summary conviction to imprisonment for a term not exceeding 6 months or a fine not exceeding level 5 on the standard scale or both.][308]

5. Harassment, alarm or distress

(1) A person is guilty of an offence if he—

(a) uses threatening, abusive or insulting words or behaviour, or disorderly behaviour, or

(b) displays any writing, sign or other visible representation which is threatening, abusive or insulting,

within the hearing or sight of a person likely to be caused harassment, alarm or distress thereby.

(2) An offence under this section may be committed in a public or a private place, except that no offence is committed where the words or behaviour are used, or the writing, sign or other visible representation is displayed, by a person inside a dwelling and the other person is also inside that or another dwelling.

(3) It is a defence for the accused to prove—

(a) that he had no reason to believe that there was any person within hearing or sight who was likely to be caused harassment, alarm or distress, or

(b) that he was inside a dwelling and had no reason to believe that the words or behaviour used, or the writing, sign or other visible representation displayed, would be heard or seen by a person outside that or any other dwelling, or

(c) that his conduct was reasonable....

(6) A person guilty of an offence under this section is liable on summary conviction to a fine not exceeding level 3 on the standard scale.

6. Mental element: miscellaneous

(1) A person is guilty of riot only if he intends to use violence or is aware that his conduct may be violent.

(2) A person is guilty of violent disorder or affray only if he intends to use or threaten violence or is aware that his conduct may be violent or threaten violence.

(3) A person is guilty of an offence under section 4 only if he intends his words or behaviour, or the writing, sign or other visible representation, to be threatening, abusive or insulting, or is aware that it may be threatening, abusive or insulting.

(4) A person is guilty of an offence under section 5 only if he intends his words or behaviour, or the writing, sign or other visible representation, to be threatening, abusive or insulting, or is aware that it may be threatening, abusive or insulting or (as the case may be) he intends his behaviour to be or is aware that it may be disorderly.

(5) For the purposes of this section a person whose awareness if impaired by intoxication shall be taken to be aware of that of which he would be aware if not intoxicated, unless he shows either that his intoxication was not self-induced or that it was caused solely by the taking or administration of a substance in the course of medical treatment.

(6) In subsection (5) 'intoxication' means any intoxication, whether caused by drink, drugs or other means, or by a combination of means.

(7) Subsections (1) and (2) do not affect the determination for the purposes of riot or violent disorder of the number of persons who use or threaten violence.

---

[308] Inserted by the Criminal Justice and Public Order Act 1994, s. 154.

7. Procedure: miscellaneous

(1) No prosecution for an offence of riot or incitement to riot may be instituted except by or with the consent of the Director of Public Prosecutions.

(2) For the purposes of the rule against charging more than one offence in the same count or information, each of sections 1 to 5 creates one offence.

(3) If on the trial on indictment of a person charged with violent disorder or affray the jury find him not guilty of the offence charged, they may (without prejudice to section 6(3) of the Criminal Law Act 1967) find him guilty of an offence under section 4.

(4) The Crown Court has the same powers and duties in relation to a person who is by virtue of subsection (3) convicted before it of an offence under section 4 as a magistrates' court would have on convicting him of the offence.

8. Interpretation

In this Part—

'dwelling' means any structure or part of a structure occupied as a person's home or as other living accommodation (whether the occupation is separate or shared with others) but does not include any part not so occupied, and for this purpose 'structure' includes a tent, caravan, vehicle, vessel or other temporary or movable structure;

'violence' means any violent conduct, so that—

(a) except in the context of affray, it includes violent conduct towards property as well as violent conduct towards persons, and

(b) it is not restricted to conduct causing or intended to cause injury or damage but includes any other violent conduct (for example, throwing at or towards a person a missile of a kind capable of causing injury which does not hit or falls short).

9. Offences abolished

(1) The common law offences of riot, rout, unlawful assembly and affray are abolished.

(2) The offences under the following enactments are abolished—

(a) section 1 of the Tumultuous Petitioning Act 1661 (presentation of petition to monarch or Parliament accompanied by excessive number of persons),

(b) section 1 of the Shipping Offences Act 1793 (interference with operation of vessel by persons riotously assembled),

(c) section 23 of the Seditious Meetings Act 1817 (prohibition of certain meetings within one mile of Westminster Hall when Parliament sitting), and

(d) section 5 of the Public Order Act 1936 (conduct conducive to breach of the peace).

(III) RIOT, VIOLENT DISORDER AND AFFRAY

NOTES

1. Part I of the 1986 Act[309] replaces the common law offences of riot, rout, unlawful assembly and affray and (*inter alia*) the statutory offence under s. 5 of the Public Order Act 1936 (the use of threatening, abusive or insulting words or behaviour with intent to provoke a breach

---

[309] See A.T.H. Smith [1987] Crim LR 156.

of the peace or whereby a breach of the peace is likely to be occasioned). It was based on the recommendations of the Law Commission,[310] with some modifications.

2. *Riot.* At common law, there were five necessary elements: (1) three or more persons; (2) a common purpose; (3) execution or inception of the common purpose; (4) an intent to help one another by force if necessary against any person who might oppose them in the execution of their common purpose; and (5) force or violence displayed in such a manner as to alarm at least one person of reasonable firmness and courage.[311] The statutory offence is similar, but with a requirement of 12 or more persons rather than three. By contrast with the offence of violent disorder (below), the riot offence applies only to those who use violence. It is the most serious of the public order offences, being triable only on indictment. The consent of the DPP is required, but; that may be expressed by any Crown Prosecutor.[312]

The Law Commission regarded riot charges as appropriate where there is evidence of prolonged, active and direct participation in the organisation of a major public disturbance.[313] 'In many respects, riot is simply an aggravated form of violent disorder.'[314] The distinguishing features are (1) its scale, with the involvement of 12 or more; (2) the requirement of common purpose; and (3) the requirement that the defendant be shown to have *used* or threatened unlawful violence.[315] The common purpose relates to the violence, not the presence of the 12. A defendant who does not *use* unlawful violence may, nevertheless, be convicted of riot as an aider and abettor if he encourages the use of violence by others: *R v Jefferson*,[316] where the court confirmed that s. 8 of the Accessories and Abettors Act 1861 was potentially applicable to each of the offences in ss. 1–5 of the 1986 Act.

The requirement of 'common purpose' may be very general, for example 'celebrating the victory of England over Egypt in their World Cup match',[317] and 'demonstrating against the poll tax'.[318] The purpose may be of any character, it does not matter whether it is public or private, lawful or unlawful.[319] It does not matter that some of the 12 are acting without the intent to use violence or awareness that conduct is violent if they use violence for the common purpose. The hypothetical person of reasonable firmness who must fear for his personal safety need not be present at the scene. This is an important aspect of the offence, reflecting the fact that the offence is against the state rather than an individual victim. The section, read in conjunction with s. 6, renders voluntarily intoxicated offenders very easily prosecuted, even where their intoxication through drink or drugs is such that they were unaware of what they were doing. Section 6(5) is likely to be regarded as imposing an evidential burden on D.[320]

3. In practice the authorities have found difficulty in securing convictions for riot following outbreaks of serious disorder. For example, in the riots in the St Paul's district of Bristol in 1980, 134 arrests were made. The DPP decided that 16 should be charged with the common law offence of riotous assembly.[321] The trial lasted over seven weeks. The judge directed the acquittal of three defendants for lack of evidence, the jury acquitted five and failed to agree a verdict on the rest: the trial collapsed, having cost around £500,000 (the same as the cost of the riot damage). The result was seen as a 'resounding victory for black

---

[310] Law Com. No. 123.   [311] *Field v Metropolitan Police Receiver* [1907] 2 KB 853.

[312] Prosecution of Offences Act 1985, s. 7(1).

[313] Law Com. No. 123, paras 6.7–6.10. See also the CPS charging standards, cited in *Smith and Hogan*, p. 1064.

[314] *Smith*, p. 78.   [315] *White Paper*, p. 17.   [316] [1994] 1 All ER 270, CA (Cr D).

[317] *Jefferson*, above.   [318] *R v Tyler* (1993) 96 Cr App R 332, CA (Cr D).

[319] Law Com. No. 123, paras 6.24, 6.25.   [320] *Smith and Hogan*, p. 974.

[321] See M. Kettle and L. Hodges, *Uprising!* (1982), pp. 34–38.

people and the rioters, and led the DPP…to comment that it may have been a mistake to bring riot charges'. It appeared that a number of the jurors were not convinced that a common purpose of 'a show of strength against the police' was sufficient to constitute a riot, even though the judge had directed that it could be.[322] Similarly, all the charges of riotous assembly (and most of those of unlawful assembly) brought in consequence of violence during the 1984/5 miners' strike failed.[323] The Attorney-General commented that 'the law of riot creates some grave evidential problems'.[324] Several convictions followed the 'Tottenham Riots', but these are a rare example of prosecutors overcoming the problems. These problems appear to remain under the 1986 Act. The number found guilty of riot each year has remained small, although the number of public order offences generally has risen.[325]

4. Most of the recent reported cases on riot have concerned claims under the Riot (Damages) Act 1886,[326] as amended by the Police Act 1996, ss. 103(1) and 63. That Act was passed to remedy defects in the previous legislation[327] under which compensation was paid by the hundred only in cases of the felonious destruction of certain specified kinds of property by persons riotously and tumultuously assembled. Pressure from people whose property was damaged in the Trafalgar Square riots of 8 February 1886, and who had no claim under the previous legislation, led to special provision being made for them by the Metropolitan Police (Compensation) Act 1886. The general legislation followed shortly afterwards. Claims are met by the police authority.

Other cases under this Act include *Gunter v Metropolitan Police District Receiver*;[328] *Rance v Hastings Corpn*[329] (attack on a hotel where three ladies, wrongly thought by the mob to be militant suffragettes, had taken refuge: claim successful); *Ford v Metropolitan Police District Receiver*[330] (a 'good humoured' crowd, some armed with crowbars and pickaxes, took woodwork and floorboards from an empty house as fuel for a 'peace night' bonfire; a neighbour gave evidence that he was afraid: claim successful); *Munday v Metropolitan Police District Receiver*[331] (crowd unable to get into Chelsea FC's ground to see a match against Moscow Dynamo broke into neighbouring premises in order to watch from there, the owner's daughter was held against a wall, and gave evidence that she was afraid: claim successful). In order to establish a claim, the conduct must be 'tumultuous' as well as 'riotous' (*JW Dwyer Ltd v Metropolitan Police District Receiver*).[332] This was endorsed by the Court of Appeal in *D H Edmonds Ltd v East Sussex Police Authority*,[333] when holding that the three or four robbers who had committed a smash and grab raid at the plaintiff's jewellery shop were assembled 'riotously' but not 'tumultuously'. To be 'tumultuous' an assembly should be of considerable size, excited and emotionally aroused and, generally although not necessarily, accompanied by noise. 'Riot' and 'riotously' in the 1886 Act are to be interpreted in accordance with s. 1: 1986 Act, s. 10(1).

---

[322] Kettle and Hodges, op. cit., p. 38.

[323] See S. McCabe and P. Wallington, *The Police, Public Order and Civil Liberties* (1988), pp. 99–100; S. Kavanagh and R. Malcolm, *Legal Action*, September 1985, p. 6.

[324] 63 HC Deb, 9 July 1984, col. 691.

[325] Between 1997 and 2006/7, the number of recorded riot offences was in single figures each year; violent disorder offences were normally between 2,000 and 3,000 each year, but fell to 1,744 in 2006/7; other offences against the state or public order more than doubled from 16,240 to 35,777: S. Nicholas et al. (eds), *Crime in England and Wales 2006/07* (July 2007), p. 40.

[326] See A. Samuels [1970] Crim LR 336 and recent cases noted in the Preface.

[327] 1827, 7 & 8 Geo IV c 31.

[328] (1888) 53 JP 249, Mathews J.   [329] (1913) 136 LT Jo 117, Hastings County Ct.

[330] [1921] 2 KB 344, Bailhache J.   [331] [1949] 1 All ER 337, Pritchard J.

[332] [1967] 2 QB 970, Lyell J.   [333] (1988) Times, 15 July.

5. *Violent disorder.* The violent disorder offence replaced the common law offence of unlawful assembly. This offence required (1) an assembly of three or more persons; (2) a common
purpose (a) to commit a crime of violence or (b) to achieve some other object, whether lawful
or not, in such a way as to cause reasonable men to apprehend a breach of the peace; and (3)
an intention to use or abet the use of violence, or to do or abet acts which D knows to be likely
to cause a breach of the peace.[334] There was, however, some uncertainty as to its exact scope.
It was used as a charge following serious outbreaks of disorder such as Chartist disturbances
in Newport;[335] the Trafalgar Square riots on 'Bloody Sunday', 13 November 1887;[336] the disturbance at the Garden House Hotel, Cambridge;[337] the Shrewsbury pickets case.[338] *Beatty
v Gillbanks*[339] was also commonly regarded as an authority on unlawful assembly.

6. The White Paper stated:[340]

3.13. Violent disorder will be the main successor offence to unlawful assembly, and to some cases currently charged as riot. Like the Law Commission, the Government anticipates that it will be used in the
future as the normal charge for serious outbreaks of public disorder. But it will be capable of being applied
over a wide spectrum of situations ranging from major public disorder to minor group disturbances involving some violence.

The offence is triable either way, but the *Consolidated Criminal Practice Direction*[341] states
that cases of violent disorder 'should generally be committed for trial'. In practice, it has been
used as a charge much more frequently than unlawful assembly was.

7. The violent disorder offence requires three or more persons together using or threatening
violence. It is not necessary for three or more to be named in the indictment, but the defence
must be apprised of the case they have to meet; the best way of achieving this is by adding
the words 'and others' to the indictment, enabling the defence then to seek particulars.[342]
The defences of self-defence, reasonable defence of another person and the 'taking of necessary steps to preserve the peace' may be raised.[343] Where D does not use or threaten violence
personally, but gives overt encouragement to others to do so, he or she may be convicted
under s. 2.[344] In sentencing a participant in public disorder the court must consider not
only the defendant's precise individual acts, but also the fact that these were part of a wider
disturbance.[345]

8. *Affray.* This offence is typically used in respect of fights, although cases involving very
serious violence are likely to lead to charges of violent disorder or riot rather than affray.
Before the 1986 Act, affray was 'by far the most important of the common law public order
offences, charged against some 1,000 people per year'.[346] It covered unlawful fighting or

---

[334] J.C. Smith and B. Hogan, *Criminal Law* (6th edn, 1988), p. 745.

[335] *R v Vincent* (1839) 9 C&P 91.

[336] See *R v Cunninghame Graham and Burns* (1888) 16 Cox CC 420; V. Bailey (ed.), *Policing and Punishment
in Nineteenth Century Britain* (1981), Chap. 5.

[337] See *R v Caird* (1970) 54 Cr App R 499.   [338] *R v Jones* [1974] ICR 310, CA (Cr D).

[339] Below p. 394.   [340] P. 15.   [341] V.51.11(a).

[342] *R v Mahroof* (1988) 88 Cr App R 317, CA (Cr D). Applied in *R v Fleming and Robinson* (1989) 153 JP 517, CA
(Cr D); *R v Worton* (1989) 154 JP 201, CA (Cr D). See also *R v Morris* [2005] EWCA Crim 609.

[343] *R v Rothwell and Barton* [1993] Crim LR 662, CA (Cr D).

[344] *R v Blackwood* [2002] EWCA Crim 3102 (applying an affray case, *Allan v Ireland* (1984) 79 Cr
App R 206; judge must direct properly as to the mental element necessary for conviction on the basis of
encouragement).

[345] *R v Hebron and Spencer* (1989) 11 Cr App R (S) 226.

[346] *White Paper*, p. 16.

violence or an unlawful display of force, in such a manner that a bystander of reasonably firm character might reasonably be expected to be terrified. Statutory affray is triable either way and carries a maximum sentence (when tried on indictment) of three years (in comparison with life imprisonment at common law).

Section 3(1) appears to contemplate both a person to whom the violence or threat is directed and a hypothetical third party of reasonable firmness as well as the defendant. It is this requirement that keeps all fights between just two participants from becoming an affray. It has been emphasised on a number of occasions that the hypothetical person is the one who must fear for his safety not the victim.[347] Accordingly, the offence will not cover every case of assault, as the circumstances may not be such as to cause a third party to fear for his own safety. The offence may be committed in the course of domestic incidents and not just occasions of public disorder.[348]

On the limitation in s. 3(3) that for the purposes of affray a threat cannot be made by words alone, see *R v Dixon*[349] (encouragement of dog to attack police officers sufficient even in the absence of evidence that the dog's subsequent attack was in response to the encouragement), and *R v Robinson*[350] (adoption of an aggressive tone of voice insufficient). Carrying a concealed weapon or the mere possession of a weapon without threatening circumstances cannot alone constitute a threat of unlawful violence; however, the carrying of dangerous weapons such as primed petrol bombs can constitute such a threat, without there being waved or brandished.[351] However, there has to be a threat directed towards a person or persons present at the scene.[352]

(IV) FEAR OR PROVOCATION OF VIOLENCE

Section 4 of the 1986 Act was considered in *Atkin v DPP*[353] and *R v Horseferry Road Metropolitan Stipendiary Magistrate, ex p Siadatan*.[354] Section 5 was considered in *Norwood*.[355] Section 4A, an offence of intentionally causing harassment, alarm or distress, was added by the Criminal Justice and Public Order Act 1994, s. 154. The aim was to provide higher penalties where harassment etc was deliberately inflicted, and to 'enable the courts to deal more effectively with serious racial harassment, particularly where it is persistent'.[356]

- **R v Horseferry Road Metropolitan Stipendiary Magistrate, ex p Siadatan**
  [1991] 1 QB 260, [1990] 3 WLR 1006, [1991] 1 All ER 324, Queen's
  Bench Divisional Court

The applicant, Sayid Mehdie Siadatan, laid an information against Penguin Books Ltd, the publishers of *Satanic Verses* by Salman Rushdie, and sought a summons accusing them of

---

[347] *R v Sanchez* (1996) JP 321, [1996] Crim LR 572, CA (S attacked V, her former partner with whom she was arguing in a car park in the early hours—hypothetical reasonable bystander unlikely to be threatened; this was a very personal fight).

[348] See *R v Davison* [1992] Crim LR 31 and Commentary by Sir John Smith, and *DPP v Cotcher and Cotcher* [1993] COD 181. In *R v Connor* (2000) 13 March, CA (Cr D) Buxton LJ reiterated the view in *R v Davison* that simple assaults ought not to be elevated to public order charges.

[349] [1993] Crim LR 579, CA (Cr D), commentary by Sir John Smith.

[350] [1993] Crim LR 581, CA (Cr D), commentary by Sir John Smith.

[351] *I v DPP* [2001] 2 WLR 765, HL

[352] Ibid. (no offence committed where about eight youths in a gang of 40 to 50 youths were armed with primed petrol bombs; the only others present were the police and no threat was made towards them).

[353] Below, p. 341.   [354] Below.   [355] Below, p. 342.

[356] Earl Ferrers, 555 HL Deb, 16 June 1994, col. 1864.

distributing a book written by the author which contained abusive and insulting writing whereby it was likely that unlawful violence would be provoked, contrary to s. 4(1) of the Public Order Act 1986. The book was offensive to many Muslims and a bookshop owned by the publishers was subjected to a fire bomb attack while the book was on sale. The magistrate hearing the information refused to issue the summons on the ground that the information disclosed no offence because it was not alleged that 'immediate' unlawful violence would be provoked. The applicant applied for judicial review to quash the magistrate's decision, but the Divisional Court dismissed the application.

The judgment of the court (**Watkins** and **Stuart-Smith LJJ** and **Roch J**) was delivered by **Watkins LJ**:...

[His Lordship noted that it was not contended that distribution of the book would provoke 'immediate' unlawful violence, and continued:]

Mr Nice [counsel for the applicant] referred to the short history of the legislation as follows. Section 4(1) of the 1986 Act replaced s. 5 of the Public Order Act 1936.... Section 5...did not require that the breach of the peace which was either intended or likely to be occasioned should follow immediately upon the actions of the defendant....

[His Lordship read s. 6(3) of the 1986 Act]

In the light of those provisions Mr Nice submits that a person who intends written words to be threatening, abusive or insulting, or who is aware that written words may be threatening, abusive or insulting, should not escape criminal liability under s. 4(1) simply because the violence which the written words are likely to provoke will not be immediate. If, he said, the construction of the section for which he contended is rejected, there will be a gap in the law which did not exist under the 1936 Act, a gap which Parliament, when passing the 1986 Act, could not have intended to create.

A consequence of construing the words 'such violence' in s. 4(1) as meaning 'immediate unlawful violence' will be that leaders of an extremist movement who prepare pamphlets or banners to be distributed or carried in public places by adherents to that movement will not be committing any offence under s. 4(1) albeit that they intend the words in the pamphlets or on the banners to be threatening, abusive or insulting and it is likely that unlawful violence will be provoked by the words in the pamphlet or on the banners.

Thus, whilst recognising the right to freedom of expression which the law confers on all persons within the United Kingdom, Mr Nice argues that such rights do not include a freedom to insult or abuse other persons in such a way that it is likely that violence will be provoked. Section 4(1) provides, he said, only a partial and imperfect protection against conduct which is insulting and abusive and likely to lead to violence unless his construction of the section is correct.

He argued strongly that, whether the court seeks the 'natural and ordinary meaning' of the words of s. 4(1) or whether we construe the words of s. 4(1) 'according to the plain literal and grammatical meaning of the words', the proper construction is that 'such violence' means 'unlawful violence' unqualified in any other way.

He divided the second part of the subsection into these four parts:

'With intent:(i) to cause that person to believe that immediate unlawful violence will be used against him or another by any person, or (ii) to provoke the immediate use of unlawful violence by that person or another, or whereby:(iii) that person is likely to believe that such violence will be used, or (iv) it is likely that such violence will be provoked.'

That makes plain, he said, that the words in part (iv) 'such violence' refer back to a previous use of the word 'violence', that the normal rules of grammatical construction require a reader to look at the most recent use of the word 'violence' prior to the phrase 'such violence'. The most recent use of that word appears in part (ii), where the word 'violence' is qualified only by the word 'unlawful'.

Furthermore, he argued that the phrase 'immediate unlawful violence' could have been used expressly in each of the parts (i) to (iv). Alternatively, the phrase 'immediate unlawful violence' having been used in part (i) the words 'such violence' could have been used in parts (ii), (iii) and (iv). The change from 'immediate unlawful violence' in part (i) to 'immediate use of unlawful violence' in part (ii) can only be explained because Parliament intended the words 'such violence' where they occurred in the remainder of the subsection to refer to 'unlawful violence' and not to 'immediate unlawful violence'.

Persuasive though those somewhat intricate arguments appeared to be, as presented by Mr Nice, the contrary construction advanced for the respondents by Mr Fitzgerald and by the amicus curiae, Mr Paget, is, we think, to be preferred. In our judgment the phrase 'such violence' in s. 4(1) means 'immediately unlawful violence'. We now give our reasons for that conclusion.

We were referred to the Law Commission's report entitled *Criminal Law Offences Relating to Public Order* (Law Com No. 123 (1983)). The content and structure of s. 4(1) is foreshadowed in the very clearly expressed para 5.43 of that report thus:

> '*Fear of violence and provoking violence*:
>   5.43 The offence requires that each defendant use threatening etc. words or behaviour which is intended or is likely—(a) to cause another person to fear immediate unlawful violence, or (b) to provoke the immediate use of unlawful violence by another person.'

That the parliamentary draftsman, when drafting the last part of s. 4(1), did not achieve the same clarity and precision found in that paragraph is, we think, most regrettable.

The context in which s. 4(1) appears in the 1986 Act is the first matter which leads us to our conclusion. The title to the Act recounts that it is 'An Act to abolish...certain statutory offences relating to public order; to create new offences relating to public order...' Section 4 appears in the first part of the Act together with the creation of new offences, namely riot by s. 1, violent disorder by s. 2, affray by s. 3, harassment, alarm or distress by s. 5. The provisions of those sections are such that the conduct of the defendants must produce in an actual or notional person of reasonable firmness fear in relation to ss. 1, 2 and 3 which is contemporaneous with the unlawful violence being used by the defendants or harassment, alarm or distress which is contemporaneous with the threatening, abusive or insulting conduct under s. 5. We consider it most unlikely that Parliament could have intended to include, among sections which undoubtedly deal with conduct having an immediate impact on bystanders, a section creating an offence for conduct which is likely to lead to violence at some unspecified time in the future.

The second reason is that, in our view, by itself a proper reading of s. 4(1) leads to this conclusion. We accept the submission of Mr Paget that the words 'immediate unlawful violence' and the words 'the immediate use of unlawful violence' have precisely the same meaning. The change in the phraseology used by Parliament is simply a matter of style. The only violence mentioned in s. 4(1) is 'immediate unlawful violence'. The words 'such violence' refer back to the earlier use or uses of the word 'violence' in the subsection as qualified by the other words which appear in the same phrases as the word 'violence'. On the first occasion that the word 'violence' is used it is qualified by the words 'immediate unlawful' and on the second it is qualified by the words 'the immediate use of unlawful'. In our opinion, praying in aid Mr Nice's useful partition of the subsection, it is not possible in construing the words 'such violence' in part (iv), which reads 'it is likely that such violence will be provoked', to return to part (ii) and ignore the words 'the immediate use'. Parts (iii) and (iv) must have been intended by Parliament to be mirror images of parts (i) and (ii) of the subsection.

A third and very compelling reason for our conclusion on the correct construction of this subsection is that here we are construing a penal statute, of which there are, or may be, two possible readings. It is an elementary rule of statutory construction that, in a penal statute where there are two possible readings, the meaning which limits the scope of the offence thus created is that which the court should adopt. It would surely be strange indeed, if, where it could be shown that a defendant has an intent to provoke unlawful violence by another person, Parliament required the prosecution to establish an intent to provoke the immediate use of unlawful violence, but in a situation where a defendant had no such intent, but nevertheless it was likely that violence would be provoked, there was no requirement that such violence be immediate.

For these reasons we hold that the magistrate was right to refuse to issue a summons.

Finally, we consider it advisable to indicate our provisional view on the meaning of the word 'immediate'. In the Law Commission's report to which reference has already been made, at para 5.46 the Law Commission indicated that in their opinion the new offence to replace that created by s. 5 of the 1936 Act should include the element of immediacy; in the case of behaviour provoking the use of violence, it must be the immediate use of such violence. Nevertheless, the Law Commission in para 5.44 gave an example of a gang in one part of a town uttering threats directed at persons, for example, of a particular ethnic or religious group resident in another part, and stated that that would be an offence, although the threat would not be capable of being performed until the gang arrived in the other part of the town. So the Law Commission recommended there that Parliament enact a law to create an offence of the making of threats which lead to the fear of violence to the person simpliciter as opposed to an offence of the making of threats, causing fear of violence to the person hearing the threats.

It seems to us that the word 'immediate' does not mean 'instantaneous', that a relatively short time interval may elapse between the act which is threatening, abusive or insulting and the unlawful violence. 'Immediate' connotes proximity in time and proximity in causation, that it is likely that violence will result within a relatively short period of time and without any other intervening occurrence. . . .

Application dismissed.

NOTES

1. Section 4 was designed to be the direct replacement for s. 5 of the Public Order Act 1936, as amended. This had provided as follows:

Any person who in any public place or at any public meeting—

    (*a*) uses threatening, abusive or insulting words or behaviour, or

    (*b*) distributes or displays any writing, sign or visible representation which is threatening, abusive or insulting,

with intent to provoke a breach of the peace or whereby a breach of the peace is likely to be occasioned, shall be guilty of an offence.

'Public place' was defined in s. 9.[357] Section 5 was modelled on the Metropolitan Police Act 1839, s. 15(13) and similar offences in local legislation. It was the key public order offence and used in preference to the more serious charges of riot, unlawful assembly and affray.

The main changes appearing in the new s. 4 were: (a) that the offence can be committed in a public or *private* place (except inside a dwelling house); (b) that it is not confined to situations where a third party is likely to be *provoked* into violence, but extends also to cases where a third party *fears* violence; and (c) that the 'breach of the peace' concept is not employed. The first point was in response to the dismissal by magistrates of charges under the old s. 5 during the miners' dispute where the defendants showed that they were on National Coal Board or other private property, while the victims of the threats were

---

[357] Above, p. 288.

on the public highway.[358] Threatening behaviour may be committed in a public or private place under s. 4. But, if the threatening words and behaviour are used by an accused inside a dwelling house, the offence cannot be committed if the other person is also inside that (or another) dwelling.[359] In this sense it is a truly 'public' order crime, unlike riot, violent disorder and affray.

The second point responded to case law such as *Marsh v Arscott*[360] and *Parkin v Norman*[361] which suggested 'that in certain circumstances intimidatory conduct may not be caught by section 5 if the victim (for example, a policeman, or an elderly lady) is someone who is not likely to be provoked into violence by the defendant's behaviour. This is clearly a loop-hole which needs to be closed....'[362] The requirement of immediacy was found in the Law Commission's proposals, rejected in the *White Paper*[363] but restored to the Bill.[364]

2. The phrase 'threatening, abusive or insulting' is common to both the old s. 5 and the new s. 4. Authorities on this aspect of the old s. 5 accordingly appear still to be relevant. See *Brutus v Cozens*[365] and *Parkin v Norman*.[366] The phrase 'uses towards another person' did not appear in the old s. 5, and has the effect of narrowing s. 4 by comparison.[367] It means 'uses in the presence of and in the direction of another person directly' and not merely 'concerning another person' or 'in regard to another person'.[368] The 'other person' in s. 4(2) is the person to whom the threat is directed under s. 4(1).[369]

3. Under the old s. 5, it was held by Lord Parker CJ in *Jordan v Burgoyne*[370]

if words are used which threaten, abuse or insult...then that person must take his audience as he finds them, and if those words to that audience or that part of the audience are likely to provoke a breach of the peace, then the speaker is guilty of an offence.

Here, J, a leader of the National Socialist movement, was addressing a rally in Trafalgar Square. The crowd included a group of young people near the speakers' platform that contained many Jews, CND supporters and communists who intended to prevent the meeting. J referred *inter alia* to the 'red rabble' some of whom were 'looking far from wholesome' and continued:

more and more people every day...are opening their eyes and coming to say that Hitler was right [and] that our real enemies were not Hitler and the National Socialists of Germany but world Jewry and its associates in this country.

There was complete disorder and the police stopped the meeting. The court rejected an argument that while the words were highly insulting, they were not likely to lead ordinary

---

[358] *White Paper*, p. 14. In fact, there was clear authority that s. 5 applied where threats etc. were directed to a person in a public place: *Ward v Holman* [1964] 2 QB 580.

[359] *R v Barber* [2001] EWCA Crim 838.   [360] (1982) 75 Cr App R 211.

[361] [1983] QB 92.   [362] *White Paper*, p. 14.   [363] P. 15.

[364] See *R v Horseferry Road Metropolitan Stipendiary Magistrates, ex p Siadatan*, above.

[365] Below, p. 351.   [366] Below, p. 353.

[367] See *Smith*, pp. 98–99 and *Atkin v DPP*, below.

[368] *Atkin v DPP* (1989) 89 Cr App R 199 (bailiff was in a car outside a farmhouse; D, inside, and with a gun in the corner of the room, said to Customs and Excise officers 'If the bailiff gets out of the car he's a dead 'un': no offence committed as the words were 'used towards' the officers, who were inside the dwelling). The exception in s. 4(2) was also applied in *R v Va Kun Hau* [1990] Crim LR 518, CA (Cr D). See also *R v Barber* [2001] EWCA Crim 838.

[369] Ibid.   [370] [1963] 2 QB 744.

reasonable persons to commit breaches of the peace. The offence was committed even on the assumption that the group were 'hooligans' ('I am not saying they were') who had come with the preconceived idea of preventing him from speaking. This decision gave rise to concern that the doctrine 'that the speaker must take his audience as he finds them' effectively conferred on those who sought to disrupt a 'heckler's veto'.[371] However, all that was decided was that the likelihood of a breach of the peace being occasioned was to be judged by reference to the people there, not a hypothetical reasonable person. This was, it is submitted, entirely right. Indeed the latter suggestion is an odd argument, that rests on the notion that a reasonable person might sometimes behave unlawfully (but would he or she still be a 'reasonable' person?). Otherwise, the offence could never be committed. However, it is clear that the doctrine cannot properly be applied to the prior question whether words used are 'insulting',[372] and whether D has the necessary mens rea as to the words being insulting.[373] The mens rea requirement for ss. 4, 4A and 5 would seem to exclude the operation of any general doctrine that defendants take their audiences as they find them.

4. The communal landing outside the front door of a flat in a block of flats is not part of a 'dwelling' for the purposes of s. 4(2).[374] Neither is a police cell.[375]

5. On the question of what constitutes immediacy for the purposes of s. 4, in *DPP v Ramos*[376] the defendant had written letters containing threats of violence to an Asian support group shortly after the Brixton nail bomb attack in 1999. The question arose as to whether the letters gave rise to a fear of immediate violence. The Divisional Court held that the magistrates were entitled to infer that from the facts. The court referred to the width of the definition of assault following the House of Lords ruling in *R v Ireland*,[377] and that the 1986 Act deals with 'the state of mind of the victim which is crucial rather than the statistical risk of violence actually occurring within a very short space of time'.[378] A similarly broad interpretation was taken in *Valentine v DPP*,[379] where V had said to a neighbouring family 'next time you go [to work] we're going to burn your house. You are all going to fucking die.' The court held that the magistrates were entitled to infer that these words gave rise to a fear of immediate violence.

(V) HARASSMENT, ALARM AND DISTRESS

- **Norwood v Director of Public Prosecutions** [2002] EWHC 1564 (Admin), Queen's Bench Divisional Court

N displayed a poster, measuring about 24 inches wide and 15 inches deep, in the first-floor window of his flat in Gobowen, a small rural town in Shropshire, containing words in very large print 'Islam out of Britain' and 'Protect the British people'. It bore a reproduction of a photograph of one of the twin towers of the World Trade Center in flames on 11 September 2001 and a crescent and star surrounded by a prohibition sign. The poster had been supplied by, and bore the initials of, the British National Party, of which the appellant was the regional organiser for Shropshire. It was displayed continuously from November 2001, and reported to the police on 9 January 2002, by an offended member of the public. N was convicted of an offence of causing alarm or distress under s. 5 (1)(b) of the Public Order Act 1986, racially or

---

[371] *Smith*, p. 13. See also D.G.T. Williams (1963) 26 MLR 425; A. Dickey [1971] Crim LR 265, 272–275.
[372] See *Smith* at p.14.   [373] Cf. D.G.T. Willliams (1963) 26 MLR 425, 429.
[374] *Rukwira v DPP* (1993) 158 JP 65, DC.
[375] *R v Francis* [2006] EWCA Civ 3323, [2007] 1 WLR 1021 (in respect of a prosecution under s. 4A).
[376] [2000] Crim LR 768.   [377] [1997] AC 148.
[378] Per Kennedy LJ.   [379] [1997] COD 339, DC.

religiously aggravated as provided by ss. 28 and 31 of the Crime and Disorder Act 1998 (as amended by s. 39 of the Anti-terrorism, Crime and Security Act 2001). He was fined £300 and appealed by case stated.

Auld LJ:

THE CASE STATED AND THE STRUCTURE OF THE STATUTORY OFFENCE

[His Lordship summarised the ingredients of the offence and noted counsel for the appellant's argument, which nevertheless she did not develop, that the defences in s. 5(3)(a), (b) and (c) placed an evidential and not a legal burden on the defendant.]

20. However, in this statutory context, whatever the nature of the burden cast on the defence, it is, in any event, hard to find much of a role for any of the section 5(3) defences, directed, as they are, to an objective *assessment* by the court of the reasonableness of the accused's conduct. That is because the essentials of the basic section 5 offence require the court to be satisfied as to the accused's *subjective* state of mind, namely that he intended that the representation should be, or was aware that it might be, threatening, abusive or insulting. See e.g. *DPP v. Clarke & Ors.*, 30th July 1991, DC, The Times 18th September 1991, per Nolan LJ. If the section 5(3) burden on the defence is to be 'read down' to an evidential burden so as to make it Convention compliant, with the result of casting upon the prosecution the burden of disproving it, it would be harder to find any sensible role for section 5(3)....

21. Add now the... element that the prosecution must prove on this religiously aggravated charge, that the appellant, in displaying the poster within the hearing or sight of a person to whom it was likely to cause harassment, harm or distress, *was motivated by hostility towards a religious group*, and it is even harder to see much of a role for section 5(3) once the prosecution has proved its case under section 5(1) and 6(4).

22. It is well established that the restrictions in Article 10.2 are to be narrowly construed. In *Redmond-Bate v. DPP* [2000] HRLR 249, Div. Ct, which concerned a breach of the peace, Sedley LJ, developing a train of thought of the European Court of Human Rights in *Handyside v. UK* (1976) 1 EHRR 737, at para. 49, said, at para. 20:

'... Free speech includes not only the inoffensive, but the irritating, the contentious, the eccentric, the heretical, the unwelcome and the provocative provided it does not tend to provoke violence. Freedom only to speak inoffensively is not worth having....'...

23. Transposed to the nature of the offence with which this appeal is concerned, which is not far from conduct likely to cause a breach of the peace, the question is whether conduct the subject matter of a prosecution under section 5, in its basic or aggravated form, is unreasonable taking into account Article 10.2, in its provision of permissible restrictions necessary in a democratic society for protection of the rights of others and/or for the prevention or disorder or crime....

CONCLUSIONS

PROOF OF THE SECTION 5 OFFENCE IN ITS AGGRAVATED FORM

33. In my view, on the evidence of the content of the poster and of the circumstances of its display, the District Judge was entitled to find that the first limb of the aggravated section 5 offence was made out, namely that the appellant had displayed the poster intending it to be, or being at least aware that it might be, insulting. The words of the poster alone, and even more so when considered alongside the symbols of one of twin towers of the World Trade centre in flames and the crescent and star surrounded by a prohibition sign, were clearly racially directed and racially insulting. The poster was a public expression of attack on all Muslims in this country, urging all who might read it that followers of the Islamic religion here should be removed from it and warning that their presence here was a threat or a danger to the British people. In my view, it could not, on any reasonable basis be dismissed as merely an intemperate

criticism or protest against the tenets of the Muslim religion, as distinct from an unpleasant and insulting attack on its followers generally.... Accordingly, in my view, the District Judge, on the evidence before him, was entitled to find the first limb of section 5 in its aggravated form proved, namely that the display of the poster was racially insulting to Muslims.

34. Similarly, in relation to the second limb of the offence that the prosecution had to prove, namely that the display of the poster was within the hearing or sight of a person likely to be caused harassment, alarm or distress, I agree with Mrs. Pitt-Lewis's submission that...the terms of the poster and the circumstances and location of its display were, as matter of plain common sense capable of causing harassment, alarm or distress to those passing by who might see it in the appellant's window. As she said, that would be the reaction of any right-thinking member of society concerned with the preservation of peace and tolerance and the avoidance of religious and racial tension, as well as to any follower of the Islamic religion. In my view, on the evidence before him, the District Judge was entitled so to find. I should add, by way of emphasis—for it is plain from the wording section 5(1)—that the prosecution do not have to prove that the display of the poster in fact caused anyone harassment, alarm or distress.

ARTICLE 10 AND THE SECTION 5(3) DEFENCE

35. I have combined Article 10 and the section 5(3) defence under one heading because often, and certainly in the circumstances of this case, the question whether a defendant's conduct is objectively reasonable necessarily includes consideration of his right to freedom of expression under Article 10. [His Lordship read Article 10.]

36. I have already mentioned that Miss Miskin did not persist with the ground of appeal that section 5, as amended to create the aggravated form of offence, was incompatible with the Convention, in particular, Article 10. Her argument was rather that, in construing section 5 in its aggravated form and in its application to the facts, courts should give proper weight to the individual's right to freedom of expression in Article 10.1 when deciding where to draw the line between, on the one hand, racial or religious threats, abuse or insults intended as such or with an awareness that they might be such, and, on the other, the right to speak openly and frankly, and to express opinions or convey ideas on matters, including those that may be of public interest or concern. She added that courts should also bear in mind, when drawing the line, not only the words of Sedley LJ in *Redmond-Bate*, but that it is for the prosecution to prove its case.

37. As this Court said in *Percy*,[380] a prosecution under section 5 does not per se engage Article 10. It depends on the facts and the drawing of an appropriate balance of competing interests under Article 10.1 and 10.2, bearing always in mind that the restrictions in Article 10.2 should be narrowly construed and convincingly established. As I have indicated earlier in this judgment, in the absence of a challenge to the compatibility of section 5 with the Convention, the mechanics of the Article's operation on a prosecution under it seem to me to be confined to the objective defence of reasonableness in section 5(3). It cannot bear in any reasoned way on whether the prosecution have proved the two limbs under section 5(1), first, intentional or foreseen insulting conduct and, second, an objective likelihood of harassment, alarm or distress. Putting aside for the moment, questions as to the nature of the reverse burden of proof provided by section 5(3), the way in which Article 10 intrudes on the operation of a section 5 prosecution is whether the defendant's conduct was objectively reasonable, having regard to all the circumstances, including importantly those for which the Article 10.2 itself provides. These will include consideration whether to mark as criminal the accused's conduct in displaying the poster as a necessary restriction of his freedom of expression for the prevention of disorder or crime and/or for the protection of the rights of others. Hallett J, who gave the leading judgment in *Percy*, identified, at paragraph 11 of her judgment, two of a number of relevant factors in that case, which seem to me to be of general application in this

---

380 [*Percy v DPP*, see p. 349 below.]

context: namely: whether the accused's conduct went beyond legitimate protest and whether the behaviour had not formed part of an open expression of opinion on a matter of public interest, but had become disproportionate and unreasonable.

38. I do not consider it necessary to give a view on the precise nature of the reverse burden or proof for which section 5(3) provides, or, depending what it is, whether it is proportionate in Convention terms in the light of Lord Hope's observations in *Kebilene*, at 377G–380D, other than to indicate my predilection for a legal burden, at any rate as to any factual issue going to the court's value judgment as to the reasonableness of the accused's conduct. As the matter has not been argued before us, it would, in any event, be inappropriate to do so. There is also the difficulty, to which I have referred in paragraph 20, of finding much of a role for the section 5(3) defence, as one for an accused to 'to prove' in whatever form, once a court has reached the stage in its thought process calling for consideration of the defence, namely that the two limbs of section 5(1) in their various alternative forms are proved by the prosecution on the criminal standard of proof.

39. Nevertheless, reasonableness or unreasonableness of an accused's conduct in an objective sense goes to the root of the court's decision whether or not raised as a section 5(3) defence. If the prosecution has proved, as it must to obtain a conviction, that an accused's conduct was insulting and that he intended it to be, or was aware that it might be so, it would in most cases follow that his conduct was objectively unreasonable, especially where, in the aggravated form, the prosecution have proved that his conduct was 'motivated (wholly or partly) by hostility towards members of a religious group based on their membership of that group'. If the prosecution fails to prove either state of mind, then the question of reasonableness does not arise because the offence cannot be proved. Accordingly, whatever the nature of the burden of proof on the appellant in raising the defence, the District Judge, in my view, in the circumstances of his findings on the two limbs in section 5(1) could not sensibly have found that the appellant's conduct was reasonable so as to enable him to secure an acquittal through the route of section 5(3). In other circumstances, as the District Judge observed in paragraph 26 of his judgment, it may be that, even where a court finds that conduct was intentionally insulting and had in fact caused alarm or distress, an accused's conduct could still be reasonable. Such circumstances are difficult to envisage but, as always it depends on the facts.

40. In my view, the District Judge was entitled on the evidence before him, and again, regardless of any of the inadmissible opinion evidence of which Miss Miskin complained, to conclude, in the light of his findings on the first two limbs of section 5, that the offence had been made out — in effect that the appellant's conduct was unreasonable, having regard to the clear legitimate aim, of which the section was itself a necessary vehicle, to protect the rights of others and/or to prevent crime and disorder. There are also, as Mrs. Pitt-Lewis submitted, considerations under Articles 9 and 17, weighing against permitting the appellant to rely on his right under Article 10.1 in the circumstances of this case.

41. Accordingly, I would...dismiss the appeal.

Goldring J agreed.

NOTES

1. Section 5 of the Public Order Act 1986 was a controversial extension of the law, designed to deal with 'minor acts of hooliganism'.[381] Instances of such behaviour might include:

hooligans on housing estates causing disturbances in the common parts of blocks of flat, blockading entrances, throwing things down the stairs, banging on doors, peering in at windows, and knocking over dustbins; groups of youths persistently shouting abuse and obscenities or pestering people waiting to

---

[381] *White Paper*, p. 18.

catch public transport or to enter a hall or cinema; someone turning out the lights in a crowded dance hall, in a way likely to cause panic; rowdy behaviour in the streets, late at night which alarms local residents.[382]

This control was:

particularly needed when the behaviour is directed at the elderly and others who may feel especially vulnerable, including members of ethnic minority communities.[383]

Thus, the new s. 5 extends to cover 'disorderly' behaviour as well as threatening, abusive or insulting words or behaviour, provided it is within the hearing or sight of a person likely to be caused harassment, alarm or distress thereby. The *White Paper* had suggested that the behaviour must *actually* cause someone to feel harassed etc., and described this as a safe-guard lest the criminal law be extended widely to cover conduct not deserving of criminal sanctions;[384] the Act's provisions on this point are weaker, and avoid any need to call the victim as a witness. Victims may well be reluctant to testify in the kinds of case for which s. 5 was purportedly designed. Unlike s. 4, the words or behaviour need not be shown to be 'used towards' a particular person, but note that there is no strict requirement that the victim is called to testify in a prosecution under s. 4.[385]

2. In the House of Lords debate, Lord Denning welcomed the new offence, saying that it was 'high time that our law did something to put down disorderly behaviour'. He gave as examples of cases that would be covered: the conduct of the defendant in *Brutus v Cozens*;[386] disorderly pickets; hippies invading a person's land against the owner's will; and students who do all they can to stop freedom of speech in the universities. Lord Scarman opposed the introduction of the offence:

A very good reason for that submission I find in the entertaining and fascinating account of cases that the noble and learned Lord, Lord Denning has just given to the Committee. The Committee will have noted the extraordinary range of activities which are covered by those cases and, which it is said that this clause would cover.[387]

3. In practice, there were many examples of cases where magistrates had convicted defendants under the old s. 5 without sufficient regard to the requirements (a) that the defendant's conduct had been more than merely 'offensive' or 'annoying' and (b) that there had been some threat to the peace.[388] In the more recent cases, the Divisional Court took steps to reassert these requirements, particularly the latter.[389]

There are indications that the fears expressed at the time of its enactment concerning the breadth of the new s. 5 have been borne out. According to Peter Thornton, a former NCCL chair:

In fact it had been used quite indiscriminately, for example against juveniles for throwing fake snowballs, against a man who had a birthday party for his son in his back garden (he was charged even though he

---

[382] Ibid.   [383] Ibid.   [384] P. 19.
[385] *Swanston v DPP* (1996) 161 JP 203, DC.   [386] Below, p. 351.
[387] 478 HL Deb, 16 July 1986, cols 935–938.
[388] D.G.T. Williams [1967] Crim LR 385; A.Dickey [1971] Crim LR 265.
[389] See *Marsh v Arscott* (1982) 75 Cr App R 211 (above, p. 341).

agreed to turn the music down), against two 19 year old males for kissing in the street, against a nudist on a beach and against another nudist in his own house, and, most sinisterly, in the so-called Madame M case (successfully taken up by NCCL) against four students who were in the process of putting up a satirical poster during the last general election. It depicted the Prime Minister as a sadistic dominatrix.[390]

It is not clear how many of these cases ended in convictions. The *Madame M* case did not, the police officers who saw the poster testified to no more than an attack of mirth (rather than harassment, alarm or distress).[391]

A survey of 470 public order cases from the 1988 records at five police stations in two force areas showed that 56 per cent of the sample led to charges under s. 5 and 24 per cent under s. 4.[392] The authors note that during the period 1986–88 the number of prosecutions for public order offences doubled. Generally, the officers they interviewed did not feel that there had been a rise in public disorder, and suggested that the rise in the number of prosecutions was due more to the nature of the new legislation. The research supported the view 'that low-level nuisances of widely varying kinds have increasingly been brought within the ambit of the law'.

4. For an offence under s. 5, the conduct in question must take place in the sight of a person: *Holloway v DPP*.[393] In this case Silber J stated[394] that 'some person must actually have seen' the behaviour; Collins J stated[395] that there had to be evidence that there was someone who could see, or hear, at the material time what the individual was doing; it was necessary to call a witness to say that they saw the behaviour.[396] There is then a series of words in s. 5 that may give rise to difficulties in their application: 'threatening', 'abusive,' 'insulting', 'disorderly', 'harassment', 'alarm', and 'distress' and 'reasonable excuse'. The first three have been held under cognate legislation to be 'ordinary English words'.[397] In *Chambers and Edwards v DPP*[398] the Divisional Court held that the same approach applied to the new word 'disorderly'. Here defendants standing peacefully to block a surveyor's theodolite were convicted despite the absence of a threat or fear of violence.

An important change from the position under the old s. 5 is that conduct only in the presence of a police officer can now give rise to an offence; while a police officer was unlikely to commit a breach of the peace in response to threats, abuse or insults,[399] an officer may be caused harassment, alarm or distress: *DPP v Orum*.[400] In *Lodge v DPP*[401] the Divisional Court held that the person caused 'alarm' for the purposes of s. 5 need not be concerned at physical danger to himself; it can be alarm about the safety of an unconnected third party. A policeman saw L walking into the middle of the road, shouting, kicking and gesticulating.

---

390 *Decade of Decline: Civil Liberties in the Thatcher Years* (Liberty, 1990), p. 37.

391 (1988) 17(8) *Index on Censorship*, pp. 12. 13. See C. Douzinas et al., 'The shrinking scope of public protest'.

392 T. Newburn et al., 'Policing the Streets' (1990) 29 HORB 10 and 'Increasing Public Order' (1991) 7 Policing 22.

393 [2004] EWHC 2621 (Admin), (2005) 169 JP 14 (H's conviction for disorderly conduct quashed; police had found a video film he had made of himself standing naked while watching school children engaged in sports activities in a playing field nearby; there was no evidence that anyone saw him in his naked state).

394 Para. [17].   395 Paras [29], [32].

396 For a discussion of the possible differences in these approaches see *Taylor v DPP* [2006] EWHC 1202 (Admin), (2006) 170 JP 485.

397 *Brutus v Cozens*, below, p. 351.

398 [1995] Crim LR 896. See P. Sefton (1988) 39 NILQ 292 for the argument that decisions on differently worded 'disorderly behaviour' offences in other jurisdictions are not likely to be appropriate authorities.

399 *Marsh v Arscott* (1982) 75 Cr App R 211.   400 [1989] 1 WLR 88, DC.

401 (1988) Times, 26 October.

A car approached and the police officer was seriously concerned that an accident might happen. L appeared to be at risk and a danger to traffic and he was arrested. The Divisional Court upheld L's conviction under s. 5, holding that there was ample evidence on which the justices could have concluded that alarm was likely to have been caused so far as both the policeman and the driver were concerned. As to 'distress' Toulson J in *R (on the application of R) v DPP*[402] said:

The word 'distress' in s.4A[403] takes its colour from its context. It is part of a trio of words: harassment, alarm or distress. They are expressed as alternatives, but in combination they give a sense of the mischief which the section is aimed at preventing. They are relatively strong words befitting an offence which may carry imprisonment or a substantial fine. I would hold that the word 'distress' in this context requires emotional disturbance or upset. The statute does not attempt to define the degree required. It does not have to be grave but nor should the requirement be trivialized. There has to be something which amounts to real emotional disturbance or upset.

Here, D, a boy of 12, made masturbation gestures at police officers, calling them 'wankers'. An officer testified that he found this offensive, but was not 'annoyed' by it; he found it 'distressing' that a lad of that age was out at that hour and acting in that manner. The DC held that the magistrates had not been entitled to conclude that the officer had been caused distress, or that D had intended to do so. This is a welcome decision, although it has been held subsequently that there is no need to show the likelihood of real emotional disturbance to establish 'harassment': *Southard v DPP*.[404] A person can be distressed by watching an incident directed at him on CCTV.[405]

5. The exception enshrined in s. 5(2) was considered by the Divisional Court in *Chappell v DPP*,[406] in holding that the deposit of a letter containing threatening, abusive or insulting words through the letter box of a house, with its recipient reading it and being alarmed or distressed by it, could not constitute an offence under s. 5(1)(a) in view of the exception.[407] Other points made in *Chappell* were (a) that the justices had been right to hold that the deposit of the letter had been a 'display in writing' within the meaning of s. 5(1)(b); and (b) that a person writing and/or delivering a letter to another, who opens it in the absence of the sender, cannot be said to be a person who 'uses… words or behaviour… within the hearing or sight of a person …' who receives it. The court noted that the conduct would now fall within the provisions of the Malicious Communications Act 1988.

6. The reasonableness of the defendant's conduct under s. 5(3) must be judged objectively: *DPP v Clarke*.[408] Here, the DC upheld the acquittal of anti-abortion protesters (in a peaceful and orderly group) in respect of the display to a police officer of pictures of aborted foetuses. The justices accepted the officer's evidence that he 'found the pictures insulting to him as a father and felt abused by them and found them distressing'. Applying the objective test, they found that Ds' conduct was not 'reasonable'. However, applying a subjective test, they found that Ds did not intend the displays to be threatening, abusive or insulting, nor were

---

[402] [2006] EWHC 1375 (Admin), (2006) 170 JP 661.

[403] The approach would be the same under s. 5: ed.

[404] [2006] EWHC 3449 (Admin) (D convicted on this basis for swearing at officers who were dealing with his brother, using the words 'fuck' or 'fucking' at least twice; the court held the magistrates were entitled to find these words abusive).

[405] *Rogers v DPP* (unreported) 22 July 1999, DC (farmer watched pictures of a disorderly demonstration at his farm, objecting to his cat breeding activities).

[406] (1988) 89 Cr App R 82.   [407] Cf. *Atkin v DPP* (above, p. 341) under s. 4.

[408] (1992) 94 Cr App R 359, DC.

they aware that they might be so. In *Morrow, Beach and Thomas v DPP,*[409] by contrast, anti-abortion protesters' conduct in shouting slogans, waving banners and preventing staff and patients from entering a clinic found to be disorderly and to have caused distress; there was no defence established under s. 5(3)(c) or s. 3 of the Criminal Law Act 1967. See also *Poku v DPP,*[410] where the Divisional Court held that it was open to D to argue in defence to a s. 5 charge arising out of his resistance to the seizure of his ice cream van by police ('You're not taking my fucking van' etc.) that the seizure (for unlicensed street trading) was in fact unlawful and his response therefore reasonable.

Norwood is one of a number of cases that have applied s. 5 (or s. 4A) of the 1986 Act after implementation of the Human Rights Act 1998. In *Percy v DPP,*[411] P was an experienced protester against weapons of mass destruction and American military policy. At an American air base at RAF Fretwell, she defaced the American flag by putting a stripe across the stars and writing the words 'Stop Star Wars' across the stripes. She stepped in front of a vehicle, placed the flag down in front of it and stood upon it. A number of American service personnel or family members gave evidence that they were distressed by this, which they regarded as the desecration of their national flag. P was convicted under s. 5 and fined £300, The district judge held that the behaviour was insulting and that P was aware of the likely effect of her conduct. P appealed, arguing that the conviction was incompatible with Art. 10 ECHR. A claim for a declaration that s. 5 was incompatible was dropped. It was accepted that it was for the court to determine whether the interference with freedom of expression was proportionate. Hallett J stated[412] that ss. 5 and 6 of the 1986 Act

contain the necessary balance between the right of freedom of expression and the right of others not to be insulted and distressed.

Where Art. 10 was engaged,

the justification for any interference with that right must be convincingly established.... In this case, therefore, the court had to presume that the appellant's conduct in relation to the American flag was protected by Article 10 unless and until it was established that a restriction on her freedom of expression was strictly necessary.[413]

Hallett J was prepared to accept that there might well be a pressing social need to protect citizens of the UK and foreign nationals from intentionally and gratuitously insulting behaviour, causing them alarm or distress. This was accordingly a lawful aim, provided the restriction was proportionate, and in striking the balance due weight had to be given to the 'presumption in the accused's favour of the right to freedom of expression'.[414] Protesting against the Star Wars project was a matter of legitimate public debate' and the message 'Stop Star Wars' a 'perfectly lawful, political message'.[415] The district judge had been entitled to find that there was a

pressing social need in a multi-cultural society to prevent the denigration of objects of veneration and symbolic importance for one cultural group.[416]

---

[409] [1994] Crim LR 58. See also *Morrow v DPP* [1993] Crim LR 58 (1991) 94 Cr App R 359. Cf. *Lewis v DPP* (1995) unreported, DC (held that display of placards including one of an aborted 21-week-old foetus could constitute abusive and insulting behaviour). Convictions upheld where a clinic was invaded.

[410] [1993] Crim LR 705.   [411] [2001] EWHC 1125 (Admin).   [412] Para. [25].

[413] Para. [27].   [414] Para. [28].   [415] Para. [29].   [416] Para. [30].

However, in determining whether the interference was proportionate, the sole factor mentioned was that Ms Percy could have demonstrated her message without use of the national flag. This gave insufficient weight to the presumption in favour of freedom of expression, and failed adequately to address the proportionality issue: 'merely stating that interference is proportionate is not sufficient'.[417] The conviction was accordingly incompatible.

It is submitted that the recognition that insulting etc behaviour may well be entitled to protection is welcome; how the balance should ultimately be drawn was left unclear, the case not being remitted for a fresh hearing as P had also been convicted for obstructing the highway.[418]

This case was distinguished in *Norwood*.[419] Then in *Hammond v DPP*[420] H was convicted under s. 5. He was an Evangelical Christian and preacher, found by the justices to be a sincere man with deeply held religious beliefs. He prepared a large double-sided sign with the words 'Stop Immorality', 'Stop Homosexuality' and 'Stop Lesbianism' on each side. On at least one previous occasion he had preached while displaying the sign, which caused a hostile reaction from members of the public, one of whom tried to set it on fire. On the present occasion he preached in Bournemouth town centre. A group of 30 or 40 gathered arguing and shouting. Someone tried to pull the placard away from H, who fell down, got up and carried on. Police officers attended, asked him to take the sign down and leave. He refused and was arrested for breach of the peace, and then prosecuted under s. 5.

The justices found that the words were insulting and caused distress to persons present (some of whom were homosexual); that H was aware of this; the restriction on free expression had the legitimate aim of preventing disorder; there was a pressing social need for the restriction and the restriction corresponded to that need. The words were directed to homosexual and lesbian communities implying they were immoral. Prosecuting H under s. 5 was a proportionate response in view of the fact that his behaviour went beyond legitimate protest and was provoking violence and disorder. Although he knew that insult, distress and disturbance was likely to be caused having received a similar reaction in the past, he refused to take the sign down in response to the police request. In these circumstances his conduct was not reasonable. In the Divisional Court, May LJ held that Art. 10 considerations were relevant both to (a) the question whether the words were insulting and (b) the question whether the reasonableness defence was established. He did not agree with the statement in *Percy* that Art. 10 considerations were only relevant to (b). On the facts, the justices had indeed taken Art. 10 (and in effect Art. 9) considerations into account, and were entitled to come to the conclusion they did. The justices were entitled to find the words insulting, particularly as they implied that homosexuals and lesbians were immoral, and that his conduct was unreasonable. How satisfactory is this conclusion? Is it not a matter of opinion or belief whether particular acts (waging war; homosexual acts) are immoral? Should not Art. 10 protect the right to express those opinions publicly? Is there a difference between saying that politicians who wage war are immoral and saying that homosexuality is immoral? There may be good reasons why the police should have the right to stop H's behaviour in order to preserve the peace;[421] it does not follow that H's behaviour should be criminalised.

---

[417] Para. [33]

[418] For comments, see A. Geddis [2004] PL 853, 859–861, noting that there was no finding that the conduct *was* reasonable and that a lower court after canvassing the relevant factors might have come to the conclusion that it was not The real point seemed to be 'whether or not the expressive value given to the appellant's message by virtue of her chosen method of conveying it outweighs the upset feelings caused to the particular persons viewing it' (p. 861).

[419] See above.   [420] [2004] EWHC 69 (Admin).

[421] See pp. 376–397.

It is submitted that the approaches in *Norwood* and *Hammond* come near to empty-ing the reasonableness defence of meaningful content.[422] It does not follow that because A insults B, A is not also making a political point that deserves protection.

In *Dehal v Crown Prosecution Service*[423] D was convicted by the justices under s. 4A of the 1986 Act for displaying writing, a sign, or visible representation which was threatening, abusive or insulting, with intent to cause JSN harassment, alarm or distress. D had entered a Sikh temple and affixed to the noticeboard a notice in Punjabi. D had attended the temple for many years and had repeatedly expressed disagreement with its religious teachings. JSN, the president of the temple, interpreted the notice as referring to him and the other members of the committee, and as describing him as a hypocrite, a liar, a maker of false statements to the police, in order to have D arrested, and to the press, a proud mad dog, a man who with others had assaulted D and who exploited the temple's congregation in order to satisfy his own greed. The Crown Court dismissed an appeal by way of rehearing. The Divisional Court allowed an appeal on the grounds that the Crown Court had not given reasons for the view that the prosecution was proportionate; it had simply asserted that the terms of the notice could not be regarded as objectively reasonable. What was needed was 'a careful analysis of the reasons why it was necessary to bring a criminal prosecution at all'.[424] It is submitted that this should be regarded as shorthand for a requirement that the decision address whether the conviction was proportionate; it would be odd to require in addition that the *decision to prosecute* was proportionate as if that raised different considerations.

7. Mr Norwood's challenge to his conviction before the ECtHR failed. The Court referred to Art. 17,[425] and noted that its general purpose was to prevent individuals or groups with totalitarian aims from exploiting in their own interests the principles enunciated by the Convention. 'The poster amounted to a public expression of attack on all Muslims in the United Kingdom. Such a general, vehement attack against a religious group, linking the group as a whole with a grave act of terrorism, is incompatible with the values proclaimed and guaranteed by the Convention, notably tolerance, social peace and non-discrimination.' The display of the poster constituted an act within the meaning of Art. 17, which did not, therefore, enjoy the protection of Art. 10 or 14. The application was 'rejected as being incom-patible *ratione materiae* with the provisions of the Convention, pursuant to Article 35 §§ 3 and 4.' Note Turenne's argument that Art. 17 'should be limited to cases where the action of the defendant is intended to have a direct and substantial effect upon the enjoyment of Convention rights of others'. Otherwise, this would 'do much to undermine the idea that even unpopular speech is prima facie protected by Art. 10'.[426]

- **Brutus v Cozens** [1973] AC 854, [1972] 2 All ER 1297, [1972] 2 WLR 521, 56 Cr App R 799, House of Lords

Members of the public were admitted to watch the annual open tennis tournament at Wimbledon from stands around the courts. They were not allowed access to the courts. During a tennis match involving Drysdale, a South African, B stepped on to No. 2 court blowing a whistle. He threw around leaflets, attempted to give one to a player and sat down on the court. Upon the blowing of the whistle other persons, some bearing banners or plac-ards on which slogans were written, came on to the court and more leaflets were distrib-uted. Play was stopped. The appellant was charged with using insulting behaviour whereby a

422 See A. Geddis [2004] PL 853, 861–866, and generally, S. Turenne [2007] Crim LR 866.
423 [2005] EWHC 2154 (Admin), (2005) 169 JP 581.   424 Per Moses J at para. [19].
425 Above, p. 30.   426 S. Turenne [2007] Crim LR 866, 874.

breach of the peace was likely to be occasioned contrary to s. 5 of the Public Order Act 1936. The justices held that his behaviour had not been insulting, and dismissed the information without calling on him to give evidence.

On appeal by the respondent prosecutor, the Divisional Court held that 'insulting...behaviour' in s. 5 of the 1936 Act was behaviour which affronted other people and evidenced a disrespect or contempt for their rights, and which reasonable persons would foresee as likely to cause resentment or protest; that on the findings of the justices, which were to be regarded as provisional, insulting behaviour by the appellant had been established and the case would be sent back to them to continue the hearing. B appealed to the House of Lords.

Lord Reid: ...It appears that the object of this demonstration was to protest against the apartheid policy of the Government of South Africa. But it is not said that that government was insulted. The insult is said to have been offered to or directed at the spectators.

The spectators at No. 2 Court were upset: they made loud shouts, gesticulated and shook their fists and while the appellant was being removed some showed hostility and attempted to strike him....

It is not clear to me what precisely is the point of law which we have to decide. The question in the case stated for the opinion of the court is, 'Whether, on the above statement of facts, we came to a correct determination and decision in point of law.' This seems to assume that the meaning of the word 'insulting' in section 5 is a matter of law. And the Divisional Court appear to have proceeded on that footing.

In my judgment that is not right. The meaning of an ordinary word of the English language is not a question of law. The proper construction of a statute is a question of law. If the context shows that a word is used in an unusual sense the court will determine in other words what that unusual sense is. But here there is in my opinion no question of the word 'insulting' being used in any unusual sense. It appears to me, for reasons which I shall give later, to be intended to have its ordinary meaning. It is for the tribunal which decides the case to consider, not as law but as fact, whether in the whole circumstances the words of the statute do or do not as a matter of ordinary usage of the English language cover or apply to the facts which have been proved. If it is alleged that the tribunal has reached a wrong decision then there can be a question of law but only of a limited character. The question would normally be whether their decision was unreasonable in the sense that no tribunal acquainted with the ordinary use of language could reasonably reach that decision.

Were it otherwise we should reach an impossible position. When considering the meaning of a word one often goes to a dictionary. There one finds other words set out. And if one wants to pursue the matter and find the meaning of those other words the dictionary will give the meaning of those other words in still further words which often include the word for whose meaning one is searching.

No doubt the court could act as a dictionary. It could direct the tribunal to take some word or phrase other than the word in the statute and consider whether that word or phrase applied to or covered the facts proved. But we have been warned time and again not to substitute other words for the words of a statute. And there is very good reason for that. Few words have exact synonyms. The overtones are almost always different.

Or the court could frame a definition. But then again the tribunal would be left with words to consider. No doubt a statute may contain a definition—which incidentally often creates more problems than it solves—but the purpose of a definition is to limit or modify the ordinary meaning of a word and the court is not entitled to do that.

So the question of law in this case must be whether it was unreasonable to hold that the appellant's behaviour was not insulting. To that question there could in my view be only one answer—No.

But as the Divisional Court [1972] 1 WLR 484, have expressed their view as to the meaning of 'insulting' I must, I think, consider it. It was said at 487:

'The language of section 5, as amended, of the Public Order Act 1936, omitting words which do not matter for our present purpose, is: "Any person who in any public place…uses…insulting…behaviour,…with intent to provoke a breach of the peace or whereby a breach of the peace is likely to be occasioned, shall be guilty of an offence." It therefore becomes necessary to consider the meaning of the word "insulting" in its context in that section. In my view it is not necessary, and is probably undesirable, to try to frame an exhaustive definition which will cover every possible set of facts that may arise for consideration under this section. It is, as I think, quite sufficient for the purpose of this case to say that behaviour which affronts other people, and evidences a disrespect or contempt for their rights, behaviour which reasonable persons would foresee is likely to cause resentment or protest such as was aroused in this case, and I rely particularly on the reaction of the crowd as set out in the case stated, is insulting for the purpose of this section.'

I cannot agree with that. Parliament had to solve the difficult question of how far freedom of speech or behaviour must be limited in the general public interest. It would have been going much too far to prohibit all speech or conduct likely to occasion a breach of the peace because determined opponents may not shrink from organising or at least threatening a breach of the peace in order to silence a speaker whose views they detest. Therefore vigorous and it may be distasteful or unmannerly speech or behaviour is permitted so long as it does not go beyond any one of three limits. It must not be threatening. It must not be abusive. It must not be insulting. I see no reason why any of these should be construed as having a specially wide or a specially narrow meaning. They are all limits easily recognisable by the ordinary man. Free speech is not impaired by ruling them out. But before a man can be convicted it must be clearly shown that one or more of them has been disregarded.

We were referred to a number of dictionary meanings of 'insult' such as treating with insolence or contempt or indignity or derision or dishonour or offensive disrespect. Many things otherwise unobjectionable may be said or done in an insulting way. There can be no definition. But an ordinary sensible man knows an insult when he sees or hears it.

Taking the passage which I have quoted, 'affront' is much too vague a word to be helpful; there can often be disrespect without insult, and I do not think that contempt for a person's rights as distinct from contempt of the person himself would generally be held to be insulting. Moreover, there are many grounds other than insult for feeling resentment or protesting. I do not agree that there can be conduct which is not insulting in the ordinary sense of the word but which is 'insulting for the purpose of this section'. If the view of the Divisional Court was that in this section the word 'insulting' has some special or unusually wide meaning, then I do not agree. Parliament has given no indication that the word is to be given any unusual meaning. Insulting means insulting and nothing else.

If I had to decide, which I do not, whether the appellant's conduct insulted the spectators in this case, I would agree with the magistrates. The spectators may have been very angry and justly so. The appellant's conduct was deplorable. Probably it ought to be punishable. But I cannot see how it insulted the spectators.

I would allow the appeal with costs.

Lords Morris of Borth-y-Gest and **Kilbrandon** and **Viscount Dilhorne** delivered concurring speeches. **Lord Diplock** agreed.

Appeal allowed.

NOTES

1. In *Parkin v Norman; Valentine v Lilley*,[427] in separate incidents, each of the defendants, P and V, was found masturbating in a public lavatory in a manner which clearly indicated that he wanted his behaviour to be seen only by the one other person present there at the

---

[427] [1983] QB 92.

time. Unknown to P and V, the other person present in each case was a police officer in plain clothes. Each was convicted under s. 5 of the Public Order Act 1936. The Divisional Court held that the justices were entitled to find that this was 'insulting' behaviour, on the basis that the behaviour was 'tantamount to a statement: "I believe you are another homosexual", which the average heterosexual would surely regard as insulting'. This was so notwithstanding that 'the defendant did not intend to insult, nor by the fact that no one was insulted, nor by his having taken steps to ensure that no third person saw what he was doing'. The conviction in *Parkin* was nevertheless quashed on the ground that a breach of the peace was not likely to result and *Valentine* on other grounds. Note that ss. 4 and 5 require D to intend his words etc. to be threatening, abusive or insulting etc. or to be aware that they may be.[428]

2. The decision of magistrates on a question of fact will only be reversed on appeal to the High Court if it is one which no reasonable bench of magistrates could reach or if it is totally unsupported by evidence (*Bracegirdle v Oxley*).[429] In most cases it is accepted that different magistrates may reasonably come to different conclusions, and the court will not interfere solely because the judges would personally have taken a different view. On occasion, decisions are overturned.[430]

More doubtful cases where the High Court has declined to interfere with the justices' decision are *DPP v Clarke*;[431] and *Herrington v DPP*.[432] In the latter case, H stood naked in his back garden, staring for some time in the direction of his neighbour's kitchen window, where he was observed by her while at her kitchen sink. This was found to be 'threatening' behaviour; although H could not have seen her at that distance as he was without his glasses, he must have been aware that his behaviour might be threatening. A further highly doubtful case was *Masterson v Holden*[433] where two men were convicted under the Metropolitan Police Act 1839, s. 54(13),[434] for overt homosexual behaviour (kissing and cuddling, and one fondling the other) at 2 a.m. in Oxford Street, London. They were seen by two young women and two young men, one of whom shouted at them. (They were given absolute discharges and bound over to keep the peace.) The Divisional Court held that the justices were entitled to find this to be 'insulting', on the basis that overt homosexual (or heterosexual) conduct in a public street

may well be considered by many persons to be objectionable, to be conduct which ought to be confined to a private place. The fact it is objectionable does not constitute an offence. But the display of such objectionable conduct in a public street may well be regarded by another person, particularly by a young woman, as conduct which insults her by suggesting that she is somebody who would find such conduct in public acceptable herself. The magistrates do not say that that was the reason for their finding.

---

[428] 1986 Act, s. 6(3), (4).   [429] [1947] KB 349, DC.

[430] See, e.g., *Hudson v Chief Constable, Avon and Somerset Constabulary* [1976] Crim LR 451 (H on the terraces at football became excited, jumped up and down clapping his hands above his head and fell forward, knocking the persons in front; justices not entitled to find that this was 'threatening'); cf. *Maile v McDowell* [1980] Crim LR 586. (D one of a crowd of 'away' supporters at football match, jumping up and down, waving their fists and shouting aggressive slogans; justices' finding that this was 'not... threatening since the crowd habitually behaved that way' was perverse.)

[431] Above, p. 348: display of photograph of aborted foetus found to be 'insulting'.

[432] 23 June 1992, unreported, DC.   [433] [1986] 3 All ER 39.

[434] This was similar in terms to the old s. 5. See also *Bryan v Robinson* [1960] 1 WLR 508 (conduct of hostss at non-alcoholic refreshment house who stood at the doorway, leaned out, smiled and beckoned and spoke to three men in the street could not be held to be insulting, even though it might be regarded as annoying).

We cannot say for certain that that was their reasoning. Certainly it may have been. I content myself with saying that in my view in the ordinary use of the word 'insulting' on the material in this case they were perfectly entitled to conclude that the conduct was insulting.'

Could this argument not be used to turn any objectionable conduct into 'insulting' conduct? Consider whether the defendants here would have been guilty under s. 4 or s. 5 of the 1986 Act. Could this interpretation withstand scrutiny under the Human Rights Act 1998? Is it realistic to claim that the overt displays of heterosexual behaviour would be prosecuted?

3. In determining a defendant's awareness under s. 6(4), a subjective test should be applied: *DPP v Clarke.*[435]

(VI) RACIALLY AGGRAVATED DISORDER

The Crime and Disorder Act 1998[436] creates new offences where a person commits a s. 4, 4A or 5 offence where the offence is 'racially aggravated'. This is defined in as follows:

- **Crime and Disorder Act 1998**

28 Meaning of '[racially or religiously aggravated]'

(1) An offence is [racially or religiously aggravated] for the purposes of sections 29 to 32 below if—

  (a) at the time of committing the offence, or immediately before or after doing so, the offender demonstrates towards the victim of the offence hostility based on the victim's membership (or presumed membership) of a [racial or religious group]; or

  (b) the offence is motivated (wholly or partly) by hostility towards members of a [racial or religious group] based on their membership of that group.

(2) In subsection (1)(a) above—

  'membership', in relation to a [racial or religious group], includes association with members of that group;

  'presumed' means presumed by the offender.

(3) It is immaterial for the purposes of paragraph (a) or (b) of subsection (1) above whether or not the offender's hostility is also based, to any extent, [on any other factor not mentioned in that paragraph].

(4) In this section 'racial group' means a group of persons defined by reference to race, colour, nationality (including citizenship) or ethnic or national origins.

[(5) In this section 'religious group' means a group of persons defined by reference to religious belief or lack of religious belief.]

NOTES

1. The racially aggravated offence carries a maximum sentence on summary conviction of six months' imprisonment or a fine not exceeding the statutory maximum or both, and on indictment to a maximum sentence of two years' imprisonment to both.

---

[435] (1992) Cr App R 359.

[436] S. 31, as amended by the Anti-terrorism, Crime and Security Act 2001, s. 39 (1), (2) extending the provision to religiously aggravated offences.

2. On race crimes generally, see Jacobs and Potter.[437] Brennan[438] argued that the provisions in the 1998 Act were well intentioned, but fraught with difficulty.[439] One problem was the point that this did not extend to 'Muslimophobia'. This gap was subsequently filled by the amendment in 2001 that followed the 9/11 attacks in the US.[440]

3. The expression 'racial group' has been interpreted broadly. In *R v Rogers*[441] the House of Lords held that it can apply to a group defined exclusively, as in 'bloody foreigners'[442] as well as to a group defined inclusively.[443] As explained by Baroness Hale of Richmond:[444]

> This flexible non-technical approach makes sense, not only as a matter of language, but also in policy terms. The mischiefs attacked by the aggravated versions of these offences are racism and xenophobia. Their essence is the denial of equal respect and dignity to people who are seen as 'other'. This is more deeply hurtful, damaging and disrespectful to the victims than the simple versions of these offences. It is also more damaging to the community as a whole, by denying acceptance to members of certain groups not for their own sake but for the sake of something they can do nothing about. This is just as true if the group is defined exclusively or if it is defined inclusively.

The House doubted a decision[445] where it had been found that no hostility to Asians was shown where one Asian called another a 'white man's arse licker' and a 'brown Englishman'; the case might have been argued on the basis that others demonstrated hostility to a person based on their association with Whites.[446]

Hostility to a victim need not be demonstrated in the victim's presence,[447] but must be 'immediate'.[448] The racial factor need not be the sole or even main motivation for the hostility.[449]

How would the courts respond to a neo-Nazi group claiming that they were a race (Aryan?) that was being harassed by anti-Nazi protesters?[450]

4. It is questionable why racial and religious aggravation should attract special attention from the criminal law when other types of discrimination evident when crimes are committed do not: e.g. gender and homophobic prejudices. Sentencing practice seems to be an adequate method of dealing with the problem. Racially and religiously aggravated crimes are monitored by the Racist and Religious Incident Monitoring Scheme. The CPS produces Annual Reports on Racist and Religious Incident Monitoring.[451] In sentencing, the judge

---

[437] *Hate Crimes, Criminal Law and Identity Politics* (1998).   [438] [1999] Crim LR 17.

[439] Pp. 27, 24.   [440] See M. Idriss [2002] Crim LR 890.

[441] [2007] UKHL 7, [2007] 2 AC 62.

[442] Endorsing *DPP v M* [2004] EWHC 1453 (Admin), [2004] 1 WLR 2758 ('bloody foreigners'); cf. *R v White (Anthony)* [2001] EWCA Crim 216, [2001] 1 WLR 1352 ('African' can demonstrate hostility to a racial group because it would generally be taken to mean Black African).

[443] As in 'fucking Paki go home': *R v Arnold* [2008] EWCA Civ 705; or calling a police officer a 'fucking English ****': *R v Jones* [2008] EWCA Civ 781.

[444] [2007] UKHL 7, para. [12].   [445] *DPP v Pal* [2000] Crim LR 756.

[446] See Baroness Hale in *Rogers* at para. [15].   [447] *Parry v DPP* [2004] EWHC 3112 (Admin).

[448] Not at least 20 minutes later: *Parry*.

[449] *R v Woods* [2002] EWHC 85 (Admin); *DPP v Green* [2004] EWHC 1225 (Admin) (G's hostility to WPC both racial and based on antagonism to police officers arresting her; DC directed conviction).

[450] See also the discussion by M. Malik (1999) 62 MLR 409, and see the discussion of race in Chaps 13 and 14 below.

[451] www.cps.gov.uk. The numbers prosecuted in respect of racial incidents each year have steadily increased: 2006/07 Annual Report, p. 11. In 2006/07 there were 22 prosecutions for religiously aggravated incidents out of 27 cases; ibid., p. 44; of the 27 cases, 17 were Muslim, 3 Christian, 1 Sikh, 2 Jewish and 4 unknown: ibid., p. 51.

should state publicly the appropriate sentence for the offence without the racial aggravation and then the additional element.[452] Section 145 of the Criminal Justice Act 2003[453] requires the court to treat the fact that an offence other than one covered by the 1998 Act was racially or religiously motivated as an aggravating faction in sentencing.

5. One of the more controversial recommendations of the Macpherson report was that consideration should be given to amending the law to allow for the prosecution of offences involving racist language or behaviour.[454] Some interpreted this as an attempt to outlaw racist language *per se*, even when spoken in a private dwelling and causing no offence to those present. Michael Mansfield QC, in a letter to the *Guardian,* wrote that the present private dwelling exceptions allow:

racist organisations and individuals who do intend to stir up racial hatred (viz video surveillance material in the Lawrence case) to evade prosecution. Either we are serious about the eradication of deep-seated racism, or the battle that was fought to place this on the statute book in the first place will have been in vain.[455]

Should use of racist language be an offence irrespective of whether it causes harassment etc.? Can criminal offences of such a nature be investigated and enforced without inappropriate intrusive policing?

(VII) HARASSMENT

In recent years the Government has sought to tackle low-level disorder and harassment through a number of legislative measures. One of the most controversial was the response to the media-fuelled panic about stalking.

- **Protection from Harassment Act 1997**

1. Prohibition of harassment

(1) A person must not pursue a course of conduct—

    (*a*) which amounts to harassment of another, and

    (*b*) which he knows or ought to know amounts to harassment of the other.

[(1A) A person must not pursue a course of conduct—

    (a) which involves harassment of two or more persons, and

    (b) which he knows or ought to know involves harassment of those persons, and

    (c) by which he intends to persuade any person (whether or not one of those mentioned above)—

        (i) not to do something that he is entitled or required to do, or

        (ii) to do something that he is not under any obligation to do.][456]

---

[452] *R v Bridger* [2006] EWCA Crim 3169, endorsing the view on this point of the Sentencing Advisory Panel. See further on sentencing, *R v Saunders* [2000] 1 Cr App R 458; *R v Kelly and Donnelly* [2001] 2 Cr App R (S) 73.

[453] Successor to s. 82 of the 1998 Act and s. 153 of the Powers of Criminal Courts (Sentencing) Act 2000.

[454] No. 39.

[455] 25 March 1999. See more generally on hate speech crimes, I. Hare (1997) 17 OJLS 415.

[456] The words in square brackets in s. 1 were inserted by the Serious Organised Crime and Police Act 2005, s. 125(1), (2).

(2) For the purposes of this section, the person whose course of conduct is in question ought to know that it amounts to [or involves] harassment of another if a reasonable person in possession of the same information would think the course of conduct amounted to [or involved] harassment of the other.

(3) Subsection (1) [or (1A)]does not apply to a course of conduct if the person who pursued it shows—

   (a) that it was pursued for the purpose of preventing or detecting crime.

   (b) that it was pursued under any enactment or rule of law or to comply with any condition or requirement imposed by any person under any enactment, or

   (c) that in the particular circumstances the pursuit of the course of conduct was reasonable.

2. Offence of harassment

(1) A person who pursues a course of conduct in breach of section 1 is guilty of an offence.

(2) A person guilty of an offence under this section is liable on summary conviction to imprisonment for a term not exceeding six months, or a fine not exceeding level 5 on the standard scale, or both…

3. Civil remedy

(1) An actual or apprehended breach of [section 1(1)] may be the subject of a claim in civil proceedings by the person who is or may be the victim of the course of conduct in question.

(2) On such a claim, damages may be awarded for (among other things) any anxiety caused by the harassment and any financial loss resulting from the harassment.

(3) Where—

   (a) in such proceedings the High Court or a county court grants an injunction for the purpose of restraining the defendant from pursuing any conduct which amounts to harassment, and

   (b) the plaintiff considers that the defendant has done anything which he is prohibited from doing by the injunction,

the plaintiff may apply for the issue of a warrant for the arrest of the defendant.

(4) An application under subsection (3) may be made—

   (a) where the injunction was granted by the High Court, to a judge of that court, and

   (b) where the injunction was granted by a county court, to a judge or district judge of that or any other county court.

(5) The judge or district judge to whom an application under subsection (3) is made may only issue a warrant if—

   (a) the application is substantiated on oath, and

   (b) the judge or district judge has reasonable grounds for believing that the defendant has done anything which he is prohibited from doing by the injunction….

4. Putting people in fear of violence

(1) A person whose course of conduct causes another to fear, on at least two occasions, that violence will be used him is guilty of an offence if he knows or ought to know that his course of conduct will cause the other so to fear on each of those occasions.

(2) For the purposes of this section, the person whose course of conduct is in question ought to know that it will cause another to fear that violence will be used against him on any occasion if a reasonable person in possession of the same information would think the course of conduct would cause the other so to fear on that occasion.

(3) It is a defence for a person charged with an offence under this section to show that—

   (a) his course of conduct was pursued for the purpose of preventing or detecting crime.

   (b) His course of conduct was pursued under any enactment or rule of law or to comply with any condition or requirement imposed by any person under any enactment, or

   (c) the pursuit of his course of conduct was reasonable for the protection of himself or another or for the protection of his or another's property....

7 Interpretation of this group of sections

(1) This section applies for the interpretation of sections 1 to 5.

(2) References to harassing a person include alarming the person or causing the person distress.

[(3) A "course of conduct" must involve—

   (a) in the case of conduct in relation to a single person (see section 1(1)), conduct on at least two occasions in relation to that person, or

   (b) in the case of conduct in relation to two or more persons (see section 1(1A)), conduct on at least one occasion in relation to each of those persons.]

[(3A) A person's conduct on any occasion shall be taken, if aided, abetted, counselled or procured by another—

   (a) to be conduct on that occasion of the other (as well as conduct of the person whose conduct it is); and

   (b) to be conduct in relation to which the other's knowledge and purpose, and what he ought to have known, are the same as they were in relation to what was contemplated or reasonably foreseeable at the time of the aiding, abetting, counselling or procuring.]

(4) "Conduct" includes speech.

[(5) References to a person, in the context of the harassment of a person, are references to a person who is an individual.][457]

NOTES

1. The courts had developed a tort of harassment at common law.[458] In *Burris v Azadani*[459] the then Master of the Rolls, Sir Thomas Bingham, stated that 'in the light of...authority' it can no longer be claimed 'that there is no tort of harassment'.[460] Further, his Lordship referred to the victim being 'adequately protected by an injunction which restrains the tort which is or is likely to be committed, whether trespass to the person or to land, interference with goods, harassment, intimidation or as the case may be'.[461] However, the use of the tort to tackle behaviour which amounted to stalking was severely curtailed by the decision of the House of Lords in *Hunter v Canary Wharf*[462] The House held that only those who had a right to exclusive possession of the land could sue in nuisance.

[457] Sub-ss. (3) and (5) were substituted by the Serious Organised Crime and Police Act 2005, s. 125(1), (7); sub-s. (3A) was inserted by the Criminal Justice and Police Act 2001, s. 44(1).

[458] N. Fricker [1992] Fam Law 158; M. Brazier [1992] Fam Law 346. See further A. Cooke (1994) 57 MLR 289.

[459] [1995] 1 WLR 1372.   [460] At 1378.

[461] At 1380. On the civil law generally, see J. Bridgman and M. Jones 'Harassing Conduct and outrageous acts: a cause of action for intentionally inflicted mental distress' (1994) LS 180. See also R. Townshend-Smith 'Harassment as a tort in English and American Law: The Boundaries of *Wilkinson v Downton*' (1995) Anglo-American LR 299.

[462] [1997] 2 All ER 426. See below, p. 535.

2. The continued existence of the common law criminal offence of causing a public nuisance has been confirmed by the House of Lords,[463] although the House also held that a series of acts that injured individuals separately rather than the community or significant section of the community was not sufficient. Multiple indecent telephone calls to separate women did not, accordingly, constitute this offence.[464] The position is different where a group is targeted. Accordingly there have been successful prosecutions in respect of multiple sexually explicit calls to female staff at a gym;[465] a prolonged campaign of harassment against individuals involved with the assessment of D's mental state,[466] and malicious telephone calls to employees and shareholders of Covance Laboratories and Huntingdon Life Sciences.[467] See also the charges of conspiracy to commit public nuisance in *R v Chee Kew Ong*,[468] where C agreed to switch off floodlights at a premiership football match.

3. The 1997 Act was badly drafted and displays many of the deficiencies typical of over-hasty legislative response to moral panics. Part of the problem lies in the intractable difficulty of trying to define the prohibited conduct:

Stalkers do not stick to activities on a list. Stalkers and other weirdos who pursue women, [sic] cause racial harassment and annoy their neighbours have a wide range of activity which it is impossible to define.[469]

The Act was preceded by the Home Office/Lord Chancellor's Department consultation paper, *Stalking—the solutions*.[470] The Act has been used in a range of contexts, protecting individuals and their privacy in a variety of contexts ranging from mass demonstrations to harassment at work to domestic disputes.

4. Celia Wells wrote that the Act 'follows a pattern witnessed in other areas (hunt saboteurs, joy riding and dangerous dogs come to mind) of addressing a narrowly conceived social harm with a widely drawn provision often supplementing and overlapping with existing offences'.[471] Home Office research found that the CPS, police and magistrates were generally positive about the Act.[472]

5. *Harassment.* Section 1 of the Act defines the conduct of harassment which is then applicable for both criminal and civil proceedings by ss. 2 and 3 respectively. Note that the offence and tort are objectively determined. The blurring of the crime/civil law divide is unsatisfactory, and Harris found that there was a lack of consensus among members of the police and CPS as to when a civil claim should be adequate.[473] The effect of this was reported to have created a 'degree of inconsistency in decision-making between police, CPS magistrates and judges'.[474]

There is no requirement that the harasser intended or directed his conduct; it is sufficient that 'a reasonable person in possession of the same information would think the course of

---

[463] *R v Rimmington; R v Goldstein* [2005] UKHL 63, [2006] 1 AC 459. See above, p. 294 and generally *Smith and Hogan*, pp. 1089–1094.

[464] The court overruled *R v Johnson* [1997] 1 WLR 367.

[465] *R v Kavanagh* [2008] EWCA Crim 855.

[466] *R v Jan* [2006] EWCA Crim 2314 and [2007] EWCA Crim 3223.

[467] *R v Holliday* [2004] EWCA Crim 1847.   [468] [2001] 1 Cr App R (S) 117.

[469] D. Maclean, Home Office Minister, HC, 17 December 1996, col. 827.

[470] (1996). For a comparative analysis of stalking legislation, see B. MacFarlane (1997) UBC LR 37.

[471] [1997] Crim LR 463, 464.

[472] J. Harris, *An Evaluation of the Use and effectiveness of the Protection from Harassment Act 1997* (2000), p. 41.

[473] P. 44.   [474] P. 53.

conduct amounted to harassment of another'.[475] The test in s. 1(2) is an objective one, with no requirement that the reasonable person be endowed with any of the defendant's characteristics: *R v Colohan*[476] (schizophrenic who could not help sending threatening letters to his MP). The word 'harassment' is not defined except in that it includes alarming or distressing (s. 7); it is not limited to that:

it may also be harassment to wear out a person, to beset a person, or to constantly trouble, annoy or pester him or her.[477]

Furthermore

a course of conduct which is unattractive and unreasonable does not of itself necessarily constitute the criminal offence under s.2; it must be unacceptable and oppressive conduct such that it should sustain criminal liability.[478]

Many of the cases involve threats, abuse, intimidation, persistent following and the like that are clearly harassment; as was delivering art work consisting of explicit, bizarre sexual fantasies to nursing homes, which repulsed and frightened the residents;[479] failing to control barking dogs;[480] and flying banners referring to the claimant in abusive and derogatory terms.[481] They include classic 'stalking' behaviour.[482] There is no doubt that harassment may occur by a course of conduct involving speech (only) or even silence (e.g., silent telephone calls). However, simply to withdraw the social grace of speaking to one's neighbour is not.[483] Other examples of conduct that have been held to fall short include offering a plant and sending a letter to the victim;[484] a loss of temper without any physical threat,[485] and chants of 'Stop the Oxford animal labs' outside a degree ceremony.[486] The publication of press articles is capable of amounting to harassment, but in only very rare circumstances in view of Art. 10 ECHR.[487] These would include the publication of articles calculated to incite racial hatred of an individual.[488]

Furthermore, there is no requirement that any violence is threatened (or feared) for the offence under s. 2. This criminalises conduct such as that in *Chambers and*

---

[475] S. 1(2).   [476] [2001] EWCA Crim 1251, [2001] 3 FCR 409.

[477] Per Beatson J in *The Church of Jesus Christ of Latter Day Saints v Price* [2004] EWHC 3245 (QB) (P found to have persistently harassed members of the Mormon church; injunction granted preventing him from coming within 30 metres of Church properties (apart from one) or contacting Church missionaries on their mobile phones, without express permission).

[478] Thomas LJ in *C v CPS* [2008] EWHC 148 (Admin) at para. [55], citing Lord Nicholls in *Majrowski v Guy's and St Thomas's NHS Trust* [2006] UKHL 34, [2007] 1 AC 224 at para. [30]; *Sunderland City Council v Conn* [2007] EWCA Civ 1492.

[479] *R v Surayzi* [1998] EWCA Crim 3460.

[480] *R (on the application of Taffurelli) v DPP* [2004] EWHC 2791 (Admin).

[481] *Howlett v Holding* [2006] EWHC 41 (QB).

[482] *Hall v Tanner* (2000) 20 July, CA (CD) (female harassed her ex partner with 41 telephone calls in two hours on one occasion; *R v Miah* [2001] EWCA Crim 228 (assault, abuse and threats to 15-year-old schoolgirl).

[483] *Morris v Knight* (1998) 22 October (Bournemouth County Court).

[484] *King v DPP* (2000) 20 June, DC.   [485] *Sunderland City Council v Conn* [2007] EWCA Div 1492.

[486] *University of Oxford v Broughton* [2008] EWHC 75 (QB)

[487] *Thomas v News Group Newspapers Ltd* [2001] EWCA Civ 1233; (2001) Times, 25 July (rejecting the argument that they were implicitly outside the 1997 Act).

[488] *Thomas*, above. Here, the CA refused to strike out a claim by T arising out of articles in *The Sun* criticising her (describing her as a 'black clerk') for reporting two police constables for making racist jokes, and publishing the address of her place of work; she received hate mail.

Edwards v DPP,[489] where protestors persistently but non-violently blocked a surveyor's the-odolite beam, since the Divisional Court held that such conduct would amount to harass-ment for the purposes of the Public Order Act 1986.

5. *The course of conduct.* At the core of both the crime and the tort is a 'course of conduct', which is further explained in s. 7(3) As originally enacted, it was an offence to pursue a course of conduct which amounted to harassment of 'another'. Section 7(3) provided that 'a "course of conduct" must involve conduct on at least two occasions'. This gave rise to two issues. First, could the Act apply to harassment of a corporate body, so that, *inter alia,* it could bring proceedings for an injunction under s. 3 as the 'victim'? The authorities were divided on this issue.[490] Secondly, was 'another' to be read as if the singular included the plural, so that a group of persons could be harassed? The answer here was yes.[491] However, an information alleging harassment of more than one person would be bad for duplicity unless those persons were a 'close knit definable group'.[492] An information alleging that D, an animal rights protestor, harassed 'the employees of B & K Universal Group Ltd' (by shouting abuse and pretending to film them outside their premises) was held to be bad for duplicity.[493] In addition it was not shown that any single employee was harassed on more than one occasion.[494]

These problems have now been alleviated by the amendments to the 1997 Act effected by s. 125 of the Serious Organised Crime and Police Act 2005.[495] Section 1(1A) now makes it clear that harassment of two or more persons by which he intends to persuade any person (whether or not one of the harassed persons) not to do or to do something is an covered; here, it is sufficient that there is conduct on at least one occasion in relation to each of the persons harassed.[496] Furthermore, s. 3A enables injunctions to be sought by either a victim or a person intended to be 'persuaded' under s. 1(1A)(c). Section 7(5) states that references to a person, in the context of the harassment of a person, are references to a person who is an individual. Apart from that, reference to a 'person' in the Act will be subject to the general provision in Sch. 1 to the Interpretation Act 1978 that '"person" includes a body of persons corporate or unincorporated'. All this means that a body corporate cannot itself be the 'victim' of harassment,[497] but can be a 'person' under s. 1(1A)(c) (as where D harasses the employees of firm X in order to persuade X to stop animal experimentation).

The Joint Committee on Human Rights[498] expressed concern that the new provisions were not limited to 'the situations primarily envisaged as the object of the measures' and that there was a 'danger they could be used to inhibit ordinary political demonstrations'. The Government's view was that the amendments did not criminalise lawful campaigning.[499]

---

[489] [1995] Crim LR 896.

[490] *Huntingdon Life Sciences v Curtin* (1997) 15 October, CA (yes); *DPP v Dziurzynski* [2002] EWHC 1380 (Admin) at paras [29]–[33]; *Daiichi UK v Stop Huntingdon Animal Cruelty* [2003] EWHC 2337 (QB).

[491] *DPP v Williams* (1998) 27 July, DC; *Mills v DPP* (1998) 17 December DC; *DPP v Dunn* [2001] 1 Cr App R 352.

[492] *Mills v DPP,* above (harassment of two neighbours living in different houses could not be included in one information); *DPP v Dunn,* above (information alleging harassment of married couple living together not bad for duplicity; see commentary by DCO [2001] Crim LR 130, noting the vagueness of this expression including the difficulties that would arise if D had a s. 1(3) defence in respect of one of the members of the group).

[493] *DPP v Dziurzynski* [2002] EWHC 1380 (Admin).

[494] Ibid. paras [13]–[14]. This point is now met by the amendment to s. 1 effected by the 2005 Act.

[495] See Home Office Circular 34/2005.   [496] S. 7(3)(b) as substituted.

[497] Assuming the word 'another' in s. 1(1) is read as 'another person', which is the more natural reading.

[498] 4th Report, 2004–05 HL 26/HC224, paras 1.109–1.113.

[499] Home Office Circular 34/2005, paras 33–36.

How closely connected must the incidents forming the course of conduct be? All turns on the precise facts.[500] In *Lau v DPP*[501] two incidents four months apart were held to be capable of amounting to a course of conduct: '... the fewer the occasions and the wider they are spread the less likely it would be that a finding of harassment can reasonably be made. One can conceive of circumstances where incidents, as far apart as a year, could constitute a course of conduct'. The example given was of racial harassment outside a synagogue on the Day of Atonement. Other examples include: where D followed his former partner on a bus journey and then immediately when she alighted he remonstrated with her;[502] and three telephone calls within five minutes.[503] The fact that incidents are unplanned and spontaneous does not prevent them being found to be a course of conduct where there is a background of family solidarity in actions against the victims.[504] By contrast, there was no course of conduct where there were two assaults by D on a long-standing partner, but between the assaults they got on well together.[505]

6. *The s. 4 offence.* The offence in s. 4 is much more serious, although research found that not all officers were aware of the difference between ss. 2 and 4.[506] The essential difference between this offence and the crime in s. 2 (and the tort in s. 3) is that the victim must be caused to fear, on at least two occasions, that violence will be used against him. The other important difference is that the defences available to this charge are that the harasser proves that his conduct was for the purpose of preventing or detecting crime, was lawfully authorised, or was reasonable for the protection of himself or another or of property. Section 4 has no requirement of immediacy as found in the offence of assault, and offences of 'violence' under Part 1 of the Public Order Act 1986. Whereas violence is defined in s. 8 of the Public Order Act 1986 for the purposes of that Act, no such definition appears in the Protection from Harassment Act 1997. In *R v Henley*[507] H's harassment of the complainant and her family included threats to kill. He was charged under s. 4. The trial judge failed to direct the jury on the section and confused the word 'violence' by telling the jury that an intention to 'seriously frighten her as to what might happen' was sufficient. The judge also confused the jury by failing to clarify that the person must fear violence against himself, not violence towards others.

In *R v DPP*,[508] D was convicted of the offence under s. 4 when he threatened to cut V's throat and threatened (in her presence) to blow her dogs' brains out. The DC held that the stipendiary magistrate was entitled to conclude that the threat to the dogs gave rise to a fear on the part of V for her own safety, this being a question of fact.[509]

7. Section 44 of the Criminal Justice and Police Act 2001 amended s. 7 to introduce unsatisfactorily broad provision for aiding, abetting, counselling and procuring.

---

[500] Where there is a jury trial, the jury must be properly directed on this issue: *R v Patel* [2004] EWCA Crim 3284, (2005) 169 JP 93.

[501] [2001] 1 FLR 799, [2000] Crim LR 580–582. See also *Pratt v DPP* [2001] EWHC 483 (Admin), (2001) 165 JP 800.

[502] *R v Wass* (2000) 11 May, CA (Cr D). See also *Buckley v DPP* [2008] EWHC 136 (Admin).

[503] *Kelly v DPP* [2002] EWHC 1428 (Admin), (2002) 166 JP 621.

[504] *Hipgrave v Jones* [2004] EWHC 2901 (QB), [2005] 2 FLR 174.

[505] *R v Hills* [2001] 1 FLR 580, CA (Cr D).

[506] J. Harris, *An Evaluation of the Use and Effectiveness of the Protection from Harassment Act 1997* (2000), p. 25.

[507] [2000] Crim LR 582–584.   [508] [2001] EWHC 1 (Admin).

[509] See further the commentary at [2001] Crim LR 397, noting the uncertainty as to whether it is sufficient that the victim fears that personal violence *will* occur by some unspecified means at some unspecified time in the future.

8. *Defences.* The defences in s. 1(3) are very important in enabling compliance with the ECHR. Section 1(3)(a) clearly protects state law enforcement agencies and it was argued in *Howlett v Holding*[510] that it is confined to them. Eady J did not have to determine the point, holding that a private citizen seeking to rely on s. 1(3)(a) 'would at least have to show that there was, objectively judged, some rational basis for the surveillance' which there was not. Unlike s. 1(3)(c),[511] s. 1(1)(a) imports a subjective rather than objective test.[512] There is no need to establish that an offence was actually committed or contemplated, provided that the course of conduct was genuinely pursued for the purpose of preventing crime; the defence extends to harassing X in order to prevent a crime by Y; but the crime must be 'both specific, in the sense that a particular victim or victims and a particular danger could be identified, and immediate or imminent'.[513] Section 1(3)(b) gives effect, *inter alia*, to the right of free expression.[514] Convictions or findings of tort liability under the Act that interfere with free expression must be proportionate.[515] The defence of reasonableness under s. 1(3)(c) is to be judged objectively.[516] Conduct that is in breach of an injunction cannot be reasonable.[517]

9. *Damages.* Where the tort of harassment is proved, the court is empowered to award damages under s. 3 for 'any anxiety caused by the harassment and any financial loss resulting from the harassment'. In addition, the court can issue an injunction restraining the defendant from behaving in any particular way. These remedies are available where the court is satisfied that there has been 'an actual or apprehended' breach of s. 1. Nuisance had been used by claimants as a cause of action against stalkers before the protection from Harassment Act 1997. In *Perharic v Hennessey*[518] the Court of Appeal upheld the claimant's injunction and awarded £5,000 for abusive calls. In *Martins v Choudhary*[519] the Court of Appeal upheld an award of £10,000 for injury to feelings in respect of a racially motivated campaign of harassment. An employer may be vicariously liable for a harassment tort committed by an employee.

10. *Injunctions.* In deciding whether to grant an interim injunction that would interfere with free expression, the court must apply s. 12(3) of the Human Rights Act 1998. This provides that no such relief is to be granted to restrain publication before trial unless the court is satisfied 'that the applicant is likely to establish that publication should not be allowed'. The applicants' prospects of success at the trial have to be

sufficiently favourable to justify such an order being made in the particular circumstances of the case. As to what degree of likelihood makes the prospects of success 'sufficiently favourable', the general approach should be that courts will be exceedingly slow to make interim restraint orders where the applicant has not satisfied the court that he will probably ('more likely than not') succeed at trial. In general, that should be the threshold an applicant must cross before the court embarks on exercising its discretion, duly taking into account the relevant jurisprudence on Article 10 and nay countervailing convention rights.[520]

---

[510] [2006] EWHC 41 (QB). See p. 365.   [511] Below.

[512] *EDO MBM Technology Ltd v Axworthy* [2005] EWHC 2490 (QB).

[513] Ibid. Section 1(1)(a) defence not available in respect of protest campaign against company that made weapons sold to the UK and US Governments which would be used in Iraq and Israel; on the facts the protests were not intended to prevent particular events.

[514] *Baron v DPP* (2000) 13 June, DC.   [515] See, e.g., *Howlett v Holding*, above.

[516] *R v Colahan* [2001] EWCA Crim 1251, [2001] 2 FLR 757.

[517] *R v DPP, ex p Moseley* (1999) 9 June, DC (protests outside a mink farm).

[518] [1997] CLY 4859.   [519] [2007] EWCA Civ 1379.

[520] Per Lord Nicholls of Birkenhead in *Cream Holdings v Banerjee* [2004] UKHL 44, [2005] 1 AC 253 at para. [22].

The civil standard of proof is to be applied when determining whether facts are established that would justify the grant of an injunction.[521] An injunction can be designed to catch acts that are less than the full offence and so may be granted in wide terms to prevent the harassment of a class of persons, such as employees of a particular organisation; these individuals need not be named.[522] In *Howlett v Holding*[523] Eady J granted an injunction restraining Holding, 'a rich man who is prepared to use his wealth to victimise a woman of modest means' from a campaign of harassment including flying abusive derogatory banners and placing her under surveillance. This followed earlier comments by C, in her capacity as a councilor, on a planning application by D's company. D was not protected by Art. 10 in view of the effect of his conduct on C's privacy, and the anguish caused to her.

Injunctions have been sought in a series of high profile cases where organisations have been the targets of ongoing organised protest, commonly by animal right protestors. Examples include the campaign against the building of an animal research laboratory at Oxford University, orchestrated by a range of individuals and organisations, who used a wide variety of tactics, from peaceful protests and the dissemination of information to trespass, serious criminal damage (including by firebombs) and threats and assaults on and defamation of laboratory and construction workers. The original contractors resigned in 2004. A campaign to stop such a laboratory in Cambridge (that had included unlawful means) had previously succeeded. In *University of Oxford v Broughton*[524] Grigson J continued an interlocutory injunction[525] against SPEAK, the Animal Liberation Front (ALF), Stop Hunting Animal Cruelty (SHAC) and an individual (John Curtin) who was found to endorse the use of illegal means, and accepted personal undertakings from two others. The injunctions restrained a range of actions including harassment, photographing or filming protected persons without consent, abusive communications to protected persons (including university and contractors' employees and shareholders and their families), and knowingly by trespassing on university property or the residence of a protected person. Demonstrating within specified exclusion zones was prohibited except that there could be a protest in a designated area once a week. This was held to be a proportionate restriction on the defendants' right of free expression, and there was no other way of preventing tortious and criminal activities. The terms were subsequently varied.[526] There have been many other similar examples.[527] Most recently Heathrow Airport Ltd sought injunctions to restrain threatened unlawful disruption of the airport by protestors against aviation expansion,

---

[521] *Hipgrave v Jones* [2004] EWHC 2901 (QB), [2005] 2 FLR 174. Cf. *Heathrow Airport Ltd v Garman* [2007] EWHC 1957 (QB), where Swift J. accepted D's submission that as this was in effect an application for a final order, 'the standard of proof should be the highest civil standard, effectively equivalent to the criminal standard' (paras [79], [80]).

[522] *University of Oxford v Broughton* [2004] EWHC 2543 (QB), per Grigson J at paras [39], [42].

[523] [2006] EWHC 3758 (QB).   [524] [2004] EWHC 2543 (QB).

[525] There was an underlying claim for harassment, conspiracy and nuisance.

[526] See *University of Oxford v Broughton* [2006] EWHC 1233 (QB), [2008] EWHC 75 (QB). The 2008 version is included (by the terms of the injunction) on the SPEAK website: www.speakcampaigns.org. One of the personal undertakings was breached and the individual was made subject to the injunction: *University of Oxford v Broughton* [2006] EWCA Civ 1305. ALF (as represented by their press officer and the press officer personally), were confirmed as parties in *University of Oxford v Webb* [2006] EWHC 2490 (QB).

[527] *Huntingdon Life Sciences Group plc v Stop Huntingdon Animal Cruelty 'SHAC'* [2003] EWHC 1967; *Daiichi UK Ltd v SHAC* [2003] EWHC 2337 (QB); *Emerson Developments (Holdings) Ltd v Avery* [2004] EWHC 194; *Phytopharm plc v Avery* [2004] EWHC 503; *Chiron Corporation v Avery* [2004] EWHC 493; *Hall v Save New Church Guinea Pigs (Campaign)* [2005] EWHC 372 (QB); *EDO MBM Technology Ltd v Campaign to Smash EDO* [2005] EWHC 837 (QB); *RWE Npower plc v Carrol* [2007] EWHC 947 (QB); *Smithkline Beecham plc v Avery* [2007] EWHC 948 (QB).

arising out of a planned 'climate camp' nearby. A claim based on the 1997 Act was dismissed on the ground that evidence of the threat was insufficiently cogent; a more limited claim based on trespass, nuisance and/or breach of its byelaws succeeded, the court excluding protestors from a specified area during the month of August.[528] The group stated that it obeyed the injunction and set up a climate camp, on a barge carrying the wing of an Airbus 380, many miles from Heathrow.[529]

A recurring issue is that an unincorporated association can only be sued where there is a representative, and that this cannot apply where there is a divergence of interests among the members, as between those who endorse the use of unlawful means and those that do not.[530]

11. *Sentencing.* The offence under s. 2 of the Act is triable summarily only and carries a maximum six months or fine exceeding level 5 or both. The s. 4 offence is triable either way, carrying a maximum sentence on indictment of five years or a fine or both. Further guidance on sentencing was provided by Curtis J for the Court of Appeal in *R v Liddle, R v Hayes*.[531]

A court may also issue a restraining order protecting the victim by prohibiting the defendant from behaving in the prescribed way (e.g. visiting home or work of victim): s. 5.[532] Penalties for breaching restraining orders are criminal with maxima as with s. 4. Of those convicted, restraining orders were issued in 56 per cent of cases.[533]

Where there are successive applications to discharge a restraining order, the court on the later application is enabled to treat whether there has been a material change of circumstances as a primary consideration.[534] Similarly, where there is a change of circumstances the prosecution or complainant may apply to extend the duration of an order.[535] The s. 5(5) offence is one of strict liability.[536] The meaning of 'abusive', in a restraining order prohibiting D from being abusive towards her nextdoor neighbour, has been held to be an 'ordinary English word' and capable of covering D's conduct in parking her car so as to block her neighbour's visitor's car.[537]

12. Research by the Home Office[538] examined 167 prosecutions during 1998. The study found that the Act is 'being used to deal with a variety of behaviour other than stalking, including domestic violence and inter-neighbour disputes, and rarely for stalking itself'.[539] A much higher proportion of cases charged were later dropped by the CPS than with other offences—this was often as. a result of the complainant withdrawing the complaint.[540] The report concludes that the:

use being made of the Act's criminal provisions is valid but that there is a need to clear up the confusion that exists among practitioners. This might be achieved by issuing some form of guidance or clarification

[528] *Heathrow Airport Ltd v Garman* [2007] EWHC 1957 (QB).

[529] www.planestupid.com: Notice issued on 13 August 2007.

[530] Ibid.: discharging representation orders in respect of three groups, but leaving one in respect of Plane Stupid, and organisation the judge was satisfied had carried out unlawful direct action in the past and intended to do so at Heathrow.

[531] [1998] 3 All ER 816.

[532] To be amended by the Domestic Violence, Crime and Victims Act 2004, s. 60. Section 60 will also insert a new s. 5A enabling a restraining order to be made on an acquittal.

[533] J. Harris, *An Evaluation of the Use and Effectiveness of the Protection from Harassment Act 1997* (2000), p. 37.

[534] *Shaw v DPP* [2005] EWHC 1215 (Admin).

[535] *DPP v Hall* [2005] EWHC 2612 (Admin), [2006] 1 WLR 1000.

[536] *Barker v DPP* [2004] All ER (D) 339 (Oct).

[537] *R v Evans* [2004] EWCA Crim 3102, (2005) 169 JP 129.

[538] J. Harris, *An Evaluation of the Use and Effectiveness of the Protection from Harassment Act 1997* (2000).

[539] P. v.   [540] P. viii.

from the centre about what the Act is intended to cover and through enhanced training for all practitioners, as and when opportunities arise.[541]

13. The Crime and Disorder Act 1998, s. 32[542] included a new offence of religiously and racially aggravated harassment (contrary to ss. 2 and 4).[543]

(VIII) PROTECTION FROM ANIMAL RIGHTS EXTREMISM

In 2004, the Government set out its strategy for countering animal rights extremism.[544] This noted that changes had already been made in response to the campaign against Huntingdon Life Science.[545] Section 42 of the Criminal Justice and Police Act 2001 gave the police a new power to direct protestors away from homes, where such protests might cause harassment, alarm or distress. The definition of public assembly in s. 16 of the Public Order Act 1986 had been broadened.[546] The offence of aggravated trespass had been extended to buildings.[547] Furthermore, the use of injunctions[548] had 'been successful in controlling overt protests at company premises and outside homes'.[549] Furthermore, ACPO had formed the National Extremism Tactical Co-ordinating Unit (NECTU) to provide tactical advice and guidance to police forces and to act as a liaison point for industry. Steps had been taken to co-ordinate investigations.[550]

However, further new offences were needed. The charges were effected by ss. 125–127 of the Serious Organised Crime and Police Act 2005.[551] The 1997 Act was extended, inter alia to make it clear that companies could seek remedies to protect their employees.[552] Harassment of a person in his home has become an offence,[553] and the powers of the police to give directions to stay away from a person's home extended.[554]

The 2005 Act also introduced (with effect from 11 July 2005) new criminal offences directed at animal rights extremists. Section 145 makes it an offence for A, with the intention of harming an animal research organisation,[555] to commit a criminal offence, or a tortious act causing B to suffer loss or damage of any description (threatening to do so), in circumstances where that act or threat is intended or likely to cause B not to perform a contractual obligation owed by B to C, to terminate any contract B has with C, or not to enter into a contract with C.[556] Section 146 provides that A commits an offence if, with the intention of causing B to abstain from doing something B is entitled to do (or to do something which B is entitled to abstain from doing), A threatens B that someone else will do a relevant act, and A does so wholly or mainly because B is connected with an animal research organisation; a 'relevant act' is an act amounting to a criminal offence or a tortious act causing B or another person to suffer loss or damage of any description. The Joint Committee on

---

[541] P. x.   [542] As amended by the Anti-terrorism, Crime and Security Act 2001, s. 39(1), (5), (6).

[543] See above, p. 355.

[544] Home Office, AG, DTI, *Animal Welfare—Human Rights: protecting people from animal rights extremists* (2004).

[545] Para. 61.   [546] See p. 314.   [547] See p. 371.   [548] See p. 364.

[549] Para. 67.   [550] Para. 71–74.   [551] See Home Office Circular 34/2005.

[552] See p. 362.

[553] Criminal Justice and Police Act 2001, s. 42A, inserted by the 2005 Act, s. 126.

[554] 2001 Act, s. 42, amended by the 2005 Act, s. 127.

[555] Defined in s. 148. The provisions may be extended to other organisations who have been subjected to similar acts, by order of the Secretary of State: s. 149. This power has not yet been exercised.

[556] See *AG's Reference (No. 113 of 2007); R v Morrison* [2008] EWCA Civ 22 (two-year sentences substituted for offences of blackmail and for s. 145 offences); *R v Harris* [2006] EWCA Crim 3303.

Human Rights[557] was not convinced that the new s. 145 offence was needed, and doubted whether it met the test of legal certainty.

(IX) ANTI-SOCIAL BEHAVIOUR ORDERS

The Crime and Disorder Act 1998[558] introduced a novel form of quasi criminal order: the anti-social behaviour order, designed to deal with low level repeated disorder. Under s. 1 of the Act a local authority or police force can apply for an anti-social behaviour order (ASBO).[559] The application is made to the magistrates' court and, if successful, will prohibit the specified person from behaving in an anti social manner for two or more years. These are based on the model of the community safety order.

Section 1[560] provides:

(1) An application for an order under this section may be made by a relevant authority if it appears to the authority that the following conditions are fulfilled with respect to any person aged 10 or over, namely—

   (a) that the person has acted, since the commencement date, in a manner that caused or was likely to cause harassment, alarm or distress to one or more persons not of the same household as himself; and

   [(b) that such an order is necessary to protect relevant persons in from further anti-social acts by him.]

NOTES

1. In this section 'relevant authority' means the council for the local government area, any chief officer of police any part of whose area lies within that area, a registered social landlord or housing action trust. 'Relevant persons' are persons in the local government area, police area or other specified place respectively. Failure to comply with such an order without reasonable excuse makes the person liable to a term of imprisonment. The application is civil in nature in that it requires proof only on the balance of probabilities. The prohibitions that may be imposed are those necessary for the purpose of protecting persons (whether relevant persons or persons elsewhere in England and Wales) from further anti-social acts by D.[561] An order must be prohibitory and not mandatory in both substance and form.[562] In certain circumstances, an order in respect of a child or young person must also make an individual support order, which may include requirements to participate in activities,

---

[557] Fifteenth Report 2004/05 HL 97/HC 496, paras 2.1–2.7.

[558] See R. Leng, R. Taylor and M. Wasik, *Blackstone's Guide to the Crime and Disorder Act 1998* (1998); Home Office, *A guide to anti-social behaviour orders* (August 2006): www.crimereduction.homeoffice.gov.uk/ antisocialbehaviour/antisocialbehaviour55.htm. The regime has been amended on a number of occasions, most notably by the Anti-social Behaviour Act 2003, ss. 85–86, the Serious Organised Crime and Police Act 2005, ss. 139–140, and the Criminal Justice and Immigration Act 2008, ss. 123–124.

[559] See generally on ASBOs, D. Hughes, V. Karn and R. Lickliss [1994] JSWFL 201; S. Cracknell [2000] JSWFL 108.

[560] As amended by the Police Reform Act 2002, s. 61.

[561] 1998 Act, s. 1(6), substituted by the Police Reform Act 2002, s. 61(7).

[562] *R (on the application of Lonergan) v Lewes Crown Court* [2005] EWHC 457 (Admin), [2005] 2 All ER 362 (curfew provisions held to be prohibitory).

comply with education arrangements or present him or herself at a specified place and time.[563]

A similar order may be made in county court proceedings and a criminal court has power to make a similar order following a conviction.[564] An application may be made for an interim ASBO.[565]

2. An application for an ASBO under s. 1 is a civil proceeding under domestic law and not a criminal proceeding for the purposes of Art. 6 ECHR; nevertheless it engages the right to a fair trial under Art. 6(1).[566] Hearsay evidence is admissible.[567] It must be established to the criminal standard of proof that D has acted in an anti-social manner,[568] including, where relevant, that D's conduct was likely to cause harassment, alarm or distress.[569] The question whether an order is necessary is, however, not a matter of standard of proof but involves an exercise of judgment.[570]

3. ASBOs have been used in respect of a wide variety of conduct, including animal rights protesters, but District Judge Roy Anderson refused to make one in respect of Grandmother Lindis Percy in respect of her regular protests at Menwith Hill, saying that the courts ought not to allow ASBOs.

to be used as a club to beat down the expression of legitimate comment and the dissemination of views of matters of public concern.

(A curfew and electronic tagging were imposed following convictions for obstruction of the highway and of the police.[571])

4. Anti-social behaviour injunctions may be granted to a local authority, housing action trust or registered social landlord in respect of conduct capable of causing nuisance or annoyance to neighbourhood residents, persons employed in connection with the landlord's housing management function, and others; the unlawful the landlord's premises and breaches of tenancy agreements capable of causing nuisance or annoyance to any person.[572]

5. The stream of measures aimed at anti-social behaviour has continued unabated. Apart from measures already mentioned, the kinds of control techniques that have been made available to the police include powers to confiscate alcohol;[573] to close premises;[574] and to

---

[563] 1998 Act, ss. 1AA, 1AB, inserted by the Criminal Justice Act 2003, s. 322. A similar 'intervention order' may be made in respect of persons over 18 whose behaviour is affected by controlled drugs: 1998 Act, ss. 1G, 1H, inserted by the Drugs Act 2005, s. 20.

[564] 1998 Act, ss. 1B and 1C, inserted by the 2002 Act, ss. 63, 64. See *R v Boness; R v Bebbington* [2005] EWCA Crim 2395, (2005) 169 JP 621 on the latter.

[565] 1998 Act, s. 1D, inserted by the 2002 Act, s. 65.

[566] *R (on the application of McCann) v Manchester Crown Court* [2002] UKHL 39, [2003] 1 AC 787.

[567] *McCann*, per Lord Hutton at para. [113].

[568] *McCann*, per Lord Steyn at para. [27], Lord Hope at para. [83].

[569] *Chief Constable of Lancashire v Potter* [2003] EWHC 2272 (Admin).

[570] *R (on the application of W) v Acton Youth Court* [2005] EWHC 954 (Admin), per Pitchers J at para. [36].

[571] BBC News, 17 May 2005.

[572] Housing Act 1996, ss. 153A–153E, inserted by the Anti-social Behaviour Act 2003, s. 13, and amended by the Police and Justice Act 2006, s. 26.

[573] Confiscation of Alcohol (Young Persons) Act 1997 (under 18s in any public place other than licensed premises; see Home Office Circular 38/97); Criminal Justice and Police Act 2001, ss. 12–16 (any person in any public place (not licensed premises) designated by the local authority).

[574] Anti-social Behaviour Act 2003, ss. 1–11 (drugs) and ss. 40, 41 (noise); Licensing Act 2003, ss. 160–171 (licensed premises in an area experiencing disorder); Criminal Justice and Immigration Act 2008, Sch. 20

direct people to leave the area.[575] There is a new offence of causing nuisance or disturbance on NHS premises.[576] Fixed penalty notices are widely applicable.[577]

(X) DISRUPTION OF LAWFUL ACTIVITIES

The statutory provisions given below afford a measure of protection to lawful meetings. Those who disrupt lawful meetings may commit other criminal offences not related in particular to meetings.[578] They may be ejected, and those who organise a meeting on private premises may employ stewards to preserve order.[579] It is arguable that the police should act first against persons who disrupt or threaten to disrupt a lawful meeting, and disperse the meeting itself only if necessary in the last resort.[580] As to police powers of entry to prevent disorder, see *Thomas v Sawkins*.[581] The Criminal Justice and Public Order Act 1994[582] introduced new provisions in respect of disruptive trespasses.

- **Public Meetings Act 1908**

1. Penalty on endeavour to break up public meeting

(1) Any person who at a lawful public meeting acts in a disorderly manner for the purpose of preventing the transaction of the business for which the meeting was called together shall be guilty of an offence....

(2) Any person who incites others to commit an offence under this section shall be guilty of a like offence.

(3) If any constable reasonably suspects any person of committing an offence under the foregoing provisions of this section, he may if requested so to do by the chairman of the meeting require that person to declare to him immediately his name and address and, if that person refuses or fails so to declare his name and address or gives a false name and address he shall be guilty of an offence under this subsection and liable on summary conviction there of to a fine not exceeding [level 1 on the standard scale.]

(4) This section does not apply as respects meetings to which section 97 of the Representation of the People Act 1983 applies.

NOTES

1. Subsection (3) was added by the Public Order Act 1936, s. 6. The maximum penalty under s. 1(1) is now six months' imprisonment, a fine not exceeding level 5 on the standard scale. The Act does not apply to election meetings, but they are protected by analogous provisions in the Representation of the People Act 1983.[583] Breach of s. 97 is an 'illegal practice' under election law.[584]

(premises associated with persistent disorder or nuisance). A closure order has to be made by a magistrates' court on application by the police.

[575] Violent Crime Reduction Act 2006, s. 27 (directions to individuals over 16 in a public place who represent a risk of alcohol-related disorder).

[576] Criminal Justice and Immigration Act 2008, s. 119; a constable may remove a (reasonably suspected) offender: s. 120.

[577] Criminal Justice and Police Act 2001, ss. 1–11, as amended; see above p. 277.

[578] See above, pp. 330–357.   [579] Public Order Act 1936, s. 2(6), above. p. 290.

[580] See below, pp. 376–397.   [581] Below, pp. 401–406.   [582] Below.

[583] S. 97, as amended by the Representation of the People Act 1985, Sch. 4, para. 39.

[584] See the 1983 Act, ss. 169, 173, 174.

2. In *Burden v Rigler*[585] justices hearing a prosecution brought under the Act held that any meeting on the highway was *ipso facto* unlawful. The Divisional Court held that the justices had 'no right to assume that, simply because the meeting was held on a highway it could be interrupted notwithstanding the provisions of the Public Meeting Act 1908'.[586] The case was remitted for the justices to consider *inter alia* whether there was an obstruction.

- **Criminal Justice and Public Order Act 1994**

Disruptive trespassers

68. Offence of aggravated trespass

(1) A person commits the offence of aggravated trespass if he trespasses on land...[587] and, in relation to any lawful activity which persons are engaging in or are about to engage in on that or adjoining land...[588] does there anything which is intended by him to have the effect—

    (a) of intimidating those persons or any of them so as to deter them or any of them from engaging in that activity,

    (b) of obstructing that activity, or

    (c) of disrupting that activity.

(2) Activity on any occasion on the part of a person or persons on land is 'lawful' for the purposes of this section if he or they may engage in the activity on the land on that occasion without committing an offence or trespassing on the land....

(5) In this section 'land' does not include—

    (a) the highways and roads excluded from the application of section 61 by paragraph (b) of the definition of 'land' in subsection (9) of that section;[589]...

69. Powers to remove persons committing or participating in aggravated trespass

(1) If the senior police officer present at the scene reasonably believes—

    (a) that a person is committing, has committed or intends to commit the offence of aggravated trespass on land...; or

    (b) that two or more persons are trespassing on land...and are present there with the common purpose of intimidating persons so as to deter them from engaging in a lawful activity or of obstructing or disrupting a lawful activity, he may direct that person or (as the case may be) those persons (or any of them) to leave the land.

(2) A direction under subsection (1) above, if not communicated to the persons referred to in subsection (1) by the police officer giving the direction, may be communicated to them by any constable at the scene.

(3) If a person knowing that a direction under subsection (1) above has been given which applies to him—

    (a) fails to leave the land as soon as practicable, or

---

585 [1911] 1 KB 337, DC.   586 Lord Alverstone CJ at 340.

587 The words 'in the open air' were omitted from s. 68(1) by the Anti-social Behaviour Act 2003, ss. 59(1), (2), 92, Sch. 3.

588 The words 'in the open air' were omitted from s. 68(1) by the Anti-social Behaviour Act 2003, ss. 59(1), (2), 92, Sch. 3.

589 I.e. highways other than a footpath, bridleway, by-way open to all traffic, road used as a public place or cycle track.

(b) having left again enters the land as a trespasser within the period of three months beginning with the day on which the direction was given, he commits an offence....

(4) In proceedings for an offence under subsection (3) it is a defence for the accused to show—

(a) that he was not trespassing on the land, or

(b) that he had a reasonable excuse for failing to leave the land as soon as practicable or, as the case may be, for again entering the land as a trespasser....

(6) In this section 'lawful activity' and 'land' have the same meaning as in section 68.

NOTES

1. The penalties for offences under ss. 68 and 69 are three months' imprisonment or a fine not exceeding level 4 on the standard scale or both (ss. 68(3), 69(3)).

2. Where the activity being disrupted is lawful in principle, the fact that minor breaches of laws of a collateral nature will not be a defence for someone charged under s. 68. Thus, the courts rejected an argument from demonstrators that the constructors at the Newbury bypass were acting unlawfully where one of the chainsaw operators was not wearing gloves contrary to Health and Safety Regulations.[590]

3. Note that s. 68 creates a single offence capable of being committed by either intimidation, obstruction or disruption: see *Nelder v DPP*.[591] Note that the Trade Union and Labour Relations (Consolidation) Act 1992, s. 241 creates an offence of (*inter alia*) hindering another in that other's work, wrongfully and without legal authority, with a view to compelling him to abstain from that work. In *Todd v DPP*[592] T was arrested for the offence when in protesting at a motorway construction site, he prevented a crane operator from working. The magistrates held that the offence only applied in trade disputes, but the Divisional Court reversed that decision, holding that the offence should not be artificially confined. The offence is triable only summarily and carries a six-month maximum sentence.

4. In the debates on the 1994 Act in the House of Commons, the Home Secretary, Michael Howard, noted:[593]

In recent months we have seen many examples of disruptive and threatening behaviour—at the Grand National, during country sports and even fishing. Those who dislike such activities have a perfect right to campaign to change the law, but they do not have the right to trespass, threaten and intimidate.

The main target, however, appears to have been hunt saboteurs, and the new powers were so employed immediately when they came into force on the passing of the Act on 3 November 1994.[594] Note that a *trespassing* hunt is not a lawful activity. In *Nelder v DPP*[595] a group of protestors had sought to disrupt a fox hunt. They had done so when a section of the hunt was crossing a railway which the hunt had no right to do. The hunt had the authority to use all the adjoining land. The magistrate concluded that, since the initial purpose of the demonstration was to disrupt the hunt in general, and that was achieved while the hunt was, as a whole, still in progress, the fact that the disruption occurred in relation to only one part of the hunt at a point when that part of the hunt was trespassing,

---

[590] *Hibberd v DPP* (1996) 27 November.   [591] (1998) Times, 11 June. DC.

[592] [1996] Crim LR 344.

[593] 235 HC Deb, 11 January 1994, col. 29.   [594] See *Civil Liberty Agenda*, 13 March 1995, p. 7.

[595] (1998) Times, 11 June, DC.

was not fatal to the charge. The court also held that there was no need to charge obstructing or disrupting as two separate offences. Does this mean that obstructing one horse or one hound is sufficient?

5. How will an officer know, under s. 68, whether someone is a trespasser unless he has the express information from the landowner? By requiring that the activity being disrupted is lawful, the Act raises the familiar issue of whether the activity must be something that is not expressly forbidden, or whether it is necessary for the those taking part in the activity to point to a specific legal right to act in that way. Note the ambiguity of the protection—it is afforded where people are 'about to engage in' the activity in question. Does this allow pre-emptive arrests the day before a hunt? Other words in the offence are equally vague—i.e. doing 'anything' intended to 'obstruct or disrupt'. Was the new offence necessary given the full breadth of s. 5 and the extremely broad powers of arrest for breach of the peace? Do all 'streakers' at cricket or other sporting events commit offence? If the senior police officer's 'reasonable belief' is in fact incorrect, could that be raised as a matter of 'reasonable excuse' under sub-s. (4)? A person cannot be convicted under s. 68 unless the person engaged in the relevant lawful activity was present on the land at the time of the alleged trespass.[596]

6. The s. 68 offence has been used extensively in relation to anti-hunt demonstrators. In *Winder v DPP*[597] it was held that running towards a hunt in order to prevent it happening amounted to disruption. In that case the Divisional Court gave two examples of the breadth of the offences:

Suppose a trespasser on open land says to a third party "go over the brow of that hill and there throw some stink bombs" so as to disrupt the lawful activity—be it a hunt, be it a concert, be it a birthday celebration for the farmer's daughter which is going on there. Is the trespasser guilty of the s. 68 offence, whether or not the third party throws the stink bombs and whether or no the members of the hunt know of the trespassers existence? Clearly the act of giving the instruction does not in itself disrupt but it is intended in due course to result in acts which have that effect. We think that the trespasser is guilty.

The same goes for a trespasser who, wishing to disrupt a lawful activity, but out of sight, picks up a stone with a view to throwing it in the midst of those carrying out the lawful activity. We do not consider that the drafting of the section would require a court to hold that since picking up a stone in itself harmed no-one no offence was committed.

The protesters in that case were trespassing, had an intention to disrupt the hunt and were running to the hunt to fulfil that purpose. The running, although not itself intended to disrupt the hunt, was sufficiently closely connected. An overt act which is intended to have the effect either of intimidating persons doing a lawful activity so as to deter them from engaging in it, or of disrupting or obstructing the activity is required in addition to trespass on land: *DPP v Barnard*[598] (mere 'occupation' of an open cast mine without proof of intimidation was insufficient).

7. A defendant charged under s. 68 may raise a defence that the conduct was reasonable in the circumstances to prevent crime (Criminal Law Act 1967, s. 3) or to protect property. In *DPP v Bayer*,[599] the defendants trespassed on private land which was being drilled with genetically modified maize, attached themselves to tractors, and disrupted the drilling process.

---

[596] *DPP v Tilly* [2001] EWHC 821 (Admin), (2001) 166 JP 22 (T had damaged a quantity of genetically modified crops in the absence of the farmer or any of his representatives).
[597] (1996) 160 JP 713.   [598] (1999) Times, 9 November, DC.
[599] [2003] EWHC 2567 (Admin), [2004] 1 WLR 2856.

The district judge held that these were reasonable actions in defence of property, as they held genuine beliefs on reasonable grounds concerning the dangers of GM crops for neighbouring property through pollen distribution, animal transfer and soil transfer. The Divisional Court held that the defence was not available as Ds knew that there was nothing unlawful about the drilling. See also *R v Jones (Margaret)*,[600] where it was held in the conjoined case of *Ayliffe v DPP* that it was no defence to charges under s. 68 in respect of activities at military bases in protest against the Iraq war that the activities at the bases were unlawful as they were carried on in pursuit of an unlawful war of aggression; even if established, 'aggression' did not constitute a crime for the purposes of s. 68(2); and even if it did, Ds' actions were not reasonable.

8. In *Capon v DPP*[601] it was held that the actual commission of an offence of aggravated trespass was not a pre-condition to an officer issuing a direction under s. 69. The direction would be lawful where the officer had a genuine belief that the lawful activity would be obstructed. Anti-hunt campaigners stood by with a video camera to record a huntsman digging out a fox and were arrested for refusing to leave the land. The huntsman claimed that the video recording and presence was intimidating. The fact that the officer did not give details of the reason for arrest over and above a reference to 'aggravated trespass' did not render it invalid. The Crown Court held that the protesters were not in fact committing an offence under s. 68, but that did not affect the validity of the officers direction or arrest for failure to comply. The Divisional Court held that there was evidence to support the officer's belief that the protesters were committing the offence under s. 68. Furthermore, the officer's instruction, 'you either leave the land or you are arrested', was sufficient for a s. 69 direction. The case is discussed by Mead,[602] who is critical of the opportunity provided to the police to use vague language of this type to direct under the statute. He also points to the opportunity for the police to have 'two bites at the cherry' where the fact that they have arrested under the wrong power does not affect the validity of their action. This is inconsistent with other arrest powers where the courts have required the correct offence to be specified.[603] He concludes that the case 'indicates a dangerous erosion by the higher courts of the freedom to protest peacefully by widening broad statutory wording even further and increasing the ambit of police discretion'. Would the case withstand challenge under Arts 10 and 11?

9. The application of the sections has focused on the activities of hunt saboteurs and environmental protesters.[604] The introduction of the provisions has been reported as leading hunters to have high expectations about policing saboteurs.[605] Violence between hunt saboteurs and field sports enthusiasts nevertheless continued to occur.[606] Notwithstanding the ban on hunting with hounds introduced by the Hunting Act 2004, hunts have continued, together with allegations that these do not conform to the law. The activities of the Hunt Saboteurs

---

[600] [2006] UKHL 16, [2007] 1 AC 136.   [601] (1998) Independent, 23 March, DC.

[602] D. Mead [1998] Crim LR 870.   [603] See above, p. 205.

[604] For an outline of the background regarding hunting and hunt saboteurs, see T. Bucke and Z. James, *Trespass and protest: policing under the Criminal Justice and Public Order Act 1994* (Home Office Research Study 190, 1998), pp. 34–36.

[605] T. Bucke and Z. James, op. cit., p. 37.

[606] See also details published on the Hunt Saboteurs Association website, www.enviroweb.org/has/. See also the Hunt Saboteurs Association comments on the aggravated trespass sections of the 1994 Act: www.hsa.enviroweb.org/legal/endterm.html, claiming that arrests have been made under the Act on public roads.

Association have continued.[607] The Countryside Alliance campaigns for repeal or modification of the 2004 Act.[608]

Sections 68–69 have also been used in relation to many high-profile environmental protests, notably the Newbury Bypass protests in 1996. The protest led to 988 arrests, including 356 for aggravated trespass.[609] Two hundred and fifty-eight were prosecuted and 59 cautioned. Bail conditions were imposed so as to prevent those charged returning to the site.[610] The conviction rate was 83 per cent.[611] The s. 69 powers were less commonly applied, partly because of trespassers 'resident' at the site.[612] Only four people of those convicted received a prison sentence. T. Bucke and Z. James concluded that the power to issue directions was vital. It was used frequently, and meant that few arrests and prosecutions had to take place.[613]

Contrary to what is sometimes thought, the CJPOA does not appear to have brought a wider range of public disorder within the orbit of policing. Nor does the CJPOA appear to have led to a significant change in the police preparedness to take action in those public order situations.[614]

To what extent are these powers necessary? Are they compatible with Art. 11?

10. A problem with aggravated trespass powers (as with those in relation to removing trespassers) is that the arrest power, although a useful threat, is in practice unusable because it requires too many officers to be removed from the incident to escort arrestees.[615] The effect is that officers 'sought to keep the peace rather than enforce the law' when policing trespass. An alternative approach adopted in some forces was to negotiate and coerce the parties and encourage the use of stewards at hunts. The Criminal Justice and Public Order Act 1994 provides a 'bargaining chip' for police in such negotiations.[616] Some officers regarded the provisions as extremely successful, others as 'difficult to enforce' and 'poorly worded'.[617] The evidential difficulties have been overcome in part by video-recording saboteurs.[618] The provisions are capable of very wide interpretation; the forms of intimidation referred to in the research conducted by Bucke and James included 'wearing balaclavas'.[619]

The s. 69 power to direct protesters to leave has also proved difficult for the police to use, with saboteurs video recording the direction to challenge discrepancies and this has led the police to use a pre-printed form of words.[620] There has been controversy over who was the senior officer present at the scene, with some cases collapsing because magistrates interpreted that as meaning the officer in charge of the operation. One magistrate also took into account length of service in deciding the issue.[621] The power to arrest for returning to land after a direction to leave is very difficult to enforce because no personal details are recorded at the time (only one arrest was recorded by Bucke and James).[622]

---

[607] They claim that 'most hunts are carrying on as they did before'.

[608] www.countryside-alliance.org.uk. The website reports that the Crawley and Horsham Hunt and 86 farmers and landowners over whose land the hunt had brought proceedings for an injunction against the West Sussex Wildlife Protection Group and its two main organisers, alleging trespass and harassment.

[609] T. Bucke and Z. James, op. cit., p. 49.

[610] P. 50. See also the orders for costs against 75 defendants in *Department of Trade v Williams* (1995) 31 July, unreported.

[611] P. 51.

[612] See also Criminal Law Act 1977, s. 6 (on restrictions regarding violent removal from premises). T. Bucke and Z. James, op. cit., p. 50.

[613] P. 57.   [614] P. 6.   [615] Bucke and James, op. cit., pp. 38–39.

[616] Pp. 40–41.   [617] P. 42.   [618] P. 46.   [619] P. 43.   [620] P. 44.

[621] P. 45.   [622] P. 45.

11. In *Percy v Hall*[623] P claimed that he had been falsely imprisoned by Ministry of Defence officers when present at the Menwith Hill Station. The arrests made by the officers under the relevant byelaws were held to be void for uncertainty in the earlier case of *Bugg v DPP*,[624] and P claimed that this rendered the arrests unlawful. The Court of Appeal reversed the trial judge's decision to follow *Bugg* and held the byelaws invalid. The fact that the byelaws were declared void in later proceedings did not render the officers liable for the tort of false imprisonment if they reasonably believed that byelaws were being broken. The court also rejected the decision in *Bugg* that the failure to define adequately the boundary of the area protected by the byelaw rendered it void for uncertainty.

(C) PREVENTIVE POWERS

(I) BREACH OF THE PEACE AND POWERS OF DISPERSAL

This section considers the powers of the police (and others) to arrest for breach of the peace, and to take direct action against persons not acting unlawfully where necessary to preserve the peace. This action may include committing what would otherwise be assaults.[625] *Duncan v Jones*[626] went one step further: it supports the proposition that resistance to a police order to disperse may constitute the offence of obstruction of the police in the execution of their duty. These cases were adversely criticised by commentators. The whole area has been reconsidered by the House of Lords in a case of fundamental importance, *R (on the application of Laporte) v Chief Constable of Gloucestershire*;[627] complemented by the decision of the Court of Appeal in *Austin v Metropolitan Police Comr*.[628]

- **R (on the application of Laporte) v Chief Constable of Gloucestershire Constabulary** [2006] UKHL 55, [2007] 2 AC 105

The claimant, Jane Laporte, was a passenger on a coach travelling from London to an organised protest demonstration against the Iraq war at an air base in Gloucestershire used by the US Air Force, RAF Fulford. It was not suggested that her conduct and intentions were at any time other than entirely peaceful. There had been previous demonstrations at the base, including one involving a group known as the 'Wombles' (White Overalls Movement Building Libertarian Effective Struggles) that had ended in serious disorder and an incursion into the base. The defendant chief constable (or officers acting on his behalf) had information that passengers on three coaches from London were likely to cause a breach of the peace at the demonstration. He chose not to seek an order under s. 13 of the Public Order Act 1986[629] but did issue a direction under s. 12[630] prescribing the time and place for the assembly and procession route. A senior officer, Chief Superintendent Lambert, on the morning of the demonstration also instructed police officers to intercept the coaches before they reached their destination and, pursuant to a stop and search authorisation made under s. 60 of the Criminal Justice and Public Order Act 1994,[631] to search the coaches and the passengers. He directed that they were not to be arrested at that particular time to prevent a breach of the peace as he did not consider there to be an imminent breach of the peace.

---

[623] [1997] QB 924.   [624] [1993] QB 473.
[625] *Humphries v Connor*, below p. 392; *O'Kelly v Harvey*, below, p. 386.   [626] Below, p. 392.
[627] [2006] UKHL 55, [2007] 2 AC 105.
[628] [2007] EWCA Civ 989, [2008] 2 WLR 415. See below, p. 391.   [629] See p. 311.
[630] See p. 310.   [631] See p. 159.

The coaches were stopped at Lechlade, 5km from the base by road, 2km across the fields. As a result of their search the officers found items including masks, crash helmets, hoods, hard hats, a can of red spray paint and some shields. Eight were identified as Wombles. One was arrested. The police concluded that some, but not necessarily all, of the passengers intended to cause a breach of the peace at the demonstration and ordered them all (apart from three designated speakers) to return to the coaches. The police escorted the coaches back to London in such a way as to prevent the passengers from disembarking until they arrived there. (Some suffered acute physical discomfort and embarrassment as no stops were permitted.)

In judicial review proceedings the claimant asserted that the defendant's actions preventing her from demonstrating at the air base and forcibly returning her to London constituted unlawful interference with the exercise of her rights of freedom of expression and assembly protected by Arts 10 and 11 ECHR. The Queen's Bench Divisional Court[632] concluded that the measures short of arrest had been legitimate, that the decision preventing participation in the demonstration had been necessary and proportionate but that detention on the coach had been unlawful since there had not been an immediately apprehended breach of the peace sufficient to justify even transitory detention. The Court of Appeal[633] affirmed that decision. As to the chief constable's appeal, the court considered (para. 52) that the passengers were 'virtually prisoners' on the returning coaches, that (para. 53) the action taken went well beyond anything held to be justified by the existing common law authorities and that (paras 54–55) it was not shown that there were no less intrusive measures that could have been taken. The court did not think it necessary to address Art. 5 of the Convention. The claimant appealed and the defendant cross-appealed.

Lord Bingham of Cornhill:

THE STATUTORY POWERS OF THE POLICE TO CONTROL PUBLIC PROCESSIONS AND ASSEMBLIES

[His Lordship summarised the Public Order Acts 1926 and 1986 and s. 60 of the Criminal Justice and Public Order Act 1994.]

26 ...[N]either during the consideration which preceded the 1986 Act, nor since, has any review been undertaken of powers to prevent a breach of the peace. Those powers depend on the common law, which must now be examined.

BREACH OF THE PEACE

27 The legal concept of a breach of the peace, although much used, was for many years understood as a term of broad but somewhat indeterminate meaning. In *R v Howell (Errol)* [1982] QB 416, the Court of Appeal heard detailed argument on the meaning of the expression, an issue raised by the facts of the case. The court concluded that the essence of the concept was to be found in violence or threatened violence. It ruled, at p 427:

'We are emboldened to say that there is a breach of the peace whenever harm is actually done or is likely to be done to a person or in his presence to his property or a person is in fear of being so harmed through an assault, an affray, a riot, unlawful assembly or other disturbance. It is for this breach of the peace when done in his presence or the reasonable apprehension of it taking place that a constable, or anyone else, may arrest an offender without warrant.'

---

632 [2004] 2 All ER 874.   633 [2005] QB 678.

28 In *Steel v United Kingdom* (1998) 28 EHRR 603, the five applicants had all been arrested for breach of the peace and contended, as one of the grounds of their applications to the authorities in Strasbourg, that breach of the peace was too ill-defined a concept to meet the requirement that the ground of their arrest be 'prescribed by law' within the meaning of article 10(2) of the European Convention. This complaint was successfully repelled by the British Government. The commission (pp 627–628, paras 146–148) considered that the concept had been defined by the passage in *R v Howell* [1982] QB 416, 427. The court, also citing that passage (28 EHRR 603, 610, para 25), considered that the concept had been clarified by the English courts over the past two decades, and now had a meaning which was sufficiently established: p 637, para 55. The accuracy of this definition has been generally accepted, and was not in issue before the House. A breach of the peace is not, as such, a criminal offence, but founds an application to bind over.

THE COMMON LAW POWER TO PREVENT A FUTURE BREACH OF THE PEACE

29 Every constable, and also every citizen, enjoys the power and is subject to a duty to seek to prevent, by arrest or other action short of arrest, any breach of the peace occurring in his presence, or any breach of the peace which (having occurred) is likely to be renewed, or any breach of the peace which is about to occur. This appeal is only concerned with the third of these situations.

30 The leading authority, from which the House has not been invited to depart and which there-fore binds it and all lower courts in England and Wales, is *Albert v Lavin* [1982] AC 546. But that case, decided in December 1981, reflected the trend of existing authority. Thus in *Humphries v Connor* (1864) 17 ICLR 1, 8–9, Fitzgerald J, although doubtful about the outcome of the case, accurately summarised a constable's duty:

'With respect to a constable, I agree that his primary duty is to preserve the peace; and he may for that pur-pose interfere, and, in the case of an affray, arrest the wrongdoer; or, if a breach of the peace is imminent, may, if necessary, arrest those who are about to commit it, if it cannot otherwise be prevented.'

(This case is one of a number where the conduct restrained is not in itself disorderly but is likely to provoke disorder by others. Such cases are not directly relevant to the present case.) Professor Glanville Williams ('Arrest for Breach of the Peace' [1954] Crim LR 578, 586) observed:

'It seems clear that there may be an arrest for breach of the peace which is reasonably apprehended in the immediate future, even though the person arrested has not yet committed any breach.'

In a summary of *King v Hodges* [1974] Crim LR 424, 425, the police officer's powers were said to be exercisable when he reasonably believed that a breach of the peace was about to take place, and refer-ence was made in the commentary to the existence of numerous examples of actions other than arrest to prevent a breach of the peace. In his Divisional Court judgment in *Albert v Lavin* Hodgson J ruled [1982] AC 546, 553:

'It is however clear law that a police officer, reasonably believing that a breach of the peace is about to take place, is entitled to take such steps as are necessary to prevent it, including the reasonable use of force: *King v Hodges* [1974] Crim LR 424 and *Piddington v Bates* [1961] 1 WLR 162.
  If those steps include physical restraint of someone then that restraint is not an unlawful detention but a reasonable use of force. It is a question of fact and degree when a restraint has continued for so long that there must be either a release or an arrest, but on the facts found in this case it seems to me to be clear that that point had not been reached. Obviously where a constable is restraining someone to prevent a breach of the peace he must release (or arrest) him as soon as the restrained person no longer presents a danger to the peace. In this case the justices found that the defendant continued in breach of the peace up to the time when he assaulted the constable.'

This judgment was given before, and was cited to the court although not referred to in the judgment in, *R v Howell* [1982] QB 416. In that case it was recognised, p 426, that a constable, or an ordinary citizen, has a power of arrest where there is reasonable apprehension of imminent danger of a breach of the peace:

'We hold that there is power of arrest for breach of the peace where: (1) a breach of the peace is committed in the presence of the person making the arrest or (2) the arrestor reasonably believes that such a breach will be committed in the immediate future by the person arrested although he has not yet committed any breach or (3) ...'

31 In *Albert v Lavin* [1982] AC 546 both the defendant (Mr Albert) and the prosecutor (Mr Lavin, a constable who was at the time off duty and in plain clothes) were waiting for a bus. When the bus arrived, the defendant pushed past a number of people ahead of him in the queue, who not surprisingly objected, and the constable tried to obstruct his entry to the bus by standing in his way. The defendant pushed past onto the step of the bus, turned, grabbed the constable's lapel and made to hit him. The constable, to protect himself, pulled the defendant from the bus and away from the queue. The defendant again tried to hit the constable, who said he would arrest him unless he stopped struggling, but he struck the constable several times and the constable arrested him for assaulting a constable in the execution of his duty. Before the justices, the defendant contended that the constable had not been acting in the execution of his duty. In convicting the defendant (whom they conditionally discharged) the justices found, at pp 549, 551, that because of the reactions of the other members of the queue when the defendant pushed past them the constable had reasonably expected a breach of the peace to be about to take place and so he had been entitled to use reasonable force to prevent the breach of the peace. Much of the judgment of Hodgson J in the Divisional Court relied on a supposed principle that only a constable could detain a man against his will without arresting him, and addressed the question whether the defendant knew or should have known that Mr Lavin was a constable. This, as Lord Diplock pointed out at p 565, with the agreement of all other members of the House, was a question that did not arise, since the true principle was

'that every citizen in whose presence a breach of the peace is being, or reasonably appears to be about to be, committed has the right to take reasonable steps to make the person who is breaking or threatening to break the peace refrain from doing so; and those reasonable steps in appropriate cases will include detaining him against his will. At common law this is not only the right of every citizen, it is also his duty, although, except in the case of a citizen who is a constable, it is a duty of imperfect obligation.'

32 It is uncertain whether the Divisional Court was referred to *Albert v Lavin* in *Moss v McLachlan* [1985] IRLR 76, an authority on which the chief constable strongly relied and which is discussed in more detail below. But the court in *Moss* was referred to *R v Howell* and cited the ruling that

'there is power of arrest for breach of the peace where...(2) the arrestor reasonably believes that such a breach will be committed in the immediate future by the person arrested although he has not yet committed any breach ...'

33 In *Foulkes v Chief Constable of the Merseyside Police* [1998] 3 All ER 705 the plaintiff, a husband, father and joint owner of the matrimonial home, was locked out of it at 9 o'clock in the morning following a family argument which began the night before and was resumed in the morning. He wished to re-enter the house, and summoned the police to assist him, but they discouraged him from seeking to re-enter and in the end arrested him, fearing that his actions outside the property would cause a breach of the peace. His claim for wrongful arrest and false imprisonment failed in the county court but succeeded on appeal. Beldam LJ, giving the leading judgment in the Court of Appeal, cited Lord Diplock's ruling in *Albert v Lavin* and continued, at p 711:

'In my view, the words used by Lord Diplock and in the other authorities show that where no breach of the peace has taken place in his presence but a constable exercises his power of arrest because he fears a [future] breach, such apprehended breach must be about to occur or be imminent. In the present case PC McNamara acted with the best of intentions. He had tried persuasion but the plaintiff refused to be persuaded or to accept the sensible guidance he had been given but in my judgment that was not a sufficient basis to conclude that a breach of the peace was about to occur or was imminent. There must, I consider, be a sufficiently real and present threat to the peace to justify the extreme step of depriving of his liberty a citizen who is not at the time acting unlawfully. The factors identified by the recorder in the present case do not in my judgment measure up to a sufficiently serious or imminent threat to the peace to justify arrest.'

The case raised no issue about the lawfulness of coercive action other than arrest. In *Redmond-Bate v Director of Public Prosecutions* (1999) 163 JP 789, 791, the agreed issue was whether it was reasonable for a constable, in the light of what he perceived, to believe that the appellant, a female lay preacher, was 'about to cause' a breach of the peace, a test equated with imminence. In other cases, of which *Williamson v Chief Constable of the West Midlands Police* [2004] 1 WLR 14, para 19, is an example, Lord Diplock's ruling in *Albert v Lavin* has been cited and applied.

FREEDOM OF EXPRESSION AND ASSEMBLY

34 The approach of the English common law to freedom of expression and assembly was hesitant and negative, permitting that which was not prohibited. Thus although Dicey in *An Introduction to the Study of the Law of the Constitution*, 10th ed (1959), in Part II on the 'Rule of Law', included chapters VI and VII entitled 'The Right to Freedom of Discussion' and 'The Right of Public Meeting', he wrote of the first, at pp 239–240, that 'at no time has there in England been any proclamation of the right to liberty of thought or to freedom of speech' and of the second, at p 271, that 'it can hardly be said that our constitution knows of such a thing as any specific right of public meeting'. Lord Hewart CJ reflected the then current orthodoxy when he observed in *Duncan v Jones* [1936] 1 KB 218, 222, that 'English law does not recognise any special right of public meeting for political or other purposes'. The Human Rights Act 1998, giving domestic effect to articles 10 and 11 of the European Convention, represented what Sedley LJ in *Redmond-Bate v Director of Public Prosecutions* 163 JP 789, 795, aptly called a 'constitutional shift'.

35 Article 10 confers a right to freedom of expression and article 11 to freedom of peaceful assembly. Neither right is absolute. The exercise of these rights may be restricted if the restriction is prescribed by law, necessary in a democratic society and directed to any one of a number of specified ends.

36 The Strasbourg court has recognised that exercise of the right to freedom of assembly and exercise of the right to free expression are often, in practice, closely associated: see, for example, *Ezelin v France* (1991) 14 EHRR 362, paras 37, 51; *Djavit An v Turkey* Reports of Judgments and Decisions, 2003-III, p 231, para 39; *Christian Democratic People's Party v Moldova* (Application No 28793/02) (unreported) 14 May 2006, para 62; *Öllinger v Austria* (Application No 76900/01) (unreported) 29 June 2006, para 38. The fundamental importance of these rights has been stressed. Thus in *Steel v United Kingdom* 28 EHRR 603, para 101, freedom of expression was said to constitute: 'an essential foundation of democratic society and one of the basic conditions for its progress and for each individual's self-fulfilment.' In *Ezelin v France*, para 53, the court considered

'that the freedom to take part in a peaceful assembly-in this instance a demonstration that had not been prohibited-is of such importance that it cannot be restricted in any way, even for an *avocat*, so long as the person concerned does not himself commit any reprehensible act on such an occasion.'

In *Ziliberberg v Moldova* (Application No 61821/00) (unreported) 4 May 2004, para 2, the court observed at the outset that: 'the right to freedom of assembly is a fundamental right in a democratic society and, like the right to freedom of expression, is one of the foundations of such a society.' It is the duty of member states to take reasonable and appropriate measures to enable lawful demonstrations to proceed peacefully: *Plattform 'Ärzte für das Leben' v Austria* (1988) 13 EHRR 204, para 34; *Steel v United Kingdom* 28 EHRR 603, 632, para 170 (commission).

37 Thus the protection of the articles may be denied if the demonstration is unauthorised and unlaw-ful (as in *Ziliberberg*) or if conduct is such as actually to disturb public order (as in *Chorherr v Austria* (1993) 17 EHRR 358). But (*Ziliberberg*, para 2):

> 'an individual does not cease to enjoy the right to peaceful assembly as a result of sporadic violence or other punishable acts committed by others in the course of the demonstration, if the individual in question remains peaceful in his or her own intentions or behaviour.'

Any prior restraint on freedom of expression calls for the most careful scrutiny: *Sunday Times v United Kingdom (No 2)* (1991) 14 EHRR 229, para 51; *Hashman and Harrup v United Kingdom* (1999) 30 EHRR 241, para 32. The Strasbourg court will wish to be satisfied not merely that a state exercised its discretion reasonably, carefully and in good faith, but also that it applied standards in conformity with Convention standards and based its decisions on an acceptable assessment of the relevant facts: *Christian Democratic People's Party v Moldova*, para 70.

THE APPEAL: THE ARGUMENT

[His Lordship summarised counsels' arguments. It was accepted that the police actions interfered with L's Art. 10 and 11 rights and had to be justified by the chief constable. It was common ground that the chief constable acted in the interests of national security, for the prevention of disorder or crime or for the protection of the rights of others, these being legitimate purposes under Arts 10(2) and 11(2). L argued that the actions were not prescribed by law as (1) they were not warranted under domestic law and (2) premature and indiscriminate and accordingly disproportionate. As to (1), the test whether a breach of the peace was 'imminent' was the same whether to justify an arrest or action short of arrest. Furthermore, domestic law only permitted action to prevent a breach of the peace 'by the person arrested' (*R v Howell*, at p. 426) or against 'the person who is…threatening to break the peace': *Albert v Lavin* [1982] AC 546, 565, per Lord Diplock. The Chief Constable argued that there was no absolute requirement of imminence before the power to take reasonable steps arose, although questions of imminence would be relevant to what was reasonable. There was also the impracticability of differentiating, at Lechlade, between those (if any) who were and those who were not about to breach the peace.]

42 [Counsel for the chief constable] relied…on *Moss v McLachlan* [1985] IRLR 76. The factual back-ground to this case was the violent conflict in the Nottinghamshire coalfields between striking miners who were members of the National Union of Mine Workers, and working miners, many of them members of the Union of Democratic Mine Workers. The latter were determined to continue working, the former equally determined to stop them. The police struggled to keep the peace. There had been some ugly clashes. The appellants were four of about 60 striking miners intent on a mass demonstration at one of several nearby collieries. They were stopped by the police when less than five minutes' journey from the nearest pit, where the police feared a violent episode. The men tried to push on and were arrested. *Albert v Lavin*, if cited, was not referred to in the judgment of the court given by Skinner J, but he accepted (para 20) a test of 'close proximity both in place and time' and a breach of the peace was held to be 'imminent and immediate'. The court cited with approval the observation of Lord Parker CJ in *Piddington v Bates* that the police must anticipate a real, not a remote, possibility of breach, preferring that test, if different, to the 'immediate future test' put forward in *R v Howell* [1982] QB 416, 426….

45 I am persuaded, for very much the reasons advanced by Mr Emmerson…above), that the chief con-stable's interference with the claimant's right to demonstrate at a lawful assembly at RAF Fairford was not prescribed by law. I attach weight to certain considerations in particular.

46 First, in the 1986 Act Parliament conferred carefully defined powers and imposed carefully defined duties on chief officers of police and the senior police officer. Offences were created and defences pro-vided. Parliament plainly appreciated the need for appropriate police powers to control disorderly demon-strations but was also sensitive to the democratic values inherent in recognition of a right to demonstrate.

It would, I think, be surprising if, alongside these closely defined powers and duties, there existed a common law power and duty, exercisable and imposed not only by and on any constable but by and on every member of the public, bounded only by an uncertain and undefined condition of reasonableness.

47 Secondly, and subject to the possible exception of *Piddington v Bates* [1961] 1 WLR 162 I find little trace of a broad reasonableness test in any of the authorities. It is not a test prescribed by the law as it stands. I respectfully regard *Piddington v Bates* as an aberrant decision: the judgment showed no recognition that the police, in this context, enjoyed no powers not enjoyed by the private citizen, and the test applied was inconsistent both with earlier authority and that later laid down authoritatively in *Albert v Lavin.* It is not enough to justify action that a breach of the peace is anticipated to be a real possibility, and neither constables nor private citizens are empowered or bound to take such steps as on the evidence before them they think proper.

48 Thirdly, I cannot accept that a general test of reasonableness is to be read into section 24 of the Police and Criminal Evidence Act 1984. At the relevant time, section 24(7) of the Act provided:

'A constable may arrest without a warrant-(a) anyone who is about to commit an arrestable offence; (b) anyone whom he has reasonable grounds for suspecting to be about to commit an arrestable offence.'

This propounds a simple and readily intelligible test, however difficult the judgment for which it will on occasion call. It plainly reflects the common law rule where a breach of the peace is apprehended. Had Parliament intended to confer a power of anticipatory arrest whenever it was reasonable to make an arrest, it would have laid down that rule. As it is, there is no ground for glossing the statute.

49 I would observe, fourthly, that *Albert v Lavin* laid down a simple and workable test readily applicable to constable and private citizen alike. It recognises the power and duty to act in an emergency to prevent something which is about to happen. There is very unlikely to be doubt about who to take action against, since this will be apparent to the senses of the intervener. Thus the difficulty which confronted the police at Lechlade can scarcely arise.

50 Fifthly, and despite the significance attached to this distinction by the courts below, I find little support in the authorities for the proposition that action short of arrest may be taken to prevent a breach of the peace which is not sufficiently imminent to justify arrest. As I read the authorities they assimilate the two situations, while of course recognising the desirability of taking action no more intrusive than is reasonably necessary to prevent the apprehended breach of the peace. Mr Lambert did not, quite correctly in my opinion, consider that the claimant could properly be arrested at Lechlade. It followed that he could not lawfully take action short of arrest either.

51 Sixthly, I would respectfully differ from the Court of Appeal's conclusion [2005] QB 678, para 45 that the present case is 'very much on all fours with the decision in [*Moss v McLachlan*]'. With four members of one belligerent faction within less than five minutes of confronting another belligerent faction, and no designated, police-controlled, assembly point separated from the scene of apprehended disorder, as in the centre of Fairford, it could plausibly be held in *Moss* that a breach of the peace was about to be committed by those whose onward progress the police decided to block. *Albert v Lavin* was not expressly relied on, but a very similar test was applied (although reliance was also placed on what I have described as the aberrant decision in *Piddington v Bates*). The court's judgment was one which, as my noble and learned friend Lord Brown of Eaton-under-Heywood suggests, carried the notion of imminence to extreme limits, but was, I think, open to it. It was a situation very different from the present when 120 passengers, by no means all of whom were or were thought to be Wombles members, were prevented from proceeding to an assembly point which was some distance away from the scene of a lawful demonstration.

52 I would add, lastly, that if (on which I express no opinion) the public interest requires that the power of the police to control demonstrations of this kind should be extended, any such extension should in my opinion be effected by legislative enactment and not judicial decision. As the Strasbourg authorities referred to in paras 35 to 37 above make clear, article 10 and 11 rights are fundamental rights,

to be protected as such. Any prior restraint on their exercise must be scrutinised with particular care. The Convention test of necessity does not require that a restriction be indispensable, but nor is it enough that it be useful, reasonable or desirable: *Handyside v United Kingdom* (1976) 1 EHRR 737, para 48; *Silver v United Kingdom* (1983) 5 EHRR 347, para 97. Assessment of whether a new restriction meets the exacting Convention test of necessity calls in the first instance for the wide consultation and inquiry and democratic consideration which should characterise the legislative process, not the more narrowly focused process of judicial decision. This is not a field in which judicial development of the law is at all appropriate.

53 In contending that the police action at Lechlade failed the Convention test of proportionality because it was premature and indiscriminate, Mr Emmerson relied on many of the matters already referred to. The action was premature because there was no hint of disorder at Lechlade and no reason to apprehend an immediate outburst of disorder by the claimant and her fellow passengers when they left their coaches at the designated drop-off points in Fairford and gathered in the designated assembly area before processing to the base. Because the action was premature it was necessarily indiscriminate because the police could not at that stage identify those (if any) of the passengers who appeared to be about to commit a breach of the peace. By taking action when no breach of the peace was in the offing, the police were obliged to take action against the sheep as well as the goats.

54 Mr Freeland resisted this contention also. He relied on Mr Lambert's belief, held by the courts below to be reasonable, that there would be disorder once the coaches reached Fairford. Given the intelligence known to the police about the Wombles, the items found on the coaches and the unwilling-ness of the passengers to acknowledge ownership of these items or (in many cases) give their names, Mr Lambert was entitled to find that the 120 passengers had a collective intent to cause a breach of the peace. These considerations justified him in acting when and as he did. Reliance was placed on *Cumming v Chief Constable of Northumbria Police* [2003] EWCA Civ 1844.

55 I would acknowledge the danger of hindsight, and I would accept that the judgment of the officer on the spot, in the exigency of the moment, deserves respect. But making all allowances, I cannot accept the chief constable's argument. It was entirely reasonable to suppose that some of those on board the coaches might wish to cause damage and injury to the base at RAF Fairford, and to enter the base with a view to causing further damage and injury. It was not reasonable to suppose that even these passengers simply wanted a violent confrontation with the police, which they could have had in the lay-by. Nor was it reasonable to anticipate an outburst of disorder on arrival of these passengers in the assembly area or during the procession to the base, during which time the police would be in close attendance and well able to identify and arrest those who showed a violent propensity or breached the conditions to which the assembly and procession were subject. The focus of any disorder was expected to be in the bell-mouth area outside the base, and the police could arrest trouble-makers then and there. Mr Lambert was quite wrong to suppose, as he apparently did (see para 13 above) that there was any question of the coaches proceeding to RAF Fairford. Limited weight can in my opinion be given to one consideration on which Mr Freeland relied, the logistical problems inherent in making multiple arrests, since the chief con-stable, by deciding not to seek an order under section 13 of the 1986 Act, had judged the demonstration to be controllable. There was no reason (other than her refusal to give her name, which however irritating to the police was entirely lawful) to view the claimant as other than a committed, peaceful demonstra-tor. It was wholly disproportionate to restrict her exercise of her rights under articles 10 and 11 because she was in the company of others some of whom might, at some time in the future, breach the peace. *Cumming* does not justify such restriction. In that case, it was thought that a crime had been committed. The number of possible culprits had been reduced so far as was possible, leaving a pool of six suspects who could have committed the crime. All of these were arrested on suspicion of committing it, although only one of them might have done so. They challenged the lawfulness of their arrest and detention. The challenge failed because, as the Court of Appeal held (para 41), affirming the judge below, each of the six was reasonably suspected of having committed the crime, although this conclusion gravely concerned

one member of the court: para 46. There is, I think, no useful analogy with the present case, where no crime had been committed and the claimant was not suspected of having personally committed or of being about to commit any crime, or any breach of the peace.

56 I would accordingly allow the claimant's appeal, set aside the orders of the Court of Appeal and the Divisional Court dismissing the claimant's first complaint, and grant the claimant a declaration that the chief constable's actions which are the subject of her first complaint were unlawful because they were not prescribed by law and were disproportionate. I would remit any ancillary claim for relief to the Divisional Court.

57 The chief constable accepted that his cross-appeal must fail if the claimant's appeal were to succeed. I would accordingly uphold the Court of Appeal's decision on this matter, and dismiss the cross-appeal on the grounds given by that court. I do not think it useful to explore the cross-appeal further.

Lord Rodger of Earlsferry:

....67 In these situations a police officer like Mr Lambert is called on to predict what is going to happen in the near future. If he merely thinks that, while a breach of the peace may happen, the chances are that it won't, then he will not regard it as imminent. He will only regard it as imminent if he thinks that it is *likely* to happen. I doubt whether Lord Parker CJ intended to say anything different in *Piddington v Bates* [1961] 1 WLR 162, 170, when he referred to 'a real danger' and 'a real possibility' of a breach of the peace. The police officer's view of the matter will depend on the information he has and on his assessment of that information. In former times, when a police officer patrolled the streets without any of the modern means of communication, he would often have no more information than any ordinary citizen walking beside him. So, for the most part, he would only apprehend the occurrence of breaches of the peace which were brewing and about to break out in his presence. These would be the ones which he would regard as imminent. But, today, officers on the ground can be supplied by radio with information about what lies round the corner or what people are doing a few miles down the road. Armed with such information, they may have good reason to anticipate that people in front of them are intending to take part in a breach of the peace, or are likely to become involved in one, a short time later or a short car ride away. Intervention to prevent that breach of the peace may therefore be justified. A fortiori, a senior officer at the centre of a police operation, receiving reports from his officers on the ground, plus intelligence and advice on how to interpret the data, may have good reason to appreciate that a breach of the peace is 'imminent' or 'about to happen', even though that would not be apparent to officers lacking these advantages. The precondition for intervention remains the same but the test has to be applied in the conditions of today.

68 In para 62 I gave examples of the kinds of expression which judges have used to describe the stage at which the power and duty to intervene arise.[634] The expressions are not precise and most can be used to refer to very different periods of time, depending on the context. For example, if someone telephones and you say you will ring back because you are 'about to' have dinner, you mean that the food is on the table or is just about to be served. But if you say that Janet was injured when she was 'about to' go to university, the injury could have occurred days or even weeks before the start of term. In the present context, however, a shorter, rather than a longer period is clearly meant: the event must be going to happen in the near future.

69 This does not mean that the officer must be able to say that the breach is going to happen in the next few seconds or next few minutes. That would be an impossible standard to meet, since a police

---

[634] 'The common law guards against this danger by insisting that the duty arises only when the police officer apprehends that a breach of the peace is "imminent" (*O'Kelly v Harvey* (1883) 14 LR Ir 105, 109; *Foulkes v Chief Constable of the Merseyside Police* [1998] 3 All ER 705, 711b–c) or is "about to take place" or is "about to be committed" (*Albert v Lavin*) or will take place "in the immediate future": *R v Howell* [1982] QB 416, 426. His apprehension "must relate to the near future": *McLeod v Comr of Police of the Metropolis*.'

officer will rarely be able to predict just when violence will break out. The protagonists may take longer than expected to resort to violence or it may flare up remarkably quickly. Or else, as in *O'Kelly v Harvey* (1883) 14 LR Ir 105, the breach of the peace may be likely to occur when others arrive on the scene and there is no way of knowing exactly when that will happen. There is no need for the police officer to wait until the opposing group hoves in sight before taking action. That would be to turn every intervention into an exercise in crisis management. As Cooke P observed in *Minto v Police* [1987] 1 NZLR 374, 377, 'It would be going too far to say as a matter of law that the powers of the police at common law can be exercised only when an instantaneous breach of the peace is apprehended …' In *Steel v United Kingdom* (1998) 28 EHRR 603, after a morning of disruption, the first applicant, a protester against blood sports, was arrested when, in the course of a grouse shoot, she walked in front of a person armed with a gun in order to prevent him from shooting. The second applicant, who was trying to stop the construction of a motorway, was arrested when she stood underneath the bucket of a mechanical digger, towards the end of a day during which protesters had repeatedly obstructed the work of the road-builders. In neither case could the police officers have predicted exactly when the violent reaction provoked by the protests would occur. But I have no doubt that the police officers were entitled to take preventive action on the view that it was likely that a breach of the peace would occur some time in the near future, if the protesters persisted. The European court held, at p 638, paras 60–61, that arresting the protesters to prevent a violent reaction had been justified and that there had been no breach of article 5(1) of the European Convention.

71 … In the present case, on the basis of the information and advice available to him, Chief Superintendent Lambert considered that a breach of the peace would occur if the coaches and the protesters reached Fairford. It was only just over three miles away-a few minutes by coach. In these circumstances, if Mr Lambert had concluded that a breach of the peace at Fairford was imminent, I might have been disposed to accept that. But it is unnecessary to decide the point since Mr Lambert, who knew all the relevant circumstances, in fact considered that, when the coaches reached Lechlade, a breach of the peace was not imminent. That being so, he had no power, and was under no duty, to take steps to prevent the breach of the peace. It follows that stopping the coaches from proceeding further was unlawful.

72 That is sufficient to dispose of the appeal in the claimant's favour but, since the second and third issues were fully argued, I think it right to consider them. Assuming that Mr Lambert had been entitled to take the steps which were reasonably necessary to prevent the breach of the peace, would those steps have included stopping the coaches and their passengers from travelling on to Fairford? Would that step have been a proportionate restriction on the claimant's article 10 and 11 rights?

73 In many straightforward cases the steps which are reasonably necessary will be obvious. Where the officer believes, for instance, that an individual is about to punch someone else, then it may well be necessary for the officer to restrain and arrest the potential aggressor. But, sometimes, all that may be required is to advise the potential aggressor or the potential victim to leave as quickly as possible.

74 In other cases, perhaps involving rival gangs or rival groups of football supporters, the police officer may see that the members of one gang or group are making offensive remarks with the intention of provoking the other side to a fight. Then the officer may prevent the breach of the peace by ordering the first group to desist and, if they fail to do so, arresting them for obstructing a police officer in the execution of his duty under section 89(2) of the Police Act 1996.

75 Even where someone does not actually intend to provoke others into a violent reaction but behaves in an outrageous way which is liable to produce such a reaction, he can be stopped. That was the position in *Wise v Dunning* [1902] 1 KB 167. When addressing meetings in a public place in Liverpool the appellant used gestures and language which were highly insulting to the Roman Catholic population. His actions had caused, and were liable to cause, breaches of the peace by his opponents and supporters. The Divisional Court held that the magistrate's decision to bind him over to keep the peace had been fully justified.

In doing so, the court rejected his argument that he could not be held responsible for any breaches of the peace that occurred since an unlawful act could not be regarded as the natural consequence of his insulting or abusive language or conduct.

76 *Albert v Lavin* [1982] AC 546 was essentially a case of the same kind, though the circumstances were very different. Mr Albert tried to jump the queue and board a bus out of turn. This naturally caused resentment and several people in the queue objected to his conduct. The reaction of the other members of the queue caused Mr Lavin, an off-duty police officer, reasonably to expect that a breach of the peace was liable to take place. He intervened to prevent it by obstructing Mr Albert's access to the bus. Lord Diplock, with whom the other members of the House agreed, held that, both as a constable and as a citizen, Mr Lavin had been entitled, indeed bound, to take this reasonable step to prevent the breach of the peace. When, in the passage quoted in para 61 above, Lord Diplock referred to a citizen having the right and duty to take reasonable steps to make the person who is breaking or threatening to break the peace refrain from doing so, this included taking such steps against a person, like Mr Albert, whose conduct is liable to cause others to do acts which would constitute a breach of the peace. Of course, it would have been wrong for the other people in the queue to resort to violence, but the reality was that this was likely to happen. In the circumstances Mr Lavin was entitled to prevent the breach of the peace by stopping Mr Albert from boarding the bus out of turn.

77 Some forms of protest involve actions which are almost certain eventually to provoke a violent reaction from their targets. That was the case with the two applicants in *Steel v United Kingdom* 28 EHRR 603 whose protests I described in para 69. The police arrested them because they feared that, after enduring some hours of disruptive protests, the other side would react violently. The applicants complained that their rights under article 10 of the Convention had been violated. The European court held, however, at pp 645–647, paras 102–109, that, in view of the risks involved if their protests had continued, the measures taken could not be regarded as disproportionate. There was accordingly no breach of article 10.

78 The common law goes further, however. Sometimes, lawful and proper conduct by A may be liable to result in a violent reaction from B, even though it is not directed against B. If B's resort to violence can be regarded as the natural consequence of A's conduct, and there is no other way of preserving the peace, a police officer may order A to desist from his conduct, even though it is lawful. If A refuses, he may be arrested for obstructing a police officer in the execution of his duty.

79 In *O'Kelly v Harvey* 14 LR Ir 105, the plaintiff, a nationalist Member of Parliament, sued the defendant for assault and battery. The incident arose out of a meeting of the Land League which was to be held at Brookeborough near Enniskillen on 7 December 1880. The previous day a placard appeared summoning local Orangemen to assemble and oppose the meeting. The defendant, who was a justice of the peace for the district, was present at the meeting. According to his pleadings, (1882) 10 LR Ir 285, 287–289, he knew of the placard and believed on reasonable and probable grounds that the only way of preventing a breach of the peace when the Orangemen arrived was to order the meeting to separate and disperse. The defendant asked the plaintiff and the other persons who were assembled to disperse and, when they failed to do so, he laid his hand on the plaintiff in order to disperse the meeting. On a demurrer the Court of Appeal held that, if made out, these averments would constitute a sufficient defence to the action. Law C explained the position in this way 14 LR Ir 105, 109–110:

'The question then seems to be reduced to this:-assuming the plaintiff and others assembled with him to be doing nothing unlawful, but yet that there were reasonable grounds for the defendant believing, as he did, that there would be a breach of the peace if they continued so assembled, and that there was no other way in which the breach of the peace could be avoided but by stopping and dispersing the plaintiff's meeting-was the defendant justified in taking the necessary steps to stop and disperse it? In my opinion he was so justified, under the peculiar circumstances stated in the defence, and which for the present must be taken as admitted to be there truly stated. Under such circumstances the defendant was not to defer action until a breach of the peace had actually been committed. His paramount duty was to *preserve the peace unbroken*, and that, by whatever means were available for the purpose. Furthermore, the duty of a justice of the peace being to preserve the peace unbroken he is, of course, entitled, and in part bound, to intervene the moment he has reasonable apprehensions of a breach of the peace being imminent; and, therefore, he must in such cases necessarily act on his own *reasonable* and *bona fide belief*, as to what is *likely* to occur. Accordingly in the present case, even assuming that the danger to the public peace arose altogether from the threatened attack of another body on the plaintiff and his friends, still if the defendant believed and had just grounds for believing that the peace *could only be preserved* by withdrawing the plaintiff and his friends from the attack with which they were threatened, it was, I think, the duty of the defendant to take that course.'

He added, at p 112:

'I assume here that the plaintiff's meeting was not unlawful. But the question still remains-was not the defendant justified in separating and dispersing it *if he had reasonable ground* for his belief that by no other possible means could he perform his duty of preserving the public peace. For the reasons already given, I think he was so justified, and therefore that the defence in question is good ...'

80 I need not examine the fairly extensive later case law in which this topic has been explored since, like Simon Brown LJ in *Nicol v Director of Public Prosecutions* (1995) 160 JP 155, 162, I accept that Lord Alverstone CJ put the position correctly when he said in *Wise v Dunning* [1902] 1 KB 167, 175–176: 'there must be an act of the defendant, the natural consequence of which, if his act be not unlawful in itself, would be to produce an unlawful act by other persons.' It is also unnecessary to try to determine the precise boundaries of the rule, which were discussed both by Simon Brown LJ in *Nicol* 160 JP 155, 162–163, and by Sedley LJ in *Redmond-Bate v Director of Public Prosecutions* (1999) 163 JP 789, 791–793. What does need to be stressed, however, is that, as *Dicey, An Introduction to the Study of the Law of the Constitution*, 10th ed by E C S Wade (1959), pp 278–279, emphasised, using the familiar example of the Salvationists and the Skeleton Army:

'the only justification for preventing the Salvationists from exercising their legal rights is the *necessity of the case*. If the peace can be preserved, not by breaking up an otherwise lawful meeting, but by arresting the wrongdoers-in this case the Skeleton Army-the magistrates or constables are bound, it is submitted, to arrest the wrongdoers and to protect the Salvationists in the exercise of their lawful rights.'

81 In *Chorherr v Austria* (1993) 17 EHRR 358 the applicant was one of two men who had been arrested when demonstrating against the Austrian armed forces on the occasion of a military parade. They had rucksacks on their backs, with slogans on them. The rucksacks were so large that they blocked other spectators' view of the parade. This caused 'a commotion' among the spectators who were protesting loudly at the obstruction. The demonstrators were arrested to prevent disorder. By a majority, the European court held, at pp 375–377, paras 27–34, that in the circumstances it could not say that the arrests had not been a proportionate way of preventing disorder. There had accordingly been no violation of the applicant's article 10 rights.

82 Here, of course, the claimant and those like her were not going to take any part in any breach of the peace. Nor was their conduct likely to lead to one. But, as *O'Kelly v Harvey* shows, where it is necessary in order to prevent a breach of the peace, at common law police officers can take action (in that case dispersing a meeting) which affects people who are not themselves going to be actively involved in the breach. Similarly, as Mr Pannick reminded the House, under section 13(1) of the Public Order Act 1986, where his other powers are inadequate, a chief constable must ask the district council to prohibit a procession which is liable to lead to serious public disorder-even if many of those taking part would not be involved in the disorder. A prior authorisation procedure for public meetings is in keeping with the requirements of article 11, if only so that the authorities may be in a position to ensure the peaceful nature of the meetings: *Ziliberberg v Moldova* (Application No 61821/00), admissibility decision, European Court, Fourth Section,

(unreported) 4 May 2004. By contrast, a peaceful protester does not cease to enjoy the right to peaceful assembly as a result of sporadic violence or other punishable acts committed by others in the course of a demonstration: *Ziliberberg v Moldova* and *Ezelin v France* (1991) 14 EHRR 362, 375, para 34 of the commission's decision.

83 On the same principle, where they need to do so in order, say, to reach the scene of an imminent breach of the peace, police officers must be able to clear a path through a crowd of innocent bystanders. Indeed, where necessary, a police officer is entitled to go further and call on any able-bodied bystanders for their active assistance in suppressing a breach of the peace. If, without any lawful excuse, they refuse to give it, they are guilty of an offence. See *Archbold, Criminal Pleading Evidence and Practice 2006*, para 19–277. The law proceeds on the basis that 'it is no unimportant matter that the Queen's subjects should assist the officers of the law, when duly required to do so, in preserving the public peace': *R v Brown* (1841) C & Mar 314, 318 per Alderson B. In the eyes of the law therefore innocent bystanders caught up in a breach of the peace are to be regarded as potential allies of the police officers who are trying to suppress the violence.

84 In the light of these authorities I would reject Mr Emmerson's submission that there has to be a causal nexus between the persons affected by any measure taken by the police and the potential breach of the peace. In some circumstances a requirement of that kind would make it impossible for police officers to discharge their primary duty to preserve the peace. In a case like the present, therefore, provided that there was no other way of preventing an imminent breach of the peace, under the common law a police officer could stop a coachload of protesters from proceeding further, even although those on board included entirely peaceful protesters. The proviso is, however, vital.

85 Under the Human Rights Act 1998 the police must have regard to the rights to freedom of expression and freedom of assembly which protesters, such as the claimant, are entitled to assert under articles 10 and 11 of the Convention. Article 10 is the lex generalis, article 11 a lex specialis. In *Steel v United Kingdom* 28 EHRR 603, para 101, the European court described the right to freedom of expression as

'an essential foundation of democratic society and one of the basic conditions for its progress and for each individual's self-fulfilment.'

To be permissible, any restriction on these essential rights in articles 10 and 11 must be necessary in a democratic society. The proportionality principle demands that a balance be struck between the requirements of the purposes listed in articles 10(2) and 11(2) and the freedom to express opinions and to assemble. See *Ezelin v France* 14 EHRR 362, 389, paras 51–52. Here the police were pursuing the legitimate aim of preventing disorder. So the court has to determine whether the police action was proportionate to that legitimate aim, having regard to the special importance of freedom of peaceful assembly and freedom of expression. In the familiar trinity in *de Freitas v Permanent Secretary of the Ministry of Agriculture, Fisheries, Lands and Housing* [1999] AC 69, 80f-g, assuming that the breach of the peace was imminent, the critical question is whether the means which the police used to impair the claimant's article 10 rights were no more than was necessary to accomplish their objective of preventing the breach of the peace which they anticipated. In this case the Convention standard is basically the same as that set by the common law rule formulated by Dicey. Under the Convention, however, as the chief constable accepts, the onus is on the police to show that what was done was no more than was necessary.

Lords Rodger of Earlsferry, Carswell, Brown of Eaton-under-Heywood and **Mance** delivered concurring speeches. Lord Mance expressed full agreement with Lord Bingham subject to some observations on *Moss v McLachlan*.

Appeal allowed; cross-appeal dismissed.

NOTES

1. The speeches of the other members of the House of Lords contained some differences of emphasis.

(a)   All were agreed that the distinction drawn in *Moss v McLachlan* between arrest and actions short of arrest was wrong. As Lord Rodger said[635] the *Moss* reformulation would 'weaken the long-standing safeguard against unnecessary and inappropriate interventions by the police—and indeed, in theory at least, by ordinary citizens'.

(b)   All were agreed that the actions of the police in turning the coaches back were disproportionate.[636]

(c)   *Moss* was regarded by the majority as correctly decided on its facts even though the test propounded was wrong.[637]

(d)   What does 'imminent' mean? This was considered by Lord Rodger.[638] Lord Carswell[639] added:

> I do consider, however, that it [the imminence test] can properly be applied with a degree of flexibility which recognises the relevance of the circumstances of the case. In particular it seems to me rational and principled to accept that where events are building up inexorably to a breach of the peace it may be possible to regard it as imminent at an earlier stage temporally than in the case of other more spontaneous breaches.

Lord Mance said[640]

> The requirement of imminence is relatively clear-cut and appropriately identifies the common law power (or duty) of any citizen including the police to take preventive action as a power of last resort catering for situations about to descend into violence. That is not to suggest that imminence falls to be judged in absolute and purely temporal terms, according to some measure of minutes. What is imminent has to be judged in the context under consideration, and the absence of any further opportunity to take preventive action may thus have relevance.

(e)   On the facts was a breach of the peace 'imminent'? No, said Lords Bingham, Brown and Mance.[641] Lord Mance pointed out that there was no imminent breach of the peace when the coaches arrived at Lechlade, and that there was still none on the assumption that the coaches had proceeded to Fairford; here there were extensive precautions in place, there being a plan to deal with 10,000, although the police estimates of numbers actually arriving on the day lay between 1,200 and 3,000. Lord Rodger[642] thought it might have been, but as Mr Lambert believed otherwise, the power could not be exercised. (This was

---

635 At para. [66].

636 Lord Bingham at paras [53]–[55]; Lord Rodger at paras [85]–[90] (the police could have dealt with any trouble at Fairford or removed known Wombles at Lechlade); Lord Carswell at paras [105]–[106]; Lord Brown at para. [129]; Lord Mance at paras [152]–[155] (no opportunity was given to individuals to explain their affiliations or intentions).

637 See Lord Bingham at [51], Lord Rodger at [70]–[71], Lord Carswell at [102]. Lord Brown (paras [116]–[118]) thought it 'just sustainable' and then only on the basis (which may not have been the case) that those stopped were 'manifestly intent on violence'. Lord Mance (para. [150]) was very doubtful.

638 At paras [67]–[71].   639 At para. [102].   640 At para. [141].

641 Paras [50], [118], [142]. Their Lordships also attached weight to the point that Mr Lambert did not regards a breach as imminent.

642 At para. [71].

asserted rather than explained, but is presumably analogous to the point that a police officer may not arrest someone he does not suspect, even if he has reasonable grounds.[643]) Lord Carswell said:[644]

It might well be said that when the coaches arrived at Lechlade, only three miles from the base at Fairford, with some members of the Wombles on board and containing a number of items quite inconsistent with peaceful demonstrations, a breach of the peace was imminent. Mr Lambert's opinion on the point is not conclusive, but, like Lord Rodger, I do not find it necessary to pronounce on that issue.

His Lordship then proceeded to hold that the police actions were not proportionate and it may be that this was the reason why he did not express a view on imminence, rather than Lord Rodger's reason.

(f) What is the correct definition of the power and duty to deal with a breach of the peace? Lord Brown stated[645] that Lord Bingham's formulation at para. [29] was preferable to that in *Howell* (cited at para. [27]):

which seems to me to confuse a breach of the peace with a reasonable apprehension of such a breach (a confusion by no means confined to that judgment). A breach of the peace, as I understand it, involves actual harm done either to a person or to a person's property in his presence or some other form of violent disorder or disturbance and itself necessarily involves a criminal offence. Whilst, therefore, it is accurate for the European Court of Human Rights to say in *Steel v United Kingdom* (1998) 28 EHRR 603, para 29

'A person may be arrested without warrant by exercise of the common law power of arrest, for causing a breach of the peace or where it is reasonably apprehended that he is likely to cause a breach of the peace'

it is at first blush puzzling to find at para 25 of the same judgment (restated at para 48) the suggestion that 'Breach of the peace...does not constitute a criminal offence', for which the authority of *R v County of London Quarter Sessions Appeals Committee, Ex p Metropolitan Police Comr* [1948] 1 KB 670 is cited—an authority perhaps more appropriately cited at footnote 15...to para 31 of the judgment for the proposition that 'a binding over order is not a criminal conviction'. When Lord Bingham says at para 28 of his opinion: 'A breach of the peace is not, *as such*, a criminal offence, but founds an application to bind over' (my emphasis), he is there referring to the *concept* of breach of the peace as sometimes the Strasbourg court does....

Lord Mance stated[646] that it was not necessary to consider whether a breach of the peace must involve some identifiable domestic criminal offence.

(g) Could the police take any action against those not themselves committing or reasonably apprehended of being about to commit a breach of the peace? Lords Rodger and Brown said yes.[647] Lord Carswell appeared to take the same view.[648] Lord Mance was prepared to assume that such a principle existed, but was confined to rare situations.[649] Lord Bingham did not deal with the issue of principle, without really explaining why.[650]

---

[643] See p. 146.   [644] At para. [111].   [645] At para. [111].

[646] At para. [137].

[647] Paras [72]–[84], [119]–[129] ('in extreme and exceptional circumstances').

[648] Paras [95]–[100].   [649] Paras [143]–[148].

[650] At para. [30] he did say that cases on non-disorderly but provocative conduct such as *Humphries v Connor* were not directly relevant. (Note that L's actions could not be described as provocative.)

(h) Lord Brown[651] agreed with Lord Bingham[652] (and presumably therefore Lord Mance) that any extension of police powers to control demonstrations would have to be conferred by primary legislation.

2. This is a landmark decision that clarifies a number of important points. These include the meaning of breach of the peace, the point at which police powers to prevent a breach become available and the point that any power to act against a person not themselves behaving unreasonably can only be taken in the last resort. It is submitted, with respect, that the decision to reject the *Moss* reformulation is entirely right as that both unacceptably broadened and made less certain the powers of the police. The finding that the police actions were disproportionate was robust and showed little deference to the view of the officer on the spot. It is surprising that the chief constable persisted with a challenge on the point decided against him in the lower courts, given the distress it caused and the self-evident lack of proportionality in securing that the coaches did not stop on the journey back to London. There are some lingering concerns. First, there is the fact that at least one of the judges was prepared to hold that on the facts a breach of the peace was imminent, even though Mr Lambert had thought otherwise. This point is convincingly rejected by the majority, and this should be borne in mind by future decisions on the point. Second, there seems an element of strain in upholding the outcome in *Moss v McLachlan,* and Lord Mance's doubts are fully justified. Third, there remains some uncertainty as to the scope of powers to intervene against those who are not themselves committing or provoking a breach of the peace. Lords Brown and Mance seemed to place more emphasis on the need to limit them particularly narrowly than Lords Rodger and Carswell. This last issue was confronted directly by the Court of Appeal in the following case.

3. *Austin v Comr of Police of the Metropolis.*[653] This case concerned a major demonstration in London on 1 May 2001.[654] The police were aware that it was planned, but the organisers had not co-operated with police. The police had good reason to anticipate serious violence and property damage. About 3,000 people congregated on Oxford Circus. Most there at 2 p.m. were surrounded by a police cordon, and not allowed to leave except with police permission. Many were kept there for over seven hours. Conditions became increasingly unacceptable, given the absence of toilets. A number were not demonstrators, but were caught up in the cordon. The first claimant, Lois Austin, was a demonstrator; the second, Geoffrey Saxby, was not. Each had asked to leave, the first because she had an 11-month-old baby to collect and the second because he was not a protestor. Both requests were refused. Both behaved lawfully throughout. They claimed damages for false imprisonment and breach of Art. 5 ECHR. This was rejected by Tugendhat J[655] on the basis that the police reasonably suspected that everyone within the cordon, including the claimants, had been about to commit a breach of the peace. Imposing the cordon had been necessary to prevent violence and the risk of injury to persons or property. He also rejected A's claims under Arts 10 and 11 ECHR. On appeal, the Court of Appeal rejected the finding that all were reasonably suspected; the police were aware that some in the crowd would not cause a breach of the peace. This raised directly the question whether powers to prevent a breach of the peace could be used against persons not themselves

651 At para. [132].   652 Para. [52].
653 [2007] EWCA Civ 989, [2008] 2 WLR 415. See A.T.H. Smith [2008] CLJ 10.
654 This was one of a series of anti-capitalist May Day demonstrations. See www.urban75.org/mayday. At para. [132].
655 [2005] EWHC 480 (QB).

suspected to be about to commit it. The court considered the speeches in *Laporte* that considered this aspect and concluded:

35 As we read the speeches of Lord Rodger and Lord Brown they give some support for the following propositions: (i) where a breach of the peace is taking place, or is reasonably thought to be imminent, before the police can take any steps which interfere with or curtail in any way the lawful exercise of rights by innocent third parties they must ensure that they have taken all other possible steps to ensure that the breach, or imminent breach, is obviated and that the rights of innocent third parties are protected; (ii) the taking of all other possible steps includes (where practicable), but is not limited to, ensuring that proper and advance preparations have been made to deal with such a breach, since failure to take such steps will render interference with the rights of innocent third parties unjustified or unjustifiable; but (iii) where (and only where) there is a reasonable belief that there are no other means whatsoever whereby a breach or imminent breach of the peace can be obviated, the lawful exercise by third parties of their rights may be curtailed by the police; (iv) this is a test of necessity which it is to be expected can only be justified in truly extreme and exceptional circumstances; and (v) the action taken must be both reasonably necessary and proportionate.

36 While it cannot we think be said that Lord Mance expressly supports those propositions, they seem to us to be consistent with his views. They are not inconsistent with the speech of Lord Carswell and Lord Bingham did not address these questions at all.

Applying these principles, the containment was lawful. It had been lawful to leave it to the discretion of individual police officers to decide whether particular individuals should leave and the refusals to let the claimants leave were not irrational. There was no deprivation of liberty for the purposes of Art. 5. The emphasis that the powers can only be used in the last resort is welcome. Leave has been given for an appeal to the House of Lords.

4. There were a number of cases in the lower courts dealing with these matters prior to *Laporte*. They were dealt with in previous editions of this book[656] and will essentially be of historic interest only. Many of these are mentioned in Lord Rodger's speech in *Laporte*. The main ones that were not were these. In *Humphries v Connor*[657] H walked through Swanlinbar wearing a party emblem (an orange lily) the wearing of which was 'calculated[658] and tended to provoke animosity between different classes of Her Majesty's subjects'. A number of people were provoked, caused noise and disturbance, and threatened her. C, a sub-inspector of Constabulary, asked her to remove the emblem. She refused. C removed the emblem. She sued for damages. The pleadings said that this was done 'gently and quietly, and *necessarily and unavoidably*' and that C '*necessarily* committed said alleged trespass' to protect her from violence and to preserve the public peace. The court held that if these facts were made out there would be a good defence in law.

In *Duncan v Jones*[659] Mrs Katharine Duncan and about 30 others collected with a view to holding a meeting to protest against the Incitement to Disaffection Bill, near to the entrance to an unemployed training centre. D was to be one of the speakers. A box was put in the roadway. She was about to mount the box when she was told by the chief constable of the district to move to another street 175 yards away. She said 'I'm going to hold it', stepped on the box, started to address the people present, and was arrested by Inspector Jones. She was convicted of obstructing Inspector Jones in the execution of his duty. On appeal to quarter sessions it was not alleged that D or anyone at the meeting had committed, incited or provoked any breach of the peace. It was proved or admitted that about a year before a meeting

---

[656] See the 4th edn, pp. 244–247 and the 5th edn, pp. 107–121.   [657] (1864) 17 ICLR 1.
[658] I.e. 'likely' rather than 'intended'.   [659] [1936] 1 KB 218.

had been held opposite to the centre, addressed by D, following which and on the same day a disturbance took place inside the centre. The superintendent of the centre attributed the disturbance to the meeting. D had tried on subsequent occasions to hold a meeting, but had been frustrated by the police. The deputy chairman of quarter sessions found that J reasonably apprehended a breach of the peace and so it became his duty to prevent the meeting. The appeal was dismissed. The DC dismissed a further appeal by case stated holding that once it was established that there was a reasonably apprehended breach of the peace, it was J's duty 'to prevent anything which in his view would cause that breach of the peace'.[660] The case was widely condemned.[661] It was subsequently taken to extremes during the miners' strike where the police attempted to stop anyone who appeared to be a miner or who was travelling north to aid the strike from crossing the Thames via the Dartford Tunnel.[662]

In *Piddington v Bates*,[663] 18 men arrived to picket a printer's works where about eight of the normal complement of 24 were working. Chief Inspector Bates told P that two pickets at each of the two entrances were sufficient. P said he was going there, 'gently pushed past' B and was 'gently arrested'. His conviction for obstruction of the police was upheld. The court found that on the facts the police reasonably apprehended that a breach of the peace might occur; this had to be a 'real possibility'.

The final case to note is *Redmond-Bate v DPP*.[664] Here, R-B was one of a group of three fundamentalists who were preaching their beliefs from the steps of Wakefield Cathedral. A crowd gathered, some of whom were hostile. PC Tennant feared that this would provoke violence and asked them to stop. They refused and he arrested them for breach of the peace. R-B was subsequently convicted of obstructing the police, but this was quashed by the DC. She was not responsible for the threat to the peace.

> To proceed, as the Crown Court did, from the fact that the three women were preaching about morality, God and the Bible (the topic not only of sermons preached on every Sunday of the year but of at least one regular daily slot on national radio) to a reasonable apprehension that violence is going to erupt is, with great respect, both illiberal and illogical. The situation perceived and recounted by PC Tennant did not justify him in apprehending a breach of the peace, much less a breach of the peace for which the three women would be responsible.[665]

Sedley LJ[666] cited a statement by Simon Brown LJ in *R v Nicol*[667]

> Before the court can properly find that the natural consequence of lawful conduct by a defendant would, if persisted in, be to provoke another to violence, it should, it seems to me, be satisfied that in all the circumstances it is the defendant who is acting unreasonably rather than the other person...

5. *Laporte* and the forthcoming ruling in *Austin* will provide definitive guidance as to the scope of powers to deal with breaches of the peace. Many of the previous cases are in any event fail to provide clear authoritative guidance in that they are interlocutory decisions (e.g. *Humphries v Connor*), decisions of the Divisional Court only (e.g. *Duncan v Jones*) or decisions where the findings of fact are unclear or obviously unsatisfactory (e.g. *Duncan*

---

660 Per Humphrey J.

661 See E.C.S. Wade, (1937) 6 CLJ 175; *Williams*, pp. 119–123; T.C. Daintith [1966] PL 248; K.D. Ewing and C. Gearty, *The Struggle for Civil Liberties* (2000), pp. 260–270.

662 See S. Miller and M. Walker, *A State of Siege* (A Report to the Yorkshire Area NUM) (1984), pp. 19–23. Cf. *Moss v McLachlan*, discussed in *Laporte*.

663 [1961] 1 WLR 162.   664 [2000] HRLR 249.   665 Para. 21.

666 At para. 8.   667 (1996) 160 JP 155, 162.

v Jones, Piddington v Bates and *Moss v McLachlan*). *Piddington* seems now to be regarded as wrongly decided.

A typology is provided by Lord Carswell in *Laporte*,[668] who distinguished three main categories of case: first, where 'the person who is arrested, detained or otherwise prevented from continuing with his proposed course of action is himself committing or about to commit a breach of the peace' (e.g. *Moss*); second, there are cases 'whose acts are lawful and peaceful in themselves but are likely to provoke others into committing a breach of the peace' (e.g. *Albert v Lavin*; *Humphries v Connor*; *Wise v Dunning*); third, there are cases where 'the actions are not necessarily provocative per se, but a counter-demonstration is arranged of such a nature that the confluence of demonstrations is likely to lead to a breach of the peace' (e.g. *O'Kelly v Harvey*). Other well-known cases were, however, difficult to fit into these categories (e.g. *Beatty v Gillbanks*; *Duncan v Jones*). It is submitted that this is helpful, but that there are other important variables. In particular, attention must be paid to the nature of the proceedings in which the issue arises. There are three possibilities as regards the second and third of Lord Carswell's categories. First, the prosecution may seek to convict the 'innocent provoker or bystander' of a substantive criminal offence or have him or her bound over to keep the peace. Here, the decision in *Beatty v Gillbanks* that the Salvation Army members whose colourful march was opposed by the violence of the 'Skeleton Army' were not guilty of the common law offence of unlawful assembly and so should not be bound over stands as a vindication of free assembly and expression, and illustrative of a fundamental principle. As explained by Sedley LJ in *Redmond-Bate v DPP*:[669]

Field J, accepting that a person is liable for the natural consequences of what he does, held nevertheless that the natural consequences of the lawful activity of the Salvation Army did not include the unlawful activities of others, even if the accused knew that others would react unlawfully.

Second, there are cases where the police take direct action against the 'innocent provoker or bystander' and are themselves sued. Here *Austin* (and *Humphries v Connor* and *O'Kelly v Harvey*) hold that the police have a good defence. This seems acceptable provided the defence is kept within very narrow bounds. Third, there are cases where the 'innocent provoker or bystander' declines to accept a police direction to move on or disperse and is prosecuted for obstruction of the police in the execution of their duty (*Duncan v Jones*, *Redmond-Bate v DPP*). There are two points that arise in these cases. First, disobedience to an instruction to move on should only ever be regarded as unlawful where the instruction is given in the narrow circumstances recognised in *Austin*. The position in *Duncan v Jones* arguably fell well short of that and the decision should be regarded as wrong. If disobedience to an instruction to move on given simply on the basis that this was *a* way of preventing a reasonably apprehended breach of the peace (not the *only* way) could be prosecuted as obstruction, a cart and horses would have been driven through the narrow bounds of *Austin*. The second point is whether, even in a narrow 'last resort' situation, disobedience to a police instruction should constitute the offence of obstruction. It is difficult here to see a reason why not. If the police officer is entitled to use lawful force to give effect to his or her lawful instruction, then (for example) the use of force to resist would seem properly to be characterised as unlawful.

The second important variable is the nature of the 'provoker's' conduct. In Lord Carswell's middle category there are in fact a number of further possibilities. The extent to which it is objectively 'unreasonable' (while not unlawful) will vary, as will the extent to which the

---

[668] Paras [94]–[99].   [669] [2000] HRLR 249, para. 6.

individual knew or ought to have known that it would be provocative. These are no doubt factors relevant in judging the proportionality of a police intervention; the suggestion in *Nicol* that the police can only intervene if the individual's conduct is 'unreasonable' goes too far and is inconsistent with *Austin*.

6. *Breach of the peace.* Howell, subject to the observations of Lord Brown cited above[670] provides a clearer and narrower definition of 'breach of the peace' than previous case law. It is now clear that loud noises and disturbance do not of themselves constitute a breach of the peace.[671] 'Harm' for the purposes of the *Howell* definition 'must be unlawful harm'.[672] A breach of the peace can take place on private premises.[673]

7. *Arrest for breach of the peace.* This power was not removed by the Police and Criminal Evidence Act 1984; s. 26 of that Act[674] repealed only statutory powers. A person making an arrest when he or she reasonably believes a breach of the peace is about to be committed complies with the requirements of *Christie v Leachinsky*[675] if he or she says merely 'I am arresting you for breach of the peace.'[676]

Lord Bingham's statement at para. [29] in *Laporte* as to the circumstances when steps can (or indeed must) be taken to prevent a breach of the peace must also be taken as definitive. This confirms that there is no power to arrest for a past breach of the peace where it is not likely to be renewed.[677]

Can a person be *arrested* for breach of the peace where his conduct is lawful but provocative? The possibility was recognised by Beldam LJ in *Foulkes v Chief Constable of Merseyside*.[678] However, this should only rarely arise. There should only be an arrest power where the facts fall within the *Austin* parameter (cf. *Redmond-Bate v DPP*) and in such a case the person should have been asked first to desist, with arrest for obstruction following refusal. It is difficult to see that it would ever be proportionate to arrest an 'innocent provoker' with no prior warning.

In civil proceedings arising out of an arrest for breach of the peace, it is for the judge to decide whether there was the necessary reasonable cause and for the jury to decide any disputed issues of fact.[679]

8. *Other consequences.* The concept of breach of the peace is also relevant to binding-over[680] and to police powers of entry.[681]

9. *Statutory dispersal powers.* The police have been given a range of statutory powers to disperse or move on individuals in public places in specified circumstances. These are broader than the common law in that they extend beyond situations where there is imminent violence or damage to property.

---

[670] On which see G. Williams (1982) 146 JPN 199–200, 217–219; D. Nicholson and K. Reid [1996] Crim LR 764 which echo observations in *Lewis v Chief Constable of Greater Manchester* (1991) *Independent*, 24 October.

[671] *Lewis*, above (loud music and screaming).

[672] *McBean v Parker* (1983) 147 JP 205, 208, DC (not, as here, the use of reasonable force to resist an unlawful police search).

[673] *McConnell v Chief Constable of the Greater Manchester Police* [1990] 1 WLR 364 (removal of McC from carpet store); *Chief Constable of Humberside Police v McQuade* [2001] EWCA Civ 1330, [2002] 1 WLR 1347 (matrimonial dispute; no need for disturbance to member of the public off the premises).

[674] This repealed statutory powers of arrest without warrant or order, unless preserved by Sch. 2.

[675] Above, p. 205.   [676] *Howell*, above.

[677] There was previously some doubt on this although the stronger view was that there was no power here point: G. Williams [1954] Crim LR 578, 586–587.

[678] [1998] 3 All ER 705, 711.

[679] *Kelly v Chief Constable of Hampshire* (1993) *Independent*, 25 March (applying *Dallison v Caffery* [1965] 1 QB 348, 371 per Diplock CJ).

[680] See pp. 397–401.   [681] See pp. 401–406.

Section 42 of the Criminal Justice and Police Act 2001[682] provides a power for an officer to direct persons to leave the vicinity of premises used as a dwelling or to follow other directions given by the officer to prevent harassment, alarm or distress to persons in a dwelling. The power exists whenever there are people present 'in the vicinity' of a dwelling[683] and the officer has reasonable grounds to believe that those present are there for the purpose:

(by his presence or otherwise) of representing to the resident or another individual (whether or not one who uses the premises as his dwelling), or of persuading the resident or such another individual: (i) that he should not do something that he is entitled to or required to do; or (ii) that he should do something that he is not under any obligation to do

and that the officer reasonably believes that the presence of the person (alone or with others) or their behaviour is likely to cause harassment, alarm or distress to people in the dwelling. Officers exercising the power may give such directions as they consider necessary to prevent the harassment of or alarm or distress to the residents. A direction may include a requirement to leave the vicinity of the premises and to do so and not to return within such period as the officer may specify, not being longer than three months. It may include conditions as to the distance or location at which persons who do not leave the vicinity must remain and as to the number and identity of persons authorised to remain in the vicinity. It is an offence to fail to comply with such an order. Conduct that could give rise to a direction was made a substantive offence by the Serious Organised Crime and Police Act 2005.[684] This enables the behaviour to be dealt with once an incident has taken place. These provisions will commonly affect the use of the highway. The provisions were designed to deal with the animal rights protesters' tactics of standing outside the houses of employees and shareholders of relevant companies with placards of animals and vivisection activity.

A significant general power is conferred by s. 30 of the Anti-social Behaviour Act 2003. This applies when an officer of the rank of superintendent or above has reasonable grounds for believing (a) that members of the public have been intimidated, harassed, alarmed or distressed as a result of the presence or behaviour of groups of two or more persons in public places in any locality in his police area (the 'relevant locality') and (b) that anti-social behaviour[685] is a significant and persistent problem in the relevant locality. Where he does, he may give an authorisation that specified powers may be exercised by a constable in uniform for a period up to six months. These include powers to direct a group to disperse; to direct any person in the group who does not reside in a relevant locality to leave it (or any part of it); to prohibit any such persons not to return to the relevant locality for (up to) 24 hours. These directions may not, however, be given to a group engaged in conduct lawful under s. 220 of the Trade Union and Labour Relations (Consolidation) Act 1992 (peaceful picketing), or taking part in a public procession of the kind mentioned in s. 11(1) of the Public Order Act 1986[686] where written notice has been given or is not required. For a direction to be given, the constable must have reasonable grounds for believing that the presence or behaviour of a group of two or more persons in any public place in the relevant

---

[682] As amended by the Serious and Organised Crime and Police Act 2005, s. 127.

[683] As defined in the Public Order Act 1986, s. 8 to include 'any structure or part of a structure occupied as a person's home or as other living accommodation (whether the occupation is separate or shared with others) but does not include any part not so occupied ...'

[684] Inserting s. 42A in the 2001 Act. See Home Office Circular 34/2005.

[685] I.e. behaviour by a person which causes or is likely to cause harassment, alarm or distress to one or more persons not of the same household as the person: s. 36.

[686] See p. 309.

locality has resulted, or is likely to result, in any members of the public being intimidated, harassed, alarmed or distressed.[687] The authorisation must be in writing, needs the consent of the local authority and must be publicised.[688] A direction can be given orally and can be varied or withdrawn. Non-compliance is an offence.[689] It has been held that these provisions are applicable to protests. Given the specific exemptions for two kinds of protest, the natural inference is that it is applicable to others.[690] However, the police must act proportionately in each situation and 'alarm and distress' may not always be sufficient to justify a dispersal direction.[691] An authorisation given for one purpose can cover a direction given for another.[692]

Separately, if between 9 p.m. and 6 a.m. a constable in uniform finds a person in any public place in the relevant locality who he has reasonable grounds for believing is under 16 and not under the effective control of a parent or a responsible person aged 18 or over, he may remove that person to his place of residence, unless the constable has reasonable grounds for believing he would be likely to suffer significant harm there.[693] The word 'remove' means that reasonable force may be used.[694]

(II) BINDING OVER[695]

The English Law Commission has recommended the abolition of the binding over power on following grounds: (a) the criminal sanctions now applicable to many of the forms of anti-social practice for which a binding-over was formerly used (e.g. the Public Order Act, ss. 4, 5, the Sexual Offences Act 1985 (kerb crawling), the Malicious Communications Act 1988 (poison pen letters), the Telecommunications Act 1984, s. 43 (covering, *inter alia*, persistent telephoning to cause annoyance, inconvenience or distress)); (b) modern developments in cautioning and diverting anti-social offenders from the criminal court system; (c) the many defects in practice in procedure which could not satisfactorily be cured without 'depriving the procedure of the informality which is regarded as one of its main attractions'. The conclusion in favour of abolition was buttressed by the belief that binding-over fell short of the requirements of ECHR, Arts 5, 6, 10 and 11.[696]

---

687 Such grounds must normally be based, in part at least, on some behaviour of the group which indicates in some way or other harassments etc: *Bucknell MB v DPP* [2006] EWHC 1888 (Admin) (2007) 171 JP 10 no reasonable grounds on the facts where there were two well-behaved groups of youths in the Centre Court Shopping Centre, Wimbledon).

688 2003 Act, s. 31. It must specify the grounds, not merely assert there were reasonable grounds: *Sierny v DPP* [2006] EWHC 716 (Admin), (2006) 170 JP 697.

689 2003 Act, s. 32.

690 *R (on the application of Singh) v Chief Constable of West Midlands Police* [2006] EWCA Civ 1118, [2007] 2 All ER 297.

691 Per Hallett LJ at para. [89].

692 *Singh* (authorisation given on account of skateboarders could be relied on to disperse a group of Sikh protesters objecting to the stopping of a play in the city centre which they considered to be offensive to that religion and beliefs).

693 2003 Act, s. 30(6).

694 *R (on the application of W) v Metropolitan Police Comr* [2006] EWCA Civ 458, [2007] QB 399.

695 On binding-over generally see G. Williams, 'Preventive Justice and the Rule of Law' (1953) 16 MLR 417; *Williams,* Chap. 4; (1961) 25 J Cr L 220; A.D. Grunis [1976] PL 16; Law Commission Report No. 222, *Binding Over* (Cm 2439, 1994) Home Office, *Bind Overs A Power for the 21st Century*: A Consultation Document (March 2003). On the historical origins, see D. Feldman, 'The King's Peace, the Royal Prerogative and Public Order: the Roots and Early Development of Binding Over Powers' [1988] CLJ 101.

696 Op. cit., pp. 59–67.

These objections are, in summary, that the conduct which can be ground for a binding over order is too vaguely defined; that binding over orders when made are in terms which are too vague and are therefore potentially oppressive; that the power to imprison someone if he or she refuses to consent to be bound over is anomalous; that orders which restrain a subject's freedom can be made without the discharge of the criminal, or indeed any clearly defined, burden of proof; and that witnesses, complainants or even acquitted defendants can be bound over without any adequate prior information of any charge or complaint against them.[697]

The common law power of justices (and any court of record having a criminal jurisdiction)[698] to bind persons over to keep the peace, and their wider power under the Justices of the Peace Act 1361[699] to bind persons over to be of good behaviour, have frequently been employed in the context of public order. The power to require a person to enter into a recognisance to keep the peace, either generally, or towards a particular person, may be exercised where there is reasonable apprehension of a future breach of the peace.[700] The recognisance may be forfeited by any unlawful action that 'either is or tends to a breach of the peace'.[701]

The statutory power 'to take of all of them that be [not] of good fame, where they shall be found, sufficient surety and mainprise of their good behaviour towards the King and his people …', according to Blackstone,[702] may be exercised:

for causes of scandal, *contra bonos mores*, as well as *contra pacem:* as, for haunting bawdy-houses with women of bad fame; or for keeping such women in his own house; or for words tending to scandalize the government, or in abuse of the officers of justice, especially in the execution of their office. Thus also a justice may bind over all night-walkers; eavesdroppers; such as keep suspicious company, or are reported to be pilferers or robbers; such as sleep in the day, and wake in the night; common drunkards; whoremasters; the putative fathers of bastards; cheats; idle vagabonds; and other persons whose misbehaviour may reasonably bring them within the general words of the statute, as persons not of good fame…

Following the decision of the European Court of Human Rights in *Hashman and Harrys v United Kingdom*,[703] the use of the power to bind over to be 'of good behaviour' as such has effectively been discontinued.

NOTES

1. An order may be made on a complaint to a magistrates' court under s. 115 of the Magistrates' Courts Act 1980; however, the binding-over powers may be exercised by justices of the peace at any stage of other proceedings. An appeal lies against a binding-over order made by a magistrates' court to the Crown Court,[704] or, by case stated on a point of law, to the Divisional Court.[705] An order may be challenged on an application for judicial review.[706] The common law powers date back to time immemorial.[707]

---

[697] Law Commission, Report No. 222, *Binding Over* (1994), para. 6.27.

[698] Justices of the Peace Act 1968, s. 1(7); Administration of Justice Act 1973, Sch. 5.

[699] 34 Edw. III c. 1.   [700] See above, pp. 376–397.

[701] *Blackstone,* Book IV, Chap. XVIII.   [702] Ibid.   [703] Below.

[704] Magistrates' Courts (Appeals from Binding Over Orders) Act 1956; the appeal should be conducted by way of rehearing: *Shaw v Hamilton* [1982] 2 All ER 718, DC.

[705] E.g. *Beatty v Gillbanks; Wise v Dunning.* Above, pp. 394, 385.

[706] *R v Londonderry Justice* (1891) 28 LR Ir 440; *R v Central Criminal Court, ex p Boulding* [1984] 1 All ER 766; DC; *R v Ilminster Justices, ex p Hamilton* (1983) Times, 23 June, DC (binding-over orders quashed on the ground of breach of natural justice); *R v Morpeth Ward Justices, ex p Ward),* (1992) 95 Cr App R 215, DC (the court noting, however, that the appeal by case stated was normally the appropriate method of challenge).

[707] D. Feldman, op. cit.

2. The person bound over must be one who is or whose case is before the court, but no conviction is required.[708] The Justices of the Peace Act 1361 does not require any complaint to have been made before a magistrates' court has the power to bind someone over. However, under s. 115 of the Magistrates' Courts Act 1980, a binding over order can only be made after a complaint has been made and adjudged to be true.[709]

In *R v South Molton Justices, ex p Ankerson*,[710] Taylor LJ stated[711] that when justices are minded to order a binding-over (sc. to keep the peace):

(1) there should be material before them justifying the conclusion that there is a risk of a breach of the peace unless action is taken to prevent it. (2) They must indicate to the defendant their intention to bind him over and the reasons for it so that he or his lawyer can make representations. (3) They must obtain consent to the bind-over from the defendant himself. (4) Before fixing the amount of the recognisance they should inquire as to the defendant's means. (5) The binding-over should be for a finite period.

Point (4) has been emphasised on a number of occasions.[712] In *R v Clerkenwell Metropolitan Stipendiary Magistrate, ex p Hooper*[713] the Divisional Court held that legal representatives should be given an opportunity to make representations before making an order requiring a defendant to provide a surety with a term of imprisonment in default.

3. The binding over power has been subjected to scrutiny by the European Court of Human Rights on a number of occasions.[714] In *Steel v United Kingdom*[715] the ECtHR did not find that binding-over orders violated Art. 5.1 ECHR. In each case the order was imposed after a finding that S had committed a breach of the peace. Given the context, it was

sufficiently clear that the applicants were being requested to agree to refrain from causing further, similar, breaches of the peace during the ensuing twelve months.[716]

Much more significant was the decision in *Hashman and Harrup v United Kingdom*.[717] Here, the applicants blew a hunting horn and engaged in hallooing with the intention of disrupting the activities of the Portman Hunt. They were bound over to keep the peace and be of good behaviour in the sum of £100 for 12 months. The Crown Court dismissed an appeal. It found that the applicants had not committed any breach of the peace, and that their conduct had not been likely to occasion a breach of the peace. However, their behaviour had been a deliberate attempt to interfere with the Hunt and to take the hounds out of the control of the huntsman, thus exposing the hounds to danger. Their conduct was *contra bonos mores*. The ECtHR held that the case concerned the applicants' behaviour while protesting against fox hunting by disrupting the hunt, but nonetheless constituted an expression of opinion. As

---

[708] *R v Kingston upon Thames Crown Court, ex p Guarino* [1986] Crim LR 325.

[709] *CPS v Speede* (1997) 17 December, DC. See *R v Middlesex CC, ex p Khan* (1997) 161 JP 240, DC (holding that a mere belief that the defendant might pose a threat was insufficient).

[710] (1989) 90 Cr App R 158.   [711] At 162.

[712] See *R v Central Criminal Court, ex p Boulding* above; *R v Atkinson* (1988) 10 Cr App R (S) 470, CA (Cr D); *R v Crown Court at Nottingham, ex p Brace* (1989) 154 JP 161, CA; *R v Lincoln Crown Court, ex p Jude* [1998] 1 WLR 24; *R (on the application of Harlow-Hayes) v Cambridge Crown Court* [2008] EWHC 1023 (Admin).

[713] [1998] 1 WLR 800. Failure to do so also constituted a violation of Art. 6.1 ECHR: *Hooper v UK*, Judgment of 16 November 2004.

[714] See D. Mead [1999] J Civ Lib Law 7.   [715] (1998) 28 EHRR 603. Above, p. 385.

[716] Para. 12.

[717] (2000) 30 EHRR 241.

such, any limitations on their freedom of expression had to be 'prescribed by law'. The Court concluded that it was not.

> 32 ...The binding-over order in the present case thus had purely prospective effect. It did not require a finding that there had been a breach of the peace. The case is thus different from the case of Steel and Others, in which the proceedings brought against the first and second applicants were in respect of breaches of the peace which were later found to have been committed.
>
> 33. The Court must consider the question of whether behaviour *contra bonos mores* is adequately defined for the purposes of Article 10 § 2 of the Convention.
>
> 34. The Court first recalls that in its Steel and Others judgment, it noted that the expression 'to be of good behaviour' 'was particularly imprecise and offered little guidance to the person bound over as to the type of conduct which would amount to a breach of the order' (ibid., p. 2739, § 76). Those considerations apply equally in the present case, where the applicants were not charged with any criminal offence, and were found not to have breached the peace.
>
> 35. The Court next notes that conduct *contra bonos mores* is defined as behaviour which is 'wrong rather than right in the judgment of the majority of contemporary fellow citizens' (see paragraph 13 above). It cannot agree with the Government that this definition has the same objective element as conduct 'likely to cause annoyance', which was at issue in the case of *Chorherr v Austria* judgment of 25 August 1993, series A no 266-B.. The Court considers that the question of whether conduct is 'likely to cause annoyance' is a question which goes to the very heart of the nature of the conduct proscribed: it is conduct whose likely consequence is the annoyance of others. Similarly, the definition of breach of the peace given in the case of *Percy v. Director of Public Prosecutions* ... – that it includes conduct the natural consequences of which would be to provoke others to violence–also describes behaviour by reference to its effects. Conduct which is 'wrong rather than right in the judgment of the majority of contemporary citizens',[718] by contrast, is conduct which is not described at all, but merely expressed to be 'wrong' in the opinion of a majority of citizens.
>
> 36. Nor can the Court agree that the Government's other examples of behaviour which is defined by reference to the standards expected by the majority of contemporary opinion are similar to conduct *contra bonos mores* as in each case cited by the Government, the example given is but one element of a more comprehensive definition of the proscribed behaviour.
>
> 37. With specific reference to the facts of the present case, the Court does not accept that it must have been evident to the applicants what they were being ordered not do for the period of their binding over. Whilst in the case of Steel and Others the applicants had been found to have breached the peace, and the Court found that it was apparent that the bind over related to similar behaviour (ibid.), the present applicants did not breach the peace, and given the lack of precision referred to above, it cannot be said that what they were being bound over not to do must have been apparent to them.'

The decision in *Hashman* brings a welcome limitation to the use of binding-over powers. The Fifteenth Amendment to the Consolidated Criminal Practice Direction 2007 included revised provision for binding-over orders.[719] The Direction confirms the need to give the individual and the prosecutor the opportunity to make representations. The court must be satisfied beyond reasonable doubt of the matters complained of before an order may be imposed; and similarly satisfied beyond reasonable doubt that a breach has occurred before making any order for forfeiture of a recognisance.

---

[718] The test set out by Glidewell LJ in *Hughes v Holley* (1986) 86 Cr App R 130: ed.

[719] This followed a Home Office Consultation: *Bind Overs A power for the 21st Century* (March 2003). Ministers had decided that they wished to retain the flexibility of the powers but that sufficient certainty should be provided to comply with the ECHR.

4. Binding-over orders have been made in many cases following conviction for a criminal offence against public order.[720] In addition, they have been made against persons who incite disorder. The most celebrated instance is *Lansbury v Riley*[721] where George Lansbury spoke in support of militant suffragettes at a time when there were many attacks on property. He said that women 'ought to break the law on every possible occasion, short of taking human life'.[722] He was bound over in the sum of £1,000 with two sureties of £500. In the 1930s, several officers of the National Unemployed Workers' Movement were imprisoned for refusing to be bound over.[723] See also *Wise v Dunning*,[724] and *Beatty v Gillbanks*.[725]

(III) POWERS OF ENTRY TO PRESERVE THE PEACE

- **Thomas v Sawkins** [1935] 2 KB 249, 104 LJKB 572, 153 LT 419, 99 JP 295, 51 TLR 514, 33 LGR 330, 30 Cox CC, King's Bench Divisional Court

Case stated by Glamorgan (Newcastle and Ogmore) justices.

On 17 August 1934 a public meeting was held at the Large Hall of the Caerau Library to protest against the Incitement to Disaffection Bill then before Parliament and to demand the dismissal of the chief constable of the county of Glamorgan, at which meeting between 500 and 700 people were present. The principal speaker was to be Alun Thomas (the appellant). He had previously addressed meetings at Nantymoel (9 August), Caerau (14 August) and Maesteg (15 August). He had lodged a written complaint against the refusal of police officers to leave the Nantymoel meeting, had threatened physically to eject the police if they attended the meeting on 17 August, and had stated at the Maesteg meeting: 'If it were not for the presence of these people'—pointing to police officers—'I could tell you a hell of a lot more.'

The Library Hall was hired by one Fred Thomas, and the public were invited to attend, free of charge. The meeting was convened by (among others) Fred Thomas and Alun Thomas. Sergeant Sawkins (the respondent), together with Inspector Parry and Sergeant Lawrence, was refused admission by Fred Thomas. Nevertheless, the three officers entered the hall and sat on the front row. They also refused to leave on two occasions when requested to do so by Alun Thomas. Alun Thomas then stated that the police officers would be ejected, and he laid his hand on Inspector Parry to eject him. Sergeant Sawkins thereupon pushed Alun Thomas's arm and hand from Parry, saying: 'I won't allow you to interfere with my superior officer.' About 30 other police officers entered with batons drawn, and no further attempt was made to eject the police. In attempting to remove Parry, Alun Thomas used no more force than was reasonably necessary for that purpose, and Sawkins used no more force than was reasonably necessary (assuming that he and Parry had a right to be there) to protect Parry and to prevent him from being ejected.

The respondent did not allege that any criminal offence was committed. There was no breach of the peace or disorder at any time.

Alun Thomas preferred an information against Sergeant Sawkins alleging that Sawkins had committed assault and battery contrary to s. 42 of the Offences against the Person Act 1861. He claimed that the police officers were trespassers. If that was correct, he would be

---

[720] See *Williams*, pp. 94–95.   [721] [1914] 3 KB 229, DC.

[722] *Williams*, p. 97.

[723] Wal Hannington in 1922 and 1931; Sid Elias in 1931; Tom Mann and Emrhys Llewellyn in 1932: see *Williams*, pp. 99–100; J. Stevenson and C. Cook, *Society and Politics, 1929–1939, Britain in the Depression* (1994), p. 251.

[724] Above, p. 385.   [725] Above, p. 394.

entitled to use reasonable force to eject them, and forcible resistance by the police officers would be illegal. The justices concluded (33 LGR at 333):

Upon the above facts and evidence given before us we were and are of the opinion that the respondent and other police officers had reasonable grounds for believing that if they were not present at the meeting seditious speeches would be made and/or incitements to violence and/or breaches of the peace would take place and that they were entitled to enter and remain in the said hall and meeting.

They dismissed the information. Alun Thomas appealed. It was argued, *inter alia*, on behalf of Sawkins that:

The respondent was entitled to be present at the meeting. A constable by his oath swears to cause the peace to be preserved and to prevent the commission of all offences. Where, therefore, the police have reasonable grounds for believing that an offence may be committed or a breach of the peace occur, they have a right to enter private premises to prevent the commission of the offence or the occurrence of the breach of the peace. If that were not so, it would be extremely difficult for the police to exercise their powers of watch and ward and their duty of preventive justice ([1935] 2 KB at 253).

Lord Hewart CJ: It is apparent that the conclusion of the justices in this case consisted of two parts. One part was a conclusion of fact that the respondent and the police officers who accompanied him believed that certain things might happen at the meeting which was then about to be held. There were ample materials on which the justices could come to that conclusion. The second part of the justices' finding is no less manifestly an expression of opinion. Finding the facts as they do, and drawing from those facts the inference which they draw, they go on to say that the officers were entitled to enter and to remain on the premises on which the meeting was being held.

Against that determination, it is said that it is an unheard-of proposition of law, and that in the books no case is to be found which goes the length of deciding, that, where an offence is expected to be committed, as distinct from the case of an offence being or having been committed, there is any right in the police to enter on private premises and to remain there against the will of those who, as hirers or otherwise, are for the time being in possession of the premises. When, however, I look at the passages which have been cited from Blackstone's Commentaries, vol. i., p. 356, and from the judgments in *Humphries v Connor* (1864) 17 ICLR 1 [above, p. 523] and *O'Kelly v Harvey* (1883) 14 LR Ir 105 [above, p. 526] and certain observations of Avory J in *Lansbury v Riley* [1914] 3 KB 229 at 236, 237, I think that there is quite sufficient ground for the proposition that it is part of the preventive power, and, therefore, part of the preventive duty, of the police, in cases where there are such reasonable grounds of apprehension as the justices have found here, to enter and remain on private premises. It goes without saying that the powers and duties of the police are directed, not to the interests of the police, but to the protection and welfare of the public.

It was urged in one part of the argument of Sir Stafford Cripps that what the police did here amounted to a trespass. It seems somewhat remarkable to speak of trespass when members of the public who happen to be police officers attend, after a public invitation, a public meeting which is to discuss as one part of its business the dismissal of the chief constable of the county. It is elementary that a good defence to an action for trespass is to show that the act complained of was done by authority of law, or by leave and licence.

I am not at all prepared to accept the doctrine that it is only where an offence has been, or is being, committed, that the police are entitled to enter and remain on private premises. On the contrary, it seems to me that a police officer has ex virtue officii full right so to act when he has reasonable ground for believing that an offence is imminent or is likely to be committed.

I think, therefore, that the justices were right and that this appeal should be dismissed.

Avory J: I am of the same opinion. I think that it is very material in this particular case to observe that the meeting was described as a public meeting, that it was extensively advertised, and that the public were invited to attend. There can be no doubt that the police officers who attended the meeting were members of the public and were included in that sense in the invitation to attend. It is true that those who had hired the hall for the meeting might withdraw their invitation from any particular individual who was likely to commit a breach of the peace or some other offence, but it is quite a different proposition to say that they might withdraw the invitation from police officers who might be there for the express purpose of preventing a breach of the peace or the commission of an offence.

With regard to the general question regarding the right of the police to attend the meeting notwithstanding the opposition of the promoters, I cannot help thinking that that right follows from the description of the powers of a constable which Sir Stafford Cripps relies on in Stone's Justices' Manual, 1935, p. 208, where it is said that when a constable hears an affray in a house he may break in to suppress it and may, in pursuit of an affrayer, break in to arrest him. If he can do that, I cannot doubt that he has a right to break in to prevent an affray which he has reasonable cause to suspect may take place on private premises. In other words, it comes within his duty, as laid down by Blackstone (Commentaries, vol. i., p. 356), to keep the King's peace and to keep watch and ward. In my view, the right was correctly expressed in *R (Feehan) v Queen's County JJ* (1882) 10 LR Ir 294 at 301 where Fitzgerald J said: 'The foundation of the jurisdiction [to bind persons to be of good behaviour] is very remote, and probably existed prior to the statute of 1360–61; but whatever its foundation may be, or by whatever language conveyed, we are bound to regard and expound it by the light of immemorial practice and of decision, and especially of direct modem decisions. It may be described as a branch of preventive justice, in the exercise of which magistrates are invested with large judicial discretionary powers, for the maintenance of order and the preservation of the public peace.' That passage was expressly approved in *Lansbury v Riley* [1914] 3 KB 229 at 236 and the statement of the law which it contains was adopted by Lord Alverstone CJ in *Wise v Dunning* [1902] 1 KB 167 at 175; *R v Queen's County JJ* is there referred to sub nom *R v Cork JJ* (1882) 15 Cox CC 149. In principle I think that there is no distinction between the duty of a police constable to prevent a breach of the peace and the power of a magistrate to bind persons over to be of good behaviour to prevent a breach of the peace.

I am not impressed by the fact that many statutes have expressly given to police constables in certain circumstances the right to break open or to force an entrance into private premises. Those have all been cases in which a breach of the peace was not necessarily involved and it, therefore, required express statutory authority to empower the police to enter. In my opinion, no express statutory authority is necessary where the police have reasonable grounds to apprehend a breach of the peace, and in the present case I am satisfied that the justices had before them material on which they could properly hold that the police officers in question had reasonable grounds for believing that, if they were not present, seditious speeches would be made and/or that a breach of the peace would take place. To prevent any such offence or a breach of the peace the police were entitled to enter and to remain on the premises, and I agree that this appeal should be dismissed.

Lawrence J: As my Lord has pointed out, our judgment proceeds on the particular facts of this case, and on those facts I agree with the conclusion. I will only add that I am unable to follow the distinction which Sir Stafford Cripps has drawn between the present matter and the cases which have been cited. If a constable in the execution of his duty to preserve the peace is entitled to commit an assault, it appears to me that he is equally entitled to commit a trespass.

Appeal dismissed.

NOTES

1. Background information not available from the law reports is given in Williams, *Keeping the Peace*.[726] The case was adversely criticised by Goodhart.[727]

---

[726] (1967), pp. 142–149, and (1985) Cambrian LR 116.   [727] (1936–38) CLJ 22.

2. What is the ratio decidendi of the judgment of Lord Hewart CJ? Is it the ratio decidendi of the case? Is it a clear ratio? See *McLeod*.[728]

3. Where Lord Hewart states that a police officer may enter and remain on private premises 'when he has reasonable ground for believing that an offence is imminent or is likely to be committed', do you think that the point he was considering was (a) the *point of time* at which the police may intervene, or (b) the nature of the *offence* which has to be anticipated, or (c) both? Does Lord Hewart's judgment amount to an endorsement of the argument of counsel for Sawkins that there is a power to enter premises to prevent *any* offence? Note that the Police and Criminal Evidence Act 1984, s. 17(5), (6) abolishes all common law powers of entry except to deal with or prevent a breach of the peace.[729] Does s. 17(6) constitute an endorsement of *Thomas v Sawkins*?

4. Could Alun Thomas have been convicted of the offences of assaulting or obstructing a police officer in the execution of his duty?[730]

5. In principle, the occupier of land may grant or refuse permission (a 'licence') to someone seeking to go on to the land according to his own wishes, unless that other has a right to enter conferred by law. A gratuitous licence may be revoked at any time provided that reasonable notice is given.[731] A licensee must be given reasonable time to depart before his continued presence on the land constitutes trespass.[732]

Apart from the situation where there is a right to remain conferred by law, a licence will only be irrevocable where (a) it is protected by estoppel or equity; (b) the licence is coupled with a proprietary interest in other property; or (c) (in some circumstances) where the licence is granted by contract.[733] In view of this, would it be correct to say that the persons who hired the hall could *only* 'withdraw their invitation from any particular individual who was likely to commit a breach of the peace or some other offence'?[734] How is the position of the organiser of a *public* meeting different from that of a *private* meeting? Is it not simply the difference between a meeting to which there is a general invitation to the public, and one to which specific invitations are given? Can the fact that a meeting is 'public' limit the power of the *occupier* to refuse entry or to eject, as distinct (possibly) from marking the limit of the right of the *police* to enter private premises in anticipation of the commission of offences?

6. The ambiguity regarding the power to enter private premises whether or not there was a public meeting occurring was resolved by the Court of Appeal in *McLeod v MPC*.[735] The court held that there was a power to enter and remain on premises to deal with an apprehended breach of the peace. The Court of Appeal's decision as to the application of that principle to the facts was, however, rejected by the European Court.[736]

7. Consider the statement of Lawrence J that if a constable is 'entitled to commit an assault,... he is equally entitled to commit a trespass' in the light of s. 3 of the Criminal Law Act 1967.[737]

---

[728] Below.   [729] See above, p. 178.

[730] Cf. *Duncan v Jones* [1936] 1 KB 218, above, p. 392.

[731] Megarry and Wade, *The Law of Real Property* (5th edn, 1984), p. 799; N. Gravells, *Land Law: Text and Materials* (2nd edn, 1999), p. 490.

[732] *Robson v Hallett* [1967] 2 QB 939, above, p. 196; unless he makes it clear that he will not leave voluntarily (*Davis v Lisle* [1936] 2 KB 434, above, p. 195).

[733] See Megarry and Wade, pp. 801–805; N. Gravells, op. cit., pp. 489–534.

[734] Cf. Avory J.   [735] [1994] 4 All ER 553.   [736] See below, p. 405.

[737] Above, p. 151.

8. What is the position where a police officer has no legal right of entry but obtains permission to enter premises:

  (a) by concealing the fact that he is a police officer in circumstances where he knows that a policeman would not be admitted; or

  (b) by a false representation of fact (e.g. 'I thought I saw a burglar'); or

  (c) by a false representation of law (e.g. 'I have a legal power to enter'); or

  (d) by acquiescing in the self deception of the occupier (e.g. 'You've a right to come in so I suppose I'd better let you').[738]

9. In *Handcock v Baker*[739] the defendants were held entitled to break into a house where they had reasonable cause to believe that the occupier was about to kill his wife. Moreover, a constable may enter premises in fresh pursuit of a person who has committed a breach of the peace within his view.[740] The power to enter to prevent a breach of the peace can be used to deal with domestic disputes, but only to prevent an imminent breach of the peace,[741] not to investigate whether a breach of the peace was likely.[742]

10. In *Kuru v State of New South Wales*,[743] the majority of the High Court of Australia[744] stated that 'as has been cogently argued in academic commentary[745] on *Thomas v Sawkins*, the statements made by Avory J and Lord Hewart CJ ...[746] were cast in "unnecessarily wide terms" '. In any event, they did not extend to confer power to investigate 'whether a breach of the peace has occurred or determining whether one is threatened or imminent'.

11. In *McLeod v United Kingdom*[747] the applicant, Mrs McLeod, had been ordered by the court to return specified property to her former husband by a certain date as part of a divorce settlement. Mr McLeod believed that the applicant had consented to his taking the property. Owing to previous difficulties between the couple, Mr McLeod's solicitors had arranged for police officers to be present because of the potential for a breach of the peace. When Mr McLeod and the police arrived, Mrs McLeod was absent. The police entered and remained on the premises during the removal of the property by Mr McLeod. When Mrs McLeod arrived home, she objected to the removal of the property. The police ensured that Mr McLeod was allowed to remove the property and instructed Mrs McLeod that if she obstructed him, there was likely to be a breach of the peace for which she would be arrested. The applicant brought criminal proceedings against the police, but when they failed, she brought a civil action for trespass to her property—that also failed. The Court of Appeal dismissed her appeal: *McLeod v Metropolitan Police Comr.*[748] She took the case to the ECtHR alleging breach of Art. 8. The Court held that the entry onto the applicant's premises violated Art. 8 of the ECHR, and was not justifiable under Art. 8(2). The power of the police to enter private premises without a warrant to deal with or prevent a breach of the peace was defined with sufficient precision for the foreseeability criterion to be satisfied.

---

[738] Cf. above, p. 195.   [739] (1800) 2 Bos & P 260.

[740] See *R v Walker* (1854) Dears CC 358: *R v Marsden* (1868) LR 1 CCR 131.

[741] *Foulkes v Chief Constable of Merseyside Police* [1998] 3 All ER 705; *Chief Constable of Humberside Police v McQuade* [2001] EWCA Civ 1330, [2002] 1 WLR 1347 (ample grounds to arrest on the facts).

[742] *Friswell v Chief Constable of Essex Police* [2004] EWHC 3009 (QB).

[743] [2008] HCA 26, paras [46]–[51].

[744] Gleeson CJ, Gummow, Kirby and Hayne JJ.

[745] A. Goodhart (1936) 6 CLJ 22; D. Feldman, *The Law Relating to Entrty, Search and Seizure* (1986), pp. 324–331.

[746] [1935] 2 KB 249, 257, 255 respectively.   [747] (1999) 27 EHRR 493, ECtHR.

[748] [1994] 4 All ER 553, CA.

The interference was, therefore, 'in accordance with the law'. The aim of the power enabling police officers to enter private premises to prevent a breach of the peace was clearly a
legitimate one for the purposes of Art. 8, namely the prevention of disorder or crime, and
there was nothing to suggest that it was applied in the present case for any other purpose.
However, the means employed by the police officers were disproportionate to the legitimate aim pursued. The police could not be faulted for attending, as Mr McLeod's solicitors
genuinely feared a breach of the peace. However, the police did not take any steps to verify
whether Mr McLeod was entitled to enter her home on 3 October 1989 and remove his
property. They did not check the court order, which showed that it was for Mrs McLeod to
deliver the property and she had three more days to do so. The police should not have taken
it for granted, on the basis of Mr McLeod's claim, that an agreement had been reached
superseding the relevant parts of the court order. Upon being informed that Mrs McLeod
was not present, the police officers should not have entered her house, as it should have been
clear to them that there was little or no risk of disorder or crime occurring.

The two dissenting judges took the view that the police were 'fully entitled on the evidence to fear a breach of the peace'.[749] They expressed concern that the majority's ruling
may significantly weaken the position of the police in dealing with cases of domestic violence. They stated[750] that there were clear dangers of escalation in this situation. Professor
Ashworth[751] noted that the court was much more interventionist in this case than it has
been in other breach of the peace cases. He concludes that: 'All of this means that "breach
of the peace" can no longer be treated by the police as a wide-ranging justification for all
manner of actions.'

12. Before *Thomas v Sawkins*, it was generally accepted that the police had no power to enter
meetings on private premises unless they had reason to believe that a breach of the peace
was *actually taking place*. This was stated to be the position by the *Departmental Committee
on the Duties of the Police with respect to the Preservation of Order at Public Meetings*,[752] and
by the Home Secretary, Sir John Gilmour, in a debate arising out of the Fascist meeting at
Olympia on 7 June 1934 where there was considerable violence.[753] Cf. *Robson v Hallett*.[754]

13. Contrary to expectations which might be engendered by *Thomas v Sawkins*,
Williams has noted 'the apparent determination of the police to avoid wherever possible
any entanglement in the protests and demonstrations taking place on private property'.[755]
This was particularly marked in relation to sit-ins at universities in the late 1960s. Cf. *R
v Dytham*,[756] where a constable was convicted of the common law misdemeanour of misconduct of a public officer in that he failed to fulfil his duty to preserve the peace. He had
witnessed a man being beaten and kicked to death outside a club, but had taken no steps to
intervene.

---

[749] Para. 2.   [750] Para. 4.   [751] [1999] Crim LR 156.
[752] Cd 4673, 1909, p. 6.   [753] 290 HC Deb, 14 June 1934, col. 1968.
[754] Above, p. 196.   [755] D.G.T. Williams [1970] CLJ 96, 116.   [756] [1979] QB 722, CA (Cr D).

6

EMERGENCY POWERS; THE PROBLEM OF POLITICAL TERRORISM

1. INTRODUCTION

The most extreme form of emergency which the country may face is war. In earlier times, the Crown relied on prerogative powers to take steps necessary for the conduct of war.[1] Each of the two world wars saw the creation of a complex edifice of statutory powers, mostly contained in delegated legislation made under the Defence of the Realm Acts 1914–15 and the Emergency Powers (Defence) Acts 1939–40. Every aspect of national life was closely regulated. Commentators were able to poke fun at the inevitable fatuity of some of the controls.[2] The interest of civil liberties was equally inevitably and equally swiftly relegated to a lesser rank in the order of national priorities. These measures have attracted both support, inasmuch as Britain had 'created the means of preserving itself from disaster without sacrificing the essential processes of democracy'[3] and stringent criticism.[4] Economic difficulties caused certain aspects of wartime regulation to be prolonged after the cessation of hostilities.

The major statute dealing with peacetime emergencies is now the Civil Contingencies Act 2004, which enables the state to obtain extraordinarily wide-ranging powers by regulation in such circumstances.[5]

That the royal prerogative is also a source of legal powers in relation to the maintenance 'of what is popularly called the Queen's peace within the realm' was affirmed by the Court of Appeal in *R v Secretary of State for the Home Department, ex p Northumbria Police Authority*.[6]

This chapter concentrates in particular on how the pressures for additional legal powers to combat terrorism can be reconciled with legitimate demands for the protection of civil

---

[1] See A.W. Bradley and K.D. Ewing, *Constitutional and Administrative Law* (14th edn, 2007), pp. 260, 343–347.

[2] See, e.g., C.K. Allen, *Law and Disorder* (1954).   [3] C.P. Cotter (1953) 5 Stanford LR 382, 416.

[4] See C.K. Allen, *Law and Order* (1st edn, 1945); R. Kidd, *British Liberty in Danger* (1940), Part Two; N. Stammers, *Civil Liberties in Britain during the Second World War* (1983).

[5] See critique by C. Walker and J. Broderick, *The Civil Contingencies Act 2004: Risk, Resilience and the Law in the United Kingdom* (OUP, Oxford, 2006); C. Walker, 'Governance of the Critical National Infrastructure' [2008] PL 323. The Centre for the Protection of National Infrastructure (CPNI), which is accountable to the Director General of the Security Service, provides protective security advice to businesses and organisations across the national infrastructure, aiming to reduce its vulnerability to terrorist and other threats: www.cpni. gov.uk.

[6] [1989] QB 26. See p. 283.

liberties. The international standards applicable to the exercise of police powers[7] apply here, subject to the point that some may be (and have been) the subject of derogation by the UK.[8]

2. POLITICAL TERRORISM[9]

Political terrorism has been defined[10] as:

the use, or threat of use, of violence by an individual or a group, whether acting for or in opposition to established authority, when such action is designed to create extreme anxiety and/or fear-inducing effects in a target larger than the immediate victims with the purpose of coercing that group into acceding to the political demands of the perpetrators.[11]

While the systematic employment of terrorist tactics can be traced back to the French Revolution and various political movements in late nineteenth century Europe, there has over the last 30 years been both a dramatic increase in the incidence of terrorism in the world, and significant changes in its nature. These changes are related to various factors, including technological developments in weaponry, the increasing sophistication of the news media (media coverage often being a major objective of terrorists), the dependence of heavily industrialised societies on a decreasing number of critical locations or processes (e.g. commercial aircraft, gas pipelines, electric power grids, government computers) and the development of links between terrorist groups in different countries.[12] For liberal democracies, the choice of appropriate measures poses problems:

The primary objective of counter-terrorist strategy must be the protection and maintenance of liberal democracy and the rule of law. It cannot be sufficiently stressed that this aim overrides in importance even the objective of eliminating terrorism and political violence as such. Any bloody tyrant can 'solve' the problem of political violence if he is prepared to sacrifice all considerations of humanity, and to trample down all constitutional and judicial rights.[13]

This point is developed in the following extract:[14]

However serious the threat of terrorism, we must not be tempted to use repressive methods to combat it. To believe that we can 'protect' liberal democracy by suspending our normal rights and methods of government is to ignore the numerous examples in contemporary history of countries where 'temporary', 'emergency' rule has subsided quickly and irrevocably into permanent dictatorial forms of government. While we must avoid the easy move to repression as a counter to terrorism, it is equally vital that

---

[7] Above, Chap. 3.   [8] See pp. 435, 455.

[9] For general surveys, see; C. Gearty, *Terror* (Faber and Faber, London, 2001); G. Wardlaw, *Political Terrorism* (2nd edn, 1989); C. Townshend, *Terrorism* (OUP, Oxford, 2002).

[10] Cf. a 'straightforward definition', noted by Gearty (in *Can Human Rights Survive?* (CUP, Cambridge, 2006), p. 410) 'that sees as terrorist violence, the intentional or reckless killing or injuring of non-combatants, or the doing of serious damage to their property, in order to communicate a political message'. These are two of many definitions; there is much writing and little agreement on what a correct definition might be (or even if there can be a definition): see Gearty, op. cit., and Townshend, op. cit., Chap. 1.

[11] G. Wardlaw, *Political Terrorism* (2nd edn, 1989), p. 16.

[12] See G. Wardlaw, op. cit., Chap. 3.   [13] P. Wilkinson, *Terrorism and the Liberal State* (1977), p. 121.

[14] G. Wardlaw, op. cit., pp. 69–70.

we do not allow ourselves to be so overcome by our democratic sensibilities that our response is weak and vacillating, and characterised by inaction. It is as much a betrayal of our beliefs and responsibilities to do not enough as to do too much. We must uphold constitutional authority and law and order, and we must do so with firmness and determination. To do so requires political will; but most importantly it requires citizen support. To gain such support the political will must be translated into effective action. First, the government must be open and honest about its policies and objectives. As will be stressed when we come to examine the role of the army in counter-terrorism, it is particularly important in a society such as ours to spell out clearly the circumstances under which military aid to the civil power would be invoked, the rights and responsibilities of military personnel operating in an internal security role, and the lines of control and command.

Second, the government must accord full and proper support to its civil and security force personnel who are involved in counter-terrorist operations. In particular, it is necessary to avoid sudden changes in security policy which could undermine both official and public confidence in the government's ability to handle difficult situations. Policy vacillations also expose weaknesses and differences within the government ranks which can be exploited by terrorists.

Third, any anti-terrorist measures must be, and be seen to be, directed only at terrorists. The response must be limited, well-defined, and controlled. It must also, wherever at all possible, be publicly explained....

It is most important that executive control of anti-terrorist and security policy rests with the civil authorities (the elected government) who are accountable to the people for their actions. Further, it should be both policy and practice for the government and its security forces to act within the law. Not only does failure to do so place the government in a morally difficult position (if it does not obey the law, why should anyone?) but also such action is likely to undermine their support and provide valuable ammunition for a terrorist cause. Propaganda capital can very easily be made out of violations of the law by government servants, and such propaganda can be used as additional justification for a terrorist campaign. While the law can be a refuge for the law-breaker and a hindrance to the law enforcement official, the law is the basis of our system of government and must be upheld. Otherwise are we any better than the terrorist who also argues on the grounds of expediency?

It is important to note at this point that modern usage (particularly by states, both authoritarian and purportedly liberal) tends to give a broader meaning to the term:

...we have come to view terrorism not as a method of violence but rather as category of person, a kind of militant rather than a kind of tactic, the sort of thing a person is rather than the kind of thing a person does....Once a group is classified as terrorist it becomes terrorist to all intents and purposes—the label does not require evidence of specific acts of terror to be made to work.[15]

Definitions enshrined in legislation also tend to be wider[16] and

to complete this story of verbal degradation, we have so contrived matters that terrorism is now widely thought of as something of which state authorities...are incapable.

It has become a label applied indiscriminately to subversive, sub-national groups, 'regardless of the content of their actions'.[17] Further distortion has been engendered by the success of politicians and commentators in persuading public opinion of the need for a 'global war

---

15 C. Gearty, *Can Human Rights Survive?* (CUP, Cambridge, 2006), pp. 111–112.
16 See pp. 416–417.   17 Gearty, op. cit., pp 112–113.

on terror'. This both diverts attention away from the use of violence by states and facilitates the introduction of special legislation removing the protection of normal human rights standards.[18]

In the UK until relatively recently the major problem of terrorism was created by the Northern Ireland conflict, although there were a number of terrorist incidents reflecting struggles between groups of foreign nationals,[19] and, following the terrorist actions in the US on 11 September 2001, increased fears of campaigns directed at the UK Government. These fears were turned to reality by the events of July 2005 in London. On 7 July, three bombs exploded without warning on London Underground trains and a fourth bomb on a bus in Tavistock Square. The four bombers, subsequently identified as Islamic extremists, were killed. Fifty-two members of the public were killed and about 700 injured. On 21 July the detonators only of four further bombs on the underground exploded. The bombers escaped, but were subsequently arrested. Consequences have included: (a) the enactment of further legislation: the Anti-terrorism, Crime and Security Act 2000 (after 9/11); the Prevention of Terrorism Act 2005; the Terrorism Act 2006; and see now the Counter-Terrorism Bill 2008; (b) extensive reviews by the Government and its agencies of their arrangements to prevent such occurrences including a number of official reports[20] (but not a public inquiry);[21] and (c) the shooting by police of John Charles de Menezes in the mistaken belief that he was a suicide bomber.[22]

Since 2003, the Government has had a long-term Counter-terrorism strategy (CONTEST),[23] with four principal strands, Prevent, Pursue, Protect and Prepare. Its aim is to reduce the risk from international terrorism, and is not entirely a package of laws. Elements include addressing problems such as inequalities and discrimination that may contribute to radicalisation, changing the environment in which extremists can operate and engaging in the battle of ideas, primarily by helping Muslims who wish to dispute ideologies that extremists believe can justify the use of violence; pursuing terrorists and those that sponsor them; protecting the public, key national services and UK interests overseas; and preparing for the consequences. Spending was to double to £2bn by 2008. The Government also publishes an assessment of the current terrorism threat level which (in December 2008) was 'severe'.[24]

As regards the legal framework, up to the enactment of the Terrorism Act 2000, distinctly different legal regimes designed to deal with terrorism applied respectively in

---

[18] Ibid, pp. 113–139.

[19] E.g. the Iranian Embassy siege in 1980 (see G. Brock et al., *Siege* (1980)) and the Libyan Embassy siege in 1984.

[20] *Report of the Official Account of the Bombings in London on 7th July 2005* (2005–06 HC 1087, 11 May 2006) (see http://security.homeoffice.gov.uk/); *Intelligence and Security Committee Report into the London Terrorist Attacks on 7 July 2005* (Cm 6785, 2006). See also *Addressing lessons from the emergency response to the 7 July 2005 London bombings: What we learned and what we are doing about it* (Home Office, DCMS, 22 September 2006).

[21] BBC News, 14 December 2005. It was reported that ministers had decided that it would divert attention and resources away from pressing security and community issues, and take too long.

[22] See p. 501.

[23] It was published in 2006: *Countering International Terrorism: The United Kingdom's Strategy* (Cm 6888, July 2006). See also *The National Security Strategy of the United Kingdom* (Cm 7291, 2008).

[24] I.e. 'an attack is highly likely'; this is on a scale comprising low, moderate, substantial, severe and critical: www.homeoffice.gov.uk/security/current-threat-level/. See *Threat Levels: The System to Assess the Threat from International Terrorism* (Home Office, July 2006). It has been 'severe' since 1 August 2006 (the date of first publication), apart from 10–14 August 2006 (following the disruption of a major terrorist plot to target UK flights) and 30 June to 4 July 2007 (following an incident at Glasgow Airport) when it was 'critical' (i.e. 'an attack is expected imminently').

Northern Ireland and in the rest of the United Kingdom. 'Emergency powers' or 'special powers' had existed in Ireland without a break from the nineteenth century. The latest was a series of Northern Ireland (Emergency Provisions) Acts; the first was passed in 1973 and the last in 1996 (amended in 1998). Elsewhere in the United Kingdom, legislation was enacted in response to perceived threats. In 1974, Parliament passed the Prevention of Terrorism (Temporary Provisions) Act following the Birmingham pub bombings. It was, in turn, replaced by Acts of 1984 and 1989. Some of its provisions extended to Northern Ireland; others did not. Both sets of provisions were subject to annual renewal.

The Terrorism Act 2000 puts a body of measures to combat terrorism drawn from both regimes on the statute book as permanent legislation; the dual arrangement whereby certain additional powers were available in Northern Ireland was reflected in their continuation in Part VII of the Act, which was subject to annual renewal, but which has now lapsed.[25]

One of the themes of the legislation since the 2000 Act has been the need to address a particular dilemma posed by the growing threat within the UK of international terrorists. Where there is admissible evidence, whose source can be disclosed in open court, that any terrorist has committed a substantive criminal offence, then proceedings can be taken in the ordinary way.[26] Suspects can be detained for a limited period while investigations are conducted.[27] Once charged a person can be remanded in custody pending trial. Recurring problems arise where, first, there are proper concerns that disclosure of the source would be against the public interest, for example by exposing a witness to danger or compromising other operations by the investigatory authorities. The question then becomes whether an effective prosecution can be conducted that is compatible with the requirements of a fair trial. If such a prosecution cannot be conducted, and in any other case where there is insufficient admissible evidence to support a prosecution, the question then becomes what steps can be taken to prevent suspected terrorists from committing offences in the future.

A mechanism that has been employed in the past is that of detention without trial, or internment. Internment powers have existed for extended periods and have been invoked from time to time, most recently on 9 August 1971 in Northern Ireland.[28] This is widely regarded as having been a mistake, generating support for paramilitary groups. The policy was ended in 1975. The powers remained in the Northern Ireland (Emergency Provisions) Act 1991 but were never commenced. The Labour Party consistently opposed the existence of such powers.[29] The existing powers were repealed by s. 3 of the Northern Ireland (Emergency Provisions) Act 1998; they were not included in the 2000 Act, and there have been no serious proposals for their resurrection (at least as such). As regards suspected terrorists who are not British citizens, there is the possibility that they can be deported. Section 3(5) of the Immigration Act 1971[30] provides that a person who is not a British citizen is liable to deportation from the UK, *inter alia*, 'if the Secretary of State deems his deportation to be conducive to the public good'. Crucially, however, this power cannot lawfully be

---

25 See below, pp. 413–414.
26 E.g. the prosecutions of the 21/7 bombers: *R v Ibrahim* [2008] EWCA Crim 880 (upholding convictions for conspiracy to murder and 40-year sentences); *R v Jalil* [2008] EWCA Crim 2910 (conspiracy to murder).
27 See p. 438.
28 See *Ireland v UK* (1978) 2 EHRR 25; the 4th edn of this book, pp. 289–290.
29 See *Walker*, p. 31.
30 Substituted by the Immigration and Asylum Act 1999, Sch. 14, paras 43, 44(2).

exercised where there are substantial grounds for believing that an individual 'would face a real risk of being subjected to treatment contrary to Art. 3 ([ECHR]) if removed to another state'.[31] Furthermore,

in these circumstances, the activities of the individual in question, however undesirable or dangerous, cannot be a material consideration.[32]

This leaves a significant number of suspected terrorists who cannot lawfully be deported, and who therefore cannot be detained under immigration law pending deportation.[33] The first attempt of the Government to plug the gap came in the form of orders for the detention of suspected international terrorists (who could not be deported) under ss. 21–32 of the Anti-terrorism, Crime and Security Act 2001. The UK derogated from the ECHR in respect of these powers. In the landmark case of *A v Secretary of State for the Home Department*,[34] the House of Lords upheld the validity of the derogation order but held that the detention order regime was incompatible with the ECHR. The regime lapsed, but the case remains a key authority on the proper approach of the courts to these issues. This in turn led to the introduction of control orders under the Terrorism Act 2005, which have led to a stream of cases testing the limits of their compatibility with Art. 5 ECHR.[35] One particular area that has given rise to particular controversy has been the Government's wish to extend the period of detention without charge at the investigation stage to 42 days.[36] Finally there have been further successful prosecutions for substantive criminal offences arising out of terrorist activities.[37]

In considering the materials in this chapter, attention should be paid to the underlying question whether the case has been made by the state for state powers over and above those available in, or deviations from the standards normally applicable to, the normal criminal justice process. A consistent theme of the commentators is that there is not; a consistent theme of official reviewers is that there is. There is recurrent criticism that new legislation is introduced as a hurried response to a particular incident and rushed through Parliament without adequate scrutiny, and that it is designed more to show that the Government is 'taking action' than to respond to demonstrated needs.[38] Some of the more recent legislative developments have, however, been introduced after more substantial consultation, commonly in the face of significant opposition, not least from the Joint Committee on Human Rights.[39]

---

[31] *Chahal v UK* (1996) 23 EHRR 413, para. 80.   [32] Ibid.

[33] See below, p. 455.

[34] [2004] UKHL 56, [2005] 2 AC 68. Below, p. 455.

[35] Below, pp. 475–485.   [36] Below, p. 492.

[37] See e.g. *R v Abu Hamza* [2006] EWCA Crim 2918, [2007] QB 659 (upholding convictions of AH for inciting foreign nationals to commit murder abroad: *A-G's References (Nos 85 of 2007, 86 of 2007 and 87 of 2007)*, *R v Tsouli* [2007] EWCA Crim 3300, [2008] 2 Cr App R (S) 247 (incitement to murder); *R v Barot* [2007] EWCA Crim 1119, [2008] 1 Cr App R (S) 156 (upholding discretionary life sentence for conspiracy to murder arising out of the preparation of proposals for murder in the US and the UK). Further details of prosecutions are set out on the MI5 website: www.mi5.gov.uk.

[38] Cf. the statement on the Home Office website: 'The Government has announced a tough new counter-terrorism bill.'

[39] See e.g. http://security.homeoffice.gov.uk/news-publications/publication-search/counter-terrorism-bill-2007/.

3. THE TERRORISM ACT 2000[40]

- Terrorism Act 2000

Part I
Introductory

1. Terrorism: interpretation

(1) In this Act 'terrorism' means the use or threat of action where—

    (a) the action falls within subsection (2),

    (b) the use or threat is designed to influence the government [or an international governmental organisation][41] or to intimidate the public or a section of the public, and

    (c) the use or threat is made for the purpose of advancing a political, religious or ideological cause.

(2) Action falls within this subsection if it—

    (a) involves serious violence against a person,

    (b) involves serious damage to property,

    (c) endangers a person's life, other than that of the person committing the action,

    (d) creates a serious risk to the health or safety of the public or a section of the public, or

    (e) is designed seriously to interfere with or seriously to disrupt an electronic system.

(3) The use or threat of action falling within subsection (2) which involves the use of firearms or explosives is terrorism whether or not subsection (1)(b) is satisfied.

(4) In this section—

    (a) 'action' includes action outside the United Kingdom,

    (b) a reference to any person or to property is a reference to any person, or to property, wherever situated,

    (c) a reference to the public includes a reference to the public of a country other than the United Kingdom, and

    (d) 'the government' means the government of the United Kingdom, of a Part of the United Kingdom or of a country other than the United Kingdom.

(5) In this Act a reference to action taken for the purposes of terrorism includes a reference to action taken for the benefit of a proscribed organisation.

NOTES (PART I: INTRODUCTORY)

1. The Terrorism Act 2000[42] repealed the Prevention of Terrorism (Temporary Provisions) Act 1989 and the Northern Ireland (Emergency Provisions) Act 1996. Part VII, which was derived from the EPA and contained additional measures for Northern Ireland, was to cease to have effect at the end of 12 months from its commencement, but could be extended by

---

[40] See J.J. Rowe, *Current Law Statutes Annotated 2000*; Home Office Circular 03/01, C. Walker, *Blackstone's Guide to the Anti-terrorism Legislation* (2002). See, generally, N. Whitty. T. Murphy and S. Livingstone, *Civil Liberties Law: The Human Rights Act Era* (2001), Chap. 3; D. Moeckli, *Human Rights and Non-discrimination in the 'War on Terror'* (OUP, Oxford, 2008); C. Walker [2004] Crim LR 311; B. Brandon [2004] Crim LR 981.

[41] Inserted by the Terrorism Act 2006, s. 34(a).   [42] S. 2.

order of the Secretary of State approved by an affirmative resolution of each House, subject to a maximum term of five years.[43] In the event, Part VII was renewed every year between 2002 and 2005.[44] The Terrorism (Northern Ireland) Act 2006 extended it further but provided that it should cease to have effect from the end of 31 July 2007.[45] This formed part of the process of security normalisation in Northern Ireland following an IRA statement of 28 July 2005 that its leadership had formally ordered an end to its armed campaign.[46]

The 2000 Act was enacted following a review of terrorism legislation by Lord Lloyd[47] and the publication of a consultation paper.[48] The Government agreed with Lord Lloyd that 'there will be a continuing need for counter-terrorist legislation for the foreseeable future', regardless of the threat of terrorism related to Northern Ireland, and that the time had come for it to be put on a permanent footing.[49]

2. Historical origins

(a) *Prevention of terrorism legislation.* The Prevention of Terrorism (Temporary Provisions) Act 1989 had its origins in the Prevention of Violence (Temporary Provisions) Act 1939[50] which was also designed to deal with terrorism relating to Irish affairs, and was in force between 1939 and 1954. The Prevention of Terrorism (Temporary Provisions) Act 1974[51] was passed in the aftermath of the Birmingham public house bombings of 21 November 1974 when 21 people were killed and over 180 injured. The Bill was introduced on 27 November and received the Royal Assent on 29 November. It was re-enacted, with some amendments, as the Prevention of Terrorism (Temporary Provisions) Act 1976.[52] The 1976 Act was replaced by the Prevention of Terrorism (Temporary Provisions) Act 1984 following Lord Jellicoe's *Review of the Operation of the Prevention of Terrorism (Temporary Provisions) Act 1976.*[53] The 1984 Act was in turn replaced by the 1989 Act, following Lord Colville's *Review of the Operation of the Prevention of Terrorism (Temporary Provisions) Act 1984.*[54] The Labour Party was committed to the repeal of the 1989 Act[55] but the Labour Government elected in 1997 did not take this step and, indeed, secured the passage of new permanent legislation.

(b) *Northern Ireland emergency provisions legislation.* There have been many occasions in Irish history when the government of the day has secured the enactment of wider statutory powers to deal with the problem of security than those normally available in Great Britain.[56] In the nineteenth century, for example, the protection of Persons and Property Act (Ireland) 1881,[57] the Peace Preservation (Ireland) Act 1881,[58] the Prevention of Crime (Ireland) Act 1882,[59] and the Criminal Law and Procedure (Ireland) Act 1887,[60] included many provisions similar to those contained in the Northern Ireland (Emergency Provisions) Act 1996,

---

[43] S. 112.   [44] SI 2002/365; SI 2003/427; SI 2004/431; SI 2005/350.

[45] S. 1.   [46] Explanatory Note, paras 5, 6.

[47] *Inquiry into legislation against terrorism* (Cm 3420, 1996) (hereafter, *Lloyd Inquiry*).

[48] *Legislation Against Terrorism* (Cm 4178, 1998).

[49] Ibid., Introduction. Vol. 2 of the *Lloyd Inquiry* comprised an assessment by Professor Paul Wilkinson of the current and potential future terrorist threat to the UK from both international and domestic groups.

[50] See O.G. Lomas [1980] PL 16.   [51] See H. Street [1975] Crim LR 192.

[52] The operation of the 1976 Act was reviewed by Lord Shackleton in a report for the Home Office, *Review of the Operation of the Prevention of Terrorism (Temporary Provisions) Acts 1974 and 1976* (Cmnd 7324, 1978).

[53] Cmnd 8803, 1983.

[54] Cm 264, 1987 (hereafter, *Colville Review (PTA)*). For comments on the PTA and these reviews, see the references in the previous edition of this book at pp. 567–568. See further on the background to the introduction of the 1974 PTA, D. Bonner, 'Responding to Crisis: Legislating against Terrorism' (2006) 122 LQR 602.

[55] See H. Arnott, 'Breaking the Silence', *Legal Action*, May 1990, p. 25.

[56] See, generally, C. Townshend, *Political Violence in Ireland* (1983).

[57] 44 Vict., c. 4.   [58] 45 Vict., c. 5.

[59] 45 & 46 Vict., c. 25.   [60] 50 & 51 Vict., c. 20.

including powers of detention, arrest and search, and trial without a jury for certain kinds of offence. In addition there were at various times powers to prohibit meetings, provisions as to special juries and the change of venue of trials, and provisions making intimidation an offence.

In the twentieth century, the main piece of 'emergency' legislation in Northern Ireland was the Civil Authorities (Special Powers) Act (NI) 1922 and the regulations made thereunder. This was originally intended as a temporary measure, but was renewed annually until 1928 and then for five years to 1933. It was then provided that the Act 'shall continue in force until Parliament otherwise determines' by the Civil Authorities (Special Powers) Act (NI) 1933.[61] The content of the regulations was altered from time to time, and certain features were strongly criticised.[62] One of the most objectionable provisions was s. 2(4) of the 1922 Act which provided that:

If any person does any act of such a nature as to be calculated to be prejudicial to the preservation of the peace or maintenance of order in Northern Ireland and not specifically provided for in the regulations, he shall be deemed to be guilty of an offence against the regulations.

This has had no counterpart in the successive Northern Ireland (Emergency Provisions) Acts.

The legal procedures to deal with terrorist activities were reviewed by the Diplock Commission.[63] The Northern Ireland (Emergency Provisions) Act 1973 (which repealed the Special Powers Acts) was based upon their recommendations. The legislation was amended in 1975, consolidated in 1978, amended again in 1987,[64] consolidated with yet further amendments in 1991, consolidated again in 1996 and amended in 1998. It has been the subject of major reviews.[65] One of its features was a steady increase in size and scope.

The 1991 Act was analysed by B. Dickson,[66] who argued[67] that:

Whatever the position in the early 1970s, the objective behind anti-terrorist legislation today, whether in Northern Ireland or in Great Britain, is no longer the prevention of atrocities or the detection and punishment of those who perpetrate them. Its real purpose is to placate the electorate, as well as some of the elected, who demand that some steps must be taken by the law to counteract terrorism, regardless of how effective these might prove in practice. Emergency law, in other words, is being exploited for its symbolic significance.

---

[61] S. 2.

[62] See the *Report of a Commission of Inquiry appointed to examine the purpose and effect of the Civil Authorities (Special Powers) Acts (NI) 1922 and 1933* (NCCL, 1936); *A Review of the 1936 NCCL Commission of Inquiry into the light of subsequent events* (NCCL, 1972): J. Ll. J. Edwards [1956] Crim LR 7; H. Calvert, *Constitutional Law in Northern Ireland* (1968), pp. 380–386; *Emergency Powers: A Fresh Start*, Fabian Tract 416 (1972).

[63] Report (Cmnd 5185, 1972); see W.L. Twining [1972] Crim LR 407.

[64] On the 1987 Act, see J.D. Jackson (1988) 39 NILQ 235.

[65] The Gardiner Committee (Cmnd 5847, 1975); above, p. 563; the Bennett Committee Inquiry into *Police Interrogation Procedures in Northern Ireland* (Cmnd 7497, 1989); Sir George Baker, *Review of the Operation of the Northern Ireland (Emergency Provisions) Act 1978* (Cmnd. 9222, 1984); Viscount Colville, *Review of the Northern Ireland (Emergency Provisions) Act 1978 and 1987* (Cm 1115, 1990); J. J. Rowe QC, *Review of the Northern Ireland (Emergency Provisions) Act 1991* (Cm 2706, 1995) (hereafter, *Rowe Review (EPA)*).

[66] 'Northern Ireland's Emergency Legislation' [1992] PL 592. For reviews of decisions of the House of Lords arising out of the Northern Ireland conflict, see S. Livingstone (1994) 57 MLR 333 and B. Dickson (2006) 69 MLR 383 (noting a 'sea-change' in the approach).

[67] P. 597.

3. *Statistics and monitoring.* Statistics as to the operation of the PTA 1989 were given regularly in Home Office Statistical Bulletins. Annual reviews of that Act were conducted, successively, by Sir Cyril Philips (1984–1985), Lord Colville (1986–1992) and John Rowe QC (1993–2000). Similar reviews of the EPA were conducted by Colville (1987–1992) and Rowe (1993–2000) and published by the Northern Ireland Office. These reports formed the background to the annual renewal debates. The 2000 Act requires that a report on its working be laid before Parliament at least once in every 12 months.[68] Lord Carlile of Berriew QC has been appointed Independent Reviewer under the 2000, 2005 and 2006 Acts, and was also reviewer for the detention provision under Pt 4 of the Anti-terrorism, Crime and Security Act 2001. He has generally found the provisions of the 2000 Act to be necessary and proportionate. There were also, periodically, major reviews of the PTA and EPA legislative regimes.[69]

4. *Definition of terrorism.* The definition of terrorism in s. 1 is both broader and narrower than previous definitions. Section 20 of the PTA 1989 and s. 58 of the EPA 1996 referred to 'the use of violence for political ends [including] any use of violence for the purpose of putting the public, or any section of the public in fear'. The PTA also conferred powers only in respect of terrorism connected with the affairs of Northern Ireland or international terrorism. The 2000 Act applies to *serious* violence etc. but introduces a reference to religious and ideological purposes and the Act applies to both domestic and international terrorism. In which circumstances could an industrial dispute fall within the definition? Or the disruption of fuel supplies?

In justifying the extension, the Government noted that the methods employed by terrorists and the effects of their actions were common whatever the cause espoused by them. Furthermore, there was a sufficient threat from domestic terrorists, including animal rights activists and to a lesser extent environmental rights activists, to justify special powers. The threat of Scottish and Welsh nationalist extremists had considerably diminished, but there was a possibility that terrorist groups might develop in other contexts, such as in opposition to abortion (where there had been bombings and murders in the US).[70] Subsequent events have reinforced rather than detracted from the case for at least some special measures to deal with international terrorism.

The reference in s. 1(4)(d) to the 'government' of a country other than the UK is not confined to countries 'governed by what may broadly be described as democratic or representative principles', but extends to 'countries which are governed by tyrants and dictators'.[71] There was no reason to deprive the inhabitants of such countries of the protection afforded by the Act and the general application of the legislation was consistent with the UK's ECHR obligation to take appropriate steps to safeguard life.

Lord Carlile regards the definition as 'practical and effective' and has stated that 'there is little evidence that a change to a more restricted and equal definition could be found'; however, as the definition is broad, implementation 'calls for restraint'.[72] He made a full report on the matter in 2007,[73] noting that there was no single definition that commands full international approval.[74] He identified[75] four possible approaches: (a) no definition needed, no special procedures; (b) definition needed but no special procedures or offences: adjustment to

---

[68] S. 126.   [69] See above.   [70] *Legislation against Terrorism*, Chap. 3.

[71] *R v F* [2007] EWCA Crim 243, [2007] QB 960, per Sir Igor Judge P at paras [19], [32]. See comments by C. Walker [2008] Crim LR 162; E. Metcalfe (2006) 3 JJ 62.

[72] *Review on the Operation in 2002 and 2003 of the Terrorism Act 2000*, p. 5.

[73] *The Definition of Terrorism* (Cm 7052, 2007). See C. Walker [2007] PL 331.

[74] Pp. 4, 47.   [75] P. 19.

sentencing powers adequate; (c) definition needed, including special procedure and offences, but a tighter definition than at present; and (d) as (c), but drawn broadly and to anticipate estimates of future terrorism activity. Critics of the current, broad, approach included the Joint Committee on Human Rights,[76] and Amnesty International, but they did not provide an alternative formulation.[77] Lord Carlile was

in no doubt, for the time being at least, there are groups of people dedicated to violent and lethal jihad....[W]ithin the UK there is abundant material, some of it necessarily outside the public domain for reasons of national security, to support the view that numerous terrorist cells are active.

There were also other organisations and persons with broadly terrorist purposes and means, such as animal rights extremists; generally these were dealt with under the ordinary criminal law. There were many examples of individuals who might fall inappropriately within the present definition. Nevertheless, the risk level posed by violent jihadists and some other terrorist groupings provided the primary justification for dealing with them in a special way.[78] The 2000 Act powers (apart from reservations about s. 44)[79] were necessary and proportional. Accordingly a definition was necessary. The provision of special sentencing powers for apparently ordinary offences was recommended.[80] He rejected arguments in favour of the exclusion of offences against property, or for a religious purpose, or lacking a sufficient political or ideological component/nature; and the creation of a defence in respect of terrorism in a just cause. Overall there was no demanding reason for change, apart from minor changes in wording.[81] He agreed with the view that mere preaching and glorification should not be capable of being regarded as a terrorist offence, but the Terrorism Act 2006 did not do that.[82] The creation of a defence in respect of action designed to further international humanitarian law (e.g. for freedom fighters) would be contrary to international treaty obligations.[83] Extraterritorial use should require the Attorney-General's approval.

Part II
Proscribed Organisations
PROCEDURE

3. Proscription

(1) For the purposes of this Act an organisation is proscribed if—

    (a) it is listed in Schedule 2, or

    (b) it operates under the same name as an organisation listed in that Schedule.

(2) Subsection (1)(b) shall not apply in relation to an organisation listed in Schedule 2 if its entry is the subject of a note in that Schedule.

(3) The Secretary of State may by order—

    (a) add an organisation to Schedule 2;

    (b) remove an organisation from that Schedule;

    (c) amend that Schedule in some other way.

---

[76] *Counter-Terrorism Policy and Human Rights: Terrorism Bill and related matters*, 28 November 2005.
[77] *The Definition of Terrorism*, p. 21.   [78] Ibid., pp. 22–27.
[79] See below, p. 432.   [80] P. 29.
[81] Pp. 34, 37. 'Intimidate' rather than 'influence'; possibly replacing s. 1(1)(c) with 'the use or threat is made for the purpose of advancing a political, philosophical, ideological, racial, ethnic, religious or other similar cause'.
[82] P. 40.   [83] P. 44.

(4) The Secretary of State may exercise his power under subsection (3)(*a*) in respect of an organisation only if he believes that it is concerned in terrorism.

(5) For the purposes of subsection (4) an organisation is concerned in terrorism if it—

(a) commits or participates in acts of terrorism,

(b) prepares for terrorism,

(c) promotes or encourages terrorism, or

(d) is otherwise concerned in terrorism.

[(5A) The cases in which an organisation promotes or encourages terrorism for the purposes of subsection (5)(c) include any case in which activities of the organisation—

(a) include the unlawful glorification of the commission or preparation (whether in the past, in the future or generally) of acts of terrorism; or

(b) are carried out in a manner that ensures that the organisation is associated with statements containing any such glorification.

(5B) The glorification of any conduct is unlawful for the purposes of subsection (5A) if there are persons who may become aware of it who could reasonably be expected to infer that what is being glorified, is being glorified as—

(a) conduct that should be emulated in existing circumstances, or

(b) conduct that is illustrative of a type of conduct that should be so emulated.

(5C) In this section—

'glorification' includes any form of praise or celebration, and cognate expressions are to be construed accordingly;

'statement' includes a communication without words consisting of sounds or images or both.][84]

[(6) Where the Secretary of State believes—

(a) that an organisation listed in Schedule 2 is operating wholly or partly under a name that is not specified in that Schedule (whether as well as or instead of under the specified name), or

(b) that an organisation that is operating under a name that is not so specified is otherwise for all practical purposes the same as an organisation so listed,

he may, by order, provide that the name that is not specified in that Schedule is to be treated as another name for the listed organisation.

(7) Where an order under subsection (6) provides for a name to be treated as another name for an organisation, this Act shall have effect in relation to acts occurring while—

(a) the order is in force, and

(b) the organisation continues to be listed in Schedule 2,

as if the organisation were listed in that Schedule under the other name, as well as under the name specified in the Schedule.

(8) The Secretary of State may at any time by order revoke an order under subsection (6) or otherwise provide for a name specified in such an order to cease to be treated as a name for a particular organisation.

---

[84] Inserted by the Terrorism Act 2006, s. 21.

(9) Nothing in subsections (6) to (8) prevents any liability from being established in any proceedings by proof that an organisation is the same as an organisation listed in Schedule 2, even though it is or was operating under a name specified neither in Schedule 2 nor in an order under subsection (6).][85]

4. Deproscription application

[(1) An application may be made to the Secretary of State for an order under section 3(3) or (8)—

    (a) removing an organisation from Schedule 2, or

    (b) providing for a name to cease to be treated as a name for an organisation listed in that Schedule.][86]

(2) An application may be made by—

    (a) the organisation, or

    (b) any person affected by the organisation's proscription [or by the treatment of the name as a name for the organisation].[87]

(3) The Secretary of State shall make regulations prescribing the procedure for applications under this section.

(4) The regulations shall, in particular—

    (a) require the Secretary of State to determine an application within a specified period of time, and

    (b) require an application to state the grounds on which it is made.

5. Deproscription appeal

(1) There shall be a commission, to be known as the Proscribed Organisations Appeal Commission.

(2) Where an application under section 4 has been refused, the applicant may appeal to the Commission.

(3) The Commission shall allow an appeal against a refusal to deproscribe an organisation [or to provide for a name to cease to be treated as a name for an organisation][88] if it considers that the decision to refuse was flawed when considered in the light of the principles applicable on an application for judicial review.

(4) Where the Commission allows an appeal under this section…, it may make an order under this subsection.

(5) Where an order is made under subsection (4) [in respect of an appeal against a refusal to deproscribe an organisation,] the Secretary of State shall as soon as is reasonably practicable—

    (a) lay before Parliament, in accordance with section 123(4), the draft of an order under section 3(3)
    (b) removing the organisation from the list in Schedule 2, or

    (b) make an order removing the organisation from the list in Schedule 2 in pursuance of section 123(5).

[(5A) Where an order is made under subsection (4) in respect of an appeal against a refusal to provide for a name to cease to be treated as a name for an organisation, the Secretary of State shall, as soon as is reasonably practicable, make an order under section 3(8) providing that the name in question is to cease to be so treated in relation to that organisation.]

(6) Schedule 3 (constitution of the Commission and procedure) shall have effect.

---

85 Inserted by the Terrorism Act 2006, s. 22(1), (2).
86 Substituted by the Terrorism Act 2006, s. 22(1),(3).
87 Inserted by the Terrorism Act 2006, s. 22(1), (4).
88 The words in square brackets in s. 5 were inserted by the Terrorism Act 2006, s. 22(5), (6).

[A further appeal on a point of law lies to the Court of Appeal, with the permission of the Commission or the court: s.6. Other persons convicted of an offence under ss. 11 to 13, 15 to 19 and 56 in respect of an organisation in respect of which there has been a successful appeal against a refusal to deproscribe or to provide for a name to cease to be treated as a name for the organisation and consequent order is entitled to have the conviction set aside on appeal, provided the activity took place on or after the date of refusal: s. 7.]

9. Human Rights Act 1998

(1) This section applies where rules (within the meaning of section 7 of the Human Rights Act 1998 (jurisdiction)) provide for proceedings under section 7(1) of that Act to be brought before the Proscribed Organisations Appeal Commission.[89]

(2) The following provisions of this Act shall apply in relation to proceedings under section 7(1) of that Act as they apply to appeals under section 5 of this Act—

    (a) section 5(4) [, (5) and (5A)],[90]

    (b) section 6,

    (c) section 7, and

    (d) paragraphs 4 to [7] of Schedule 3.

(3) The Commission shall decide proceedings in accordance with the principles applicable on an application for judicial review.

(4) In the application of the provisions mentioned in subsection (2)—

    (a) a reference to the Commission allowing an appeal shall be taken as a reference to the Commission determining that an action of the Secretary of State is incompatible with a Convention right,…

    (b) a reference to the refusal to deproscribe against which an appeal was brought shall be taken as a reference to the action of the Secretary of State which is found to be incompatible with a Convention right [, and

    (c) a reference to a refusal to provide for a name to cease to be treated as a name for an organisation shall be taken as a reference to the action of the Secretary of State which is found to be incompatible with a Convention right].

10. Immunity

(1) The following shall not be admissible as evidence in proceedings for an offence under any of sections 11 to 13, 15 to 19 and 56—

    (a) evidence of anything done in relation to an application to the Secretary of State under section 4,

    (b) evidence of anything done in relation to proceedings before the Proscribed Organisations Appeal Commission under section 5 above or section 7(1) of the Human Rights Act 1998,

    (c) evidence of anything done in relation to proceedings under section 6 (including that section as applied by section 9(2)), and

    (d) any document submitted for the purposes of proceedings mentioned in any of paragraphs (a) to (c).

(2) But subsection (1) does not prevent evidence from being adduced on behalf of the accused.

---

[89] See the Proscribed Organisations Appeal Commission (Human Rights Act Proceedings) Rules 2006, SI 2006/2290, which provide that the Commission is an appropriate tribunal for the purposes of s. 7 in relation to any proceedings under s. 7(1)(a) against the Secretary of State in respect of a refusal to deproscribe or to provide for a name to cease to be treated as a name for a prescribed organisation.

[90] The words in square brackets in s. 9(2) and (4) were inserted by the Terrorism Act 2006, s. 22(9).

OFFENCES

11. Membership

(1) A person commits an offence if he belongs or professes to belong to a proscribed organisation.

(2) It is a defence for a person charged with an offence under subsection (1) to prove—

(a) that the organisation was not proscribed[91] on the last (or only) occasion on which he became a member or began to profess to be a member, and

(b) that he has not taken part in the activities of the organisation at any time while it was proscribed.

(3) A person guilty of an offence under this section shall be liable—

(a) on conviction on indictment, to imprisonment for a term not exceeding ten years, to a fine or to both, or

(b) on summary conviction, to imprisonment for a term not exceeding six months, to a fine not exceeding the statutory maximum or to both.....

12. Support

(1) A person commits an offence if—

(a) he invites support for a proscribed organisation, and

(b) the support is not, or is not restricted to, the provision of money or other property (within the meaning of section 15).

(2) A person commits an offence if he arranges, manages or assists in arranging or managing a meeting which he knows is—

(a) to support a proscribed organisation,

(b) to further the activities of a proscribed organisation, or

(c) to be addressed by a person who belongs or professes to belong to a proscribed organisation.

(3) A person commits an offence if he addresses a meeting and the purpose of his address is to encourage support for a proscribed organisation or to further its activities.

(4) Where a person is charged with an offence under subsection (2)(c) in respect of a private meeting it is a defence for him to prove that he had no reasonable cause to believe that the address mentioned in subsection (2)(c) would support a proscribed organisation or further its activities.

(5) In subsections (2) to (4)—

(a) 'meeting' means a meeting of three or more persons, whether or not the public are admitted, and

(b) a meeting is private if the public are not admitted.

[Subs (6) provides for the same maximum sentences as s.11(3).]

13. Uniform

(1) A person in a public place commits an offence if he—

(a) wears an item of clothing, or

(b) wears, carries or displays an article,

in such a way or in such circumstances as to arouse reasonable suspicion that he is a member or supporter of a proscribed organisation...

---

91 I.e. for the purposes of the 2000 Act or any of the PTAs or EPAs: s. 11(4).

(3) A person guilty of an offence under this section shall be liable on summary conviction to—

    (a) imprisonment for a term not exceeding six months,

    (b) a fine not exceeding level 5 on the standard scale, or

    (c) both.

NOTES (PART II: PROSCRIBED ORGANISATIONS)

1. *Proscribed organisations.* Powers to proscribe organisations were conferred by both the EPA (in Northern Ireland) and PTA (elsewhere in the UK). They only applied in respect of terrorism related to Northern Irish affairs.

The 'Irish Republican Army' (which term covers both the 'Official' and 'Provisional' wings) was proscribed under the PTA 1974. The Irish National Liberation Army was proscribed in July 1979.[92] The group had claimed responsibility for the killing of Mr Airey Neave, Opposition spokesman on Northern Ireland. They remained proscribed throughout the operation of the PTA 1989 and are proscribed under the 2000 Act. These and a number of other organisations were proscribed by the EPA. Neither Lord Jellicoe[93] nor Lord Colville[94] saw any need for symmetry for proscription under the two regimes given that the difference reflected the activities of terrorist organisations in different parts of the UK. Such symmetry was introduced by the 2000 Act, which establishes one regime for proscribed organisations and extends its scope to cover domestic and international terrorism in addition to Northern Ireland-related terrorism.

Schedule 2 to the 2000 Act proscribes the IRA, Cumann na mBan, Fianna na hEireann, the Red Hand Commando, Saor Eire, the Ulster Freedom Fighters, the Ulster Volunteer Force, the INLA, the Irish People's Liberation Organisation, the Ulster Defence Organisation, the Loyalist Volunteer Force, the Continuity Army Council, the Orange Volunteers, and the Red Hand Defenders. All were previously proscribed under the PTA or EPA. The criteria for proscription are not set out in the Act (beyond s. 3(4), (5)). From 29 March 2001, 21 international organisations were also proscribed.[95] 25 further international organisations have been added since.[96] It was stated in Parliament that the Secretary of State would take account of such factors as the nature and scale of the group's activities, the specific threat they pose to the UK and British nationals abroad, the extent of their presence in the UK and the need to support other members of the international community in the global fight against terrorism.[97] A novel feature is that a refusal by the Secretary of State to deproscribe an organisation may be subject to an appeal to the

---

[92] SI 1979/745.　　[93] 1983 Report, paras 2–11.

[94] *Colville Review (EPA),* p. 5.

[95] Terrorism Act 2000 (Proscribed Organisations) (Amendment) Order 2001, SI 2001/1261. These include Al-Qaeda, the Liberation Tigers of Tamil Eelam (LTTE), Hizballah External Security Organisation, Hamas-Izz al-Din al-Qassem Brigades, Palestinian Islamic Jihad-Shaquaqi, Abu Nidal Organisation, and Basque Homeland and Liberty.

[96] SI 2002/2724, SI 2005/2892, SI 2006/2016, SI 2007/2184. One organisation (Mujaheddin e Khalq) has been removed: SI 2008/1645, giving effect to the decision in *Secretary of State for the Home Department v Lord Alton of Liverpool* [2008] EWCA Civ 443. Explanations for the addition or removal of organisations are set out in the Explanatory Memorandum accompanying each order. Two additional names have been specified for the Kurdistan Workers' Party (PKK): SI 2006/1919.

[97] Charles Clarke, 341 HC Deb, col. 227 (in respect of international terrorism); Adam Ingram, Standing Committee D, col. 79 (in respect of domestic terrorism). This approach was confirmed in Home Office News Release, 28 March 2001, on SI 2001/1261, and in subsequent Explanatory Memoranda.

Proscribed Organisation Appeals Commission. The Commission is to apply judicial review principles (including principles arising out of the Human Rights Act 1998). The Commission's members are appointed by the Lord Chancellor; it sits in panels of three, one of whom must be a person who holds or has held high judicial office.[98] Procedural rules are made by the Lord Chancellor, and may include limits on the reasons and evidence disclosed to the organisation or applicant concerned and provision for a lawyer to be appointed by the relevant Law Officer to represent the interests of but not be responsible to the organisation or applicant concerned.[99]

Under the PTA and EPA, convictions for membership or support of a proscribed organisation were relatively rare.[100] An offence of contributing to the resources of a proscribed organisation[101] led to more convictions.[102] The Criminal Justice (Terrorism and Conspiracy) Act 1998[103] inserted provisions into the EPA[104] and PTA[105] making the opinion of a senior police officer that a person belonged to a 'specified organisation' which was or was part of a proscribed organisation admissible as evidence of the matter stated. These were not used in practice and probably did not comply with the ECHR.[106]

The justification advanced for proscription is as follows:[107]

SHOULD THE PROSCRIPTION POWERS BE RETAINED IN RESPECT OF IRISH TERRORISM?

4.7 In Northern Ireland, in particular, proscription has come to symbolise the community's abhorrence of the kind of violence that has blighted society there for over 30 years. The indications are that the proscription provisions have made life significantly more difficult for organisations to which they have been applied. Whilst the measures may not in themselves have closed down terrorist organisations, a knock on effect has been to deny the proscribed groups legitimate publicity and with it lawful ways of soliciting support and raising funds. Many activities by, or on behalf of, such groups are made more difficult by proscription, and that in itself aids the law enforcement effort in countering them. But perhaps more importantly the provisions have signalled forcefully the government's, and society's, rejection of these organisations' claims to legitimacy.

4.8 There have been no convictions for proscription-related offences in GB since 1990, though, in the same period, 195 convictions in Northern Ireland (usually as the second count on the charge sheet). But the indications are that the provisions have produced some less quantifiable but still significant outcomes. In particular it is suggested they have led proscribed organisations to tone down overt promotion and rallies. Although it is less easy to measure what has *not* happened because the proscription provisions have been in place, or to calculate the numbers deterred from supporting proscribed organisations because of the penalties if convicted (up to 10 years' imprisonment and an unlimited fine), the government still believes these factors to be very important.

---

[98] Sch. 3, paras 1, 4.

[99] Ibid., paras 5–8. See the Proscribed Organisations Appeal Commission (Procedure) Rules 2007. SI 2007/1286. See also the Proscribed Organisations (Applications for Deproscription) Regulations 2006, SI 2006/2299. Cf. arrangements for the handling of appeals in other security-sensitive contexts: below, p. 767.

[100] In *R v Adams* [1978] 5 NIJB, Belfast City Commission, Lowry LCJ declined to infer IRA membership from the defendant's conduct in parading in a compound of the Maze prison run by the inmates on quasi-military lines.

[101] PTA 1989, s. 10.   [102] *Walker*, p. 125.   [103] Ss. 1, 2.

[104] Ss. 2A, 2B.   [105] Ss. 30A, 30B.

[106] See C. Walker, *Current Law Statutes Annotated 1998* and (1999) 62 MLR 879; J.J. Rowe, *1998 EA Report*, paras 27–29 and *1999 PTA Report*, para. 51.

[107] *Legislation against Terrorism*, paras 4.7, 4.8.

The Government thought the arguments for and against extending proscription powers to other organisations were finely balanced[108] but ultimately decided in favour of extension. Advantages in extension was that condemnation of any terrorist organisation could be signalled whatever its origin and motivation, and that it could become easier to tackle fundraising. On the other hand, a large number of groups could be candidates and it would be difficult to keep the list up to date. Only Northern Ireland related groups were specified in the Act itself.

The grounds for proscription were broadened by the Terrorism Act 2006 to include glorification activities. As regards the proscription of organisations relating to international terrorism, 'the FCO wants to send out a clear signal that the UK does not welcome terrorists'.[109]

2. *Judicial Review; appeals to POAC.* Challenges have been made by way of judicial review to decisions to proscribe or to refuse to deproscribe. However, in *R (on the application of the Kurdistan Workers' Party) v Secretary of State for the Home Department*,[110] Richards J refused permission to apply for judicial review in respect of the proscription by the 2001 order of the KWP (Partiya Karkeren Kurdistan), the People's Mojahedin Organisation of Iran and Lashkar e Tayyabah. The ground was that judicial review was not appropriate in view of the availability of appeal to POAC, which had been initiated (in two cases) but not yet concluded. The judge did, however, accept that a number of grounds were arguable. These included procedural issues (unfairness in including organisations in the draft order without prior notice and an opportunity to make representations; the discretion of the Secretary of State was insufficiently circumscribed to meet the Convention test of 'prescribed by law'; it was unlawful to include 21 organisations in a single order); whether proscription was 'necessary in a democratic society' and non-discriminatory; whether the offences gave rise to a disproportionate interference with the rights of individual claimants, particularly with the chilling effect on free speech. No further legal steps were apparently taken following this decision, but separate proceedings concerning one of the organisations were successful.

In *Secretary of State for the Home Department v Alton*[111] the Court of Appeal held that the POAC[112] had been entitled to conclude that the Home Secretary had acted perversely in refusing an application by Lord Alton and other members of Parliament for her to remove the People's Mujahidin Organisation of Iran, previously known as Mujaheddin e Khalq, from the list of proscribed organisations. The organisation had conducted military activity against the Iran regime prior to June 2001 but it then dissolved its operational units and renounced terrorism. The court held that it now lacked capacity to carry on terrorist activities and had taken no steps to acquire such capacity: the presence of a conditional intention on the part of the leaders to do so in the future was insufficient to establish that the organisation was concerned in terrorism.

3. *Offences.* In *R v Z (Attorney General for Northern Ireland's Reference)*[113] the House of Lords held unanimously that proscription of the 'Irish Republican Army' under the 2000 Act extended to cover members of the 'Real IRA'. This formula had been consistently adopted for proscription under PTAs and EPAs from 1973, and was 'intended as an

---

[108] Ibid., paras 4.12–4.17.

[109] Lord Carlile, *Report on the Operation in 2002 and 2003 of the Terrorism Act 2000* (2004), p. 7.

[110] [2002] EWHC 644 (Admin).   [111] [2008] EWCA Civ 443, (2008) Times, 13 May.

[112] POAC's decision is available at www.siac.tribunals.gov.uk/poac/. It is the only appeal it appears to have heard.

[113] [2005] UKHL 35, [2005] 2 AC 645. See C. Walker [2007] Crim LR 331.

umbrella term, capable of describing all manifestations or splinter groups'.[114] It had clearly, in the past, been Parliament's intention to proscribe the 'Provisional IRA' given that the group that became known as the Official IRA had in effect declared a ceasefire in 1972. The House, however, divided on the proper approach to s. 3(1). The majority[115] held that s. 3(1)(a) and (1)(b) were distinct and the present case fell under s. 3(1)(a). The minority held that s. 3(1) created a single composite test: 'is this the body listed in the Schedule or a part or emanation of it or does it in any event operate under the name of an organization listed in the Schedule?'[116] Lord Brown[117] expressed the view that s. 3(1)(b) was intended and apt to cover only those cases where an organisation operates under an identical name to that of a listed organisation but asserts that it is completely independent of that organisation.

The House of Lords has also held by 3 to 2[118] in *Attorney-General's Reference No. 4 of 2002*[119] that the defence in s. 11(2) was to be read by virtue of s. 3 of the HRA as imposing only an evidential burden on D. For the majority, relevant considerations included that the breadth of s. 11(1) was such that a person innocent of any blameworthy or properly criminal conduct, such as a person who joined an organisation when it was not a terrorist organisation, or not proscribed, or when, if it was, he did not know it was, or a person who now wished to disassociate himself from an organisation, but had no means to do so without exposing him to risk. It might be very difficult for D to show he had not taken part in activities at any time when the organisation was proscribed, given that terrorist organisations do not generate minutes or records and its members would be unlikely to testify on D's behalf. Imposition of a legal burden would leave the court no discretion. The possible sentence was severe.[120] The minority thought that D's difficulties were met by the point that the Crown would be likely to have difficulty in finding witnesses to contradict anything he says.[121]

An offence is committed where a person joins and participates in the activities of a UK proscribed organisation abroad in a country where it is not proscribed, but then enters the UK.[122]

4. There is also an *EU list of persons, groups and entities subject to specified measures to combat terrorism*.[123] These measures include the freezing of funds, other financial assets and economic resources. PMOI successfully challenged its inclusion on the list on the ground that the procedure adopted breeched the organisations's right to a fair hearing; there was no statement of reasons for the measures (required by Art. 253EC) and it was unable effectively

---

[114] Per Lord Carswell at para. [51].

[115] Lords Brown of Eaton-Under-Heywood, Rodger of Earlsferry and Carswell.

[116] Lord Bingham at para. [22]; Lord Woolf at para. [46].

[117] At para. [68]. Lord Rodger agreed but Lord Carswell left the point open (paras [48], [54]).

[118] Lords Bingham of Cornhill, Steyn and Phillips of Worth Matravers, Lords Rodger of Earlsferry and Carswell dissenting.

[119] [2004] UKHL 43, [2005] 1 AC 264; heard with *Sheldrake v DPP*. See D. Hamer [2007] CLJ 142. Applied to the offence of facilitating the control of terrorist funds under s. 11 of the Prevention of Terrorism Act 1989 in *R v Brogan* [2004] NICC 27, Crown Court.

[120] See Lord Bingham at para. [51].

[121] Lord Rodger at para. [76], Lord Carswell at para. [90], and further reasons at para. [91].

[122] *R v Hundal; R v Dhaliwal* [2004] EWCA Crim 389 (12-month sentences (reduced from 30 months) imposed on two members of the International Sikh Youth Federation who entered the UK without realising it was proscribed here).

[123] The latest version was published on 15 July 2008 (OJ L188 21). See EU factsheet, at www.consilium. europa.eu/vedocs/cmsUpload/080715_combat%20terrorism_EN.pdf. For monitoring by Stateswatch see www.statewatch.org/terrorlists/terrorlists.html.

to make representations.[124] However, the EU made some procedural changes and has kept it on the list. The CFI held subsequently that the statement of reasons given in respect of the PKK was inadequate, and could not be remedied by further reasons given after the judicial proceedings had commenced.[125] It is difficult to see how the UK Government could maintain its support for the listing of PMOI given the Court of Appeal's ruling under the domestic legislation.

5. Compare the offences under ss. 12 and 13 with s. 1 of the Public Order Act 1936 banning political uniforms.[126] Are these offences necessary or desirable?[127] The s. 13 offence has been held applicable to wearing a ring with UVF marked on it, this being a reference to the Ulster Volunteer Force.[128]

PART IV

TERRORIST INVESTIGATIONS

INTERPRETATION

32. Terrorist investigation

In this Act 'terrorist investigation' means an investigation of—

   (*a*) the commission, preparation or instigation of acts of terrorism,

   (*b*) an act which appears to have been done for the purposes of terrorism,

   (*c*) the resources of a proscribed organisation,

   (*d*) the possibility of making an order under section 3(3), or

   (*e*) the commission, preparation or instigation of an offence under this Act [or under Part 1 of the Terrorism Act 2006 other than an offence under section 1 or 2 of that Act].[129]

TERRORIST INVESTIGATION...

INFORMATION AND EVIDENCE...

[38B Information about acts of terrorism]

[(1) This section applies where a person has information which he knows or believes might be of material assistance—

   (a) in preventing the commission by another person of an act of terrorism, or

   (b) in securing the apprehension, prosecution or conviction of another person, in the United Kingdom, for an offence involving the commission, preparation or instigation of an act of terrorism.

(2) The person commits an offence if he does not disclose the information as soon as reasonably practicable in accordance with subsection (3).

(3) Disclosure is in accordance with this subsection if it is made—

   (a) in England and Wales, to a constable,... or

   (b) in Northern Ireland, to a constable or a member of Her Majesty's forces.

---

[124] Case T-228/02, *Organisation des Mojahedinas due peuple d'Iran v Council* [2006] ECR II–4665 ('OMPI') (Court of First Instance).

[125] Case T-229/02, *Osman Oclan, on behalf of the Kurdistan Workers' Party (PKK) v Council*, 3 April 2008.

[126] Above, pp. 287–289.

[127] See the debate in respect of the offences under PTA 1989, s. 3 by W. Finnie [1990] JR 1, 6; B. Robertson [1991] JR 250; C. Walker [1993] JR 90; and W. Finnie [1994] JR 118.

[128] *Rankin v Murray* 2004 SCCR 422.

[129] Inserted by the Terrorism Act 2006, s. 37(1).

(4) It is a defence for a person charged with an offence under subsection (2) to prove that he had a reasonable excuse for not making the disclosure.

(5) A person guilty of an offence under this section shall be liable—

(a) on conviction on indictment, to imprisonment for a term not exceeding five years, or to a fine or to both, or

(b) on summary conviction, to imprisonment for a term not exceeding six months, or to a fine not exceeding the statutory maximum or to both.

(6) Proceedings for an offence under this section may be taken, and the offence may for the purposes of those proceedings be treated as having been committed, in any place where the person to be charged is or has at any time been since he first knew or believed that the information might be of material assistance as mentioned in subsection (1).][130]

39. Disclosure of information, etc.

(1) Subsection (2) applies where a person knows or has reasonable cause to suspect that a constable is conducting or proposes to conduct a terrorist investigation.

(2) The person commits an offence if he—

(a) discloses to another anything which is likely to prejudice the investigation, or

(b) interferes with material which is likely to be relevant to the investigation.

(3) Subsection (4) applies where a person knows or has reasonable cause to suspect that a disclosure has been or will be made under any of sections 19 to [21] [or 38B].

(4) The person commits an offence if he—

(a) discloses to another anything which is likely to prejudice an investigation resulting from the disclosure under that section, or

(b) interferes with material which is likely to be relevant to an investigation resulting from the disclosure under that section.

(5) It is a defence for a person charged with an offence under subsection (2) or (4) to prove—

(a) that he did not know and had no reasonable cause to suspect that the disclosure or interference was likely to affect a terrorist investigation, or

(b) that he had a reasonable excuse for the disclosure or interference.

(6) Subsections (2) and (4) do not apply to a disclosure which is made by a professional legal adviser—

(a) to his client or to his client's representative in connection with the provision of legal advice by the adviser to the client and not with a view to furthering a criminal purpose, or

(b) to any person for the purpose of actual or contemplated legal proceedings and not with a view to furthering a criminal purpose.

[(6A) Subsections (2) and (4) do not apply if—

(a) the disclosure is of a matter within section 21D(2) or (3)(a) (terrorist property: tipping off), and

(b) the information on which the disclosure is based came to the person in the course of a business in the regulated sector.][131]

[Sub-s. (7) provides for the same penalty as s. 38B(5).]

---

130 Inserted by the Anti-terrorism, Crime and Security Act 2001, s. 117(1), (2).
131 Inserted by SI 2007/3398, reg. 2, Sch. 1, paras 1, 6(1), (3),

(8) For the purposes of this section—

(a) a reference to conducting a terrorist investigation includes a reference to taking part in the conduct of, or assisting, a terrorist investigation, and

(b) a person interferes with material if he falsifies it, conceals it, destroys it or disposes of it, or if he causes or permits another to do any of those things.

NOTES (PARTS III AND IV: TERRORIST PROPERTY AND TERRORIST INVESTIGATIONS)

1. *Terrorist property.*[132] Part III of the Act creates a series of offences concerning terrorist property. This is money or other property likely to be used for the purposes of terrorism (including any resources of a proscribed organisation), proceeds of the commission of acts of terrorism and proceeds of acts carried out for the purposes of terrorism (s. 14). There are offences relating to fund-raising: inviting another to provide, receiving or providing money or other property intending that it be used or with reasonable cause to suspect that it may be used for the purposes of terrorism (s. 15). It is an offence to use money or other property for the purposes of terrorism or to possess money or other property intending that it should be used, or having reasonable cause to suspect that it may be used, for the purposes of terrorism (s.16). It is an offence to enter a funding arrangement as a result of which money or other property is (or is to be) made available to another and he knows or has reasonable cause to suspect it will or may be used for the purposes of terrorism (s. 17). There are offences of money-laundering in respect of terrorist property (s. 18).

A person who believes or suspects that a person has committed an offence under ss. 15–18 and bases that belief on information which comes to his attention in the course of a trade, profession, business or employment (other than a business in the regulated sector), must disclose this to a constable or authorised SOCA officer as soon as is reasonably practicable; it is an offence not to do so although it is a defence for D to prove he had a reasonable excuse (s. 19). This does not require disclosure by a professional legal adviser of information covered by legal privilege (s. 19(5), (6)). Disclosures may be made notwithstanding restrictions on disclosure imposed by statute or otherwise (s. 20). No offence is committed under ss. 15–18 where D acts with the express permission of a constable or authorised SOCA officer, or disclosures are made in specified circumstances after a person has become involved in a transaction, or D intends to make a disclosure and there is a reasonable excuse for his failure to do so (s. 21).

There are defences to the ss. 15–18 offences if the person has made a disclosure to an authorised officer of SOCA before (or after if there is a reasonable excuse) becoming involved in a transaction or arrangement; or otherwise has a reasonable excuse.[133] A person commits an offence if (a) he knows or suspects or has reasonable grounds for knowing or suspecting that another person has committed or attempted to commit an offence under ss. 15–18; (b) the information came to him in the course of a business in the regulated sector; and (c) he does not disclose the information to a constable, authorised SOCA officer or nominated

---

[132] See *Lloyd Inquiry,* Chap. 13: *Legislation Against Terrorism,* Chap. 6.

[133] 2000 Act, ss. 21ZA–21ZC, inserted by the Terrorism Act 2000 and Proceeds of Crime Act 2002 (Amendment) Regulations 2007, SI 2007/3398, implementing art. 24 of Directive 2005/60/EC of the European Parliament and Council of 26 October 2005 on the prevention of the use of the financial system for the purpose of money laundering and terrorist financing.

officer as soon as practicable after it comes to him. There is a defence of reasonable excuse or where D is a professional legal adviser or professional accountant, auditor or tax adviser (or support staff) and it came to the adviser in circumstances covered by legal privilege.[134] The regulated sector includes banking, insurance, accountancy, statutory audit work, insolvency practitioner, financial or real property transactions, estate agency, trading in goods and casinos.[135] Such disclosures do not breach any restriction on the disclosure of information (however imposed).[136] Disclosure ('tipping off') that a person has made a disclosure under Pt 3 or that an investigation into allegations of offences under Pt 3 are offences.[137] There are a number of permitted disclosures.[138]

The original powers in this Part developed and added to those in PTA 1989 Pt III, and were extended to include domestic terrorism. There were new powers to seize cash in transit,[139] modelled on those in the Drug Trafficking Offences Act 1994. Sections 15–28 (and 39) may be applied to Crown servants by regulations made by the Secretary of State under s. 119.[140] Section 118, under which certain reversed burdens of proof are to be evidential only, does *not* apply to ss. 18(2), 19(3), 21(5). The s. 16 offence has been held to be Convention-compliant, as being sufficiently precise and proportionate.[141]

2. *Terrorist investigations.* Sections 33–36 enables a superintendent or above (or constable if he considers it necessary by reason of urgency) to designate a cordoned area if he considers it expedient for the purposes of a terrorist investigation. It may last for up to 14 days, but can be extended to 28. A constable in uniform may order a person to leave the area or adjacent premises or move a vehicle, or prohibit or restrict access by pedestrians or vehicles. 'Cordoning powers' were first introduced by the Prevention of Terrorism (Additional Powers) Act 1996,[142] following the IRA's ending of its ceasefire in that year with the South Quay bomb. The powers have been used in Great Britain, as well as Northern Ireland.[143]

Schedule 5[144] is modelled on Sch. 7 to the PTA 1989 and enables a constable to obtain a warrant authorising, for the purposes of a terrorist investigation,[145] entry to premises, the search of the premises and any person found there, and the seizure and retention of any 'relevant material' found. As with PACE,[146] it may be a 'specific' premises warrant' or an 'all premises warrant'.[147] The material is 'relevant' if the constable has reasonable grounds for believing that it is likely to be of substantial value[148] to a terrorist investigation and that it must be seized to prevent it from being concealed, lost, damaged, altered or destroyed. It must, not, however, be subject to legal privilege. A justice of the peace may grant a warrant

---

[134] 2000 Act, ss. 21A, inserted by the Anti-terrorism, Crime and Security Act 2001, Sch. 2, para. 5(1), (2).

[135] 2000 Act, Sch. 3A, inserted by the 2001 Act and substituted by SI 2007/3288, art. 2.

[136] 2000 Act, s. 21B, inserted by the 2001 Act, Sch. 2, Pt 3, para. 5(1), (2).

[137] 2000 Act, s. 21D, inserted by SI 2007/3398, Sch. 1, paras 1, 5.

[138] 2000 Act ss. 21E–21H, inserted by SI 2007/3398, Sch. 1, paras 1, 5.

[139] See the Code of Practice for Authorised Officers under the Terrorism Act 2000, made under Sch. 14, para. 6(1), operative by virtue of SI 2001/425.

[140] See the Terrorism Act 2000 (Crown Servants and Regulators) Regulations 2001, SI 2001/192.

[141] *R (on the application of O'Driscoll) v Secretary of State of the Home Department* [2002] EWHC 2477 (Admin) (refusing permission to apply for judicial review of decisions to arrest O'D and seize material in relation to his importation of 1,001 copies of a magazine whose proceeds, it was claimed, supported a proscribed organisation, DHKP-C.

[142] See K. Reid [1996] 4 Web JCLI.   [143] See Lord Carlile's Annual Reviews.

[144] As amended by the Terrorism Act 2006, s. 26.

[145] As defined in s. 32 of the 2000 Act.   [146] See p. 172.

[147] The latter being a warrant in respect of any premises or sets of premises controlled by a specified person.

[148] Not 'necessary' for the investigation: *R (on the application of Malik) v Manchester Crown Court* [2008] EWHC 1362 (Admin).

if satisfied: (a) that it is sought for the purposes of a terrorist investigation; (b) that there are reasonable grounds for believing that there is relevant material (other than excluded material, items subject to legal privilege or special procedure material) on premises to which the application relates; (c) that the issue of the warrant is likely to be necessary in the circumstances of the case; and (d), in the case of an application for an all premises warrant, that it is not reasonably practicable to specify in the application all the premises occupied or controlled by the specified person that might need to be searched. Where the applicant is a senior officer (superintendent or above), and the application does not relate to residential premises, condition (c) need not be satisfied.[149] A senior officer (a constable in a case of urgency) may also authorise similar searches of premises within a condoned area.[150] Access to excluded or special procedure material may be ordered by a circuit judge, and a warrant may be issued if there is non-compliance with an access order or such an order would not be appropriate.[151]

A circuit judge may by order require a person to provide an explanation of any material seized under a warrant or order.[152] A senior officer may by a written order confer the same authority as a search warrant where he has reasonable grounds for believing the case to be of 'great emergency' where 'immediate action is necessary.'[153] Note that the Sch. 5 powers are not confined to 'serious arrestable offences' or now 'indictable offences' and 'relevant material' need not be 'evidence'.[154] The powers in Sch. 5 are broader in many respects than those in PACE.[155] The judge has a discretion to permit the respondent to appear,[156] but to hold all or part of the hearing on a closed basis and in an exceptional case and as a last resort to request the appointment of a special advocate, although the latter is not necessary for compliance with Art. 6 ECHR.[157] Convention issues must properly be taken into account.[158] Disobedience to a production order is a contempt.[159] Production and explanation orders have been regularly used.[160]

Schedule 6[161] provides a new general power for a constable to obtain an order (a 'general bank circular') from a circuit judge requiring a financial institution[162] to provide 'customer information' for the purpose of a terrorist investigation. An application may only be made by an officer of the rank of superintendent or above. An order overrides any restriction on disclosure imposed by statute or otherwise. 'Customer information' means information whether

---

[149] Sch. 5, paras 1, 2, 2A. In these cases, the powers of entry and search are exercisable within 24 hours of issue of the warrant.

[150] Sch. 5, para. 3.

[151] Sch. 5, paras 5–12; to be extended in England and Wales to a district judge (magistrates' courts by the Courts Act 2003, s. 110.

[152] Sch. 5, paras 13, 14.   [153] Sch. 5, paras 15, 16.

[154] Cf. PACE, above, pp. 172–192.

[155] See the detailed analysis by J.J. Rowe, *Current Law Statutes Annotated 2000*, pp. 11.45–11.47.

[156] *Re Morris's Application under the Terrorism Act 2000, Sch 5, para. 5* [2003] NICC 1, Crown Court.

[157] *R (on the application of Malik) v Manchester Crown Court* [2008] EWHC 1362 (Admin) (concerning an order in respect of a freelance journalist who was collaborating with Hassan Butt, who had previously admitted past involvement with Al-Qaeda, in writing a book based on his experiences). It is submitted that such an appointment will not necessarily be sufficient for compliance; cf. the position in respect of control orders, below pp. 475–485.

[158] Ibid. (They were.)   [159] See *DPP v Channel 4 Television Co Ltd*, below, p. 761.

[160] 237 in GB in 1996, over 150 in 1997 and well over 100 in 1998: J.J. Rowe, *Annual Reports on the PTA 1996–98*, 'A production order played a part in almost every terrorist investigation in Great Britain': *1997 PTA Report*, para. 39.

[161] In these cases, the powers of entry and search are exercisable within 24 hours of issue of the warrant.

[162] An order may apply to all financial institutions, particular description(s) of institution or a particular institution.

a business relationship exists with a particular person, his account number, full name, date of birth, address or former address, the date on which a business relationship begins or ends, evidence of identity obtained under money laundering legislation and the identity of any person sharing an account with that person. Customer information is not admissible in evidence in criminal proceedings against the institution or its officers or employees.

These powers are designed to be used at an earlier stage than Sch. 5 powers; the latter would have to be used, for example, to obtain details of transactions. The Sch. 6 powers are similar to but broader than existing powers of investigation in Northern Ireland in respect of proceeds of crime.[163]

Schedule 6A[164] introduced new, similar, powers for account monitoring orders in respect of the accounts of specified persons held at the financial institution specified in the application. An application can be made by any police officer and an order can be for up to 90 days.

PART V

COUNTER-TERRORIST POWERS

SUSPECTED TERRORISTS

40. Terrorist: interpretation

(1) In this Part 'terrorist' means a person who—

    (a) has committed an offence under any of sections 11, 12, 15 to 18, 54 and 56 to 63, or

    (b) is or has been concerned in the commission, preparation or instigation of acts of terrorism.

(2) The reference in subsection (1)(b) to a person who has been concerned in the commission, preparation or instigation of acts of terrorism includes a reference to a person who has been, whether before or after the passing of this Act, concerned in the commission, preparation or instigation of acts of terrorism within the meaning given by section 1.

41. Arrest without warrant

(1) A constable may arrest without a warrant a person whom he reasonably suspects to be a terrorist.

(2) Where a person is arrested under this section the provisions of Schedule 8 (detention: treatment, review and extension) shall apply.

(3) Subject to subsections (4) to (7), a person detained under this section shall (unless detained under any other power) be released not later than the end of the period of 48 hours beginning—

    (a) with the time of his arrest under this section, or

    (b) if he was being detained under Schedule 7 when he was arrested under this section, with the time when his examination under that Schedule began.

(4) If on a review of a person's detention under Part II of Schedule 8 the review officer does not authorise continued detention, the person shall (unless detained in accordance with subsection (5) or (6) or under any other power) be released.

(5) Where a police officer intends to make an application for a warrant under paragraph 29 of Schedule 8 extending a person's detention, the person may be detained pending the making of the application.

---

[163] Proceeds of Crime (Northern Ireland) Order 1996, SI 1996/1299. See *Re Devine* [1999] NIJB 128 (issue of code of practice not a necessary precondition for exercise of power by investigator; investigator entitled to use a pseudonym).

[164] Inserted by the Anti-terrorism, Crime and Security Act 2001, Sch. 2, Pt 1, para. 1(2)(3).

(6) Where an application has been made under paragraph 29 or 36 of Schedule 8 in respect of a person's detention, he may be detained pending the conclusion of proceedings on the application.

(7) Where an application under paragraph 29 or 36 of Schedule 8 is granted in respect of a person's detention, he may be detained, subject to paragraph 37 of that Schedule, during the period specified in the warrant.

(8) The refusal of an application in respect of a person's detention under paragraph 29 or 36 of Schedule 8 shall not prevent his continued detention in accordance with this section.

(9) A person who has the powers of a constable in one Part of the United Kingdom may exercise the power under subsection (1) in any Part of the United Kingdom.

42. Search of premises

(1) A justice of the peace may on the application of a constable issue a warrant in relation to specified premises if he is satisfied that there are reasonable grounds for suspecting that a person whom the constable reasonably suspects to be a person falling within section 40(1)(b) is to be found there.

(2) A warrant under this section shall authorise any constable to enter and search the specified premises for the purpose of arresting the person referred to in subsection (1) under section 41...

43. Search of persons

(1) A constable may stop and search a person whom he reasonably suspects to be a terrorist to discover whether he has in his possession anything which may constitute evidence that he is a terrorist.

(2) A constable may search a person arrested under section 41 to discover whether he has in his possession anything which may constitute evidence that he is a terrorist.

(3) A search of a person under this section must be carried out by someone of the same sex.

(4) A constable may seize and retain anything which he discovers in the course of a search of a person under subsection (1) or (2) and which he reasonably suspects may constitute evidence that the person is a terrorist.

(5) A person who has the powers of a constable in one Part of the United Kingdom may exercise a power under this section in any Part of the United Kingdom.

44. Authorisations

(1) An authorisation under this subsection authorises any constable in uniform to stop a vehicle in an area or at a place specified in the authorisation and to search—

   (a) the vehicle;

   (b) the driver of the vehicle;

   (c) a passenger in the vehicle;

   (d) anything in or on the vehicle or carried by the driver or a passenger.

(2) An authorisation under this subsection authorises any constable in uniform to stop a pedestrian in an area or at a place specified in the authorisation and to search—

   (a) the pedestrian;

   (b) anything carried by him.

(3) An authorisation under subsection (1) or (2) may be given only if the person giving it considers it expedient for the prevention of acts of terrorism.

(4) An authorisation may be given—

   (a) where the specified area or place is the whole or part of a police area outside Northern Ireland other than one mentioned in paragraph (b) or (c), by a police officer for the area who is of at least the rank of assistant chief constable;

(b) where the specified area or place is the whole or part of the metropolitan police district, by a police officer for the district who is of at least the rank of commander of the metropolitan police;

(c) where the specified area or place is the whole or part of the City of London, by a police officer for the City who is of at least the rank of commander in the City of London police force;

(d) where the specified area or place is the whole or part of Northern Ireland, by a [member of the Police Service of Northern Ireland] who is of at least the rank of assistant chief constable.

[Sub-ss. (4ZA), (4A), (4B), (4BA), (4C), (5A)[165] extend the powers to adjacent internal waters (i.e. waters in the UK not in any police area, and to the British Transport Police, the Ministry of Defence Police and the Civil Nuclear Constabulary.]

(5) If an authorisation is given orally, the person giving it shall confirm it in writing as soon as is reasonably practicable.

[(5A) In this section—

'driver', in relation to an aircraft, hovercraft or vessel, means the captain, pilot or other person with control of the aircraft, hovercraft or vessel or any member of its crew and, in relation to a train, includes any member of its crew; . . .]

45. Exercise of power

(1) The power conferred by an authorisation under section 44(1) or (2)—

(a) may be exercised only for the purpose of searching for articles of a kind which could be used in connection with terrorism, and

(b) may be exercised whether or not the constable has grounds for suspecting the presence of articles of that kind.

(2) A constable may seize and retain an article which he discovers in the course of a search by virtue of section 44(1) or (2) and which he reasonably suspects is intended to be used in connection with terrorism.

(3) A constable exercising the power conferred by an authorisation may not require a person to remove any clothing in public except for headgear, footwear, an outer coat, a jacket or gloves.

(4) Where a constable proposes to search a person or vehicle by virtue of section 44(1) or (2) he may detain the person or vehicle for such time as is reasonably required to permit the search to be carried out at or near the place where the person or vehicle is stopped.

(5) Where—

(a) a vehicle or pedestrian is stopped by virtue of section 44(1) or (2), and

(b) the driver of the vehicle or the pedestrian applies for a written statement that the vehicle was stopped, or that he was stopped, by virtue of section 44(1) or (2),

the written statement shall be provided.

(6) An application under subsection (5) must be made within the period of 12 months beginning with the date on which the vehicle or pedestrian was stopped.

[(7) In this section 'driver' has the same meaning as in section 44.][166]

---

165 Inserted by the Terrorism Act 2006, s. 30(1), (2), the Anti-terrorism, Crime and Security Act 2001, s. 127(2)(f) and the Energy Act 2004, s. 57(1) (2)(a).

166 Inserted by the Terrorism Act 2006, s. 30(1)(4).

46. Duration of authorisation

(1) An authorisation under section 44 has effect, subject to subsections (2) to (7), during the period—

    (a) beginning at the time when the authorisation is given, and

    (b) ending with a date or at a time specified in the authorisation.

(2) The date or time specified under subsection (1)(*b*) must not occur after the end of the period of 28 days beginning with the day on which the authorisation is given....

(3) The person who gives an authorisation shall inform the Secretary of State as soon as is reasonably practicable.

(4) If an authorisation is not confirmed by the Secretary of State before the end of the period of 48 hours beginning with the time when it is given—

    (a) it shall cease to have effect at the end of that period, but

    (b) its ceasing to have effect shall not affect the lawfulness of anything done in reliance on it before the end of that period.

(5) Where the Secretary of State confirms an authorisation he may substitute an earlier date or time for the date or time specified under subsection (1)(*b*).

(6) The Secretary of State may cancel an authorisation with effect from a specified time.

(7) An authorisation may be renewed in writing by the person who gave it or by a person who could have given it; and subsections (1) to (6) shall apply as if a new authorisation were given on each occasion on which the authorisation is renewed.

47. Offences

(1) A person commits an offence if he—

    (a) fails to stop a vehicle when required to do so by a constable in the exercise of the power conferred by an authorisation under section 44(1);

    (b) fails to stop when required to do so by a constable in the exercise of the power conferred by an authorisation under section 44(2);

    (c) wilfully obstructs a constable in the exercise of the power conferred by an authorisation under section 44(1) or (2).

(2) A person guilty of an offence under this section shall be liable on summary conviction to—

    (a) imprisonment for a term not exceeding six months,

    (b) a fine not exceeding level 5 on the standard scale, or

    (c) both.

PARKING

[Ss. 48–52 enable a constable in uniform to be authorised by a commander or assistant chief constable if he considers it expedient for the prevention of acts of terrorism, to prohibit or restrict the parking of vehicles on a specified road.]

PORT AND BORDER CONTROLS

[S. 53 and Sch. 7 provide for port and border controls.]

NOTES (PART V: COUNTER-TERRORIST POWERS)

1. *Arrest and detention.* Sections 40 and 41 and Sch. 8 confer powers of arrest and extended detention analogous to those previously available under PTA 1989, s. 14. The arrest power by virtue of s. 40(1)(b) extends to persons not suspected of a specific crime; Sch. 8 provides for extended detention. The UK police terrorism arrest statistics (excluding Northern Ireland) from 11 September 2001–31 March 2007 show that 1,228 arrests were made (1,165 under the Terrorism Act 2000); 436 were charged with offences (241 with terrorism legislation offences); 669 were released without charge and the rest dealt with in other ways; of those charged, there were 41 Terrorism Act convictions to date, 183 convicted under other legislation, and 114 at or awaiting trial.[167]

(a) *The justification for the powers.* Lord Colville reported that the arrest power under s. 12 of the 1984 Act (see now s. 41 of the 2000 Act) was justified as it enabled the police to arrest on reasonable suspicion 'at the preparatory stage of the commission of offences of violence'; reliance on ordinary powers to arrest for an attempt would be 'leaving things rather late' and proving conspiracy 'will often be more difficult than proving an attempt' and was surrounded by jurisdictional and other difficulties.[168] There were still good reasons for permitting a period of detention of up to seven days.[169]

In 1998, the Government justified the existence of extended arrest powers as follows:[170]

Whilst the ordinary powers of arrest are extensive, the government believes they may not be sufficient to deal effectively with all the problems posed by terrorism. Terrorist groups are frequently highly organised with well practised procedures for thwarting police actions against them. Many of those who have operated in the UK (including non-Irish terrorist groups) have been trained to evade surveillance and their operations have been meticulously planned both to minimise the risk of arousing suspicion before the terrorist act is undertaken and to minimise the chance of leaving forensic evidence. Communications may be in an encrypted form and, especially where international groups are involved, foreign languages may be deployed. Information about these sorts of techniques is increasingly available (for instance on the Internet and in exchanges between like-minded activists). The police are therefore, (and are likely to continue to be) up against groups skilled in, and dedicated to, evading detection. Although some of the factors may also apply in the disruption and investigation of serious non-terrorist crime it still remains the case that terrorist crime is often of a quite different order both in terms of the sophistication of the techniques deployed and the (potential) harm caused.

(b) *Reviews of detention.* The PTA powers[171] provided for extended detention on the authority of the Secretary of State rather than a judicial officer. They were held by the European Court of Human Rights (in *Brogan v United Kingdom*)[172] to be contrary to the ECHR, Art. 5(3) and (5). The Government's response was for the UK to derogate from the relevant provisions of the ECHR and the International Covenant on Civil and Political Rights.[173] Periodic reviews of detention were introduced by Sch. 3 to PTA 1989, modelled on the provisions of PACE.[174] Under the 2000 Act, a detention must be reviewed as soon as reasonably practicable after arrest and subsequently at interviews of not more than 12 hours.[175] In contrast with PACE provisions, all reviews under the PTA were conducted by police officers, albeit senior officers not directly involved with the case; there was no requirement for authorisation by magistrates or another judicial officer at the later

---

167 www.homeoffice.gov.uk/security/terrorism-and-the-law/?version=3.
168 *Colville Review (PTA)* (1987), Chap. 4.   169 Ibid., Chap. 5.
170 *Legislation Against Terrorism*, para. 7.8.   171 PTA 1984, s. 12; PTA 1989, s. 14.
172 (1988) 11 EHRR 117. Also *O'Hara v UK*, Judgment of 16 October 2001.
173 The ECtHR held the derogation notice to be valid: *Brannigan and McBride v UK* (1993) 17 EHRR 539.
174 Ss. 40–44, above, pp. 216–223.   175 Sch. 8, para. 21.

stages of detention. Moreover, even if the review officer refused to authorise an extension of detention, an extension might still be granted by the Secretary of State.[176] However, under the 2000 Act, provision has now been made for a warrant of further detention in respect of detention beyond 48 hours up to a maximum of seven days to be granted by a judicial officer.[177] The judicial authority may order that the applicant and/or his representative be excluded from any part of the hearing and that specified information is not to be disclosed to them. This was one of three options proposed by the Government to enable there to be compliance with the ECHR and ICCPR.[178]

Do these provisions now comply with Art. 5 ECHR? The Government 's position is that an arrest power without an explicit link to a specific offence is compatible with Art. 5(1)(c), citing the decision in *Brogan* where in the circumstances of the case (where the applicants were suspected of being members of a proscribed organisation), the European Court of Human Rights held that their arrest under PTA 1984, s. 12 was not in breach of Art. 5(1)(c).[179] However, it has been pointed out that the Court noted in *Brogan* that the definition of acts of terrorism was 'well in keeping with the idea of an offence' and that after arrest the applicants were asked about specific offences. The definition of 'terrorism' is now broader and a person arrested might not of course in another case be questioned so specifically. It is accordingly doubtful that there is compliance here.[180] The Government intended by the introduction of the requirement of judicial authority for extended detention to be able to withdraw the ECHR and ICCPR derogations and this took place on 19 February 2001. However, the fact that detention may continue beyond 48 hours while a warrant is sought may itself come to be a breach of Art. 5(3).[181]

(c) *Other points.* The PTA 1989, s. 14 arrest power (then PTA 1976, s. 12) was considered by the Northern Ireland Court of Appeal in *Ex p Lynch*.[182] The court held that the arresting officer complied with the requirements of *Christie v Leachinsky*[183] by telling L that he was arresting him under s. 12 as he suspected him of being involved in terrorism:

an arrest [under s. 12] is not necessarily…the first step in a criminal proceeding against a suspected person on a charge which was intended to be judicially investigated. Rather it is usually the first step in the investigation of the suspected person's involvement in terrorism.[184]

In *Fox, Campbell and Hartley v United Kingdom*,[185] the Court of Human Rights held that the use of this formula (in respect of an arrest under EPA 1978, s. 11, since repealed) was not sufficient to comply with Art. 5(2) of the ECHR. However, it was not necessary for compliance that the required information be supplied on arrest; here, the information had been provided during interrogation, and in the present context 'intervals of a few hours [between arrest and interrogation] cannot be regarded as falling outside the constraints of time imposed by the notion of promptness in Article 5(2)'.[186] Then in *Oscar v Chief Constable of the Royal Ulster Constabulary*[187] the Northern Ireland Court of Appeal held it sufficient for an arrest under PTA for the arresting officer to say:

---

[176] PTA 1989, Sch. 3, para. 3(1)(b).
[177] There may be further extensions. See below.
[178] *Lloyd Inquiry,* Chap. 9; *Legislation Against Terrorism,* Chap. 8.
[179] Lord Bassam of Brighton, 613 HL Deb, col. 682; *Brogan v UK* (1988) 12 EHRR 371.
[180] H. Fenwick, *Civil Rights* (2000), p. 247; *Lloyd Inquiry,* para. 8.13.   [181] Ibid., p 251.
[182] [1980] NI 126 (see W. Finnie (1982) 45 MLR 215).   [183] Above, p. 205.
[184] Per Lord Lowry LCJ at 131.   [185] (1990) 13 EHRR 157.
[186] P. 171.   [187] [1992] 9 NIJB 27.

I arrest you under section 12(1)(b) of the Prevention of Terrorism (Temporary Provisions) Act 1984 as I have reasonable grounds for suspecting you have been concerned in the commission, preparation or investigation of acts of terrorism.

The arrest:

was not unlawful because the constable failed to tell him of the nature of the terrorist acts which he was suspected to have committed.[188]

The principle of *McKee v Chief Constable of the RUC*[189] that bona fide acceptance of instructions from a superior officer may amount to reasonable suspicion, has been applied in subsequent cases involving arrests under the Prevention of Terrorism legislation.[190] The outcome in *O'Hara* was that:

the information given at the briefing to the arresting officer was admissible and although [in the words of the trial judge] 'scanty', it was sufficient to constitute the required state of mind of an arresting officer under s. 12(1)(b) of the [1984] Act.[191]

The arresting officer was simply briefed that O'Hara had been 'involved in' a particular murder. The decision in *O'Hara* was upheld by the House of Lords.[192] The House held that the mere fact that the arresting officer had been instructed to effect an arrest or had been told that the person in question had been concerned in the commission etc. of acts of terrorism was not itself sufficient. However, the trial judge had been entitled to find that the information provided at the briefing was on the facts of the particular case sufficient.

2. *Conditions in detention*

(a) *PTA detention in England and Wales.*[193] Detention under the PTA in England and Wales was regulated by the PACE regime, albeit with modifications.[194] Research on PTA detentions in England and Wales[195] showed that the exercise of rights to legal advice and to have someone notified of their detention were delayed in a far higher proportion of PTA than ordinary PACE detentions (26 per cent, 44 per cent of the sample), and a far higher percentage (40 per cent) were held for more than 24 hours. The report also noted shortcomings in

---

[188] Per Hutton LCJ at 54.   [189] [1984] 1 WLR 1358.

[190] See *Clinton v Chief Constable of the Royal Ulster Constabulary* [1991] 2 NIJB 53, QBD (NI); *Bradley v Chief Constable of the Royal Ulster Constabulary* [1991] 2 NIJB 22, QBD (NI) (see 'A barrister' (1992) 43 NILQ 66); *Oscar v Chief Constable of the RUC* [1992] NI 209, CA (NI); *O'Hara v Chief Constable of the RUC* (6 May 1994, unreported, CA (NI)).

[191] Per Kelly LJ.

[192] [1997] AC 296. See p. 143. Applied in *Porter v Chief Constable of the RUC* (unreported, 24 February 1999, QBD (NI)) and *Raissi v Comr of Police of the Metropolis* [2007] EWHC 2842 (QB) (held to be reasonable grounds for suspicion of wife of prime suspect in 11/9 bombings (she had been with him in the US while he was undergoing flight training) but not for suspicion of his brother based simply on that relationship and the fact that they lived near to each other; the court confirmed (para. [48]) that the police could not rely on surmise that senior officers had additional information not passed on. The Court of Appeal dismissed an appeal in respect of the brother: [2008] EWCA Civ 1237. The ECtHR in *O'Hara* subsequently found no breach of Art. 5(1): *O'Hara v UK*, Judgment of 16 October 2001. See above, p. 148.

[193] For frequently critical views and experiences of conditions in PTA detention, see P. Hillyard, *Suspect Community* (1993), Chap. 7.

[194] See PACE, Part V and Code C.

[195] D. Brown, *Detention under the Prevention of Terrorism (Temporary Provision) Act 1989: Access to Legal Advice and Outside Contact* (HORPU Paper 75, 1993).

record-keeping. However, nearly 40 per cent of detainees successfully obtained legal advice (a far higher proportion than for PACE prisoners) and:

scrupulous attention to the detainee's physical well-being through regular medical examination and reviews by senior officers was also common, particularly where detention was lengthy.[196]

(b) *Treatment in detention in Northern Ireland.* In *Ireland v United Kingdom*[197] the European Court of Human Rights found that the adoption of 'five techniques' of sensory deprivation[198] in the operation of the policy of internment and detention in 1971 constituted inhuman treatment. The use of these techniques was officially abandoned following the Parker Report.[199] Allegations of ill-treatment in the period following that considered by the European Court were substantiated.[200] However, following implementation of a range of measures recommended by the Bennett Committee, including the coverage of interview rooms by CCTV monitored by uninformed, supervisory officers, and a right of access to a solicitor every 48 hours (albeit not during interrogations), there was a very marked reduction in allegations of physical abuse.[201] Detention at holding centres in Northern Ireland was also monitored by an Independent Commissioner for the Holding Centres (Sir Louis Blom-Cooper QC), appointed under the royal prerogative.[202]

(c) *Detention under the Terrorism Act 2000.* All detentions under the 2000 Act are regulated by the regime established by Sch. 8 to the Act, rather than by PACE. The detailed structure is, however broadly analogous. The Secretary of State must designate places at which persons may be detained under Sch. 7 or s. 41.[203] A person is deemed to be in legal custody throughout his period of detention.[204] There are rights to have one named person informed of the detention as soon as reasonably practicable and to consult a solicitor as soon as reasonably practicable, privately and at any time. A delay may be authorised by a senior officer.[205] In Northern Ireland it is now not possible to impose a delay or further delay once access is allowed, bringing the position into line with that in England and Wales. Note the restrictions on the use of evidence obtained during the period of the delay that will apply by virtue of *Magee v United Kingdom*.[206] Breach of the duty to allow access to a solicitor does not give rise to a claim for damages for breach of statutory duty, it being regarded as a public law duty only.[207] The Secretary of State (a) must issue a code of practice about the audio-recording of interviews in a police station by a constable of a person detained under Sch. 7 or s. 41 and

---

[196] P. 56.

[197] See A. Mowbray, *Cases and Materials on the European Convention on Human Rights* (2nd edn, 2007), pp. 145–154.

[198] Wall-standing, hooding, noise, deprivation of sleep, deprivation of food and drink.

[199] Cmnd 4901.

[200] See the *Report of an Amnesty International Mission to Northern Ireland* (1978), the Bennett Report (Cmnd 7497, 1979) and P. Taylor, *Beating the Terrorists?* (1980).

[201] See Lord Jellicoe's *Review of the Operation of the Prevention of Terrorism (Temporary Provisions) Act 1976* (Cmnd 8803), pp. 29–35, 39–44.

[202] See the Commissioner's Annual Reports.   [203] Sch. 8, para. 1(1).

[204] Sch. 8, para. 5.   [205] Sch. 8, paras 6–8.

[206] Judgment of 6 June 2000. Here the ECtHR held that the denial of access by M to a lawyer for more than 48 hours (including at interrogations that eventually led to a confession) violated Art. 6(1) in conjunction with Art. 6(3)(c). It was the consistent practice up to 2000 for such access to be denied.

[207] *Cullen v Chief Constable of the RUC* [2003] UKHL 39, [2003] 1WLR 1763. (Lords Hutton, Millett and Rodger of Earlsferry, Lords Bingham of Cornhill and Steyn dissenting).

must make an order requiring compliance with the Code;[208] (b) may make an order requiring video-recording of such interviews (or such interviews in a particular part of the UK), specifying whether recording is to be silent or with sound, and if he does so he must issue a code of practice and require that it be followed.[209] The Secretary of State required the video-taping with sound of such interviews at a police station in Northern Ireland.[210] Provision is made for the taking of fingerprints and intimate and non-intimate samples.[211]

A person's detention must be reviewed periodically by a 'review officer' who has not been directly involved in the investigation, reviews taking place in the first 24 hours by (at least) an inspector and thereafter by (at least) a superintendent. The first review must take place as soon as reasonably practicable after arrest, and thereafter they must (normally) be at intervals of not more than 12 hours. The review officer(s) may authorise continued detention for up to 48 hours.[212] Thereafter, detention may be continued for up to a total of seven days by a warrant of further detention granted by a designated district judge (magistrates' courts).[213] (The person may be detained for up to a further six hours beyond the 48 while an application for a warrant is made.[214]) A warrant may be extended to a total of 14 days by a designated district judge (magistrates' courts) and a total of 28 days by a High Court judge.[215] The grounds for extension are that there are reasonable grounds for believing that further detention is necessary to obtain relevant evidence, whether by questioning or otherwise, to preserve relevant evidence or, pending the result of an examination or analysis of relevant evidence; the judge must also be satisfied that the investigation is being conducted diligently and expeditiously.[216] The person to whom the application relates must be given the opportunity to make representations and is entitled to be legally represented. However, both that person and any represented may be excluded from any part of the hearing by the judge.[217] The applicant officer may apply to the judge for an order that specified information on which he or she intends to rely be withheld from them. Such an order may be made if one of a variety of grounds is established, for example that there are reasonable grounds for believing that otherwise evidence of an offence under the provisions mentioned in s. 40(1)(a) would be interfered with or harmed; or the prevention of an act of terrorism would be made more difficult as a result of a person being alerted, or a person would be interfered with or physically injured.[218] Where the ground for extension is that the police need more time to question the person in detention, it is not necessary for the police to divulge to him or her the further lines of questioning; the judge is entitled, however, to exclude him or her and any representative under para. 33(3) so that those matters can be examined by the judge, the additional scrutiny being a factor likely to be to the advantage of the detained person. The power to exclude carries with it the power not to disclose what took place during the period of exclusion; and it is not necessary to make an application under para. 34. Such an

208 See the Terrorism Act 2000 (Code of Practice on Audio Recording of Interviews) Order 2001, SI 2001/159 and (No. 2) Order 2001, SI 2001/189); *Code of Practice for the Audio Recording of Interviews under the Terrorism Act 2000.*

209 Sch. 8, paras 3, 4.

210 See the Terrorism Act 2000 (Code of Practice on Video Recording of Interviews) (Northern Ireland) Order 2001, SI 2001/402; *Code of Practice on Video Recording of Interviews.* A revised code was approved by SI 2003/1100.

211 Sch. 8, paras 10–15, as amended.

212 Sch. 8, paras 21–28, para. 23 as amended by the Terrorism Act 2006, s. 24.

213 Sch. 8, paras 29–36, as amended by the Terrorism Act 2006, s. 23.

214 Sch. 8, para. 30.   215 Sch. 8, paras 29–36.   216 Sch. 8, para. 32.

217 Sch. 8, para. 33.   218 Sch. 8, para. 34.

application would, however, be needed in cases where non-disclosure of other grounds for extending detention is sought.[219]

3. *Travel controls.*[220] Section 53 and Sch. 7[221] set out a system of travel controls based on those previously found in PTA 1989, s. 16 and Sch. 5. An 'examining officer'[222] may question a person for the purpose of determining whether he appears to be a person who is or has been concerned in the commission, preparation or instigation of acts of terrorism. The person must be at a port (including an airport or hoverport) or in the 'border area'[223] or on a ship or aircraft which has arrived in Great Britain or Northern Ireland (whether from within or outside Great Britain or Northern Ireland). There need be no prior suspicion. An examining officer may also question a person in the border area for the purpose of determining whether his presence in the area is connected with his entering or leaving Northern Ireland. For the purpose of exercising these powers an officer may stop a person or vehicle or detain a person for up to nine hours.[224] The detention regime is that prescribed by Sch. 8, Part I. There are extensive powers to search, to detain property and to require the production of information, and controls over journeys by ship or aircraft between Great Britain and the Republic of Ireland, Northern Ireland or the Islands and between Northern Ireland and any of those places. Such journeys must be to designated ports or otherwise as approved by an examining officer, or where the passengers are not carried for reward, on 12 hours' notice. Passengers may be required to complete embarkation or landing cards. However, under the 2000 Act, these arrangements now only apply where the Secretary of State has made an order subject to the affirmative resolution procedure bringing them into effect.[225]

Lord Lloyd reported that the port powers were among the less controversial of the PTA provisions and that 'there are sound strategic reasons for an island nation to carry out checks of this kind at ports. They provide a first line of defence against the entry of terrorists, and serve a useful function against crime as a by product'.[226]

- **R (on the application of Gillan) v Comr of Police of the Metropolis**
  [2006] UKHL 12, [2006] 2 AC 307, House of Lords

In August 2003 an assistant commissioner of the Metropolitan Police made an authorisation under ss. 44 and 45 of the Terrorism Act 2000 allowing police officers to stop and search members of the public at random for articles that could be used in connection with terrorism. The authorisation, which was made in relation to the whole of the Metropolitan District, lasted for 28 days, the maximum period possible, and followed a succession of authorisations that had been made since s. 44 had come into force in February 2001. The authorisation was subsequently confirmed by the Home Secretary pursuant to s. 46 of the

---

[219] *Ward v Police Service of Northern Ireland* [2007] UKHL 50, [2008] NI 138.

[220] See *Legislation Against Terrorism,* Chap. 11; *Code of Practice for Examining Officers under the Terrorism Act 2000,* made operative by SI 2001/427.

[221] As amended by the Anti-terrorism, Crime and Security Act 2001, ss 118, 119, and the Terrorism Act 2006, s. 29.

[222] I.e. a constable, immigration officer or designated customs officer. Their Sch. 7 functions may be conferred on members of HM Forces by an order made by the Secretary of State under s. 97.

[223] I.e. in an area no more than one mile from the border between Northern Ireland and the Republic of Ireland or the first stopping place for a train going into Northern Ireland from the Republic.

[224] Reduced from the PTA period of 12 hours, which could be extended where there were reasonable grounds to suspect terrorist involvement. In such a case now the person would have to be arrested under s. 41. Lord Lloyd had recommended a six-hour maximum period: *Lloyd Inquiry,* p. 66.

[225] See the Terrorism Act 2000 (Carding) Order 2001, SI 2001/426.

[226] *Lloyd Inquiry,* pp. 59–66.

Act. In September 2003 the claimants Mr Gillan, a student who was on his way to join a demonstration against an arms fair in Docklands, East London, and Ms Quinton, a journalist who was in the area to film the protest, were stopped and searched by police officers pursuant to the authorisation. Nothing incriminating was found. The claimants brought proceedings against the Commissioner of Police of the Metropolis and the Home Secretary seeking judicial review of their treatment, the authorisation and its confirmation. The Divisional Court dismissed their claims. On appeals by the claimants, the Court of Appeal made no order on the appeals as against the Commissioner and dismissed the appeals as against the Home Secretary.

Lord Bingham of Cornhill:

1 It is an old and cherished tradition of our country that everyone should be free to go about their business in the streets of the land, confident that they will not be stopped and searched by the police unless reasonably suspected of having committed a criminal offence. So jealously has this tradition been guarded that it has almost become a constitutional principle. But it is not an absolute rule. There are, and have for some years been, statutory exceptions to it. These appeals concern an exception now found in sections 44 to 47 of the Terrorism Act 2000. The appellant claimants challenge the use made of these sections and, in the last resort, the sections themselves. Since any departure from the ordinary rule calls for careful scrutiny, their challenge raises issues of general importance....

[His Lordship referred to the Terrorism Act 2000, ss. 1, 41–47 and the Guidance in PACE Code A paras 1.1, 1.2, 2.19–2.26, 3.5–3.11.]

9 In dispensing with the condition of reasonable suspicion, section 45(1)(b) departs from the ordinary and salutary rule found in provisions such as section 1 of the Police and Criminal Evidence Act 1984, section 47 of the Firearms Act 1968, section 23 of the Misuse of Drugs Act 1971 and...sections 41–43 of the 2000 Act itself. But such departure is not without precedent. A similar (although more specific and more time-limited) departure is found in section 60 of the Criminal Justice and Public Order Act 1994, where incidents involving serious violence are reasonably believed to be imminent. More pertinently, because addressed to the prevention of terrorism, a similar departure was made in section 13A of the 1989 Act, inserted by section 81 of the 1994 Act just mentioned. As originally enacted, that section contained provisions very similar to those in sections 44(1), (3) and (4), 45(1) and (5) and 47(1) and (2) of the 2000 Act, but that Act did not (until amended in 1996 by section 1(1) of the Prevention of Terrorism (Additional Powers) Act) 1996) apply to the stopping or searching of pedestrians or make any provision for confirmation by the Secretary of State. It is also noteworthy that section 45(1)(b) is not the only provision of the 2000 Act which dispenses with the condition of reasonable suspicion: Schedule 7 to the Act makes detailed provision for the stopping and questioning of those embarking and disembarking at ports and airports, without reasonable suspicion, supplemented by a power to detain for a period of up to nine hours.

III. THE ISSUES

12 ...[The argument] was presented to the House under four main heads.

A. CONSTRUCTION

13 The argument centred on the expression 'expedient' in section 44(3). The claimants pointed to the Divisional Court's description of these stop and search powers as 'extraordinary' and as 'sweeping and far beyond anything ever permitted by common law powers' (para 44 of the judgment), a description echoed by the Court of Appeal (para 8), and suggested that Parliament could not have intended to sanction police intrusion into the freedom of individuals unless it was necessary that the police have such a power. Reliance was placed on the principle of legality articulated in *R v Secretary of State for the Home Department, Ex p Simms* [2000] 2 AC 115, 130, 131. Reliance was also placed on Home Office Circular

038/2004 (1 July 2004), Authorisations of Stop and Search Powers under Section 44 of the Terrorism Act, addressed to chief officers of police, which emphasised that 'Powers should only be authorised where they are absolutely necessary to support a force's anti-terrorism operations'. The claimants submitted that section 44(3) should be interpreted as permitting an authorisation to be made only if the decision-maker has reasonable grounds for considering that the powers are necessary and suitable, in all the circumstances, for the prevention of terrorism.

14 I would for my part reject this argument for one short and simple reason. 'Expedient' has a meaning quite distinct from 'necessary'. Parliament chose the first word, also used in section 13A of the 1989 Act, not the second. There is no warrant for treating Parliament as having meant something which it did not say. But there are other reasons also for rejecting the argument. It is true, as already recognised, that section 45(1)(b), in dispensing with the condition of reasonable suspicion, departs from the normal rule applicable where a constable exercises a power to stop and search. One would therefore incline, within the permissible limits of interpretation, to give 'expedient' a meaning no wider than the context requires. But examination of the statutory context shows that the authorisation and exercise of the power are very closely regulated, leaving no room for the inference that Parliament did not mean what it said. There is indeed every indication that Parliament appreciated the significance of the power it was conferring but thought it an appropriate measure to protect the public against the grave risks posed by terrorism, provided the power was subject to effective constraints. The legislation embodies a series of such constraints. First, an authorisation under section 44(1) or (2) may be given only if the person giving it considers (and, it goes without saying, reasonably considers) it expedient 'for the prevention of acts of terrorism'. The authorisation must be directed to that overriding objective. Secondly, the authorisation may be given only by a very senior police officer. Thirdly, the authorisation cannot extend beyond the boundary of a police force area, and need not extend so far. Fourthly, the authorisation is limited to a period of 28 days, and need not be for so long. Fifthly, the authorisation must be reported to the Secretary of State forthwith. Sixthly, the authorisation lapses after 48 hours if not confirmed by the Secretary of State. Seventhly, the Secretary of State may abbreviate the term of an authorisation, or cancel it with effect from a specified time. Eighthly, a renewed authorisation is subject to the same confirmation procedure. Ninthly, the powers conferred on a constable by an authorisation under sections 44(1) or (2) may only be exercised to search for articles of a kind which could be used in connection with terrorism. Tenthly, Parliament made provision in section 126 for reports on the working of the Act to be made to it at least once a year, which have in the event been made with commendable thoroughness, fairness and expertise by Lord Carlile of Berriew QC. Lastly, it is clear that any misuse of the power to authorise or confirm or search will expose the authorising officer, the Secretary of State or the constable, as the case may be, to corrective legal action.

15 The principle of legality has no application in this context, since even if these sections are accepted as infringing a fundamental human right, itself a debatable proposition, they do not do so by general words but by provisions of a detailed, specific and unambiguous character. Nor are the claimants assisted by the Home Office circular. This may well represent a cautious official response to the claimants' challenge, and to the urging of Lord Carlile that these powers be sparingly used. But it cannot, even arguably, affect the construction of section 44(3). The effect of that sub-section is that an authorisation may be given if, and only if, the person giving it considers it likely that these stop and search powers will be of significant practical value and utility in seeking to achieve the public end to which these sections are directed, the prevention of acts of terrorism.

B. AUTHORISATION AND CONFIRMATION . . .

17 The claimants' first ground of attack on the authorisation and confirmation was based on their geographical coverage. This, they said, was excessive: even if there was justification for conferring such exceptional powers in areas of central London offering the most spectacular targets for terrorist violence, there could be no need for them in the dormitory suburbs of outer London, which offered no such targets.

This is not, in my opinion, an unattractive submission, but it founders on two major obstacles. First, the Assistant Commissioner in his witness statement, having addressed the terrorist threat to the United Kingdom in general and London in particular in August-September 2003, expressly said:

'(I was particularly conscious that the number and range of particular terrorism targets in London was numerous and geographically spread throughout the entire Metropolitan Police District).'

This aspect was also addressed in the witness statement of Catherine Byrne, a senior Home Office civil servant, on behalf of the Secretary of State:

'17. In this context it is also simply impracticable to attempt to differentiate between some parts of the Metropolitan Police area and others. As I have already indicated potential targets within the London area are not limited to central London, but exist throughout the metropolitan area. Moreover, the powers under sections 44 and 45 of the 2000 Act are aimed not simply at disrupting any attempted attack "at the last possible moment" but are intended to enable police forces, where appropriate, to ensure that any attempted attack is disrupted at an early stage, and certainly well before any serious harm could be done to members of the public or to property. It must also be remembered that the powers under sections 44 and 45 of the 2000 Act are simply one element of the strategy adopted by the Metropolitan Police (in conjunction with the City of London police) to combat the risk posed by terrorists. This is a point made in the reasons supporting both authorisations made by the Commissioner [of Police of the Metropolis]. Further, the powers under sections 44 and 45 of the 2000 Act play a legitimate part in focused intelligence-gathering operations. These can be directed either for the purpose of disrupting identified risks or (equally legitimately) as a means of obtaining information that can lead to the identification of potential risks.'

There is no evidence of any kind to contradict or undermine this testimony. Secondly, as both these witness statements make clear, the Assistant Commissioner and the Secretary of State independently paid attention to secret security intelligence when making the judgments which they respectively did. An offer to explore this evidence before the Divisional Court hearing, subject to procedural safeguards, was made to the claimants but not taken up. In the result, therefore, the House has before it what appear to be considered and informed evaluations of the terrorist threat on one side and effectively nothing save a measure of scepticism on the other. There is no basis on which the defendants' evidence can be rejected. This is not a question of deference but of what in *A v Secretary of State for the Home Department* [2005] 2 AC 68, 102, para 29, was called 'relative institutional competence'.

18 The claimants' second, and main, ground of attack was directed to the succession of authorisations which had had effect throughout the Metropolitan Police District since February 2001, continuing until September 2003. It was, they suggested, one thing to authorise the exercise of an exceptional power to counter a particular and specific threat, but quite another to authorise what was, in effect, a continuous ban throughout the London area. Again this is not an unattractive submission. One can imagine that an authorisation renewed month after month might become the product of a routine bureaucratic exercise and not of the informed consideration which sections 44 and 46 clearly require. But all the authorisations and confirmations relevant to these appeals conformed with the statutory limits on duration and area. Renewal was expressly authorised by section 46(7). The authorisations and confirmations complied with the letter of the statute. The evidence of the Assistant Commissioner and Catherine Byrne does not support, and indeed contradicts, the inference of a routine bureaucratic exercise. It may well be that Parliament, legislating before the events of September 2001, did not envisage a continuous succession of authorisations. But it clearly intended that the section 44 powers should be available to be exercised when a terrorist threat was apprehended which such exercise would help to address, and the pattern of renewals which developed up to September 2003 (it is understood the pattern has since changed) was itself a product of Parliament's principled refusal to confer these exceptional stop and search powers on a continuing, countrywide basis. Reporting on the operation of the 2000 Act during the years 2002 and 2003, Lord Carlile (Report on the Operation in 2002 and 2003 of the Terrorism Act 2000, para 86) found

that sections 44 and 45 remained necessary and proportional to the continuing and serious risk of terrorism, and regarded London as 'a special case, having vulnerable assets and relevant residential pockets in almost every borough'.

19 There is no material before the House to justify the conclusion that the authorisation of 13 August and the confirmation of 14 August 2003, or either of them, were unlawful.

C. THE HUMAN RIGHTS ACT 1998 AND THE EUROPEAN CONVENTION

20 The appellants addressed argument on articles 5, 8, 10 and 11 of the European Convention on Human Rights. It is necessary to consider these articles separately.

Article 5

21 [His Lordship referred to Art 5(1)(b).] It is unnecessary to recite the other sub-heads of exception: they provide an exhaustive list of the cases in which, in accordance with a procedure prescribed by law, a person may be deprived of his liberty (*Ireland v United Kingdom* (1978) 2 EHRR 25, 87, para 194), but none of the other exceptions is capable of applying here. Reference must, however, be made to article 2 of the Protocol No 4 to the Convention. This Protocol has not been ratified by the United Kingdom, but has been relied on by the European Court when considering what amounts to a deprivation of liberty under article 5. Article 2 of the Fourth Protocol is entitled 'Freedom of movement' and provides in para 1: 'Everyone lawfully within the territory of a state shall, within that territory, have the right to liberty of movement ...'

22 It is clear that the giving of an authorisation by a senior officer and its confirmation by the Secretary of State cannot, of themselves, infringe the Convention rights of anyone. Thus the threshold question is whether, if a person is stopped and searched in accordance with the procedure prescribed by sections 44 and 45 and Code A, he is 'deprived of his liberty' within the autonomous meaning of that expression in article 5(1). The claimants contend that he is so deprived, even if only for a short time, since the police officer has the power to require compliance with the procedure; a member of the public will not feel that his compliance is voluntary; the officer has a power to detain, which he may or may not exercise (section 45(4)); reasonable force may be used to enforce compliance (section 114(2)); and non-compliance is criminally punishable. Thus a member of the public has no effective choice but to submit, for as long as the procedure takes. The defendants for their part do not, I think, contend that compliance with the procedure is in any meaningful sense voluntary; but they submit that viewed objectively, and in the absence of special circumstances, the procedure involves a temporary restriction of movement and not anything which can sensibly be called a deprivation of liberty.

23 The House was referred to a mass of authority relied on to show that one or other of these approaches should be preferred. There is, however, no European decision on facts closely analogous with the present, and it is not in my view helpful to consider whether a stop and search under section 45 is more closely analogous with, for instance, the case of a man forcibly compelled to submit to a blood test (*X v Austria* (1979) 18 DR 154: held, deprivation of liberty) or with that of a ten-year-old girl kept at a police station for two hours for questioning, for part of the time in an unlocked cell (*X v Republic of Germany* (1981) 24 DR 158: held, no deprivation of liberty). The Strasbourg jurisprudence is closely focused on the facts of particular cases, and this makes it perilous to transpose the outcome of one case to another where the facts are different. Still more perilous is it, in my opinion, to seek to transpose the outcome of Canadian cases decided under a significantly different legislative regime.

24 The task of the House is eased by the substantial agreement of the parties on the correct approach in principle. Perhaps the clearest exposition of principle by the Strasbourg court is to be found in *Guzzardi v Italy* (1980) 3 EHRR 333, an exposition repeatedly cited in later cases. [See the discussion of this case in *Secretary of State for the Home Department y v JJ.*[227]]

---

[227] See below, p. 479.

25 It is accordingly clear, as was held in *HL v United Kingdom* (2004) 40 EHRR 761, para 89, that

'in order to determine whether there has been a deprivation of liberty, the starting-point must be the concrete situation of the individual concerned and account must be taken of a whole range of factors arising in a particular case such as the type, duration, effects and manner of implementation of the measure in question.'

I would accept that when a person is stopped and searched under sections 44 and 45 the procedure has the features on which the appellants rely. On the other hand, the procedure will ordinarily be relatively brief. The person stopped will not be arrested, handcuffed, confined or removed to any different place. I do not think, in the absence of special circumstances, such a person should be regarded as being detained in the sense of confined or kept in custody, but more properly of being detained in the sense of kept from proceeding or kept waiting. There is no deprivation of liberty. That was regarded by the Court of Appeal [2005] QB 388, 406, para 46 as 'the better view', and I agree.

26 If, however, a stop and search carried out in accordance with sections 44 and 45 and Code A, in the absence of special circumstances, does involve a deprivation of liberty, it is necessary to consider (as the Court of Appeal did) (a) whether that deprivation is in accordance with the law and, if so, (b) whether it is a lawful detention in order to secure the fulfilment of an obligation prescribed by law. Whether the deprivation is in accordance with the law and whether the relevant obligation is prescribed by law are questions separately considered in paras 31 to 35 below. If not, and if there is a deprivation of liberty, the claimants must succeed, for the defendants cannot rely on the exception. But if, for purposes of the argument at this stage, compliance with the law be assumed, the defendants in my opinion bring themselves within the exception, for the public are in my opinion subject to a clear obligation not to obstruct a constable exercising a lawful power to stop and search for articles which could be used for terrorism and any detention is in order to secure effective fulfilment of that obligation.

Article 8

27 [His Lordship read Art. 8]

28 The claimants contended that exercise of the section 45 stop and search power necessarily involves an interference with the exercise of the article 8(1) right, and therefore had to be justified under article 8(2). The defendants did not accept that there would necessarily be such interference, but accepted that there might, as where (for instance) an officer in the course of a search perused an address book, or diary, or correspondence. I have no doubt but that the defendants' concession is rightly made. I am, however, doubtful whether an ordinary superficial search of the person can be said to show a lack of respect for private life. It is true that 'private life' has been generously construed to embrace wide rights to personal autonomy. But it is clear Convention jurisprudence that intrusions must reach a certain level of seriousness to engage the operation of the Convention, which is, after all, concerned with human rights and fundamental freedoms, and I incline to the view that an ordinary superficial search of the person and an opening of bags, of the kind to which passengers uncomplainingly submit at airports, for example, can scarcely be said to reach that level.

[His Lordship held that it would be impossible to regards a lawful search in accordance with Code A to be other than proportionate when seeking to counter the great danger of terrorism.]

Articles 10 and 11

30 The power to stop and search under sections 44–45 may, if misused, infringe the Convention rights to free expression and free assembly protected by articles 10 and 11, as would be the case, for example, if the power were used to silence a heckler at a political meeting. I find it hard to conceive of circumstances in which the power, properly exercised in accordance with the statute and Code A, could be held to restrict those rights in a way which infringed either of those articles. But if it did, and subject always to compliance with the 'prescribed by law' condition discussed below, I would expect the restriction to fall within the heads of justification provided in articles 10(2) and 11(2).

D. LAWFULNESS

31 The expressions 'prescribed by law' in article 5(1), 5(1)(b), 10(2) and 11(2) and 'in accordance with the law' in article 8(2) are to be understood as bearing the same meaning. What is that meaning?

32 The claimants relied on a number of authorities such as *Malone v United Kingdom* (1984) 7 EHRR 14, paras 66–68, *Huvig v France* (1990) 12 EHRR 528, *Hafsteinsdóttir v Iceland* (Application No 40905/98), (unreported), 8 June 2004, paras 51 and 55–56 and *Enhorn v Sweden* (2005) 41 EHRR 633, para 36, to submit that the object of this requirement is to give protection against arbitrary interference by public authorities; that 'law' includes written and unwritten domestic law, but must be more than mere administrative practice; that the law must be accessible, foreseeable and compatible with the rule of law, giving an adequate indication of the circumstances in which a power may be exercised and thereby enabling members of the public to regulate their conduct and foresee the consequences of their actions; that the scope of any discretion conferred on the executive, which may not be unfettered, must be defined with such precision, appropriate to the subject matter, as to make clear the conditions in which a power may be exercised; and that there must be legal safeguards against abuse. These requirements, the claimants argued, were not met in the present case. They acknowledged, of course, that sections 44 to 47 of the 2000 Act were adequately accessible to the public. But they contended that 'law' in this context meant not only the Act but also the authorisation and confirmation, and these were not accessible. Thus a member of the public would know that the section 44 power to stop and search could be conferred on the police, but would not know at any given time or in any given place whether it had been. He could not know whether, if he went to Battersea Park, he would be liable to be stopped and searched. Nor, if stopped and searched, could he know whether the constable was authorised to stop and search him. When, unknown to a member of the public, the power had been conferred on a constable, the constable's discretion to stop and search was broad and ill-defined, requiring no grounds of suspicion and constrained only by the condition that the power could be exercised only for the purpose of searching for articles of a kind which could be used in connection with terrorism.

33 The defendants did not, I think, challenge the principles advanced by the claimants, which are indeed to be found, with minor differences of expression, in many decisions of the Strasbourg court. But they strongly challenged the claimants' application of those principles to the present facts. They did not accept that the authorisation and confirmation were 'law' in this context. They pointed to the court's acceptance in *Malone v United Kingdom*, a case concerned with the covert interception of telephonic communications, that (para 67):

> 'the requirements of the Convention, notably in regard to foreseeability, cannot be exactly the same in the special context of interception of communications for the purposes of police investigations as they are where the object of the relevant law is to place restrictions on the conduct of individuals. In particular, the requirement of foreseeability cannot mean that an individual should be enabled to foresee when the authorities are likely to intercept his communications so that he can adapt his conduct accordingly.'

The court had recognised that in some fields legal rules could not be laid down with total precision (*Bronda v Italy* (1998) 33 EHRR 81, para 54) and that a measure of vagueness was inevitable if excessive rigidity was to be avoided: *Kuijper v The Netherlands* (2005) 41 EHRR SE 16. There were, moreover, strong reasons for not publishing the details of authorisations, which would by implication reveal those places where such measures had not been put in place, thereby identifying vulnerable targets, and could undermine the ability of the police to use such powers effectively in cases where they suspected that terrorists might be operating and wished to conduct random stopping and searching in a particular area in the hope of catching them without giving them warning in advance. The defendants contended that the constable's discretion was closely constrained by the sole purpose for which the power could be properly exercised. An improper authorisation and confirmation were susceptible to challenge by judicial review. An improper stop and search would expose the constable to claims in tort for wrongful imprisonment, trespass to the person and goods, and breach of Convention rights.

34 The lawfulness requirement in the Convention addresses supremely important features of the rule of law. The exercise of power by public officials, as it affects members of the public, must be governed by clear and publicly accessible rules of law. The public must not be vulnerable to interference by public officials acting on any personal whim, caprice, malice, predilection or purpose other than that for which the power was conferred. This is what, in this context, is meant by arbitrariness, which is the antithesis of legality. This is the test which any interference with or derogation from a Convention right must meet if a violation is to be avoided.

35 The stop and search regime under review does in my opinion meet that test. The 2000 Act informs the public that these powers are, if duly authorised and confirmed, available. It defines and limits the powers with considerable precision. Code A, a public document, describes the procedure in detail. The Act and the Code do not require the fact or the details of any authorisation to be publicised in any way, even retrospectively, but I doubt if they are to be regarded as 'law' rather than as a procedure for bringing the law into potential effect. In any event, it would stultify a potentially valuable source of public protection to require notice of an authorisation or confirmation to be publicised prospectively. The efficacy of a measure such as this will be gravely weakened if potential offenders are alerted in advance. Anyone stopped and searched must be told, by the constable, all he needs to know. In exercising the power the constable is not free to act arbitrarily, and will be open to civil suit if he does. It is true that he need have no suspicion before stopping and searching a member of the public. This cannot, realistically, be interpreted as a warrant to stop and search people who are obviously not terrorist suspects, which would be futile and time-wasting. It is to ensure that a constable is not deterred from stopping and searching a person whom he does suspect as a potential terrorist by the fear that he could not show reasonable grounds for his suspicion. It is not suggested that the constables in these cases exercised their powers in a discriminatory manner (an impossible contention on the facts), and I prefer to say nothing on the subject of discrimination.

IV. THE EXERCISE OF THE POWERS IN THIS CASE

36 In summarising the facts in paras 2 and 3 above, I have deliberately omitted reference to matters mentioned by the respective claimants in their witness statements which, if accepted, might show that the stop and search powers were improperly exercised in their cases. This is an aspect which, because of the course these proceedings have taken, has not been explored in sworn evidence by the claimants, or tested in cross-examination, or made the subject of any evidence by the officers who conducted the searches. It is a matter which the claimants may, if so advised, pursue in county court proceedings which they have already issued. It is a matter which the House cannot fairly resolve at this stage in these proceedings. I therefore express no opinion upon it.

37 I would accordingly dismiss both appeals....

Lord Hope of Craighead, Lord Scott of Foscote and **Lord Brown of Eaton–under-Heywood** agreed with **Lord Bingham** and delivered concurring speeches. **Lord Walker of Gestingthorpe** agreed with Lord Bingham.

Appeal dismissed.

NOTES

1. Lords Hope of Craighead and Brown of Eaton-under-Heywood also considered obiter the possibility that the powers might not be according to law in that there were insufficient safeguards to avoid the risk of the power being abused or exercised arbitrarily. There was, for example, no way of enforcing the PACE Code A, para. 2.25 guidance that particular care must be taken 'not to discriminate against members of minority ethnic groups'. There was no way of policing that instruction unless all were stopped or stops were done on a strictly numerical basis. Lord Brown rejected this argument on the ground that it would be impossible to exercise the powers effectively in either of these ways. The legislation was to be regarded as enabling stops to be made on the basis of the intuition of a trained police officer, with experience and training in the features and circumstances of terrorism and terrorist group.[228]

The question whether there was any infringement of domestic discrimination law is considered below.[229]

2. Lord Carlile has repeatedly expressed the view that the s. 44 powers are overused, and believes this view to be shared by senior police officers with experience of terrorist work.[230] He has also noted unexplained differences between different police forces with similar risk profiles in the use of the powers.[231] In his 2004 Report, he welcomed the fact that the Metropolitan Police no longer sought blanket s. 44 authorisations for their whole area in normal circumstances.[232]

3. Compare the approach here with those concerning detention without trial and control orders.[233]

Part VI
Miscellaneous

TERRORIST OFFENCES...

56. Directing terrorist organisation

(1) A person commits an offence if he directs, at any level, the activities of an organisation which is concerned in the commission of acts of terrorism....

57. Possession for terrorist purposes

(1) A person commits an offence if he possesses an article in circumstances which give rise to a reasonable suspicion that his possession is for a purpose connected with the commission, preparation or instigation of an act of terrorism.

(2) It is a defence for a person charged with an offence under this section to prove that his possession of the article was not for a purpose connected with the commission, preparation or instigation of an act of terrorism.

(3) In proceedings for an offence under this section, if it is proved that an article—

 (a) was on any premises at the same time as the accused, or

 (b) was on premises of which the accused was the occupier or which he habitually used otherwise than as a member of the public,

the court may assume that the accused possessed the article, unless he proves that he did not know of its presence on the premises or that he had no control over it....

58. Collection of information

(1) A person commits an offence if—

 (a) he collects or makes a record of information of a kind likely to be useful to a person committing or preparing an act of terrorism, or

 (b) he possesses a document or record containing information of that kind.

---

[228] Paras [78], [79]. [229] P. 953.

[230] *The Definition of Terrorism* (Cm 7052, 2007), p. 27; see also Home Office Circular 038/2004, 1 July 2004, encouraging reduced use.

[231] See annual reviews. [232] *Review of the Operation in 2004 of the Terrorism Act 2000*, p. 27.

[233] Below, pp. 475–485.

(2) In this section 'record' includees a photographic or electronic record.

(3) It is a defence for a person charged with an offence under this section to prove that he had a reasonable excuse for his action or possession...

(5) A court by or before which a person is convicted of an offence under this section may order the forfeiture of any document or record containing information of the kind mentioned in subsection (1)(*a*).

(6) Before making an order under subsection (5) a court must give an opportunity to be heard to any person, other than the convicted person, who claims to be the owner of or otherwise interested in anything which can be forfeited under that subsection.

(7) An order under subsection (5) shall not come into force until there is no further possibility of it being varied, or set aside, on appeal (disregarding any power of a court to grant leave to appeal out of time).

INCITING TERRORISM OVERSEAS

59. England and Wales

(1) A person commits an offence if—

    (a) he incites another person to commit an act of terrorism wholly or partly outside the United Kingdom, and

    (b) the act would, if committed in England and Wales, constitute one of the offences listed in subsection (2).

(2) Those offences are—

    (a) murder,

    (b) an offence under section 18 of the Offences against the Person Act 1861 (wounding with intent),

    (c) an offence under section 23 or 24 of that Act (poison),

    (d) an offence under section 28 or 29 of that Act (explosions), and

    (e) an offence under section 1(2) of the Criminal Damage Act 1971 (endangering life by damaging property).

(3) A person guilty of an offence under this section shall be liable to any penalty to which he would be liable on conviction of the offence listed in subsection (2) which corresponds to the act which he incites.

(4) For the purposes of subsection (1) it is immaterial whether or not the person incited is in the United Kingdom at the time of the incitement.

(5) Nothing in this section imposes criminal liability on any person acting on behalf of, or holding office under, the Crown.

TERRORIST BOMBING AND FINANCE OFFENCES

62. Terrorist bombing: jurisdiction

(1) If—

    (a) a person does anything outside the United Kingdom as an act of terrorism or for the purposes of terrorism, and

    (b) his action would have constituted the commission of one of the offences listed in subsection (2) if it had been done in the United Kingdom, he shall be guilty of the offence.

(2) The offences referred to in subsection (1)(*b*) are—

    (a) an offence under section 2, 3 or 5 of the Explosive Substances Act 1883 (causing explosions, &c),

(b) an offence under section 1 of the Biological Weapons Act 1974 (biological weapons), and

(c) an offence under section 2 of the Chemical Weapons Act 1996 (chemical weapons).

63. Terrorist finance: jurisdiction

(1) If—

(a) a person does anything outside the United Kingdom, and

(b) his action would have constituted the commission of an offence under any of sections 15 to 18 if it had been done in the United Kingdom, he shall be guilty of the offence.

(2) For the purposes of subsection (1) (*b*), section 18(1)(*b*) shall be read as if for 'the jurisdiction' there were substituted 'a jurisdiction'.

NOTES (PART VI: MISCELLANEOUS)

1. *Penalties.* Offences under ss. 54, 57 and 58 carry sentences of 10 years' imprisonment or a fine or both on indictment or six months' imprisonment or a fine not exceeding the statutory maximum or both on summary conviction. Conviction (on indictment) for an offence under s. 56 carries a sentence of life imprisonment.[234]

2. *Weapons training.* Sections 54 and 55 create offences in respect of providing or receiving instruction or training in the making or use of firearms, radioactive material or weapons designed or adapted for the discharge of such material, explosives or chemical, biological or nuclear weapons, or inviting another to receive such instruction or training. It is a defence to show that D's involvement was wholly for a purpose other than assisting, preparing for or participating in terrorism. This offence (ss. 54, 55) formerly applied only in Northern Ireland[235] and has been extended to include chemical biological weapons and the use of radioactive material. It was noted in *Legislation Against Terrorism*[236] that the Kurdistan Workers Party poisoned the water supply of a Turkish military base in 1992 and the Aum Shinrikyo cult used Sarin gas in attacking the Tokyo underground in 1995. The offence has been difficult to prove.[237]

3. *Directing terrorist organisation.* This offence (s. 56) formerly applied only in Northern Ireland.[238] It was first introduced in the EPA 1991[239] and was criticised by Walker and Reid[240] on the grounds that it was too wide in that it was not limited to proscribed organisations and all directions were penalised even if lawful. By 1998 there had been two convictions, with long sentences imposed in each case.[241] Its retention was supported by Lord Lloyd who thought it had 'real value.'[242]

4. *Possession for terrorist purposes; collection of information.* These offences (ss. 57, 58) are based on the PTA, ss. 16A, 16B,[243] and the EPA, ss. 32, 33. They are controversial to the extent that they are broad and involve a reversal of the burden of proof. The possession offence enables action to be taken, for example, in respect of commonplace articles that are well known to be used in bomb manufacture.

---

[234] Ss. 54(6), 57(4), 58(4): s. 56(2).   [235] EPA, s. 34.   [236] Para. 12.13.

[237] *Lloyd Inquiry*, p. 95. In the absence of evidence that this offence would be of substantial value. Lord Lloyd did not recommend its inclusion in the permanent legislation. For further training offences, see below, p. 487.

[238] EPA, s. 29.   [239] S. 27.

[240] G. Walker and K. Reid [1993] Crim LR 669. B. Dickson [1992] PL at 617 regarded it as 'symbolic law-making'.

[241] *Legislation Against Terrorism*, para. 12.8.   [242] *Lloyd Inquiry*, para. 6.10.

[243] Introduced by the Criminal Justice and Public Order Act 1994, s. 82.

The collection of information offence would cover, for example, targeting lists. In *R v Lorenc*,[244] the Northern Ireland Court of Appeal held that the EPA offence (then s. 22 of the EPA 1978) was committed when L was found in possession of three Army Manuals pertaining to the use of rifles, booby traps and incendiaries. The court rejected an argument that the offence only applied to information likely or intended to be used in planning or carrying out an act of violence. Conversely, in *R v McLoughlin*[245] the court quashed McLoughlin's conviction under this provision in respect of his collection of a list of radio frequencies used by the RUC. The court was satisfied that he had established on the balance of probabilities the 'reasonable excuse' of being a 'radio buff' and not a terrorist.

Section 118, which applies (*inter alia*) to both provisions, expressly provides that the burden placed on the defendant is only an evidential burden.

The ss. 57 and 58 offences have rightly been given a narrow rather than broad interpretation by the Court of Appeal, although some elements of this are the subject of an appeal to the House of Lords. In *R v Zafar*,[246] four university students and a schoolboy were prosecuted under s. 57 with the possession of documents, computer discs and hard drives (on which information was electronically stored)[247] for a purpose connected with the commission etc. of an act of terrorism. The material included idealogical propaganda as well as communications between the appellants and others which, it was alleged, showed a settled plan under which the appellants would travel to Pakistan for training and thereafter commit terrorist acts in Afghanistan. It did not, the court noted, include instruction as to how to carry out a particular activity. The court held that:

> if s. 57 is to have the certainty of meaning that the law requires, it must be interpreted in a way that requires a direct connection between the object possessed and the act of terrorism. The section should be interpreted as if it reads:
>
> 'A person commits an offence if he possesses an article in circumstances which give rise to a reasonable suspicion that he intends it to be used for the purpose of the commission, preparation or instigation of an act of terrorism.'[248]

Possession for the purpose of inciting a person to commit an act of terrorism does fall within s. 57.[249] However, it would not be sufficiently direct for the information to be held for a purpose connected with the travel to Pakistan.[250] The directions to the jury had been inadequate in not emphasising the need for a direct connection.

Then in *R v K*,[251] K was prosecuted under s. 58 in respect of his possession of (a) a CD Rom with a copy of the Al-Qaeda training manual, (b) a text directed to the formation and organisation of Jihad movements, and (c) a text which argued that a Muslim was under an obligation to work for the establishment of an Islamic state. At a preparatory hearing, the judge

----

244 [1988] NI 96. Cf. the cases on s. 58, below.

245 8 October 1993, unreported, CA (Cr D) (NI).

246 [2008] EWCA Crim 184, [2008] 2 WLR 1013. See G. Virgo [2008] CLJ 236. On sentencing, see *R v Qureshi* [2008] EWCA Crim 1054.

247 It was confirmed in *R v Rowe* [2007] EWCA Crim 635, [2007] QB 975 that documents and records can be 'articles' for the purposes of s. 57 (here a notebook with instructions on how to assemble and operate a mortar and an encrypted list of potential targets for terrorist bombing). The Court of Appeal declined to follow the decision in *R v M* [2007] EWCA Crim 298 on the ground that it was *per incuriam*.

248 Per Lord Phillips of Worth Matravers (for the court) para. [29].

249 Ibid., para. [31].   250 Ibid., para. [34].

251 [2008] EWCA Crim 185, [2008] 2 WLR 1026. In *R v G* [2008] EWCA Crim 922 the CA rejected an argument that *R v K* was decided *per incuriam*.

rejected an argument that the prosecution was an abuse of process as s. 58 was insufficiently certain to comply with the common law or Art. 7 ECHR. The court rejected arguments (a) that the prosecution could rely on extrinsic evidence to show that information, which on its face was not the kind of information that would raise a reasonable suspicion that it might be intended to be used for the commission or preparation of an act of terrorism, was in fact held with that intention; (b) that for the defence of reasonable excuse to be established the purpose for which the information was held had to be lawful (so there would be no defence if it were shown that information concerning explosives was held for a planned bank robbery); and (c) that a document that exhorted the reader to commit acts of terrorism fell within the definition of a document containing information likely to be useful to a terrorist. Lord Phillips of Worth Matravers said:

13 We draw attention to the contrast between subsection (3)(a) and subsection (3)(b) [of section 58]. On Mr Sharp's submission section 58 of the 2000 Act covers documents described in either (3)(a) or (3)(b). We consider that it is plain from the language of section 58 that it covers only documents that fall within the description in (3)(b). A document or record will only fall within section 58 if it is of a kind that is likely to provide practical assistance to a person committing or preparing an act of terrorism. A document that simply encourages the commission of acts of terrorism does not fall within section 58.

14 The provisions of section 2 of the 2006 Act, and in particular those of section 2(5), require the jury to have regard to surrounding circumstances when deciding whether a publication is likely to be useful in the commission or preparation of acts of terrorism. Contrary to Mr Sharp's submission, we do not consider that the same is true of section 58 of the 2000 Act. The natural meaning of that section requires that a document or record that infringes it must contain information of such a nature as to raise a reasonable suspicion that it is intended to be used to assist in the preparation or commission of an act of terrorism. It must be information that calls for an explanation. Thus the section places on the person possessing it the obligation to provide a reasonable excuse. Extrinsic evidence may be adduced to explain the nature of the information. Thus had the defendant in *R v Rowe* [2007] QB 975 been charged under section 58, evidence could have been admitted as to the nature of the substitution code possessed by the defendant. What is not legitimate under section 58 is to seek to demonstrate, by reference to extrinsic evidence, that a document, innocuous on its face, is intended to be used for the purpose of committing or preparing a terrorist act.

15 As for the nature of a 'reasonable excuse', it seems to us that this is simply an explanation that the document or record is possessed for a purpose other than to assist in the commission or preparation of an act of terrorism. It matters not that that other purpose may infringe some other provision of the criminal or civil law.

16 If section 58 is interpreted in accordance with this judgment, its effect will not be so uncertain as to offend against the doctrine of legality.'

The overthrow of a tyrannical regime cannot constitute a 'reasonable excuse'.[252] It cannot be the case that a 'reasonable excuse for conduct which constituted a crime may be found in the commission of the very one prohibited by the statute'.[253] If Parliament had contemplated the possibility they would have used express words to provide a defence, or restricted the scope of Act to countries with a representative, democratic government. (Would such a distinction have been appropriate or workable?)

5. *Inciting terrorism overseas.* Sections 59–61 extend the circumstances in which a UK court may exercise jurisdiction in respect of offences committed abroad. The Crime (International

---

[252] *R v F* [2007] EWCA Crim 243, [2007] QB 960.   [253] Sir Igor Judge at para. [38].

Co-operation) Act 2003[254] inserted further provisions[255] that make it an offence in the UK for a UK national or resident to do anything outside the UK that would be an offence under ss. 56–61 of the 2000 Act; or other specified offences, including murder, done as an act of terrorism or for the purposes of terrorism. Similarly, it is an offence in the UK for a person outside the UK to commit such an offence for such purposes to or in relation to a UK national or resident or a protected person (such as a member of a diplomatic mission or consular post), or to commit damage offences in relation to premises or vehicles.

PART VIII

GENERAL

114. Police powers

(1) A power conferred by virtue of this Act on a constable—

    (a) is additional to powers which he has at common law or by virtue of any other enactment, and

    (b) shall not be taken to affect those powers.

(2) A constable may if necessary use reasonable force for the purpose of exercising a power conferred on him by virtue of this Act (apart from paragraphs 2 and 3 of Schedule 7).

(3) Where anything is seized by a constable under a power conferred by virtue of this Act, it may (unless the contrary intention appears) be retained for so long as is necessary in all the circumstances...

116. Powers to stop and search

(1) A power to search premises conferred by virtue of this Act shall be taken to include power to search a container.

(2) A power conferred by virtue of this Act to stop a person includes power to stop a vehicle (other than an aircraft which is airborne).

(3) A person commits an offence if he fails to stop a vehicle when required to do so by virtue of this section.

(4) A person guilty of an offence under subsection (3) shall be liable on summary conviction to—

    (a) imprisonment for a term not exceeding six months,

    (b) a fine not exceeding level 5 on the standard scale, or

    (c) both...

118. Defences

(1) Subsection (2) applies where in accordance with a provision mentioned in subsection (5) it is a defence for a person charged with an offence to prove a particular matter.

(2) If the person adduces evidence which is sufficient to raise an issue with respect to the matter the court or jury shall assume that the defence is satisfied unless the prosecution proves beyond reasonable doubt that it is not.

(3) Subsection (4) applies where in accordance with a provision mentioned in subsection (5) a court—

    (a) may make an assumption in relation to a person charged with an offence unless a particular matter is proved, or

    (b) may accept a fact as sufficient evidence unless a particular matter is proved.

---

[254] S. 52.   [255] 2000 Act, ss. 63A–63E.

(4) If evidence is adduced which is sufficient to raise an issue with respect to the matter mentioned in subsection (3)(*a*) or (*b*) the court shall treat it as proved unless the prosecution disproves it beyond reasonable doubt.

(5) The provisions in respect of which subsections (2) and (4) apply are—

(*a*) sections 12(4). 39(5)(*a*), 54, 57, 58, 77 and 103 of this Act, and

(*b*) sections 13, 32 and 33 of the Northern Ireland (Emergency Provisions) Act 1996 (possession and information offences) as they have effect by virtue of Schedule 1 to this Act.

121. Interpretation

In this Act—

'act' and 'action' include omission,

'article' includes substance and any other thing,…

['customs officer' means an officer [of Revenue and Customs],

['dwelling' means a building or part of a building used as a dwelling, and a vehicle which is habitually stationary and which is used as a dwelling,]

['explosive' means—

(*a*) an article or substance manufactured for the purpose of producing a practical effect by explosion,

(*b*) materials for making an article or substance within paragraph (*a*),

(*c*) anything used or intended to be used for causing or assisting in causing an explosion, and

(*d*) a part of anything within paragraph (*a*) or (*c*)],

'firearm' includes an air gun or air pistol,

'immigration officer' means a person appointed as an immigration officer under paragraph 1 of Schedule 2 to the Immigration Act 1971,

'the Islands' means the Channel Islands and the Isle of Man,

'organisation' includes any association or combination of persons,

'premises' [, except in section 63D,] includes any place and in particular includes—

(*a*) a vehicle,

(*b*) an offshore installation within the meaning given in section 44 of the Petroleum Act 1998, and

(*c*) a tent or moveable structure,

'property' includes property wherever situated and whether real or personal, heritable or moveable, and things in action and other intangible or incorporeal property,

'public place' means a place to which members of the public have or are permitted to have access, whether or not for payment,

'road' has the same meaning as in the Road Traffic Act 1988 (in relation to England and Wales), … and includes part of a road, and

'vehicle', except in sections 48 to 52 and Schedule 7, includes an aircraft, hovercraft, train or vessel.

124. Directions

A direction given under this Act may be varied or revoked by a further direction…

NOTE (PART VIII: GENERAL)

1. Section 115 and Sch. 14 enable an authorised officer or an examining officer to enter a vehicle and use reasonable force (other than in respect of Sch. 7, paras 2 and 3 (port and border controls) on Sch. 1 to the Anti-terrorism, Crime and Security Act 2001 (the 'terrorist cash provisions)). The Secretary of State may issue codes of practice. The consent of the DPP or DPP for Northern Ireland is necessary in respect of most offences under the Act; where it appears to him that an offence is committed for a purpose connected with the affairs of a country other than the UK, the consent of the Attorney-General or the Attorney-General for Northern Ireland is required (s. 117). Section 118 is an important provision restricting the number of provisions that impose anything more than an evidential burden on the defendant.[256]

4. THE ANTI-TERRORISM, CRIME AND SECURITY ACT 2001

In the aftermath of the 11/9 attacks in the US in which passenger airlines were hijacked by terrorists and crashed into buildings or the ground, the Government secured the speedy passage of the Anti-terrorism, Crime and Security Act 2005. It contained a range of provisions, some more directly concerned with terrorism than others.

Part 1 of the Act[257] contained more extensive powers enabling cash intended to be used for the purposes of terrorism, or which consists of resources of a prescribed organisation or is, or represents, property obtained through terrorism, to be forfeited in civil proceedings before a magistrates' court. The powers may apply to cash found anywhere in the UK and relate to terrorism anywhere in the world.[258] Part 2[259] enables the Treasury to make an order freezing the assets of persons who it reasonably believes have or are likely to take action to the detriment of the UK's economy or action constituting a threat to the life of one or more UK nationals or residents, or who have provided or are likely to provide assistance to such persons. Other topics covered by the Act include weapons of mass destruction, the security of pathogens and toxins, the security of the nuclear industry and aviation security.[260] There were some amendments to the 2000 Act.[261] The Secretary of State was required to appoint a committee to conduct a review of the Act.[262] The provisions that proved particularly controversial were those in Part 4 (ss. 21–32) concerning the ongoing detention of suspected international terrorists. These were considered by the House of Lords in the following case.

- **A and others v Secretary of State for the Home Department; X and another v Secretary of State for the Home Department** [2004] UKHL 56, [2005] 2 AC 68, House of Lords

Following the terrorist attacks in the US on 11 September 2001, for which the organisation Al-Qaeda was responsible, and in the light of threats made by that organisation specifically directed against the UK, the Government (a) secured the passage of ss. 21–32 within Pt 4 of the Anti-terrorism, Crime and Security Act 2001 and (b) made the Human Rights Act 1998

---

256 See above, p. 451.

257 Ss. 1–3 and Schs 1, 2, replacing ss. 24–31 of the Terrorism Act 2000. See generally on the Act H. Fenwick (2002) 65 MLR 724; D. Bonner (2002) 8 European Public Law 497; C. Gearty (2005) 32 JLS 18.

258 J.J. Rowe and others, *Current Law Statutes Annotated 2001*, p. 24–10.

259 Ss. 4–16. For a discussion of international responses to terrorist financing see N. Ryder [2007] JBL 821.

260 Parts 6, 7, 8, 9.   261 See ss. 117–120.   262 S. 122.

(Designated Derogation) Order 2001.[263] Section 21(1) empowered the Secretary of State to issue a certificate in respect of a person if he reasonably '(a) believes his presence in the UK is a risk to national security, and (b) suspects that the person is a terrorist'. 'Terrorist' meant a person who is or has been concerned in the commission, preparation or instigation of acts of international terrorism, or who belonged to or had links with an international terrorist group.

Normally, a non-UK national in respect of whom a deportation order has been made, and who is not charged with a crime, may only be detained for such time as is reasonably necessary for the process of deportation to be carried out.[264] Such detention is authorised by Art. 5(1)(f) ECHR. However, this does not authorise the long-term detention of a person where his return to his home country would involve a real risk of his being subjected to treatment contrary to Art. 3, and there is no other country (where there would not be such a risk) willing to take him.[265] Section 23 disapplied that rule in the case of persons certified as suspected international terrorists, enabling indefinite detention. The point that the application of this would infringe Art. 5(1) ECHR was met by a derogation notified under Art. 15 ECHR and the derogation order under the 1998 Act, s.14.

An appeal against certification lay (only) to the Special Immigration Appeals Commission,[266] which would also carry out periodic reviews.[267] SIAC also had exclusive jurisdiction in respect of challenges on derogation matters.[268] A number of persons were detained in Belmarsh prison by virtue of these provisions. They challenged the validity of the derogation order and the compatibility of the detention provisions with their Convention rights. SIAC[269] rejected a challenge to the derogation order but held that s. 23 was incompatible with Art. 14 as discriminatory on the ground of national origin and disproportionate. The Court of Appeal[270] allowed the Secretary of State's appeal. The House of Lords allowed a further appeal by the claimants. Seven members of the House (Lords Bingham of Cornhill, Nicholls of Birkenhead, Hope of Craighead, Scott of Foscote, Rodger of Earlsferry and Carswell, and Baroness Hale of Richmond) held (a) that the derogation order could not be challenged on the basis that there neither was nor is a 'public emergency threatening the life of the nation' within Art. 15(1); but (b) that the order should be quashed, and a declaration granted that s. 23 of the 2001 Act was incompatible with Arts 5 and 14 ECHR, on the ground that this was a disproportionate response to the emergency. Notwithstanding that Art. 15 ECHR, was not incorporated the Attorney-General was content to argue the case in the footing that the derogation order had to be justified by reference to it.[271] Lord Hoffmann dissented on the 'emergency' issue, and expressed no opinion on the proportionality and discrimination issues. Lord Walker of Gestingthorpe agreed on the 'emergency' issue and dissented on the proportionality and discrimination issues. The main opinion for the majority was given by Lord Bingham.

---

[263] SI 2001/3644.

[264] *Ex p Hardial Singh* [1984] 1 WLR 704. The reasonableness of the Home Secretary's view that there is a real prospect of being able to remove a person to his country in compliance with Art. 3 ECHR is to be judged by the court as the primary decision-maker, as is the reasonableness of the length of the detention bearing in mind the obligation to exercise all reasonable expedition to ensure that the steps necessary to effect a lawful return are taken in a reasonable time: *Youssef v Home Office* [2004] EWHC 1884 (QB), per Field J at para. [62] (damages for false imprisonment awarded in respect of 14 days after date on which it became clear that this would not be possible).

[265] *Chahal v UK* (1996) 23 EHRR 413. Here the Court rejected the UK's argument that the effect of Art. 3 should be qualified in a case where a state sought to deport a non-national on grounds of national security.

[266] S. 25.   [267] S. 26.   [268] S. 3.   [269] [2002] HRLR 45.

[270] [2004] QB 335.   [271] See Lord Scott of Foscote at paras [149]–[152].

Lord Bingham of Cornhill:

PUBLIC EMERGENCY

16 The appellants repeated before the House a contention rejected by both SIAC and the Court of Appeal, that there neither was nor is a 'public emergency threatening the life of the nation' within the meaning of article 15(1). Thus, they contended, the threshold test for reliance on article 15 has not been satisfied....

[His Lordship referred to the jurisprudence of the ECtHR, which had held that this test referred to 'an exceptional situation of crisis or emergency which affects the whole population and constitutes a threat to the organised life of the community of which the state is composed' (*Lawless v Ireland (No. 3)* (1961) 1 EHRR 15, at para. 28, a case where 'very low-level IRA terrorist activity in Ireland and Northern Ireland between 1954 and 1957' (in Lord Bingham's words) was held to constitute such an emergency). In *The Greek Case* (1969) 12 YBI, the Commission stated (at para. 153) that

'Such a public emergency may then be seen to have, in particular, the following characteristics: (1) It must be actual or imminent. (2) Its effects must involve the whole nation. (3) The continuance of the organised life of the Community must be threatened. (4) The crisis or danger must be exceptional, in that the normal measures or restrictions, permitted by the Convention for the maintenance of public safety, health and order, are plainly inadequate.'

In *Ireland v UK* (1978) 2 EHRR 25, the Court stated (at para. 207) that Art. 15(1) left the national authorities a wide margin of appreciation.]

20 The appellants did not seek to play down the catastrophic nature of what had taken place on 11 September 2001 nor the threat posed to western democracies by international terrorism. But they argued that there had been no public emergency threatening the life of the British nation, for three main reasons: if the emergency was not (as in all the decided cases) actual, it must be shown to be imminent, which could not be shown here; the emergency must be of a temporary nature, which again could not be shown here; and the practice of other states, none of which had derogated from the European Convention, strongly suggested that there was no public emergency calling for derogation....

[As to imminence, the appellants pointed to ministerial statements in October 2001 and March 2002: 'There is no immediate intelligence pointing to a specific threat to the UK, but we remain alert, domestically as well as internationally;' and 'it would be wrong to say that we have evidence of a particular threat.' As to temporariness, official spokesmen had declined to suggest when, if ever, the present situation might change. No state other than the UK had derogated from Art. 5, although France, Italy and Germany had all been threatened as well as the UK. The view of the Joint Committee on Human Rights was that insufficient evidence had been presented to Parliament to make it possible for them to accept that derogation was strictly required.]

25 The Attorney General, representing the Home Secretary, answered these points. He submitted that an emergency could properly be regarded as imminent if an atrocity was credibly threatened by a body such as Al-Qaeda which had demonstrated its capacity and will to carry out such a threat, where the atrocity might be committed without warning at any time. The Government, responsible as it was and is for the safety of the British people, need not wait for disaster to strike before taking necessary steps to prevent it striking. As to the requirement that the emergency be temporary, the Attorney General did not suggest that an emergency could ever become the normal state of affairs, but he did resist the imposition of any artificial temporal limit to an emergency of the present kind, and pointed out that the emergency which had been held to justify derogation in Northern Ireland in 1988 had been accepted as continuing for a considerable number of years: see *Marshall v United Kingdom* (Application No 41571/98), para 18 above. Little help, it was suggested, could be gained by looking at the practice of other states. It was for each national government, as the guardian of its own people's safety, to make its own judgment on the basis of the facts known to it. In so far as any difference of practice as between the United Kingdom and other Council of Europe members called for justification, it could be found in this country's prominent role as an enemy of Al-Qaeda and an ally of the United States. The Attorney General also made two more fundamental submissions. First, he submitted that there was no error of law in SIAC's approach to this issue and accordingly, since an appeal against its decision lay only on a point of law, there was no ground upon which any appellate court was entitled to disturb its conclusion. Secondly, he submitted that the judgment on this question was pre-eminently one within the discretionary area of judgment reserved to the Secretary of State and his colleagues, exercising their judgment with the benefit of official advice, and to Parliament.

26 The appellants have in my opinion raised an important and difficult question, as the continuing anxiety of the Joint Committee on Human Rights, the observations of the Commissioner for Human Rights and the warnings of the UN Human Rights Committee make clear. In the result, however, not without misgiving (fortified by reading the opinion of my noble and learned friend Lord Hoffmann), I would resolve this issue against the appellants, for three main reasons.

27 First, it is not shown that SIAC or the Court of Appeal misdirected themselves on this issue. SIAC considered a body of closed material, that is, secret material of a sensitive nature not shown to the parties. The Court of Appeal was not asked to read this material. The Attorney General expressly declined to ask the House to read it. From this I infer that while the closed material no doubt substantiates and strengthens the evidence in the public domain, it does not alter its essential character and effect. But this is in my view beside the point. It is not shown that SIAC misdirected itself in law on this issue, and the view which it accepted was one it could reach on the open evidence in the case.

28 My second reason is a legal one. The European Court decisions in *Ireland v United Kingdom* 2 EHRR 25; *Brannigan and McBride v United Kingdom* 17 EHRR 539; *Aksoy v Turkey* 23 EHRR 553 and *Marshall v United Kingdom* (Application No 41571/98) seem to me to be, with respect, clearly right. In each case the member state had actually experienced widespread loss of life caused by an armed body dedicated to destroying the territorial integrity of the state. To hold that the article 15 test was not satisfied in such circumstances, if a response beyond that provided by the ordinary course of law was required, would have been perverse. But these features were not, on the facts found, very clearly present in *Lawless v Ireland (No 3)* 1 EHRR 15. That was a relatively early decision of the European Court, but it has never to my knowledge been disavowed and the House is required by section 2(1) of the 1998 Act to take it into account. The decision may perhaps be explained as showing the breadth of the margin of appreciation accorded by the court to national authorities. It may even have been influenced by the generous opportunity for release given to Mr Lawless and those in his position. If, however, it was open to the Irish Government in *Lawless* to conclude that there was a public emergency threatening the life of the Irish nation, the British Government could scarcely be faulted for reaching that conclusion in the much more dangerous situation which arose after 11 September.

29 Thirdly, I would accept that great weight should be given to the judgment of the Home Secretary, his colleagues and Parliament on this question, because they were called on to exercise a pre-eminently political judgment. It involved making a factual prediction of what various people around the world might or might not do, and when (if at all) they might do it, and what the consequences might be if they did. Any prediction about the future behaviour of human beings (as opposed to the phases of the moon or high water at London Bridge) is necessarily problematical. Reasonable and informed minds may differ, and a judgment is not shown to be wrong or unreasonable because that which is thought likely to happen does not happen. It would have been irresponsible not to err, if at all, on the side of safety. As will become apparent, I do not accept the full breadth of the Attorney General's argument on what is generally called the deference owed by the courts to the political authorities. It is perhaps preferable to approach this question as one of demarcation of functions or what Liberty in its written case called 'relative institutional competence'. The more purely political (in a broad or narrow sense) a question is, the more

appropriate it will be for political resolution and the less likely it is to be an appropriate matter for judicial decision. The smaller, therefore, will be the potential role of the court. It is the function of political and not judicial bodies to resolve political questions. Conversely, the greater the legal content of any issue, the greater the potential role of the court, because under our constitution and subject to the sovereign power of Parliament it is the function of the courts and not of political bodies to resolve legal questions. The present question seems to me to be very much at the political end of the spectrum: see *Secretary of State for the Home Department v Rehman* [2003] 1 AC 153, para 62, per Lord Hoffmann. The appellants recognised this by acknowledging that the Home Secretary's decision on the present question was less readily open to challenge than his decision (as they argued) on some other questions. This reflects the unintrusive approach of the European court to such a question. I conclude that the appellants have shown no ground strong enough to warrant displacing the Secretary of State's decision on this important threshold question.

PROPORTIONALITY

30 Article 15 requires that any measures taken by a member state in derogation of its obligations under the Convention should not go beyond what is 'strictly required by the exigencies of the situation'. Thus the Convention imposes a test of strict necessity or, in Convention terminology, proportionality. The appellants founded on the principle adopted by the Privy Council in *de Freitas v Permanent Secretary of Ministry of Agriculture, Fisheries, Lands and Housing* [1999] 1 AC 69, 80. In determining whether a limitation is arbitrary or excessive, the court must ask itself:

'whether: (i) the legislative objective is sufficiently important to justify limiting a fundamental right; (ii) the measures designed to meet the legislative objective are rationally connected to it; and (iii) the means used to impair the right or freedom are no more than is necessary to accomplish the objective.'

This approach is close to that laid down by the Supreme Court of Canada in *R v Oakes* [1986] 1 SCR 103, paras 69–70, and in *Libman v Attorney General of Quebec* (1997) 3 BHRC 269, para 38. To some extent these questions are, or may be, interrelated. But the appellants directed the main thrust of their argument to the second and third questions. They submitted that even if it were accepted that the legislative objective of protecting the British people against the risk of catastrophic Al-Qaeda terrorism was sufficiently important to justify limiting the fundamental right to personal freedom of those facing no criminal accusation, the 2001 Act was not designed to meet that objective and was not rationally connected to it. Furthermore, the legislative objective could have been achieved by means which did not, or did not so severely, restrict the fundamental right to personal freedom.

31 The appellants' argument under this head can, I hope fairly, be summarised as involving the following steps.

(1) Part 4 of the 2001 Act reversed the effect of the decisions in *Ex p Hardial Singh* [1984] 1 WLR 704 and *Chahal* 23 EHRR 413 and was apt to address the problems of immigration control caused to the United Kingdom by article 5(1)(f) of the Convention read in the light of those decisions.

(2) The public emergency on which the United Kingdom relied to derogate from the Convention right to personal liberty was the threat to the security of the United Kingdom presented by Al-Qaeda terrorists and their supporters.

(3) While the threat to the security of the United Kingdom derived predominantly and most immediately from foreign nationals, some of whom could not be deported because they would face torture or inhuman or degrading treatment or punishment in their home countries and who could not be deported to any third country willing to receive them, the threat to the United Kingdom did not derive solely from such foreign nationals.

(4) Sections 21 and 23 did not rationally address the threat to the security of the United Kingdom presented by Al-Qaeda terrorists and their supporters because (a) it did not address the threat presented by

UK nationals, (b) it permitted foreign nationals suspected of being Al-Qaeda terrorists or their supporters to pursue their activities abroad if there was any country to which they were able to go, and
(c) the sections permitted the certification and detention of persons who were not suspected of presenting any threat to the security of the United Kingdom as Al-Qaeda terrorists or supporters.

(5) If the threat presented to the security of the United Kingdom by UK nationals suspected of being
Al-Qaeda terrorists or their supporters could be addressed without infringing their right to personal
liberty, it is not shown why similar measures could not adequately address the threat presented by
foreign nationals.

(6) Since the right to personal liberty is among the most fundamental of the rights protected by the
European Convention, any restriction of it must be closely scrutinised by the national court and such
scrutiny involves no violation of democratic or constitutional principle.

(7) In the light of such scrutiny, neither the Derogation Order nor sections 21 and 23 of the 2001 Act can
be justified.

32 It is unnecessary to linger on the first two steps of this argument, neither of which is controversial
and both of which are clearly correct. The third step calls for closer examination. The evidence before SIAC
was that the Home Secretary considered 'that the serious threats to the nation emanated predominantly
(albeit not exclusively) and more immediately from the category of foreign nationals'. In para 95 of its
judgment SIAC held:

'But the evidence before us demonstrates beyond argument that the threat is not so confined [to the
alien section of the population]. There are many British nationals already identified—mostly in detention
abroad—who fall within the definition of "suspected international terrorists", and it was clear from the
submissions made to us that in the opinion of the [Home Secretary] there are others at liberty in the United
Kingdom who could be similarly defined.'

This finding has not been challenged, and since SIAC is the responsible fact-finding tribunal it is unnecessary to examine the basis of it. There was however evidence before SIAC that 'upwards of a thousand
individuals from the UK are estimated on the basis of intelligence to have attended training camps in
Afghanistan in the last five years', that some British citizens are said to have planned to return from
Afghanistan to the United Kingdom and that 'The backgrounds of those detained show the high level of
involvement of British citizens and those otherwise connected with the United Kingdom in the terrorist
networks'. It seems plain that the threat to the United Kingdom did not derive solely from foreign nationals
or from foreign nationals whom it was unlawful to deport. Later evidence, not before SIAC or the Court of
Appeal, supports that conclusion. The Newton Committee recorded the Home Office argument that the
threat from Al-Qaeda terrorism was predominantly from foreigners but drew attention, at para 193, to

'accumulating evidence that this is not now the case. The British suicide bombers who attacked Tel Aviv
in May 2003, Richard Reid ('the Shoe Bomber'), and recent arrests suggest that the threat from UK citizens
is real. Almost 30% of Terrorism Act 2000 suspects in the past year have been British. We have been told
that, of the people of interest to the authorities because of their suspected involvement in international
terrorism, nearly half are British nationals.'

33 The fourth step in the appellants' argument is of obvious importance to it. It is plain that sections 21
and 23 of the 2001 Act do not address the threat presented by UK nationals since they do not provide
for the certification and detention of UK nationals. It is beside the point that other sections of the 2001
Act and the 2000 Act do apply to UK nationals, since they are not the subject of derogation, are not the
subject of complaint and apply equally to foreign nationals. Yet the threat from UK nationals, if quantita-
tively smaller, is not said to be qualitatively different from that from foreign nationals. It is also plain that
sections 21 and 23 do permit a person certified and detained to leave the United Kingdom and go to any
other country willing to receive him, as two of the appellants did when they left for Morocco and France
respectively (see para 2 above). Such freedom to leave is wholly explicable in terms of immigration

control: if the British authorities wish to deport a foreign national but cannot deport him to country A because of *Chahal* their purpose is as well served by his voluntary departure for country B. But allowing a suspected international terrorist to leave our shores and depart to another country, perhaps a country as close as France, there to pursue his criminal designs, is hard to reconcile with a belief in his capacity to inflict serious injury to the people and interests of this country. It seems clear from the language of section 21 of the 2001 Act, read with the definition of terrorism in section 1 of the 2000 Act, that section 21 is capable of covering those who have no link at all with Al-Qaeda (they might, for example, be members of the Basque separatist organisation ETA), or who, although supporting the general aims of Al-Qaeda, reject its cult of violence. The Attorney General conceded that sections 21 and 23 could not lawfully be invoked in the case of suspected international terrorists other than those thought to be connected with Al-Qaeda, and undertook that the procedure would not be used in such cases. A restrictive reading of the broad statutory language might in any event be indicated: *Padfield v Minister of Agriculture, Fisheries and Food* [1968] AC 997. The appellants were content to accept the Attorney General's concession and undertaking. It is not however acceptable that interpretation and application of a statutory provision bearing on the liberty of the subject should be governed by implication, concession and undertaking....

35 The fifth step in the appellants' argument permits of little elaboration. But it seems reasonable to assume that those suspected international terrorists who are UK nationals are not simply ignored by the authorities. When G, one of the appellants, was released from prison by SIAC on bail (*G v Secretary of State for the Home Department* (unreported) 20 May 2004) it was on condition (among other things) that he wear an electronic monitoring tag at all times; that he remain at his premises at all times; that he telephone a named security company five times each day at specified times; that he permit the company to install monitoring equipment at his premises; that he limit entry to his premises to his family, his solicitor, his medical attendants and other approved persons; that he make no contact with any other person; that he have on his premises no computer equipment, mobile telephone or other electronic communications device; that he cancel the existing telephone link to his premises; and that he install a dedicated telephone link permitting contact only with the security company. The appellants suggested that conditions of this kind, strictly enforced, would effectively inhibit terrorist activity. It is hard to see why this would not be so.

36 In urging the fundamental importance of the right to personal freedom, as the sixth step in their proportionality argument, the appellants were able to draw on the long libertarian tradition of English law, dating back to chapter 39 of Magna Carta 1215, given effect in the ancient remedy of habeas corpus, declared in the Petition of Right 1628, upheld in a series of landmark decisions down the centuries and embodied in the substance and procedure of the law to our own day. Recent statements, not in themselves remarkable, may be found in *In re S-C (Mental Patient: Habeas Corpus)* [1996] QB 599, 603 and *In re Wasfi Suleman Mahmod* [1995] Imm A R 311, 314. In its treatment of article 5 of the European Convention, the European Court also has recognised the prime importance of personal freedom. In *Kurt v Turkey* (1998) 27 EHRR 373, para 122, it referred to 'the fundamental importance of the guarantees contained in article 5 for securing the right of individuals in a democracy to be free from arbitrary detention at the hands of the authorities' and to the need to interpret narrowly any exception to 'a most basic guarantee of individual freedom'. In *Garcia Alva v Germany* (2001) 37 EHRR 335, para 39, it referred to 'the dramatic impact of deprivation of liberty on the fundamental rights of the person concerned'....

37 While the Attorney General challenged and resisted the third, fourth and fifth steps in the appellants' argument, he directed the weight of his submission to challenging the standard of judicial review for which the appellants contended in this sixth step. He submitted that as it was for Parliament and the executive to assess the threat facing the nation, so it was for those bodies and not the courts to judge the response necessary to protect the security of the public. These were matters of a political character calling for an exercise of political and not judicial judgment. Just as the European court allowed a

generous margin of appreciation to member states, recognising that they were better placed to under-stand and address local problems, so should national courts recognise, for the same reason, that matters of the kind in issue here fall within the discretionary area of judgment properly belonging to the demo-cratic organs of the state. It was not for the courts to usurp authority properly belonging elsewhere. The Attorney General drew attention to the dangers identified by Richard Ekins in 'Judicial Supremacy and the Rule of Law' (2003) 119 LQR 127. This is an important submission, properly made, and it calls for careful consideration.

38 Those conducting the business of democratic government have to make legislative choices which, notably in some fields, are very much a matter for them, particularly when (as is often the case) the interests of one individual or group have to be balanced against those of another individual or group or the interests of the community as a whole. The European court has recognised this on many occasions: *Chassagnou v France* (1999) 29 EHRR 615, para 113, and *Hatton v United Kingdom* (2003) 37 EHRR 611, paras 97–98, may be cited as recent examples. In para 97 of *Hatton* , a case which concerned aircraft noise at Heathrow, the court said:

'At the same time, the court reiterates the fundamentally subsidiary role of the Convention. The national authorities have direct democratic legitimation and are, as the court has held on many occasions, in prin-ciple better placed than an international court to evaluate local needs and conditions. In matters of general policy, on which opinions within a democratic society may reasonably differ widely, the role of the domestic policy maker should be given special weight.'

Where the conduct of government is threatened by serious terrorism, difficult choices have to be made and the terrorist dimension cannot be overlooked. This also the European commission and court have rec-ognised in cases such as *Brogan v United Kingdom* (1988) 11 EHRR 117, para 80; *Fox, Campbell & Hartley v United Kingdom* (1990) 13 EHRR 157, paras 32, 34; and *Murray v United Kingdom* (1994) 19 EHRR 193, para 47. The same recognition is found in domestic authority: see, for example, *Secretary of State for the Home Department v Rehman* [2003] 1 AC 153, paras 28, 62.

39 While any decision made by a representative democratic body must of course command respect, the degree of respect will be conditioned by the nature of the decision. As the European court observed in *Fretté v France* (2002) 38 EHRR 438, para 40:

'the contracting states enjoy a margin of appreciation in assessing whether and to what extent differences in otherwise similar situations justify a different treatment in law. The scope of the margin of appreciation will vary according to the circumstances, the subject-matter and its background; in this respect, one of the relevant factors may be the existence or non-existence of common ground between the laws of contract-ing states.'

A similar approach is found in domestic authority. In *R v Director of Public Prosecutions, Ex p Kebilene* [2000] 2 AC 326, 381, Lord Hope of Craighead said:

'It will be easier for such [a discretionary] area of judgment to be recognised where the Convention itself requires a balance to be struck, much less so where the right is stated in terms which are unqualified. It will be easier for it to be recognised where the issues involve questions of social or economic policy, much less so where the rights are of high constitutional importance or are of a kind where the courts are especially well placed to assess the need for protection.'

Another area in which the court was held to be qualified to make its own judgment is the requirement of a fair trial: *R v A (No 2)* [2002] 1 AC 45, para 36. The Supreme Court of Canada took a similar view in *Libman v Attorney General of Quebec* 3 BHRC 269, para 59. In his dissenting judgment (cited with approval in *Libman*) in *RJR-MacDonald Inc v Attorney General of Canada* [1995] 3 SCR 199, para 68, La Forest J, sit-ting in the same court, said:

'Courts are specialists in the protection of liberty and the interpretation of legislation and are, accordingly, well placed to subject criminal justice legislation to careful scrutiny. However, courts are not specialists in the realm of policy-making, nor should they be.'

See also McLachlin J in the same case, para 135. Jackson J, sitting in the Supreme Court of the United States in *West Virginia State Board of Education v Barnette* (1943) 319 US 624, para 3, stated, speaking of course with reference to an entrenched constitution:

'The very purpose of a Bill of Rights was to withdraw certain subjects from the vicissitudes of political controversy, to place them beyond the reach of majorities and officials and to establish them as legal principles to be applied by the courts...We cannot, because of modest estimates of our competence in such specialties as public education, withhold the judgment that history authenticates as the function of this court when liberty is infringed.'

40 The Convention regime for the international protection of human rights requires national authorities, including national courts, to exercise their authority to afford effective protection. The European Court made this clear in the early case of *Handyside v United Kingdom* (1976) 1 EHRR 737, para 48:

'The court points out that the machinery of protection established by the Convention is subsidiary to the national systems safeguarding human rights. The Convention leaves to each contracting state, in the first place, the task of securing the rights and freedoms it enshrines.'

Thus the European Commissioner for Human Rights had authority for saying (Opinion 1/2002, para 9):

'It is furthermore, precisely because the Convention presupposes domestic controls in the form of a preventive parliamentary scrutiny and posterior judicial review that national authorities enjoy a large margin of appreciation in respect of derogations. This is, indeed, the essence of the principle of the subsidiarity of the protection of Convention rights.'

In *Smith and Grady v United Kingdom* (1999) 29 EHRR 493 the traditional *Wednesbury* approach to judicial review (see *Associated Provincial Pictures Houses Ltd v Wednesbury Corpn* [1948] 1 KB 223) was held to afford inadequate protection. It is now recognised that 'domestic courts must themselves form a judgment whether a Convention right has been breached' and that 'the intensity of review is somewhat greater under the proportionality approach': *R (Daly) v Secretary of State for the Home Department* [2001] 2 AC 532, paras 23, 27.

41 Even in a terrorist situation the Convention organs have not been willing to relax their residual supervisory role: *Brogan v United Kingdom* 11 EHRR 117, para 80; *Fox, Campbell & Hartley v United Kingdom* 13 EHRR 157, paras 32–34. In *Aksoy v Turkey* 23 EHRR 553, para 76, the court, clearly referring to national courts as well as the Convention organs, held:

'The court would stress the importance of article 5 in the Convention system: it enshrines a fundamental human right, namely the protection of the individual against arbitrary interference by the state with his or her right to liberty. Judicial control of interferences by the executive with the individual's right to liberty is an essential feature of the guarantee embodied in article 5(3), which is intended to minimise the risk of arbitrariness and to ensure the rule of law.'

In *Korematsu v United States* (1984) 584 F Supp 1406 para 21, Judge Patel observed that the Supreme Court's earlier decision (1944) 323 US 214 'stands as a caution that in times of distress the shield of military necessity and national security must not be used to protect governmental actions from close scrutiny and accountability'. Simon Brown LJ observed in *International Transport Roth GmbH v Secretary of State for the Home Department* [2003] QB 728, para 27, that 'the court's role under the 1998 Act is as the guardian of human rights. It cannot abdicate this responsibility.' He went on to say, in para 54:

'But judges nowadays have no alternative but to apply the Human Rights Act 1998. Constitutional dangers exist no less in too little judicial activism as in too much. There are limits to the legitimacy of executive or legislative decision-making, just as there are to decision-making by the courts.'

42 It follows from this analysis that the appellants are in my opinion entitled to invite the courts to review, on proportionality grounds, the Derogation Order and the compatibility with the Convention of section 23 and the courts are not effectively precluded by any doctrine of deference from scrutinising the issues raised. It also follows that I do not accept the full breadth of the Attorney General's submissions. I do not in particular accept the distinction which he drew between democratic institutions and the courts. It is of course true that the judges in this country are not elected and are not answerable to Parliament. It is also of course true, as pointed out in para 29 above, that Parliament, the executive and the courts have different functions. But the function of independent judges charged to interpret and apply the law is universally recognised as a cardinal feature of the modern democratic state, a cornerstone of the rule of law itself. The Attorney General is fully entitled to insist on the proper limits of judicial authority, but he is wrong to stigmatise judicial decision-making as in some way undemocratic. It is particularly inappropriate in a case such as the present in which Parliament has expressly legislated in section 6 of the 1998 Act to render unlawful any act of a public authority, including a court, incompatible with a Convention right, has required courts (in section 2) to take account of relevant Strasbourg jurisprudence, has (in section 3) required courts, so far as possible, to give effect to Convention rights and has conferred a right of appeal on derogation issues. The effect is not, of course, to override the sovereign legislative authority of the Queen in Parliament, since if primary legislation is declared to be incompatible the validity of the legislation is unaffected (section 4(6)) and the remedy lies with the appropriate minister (section 10), who is answerable to Parliament. The 1998 Act gives the courts a very specific, wholly democratic, mandate. As Professor Jowell has put it 'The courts are charged by Parliament with delineating the boundaries of a rights-based democracy' ('Judicial Deference: servility, civility or institutional capacity?' [2003] PL 592, 597). See also Clayton, 'Judicial deference and 'democratic dialogue': the legitimacy of judicial intervention under the Human Rights Act 1998' [2004] PL 33.

43 The appellants' proportionality challenge to the Order and section 23 is, in my opinion, sound, for all the reasons they gave and also for those given by the European Commissioner for Human Rights and the Newton Committee. The Attorney General could give no persuasive answer. In a discussion paper 'Counter-Terrorism Powers: Reconciling Security and Liberty in an Open Society' (Cm 6147) (February 2004) the Secretary of State replied to one of the Newton Committee's criticisms in this way:

> '32. It can be argued that as suspected international terrorists their departure for another country could amount to exporting terrorism: a point made in the Newton Report at para 195. But that is a natural consequence of the fact that Part 4 powers are immigration powers: detention is permissible only pending deportation and there is no other power available to detain (other than for the purpose of police inquiries) if a foreign national chooses voluntarily to leave the UK. (Detention in those circumstances is limited to 14 days after which the person must be either charged or released.) Deportation has the advantage moreover of disrupting the activities of the suspected terrorist.'

This answer, however, reflects the central complaint made by the appellants: that the choice of an immigration measure to address a security problem had the inevitable result of failing adequately to address that problem (by allowing non-UK suspected terrorists to leave the country with impunity and leaving British suspected terrorists at large) while imposing the severe penalty of indefinite detention on persons who, even if reasonably suspected of having links with Al-Qaeda, may harbour no hostile intentions towards the United Kingdom. The conclusion that the Order and section 23 are, in Convention terms, disproportionate is in my opinion irresistible.

44 Since, under section 7 of the Special Immigration Appeals Commission Act 1997 and section 30(5) of the 2001 Act, an appeal from SIAC lies only on a point of law, that is not the end of the matter. It is necessary to examine SIAC's reasons for rejecting this part of the appellants' challenge. They are given in para 51 of SIAC's judgment, and are fourfold:

> (1) that there is an advantage to the UK in the removal of a potential terrorist from circulation in the UK because he cannot operate actively in the UK whilst he is either not in the country or not at liberty;

(2) that the removal of potential terrorists from their UK communities disrupts the organisation of terrorist activities;

(3) that the detainee's freedom to leave, far from showing that the measures are irrational, tends to show that they are to this extent properly tailored to the state of emergency; and

(4) that it is difficult to see how a power to detain a foreign national who had not been charged with a criminal offence and wished to leave the UK could readily be defended as tending to prevent him committing acts of terrorism aimed at the UK.

Assuming, as one must, that there is a public emergency threatening the life of the nation, measures which derogate from article 5 are permissible only to the extent strictly required by the exigencies of the situation, and it is for the derogating state to prove that that is so. The reasons given by SIAC do not warrant its conclusion. The first reason does not explain why the measures are directed only to foreign nationals. The second reason no doubt has some validity, but is subject to the same weakness. The third reason does not explain why a terrorist, if a serious threat to the UK, ceases to be so on the French side of the English Channel or elsewhere. The fourth reason is intelligible if the foreign national is not really thought to be a serious threat to the UK, but hard to understand if he is. I do not consider SIAC's conclusion as one to which it could properly come. In dismissing the appellants' appeal, Lord Woolf CJ broadly considered that it was sensible and appropriate for the Secretary of State to use immigration legislation, that deference was owed to his decisions (para 40) and that SIAC's conclusions depended on the evidence before it (para 43). Brooke LJ reached a similar conclusion (para 91), regarding SIAC's findings as unappealable findings of fact. Chadwick LJ also regarded SIAC's finding as one of fact (para 150). I cannot accept this analysis as correct. The European Court does not approach questions of proportionality as questions of pure fact: see, for example, *Smith and Grady v United Kingdom* 29 EHRR 493. Nor should domestic courts do so. The greater intensity of review now required in determining questions of proportionality, and the duty of the courts to protect Convention rights, would in my view be emasculated if a judgment at first instance on such a question were conclusively to preclude any further review. So would excessive deference, in a field involving indefinite detention without charge or trial, to ministerial decision. In my opinion, SIAC erred in law and the Court of Appeal erred in failing to correct its error.

DISCRIMINATION

45 As part of their proportionality argument, the appellants attacked section 23 as discriminatory. They contended that, being discriminatory, the section could not be 'strictly required' within the meaning of article 15 and so was disproportionate. The courts below found it convenient to address this discrimination issue separately, and I shall do the same.

46 The appellants complained that in providing for the detention of suspected international terrorists who were not UK nationals but not for the detention of suspected international terrorists who were UK nationals, section 23 unlawfully discriminated against them as non-UK nationals in breach of article 14 of the European Convention.... It is well established that the obligation on the state not to discriminate applies only to rights which it is bound to protect under the Convention.

The appellants claim that section 23 discriminates against them in their enjoyment of liberty under article 5. Article 14 is of obvious importance. In his influential work 'An International Bill of the Rights of Man' (1945), p 115, Professor Hersch Lauterpacht wrote: 'The claim to equality before the law is in a substantial sense the most fundamental of the rights of man.' Jackson J reflected this belief in his well-known judgment in *Railway Express Agency Inc v New York* (1949) 336 US 106, 112–113, when he said:

'I regard it as a salutary doctrine that cities, states and the Federal Government must exercise their powers so as not to discriminate between their inhabitants except upon some reasonable differentiation fairly related to the object of regulation. This equality is not merely abstract justice. The framers of the Constitution knew, and we should not forget today, that there is no more effective practical guaranty against arbitrary and unreasonable government than to require that the principles of law which officials would impose upon a minority must be imposed generally. Conversely, nothing opens the door to arbitrary action so effectively as to allow those officials to pick and choose only a few to whom they will apply legislation and thus to escape the political retribution that might be visited upon them if larger numbers were affected. Courts can take no better measure to assure that laws will be just than to require that laws be equal in operation.'

More recently, the Privy Council (per Lord Hoffmann, *Matadeen v Pointu* [1999] 1 AC 98, 109) observed, with reference to the principle of equality:

'Their Lordships do not doubt that such a principle is one of the building blocks of democracy and necessarily permeates any democratic constitution. Indeed, their Lordships would go further and say that treating like cases alike and unlike cases differently is a general axiom of rational behaviour.'

47 The United Kingdom did not derogate from article 14 of the European Convention (or from article 26 of the ICCPR, which corresponds to it). The Attorney General did not submit that there had been an implied derogation, an argument advanced to SIAC but not to the Court of Appeal or the House.

48 The foreign nationality of the appellants does not preclude them from claiming the protection of their Convention rights. By article 1 of the Convention (which has not been expressly incorporated) the contracting states undertook to secure the listed Convention rights 'to everyone within their jurisdiction'. That includes the appellants. The European Court has recognised the Convention rights of non-nationals: see, for a recent example, *Conka v Belgium* (2002) 34 EHRR 1298. This accords with domestic authority. In *R v Secretary of State for the Home Department, Ex p Khawaja* [1984] AC 74, 111–112:

'Habeas corpus protection is often expressed as limited to "British subjects". Is it really limited to British nationals? Suffice it to say that the case law has given an emphatic "no" to the question. Every person within the jurisdiction enjoys the equal protection of our laws. There is no distinction between British nationals and others. He who is subject to English law is entitled to its protection. This principle has been in the law at least since Lord Mansfield freed "the black" in *Sommersett's Case* (1772) 20 St Tr 1. There is nothing here to encourage in the case of aliens or non-patrials the implication of words excluding the judicial review our law normally accords to those whose liberty is infringed.'

49 It was pointed out that nationality is not included as a forbidden ground of discrimination in article 14. The Strasbourg court has however treated nationality as such. In *Gaygusuz v Austria* (1996) 23 EHRR 364, para 42, it said:

'However, very weighty reasons would have to be put forward before the court could regard a difference of treatment based exclusively on the ground of nationality as compatible with the Convention.'

The Attorney General accepted that 'or other status' would cover the appellants' immigration status, so nothing turns on this point. Nationality is a forbidden ground of discrimination within section 3(1) of the Race Relations Act 1976 and the Secretary of State is bound by that Act by virtue of section 19B(1). It was not argued that in the present circumstances he was authorised to discriminate by section 19D.

50 The first important issue between the parties was whether, in the present case, the Secretary of State had discriminated against the appellants on the ground of their nationality or immigration status. The court gave guidance on the correct approach in the *Belgian Linguistic Case (No 2)* (1968) 1 EHRR 252, para 10: [set out in Chap. 13, below at p. 872]…

The question is whether persons in an analogous or relevantly similar situation enjoy preferential treatment, without reasonable or objective justification for the distinction, and whether and to what extent differences in otherwise similar situations justify a different treatment in law: *Stubbings v United Kingdom* (1996) 23 EHRR 213, para 70. The parties were agreed that in domestic law, seeking to give effect to the

Convention, the correct approach is to pose the questions formulated by *Grosz, Beatson & Duffy, Human Rights: The 1998 Act and the European Convention* (2000), para C14–08, substantially adopted by Brooke LJ in *Wandsworth London Borough Council v Michalak* [2003] 1 WLR 617, para 20, and refined in the later cases of *R (Carson) v Secretary of State for Work and Pensions* [2002] 3 All ER 994, para 52; [2003] 3 All ER 577, paras 56–61, *Ghaidan v Godin-Mendoza* [2004] 2 AC 557, paras 133–134 and *R(S) v Chief Constable of the South Yorkshire Police* [2004] 1 WLR 2196. As expressed in para 42 of this last case the questions are:

'(1) Do the facts fall within the ambit of one or more of the Convention rights? (2) Was there a difference in treatment in respect of that right between the complainant and others put forward for comparison? (3) If so, was the difference in treatment on one or more of the proscribed grounds under article 14? (4) Were those others in an analogous situation? (5) Was the difference in treatment objectively justifiable in the sense that it had a legitimate aim and bore a reasonable relationship of proportionality to that aim?'

51 It is plain that the facts fall within the ambit of article 5. That is why the United Kingdom thought it necessary to derogate. The Attorney General reserved the right to argue in another place at another time that it was not necessary to derogate, but he accepted for the purpose of these proceedings that it was. The appellants were treated differently from both suspected international terrorists who were not UK nationals but could be removed and also from suspected international terrorists who were UK-nationals and could not be removed. There can be no doubt but that the difference of treatment was on grounds of nationality or immigration status (one of the proscribed grounds under article 14). The problem has been treated as an immigration problem.

52 The Attorney General submitted that the position of the appellants should be compared with that of non-UK nationals who represented a threat to the security of the UK but who could be removed to their own or to safe third countries. The relevant difference between them and the appellants was that the appellants could not be removed. A difference of treatment of the two groups was accordingly justified and it was reasonable and necessary to detain the appellants. By contrast, the appellants' chosen comparators were suspected international terrorists who were UK nationals. The appellants pointed out that they shared with this group the important characteristics (a) of being suspected international terrorists and (b) of being irremovable from the United Kingdom. Since these were the relevant characteristics for purposes of the comparison, it was unlawfully discriminatory to detain non-UK nationals while leaving UK nationals at large.

53 Were suspected international terrorists who were UK nationals, the appellants' chosen comparators, in a relevantly analogous situation to the appellants? The question, as posed by Laws LJ in *R (Carson) v Secretary of State for Work and Pensions* [2003] 3 All ER 577, para 61, is whether the circumstances of X and Y are so similar as to call (in the mind of a rational and fair-minded person) for a positive justification for the less favourable treatment of Y in comparison with X. The Court of Appeal thought not because (per Lord Woolf CJ, para 56) 'the nationals have a right of abode in this jurisdiction but the aliens only have a right not to be removed'. This is, however, to accept the correctness of the Secretary of State's choice of immigration control as a means to address the Al-Qaeda security problem, when the correctness of that choice is the issue to be resolved. In my opinion, the question demands an affirmative answer. Suspected international terrorists who are UK nationals are in a situation analogous with the appellants because, in the present context, they share the most relevant characteristics of the appellants.

54 Following the guidance given in the *Belgian Linguistic Case (No 2)* (see para 50 above) it is then necessary to assess the justification of the differential treatment of non-UK nationals 'in relation to the aim and effects of the measure under consideration'. The undoubted aim of the relevant measure, section 23 of the 2001 Act, was to protect the UK against the risk of Al-Qaeda terrorism. As noted above (para 32) that risk was thought to be presented mainly by non-UK nationals but also and to a significant extent by UK nationals also. The effect of the measure was to permit the former to be deprived of their

liberty but not the latter. The appellants were treated differently because of their nationality or immigration status. The comparison contended for by the Attorney General might be reasonable and justified in an immigration context, but cannot in my opinion be so in a security context, since the threat presented by suspected international terrorists did not depend on their nationality or immigration status. It is noteworthy that in *Ireland v United Kingdom* 2 EHRR 25 the European Court was considering legislative provisions which were, unlike section 23, neutral in their terms, in that they provided for internment of loyalist as well as republican terrorists. Even so, the court was gravely exercised whether the application of the measures had been even handed as between the two groups of terrorists. It seems very unlikely that the measures could have been successfully defended had they only been capable of application to republican terrorists, unless it were shown that they alone presented a threat.

[[55]–[65] His Lordship proceeded to reject the Attorney General's argument that the ECHR permits the differential treatment of aliens as compared with nationals. There can be such differential treatment, in the immigration content, arising from the point that nationals have the right of abode and non-nationals do not, but apart from that there was no European or other authority to support the Attorney General's argument. The Joint Committee on Human Rights had consistently expressed its concern that these provisions unjustifiably discriminated on the ground of nationality.]

68 …Article 15 requires any derogation measures to go no further than is strictly required by the exigencies of the situation and the prohibition of discrimination on grounds of nationality or immigration status has not been the subject of derogation. Article 14 remains in full force. Any discriminatory measure inevitably affects a smaller rather than a larger group, but cannot be justified on the ground that more people would be adversely affected if the measure were applied generally. What has to be justified is not the measure in issue but the difference in treatment between one person or group and another. What cannot be justified here is the decision to detain one group of suspect international terrorists, defined by nationality or immigration status, and not another. To do so was a violation of article 14. It was also a violation of article 26 of the ICCPR and so inconsistent with the United Kingdom's other obligations under international law within the meaning of article 15 of the European Convention.

[[69]–[70] His Lordship rejected the Attorney General's argument that international law sanctioned the detention of aliens in time of war or public emergency.]

73 I would allow the appeals. There will be a quashing order in respect of the Human Rights Act 1998 (Designated Derogation) Order 2001. There will also be a declaration under section 4 of the Human Rights Act 1998 that section 23 of the Anti-terrorism, Crime and Security Act 2001 is incompatible with articles 5 and 14 of the European Convention in so far as it is disproportionate and permits detention of suspected international terrorists in a way that discriminates on the ground of nationality or immigration status…

Lord Hoffmann:

86 My Lords, I have had the advantage of reading in draft the speech of my noble and learned friend, Lord Bingham of Cornhill, and I gratefully adopt his statement of the background to this case and the issues which it raises. This is one of the most important cases which the House has had to decide in recent years. It calls into question the very existence of an ancient liberty of which this country has until now been very proud: freedom from arbitrary arrest and detention. The power which the Home Secretary seeks to uphold is a power to detain people indefinitely without charge or trial. Nothing could be more antithetical to the instincts and traditions of the people of the United Kingdom.

87 At present, the power cannot be exercised against citizens of this country. First, it applies only to foreigners whom the Home Secretary would otherwise be able to deport. But the power to deport foreigners is extremely wide. Secondly, it requires that the Home Secretary should reasonably suspect the foreigners of a variety of activities or attitudes in connection with terrorism, including supporting a

group influenced from abroad whom the Home Secretary suspects of being concerned in terrorism. If the finger of suspicion has pointed and the suspect is detained, his detention must be reviewed by the Special Immigration Appeals Commission. They can decide that there were no reasonable grounds for the Home Secretary's suspicion. But the suspect is not entitled to be told the grounds upon which he has been suspected. So he may not find it easy to explain that the suspicion is groundless. In any case, suspicion of being a supporter is one thing and proof of wrongdoing is another. Someone who has never committed any offence and has no intention of doing anything wrong may be reasonably suspected of being a supporter on the basis of some heated remarks overheard in a pub. The question in this case is whether the United Kingdom should be a country in which the police can come to such a person's house and take him away to be detained indefinitely without trial.

88 The technical issue in this appeal is whether such a power can be justified on the ground that there exists a 'war or other public emergency threatening the life of the nation' within the meaning of article 15 of the European Convention on Human Rights. But I would not like anyone to think that we are concerned with some special doctrine of European law. Freedom from arbitrary arrest and detention is a quintessentially British liberty, enjoyed by the inhabitants of this country when most of the population of Europe could be thrown into prison at the whim of their rulers. It was incorporated into the European Convention in order to entrench the same liberty in countries which had recently been under Nazi occupation. The United Kingdom subscribed to the Convention because it set out the rights which British subjects enjoyed under the common law.

89 The exceptional power to derogate from those rights also reflected British constitutional history. There have been times of great national emergency in which habeas corpus has been suspended and powers to detain on suspicion conferred on the Government. It happened during the Napoleonic Wars and during both World Wars in the 20th century. These powers were conferred with great misgiving and, in the sober light of retrospect after the emergency had passed, were often found to have been cruelly and unnecessarily exercised. But the necessity of draconian powers in moments of national crisis is recognised in our constitutional history. Article 15 of the Convention, when it speaks of 'war or other public emergency threatening the life of the nation', accurately states the conditions in which such legislation has previously been thought necessary.

90 Until the Human Rights Act 1998, the question of whether the threat to the nation was sufficient to justify suspension of habeas corpus or the introduction of powers of detention could not have been the subject of judicial decision. There could be no basis for questioning an Act of Parliament by court proceedings. Under the 1998 Act, the courts still cannot say that an Act of Parliament is invalid. But they can declare that it is incompatible with the human rights of persons in this country. Parliament may then choose whether to maintain the law or not. The declaration of the court enables Parliament to choose with full knowledge that the law does not accord with our constitutional traditions.

91 What is meant by 'threatening the life of the nation'? The 'nation' is a social organism, living in its territory (in this case, the United Kingdom) under its own form of government and subject to a system of laws which expresses its own political and moral values. When one speaks of a threat to the 'life' of the nation, the word life is being used in a metaphorical sense. The life of the nation is not coterminous with the lives of its people. The nation, its institutions and values, endure through generations. In many important respects, England is the same nation as it was at the time of the first Elizabeth or the Glorious Revolution. The Armada threatened to destroy the life of the nation, not by loss of life in battle, but by subjecting English institutions to the rule of Spain and the Inquisition. The same was true of the threat posed to the United Kingdom by Nazi Germany in the Second World War. This country, more than any other in the world, has an unbroken history of living for centuries under institutions and in accordance with values which show a recognisable continuity.

92 This, I think, is the idea which the European Court of Human Rights was attempting to convey when it said (in *Lawless v Ireland (No 3)* (1961) 1 EHRR 15) that it must be a 'threat to the organised life of the

community of which the state is composed', although I find this a rather desiccated description. Nor do I find the European cases particularly helpful. All that can be taken from them is that the Strasbourg court allows a wide 'margin of appreciation' to the national authorities in deciding 'both on the presence of such an emergency and on the nature and scope of derogations necessary to avert it': *Ireland v United Kingdom* (1978) 2 EHRR 25, at para 207. What this means is that we, as a United Kingdom court, have to decide the matter for ourselves.

93 Perhaps it is wise for the Strasbourg court to distance itself from these matters. The institutions of some countries are less firmly based than those of others. Their communities are not equally united in their loyalty to their values and system of government. I think that it was reasonable to say that terrorism in Northern Ireland threatened the life of that part of the nation and the territorial integrity of the United Kingdom as a whole. In a community riven by sectarian passions, such a campaign of violence threatened the fabric of organised society. The question is whether the threat of terrorism from Muslim extremists similarly threatens the life of the British nation.

94 The Home Secretary has adduced evidence, both open and secret, to show the existence of a threat of serious terrorist outrages. The Attorney General did not invite us to examine the secret evidence, but despite the widespread scepticism which has attached to intelligence assessments since the fiasco over Iraqi weapons of mass destruction, I am willing to accept that credible evidence of such plots exist. The events of 11 September 2001 in New York and Washington and 11 March 2003 in Madrid make it entirely likely that the threat of similar atrocities in the United Kingdom is a real one.

95 But the question is whether such a threat is a threat to the life of the nation. The Attorney General's submissions and the judgment of the Special Immigration Appeals Commission treated a threat of serious physical damage and loss of life as necessarily involving a threat to the life of the nation. But in my opinion this shows a misunderstanding of what is meant by 'threatening the life of the nation'. Of course the Government has a duty to protect the lives and property of its citizens. But that is a duty which it owes all the time and which it must discharge without destroying our constitutional freedoms. There may be some nations too fragile or fissiparous to withstand a serious act of violence. But that is not the case in the United Kingdom. When Milton urged the government of his day not to censor the press even in time of civil war, he said: 'Lords and Commons of England, consider what nation it is whereof ye are, and whereof ye are the governours'

96 This is a nation which has been tested in adversity, which has survived physical destruction and catastrophic loss of life. I do not underestimate the ability of fanatical groups of terrorists to kill and destroy, but they do not threaten the life of the nation. Whether we would survive Hitler hung in the balance, but there is no doubt that we shall survive Al-Qaeda. The Spanish people have not said that what happened in Madrid, hideous crime as it was, threatened the life of their nation. Their legendary pride would not allow it. Terrorist violence, serious as it is, does not threaten our institutions of government or our existence as a civil community.

97 For these reasons I think that the Special Immigration Appeals Commission made an error of law and that the appeal ought to be allowed. Others of your Lordships who are also in favour of allowing the appeal would do so, not because there is no emergency threatening the life of the nation, but on the ground that a power of detention confined to foreigners is irrational and discriminatory. I would prefer not to express a view on this point. I said that the power of detention is at present confined to foreigners and I would not like to give the impression that all that was necessary was to extend the power to United Kingdom citizens as well. In my opinion, such a power in any form is not compatible with our constitution. The real threat to the life of the nation, in the sense of a people living in accordance with its traditional laws and political values, comes not from terrorism but from laws such as these. That is the true measure of what terrorism may achieve. It is for Parliament to decide whether to give the terrorists such a victory.

Appeal allowed.

NOTES

1. This decision[272] caused great political difficulty for the Government. It secured, amid much contentious debate, the passage of the Prevention of Terrorism Act 2005, which provided for the making of control order imposing obligations on individuals suspected of involvement in terrorist related activities.[273] Sections 21–23 of the 2001 Act lapsed on 14 March 2005 when not continued by order under s. 29.

The House was not asked to rule on the question whether the detention (or continued detention) of the suspected terrorists was unlawful. They were released after a further period in detention while the legislation was reconsidered by Parliament.

2. The decision is of significance on many points, including the extent of 'deference' (or recognition of 'relative institutional competence') appropriate in different contexts, the application of the requirement of proportionality and the approach to discrimination under Art. 14 (as to which see further below, Chap. 14). As to relative institutional competence, compare the approaches to the derogation and proportionality issues. Why is a 'less intrusive' approach justified on the first issue? Why do the difficulties of predicting human behaviour turn the matter into one of a 'pre-eminently political judgment'? Compare the interpretations of Lord Bingham and Lord Hoffmann of 'threatening the life of the nation'. Although not subsequently doubted by the ECtHR it is difficult to square the outcome in *Lawless* with either the wording of Art. 15(1) ECHR or subsequent comments of the Commission and Court. The HRA 1998 requires English courts to take *Lawless* into account, but does not require it to be accepted as setting the threshold for the purposes of UK law. If there were really strong evidence of an imminent threat to the life of the nation, should the view on the proportionality and discrimination issue change? Compare the extent of deference shown in cases such as *Rehman* and *Gillan*.[274] The cases reveal a variety of approaches to Government arguments that responses are need to meet the *risk* of terrorism: these include deference to the Government's assessment; applying a presumption of good faith on the part of Government; and ignoring it where it is not relevant, as to the question whether a person has been subject to a deprivation of liberty.[275]

3. Lord Hoffmann's robust approach on the derogation issue places much emphasis on constitutional freedoms protected by the common law and to be protected by an appropriate interpretation of legislative provisions that violate them. The dismissive references to 'European law' (and some Europeans), however, seem ungenerous given that it has only been the measure of incorporation of the ECHR by the HRA 1998 that has strengthened the power of the judges in the face of legislation designed to interfere with human rights and fundamental freedoms. The UK and the common law can hardly claim whole credit for the ECHR.[276] It is also to be expected that Lord Hoffmann would adopt a more conventional approach to the style and content of his arguments in a case where he was delivering a

---

[272] See also *M v Secretary of State for the Home Department* [2004] EWCA Civ 324, [2004] 2 All ER 863 (CA held that SIAC was entitled to conclude that suspicious circumstances did not amount to reasonable suspicion for the purposes of detention under the 2001 Act).

[273] See below, pp 475–485.

[274] See pp. 440, 472. Poole regards these cases as illustrating 'deferential accommodation' with 'reasserting public law principles' evident in the *Belmarsh, Torture Evidence* and *MB* cases (see pp. 455, 474 and 483): T. Poole, 'Courts and Conditions of Uncertainty in "Times of Crisis"' [2008] PL 234, 237–243. On the tensions between politicians and judges in this area, see D. Feldman, 'Human Rights, Terrorism and Risk: The Roles of Politicians and Judges' [2006] PL 364.

[275] Poole, op. cit., pp. 248–258.

[276] See T. Poole (2005) 32 JLS 534, for an analysis of Lord Hoffmann's speech.

major opinion for all or the majority of the House. For further comments, see Tomkins,[277] welcoming 'the beginnings of a much belated judicial awakening to the fact that even in the context of national security the courts have a responsibility to ensure that the rule of law is respected'.[278]

4. *Deportation.* A range of legal issues may arise where it is proposed that a person be deported as conducive to the public good.[279] This expression is not further defined by the Immigration Rules.[280] A decision to make or to refuse to revoke a deportation order may be the subject of an appeal to the Asylum and Immigration Tribunal.[281] The grounds include that the decision is not in accordance with the immigration rules; unlawful under s. 19B of the Race Relations Act 1976 or under s. 6, HRA 1998 as being incompatible with Convention rights; otherwise not in accordance with the law; or that the person taking the decision should have exercised differently a discretion conferred by immigration rules; or removal from the UK would breach the UK's obligations under the Refugee Convention or be unlawful under s. 6, HRA.[282] However, the Secretary of State may certify that the decision was taken in person by the Secretary of State wholly or partly on the ground that the person's removal from the UK is in the interests of national security, or in the interests of the relationship between the UK and another country; and the Secretary of State in person may certify that the decision was taken wholly or partly in reliance on information which in his opinion should not be made public in those interests, or otherwise in the public interest.[283] Here the appeal was instead to the Special Immigration Appeals Commission (SIAC).[284] This is a superior court of record. A panel comprises a senior judge, a senior legally-qualified member of the AIT and a third member, usually with experience of national security matters.[285] There may be both open and closed sessions, and there is provision for appointment of a special advocate.[286] A further appeal lies on a point of law, to the Court of Appeal, with the leave of SIAC or the Court of Appeal.[287] Further restrictions apply to appeals in national security cases.[288]

The House of Lords in *Secretary of State for the Home Department v Rehman*[289] held, first, that for a lawful deportation in the interests of national security

---

[277] A. Tomkins [2005] PL 259. See also comments by T. Hickman et al. (2005) 68 MLR 655–680; M. Arden (2005) 121 LQR 604; D. Bonner (2006) 12 European Public Law 45; S. Shah (2005) 5 HRL Rev 403; C. Walker (2005) Eur HRL Rev 50.

[278] P. 263. See also the discussion of the applicability of Art. 15 at pp. 261–262.

[279] Under the power conferred by s. 3(5) of the Immigration Act 1971, substituted by the Immigration and Asylum Act 1999, Sch. 14, paras 43, 44(2). The same ground may be used to deprive a person of citizenship status: British Nationality Act 1981, s. 40(2), substituted by the Immigration, Asylum and Nationality Act 2006, s. 56(1); or of the right of abode: 1971 Act, s. 2A, inserted by the 2006 Act, s. 57(1). The guidelines on exercise of the power have been amended to expand the list of examples of 'unacceptable behaviours': see C. Walker (2007) 70 MLR 427, 434–437.

[280] See generally on deportation 1993–94 HC 395, Part 13, rr. 362–395F, as amended.

[281] Nationality, Immigration and Asylum Act 2002, s. 82(1), (2)(j), (k).

[282] 2002 Act, s. 84.   [283] 2002 Act, s. 97.

[284] Special Immigration Appeals Commission Act 1997, s. 2. See the Special Immigration Appeals Commission (Procedure) Rules 2003, SI 2003/1034, as amended by SIs 2007/1285 and 3370.

[285] www.siac.tribunals.gov.uk/aboutus.htm.

[286] 1997 Act, s. 6.   [287] 1997 Act, s. 7.

[288] 2002 Act, s. 97A, inserted by the 2006 Act, s. 7. An order may be made before any appeal is disposed of; appeals can normally only be made from outside the UK unless there is a human rights claim, and the Secretary of State does not certify that removal would not breach the UK's ECHR obligations. An appeal against such a certificate lies to SIAC.

[289] [2001] UKHL 47, [2003] 1 AC 153, upholding the decision of the CA, which reversed the decision of SIAC [1999] INLR 517. See A. Tomkins (2002) 118 LQR 200.

there must be some possibility of risk or danger to the security or well-being of the nation which the Secretary of State considers makes it desirable for the public good that the individual should be deported.[290]

However, the risk did not have to be the result of a 'direct threat' to the UK and the interests of national security are not

limited to action by an individual which can be said to be 'targeted at' the United Kingdom, its system of government or its people

as SIAC had considered. Action against a foreign state may be capable of indirectly affecting the security of the UK. Furthermore, it was not necessary for the Secretary of State to be satisfied that his conclusion was justified 'to a high degree of civil probability'. There had to be material on which, proportionately and reasonably, he could conclude that there was a real possibility of activities harmful to national security. Disputed facts should be established on the balance of probability. However, establishing a degree of probability did not seem relevant to reaching a conclusion on whether there should be a deportation. In exercising its powers, SIAC

must give due weight to the assessment and conclusions of the Secretary of State in the light at any particular time of his responsibilities, or of government policy and the means at his disposal of being informed of and understanding the problems involved. He is undoubtedly in the best position to judge what national security requires even if his decision is open to review. The assessment of what is needed in the light of changing circumstances is primarily for him.[291]

5. One issue that may arise is whether deportation to a particular country will give rise to substantial grounds for believing that the person concerned faced a real risk of suffering treatment contrary of Art. 3 ECHR.[292] The UK has entered a Memorandum of Understanding with each of a number of countries under which the country concerned has given assurances that anyone deported from the UK will be properly treated.[293] However, SIAC, in a case concerning Libya,[294] has held that such a memorandum is not conclusive on the point and that while the assurance here had been made in good faith, motivated by self-interest and pragmatic reasons, Libya's motivation and reasoning might change and it might not honour the MoU. On appeal, the Court of Appeal found no error of law.[295] There has to be a proper evidential basis for concluding that there was a 'real risk', which was more than a 'mere possibility' but something less than a balance of probabilities.

---

[290] Per Lord Slynn at para. [15].

[291] Lord Slynn at paras [22], [26]. See also Lord Hoffmann at para. [55].

[292] *Soering v UK*, above p. 83. An analogous issue may arise in respect of the risk of a 'complete denial or nullification' of other convention rights: see *R (on the application of Ullah) v Special Adjudicator* [2004] UKHL 26, [2004] 2 AC 323 (Art. 9); *EM (Lebanon) v Secretary of State for the Home Department* [2006] EWCA Civ 1531.

[293] There are MoUs with Jordan, Lebanon and Libya; separate arrangements have been made with Algeria: see www.fco.gov.uk; C.Walker (2007) 70 MLR 427, 441–450.

[294] *DD and AS v Secretary of State for the Home Department* (27 April 2007).

[295] *AS (Libya) v Secretary of State for the Home Department* [2008] EWCA Civ 289, [2008] HRLR 28. As to the proper approach to an appeal, the court applied a dictum of Baroness Hale of Richmond in *AH (Sudan) v Secretary of State for the Home Department* [2007] UKHL 49, [2007] 3 WLR 832.

It has also been held that the rigorous scrutiny required where Art. 3 ill-treatment was alleged dose not require the presence of the person concerned throughout the proceedings; use of the special advocate procedure can accordingly be compatible.[296]

In considering whether there might be a risk of an unfair trial in the country to which a person is to be returned, SIAC must not treat the possible use of evidence obtained by torture as giving rise simply to issues about its reliability; the use of such evidence would in any event be inconsistent with Art. 6.[297]

6. *The use of information derived from torture.* In *A v Secretary of State to the Home Department (No. 2)*[298] the House of Lords held, reversing the Court of Appeal,[299] that evidence obtained by torture was inadmissible in civil proceedings, including those before SIAC.[300] Once an appellant raised in a general way a plausible reason why evidence adduced might have been procured by torture, it was for SIAC to consider and if necessary investigate the matter. It was not simply to be left for the appellant to prove, with SIAC confined to an adjudicatory role. The majority[301] held that then SIAC should ask itself whether it was established on a balance of probabilities that the information was obtained under torture. This was the approach adopted in Art. 15 of the UN Torture Convention. The minority[302] took the view that the evidence should be excluded if SIAC was unable to conclude that there was not a real risk that the evidence had been obtained by torture. Lord Hope's view[303] was that the terms on which information was passed to the intelligence services would make it impossible for these to be met in practice.

7. *Facilitation of breaches of human rights abroad.* The US in its so-called 'War on Terror' has seen fit to detain, incommunicado, suspected terrorists at various locations outside the US, including at Guantanamo Bay in Cuba. It has also authorised the use of coercive interrogation techniques, alleged to amount to inhuman or degrading treatment or torture. Any trials would be conducted by military commissions.[304] Suspects have been transferred from one country to another ('rendition') without going through established extradition procedures. This conduct has generated significant litigation and widespread condemnation.[305]

---

[296] *MT (Algeria) v Secretary of State for the Home Department* [2007] EWCA Civ 808, [2008] QB 534 (the case was nevertheless remitted to SIAC).

[297] *Othman (Jordan) v Secretary of State for the Home Department* [2008] EWCA Civ 290 (not open on the evidence to SIAC to conclude that the risk of the total denial of justice represented by the use of evidence obtained by torture had adequately been excluded).

[298] [2005] UKHL 71, [2006] 2 AC 221. See N. Rasiah (2006) 69 MLR 995; S. Shah (2006) 6 HRL Rev 416.

[299] [2004] EWCA Civ 1125, [2005] 1 WLR 414.

[300] Evidence obtained by ill-treatment short of torture may be excluded under s. 78 PACE: see Lord Bingham at para. [53].

[301] Lords Hope of Craighead, Rodger of Earlsferry, Carswell and Brown of Eaton-under-Heywood.

[302] Lords Bingham, Nicholls of Birkenhead and Hoffmann. Lord Nicholls at para. [80] noted that the majority's approach in practice largely nullified the principle.

[303] Para. [125].

[304] The procedure of these Commissions was held to be unconstitutional in *Harndon v Rumsfeld* (2006) 548 US 557 and a new Military Commissions Act 2006 was passed.

[305] On the adoption by the US Government of new interrogation techniques that violated Art. 3 of the Geneva Convention, see P. Sands, *Torture Team* (Allen Lane, London, 2008); G. Robertson, *Crimes against Humanity* (Penguin Books, London, 3rd edn, 2006), pp. 530–548. For further background, see *R (on the application of Abbasi) v Secretary of State for Foreign and Commonwealth Affairs* [2002] EWCA Civ 1598, [2003] UKHRR 76 (no duty on Secretary of State to take all reasonable steps, including the making of representations to the US Government to secure the release of A, a British national, from detention at Guantanamo Bay; there had been some discussions between the governments; see S. Palmer [2003] CLJ 6); *R (on the application of Al Rawi) v Secretary of State for Foreign and Commonwealth Affairs* [2006] EWCA Civ 1279, [2008] QB 289 (no duty to make representations on behalf of British-associated detainees who were not British nationals, to the same extent as those that

In *R (on the application of Mohamed) v Secretary of State for Foreign and Commonwealth Affairs*[306] the Divisional Court held that the Secretary of State was obliged to make information available to M (an Ethiopian national) for the purposes of his forthcoming trial by a military commission.[307] It was accepted that the Security Services held material that might arguably assist M in arguing that statements made by him were inadmissible. The Secretary of State claimed its disclosure would cause serious damage to national security. M had been arrested in 2002 in Pakistan and detained incommunicado. He alleged he was moved, by extraordinary rendition, to Morocco and then Afghanistan. He was transferred to Guantanamo Bay and held there. He made statements at various times and claimed they resulted from the use of torture or cruel, inhuman or degrading treatment. The court held that the UK Security Services had facilitated alleged wrongdoing through their supply of information and participation in a number of interrogations (albeit that coercive methods were not used during those interrogations). They must have been aware that M was not being held in a regular US facility and that they were supplying information for use at other interrogations while M was being detained incommunicado and without access to a lawyer. The information was necessary for the proceedings. It would then be open to the Secretary of State to make a public interest immunity claim.[308]

5. THE PREVENTION OF TERRORISM ACT 2005

This Act was passed as the response to the decision in *A v Secretary of State for the Home Department*. It repealed the detention provisions of the 2001 Act and introduced the regime of control orders.

● **Secretary of State for the Home Department v JJ and others**
  [2007] UKHL 45, [2008] 1 AC 385, House of Lords

The Secretary of State, in purported exercise of his power conferred by s. 1(2)(a) of the Prevention of Terrorism Act 2005, made non-derogating control orders in respect of six persons (JJ to LL), who were Iraqi or Iranian nationals, on the basis, set out in s. 2 of the Act, that he had reasonable grounds for suspecting them of involvement in terrorism-related activity and considered the orders to be necessary for purposes connected with protecting members of the public from a risk of terrorism. The orders, in particular, obliged each controlled person at all times to wear an electronic tagging device, to remain within his specified residence, a one-bedroom flat, except between 10 a.m. and 4 p.m., and to permit police searches of the premises at any time. Visitors to the premises were permitted only where prior Home Office

---

had been made in respect of British nationals; see K. Parlett [2007] CLJ 1). All detained British nationals were returned by January 2005. In 2007, the Foreign and Commonwealth Office made representations on behalf of five non-nationals, and three were returned to the UK (Ministerial Statement, 13 December 2007, www.fco.gov.uk). See also 'Second Report of the Foreign Affairs Committee, HC, *Visit to Guantanamo Bay* and the Government response, Cm 7063, 2007; J. Steyn, 'Guantanamo Bay: The Legal Black Hole' (2004) 53 ICLQ 1. The Government believes that the facility should be closed. This step is to be taken under Barack Obama's presidency.

306 [2008] EWHC 2048 (Admin).

307 Under the principle of *Norwich Pharmacal v Customs and Excise Comrs* [1974] AC 133 (but not, as also claimed, under a rule of customary public international law).

308 For subsequent proceedings see [2008] EWHC 2100 (Admin), where the court noted a softening of the stance of the US Government and extending time for a P11 claim.

permission had been given. During the six hours when the controlled persons were permitted to leave their residences they were confined to restricted urban areas, which deliberately did not extend, except in one case, to any area where they had previously lived. Each area contained a mosque, health care facilities, shops and entertainment and sporting facilities. Each controlled person was prohibited from meeting anyone by pre-arrangement without prior Home Office approval. On a hearing pursuant to s. 3(10) of the 2005 Act to determine whether the Secretary of State's decisions under s. 2 were flawed the judge considered that the cumulative impact of the obligations imposed by the orders amounted to a deprivation of liberty contrary to Art. 5 ECHR. He concluded that the orders could not have been made by the Secretary of State under the 2005 Act and that they should be quashed. On the Secretary of State's appeal the Court of Appeal[309] affirmed the decision. The House of Lords dismissed an appeal by 3 to 2, Lords Hoffmann and Carswell dissenting.

Lord Bingham of Cornhill:

4 …At the forefront of his argument the Secretary of State stresses the grave threat presented to the public by the criminal activity of terrorists; the imperative duty of democratic governments to do what can lawfully be done to protect the public against that threat; and the balance inherent in the European Convention between the rights of individuals and the rights of the community as a whole. These considerations provide the important backdrop to these appeals, but they need not be elaborated since they are not controversial…

It is common ground that none of the cases subject to this appeal falls within any of the categories listed in (a) to (f) of article 5 of the Convention, and the United Kingdom has not derogated from its obligation to comply with that article. It necessarily follows that if, as the controlled persons (with the support of JUSTICE) contend and the Secretary of State strongly denies, the effect of the obligations imposed on the controlled persons under the control orders is to deprive them of their liberty, such orders are inconsistent with article 5 of the Convention.

THE 2005 ACT

6 The core of the 2005 Act is found in section 1. Subsection (1) defines a control order as meaning 'an order made against an individual that imposes obligations on him for purposes connected with protecting members of the public from a risk of terrorism'. Subsection (4) specifies the obligations which a control order 'may include, in particular'. It is not therefore an exclusive list. But it is a detailed list, containing 16 potential obligations running from (a) to (p). It is unnecessary to recite the full list. Among the listed obligations are:

'(d) a restriction on his association or communications with specified persons or with other persons generally; (e) a restriction in respect of his place of residence or on the persons to whom he gives access to his place of residence; (f) a prohibition on his being at specified places or within a specified area at specified times or on specified days; (g) a prohibition or restriction on his movements to, from or within the United Kingdom, a specified part of the United Kingdom or a specified place or area within the United Kingdom…(j) a requirement on him to give access to specified persons to his place of residence or to other premises to which he has power to grant access; (k) a requirement on him to allow specified persons to search that place or any such premises for the purpose of ascertaining whether obligations imposed by or under the order have been, are being or are about to be contravened.'

A person who, without reasonable excuse, contravenes an obligation imposed on him by a control order is guilty of an offence punishable, on conviction on indictment to imprisonment for a term of up to five years: section 9(1)(4)(a).

---

[309] [2007] QB 446.

7 The Act draws a categorical distinction between what it calls a 'derogating control order' and what it calls a 'non-derogating control order'. The former is defined in section 15(1) to mean 'a control order imposing obligations that are or include derogating obligations' and a 'derogating obligation' is defined in section 1(10) to mean

'an obligation on an individual which—(a) is incompatible with his right to liberty under article 5 of the Human Rights Convention; but (b) is of a description of obligations which, for the purposes of the designation of a designated derogation, is set out in the designation order.'

A 'non-derogating control order' is defined in section 15(1) to mean 'a control order made by the Secretary of State': it is one that does not consist of or include derogating obligations. Thus the premise of the Act is that control orders made under section 1 of the Act and including obligations within the scope of section 1(4) may, or of course may not, be incompatible with the controlled person's right to liberty under article 5 of the Convention.

8 The power to make a control order against an individual, in the case of an order imposing obligations that are or include derogating obligations, is exercisable by the court on an application by the Secretary of State (section 1(2)(b)); save where the order imposes obligations that are incompatible with the individual's right to liberty under article 5, the power is exercisable by the Secretary of State (section 1(2)(a)), with the permission of the court (section 3(1)(a)) save where the urgency of the case requires an order to be made without permission: section 3(1)(b). In each case there is a preliminary hearing by the court, but the procedure differs (section 4(1) applies to derogating control orders, section 3(1)(a)(2)(3)(5)(6) to non-derogating control orders). The threshold conditions for making an order are different. At the preliminary hearing, the court may make a derogating control order against the individual in question under section 4(3) if it appears to the court

'(a) that there is material which (if not disproved) is capable of being relied on by the court as establishing that the individual is or has been involved in terrorism-related activity; (b) that there are reasonable grounds for believing that the imposition of obligations on that individual is necessary for purposes connected with protecting members of the public from a risk of terrorism; (c) that the risk arises out of, or is associated with, a public emergency in respect of which there is a designated derogation from the whole or a part of article 5 of the Human Rights Convention; and (d) that the obligations that there are reasonable grounds for believing should be imposed on the individual are or include derogating obligations of a description set out for the purposes of the designated derogation in the designation order.'

By contrast, under section 2(1) the Secretary of State may make a non-derogating control order against an individual if he

'(a) has reasonable grounds for suspecting that the individual is or has been involved in terrorism-related activity; and (b) considers that it is necessary, for purposes connected with protecting members of the public from a risk of terrorism, to make a control order imposing obligations on that individual.'

At the preliminary hearing before such an order is made, or immediately after in case of urgency, the court's function is to consider whether the Secretary of State's decision is 'obviously flawed': section 3(2)(3).

9 On the full hearing the function of the court is again different. In the case of a derogating control order the test reflects that set out in section 4(3) quoted above: the court may confirm the order, with or without modifications, only if (section 4(7))

'(a) it is satisfied, on the balance of probabilities, that the controlled person is an individual who is or has been involved in terrorism-related activity; (b) it considers that the imposition of obligations on the controlled person is necessary for purposes connected with protecting members of the public from a risk of terrorism; (c) it appears to the court that the risk is one arising out of, or is associated with, a public emergency in respect of which there is a designated derogation from the whole or a part of article 5 of the Human Rights Convention; and (d) the obligations to be imposed by the order or (as the case may be) by the order as modified are or include derogating obligations of a description set out for the purposes of the designated derogation in the derogation order.'

In the case of a non-derogating order the function of the court is to decide, applying the principles applicable on an application for judicial review, whether any relevant decision of the Secretary of State was 'flawed': section 3(10)(11).

10 A derogating control order has effect for six months unless revoked or renewed (section 4(8)), provided the derogation remains in force and the designation order was not made more than 12 months earlier (section 6(1)), and may be revoked or modified by the court: section 7(5)-(7). A non-derogating control order has effect for a period of 12 months (section 2(4)), renewable indefinitely for 12 months at a time if the Secretary of State considers that the conditions for making it continue to obtain: section 2(6). It may be revoked or modified by the Secretary of State (section 7(1)(2)), but he may not make any modification which converts a non-derogating control order into a derogating control order: section 7(3). A power of arrest exists in relation to derogating but not non-derogating control orders: section 5.

11 In some respects the Act does not distinguish between the two types of order. Thus the duty on the Secretary of State and the chief officer of police in relation to prosecution, considered in more detail in the case of *E* [2007] 3 WLR 720, is the same in the two cases (section 8), as are the criminal consequences of contravening an obligation: section 9. The procedural provisions laid down in the Schedule to the Act apply to both types of control order proceedings (section 11), although the rules made pursuant to the rule-making power conferred by the Act distinguish between derogating control orders (section II of CPR Pt 76) and non-derogating control orders: section III. No appeal lies to the Court of Appeal from any determination of the court in control order proceedings, except on a question of law: section 11(3).

DEPRIVATION OF LIBERTY

12 In ordinary parlance a person is taken to be deprived of his or her liberty when locked up in a prison cell or its equivalent. This common sense approach is, unsurprisingly, reflected in the Convention jurisprudence. Thus in *Engel v The Netherlands (No 1)* 1 EHRR 647, para 58, the European court has recognised that 'In proclaiming the 'right to liberty', paragraph 1 of article 5 is contemplating individual liberty in its classic sense, that is to say the physical liberty of the person', a ruling repeated in *Guzzardi v Italy* (1980) 3 EHRR 333, para 92. It has also referred to 'classic detention in prison or strict arrest': *Guzzardi*, para 95. Further, the court has recognised the distinction between deprivation of liberty and restriction of movement and freedom of a person to choose his residence. The latter are the subject of article 2 of Protocol 4 to the Convention, a provision which the United Kingdom has not ratified but which is accepted as relevant in interpreting the scope of the prohibition in article 5.

13 It is, however, common ground between the parties that the prohibition in article 5 on depriving a person of his liberty has an autonomous meaning: that is, it has a Council of Europe-wide meaning for purposes of the Convention, whatever it might or might not be thought to mean in any member state. For guidance on the autonomous Convention meaning to be given to the expression, national courts must look to the jurisprudence of the commission and the European Court of Human Rights in Strasbourg, which United Kingdom courts are required by section 2(1) of the Human Rights Act 1998 to take into account. But that jurisprudence must be used in the same way as other authority is to be used, as laying down principles and not mandating solutions to particular cases. It is, as observed in *R (Gillan) v Comr of Police of the Metropolis* [2006] 2 AC 307, para 23, perilous to transpose the outcome of one case to another where the facts are different. The case law shows that the prohibition in article 5 has fallen to be considered in a very wide range of factual situations. It is to the principles laid down by the court in *Engel* and *Guzzardi* particularly, reiterated by the court on many occasions (see, for instance, *Ashingdane v United Kingdom* (1985) 7 EHRR 528, para 41, *Amuur v France* (1996) 22 EHRR 533, para 42), that national courts must look for guidance.

14 A series of Strasbourg decisions establishes that 24-hour house arrest has been regarded as tantamount to imprisonment and so as depriving the subject of his or her liberty: see, for example, *Mancini v Italy* Reports of Judgments and Decisions 2001-IX, p 109, para 17....

15 Continuous house arrest may reasonably be regarded as resembling, save as to the place of confinement, conventional modes of imprisonment or detention. But the court has made clear (*Guzzardi*, para 95) that deprivation of liberty may take numerous forms other than classic detention in prison or strict arrest. The variety of such forms is being increased by developments in legal standards and attitudes, and the Convention must be interpreted in the light of notions prevailing in democratic states: ibid. What has to be considered is the concrete situation of the particular individual: *Engel*, para 59; *Guzzardi*, para 92; *HL v United Kingdom* (2004) 40 EHRR 761, para 89. Thus the task of a court is to assess the impact of the measures in question on a person in the situation of the person subject to them. The Strasbourg court has been true to this guiding principle. Thus in *Engel*, at para 59, the court recognised that

'A disciplinary penalty or measure which on analysis would unquestionably be deemed a deprivation of liberty were it to be applied to a civilian may not possess this characteristic when imposed upon a serviceman.'

In *Ashingdane* 7 EHRR 528 the applicant had been transferred from a high security mental hospital to an ordinary psychiatric hospital but was, it seems, still held to be detained and so deprived of his liberty (albeit legitimately) during the latest phase of his stay in the psychiatric hospital when he was on an open ward, was free to make regular unescorted visits to his family, was going home every weekend from Thursday to Sunday and was free to leave the hospital as he pleased on Monday to Wednesday provided only that he returned to his ward at night: see pp 536, 543–544.

16 Thus the court has insisted that account should be taken of a whole range of factors such as the nature, duration, effects and manner of execution or implementation of the penalty or measure in question: *Engel*, para 59; *Guzzardi*, paras 92, 94. There may be no deprivation of liberty if a single feature of an individual's situation is taken on its own but the combination of measures considered together may have that result: *Guzzardi*, para 95. Consistently with this approach, account was taken in *Guzzardi* of a number of aspects of the applicant's stay on the island of Asinara: the locality; the possibilities of movement; his accommodation; the availability of medical attention; the presence of his family; the possibilities of attending worship; the possibilities of obtaining work; the possibilities for cultural and recreational activities; and communications with the outside: pp 342–345. In the result, the court on the facts attached weight, at para 95, to the small area of the island open to him, the dilapidated accommodation, the lack of available social intercourse, the strictness of the almost constant supervision, a nine-hour overnight curfew, the obligation on him to report to the authorities twice a day and inform them of any person he wished to telephone, the need for consent to visit Sardinia on the mainland, the liability to punishment by arrest for breach of any obligation and the 16-month period during which he was subject to these restrictions. Some of these matters plainly fall within the purview of other articles of the Convention. Because account must be taken of an individual's whole situation it seems to me inappropriate to draw a sharp distinction between a period of confinement which will, and one which will not, amount to a deprivation of liberty, important though the period of daily confinement will be in any overall assessment.

17 The Strasbourg court has realistically recognised that 'The difference between deprivation of and restriction upon liberty is none the less merely one of degree or intensity, and not one of nature or substance': *Guzzardi*, para 93. There is no bright line separating the two. The court acknowledges (ibid) the difficulty attending the process of classification in borderline cases, suggesting that in such cases the decision is one of pure opinion or what may, rather more aptly, be called judgment.

18 In assessing the impact of the measures in question on a person in the situation of the person subject to them, the court has assessed the effect of the measures on the life the person would have been living otherwise. Thus no deprivation of liberty was held to result from light arrest of serving soldiers

(*Engel*, para 61) since they continued to perform their duties and remained more or less within the ordinary framework of their army life. The decisions of the court on curfews during the night hours is consistent with that approach. The curfew from 9 p m to 7 a m imposed in *Raimondo v Italy* (1994) 18 EHRR 237 and the obligation imposed on him not to leave home without informing the police did not prevent him living a normal life and did not deprive him of his liberty.... In *Ciancimino v Italy* (1991) 70 DR 103 the applicant was obliged to live in a nominated commune which he was not permitted to leave, was obliged to report to the police daily at 11 a m and was subject to a curfew from 8 p m to 7 a m, but this did not amount to a deprivation of liberty. The same result followed in *Trijonis*, 17 March 2005, in which from 11 January 2001 until 6 May 2002, the applicant was permitted to be at his work-place during week-days, subject to a curfew at his home from 7 p m to 7 a m on week-days and for the whole day at the weekend. The court pointed out, contrasting the case with *Guzzardi*, that the applicant was allowed to spend time at work as well as at home during this period.

19 It is not, I think, suggested that the Strasbourg court has had to rule on any case at all closely comparable with the present. It is inappropriate to seek to align this case with the least dissimilar of the reported cases. The task of the English courts is to seek to give fair effect, on the facts of this case, to the principles which the Strasbourg court has laid down.

THE OBLIGATIONS IMPOSED ON THE CONTROLLED PERSONS

20 The obligations imposed on the controlled persons by the non-derogating control orders made by the Secretary of State in each of their respective cases were in more or less standard form. Lord Carlile of Berriew QC, the independent reviewer appointed under section 14 of the Act, annexed to his First Report (2006) a pro forma of the schedule of obligations 'imposed on most but not quite all of the controlees so far' (Report, para 42), and Sullivan J annexed to his judgment a list, in almost identical terms, of the obligations imposed on the controlled persons in this case. An obligation was imposed under almost all the heads specifically identified in the paragraphs of section 1(4) of the Act, and some under heads not so identified. The general effect of the obligations was helpfully summarised by the Court of Appeal [2007] QB 446 in para 4 of its judgment:

> 'The obligations imposed by the control orders are set out in annex I to Sullivan J's judgment. They are essentially identical. Each respondent is required to remain within his 'residence' at all times, save for a period of six hours between 10 a m and 4 p m. In the case of GG the specified residence is a one-bedroom flat provided by the local authority in which he lived before his detention. In the case of the other five respondents the specified residences are one-bedroom flats provided by the National Asylum Support Service. During the curfew period the respondents are confined in their small flats and are not even allowed into the common parts of the buildings in which these flats are situated. Visitors must be authorised by the Home Office, to which name, address, date of birth and photographic identity must be supplied. The residences are subject to spot searches by the police. During the six hours when they are permitted to leave their residences, the respondents are confined to restricted urban areas, the largest of which is 72 square kilometres. These deliberately do not extend, save in the case of GG, to any area in which they lived before. Each area contains a mosque, a hospital, primary health care facilities, shops and entertainment and sporting facilities. The respondents are prohibited from meeting anyone by pre-arrangement who has not been given the same Home Office clearance as a visitor to the residence.'

It may be added that the controlled persons were required to wear an electronic tag and to report to a monitoring company on first leaving their flat after a curfew period and on returning to it before a curfew period. They were forbidden to use or possess any communications equipment of any kind save for one fixed telephone line in their flat maintained by the monitoring company. They could attend a mosque of their choice if it was in their permitted area and approved in advance by the Home Office. Some of the controlled persons are not permitted, because of their immigration status, to work; those who are permitted have not done so in the six-hour period between 10 a m and 4 p m. They received benefits of £30–£35 per week, mostly in vouchers, but in JJ's case £57·45. A request by JJ to study English at a college outside his area was refused.

21 …Sullivan J…regarded the orders made in these cases, although in force for only 12 months at a time, as of indefinite duration: para 48. He confined himself to facts which were agreed or were apparent on the face of the control orders: paras 57–58. He took as his starting point the confinement of the controlled persons for 18 hours each day of the week in a small flat where (save in the case of GG) they had not previously lived in a significantly different location: paras 60–62. He noted that the controlled persons were all single men, and accepted that the requirement to supply the name, address, date of birth and photographic identification to obtain prior Home Office approval of anyone wishing to visit the flat for social purposes during curfew hours deterred all but the most courageous of visitors: para 66. He expressed his conclusion in para 73 of his judgment:

'Drawing these threads together, and bearing in mind the type, duration, effects and manner of implementation of the obligations in these control orders, I am left in no doubt whatsoever that the cumulative effect of the obligations has been to deprive the respondents of their liberty in breach of article 5 of the Convention. I do not consider that this is a borderline case. The collective impact of the obligations in Annex I could not sensibly be described as a mere restriction upon the respondents' liberty of movement. In terms of the length of the curfew period (18 hours), the extent of the obligations, and their intrusive impact on the respondents' ability to lead anything resembling a normal life, whether inside their residences within the curfew period, or for the six-hour period outside it, these control orders go far beyond the restrictions in those cases where the European Court of Human Rights has concluded that there has been a restriction upon but not a deprivation of liberty.'

He regarded the controlled persons' concrete situation, at para 74, as the antithesis of liberty and more akin to detention in an open prison…

24 …No legal error in the reasoning of the judge or the Court of Appeal is shown, and it is not for the House to make a value judgment of its own. I would, however, add that on the agreed facts of these individual cases I would have reached the same conclusion. The effect of the 18-hour curfew, coupled with the effective exclusion of social visitors, meant that the controlled persons were in practice in solitary confinement for this lengthy period every day for an indefinite duration, with very little opportunity for contact with the outside world, with means insufficient to permit provision of significant facilities for self-entertainment and with knowledge that their flats were liable to be entered and searched at any time. The area open to them during their six non-curfew hours was unobjectionable in size, much larger than that open to Mr Guzzardi. But they were (save for GG) located in an unfamiliar area where they had no family, friends or contacts, and which was no doubt chosen for that reason. The requirement to obtain prior Home Office clearance of any social meeting outside the flat in practice isolated the controlled persons during the non-curfew hours also. Their lives were wholly regulated by the Home Office, as a prisoner's would be, although breaches were much more severely punishable. The judge's analogy with detention in an open prison was apt, save that the controlled persons did not enjoy the association with others and the access to entertainment facilities which a prisoner in an open prison would expect to enjoy.

REMEDY

[His Lordship held that as the order was a nullity it was not open to the court to quash particular restrictions so as to make it compatible.]

NOTES

1. Lord Hoffmann dissented. In his view, the correct position[310] was that

article 5…guaranteed the individual against illegitimate imprisonment, or confinement so close as to amount to the same thing—in sum against deprivation of liberty stricto sensu.

---

[310] As stated by Sir Gerald Fitzmaurice in a dissenting judgment in *Guzzardi* at para. 6.

He found it

impossible to say that a person in the position of LL is for practical purposes in prison. To describe him in such a way would be an extravagant metaphor. A person who lives in his own flat, has a telephone and whatever other conveniences he can afford, buys, prepares and cooks his own food, and is free on any day between 10 a m and 4 p m to go at his own choice to walk the streets, visit the shops, places of entertainment, sports facilities and parks of a London borough, use public transport, mingle with the people and attend his place of worship, is not in prison or anything that can be called an approximation to prison. True, his freedom of movement, communication and association is greatly restricted compared with an ordinary person. But that is not the comparison which the law requires to be made. The question is rather whether he can be compared with someone in prison and in my opinion he cannot.

It did not appear that Sullivan J and the Court of Appeal had applied the right test. Furthermore, if he had been of a different view, he would have remitted the case for consideration by the judge under s. 3(12) as that power was exercisable even if the order was a nullity. Lord Carswell also dissented on the first point but agreed with Lord Bingham on the second. Baroness Hale of Richmond and Lord Brown of Eaton-under-Heywood delivered speeches concurring with Lord Bingham.

2. Further points were clarified in two other cases heard at the same time.
(a) Lesser restrictions imposed in other cases were held to fall on the other side of the line. AF was required to remain in the flat where he was already living save for 10 hours between 8 a.m. and 6 p.m.; the 14-hour curfew was not regarded as sufficient to amount to a deprivation of liberty.[311] The position in the case of E was set out as follows by Lord Bingham:[312]

6 ...the control order...contains a number of obligations similar to those noted in the *JJ* case [2008] 1 AC 385. Thus, for example, he must wear an electronic tag; he must reside at a specified address; he must report to a monitoring company each day on first leaving his residence and on his last return to it; the permission of the Home Office is required in advance (with name, address, date of birth and photographic evidence of identity supplied) for most visitors to the residence; he must obtain the agreement of the Home Office in advance to attend most pre-arranged meetings outside his residence; his residence is liable to be searched by the police at any time; and he is permitted to have no communications equipment of any kind save for one fixed telephone line and one or more computers, provided any computer is disabled from connecting to the internet.

7 The obligations imposed on E do, however, differ from those imposed on JJ and others in respects accepted by the courts below as material. The curfew to which he is subject is of 12 hours' duration, from 7 pm to 7 am, not 18 hours. The residence specified in the order is his own home, where he had lived for some years, in a part of London with which he is familiar. By a variation of the order his residence is

---

[311] *Secretary of State for the Home Department v MB; Secretary of State for the Home Department v AF* [2007] UKHL 46, [2008] 1 AC 440. Control orders have also been upheld in *AL v Secretary of State for the Home Department* [2007] EWHC 1970 (Admin); *Abu Rideh v Secretary of State for the Home Department* [2007] EWHC 2237; *Secretary of State for the Home Department v AE* [2008] EWHC 585 (Admin); *Secretary of State for the Home Department v AH* [2008] EWHC 1018 (Admin); *AE v Secretary of State for the Home Department* [2008] EWHC 1743 (upholding refusal to permit AS level courses in Chemistry and Human Biology); *AV v Secretary of State for the Home Department* [2008] EWHC 1895 (Admin). Modifications were ordered in *Abu Rideh v Secretary of State for the Home Department* [2008] EWHC 2019 (Admin). In *Secretary of State for the Home Department v Bullivant* an order was quashed where the reasonable suspicion generated by the original evidence was dispelled by further information.

[312] *Secretary of State for the Home Department v E* [2007] UKHL 47, [2008] 1 AC 499.

defined to include his garden, to which he thus has access at any time. He lives at his home with his wife and family, and Home Office permission is not required in advance to receive visitors under the age of ten. Five members of his wider family live in the area, and have been approved as visitors. He is subject to no geographical restriction during non-curfew hours, is free to attend a mosque of his choice, and is not prohibited from associating with named individuals. The judge found...that E does not lack a social network, goes to the mosque, takes his older children to school, picks them up, goes shopping and sees family members who live in the area.

(b) Non-derogating control order proceedings did not involve determination of a criminal charge for the purposes of Art. 6 ECHR:

there is no assertion of criminal conduct, only a foundation of suspicion; no identification of any specific criminal offence is provided for; the order made is preventative in purpose, not punitive or retributive; and the obligations imposed must be no more restrictive than are judged necessary to achieve the preventative object of the order.[313]

(c) However,

in any case in which a person is at risk of an order containing obligations of the stringency found in this case, or the cases of *JJ* [2008] 1 AC 385 and *E* [2008] 1 AC 499, the application of the civil limb of article 6(1) does in my opinion entitle such person to such measure of procedural protection as is commensurate with the gravity of the potential consequences.[314]

This gave rise to difficulties in so far as the basis for the order was set out not in the open part of the hearing but in the closed part where the person concerned was represented by a special advocate. The special advocate would not be able to disclose that material to his or her client or take instructions on it. Lord Hoffmann took the view that recourse to the special advocate procedure would always be sufficient for compliance with Art. 6. The majority[315] took a different view, accepting that in some cases, so little would be disclosed to the persons subject to the order that they would be unable effectively to meet the allegations against them. This was heavily fact-sensitive, and the cases raising the point should be remitted to the Administrative Court for further consideration. In *MB*, the evidence implicating MB in terrorist activities was wholly contained in the closed material; in *AF*, no, or at least no clear or significant, allegations of involvement in terrorist-based activities were disclosed by the open material, nor had the gist of any such allegations been given. Paragraph 4(2)(a) of the Schedule to the 2005 Act stated that rules of court may:

make provision enabling control order proceedings or relevant appeal proceedings to take place without full particulars of the reasons for decisions to which the proceedings relate being given to a relevant party to the proceedings or his legal representative (if he has one)....

Paragraph 4(3)(d) provided that rules of court *must secure* 'that the relevant court is required to give permission for material not to be disclosed where it considers that disclosure of the material would be contrary to the public interest', and CPR r. 76.2(2) that: 'The court must ensure that information is not disclosed contrary to the public interest.' These provisions

---

313 Per Lord Bingham, ibid., at para. [24].   314 Ibid.
315 Lords Bingham, Carswell and Brown of Eaton-under-Heywood and Baroness Hale of Richmond.

apparently prioritised non-disclosure over fairness. Nevertheless, the majority held that by virtue of s. 3 of the HRA, they were to be read as modified:[316]

In my view, therefore, paragraph 4(3)(d) of the Schedule to the 2005 Act, should be read and given effect 'except where to do so would be incompatible with the right of the controlled person to a fair trial'. Paragraph 4(2)(a) and rule 76.29(8) would have to be read in the same way. This would then bring into play rule 76.29(7), made under paragraph 4(4) of the Schedule. Where the court does not give the Secretary of State permission to withhold closed material, she has a choice. She may decide that, after all, it can safely be disclosed (experience elsewhere in the world has been that, if pushed, the authorities discover that more can be disclosed than they first thought possible). But she may decide that it must still be withheld. She cannot then be required to serve it. But if the court considers that the material might be of assistance to the controlled person in relation to a matter under consideration, it may direct that the matter be withdrawn from consideration by the court. In any other case, it may direct that the Secretary of State cannot rely upon the material. If the Secretary of State cannot rely upon it, and it is indeed crucial to the decision, then the decision will be flawed and the order will have to be quashed.

(d) Section 8(2) of the 2005 Act provides that 'before making or applying for the making of, a control order against the individual, the Secretary of State must consult the chief officer of the police force about whether there is evidence available that could realistically be used for the purposes of a prosecution of the individual for an offence relating to terrorism'. This does not constitute a condition precedent to the making of a lawful order, although if it has not been fulfilled there would have to be very convincing reasons for the omission.[317] There is a continuing duty to review the possibility of prosecution.[318]

3. The adoption of a broader rather than narrower interpretation of deprivation of liberty and rejection of the view that recourse to the special advocate procedure is always sufficient to guarantee fairness is welcome. Would the lesser restrictions of the kind adopted in *AF* and *E* be regarded as lawful interferences with freedom of movement?

4. In *Secretary of State for the Home Department v AF (No. 3)*[319] Stanley Burnton J held that a *dictum* of Lord Brown in *MB*[320] that a court that took the view that the right to a fair hearing had been impaired could nevertheless dismiss an appeal if it felt 'quite sure that in any event no possible challenge could conceivably have succeeded', had not been endorsed by other members of the House and did not represent the law.

5. Further judgments have addressed the question of what has to be done to ensure procedural fairness. In *Secretary of State for the Home Department v AF*,[321] Stanley Burnton J cited with approval a *dictum* of Mitting J:[322]

unless, at a minimum, the special advocates are able to challenge the Secretary of State's grounds for suspicion on the basis of instructions from the controlled person which directly address their essential features, the controlled person will not receive a fair hearing.... In practice, this means he must be told their gist. This means that, if he chooses to do so, he can give and call evidence about the issues himself.

---

[316] Per Baroness Hale of Richmond at para. [72].
[317] *Secretary of State for the Home Department v E* [2007] UKHL 47, [2008] 1 AC 499.
[318] Ibid.   [319] [2008] EWHC 689 (Admin).   [320] At para. [90].
[321] [2008] EWHC 453 (Admin). This was one of the cases remitted by the HL in *MB* (above).
[322] In *Secretary of State for the Home Department v AN* [2008] EWHC 372 (Admin), at para. [9].

In *AF*, the case against him depended entirely on the closed material and the previous procedure did not comply with Art. 6. The Secretary of State would now be put to her election as to whether to disclose more information.[323]

It has also been held, however, that there is no minimum amount of material that has invariably to be disclosed to the controlled person in open proceedings to ensure that Art. 6 rights are preserved; and that it will be exceptional for there to be a finding of infringement when the special advocate procedure is used.[324]

6. The Joint Committee on Human Rights takes the view that the control order regime continues to give rise to breaches of Arts 5 and 6, and has made proposals for amending the legislation, including more detailed provision for parliamentary oversight and a maximum daily curfew limit of 12 hours.[325] The Government disagrees.[326] The control order regime is the subject of quarterly reports to Parliament by the Government and to reviews by Lord Carlile of Berriew QC.[327] Lord Carlile is of the view that the system as operated currently in its non-derogating form 'remains necessary given the nature of the risks of terrorist attacks' and is 'a justifiable and proportional safety valve for the proper protection of civil society'.[328] As at 10 June 2008, there were 15 control orders currently in force, three of which were in respect of British citizens.

6. THE TERRORISM ACT 2006

The stream of legislation continued with this Act, which introduced some additional offences and amended aspects of the existing legislation. One of the motivations was to find ways of convicting suspected terrorists of substantive offences so as to avoid the difficulties of securing on-going detention without trial.[329] It was passed in the aftermath of the 7/7 London bombings. The legislative process was difficult for the Government. The provisions in the Bill first presented were narrower in some respects than those in the Government's original proposals and those ultimately passed narrower still.[330] Most notably, a proposal to allow up to 90 days' detention without charge was defeated in the House of Commons at the Report stage, and the period reduced to 28 days.[331] The Government has since returned to this issue.[332] The offence of the encouragement or glorification of terrorism just survived when the House of Lords reluctantly withdrew its opposition.

---

[323] There was a similar outcome in *AN*, above, where AN did not know the gist of significant grounds of suspicion raised against him. The Court of Appeal allowed appeals: see Preface.

[324] *Secretary of State for the Home Department v AE* [2008] EWHC 585 (Admin).

[325] *Counter-Terrorism Policy and Human Rights (Ninth Report): Annual Renewal of Control Orders Legislation 2008* (Tenth Report, Session 2007–08 HL 57/HC 356).

[326] *Government Reply* (Cm 7368, April 2008).

[327] http://security.homeoffice.gov.uk/legislation/current-legislation/prevention-terrorism-act-2005/.

[328] Second Report of the Independent Reviewer pursuant to s. 14(3) of the Prevention of Terrorism Act 2005 (19 February 2007), paras 7, 59.

[329] D. Hoffman, *Current Law Statutes Annotated 2006*, p. 11.3; House of Commons Library Research Paper 05/66, 20 October 2005, *The Terrorism Bill 2005–06*; A. Jones, et al., *The Terrorism Act 2006* (OUP, Oxford, 2006).

[330] Ibid., pp. 11.3–11.4.

[331] Section 23. See p. 439. By virtue of s. 25, this is to revert to a 14-day maximum (with no involvement of a senior judge) unless s. 25 is disapplied annually by an order made by the Secretary of State. This has been done by SI 2007/2181 and SI 2008/1745.

[332] See p. 492.

Part 2 of the Act made a number of further changes to existing legislation including broadening the grounds of proscription[333] and providing for change of name;[334] adding to the grounds for extending detention;[335] the introduction of all premises warrants;[336] the extension to internal waters of authorisations to stop and search.[337] A person must be appointed to review the 2000 Act and Part 1 of the 2006 Act.[338]

NOTES

1. *Encouragement of terrorism and dissemination of terrorist publications.* The original proposals included separate offences of encouragement and glorification of terrorism. There was no intention requirement, the offence being committed where a person published a statement knowing or believing or having reasonable grounds for believing that members of the public to whom it was or was to be published were likely to understand it as a direct or indirect encouragement or other inducement to the Commission, preparation or instigation of acts of terrorism.[339] The inclusion of a significant mens rea requirement was clearly an improvement. The reference to recklessness was regarded as involving a subjective rather than objective test.[340] There remain significant concerns that the offence that emerged is overbroad. At the core is the point that it is not necessary to show that any person was in fact encouraged or induced to commit an offence; if this can be shown the position was already covered by existing offences. This means in turn that whether the offence is committed will turn on speculation as to what members of the public are likely to understand or reasonably infer, which is unusually vague for a criminal offence. Convictions are likely to be closely scrutinised for conformity to the ECHR, Arts 7, 9 and 10.

2. The Government stated that one of the intentions behind s. 1 was to implement Art. 5 of the Prevention of Terrorism Convention,[341] which requires parties to the Convention to establish an offence of 'public provocation to commit a terrorist offence', covering the publishing of messages with intent to invite the commission of a terrorist offence and when that causes a danger that one or more such offences may be committed. The offence enacted is clearly broader, with the inclusion of recklessness and the lack of a requirement that the conduct 'causes a danger'.[342]

3. *Dissemination of terrorist publications.* As with s. 1, the s. 2 offences originally drafted also lacked a significant mens rea requirement. A JP may issue a warrant authorising entry, search and seizure in respect of articles likely to be the subject of conduct within s. 2(2)(a)–(e) and which would fall to be treated as a terrorist publication for the purposes of s. 2.[343] Forfeiture proceedings may be taken.[344] Section 2(7) and (8) do not restrict the considerations relevant to the assessment of the seriousness of an offence for the purposes of sentencing.[345]

4. Section 3 applies ss. 1 and 2 to statements or conduct (under s. 2(2)) in the course of or in connection with the provision or use of a service provided electronically. A statement, or the

---

[333] Ss. 21, 22. See p. 418.   [334] Ss. 21, 22. See p. 418.   [335] S. 24. See p. 439.

[336] S. 26. See p. 429.   [337] S. 30. See p. 433.   [338] 2006 Act, s. 36.

[339] HC Bill 55, 12 October 2005, cl. 1.

[340] D. Hoffman, op. cit., p. 11.10, citing *R v G* [2003] UKHL 50, [2004] 1 AC 1034, and noting that the offence will have to be interpreted accordingly if it is not to be overbroad. See also A. Hunt [2007] Crim LR 441.

[341] Council of Europe Convention for the Prevention of Terrorism 2005, CETS No. 196. It has been signed by the UK but not yet ratified (as at 10 August 2008) (see www.conventions.coe.int).

[342] D. Hoffman, op. cit., p. 11.10.   [343] 2006 Act, s. 28.   [344] 2006 Act, Sch. 2.

[345] *R v Rahman; R v Mohammed* [2008] EWCA Civ 1465.

article or record to which the conduct relates, is to be regarded as having the endorsement of a person where he or she fails to comply within two working days with a notice given by a constable requiring the statement etc. to be withdrawn or modified so as no longer to be unlawfully terrorism-related. A repeat statement etc. that is for all practical purposes the same is to be regarded as covered by the original notice, but there is a defence that D has taken every reasonable step to prevent it from becoming available to the public and to ascertain whether it does, was not aware of its publication and having become aware took every reasonable step to secure that it either ceased to become available or was modified. A statement is unlawfully terrorism-related is defined in similar terms to the provisions in s. 2(3) and (4). Section 4 governs the giving of notices under s. 3.

5. *Preparation of terrorism.* Section 5 covers preparatory acts which have not reached the stage of attempts or conspiracy to commit an offence.[346]

6. *Other offences.* Further offences created by the 2006 Act cover the following. Section 6 makes it an offence to provide or receive instruction or training in specified skills. These include handling noxious substances; the use of any method or technique for doing anything else capable of being done for the purposes of terrorism or in connection with the commission or preparation of an act of terrorism, or assisting such commission or preparation; and the design or adaptation for such purposes of any method or technique for doing anything. D must know that the trainee (or him or herself if the recipient) intends to use the skills for or in connection with the commission or preparation of acts of terrorism or Convention offences, or assisting such commission or preparation. It is, however, irrelevant whether any instruction or training is provided to particular persons or generally and whether the acts or offences intended are particular acts or offences or acts of terrorism or Convention offences generally. This ensures compliance with Art. 7 of the Prevention of Terrorism Convention 2005. Section 7 confers powers of forfeiture in respect of s. 6 offences.

Section 8 makes it an offence to attend at any place, whether in the UK or elsewhere, while instruction or training as mentioned in s. 6(1) of the 2006 Act or s. 54(1) of the Terrorism Act 2000[347] as produced or made available there. The instruction or training must be provided or made available there wholly or partly for purposes connected with the commission or preparation of acts of terrorism or Convention offences,[348] and it must be shown either that D knows or believes that that is the case, or a person attending at that place throughout the periods of that person's attendance could not reasonably have failed to understand that. It is immaterial whether the person concerned receives the instruction or training him or herself, and whether it is provided or made available in respect of particular acts or offences or acts of terrorism or Convention offences generally. There is then a series of offences covering specific acts in the course of or in connection with the commission or preparation of an act of terrorism or for the purposes of terrorism.[349] The acts are making or possessing a radioactive device or possessing radioactive material; using such devices or materials; using or damaging a nuclear facility in a manner which causes or increases a risk of the release of radioactive material; or the use of a range of threats or demands in respect of such devices, materials or facilities.[350]

---

[346] D. Hoffman, op. cit., p. 11.17.   [347] See p. 450.

[348] I.e. offences listed in Sch. 1 or an equivalent offence under the law of a country or territory outside the UK: s. 20(2).

[349] Or in the case of s. 9, making the device or material available to be so used.

[350] Ss. 9–11, enabling the UK to ratify the (UN) International Convention on the Suppression of Acts of Nuclear Terrorism.

7. *Other matters.* Offences under ss. 5, 9, 10 and 11 are indictable only and punishable by life imprisonment. Offences under ss. 1, 6 and 8 are triable either way with maximum sentences on indictment of seven (s. 1) or 10 (ss. 6, 8) years' imprisonment or a fine or both and on summary conviction of 12 months' imprisonment, a fine not exceeding the statutory maximum or both. A further range of acts done outside the UK which if done in the UK would be one of a list of offences[351] are to be offences against UK law.[352] The consent of the Director of Public Prosecutions is necessary for proceedings under Pt 1; the Attorney-General's consent is needed if it appears to the DPP that an offence has been committed for a purpose wholly or partly connected with the affairs of a country other than the UK.

- **Terrorism Act 2006**

Part 1 Offences

ENCOURAGEMENT ETC OF TERRORISM

1 Encouragement of terrorism

(1) This section applies to a statement that is likely to be understood by some or all of the members of the public to whom it is published as a direct or indirect encouragement or other inducement to them to the commission, preparation or instigation of acts of terrorism or Convention offences.

(2) A person commits an offence if—

   (a) he publishes a statement to which this section applies or causes another to publish such a statement; and

   (b) at the time he publishes it or causes it to be published, he—

      (i) intends members of the public to be directly or indirectly encouraged or otherwise induced by the statement to commit, prepare or instigate acts of terrorism or Convention offences; or

      (ii) is reckless as to whether members of the public will be directly or indirectly encouraged or otherwise induced by the statement to commit, prepare or instigate such acts or offences.

(3) For the purposes of this section, the statements that are likely to be understood by members of the public as indirectly encouraging the commission or preparation of acts of terrorism or Convention offences include every statement which—

   (a) glorifies the commission or preparation (whether in the past, in the future or generally) of such acts or offences; and

   (b) is a statement from which those members of the public could reasonably be expected to infer that what is being glorified is being glorified as conduct that should be emulated by them in existing circumstances.

(4) For the purposes of this section the questions how a statement is likely to be understood and what members of the public could reasonably be expected to infer from it must be determined having regard both—

   (a) to the contents of the statement as a whole; and

   (b) to the circumstances and manner of its publication.

---

[351] Including offences under ss. 1, 6 of the 2006 Act (in respect of Convention offences) ss. 8–11 of this Act; ss. 11(1) and 54 of the 2000 Act.

[352] 2006 Act, s. 17.

(5) It is irrelevant for the purposes of subsections (1) to (3)—

    (a) whether anything mentioned in those subsections relates to the commission, preparation or instigation of one or more particular acts of terrorism or Convention offences, of acts of terrorism or Convention offences of a particular description or of acts of terrorism or Convention offences generally; and,

    (b) whether any person is in fact encouraged or induced by the statement to commit, prepare or instigate any such act or offence.

(6) In proceedings for an offence under this section against a person in whose case it is not proved that he intended the statement directly or indirectly to encourage or otherwise induce the commission, preparation or instigation of acts of terrorism or Convention offences, it is a defence for him to show—

    (a) that the statement neither expressed his views nor had his endorsement (whether by virtue of section 3 or otherwise); and

    (b) that it was clear, in all the circumstances of the statement's publication, that it did not express his views and (apart from the possibility of his having been given and failed to comply with a notice under subsection (3) of that section) did not have his endorsement....

2 Dissemination of terrorist publications

(1) A person commits an offence if he engages in conduct falling within subsection (2) and, at the time he does so—

    (a) he intends an effect of his conduct to be a direct or indirect encouragement or other inducement to the commission, preparation or instigation of acts of terrorism;

    (b) he intends an effect of his conduct to be the provision of assistance in the commission or preparation of such acts; or

    (c) he is reckless as to whether his conduct has an effect mentioned in paragraph (a) or (b).

(2) For the purposes of this section a person engages in conduct falling within this subsection if he—

    (a) distributes or circulates a terrorist publication;

    (b) gives, sells or lends such a publication;

    (c) offers such a publication for sale or loan;

    (d) provides a service to others that enables them to obtain, read, listen to or look at such a publication, or to acquire it by means of a gift, sale or loan;

    (e) transmits the contents of such a publication electronically; or

    (f) has such a publication in his possession with a view to its becoming the subject of conduct falling within any of paragraphs (a) to (e).

(3) For the purposes of this section a publication is a terrorist publication, in relation to conduct falling within subsection (2), if matter contained in it is likely—

    (a) to be understood, by some or all of the persons to whom it is or may become available as a consequence of that conduct, as a direct or indirect encouragement or other inducement to them to the commission, preparation or instigation of acts of terrorism; or

    (b) to be useful in the commission or preparation of such acts and to be understood, by some or all of those persons, as contained in the publication, or made available to them, wholly or mainly for the purpose of being so useful to them.

(4) For the purposes of this section matter that is likely to be understood by a person as indirectly encouraging the commission or preparation of acts of terrorism includes any matter which—

   (a) glorifies the commission or preparation (whether in the past, in the future or generally) of such acts; and

   (b) is matter from which that person could reasonably be expected to infer that what is being glorified is being glorified as conduct that should be emulated by him in existing circumstances.

(5) For the purposes of this section the question whether a publication is a terrorist publication in relation to particular conduct must be determined—

   (a) as at the time of that conduct; and

   (b) having regard both to the contents of the publication as a whole and to the circumstances in which that conduct occurs.

(6) In subsection (1) references to the effect of a person's conduct in relation to a terrorist publication include references to an effect of the publication on one or more persons to whom it is or may become available as a consequence of that conduct.

(7) It is irrelevant for the purposes of this section whether anything mentioned in subsections (1) to (4) is in relation to the commission, preparation or instigation of one or more particular acts of terrorism, of acts of terrorism of a particular description or of acts of terrorism generally.

(8) For the purposes of this section it is also irrelevant, in relation to matter contained in any article whether any person—

   (a) is in fact encouraged or induced by that matter to commit, prepare or instigate acts of terrorism; or

   (b) in fact makes use of it in the commission or preparation of such acts.

(9) In proceedings for an offence under this section against a person in respect of conduct to which subsection (10) applies, it is a defence for him to show—

   (a) that the matter by reference to which the publication in question was a terrorist publication neither expressed his views nor had his endorsement (whether by virtue of section 3 or otherwise); and

   (b) that it was clear, in all the circumstances of the conduct, that that matter did not express his views and (apart from the possibility of his having been given and failed to comply with a notice under subsection (3) of that section) did not have his endorsement.

(10) This subsection applies to the conduct of a person to the extent that—

   (a) the publication to which his conduct related contained matter by reference to which it was a terrorist publication by virtue of subsection (3)(a); and

   (b) that person is not proved to have engaged in that conduct with the intention specified in subsection (1)(a)....

(13) In this section—

'lend' includes let on hire, and 'loan' is to be construed accordingly;

'publication' means an article or record of any description that contains any of the following, or any combination of them—

   (a) matter to be read;

   (b) matter to be listened to;

   (c) matter to be looked at or watched.

PREPARATION OF TERRORIST ACTS AND TERRORIST TRAINING

5 Preparation of terrorist acts

(1) A person commits an offence if, with the intention of—

    (a) committing acts of terrorism, or

    (b) assisting another to commit such acts,

he engages in any conduct in preparation for giving effect to his intention.

(2) It is irrelevant for the purposes of subsection (1) whether the intention and preparations relate to one or more particular acts of terrorism, acts of terrorism of a particular description or acts of terrorism generally.

(3) A person guilty of an offence under this section shall be liable, on conviction on indictment, to imprisonment for life.

20 Interpretation of Part 1

(1) Expressions used in this Part and in the Terrorism Act 2000 (c 11) have the same meanings in this Part as in that Act.

(2) In this Part—

    'act of terrorism' includes anything constituting an action taken for the purposes of terrorism, within the meaning of the Terrorism Act 2000 (see section 1(5) of that Act);

    'article' includes anything for storing data;

    'Convention offence' means an offence listed in Schedule 1 or an equivalent offence under the law of a country or territory outside the United Kingdom;

    'glorification' includes any form of praise or celebration, and cognate expressions are to be construed accordingly;

    'public' is to be construed in accordance with subsection (3);

    'publish' and cognate expressions are to be construed in accordance with subsection (4);

    'record' means a record so far as not comprised in an article, including a temporary record created electronically and existing solely in the course of, and for the purposes of, the transmission of the whole or a part of its contents;

    'statement' is to be construed in accordance with subsection (6).

(3) In this Part references to the public—

    (a) are references to the public of any part of the United Kingdom or of a country or territory outside the United Kingdom, or any section of the public; and

    (b) except in section 9(4), also include references to a meeting or other group of persons which is open to the public (whether unconditionally or on the making of a payment or the satisfaction of other conditions).

(4) In this Part references to a person's publishing a statement are references to—

    (a) his publishing it in any manner to the public;

    (b) his providing electronically any service by means of which the public have access to the statement; or

    (c) his using a service provided to him electronically by another so as to enable or to facilitate access by the public to the statement;

but this subsection does not apply to the references to a publication in section 2.

(5) In this Part references to providing a service include references to making a facility available; and references to a service provided to a person are to be construed accordingly.

(6) In this Part references to a statement are references to a communication of any description, including a communication without words consisting of sounds or images or both.

(7) In this Part references to conduct that should be emulated in existing circumstances include references to conduct that is illustrative of a type of conduct that should be so emulated.

(8) In this Part references to what is contained in an article or record include references—

(a) to anything that is embodied or stored in or on it; and

(b) to anything that may be reproduced from it using apparatus designed or adapted for the purpose....

7. THE COUNTER-TERRORISM BILL 2007-08

EXPLANATORY NOTES

These Notes refer to the Counter-Terrorism Bill as brought from the House of Commons on 12th June 2008 [HL Bill 65]

OVERVIEW

5. The Bill's Parts and Schedules are as follows.

6. Part 1 (powers to gather and share information) contains provisions for new powers relating to the removal of documents for examination in the context of a search under existing terrorism legislation. It also provides a power for a constable to take fingerprints and samples from individuals subject to control orders and amends the law relating to the retention and use of fingerprints and DNA samples. It also contains provisions on the disclosure of information to and by the intelligence services and their use of such information.

7. Part 2 (detention and questioning of terrorist suspects) provides for a temporary extension to the maximum amount of time that terrorist suspects can be held before being charged to 42 days.[353] This extension may be made available by order by the Secretary of State in defined circumstances. This Part also provides that terrorist suspects may be questioned after they have been charged. The questioning will be limited to the offence for which the person has been charged with and adverse inferences from the silence of the suspect may be drawn by a court in England, Wales or Northern Ireland.[354]

8. Part 3 (prosecution and punishment of offences) provides for specified terrorism offences committed anywhere in the UK to be tried in any part of the UK. It also requires the Attorney General's or Advocate General for Northern Ireland's consent for prosecution of specified terrorism offences committed outside the UK. This Part also deals with sentences for cases tried under the general criminal law: the court is to consider a terrorist connection as an aggravating factor when considering sentence. It also extends the forfeiture regime applicable in terrorist cases.

---

[353] Opposed by, amongst others, the Joint Committee on Human Rights, on the basis that: '(i) it can find no clear evidence of likely need in the near future;(ii) alternatives to extension do enough, in combination, to protect the public and are much more proportionate;(iii) the proposed parliamentary mechanism would create a serious risk of prejudice to the fair trial of suspects;(iv) the existing judicial safeguards for extensions even up to 28 days are inadequate': *Counter-terrorism Policy and Human Rights: 42 days* (Second report, 2007–08 HL23/HC156).

[354] On the issues concerning post-charge questioning, see C. Walker [2008] Crim LR 509.

9. Part 4 (notification requirements) makes provision about notification of certain information to the police by individuals who are convicted of, and sentenced to 12 months or more for, a terrorism or terrorism-related offence. They must provide the police with certain personal information when they are not in custody, notify any subsequent changes to this information and confirm its accuracy annually. And under Schedule 6, courts may make foreign travel restriction orders which will enable restrictions to be placed on the overseas travel of those subject to the notification requirements.

10. Part 5 (asset freezing proceedings) amends the Regulation of Investigatory Powers Act 2000 so that intercept material can be used in asset freezing cases relating to terrorism (cases in which assets are frozen for the purposes of a UN terrorism order). It also provides an enabling power for the Lord Chancellor (in the first instance) to make court procedure rules about the use of special advocates, closed hearings and the withholding of evidence in civil court proceedings relating to asset freezing decisions.

11. Part 6 (inquests and inquiries) creates provisions for coroners' inquests to take place without a jury if the Secretary of State has certified that the inquest will involve the consideration of material that should not be made public in the interests of national security, the relationship between the United Kingdom and another country, or otherwise in the public interest. This Part also amends the Regulation of Investigatory Powers Act 2000 to allow intercept material to be disclosed in exceptional circumstances to: (i) coroners and counsel to the inquest in cases where the Secretary of State has issued a certificate requiring the inquest to he held without a jury; and (ii) to counsel to an inquiry held under the Inquiries Act 2005 (in addition to the inquiry panel).

12. Part 7 (miscellaneous) amends the definition of terrorism in section 1 of the Terrorism Act 2000 (and various other pieces of terrorism legislation) by inserting a reference to a racial cause. This Part also creates an offence of eliciting, publishing or communicating information about members of the armed forces, members of the intelligence and security agencies or police constables which is likely to be of use to terrorists, and amends the offence of failing to disclose information about a suspected terrorist finance offence. It also includes some amendments to the control order system, amendments to provisions on forfeiture of terrorist cash, a new scheme relating to the recovery of costs of policing at gas facilities and a provision on the appointment of special advocates in Northern Ireland.

NOTES

1. The provisions concerning extended detention and the removal of juries from some coroners' inquests have been particularly controversial.

2. The provisions concerning freezing orders implementing UN Resolutions are designed to fill the gap created by the decision in *A v HM Treasury*[355] Here, Collins J quashed two orders in council made under the United Nations Act 1946[356] implementing UN measures requiring member states to prevent and suppress the financing of terrorist acts, and take other steps including freezing the assets of persons who commit or attempt to commit or participate in or facilitate the commission of terrorist acts; and to freeze the assets of persons listed by a UN committee. Freezing orders had been made on the applicant under these orders. The orders were held to be *ultra vires*. It was unlawful to use the procedure in the 1946 Act, under which orders had merely to be laid before Parliament and there was no opportunity for Parliament to scrutinise the order. It could not be said that it was 'necessary and expedient' for this route to be used, are required by s. 1 of the 1946 Act. Under the orders, a person could be affected where there were 'reasonable grounds for suspecting that

---

[355] [2008] EWHC 869 (Admin).
[356] Terrorism (United Nations Measures) Order 2006, SI 2006/2657; Al-Qaida and Taliban (United Nations Measures) Order 2006, SI 2006/2952.

the person is or *may be* a person who commits etc' (judge's emphasis). This was a very low threshold. A further point was that ss. 17 and 18 of the Regulation of Investigatory Powers Act 2000 would prevent a court hearing a challenge to a freezing order on an appeal or judicial review from considering intercepted material, which would usually be relevant; this would mean that 'a fair and just consideration of the question whether the individual applicant is one who should be subjected to an order is likely to be impossible in most cases'. This would affect both the applicant and the Crown (who would not be able to rely on inculpatory intercept evidence). There were also concerns about the scope of the offences which were matters appropriate for Parliamentary consideration. The Court of Appeal allowed an appeal (see Preface).

8.   THE USE OF FORCE[357]

- **Attorney-General for Northern Ireland's Reference (No. 1 of 1975)** [1977]
  AC 105, [1976] 2 All ER 937, [1976] 3 WLR 235, House of Lords (NI)

A British soldier on patrol in Northern Ireland in the exercise of his power to prevent crime under s. 3(1) of the Criminal Law Act (NI) 1967 (which is in the same terms as the Criminal Law Act 1967, s. 3(1))[358] shot and killed an unarmed man, who had run away when challenged. The soldier had the honest and reasonable, though mistaken, belief that he was a terrorist. A judge sitting without a jury acquitted him of murder holding that he had no conscious intention to kill or seriously injure and that the killing was justifiable. The Attorney-General referred two matters to the Court of Criminal Appeal in Northern Ireland, and an appeal was taken to the House of Lords. The House held that the first matter raised no point of law, since it was in essence whether or not the soldier had used reasonable force, and that was a question of fact for the judge. The second matter accordingly did not arise. Lord Diplock made some observations as to the legal position.

Lord Diplock: . . . There is little authority in English law concerning the rights and duties of a member of the armed forces of the Crown when acting in aid of the civil power; and what little authority there is relates almost entirely to the duties of soldiers when troops are called upon to assist in controlling a riotous assembly. Where used for such temporary purposes it may not be inaccurate to describe the legal rights and duties of a soldier as being no more than those of an ordinary citizen in uniform. But such a description is in my view misleading in the circumstances in which the army is currently employed in aid of the civil power in Northern Ireland. . . . In theory it may be the duty of every citizen when an arrestable offence is about to be committed in his presence to take whatever reasonable measures are available to him to prevent the commission of the crime; but the duty is one of imperfect obligation and does not place him under any obligation to do anything by which he would expose himself to risk of personal injury, nor is he under any duty to search for criminals or seek out crime. In contrast to this a soldier who is employed in aid of the civil power in Northern Ireland is under a duty, enforceable under military law, to search for criminals if so ordered by his superior officer and to risk his own life should this be necessary in preventing terrorist acts. For the performance of this duty he is armed with a firearm, a self-loading rifle, from which a bullet, if it hits the human body, is almost certain to cause serious injury if not death. . . .

What amount of force is 'reasonable in the circumstances' for the purpose of preventing crime, is in my view, always a question for the jury in a jury trial, never a 'point of law' for the judge.

---

[357] See also pp. 151–154.   [358] Above, p. 151.

The form in which the jury would have to ask themselves the question in a trial for an offence against the person in which this defence was raised by the accused, would be: Are we satisfied that no reasonable man (a) with knowledge of such facts as were known to the accused or reasonably believed by him to exist (b) in the circumstances and time available to him for reflection (c) could be of opinion that the prevention of the risk of harm to which others might be exposed if the suspect were allowed to escape justified exposing the suspect to the risk of harm to him that might result from the kind of force that the accused contemplated using?

The jury would have also to consider how the circumstances in which the accused had to make his decision whether or not to use force and the shortness of the time available to him for reflection, might affect the judgment of a reasonable man. In the facts that are to be assumed for the purposes of the reference there is material upon which a jury might take the view that the accused had reasonable grounds for apprehension of imminent danger to himself and other members of the patrol if the deceased were allowed to get away and join armed fellow-members of the Provisional IRA who might be lurking in the neighbourhood, and that the time available to the accused to make up his mind what to do was so short that even a reasonable man could only act intuitively. This being so, the jury in approaching the final part of the question should remind themselves that the postulated balancing of risk against risk, harm against harm, by the reasonable man is not undertaken in the calm analytical atmosphere of the court-room after counsel with the benefit of hindsight have expounded at length the reasons for and against the kind and degree of force that was used by the accused; but in the brief second or two which the accused had to decide whether to shoot or not and under all the stresses to which he was exposed.

In many cases where force is used in the prevention of crime or in effecting an arrest there is a choice as to the degree of force to use. On the facts that are to be assumed for the purposes of the reference the only options open to the accused were either to let the deceased escape or to shoot at him with a service rifle. A reasonable man would know that a bullet from a self loading rifle if it hit a human being, at any rate at the range at which the accused fired, would be likely to kill him or to injure him seriously. So in one scale of balance the harm to which the deceased would be exposed if the accused aimed to hit him was predictable and grave and the risk of its occurrence high. In the other scale of the balance it would be open to the jury to take the view that it would not be unreasonable to assess the kind of harm to be averted by preventing the accused's escape as even graver—the killing or wounding of members of the patrol by terrorists in ambush, and the effect of this success by members of the Provisional IRA in encouraging the continuance of the armed insurrection and all the misery and destruction of life and property that terrorist activity in Northern Ireland has entailed. The jury would have to consider too what was the highest degree at which a reasonable man could have assessed the likelihood that such consequences might follow the escape of the deceased if the facts had been as the accused knew or believed them reasonably to be.

Lords Simon of Glaisdale, Edmund-Davies and **Russell of Killowen** expressed their agreement with Lord Diplock's opinion.

NOTES

1. In *Farrell v Secretary of State for Defence* [359] the commanding officer of an army unit (X) received information that a bomb attack would be made by three men on a bank in Newry. He instructed an NCO, soldier A and three other soldiers to take up a position on the roof

[359] [1980] 1 All ER 1667. See also *R v MacNaughton* [1975] NI 203; *R v Bohan* [1979] 5 NIJB, Belfast Crown Court; *McLaughlin v Ministry of Defence* [1978] 7 NIJB, (NI CA): on appeal, *Farrell v Secretary of State for Defence* [1980] 1 All ER 1667, HL; *McGuigan v Ministry of Defence* [1982] 19 NIJB, QBD (NI); *Lynch v Ministry of Defence* [1983] NI 216; *R v Hegarty* [1986] NI 343; *Magill v Ministry of Defence* [1987] NI 194; *Hegarty, Doyle and Kelly v Ministry of Defence* [1989] 9 NIJB 88.

of a building opposite the bank. During the night, soldier B saw two men attempt to open the bank's night safe; they were then attacked by three other men. B called soldier A, who saw only the second group. He called on them to halt. They stopped and looked up and down the street. One of them shouted 'run' and they made off. Soldier A shouted 'Halt, I am ready to fire'. They did not stop. A opened fire, as did his colleagues, and all three were killed. The widow of one of them sued the Secretary of State. The jury held that the soldiers had reasonable cause to suspect that the three men were attempting to place at the bank an explosive device that would endanger life, and that it was reasonable in the circumstances for the soldiers to shoot to kill, in the prevention of crime or in effecting a lawful arrest.[360] The Northern Ireland Court of Appeal ordered a new trial on the ground that the jury should have been invited to consider whether there had been negligence in the planning of the operation: it had emerged that X had only given instructions to one soldier, A; that he had given no instructions about summoning help; that there was no agreed procedure for the four soldiers reporting back to base; only four soldiers out of 80 in X's command were selected for the operation; all four were ordered to go on the roof; they did not have a loud hailer; they were left in a situation where the only way to stop a suspected terrorist if he refused to stop was by firing at him. The House of Lords allowed an appeal, holding (1) that the term 'circumstances' in s. 3(1) did not extend to include the planning of the operation; and (2) that negligence had not been pleaded against any person other than the four soldiers at the scene. On the first point, Viscount Dilhorne stated:[361]

> I am unable to agree that the phrase 'in the circumstances' in s. 3(1) should be given the wide interpretation given to it in the Court of Appeal. That section is contained in a statute dealing with the criminal law. It may provide a defence for a person sued. In each case when such a defence is put forward the question to be determined is whether the person who is accused or sued used such force as was reasonable in the circumstances in which he was placed in the prevention of crime or in bringing about a lawful arrest of an offender or suspected offender.
>
> Section 3(1) would provide no defence to soldier X in respect of a claim for negligence in the planning of the operation. It can only provide a defence for those who have used force and if the force the four soldiers used was reasonable in the circumstances in which they used it, the defects, if there were any, in the planning of the operation would not deprive them of that defence and render the force used unreasonable.

This narrow approach has been criticised.[362] Many commentators, including Greer, Walker and the Standing Advisory Commission on Human Rights[363] have argued that s. 3(1) provides insufficient guidance on the general nature of the circumstances in which potentially lethal force may be used.[364] It has, furthermore, been argued that different standards should be applicable to the use of force by agents of the state as distinct from other citizens.[365] Can

---

[360] S. 3(1) of the Criminal Law Act (Northern Ireland) 1967: in the same terms as s. 3(1) of the Criminal Law Act 1967, above, p. 151.

[361] At p. 172.

[362] D.S. Greer (1980) 31 NILQ 151, 154–155. See also on the *Farrell* case C.P. Walker (1980) 43 MLR 591.

[363] 9th Annual Report for 1982–83 (1983–84 HC 262), pp. 21–23 and Appendix B.

[364] See also G. Williams, *Textbook of Criminal Law* (2nd edn, 1983), pp. 493–500; D.C. Ormerod, *Smith and Hogan Criminal Law* (12th edn, 2008), pp. 358–376; P.J. Rowe and C.J. Whelan (eds), *Military Intervention in Democratic Societies* (1985), Chap. 9; *Hogan and Walker*, pp. 64–69; R.J. Spjut [1986] PL 38; J.C. Smith (1994) 47(2) CLP 101 and [2002] Crim LR 958; F. Leverick [2002] Crim LR 347, 963.

[365] See J. Rogers (1998) 18 LS 486 and S. Skinner [2000] PL 266. Skinner argues that the 'citizen in uniform' concept applied to soldiers and police officers is 'based on an anachronistic fiction' and is 'an historically dubious precedent'.

this be right? If Art. 2 ECHR[366] requires a certain standard in the case of the taking of life by state agents should the state not protect citizens by applying the same standards in its domestic law to the taking of life by a citizen?

2. The *Farrell* case was taken to Strasbourg and a claim under Art. 2 ECHR admitted for consideration on the merits.[367] The case was then the subject of a friendly settlement, the British Government agreeing to pay substantial damages to Mrs Farrell. In *Stewart v United Kingdom*[368] the applicant's son died after being struck on the head by a plastic bullet fired by a British soldier in Northern Ireland. It was held that the use of plastic bullets was not *per se* contrary to Art. 2 or 3 ECHR. Then, in *Kelly v United Kingdom*[369] the Commission found that the shooting dead of a joyrider attempting to evade an army checkpoint did not contravene Art. 2 ECHR, as the soldiers had a genuine and reasonable belief that the youth was a terror- ist and had fired 'in order to effect a lawful arrest' within Art. 2(2). This has been cogently criticised[370] on the ground that the national court had rejected a claim for damages on the basis of the force being reasonable force in the prevention of crime (a basis not found in Art. 2), and that the soldiers were neither seeking nor had power to arrest in the circumstances. The key decision of the ECtHR is now that in *McCann v United Kingdom*.[371]

It is argued that s. 3 is broader than the test prescribed by Art. 2 ECHR.[372] However, it must by virtue of the Human Rights Act 1998 now be interpreted and applied so as to conform with Art. 2 ECHR.

3. According to Jennings,[373] writing in 1988, over 270 individuals, at least 155 of them 'civil- ians', had been killed by the security forces in Northern Ireland since 1969. Between 1982 and 1985, 35 individuals were so killed, 23 in covert operations. Twenty-one members of the secu- rity forces had been prosecuted for killings using firearms on duty, of whom one was convicted of manslaughter[374] and one of murder.[375] There were suspicions of the existence of a 'shoot-to- kill' policy in the 1982/5 period, associated particularly with undercover surveillance units. John Stalker, then Deputy Chief Constable of Greater Manchester, conducted an inquiry into a series of killings, including those at two incidents where prosecutions of members of the secu- rity forces ended in acquittals.[376] The terms of reference did not, however, include an investiga- tion of the existence of a shoot-to-kill policy. The inquiry was completed by Colin Sampson, Chief Constable of West Yorkshire, following Stalker's suspension for alleged disciplinary offences. The outcome of the inquiry was not made public. However, the Attorney-General announced in 1988 that eight RUC officers involved in a conspiracy to pervert the course of justice and responsible for obstructing the Stalker inquiry would not be prosecuted for reasons of national security. There was no evidence of a shoot-to-kill policy.[377]

John Stalker has subsequently suggested that there was:

no written instruction, nothing pinned upon a noticeboard. But there was a clear understanding on the part of the men whose job it was to pull the trigger that that was what was expected of them.[378]

---

[366] See above, pp. 69–81.   [367] *Farrell v UK* (1983) 5 EHRR 466.

[368] Decn admiss of 10 July 1984.   [369] App. No. 17579/90.

[370] Sir John Smith (1994) 144 NLJ 354; D.J. Harris (1994) 1 Maastricht J European and Comparative Law 123 at 134–137.

[371] Above, p. 69.   [372] See, e.g., SACHR, 18th Report, 1992–93 HC 739, p. 12, and n. 7, below.

[373] A. Jennings, 'Shoot to Kill: The Final Courts of Justice' in Jennings (ed.), *Justice under Fire* (revd edn, 1990), Chap. 5.

[374] *R v Davidson* (1981, unreported).   [375] *R v Thain* [1985] NI 457.

[376] *R v Robinson* [1984] 4 NIJB; *R v Montgomery* (1984, unreported).

[377] 126 HC Deb, 25 January 1958, cols 21–35.

[378] *The Times*, 9 February 1988, cited by A. Jennings, op. cit., p. 120.

Jennings concludes that:

The sheer number of incidents and the circumstances in which they occurred during 1977–78 and 1982–85 points towards the deliberate planning of operations in which opportunities for the use of lethal force would arise.[379]

Similar controversy was caused by the killing by the army of three members of the Provisional IRA in Gibraltar in 1988, and the programme about the shootings, 'Death on the Rock', subsequently made by Thames Television. An inquest jury returned majority verdicts of lawful killing.[380] The Court of Human Rights subsequently found, on narrow grounds, there to have been a violation of Art. 2 ECHR.[381]

In 1993, one member of the Parachute Regiment was convicted of murder and another of attempted murder.[382] In this case 'the crucial evidence…came from a policeman, on patrol with the army unit on the night the incident occurred, who was unable to sustain the army's version of events'.[383] The victims were teenage joyriders in a stolen car. Campbell J held that the defendants were justified in firing shots at the car when speeding towards them, but not in shooting after the car had passed their patrol. On appeal, the Northern Ireland Court of Appeal dismissed C's appeal but substituted a conviction for malicious wounding for A's conviction for attempted murder.[384] The House of Lords dismissed an appeal.[385] Following a campaign on his behalf, C was released on licence in July 1995. The case was referred back to the Court of Appeal (Criminal Division) in Northern Ireland, which ordered a new trial in the light of fresh forensic evidence which cast doubt on whether C had indeed shot the deceased from behind.[386] At the retrial C was acquitted of murder but convicted of attempting to wound the driver of the car by firing from behind. This conviction was set aside by the Court of Appeal (Criminal Division) on the ground that it was unsafe.[387]

In 1995, two members of the Scots Guards (Fisher and Wright) were convicted of the murder of Peter McBride while on patrol. Kelly LJ found that they had lied about critical elements of their version of events, and that both had had sufficient time to decide whether or not to fire and had been aware when they discharged aimed shots at PM that he posed no threat to them. The Court of Appeal rejected an appeal and the House of Lords refused leave to appeal. An Army Board subsequently decided that they should not be discharged from the army but this was quashed on an application for judicial review brought by PM's mother on the ground that the Board had misinterpreted the findings of the trial judge.[388] The Board subsequently reached the same decision and this too was challenged on judicial review.[389]

It has been reported that overall there were 3,703 deaths attributable to the security situation in Northern Ireland between 1966 and 2003, with responsibility attributed

---

[379] Op. cit., p. 123. See also *Shoot to Kill? International Lawyers' Inquiry into the Lethal Use of Firearms by the Security Forces in Northern Ireland* (Chairman, Kader Asmal, 1985) and M. Urban, *Big Boys' Rules* (1992). On the Stalker affair, see J. Stalker, *Stalker* (1988); P. Taylor, *Stalker: The Search for the Truth* (1987); K. Taylor, *The Poisoned Tree* (1990); D. Murphy, *The Stalker Affair and the Press* (1991).

[380] See A. Jennings (ed.), *Justice under Fire* (revd edn, 1990), pp. xx–xxii; Amnesty International, *Investigating Lethal Shootings: the Gibraltar Inquest* (1989); *The Windelsham/ Rampton Report on 'Death on the Rock'* (1989); NCCL, *The Gibraltar Report*; R. Bolton, *Death on the Rock and other stories* (1990).

[381] Above, p. 69.   [382] *R v Clegg and Aindow* (4 June 1993, unreported, Cr Ct).

[383] *Just News* (1993) Vol. 8 No. 6, p. 3.   [384] Unreported, 30 March 1994.

[385] [1995] 1 All ER 334.   [386] Unreported, 27 February 1998.

[387] *R v Clegg* [2000] NI 305.   [388] *Re McBride's Application for Judicial Review* [1999] NI 299.

[389] *Just News* Vol. 16 No. 2, pp. 4–5. For a critical overview, see Amnesty International, *Political Killings in Northern Ireland* (1994), and F. Ní Aoláin. *The Politics of Force* (2000).

as: republican paramilitaries 2,158 deaths; loyalist paramilitaries 1,099 deaths; and the security forces 365 deaths, most of which were not attributed to criminal activity.[390]

4. Of enormous and lasting significance in the history of Northern Ireland has been the killing by members of the Parachute Regiment (and, it is alleged, another regiment) on 30 January 1972 of 13 persons attending a peaceful civil rights protest in Derry/Londonderry. The subsequent inquiry by Lord Widgery CJ largely exonerated the army, although firing by some soldiers 'bordered on the reckless.[391] No prosecutions followed. The Government subsequently settled civil actions and formally acknowledged that all those killed 'should be regarded as having been found not guilty of the allegation of having been shot whilst handling a firearm or bomb'.[392]

The Widgery Report has been subjected to devastating criticism[393] and a new Tribunal of Inquiry has been appointed, chaired by Lord Saville of Newdigate. It began its work in 1998. The families and the wounded have been accorded extended legal representation. The tribunal was required to reconsider a decision to withdraw anonymity from individual soldiers who admitted firing, or were alleged to have fired, live rounds.[394] At the time of writing (December 2008) it had still not reported.

5. On the possible liability of members of the armed forces in negligence see the Court of Appeal in *McLaughlin v Ministry of Defence*.[395] In *McGuigan*, Hutton J noted that while in a criminal case, once the accused has raised by evidence the defence of reasonable force under s. 3(1) the onus rests on the *prosecution* to prove beyond a reasonable doubt that the force used was not reasonable in the circumstances, in a civil case the onus lies on the *defence* to establish a defence of reasonable force on the balance of probabilities. In *Copeland v Ministry of Defence*[396] Shiel J held the Ministry of Defence vicariously liable: (a) in trespass, in respect of the shooting of the plaintiff by Private Clarke from an army land rover without any justification; and (b) in negligence in respect of the failure of the Corporal in charge of the vehicle to disarm C following an earlier comment 'I'm going to get them when we go round next'. The judge based this on ordinary principles of vicarious liability but also stated that he considered that:

as a matter of public policy...when the State sends out a soldier or police officer armed with a lethal weapon which he is authorised to use in certain circumstances and that soldier or police officer, while on duty, intentionally or otherwise fires that weapon injuring a third party in circumstances which are not authorised and in which, as in the present case, there is no justification or defence for so doing, the State should be liable in damages at common law for any injury, loss or damage sustained by that third party.

---

[390] D. McKittrick, et al., *Lost Lives* (Mainstream Publishing Co, 2nd edn, 2004), cited by the HC Select Committee on Northern Ireland Affairs, Third Report *Policing and Criminal Justice in Northern Ireland: the Cost of Policing the Past* (2007–08 HC 333), para. 8.

[391] *Report of the Tribunal appointed to inquire into the events on Sunday, 30 January 1972, which led to the loss of life in connection with the procession in Londonderry on that day by the Rt Hon Lord Widgery* (1972) HC (22).

[392] Dermot P.J. Walsh, *Bloody Sunday and the Rule of Law in Northern Ireland* (2000), p. 285.

[393] S. Dash, *Justice Denied* (NCCL, 1972); E. McCann, *Bloody Sunday in Derry* (1992); D. Mullan, *Eyewitness Bloody Sunday: The Truth* (1997); P. Pringle and P. Jacobson, *Those are real bullets aren't they?* (2000); Walsh, op. cit.; B.M.E. McMahon (1974) *The Human Context*, p. 681. See also *Ireland v UK* (App. No. 5310/7141) CDE Comm HR, p. 3 (1972) (application under Art. 2 ECHR in respect of the death of certain persons in Northern Ireland declared inadmissible).

[394] *R v Lord Saville of Newdigate, ex p B (No. 2)* [1999] 4 All ER 860, CA.

[395] (1978) 7 NIJB; Greer (1980) 31 NILQ 151, 156–159; *Doherty v Ministry of Defence* (1980, unreported, HL), noted by P.J. Rowe (1981) 44 MLR 466; *McGuigan v Ministry of Defence* [1982] 19 NIJB.

[396] 19 May 1999, unreported, QBD (NI).

6. Where a plaintiff establishes a case in trespass against the police, the damages may be reduced on account of the plaintiff's contributory negligence. Thus in *Wasson v Chief Constable of the Royal Ulster Constabulary*[397] the plaintiff was taking part in a 'very serious' riot, when he was struck on the head by a baton round and badly injured. The police were held liable in trespass, having failed to show on a balance of probabilities that the baton round was not fired above leg level, and, as a result, being unable to establish a defence under s. 3(1) of the 1967 Act. However, the plaintiff's damages were halved in view of his participation in the riot.[398]

7. The absence of clear guidelines has been criticised by a number of commentators.[399] The SACHR recommended that a specific code of conduct to govern the use of legal force should be introduced, and prepared a draft code for consideration.[400] This code is based in part on the *Yellow Card* for 1972 and for 1980 (internal guidance for the armed forces) and on the terms of the *United Nations Instrument on Basic Principles on the Use of Force and Firearms by Law Enforcement Officials.*[401]

In *R v Clegg and Aindow*[402] the Northern Ireland Court of Appeal endorsed the view that Parliament should consider a change in the existing law to permit a conviction for manslaughter where a soldier or police officer causes death with the intention to kill or cause grievous bodily harm, reacting wrongly but without malice or evil motive to a situation arising in the course of his duty. The House of Lords stated that any change should be made by Parliament and not by the House in its judicial capacity.[403] A measure of reform is now in prospect. The Law Commission did not support the creation of a separate partial defence (reducing murder to manslaughter) applicable where excessive force is used in self defence.[404] Instead they favoured the adoption of a defence replacing provocation which would apply where D acted in response to a fear of serious violence towards D or another and a person of D's age and of ordinary temperament (i.e. ordinary tolerance and self restraint), in the circumstances of D, might have reacted in the same or a similar way.[405] The Government is currently[406] consulting on a modified version of this proposal.[407]

8. The law relating to coroners and inquests in England and Wales is to be substantially reformed in view of a range of factors, including the Report of the Shipman Inquiry and

---

[397] [1987] NI 420.

[398] Cf. *Tumelty v Ministry of Defence* [1988] 3 NIJB 51, where in a somewhat similar case, an 80 per cent reduction in damages was made.

[399] See p. 496, above.

[400] 16th Report, 1990–91 HC 488, Annex C, Appendix 2. See also 18th Report, 1992–93 HC 739, pp. 11–15.

[401] Adopted in the 8th UN Congress on the Prevention of Crime and the Treatment of Offenders, Havana, 7 September 1990.

[402] Above, p. 498. See further S. Doran, 'The doctrine of excessive defence: developments past, present and potential' (1985) 36 NILQ 314 and 'The use of force by the security forces in Northern Ireland: a legal perspective' (1987) 7 LS 291; Lord Colville's Annual Reports on the Northern Ireland (Emergency Provisions) Acts for 1987, pp. 28–30, 1988, pp. 34–38; paper by T. Hadden, SACHR 18th Report, Annex E.

[403] [1995] 1 All ER 334 at 345–347.

[404] *Final Report: Partial Defences to Murder* (Law Com 290, 2004), pp. 79–80.

[405] Ibid. This was taken forward into their later report, *Murder, Manslaughter and Infanticide* (Law Com 304, 2006).

[406] To October 2008.

[407] *Murder, manslaughter and infanticide: proposals for reform of the law* (Ministry of Justice, Attorney-General, Home Office Consultation Paper CP 19/08, 28 July 2008).

the need for compliance with Art. 2 ECHR. A draft Bill has been published and revised in the light of the consultation outcomes.[408] It is in the draft legislative programme for 2008/9.

9. Great concern was generated by the shooting of Jean Charles de Menezes by Metropolitan Police officers at Stockwell tube station on 22 July 2005, the day after failed suicide bombings in London. Officers were conducting a surveillance of a block of flats, suspecting it to be the address of one of the bombers. M left the flat, was followed to the tube and was wrongly identified as a suspected bomber. He took a seat on the train. Armed officers entered the train. There was a conflict of evidence as to whether they shouted 'police' or 'armed police' or indeed whether anything at all was shouted. M was shot 11 times, the officers subsequently stating they believed that he was a suicide bomber and that the shooting was necessary to prevent the detonation of a bomb. Two investigations were conducted by the Independent Police Complaints Commission. The first[409] concerned the shooting. It concluded that, if applied in appropriate circumstances, it was lawful for the police to adopt a national policy for dealing with suspected suicide bombers under which in some circumstances it may be necessary to shoot a suspected suicide bomber in the head, without a warning, to prevent detonation of a device. A decision to shoot may have to be taken on the command of a senior officer who has sufficient information to justify the use of lethal force.[410] However, the shooting on the facts was not the product of a formal KRATOS decision. The CPS should, however, consider possible charges of murder and gross negligence manslaughter. A series of operational recommendations was made.

The CPS decided that no individual should face criminal proceedings, but that the Office of the Commissioner of the Metropolis should be prosecuted for a breech of the Health and Safety at Work etc. Act 1974, s. 3(1).[411] On 1 November 2007, these proceedings ended in a conviction, the jury adding a rider that no personal culpability attached to the officer in charge of the operation, DAC (then Commander) Cressida Dick. A fine of £175,000 was imposed, with £385,000 costs.[412] At the inquest in 2008, 44 officers were granted anonymity.[413]

The IPCC ultimately concluded that no disciplinary proceedings should be taken against any of the frontline officers involved, apart from one officer who received words of advice in respect of an alteration to the surveillance log.

10. By s. 134(1) of the Criminal Justice Act 1988, 'a public official or person acting in an official capacity, whatever his nationality, commits the offence of torture if in the United

---

[408] *Coroner Reform: The Government's Draft Bill Improving death investigation in England and Wales* (Cm 6849, 2006); Coroners Bill—Changes made resulting from consultation (Ministry of Justice, 27 March 2008). On Art. 2, see above, p. 69.

[409] *Stockwell One* (IPCC, 8 November 2007). *Stockwell Two* (IPCC, July 2007) concerned complaints about the MPs' handling of public statements. This concluded that inaccurate information about the events had been released, but not knowingly, and that there had then been a communication breakdown delaying the release of correct information about M's clothing; an assistant commissioner had misled the Commissioner, leading to the issue of inaccurate press releases (this was denied).

[410] 'Operation KRATOS': see ibid., Part 9.

[411] This imposes a duty on every employer to conduct his undertaking in such a way as to ensure, so far as reasonably practicable, that persons not in his employment who may be affected thereby are not thereby exposed to risks to their health or safety. A challenge by way of judicial review to the decision not to prosecute far more serious offences was rejected: *R (on the application of Da Silva) v DPP* [2006] EWHC 3204 (Admin).

[412] *The Times*, 1 November 2007: the prosecution alleged there had been a 'string of errors' by Scotland Yard commanders.

[413] *Daily Telegraph*, 1 July 2008. See also the Preface.

Kingdom or elsewhere he intentionally inflicts severe pain or suffering on another in the performance or purported performance of his official duties'.

11. The gap between theory and practice as regards military aid to the civil power is discussed by Evelegh.[414] 'By contrast with 19th century practice, the "civil power" that may call in the armed forces appears no longer to be the local magistracy, but the Home Secretary, acting on a request from a chief officer of police.'[415]

---

[414] Op. cit.

[415] A.W. Bradley and K. Ewing, *Wade and Bradley: Constitutional and Administrative Law* (12th edn, 1997), pp. 668–669. For further references, see the 5th edn of this book at p. 633.

PART THREE: Privacy

7

ECHR PROTECTION
OF PRIVACY: ARTICLE 8[1]

Despite the fact that a right to privacy is contained in many international legal documents and national declarations of rights it remains a concept of which everybody has some understanding but few are able to comprehensively define. 'Perhaps the most striking thing about privacy is that nobody seems to have any very clear idea about what it is.'[2] From Cooley's basic definition of privacy as 'the right to be let alone',[3] many interpretations of what underpins privacy as a concept have been advanced, and these include: the control over personal information;[4] secrecy;[5] anonymity;[6] intimacy; self fulfilment; dignity;[7] and autonomy[8] to name but a few. The European Court of Human Rights has consistently refused to provide a comprehensive definition of privacy or private life which has led to a large body of jurisprudence under Art. 8 covering a disparate range of issues which continue to widen.[9] This chapter seeks to provide a brief introduction to the European Court's treatment of Art. 8 in order that it can provide a context within which one can then view the development of domestic law in the following chapter.

The structure of Art. 8 is as follows:

(1) Everyone has the right to respect for his private and family life, his home and his correspondence.

(2) There shall be no interference by a public authority with the exercise of this right except such as is in accordance with the law and is necessary in a democratic society in the interests of national security, public safety or the economic well being of the country, for the prevention of disorder or crime, for the protection of health or morals, or for the protection of the rights and freedoms of others.

Article 8(1) provides a statement of the primary right which must be engaged before one moves to a consideration of Art. 8(2) which states the grounds for legitimate interferences with the primary right.

---

[1] See, generally, A. Lestor and D. Pannick, *Human Rights Law and Practice* (2004); R. Clayton and H. Tomlinson, *The Law of Human Rights* (2nd edn, 2008); A. Mowbray, *Cases and Materials on the European Convention on Human Rights* (2nd edn, 2007); M. O'Boyle, C. Warbrick, E. Bates, and D. Harris, *Law of the European Convention on Human Rights* (2nd edn, 2008); C. Ovey and R. White, *Jacobs and White: The European Convention on Human Rights* (4th edn, 2006); M. Janis, R. Kay and A. Bradley, *European Human Rights Law* (3rd edn, 2007).

[2] J.J. Thomson quoted in D.J. Solove [2002] 90 California Law Review 1087 at 1089; see also, R. Wacks (1980) 96 LQR 73.

[3] *Torts* (2nd edn, 1888), p. 29.   [4] A. Westin, *Privacy and Freedom* (1967).

[5] S.M. Jourard (1966) 31 Law and Contemporary Problems 307.

[6] R. Gavison (1980) 89 Yale LJ 421.

[7] On the different emphases in Europe and the US see J.Q. Whitman (2004) 113 Yale LJ 1151.

[8] D. Feldman (1994) 47(2) CLP 41.   [9] D. Feldman [1997] EHRLR 264.

- **Niemietz v Germany, App. No. 13710/88** (1992) 16 EHRR 97,
  European Court of Human Rights

A letter was sent from a member of a pressure group to a judge in the local district court seeking to put pressure on him to reach an acquittal in a criminal case before him. The applicant was a lawyer who had links to the same pressure group. A wide-ranging search of the lawyer's office was undertaken under warrant to seek to discover the author of the letter. The applicant complained that this represented a breach of Art. 8. The Government contended that the applicant's private life was not affected by a search of business premises.

A. WAS THERE AN 'INTERFERENCE'?

27. In contesting the Commission's conclusion, the Government maintained that Article 8 did not afford protection against the search of a lawyer's office. In their view, the Convention drew a clear distinction between private life and home, on the one hand, and professional and business life and premises, on the other.

28. In arriving at its opinion that there had been an interference with Mr Niemietz's 'private life' and 'home', the Commission attached particular significance to the confidential relationship that exists between lawyer and client. The Court shares the Government's doubts as to whether this factor can serve as a workable criterion for the purposes of delimiting the scope of the protection afforded by Article 8. Virtually all professional and business activities may involve, to a greater or lesser degree, matters that are confidential, with the result that, if that criterion were adopted, disputes would frequently arise as to where the line should be drawn.

29. The Court does not consider it possible or necessary to attempt an exhaustive definition of the notion of 'private life'. However, it would be too restrictive to limit the notion to an 'inner circle' in which the individual may live his own personal life as he chooses and to exclude therefrom entirely the outside world not encompassed within that circle. Respect for private life must also comprise to a certain degree the right to establish and develop relationships with other human beings.

There appears, furthermore, to be no reason of principle why this understanding of the notion of 'private life' should be taken to exclude activities of a professional or business nature since it is, after all, in the course of their working lives that the majority of people have a significant, if not the greatest, opportunity of developing relationships with the outside world. This view is supported by the fact that, as was rightly pointed out by the Commission, it is not always possible to distinguish clearly which of an individual's activities form part of his professional or business life and which do not. Thus, especially in the case of a person exercising a liberal profession, his work in that context may form part and parcel of his life to such a degree that it becomes impossible to know in what capacity he is acting at a given moment of time.

To deny the protection of Article 8 on the ground that the measure complained of related only to professional activities—as the Government suggested should be done in the present case—could moreover lead to an inequality of treatment, in that such protection would remain available to a person whose professional and non-professional activities were so intermingled that there was no means of distinguishing between them. In fact, the Court has not heretofore drawn such distinctions: it concluded that there had been an interference with private life even where telephone tapping covered both business and private calls (see the *Huvig v. France* judgment of 24 April 1990, Series A no. 176-B, p. 41, para. 8, and p. 52, para. 25); and, where a search was directed solely against business activities, it did not rely on that fact as a ground for excluding the applicability of Article 8 under the head of 'private life' (see the *Chappell v. the United Kingdom* judgment of 30 March 1989, Series A no. 152-A, pp. 12–13, para. 26, and pp. 21–22, para. 51.)

30. As regards the word 'home', appearing in the English text of Article 8, the Court observes that in certain Contracting States, notably Germany (see paragraph 18 above), it has been accepted as extending to business premises. Such an interpretation is, moreover, fully consonant with the French text, since the

word 'domicile' has a broader connotation than the word 'home' and may extend, for example, to a professional person's office.

In this context also, it may not always be possible to draw precise distinctions, since activities which are related to a profession or business may well be conducted from a person's private residence and activities which are not so related may well be carried on in an office or commercial premises. A narrow interpretation of the words 'home' and 'domicile' could therefore give rise to the same risk of inequality of treatment as a narrow interpretation of the notion of 'private life' (see paragraph 29 above).

31. More generally, to interpret the words 'private life' and 'home' as including certain professional or business activities or premises would be consonant with the essential object and purpose of Article 8, namely to protect the individual against arbitrary interference by the public authorities (see, for example, the *Marckx v. Belgium* judgment of 13 June 1979, Series A no. 31, p. 15, para. 31). Such an interpretation would not unduly hamper the Contracting States, for they would retain their entitlement to 'interfere' to the extent permitted by paragraph 2 of Article 8; that entitlement might well be more far-reaching where professional or business activities or premises were involved than would otherwise be the case.

...

33. Taken together, the foregoing reasons lead the Court to find that the search of the applicant's office constituted an interference with his rights under Article 8.

NOTES

1. The Court found that under German law the search of a lawyer's office was not accompanied by any special safeguards despite the clear infringement of professional secrecy. As such, the search was not a proportionate interference with private life and therefore there was a breach of Art. 8.

2. The Court was clear in not limiting the notion of private life to traditional spatial boundaries of public and private but saw Art. 8 as including the right to establish and develop relationships with others. However, the Court also noted that it was not possible or necessary to attempt an exhaustive definition of private life.

3. Though a single definition is not possible, what other areas has the Strasbourg Court deemed to be within the remit of Art. 8? In *Pretty v United Kingdom*[10] the Court stated:

As the Court has had previous occasion to remark, the concept of 'private life' is a broad term not susceptible to exhaustive definition. It covers the physical and psychological integrity of a person (see *X and Y v. the Netherlands*, judgment of 26 March 1985, Series A no. 91, p. 11, § 22). It can sometimes embrace aspects of an individual's physical and social identity (see *Mikulic v. Croatia*, no. 53176/99, § 53, ECHR 2002-I). Elements such as, for example, gender identification, name and sexual orientation and sexual life fall within the personal sphere protected by Article 8 (see, for example, *B. v. France*, judgment of 25 March 1992, Series A no. 232-C, pp. 53–54, § 63; *Burghartz v. Switzerland*, judgment of 22 February 1994, Series A no. 280-B, p. 28, § 24; *Dudgeon v. the United Kingdom*, judgment of 22 October 1981, Series A no. 45, pp. 18–19, § 41; and *Laskey, Jaggard and Brown*, cited above, p. 131, § 36). Article 8 also protects a right to personal development, and the right to establish and develop relationships with other human beings and the outside world (see, for example, *Burghartz*, cited above, opinion of the Commission, p. 37, § 47, and *Friedl v. Austria*, judgment of 31 January 1995, Series A no. 305-B, opinion of the Commission, p. 20, § 45). Although no previous case has established as such

---

[10] App. No. 2346/02.

any right to self-determination as being contained in Article 8 of the Convention, the Court considers that the notion of personal autonomy is an important principle underlying the interpretation of its guarantees.[11]

Certainly the categories are not closed. Clayton and Tomlinson have suggested that private life interests under Art. 8 include: respect for moral and physical integrity; personal identity; personal information; personal sexuality; and personal or private space.[12] The range of circumstances that have occurred within these loose categories and thus have appeared before the Court are extremely broad. For example, in *Pretty*, where personal autonomy was recognised as a key underlying principle, the European Court suggested that non consensual medical treatment would impact upon physical integrity and therefore Art. 8:

In the sphere of medical treatment, the refusal to accept a particular treatment might, inevitably, lead to a fatal outcome, yet the imposition of medical treatment, without the consent of a mentally competent adult patient, would interfere with a person's physical integrity in a manner capable of engaging the rights protected under Article 8 § 1 of the Convention.[13]

In *Bensaid v United Kingdom*, the Court noted:

Not every act or measure which adversely affects moral or physical integrity will interfere with the right to respect to private life guaranteed by Article 8. However, the Court's case-law does not exclude that treatment which does not reach the severity of Article 3 treatment may nonetheless breach Article 8 in its private-life aspect where there are sufficiently adverse effects on physical and moral integrity (see *Costello-Roberts v. the United Kingdom*, judgment of 25 March 1993, Series A no. 247-C, pp. 60–61, § 36).[14]

With regard to personal identity, the Court has stated that a failure to recognise the post-operative identity of transsexuals represents a failure to respect private life.[15] In *Burghartz v Switzerland* the Court dealt with the issue of whether an individual could exist under a name of their choice:

Unlike some other international instruments, such as the International Covenant on Civil and Political Rights (Article 24 para. 2), the Convention on the Rights of the Child of 20 November 1989 (Articles 7 and 8) or the American Convention on Human Rights (Article 18), Article 8 (Article 8) of the Convention does not contain any explicit provisions on names. As a means of personal identification and of linking to a family, a person's name none the less concerns his or her private and family life. The fact that society and the State have an interest in regulating the use of names does not exclude this, since these public-law aspects are compatible with private life conceived of as including, to a certain degree, the right to establish and develop relationships with other human beings, in professional or business contexts as in others (see, mutatis mutandis, the *Niemietz v. Germany* judgment of 16 December 1992, Series A no. 251-B, p. 33, para. 29). In the instant case, the applicant's retention of the surname by which, according to him, he has become known in academic circles may significantly affect his career. Article 8 (Article 8) therefore applies.[16]

---

[11] Para. 61.

[12] Clayton and Tomlinson (2008). These categories are also broadly in line with those recognised by Lestor and Pannick (2004), para. 4.8.18 and N. Moreham [2008] EHRLR 44. On personal autonomy and Art. 8 see, J. Marshall [2008] EHRLR 337.

[13] Para. 63.   [14] (2001) 33 EHRR 205, para. 46

[15] *Goodwin v UK* (2002) 35 EHRR 18.   [16] (1994) 18 EHRR 101, para. 24.

Personal sexuality is seen as a core aspect of the exercise of moral autonomy and is clearly encapsulated within the protection offered by Art. 8. In *Dudgeon v United Kingdom*,[17] the applicant was a homosexual living in Northern Ireland where, unlike the rest of the UK, homosexual conduct was an offence, even if conducted in private and between mature and consenting adults. In upholding the applicant's claim that his privacy had been breached, the Court noted:

...the maintenance in force of the impugned legislation constitutes a continuing interference with the applicant's right to respect for his private life (which includes his sexual life) within the meaning of Article 8 par. 1 (Article 8–1). In the personal circumstances of the applicant, the very existence of this legislation continuously and directly affects his private life (see, mutatis mutandis, the *Marckx* judgment of 13 June 1979, Series A no. 31, p. 13, par. 27): either he respects the law and refrains from engaging—even in private with consenting male partners—in prohibited sexual acts to which he is disposed by reason of his homosexual tendencies, or he commits such acts and thereby becomes liable to criminal prosecution.[18]

...the moral attitudes towards male homosexuality in Northern Ireland and the concern that any relaxation in the law would tend to erode existing moral standards cannot, without more, warrant interfering with the applicant's private life to such an extent. 'Decriminalisation' does not imply approval, and a fear that some sectors of the population might draw misguided conclusions in this respect from reform of the legislation does not afford a good ground for maintaining it in force with all its unjustifiable features.[19]

However, in *Laskey, Jaggard and Brown v United Kingdom*:[20]

The Court observes that not every sexual activity carried out behind closed doors necessarily falls within the scope of Article 8 (Article 8). In the present case, the applicants were involved in consensual sado-masochistic activities for purposes of sexual gratification. There can be no doubt that sexual orientation and activity concern an intimate aspect of private life (see, mutatis mutandis, the *Dudgeon v. the United Kingdom* judgment of 22 October 1981, Series A no. 45, p. 21, para. 52). However, a considerable number of people were involved in the activities in question which included, inter alia, the recruitment of new 'members', the provision of several specially equipped 'chambers', and the shooting of many videotapes which were distributed among the 'members' (see paragraphs 8 and 9 above). It may thus be open to question whether the sexual activities of the applicants fell entirely within the notion of 'private life' in the particular circumstances of the case.[21]

The collection, storage and dissemination of personal information have formed the subject of many cases before the European Court.

- **Peck v United Kingdom, App. No. 44647/98** (2003) 36 EHRR 719

In 1995 the applicant was seen by local authority CCTV operators in the centre of Brentwood in the early hours of the morning carrying a knife. He was in a state of mental distress. The police were called and the applicant was detained under the Mental Health Act 1983. The following month the Council agreed to allow the regular release of CCTV related stories to the media. This would also include material that might be useful to third parties making factual programmes concerning the CCTV system. This was done in order to enhance the crime prevention features of the CCTV system by emphasising its efficiency to the local population. Photographs and film footage of the incident involving the applicant were

[17] (1981) 4 EHRR 149.   [18] Para. 41.   [19] Para. 61.
[20] (1997) 24 EHRR 39.   [21] Para. 36.

disseminated to both local and national media whereupon it was used without sufficient masking to anonymise the applicant. The applicant sought judicial review[22] of the local authority's decision to release the footage, but his claim was rejected, Harrison J stating:

I have some sympathy with the applicant who has suffered an invasion of his privacy, as is borne out by the findings of the Independent Television Commission, and the Broadcasting Standards Commission. However, if I am right in deciding that the Council does have the power to distribute the film footage from its CCTV system, there may on occasion be undesirable invasions of privacy. Unless and until there is a general right of privacy recognised by English law (and the indications are that there may soon be so by the incorporation of the European Convention on Human Rights into our law), reliance must be placed on effective guidance being issued by Codes of practice or otherwise, in order to try and avoid such undesirable invasions of a person's privacy.[23]

The applicant took his case before the Strasbourg Court claiming that his private life had been infringed.

JUDGMENT OF THE COURT

1. ...There is...a zone of interaction of a person with others, even in a public context, which may fall within the scope of 'private life' (see *P.G. and J.H. v. the United Kingdom*, no. 44787/98, § 56, ECHR 2001-IX, with further references).

2. In *P.G. and J.H.* (§ 57) the Court further noted as follows:

'There are a number of elements relevant to a consideration of whether a person's private life is concerned in measures effected outside a person's home or private premises. Since there are occasions when people knowingly or intentionally involve themselves in activities which are or may be recorded or reported in a public manner, a person's reasonable expectations as to privacy may be a significant, although not necessarily conclusive, factor. A person who walks down the street will, inevitably, be visible to any member of the public who is also present. Monitoring by technological means of the same public scene (for example, a security guard viewing through closed-circuit television) is of a similar character. Private life considerations may arise, however, once any systematic or permanent record comes into existence of such material from the public domain.'

3. The monitoring of the actions of an individual in a public place by the use of photographic equipment which does not record the visual data does not, as such, give rise to an interference with the individual's private life (see, for example, *Herbecq and the association 'Ligue des droits de l'homme' v. Belgium*, applications nos. 32200/96 and 32201/96, Commission decision of 14 January 1998, DR 92-B, p. 92). On the other hand, the recording of the data and the systematic or permanent nature of the record may give rise to such considerations. Accordingly, in both *Rotaru* and *Amann* (to which *P.G. and J.H.* referred) the compilation of data by security services on particular individuals, even without the use of covert surveillance methods, constituted an interference with the applicants' private lives (*Rotaru v. Romania* [GC], no. 28341/95, §§ 43–44, ECHR 2000-V, and *Amann v. Switzerland* [GC], no. 27798/95, §§ 65–67, ECHR 2000-II). While the permanent recording of the voices of P.G. and J.H. was made while they answered questions in a police cell as police officers listened to them, the recording of their voices for further analysis was regarded as the processing of personal data about them amounting to an interference with their right to respect for their private lives (see *P.G. and J.H.*, cited above, §§ 59–60).

4. However, the Court notes that the present applicant did not complain that the collection of data through the CCTV-camera monitoring of his movements and the creation of a permanent record of itself amounted to an interference with his private life. Indeed, he admitted that that function of the

---

[22] *R v Brentwood Borough Council, ex p Peck* [1998] EMLR 697.   [23] Ibid., at p. 707.

CCTV system, together with the consequent involvement of the police, may have saved his life. Rather, he argued that it was the disclosure of that record of his movements to the public in a manner in which he could never have foreseen which gave rise to such an interference.

5. In this connection, the Court recalls both *Lupker* and *Friedl* decided by the Commission, which concerned the unforeseen use by the authorities of photographs which had been previously voluntarily submitted to them (*Lupker and Others v. the Netherlands*, no. 18395/91, Commission decision of 7 December 1992, unreported) and the use of photographs taken by the authorities during a public demonstration (*Friedl v. Austria*, judgment of 31 January 1995, Series A no. 305-B, opinion of the Commission, p. 21, §§ 49–52). In those cases, the Commission attached importance to whether the photographs amounted to an intrusion into the applicant's privacy (as, for instance, by entering and taking photographs in a person's home), whether the photograph related to private or public matters and whether the material thus obtained was envisaged for a limited use or was likely to be made available to the general public. In *Friedl* the Commission noted that there was no such intrusion into the 'inner circle' of the applicant's private life, that the photographs taken of a public demonstration related to a public event and that they had been used solely as an aid to policing the demonstration on the relevant day. In this context, the Commission attached weight to the fact that the photographs taken remained anonymous in that no names were noted down, the personal data recorded and photographs taken were not entered into a data-processing system and no action had been taken to identify the persons photographed on that occasion by means of data processing (ibid.). Similarly, in *Lupker*, the Commission specifically noted that the police used the photographs to identify offenders in criminal proceedings only and that there was no suggestion that the photographs had been made available to the general public or would be used for any other purpose.

6. The present applicant was in a public street but he was not there for the purposes of participating in any public event and he was not a public figure. It was late at night, he was deeply perturbed and in a state of distress. While he was walking in public wielding a knife, he was not later charged with any offence. The actual suicide attempt was neither recorded nor therefore disclosed. However, footage of the immediate aftermath was recorded and disclosed by the Council directly to the public in its *CCTV News* publication. In addition, the footage was disclosed to the media for further broadcasting and publication purposes. Those media included the audiovisual media: Anglia Television broadcast locally to approximately 350,000 people and the BBC broadcast nationally, and it is 'commonly acknowledged that the audiovisual media have often a much more immediate and powerful effect than the print media' (*Jersild v. Denmark*, judgment of 23 September 1994, Series A no. 298, pp. 23–24, § 31). The *Yellow Advertiser* was distributed in the applicant's locality to approximately 24,000 readers. The applicant's identity was not adequately, or in some cases not at all, masked in the photographs and footage so published and broadcast. He was recognised by certain members of his family and by his friends, neighbours and colleagues.

As a result, the relevant moment was viewed to an extent which far exceeded any exposure to a passer-by or to security observation (as in *Herbecq and the association 'Ligue des droits de l'homme'*, cited above) and to a degree surpassing that which the applicant could possibly have foreseen when he walked in Brentwood on 20 August 1995.

7. Accordingly, the Court considers that the disclosure by the Council of the relevant footage constituted a serious interference with the applicant's right to respect for his private life.

NOTES

1. The applicant was awarded compensation of €11.800.

2. The applicant did not complain that the recording of the images *per se* infringed his private life. Subject to possible justification under Art. 8(2) do you think his privacy was engaged in this regard? The Court suggests that it is the recording of data which is key, but does that include overt public space surveillance? Given that the subject of the observation or

surveillance is unlikely to know whether recording is in fact taking place does this have any bearing upon his sense of privacy loss?

3. The case illustrates that by finding a breach of Art. 8 the European Court was willing to take privacy beyond spatial boundaries and into what might be termed the traditionally 'public domain', extending the principle outlined in *Niemietz*. Provided that the claimant did not expose himself to publicity (for example by taking part in a public demonstration)[24] or reasonably foresee that his actions would be recorded and given widespread publicity, the location of his or her actions will not be determinative of his or her Art. 8 claim. Applying this test strictly, would it rob a 'celebrity' of privacy in that they would expect to be photographed in public?[25]

4. The fact that the various media commissions (Press Complaints Commission, Independent Television Commission, Broadcasting Standards Commission) did not have the legal power to award damages meant that they could not supply the applicant with an effective remedy as required by Art. 13. Following the enactment of the Human Rights Act 1998 the status and powers of all of these bodies have changed considerably (see next chapter). However, the new regulatory body, Ofcom, still does not have the power to prevent a particular broadcast or award damages to a claimant. In framing the case as one involving inadequate remedies the Court did not need to address the issue of whether there was not merely a negative duty on the state not to interfere with Art. 8 but whether on these facts there was a *positive* duty on the state to prevent the infringement taking place.

5. The case played an important role in the development of the action for misuse of personal information in domestic law (see the following chapter). In *Douglas v Hello!*[26] Lindsay J stated that the *Peck* judgment 'shows that in circumstances where the law of confidence did not operate our domestic law has already been held to be inadequate. That inadequacy will have to be made good and if Parliament does not step in the Courts will be obliged to.'[27]

- **Von Hannover v Germany, App. No. 59320/00** (2005) 40 EHRR 1

The applicant was the eldest daughter of Prince Rainier III of Monaco but did not undertake official duties on behalf of the state. Her photograph regularly appeared in the tabloid press and she had attempted to take action against some newspapers on a number of occasions. The photographs that formed the substance of this case were published in German newspapers and magazines, and included scenes of her on horseback; at the far end of a restaurant; shopping; and on a bicycle. In the domestic German court it was held that as a figure of contemporary society '*par excellence*', she had to tolerate this kind of publication. All the photographs were taken in public places and although even figures '*par excellence*' had privacy that extended beyond the home, to exercise privacy she would have had to have retreated to a secluded place. The applicant took the case to the ECtHR claiming a breach of Art. 8.

JUDGMENT OF THE COURT

50. The Court reiterates that the concept of private life extends to aspects relating to personal identity, such as a person's name (see *Burghartz v. Switzerland*, judgment of 22 February 1994, Series A no. 280-B, p. 28, § 24), or a person's picture (see *Schüssel v. Austria* (dec.), no. 42409/98, 21 February 2002).

Furthermore, private life, in the Court's view, includes a person's physical and psychological integrity; the guarantee afforded by Article 8 of the Convention is primarily intended to ensure the development,

---

24 See *Friedl v Austria* (1996) 21 EHRR 83.   25 See N. Moreham (2006) CLJ 606.
26 [2003] EWHC 786.   27 Para. 229.

without outside interference, of the personality of each individual in his relations with other human beings (see, *mutatis mutandis, Niemietz v. Germany*, judgment of 16 December 1992, Series A no. 251-B, pp. 33–34, § 29, and *Botta v. Italy*, judgment of 24 February 1998, *Reports of Judgments and Decisions* 1998-I, p. 422, § 32). There is therefore a zone of interaction of a person with others, even in a public context, which may fall within the scope of 'private life' (see, *mutatis mutandis, P.G. and J.H. v. the United Kingdom*, no. 44787/98, § 56, ECHR 2001-IX, and *Peck v. the United Kingdom*, no. 44647/98, § 57, ECHR 2003-I).

51. The Court has also indicated that, in certain circumstances, a person has a 'legitimate expectation' of protection and respect for his or her private life. Accordingly, it has held in a case concerning the interception of telephone calls on business premises that the applicant 'would have had a reasonable expectation of privacy for such calls' (see *Halford v. the United Kingdom*, judgment of 25 June 1997, *Reports* 1997-III, p. 1016, § 45).

52. As regards photos, with a view to defining the scope of the protection afforded by Article 8 against arbitrary interference by public authorities, the European Commission of Human Rights had regard to whether the photographs related to private or public matters and whether the material thus obtained was envisaged for a limited use or was likely to be made available to the general public (see, *mutatis mutandis, Friedl v. Austria*, judgment of 31 January 1995, Series A no. 305-B, opinion of the Commission, p. 21, §§ 49–52; *P.G. and J.H. v. the United Kingdom*, cited above, § 58; and *Peck*, cited above, § 61).

53. In the present case there is no doubt that the publication by various German magazines of photos of the applicant in her daily life either on her own or with other people falls within the scope of her private life.

3. COMPLIANCE WITH ARTICLE 8

(a) The domestic courts' position

54. The Court notes that, in its landmark judgment of 15 December 1999, the Federal Constitutional Court interpreted sections 22 and 23 of the Copyright (Arts Domain) Act (see paragraphs 40–41 above) by balancing the requirements of the freedom of the press against those of the protection of private life, that is, the public interest in being informed against the legitimate interests of the applicant. In doing so the Federal Constitutional Court took account of two criteria under German law, one functional and the other spatial. It considered that the applicant, as a figure of contemporary society '*par excellence*', enjoyed the protection of her private life even outside her home but only if she was in a secluded place out of the public eye to which persons retire 'with the objectively recognisable aim of being alone and where, confident of being alone, they behave in a manner in which they would not behave in public'. In the light of those criteria, the Federal Constitutional Court held that the Federal Court of Justice's judgment of 19 December 1995 regarding publication of the photos in question was compatible with the Basic Law. The court attached decisive weight to the freedom of the press, even the entertainment press, and to the public interest in knowing how the applicant behaved outside her representative functions (see paragraph 25 above).

55. Referring to its landmark judgment, the Federal Constitutional Court did not entertain the applicant's appeals in the subsequent proceedings brought by her (see paragraphs 32 and 38 above).

(b) General principles governing the protection of private life and the freedom of expression

56. In the present case the applicant did not complain of an action by the State, but rather of the lack of adequate State protection of her private life and her image.

57. The Court reiterates that, although the object of Article 8 is essentially that of protecting the individual against arbitrary interference by the public authorities, it does not merely compel the State to abstain from such interference: in addition to this primarily negative undertaking, there may be positive obligations inherent in an effective respect for private or family life. These obligations may involve the

adoption of measures designed to secure respect for private life even in the sphere of the relations of individuals between themselves (see, *mutatis mutandis*, *X and Y v. the Netherlands*, judgment of 26 March 1985, Series A no. 91, p. 11, § 23; *Stjerna v. Finland*, judgment of 25 November 1994, Series A no. 299-B, pp. 60–61, § 38; and *Verliere v. Switzerland* (dec.), no. 41953/98, ECHR 2001-VII). That also applies to the protection of a person's picture against abuse by others (see *Schüssel*, cited above).

The boundary between the State's positive and negative obligations under this provision does not lend itself to precise definition. The applicable principles are, nonetheless, similar. In both contexts regard must be had to the fair balance that has to be struck between the competing interests of the individual and of the community as a whole; and in both contexts the State enjoys a certain margin of appreciation (see, among many other authorities, *Keegan v. Ireland*, judgment of 26 May 1994, Series A no. 290, p. 19, § 49, and *Botta*, cited above, p. 427, § 33).

58. That protection of private life has to be balanced against the freedom of expression guaranteed by Article 10 of the Convention.

In that context, the Court reiterates that freedom of expression constitutes one of the essential foundations of a democratic society. Subject to paragraph 2 of Article 10, it is applicable not only to 'information' or 'ideas' that are favourably received or regarded as inoffensive or as a matter of indifference, but also to those that offend, shock or disturb. Such are the demands of that pluralism, tolerance and broadmindedness without which there is no 'democratic society' (see *Handyside v. the United Kingdom*, judgment of 7 December 1976, Series A no. 24, p. 23, § 49).

In that connection, the press plays an essential role in a democratic society. Although it must not overstep certain bounds, in particular in respect of the reputation and rights of others, its duty is nevertheless to impart—in a manner consistent with its obligations and responsibilities—information and ideas on all matters of public interest (see, among many authorities, Observer *and* Guardian *v. the United Kingdom*, judgment of 26 November 1991, Series A no. 216, pp. 29–30, § 59, and Bladet Tromsø *and Stensaas v. Norway* [GC], no. 21980/93, § 59, ECHR 1999-III). Journalistic freedom also covers possible recourse to a degree of exaggeration, or even provocation (see *Prager and Oberschlick v. Austria*, judgment of 26 April 1995, Series A no. 313, p. 19, § 38; *Tammer v. Estonia*, no. 41205/98, §§ 59–63, ECHR 2001-I; and *Prisma Presse v. France* (dec.), nos. 66910/01 and 71612/01, 1 July 2003).

59. Although freedom of expression also extends to the publication of photos, this is an area in which the protection of the rights and reputation of others takes on particular importance. The present case does not concern the dissemination of 'ideas', but of images containing very personal or even intimate 'information' about an individual. Furthermore, photos appearing in the tabloid press are often taken in a climate of continual harassment which induces in the person concerned a very strong sense of intrusion into their private life or even of persecution.

60. In the cases in which the Court has had to balance the protection of private life against freedom of expression, it has always stressed the contribution made by photos or articles in the press to a debate of general interest (see, as a recent authority, *Tammer*, cited above, §§ 59 et seq.; *News Verlags GmbH & Co. KG v. Austria*, no. 31457/96, §§ 52 et seq., ECHR 2000-I; and *Krone Verlag GmbH & Co. KG v. Austria*, no. 34315/96, §§ 33 et seq., 26 February 2002). The Court thus found, in one case, that the use of certain terms in relation to an individual's private life was not 'justified by considerations of public concern' and that those terms did not '[bear] on a matter of general importance' (see *Tammer*, cited above, § 68) and went on to hold that there had not been a violation of Article 10. In another case, however, the Court attached particular importance to the fact that the subject in question was a news item of 'major public concern' and that the published photographs 'did not disclose any details of [the] private life' of the person in question (see *Krone Verlag GmbH & Co. KG*, cited above, § 37) and held that there had been a violation of Article 10. Similarly, in a recent case concerning the publication by President Mitterrand's former private doctor of a book containing revelations about the President's state of health, the Court held that 'the more time that elapsed, the more the public interest in discussion of the history of President Mitterrand's two terms

of office prevailed over the requirements of protecting the President's rights with regard to medical confidentiality' (see *Editions Plon v. France*, no. 58148/00, § 53, ECHR 2004-IV) and held that there had been a breach of Article 10.

(c) Application of these general principles by the Court

61. The Court notes at the outset that in the present case the photos of the applicant in the various German magazines show her in scenes from her daily life, thus involving activities of a purely private nature such as engaging in sport, out walking, leaving a restaurant or on holiday. The photos, in which the applicant appears sometimes alone and sometimes in company, illustrate a series of articles with such innocuous titles as 'Pure happiness', 'Caroline... a woman returning to life', 'Out and about with Princess Caroline in Paris' and 'The kiss. Or: they are not hiding anymore' (see paragraphs 11–17 above).

62. The Court also notes that the applicant, as a member of the Prince of Monaco's family, represents the ruling family at certain cultural or charitable events. However, she does not exercise any function within or on behalf of the State of Monaco or any of its institutions (see paragraph 8 above).

63. The Court considers that a fundamental distinction needs to be made between reporting facts—even controversial ones—capable of contributing to a debate in a democratic society relating to politicians in the exercise of their functions, for example, and reporting details of the private life of an individual who, moreover, as in this case, does not exercise official functions. While in the former case the press exercises its vital role of 'watchdog' in a democracy by contributing to 'impart[ing] information and ideas on matters of public interest (see Observer *and* Guardian, loc. cit.), it does not do so in the latter case.

64. Similarly, although the public has a right to be informed, which is an essential right in a democratic society that, in certain special circumstances, can even extend to aspects of the private life of public figures, particularly where politicians are concerned (see *Editions Plon*, loc. cit.), this is not the case here. The situation here does not come within the sphere of any political or public debate because the published photos and accompanying commentaries relate exclusively to details of the applicant's private life.

65. As in other similar cases it has examined, the Court considers that the publication of the photos and articles in question, the sole purpose of which was to satisfy the curiosity of a particular readership regarding the details of the applicant's private life, cannot be deemed to contribute to any debate of general interest to society despite the applicant being known to the public (see, *mutatis mutandis*, *Campmany y Diez de Revenga and Lopez Galiacho Perona v. Spain* (dec.), no. 54224/00, ECHR 2000-XII; *Julio Bou Gibert and El Hogar Y La Moda J.A. v. Spain* (dec.), no. 14929/02, 13 May 2003; and *Prisma Presse*, cited above).

66. In these conditions freedom of expression calls for a narrower interpretation (see *Prisma Presse*, cited above, and, by converse implication, *Krone Verlag GmbH & Co. KG*, cited above, § 37).

67. In that connection, the Court also takes account of the resolution of the Parliamentary Assembly of the Council of Europe on the right to privacy, which stresses the 'one-sided interpretation of the right to freedom of expression' by certain media which attempt to justify an infringement of the rights protected by Article 8 of the Convention by claiming that 'their readers are entitled to know everything about public figures' (see paragraph 42 above, and *Prisma Presse*, cited above).

68. The Court finds another point to be of importance: even though, strictly speaking, the present application concerns only the publication of the photos and articles by various German magazines, the context in which these photos were taken—without the applicant's knowledge or consent—and the harassment endured by many public figures in their daily lives cannot be fully disregarded (see paragraph 59 above).

In the present case this point is illustrated in particularly striking fashion by the photos taken of the applicant at the Monte Carlo Beach Club tripping over an obstacle and falling down (see paragraph 17 above). It appears that these photos were taken secretly at a distance of several hundred metres, probably from a neighbouring house, whereas journalists' and photographers' access to the club was strictly regulated (see paragraph 33 above).

69. The Court reiterates the fundamental importance of protecting private life from the point of view of the development of every human being's personality. That protection—as stated above—extends beyond the private family circle and also includes a social dimension. The Court considers that anyone, even if they are known to the general public, must be able to enjoy a 'legitimate expectation' of protection of and respect for their private life (see paragraph 51 above and, *mutatis mutandis, Halford*, cited above, p. 1016, § 45).

70. Furthermore, increased vigilance in protecting private life is necessary to contend with new communication technologies which make it possible to store and reproduce personal data (see point 5 of the Parliamentary Assembly's resolution on the right to privacy, paragraph 42 above, and, *mutatis mutandis, Amann v. Switzerland* [GC], no. 27798/95, §§ 65–67, ECHR 2000-II; *Rotaru v. Romania* [GC], no. 28341/95, §§ 43–44, ECHR 2000-V; *P.G. and J.H. v. the United Kingdom*, cited above, §§ 57–60; and *Peck*, cited above, §§ 59–63 and 78). This also applies to the systematic taking of specific photos and their dissemination to a broad section of the public.

71. Lastly, the Court reiterates that the Convention is intended to guarantee not rights that are theoretical or illusory but rights that are practical and effective (see *Artico v. Italy*, judgment of 13 May 1980, Series A no. 37, pp. 15–16, § 33).

72. The Court finds it hard to agree with the domestic courts' interpretation of section 23(1) of the Copyright (Arts Domain) Act, which consists in describing a person as such as a figure of contemporary society '*par excellence*'. Since that definition affords the person very limited protection of their private life or the right to control the use of their image, it could conceivably be appropriate for politicians exercising official functions. However, it cannot be justified for a 'private' individual, such as the applicant, in whom the interest of the general public and the press is based solely on her membership of a reigning family, whereas she herself does not exercise any official functions.

In any event the Court considers that, in these conditions, the Act has to be interpreted narrowly to ensure that the State complies with its positive obligation under the Convention to protect private life and the right to control the use of one's image.

73. Lastly, the distinction drawn between figures of contemporary society '*par excellence*' and 'relatively' public figures has to be clear and obvious so that, in a State governed by the rule of law, the individual has precise indications as to the behaviour he or she should adopt. Above all, they need to know exactly when and where they are in a protected sphere or, on the contrary, in a sphere in which they must expect interference from others, especially the tabloid press.

74. The Court therefore considers that the criteria on which the domestic courts based their decisions were not sufficient to protect the applicant's private life effectively. As a figure of contemporary society '*par excellence*' she cannot—in the name of freedom of the press and the public interest—rely on protection of her private life unless she is in a secluded place out of the public eye and, moreover, succeeds in proving it (which can be difficult). Where that is not the case, she has to accept that she might be photographed at almost any time, systematically, and that the photos are then very widely disseminated even if, as was the case here, the photos and accompanying articles relate exclusively to details of her private life.

75. In the Court's view, the criterion of spatial isolation, although apposite in theory, is in reality too vague and difficult for the person concerned to determine in advance. In the present case, merely classifying the applicant as a figure of contemporary society '*par excellence*' does not suffice to justify such an intrusion into her private life.

(d) Conclusion

76. As the Court has stated above, it considers that the decisive factor in balancing the protection of private life against freedom of expression should lie in the contribution that the published photos and articles make to a debate of general interest. It is clear in the instant case that they made no such contribution,

since the applicant exercises no official function and the photos and articles related exclusively to details of her private life.

77. Furthermore, the Court considers that the public does not have a legitimate interest in knowing where the applicant is and how she behaves generally in her private life even if she appears in places that cannot always be described as secluded and despite the fact that she is well known to the public.

Even if such a public interest exists, as does a commercial interest of the magazines in publishing these photos and these articles, in the instant case those interests must, in the Court's view, yield to the applicant's right to the effective protection of her private life.

78. Lastly, in the Court's opinion the criteria established by the domestic courts were not sufficient to ensure the effective protection of the applicant's private life and she should, in the circumstances of the case, have had a 'legitimate expectation' of protection of her private life.

79. Having regard to all the foregoing factors, and despite the margin of appreciation afforded to the State in this area, the Court considers that the German courts did not strike a fair balance between the competing interests.

80. There has therefore been a breach of Article 8 of the Convention.

NOTES

1. Judge Cabral Barreto and Judge Zupančič concurred with the decision as to the breach of Art. 8 but did not agree with the reasoning of the majority. Instead, they found that the applicant was a public figure in whom there was public interest. Information about the applicant's life was of general interest and that did not have to contribute to political debate. Judge Cabral Barreto stated: 'In my view, whenever a public figure has a "legitimate expectation" of being safe from the media, his or her right to private life prevails over the right to freedom of expression or the right to be informed. It will never be easy to define in concrete terms the situations that correspond to this "legitimate expectation" and a case-by-case approach is therefore justified.' Judge Zupančič stated: 'I agree with the outcome of this case. However, I would suggest a different determinative test: the one we have used in *Halford v. the United Kingdom* (judgment of 25 June 1997, *Reports of Judgments and Decisions* 1997-III), which speaks of "reasonable expectation of privacy".' He further stated that under the test the dilemma as to whether the person is a public figure then ceases to exist. Do you agree?

2. At para. 53 the Court stated: 'there is no doubt that the publication by various German magazines of photos of the applicant in her daily life either on her own or with other people falls within the scope of her private life.' Do you agree? Can daily life be so readily equated to private life? Despite this potentially far reaching statement there is a lack of articulation on the part of the Court as to the principles which underpin the decision.

3. The case was decided soon after the House of Lords decision in *Campbell* (see following chapter) and the two cases appear to have some differences. For example, in *Campbell* it was suggested that the claimant would need to be carrying out a private activity albeit in public before privacy could attach itself. As yet there has been no decision in domestic law that has sat squarely with the *von Hannover* position. Do you think it is possible for domestic courts to reconcile the two decisions?

4. The decision provides an example of the positive obligation required by Art. 8. This was not a case involving the state infringing rights but involved a scenario in which the state

failed in its positive duty to protect the rights of an individual against abuse by others.[28] In *Stubbings v United Kingdom*[29] the ECtHR said:

It is to be recalled that although the object of Article 8 is essentially that of protecting the individual against arbitrary interference by the public authorities, it does not merely compel the state to abstain from such interference: there may, in addition to this primary negative undertaking, be positive obligations inherent in an effective respect for private or family life. These obligations may involve the adoption of measures designed to secure respect for private life even in the sphere of the relations of individuals between themselves.[30]

Thus, it is the need to *respect* private and family life that arguably creates such a positive obligation, an area which is increasingly the subject of attention in Strasbourg.[31] However, such positive obligations are not uncontroversial. Do signatory states to the ECHR really agree to advance social and economic measures that they may not support in order to fulfil a positive obligation? Does the notion of 'respect' necessitate positive obligations or have they been implied? By way of contrast, Singh has argued that 'to be effective even civil and political rights have to be protected—and protection has a price'.[32] Fredman outlines the basic problem: 'Duties of restraint are said to be determinate, immediately realizable, and resource free. Positive duties are said to be indeterminate, programmatic, and resource intensive. While duties of restraint must be fulfilled immediately, positive duties are said to require only progressive realization as resources become available...these contrasts are overdrawn. Nevertheless, positive duties pose specific challenges, which need to be met.'[33]

The need to balance competing issues when responding to positive obligations also raises the issue of the margin of appreciation. In *Dickson v United Kingdom*, the European Court stated:

Since the national authorities make the initial assessment as to where the fair balance lies in a case before a final evaluation by this Court, a certain margin of appreciation is, in principle, accorded by this Court to those authorities as regards that assessment. The breadth of this margin varies and depends on a number of factors including the nature of the activities restricted and the aims pursued by the restrictions (*Smith and Grady v. the United Kingdom*, nos. 33985/96 and 33986/96, § 88, ECHR 1999-VI).

Accordingly, where a particularly important facet of an individual's existence or identity is at stake (such as the choice to become a genetic parent), the margin of appreciation accorded to a State will in general be restricted.

Where, however, there is no consensus within the Member States of the Council of Europe, either as to the relative importance of the interest at stake or as to how best to protect it, the margin will be wider. This is particularly so where the case raises complex issues and choices of social strategy: the authorities' direct knowledge of their society and its needs means that they are in principle better placed than the international judge to appreciate what is in the public interest. In such a case, the Court would generally

---

[28] A. Mowbray, *The Development of Positive Obligations Under the European Convention of Human Rights by the European Court of Human Rights* (2004), Chap. 6. See also K. Starmer, *European Human Rights Law* (1999).
[29] (1996) 23 EHRR 213.   [30] Para. 62.
[31] See, e.g., *Dickson v UK* [2006] ECHR 430, para. 69.
[32] R. Singh, *The Future of Human Rights in the United Kingdom: Essays on Law and Practice* (1997), p. 54.
[33] S. Fredman, *Human Rights Transformed: Positive Rights and Positive Duties* (2008), p. 70.

respect the legislature's policy choice unless it is 'manifestly without reasonable foundation'. There will also usually be a wide margin accorded if the State is required to strike a balance between competing private and public interests or Convention rights (*Evans*, cited above, § 77).[34]

Family life, home and correspondence are rather less nebulous concepts than private life. Family life is very broadly defined and covers *de facto* family ties such as cohabiting couples.[35] It also covers relations with grandparents, and aunts and uncles depending upon the strength of the particular relationships. The question of family life is ultimately one of fact. In *X, Y and Z v United Kingdom*[36] the applicant who was a female to male transsexual sought to be named as the child's father on the birth certificate. After looking at the particular circumstances the Court stated:

> ... the Court notes that X is not prevented in any way from acting as Z's father in the social sense. Thus, for example, he lives with her, providing emotional and financial support to her and Y, and he is free to describe himself to her and others as her 'father' and to give her his surname. Furthermore, together with Y, he could apply for a joint residence order in respect of Z, which would automatically confer on them full parental responsibility for her in English law.
>
> It is impossible to predict the extent to which the absence of a legal connection between X and Z will affect the latter's development. As previously mentioned, at the present time there is uncertainty with regard to how the interests of children in Z's position can best be protected and the Court should not adopt or impose any single viewpoint.
>
> In conclusion, given that transsexuality raises complex scientific, legal, moral and social issues, in respect of which there is no generally shared approach among the Contracting States, the Court is of the opinion that Article 8 cannot, in this context, be taken to imply an obligation for the respondent State formally to recognise as the father of a child a person who is not the biological father. That being so, the fact that the law of the United Kingdom does not allow special legal recognition of the relationship between X and Z does not amount to a failure to respect family life within the meaning of that provision.
>
> It follows that there has been no violation of Article 8 of the Convention.[37]

The interpretation of 'home' similarly depends upon factual circumstances rather than depending upon legal property interests, the latter contention being rejected in *Buckley v United Kingdom*.[38] Interference with the right to respect for one's home has encompassed environmental interference, though the court has emphasised the need for a balance to be struck between the individual and community interests. In *Lopez Ostra v Spain*[39] the Court commented:

> Naturally, severe environmental pollution may affect individuals' well-being and prevent them from enjoying their homes in such a way as to affect their private and family life adversely, without, however, seriously endangering their health. Whether the question is analysed in terms of a positive duty on the State—to take reasonable and appropriate measures to secure the applicant's rights under paragraph 1 of Article 8 (art. 8-1)—as the applicant wishes in her case, or in terms of an 'interference by a public authority' to be justified in accordance with paragraph 2 (art. 8-2), the applicable principles are broadly similar. In both contexts regard must be had to the fair balance that has to be struck between the competing interests of the individual and of the community as a whole, and in any case the State enjoys a certain margin of appreciation.[40]

Environmental rights are not, however, accorded any special status.[41]

---

[34] Paras 77–78.
[35] See, e.g., *Kroon v Netherlands* (1995) 19 EHRR 263.   [36] (1997) 24 EHRR 143.
[37] Paras 50–52.   [38] (1996) 23 EHRR 101.   [39] (1994) 20 EHRR 277.
[40] Para. 51.   [41] See *Hatton v UK* (2003) 37 EHRR 611.

Correspondence has included a number of cases dealing with surveillance operations, telephone tapping and the exercise of search warrants. In *Halford v United Kingdom*,[42] the applicant claimed that the interception of her office telephone amounted to a breach of Art. 8. The Court agreed: 'In the Court's view, it is clear from its case-law that telephone calls made from business premises as well as from the home may be covered by the notions of "private life" and "correspondence" within the meaning of Article 8.'[43]

In many circumstances the action of the state will clearly engage with the very broad scope of Art. 8(1). The key question will therefore be whether such interference can be justified under Art. 8(2).

Article 8(2) requires a justifiable interference to be 'in accordance with law'. The European Court explained what this required in *Silver v United Kingdom*,[44] in which the applicants, prisoners, claimed their mail, was being stopped by the authorities under confidential Home Office standing orders.

A first principle that emerges from the Sunday Times judgment is that the interference in question must have some basis in domestic law (ibid., p. 30, § 47). In the present case, it was common ground between Government, Commission and applicants that a basis for the interferences was to be found in the Prison Act and the Rules, but not in the Orders and Instructions which lacked the force of law (see paragraph 26 above). There was also no dispute that the measures complained of were in conformity with English law.

A second principle is that 'the law must be adequately accessible: the citizen must be able to have an indication that is adequate, in the circumstances, of the legal rules applicable to a given case'. Clearly, the Prison Act and the Rules met this criterion, but the Orders and Instructions were not published.

A third principle is that 'a norm cannot be regarded as a 'law' unless it is formulated with sufficient precision to enable the citizen to regulate his conduct: he must be able—if need be with appropriate advice—to foresee, to a degree that is reasonable in the circumstances, the consequences which a given action may entail'.

A law which confers a discretion must indicate the scope of that discretion. However, the Court has already recognised the impossibility of attaining absolute certainty in the framing of laws and the risk that the search for certainty may entail excessive rigidity. These observations are of particular weight in the 'circumstances' of the present case, involving as it does, in the special context of imprisonment, the screening of approximately ten million items of correspondence in a year (see paragraph 57 above). It would scarcely be possible to formulate a law to cover every eventuality. Indeed, the applicants themselves did not deny that some discretion should be left to the authorities.

In view of these considerations, the Court points out once more that 'many laws are inevitably couched in terms which, to a greater or lesser extent, are vague and whose interpretation and application are questions of practice' (ibid.). And in the present case the operation of the correspondence control system was not merely a question of practice that varied in each individual instance: the Orders and Instructions established a practice which had to be followed save in exceptional circumstances (see paragraphs 26 and 27 above). In these conditions, the Court considers that although those directives did not themselves have the force of law, they may—to the admittedly limited extent to which those concerned were made sufficiently aware of their contents—be taken into account in assessing whether the criterion of foreseeability was satisfied in the application of the Rules.[45]

---

[42] (1997) 24 EHRR 523.   [43] Para. 44.
[44] (1983) 5 EHRR 347.   [45] Paras 86–88.

Later in the same judgment the Court also gave guidance as to the meaning of 'necessary in a democratic society'.

On a number of occasions, the Court has stated its understanding of the phrase 'necessary in a democratic society', the nature of its functions in the examination of issues turning on that phrase and the manner in which it will perform those functions. It suffices here to summarise certain principles:

(a) the adjective 'necessary' is not synonymous with 'indispensable', neither has it the flexibility of such expressions as 'admissible', 'ordinary', 'useful', 'reasonable' or 'desirable' (see the Handyside (1976), para. 48);

(b) the Contracting States enjoy a certain but not unlimited margin of appreciation in the matter of the imposition of restrictions, but it is for the Court to give the final ruling on whether they are compatible with the Convention (ibid., para. 49);

(c) the phrase 'necessary in a democratic society' means that, to be compatible with the Convention, the interference must, inter alia, correspond to a 'pressing social need' and be 'proportionate to the legitimate aim pursued' (ibid., paras. 48–49);

(d) those paragraphs of Articles of the Convention which provide for an exception to a right guaranteed are to be narrowly interpreted (see the above-mentioned Klass and others para. 42).

The 'proportionality' of the interference by the state will often be central to the case. Clearly, by its very nature it will vary from case to case but some relevant considerations can be extracted from the case law.

- **Campbell v United Kingdom, App. No. 13590/88** (1992) 15 EHRR 137

The applicant contested the necessity of opening and examining letters to and from his solicitor. He pointed out that many of the items of correspondence with his solicitor concerned legal actions or complaints against prison officials who had an interest in protecting their positions. It was unjust that they and their colleagues should be allowed access to what was essentially private information and legal advice. Such access was susceptible to abuse in view of the solidarity which existed amongst prison staff.

He further submitted that the rights, duties and privileges of lawyers were specifically developed to protect the liberty and privacy of the individual as well as the right to a fair trial and the proper administration of justice. He pointed out that the purpose of the principle of confidentiality between lawyer and client is to enable a person to consult his solicitor freely without the risk that information would be communicated to his opponent.

The Government did not contest that, if correspondence relating to pending proceedings had been routinely opened, there would have been a breach of Article 8. They limited their plea in this context to maintaining that the applicant had not substantiated his complaint (see paragraph 32 above). Nor did they seek to argue that there existed any particular suspicion in respect of the applicant's mail on account of his own or his solicitor's personal circumstances.

However, they argued that it was necessary inter alia in the interests of prison security to open letters to and from a solicitor concerning contemplated legal proceedings, as well as general correspondence, with a view to determining whether or not they contained prohibited material. In addition, it was contended that Contracting States enjoy a certain margin of appreciation in striking a balance between the protection of prison security and respect for the confidentiality of correspondence. How the balance was to be struck was a matter of judgment best made by those familiar with the Scottish prison system who had experience in dealing with both prisoners and solicitors in Scotland. The prison authorities were entitled to strike a different balance in relation to correspondence between prisoners and solicitors which concerned matters other than pending legal proceedings.

The Court recalls that the notion of necessity implies that the interference corresponds to a pressing social need and, in particular, that it is proportionate to the legitimate aim pursued. In determining whether an interference is 'necessary in a democratic society' regard may be had to the State's margin of appreciation (see, amongst other authorities, *The Sunday Times v. the United Kingdom (no. 2)* 1991, para. 50).

It has also been recognised that some measure of control over prisoners' correspondence is called for and is not of itself incompatible with the Convention, regard being paid to the ordinary and reasonable requirements of imprisonment (see the *Silver and Others v. the United Kingdom* 1983, para. 98). In assessing the permissible extent of such control in general, the fact that the opportunity to write and to receive letters is sometimes the prisoner's only link with the outside world should, however, not be overlooked.

It is clearly in the general interest that any person who wishes to consult a lawyer should be free to do so under conditions which favour full and uninhibited discussion. It is for this reason that the lawyer-client relationship is, in principle, privileged. Indeed, in its *S. v. Switzerland* 1991 the Court stressed the importance of a prisoner's right to communicate with counsel out of earshot of the prison authorities. It was considered, in the context of Article 6, that if a lawyer were unable to confer with his client without such surveillance and receive confidential instructions from him his assistance would lose much of its usefulness, whereas the Convention is intended to guarantee rights that are practical and effective (para. 48; see also, in this context, the *Campbell and Fell v. the United Kingdom* 1984, paras. 111–113).

In the Court's view, similar considerations apply to a prisoner's correspondence with a lawyer concerning contemplated or pending proceedings where the need for confidentiality is equally pressing, particularly where such correspondence relates, as in the present case, to claims and complaints against the prison authorities. That such correspondence be susceptible to routine scrutiny, particularly by individuals or authorities who may have a direct interest in the subject matter contained therein, is not in keeping with the principles of confidentiality and professional privilege attaching to relations between a lawyer and his client.

Admittedly, as the Government pointed out, the borderline between mail concerning contemplated litigation and that of a general nature is especially difficult to draw and correspondence with a lawyer may concern matters which have little or nothing to do with litigation. Nevertheless, the Court sees no reason to distinguish between the different categories of correspondence with lawyers which, whatever their purpose, concern matters of a private and confidential character. In principle, such letters are privileged under Article 8.

This means that the prison authorities may open a letter from a lawyer to a prisoner when they have reasonable cause to believe that it contains an illicit enclosure which the normal means of detection have failed to disclose. The letter should, however, only be opened and should not be read. Suitable guarantees preventing the reading of the letter should be provided, e.g. opening the letter in the presence of the prisoner. The reading of a prisoner's mail to and from a lawyer, on the other hand, should only be permitted in exceptional circumstances when the authorities have reasonable cause to believe that the privilege is being abused in that the contents of the letter endanger prison security or the safety of others or are otherwise of a criminal nature. What may be regarded as 'reasonable cause' will depend on all the circumstances but it presupposes the existence of facts or information which would satisfy an objective observer that the privileged channel of communication was being abused (see, mutatis mutandis, the *Fox, Campbell and Hartley v. the United Kingdom* 1990, para. 32).

The Government have argued that the opening of the applicant's correspondence did not prevent him from having an effective opportunity to communicate in confidence with his solicitor during prison visits. By way of analogy they pointed out that Article 3 para. 2 (c) of the European Agreement only guaranteed, in the context of proceedings before the Strasbourg organs, the confidentiality of legal consultations with a prisoner during a visit. In a commentary to the Agreement, the Committee of Experts on Human Rights considered that correspondence between a prisoner and his lawyer, in this context, was susceptible to examination by the competent authorities (report to the Committee of Ministers, 27 October 1969, para. 58, H (69)15.)

However, these arguments do not answer the applicant's complaint. In the first place, the provisions of the European Agreement are not to be interpreted as limiting the obligations assumed under the Convention, as indicated by Article 6 of the Agreement. They thus cannot be interpreted as prejudicing the rights guaranteed in the Convention (see, mutatis mutandis, the Ekbatani v. Sweden 1988, para. 26). Moreover, the application of Article 3 para. 2 (c) is subject to the safeguards contained in Article 3 para. 3 which raise problems of interpretation similar to those raised by Article 8 para. 2 of the Convention. It therefore offers little clarification of the point at issue and cannot be construed as permitting the opening of such correspondence under Article 8.

Further, correspondence is a different medium of communication which is afforded separate protection under Article 8. The right to respect for correspondence is of special importance in a prison context where it may be more difficult for a legal adviser to visit his client in person because, as in the present case, of the distant location of the prison (see paragraph 8 above). Finally, the objective of confidential communication with a lawyer could not be achieved if this means of communication were the subject of automatic control.

The Government have also argued that the professional competence and integrity of solicitors could not always be relied on. The Government added that they not infrequently broke their disciplinary rules and various abuses had come to light since the coming into force of the new rules in respect of correspondence relating to pending proceedings. Moreover, if it were known that all correspondence with solicitors would pass unopened there existed a risk that they would become the target of pressure from those wishing to smuggle forbidden material into or out of prisons. Since drugs or even explosives could be concealed within an ordinary letter this was a real risk. It was thus wholly proportionate for the authorities to minimise risks of this kind by opening such letters.

The Court, however, is not persuaded by these submissions. The possibility of examining correspondence for reasonable cause (see paragraph 48 above) provides a sufficient safeguard against the possibility of abuse. It must also be borne in mind that solicitors in Scotland are officers of the court and are subject to disciplinary sanctions by the Law Society of Scotland for professional misconduct. It has not been suggested that there was any reason to suspect that the applicant's solicitor was not complying with the rules of his profession. In sum, the mere possibility of abuse is outweighed by the need to respect the confidentiality attached to the lawyer-client relationship.

There being no further room for allowing for a margin of appreciation, the Court finds that there was no pressing social need for the opening and reading of the applicant's correspondence with his solicitor and that, accordingly, this interference was not 'necessary in a democratic society' within the meaning of Article 8 para. 2.

Accordingly, there has been a breach of Article 8 in this respect.

NOTES

1. This case provides a good example of how the European Court considers the issue of proportionality which might be summarised as the least intrusive means to secure the legitimate objective. In *W v United Kingdom* the Court stated:[46]

It is true that Article 8 contains no explicit procedural requirements, but this is not conclusive of the matter. The [state's] decision-making process clearly cannot be devoid of influence on the substance

---

[46] (1988) 10 EHRR 29.

of the decision, notably by ensuring that it is based on the relevant considerations and is not one-sided and, hence, neither is nor appears to be arbitrary.

Furthermore, in *Klass v Germany*[47] the Court noted the importance of having in place sufficient safeguards against abuse. For example, in the context of police surveillance is there an effective system of control and review to ensure the measures adopted are proportionate.

2. Since the Human Rights Act 1998 domestic regulation providing for potentially intrusive powers for state bodies often explicitly refers to the need for that body to demonstrate proportionality.[48] Unfortunately, clear guidance on the meaning of proportionality is less forthcoming. Is it possible to formulate guidance in an area that is so clearly fact specific?

Although the legitimate aims in Art. 8(2) must be interpreted strictly they are broadly drafted. It has been argued that the interpretation of the legitimate exceptions is key to how the right works in practice.[49]

The following chapter will consider how domestic law seeks to reflect the demands of Art. 8.

---

[47] (1979–80) 2 EHRR 214.   [48] N. Taylor [2003] EHRLR Special Issue 86.
[49] A. McHarg (1999) MLR 671.

8

THE PROTECTION OF PRIVACY

1. INTRODUCTION[1]

As noted in the previous chapter, the meaning of privacy is somewhat elusive. Both the Justice Report[2] and the Younger Committee Report[3] pointed out the difficulty of finding 'a precise or logical formula which could either circumscribe the meaning of the word "privacy" or define it exhaustively'.[4] Each, however, suggested a working definition. The Justice Report[5] understood privacy as meaning

that area of a man's life which, in any given circumstances, a reasonable man with an understanding of the legitimate needs of the community would think it wrong to invade.

Cf. the definition adopted by Westin:[6]

Privacy is the claim of individuals, groups, or institutions to determine for themselves when, how, and to what extent information about them is communicated to others. Viewed in terms of the relation of the individual to social participation, privacy is the voluntary and temporary withdrawal of a person from the general society through physical or psychological means, either in a state of solitude or small-group intimacy or, when among larger groups, in a condition of anonymity or reserve.

The Younger Committee[7] 'conceived of the right of privacy as having two main aspects':

The first of these is freedom from intrusion upon oneself, one's home, family and relationships. The second is privacy of information, that is the right to determine for oneself how and to what extent information about oneself is communicated to others.

---

[1] On the right to privacy, see P. Birks (ed.), *Privacy and Loyalty* (1997), particularly the chapters by E. Barendt, D. Feldman and R. Bagshaw: D. Feldman (1994) 47(2) CLP 41; S. Goode, *The Right to Privacy* (1983); B. Markesenis (1990) 53 MLR 802; D. McLean, *Privacy and its Invasion* (1995); H. Nissenbaum (1998) 17 Law and Philosophy 559; E. Paton-Smith (1998) 61 MLR 318; F.D. Schoman, *Privacy and Social Freedom* (1992); D.J. Siepp (1983) 3 OJLS 325; R. Wacks. *The Protection of Privacy* (1980); ibid., *Personal Information: Privacy and the Law* (1989): ibid., *Privacy and Press Freedom* (1995); R. Gavison (1980) 89(3) Yale LJ 421; G. Phillipson [2003] EHRLR 54; ibid., [2003] MLR 726; G. Phillipson and H. Fenwick [2000] MLR 660; M Tugendhat and I Christie, *The Law of Privacy and the Media* (2002); M. Colvin, *Developing Key Privacy Rights* (2002); A. Etzioni, *The Limits of Privacy* (1999).

[2] *Privacy and the Law* (1970), p. 5.   [3] *Report of the Committee on Privacy* (Cmnd 5012, 1972), p. 17.
[4] Justice Report, p. 5.   [5] Ibid.   [6] A.F. Westin, *Privacy and Freedom* (1970), p. 7.
[7] Report, p. 10.

The concept underlying and justifying the right to privacy is a matter of debate. Writers have championed, *inter alia,* the notions of seclusion, individual autonomy and human dignity.[8] In *Douglas v Hello! Ltd,*[9] Sedley LJ suggested that privacy is a 'legal principle drawn from the fundamental value of personal autonomy', and in *Campbell,*[10] Lord Hoffmann recognised that 'what human rights law has done is to identify private information as something worth protecting as an aspect of human autonomy and dignity'.[11]

In the absence of a general right to privacy,[12] the protection afforded to privacy by English law has been piecemeal, incomplete and indirect.

2. A GENERAL RIGHT OF PRIVACY?

● Kaye v Robertson [1991] FSR 62, Court of Appeal

The plaintiff, the star of *Allo! Allo!,* a popular television comedy series, underwent extensive surgery to his head and brain after injuries resulting from storm debris falling on his car. In the interests of Mr Kaye's health, which remained a matter of serious concern, the hospital authorities placed a notice on the door of Mr Kaye's private room asking visitors to contact a member of the hospital staff before visiting. Acting on the instructions of their editor, a journalist and a photographer from *Sunday Sport,* a national newspaper, went to the hospital and, ignoring the notice on the door, entered Mr Kaye's room. They interviewed him and took photographs showing the injuries to his head. This, the editor claimed, was a 'great old-fashioned scoop'. The plaintiff obtained an injunction, based mainly upon *Tolley v J S Fry & Sons Ltd,*[13] requiring the first and second defendants, the newspaper editor and publisher respectively, to refrain from publishing the interview and photographs. The defendants appealed to the Court of Appeal.

Glidewell LJ: It is well-known that in English law there is no right to privacy, and accordingly there is no right of action for breach of a person's privacy. The facts of the present case are a graphic illustration of the desirability of Parliament considering whether and in what circumstances statutory provision can be made to protect the privacy of individuals.

In the absence of such a right, the plaintiff's advisers have sought to base their claim to injunctions upon other well-established rights of action....

1. LIBEL

The basis of the plaintiff's case under this head is that the article as originally written clearly implied that Mr. Kaye consented to give the first 'exclusive' interview to *Sunday Sport,* and to be photographed by their photographer. This was untrue: [according to medical evidence] Mr. Kaye was in no fit condition to give any informed consent, and such consent as he may appear to have given was, and should have been known by *Sunday Sport's* representative to be, of no effect. The implication in the article would have the effect of lowering Mr. Kaye in the esteem of right-thinking people, and was thus defamatory.

The plaintiff's case is based on the well-known decision in *Tolley v J S Fry & Sons Ltd*...Mr. Milmo for the defendants submits that, assuming that the article was capable of having the meaning alleged, this would

---

[8] For differing views, see E. Bloustein (1964) 39 NYULR 962; D. Feldman (1994) 47(2) CLP 41; P. Jones (2000) 6 EPL 275; R. Gavison (1980) 89(3) Yale LJ 421; and J. Inness, *Privacy, Intimacy and Isolation* (1992), p. 46.

[9] [2001] 2 All ER 289.   [10] [2004] UKHL 22, para. 50.

[11] See also Fifth Report of the Culture, Media and Sport Select Committee on *Privacy and Media Intrusion,* Session 2002–03 (Cm 5985), para. 9.

[12] See below: *Wainwright v Home Office* [2004] 2 AC 406.   [13] [1931] AC 333, HL.

not be a sufficient basis for interlocutory relief. In *William Coulson & Sons v James Coulson & Co* (1887) 3 TLR 846, this court held that, though the High Court has jurisdiction to grant an interim injunction before the trial of a libel action, it is a jurisdiction to be exercised only sparingly.[14] ...

This is still the rule in actions for defamation, despite the decision of the House of Lords in *American Cyanamid Co v Ethicon Ltd* [1975] AC 396 in relation to interim injunctions generally. This court so decided in *Herbage v Times Newspapers Ltd*, unreported but decided on 1 May 1981.[15] ...

It is in my view certainly arguable that the intended article would be libellous, on the authority of *Tolley v Fry*. I think that a jury would probably find that Mr. Kaye had been libelled, but I cannot say that such a conclusion is inevitable. It follows that I agree with Mr. Milmo's submission and in this respect I disagree with the learned judge; I therefore would not base an injunction on a right of action for libel.

2. MALICIOUS FALSEHOOD

The essentials of this tort are that the defendant has published about the plaintiff words which are false, that they were published maliciously, and that special damage has followed as the direct and natural result of their publication. As to special damage, the effect of section 3(1) of the Defamation Act 1952 is that it is sufficient if the words published in writing are calculated to cause pecuniary damage to the plaintiff. Malice will be inferred if it be proved that the words were calculated to produce damage and that the defendant knew when he published the words that they were false or was reckless as to whether they were false or not.

The test in *Coulson v Coulson (supra)* applies to interlocutory injunctions in actions for malicious falsehood as it does in actions for defamation. However, in relation to this action, the test applies only to the requirement that the plaintiff must show that the words were false. In the present case I have no doubt that any jury which did not find that the clear implication from the words contained in the defendants' draft article were false would be making a totally unreasonable finding. Thus the test is satisfied in relation to this cause of action.

As to malice I equally have no doubt from the evidence, including the transcript of the tape-recording of the 'interview' with Mr. Kaye in his hospital room which we have read, that it was quite apparent to the reporter and photographer from *Sunday Sport* that Mr. Kaye was in no condition to give any informed consent to their interviewing or photographing him. Moreover, even if the journalists had been in any doubt about Mr. Kaye's fitness to give his consent, Mr. Robertson [the first defendant] could not have entertained any such doubt after he read the affidavit sworn on behalf of Mr. Kaye in these proceedings. Any subsequent publication of the falsehood would therefore inevitably be malicious.

As to damage, I have already recorded that Mr. Robertson appreciated that Mr. Kaye's story was one for which other newspapers would be willing to pay 'large sums of money'. It needs little imagination to appreciate that whichever journal secured the first interview with Mr. Kaye would be willing to pay the most. Mr. Kaye thus has a potentially valuable right to sell the story of his accident and his recovery when he is fit enough to tell it. If the defendants are able to publish the article they proposed, or one anything like it, the value of this right would in my view be seriously lessened, and Mr. Kaye's story thereafter be worth much less to him.

I have considered whether damages would be an adequate remedy in these circumstances. They would inevitably be difficult to calculate, would also follow some time after the event, and in my view would in no way be adequate. It thus follows that in my opinion all the preconditions to the grant of an interlocutory injunction in respect of this cause of action are made out....

---

14 *Ed.* Cf. *Bonnard v Perryman* [1891] 2 Ch 269.
15 *Ed.* See also *Herbage v Pressdram* [1984] 2 All ER 769, CA.

3. TRESPASS TO THE PERSON

... The plaintiff's case in relation to this cause of action is that the taking of the flashlight photographs may well have caused distress to Mr. Kaye and set back his recovery, and thus caused him injury. In this sense it can be said to be a battery.... I am prepared to accept that it may well be the case that if a bright light is deliberately shone into another person's eyes and injures his sight, or damages him in some other way, this may be in law a battery. But in my view the necessary effects are not established by the evidence in this case. Though there must have been an obvious risk that any disturbance to Mr. Kaye would set back his recovery, there is no evidence that the taking of the photographs did in fact cause him any damage.

Moreover, the injunction sought in relation to this head of action would not be intended to prevent another anticipated battery, since none was anticipated. The intention here is to prevent the defendants from profiting from the taking of the photographs, i.e. from their own trespass. Attractive though this argument may appear to be, I cannot find as a matter of law that an injunction should be granted in these circumstances....

4. PASSING OFF

Mr. Caldecott submits...that the essentials of the tort of passing off, as laid down by the speeches in the House of Lords in *E Warnink BV v J Townend & Sons (Hull) Ltd* [1979] AC 731, are satisfied here.... I think that the plaintiff is not in the position of a trader in relation to his interest in his story about his accident and his recovery, and thus fails from the start to have a right of action under this head....

Bingham LJ: The defendants' conduct towards the plaintiff here was 'a monstrous invasion of his privacy' (to adopt the language of Griffiths J in *Bernstein v Skyviews Ltd* [1978] QB 479 at 489G). If ever a person has a right to be let alone by strangers with no public interest to pursue, it must surely be when he lies in hospital recovering from brain surgery and in no more than partial command of his faculties. It is this invasion of his privacy which underlies the plaintiff's complaint. Yet it alone, however gross, does not entitle him to relief in English law.

Leggatt LJ:...In view of the importance of the topic I add a note about the way in which the common law has developed in the United States to meet the need which in the present case we are unable to fulfil satisfactorily....

It [the right to privacy] is manifested in several forms.... One example is such intrusion upon physical solitude as would be objectionable to a reasonable man. So when in *Barber v Time Inc* 159 SW 2d 291 (1942) the plaintiff was confined to a hospital bed, the publication of her photograph taken without consent was held to be an invasion of a private right of which she was entitled to complain. Similarly, a so-called 'right of publicity' has developed to protect the commercial interest of celebrities in their identities.... *Carson v Here's Johnny Portable Toilets Inc* 698 F 2d 831 (1983) at page 835.

We do not need a First Amendment to preserve the freedom of the press, but the abuse of that freedom can be ensured only by the enforcement of a right to privacy. This right has so long been disregarded here that it can be recognised now only by the legislature. Especially since there is available in the United States a wealth of experience of the enforcement of this right both at common law and also under statute, it is to be hoped that the making good of this signal shortcoming in our law will not be long delayed.

NOTES

1. Although the Court of Appeal was unanimously of the opinion that an interlocutory injunction should be granted on the basis of malicious falsehood, the appeal was allowed in part, the original injunction being discharged as having been wrongly granted on the basis of the claim of libel.[16] In accordance with the law of malicious falsehood, the new injunction was more limited than the original one. It allowed the publication of the story and certain less objectionable photographs (one of Mr Kaye lying in bed asleep was published) provided that it was not claimed that the plaintiff had given his consent.

2. The Court of Appeal's acknowledgement in *Kaye v Robertson* that there is no right to privacy in English Law followed similar pronouncements by judges in earlier cases.[17] In 1996, in *R v Brown*[18] Lord Hoffmann stated that 'English common law does not know a general right of privacy and Parliament has been reluctant to enact one'. Soon afterwards, however, three members of the House of Lords preferred to leave the question open in *R v Khan*[19] and the UK Government position in the Strasbourg case of *Spencer v United Kingdom*[20] caused others to think again. In view of the *Spencer* case and following the enactment of the Human Rights Act 1998, the Court of Appeal in *Douglas v Hello!*[21] indicated that the time might have come for the judicial development of a tort of invasion of privacy.

86. ...A photograph of Lady Spencer had been taken with a telephoto lens while she was walking in the grounds of a private clinic at which she was receiving treatment. This photograph was published under the caption: 'SO THIN: Victoria walks in the clinic grounds this week.' Relying on the decision of this court in *Kaye v Robertson*, she did not pursue a claim in the English courts, but the commission held that she should have pursued her remedies in these courts first. It appears that the eloquence of the advocate for the United Kingdom government persuaded the commission that English law provided her with a potentially satisfactory remedy in an action for breach of confidence.

87. In this respect the commission relied heavily on the strong and detailed case of the applicants in the domestic proceedings which pointed to their former friends as the direct source of the essential confidential information that had been published. Its determination ended in these terms:

'Accordingly, the Commission considers that the parties' submissions indicate that the remedy of breach of confidence (against the newspapers and their sources) was available to the applicants and that the applicants have not demonstrated that it was insufficient or ineffective in the circumstances of their cases. It considers that, in so far as relevant doubts remain concerning the financial awards to be made following a finding of a breach of confidence, they arc not such as to warrant a conclusion that the breach of confidence action is ineffective or insufficient but rather a conclusion that the matter should be put to the domestic courts for consideration in order to allow those courts, through the common law system in the United Kingdom, the opportunity to develop existing rights by way of interpretation.' (See (1998) 25 EHRR CD 105 at 117–118.)

88. The commission appears to be saying that since the authorities in this country have been content to leave it to the judges to develop the law in this sensitive field, it is the judges who must develop the law so that it gives appropriate recognition to art 8(1) rights. Whether they do so in future by an extension of the existing frontiers of the law of confidence, or by recognising the existence of new relationships which give rise to enforceable legal rights (as has happened in relation to the law of negligence ever since the 3–2 decision of the House of Lords in *Donoghue (or M'Alister) v Stevenson* [1932] AC 562, [1932] All ER Rep 1) is not for this court, on this occasion, to predict...

---

[16] On *Kaye v Robertson*, see D. Bedingfield (1992) 55 MLR 111; B.S. Markensis (1992) 55 MLR 118; and P. Prescott (1991) 54 MLR 451.

[17] E.g. per Sir Robert Megarry V-C in *Malone v Metropolitan Police Comr* [1979] 1 Ch 344, Ch D and Lord Denning MR in *Re X (a minor)* [1975] Fam 47, CA.

[18] [1996] 1 All ER 545 at 556, HL.

[19] [1997] AC 558, HL, Lords Browne-Wilkinson, Slynn and Nicholls.

[20] App. No. 28851/95; (1998) 25 EHRR CD 105.   [21] [2001] QB 967.

3. The frontiers of the law of confidence have indeed been extended and this is considered below. The development of a wider free-standing tort of breach of privacy was considered by the House of Lords in the following case.

- **Wainwright v Home Office** [2003] UKHL 53, [2004] 2 AC 406,
  [2003] 3 WLR 1137, [2003] 4 All ER 969, House of Lords

In 1996 prison authorities at Armley Prison suspected that a remand prisoner was dealing in drugs and ordered that all of his visitors should be strip searched. Internal rules at Armley Prison were modelled on a code of practice issued to the police in order to reduce the embarrassment of those searched. In 1997, the prisoner's mother (W) and half brother (A) visited him. Both were strip searched and both found the experience upsetting. Some time later they consulted a solicitor who recommended that they both be examined by a psychiatrist. A, who had physical and learning difficulties, was found to be suffering from post-traumatic stress, whilst W suffered emotional distress. Action was commenced against the Home Office. It transpired that the search had not taken place in accordance with the guidelines. The County Court found that the strip search was an invasion of privacy which exceeded what was necessary and proportionate to deal with the drug smuggling problem. Secondly, the prison authorities had not adhered to their own rules. The Court of Appeal agreed with the second reason but not the first. The searches were not protected by statutory authority. But that was not enough to give rise to a claim to compensation. The acts of the prison officers needed statutory authority only if they would otherwise have been tortious or in breach of a statutory duty. The House considered whether the searches themselves or the manner in which they were conducted gave a cause of action. After dealing with the issue of assault their Lordships' turned to consider privacy.

Lord Hoffmann:

15. My Lords, let us first consider the proposed tort of invasion of privacy. Since the famous article by Warren and Brandeis (*The Right to Privacy* (1890) 4 Harvard LR 193) the question of whether such a tort exists, or should exist, has been much debated in common law jurisdictions. Warren and Brandeis suggested that one could generalise certain cases on defamation, breach of copyright in unpublished letters, trade secrets and breach of confidence as all based upon the protection of a common value which they called privacy or, following Judge Cooley (*Cooley on Torts*, 2nd ed (1888), p 29) 'the right to be let alone'. They said that identifying this common element should enable the courts to declare the existence of a general principle which protected a person's appearance, sayings, acts and personal relations from being exposed in public.

16. Courts in the United States were receptive to this proposal and a jurisprudence of privacy began to develop. It became apparent, however, that the developments could not be contained within a single principle; not, at any rate, one with greater explanatory power than the proposition that it was based upon the protection of a value which could be described as privacy. Dean Prosser, in his work on *The Law of Torts*, 4th ed (1971), p 804, said that:

> 'What has emerged is no very simple matter…it is not one tort, but a complex of four. To date the law of privacy comprises four distinct kinds of invasion of four different interests of the plaintiff, which are tied together by the common name, but otherwise have almost nothing in common except that each represents an interference with the right of the plaintiff 'to be let alone'.

17. Dean Prosser's taxonomy divided the subject into (1) intrusion upon the plaintiff's physical solitude or seclusion (including unlawful searches, telephone tapping, long-distance photography and telephone harassment) (2) public disclosure of private facts and (3) publicity putting the plaintiff in a false light and

(4) appropriation, for the defendant's advantage, of the plaintiff's name or likeness. These, he said, at p 814, had different elements and were subject to different defences.

18. The need in the United States to break down the concept of 'invasion of privacy' into a number of loosely-linked torts must cast doubt upon the value of any high-level generalisation which can perform a useful function in enabling one to deduce the rule to be applied in a concrete case. English law has so far been unwilling, perhaps unable, to formulate any such high-level principle. There are a number of common law and statutory remedies of which it may be said that one at least of the underlying values they protect is a right of privacy. Sir Brian Neill's well known article 'Privacy: a challenge for the next century' in *Protecting Privacy* (ed B Markesinis, 1999) contains a survey. Common law torts include trespass, nuisance, defamation and malicious falsehood; there is the equitable action for breach of confidence and statutory remedies under the Protection from Harassment Act 1997 and the Data Protection Act 1998. There are also extra-legal remedies under Codes of Practice applicable to broadcasters and newspapers. But there are gaps; cases in which the courts have considered that an invasion of privacy deserves a remedy which the existing law does not offer. Sometimes the perceived gap can be filled by judicious development of an existing principle. The law of breach of confidence has in recent years undergone such a process: see in particular the judgment of Lord Phillips of Worth Matravers MR in *Campbell v MGN Ltd* [2003] QB 633. On the other hand, an attempt to create a tort of telephone harassment by a radical change in the basis of the action for private nuisance in *Khorasandjian v Bush* [1993] QB 727 was held by the House of Lords in *Hunter v Canary Wharf Ltd* [1997] AC 655 to be a step too far. The gap was filled by the 1997 Act.

19. What the courts have so far refused to do is to formulate a general principle of 'invasion of privacy' (I use the quotation marks to signify doubt about what in such a context the expression would mean) from which the conditions of liability in the particular case can be deduced. The reasons were discussed by Sir Robert Megarry V-C in *Malone v Metropolitan Police Comr* [1979] Ch 344, 372–381. I shall be sparing in citation but the whole of Sir Robert's treatment of the subject deserves careful reading. The question was whether the plaintiff had a cause of action for having his telephone tapped by the police without any trespass upon his land. This was (as the European Court of Justice subsequently held in *Malone v United Kingdom* (1984) 7 EHRR 14) an infringement by a public authority of his right to privacy under article 8 of the Convention, but because there had been no trespass, it gave rise to no identifiable cause of action in English law. Sir Robert was invited to declare that invasion of privacy, at any rate in respect of telephone conversations, was in itself a cause of action. He said, at p 372:

'I am not unduly troubled by the absence of English authority: there has to be a first time for everything, and if the principles of English law, and not least analogies from the existing rules, together with the requirements of justice and common sense, pointed firmly to such a right existing, then I think the court should not be deterred from recognising the right. On the other hand, it is no function of the courts to legislate in a new field. The extension of the existing laws and principles is one thing, the creation of an altogether new right is another.'

20. As for the analogy of construing statutes in accordance with the Convention, which appealed to the judge in the present case, Sir Robert said, at p 379:

'I readily accept that if the question before me were one of construing a statute enacted with the purpose of giving effect to obligations imposed by the Convention, the court would readily seek to construe the legislation in a way that would effectuate the Convention rather than frustrate it. However, no relevant legislation of that sort is in existence. It seems to me that where Parliament has abstained from legislating on a point that is plainly suitable for legislation, it is indeed difficult for the court to lay down new rules of common law or equity that will carry out the Crown's treaty obligations, or to discover for the first time that such rules have always existed.'

21. Sir Robert pointed out, at p 380, that the problem about telephone tapping was not in formulating the generalisation that the state should not ordinarily listen to one's telephone calls but in specifying the

circumstances under which it should be allowed to do so. This required detailed rules and not broad common law principles:

> 'Give full rein to the Convention, and it is clear that when the object of the surveillance is the detection of crime, the question is not whether there ought to be a general prohibition of all surveillance, but in what circumstances, and subject to what conditions and restrictions, it ought to be permitted. It is those circumstances, conditions and restrictions which are at the centre of this case; and yet it is they which are the least suitable for determination by judicial decision.'

22. Once again, Parliament provided a remedy, subject to a detailed code of exceptions, in the Interception of Communications Act 1985. A similar problem arose in *R v Khan (Sultan)* [1997] AC 558, in which the defendant in criminal proceedings complained that the police had invaded his privacy by using a listening device fixed to the outside of a house. There was some discussion of whether the law should recognise a right to privacy which had been prima facie infringed, but no concluded view was expressed because all their Lordships thought that any such right must be subject to exceptions, particularly in connection with the detection of crime, and that the accused's privacy had been sufficiently taken into account by the judge when he exercised his discretion under section 78 of the Police and Criminal Evidence Act to admit the evidence obtain by the device at the criminal trial. The European Court of Human Rights subsequently held (*Khan v United Kingdom* The Times, 23 May 2000) that the invasion of privacy could not be justified under article 8 because, in the absence of any statutory regulation, the actions of the police had not been 'in accordance with law'. By that time, however, Parliament had intervened in the Police Act 1997 to put the use of surveillance devices on a statutory basis.

23. The absence of any general cause of action for invasion of privacy was again acknowledged by the Court of Appeal in *Kaye v Robertson*...at the time of the judgment (16 March 1990) a Committee under the chairmanship of Sir David Calcutt QC was considering whether individual privacy required statutory protection against intrusion by the press. Glidewell LJ said, at p 66:

> 'The facts of the present case are a graphic illustration of the desirability of Parliament considering whether and in what circumstances statutory provision can be made to protect the privacy of individuals.'

24. Bingham LJ likewise said, at p 70:

> 'The problems of defining and limiting a tort of privacy are formidable but the present case strengthens my hope that the review now in progress may prove fruitful.'

25. Leggatt LJ, at p 71, referred to Dean Prosser's analysis of the development of the law of privacy in the United States and said that similar rights could be created in England only by statute: 'it is to be hoped that the making good of this signal shortcoming in our law will not be long delayed.'

26. All three judgments are flat against a judicial power to declare the existence of a high-level right to privacy and I do not think that they suggest that the courts should do so. The members of the Court of Appeal certainly thought that it would be desirable if there was legislation to confer a right to protect the privacy of a person in the position of Mr Kaye against the kind of intrusion which he suffered, but they did not advocate any wider principle. And when the Calcutt Committee reported in June 1990, they did indeed recommend that 'entering private property, without the consent of the lawful occupant, with intent to obtain personal information with a view to its publication' should be made a criminal offence: see *Report of the Committee on Privacy and Related Matters* (1990) Cm 1102, para 6.33 The Committee also recommended that certain other forms of intrusion, like the use of surveillance devices on private property and long-distance photography and sound recording, should be made offences.

27. But the Calcutt Committee did not recommend, even within their terms of reference (which were confined to press intrusion) the creation of a generalised tort of infringement of privacy: paragraph 12.5. This was not because they thought that the definitional problems were insuperable. They said that if

one confined the tort to 'publication of personal information to the world at large' (paragraph 12.12) it should be possible to produce an adequate definition and they made some suggestions about how such a statutory tort might be defined and what the defences should be. But they considered that the problem could be tackled more effectively by a combination of the more sharply-focused remedies which they recommended: paragraph 12.32. As for a 'general wrong of infringement of privacy', they accepted, at paragraph 12.12, that it would, even in statutory form, give rise to 'an unacceptable degree of uncertainty'. There is nothing in the opinions of the judges in *Kaye v Robertson* [1991] FSR 62 which suggests that the members of the court would have held any view, one way or the other, about a general tort of privacy.

28. The claimants placed particular reliance upon the judgment of Sedley LJ in *Douglas v Hello! Ltd* [2001] QB 967. Sedley LJ drew attention to the way in which the development of the law of confidence had attenuated the need for a relationship of confidence between the recipient of the confidential information and the person from whom it was obtained—a development which enabled the UK Government to persuade the European Human Rights Commission in *Earl Spencer v United Kingdom* (1998) 25 EHRR CD 105 that English law of confidence provided an adequate remedy to restrain the publication of private information about the applicants' marriage and medical condition and photographs taken with a telephoto lens. These developments showed that the basic value protected by the law in such cases was privacy. Sedley LJ said, at p 1001, para 126:

'What a concept of privacy does, however, is accord recognition to the fact that the law has to protect not only those people whose trust has been abused but those who simply find themselves subjected to an unwanted intrusion into their personal lives. The law no longer needs to construct an artificial relationship of confidentiality between intruder and victim: it can recognise privacy itself as a legal principle drawn from the fundamental value of personal autonomy.'

29. I read these remarks as suggesting that, in relation to the publication of personal information obtained by intrusion, the common law of breach of confidence has reached the point at which a confidential relationship has become unnecessary. As the underlying value protected is privacy, the action might as well be renamed invasion of privacy. 'To say this' said Sedley LJ, at p 1001, para 125, 'is in my belief to say little, save by way of a label, that our courts have not said already over the years.'

30. I do not understand Sedley LJ to have been advocating the creation of a high-level principle of invasion of privacy. His observations are in my opinion no more (although certainly no less) than a plea for the extension and possibly renaming of the old action for breach of confidence. As Buxton LJ pointed out in this case in the Court of Appeal, at [2002] QB 1334, 1361–1362, paras 96–99, such an extension would go further than any English court has yet gone and would be contrary to some cases (such as *Kaye v Robertson* [1991] FSR 62) in which it positively declined to do so. The question must wait for another day. But Sedley LJ's dictum does not support a principle of privacy so abstract as to include the circumstances of the present case.

31. There seems to me a great difference between identifying privacy as a value which underlies the existence of a rule of law (and may point the direction in which the law should develop) and privacy as a principle of law in itself. The English common law is familiar with the notion of underlying values—principles only in the broadest sense—which direct its development. A famous example is *Derbyshire County Council v Times Newspapers Ltd* [1993] AC 534, in which freedom of speech was the underlying value which supported the decision to lay down the specific rule that a local authority could not sue for libel. But no one has suggested that freedom of speech is in itself a legal principle which is capable of sufficient definition to enable one to deduce specific rules to be applied in concrete cases. That is not the way the common law works.

32. Nor is there anything in the jurisprudence of the European Court of Human Rights which suggests that the adoption of some high level principle of privacy is necessary to comply with article 8 of the Convention. The European Court is concerned only with whether English law provides an adequate

remedy in a specific case in which it considers that there has been an invasion of privacy contrary to article 8(1) and not justifiable under article 8(2). So in *Earl Spencer v United Kingdom* 25 EHRR CD 105 it was satisfied that the action for breach of confidence provided an adequate remedy for the Spencers' complaint and looked no further into the rest of the armoury of remedies available to the victims of other invasions of privacy. Likewise, in *Peck v United Kingdom* (2003) 36 EHRR 41 the court expressed some impatience, at paragraph 103, at being given a tour d'horizon of the remedies provided and to be provided by English law to deal with every imaginable kind of invasion of privacy. It was concerned with whether Mr Peck (who had been filmed in embarrassing circumstances by a CCTV camera) had an adequate remedy when the film was widely published by the media. It came to the conclusion that he did not.

33. Counsel for the Wainwrights relied upon *Peck's* case as demonstrating the need for a general tort of invasion of privacy. But in my opinion it shows no more than the need, in English law, for a system of control of the use of film from CCTV cameras which shows greater sensitivity to the feelings of people who happen to have been caught by the lens. For the reasons so cogently explained by Sir Robert Megarry in *Malone v Metropolitan Police Comr* [1979] Ch 344, this is an area which requires a detailed approach which can be achieved only by legislation rather than the broad brush of common law principle.

34. Furthermore, the coming into force of the Human Rights Act 1998 weakens the argument for saying that a general tort of invasion of privacy is needed to fill gaps in the existing remedies. Sections 6 and 7 of the Act are in themselves substantial gap fillers; if it is indeed the case that a person's rights under article 8 have been infringed by a public authority, he will have a statutory remedy. The creation of a general tort will, as Buxton LJ pointed out in the Court of Appeal, at [2002] QB 1334, 1360, para 92, pre-empt the controversial question of the extent, if any, to which the Convention requires the state to provide remedies for invasions of privacy by persons who are not public authorities.

35. For these reasons I would reject the invitation to declare that since at the latest 1950 there has been a previously unknown tort of invasion of privacy.

48. Counsel for the Wainwrights submit that unless the law is extended to create a tort which covers the facts of the present case, it is inevitable that the European Court of Human Rights will find that the United Kingdom was in breach of its Convention obligation to provide a remedy for infringements of Convention rights. In addition to a breach of article 8, they say that the prison officers infringed their Convention right under article 3 not to be subjected to degrading treatment.

49. I have no doubt that there was no infringement of article 3 …

51. Article 8 is more difficult. Buxton LJ thought, at [2002] QB 1334, 1352, para 62, that the Wainwrights would have had a strong case for relief under section 7 if the 1998 Act had been in force. Speaking for myself, I am not so sure. Although article 8 guarantees a right of privacy, I do not think that it treats that right as having been invaded and requiring a remedy in damages, irrespective of whether the defendant acted intentionally, negligently or accidentally. It is one thing to wander carelessly into the wrong hotel bedroom and another to hide in the wardrobe to take photographs. Article 8 may justify a monetary remedy for an intentional invasion of privacy by a public authority, even if no damage is suffered other than distress for which damages are not ordinarily recoverable. It does not follow that a merely negligent act should, contrary to general principle, give rise to a claim for damages for distress because it affects privacy rather than some other interest like bodily safety: compare *Hicks v Chief Constable of the South Yorkshire Police* [1992] 2 All ER 65.

52. Be that as it may, a finding that there was a breach of article 8 will only demonstrate that there was a gap in the English remedies for invasion of privacy which has since been filled by sections 6 and 7 of the 1998 Act. It does not require that the courts should provide an alternative remedy which distorts the principles of the common law.

I would therefore dismiss the appeal.

Lord Bingham of Cornhill, Lord Hope of Craighead, Lord Hutton and **Lord Scott of Foscote** agreed.

Appeal dismissed.

NOTES

1. The House of Lords concluded that there was no general cause of action for breach of privacy in English law and further confirmed that Art. 8 did not require that one be developed. The comments of Sedley LJ in *Douglas* were confined to personal information (para. 29). Should the law continue to develop incrementally filling in gaps in privacy protection? What are the advantages in such an approach?

2. Lord Hoffmann suggests that if a breach of Art. 8 were established this need not necessarily lead to a monetary remedy for distress if the breach was not intentional. Do you agree with this proposition?

3. At Strasbourg[22] the claimants were awarded £3,000 non-pecuniary damages after the Court found that the search amounted to a disproportionate interference with their Art. 8 right. The case was, of course, pre-HRA and, as Lord Hoffmann recognised, this gap in domestic law will be closed by HRA, s. 6 and s. 7.

4. It had been suggested[23] that the tort of *intentional infliction of physical harm* (other than by trespass) established in *Wilkinson v Downton*,[24] could be developed to provide an indirect remedy for some invasions of privacy. In that case, as a practical joke the defendant told the plaintiff that the plaintiff's husband had broken his legs in an accident. The plaintiff suffered nervous shock causing 'serious and permanent physical consequences'. However, in *Wainwright* Lord Hoffmann suggested that such a development should go no further in light of developments in negligence and the enactment of the Protection form Harassment Act 1997.

3. INDIRECT REMEDIES IN LAW FOR INVASION OF PRIVACY

The established remedies relevant to the protection of privacy that exist in English law are found in various parts of the criminal and, particularly, the civil law. In terms of the two main kinds of invasion of privacy, protection from physical intrusion is offered mainly by the torts of trespass and nuisance. Informational privacy has been given increased protection recently through develops in breach of confidence, and is also safeguarded to varying degrees by the law of defamation, the court's jurisdiction to protect juveniles, breach of copyright and data protection legislation. Comprehensive legislation to regulate surveillance has also developed in the wake of the HRA.

(A) TRESPASS

In *Baron Bernstein of Leigh v Skyviews and General Ltd*,[25] the plaintiff's land was flown over and an aerial photograph of his house taken without his knowledge or consent. He refused

---

[22] *Wainwright v UK*, App. No. 12350/04; (2007) 44 EHRR 40.

[23] See Dworkin (1967) 2 U Tas LR 418, 444, and Neill (1962) 25 MLR 393, 402.

[24] [1897] 2 QB 57, QBD.

[25] [1978] QB 479. See R. Wacks (1977) 93 LQR 491. For doubts about this case, see Sedley LJ in *Douglas v Hello!* [2001] QB 967.

the offer to sell him the photograph and sued the defendant in trespass and invasion of privacy instead. Rejecting the claim, Griffiths J stated:

I can find no support in authority for the view that a landowner's rights in the air space above his property extend to an unlimited height. In *Wandsworth Board of Works v United Telephone Co Ltd* [1884] 13 QBD 904 Bowen LJ described the maxim, usque ad coelum, as a fanciful phrase, to which I would add that if applied literally it is a fanciful notion leading to the absurdity of a trespass at common law being committed by a satellite every time it passes over a suburban garden.... The problem is to balance the rights of an owner to enjoy the use of his land against the rights of the general public to take advantage of all that science now offers in the use of air space. This balance is in my judgment best struck in our present society by restricting the rights of an owner in the air space above his land to such height as is necessary for the ordinary use and enjoyment of his land and the structures upon it, and declaring that above that height he has no greater rights in the air space than any other member of the public.

Applying this test to the facts of this case, I find that the defendants' aircraft did not infringe any rights in the plaintiff's air space, and thus no trespass was committed. It was on any view of the evidence flying many hundreds of feet above the ground and it is not suggested that by its mere presence in the air space it caused any interference with any use to which the plaintiff put or might wish to put his land. The plaintiff's complaint is not that the aircraft interfered with the use of his land but that a photograph was taken from it. There is, however, no law against taking a photograph, and the mere taking of a photograph cannot turn an act which is not a trespass into the plaintiff's air space into one that is a trespass.

The present action is not founded in nuisance for no court would regard the taking of a single photograph as an actionable nuisance. But if the circumstances were such that a plaintiff was subjected to the harassment of constant surveillance of his house from the air, accompanied by the photographing of his every activity, I am far from saying that the court would not regard such a monstrous invasion of his privacy as an actionable nuisance for which they would give relief.

NOTES

1. See also the case of *Hickman v Maisey*,[26] considered in the judgment of *DPP v Jones* which is reproduced in Chap. 5. The case illustrates that the person in possession of the land must bring the claim. Therefore, in *Kaye v Robertson,* the hospital authorities, but not the patient or his family, could have brought proceedings in trespass.

2. The public opinion survey done for the Younger Committee[27] showed that 'callers at the door' were regarded as invading privacy, with Jehovah's Witnesses being mentioned in particular. In *Robson v Hallett*[28] Diplock LJ stated that:

when a householder lives in a dwelling house to which there is a garden in front and does not lock the gate of the garden, it gives an implied licence to any member of the public who has lawful reason for doing so to proceed from the gate to the front door or back door, and to inquire whether he may be admitted and to conduct his lawful business.

Diplock LJ stated that such an implied licence may be rebutted, as by a notice on the gate (e.g. 'No hawkers').

3. The above materials concern trespass to land. With statutory exceptions,[29] trespass to land is not a criminal offence. When Michael Fagan climbed into Buckingham Palace and

---

[26] [1900] 1 QB 752.   [27] Report, Appendix E.   [28] [1967] 2 QB 939 at 953–954, DC.
[29] E.g. trespass using violence to secure entry (Criminal Law Act 1977, s. 6) and aggravated trespass (Criminal Justice and Public Order Act 1994, ss. 68–69).

surprised the Queen by sitting on her bed, he thereby committed no offence. He was charged and acquitted of burglary in respect of an entry into the Palace a month earlier when he had stolen wine.[30] Following the second incident, the enactment of an offence of trespassing on residential property in a 'manner likely to cause the occupier alarm or distress', was considered but no government bill resulted.[31] Trespass to goods may also occasionally provide a remedy for invasion of privacy, as where a document is taken.

(B) NUISANCE

Private nuisance, giving rise to a civil action at the suit of an aggrieved individual, has on occasions been very widely defined to cover virtually any unreasonable interference with that individual's enjoyment of land which he occupies. But an action for private nuisance is normally brought for *some physical invasion of the plaintiffs land by some deleterious subject matter*—such as noise, smell, water or electricity—in circumstances which would not amount to trespass to land. It is much more doubtful if it would cover an activity which had no physical effects on the plaintiff's land, although it detracts from the plaintiff's enjoyment of that land. Thus spying on one's neighbour is probably not in itself a private nuisance although watching and besetting a man's house with a view to compelling him to pursue (or not to pursue) a particular course of conduct has been said to be a nuisance at common law. With regard to the latter type of conduct, however, it must be admitted that it is concerned with a situation very different from the typical case in which complaint is made of an invasion of privacy. The eavesdropper or spy does not seek to change the behaviour of his victim; on the contrary he hopes that it will continue unchanged, so that he may have the opportunity of noting it unobserved....

As a remedy for invasions of privacy private nuisance has the same basic disadvantages as the action for trespass to land, namely that it can only be brought by the person who is from a legal point of view the 'occupier' of the land, enjoyment of which is affected by the nuisance.[32]

NOTES

1. In *Khorasandjian v Bush*[33] the Court of Appeal allowed a person who had no proprietary interest in the land to bring a claim in private nuisance as a victim of persistent telephone calls to her in her parents' home. The case was overruled by the House of Lords in *Hunter v Canary Wharf*[34] on this point on the basis that it was inappropriate to extend the tort of nuisance beyond its purpose of protecting the quiet enjoyment of a person's land; the remedy was to develop a tailor-made remedy focusing on harassment. Nuisance remains available as a remedy for a householder for persistent[35] telephone calls.[36]

2. As noted by Lord Goff in *Hunter*, the Protection from Harassment Act 1997, s. 3, establishes a statutory tort of harassment. Under this, a course of conduct which the defendant knows or ought to know constitutes harassment is actionable for damages for, *inter alia*,

---

[30] *The Times*, 24 September 1982.

[31] Calcutt Report, *Report of the Committee on Privacy and Related Matters* (Cm 1102, 1990), p. 10.

[32] Younger Committee Report Appendix I, para. 18.

[33] [1993] 3 All ER 669.   [34] [1997] 2 All ER 426.

[35] A single telephone call, even in the middle of the night (see 11th Press Council Report 1964, pp. 32, 35), is not a nuisance.

[36] Cf. *Stokes v Brydges* (1958) 5 S Ct Queensland, in which the defendant, annoyed by the noise made by milkmen, retaliated by making telephone calls to the homes of the directors of the milk company to disturb their sleep. The directors were granted an injunction.

'any anxiety caused by the harassment and any financial loss resulting' therefrom. As well as persistent telephone calling, this covers conduct such as stalking. As Lord Goff noted, the result of the statutory tort was that the development of a common law tort of harassment was unnecessary.[37] Recent developments have also widened the ambit of harassment to include acting outside a person's home in a way which would cause harassment to a resident or neighbour.[38]

3. In *Robbins v Canadian Broadcasting Corpn*,[39] the plaintiff wrote to the producer of a television programme criticising it. The letter was read on the programme and viewers were invited to telephone (the number was given) or write to the plaintiff to cheer him up. For three days afterwards, the plaintiff's telephone rang non-stop until he was obliged to change his number. He also received 102 letters and had pranks played upon him. He was awarded damages by the Quebec Superior Court under the Quebec Civil Code for damage caused by the fault of another.

4. The criminal law also controls improper use of public electronic communications network under s. 127 of the Communications Act 2003:

(1) A person is guilty of an offence if he—

    (a) sends by means of a public electronic communications network a message or other matter that is grossly offensive or of an indecent, obscene or menacing character; or

    (b) causes any such message or matter to be so sent.

(2) A person is guilty of an offence if, for the purpose of causing annoyance, inconvenience or needless anxiety to another, he—

    (a) sends by means of a public electronic communications network, a message that he knows to be false,

    (b) causes such a message to be sent; or

    (c) persistently makes use of a public electronic communications network.

In *DPP v Collins*,[40] the House of Lords determined that gross offence did not depend upon the reaction of the recipient to the calls, but was based upon the standards of reasonable people in an open and just multicultural society. Therefore, the conversations of two racists might be caught by the provision as both would be aware that there terminology was grossly offensive. Does this provision effectively outlaw the use of telephone sex lines?

(C) DEFAMATION

● **Corelli v Wall** (1906) 22 TLR 532, Chancery Division, Swinfen Eady J

The plaintiff, a well-known authoress and a resident of Stratford-on-Avon, sought an interlocutory injunction to restrain the defendants, publishers in the same town, from publishing a series of postcards depicting imaginary scenes in the private life of the plaintiff. The injunction was sought pending the hearing of a libel action based upon the cards. The scenes

---

[37] For an earlier move in that direction, see *Burris v Azadani* [1995] 1 WLR 1372, CA.

[38] Criminal Justice Act 2001, s. 42A, as amended by the Serious Organised Crime and Police Act 2005, ss. 125–127.

[39] (1958) 12 DLR (2d) 35, Quebec Sup Ct.

[40] [2006] UKHL 40. See also Ofcom, *Statement of Policy on the Persistent Misuse of an Electronic Communications Network or Service* (2006), available at www.OFCOM.org.uk.

included the plaintiff feeding ponies, on the river Avon in a gondola, and in an imaginary garden. The plaintiff's annoyance reached its height when the defendants hired sandwich men to parade through Stratford, particularly near the plaintiff's home, to advertise the postcards.

> **Swinfen Eady J:** The real ground of the plaintiff's motion is that the cards constitute a libel upon her and that their sale ought to be restrained on that ground. Although it is well settled that a person may be defamed as well by a picture or effigy as by written or spoken words, I am not satisfied that the cards are libellous; and in any event the case is not so clear as to justify the Court in intervening before the fact of libel has been established. The case of *Bonnard v Perryman* [1891] 2 Ch 269 shows how careful the Court should be in granting interlocutory injunctions in cases of alleged libel. It is also urged that the plaintiff as a private person was entitled to restrain the publication of a portrait of herself which had been made without her authority and which, although professing to be her portrait, was totally unlike her. No authority in support of this proposition was cited. The plaintiff has not established, for the purpose of this motion, that she has any such right. Under these circumstances I do not see my way to grant any interlocutory injunction. When it is known that the sale of the postcards is in direct opposition to the plaintiff's wishes, and is the subject of grave annoyance to her, most respectable persons will probably do as Messrs. W. H. Smith and Son have done, and refuse to have anything to do with them.
>
> *Motion dismissed.*

NOTES

1. The case illustrates that even if an action in defamation is available, the remedy may be limited to damages. Although an interlocutory injunction will often be much the more effective remedy from the privacy point of view, one will only be granted under the rule in *Bonnard v Perryman*[41] 'in the clearest cases, where any jury would say that the matter complained of was libellous...'. An interlocutory injunction will not be granted if the defendant's defence is justification.[42]

2. Did *Corelli v Wall* decide that there was no remedy in English law for invasion of privacy in the form of the 'appropriation' of a person's 'name or likeness'?[43] Or only that an injunction could not be granted on the facts of the case?

3. In *Tolley v J S Fry & Sons Ltd*,[44] the defendants published an advertisement for their chocolate showing, without his knowledge or consent, a caricature of the plaintiff, a well-known amateur golfer, playing golf with a packet of their chocolate in his pocket. The plaintiff recovered damages in defamation on the basis that the advertisement carried an innuendo that he had prostituted his amateur status by advertising the defendant's goods for reward. On the question whether a remedy would have existed if the advertisement had not been defamatory, Greer LJ stated in the Court of Appeal:[45]

> Some men and women voluntarily enter professions which by their nature invite publicity, and public approval or disapproval. It is not unreasonable in their case that they should submit without complaint to their names and occupations and reputations being treated as matters of public interest, and almost as

[41] [1891] 2 Ch 269 at 284, CA.
[42] See, e.g., Fox LJ in *Francome v Mirror Newspapers* [1984] 2 All ER 408 at 414, CA; see also *Greene v Associated Newspapers Ltd* [2005] 1 All ER 30.
[43] *Restatement, 2d. Torts*, above, p. 914.   [44] [1931] AC 333, HL.
[45] [1930] 1 KB at 477–478.

public property. On the other hand a great many people outside the professions I have referred to resent any attempt to utilize their names or their doings as public property. And I can very well imagine that an amateur sportsman, though success necessarily brings about a certain amount of publicity, strongly objecting to the use of his name in connection with an advertising campaign aimed at increasing the sales of a commodity which he may either dislike, or at any rate in which he is not the least interested. I have no hesitation in saying that in my judgment the defendants in publishing the advertisement in question, without first obtaining Mr. Tolley's consent, acted in a manner inconsistent with the decencies of life, and in doing so they were guilty of an act for which there ought to be a legal remedy. But unless a man's photograph, caricature, or name be published in such a context that the publication can be said to be defamatory within the law of libel, it cannot be made the subject-matter of complaint by action at law: *Dockrell v Dougall* and *Corelli v Wall* [above].

4. The use of photographs and other personal information must now be considered in the light of the development of the action for misuses of personal information: see below, p. 539.

(D) BREACH OF COPYRIGHT

● **Williams v Settle** [1960] 1 WLR 1072, [1960] 2 All ER 806, Court of Appeal

The defendant, a professional photographer, took the photographs at the plaintiff's wedding. Two years later, when the plaintiff's wife was pregnant, her father was murdered. The case attracted publicity and, when the national press came looking for photographs, the defendant sold them copies of the wedding photographs. He did so without the knowledge or consent of the plaintiff, who held the copyright. One of the photographs—a family group with the father in it—was published five days after the wife gave birth with captions identifying the persons in it. One newspaper gave a particular description of the plaintiff's wife. The plaintiff successfully sued the defendant for breach of copyright in the county court. He was awarded £1,000 damages. The defendant's appeal to the Court of Appeal on the ground that the county court had lacked jurisdiction to award such a high amount of damages was rejected. The following extract concerns the appeal on the amount of damages.

Sellers LJ: In the present action the judge was clearly justified, in the circumstances in which the defendant, in breach of the plaintiff's copyright, handed these photographs to the press knowing the use to which they were going to be put, in awarding substantial and heavy damages of a punitive nature. The power so to do, quite apart from the ordinary law of the land, is expressly given by statute. By section 17(3) of the Copyright Act 1956, it is provided: 'Where in an action under this section an infringement of copyright is proved or admitted, and the court, having regard (in addition to all other material considerations) to—(*a*) the flagrancy of the infringement, and (*b*) any benefit shown to have accrued to the defendant by reason of the infringement, is satisfied that effective relief would not otherwise be available to the plaintiff, the court, in assessing damages for the infringement, shall have power to award such additional damages by virtue of this subsection as the court may consider appropriate in the circumstances.' It seems that this is not a case where there is any effective relief which could be given. The benefit which can be shown to have accrued to the defendant is meagre ... It is the flagrancy of the infringement which calls for heavy damages, because this was a scandalous matter in the circumstances, which I do not propose to elaborate and about which I do not propose to express a view. It is sufficient to say that it was a flagrant infringement of the right of the plaintiff, and it was scandalous conduct and in total disregard not only of the legal rights of the plaintiff regarding copyright but of his feelings and his sense of family dignity and pride. It was an intrusion into his life, deeper and graver than an intrusion into a man's property.

Willmer and **Harman LJJ** delivered concurring judgments.

Appeal dismissed.

NOTES

1. The plaintiff also obtained £52 10s damages and costs from the *Daily Express,* an apology and undertakings from the *Daily Mail* and a ruling in his favour from the Press Council.[46] The power to award 'additional damages' in s. 17(3) of the 1956 Act has been re-enacted in similar terms in s. 97(2), Copyright, Designs and Patents Act 1988.

2. The first owner of the copyright in a 'work', including a photograph or letter, is its author (other than in the case of an employee acting in the course of his employment): Copyright, Designs and Patents Act 1988, s. 11. A person 'who for private and domestic purposes commissions the taking of a photograph or the making of a film has, where copyright subsists in the resulting work, the right not to have', *inter alia,* 'copies of the work issued to the public' or 'the work exhibited or shown in public'.[47] This right may, however, be waived, by contract or otherwise.[48]

3. In *Barrymore v News Group Newspapers Ltd*[49] the *Sun* printed extracts from letters written by a TV personality, 'in which he plainly owns the copyright', to a homosexual friend who had given them to the newspaper. Jacobs J stated:

The Sun newspaper, manifestly knowing that what they were doing was likely to be a breach of copyright, nonetheless decided to publish portions of those letters. The financial consequences will no doubt be a matter for the court to decide in due course. I can say no more at this stage other than that newspapers which think that they can pay their way out of breach of copyright may find it more expensive than it is worth to print the material.[50]

4. In *Ashdown v Telegraph Group Ltd*[51] the Court of Appeal determined that application of the Copyright, Designs and Patents Act 1988 could be interpreted so as to draw an adequate balance between freedom of expression and copyright for the purposes of the HRA.

(E) BREACH OF CONFIDENCE[52]

- **Prince Albert v Strange** (1849) 1 Mac and G 25, 1 H & TW 1, Court of Chancery

Queen Victoria and the plaintiff had for their private amusement made etchings of their children and other subjects of personal interest. The defendant obtained copies and planned

---

46 See [1960] 1 WLR 1074–1075. On the case, see (1961) 77 LQR 12 and G. Dworkin (1961) 24 MLR 185. On the public interest defence available in breach of copyright cases, see the *Woolgar* case, below, p. 982.

47 1988 Act, s. 85.   48 1988 Act, s. 87.

49 [1997] FSR 600, Ch D.

50 At 601.   51 [2001] 4 All ER 666.

52 See on breach of confidence, H. Fenwick and G. Phillipson [1996] 55 CLJ 447; F. Gurry, *Breach of Confidence* (1984, reissued in 1991); and M. Richardson (1994) 19 MULR 673: Meagher, Gummow and Lehane, *Equity Doctrines and Remedies* (3rd edn, 1992), Chap. 41: And see Law Commission Report on Breach of Confidence

to exhibit them and to publish a catalogue listing and describing the etchings for profit. The etchings had been kept privately by the Royal Family, although a few copies had been given to friends. The plates for the etchings had been entrusted to a printer in Windsor for him to make further impressions. It appeared that, without the printer's knowledge or consent, one of his employees had made unauthorised copies of the etchings and the defendant had purchased these. The plaintiff obtained an injunction preventing the exhibition and the publication of the catalogue. In these proceedings, the defendant, who accepted that the exhibition should not proceed, applied to have the injunction amended to allow him to publish the catalogue. He appealed to the Lord Chancellor against the refusal of his application by Knight Bruce V-C[53] who had referred in his judgment to 'sordid spying into the privacy of domestic life':

Lord Cottenham LC: ...the Defendant insists that he is entitled to publish a catalogue of the etchings, that is to say, to publish a description or list of works or compositions of another, made and kept for the private use of that other, the publication of which was never authorised, and the possession of copies of which could only have been obtained by surreptitious and improper means. If was said by one of the learned counsel for the Defendant, that the injunction must rest upon the ground of property or breach of trust; both appear to me to exist. The property of an author or composer of any work, whether of literature, art, or science, in such work unpublished and kept for his private use or pleasure, cannot be disputed...the Plaintiff is entitled to the injunction of this Court to protect him against the invasion of such right and interest by the Defendant, which the publication of any catalogue would undoubtedly be; but this case by no means depends solely upon the question of property, for a breach of trust, confidence, or contract, would of itself entitle the Plaintiff to an injunction...and upon the evidence on behalf of the Plaintiff, and in the absence of any explanation on the part of the Defendant, I am bound to assume that the possession of the etchings by the Defendant...has its foundation in a breach of trust, confidence, or contract...upon this ground also I think the Plaintiff's title to the injunction sought to be discharged, fully established. The observations of Vice-Chancellor Wigram in *Tipping v Clarke* ((1843) 2 Hare 383) are applicable to this part of the case. He says: 'Every clerk employed in a merchant's counting-house is under an implied contract that he will not make public that which he learns in the execution of his duty as clerk. If the Defendant has obtained copies of books, it would very probably be by means of some clerk or agent of the Plaintiff; and if he availed himself surreptitiously of the information which he could not have had except from a person guilty of a breach of contract in communicating it, I think he could not be permitted to avail himself of that breach of contract.

...This was the opinion of Lord Eldon, expressed in the case of *Wyatt v Wilson* in 1820, respecting an engraving of George the Third during his illness, in which, according to a note with which I have been favoured by Mr. Cooper, he said, 'If one of the late king's physicians had kept a diary of what he heard and saw, this court would not, in the king's lifetime, have permitted him to print and publish it.'

Motion refused.

(Cmnd 8388, 1981), Report No. 110. On the Law Commission Report, see M.W. Bryan [1982] PL 188; G. Jones [1982] CLJ 40; J. Michael (1981) 131 NLJ 1201; A.M. Tettenborn (1983) 34 NILQ 248. The development of breach of confidence towards a remedy for misuse of private information can be followed in H. Fenwick and G. Phillipson [2000] 63(5) MLR 660; G. Phillipson [2003] EHRLR 54; G. Phillipson [2003] 66(5) MLR 726; R. Singh and J. Strachan [2002] EHRLR 129; R. Singh and J. Strachan [2003] EHRLR 12; R. Mulheron (2006) 69(5) MLR 679; A. Sims (2005) 1 IPQ 27; T. Alpin (2007) 1 IPQ 19.

[53] (1848) 2 De G and Sm 652 at 698.

NOTES

1. The Younger Committee[54] considered that the 'law on breach of confidence offers the most effective protection of privacy in the whole of our existing law, civil or criminal'. In its opinion 'the extent of its potential effectiveness is not widely recognised'. Although this has been shown to be true by recent cases, the value of breach of confidence as a remedy is inevitably limited in that it only concerns informational privacy; it does not extend to physical intrusion.

2. *Prince Albert v Strange* is a seminal case in the development of the equitable doctrine of breach of confidence. In so far as judgment was given for the plaintiff on a basis other than that of his property right in the etchings, was it given purely because of breach of confidence or because of an implied term in the rogue employee's contract of employment? As the cases Lord Cottenham refers to at the end of the above extract indicate, the common law has, in the absence of an express term, implied a term in a contract of employment by which an employee may not divulge confidential information obtained during employment to any third party without consent while he is still employed and thereafter. In practice for many years this was mainly relevant in the context of trade secrets, but developments in the years before the implementation of the HRA illustrated that it could apply to more personal matters.

3. In *Coco v A N Clark (Engineers) Ltd*,[55] Megarry J listed the three elements that were required for a claim in breach of confidence to be made:

> In my judgment, three elements are normally required if, apart from contract, a case of breach of confidence is to succeed. First, the information itself, in the words of Lord Greene MR in the *Saltman* case on p. 215, must 'have the necessary quality of confidence about it.' Secondly, that information must have been imparted in circumstances importing an obligation of confidence. Thirdly, there must be an unauthorised use of that information to the detriment of the party communicating it....

A defence of public interest might still provide for publication even though the three conditions might be made out.

4. *Quality of confidence. Argyll v Argyll*[56] had illustrated that information having a necessary quality of confidence was expanding from trade secrets to include personal information (in this case marital secrets) and thus was becoming a more effective protector of personal privacy. Further, whereas the decision in *Argyll* was predicated upon the fact that the information was disclosed during marriage, an institution which the law seeks to protect, this was not the basis for the decision in *Stephens v Avery*,[57] where details of a sexual relationship outside marriage was protected. The court in *Stephens* supposed instead that it is the policy of the law to uphold the moral quality of an undertaking not to disclose information given in confidence, whatever the existing relationship between the persons concerned. Provided that the information was not already in the public domain (thus lacking 'confidence') and was more than mere 'tittle-tattle' (which equity would not protect) it might be capable of being protected. However, it was the impetus of the HRA, s. 6 and the

---

54 Report, p. 26.

55 [1969] RPC 41, 47. Cf. the same judge, Sir Robert Megarry V-C, in *Malone v Metropolitan Police Comr* [1979] Ch 344, 375.

56 [1965] 1 All ER 611.

57 [1988] 2 All ER 477, Ch. See also *Barrymore v News Group Newspapers Ltd* [1997] FSR 600, Ch D.

need to develop confidence as a remedy in line with the requirements of Art. 8 that enabled the courts to develop the action beyond the confines of what was considered 'confidential' into the realms of what was considered to be 'private'. The question of what is 'private information' is addressed in *Campbell* below at p. 545.[58]

5. *Obligation of confidence.* The need for a confidential relationship to exist between confider and confidant inevitably reduced the potential for confidence to act as a protector of privacy, given that in many circumstances in which there will be an apparent breach of privacy there will not be an obligation of confidence. However, as with the quality of confidence, the requirements of an obligation of confidence were being developed as reflected in the dictum of Lord Goff in *A-G v Guardian Newspapers Ltd (No. 2)*:[59]

I start with the broad general principle (which I do not intend in any way to be definitive) that a duty of confidence arises, when confidential information comes to the knowledge of a person (the confidant) in circumstances where he has notice, or is held to have agreed, that the information is confidential, with the effect that it would be just in all the circumstances that he should be precluded from disclosing the information to others. I have used the word 'notice' advisedly, in order to avoid the (here unnecessary) question of the extent to which actual knowledge is necessary; though I of course understand knowledge to include circumstances where the confidant has deliberately closed his eyes to the obvious. The existence of this broad general principle reflects the fact that there is such a public interest in the maintenance of confidences, that the law will provide remedies for their protection.

I realise that, in the vast majority of cases, in particular those concerned with trade secrets, the duty of confidence will arise from a transaction or relationship between the parties—often a contract, in which event the duty may arise by reason of either an express or an implied term of that contract. It is in such cases as these that the expressions 'confider' and 'confidant' are perhaps most aptly employed. But it is well settled that a duty of confidence may arise in equity independently of such cases; and I have expressed the circumstances in which the duty arises in broad terms, not merely to embrace those cases where a third party receives information from a person who is under a duty of confidence in respect of it, knowing that it has been disclosed by that person to him in breach of his duty of confidence, but also to include certain situations, beloved of law teachers—where an obviously confidential document is wafted by an electric fan out of a window into a crowded street, or where an obviously confidential document, such as a private diary, is dropped in a public place, and is then picked up by a passer-by. I also have in mind the situations where secrets of importance to national security come into the possession of members of the public…

Subsequent cases, such as *Shelley Films v Rex Features Ltd*[60] indicated that the obligation of confidence could be imposed unilaterally without the need for communication between the parties.[61] As recognised in *Creation Records v News Group Newspapers*[62] the obligation could be imposed on the basis of when a reasonable man would be considered to be bound by an obligation of confidence. This had the potential to cover the classic breach of privacy case where information is taken surreptitiously. These were radical developments but again it was the impetus of the HRA that enabled the courts to develop the law still further. In *Douglas v Hello!*[63] Sedley LJ found some difficulty in stretching confidence beyond recognition but stated:

---

58 See, e.g., the comments of Lord Nicholls at para. 21.   59 [1990] 1 AC 109 at 281, HL.
60 [1994] EMLR 134.
61 See also *Hellewell v Chief Constable of Derbyshire* [1995] 1 WLR 804.
62 [1997] EMLR 444.   63 [2001] QB 967.

126. What a concept of privacy does, however, is accord recognition to the fact that the law has to protect not only those people whose trust has been abused but those who simply find themselves subjected to an unwanted intrusion into their personal lives. The law no longer needs to construct an artificial relationship of confidentiality between intruder and victim: it can recognise privacy itself as a legal principle drawn from the fundamental value of personal autonomy.[64]

A more radical development of this limb of confidence came in the case of *Venables v News Group Newspapers*[65] where the court granted an injunction against the whole world in relation to information that might lead to the identification or whereabouts following release from prison of those responsible for the murder of two-year-old James Bulger. Butler-Sloss P stated:

80. I am satisfied that, taking into account the effect of the convention on our law, the law of confidence can extend to cover the injunctions sought in this case and, therefore, the restrictions proposed are in accordance with the law. There is a well-established cause of action in the tort of breach of confidence in respect of which injunctions may be granted. The common law continues to evolve, as it has done for centuries, and it is being given considerable impetus to do so by the implementation of the convention into our domestic law. I am encouraged in that view by the observations of Brooke LJ in *Douglas v Hello! Ltd* [2001] IP & T 391 at 405–406 (para. 61):

'It is well known that this court in *Kaye v Robertson* [1991] FSR 62 said in uncompromising terms that there was no tort of privacy known to English law. In contrast, both academic commentary and extra-judicial commentary by judges over the last ten years have suggested from time to time that a development of the present frontiers of a breach of confidence action could fill the gap in English law which is filled by privacy law in other developed countries. This commentary was given a boost recently by the decision of the European Commission on Human Rights in *Earl Spencer v UK* (1998) 25 EHRR CD 105, and by the coming into force of the Human Rights Act 1998.'

Keene LJ said:

'…breach of confidence is a developing area of the law, the boundaries of which are not immutable but may change to reflect changes in society, technology and business practice.' (See [2001] IP & T 391 at 433 (para. 165).)

81. The duty of confidence may arise in equity independently of a transaction or relationship between parties. In this case it would be a duty placed upon the media. A duty of confidence does already arise when confidential information comes to the knowledge of the media, in circumstances in which the media have notice of its confidentiality. An example is the medical reports of a private individual which are recognised as being confidential. Indeed it is so well known that medical reports are confidential that Mr. Desmond Browne submitted that it was not necessary to protect that information by an injunction. It is also recognised that it is just in all the circumstances that information known to be confidential should not be disclosed to others, in this case by publication in the press (see Lord Goff in *A-G v Guardian Newspapers (No 2)*). The issue is whether the information leading to disclosure of the claimants' identity and location comes within the confidentiality brackets. In answering that crucial question, I can properly rely upon the European case law and the duty on the court, where necessary, to take appropriate steps to safeguard the physical safety of the claimants, including the adoption of measures even in the sphere of relations of individuals and/or private organisations between themselves. Under the umbrella of confidentiality there will be information which may require a special quality of protection. In the present case the reason for

---

[64] At para. 126. [65] [2001] 1 All ER 908.

advancing that special quality is that, if the information was published, the publication would be likely to lead to grave and possibly fatal consequences. In my judgment, the court does have the jurisdiction, in exceptional cases, to extend the protection of confidentiality of information, even to impose restrictions on the press, where not to do so would be likely to lead to serious physical injury, or to the death, of the person seeking that confidentiality, and there is no other way to protect the applicants other than by seeking relief from the court....

This appeared to recognise that the nature of the information itself may be enough to import the obligation of confidence, potentially radically developing the second limb of the confidence requirements. However, that this particular information would place in jeopardy the most basic rights of those seeking the injunction was a determining factor. Nevertheless, it was arguable that the type of information itself might now be sufficient to satisfy both the first and second limbs of the *Coco* test and develop the law well beyond its traditional confines of confidentiality. The House of Lords addressed these issues in *Campbell* below.

6. *The need for detriment.* The 'detriment' part of the third of Megarry J's three requirements in the *Coco* case had been doubted by some and given a very modest meaning by others.[66] In *A-G v Guardian Newspapers Ltd (No. 2),* Lord Keith took the view that 'it is in the public interest that confidences should be respected', so that there was no need for the plaintiff to show 'specific detriment to himself'. The requirement was explained and applied by Rose J in *X v Y,*[67] as follows:

In my judgment detriment *in the use of* the information is not a necessary precondition to injunctive relief. Although in *Seager v Copydex Ltd* the Court of Appeal held, by reference to the facts of that case, that the confidential information could not be used as a springboard for activities detrimental to the plaintiff, I do not understand any member of the court to have been saying that detrimental use is always necessary. I respectfully agree with Megarry V-C that an injunction may be appropriate for breach of confidence where the plaintiff may not suffer from the use of the information and that is borne out by more recent observations in the Court of Appeal and House of Lords...(in particular in *Lion Laboratiries Ltd v Evans* [1984] 2 All ER 417, [1985] QB 526, *Schering Chemicals Ltd v Falkman Ltd* [1981] 2 All ER 321, [1982] QB 1 and *British Steel Corp v Granada Television Ltd* [1981] 1 All ER 417, [1981] AC 1096), which contain no reference to the necessity for detriment in use and, indeed, point away from any such principle. In the present case, detriment occurred to the plaintiffs because patients' records were leaked to the press in breach of contract and breach of confidence, with the consequences, even without publication, to the plaintiffs and the patients listed by counsel for the plaintiffs. If use were made of that information in such a way as to demonstrate to the public (by identifying the hospital) the source of the leak, the plaintiffs would suffer further detriment. But use of the information (as the defendants now seek) in a way which identifies neither the hospital nor the patients does not mean that the plaintiffs have suffered no detriment. Significant damage, about which the plaintiffs are entitled to complain, has already been done. This is also the answer to the additional submission of counsel for the first defendant that, though there was a breach of confidence in obtaining the information there is, on the evidence, none in publishing it, if the doctors are not identified. In my judgment it is, in the present case, the initial disclosure and its immediate consequences, not subsequent publication, which found the plaintiffs' claim in breach of contract and breach of confidence.

---

[66] As noted by Simon Brown LJ in *R v Department of Health, ex p Source Informatics Ltd* [2000] 1 All ER 786 at 790, CA, on 'the very next page of his judgment' in the *Coco* case, 'Megarry J expressly kept open the possibility that "detriment" was not, after all, required'.

[67] [1988] 2 All ER 648.

7. The developments of the requirements for an action in confidence were radical and brought about what some argued was a *de facto* tort of privacy. That was rejected by the House of Lords in *Wainwright* (above) but the protection for personal information was confirmed and clarified in the following case.

- **Campbell v Mirror Group Newspapers** [2004] UKHL 22, [2004] 2 AC 457, [2004] 2 WLR 1232, House of Lords

Naomi Campbell, a well-known fashion model, took action for breach of confidence against the *Daily Mirror* in relation to a story and accompanying photographs contradicting the model's claims that she was not a drug addict. The article sought to contradict her previous assertions by discussing her visits to Narcotics Anonymous and showing photographs of her leaving NA meetings. At trial the judge found that the newspaper was entitled to put the record straight regarding Campbell's previous statements but that details and photographs regarding her visits to NA were not necessary in order to do this. She was awarded damages. The Court of Appeal similarly held that the newspaper was entitled to put the record straight but they went further in stating that the details of the visits to NA and the photographs were a legitimate part of the package in putting the record straight. Once it was determined that the story was in the public interest then newspapers should be given a degree of latitude as to how they formulate their report. Campbell appealed to the House of Lords, who, by a majority of 3 to 2 restored the order of the trial judge.

Lord Nicholls:

12. The present case concerns one aspect of invasion of privacy: wrongful disclosure of private information. The case involves the familiar competition between freedom of expression and respect for an individual's privacy. Both are vitally important rights. Neither has precedence over the other. The importance of freedom of expression has been stressed often and eloquently, the importance of privacy less so. But it, too, lies at the heart of liberty in a modern state. A proper degree of privacy is essential for the well-being and development of an individual. And restraints imposed on government to pry into the lives of the citizen go to the essence of a democratic state: see La Forest J in *R v Dymont* [1988] 2 SCR 417, 426.

13. The common law or, more precisely, courts of equity have long afforded protection to the wrongful use of private information by means of the cause of action which became known as breach of confidence. A breach of confidence was restrained as a form of unconscionable conduct, akin to a breach of trust. Today this nomenclature is misleading. The breach of confidence label harks back to the time when the cause of action was based on improper use of information disclosed by one person to another in confidence. To attract protection the information had to be of a confidential nature. But the gist of the cause of action was that information of this character had been disclosed by one person to another in circumstances 'importing an obligation of confidence' even though no contract of non-disclosure existed: see the classic exposition by Megarry J in *Coco v A N Clark (Engineers) Ltd* [1969] RPC 41, 47–48. The confidence referred to in the phrase 'breach of confidence' was the confidence arising out of a confidential relationship.

14. This cause of action has now firmly shaken off the limiting constraint of the need for an initial confidential relationship. In doing so it has changed its nature. In this country this development was recognised clearly in the judgment of Lord Goff of Chieveley in *Attorney-General v Guardian Newspapers Ltd (No 2)* [1990] 1 AC 109, 281. Now the law imposes a 'duty of confidence' whenever a person receives information he knows or ought to know is fairly and reasonably to be regarded as confidential. Even this formulation is awkward. The continuing use of the phrase 'duty of confidence' and the description of the information as 'confidential' is not altogether comfortable. Information about an individual's private life would not, in ordinary usage, be called 'confidential'. The more natural description today is that such information is private. The essence of the tort is better encapsulated now as misuse of private information.

15. In the case of individuals this tort, however labelled, affords respect for one aspect of an individual's privacy. That is the value underlying this cause of action. An individual's privacy can be invaded in ways not involving publication of information. Strip-searches are an example. The extent to which the common law as developed thus far in this country protects other forms of invasion of privacy is not a matter arising in the present case. It does not arise because, although pleaded more widely, Miss Campbell's common law claim was throughout presented in court exclusively on the basis of breach of confidence, that is, the wrongful *publication* by the 'Mirror' of private *information*.

16. The European Convention on Human Rights, and the Strasbourg jurisprudence, have undoubtedly had a significant influence in this area of the common law for some years. The provisions of article 8, concerning respect for private and family life, and article 10, concerning freedom of expression, and the interaction of these two articles, have prompted the courts of this country to identify more clearly the different factors involved in cases where one or other of these two interests is present. Where both are present the courts are increasingly explicit in evaluating the competing considerations involved. When identifying and evaluating these factors the courts, including your Lordships' House, have tested the common law against the values encapsulated in these two articles. The development of the common law has been in harmony with these articles of the Convention: see, for instance, *Reynolds v Times Newspapers Ltd* [2001] 2 AC 127, 203–204.

17. The time has come to recognise that the values enshrined in articles 8 and 10 are now part of the cause of action for breach of confidence. As Lord Woolf CJ has said, the courts have been able to achieve this result by absorbing the rights protected by articles 8 and 10 into this cause of action: *A v B plc* [2003] QB 195, 202, para 4. Further, it should now be recognised that for this purpose these values are of general application. The values embodied in articles 8 and 10 are as much applicable in disputes between individuals or between an individual and a non-governmental body such as a newspaper as they are in disputes between individuals and a public authority.

21. Accordingly, in deciding what was the ambit of an individual's 'private life' in particular circumstances courts need to be on guard against using as a touchstone a test which brings into account considerations which should more properly be considered at the later stage of proportionality. Essentially the touchstone of private life is whether in respect of the disclosed facts the person in question had a reasonable expectation of privacy.

22. Different forms of words, usually to much the same effect, have been suggested from time to time. The second Restatement of Torts in the United States (1977), article 652D, p 394, uses the formulation of disclosure of matter which 'would be highly offensive to a reasonable person'. In *Australian Broadcasting Corporation v Lenah Game Meats Pty Ltd* (2001) 185 ALR 1, 13, para 42, Gleeson CJ used words, widely quoted, having a similar meaning. This particular formulation should be used with care, for two reasons. First, the 'highly offensive' phrase is suggestive of a stricter test of private information than a reasonable expectation of privacy. Second, the 'highly offensive' formulation can all too easily bring into account, when deciding whether the disclosed information was private, considerations which go more properly to issues of proportionality; for instance, the degree of intrusion into private life, and the extent to which publication was a matter of proper public concern. This could be a recipe for confusion.

23. I turn to the present case and consider first whether the information whose disclosure is in dispute was private. Mr Caldecott QC placed the information published by the newspaper into five categories: (1) the fact of Miss Campbell's drug addiction; (2) the fact that she was receiving treatment; (3) the fact that she was receiving treatment at Narcotics Anonymous; (4) the details of the treatment—how long she had been attending meetings, how often she went, how she was treated within the sessions themselves, the extent of her commitment, and the nature of her entrance on the specific occasion; and (5) the visual portrayal of her leaving a specific meeting with other addicts.

24. It was common ground between the parties that in the ordinary course the information in all five categories would attract the protection of article 8. But Mr Caldecott recognised that, as he put it,

Miss Campbell's 'public lies' precluded her from claiming protection for categories (1) and (2). When talking to the media Miss Campbell went out of her way to say that, unlike many fashion models, she did not take drugs. By repeatedly making these assertions in public Miss Campbell could no longer have a reasonable expectation that this aspect of her life should be private. Public disclosure that, contrary to her assertions, she did in fact take drugs and had a serious drug problem for which she was being treated was not disclosure of private information. As the Court of Appeal noted, where a public figure chooses to present a false image and make untrue pronouncements about his or her life, the press will normally be entitled to put the record straight: [2003] QB 633, 658. Thus the area of dispute at the trial concerned the other three categories of information.

25. Of these three categories I shall consider first the information in categories (3) and (4), concerning Miss Campbell's attendance at Narcotics Anonymous meetings. In this regard it is important to note this is a highly unusual case. On any view of the matter, this information related closely to the fact, which admittedly could be published, that Miss Campbell was receiving treatment for drug addiction. Thus when considering whether Miss Campbell had a reasonable expectation of privacy in respect of information relating to her attendance at Narcotics Anonymous meetings the relevant question can be framed along the following lines: Miss Campbell having put her addiction and treatment into the public domain, did the further information relating to her attendance at Narcotics Anonymous meetings retain its character of private information sufficiently to engage the protection afforded by article 8?

26. I doubt whether it did. Treatment by attendance at Narcotics Anonymous meetings is a form of therapy for drug addiction which is well known, widely used and much respected. Disclosure that Miss Campbell had opted for this form of treatment was not a disclosure of any more significance than saying that a person who has fractured a limb has his limb in plaster or that a person suffering from cancer is undergoing a course of chemotherapy. Given the extent of the information, otherwise of a highly private character, which admittedly could properly be disclosed, the additional information was of such an unremarkable and consequential nature that to divide the one from the other would be to apply altogether too fine a toothcomb. Human rights are concerned with substance, not with such fine distinctions.

27. For the same reason I doubt whether the brief details of how long Miss Campbell had been undergoing treatment, and how often she attended meetings, stand differently. The brief reference to the way she was treated at the meetings did no more than spell out and apply to Miss Campbell common knowledge of how Narcotics Anonymous meetings are conducted.

28. But I would not wish to found my conclusion solely on this point. I prefer to proceed to the next stage and consider how the tension between privacy and freedom of expression should be resolved in this case, on the assumption that the information regarding Miss Campbell's attendance at Narcotics Anonymous meetings retained its private character. At this stage I consider Miss Campbell's claim must fail. I can state my reason very shortly. On the one hand, publication of this information in the unusual circumstances of this case represents, at most, an intrusion into Miss Campbell's private life to a comparatively minor degree. On the other hand, non-publication of this information would have robbed a legitimate and sympathetic newspaper story of attendant detail which added colour and conviction. This information was published in order to demonstrate Miss Campbell's commitment to tackling her drug problem. The balance ought not to be held at a point which would preclude, in this case, a degree of journalistic latitude in respect of information published for this purpose.

29. The need to be free to disseminate information regarding Miss Campbell's drug addiction is of a lower order than the need for freedom to disseminate information on some other subjects such as political information. The degree of latitude reasonably to be accorded to journalists is correspondingly reduced, but it is not excluded altogether.

30. There remains category (5): the photographs taken covertly of Miss Campbell in the road outside the building she was attending for a meeting of Narcotics Anonymous. I say at once that I wholly understand why Miss Campbell felt she was being hounded by the 'Mirror'. I understand also that this could

be deeply distressing, even damaging, to a person whose health was still fragile. But this is not the subject of complaint. Miss Campbell, expressly, makes no complaint about the taking of the photographs. She does not assert that the taking of the photographs was itself an invasion of privacy which attracts a legal remedy. The complaint regarding the photographs is of precisely the same character as the nature of the complaints regarding the text of the articles: the information conveyed by the photographs was private information. Thus the fact that the photographs were taken surreptitiously adds nothing to the only complaint being made.

31. In general photographs of people contain more information than textual description. That is why they are more vivid. That is why they are worth a thousand words. But the pictorial information in the photographs illustrating the offending article of 1 February 2001 added nothing of an essentially private nature. They showed nothing untoward. They conveyed no private information beyond that discussed in the article.

32. For these reasons and those given by my noble and learned friend Lord Hoffmann, I agree with the Court of Appeal that Miss Campbell's claim fails. It is not necessary for me to pursue the claim based on the Data Protection Act 1998. The parties were agreed that this claim stands or falls with the outcome of the main claim.

34. That Miss Campbell should suffer real distress under all these heads is wholly understandable. But in respect of none of these causes of distress does she have reason for complaint against the newspaper for misuse of private information. Against this background I find it difficult to envisage Miss Campbell suffered any significant additional distress based on public disclosure that her chosen form of treatment was attendance at Narcotics Anonymous meetings.

Lord Hoffmann:

36. The House is divided as to the outcome of this appeal, but the difference of opinion relates to a very narrow point which arises on the unusual facts of this case. The facts are unusual because the plaintiff is a public figure who had made very public false statements about a matter in respect of which even a public figure would ordinarily be entitled to privacy, namely her use of drugs. It was these falsehoods which, as was conceded, made it justifiable, for a newspaper to report the fact that she was addicted. The division of opinion is whether in doing so the newspaper went too far in publishing associated facts about her private life. But the importance of this case lies in the statements of general principle on the way in which the law should strike a balance between the right to privacy and the right to freedom of expression, on which the House is unanimous.

50. What human rights law has done is to identify private information as something worth protecting as an aspect of human autonomy and dignity. And this recognition has raised inescapably the question of why it should be worth protecting against the state but not against a private person. There may of course be justifications for the publication of private information by private persons which would not be available to the state—I have particularly in mind the position of the media, to which I shall return in a moment—but I can see no logical ground for saying that a person should have less protection against a private individual than he would have against the state for the publication of personal information for which there is no justification. Nor, it appears, have any of the other judges who have considered the matter.

51. The result of these developments has been a shift in the centre of gravity of the action for breach of confidence when it is used as a remedy for the unjustified publication of personal information. It recognises that the incremental changes to which I have referred do not merely extend the duties arising traditionally from a relationship of trust and confidence to a wider range of people. As Sedley LJ observed in a perceptive passage in his judgment in *Douglas v Hello! Ltd* [2001] QB 967, 1001, the new approach takes a different view of the underlying value which the law protects. Instead of the cause of action being based upon the duty of good faith applicable to confidential personal information and trade secrets alike, it focuses upon the protection of human autonomy and dignity—the right to control the dissemination of information about one's private life and the right to the esteem and respect of other people.

52. These changes have implications for the future development of the law. They must influence the approach of the courts to the kind of information which is regarded as entitled to protection, the extent and form of publication which attracts a remedy and the circumstances in which publication can be justified.

53. In this case, however, it is unnecessary to consider these implications because the cause of action fits squarely within both the old and the new law.

58. The reason why Mr Caldecott concedes that the *Mirror* was entitled to publish the fact of her drug dependency and the fact that she was seeking treatment is that she had specifically given publicity to the very question of whether she took drugs and had falsely said that she did not. I accept that this creates a sufficient public interest in the correction of the impression she had previously given.

59. The question is then whether the *Mirror* should have confined itself to these bare facts or whether it was entitled to reveal more of the circumstantial detail and print the photographs. If one applies the test of necessity or proportionality which I have suggested, this is a matter on which different people may have different views. That appears clearly enough from the judgments which have been delivered in this case. But judges are not newspaper editors. It may have been possible for the *Mirror* to satisfy the public interest in publication with a story which contained less detail and omitted the photographs. But the *Mirror* said that they wanted to show themselves sympathetic to Ms Campbell's efforts to overcome her dependency. For this purpose, some details about her frequency of attendance at NA meetings were needed. I agree with the observation of the Court of Appeal, at p 660, para 52, that it is harsh to criticise the editor for "painting a somewhat fuller picture in order to show her in a sympathetic light".

60. To someone who started with the (legitimately communicated) knowledge that she was seeking treatment, there was nothing special about the additional details. The fact that she was going to NA would come as no surprise; there are, according to its web-site, 31,000 NA meetings a week in 100 different countries. The anonymity of participants and the general nature of the therapy is common knowledge. The details of her frequency of attendance (which were in fact inaccurate) could not be said to be discreditable or embarrassing. The relatively anodyne nature of the additional details is in my opinion important and distinguishes this case from cases in which (for example) there is a public interest in the disclosure of the existence of a sexual relationship (say, between a politician and someone whom she has appointed to public office) but the addition of salacious details or intimate photographs is disproportionate and unacceptable. The latter, even if accompanying a legitimate disclosure of the sexual relationship, would be too intrusive and demeaning.

61. That brings me to what seems to be the only point of principle which arises in this case. Where the main substance of the story is conceded to have been justified, should the newspaper be held liable whenever the judge considers that it was not necessary to have published some of the personal information? Or should the newspaper be allowed some margin of choice in the way it chooses to present the story?

62. In my opinion, it would be inconsistent with the approach which has been taken by the courts in a number of recent landmark cases for a newspaper to be held strictly liable for exceeding what a judge considers to have been necessary. The practical exigencies of journalism demand that some latitude must be given. Editorial decisions have to be made quickly and with less information than is available to a court which afterwards reviews the matter at leisure. And if any margin is to be allowed, it seems to me strange to hold the *Mirror* liable in damages for a decision which three experienced judges in the Court of Appeal have held to be perfectly justified.

65. In my opinion the Court of Appeal was right in the present case to say [2003] QB 633, 662, para 64:

'Provided that publication of particular confidential information is justifiable in the public interest, the journalist must be given reasonable latitude as to the manner in which that information is conveyed to the public or his article 10 right to freedom of expression will be unnecessarily inhibited.'

71. As for the Court of Appeal's own approach, I do not understand the submission that it erred in saying, at p 659, para 48, that it did not equate 'the information that Miss Campbell was receiving therapy from

[NA]…with disclosure of clinical details of medical treatment'. I do not imagine that the Court of Appeal was unaware of the nature of the therapy provided by NA or was attempting some obscure metaphysical distinction. It was saying only that the support provided by NA for large numbers of drug addicts is so well known that it cannot be compared with the details of individual clinical treatment. This seems to me no more than common sense.

72. That leaves the question of the photographs. In my opinion a photograph is in principle information no different from any other information. It may be a more vivid form of information than the written word ('a picture is worth a thousand words'). That has to be taken into account in deciding whether its publication infringes the right to privacy of personal information. The publication of a photograph cannot necessarily be justified by saying that one would be entitled to publish a verbal description of the scene: see *Douglas v Hello! Ltd* [2001] QB 967. But the principles by which one decides whether or not the publication of a photograph is an unjustified invasion of the privacy of personal information are in my opinion the same as those which I have already discussed.

73. In the present case, the pictures were taken without Ms Campbell's consent. That in my opinion is not enough to amount to a wrongful invasion of privacy. The famous and even the not so famous who go out in public must accept that they may be photographed without their consent, just as they may be observed by others without their consent. As Gleeson CJ said in *Australian Broadcasting Corporation v Lenah Game Meats Pty Ltd* (2001) 185 ALR 1, 13, para 41:

'Part of the price we pay for living in an organised society is that we are exposed to observation in a variety of ways by other people.'

74. But the fact that we cannot avoid being photographed does not mean that anyone who takes or obtains such photographs can publish them to the world at large. In the recent case of *Peck v United Kingdom* (2003) 36 EHRR 41 Mr Peck was filmed on a public street in an embarrassing moment by a CCTV camera. Subsequently, the film was broadcast several times on the television. The Strasbourg court said (at p. 739) that this was an invasion of his privacy contrary to article 8:

'the relevant moment was viewed to an extent which far exceeded any exposure to a passer-by or to security observation and to a degree surpassing that which the applicant could possibly have foreseen when he walked in Brentwood on August 20, 1995.'

75. In my opinion, therefore, the widespread publication of a photograph of someone which reveals him to be in a situation of humiliation or severe embarrassment, even if taken in a public place, may be an infringement of the privacy of his personal information. Likewise, the publication of a photograph taken by intrusion into a private place (for example, by a long distance lens) may in itself by such an infringement, even if there is nothing embarrassing about the picture itself: *Hellewell v Chief Constable of Derbyshire* [1985] 1 WLR 804, 807. As Lord Mustill said in *R v Broadcasting Standards Commission, Ex p BBC* [2001] QB 885, 900, 'An infringement of privacy is an affront to the personality, which is damaged both by the violation and by the demonstration that the personal space is not inviolate.'

76. In the present case, however, there was nothing embarrassing about the picture, which showed Ms Campbell neatly dressed and smiling among a number of other people. Nor did the taking of the picture involve an intrusion into private space.

I would therefore dismiss the appeal.

Lord Hope of Craighead:
92. The underlying question in all cases where it is alleged that there has been a breach of the duty of confidence is whether the information that was disclosed was private and not public. There must be some interest of a private nature that the claimant wishes to protect: *A v B Ltd* [2003] QB 195, 206, para 11 (vii). In some cases, as the Court of Appeal said in that case, the answer to the question whether the information is public or private will be obvious. Where it is not, the broad test is whether disclosure of the information

about the individual ('A') would give substantial offence to A, assuming that A was placed in similar circumstances and was a person of ordinary sensibilities.

93. The trial judge applied the test which was suggested by Gleeson CJ in *Australian Broadcasting Corporation v Lenah Game Meats Pty Ltd* (2001) 185 ALR 1.... At p 13, para 41 he observed that there was a large area in between what was necessarily public and what was necessarily private:

> 'An activity is not private simply because it is not done in public. It does not suffice to make an act private that, because it occurs on private property, it has such measure of protection from the public gaze as the characteristics of the property, the nature of the activity, the locality, and the disposition of the property owner combine to afford. Certain kinds of information about a person, such as information relating to health, personal relationships, or finances, may be easy to identify as private, as may certain kinds of activity which a reasonable person, applying contemporary standards of morals and behaviour, would understand to be meant to be unobserved. The requirement that disclosure or observation of information or conduct would be highly offensive to a reasonable person of ordinary sensibilities is in many circumstances a useful practical test of what is private.'

Applying to the facts of the case the test which he had described in the last sentence of this paragraph, he said in para 43 that the problem for the respondent was that the activities secretly observed and filmed were not relevantly private.

94. The test which Gleeson CJ has identified is useful in cases where there is room for doubt, especially where the information relates to an activity or course of conduct such as the slaughtering methods that were in issue in that case. But it is important not to lose sight of the remarks which preceded it. The test is not needed where the information can easily be identified as private.

96. If the information is obviously private, the situation will be one where the person to whom it relates can reasonably expect his privacy to be respected. So there is normally no need to go on and ask whether it would be highly offensive for it to be published. The trial judge nevertheless asked himself, as a check, whether the information that was disclosed about Miss Campbell's attendance at these meetings satisfied Gleeson CJ's test of confidentiality. His conclusion, echoing the words of Gleeson CJ, was that disclosure that her therapy for drug addiction was by regular attendance at meetings of Narcotics Anonymous would be highly offensive to a reasonable person of ordinary sensibilities. The Court of Appeal disagreed with this assessment.

99. The approach which the Court of Appeal took to this issue seems to me, with great respect, to be quite unreal. I do not think that they had a sound basis for differing from the conclusion reached by the trial judge as to whether the information was private. They were also in error, in my opinion. when they were asking themselves whether the disclosure would have offended the reasonable man of ordinary susceptibilities. The mind that they examined was the mind of the reader: para 54. This is wrong. It greatly reduces the level of protection that is afforded to the right of privacy. The mind that has to be examined is that, not of the reader in general, but of the person who is affected by the publicity. The question is what a reasonable person of ordinary sensibilities would feel if she was placed in the same position as the claimant and faced with the same publicity.

112. There is no doubt that the presentation of the material that it was legitimate to convey to the public in this case without breaching the duty of confidence was a matter for the journalists. The choice of language used to convey information and ideas, and decisions as to whether or not to accompany the printed word by the use of photographs, are pre-eminently editorial matters with which the court will not interfere. The respondents are also entitled to claim that they should be accorded a reasonable margin of appreciation in taking decisions as to what details needed to be included in the article to give it credibility. This is an essential part of the journalistic exercise.

113. But decisions about the publication of material that is private to the individual raise issues that are not simply about presentation and editing. Any interference with the public interest in disclosure has to be balanced against the interference with the right of the individual to respect for their private life.

The decisions that are then taken are open to review by the court. The tests which the court must apply are the familiar ones. They are whether publication of the material pursues a legitimate aim and whether the benefits that will be achieved by its publication are proportionate to the harm that may be done by the interference with the right to privacy. The jurisprudence of the European Court of Human Rights explains how these principles are to be understood and applied in the context of the facts of each case. Any restriction of the right to freedom of expression must be subjected to very close scrutiny. But so too must any restriction of the right to respect for private life. Neither article 8 nor article 10 has any pre-eminence over the other in the conduct of this exercise.

114. In the present case it is convenient to begin by looking at the matter from the standpoint of the respondents' assertion of the article 10 right and the court's duty as a public authority under section 6(1) of the Human Rights Act 1998, which section 12(4) reinforces, not to act in a way which is incompatible with that Convention right.

115. The first question is whether the objective of the restriction on the article 10 right—the protection of Miss Campbell's right under article 8 to respect for her private life—is sufficiently important to justify limiting the fundamental right to freedom of expression which the press assert on behalf of the public. It follows from my conclusion that the details of Miss Campbell's treatment were private that I would answer this question in the affirmative. The second question is whether the means chosen to limit the article 10 right are rational, fair and not arbitrary and impair the right as minimally as is reasonably possible. It is not enough to assert that it would be reasonable to exclude these details from the article. A close examination of the factual justification for the restriction on the freedom of expression is needed if the fundamental right enshrined in article 10 is to remain practical and effective. The restrictions which the court imposes on the article 10 right must be rational, fair and not arbitrary, and they must impair the right no more than is necessary.

116. In my opinion the factors that need to be weighed are, on the one hand, the duty that was recognised in *Jersild v Denmark* (1994) 19 EHRR 1, para 31 to impart information and ideas of public interest which the public has a right to receive, and the need that was recognised in *Fressoz v France* (2001) 31 EHRR 28, para 54 for the court to leave it to journalists to decide what material needs to be reproduced to ensure credibility; and, on the other hand, the degree of privacy to which Miss Campbell was entitled under the law of confidence as to the details of her therapy. Account should therefore be taken of the respondents' wish to put forward a story that was credible and to present Miss Campbell in a way that commended her for her efforts to overcome her addiction.

117. But it should also be recognised that the right of the public to receive information about the details of her treatment was of a much lower order than the undoubted right to know that she was misleading the public when she said that she did not take drugs. In *Dudgeon v United Kingdom* (1981) 4 EHRR 149, para 52 the European Court said that the more intimate the aspects of private life which are being interfered with, the more serious must be the reasons for doing so before the interference can be legitimate. *Clayton and Tomlinson, The Law of Human Rights* (2000), para 15.162, point out that the court has distinguished three kinds of expression: political expression, artistic expression and commercial expression, and that it consistently attaches great importance to political expression and applies rather less rigorous principles to expression which is artistic and commercial.... But there were no political or democratic values at stake here, nor has any pressing social need been identified: contrast *Goodwin v United Kingdom* (1996) 22 EHRR 123, para 40.

118. As for the other side of the balance, Keene LJ said in *Douglas v Hello! Ltd* [2001] QB 967, para 168, that any consideration of article 8 rights must reflect the fact that there are different degrees of privacy. In the present context the potential for disclosure of the information to cause harm is an important factor to be taken into account in the assessment of the extent of the restriction that was needed to protect Miss Campbell's right to privacy.

119. Looking at the matter from Miss Campbell's point of view and the protection of her article 8 Convention right, publication of details of the treatment which she was undertaking to cure her addiction—that she was attending Narcotics Anonymous, for how long, how frequently and at what times of day she had been attending this therapy, the nature of it and extent of her commitment to the process and the publication of the covertly taken photographs (the third, fourth and fifth of the five elements contained in the article)—had the potential to cause harm to her, for the reasons which I have already given. So I would attach a good deal of weight to this factor.

120. As for the other side of the balance, a person's right to privacy may be limited by the public's interest in knowing about certain traits of her personality and certain aspects of her private life, as L'Heureux-Dub and Bastarache JJ in the Supreme Court of Canada recognised in *Aubry v Les Editions Vice-Versa Inc* [1998] 1 SCR 591, paras 57–58. But it is not enough to deprive Miss Campbell of her right to privacy that she is a celebrity and that her private life is newsworthy. A margin of appreciation must, of course, be given to the journalist. Weight must be given to this. But to treat these details merely as background was to undervalue the importance that was to be attached to the need, if Miss Campbell was to be protected, to keep these details private. And it is hard to see that there was any compelling need for the public to know the name of the organisation that she was attending for the therapy, or for the other details of it to be set out. The presentation of the article indicates that this was not fully appreciated when the decision was taken to publish these details. The decision to publish the photographs suggests that greater weight was being given to the wish to publish a story that would attract interest rather than to the wish to maintain its credibility.

121. Had it not been for the publication of the photographs, and looking to the text only, I would have been inclined to regard the balance between these rights as about even. Such is the effect of the margin of appreciation that must, in a doubtful case, be given to the journalist. In that situation the proper conclusion to draw would have been that it had not been shown that the restriction on the article 10 right for which Miss Campbell argues was justified on grounds of proportionality. But the text cannot be separated from the photographs. The words 'Therapy: Naomi outside meeting' underneath the photograph on the front page and the words 'Hugs: Naomi, dressed in jeans and baseball hat, arrives for a lunchtime group meeting this week' underneath the photograph on page 13 were designed to link that what might otherwise have been anonymous and uninformative pictures with the main text. The reader would undoubtedly make that link, and so too would the reasonable person of ordinary sensibilities. The reasonable person of ordinary sensibilities would also regard publication of the covertly taken photographs, and the fact that they were linked with the text in this way, as adding greatly overall to the intrusion which the article as a whole made into her private life.

122. The photographs were taken of Miss Campbell while she was in a public place, as she was in the street outside the premises where she had been receiving therapy. The taking of photographs in a public street must, as Randerson J said in *Hosking v Runting* [2003] 3 NZLR 385, 415, para 138, be taken to be one of the ordinary incidents of living in a free community. The real issue is whether publicising the content of the photographs would be offensive: Gault and Blanchard JJ in the Court of Appeal (25 March 2004), para 165. A person who just happens to be in the street when the photograph was taken and appears in it only incidentally cannot as a general rule object to the publication of the photograph, for the reasons given by L'Heureux-Dub and Bastarache JJ in *Aubry v Editions Vice-Versa Inc* [1998] 1 SCR 591, para 59. But the situation is different if the public nature of the place where a photograph is taken was simply used as background for one or more persons who constitute the true subject of the photograph. The question then arises, balancing the rights at issue, where the public's right to information can justify dissemination of a photograph taken without authorisation: *Aubry*, para 61. The European Court has recognised that a person who walks down a public street will inevitably be visible to any member of the public who is also present and, in the same way, to a security guard viewing the scene through closed

circuit television: *PG v JH v United Kingdom*, App No. 44787/98, para 57. But, as the court pointed out in the same paragraph, private life considerations may arise once any systematic or permanent record comes into existence of such material from the public domain. In *Peck v United Kingdom* [2003] 36 EHRR 719, para 62 the court held that the release and publication of CCTV forage which showed the applicant in the process of attempting to commit suicide resulted in the moment being viewed to an extent that far exceeded any exposure to a passer-by or to security observation that he could have foreseen when he was in that street.

123. The same process of reasoning that led to the findings in *Peck* that the article 8 right had been violated and by the majority in *Aubry* that there had been an infringement of the claimant's right to respect for her private life can be applied here. Miss Campbell could not have complained if the photographs had been taken to show the scene in the street by a passer-by and later published simply as street scenes. But these were not just pictures of a street scene where she happened to be when the photographs were taken. They were taken deliberately, in secret and with a view to their publication in conjunction with the article. The zoom lens was directed at the doorway of the place where the meeting had been taking place. The faces of others in the doorway were pixilated so as not to reveal their identity. Hers was not, the photographs were published and her privacy was invaded. The argument that the publication of the photograph added credibility to the story has little weight. The photograph was not self-explanatory. Neither the place nor the person were instantly recognisable. The reader only had the editor's word as to the truth of these details.

125. Despite the weight that must be given to the right to freedom of expression that the press needs if it is to play its role effectively, I would hold that there was here an infringement of Miss Campbell's right to privacy that cannot be justified. In my opinion publication of the third, fourth and fifth elements in the article (see para 88) was an invasion of that right for which she is entitled to damages. I would allow the appeal and restore the orders that were made by the trial judge.

Baroness Hale of Richmond:

126. This case raises some big questions. How is the balance to be struck between everyone's right to respect for their private and family life under Article 8 of the European Convention on Human Rights and everyone's right to freedom of expression, including the freedom to receive and impart information and ideas under Article 10? How do those rights come into play in a dispute between two private persons? But the parties are largely agreed about the answers to these. They disagree about where that balance is to be struck in the individual case. In particular, how far is a newspaper able to go in publishing what would otherwise be confidential information about a celebrity in order to set the record straight? And does it matter that the article was illustrated by a covertly taken photograph?

132. Neither party to this appeal has challenged the basic principles which have emerged from the Court of Appeal in the wake of the Human Rights Act 1998. The 1998 Act does not create any new cause of action between private persons. But if there is a relevant cause of action applicable, the court as a public authority must act compatibly with both parties' Convention rights. In a case such as this, the relevant vehicle will usually be the action for breach of confidence, as Lord Woolf CJ held in *A v B plc* [2002] EWCA Civ 337, [2003] QB 195, 202, para 4:

'[Articles 8 and 10] have provided new parameters within which the court will decide, in an action for breach of confidence, whether a person is entitled to have his privacy protected by the court or whether the restriction of freedom of expression which such protection involves cannot be justified. The court's approach to the issues which the applications raise has been modified because, under section 6 of the 1998 Act, the court, as a public authority, is required not to "act in a way which is incompatible with a Convention right". The court is able to achieve this by absorbing the rights which articles 8 and 10 protect into the long-established action for breach of confidence. This involves giving a new strength and breadth to the action so that it accommodates the requirements of these articles.'

133. The action for breach of confidence is not the only relevant cause of action: the inherent jurisdiction of the High Court to protect the children for whom it is responsible is another example: see *In re S (a child) (identification: restrictions on publication)* [2003] EWCA Civ 963[2003] 3 WLR 1425. But the courts will not invent a new cause of action to cover types of activity which were not previously covered: see *Wainwright v Home Office* [2003] 3 WLR 1137.

134. The position we have reached is that the exercise of balancing article 8 and article 10 may begin when the person publishing the information knows or ought to know that there is a reasonable expectation that the information in question will be kept confidential.

137. It should be emphasised that the 'reasonable expectation of privacy' is a threshold test which brings the balancing exercise into play. It is not the end of the story. Once the information is identified as 'private' in this way, the court must balance the claimant's interest in keeping the information private against the countervailing interest of the recipient in publishing it. Very often, it can be expected that the countervailing rights of the recipient will prevail.

140. The application of the proportionality test is more straightforward when only one Convention right is in play: the question then is whether the private right claimed offers sufficient justification for the degree of interference with the fundamental right. It is much less straightforward when two Convention rights are in play, and the proportionality of interfering with one has to be balanced against the proportionality of restricting the other. As each is a fundamental right, there is evidently a 'pressing social need' to protect it. The Convention jurisprudence offers us little help with this. .. In the national court, the problem of balancing two rights of equal importance arises most acutely in the context of disputes between private persons.

141. Both parties accepted the basic approach of the Court of Appeal in *In re S* [2003] 3 WLR 1425, 1451–1452, at paras 54 to 60. This involves looking first at the comparative importance of the actual rights being claimed in the individual case; then at the justifications for interfering with or restricting each of those rights; and applying the proportionality test to each. The parties in this case differed about whether the trial judge or the Court of Appeal had done this, the appellant arguing that the Court of Appeal had assumed primacy for the Article 10 right while the respondent argued that the trial judge had assumed primacy for the Article 8 right.

145. It has always been accepted that information about a person's health and treatment for ill-health is both private and confidential. This stems not only from the confidentiality of the doctor-patient relationship but from the nature of the information itself.

146. The Court of Appeal in this case held that the information revealed here was not in the same category as clinical medical records. That may be so, in the sense that it was not the notes made by a doctor when consulted by a patient. But the information was of exactly the same kind as that which would be recorded by a doctor on those notes: the presenting problem was addiction to illegal drugs, the diagnosis was no doubt the same, and the prescription was therapy, including the self-help group therapy offered by regular attendance at Narcotics Anonymous.

147. I start, therefore, from the fact—indeed, it is common ground—that *all* of the information about Miss Campbell's addiction and attendance at NA which was revealed in the Daily Mirror article was both private and confidential, because it related to an important aspect of Miss Campbell's physical and mental health and the treatment she was receiving for it. It had also been received from an insider in breach of confidence. That simple fact has been obscured by the concession properly made on her behalf that the newspaper's countervailing freedom of expression did serve to justify the publication of some of this information. But the starting point must be that it was all private and its publication required specific justification.

148. What was the nature of the freedom of expression which was being asserted on the other side? There are undoubtedly different types of speech, just as there are different types of private information, some of which are more deserving of protection in a democratic society than others. Top of the list is

political speech. The free exchange of information and ideas on matters relevant to the organisation of the economic, social and political life of the country is crucial to any democracy. Without this, it can scarcely be called a democracy at all. This includes revealing information about public figures, especially those in elective office, which would otherwise be private but is relevant to their participation in public life. Intellectual and educational speech and expression are also important in a democracy, not least because they enable the development of individuals' potential to play a full part in society and in our democratic life. Artistic speech and expression is important for similar reasons, in fostering both individual originality and creativity and the free-thinking and dynamic society we so much value. No doubt there are other kinds of speech and expression for which similar claims can be made.

149. But it is difficult to make such claims on behalf of the publication with which we are concerned here. The political and social life of the community, and the intellectual, artistic or personal development of individuals, are not obviously assisted by pouring over the intimate details of a fashion model's private life. However, there is one way in which the article could be said to be educational. The editor had considered running a highly critical piece, adding the new information to the not inconsiderable list of Miss Campbell's faults and follies detailed in the article, emphasising the lies and hypocrisy it revealed. Instead he chose to run a sympathetic piece, still listing her faults and follies, but setting them in the context of her now-revealed addiction and her even more important efforts to overcome it. Newspaper and magazines often carry such pieces and they may well have a beneficial educational effect.

150. The crucial difference here is that such pieces are normally run with the co-operation of those involved. Private people are not identified without their consent. It is taken for granted that this is otherwise confidential information. The editor did offer Miss Campbell the opportunity of being involved with the story but this was refused. Her evidence suggests that she was concerned for the other people in the group. What entitled him to reveal this private information about her without her consent?

151. The answer which she herself accepts is that she had presented herself to the public as someone who was not involved in drugs. It would have been a very good thing if she were not. If other young women do see her as someone to be admired and emulated, then it is all to the good if she is not addicted to narcotic substances. It might be questioned why, if a role model has adopted a stance which all would agree is beneficial rather than detrimental to society, it is so important to reveal that she has feet of clay. But the possession and use of illegal drugs is a criminal offence and a matter of serious public concern. The press must be free to expose the truth and put the record straight.

152. That consideration justified the publication of the fact that, contrary to her previous statements, Miss Campbell had been involved with illegal drugs. It also justified publication of the fact that she was trying to do something about it by seeking treatment. It was not necessary for those purposes to publish any further information, especially if this might jeopardise the continued success of that treatment.

154. Publishing the photographs contributed both to the revelation and to the harm that it might do. By themselves, they are not objectionable. Unlike France and Quebec, in this country we do not recognise a right to one's own image: cf *Aubry v Editions Vice-Versa Inc* [1998] 1 SCR 591. We have not so far held that the mere fact of covert photography is sufficient to make the information contained in the photograph confidential. The activity photographed must be private. If this had been, and had been presented as, a picture of Naomi Campbell going about her business in a public street, there could have been no complaint. She makes a substantial part of her living out of being photographed looking stunning in designer clothing. Readers will obviously be interested to see how she looks if and when she pops out to the shops for a bottle of milk. There is nothing essentially private about that information nor can it be expected to damage her private life. It may not be a high order of freedom of speech but there is nothing to justify interfering with it. (This was the view of Randerson J in *Hosking v Runting* [2003] 3 NZLR 385, which concerned a similarly innocuous outing; see now the decision of the Court of Appeal, 25 March 2004.)

155. But here the accompanying text made it plain that these photographs were different. They showed her coming either to or from the NA meeting. They showed her in the company of others, some

of whom were undoubtedly part of the group. They showed the place where the meeting was taking place, which will have been entirely recognisable to anyone who knew the locality. A picture is 'worth a thousand words' because it adds to the impact of what the words convey; but it also adds to the information given in those words. If nothing else, it tells the reader what everyone looked like; in this case it also told the reader what the place looked like. In context, it also added to the potential harm, by making her think that she was being followed or betrayed, and deterring her from going back to the same place again.

156. There was no need to do this. The editor accepted that even without the photographs, it would have been a front page story.

157. The weight to be attached to these various considerations is a matter of fact and degree. Not every statement about a person's health will carry the badge of confidentiality or risk doing harm to that person's physical or moral integrity. The privacy interest in the fact that a public figure has a cold or a broken leg is unlikely to be strong enough to justify restricting the press's freedom to report it. What harm could it possibly do? Sometimes there will be other justifications for publishing, especially where the information is relevant to the capacity of a public figure to do the job. But that is not this case and in this case there was, as the judge found, a risk that publication would do harm. The risk of harm is what matters at this stage, rather than the proof that actual harm has occurred. People trying to recover from drug addiction need considerable dedication and commitment, along with constant reinforcement from those around them. That is why organisations like Narcotics Anonymous were set up and why they can do so much good. Blundering in when matters are acknowledged to be at a 'fragile' stage may do great harm.

160. I would therefore allow this appeal and restore the order of the judge.

Lord Carswell:

161. I have had the advantage of reading in draft the opinions of my noble and learned friends, Lord Hope of Craighead and Baroness Hale of Richmond, and I agree with them that the appeal should be allowed.

Appeal allowed.

NOTES

1. This important case reaffirms that whilst there is no overarching privacy tort (see *Wainwright* above)[68] the developed law of confidence can be used to provide a remedy against the unauthorised use of private information. Though the House was divided over the precise details of the case there was agreement that developments in breach of confidence made it applicable to this case. Their Lordships and Baroness Hale all agreed that there was the publication of private information but the disagreement pertained to the extent of what was justifiably published by the media. Following *Campbell* the action is no longer limited by the need to discover an initial confidential relationship, Lord Hoffmann recognising that the protection of confidences was not the key but the protection of individual dignity and autonomy. Lord Nicholls further recognised the inherent difficulties in continuing to use the lexicon of confidence and sought to rename the action as misuse of private information. This renaming has since found support in subsequent cases, for example, *McKennitt v Ash*[69] and *Douglas v Hello! (No. 3)*.[70]

2. Breach of confidence provided a relevant vehicle for the courts to develop the law. In an action between two private parties the court must act compatibly with both parties'

---

[68] The point was reiterated by Buxton LJ in *McKennitt v Ash* [2006] EWCA Civ 1714, at para. 8.

[69] Ibid., per Longmore LJ at para. 86.

[70] [2005] EWCA Civ 595, per Lord Phillips at para. 77.

rights, and thus an existing cause of action may be developed. However, the House of Lords reiterated that the HRA 1998 does not allow for the creation of a new cause of action between private parties. Interestingly, privacy is coming to be seen as being independent of breach of confidence.[71]

3. From the three-stage test developed in *Coco v Clark* 'new confidence' (or, more appropriately, the action for misuse of personal information) is triggered by the claimant identifying that he or she has a reasonable expectation of privacy in the relevant information. What amounts to a reasonable expectation will be, in many circumstances straightforward. For example, a claimant clearly has a reasonable expectation of privacy in medical records or a private diary. In more difficult cases the test espoused by Gleeson CJ in *Australian Broadcasting Corpn v Lenah Game Meats Pty Ltd* may be useful, specifically, whether disclosure or observation of information or conduct would be highly offensive to a reasonable person of ordinary sensibilities. However, this is subject to the comments made by their Lordships:

> Chief Justice [Gleeson] did not intend those last words to be the only test, particularly in respect of information which is obviously private, including information about health, personal relationships or finance. It is also apparent that he was referring to the sensibilities of a reasonable person placed in the situation of the subject of the disclosure rather than to its recipient.[72]

Is *highly* offensive too high a threshold? The most appropriate measure of what might amount to private information is to consider the jurisprudence of the Strasbourg Court in relation to Art. 8. In *Douglas (No. 3)* Lord Phillips stated:

> In considering the nature of those rights, account should be taken of the Strasbourg jurisprudence. In particular, when considering what information should be protected as private pursuant to article 8, it is right to have regard to the decisions of the European Court of Human Rights.[73]

Additionally, it should be noted that the interference with privacy must be more than trivial before privacy is engaged.[74]

4. Historically, considerable weight has been attached to the importance of free speech in the UK, certainly when compared to the scant regard afforded to privacy. However, *Campbell* is very clear in stating that restrictions on both rights must be given close scrutiny and neither is given pre-eminence over the other. Once the information has been identified as 'private' then the court must balance the claimant's interest in keeping the information private against the recipient's countervailing interest in publishing it. This involves a consideration of the relative importance of the rights being claimed followed by consideration of the justifications for interfering with those rights. The proportionality test which follows a restriction of Art. 8 or 10 must then be considered in relation to both rights at issue. This approach has been referred to as the 'parallel analysis'.

5. Though the media have expressed justifiable concern that developments in the realm of privacy might restrict the right to freedom of expression, issues of public interest in publication can, in appropriate circumstances, clearly outweigh a privacy claim when considered

---

[71] See *HRH Prince of Wales v Mirror Group Newspapers Limited* [2006] EWCA Civ 1776.
[72] Per Baroness Hale at para. 136.   [73] [2006] EWCA Civ 1776, para. 53.
[74] See, e.g., *M v Secretary of State for Work and Pensions* [2006] 2 AC 91 per Lord Walker of Gestingthorpe at 83.

in the balancing exercise. In *Campbell* the division of issues into five categories illustrated the nuanced approach that the courts can and will take to considering where the appropriate balance should be struck.

6. The form in which the information is captured is a relevant factor in the balancing exercise. For example, information marked as 'confidential' will clearly have added weight when one considers its 'privacy value'.[75] It is clear from *Campbell* that photographs can pose a particular problem. This has been further reinforced by the Strasbourg Court in both *Peck*[76] and *von Hannover*.[77] Photographs can present graphic and intimate details in a permanent form which simply cannot be described in words with the same effect. In *D v L*,[78] Waller LJ remarked:

A court may restrain the publication of an improperly obtained photograph even if the taker is free to describe the information which the photographer provides or even if the information revealed by the photograph is in the public domain. It is no answer to the claim to restrain the publication of an improperly obtained photograph that the information portrayed by the photograph is already available in the public domain.

In *Campbell* the photographs 'added to the potential harm, by making her think that she was being followed or betrayed, and deterring her from going back to the same place again'. In *Peck* the images were both embarrassing and distressing. On one view therefore, these incidents in public locations had a clear element of privacy about them—they were not simply ordinary daily activities. In *Campbell*, Baroness Hale explicitly rejects the notion that covert photography of itself engages with an individual's privacy (para. 154). However, in *von Hannover* the privacy claim did succeed in relation to images of everyday activities carried out in public. To date, UK courts under the normal rules of judicial precedent[79] are bound to follow the decision in *Campbell* but is there a difference between domestic and European approaches? This question has not as yet been tackled at the highest level but it would appear that consistency is being found through a concentration not solely upon the expectation of privacy but on 'informational autonomy'—the right of an individual to control the dissemination of personal information. This is a consistent thread through the cases above and also finds resonance in more recent *dicta*.

- **Murray v Express Newspapers plc** [2008] EWCA Civ 446, [2008] NLJR 706, (2008) Times, 12 May, [2008] All ER (D) 70, Court of Appeal

The claimant was the one-year-old son of a well-known author. The defendant covertly photographed the claimant being pushed in a buggy along a public street by his parents. The parents did not consent to the photograph, which subsequently appeared in a magazine. Proceedings were issued against the defendants seeking an injunction to restrain further publication of the photograph, and for damages or an account of profits for breach of confidence, the infringement his right to privacy under Art. 8, and the misuse of private information resulting from the taking, recording, holding and publication of the photograph. The trial judge stated, 'I start with a strong predisposition to the view that routine acts such as the visit to the shop or the ride on the bus should not attract any reasonable expectation of

---

[75] See *HRH Prince of Wales v Mirror Group Newspapers Ltd* [2006] EWCA Civ 1776.
[76] (2003) 36 EHRR 41: reported in Chap. 7.   [77] (2005) 40 EHRR 1: reported in Chap. 7.
[78] [2004] EMLR 1, para. 23.   [79] See *Kay v Lambeth LBC* [2006] UKHL 10.

privacy.' He found that Art. 8 was not engaged and thus the privacy claim should be struck out. The claimant appealed.

Sir Anthony Clarke MR:

54 …As we indicated earlier, it is our opinion that the focus should not be on the taking of a photograph in the street, but on its publication. In the absence of distress or the like caused when the photograph is taken, the mere taking of a photograph in the street may well be entirely unobjectionable. We do not therefore accept, as the judge appears to suggest in [65], that, if the claimant succeeds in this action, the courts will have created an image right.

55 We recognise that there may well be circumstances in which there will be no reasonable expectation of privacy, even after Von Hannover . However, as we see it all will (as ever) depend upon the facts of the particular case. The judge suggests that a distinction can be drawn between a child (or an adult) engaged in family and sporting activities and something as simple as a walk down a street or a visit to the grocers to buy the milk. This is on the basis that the first type of activity is clearly part of a person's private recreation time intended to be enjoyed in the company of family and friends and that, on the test deployed in Von Hannover , publicity of such activities is intrusive and can adversely affect the exercise of such social activities. We agree with the judge that that is indeed the basis of the ECtHR's approach but we do not agree that it is possible to draw a clear distinction in principle between the two kinds of activity. Thus, an expedition to a café of the kind which occurred here seems to us to be at least arguably part of each member of the family's recreation time intended to be enjoyed by them and such that publicity of it is intrusive and such as adversely to affect such activities in the future.

56 We do not share the predisposition identified by the judge in [66] that routine acts such as a visit to a shop or a ride on a bus should not attract any reasonable expectation of privacy. All depends upon the circumstances. The position of an adult may be very different from that of a child. In this appeal we are concerned only with the question whether David, as a small child, had a reasonable expectation of privacy, not with the question whether his parents would have had such an expectation. Moreover, we are concerned with the context of this case, which was not for example a single photograph taken of David which was for some reason subsequently published.

57 It seems to us that, subject to the facts of the particular case, the law should indeed protect children from intrusive media attention, at any rate to the extent of holding that a child has a reasonable expectation that he or she will not be targeted in order to obtain photographs in a public place for publication which the person who took or procured the taking of the photographs knew would be objected to on behalf of the child. That is the context in which the photographs of David were taken.

58 It is important to note that so to hold does not mean that the child will have, as the judge puts it in [66], a guarantee of privacy. To hold that the child has a reasonable expectation of privacy is only the first step. Then comes the balance which must be struck between the child's rights to respect for his or her private life under article 8 and the publisher's rights to freedom of expression under article 10. This approach does not seem to us to be inconsistent with that in Campbell, which was not considering the case of a child.

59 In these circumstances we do not think that it is necessary for us to analyse the decision in Von Hannover in any detail, especially since this is not an appeal brought after the trial of the action but an appeal against an order striking the action out. Suffice it to say that, in our opinion, the view we have expressed is consistent with that in Von Hannover, to which, as *McKennitt v Ash* makes clear, it is permissible to have regard. We do not disagree with the judge's summary of the decision in Von Hannover which we have quoted at [43 ix)] above. Mr Warby drew our attention to the oral submissions made to the ECtHR by Mr Prinz on behalf Princess Caroline, where he emphasised the campaign of harassment conducted against her by the German media. That was indeed part of the context in which the decision was made. For his part Mr Spearman stressed the fact that some of the photographs, the publication of which was held to infringe Princess Caroline's rights under article 8, showed her doing no more than walking in public.

60 The context of Von Hannover was therefore different from this but we have little doubt that, if the assumed facts of this case were to be considered by the ECtHR, the court would hold that David had a reasonable expectation of privacy and it seems to us to be more likely than not that, on the assumed facts, it would hold that the article 8/10 balance would come down in favour of David.

Appeal allowed.

NOTES

1. Routine activities of daily life carried out in public can, it would appear, fall within the ambit of an individual's private life. All, the court argued, depends upon the circumstances, which in this case followed the seemingly consistent line that it was clear that dissemination of the images would be objected to.

2. Clearly there will be much case law to follow but the comments of Lord Phillips in *Douglas v Hello! (No. 3)*[80] provide a useful summary of the present position:

83 Megarry J in *Coco v A N Clark (Engineers) Ltd* [1969] RPC 41 identified two requirements for the creation of a duty of confidence. The first was that the information should be confidential in nature and the second was that it should have been imparted in circumstances importing a duty of confidence. As we have seen, it is now recognised that the second requirement is not necessary if it is plain that the information is confidential, and for the adjective 'confidential' one can substitute the word 'private'. What is the nature of 'private information'? It seems to us that it must include information that is personal to the person who possesses it and that he does not intend shall be imparted to the general public. The nature of the information, or the form in which it is kept, may suffice to make it plain that the information satisfies these criteria.[81]

3. To date the damages awarded to successful claimants under the new action for misuse of personal information have been relatively modest. Naomi Campbell for example, was awarded £2,500 plus aggravated damages amounting to a further £1,000.[82]

● **Mosley v News Group Newspapers Ltd** [2008] EWHC 1777, Queen's Bench

In 2008 Max Mosley, President of the Fédération Internationale de l'Automobile, sued News Group Newspapers Ltd for misuse of personal information following an article in the *News of the World* headed 'F1 Boss Has Sick Nazi Orgy with Five Hookers' accompanied by the subheading 'Son of Hitler-loving fascist in sex shame'. In a straightforward application of the new action the claimant succeeded in his claim in the High Court. Eady J suggested that the case was not a 'landmark ruling' but he did provide useful guidance as to the applicability of exemplary damages to this area.

Eady J:
173. My primary reason for not extending the scope of this anomalous form of relief into a new area of law was that such a step could not be justified by reference to the matters identified in art 10(2) of the Convention. It could not be said to be either 'prescribed by law' or necessary in a democratic society. That is to say, I was not satisfied that English law requires, *in addition* to the availability of compensatory damages and injunctive relief, that the media should also be exposed to the somewhat unpredictable

80 [2006] QB 125.   81 Para. 83.   82 L. Clarke (2005) 24 CJQ 316.

risk of being 'fined' on a quasi-criminal basis. There is no 'pressing social need' for this. The 'chilling effect' would be obvious.

212. So far there have been very few awards of **damages** for infringement of **privacy** and they have all been pitched at relatively modest levels compared with some defamation awards: see eg *Campbell* (cited above), *Lady Archer v Williams* [2003] EMLR 38; *Douglas v Hello! Ltd* [2003] EWHC 786 (Ch), [2003] 3 All ER 996, [2003] NLJR 595 and *McKennitt v Ash* [2005] EWHC 3003 (QB), [2006] IP & T 605, [2006] EMLR 178. There have been some settlements which have been mentioned in the newspapers, but those are of no value as precedents or as setting any kind of tariff.

214. Because both libel and breach of **privacy** are concerned with compensating for infringements of art 8, there is clearly some scope for analogy. On the other hand, it is important to remember that this case is not directly concerned with compensating for, or vindicating, injury to *reputation*. The claim was not brought in libel. The distinctive functions of a defamation claim do not arise. The purpose of **damages,** therefore, must be to address the specific public policy factors in play when there has been 'an old fashioned breach of confidence' and/or an unauthorised revelation of personal information. It would seem that the law is concerned to protect such matters as personal dignity, autonomy and integrity.

...

217. If the objective is to provide an adequate remedy for the infringement of a right, it would not be served effectively if the court were merely to award nominal **damages** out of distaste for what the newspaper had revealed. As I have said, that should not be the court's concern. It would demonstrate that the judge had been distracted from the main task. The danger would be that the more unconventional the taste, and the greater the embarrassment caused by the revelation, the less effective would be the vindication. The easier it would be for the media to hound minorities.

222. It must be recognised that it may be appropriate to take into account any aggravating conduct in **privacy** cases on the part of the Defendant which increases the hurt to the Claimant's feelings or 'rubs salt in the wound'. As Lord Reid said, in the context of defamation, in *Cassell v Broome* at p 1085:

'It has long been recognised that in determining what sum within that bracket should be awarded, a jury, or other tribunal, is entitled to have regard to the conduct of the Defendant. He may have behaved in a highhanded, malicious, insulting or oppressive manner in committing the tort or he or his counsel may at the trial have aggravated the injury by what they there said. That would justify going to the top of the bracket and awarding as **damages** the largest sum that could fairly be regarded as compensation.'

224. So too, it may be appropriate that a Claimant's conduct should be taken into account (as it is in libel cases). Logically, it may be said, a Claimant's conduct has nothing to do with whether or not his **privacy** has been invaded or the impact upon his feelings caused by such an intrusion. There is no doctrine of contributory negligence. On the other hand, the extent to which his own conduct has contributed to the nature and scale of the distress *might* be a relevant factor on causation. Has he, for example, put himself in a predicament by his own choice which contributed to his distress and loss of dignity?

225. To what extent is he the author of his own misfortune? Many would think that if a prominent man puts himself, year after year, into the hands (literally and metaphorically) of prostitutes (or even professional dominatrices) he is gambling in placing so much trust in them. There is a risk of exposure or blackmail inherent in such a course of conduct....

226. To a casual observer, therefore, and especially with the benefit of hindsight, it might seem that the Claimant's behaviour was reckless and almost self-destructive. This does not excuse the intrusion into his **privacy** but it might be a relevant factor to take into account when assessing causal responsibility for what happened. It could be thought unreasonable to absolve him of all responsibility for placing himself and his family in the predicament in which they now find themselves...

227. An issue to which attention was directed in counsel's submissions was that of deterrence. Passing reference has been made in the authorities from time to time to this concept, but it seems at least questionable whether deterrence should have a distinct (as opposed to a merely incidental) role to play in

the award of compensatory **damages**. It is a notion more naturally associated with punishment. It often comes into the court's assessment of an appropriate punishment for prevalent criminal offences. There is also the anomaly to be considered, already mentioned in the context of exemplary **damages**; namely, that if **damages** are paid to an individual for the purpose of deterring the Defendant (or others) it would naturally be seen as an undeserved windfall.

228. Furthermore, if deterrence is to have any prospect of success it would be necessary to take into account (as with exemplary **damages**) the means of the relevant Defendant (often a newspaper group). Any award against the present Defendant would have to be so large that it would fail the test of proportionality when seen as fulfilling a compensatory function. There is also a concomitant danger in including a large element of deterrence by way of 'chilling effect'.

231. …it has to be accepted that an infringement of **privacy** cannot ever be effectively compensated by a monetary award. Judges cannot achieve what is, in the nature of things, impossible. That unpalatable fact cannot be mitigated by simply adding a few noughts to the number first thought of. Accordingly, it seems to me that the only realistic course is to select a figure which marks the fact that an unlawful intrusion has taken place while affording some degree of *solatium* to the injured party. That is all that can be done in circumstances where the traditional object of *restitutio* is not available. At the same time, the figure selected should not be such that it could be interpreted as minimising the scale of the wrong done or the **damage** it has caused.

235. It is necessary, therefore, to afford an adequate financial remedy for the purpose of acknowledging the infringement and compensating, to some extent, for the injury to feelings, the embarrassment and distress caused. I am not persuaded that it is right to extend the application of exemplary (or punitive) **damages** into this field or to include an additional element specifically directed towards 'deterrence'. That does not seem to me to be a legitimate exercise in awarding compensatory **damages**.

236. It has to be recognised that no amount of **damages** can fully compensate the Claimant for the **damage** done. He is hardly exaggerating when he says that his life was ruined. What can be achieved by a monetary award in the circumstances is limited. Any award must be proportionate and avoid the appearance of arbitrariness. I have come to the conclusion that the right award, taking all these considerations into account, is £60,000.

NOTES

1. It is clearly accepted that damages can never appropriately compensate a breach of privacy. However, in awarding a sum greater than many seen to date in 'privacy' cases, 'the only realistic course is to select a figure which marks the fact that an unlawful intrusion has taken place while affording some degree of *solatium* to the injured party'. Does the sum of £60,000 provide any discouragement to the tabloid press in seeking to publish such stories?

2. Though the story was of interest to the public it was found to be not in the public interest. Does this reflect a narrowing of the categories of 'public interest' as far as issues that the tabloid press wish to publish? Does the case represent a genuine threat to press freedom?

(F) COURT JURISDICTION TO PROTECT MINORS

In *R v Central Independent Television plc*[83] the court was concerned with the prerogative power of the Crown *parens patriae*, exercisable through the courts, to protect children. This power is normally used in respect of a child whom a court has decided to make a ward of court but *Central Independent Television* illustrated that it may also be invoked to request

---

[83] [1994] Fam 192.

a court order to protect other children. Although the power was invoked unsuccessfully, the courts have in several cases used their wardship jurisdiction to make orders protecting children in cases raising privacy or related issues. In the *Central Independent Television* case, the Court of Appeal drew a distinction between cases where the publication that is challenged contains information (e.g. concerning the child's medical treatment) that has a direct bearing upon a child and his welfare, for which the courts are responsible, and cases where the publication has a less direct connection (e.g. where personal details are given about a close relative). In the former kind of case, the prerogative jurisdiction *parens patriae* is available to censor a publication provided that on balance this should be done. In other kinds of cases, such as the *Central Independent Television plc* case, it was suggested that no balancing act is called for: freedom of expression simply prevails. This is an important decision in effectively developing a privacy right for children. However, the inherent jurisdiction must now be considered in light of the interpretation of the relationship between Arts 8 and 10 of the ECHR.

- **Re S (a child)** [2004] UKHL 47, [2005] 1 AC 593, [2004] 3 WLR 1129, [2004] 4 All ER 83, [2005] EMLR 2, House of Lords

The case concerned eight-year-old CS whose older brother, DS, died of acute salt poisoning whilst in hospital. Press reports about the death appeared soon afterwards. All the reports named the dead child and where he lived. The local paper also named his parents, his younger brother and his school in their earlier reports. Shortly after DS died and his mother was charged with murder. Hedley J in the Family Division dismissed an application for an injunction restraining the publication by newspapers of the identity of CS's mother which was designed to protect the privacy of CS. The Court of Appeal dismissed an appeal against the refusal to grant the injunction. The Court of Appeal placed emphasis upon the primacy in a democratic society of the open reporting of proceedings on serious criminal charges and held that where circumstances arose which were not covered by statutory exceptions (such as the Children and Young Persons Act 1933, s. 39) the courts should be slow to extend restrictions upon the right of free speech by use of the inherent jurisdiction of the court. Furthermore, grounds under Art. 10(2) had been made out in balancing CS's rights of privacy under Art. 8 with the right to publish under Art. 10. It was submitted on appeal that the principle of proportionality in a case of competing rights under the Convention had been misapplied and that CS had a right to respect for private and family life including a right to protection from publicity which could damage his health and well-being.

Lord Steyn:

13. Through his guardian the child now challenges the decision of the majority of the Court of Appeal. Counsel for the child submitted that the majority misapplied the principle of proportionality in a case of competing rights under the ECHR and in so doing exposed a vulnerable child to interference with his private and family rights. In outline her submissions were as follows. The child had a right to respect for his private and family life in that he was entitled to expect the state to provide, by way of his access to the court, protection against harmful publicity concerning his family. The child has a right to protection from publicity which could damage his health and well-being and risk emotional and psychiatric harm. Recognising that the subject matter of the trial is a matter of public interest counsel for the child submitted that a proportionate response would be to permit only newspaper reports which do not refer to the family name or incorporate photographs of family members or the deceased.

17. The interplay between articles 8 and 10 has been illuminated by the opinions in the House of Lords in *Campbell v MGN Ltd* [2004] 2 WLR 1232. For present purposes the decision of the House on the facts of *Campbell* and the differences between the majority and the minority are not material. What does, however, emerge clearly from the opinions are four propositions. First, neither article has *as such* precedence over the other. Secondly, where the values under the two articles are in conflict, an intense focus on the comparative importance of the specific rights being claimed in the individual case is necessary. Thirdly, the justifications for interfering with or restricting each right must be taken into account. Finally, the proportionality test must be applied to each. For convenience I will call this the ultimate balancing test. This is how I will approach the present case.

18. In oral argument it was accepted by both sides that the ordinary rule is that the press, as the watchdog of the public, may report everything that takes place in a criminal court. I would add that in European jurisprudence and in domestic practice this is a strong rule. It can only be displaced by unusual or exceptional circumstances. It is, however, not a mechanical rule. The duty of the court is to examine with care each application for a departure from the rule by reason of rights under article 8.

22. At all stages in this litigation the provisions of the ECHR have been carefully taken into account. But at first instance, and in the Court of Appeal, much of the debate centred on the inherent jurisdiction of the High Court to restrain publicity. Hedley J and the Court of Appeal were asked to exercise this inherent jurisdiction. Hale LJ (with the agreement of the other members of the court) observed (para 40):

'Now that the Human Rights Act 1998 is in force, the relevance of the jurisdiction may simply be to provide the vehicle which enables the court to conduct the necessary balancing exercise between the competing rights of the child under Article 8 and the media under Article 10.'

In their printed cases, and in oral argument, both counsel adopted this approach. This is the context in which in oral argument the House was taken on a tour of the following decisions on the inherent jurisdiction: *In re X (A Minor) (Wardship: Jurisdiction)* [1975] Fam 47; *In re C (A Minor) (Wardship: Medical Treatment) (No. 2)* [1990] Fam 39; *In re M and N (Minors) (Wardship: Publication of Information)* [1990] Fam 211; *In re W (A Minor) (Wardship: Restrictions on Publication)* [1992] 1 WLR 100; *In re H (Minors) (Injunction: Public Interest)* [1994] 1 FLR 519; *R v Central Independent Television PLC* [1994] Fam 192; *In re R (Wardship: Restrictions on Publication)* [1994] Fam 254; *In re Z (A Minor) (Identification: Restrictions on Publications)* [1997] Fam 1. The question arises whether such an exercise, in a case such as the present, is still necessary or useful.

23. The House unanimously takes the view that since the 1998 Act came into force in October 2000, the earlier case law about the existence and scope of inherent jurisdiction need not be considered in this case or in similar cases. The foundation of the jurisdiction to restrain publicity in a case such as the present is now derived from convention rights under the ECHR. This is the simple and direct way to approach such cases. In this case the jurisdiction is not in doubt. This is not to say that the case law on the inherent jurisdiction of the High Court is wholly irrelevant. On the contrary, it may remain of some interest in regard to the ultimate balancing exercise to be carried out under the ECHR provisions. My noble and learned friend Lord Bingham of Cornhill invited the response of counsel to this approach. Both expressed agreement with it. I would affirm this approach. Before passing on I would observe on a historical note that a study of the case law revealed that the approach adopted in the past under the inherent jurisdiction was remarkably similar to that to be adopted under the ECHR. Indeed the ECHR provisions were often cited even before it became part of our law in October 2000. Nevertheless, it will in future be necessary, if earlier case law is cited, to bear in mind the new methodology required by the ECHR as explained in *Campbell*.

24. On the evidence it can readily be accepted that article 8 is engaged. Hedley J observed (para 18) 'that these will be dreadfully painful times for the child'. Everybody will sympathise with that observation.

25. But it is necessary to measure the nature of the impact of the trial on the child. He will not be involved in the trial as a witness or otherwise. It will not be necessary to refer to him. No photograph of

him will be published. There will be no reference to his private life or upbringing. Unavoidably, his mother must be tried for murder and that must be a deeply hurtful experience for the child. The impact upon him is, however, essentially indirect.

26. While article 8.1 is engaged, and none of the factors in article 8.2 justifies the interference, it is necessary to assess realistically the nature of the relief sought. This is an application for an injunction beyond the scope of section 39, the remedy provided by Parliament to protect juveniles directly affected by criminal proceedings. No such injunction has in the past been granted under the inherent jurisdiction or under the provisions of the ECHR. There is no decision of the Strasbourg court granting injunctive relief to non-parties, juvenile or adult, in respect of publication of criminal proceedings. Moreover, the Convention on the Rights of the Child, which entered into force on 2 September 1990, protects the privacy of children directly involved in criminal proceedings, but does not protect the privacy of children if they are only indirectly affected by criminal trials: articles 17 and 40.2(vii); see also Geraldine Van Bueren, *The International Law on the Rights of the Child,* 1994, 141 and 182. The verdict of experience appears to be that such a development is a step too far.

27. The interference with article 8 rights, however distressing for the child, is not of the same order when compared with cases of juveniles, who are directly involved in criminal trials. In saying this I have not overlooked the fact that the mother, the defendant in the criminal trial, has waived her right to a completely public trial, and supports the appeal of the child. In a case such as the present her stance can only be of limited weight.

28. Article 10 is also engaged. This case is concerned with the freedom of the press, subject to limited statutory restrictions, to report the proceedings at a criminal trial without restriction. It is necessary to assess the importance of this freedom. I start with a general proposition. In *Reynolds v Times Newspapers Limited* [2001] 2 AC 127 Lord Nicholls of Birkenhead described the position as follows (200G–H):

'It is through the mass media that most people today obtain their information on political matters. Without freedom of expression by the media, freedom of expression would be a hollow concept. The interest of a democratic society in ensuring a free press weighs heavily in the balance in deciding whether any curtailment of this freedom bears a reasonable relationship to the purpose of the curtailment.'

These observations apply with equal force to the freedom of the press to report criminal trials in progress and after verdict.

29. The importance of the freedom of the press to report criminal trials has often been emphasised in concrete terms. In *R v Legal Aid Board ex parte Kaim Todner (A firm)* [1999] QB 966, Lord Woolf MR explained (at 977):

'The need to be vigilant arises from the natural tendency for the general principle to be eroded and for exceptions to grow by accretion as the exceptions are applied by analogy to existing cases. This is the reason it is so important not to forget why proceedings are required to be subjected to the full glare of a public hearing. It is necessary because the public nature of the proceedings deters inappropriate behaviour on the part of the court. It also maintains the public's confidence in the administration of justice. It enables the public to know that justice is being administered impartially. It can result in evidence becoming available which would not become available if the proceedings were conducted behind closed doors or with one or more of the parties' or witnesses' identity concealed. It makes uninformed and inaccurate comment about the proceedings less likely…Any interference with the public nature of court proceedings is therefore to be avoided unless justice requires it. However Parliament has recognised there are situations where interference is necessary.'

These are valuable observations. It is, however, still necessary to assess the importance of unrestricted reporting in specifics relating to this case.

30. Dealing with the relative importance of the freedom of the press to report the proceedings in a criminal trial Hale LJ drew a distinction. She observed (at para 56):

'The court must consider what restriction, if any, is needed to meet the legitimate aim of protecting the rights of CS. If prohibiting publication of the family name and photographs is needed, the court must consider how great an impact that will in fact have upon the freedom protected by Article 10. It is relevant here that restrictions on the identification of defendants before conviction are by no means unprecedented. The situation may well change if and when the mother is convicted. There is a much greater public interest in knowing the names of persons convicted of serious crime than of those who are merely suspected or charged. These considerations are also relevant to the extent of the interference with CS's rights.'

I cannot accept these observations without substantial qualification. A criminal trial is a public event. The principle of open justice puts, as has often been said, the judge and all who participate in the trial under intense scrutiny. The glare of contemporaneous publicity ensures that trials are properly conducted. It is a valuable check on the criminal process. Moreover, the public interest may be as much involved in the circumstances of a remarkable acquittal as in a surprising conviction. Informed public debate is necessary about all such matters. Full contemporaneous reporting of criminal trials in progress promotes public confidence in the administration of justice. It promotes the values of the rule of law.

31. For these reasons I would, therefore, attribute greater importance to the freedom of the press to report the progress of a criminal trial without any restraint than Hale LJ did.

32. There are a number of specific consequences of the grant of an injunction as asked for in this case to be considered. First, while counsel for the child wanted to confine a ruling to the grant of an injunction restraining publication *to protect a child*, that will not do. The jurisdiction under the ECHR could equally be invoked by an adult non-party faced with possible damaging publicity as a result of a trial of a parent, child or spouse. Adult non-parties to a criminal trial must therefore be added to the prospective pool of applicants who could apply for such injunctions. This would confront newspapers with an ever wider spectrum of potentially costly proceedings and would seriously inhibit the freedom of the press to report criminal trials.

33. Secondly, if such an injunction were to be granted in this case, it cannot be assumed that relief will only be sought in future in respect of the name of a defendant and a photograph of the defendant and the victim. It is easy to visualise circumstances in which attempts will be made to enjoin publicity of, for example, the gruesome circumstances of a crime. The process of piling exception upon exception to the principle of open justice would be encouraged and would gain in momentum.

34. Thirdly, it is important to bear in mind that from a newspaper's point of view a report of a sensational trial without revealing the identity of the defendant would be a very much disembodied trial. If the newspapers choose not to contest such an injunction, they are less likely to give prominence to reports of the trial. Certainly, readers will be less interested and editors will act accordingly. Informed debate about criminal justice will suffer.

35. Fourthly, it is true that newspapers can always contest an application for an injunction. Even for national newspapers that is, however, a costly matter which may involve proceedings at different judicial levels. Moreover, time constraints of an impending trial may not always permit such proceedings. Often it will be too late and the injunction will have had its negative effect on contemporary reporting.

36. Fifthly, it is easy to fall into the trap of considering the position from the point of view of national newspapers only. Local newspapers play a huge role. In the United Kingdom according to the website of The Newspaper Society there are 1301 regional and local newspapers which serve villages, towns and cities. Apparently, again according to the website of The Newspaper Society, over 85% of all British adults read a regional or local newspaper compared to 70% who read a national newspaper. Very often a sensational or serious criminal trial will be of great interest in the community where it took place. A regional or local newspaper is likely to give prominence to it. That happens every day up and down the country. For local newspapers, who do not have the financial resources of national newspapers, the spectre of being involved in costly legal proceedings is bound to have a chilling effect. If local

newspapers are threatened with the prospect of an injunction such as is now under consideration it is likely that they will often be silenced. Prudently, the Romford Recorder, which has some 116,000 readers a week, chose not to contest these proceedings. The impact of such a new development on the regional and local press in the United Kingdom strongly militates against its adoption. If permitted, it would seriously impoverish public discussion of criminal justice.

37. In agreement with Hale LJ the majority of the Court of Appeal took the view that Hedley J had not analysed the case correctly in accordance with the provisions of the ECHR. I do not agree. In my view the judge analysed the case correctly under the ECHR. Given the weight traditionally given to the importance of open reporting of criminal proceedings it was in my view appropriate for him, in carrying out the balance required by the ECHR, to begin by acknowledging the force of the argument under article 10 before considering whether the right of the child under article 8 was sufficient to outweigh it. He went too far in saying that he would have come to the same conclusion even if he had been persuaded that this was a case where the child's welfare was indeed the paramount consideration under section 1(1) of the Children Act 1989. But that was not the shape of the case before him.

38. I would dismiss the appeal. The effect of the opinions delivered in the House today is that there is no injunction in respect of publication of the identity of the defendant or of photographs of the defendant or her deceased son.

Lords Bingham, Nicholls, Hoffman and **Carswell** concurred.

Appeal dismissed.

NOTES

1. At first instance, Hedley J had taken Art. 10 to have presumptive priority, with Art. 8 acting as an exception. However, in correctly outlining the test to be applied in these circumstances (at para. 17) Lord Steyn suggests that Hedley J was correct in his analysis (para. 37). Can this be right?

2. The inherent jurisdiction of the courts in this field is now more appropriately known as the Convention jurisdiction.

3. In cases such as *Central Independent Television plc* freedom of expression clearly cannot now be taken by presumption to override individual privacy. A balancing exercise must take place between Arts 8 and 10, though it is accepted that given similar facts it is likely that free expression claims are likely to hold considerable weight within the balance.

4. In *Venables v News Group Newspapers Ltd*[84] an injunction was granted under the law of breach of confidence to continue beyond the age of 18 a ban on media publicity about the two persons convicted of a notorious child murder.

(G) OTHER REMEDIES IN LAW

Breach of contract may provide a remedy in some cases.[85]

In *criminal law,* eavesdroppers and 'peeping Toms' may be bound over to be of good behaviour.[86] A compulsive 'nosey parker' who had been seen peeping through many a window and who had been trapped with her hand in someone's letter box was bound over to keep

---

[84] [2001] 1 All ER 908.   [85] See, e.g., *Pollard v Photographic Co* (1889) 40 Ch D 345.
[86] See *R v Wyres* (1956) 2 *Russell on Crime* (12th edn, 1964) 1397 (spying on woman undressing).

the peace. She had earlier had buckets of water and snowballs thrown at her by neighbours.[87] Eavesdropping is not a criminal offence.[88]

The Sexual Offences Act 2003 provides an offence of voyeurism.

67 Voyeurism

(1) A person commits an offence if—

    (a) for the purpose of obtaining sexual gratification, he observes another person doing a private act, and

    (b) he knows that the other person does not consent to being observed for his sexual gratification.

(2) A person commits an offence if—

    (a) he operates equipment with the intention of enabling another person to observe, for the purpose of obtaining sexual gratification, a third person (B) doing a private act, and

    (b) he knows that B does not consent to his operating equipment with that intention.

(3) A person commits an offence if—

    (a) he records another person (B) doing a private act,

    (b) he does so with the intention that he or a third person will, for the purpose of obtaining sexual gratification, look at an image of B doing the act, and

    (c) he knows that B does not consent to his recording the act with that intention.

(4) A person commits an offence if he instals equipment, or constructs or adapts a structure or part of a structure, with the intention of enabling himself or another person to commit an offence under subsection (1).

(5) A person guilty of an offence under this section is liable—

    (a) on summary conviction, to imprisonment for a term not exceeding 6 months or a fine not exceeding the statutory maximum or both;

    (b) on conviction on indictment, to imprisonment for a term not exceeding 2 years.

68 Voyeurism: interpretation

(1) For the purposes of section 67, a person is doing a private act if the person is in a place which, in the circumstances, would reasonably be expected to provide privacy, and—

    (a) the person's genitals, buttocks or breasts are exposed or covered only with underwear,

    (b) the person is using a lavatory, or

    (c) the person is doing a sexual act that is not of a kind ordinarily done in public.

(2) In section 67, 'structure' includes a tent, vehicle or vessel or other temporary or movable structure.

In *R v Bassett*[89] the Court of Appeal stated that it was for the jury to determine whether there was a reasonable expectation of privacy and the nature of the observation rather than its purpose would be relevant. The court further held that the word 'breasts' in s. 68(1)(a) did not extend to the male chest.

---

[87] *Guardian*, 6 November 1979.

[88] Criminal Law Act 1967, s. 13(1)(a). The Official Secrets Acts 1911–89, below, pp. 768ff. protect confidential information about private individuals in official hands. For other statutory provisions, see the Younger Committee Report, Appendix I.

[89] [2008] EWCA Crim 1174.

4. PRIVACY AND MEDIA REGULATION

In addition to such remedies at law as may exist, the following regulatory bodies have powers to receive and pronounce upon (in a legally non-binding way) invasions of privacy by the press and in broadcasting.

(A) PRESS COMPLAINTS COMMISSION

The PCC Code so far as it affects privacy includes the following statements:

Clauses marked* are covered by exceptions relating to the public interest.

All members of the press have a duty to maintain the highest professional standards. The Code, which includes this preamble and the public interest exceptions below, sets the benchmark for those ethical standards, protecting both the rights of the individual and the public's right to know. It is the cornerstone of the system of self-regulation to which the industry has made a binding commitment. It is essential that an agreed code be honoured not only to the letter but in the full spirit. It should not be interpreted so narrowly as to compromise its commitment to respect the rights of the individual, nor so broadly that it constitutes an unnecessary interference with freedom of expression or prevents publication in the public interest. It is the responsibility of editors and publishers to apply the Code to editorial material in both printed and online versions of publications. They should take care to ensure it is observed rigorously by all editorial staff and external contributors, including non-journalists, in printed and online versions of publications. Editors should co-operate swiftly with the PCC in the resolution of complaints. Any publication judged to have breached the Code must print the adjudication in full and with due prominence, including headline reference to the PCC.

1 ACCURACY

i) The press must take care not to publish inaccurate, misleading or distorted information, including pictures.

ii) A significant inaccuracy, misleading statement or distortion once recognized must be corrected, promptly and with due prominence, and—where appropriate—an apology published.

iii) The press, whilst free to be partisan, must distinguish clearly between comment, conjecture and fact.

iv) A publication must report fairly and accurately the outcome of an action for defamation to which it has been a party, unless an agreed settlement states otherwise, or an agreed statement is published.

2 OPPORTUNITY TO REPLY

A fair opportunity for reply to inaccuracies must be given when reasonably called for.

3 * PRIVACY

i) Everyone is entitled to respect for his or her private and family life, home, health and correspondence, including digital communications. Editors will be expected to justify intrusions into any individual's private life without consent.

ii) It is unacceptable to photograph individuals in a private place without their consent.

Note—Private places are public or private property where there is a reasonable expectation of privacy.

4 * HARASSMENT

i) Journalists must not engage in intimidation, harassment or persistent pursuit.

ii) They must not persist in questioning, telephoning, pursuing or photographing individuals once asked to desist; nor remain on their property when asked to leave and must not follow them.

iii) Editors must ensure these principles are observed by those working for them and take care not to use non-compliant material from other sources.

5 INTRUSION INTO GRIEF OR SHOCK

i) In cases involving personal grief or shock, enquiries and approaches must be made with sympathy and discretion and publication handled sensitively. This should not restrict the right to report legal proceedings, such as inquests.

* ii) When reporting suicide, care should be taken to avoid excessive detail about the method used.

6 * CHILDREN

i) Young people should be free to complete their time at school without unnecessary intrusion.

ii) A child under 16 must not be interviewed or photographed on issues involving their own or another child's welfare unless a custodial parent or similarly responsible adult consents.

iii) Pupils must not be approached or photographed at school without the permission of the school authorities.

iv) Minors must not be paid for material involving children's welfare, nor parents or guardians for material about their children or wards, unless it is clearly in the child's interest.

v) Editors must not use the fame, notoriety or position of a parent or guardian as sole justification for publishing details of a child's private life.

7 * CHILDREN IN SEX CASES

1. The press must not, even if legally free to do so, identify children under 16 who are victims or witnesses in cases involving sex offences.

2. In any press report of a case involving a sexual offence against a child—

   i) The child must not be identified.

   ii) The adult may be identified.

   iii) The word 'incest' must not be used where a child victim might be identified.

   iv) Care must be taken that nothing in the report implies the relationship between the accused and the child.

8 * HOSPITALS

i) Journalists must identify themselves and obtain permission from a responsible executive before entering non-public areas of hospitals or similar institutions to pursue enquiries.

ii) The restrictions on intruding into privacy are particularly relevant to enquiries about individuals in hospitals or similar institutions.

9 * REPORTING OF CRIME

i) Relatives or friends of persons convicted or accused of crime should not generally be identified without their consent, unless they are genuinely relevant to the story. ii) Particular regard should be paid to the potentially vulnerable position of children who witness, or are victims of, crime. This should not restrict the right to report legal proceedings.

10 * CLANDESTINE DEVICES AND SUBTERFUGE

i) The press must not seek to obtain or publish material acquired by using hidden cameras or clandestine listening devices; or by intercepting private or mobile telephone calls, messages or emails; or by the unauthorized removal of documents, or photographs; or by accessing digitally-held private information without consent.

ii) Engaging in misrepresentation or subterfuge, including by agents or intermediaries, can generally be justified only in the public interest and then only when the material cannot be obtained by other means.

11 VICTIMS OF SEXUAL ASSAULT

The press must not identify victims of sexual assault or publish material likely to contribute to such identification unless there is adequate justification and they are legally free to do so.

THE PUBLIC INTEREST

There may be exceptions to the clauses marked *where they can be demonstrated to be in the public interest.

1. The public interest includes, but is not confined to:

    i) Detecting or exposing crime or serious impropriety.

    ii) Protecting public health and safety.

    iii) Preventing the public from being misled by an action or statement of an individual or organisation.

2. There is a public interest in freedom of expression itself.

3. Whenever the public interest is invoked, the PCC will require editors to demonstrate fully how the public interest was served.

4. The PCC will consider the extent to which material is already in the public domain, or will become so.

5. In cases involving children under 16, editors must demonstrate an exceptional public interest to override the normally paramount interest of the child.

NOTES

1. Established in 1991 following the Calcutt Committee Report, the Press Complaints Commission replaced the Press Council, which had existed since 1953. The Council had an independent chairman and an otherwise equal number of press and lay members. It was the subject of much criticism because of its limited powers and impact in curbing press intrusion into individual privacy.

2. Like its predecessor, the Press Complaints Commission is a non-statutory body established by the newspapers and periodicals industry with the object, *inter alia,* of hearing complaints about the conduct of the press, representing an alternative to the legal process. It does not usually pursue complaints that are also the subject of ongoing legal action. It has an independent chairman (Sir Christopher Meyer) and 16 members, including editors and non-press members. Any person may complain to the Commission of an invasion of privacy, whether personally affected or not. The Commission does not conduct oral hearings. It does not require a complainant to waive any legal right of action, as the Press Council was criticised for doing. Instead, the Commission may call upon a complainant to wait until his case has been heard before resorting to law. The Commission has the same limited sanctions as the Press Council formerly had. It may censure a newspaper or journalist, but it has no power to fine or award compensation. In the absence of such a power the PCC cannot alone provide an effective remedy for a breach of Art. 8.[90] Newspapers are expected to publish an adverse adjudication 'in full and with due prominence', although they are under no legal obligation to do so. In fact, newspapers normally co-operate.

[90] *Peck v UK* (2003) 36 EHRR 41, para. 109.

3. The number of complaints of invasion of privacy dealt with by the Press Council was not high. The same is true of the Press Complaints Commission. In its first year of operation, only 80 of the 1,000 or so complaints found to present a prima facie case concerned privacy. Even so, as the Younger Committee Report, p. 44, stated in respect of the Press Council, although the percentage of complaints which the Council received that were on privacy are 'a tiny proportion of the whole', they are sufficient in number and diversity to indicate the hazards that press coverage present for the protection of privacy. In 2007 there were a total of 245 privacy rulings, most of which are dealt with within 35 days. Over 52 per cent of privacy rulings were made against the regional press.[91] Once a breach of privacy has occurred might the aggrieved feel it is counterproductive to keep the issue alive with a claim before the PCC?

4. The PCC's definition of private place now accords with domestic law, with location not being the determinative factor. It states: 'Private places are public or private property where there is a reasonable expectation of privacy.' In 2007 the model Elle MacPherson had upheld by the PCC her complaint that innocuous photographs taken of her and her family on a public beach were an invasion of her privacy.[92]

5. In 2006, 75 per cent of complainants surveyed thought that their complaint had been handled 'very satisfactorily' or 'satisfactorily', and 81 per cent claimed that their case had been considered 'very thoroughly' or 'thoroughly'.[93] However, it should be noted that many of those claiming breach of privacy would seek recourse to law and the potential for an injunction rather than an apology from the PCC.

6. In January 2007 one of the most serious breaches of the Code to date occurred.[94] Clive Goodman, the former royal editor of the *News of the World*, and a private investigator, Glenn Mulcaire, were convicted of conspiracy to intercept communications without lawful authority and received custodial sentences. The Editor of the *News of the World*, Andy Coulson, took ultimate responsibility for Goodman's actions and resigned. The Culture, Media and Sport Select Committee stated that 'a clear message has been sent that breaches of this kind cannot be tolerated and that editors must accept final responsibility for what happens on their watch'.[95]

7. A Select Committee Report in 2002/3[96] recognised the problem that the PCC was not raising its own complaints where appropriate, and cited the following examples:

i) In October 1997 *The Observer* reported that a private detective had pleaded guilty to 12 offences under the Data Protection Act whereby she had extracted ex-directory phone numbers and telephone bills out of BT. The article reported her clients as *The News of the World*, *The People*, *The Sunday Express* and *The Mail on Sunday*.

ii) In January 2002 *The Daily Telegraph* reported that a solicitor's employee had stolen sensitive documents relating to a murder case from work and sold them to *The Sun*, *The Daily Mirror* and *The Express* (and was only prevented by arrest from keeping an appointment with *The Daily Mail*). *The Guardian* reported that *The Sun* was accused of prompting the man to steal the documents.

---

[91] Press Complaints Commission, *The Review* (2007), p. 26.

[92] Ibid., p. 8.   [93] See www.pcc.org.uk.

[94] See Select Committee on Culture, Media and Sport, Seventh Report of Session 2006–7, *Self Regulation of the Press*, HC 375, paras 17–26.

[95] Ibid., para. 22.

[96] Select Committee on Culture, Media and Sport, Fifth Report of Session 2002–3, *Privacy and Media Intrusion*, HC 458–1.

iii) In September 2002 *The Guardian* reported that there was a data 'black market' and referred to a private detective agency called 'Southern Investigations' which had been found to be selling information from police sources to *The News of the World, The Daily Mirror and The Sunday Mirror*.

iv) In December 2002 *The Sunday Telegraph* reported that private detective agencies routinely tapped private telephone calls for the tabloid press, with some agencies deriving the bulk of their income from such work and such clients.

v) In January 2003 *The Times* reported the Human Resources directorate at the Inland Revenue admitting that there was evidence that some employees had sold confidential information from tax returns to outside agencies (but without identifying which agencies)…

We regard this as a depressing catalogue of deplorable practices.

The Office of the Information Commissioner considered similar incidents to the extent that they breached data protection legislation and issued reports in 2006[97] and 2007.[98] The Information Commissioner said that he was 'a little disappointed that there was not a more strident denunciation of the activity' by the PCC. However, the PCC did respond by redrafting cl. 10 of the Code to emphasise that illegal trading in confidential information was a breach of press standards.

8. Despite the development of the new action for misuse of private information the PCC Code continues to have an important role. Under s. 32(3) of the Data Protection Act compliance with the Code presents a defence for journalists against action taken by the Information Commissioner. Furthermore, under HRA, s. 12(4)(b) a court must take into account a newspaper's compliance with the Code when assessing a defence based upon freedom of expression.

9. A hotline has been established to enable individuals to register their concerns. This may provide the advantage that an individual can contact the PCC more quickly with the result that the PCC itself may be able to act more quickly thus reducing a potential breach of privacy.

10. In 2007 the Select Committee on Culture, Media and Sport stated:

54. We do not believe that there is a case for a statutory regulator for the press, which would represent a very dangerous interference with the freedom of the press. We continue to believe that statutory regulation of the press is a hallmark of authoritarianism and risks undermining democracy. We recommend that self-regulation should be retained for the press, while recognising that it must be seen to be effective if calls for statutory intervention are to be resisted.

(B) BROADCASTING STANDARDS AND OFCOM

OFCOM, the Office of Communications, is a statutory body established under the Communications Act 2003, taking over the role of the Broadcasting Standards Commission. It is a body independent of the Government, which must produce annual reports to Parliament. Its functions and duties are laid down in the 2003 Act, but in respect of privacy issues, Ofcom is required to 'consider and where appropriate, adjudicate on fairness and privacy complaints'. Under s. 319 of the 2003 Act Ofcom must publish a standards

---

[97] The Information Commissioner's Office, *What price privacy?* (2006) HC 1056.
[98] The Information Commissioner's Office, *What price privacy now?* (2007) HC 36.

Code, the most recent of which came into force in July 2005. Rule 8 of the Code concerns privacy.

8.1 Any infringement of privacy in programmes, or in connection with obtaining material included in programmes, must be warranted. Meaning of 'warranted':

In this section 'warranted' has a particular meaning. It means that where broadcasters wish to justify an infringement of privacy as warranted, they should be able to demonstrate why in the particular circumstances of the case, it is warranted. If the reason is that it is in the public interest, then the broadcaster should be able to demonstrate that the public interest outweighs the right to privacy. Examples of public interest would include revealing or detecting crime, protecting public health or safety, exposing misleading claims made by individuals or organisations or disclosing incompetence that affects the public.

Legitimate expectations of privacy will vary according to the place and nature of the information, activity or condition in question, the extent to which it is in the public domain (if at all) and whether the individual concerned is already in the public eye. There may be circumstances where people can reasonably expect privacy even in a public place. Some activities and conditions may be of such a private nature that filming or recording, even in a public place, could involve an infringement of privacy. People under investigation or in the public eye, and their immediate family and friends, retain the right to a private life, although private behaviour can raise issues of legitimate public interest.

NOTES

1. The code replaces codes set by the previous broadcasting regulators, including the Independent Television Commission for commercial television, the Radio Authority for commercial radio and the Broadcasting Standards Commission on matters relating to taste, decency, fairness and privacy. However, Ofcom does not provide an overarching code for the media with, for example, the BBFC and PhonepayPlus (previously ICSTIS) retaining their own regulatory powers. Should there be one regulatory authority covering the media?

2. Rule 8 on privacy reflects the demands and jurisprudence of the European Convention in recognising the flexibility of an individual's expectations of privacy and their location. This also follows case law decided under the Broadcasting Standards Committee regime. In *R v Broadcasting Complaints Commission, ex p Granada Television Ltd,*[99] it was held that the Commission had not acted unreasonably under the *Wednesbury* principle in taking the view that there was an unwarranted infringement of privacy even though the material that was broadcast was in the public domain. In that case, parents of deceased children had complained to the Commission of a television programme called 'The Allergy Business' that had shown clips of their children without forewarning them, causing them great distress. Dismissing an application for judicial review of a decision made under s. 143, 1990 Act, Popplewell J held that it was not unreasonable for the Commission to decide that the recall in the film of what was in the public domain could intrude upon the parents' privacy. The secret filming of transactions in a shop for the purposes of a consumer protection programme (*Watchdog*) could amount to an invasion of privacy even though the public had access to the shop and the events filmed were not private in character.[100] However, it is suggested that

---

[99] (1993) Times, 31 May, QBD.

[100] *R v Broadcasting Standards Commission, ex p BBC* [2000] EMLR 587, CA. It was also held that a company may complain of invasion of privacy.

r. 8.11 might require redrafting or, at least be given restrictive interpretation in light of the decision in *von Hannover*. Rule 8.11 states:

> Doorstepping for factual programmes should not take place unless a request for an interview has been refused or it has not been possible to request an interview, or there is good reason to believe that an investigation will be frustrated if the subject is approached openly, and it is warranted to doorstep. However, normally broadcasters may, without prior warning interview, film or record people in the news when in public places.

3. Rule 8 also provides guidance notes. For example, 'Some activities and conditions may be of such a private nature that filming, even in a public place where there was normally no reasonable expectation of privacy, could involve an infringement of privacy. For example, a child in state of undress, someone with disfiguring medical condition or CCTV footage of suicide attempt.'

4. Rules 8.20–8.22 state that particular attention must be paid to the privacy of vulnerable people and those under 16. Vulnerable 'may include those with learning difficulties, those with mental health problems, the bereaved, people with brain damage or forms of dementia, people who have been traumatised or who are sick or terminally ill'.

5. Ofcom's 2007/8 Annual Report[101] disclosed that 67,548 complaints were received in relation to programme standards. Of those, 124 related to fairness and/or privacy with a total of 23 being upheld and 20 partially upheld.

6. Unlike its predecessor, Ofcom has the power to fine in addition to requiring broadcasters to outline Ofcom decisions and carry apologies where appropriate. These sanctions also apply for the first time to the BBC (as regards issues of privacy). Ofcom publishes six-monthly bulletins of its decisions on complaints and disputes.[102]

5. SURVEILLANCE

In recent years surveillance has grown enormously both in the public and private sectors. In 2006 the Surveillance Studies Network produced a report for the Information Commissioner.[103] It stated:

> 1.1. We live in a surveillance society. It is pointless to talk about surveillance society in the future tense. In all the rich countries of the world everyday life is suffused with surveillance encounters, not merely from dawn to dusk but 24/7. Some encounters obtrude into the routine, like when we get a ticket for running a red light when no one was around but the camera. But the majority are now just part of the fabric of daily life. Unremarkable.

Being compliant in various types of surveillance is now essential if an individual is to take part fully in a modern society. In 2008 The Home Affairs Select Committee[104] recognised the potential pitfalls of the increase in surveillance and the need to ensure that public trust in maintained.

---

[101] Annual Reports are available at www.ofcom.org.uk.
[102] www.ofcom.org.uk/bulletins/.
[103] Surveillance Studies Network, *A Report on the Surveillance Society* (2006), available at www.ico.gov.uk.
[104] Home Affairs Select Committee Fifth Report of 2007–8, *A Surveillance Society?* (2008) HC 58.

1. We reject crude characterisations of our society as a surveillance society in which all collections and means of collecting information about citizens are networked and centralised in the service of the state. Yet the potential for surveillance of citizens in public spaces and private communications has increased to the extent that ours could be described as a surveillance society unless trust in the Government's intentions in relation to data and data sharing is preserved. The Home Office in particular and Government in general must take every possible step to maintain and build on this trust.

123. The technological developments which facilitate the collection, storage and use of information about individuals and their activities have clear benefits for the individual as a consumer and a user of public services. If collected accurately and used properly databases of personal information can support both 'de-personalised', impartial decision-making processes and the delivery of 'personalised' services tailored to the needs of the individual.

124. However, the risks associated with the collection and use of personal information in databases in particular and the monitoring of individuals' behaviour in general, should not be underestimated. Mistakes or misuse of data can result in serious practical harm to individuals. Those less demonstrable risks which relate to the erosion of one's sense of privacy or individual liberty also have a practical aspect and a broad application in that they affect the way in which citizens interact with the state.

125. The risks associated with surveillance increase with the range and volume of information collected. The Government has a crucial role to play in maintaining the trust of the public: any evaluation of the use of surveillance must take into account the potential risk to this relationship with the public.

126. Technological capabilities continue to expand, increasing our means both of generating information about ourselves and of using that information for different purposes. But the drive to make the most of these capabilities should be tempered by an evaluation of the risks involved in collecting more information. Particular consideration should be given to situations in which individuals might suffer as a result of their lack of awareness or ability to take advantage of opportunities to exercise choice over how information about them is used, or to check that it is accurate.

(A) OVERT VIDEO SURVEILLANCE

The use of CCTV is regulated by the Data Protection Act 1998 (see below) and the Code of Practice for users of Close Circuit Television published by the Information Commissioner. The CCTV Code recognises that:

CCTV surveillance has become a common feature of our daily lives. We are caught on numerous CCTV cameras as we move around our towns and cities, visit shops and offices, and travel on the road and other parts of the public transport network. Whilst the use of CCTV continues to enjoy general public support, it necessarily involves intrusion into the lives of ordinary individuals as they go about their day to day business. Our research has shown that the public expect it to be used responsibly with effective safeguards in place. Maintaining public trust and confidence in its use is essential if its benefits are to be realised and its use is not to become increasingly viewed with suspicion as part of a surveillance society.[105]

There is an ongoing debate as to its effectiveness in reducing crime[106] and the development of surveillance technology, particularly digitalisation, brings issues of effective accountability

---

105 Information Commissioner, *CCTV Code of Practice* (2008), available at www.ico.gov.uk.

106 See, e.g., J. Ditton, E. Short, S. Phillips, C. Norris and G. Armstrong, *The Effect of Closed Circuit Television on Recorded Crime Rates, and on the Fear of Crime in Glasgow* (Central Research Unit, Scottish Office, Edinburgh, 1999); M. Gill, A. Spriggs, J. Allen, J. Argomaniz, J. Bryan, M. Hemming, P. Jessiman, D. Kara, J. Kilworth, R. Little, D. Swain and S. Waples, *The Impact of CCTV: Fourteen Case Studies* (Home Office;

and security to the fore.[107] The Data Protection Act 1998 (see further below) requires that CCTV cameras which capture identifiable images[108] of individuals must be registered with the Information Commissioner's Office, though household users are largely exempt. CCTV users must then abide by the Data Protection principles which impact upon issues such as the collection of information, its storage and dissemination. The European Court of Human Rights has stated that:

> The monitoring of the actions of an individual in a public place by the use of photographic equipment which does not record the visual data does not, as such, give rise to an interference with the individual's private life.[109]

Therefore, the recording of video images must be regulated. Is regulation by a Code issued by the Office of the Information Commissioner sufficient given the widespread use of such surveillance? The case of *Peck v United Kingdom*[110] further illustrates that the publication of images beyond what might reasonably be expected can amount to an interference with Art. 8.

Since the evidence generated by CCTV is likely to be very cogent and reliable there is a strong incentive to admit it at trial, and the potential dangers of privacy infringements will be unlikely to lead to exclusion.

(B) COVERT SURVEILLANCE

(I) THE POLICE ACT 1997, PT III

In the House of Lords in *Khan v United Kingdom*,[111] Lord Nicholls expressed 'astonishment' that there was then no statutory regulation of the use of devices such as that used in the case to listen to conversations of K via a bugging device covertly fitted to an associate's house (the police committing a trespass, criminal damage and breaching Art. 8 of the ECHR in the process),[112] rendering English law incompatible with Art. 8. Under Art. 8, secret surveillance must be prescribed by law, necessary, and proportionate: *Kopp v Switzerland*;[113] *Klass v Germany*.[114] Partly in response to this the Police Act 1997 was enacted.[115] Part III of the Act provides the police with the power to authorise entry to and interference with property, and carry out surveillance by means of wireless telegraphy. Authorisation officers include chief constables and the Director General of the Serious Organised Crime Agency.[116] An assist-

---

NACRO, Home Office Online Report, London, 2002); B. Welsh and D. Farrington, *Crime Prevention Effects of Closed Circuit Television: A Systematic Review* (HMSO, London, Home Office Research Study No. 252, 2002).

[107] M. Gill, A. Spriggs, J. Allen, M. Hemming, P. Jessiman, D. Kara, J. Kilworth, R. Little and D. Swain, *Control Rooms: Findings from Control Room Observations* (Home Office, London, Home Office Online Report, 2005). On attitudes to CCTV see: T. Levesley and A. Martin, *Police Attitudes to and use of CCTV* (Home Office, London, Online Report, 2005); A. Spriggs, M. Gill, J. Argomaniz and J. Bryan, *Public Attitudes Towards CCTV: Results from the Pre-Intervention Public Attitude Survey carried out in areas Implementing CCTV* (Home Office, London, Home Office Online Report, 2005); House of Lords Select Committee on Science and Technology, *Digital Images as Evidence*, Eighth Report (1998) HL 121.

[108] But note the interpretation of personal data below.

[109] *Perry v UK* (2004) 39 EHRR 3 at para. 38; see also *Herbecq v Belgium*, App. No. 32200/96.

[110] *Peck v UK* (2003) 36 EHRR 41.   [111] [1997] AC 558.

[112] See *Khan v UK* [2000] Crim LR 684.   [113] (1998) 27 EHRR 91.

[114] (1978) 2 EHRR 24.

[115] See also Home Affairs Select Committee Third Report for 1994–5, *Organised Crime* (1995) HC 18.

[116] S. 93(5).

ant chief constable may authorise in cases of urgency.[117] The grounds for authorisation are contained in s. 93:

(2) This subsection applies where the authorising officer believes—

    (a) that it is necessary for the action specified to be taken [for the purpose of preventing or detecting][118] serious crime, and

    [(b) that the taking of the action is proportionate to what the action seeks to achieve].[119]

(4) For the purposes of subsection (2), conduct which constitutes one or more offences shall be regarded as serious crime if, and only if,—

    (a) it involves the use of violence, results in substantial financial gain or is conduct by a large number of persons in pursuit of a common purpose, or

    (b) the offence or one of the offences is an offence for which a person who has attained the age of twenty-one [(eighteen in relation to England and Wales)[120]] and has no previous convictions could reasonably be expected to be sentenced to imprisonment for a term of three years or more,

and, where the authorising officer is within subsection (5)(h), it relates to an assigned matter within the meaning of section 1(1) of the Customs and Excise Management Act 1979.

NOTES

1. By s. 92: 'No entry on or interference with property or with wireless telegraphy shall be unlawful if it is authorised by an authorisation having effect under this Part.' The Act therefore provides immunity from civil and criminal liability for those acting under its terms.

2. In many ways, Pt III of the Police Act 1997 was a very short-sighted piece of legislation since it failed to deal with many types of surveillance that are claimed to be vital in the fight against crime; most notably those relating to access of electronic communication. The Act was narrowly focused, effectively replicating the previous non-statutory Home Office Guidelines rather than seeking to provide a comprehensive surveillance code.[121] One major difference however, was that the Act provided for wider grounds of authorisation. Should s. 93(4)(a) justify the bugging of peaceful protesters?

3. Authorisation should be in writing except in urgent cases and will last for three months in written cases and 72 hours in oral cases. Once the authorisation has been given, it must be reported to the Surveillance Commissioners for scrutiny who may, if they believe that there were not reasonable grounds that the conditions of issue were satisfied, quash the authorisation or order the destruction of material derived from the operation (unless that material is already required for pending legal action).

4. Approval by a Commissioner may be needed where the authorising officer believes that material subject to legal privilege, confidential journalistic material or confidential personal information might be obtained. All authorisations are reviewed by an independent

---

117 S. 94.
118 Substituted by the Regulation of Investigatory Powers Act 2000, s. 75(1), (4)(a).
119 Ibid., s. 75(1), (4)(b).
120 Inserted by the Criminal Justice and Court Services Act 2000, s. 74, Sch. 7, Pt II, para. 149.
121 See S. Uglow [1999] Crim LR 287.

commission, but some of those reviews are conducted *after* the authorisation has been given by senior police officers. Is this a sufficient safeguard?

5. In 2005/6 2,311 authorisations were made under Pt III of the Police Act 1997, 188 of which required the prior approval of a Commissioner. This number has remained relatively stable. By far the majority of authorisations were made in relation to suspected drug trafficking.

Prompted by the passage of the Human Rights Act 1998 and the increasing use of covert policing techniques, a more comprehensive system of covert surveillance regulation emerged.[122]

(II) THE REGULATION OF INVESTIGATORY POWERS ACT 2000

The Regulation of Investigatory Powers Act 2000 was designed to represent a comprehensive code for surveillance. The Home Secretary assured the public that RIPA would ensure that [covert policing]:

... will be properly regulated by law and externally supervised, not least to ensure that law enforcement operations are consistent with the duties imposed on public authorities by the European Convention on Human Rights.[123]

The 2000 Act sought to regulate surveillance of the types of communication not dealt with in the Police Act 1997: pagers, e-mails, mobile phones, etc. It extended the powers in relation to post and telecommunications surveillance by replacing the Interception of Communications Act 1985.

Part I of the 2000 Act deals with the extension of the powers of surveillance over post and telecommunications. Part II deals with surveillance and the regulation of covert human policing (undercover officers, informers entrapment, etc.). Part III governs controversial powers to maintain effective policing by allowing enforcement agencies to require the disclosure of encryption keys for material or for a plain text copy. The Government stated its considerable concern that the electronic commerce that is now so vital to the country's economy was inadequately protected from fraud.[124] Part IV provides for the appointment of Commissioners and a complaints tribunal. The Act is a complex and lengthy piece of legislation, extracts of which are reproduced below.

(III) REGULATION OF INVESTIGATIVE POWERS ACT 2000

PART I: CHAPTER I

1 Unlawful interception

(1) It shall be an offence for a person intentionally and without lawful authority to intercept, at any place in the United Kingdom, any communication in the course of its transmission by means of—

(a) a public postal service; or

(b) a public telecommunication system.

---

[122] A number of adverse judgments in Strasbourg also prompted reform. See especially *Govell v UK*, App. No. 27237/95; *Khan v UK*, App. No. 35394/97; *Halford v UK*, App. No. 20605/92.

[123] HC Debs, vol. 345, col. 677.

[124] See the Home Office, *Building Confidence in Electronic Commerce: A Consultation Document* (1999).

(2) It shall be an offence for a person—

   (a) intentionally and without lawful authority, and

   (b) otherwise than in circumstances in which his conduct is excluded by subsection (6) from criminal liability under this subsection,

to intercept, at any place in the United Kingdom, any communication in the course of its transmission by means of a private telecommunication system.

(3) Any interception of a communication which is carried out at any place in the United Kingdom by, or with the express or implied consent of, a person having the right to control the operation or the use of a private telecommunication system shall be actionable at the suit or instance of the sender or recipient, or intended recipient, of the communication if it is without lawful authority and is either—

   (a) an interception of that communication in the course of its transmission by means of that private system; or

   (b) an interception of that communication in the course of its transmission, by means of a public telecommunication system, to or from apparatus comprised in that private telecommunication system.

(4) Where the United Kingdom is a party to an international agreement which—

   (a) relates to the provision of mutual assistance in connection with, or in the form of, the interception of communications,

   (b) requires the issue of a warrant, order or equivalent instrument in cases in which assistance is given, and

   (c) is designated for the purposes of this subsection by an order made by the Secretary of State,

it shall be the duty of the Secretary of State to secure that no request for assistance in accordance with the agreement is made on behalf of a person in the United Kingdom to the competent authorities of a country or territory outside the United Kingdom except with lawful authority.

(5) Conduct has lawful authority for the purposes of this section if, and only if—

   (a) it is authorised by or under section 3 or 4;

   (b) it takes place in accordance with a warrant under section 5 ('an interception warrant'); or

   (c) it is in exercise, in relation to any stored communication, of any statutory power that is exercised (apart from this section) for the purpose of obtaining information or of taking possession of any document or other property;

and conduct (whether or not prohibited by this section) which has lawful authority for the purposes of this section by virtue of paragraph (a) or (b) shall also be taken to be lawful for all other purposes.

(6) The circumstances in which a person makes an interception of a communication in the course of its transmission by means of a private telecommunication system are such that his conduct is excluded from criminal liability under subsection (2) if—

   (a) he is a person with a right to control the operation or the use of the system; or

   (b) he has the express or implied consent of such a person to make the interception.

(7) A person who is guilty of an offence under subsection (1) or (2) shall be liable—

   (a) on conviction on indictment, to imprisonment for a term not exceeding two years or to a fine, or to both;

   (b) on summary conviction, to a fine not exceeding the statutory maximum.

(8) No proceedings for any offence which is an offence by virtue of this section shall be instituted—

    (a) in England and Wales, except by or with the consent of the Director of Public Prosecutions;

...

2 Meaning and location of 'interception' etc

(1) In this Act—

'postal service' means any service which—

    (a) consists in the following, or in any one or more of them, namely, the collection, sorting, conveyance, distribution and delivery (whether in the United Kingdom or elsewhere) of postal items; and

    (b) is offered or provided as a service the main purpose of which, or one of the main purposes of which, is to make available, or to facilitate, a means of transmission from place to place of postal items containing communications;

'private telecommunication system' means any telecommunication system which, without itself being a public telecommunication system, is a system in relation to which the following conditions are satisfied—

    (a) it is attached, directly or indirectly and whether or not for the purposes of the communication in question, to a public telecommunication system; and

    (b) there is apparatus comprised in the system which is both located in the United Kingdom and used (with or without other apparatus) for making the attachment to the public telecommunication system;

...

(2) For the purposes of this Act, but subject to the following provisions of this section, a person intercepts a communication in the course of its transmission by means of a telecommunication system if, and only if, he—

    (a) so modifies or interferes with the system, or its operation,

    (b) so monitors transmissions made by means of the system, or

    (c) so monitors transmissions made by wireless telegraphy to or from apparatus comprised in the system,

as to make some or all of the contents of the communication available, while being transmitted, to a person other than the sender or intended recipient of the communication.

...

3 Lawful interception without an interception warrant

(1) Conduct by any person consisting in the interception of a communication is authorised by this section if the communication is one which, or which that person has reasonable grounds for believing, is both—

    (a) a communication sent by a person who has consented to the interception; and

    (b) a communication the intended recipient of which has so consented.

(2) Conduct by any person consisting in the interception of a communication is authorised by this section if—

    (a) the communication is one sent by, or intended for, a person who has consented to the interception; and

    (b) surveillance by means of that interception has been authorised under Part II.

(3) Conduct consisting in the interception of a communication is authorised by this section if—

    (a) it is conduct by or on behalf of a person who provides a postal service or a telecommunications service; and

    (b) it takes place for purposes connected with the provision or operation of that service or with the enforcement, in relation to that service, of any enactment relating to the use of postal services or telecommunications services.

...

4 Power to provide for lawful interception

(1) Conduct by any person ('the interceptor') consisting in the interception of a communication in the course of its transmission by means of a telecommunication system is authorised by this section if—

    (a) the interception is carried out for the purpose of obtaining information about the communications of a person who, or who the interceptor has reasonable grounds for believing, is in a country or territory outside the United Kingdom;

    (b) the interception relates to the use of a telecommunications service provided to persons in that country or territory which is either—

        (i) a public telecommunications service; or

        (ii) a telecommunications service that would be a public telecommunications service if the persons to whom it is offered or provided were members of the public in a part of the United Kingdom;

    (c) the person who provides that service (whether the interceptor or another person) is required by the law of that country or territory to carry out, secure or facilitate the interception in question;

    (d) the situation is one in relation to which such further conditions as may be prescribed by regulations made by the Secretary of State are required to be satisfied before conduct may be treated as authorised by virtue of this subsection; and

    (e) the conditions so prescribed are satisfied in relation to that situation.

(2) Subject to subsection (3), the Secretary of State may by regulations authorise any such conduct described in the regulations as appears to him to constitute a legitimate practice reasonably required for the purpose, in connection with the carrying on of any business, of monitoring or keeping a record of—

    (a) communications by means of which transactions are entered into in the course of that business; or

    (b) other communications relating to that business or taking place in the course of its being carried on.

(3) Nothing in any regulations under subsection (2) shall authorise the interception of any communication except in the course of its transmission using apparatus or services provided by or to the person carrying on the business for use wholly or partly in connection with that business.

...

5 Interception with a warrant

(1) Subject to the following provisions of this Chapter, the Secretary of State may issue a warrant authorising or requiring the person to whom it is addressed, by any such conduct as may be described in the warrant, to secure any one or more of the following—

    (a) the interception in the course of their transmission by means of a postal service or telecommunication system of the communications described in the warrant;

(b) the making, in accordance with an international mutual assistance agreement, of a request for the provision of such assistance in connection with, or in the form of, an interception of communications as may be so described;

(c) the provision, in accordance with an international mutual assistance agreement, to the competent authorities of a country or territory outside the United Kingdom of any such assistance in connection with, or in the form of, an interception of communications as may be so described;

(d) the disclosure, in such manner as may be so described, of intercepted material obtained by any interception authorised or required by the warrant, and of related communications data.

(2) The Secretary of State shall not issue an interception warrant unless he believes—

(a) that the warrant is necessary on grounds falling within subsection (3); and

(b) that the conduct authorised by the warrant is proportionate to what is sought to be achieved by that conduct.

(3) Subject to the following provisions of this section, a warrant is necessary on grounds falling within this subsection if it is necessary—

(a) in the interests of national security;

(b) for the purpose of preventing or detecting serious crime;

(c) for the purpose of safeguarding the economic well-being of the United Kingdom; or

(d) for the purpose, in circumstances appearing to the Secretary of State to be equivalent to those in which he would issue a warrant by virtue of paragraph (b), of giving effect to the provisions of any international mutual assistance agreement.

(4) The matters to be taken into account in considering whether the requirements of subsection (2) are satisfied in the case of any warrant shall include whether the information which it is thought necessary to obtain under the warrant could reasonably be obtained by other means.

(5) A warrant shall not be considered necessary on the ground falling within subsection (3)(c) unless the information which it is thought necessary to obtain is information relating to the acts or intentions of persons outside the British Islands.

...

8 Contents of warrants

(1) An interception warrant must name or describe either—

(a) one person as the interception subject; or

(b) a single set of premises as the premises in relation to which the interception to which the warrant relates is to take place.

(2) The provisions of an interception warrant describing communications the interception of which is authorised or required by the warrant must comprise one or more schedules setting out the addresses, numbers, apparatus or other factors, or combination of factors, that are to be used for identifying the communications that may be or are to be intercepted.

(3) Any factor or combination of factors set out in accordance with subsection (2) must be one that identifies communications which are likely to be or to include—

(a) communications from, or intended for, the person named or described in the warrant in accordance with subsection (1); or

(b) communications originating on, or intended for transmission to, the premises so named or described.

(4) Subsections (1) and (2) shall not apply to an interception warrant if—

    (a) the description of communications to which the warrant relates confines the conduct authorised or required by the warrant to conduct falling within subsection (5); and

    (b) at the time of the issue of the warrant, a certificate applicable to the warrant has been issued by the Secretary of State certifying—

        (i) the descriptions of intercepted material the examination of which he considers necessary; and

        (ii) that he considers the examination of material of those descriptions necessary as mentioned in section 5(3)(a), (b) or (c).

(5) Conduct falls within this subsection if it consists in—

    (a) the interception of external communications in the course of their transmission by means of a telecommunication system; and

    (b) any conduct authorised in relation to any such interception by section 5(6).

(6) A certificate for the purposes of subsection (4) shall not be issued except under the hand of the Secretary of State.

9 Duration, cancellation and renewal of warrants

(1) An interception warrant—

    (a) shall cease to have effect at the end of the relevant period; but

    (b) may be renewed, at any time before the end of that period, by an instrument under the hand of the Secretary of State [or, in the case of a warrant issued by the Scottish Ministers (by virtue of provision made under section 63 of the Scotland Act 1998), a member of the Scottish Executive][125] or, in a case falling within section 7(2)(b), under the hand of a senior official.

(2) An interception warrant shall not be renewed under subsection (1) unless the Secretary of State believes that the warrant continues to be necessary on grounds falling within section 5(3).

(3) The Secretary of State shall cancel an interception warrant if he is satisfied that the warrant is no longer necessary on grounds falling within section 5(3).

(4) The Secretary of State shall cancel an interception warrant if, at any time before the end of the relevant period, he is satisfied in a case in which—

    (a) the warrant is one which was issued containing the statement set out in section 7(5)(a) or has been renewed by an instrument containing the statement set out in subsection (5)(b)(i) of this section, and

    (b) the latest renewal (if any) of the warrant is not a renewal by an instrument under the hand of the Secretary of State,

that the person named or described in the warrant as the interception subject is in the United Kingdom.

(5) An instrument under the hand of a senior official that renews an interception warrant must contain—

    (a) a statement that the renewal is for the purposes of a request for assistance made under an international mutual assistance agreement by the competent authorities of a country or territory outside the United Kingdom; and

---

125 Inserted by SI 2000/3253, art. 4(1), Sch. 3, Pt II, paras 3, 5.

    (b) whichever of the following statements is applicable—

        (i) a statement that the interception subject appears to be outside the United Kingdom;

        (ii) a statement that the interception to which the warrant relates is to take place in relation only to premises outside the United Kingdom.

…

17 Exclusion of matters from legal proceedings

(1) Subject to section 18, no evidence shall be adduced, question asked, assertion or disclosure made or other thing done in, for the purposes of or in connection with any legal proceedings [or Inquiries Act proceedings][126] which (in any manner)—

    (a) discloses, in circumstances from which its origin in anything falling within subsection (2) may be inferred, any of the contents of an intercepted communication or any related communications data; or

    (b) tends (apart from any such disclosure) to suggest that anything falling within subsection (2) has or may have occurred or be going to occur.

…

21 Lawful acquisition and disclosure of communications data

(1) This Chapter applies to—

    (a) any conduct in relation to a postal service or telecommunication system for obtaining communications data, other than conduct consisting in the interception of communications in the course of their transmission by means of such a service or system; and

    (b) the disclosure to any person of communications data.

(2) Conduct to which this Chapter applies shall be lawful for all purposes if—

    (a) it is conduct in which any person is authorised or required to engage by an authorisation or notice granted or given under this Chapter; and

    (b) the conduct is in accordance with, or in pursuance of, the authorisation or requirement.

(3) A person shall not be subject to any civil liability in respect of any conduct of his which—

    (a) is incidental to any conduct that is lawful by virtue of subsection (2); and

    (b) is not itself conduct an authorisation or warrant for which is capable of being granted under a relevant enactment and might reasonably have been expected to have been sought in the case in question.

(4) In this Chapter 'communications data' means any of the following—

    (a) any traffic data comprised in or attached to a communication (whether by the sender or otherwise) for the purposes of any postal service or telecommunication system by means of which it is being or may be transmitted;

    (b) any information which includes none of the contents of a communication (apart from any information falling within paragraph (a)) and is about the use made by any person—

        (i) of any postal service or telecommunications service; or

        (ii) in connection with the provision to or use by any person of any telecommunications service, of any part of a telecommunication system;

---

[126] Inserted by the Inquiries Act 2005, s. 48(1), Sch. 2, Pt 1, para. 20(1), (2).

(c) any information not falling within paragraph (a) or (b) that is held or obtained, in relation to persons to whom he provides the service, by a person providing a postal service or telecommunications service.

...

22 Obtaining and disclosing communications data

(1) This section applies where a person designated for the purposes of this Chapter believes that it is necessary on grounds falling within subsection (2) to obtain any communications data.

(2) It is necessary on grounds falling within this subsection to obtain communications data if it is necessary—

(a) in the interests of national security;

(b) for the purpose of preventing or detecting crime or of preventing disorder;

(c) in the interests of the economic well-being of the United Kingdom;

(d) in the interests of public safety;

(e) for the purpose of protecting public health;

(f) for the purpose of assessing or collecting any tax, duty, levy or other imposition, contribution or charge payable to a government department;

(g) for the purpose, in an emergency, of preventing death or injury or any damage to a person's physical or mental health, or of mitigating any injury or damage to a person's physical or mental health; or

(h) for any purpose (not falling within paragraphs (a) to (g)) which is specified for the purposes of this subsection by an order made by the Secretary of State.

(3) Subject to subsection (5), the designated person may grant an authorisation for persons holding offices, ranks or positions with the same relevant public authority as the designated person to engage in any conduct to which this Chapter applies.

(4) Subject to subsection (5), where it appears to the designated person that a postal or telecommunications operator is or may be in possession of, or be capable of obtaining, any communications data, the designated person may, by notice to the postal or telecommunications operator, require the operator—

(a) if the operator is not already in possession of the data, to obtain the data; and

(b) in any case, to disclose all of the data in his possession or subsequently obtained by him.

(5) The designated person shall not grant an authorisation under subsection (3), or give a notice under subsection (4), unless he believes that obtaining the data in question by the conduct authorised or required by the authorisation or notice is proportionate to what is sought to be achieved by so obtaining the data.

(6) It shall be the duty of the postal or telecommunications operator to comply with the requirements of any notice given to him under subsection (4).

(7) A person who is under a duty by virtue of subsection (6) shall not be required to do anything in pursuance of that duty which it is not reasonably practicable for him to do.

(8) The duty imposed by subsection (6) shall be enforceable by civil proceedings by the Secretary of State for an injunction, or for specific performance of a statutory duty under section 45 of the Court of Session Act 1988, or for any other appropriate relief.

(9) The Secretary of State shall not make an order under subsection (2)(h) unless a draft of the order has been laid before Parliament and approved by a resolution of each House.

NOTES

1. *Warrants for interception.* RIPA 2000, s. 1, makes it an offence 'intentionally and without lawful authority' to intercept in the UK any communication in the course of its transmission by means of a 'public' or 'private telecommunications system', or by means of a 'public postal service'.[127] Private telephone communications systems include 'an office or hotel network, or the telephones in a domestic household'.

2. An interception is 'without lawful authority' unless: (a) it is authorised by warrant;[128] or (b) there are reasonable grounds to believe that it is with the consent of the sender and the intended recipient;[129] or (c) it is with the consent of either the sender or the recipient and it is authorised under the surveillance provisions of Part II the RIPA 2000;[130] or (d) in certain other cases.[131]

3. Applications for a warrant may be made by a police chief constable or other similar office-holder listed in s. 6. The Act leaves the authority to issue a warrant with the competent Secretary of State (s. 5); proposals[132] that warrants should be issued by a judge were not accepted.[133]

4. The grounds for issuing a warrant are indicated in s. 5(3). A 'serious crime' is defined in s. 81(3) as one that satisfies either of the following tests:[134]

(*a*) that the offence is one of the offences that is or would be constituted by the conduct is an offence for which a person who has attained the age of twenty-one and has no previous convictions could reasonably be expected to be sentences to imprisonment for a term of three years or more;

(*b*) that the conduct involves the use of violence, results in substantial financial gain or is conduct by a large number of persons in pursuit of a common purpose.

As to 'economic well-being', a Government spokesman[135] stated during the passage of the same wording in the earlier Interception of Communications Act 1985:

It is concerned with the interception that is necessary for the effective protection of the country's economic interests at the international level. It is an important part of our foreign policy to protect the country from adverse developments overseas which may not necessarily affect our national security so directly as to justify interception on that ground but which may have damaging consequences for our economic well-being... If I refer in a general way to a threat to the supply from abroad of a commodity [e.g. oil] on which our economy is particularly dependent, I hope that your Lordships will accept that I have gone... as far as I can by way of offering an example.

The term 'national security' is not defined.

Warrants may be issued only when the Secretary of State considers that the warrant is 'necessary' on one of the above grounds and the authorised conduct is 'proportionate to what is sought to be achieved'.[136]

---

[127] These terms are defined in RIPA 2000, s. 2. Prosecution for the s. 1 offence is only with the consent of the DPP. The penalty is up to two years' imprisonment or an unlimited fine.

[128] RIPA 2000, s. 5.   [129] RIPA 2000, s. 3(1).   [130] RIPA 2000, s. 3(2).

[131] RIPA 2000, s. 3(3).   [132] See the Justice Report, *Under Surveillance* (1998), p. 21.

[133] A proposal that judicial authorisation be introduced was made by the Joint Committee of Human Rights, *Nineteenth Report of Session 2006–7* (2007) HC 394, para. 38.

[134] Cf. the identical definition of 'serious crime' in s. 93(4) of the Police Act 1997.

[135] Lord President of the Council (Lord Hailsham) HL Deb 6, 6 June 1985, col. 879.

[136] RIPA 2000, s. 5(2). The terms 'necessary' and 'proportionate' echo the limitations on interferences with privacy in Art. 8(2) ECHR.

5. Warrants may be issued under the RIPA 2000 for the interception of communications to or from the persons or to or from the premises described in the warrant.[137] In 1966, the Prime Minister (Mr Wilson) announced that he had given instructions after taking office that MPs' telephones were to be immune from tapping.[138] The Secretary of State may certify that the required description in the warrant of the person or premises to be targeted may be dispensed in the case of 'external communications',[139] i.e. communications to or from outside the British Isles.[140] Warrants are issued for three months, renewable for a further six months.[141]

6. At the close of 2006, 754 warrants were in force. During the period of April to December 2006 1,333 warrants were issued.[142] Within that same period 24 interception errors were noted, none of which were said to be deliberate.[143]

7. Under RIPA 2000, s. 17, evidence obtained from interceptions of communications made under a warrant issued under the RIPA 2000 is inadmissible in legal proceedings.[144] This section has been the source of much recent controversy.[145] As Ormerod and McKay point out 'there is something inherently incoherent and illogical in a scheme which seeks to author-ise an activity (ss. 1–9), recognises that that activity must lead to material which will be relevant at trial (s. 18), and yet seeks to suppress that material and even the fact of its exist-ence (s. 17)'.[146] Intercept evidence can be compelling evidence and possibly the only evidence available. Thus, there have been many calls for the law to be changed. In 2006 the Home Secretary stated that the Government was working 'to find, if possible, a legal model that would provide the necessary safeguards to allow intercept material to be used as evidence'.[147] In support of the rule of inadmissibility is the argument that the security forces need to keep secret their techniques and sources.[148]

8. *Metering.* RIPA 2000, ss. 21–25 regulate the disclosure of telephone or postal com-munications data resulting from metering[149] to a 'relevant public authority', such as the police and Revenue and Customs.[150] Access to communications data may be authorised

---

[137] RIPA 2000, s. 8(1).

[138] 736 HC Deb, 17 November 1966, col. 639. Cf. Mr. Heath 803 HC Deb, 16 July 1970, col. 1723. In February 2008 the Wilson doctrine was alleged to have been breached following the discovery that a Labour MP had had his conversations with a constituent bugged: see, *The Times*, 3 February 2008. An inquiry conducted by the Chief Surveillance Commissioner however found that the 'interception' did not come within the statutory def-inition and thus did not breach the Wilson doctrine: see, *The Times*, 5 February 2008.

[139] RIPA 2000, s. 8(4). For safeguards in respect of such certified warrants, see s. 16 RIPA 2000.

[140] RIPA 2000, s. 20.   [141] RIPA 2000, s. 9(6).

[142] *Report of the Interception of Communications Commissioner for 2006* (2008) HC 252, Annex.

[143] Ibid., para. 42.

[144] Certain exceptions are allowed by RIPA, s. 18. The contents of lawful interceptions made under RIPA 2000, s. 1(5)(c), (3), (4) fall within these exceptions: RIPA 2000, s. 18(4).

[145] On s. 17. see *Attorney-General's Reference (No. 5 of 2002)* [2004] UKHL 40; The Joint Committee on Human Rights Twenty-fourth Report 2005–06, *Counter-Terrorism Policy and Human Rights: Prosecution and Pre-Charge Detention* (2006) HL 240/HC 1576; Liberty's response to the Joint Committee on Human Rights: Relaxing the Ban on the Admissibility of Intercept Evidence (2007); The Government Reply to the Twenty-Fourth Report from the Joint Committee on Human Rights (2006); JUSTICE, *Intercept Evidence: Lifting the Ban* (2006); Privy Counsellor Review Committee, *Anti-terrorism, Crime and Security Act Review: Report* (2003), para. 208.

[146] [2004] Crim LR 15 at 31.   [147] HC Deb, 2 February 2006, col. 479.

[148] See further, House of Lords Liaison Committee, *First Report Session 2005–6* (2006) HL 29, Appendix B.

[149] I.e. data resulting from the collection of information about, for example, the traffic on a telephone, includ-ing the numbers dialled and the time and duration of calls, or the address on a postal communication.

[150] The system under RIPA 2000, ss. 21–25 replaces the less rigorous, permissive system under the Telecommunications Act 1984, s. 45 and the Data Protection Act 1998, s. 29. In *Malone v UK* (1984) 7 EHRR

on grounds of the detection of crime, etc.[151] by a 'designated person' within the 'relevant public authority'.[152] There is no provision for authorisation or approval by a judge or other independent person.

9. *Interception of Communications Commissioner.* RIPA 2000 provides for independent supervision of the operation of the warrant procedure for the interception of communications and authorisations for the disclosure of communications data in Pt I of the Act. The supervision is the responsibility of an Interception of Communications Commissioner appointed by the Prime Minister.[153] The Commissioner must report annually to the Prime Minister, the report being presented to Parliament and published as a command paper.[154] A part of the report need not be presented to Parliament if its presentations would be 'contrary to the public interest' or 'prejudicial to—(a) national security, (b) the prevention or detection of serious crime, (c) the economic well-being of the United Kingdom, or (d) the continued discharge of the functions of any public authority whose activities include activities that are subject to review'.[155] The Commissioner has no power to authorise, approve or cancel warrants, etc. Instead his function is to monitor and report upon practice.

10. RIPA 2000, s. 65 establishes a Tribunal that has jurisdiction to hear complaints from individuals arising out of the operation of the arrangements for: (a) the interception of communications and the disclosure of communications data under Pt I, RIPA; and (b) the release of encrypted data under Pt II of RIPA 2000.[156] Tribunal members must hold or have held 'high judicial office' and are appointed for five-year terms.[157] If the Tribunal finds, applying judicial review principles, that the required procedures have not been complied with, it may make an order awarding compensation, or quashing the warrant or authorisation, or requiring the destruction of the intercepted material.[158] The remedy before the Tribunal is final; it is not subject to appeal or judicial review in the courts.[159]

11. RIPA 2000, s. 1(3) creates a statutory tort of unlawful interception of a communication by means of a private telecommunications system by or with the consent of a person with the right to control the system. The tort might, for example, be committed by an employer

---

14, the disclosure to the police by the Post Office of its records of metering was a breach of Art. 8 ECHR because there was no legal regulation of this interference with privacy.

[151] The list of grounds is longer than that for the interception of communications. It includes 'national security', 'preventing or detecting crime', 'preventing disorder', 'economic well-being', 'public safety', 'public health', collecting tax and preventing death or injury in an emergency: RIPA 2000, s. 22(2). Requirements of 'necessity' and 'proportionality' apply: RIPA 2000, ss. 22(5), 23(8).

[152] For definitions, see RIPA 2000, s. 25. The data may be ordered to be disclosed by a postal or telecommunications operator to, for example, the police by the designated police officer, or it may already be in the hands of the police as a result of a lawful police operation, with the self-authorisation providing a legal safeguard.

[153] RIPA 2000, s. 57(1). The Commissioner must hold or have held 'high judicial office': RIPA 2000. s. 57(5). A similar office existed previously under the 1988, Act. The current Commissioner is Sir Paul Kennedy.

[154] RIPA 2000, s. 58.   [155] RIPA 2000, s. 58(7).

[156] The Tribunal also has jurisdiction in complaints arising out of the operation of the surveillance system in RIPA 2000, Part II. The Tribunal is exclusively competent to determine any action brought under s. 7(1)(a) of the Human Rights Act 1998 claiming that conduct under the RIPA 2000 is incompatible with Convention rights (e.g. the right to privacy) RIPA 2000, s. 65(2). The Tribunal established by s. 65 is the successor to the one that operated under the Interception of Communications Act 1985. It also has jurisdiction to consider complaints under the Security Services Act 1989, the Intelligence Services Act 1994 and the Police Act 1997. The tribunals that formerly considered complaints under these other statutes are replaced by the present Tribunal established by the RIPA.

[157] RIPA 2000, Sch. 3, para. 1.   [158] RIPA 2000, s. 67(7).

[159] RIPA 2000, s. 67(8). The remedy before the Tribunal is also the exclusive first instance judicial remedy to challenge compliance with the relevant statutory procedures.

who unlawfully intercepts communications made by employees on an internal office system, as where employees are not made aware that monitoring may take place. The statutory tort established by s. 1(3) applies in situations where the tortfeasor is exempt from the offence in RIPA 2000, s. 1(3).[160]

Part II of the 2000 Act provides a statutory framework governing the authorisation and use of covert surveillance, agents, informants and undercover officers. It is designed to provide appropriate regulation of the use of covert policing techniques and meet the demands of the Human Rights Act 1998 by providing adequate protection against invasions of privacy.

PART II

26 Conduct to which Part II applies

(1) This Part applies to the following conduct—

   (a) directed surveillance;

   (b) intrusive surveillance; and

   (c) the conduct and use of covert human intelligence sources.

(2) Subject to subsection (6), surveillance is directed for the purposes of this Part if it is covert but not intrusive and is undertaken—

   (a) for the purposes of a specific investigation or a specific operation;

   (b) in such a manner as is likely to result in the obtaining of private information about a person (whether or not one specifically identified for the purposes of the investigation or operation); and

   (c) otherwise than by way of an immediate response to events or circumstances the nature of which is such that it would not be reasonably practicable for an authorisation under this Part to be sought for the carrying out of the surveillance.

(3) Subject to subsections (4) to (6), surveillance is intrusive for the purposes of this Part if, and only if, it is covert surveillance that—

   (a) is carried out in relation to anything taking place on any residential premises or in any private vehicle; and

   (b) involves the presence of an individual on the premises or in the vehicle or is carried out by means of a surveillance device.

(4) For the purposes of this Part surveillance is not intrusive to the extent that—

   (a) it is carried out by means only of a surveillance device designed or adapted principally for the purpose of providing information about the location of a vehicle; or

   (b) it is surveillance consisting in any such interception of a communication as falls within section 48(4).

(5) For the purposes of this Part surveillance which—

   (a) is carried out by means of a surveillance device in relation to anything taking place on any residential premises or in any private vehicle, but

   (b) is carried out without that device being present on the premises or in the vehicle,

is not intrusive unless the device is such that it consistently provides information of the same quality and detail as might be expected to be obtained from a device actually present on the premises or in the vehicle.

---

[160] See RIPA 2000, s. 1(6).

(6) For the purposes of this Part surveillance which—

  (a) is carried out by means of apparatus designed or adapted for the purpose of detecting the instal-lation or use in any residential or other premises of a television receiver (within the meaning of [Part 4 of the Communications Act 2003)],[161] and

  (b) is carried out from outside those premises exclusively for that purpose,

  is neither directed nor intrusive.

(7) In this Part—

  (a) references to the conduct of a covert human intelligence source are references to any conduct of such a source which falls within any of paragraphs (a) to (c) of subsection (8), or is incidental to anything falling within any of those paragraphs; and

  (b) references to the use of a covert human intelligence source are references to inducing, asking or assisting a person to engage in the conduct of such a source, or to obtain information by means of the conduct of such a source.

(8) For the purposes of this Part a person is a covert human intelligence source if—

  (a) he establishes or maintains a personal or other relationship with a person for the covert purpose of facilitating the doing of anything falling within paragraph (b) or (c);

  (b) he covertly uses such a relationship to obtain information or to provide access to any information to another person; or

  (c) he covertly discloses information obtained by the use of such a relationship, or as a consequence of the existence of such a relationship.

(9) For the purposes of this section—

  (a) surveillance is covert if, and only if, it is carried out in a manner that is calculated to ensure that persons who are subject to the surveillance are unaware that it is or may be taking place;

  (b) a purpose is covert, in relation to the establishment or maintenance of a personal or other rela-tionship, if and only if the relationship is conducted in a manner that is calculated to ensure that one of the parties to the relationship is unaware of the purpose; and

  (c) a relationship is used covertly, and information obtained as mentioned in subsection (8)(c) is disclosed covertly, if and only if it is used or, as the case may be, disclosed in a manner that is calculated to ensure that one of the parties to the relationship is unaware of the use or disclosure in question.

(10) In this section 'private information', in relation to a person, includes any information relating to his private or family life.

(11) References in this section, in relation to a vehicle, to the presence of a surveillance device in the vehicle include references to its being located on or under the vehicle and also include references to its being attached to it.

27 Lawful surveillance etc

(1) Conduct to which this Part applies shall be lawful for all purposes if—

  (a) an authorisation under this Part confers an entitlement to engage in that conduct on the person whose conduct it is; and

  (b) his conduct is in accordance with the authorisation.

---

161 Substituted by the Communications Act 2003, s. 406(1), Sch. 17, para. 161(1), (2).

(2) A person shall not be subject to any civil liability in respect of any conduct of his which—

(a) is incidental to any conduct that is lawful by virtue of subsection (1); and

(b) is not itself conduct an authorisation or warrant for which is capable of being granted under a relevant enactment and might reasonably have been expected to have been sought in the case in question.

(3) The conduct that may be authorised under this Part includes conduct outside the United Kingdom.

(4) In this section 'relevant enactment' means—

(a) an enactment contained in this Act;

(b) section 5 of the Intelligence Services Act 1994 (warrants for the intelligence services); or

(c) an enactment contained in Part III of the Police Act 1997 (powers of the police and of [officers of Revenue and Customs)].[162]

NOTES

1. Part II of the Act, particularly the use of 'directed surveillance' is utilised by a wide variety of public bodies. The Surveillance Commissioner in the *2006-7 Annual Report*[163] commented that:

My prevailing impression is that the legislation has greatly improved the management and oversight of covert activity by public authorities. There is no room for complacency but it should provide confidence to the general public that the privacy of individuals is not being interfered with without proper regard for the law.[164]

2. Whether surveillance is directed or intrusive will determine which bodies can use it and who must authorise it. To what extent is the division of surveillance into 'directed' and 'intrusive' appropriate in terms of respect for privacy and is it successfully achieved by the Act?

3. Section 26(2), which defines directed surveillance, presents some difficulties of interpretation for an authorising officer. For example, directed surveillance must be 'likely to result in the obtaining of private information about a person'. If the police set up video surveillance in a car park which is a 'hot spot' for thefts from cars, is private information *likely* to be gathered? If not, such an operation will not require authorisation. However, should such covert surveillance by the state be legally unregulated? Considering the issue of when private life might be engaged in a public setting in *PG and JH v United Kingdom*[165] the Strasbourg Court noted:

There are a number of elements relevant to a consideration of whether a person's private life is concerned by measures effected outside a person's home or private premises. Since there are occasions when people knowingly or intentionally involve themselves in activities which are or may be recorded or reported in a public manner, a person's reasonable expectations as to privacy may be a significant, although not necessarily conclusive, factor. A person who walks down the street will, inevitably, be visible to any member of the public who is also present. Monitoring by technological means of the same public scene (for example, a

162 Substituted by the Serious Crime Act 2007, s. 88, Sch. 12, paras 5, 9.
163 Office of the Surveillance Commissioner, *Annual Report 2006-7* (2007) HC 713.
164 Ibid., para. 14.1.   165 App. No. 44787/98. See also *Perry v UK* (2004) 39 EHRR 3.

security guard viewing through closed-circuit television) is of a similar character. Private-life considerations may arise, however, once any systematic or permanent record comes into existence of such material from the public domain.[166]

This would suggest that the authorising officer should pay attention to the nature of the record being made rather than merely an analysis of the location alone.[167]

4. Directed surveillance must also be 'otherwise than by way of an immediate response to events'. If the police were involved in an armed siege which continued for several hours or even days would it require authorisation at some point?

5. Further difficulties arise under s. 26(5) and the ambiguity of the protection turning on the quality of the device rather than the degree of intrusion. Should a citizen's freedom from intrusion depend on how strong the officer anticipates the signal from the bug will be?

6. Under s. 26(9)(a) covert surveillance is surveillance carried out in a 'manner that is calculated to ensure that persons who are subject to the surveillance are unaware that it is or may be taking place'. The overt or covert nature of the device is not decisive but the manner in which it is used. For example, if a neighbour has a telescope in his window visible to other neighbours they would not presume that surveillance was taking place. However, was the telescope to be used by the local authority for surveillance purposes it is suggested that this would be calculated to ensure people were unaware of its use despite it being clearly visible to them.

7. If a member of the public carries out visual recordings of others to pass to the police or other public body this does not require RIPA authorisation. However, should the public body 'initiate or encourage' the surveillance then the protection provided by RIPA authorisation and review cannot be sidestepped.[168]

8. In the 2006/7 Surveillance Commissioner's Report stated that in relation to law enforcement agencies 19,651 directed surveillance authorisations were granted between 1 April 2006 and 31 March 2007, and 2,526 were still in place at the end of that period. This compares with 23,628 and 3,073 respectively in the previous year. Clearly this indicates a significant decrease in the use of these powers, but it must be noted that this figure pertains to authorisations and not operations. There may be as many surveillance operations but authorising officers may determine that these fall outside the realms of RIPA. Indeed, there has been criticism that the police have adopted a risk-averse approach to RIPA resulting in the authorisation of practices that are not intended to be within the remit of the legislation. In 2008 the Flanagan Report stated 'in some instances excessive bureaucracy is created by a combination of misunderstanding and sometimes over-interpretation of the relevant rules'.[169] Public authority use of directed surveillance has increased over the same period. Some 12,494 authorisations were granted during the year, of which 1,800 were still in place at the end of the reporting year. The figures for the previous year were 6,924 and 1,340 respectively. It is argued that this substantial increase reflects a greater awareness by public authorities of their powers under the Act. However, in June 2008 the Chair of the Local Government Association wrote to all local authorities recommending that they review their surveillance

---

[166] Ibid., para. 57.

[167] See also *Wood v Comr of Police for the Metropolis* [2008] EWHC 1105 (Admin).

[168] *MM v The Netherlands* (2004) 39 EHRR 19; see also the commentary to *R v Rosenberg* [2006] Crim LR 540.

[169] Sir Ronnie Flanagan, *The Review of Policing Final Report* (2008), para. 5.55.

practices under RIPA following media attention that covert surveillance was being used in an over-zealous manner.[170]

9. Intrusive surveillance is available to fewer bodies and can be authorised on narrower criteria than directed surveillance. Normally, approval must be sought from the Surveillance Commissioner who must be satisfied that the relevant grounds exist (s. 36(4)). Note the exception for urgent cases. Can there be an effective safeguard against abuse of such an exception? What is noticeable is that there is no criminal offence of unlawful intrusive surveillance—should there have been? What would be an appropriate remedy for unlawful police surveillance? Who would police such an offence?[171] In what circumstances should the Home Secretary have the power to authorise intrusive surveillance to 'protect the economic well being of the country' if that is not also a serious crime? Would this allow for the surveillance of fuel protestors?

10. The relevant grounds for authorisation are the same for directed surveillance and covert sources, namely: (a) in the interests of national security; for the purpose of preventing or detecting crime or of preventing disorder; in the interests of the economic well-being of the UK; in the interests of public safety; for the purpose of protecting public health; for the purpose of assessing or collecting any tax, duty, levy or other imposition, contribution or charge payable to a government department; or for any purpose (not falling within the preceding categories which is specified by an order made by the Secretary of State). Section 30 requires only that the authorising officer is satisfied that, *inter alia,* the surveillance is necessary to detect crime, not *serious* crime. In *Kopp v Switzerland,*[172] the practice of internal authorisation of surveillance activities without judicial authorisation was severely criticised. In the case of serious crime is internal supervision a sufficient safeguard? The authorisation of intrusive surveillance is on rather narrower grounds: the interests of national security; for the purpose of preventing or detecting serious crime; or in the interests of the economic well-being of the UK. For all authorisations the tests of necessity and proportionality must be satisfied.

11. There were 350 intrusive surveillance authorisations during 2006/7, again representing a fall in comparison with the previous years in which there were 435.[173] The police have voiced concerns over the lack of training and personnel to utilize intrusive surveillance.

12. The Code of Practice[174] issued under RIPA reminds users of the need to respect the Convention requirements of necessity and proportionality.

> If the activities are necessary, the person granting the authorisation must believe that they are proportionate to what is sought to be achieved by carrying them out. This involves balancing the intrusiveness of the activity on the target and others who might be affected by it against the need for the activity in operational terms. The activity will not be proportionate if it is excessive in the circumstances of the case or if the information which is sought could reasonably be obtained by other less intrusive means. All such activity should be carefully managed to meet the objective in question and must not be arbitrary or unfair.[175]

---

[170] See www.lga.gov.uk media release, June 2008. Particular media attention was given to a local authority who had used directed surveillance to confirm whether a family was living within a school catchment area: see HC Written Answers 22 May 2008, col. 478w.

[171] See P. Mirfield [2001] Crim LR 91 who considers the evidential difficulties created by the Act and the many methods by which the admissibility of evidence discovered under the Act could be challenged.

[172] App. No. 23224/94, 1998-II.   [173] *Annual Report* (2007), para. 6.7.

[174] The various codes issued under RIPA can be accessed at: http://security.homeoffice.gov.uk/ripa/publication-search/ripa-cop/.

[175] Ibid., para. 2.5. See also N. Taylor [2006] Covert Policing 22.

13. Covert human intelligence sources (CHIS) are placed on a statutory footing for the first time in s. 26(7). The necessity for legal regulation in this area was highlighted in the case of *Texeira de Castro v Portugal*.[176]

14. There were 4,373 CHIS recruited by law enforcement agencies during 2006/7; 4,800 were cancelled during the year (some of whom were recruited in the previous year); and 3,705 were in place at the end of March 2007. For the same period, 429 CHIS were recruited by local authorities and other government departments, of whom 143 were in place at the end of March 2007.[177]

15. The Office of the Surveillance Commissioner, a tribunal of 26, provides oversight of the surveillance operations carried out under the Police Act 1997, Pt III and RIPA, Pts II and III. The Chief Surveillance Commissioner reports annually to Parliament. The Tribunal represents the only route for complaints. If the Tribunal decides that there has been contravention of any relevant legislation and the organisation concerned has not acted reasonably, they may uphold the complaint. Remedial measures such as the quashing of any warrants, destruction of any records held or financial compensation, may be imposed at the Tribunal's discretion.

The explanation behind the introduction of powers in Pt III of RIPA was that society would suffer if 'criminals are able to use such technology without law enforcement having corresponding powers of decryption'.[178] With this in mind it is perhaps surprising that Part III was not brought into force until 2007.[179]

PART III

49 Notices requiring disclosure

(1) This section applies where any protected information—

(a) has come into the possession of any person by means of the exercise of a statutory power to seize, detain, inspect, search or otherwise to interfere with documents or other property, or is likely to do so;

(b) has come into the possession of any person by means of the exercise of any statutory power to intercept communications, or is likely to do so;

(c) has come into the possession of any person by means of the exercise of any power conferred by an authorisation under section 22(3) or under Part II, or as a result of the giving of a notice under section 22(4), or is likely to do so;

(d) has come into the possession of any person as a result of having been provided or disclosed in pursuance of any statutory duty (whether or not one arising as a result of a request for information), or is likely to do so; or

(e) has, by any other lawful means not involving the exercise of statutory powers, come into the possession of any of the intelligence services, the police[, SOCA][180] [, SCDEA][181] or [Her Majesty's Revenue and Customs],[182] or is likely so to come into the possession of any of those services, the police[, SOCA][, SCDEA] or [Her Majesty's Revenue and Customs].

---

[176] App. No. 25829/94 (1999) 28 EHRR 101.   [177] *Annual Report* (2007) paras 7.4–7.5.
[178] DTI, Summary of Responses to 'Promoting Electronic Commerce' Consultation on Draft Legislation and the Government's Response to the Trade and Industry Committee's Report (Cm 4417, 1999).
[179] Regulation of Investigatory Powers Act 2000 (Commencement No. 4) Order 2007.
[180] Inserted by the Serious Organised Crime and Police Act 2005, s. 59, Sch. 4, paras 131, 145.
[181] Inserted by SI 2007/1098, art. 6, Sch., Pt 1, para. 4(1), (8).
[182] Substituted by the Serious Crime Act 2007, s. 88, Sch. 12, paras 5, 19.

(2) If any person with the appropriate permission under Schedule 2 believes, on reasonable grounds—

(a) that a key to the protected information is in the possession of any person,

(b) that the imposition of a disclosure requirement in respect of the protected information is—

(i) necessary on grounds falling within subsection (3), or

(ii) necessary for the purpose of securing the effective exercise or proper performance by any public authority of any statutory power or statutory duty,

(c) that the imposition of such a requirement is proportionate to what is sought to be achieved by its imposition, and

(d) that it is not reasonably practicable for the person with the appropriate permission to obtain possession of the protected information in an intelligible form without the giving of a notice under this section,

the person with that permission may, by notice to the person whom he believes to have possession of the key, impose a disclosure requirement in respect of the protected information.

(3) A disclosure requirement in respect of any protected information is necessary on grounds falling within this subsection if it is necessary—

(a) in the interests of national security;

(b) for the purpose of preventing or detecting crime; or

(c) in the interests of the economic well-being of the United Kingdom.

(4) A notice under this section imposing a disclosure requirement in respect of any protected information—

(a) must be given in writing or (if not in writing) must be given in a manner that produces a record of its having been given;

(b) must describe the protected information to which the notice relates;

(c) must specify the matters falling within subsection (2)(b)(i) or (ii) by reference to which the notice is given;

(d) must specify the office, rank or position held by the person giving it;

(e) must specify the office, rank or position of the person who for the purposes of Schedule 2 granted permission for the giving of the notice or (if the person giving the notice was entitled to give it without another person's permission) must set out the circumstances in which that entitlement arose;

(f) must specify the time by which the notice is to be complied with; and

(g) must set out the disclosure that is required by the notice and the form and manner in which it is to be made;

and the time specified for the purposes of paragraph (f) must allow a period for compliance which is reasonable in all the circumstances.

(5) Where it appears to a person with the appropriate permission—

(a) that more than one person is in possession of the key to any protected information,

(b) that any of those persons is in possession of that key in his capacity as an officer or employee of any body corporate, and

(c) that another of those persons is the body corporate itself or another officer or employee of the body corporate, a notice under this section shall not be given, by reference to his possession of the key, to any officer or employee of the body corporate unless he is a senior officer of the body corporate or it appears to the person giving the notice that there is no senior officer of the body corporate and (in the case of an employee) no more senior employee of the body corporate to whom it is reasonably practicable to give the notice.

(6) Where it appears to a person with the appropriate permission—

(a) that more than one person is in possession of the key to any protected information,

(b) that any of those persons is in possession of that key in his capacity as an employee of a firm, and

(c) that another of those persons is the firm itself or a partner of the firm,

a notice under this section shall not be given, by reference to his possession of the key, to any employee of the firm unless it appears to the person giving the notice that there is neither a partner of the firm nor a more senior employee of the firm to whom it is reasonably practicable to give the notice.

(7) Subsections (5) and (6) shall not apply to the extent that there are special circumstances of the case that mean that the purposes for which the notice is given would be defeated, in whole or in part, if the notice were given to the person to whom it would otherwise be required to be given by those subsections.

(8) A notice under this section shall not require the making of any disclosure to any person other than—

(a) the person giving the notice; or

(b) such other person as may be specified in or otherwise identified by, or in accordance with, the provisions of the notice.

(9) A notice under this section shall not require the disclosure of any key which—

(a) is intended to be used for the purpose only of generating electronic signatures; and

(b) has not in fact been used for any other purpose.

(10) In this section 'senior officer', in relation to a body corporate, means a director, manager, secretary or other similar officer of the body corporate; and for this purpose 'director', in relation to a body corporate whose affairs are managed by its members, means a member of the body corporate.

(11) Schedule 2 (definition of the appropriate permission) shall have effect.

50 Effect of notice imposing disclosure requirement

(1) Subject to the following provisions of this section, the effect of a section 49 notice imposing a disclosure requirement in respect of any protected information on a person who is in possession at a relevant time of both the protected information and a means of obtaining access to the information and of disclosing it in an intelligible form is that he—

(a) shall be entitled to use any key in his possession to obtain access to the information or to put it into an intelligible form; and

(b) shall be required, in accordance with the notice imposing the requirement, to make a disclosure of the information in an intelligible form.

(2) A person subject to a requirement under subsection (1)(b) to make a disclosure of any information in an intelligible form shall be taken to have complied with that requirement if—

(a) he makes, instead, a disclosure of any key to the protected information that is in his possession; and

(b) that disclosure is made, in accordance with the notice imposing the requirement, to the person to whom, and by the time by which, he was required to provide the information in that form.

(3) Where, in a case in which a disclosure requirement in respect of any protected information is imposed on any person by a section 49 notice—

(a) that person is not in possession of the information,

(b) that person is incapable, without the use of a key that is not in his possession, of obtaining access to the information and of disclosing it in an intelligible form, or

(c) the notice states, in pursuance of a direction under section 51, that it can be complied with only by the disclosure of a key to the information,

the effect of imposing that disclosure requirement on that person is that he shall be required, in accordance with the notice imposing the requirement, to make a disclosure of any key to the protected information that is in his possession at a relevant time.

(4) Subsections (5) to (7) apply where a person ('the person given notice')—

(a) is entitled or obliged to disclose a key to protected information for the purpose of complying with any disclosure requirement imposed by a section 49 notice; and

(b) is in possession of more than one key to that information.

(5) It shall not be necessary, for the purpose of complying with the requirement, for the person given notice to make a disclosure of any keys in addition to those the disclosure of which is, alone, sufficient to enable the person to whom they are disclosed to obtain access to the information and to put it into an intelligible form.

(6) Where—

(a) subsection (5) allows the person given notice to comply with a requirement without disclosing all of the keys in his possession, and

(b) there are different keys, or combinations of keys, in the possession of that person the disclosure of which would, under that subsection, constitute compliance,

the person given notice may select which of the keys, or combination of keys, to disclose for the purpose of complying with that requirement in accordance with that subsection.

(7) Subject to subsections (5) and (6), the person given notice shall not be taken to have complied with the disclosure requirement by the disclosure of a key unless he has disclosed every key to the protected information that is in his possession at a relevant time.

(8) Where, in a case in which a disclosure requirement in respect of any protected information is imposed on any person by a section 49 notice—

(a) that person has been in possession of the key to that information but is no longer in possession of it,

(b) if he had continued to have the key in his possession, he would have been required by virtue of the giving of the notice to disclose it, and

(c) he is in possession, at a relevant time, of information to which subsection (9) applies,

the effect of imposing that disclosure requirement on that person is that he shall be required, in accordance with the notice imposing the requirement, to disclose all such information to which subsection (9) applies as is in his possession and as he may be required, in accordance with that notice, to disclose by the person to whom he would have been required to disclose the key.

(9) This subsection applies to any information that would facilitate the obtaining or discovery of the key or the putting of the protected information into an intelligible form.

(10) In this section 'relevant time', in relation to a disclosure requirement imposed by a section 49 notice, means the time of the giving of the notice or any subsequent time before the time by which the requirement falls to be complied with.

NOTES

1. RIPA, ss. 49–56 regulate access by investigating authorities to encrypted electronic data ('protected information'). They cover the situation, for example, where the police gain access to computer files by a lawful search but are unable to read them because they are encrypted. Where a 'person with appropriate permission' within an investigating authority (the police, customs and excise, the intelligence services) has reasonable grounds to believe that 'a key to the protected information is in the possession of any person, a disclosure notice may be issued under RIPA 2000, s. 49(2), requiring that the person in possession disclose the encrypted information or the key to gain access to it. The notice may be issued only where disclosure is 'necessary' in the interests of 'national security', the prevention or detection of crime, or the 'economic well-being' of the UK.[183] A notice under s. 49 must be issued by a circuit court judge, except where access to the encrypted data has been obtained through the use of a lawful search, interception, surveillance or other warrant which grants the required permission to have access to encrypted electronic data.

2. Section 52 deals with the arrangements for payments for disclosure. The Secretary of State must ensure that such arrangements are in force as he thinks appropriate for authorising, in such cases as he thinks fit, the making to persons to whom s. 49 notices are given of appropriate contributions towards the costs incurred by them in complying with such notices.

3. A person to whom a s. 49 notice has been given will be guilty of an offence (with a maximum penalty of two years' imprisonment) if he knowingly fails, in accordance with the notice, to make the disclosure required by virtue of the giving of the notice under s. 53(1). A person served with a s. 49 notice, or every other person who becomes aware of it or of its contents, is required to keep secret the giving of the notice, its contents and the things done in pursuance of it. The 'tipping-off offence' carries a five-year maximum penalty.

6. PERSONAL DATA: ITS ELECTRONIC AND MANUAL STORAGE AND PRIVACY

NOTES

1. The question of safeguarding privacy in the use of computerised data banks containing personal information about individuals in the private sector was considered in 1970 by the Younger Committee.[184] The Committee stated that 'of all the forms of invasion of privacy which have been cited in evidence to us that involving the use or misuse of computers has been the least supported in concrete terms'.[185] The Committee could not on the evidence before it 'conclude that the computer as used in the private sector is at present a threat to privacy, but we recognise that there is a possibility of such a threat becoming a reality in the

---

[183] RIPA 2000, s. 49(3). There is also a 'proportionality' requirement: RIPA 2000, s. 49(2).
[184] Report, Chap. 20.   [185] Ibid., p. 179.

future'.[186] In recognition of the potential threat, the Committee formulated 10 principles—the Younger Principles—which it proposed computer users should adopt in the handling of personal information. In 1975, the Government published a White Paper in which it stated that 'the time had come when those who use computers to handle personal information, however responsible they are, can no longer remain the sole judges of whether their own systems adequately safeguard privacy'.[187] The Government therefore established the Data Protection Committee (the Lindop Committee), which reported in 1978 on the form that legislation should take.[188] Not all of its recommendations were followed in subsequent legislation.

2. In 2008 the Home Affairs Committee produced a report on the 'Surveillance Society'. It recognised that there were clear benefits to consumers and users of public services from the growth in data collection and use. This included more efficient targeting of health care and other public services, potential reductions in crime, and more personalised consumer services. However, there are also clear disadvantages and problems attached to greater surveillance. The Report noted:

34. A survey conducted by the Information Commissioner's Office in 2005–06 found high levels of concern amongst individuals about the use, transfer and security of their personal information. In 2005–06 the survey found that 80% of individuals held such concerns.[189] In another survey, conducted in February 2008, after the HMRC incident and other high-profile data losses from public bodies, 85% of respondents said that they worried more about the safety of their personal details than they used to and 72% said that they felt powerless over how their personal information was looked after.[190]

96. At the beginning of our inquiry the Information Commissioner outlined the risks to the individual which may be associated with 'excessive' surveillance whether by means of cameras or other monitoring techniques such as the collection of information on databases. For individuals, the Commissioner told us, the risk is that they will suffer harm because information about them is:

- inaccurate, insufficient or out of date

- excessive or irrelevant

- kept for too long

- disclosed to those who ought not to have it

- used in unacceptable or unexpected ways beyond their control, or

- not kept securely.

101. The International Association of Privacy Professionals (IAPP) drew a distinction between security breaches as a result of criminal activity and those occasions on which 'people just lose disks or other back-up tapes'. During our inquiry, however, a series of high-profile incidents of data loss by Government agencies served to underline the risks associated not only with the abuse of surveillance by criminals but also with the collection and sharing of personal information for the purpose of delivering public services.

102. In terms of the amount of data lost, the incident reported to the House of Commons in a statement by the Chancellor of the Exchequer on 20 November 2007 was the most serious. Two password-protected discs containing a full copy of HM Revenue and Customs 'entire data' in relation to the payment

---

186 Ibid., p. 191.   187 *Computers and Privacy* (Cmnd 6353), p. 8.   188 Cmnd 7341.
189 Information Commissioner's Office, *Annual Report Summary 2005–06* (2006), p. 13.
190 Personal Information Survey, prepared on behalf of Tri Media by ICM Research for the Information Commissioner's Office. Available at: www.ico.gov.uk/tools_and_resources/document_library/data_protection.aspx.

of child benefit—records for 25 million individuals and 7.25 million families—were sent to the National Audit Office by HMRC's internal post system (operated by the courier TNT). The discs failed to reach the NAO and were not recovered.

106. Another risk associated with surveillance is the danger that an individual will suffer harm not because he or she has been impersonated by someone else but because an organisation or individual targets him or her by mistake or makes decisions based on incorrect information. Where these decisions involve targeted marketing, harm to an individual might amount only to inconvenience or to missed opportunities to choose a more appropriate product or service—although concerns have been raised about the implications for individual privacy of new internet advertising services which collect information about users' internet searches—but where financial, health or security decisions are concerned the potential for harm is much greater.

108. Whilst there are steps that individuals themselves can take to protect their privacy, and to gain access to the information held about them under the rights afforded by the Data Protection Act, to check that information is correct or to limit its disclosure to suit their needs, taking these steps requires individuals to exercise an informed choice in relation to surveillance. Those without the degree of awareness or the means to exercise this choice may therefore be at greater risk of suffering harm as a result of misuse or mistakes in information held about them; where no such choice is available their vulnerability may be compounded.

3. The Data Protection Act 1998 gives effect in UK law to European Data Protection Directive 95/46/EC, on the protection of individuals with regard to the processing of personal data and the free movement of such data.

- **Data Protection Act 1998**[191]

1 Basic interpretative provisions

(1) In this Act, unless the context otherwise requires—

'data' means information which—

(a) is being processed by means of equipment operating automatically in response to instructions given for that purpose,

(b) is recorded with the intention that it should be processed by means of such equipment,

(c) is recorded as part of a relevant filing system or with the intention that it should form part of a relevant filing system,...[192]

(d) does not fall within paragraph (a), (b) or (c) but forms part of an accessible record as defined by section 68; [or

(e) is recorded information held by a public authority and does not fall within any of paragraphs (a) to (d);][193]

'data controller' means, subject to subsection (4), a person who (either alone or jointly or in common with other persons) determines the purposes for which and the manner in which any personal data are, or are to be, processed;

'data processor', in relation to personal data, means any person (other than an employee of the data controller) who processes the data on behalf of the data controller;

---

[191] See P. Carey, *Data Protection: A Practical Guide to UK and EU Law* (2004).

[192] See SI 2004/1909, art. 2(1), (2)(f), (3).

[193] Inserted by the Freedom of Information Act 2000, s. 68(1), (2)(a). Date in force: 1 January 2005; see SI 2004/1909, art. 2(1), (2)(f), (3).

'data subject' means an individual who is the subject of personal data;

'personal data' means data which relate to a living individual who can be identified—

(a) from those data, or

(b) from those data and other information which is in the possession of, or is likely to come into the possession of, the data controller,

and includes any expression of opinion about the individual and any indication of the intentions of the data controller or any other person in respect of the individual;

'processing', in relation to information or data, means obtaining, recording or holding the information or data or carrying out any operation or set of operations on the information or data, including—

(a) organisation, adaptation or alteration of the information or data,

(b) retrieval, consultation or use of the information or data,

(c) disclosure of the information or data by transmission, dissemination or otherwise making available, or

(d) alignment, combination, blocking, erasure or destruction of the information or data;

['public authority' means a public authority as defined by the Freedom of Information Act 2000 or a Scottish public authority as defined by the Freedom of Information (Scotland) Act 2002;][194]

'relevant filing system' means any set of information relating to individuals to the extent that, although the information is not processed by means of equipment operating automatically in response to instructions given for that purpose, the set is structured, either by reference to individuals or by reference to criteria relating to individuals, in such a way that specific information relating to a particular individual is readily accessible.

(2) In this Act, unless the context otherwise requires—

(a) 'obtaining' or 'recording', in relation to personal data, includes obtaining or recording the information to be contained in the data, and

(b) 'using' or 'disclosing', in relation to personal data, includes using or disclosing the information contained in the data.

(3) In determining for the purposes of this Act whether any information is recorded with the intention—

(a) that it should be processed by means of equipment operating automatically in response to instructions given for that purpose, or

(b) that it should form part of a relevant filing system,

it is immaterial that it is intended to be so processed or to form part of such a system only after being transferred to a country or territory outside the European Economic Area.

(4) Where personal data are processed only for purposes for which they are required by or under any enactment to be processed, the person on whom the obligation to process the data is imposed by or under that enactment is for the purposes of this Act the data controller.

[(5) In paragraph (e) of the definition of 'data' in subsection (1), the reference to information 'held' by a public authority shall be construed in accordance with section 3(2) of the Freedom of Information Act 2000 [or section 3(2), (4) and (5) of the Freedom of Information (Scotland) Act 2002].[195]

---

194 Definition 'public authority' (inserted by the Freedom of Information Act 2000, s. 68(1), (2)(b)) substituted by SI 2004/3089, art. 2(1), (2)(a). See SI 2004/3089, art. 1.

195 Inserted by SI 2004/3089, art. 2(1), (2)(b). See SI 2004/3089, art. 1.

(6) Where

[(a)] section 7 of the Freedom of Information Act 2000 prevents Parts I to V of that Act [or

(b) section 7(1) of the Freedom of Information (Scotland) Act 2002 prevents that Act,][196]

from applying to certain information held by a public authority, that information is not to be treated for the purposes of paragraph (e) of the definition of 'data' in subsection (1) as held by a public authority.][197]

2 Sensitive personal data

In this Act 'sensitive personal data' means personal data consisting of information as to—

(a) the racial or ethnic origin of the data subject,

(b) his political opinions,

(c) his religious beliefs or other beliefs of a similar nature,

(d) whether he is a member of a trade union (within the meaning of the Trade Union and Labour Relations (Consolidation) Act 1992,

(e) his physical or mental health or condition,

(f) his sexual life,

(g) the commission or alleged commission by him of any offence, or

(h) any proceedings for any offence committed or alleged to have been committed by him, the disposal of such proceedings or the sentence of any court in such proceedings.

3 The special purposes

In this Act 'the special purposes' means any one or more of the following—

(a) the purposes of journalism,

(b) artistic purposes, and

(c) literary purposes.

4 The data protection principles

(1) References in this Act to the data protection principles are to the principles set out in Part I of Schedule 1.

(2) Those principles are to be interpreted in accordance with Part II of Schedule 1.

(3) Schedule 2 (which applies to all personal data) and Schedule 3 (which applies only to sensitive personal data) set out conditions applying for the purposes of the first principle; and Schedule 4 sets out cases in which the eighth principle does not apply.

(4) Subject to section 27(1), it shall be the duty of a data controller to comply with the data protection principles in relation to all personal data with respect to which he is the data controller.

7 Right of access to personal data

(1) Subject to the following provisions of this section and to [sections 8, 9 and 9A],[198] an individual is entitled—

(a) to be informed by any data controller whether personal data of which that individual is the data subject are being processed by or on behalf of that data controller,

---

[196] Numbered as such by SI 2004/3089, art. 2(1), (2)(c). See SI 2004/3089, art. 1.

[197] Inserted by the Freedom of Information Act 2000, s. 68(1), (3). See SI 2004/1909, art. 2(1), (2)(f), (3).

[198] Substituted by the Freedom of Information Act 2000, s. 69(1). See SI 2004/1909, art. 2(1), (2)(f), (3).

(b) if that is the case, to be given by the data controller a description of—

    (i) the personal data of which that individual is the data subject,

    (ii) the purposes for which they are being or are to be processed, and

    (iii) the recipients or classes of recipients to whom they are or may be disclosed,

(c) to have communicated to him in an intelligible form—

    (i) the information constituting any personal data of which that individual is the data subject, and

    (ii) any information available to the data controller as to the source of those data, and

(d) where the processing by automatic means of personal data of which that individual is the data subject for the purpose of evaluating matters relating to him such as, for example, his performance at work, his creditworthiness, his reliability or his conduct, has constituted or is likely to constitute the sole basis for any decision significantly affecting him, to be informed by the data controller of the logic involved in that decision-taking.

(2) A data controller is not obliged to supply any information under subsection (1) unless he has received—

(a) a request in writing, and

(b) except in prescribed cases, such fee (not exceeding the prescribed maximum) as he may require.

[(3) Where a data controller—

(a) reasonably requires further information in order to satisfy himself as to the identity of the person making a request under this section and to locate the information which that person seeks, and

(b) has informed him of that requirement,

the data controller is not obliged to comply with the request unless he is supplied with that further information.][199]

(4) Where a data controller cannot comply with the request without disclosing information relating to another individual who can be identified from that information, he is not obliged to comply with the request unless—

(a) the other individual has consented to the disclosure of the information to the person making the request, or

(b) it is reasonable in all the circumstances to comply with the request without the consent of the other individual.

(5) In subsection (4) the reference to information relating to another individual includes a reference to information identifying that individual as the source of the information sought by the request; and that subsection is not to be construed as excusing a data controller from communicating so much of the information sought by the request as can be communicated without disclosing the identity of the other individual concerned, whether by the omission of names or other identifying particulars or otherwise.

(6) In determining for the purposes of subsection (4)(b) whether it is reasonable in all the circumstances to comply with the request without the consent of the other individual concerned, regard shall be had, in particular, to—

(a) any duty of confidentiality owed to the other individual,

---

199 Substituted by the Freedom of Information Act 2000, s. 73, Sch. 6, para. 1. See SI 2001/1637, art. 2(d).

(b) any steps taken by the data controller with a view to seeking the consent of the other individual,

(c) whether the other individual is capable of giving consent, and

(d) any express refusal of consent by the other individual.

(7) An individual making a request under this section may, in such cases as may be prescribed, specify that his request is limited to personal data of any prescribed description.

(8) Subject to subsection (4), a data controller shall comply with a request under this section promptly and in any event before the end of the prescribed period beginning with the relevant day.

(9) If a court is satisfied on the application of any person who has made a request under the foregoing provisions of this section that the data controller in question has failed to comply with the request in contravention of those provisions, the court may order him to comply with the request.

(10) In this section—

'prescribed' means prescribed by the [Secretary of State][200] by regulations;

'the prescribed maximum' means such amount as may be prescribed;

'the prescribed period' means forty days or such other period as may be prescribed;

'the relevant day', in relation to a request under this section, means the day on which the data controller receives the request or, if later, the first day on which the data controller has both the required fee and the information referred to in subsection (3).

(11) Different amounts or periods may be prescribed under this section in relation to different cases.

10 Right to prevent processing likely to cause damage or distress

(1) Subject to subsection (2), an individual is entitled at any time by notice in writing to a data controller to require the data controller at the end of such period as is reasonable in the circumstances to cease, or not to begin, processing, or processing for a specified purpose or in a specified manner, any personal data in respect of which he is the data subject, on the ground that, for specified reasons—

(a) the processing of those data or their processing for that purpose or in that manner is causing or is likely to cause substantial damage or substantial distress to him or to another, and

(b) that damage or distress is or would be unwarranted.

(2) Subsection (1) does not apply—

(a) in a case where any of the conditions in paragraphs 1 to 4 of Schedule 2 is met, or

(b) in such other cases as may be prescribed by the [Secretary of State][201] by order.

(3) The data controller must within twenty-one days of receiving a notice under subsection (1) ('the data subject notice') give the individual who gave it a written notice—

(a) stating that he has complied or intends to comply with the data subject notice, or

(b) stating his reasons for regarding the data subject notice as to any extent unjustified and the extent (if any) to which he has complied or intends to comply with it.

(4) If a court is satisfied, on the application of any person who has given a notice under subsection (1) which appears to the court to be justified (or to be justified to any extent), that the data controller in question has failed to comply with the notice, the court may order him to take such steps for complying with the notice (or for complying with it to that extent) as the court thinks fit.

---

[200] Substituted by SI 2003/1887, art. 9, Sch. 2, para. 9(1)(a). See SI 2003/1887, art. 1(2).
[201] Substituted by SI 2003/1887, art. 9, Sch. 2, para. 9(1)(a). See SI 2003/1887, art. 1(2).

(5) The failure by a data subject to exercise the right conferred by subsection (1) or section 11(1) does not affect any other right conferred on him by this Part.

13 Compensation for failure to comply with certain requirements

(1) An individual who suffers damage by reason of any contravention by a data controller of any of the requirements of this Act is entitled to compensation from the data controller for that damage.

(2) An individual who suffers distress by reason of any contravention by a data controller of any of the requirements of this Act is entitled to compensation from the data controller for that distress if—

    (a) the individual also suffers damage by reason of the contravention, or

    (b) the contravention relates to the processing of personal data for the special purposes.

(3) In proceedings brought against a person by virtue of this section it is a defence to prove that he had taken such care as in all the circumstances was reasonably required to comply with the requirement concerned.

14 Rectification, blocking, erasure and destruction

(1) If a court is satisfied on the application of a data subject that personal data of which the applicant is the subject are inaccurate, the court may order the data controller to rectify, block, erase or destroy those data and any other personal data in respect of which he is the data controller and which contain an expression of opinion which appears to the court to be based on the inaccurate data.

(2) Subsection (1) applies whether or not the data accurately record information received or obtained by the data controller from the data subject or a third party but where the data accurately record such information, then—

    (a) if the requirements mentioned in paragraph 7 of Part II of Schedule 1 have been complied with, the court may, instead of making an order under subsection (1), make an order requiring the data to be supplemented by such statement of the true facts relating to the matters dealt with by the data as the court may approve, and

    (b) if all or any of those requirements have not been complied with, the court may, instead of making an order under that subsection, make such order as it thinks fit for securing compliance with those requirements with or without a further order requiring the data to be supplemented by such a statement as is mentioned in paragraph (a).

(3) Where the court

    (a) makes an order under subsection (1), or

    (b) is satisfied on the application of a data subject that personal data of which he was the data subject and which have been rectified, blocked, erased or destroyed were inaccurate,

it may, where it considers it reasonably practicable, order the data controller to notify third parties to whom the data have been disclosed of the rectification, blocking, erasure or destruction.

(4) If a court is satisfied on the application of a data subject—

    (a) that he has suffered damage by reason of any contravention by a data controller of any of the requirements of this Act in respect of any personal data, in circumstances entitling him to compensation under section 13, and

    (b) that there is a substantial risk of further contravention in respect of those data in such circumstances,

the court may order the rectification, blocking, erasure or destruction of any of those data.

(5) Where the court makes an order under subsection (4) it may, where it considers it reasonably practicable, order the data controller to notify third parties to whom the data have been disclosed of the rectification, blocking, erasure or destruction.

(6) In determining whether it is reasonably practicable to require such notification as is mentioned in subsection (3) or (5) the court shall have regard, in particular, to the number of persons who would have to be notified.

32 Journalism, literature and art

(1) Personal data which are processed only for the special purposes are exempt from any provision to which this subsection relates if—

   (a) the processing is undertaken with a view to the publication by any person of any journalistic, literary or artistic material,

   (b) the data controller reasonably believes that, having regard in particular to the special importance of the public interest in freedom of expression, publication would be in the public interest, and

   (c) the data controller reasonably believes that, in all the circumstances, compliance with that provision is incompatible with the special purposes.

(2) Subsection (1) relates to the provisions of—

   (a) the data protection principles except the seventh data protection principle,

   (b) section 7,

   (c) section 10,

   (d) section 12, and

   (e) section 14(1) to (3).

(3) In considering for the purposes of subsection (1)(b) whether the belief of a data controller that publication would be in the public interest was or is a reasonable one, regard may be had to his compliance with any code of practice which—

   (a) is relevant to the publication in question, and

   (b) is designated by the [Secretary of State][202] by order for the purposes of this subsection.

(4) Where at any time ('the relevant time') in any proceedings against a data controller under section 7(9), 10(4), 12(8) or 14 or by virtue of section 13 the data controller claims, or it appears to the court, that any personal data to which the proceedings relate are being processed—

   (a) only for the special purposes, and

   (b) with a view to the publication by any person of any journalistic, literary or artistic material which, at the time twenty-four hours immediately before the relevant time, had not previously been published by the data controller,

   the court shall stay the proceedings until either of the conditions in subsection (5) is met.

(5) Those conditions are—

   (a) that a determination of the Commissioner under section 45 with respect to the data in question takes effect, or

   (b) in a case where the proceedings were stayed on the making of a claim, that the claim is withdrawn.

(6) For the purposes of this Act 'publish', in relation to journalistic, literary or artistic material, means make available to the public or any section of the public.

---

[202] Substituted by SI 2003/1887, art. 9, Sch. 2, para. 9(1)(a). See SI 2003/1887, art. 1(2).

SCHEDULE 1

THE DATA PROTECTION PRINCIPLES

Part I

The Principles

1. Personal data shall be processed fairly and lawfully and, in particular, shall not be processed unless—

   (*a*) at least one of the conditions in Schedule 2 is met, and

   (*b*) in the case of sensitive personal data, at least one of the conditions in Schedule 3 is also met.

2. Personal data shall be obtained only for one or more specified and lawful purposes, and shall not be further processed in any manner incompatible with that purpose or those purposes.

3. Personal data shall be adequate, relevant and not excessive in relation to the purpose or purposes for which they are processed.

4. Personal data shall be accurate and, where necessary, kept up to date.

5. Personal data processed for any purpose or purposes shall not be kept for longer than is necessary for that purpose or those purposes.

6. Personal data shall be processed in accordance with the rights of data subjects under this Act.

7. Appropriate technical and organisational measures shall be taken against unauthorised or unlawful processing of personal data and against accidental loss or destruction of, or damage to, personal data.

8. Personal data shall not be transferred to a country or territory outside the European Economic Area unless that country or territory ensures an adequate level of protection for the rights and freedoms of data subjects in relation to the processing of personal data.

NOTES

1. Following the *Lindop Report*, Parliament enacted the Data Protection Act 1984, which incorporated the Younger Principles into the Data Protection Principles, and adopted most of the Lindop recommendations. The Data Protection Act 1998[203] replaced the Data Protection Act 1984, which it repealed.[204] The 1998 Act follows the pattern of the 1984 Act, but contains some important differences, partly in response to the EU Data Protection Directive 1995. Most significantly from a privacy standpoint, the law extends to some manually processed data, as well as data that are processed by computer, and the 'data subject' (a) has a more extensive right of access to personal information held by the 'data controller' and (b) may prevent the processing of personal data information where this would be likely to cause damage or distress or the information is of a sensitive personal kind.

2. The Act applies only to 'personal data'.[205] As well as computer-based data, the 1998 Act applies to information that 'is recorded as part of a relevant filing system or with the intention that it should form part of' such a system (s. 1(1)(c)). This includes manually prepared files, such as employee record files.[206] In *Durant v Financial Services Authority*[207] the Court of

---

[203] D. Bainbridge and G. Pearce (2000) 2 JILT.

[204] On the 1998 Act see P. Carey, *Data Protection in the UK* (2000); P. Carey, *Data Protection: A Practical Guide to UK and EU Law* (2nd edn, 2004); G. Maguire and P. Church (2002) NLJ 147.

[205] For the definition of 'personal data', see s. 1(1) of the 1998 Act.

[206] For the definition of a 'relevant filing system', see s. 1(1) of the 1998 Act.

[207] [2003] EWCA Civ 1746.

Appeal held that personal data is 'information that affects [an individual's] privacy, whether in his personal or family life, business or professional capacity'.[208] It was not enough that the claimant was named in files but he must be the focus of attention. Processing 'personal data' is what brings the protections and constraints of the Act into play. The interpretation provided by the Court of Appeal narrows the application of the Act. Do you think this interpretation reflects the spirit and purpose behind the EU Data Protection Directive, or Art. 8 ECHR?

3. A 'data subject' has a right of access to 'personal data' of which he or she is the subject.[209] Under the 1998 Act, this includes information about the source of the data. The information must be provided, for a fee, by the 'data controller', who is the person who controls the data storage operation concerned.[210] The data subject may prevent the processing of personal data that is likely to cause substantial distress or damage.[211] The processing of 'sensitive personal data'[212] is also prohibited, unless it satisfies one or more of a large number of specified conditions.[213] The data subject is entitled to compensation from a data controller for the damage or distress caused by a breach of the Act, including the storage of inaccurate information.[214] The processing of personal data must be conducted in accordance with the Data Protection Principles.[215]

4. Journalists, who have extensive personal data files, whether computer or manually based, are exempt from key parts of the Act, including those providing for the rights of the data subject to access to stored information and to prevent the publication of data that is likely to cause substantial distress or damage.[216] Interim injunctions cannot be obtained under the Act and therefore this reduces the power of the Act as a remedy for breaches of privacy by the media in any event.

5. The Act is administered by the Information Commissioner. The Commissioner maintains a register of data-processing operations, which, subject to certain exemptions, cannot be conducted unless they are notified to the Commissioner.[217] The Commissioner monitors compliance with the Act by data processors. The Information Tribunal may hear appeals against action taken by the Commissioner.

6. The DPA has been the subject of much criticism. In 2004 the Lord Chancellor stated:

The problem about the Data Protection Act is that it is almost incomprehensible. It is very difficult to understand. The precise limits of it are problematic. There are constant difficulties about what information you are allowed to share between departments for instance. I just think it needs to be looked at again at some stage to make it more simple.[218]

---

[208] Ibid., at para. 28.   [209] 1998 Act, s. 7.

[210] For the definition of a 'data controller', see s. 1(1) of the 1998 Act.

[211] 1998 Act, s. 10.

[212] For the definition of 'sensitive personal data', see s. 2 of the 1998 Act. 'Sensitive' data include data about a person's racial or ethnic origin, sexual life, health and criminal record.

[213] For the conditions, see Sch. 2 to the 1998 Act and the relevant statutory instruments. They include consent, public knowledge and statutory authority.

[214] 1998 Act, s. 13.   [215] 1998 Act, s. 3 and Sch. I.

[216] 1998 Act, s. 32.

[217] 1998 Act, s. 17. For the exemptions, see ss. 28–38, of the 1998 Act.

[218] *The Guardian*, 18 October 2004.

These criticisms followed the revelation that Soham murderer Ian Huntley's criminal record, which may have prevented him working in a school, had been deleted following a misinterpretation of the DPA.[219]

7. In April 2008 the Information Commissioner's Office announced a study of the strengths and weaknesses of EU Data Protection law, addressing 'a growing feeling that the EU Directive on data protection is becoming increasingly outdated and is more bureaucratic and burdensome than it needs to be'.[220]

---

[219] This was officially recognised in the Bichard Inquiry, *An independent inquiry arising from the Soham murders* (2004).

[220] Information Commissioner's Office, *Invitation to Tender—Review of EU Data Protection Law* (2008).

PART FOUR: Freedom of expression

9

ECHR PROTECTION OF FREEDOM OF EXPRESSION: ARTICLE 10

Chapters 9 to 12 have as a unifying theme the issue of 'freedom of expression'. This freedom is commonly considered to be of fundamental importance in Western-style democracies.[1] The First Amendment to the US Constitution includes the proposition 'Congress shall make no law...abridging the freedom of speech, or of the press'; Art. 19(2) of the International Covenant on Civil and Political Rights provides that 'everyone shall have the right to freedom of expression: this right shall include freedom to seek, receive and impart information and ideas of all kinds, regardless of frontiers, either orally, in writing or in print, in the form of art, or through any other media of his choice'; and Art. 10 of the European Convention on Human Rights proclaims: 'Everyone has the right to freedom of expression. This right shall include freedom to hold opinions and to receive and impart information and ideas without interference by public authority.'[2]

The philosophical underpinnings of this freedom have been much discussed.[3] Desire to protect freedom of speech is to an extent simply an aspect of the more general ideal that individual freedom of behaviour be protected: that incursions on an individual's liberty

---

[1] In August 1994 the French Constitutional Council held that certain recently enacted laws, designed to purge English words and phrases from the French language, were invalid as contrary to the freedom of expression guarantees of the Declaration of the Rights of Man of 1789, protected under the French Constitution. The law had purported to outlaw the use of 'unapproved' foreign words on television, on radio and in the press. The law was upheld, however, to the extent that it applied to the language which the state required to be used by its own officials in the performance of their duties.

[2] Note also decisions of the High Court of Australia which recognise the notion of 'implied' rights to freedom of expression within the Australian Constitution, such rights being implicit in the Constitution's fundamental principles of governmental accountability and representative government. See *Australian Capital Television Pty Ltd v The Commonwealth* (1992) 177 CLR 506; *Theospharious v Herald and Weekly Times Ltd* (1994) CLR 104; *Lange v Australian Broadcasting Corpn* (1997) 189 CLR 520; *Levy v Victoria* (1997) 189 CLR 579. The *Lange* case affirmed that the freedom of political communication now recognised was to be interpreted only by reference to those aspects of representative and responsible government that could be identified in the 'text and structure' of the Constitution. For criticism, see A. Stone (1999) 23 MULR 668.

[3] See, for excellent surveys, E. Barendt, *Freedom of Speech* (OUP, Oxford, 2nd edn, 2005), Chap. 1; D. Feldman, *Civil Liberties and Human Rights in England and Wales* (OUP, Oxford, 2nd edn, 2002), Part IV; H. Fenwick and G. Phillipson, *Media Freedom under the Human Rights Act* (OUP, Oxford, 2006).

should be permitted only in situations where this is necessary to prevent harm to another, or where one person's liberty must be curtailed in order to preserve the liberty of others.

However, in addition to this general reason for seeking to protect liberty of expression, other more specific justifications may be offered. Some have pointed to the importance of freedom of expression in terms of the 'fulfilment' and 'development' of the individual in society, by means of the exposure of individuals to a free and wide-ranging flow of information, experience, ideas and opinions. Such exposure should at one and the same time both provide a stimulus to individual personality development, and also act as a safeguard against an unduly restricted diet of 'information' and 'opinion' fed from official sources. It follows that there is a need, in a society which places a high value on the individual, for there to be freedom of artistic, literary and political expression. An adjunct to this is that the operation of democracy requires that there should be both open and informed discussion of issues of contemporary significance. Well known are the words of Mr Justice Brandeis of the US Supreme Court in *Whitney v California*,[4] speaking of those whose ideals had shaped the terms of the US Constitution. They:

> believed that freedom to think as you will and to speak as you think are means indispensable to the discovery and spread of political truth: that without free speech and assembly, discussion would be futile: that with them, discussion affords ordinarily adequate protection against the dissemination of noxious doctrine: that the greatest menace to freedom is an inert people: that public discussion is a political duty; and that this should be a fundamental principle of the American government....

And in the still stronger words of Alexander Meiklejohn:

> when a question of policy is 'before the house', free men choose it not with their eyes shut, but with their eyes open. To be afraid of ideas, any idea, is to be unfit for self-government.[5]

This is not, of course, to suggest that there should be no limits to this liberty: only that in assessing the limits which should be drawn it is well to remember what may be the reasons underlying this ideal. Chapter 10 we shall look at liberty of expression in the theatre, the cinema, on video and in the broadcasting media, in the published media and in the world of art. There then follows a chapter which looks at the extent to which free expression may be restricted in the interests of the due administration of justice; and this in turn is followed by a chapter which addresses these issues in the context of the 'openness' or otherwise of governmental information and activity. The proper balance between privacy and freedom of expression is considered in Part four of the book.

The structure of Art. 10, conferring a right to freedom of expression, is similar to that of Art. 8.[6] It brings into play a wide range of laws. Most of the cases turn on the question whether the restriction can be justified under Art. 10(2).

In principle, the imposition of a prior restriction on freedom of expression requires particularly strong justification.[7] Given the value of expression, the harm or offence it causes may only justify the imposition of a penalty after the event; there may not in any event be a prosecution; prior restraint substitutes the view of an (often unaccountable) censor of the worth of the material for that of society; prior restraint often takes place at an interim

---

[4] 274 US 357 (1927).   [5] *Free Speech and its Relation to Self-Government* (New York, 1948), p. 19.
[6] See Chap. 7.
[7] See E. Barendt. *Freedom of Speech* 2nd edn (2005), Chap. 4; D. Feldman, *Civil Liberties and Human Rights in England and Wales* (OUP, Oxford, 2nd edn, 2002), pp. 771–773.

stage. Nevertheless, subsequent restrictions may well of course inhibit expression, and prior restraints can be justified where there is a pressing need. Illustrations of these issues are considered below.[8] In the context of indecency and obscenity, prior restraint in the form of state censorship is now limited in England and Wales to videos, DVDs and certain computer games; the arrangements for the censorship of films are technically extra-statutory but do have a statutory underpinning in practice through the cinema licensing powers of local authorities.[9] In the US, most state visual prior censorship laws and procedures have been held unconstitutional.[10] Issues concerning prior restraint have naturally loomed large in proceedings where the state seeks an injunction to prevent the publication of matters that might interfere with the administration of justice or of government secrets.[11] Given the ease and speed of publication on the internet, such proceedings are increasingly less likely to be effective as a matter of practice, whatever the legal position.

- **Sunday Times v United Kingdom,** Judgment of 26 April 1979, ECtHRR A30
  (1979) 2 EHRR 245, European Court of Human Rights

Following the decision in *A-G v Times Newspapers Ltd*[12] the present application was brought by the publisher, editor, and a group of journalists of *The Sunday Times*. The Commission expressed the opinion, by 8 votes to 5, that the injunction granted by the House of Lords against the Sunday Times was a breach of Art. 10. The case was referred to the Court by the Commission. The Court held that Art. 10 had been infringed because the restriction, although 'prescribed by law' and imposed for a legitimate purpose, was not 'necessary in a democratic society' for the maintenance of the 'authority...of the judiciary'. The full Court reached this conclusion by 11 votes to 9.

JUDGMENT OF THE COURT

49. In the Court's opinion, the following are two of the requirements that flow from the expression 'prescribed by law'. Firstly, the law must be adequately accessible: the citizen must be able to have an indication that is adequate in the circumstances of the legal rules applicable to a given case. Secondly, a norm cannot be regarded as a law unless it is formulated with sufficient precision to enable the citizen to regulate his conduct: he must be able—if need be with appropriate advice—to foresee, to a degree that is reasonable in the circumstances, the consequences which a given action may entail. Those consequences need not be foreseeable with absolute certainty: experience shows this to be unattainable. Again, whilst certainty is highly desirable, it may bring in its train excessive rigidity and the law must be able to keep pace with changing circumstances. Accordingly, many laws are inevitably couched in terms which, to a greater or lesser extent, are vague and whose interpretation and application are questions of practice.

[The Court, having confirmed that the term 'law' in the above phrase included unwritten law such as the common law, concluded that although the English law of contempt was not as clear as it might be, the applicants 'were able to foresee to a degree that was reasonable in the circumstances, a risk that publication of the draft article' might be contempt. The Court also held that the injunction could be justified as having an aim permitted by Art. 10(2), viz. 'the maintenance of the authority...of the judiciary'. More difficult was the question whether it was 'necessary,' etc., to achieve that aim:]

---

[8] Pp. 814–817, 820–821.   [9] See below, pp. 631–637.
[10] *Kingsley International Pictures v Regents* 360 US 684 (1959) (film); *Southeastern Promotions Ltd v Conrad* 419 US 892 (1975) (theatre).
[11] See pp. 714, 814–817, 820–821.   [12] Below, p. 721.

59. ... The Court has noted[13] that, whilst the adjective 'necessary,' within the meaning of Article 10 § 2. is not synonymous with 'indispensable' neither has it the flexibility of such expressions as 'admissible', 'ordinary', 'useful', 'reasonable', or 'desirable' and that it implies the existence of a 'pressing social need...'

In the second place, the Court has underlined that the initial responsibility for securing the rights and freedoms enshrined in the Convention lies with the individual Contracting States. Accordingly, 'Article 10 § 2 leaves to the Contracting States a margin of appreciation. This margin is given both to the domestic legislator... and to the bodies, judicial amongst others, that are called upon to interpret and apply the laws in force...'

'Nevertheless, Article 10 § 2 does not give the Contracting States an unlimited power of appreciation:' 'The Court... is empowered to give the final ruling on whether a "restriction"... is reconcilable with freedom of expression as protected by Article 10...

The Court has deduced from a combination of these principles that 'it is in no way [its] task to take the place of the competent national courts but rather to review under Article 10 the decisions they delivered in the exercise of their power of appreciation...'

This does not mean that the Court's supervision is limited to ascertaining whether a respondent State exercised its discretion reasonably, carefully and in good faith. Even a Contracting State so acting remains subject to the Court's control as regards the compatibility of its conduct with the engagements it has undertaken under the Convention...

Again, the scope of the domestic power of appreciation is not identical as regards each of the aims listed in Article 10 § 2. The *Handyside* case concerned the 'protection of morals'. The view taken by the Contracting States of the 'requirements of morals', observed the Court, 'varies from time to time and from place to place, especially in our era'. Precisely the same cannot be said of the far more objective notion of the 'authority' of the judiciary. The domestic law and practice of the Contracting States reveal a fairly substantial measure of common ground in this area. This is reflected in a number of provisions of the Convention, including Article 6, which have no equivalent as far as 'morals' are concerned. Accordingly, here a more extensive European supervision corresponds to a less discretionary power of appreciation...

60. Both the minority of the Commission and the Government attach importance to the fact that the institution of contempt of court is peculiar to common-law countries and suggest that the concluding words of Article 10 § 2 were designed to cover this institution which has no equivalent in many other member States of the Council of Europe.

However, even if this were so. the Court considers that the reason for the insertion of those words would have been to ensure that the general aims of the law of contempt of court should be considered legitimate aims under Article 10 § 2 but not to make that law the standard by which to assess whether a given measure was 'necessary.'...

62. It must now be decided whether the 'interference' complained of correspond to a 'pressing social need', whether it was 'proportionate to the legitimate aim pursued ...'

63. ... The speeches in the House of Lords emphasised above all the concern that the processes of the law may be brought into disrespect and the functions of the courts usurped either if the public is led to form an opinion on the subject-matter of litigation before adjudication by the courts or if the parties to litigation have to undergo 'trial by newspaper'. Such concern is in itself 'relevant' to the maintenance of the 'authority of the judiciary.'...

Nevertheless, the proposed *Sunday Times* article was couched in moderate terms and did not present just one side of the evidence or claim that there was only one possible result at which a court could arrive... Accordingly, eve to the extent that the article might have led some readers to form an opinion on the negligence issue, this would not have had adverse consequences for the 'authority of the judiciary' especially since, as noted above, there had been a nationwide campaign in the meantime.

---

[13] *Ed.* In *Handyside v UK* (1976) 1 EHRR 737 (see A. Mowbray, *Cases and Materials on the European Convention on Human Rights* (OUP, Oxford, 2nd edn, 2007), pp. 623ff).

65. ...Whilst...[the courts] are the forum for the settlement of disputes, this does not mean that there can be no prior discussion of disputes elsewhere, be it in specialised journals, in the general press or amongst the public at large....Not only do the media have the task of imparting such information and ideas: the public also has a right to receive them....The Court observes...that, following a balancing of the conflicting interests involved, an absolute rule was formulated by certain of the Law Lords to the effect that it was not permissible to prejudge issues in pending cases....Whilst emphasising that it is not its function to pronounce itself on an interpretation of English law adopted in the House of Lords...the Court points out that it has to take a different approach. The Court is faced not with a choice between two conflicting principles but with a principle of freedom of expression [in Article 10] that is subject to a number of exceptions which must be narrowly interpreted...the Court has to be satisfied that the inter-ference was necessary having regard to the facts and circumstances prevailing in the specific case before it...the families of numerous victims of the tragedy, who were unaware of the legal difficulties involved, had a vital interest in knowing all the underlying facts and the various possible solutions. They could be deprived of this information, which was crucially important for them, only if it appeared absolutely certain that its diffusion would have presented a threat to the 'authority of the judiciary'.

66. The thalidomide disaster was a matter of undisputed public concern...fundamental issues concern-ing protection against and compensation for injuries resulting from scientific developments were raised and many facets of the existing law on these subjects were called in question.

...the facts of the case did not cease to be a matter of public interest merely because they formed a background to pending litigation. By bringing to light certain facts, the article might have served as a brake on speculative and unenlightened discussion.

67. Having regard to all the circumstances of the case...the Court concludes that the interference complained of did not correspond to a social need sufficiently pressing to outweigh the public interest in freedom of expression within the meaning of the Convention. The Court therefore finds the reasons for the restraint imposed on the applicants not to be sufficient under Article 10 § 2. That restraint proves not to be proportionate to the legitimate aim pursued; it was not necessary in a democratic society for main-taining the authority of the judiciary.

NOTES[14]

1. In their joint dissenting opinion, the nine dissenting judges, who included Judge Sir Gerald Fitzmaurice, disagreed with the majority essentially on the question whether the injunction was 'necessary' and on the latitude to be given to the defendant state under the 'margin of appreciation' doctrine. They pointed out that the 'authority and impartiality of the judiciary' exception allowed by Art. 10(2) was inserted on the proposal of the UK when the Convention was drafted to take account of the common law of contempt which is 'peculiar to the legal traditions of the common-law countries...and...is unknown in the law of most of the member states'. In the opinion of the dissenting judges, the conclusion of the majority that the 'authority...of the judiciary' was a far more objective notion than that of 'the protection of morals' (so that less discretion should be allowed to the defend-ant state) was erroneous. It was 'by no means divorced from national circumstances and cannot be determined in a uniform way'. Evidence for this was to be found in the differ-ent ways in which states went about protecting the authority. A state such as the UK that relied upon the law of contempt to protect it should be given sufficient latitude to apply it as national circumstances warranted or required.

---

[14] For casenotes see P.J. Duffy (1980) 5 H Rts Rev 17; F.A. Mann (1979) 95 LQR 348; W.W.M. Wong (1984) 17 NY Univ JIL & Pol 35.

2. The *Sunday Times* case was the first in which the Court was called upon to consider whether a judgment applying a rule of common law complied with the Convention. Crucial to the Court's decision was its understanding of the difference between the approach that it could adopt under Art. 10 and that open to the House of Lords at common law. Whereas it had to give priority to freedom of expression, the House of Lords could give equal weight to two competing freedoms. Even so. it is difficult to avoid the conclusion that had the House of Lords been applying Art. 10 (and it is interesting to note that the Convention was not referred to by any of their Lordships) it would have found the injunction to have been 'necessary' in the sense in which the Court interpreted that term. It would seem, moreover, that when applying the 'margin of appreciation' doctrine in this context, the Court reduced it almost to vanishing point. It appears to have made its own assessment of the situation *de novo* and simply to have disagreed with that of the House of Lords. This raises the question of the relationship between the Strasbourg authorities and local courts. (Cf. the *Handyside* case,[15] in which a court judgment applying statutory law was in issue.) As the Court indicated in the *Sunday Times* case,[16] it is not a court of appeal from national courts. It seems likely that the Court found confidence to disagree with the House of Lords from the lack of unanimity among English judges on the proper scope of the law of criminal contempt and its application in this case. Certainly it was affected by the fact, to which it refers, that the Phillimore Committee had suggested that the 'prejudgment' principle should be considered[17] and that the British Government White Paper[18] had not called in question this suggestion. The Contempt of Court Act 1981 was enacted partly to bring UK law into line with the Convention.

- **Lingens v Austria,** Judgment of 8 July 1986, ECtHRR A103
  (1986) 8 EHRR 407, European Court of Human Rights

The applicant published two articles in an Austrian magazine in which he criticised Mr Bruno Kreisky, an Austrian politician. The articles were written shortly after an Austrian general election in which the party of which Mr Kreisky, the retiring Chancellor (Prime Minister), was the leader had won. At a time when Mr Kreisky was forming a new government and in this connection had consulted Mr Peter, the leader of another party, Mr Kreisky defended Mr Peter in a television interview from criticism of his Nazi past by Mr Wiesenthal of the Jewish Documentation Centre. The applicant's first article accused Mr Kreisky of protecting Mr Peter and other former SS members for political reasons and described Mr Kreisky's attack in the television interview on Mr Peter's accuser as displaying 'the basest opportunism'. In the second article, the applicant criticised Mr Kreisky's accommodating attitude towards former Nazis who had taken part in politics and described his attitude as 'immoral' and 'undignified'. Following private prosecutions by Mr Kreisky, the applicant was convicted of the criminal offence of defamation for using the words 'the basest opportunism', 'immoral' and 'undignified' about Mr Kreisky. The applicant claimed a breach of Art. 10.

JUDGMENT OF THE COURT

35. It was not disputed that there was 'interference by public authority' with the exercise of the applicant's freedom of expression. This resulted from the applicant's conviction for defamation....Such interference contravenes the Convention if it does not satisfy the requirements of paragraph 2 of Article 10. It therefore falls to be determined whether the interference was 'prescribed by law', had an aim or aims that is or are legitimate under Article 10 para. 2 and was 'necessary in a democratic society' for the aforesaid aim or aims....

---

[15] (1976) 1 EHRR 737.   [16] Para. 59.   [17] Cmnd 5794, para. 111.
[18] Cmnd 7145, para. 43.

36. As regards the first two points, the Court agrees with the Commission and the Government that the conviction in question was indisputably based on Article 111 of the Austrian Criminal Code…; it was moreover designed to protect 'the reputation or rights of others' and there is no reason to suppose that it had any other purpose (see Article 18 of the Convention). The conviction was accordingly 'prescribed by law' and had a legitimate aim under Article 10 para. 2) of the Convention.…

39. The adjective 'necessary', within the meaning of Article 10 para. 2, implies the existence of a 'pressing social need'…. The Contracting States have a certain margin of appreciation in assessing whether such a need exists…, but it goes hand in hand with a European supervision, embracing both the legislation and the decisions applying it, even those given by an independent court (see the *Sunday Times* judgment of 26 April 1979, para. 59). The Court is therefore empowered to give the final ruling on whether a 'restriction' or 'penalty' is reconcilable with freedom of expression as protected by Article 10 (ibid.).

40. In exercising its supervisory jurisdiction, the Court cannot confine itself to considering the impugned court decisions in isolation; it must look at them in the light of the case as a whole, including the articles held against the applicant and the context in which they were written (see, mutatis mutandis, the *Handyside* judgment of 7 December 1976, para. 50). The Court must determine whether the interference at issue was 'proportionate to the legitimate aim pursued' and whether the reasons adduced by the Austrian courts to justify it are 'relevant and sufficient'.…

41. In this connection, the Court has to recall that freedom of expression, as secured in paragraph 1 of Article 10, constitutes one of the essential foundations of a democratic society and one of the basic conditions for its progress and for each individual's self-fulfilment. Subject to paragraph 2, it is applicable not only to 'information' or 'ideas' that are favourably received or regarded as inoffensive or as a matter of indifference, but also to those that offend, shock or disturb. Such are the demands of that pluralism, tolerance and broadmindedness without which there is no 'democratic society' (see the above-mentioned *Handyside* judgment, Series A no. 24, p. 23, para. 49).

These principles are of particular importance as far as the press is concerned. Whilst the press must not overstep the bounds set, inter alia, for the 'protection of the reputation of others', it is nevertheless incumbent on it to impart information and ideas on political issues just as on those in other areas of public interest. Not only does the press have the task of imparting such information and ideas: the public also has a right to receive them (see, mutatis mutandis, the above-mentioned *Sunday Times* judgment, para. 65). In this connection, the Court cannot accept the opinion, expressed in the judgment of the Vienna Court of Appeal, to the effect that the task of the press was to impart information, the interpretation of which had to be left primarily to the reader.…

42. Freedom of the press furthermore affords the public one of the best means of discovering and forming an opinion of the ideas and attitudes of political leaders. More generally, freedom of political debate is at the very core of the concept of a democratic society which prevails throughout the Convention.

The limits of acceptable criticism are accordingly wider as regards a politician as such than as regards a private individual. Unlike the latter, the former inevitably and knowingly lays himself open to close scrutiny of his every word and deed by both journalists and the public at large, and he must consequently display a greater degree of tolerance. No doubt Article 10 para. 2 enables the reputation of others—that is to say, of all individuals—to be protected, and this protection extends to politicians too, even when they are not acting in their private capacity; but in such cases the requirements of such protection have to be weighed in relation to the interests of open discussion of political issues.

43. The applicant was convicted because he had used certain expressions ('basest opportunism', 'immoral' and 'undignified') apropos of Mr. Kreisky, who was Federal Chancellor at the time, in two articles published in the Viennese magazine Profil on 14 and 21 October 1975.… The articles dealt with political issues of public interest in Austria which had given rise to many heated discussions concerning the attitude of Austrians in general—and the Chancellor in particular—to National Socialism and to the participation of former Nazis in the governance of the country. The content and tone of the articles were on the whole fairly balanced but the use of the aforementioned expressions in particular appeared likely to harm Mr. Kreisky's reputation.

However, since the case concerned Mr. Kreisky in his capacity as a politician, regard must be had to the background against which these articles were written. They had appeared shortly after the general election of October 1975. Many Austrians had thought beforehand that Mr. Kreisky's party would lose its absolute majority and, in order to be able to govern, would have to form a coalition with Mr. Peter's party. When, after the elections, Mr. Wiesenthal made a number of revelations about Mr. Peter's Nazi past, the Chancellor defended Mr. Peter and attacked his detractor, whose activities he described as 'mafia methods'; hence Mr. Lingens' sharp reaction. . . .

The impugned expressions are therefore to be seen against the background of a post-election political controversy . . . , in this struggle each used the weapons at his disposal; and these were in no way unusual in the hard-fought tussles of politics.

In assessing, from the point of view of the Convention, the penalty imposed on the applicant and the reasons for which the domestic courts imposed it, these circumstances must not be overlooked.

44. On final appeal the Vienna Court of Appeal sentenced Mr. Lingens to a fine; it also ordered confiscation of the relevant issues of Profil and publication of the judgment. . . .

As the Government pointed out, the disputed articles had at the time already been widely disseminated, so that although the penalty imposed on the author did not strictly speaking prevent him from expressing himself, it nonetheless amounted to a kind of censure, which would be likely to discourage him from making criticisms of that kind again in future; the Delegate of the Commission rightly pointed this out. In the context of political debate such a sentence would be likely to deter journalists from contributing to public discussion of issues affecting the life of the community. By the same token, a sanction such as this is liable to hamper the press in performing its task as purveyor of information and public watchdog. . . .

45. The Austrian courts applied themselves first to determining whether the passages held against Mr. Lingens were objectively defamatory; they ruled that some of the expressions used were indeed defamatory—'the basest opportunism', 'immoral' and 'undignified'. . . .

The defendant had submitted that the observations in question were value-judgments made by him in the exercise of his freedom of expression. . . . The Court, like the Commission, shares this view. The applicant's criticisms were in fact directed against the attitude adopted by Mr. Kreisky, who was Federal Chancellor at the time. What was at issue was not his right to disseminate information but his freedom of opinion and his right to impart ideas; the restrictions authorised in paragraph 2 of Article 10 nevertheless remained applicable.

46. The relevant courts then sought to determine whether the defendant had established the truth of his statements; this was in pursuance of Article 111 para. 3 of the Criminal Code. . . . They held in substance that there were different ways of assessing Mr. Kreisky's behaviour and that it could not logically be proved that one interpretation was right to the exclusion of all others; they consequently found the applicant guilty of defamation. . . .

In the Court's view, a careful distinction needs to be made between facts and value-judgments. The existence of facts can be demonstrated, whereas the truth of value-judgments is not susceptible of proof. The Court notes in this connection that the facts on which Mr. Lingens founded his value-judgment were undisputed, as was also his good faith. . . .

Under paragraph 3 of Article 111 of the Criminal Code, read in conjunction with paragraph 2, journalists in a case such as this cannot escape conviction for the matters specified in paragraph 1 unless they can prove the truth of their statements. . . .

As regards value-judgments this requirement is impossible of fulfilment and it infringes freedom of opinion itself, which is a fundamental part of the right secured by Article 10 of the Convention. . . .

47. From the various foregoing considerations it appears that the interference with Mr. Lingens' exercise of the freedom of expression was not 'necessary in a democratic society . . . for the protection of the reputation . . . of others'; it was disproportionate to the legitimate aim pursued. There was accordingly a breach of Article 10 of the Convention.

[The Court held unanimously that there had been a breach of Article 10.]

NOTES

1. The *Lingens* case is important because of the emphasis placed by the plenary Court upon the value of freedom of expression and also because of the distinction it draws between public and private figures, with the former being properly subject to closer scrutiny by way of comment in the public interest than the latter. There are echoes here of *New York Times v Sullivan*[19] in the US law of defamation under which a public official must prove actual malice if a defamation action is to be successful.[20] Austria's difficulty in this case was that its law did not draw a distinction between assertions of fact and expression of opinion by way of comment. A defendant had to prove the truth of the latter as well as the former; it was not sufficient just to show that a comment was made without malice. What the Court in effect requires is that a state provide a defence of fair comment on matters of public concern in its law of defamation in order to comply with Art. 10.

2. Following *Lingens*, there has been a series of cases on the application of national defamation laws to criticism of politicians. Such laws must in effect allow truth and fair comment defences, and even afford some protection to aspects the private lives of politicians that do not bear on matters of public concern.[21] Criticisms of governments carry even greater protection. In *Castells v Spain*,[22] C, a Spanish senator representing a party that supported Basque independence wrote a magazine article which accused the state of a number of murders, and 'the ruthless hunting down of Basque dissidents'. He was convicted of insulting the government; truth was not a defence. The Court unanimously found a breach of Art. 10:

42. While freedom of expression is important for everybody, it is especially so for an elected representative of the people. He represents his electorate, draws attention to their preoccupations and defends their interests. Accordingly, interferences with the freedom of expression of an opposition member of parliament, like the applicant, call for the closest scrutiny on the part of the Court....

46. The freedom of political debate is undoubtedly not absolute in nature.... The limits of permissible criticism are wider with regard to the Government than in relation to a private citizen, or even a politician. In a democratic system the actions or omissions of the Government must be subject to the close scrutiny not only of the legislative and judicial authorities but also of the press and public opinion. Furthermore, the dominant position which the Government occupies makes it necessary for it to display restraint in resorting to criminal proceedings, particularly where other means are available for replying to the unjustified attacks and criticisms of its adversaries or the media. Nevertheless it remains open to the competent State authorities to adopt, in their capacity as guarantors of public order, measures, even of a criminal law nature, intended to react appropriately and without excess to defamatory accusations devoid of foundation or formulated in bad faith.

[19] 376 US 254 (1964).   [20] Barendt, op. cit., pp. 206–210.

[21] See, e.g., *Oberschlick v Austria* (1991) 19 EHRR 389; *Tammer v Estonia* (2003) 37 EHRR 43 (ECtHR found compatible conviction of journalist for using offensive words about the lover of a former prime minister; she had resigned from a government position although was still active in the political party, but the comments were couched in offensive language and her private life was not one of the issues that affected the public); *Karhuvaara and Iltalehti v Finland*, Judgment of 16 November 2004 (breach of Art. 10 in respect of invasion of privacy conviction by reporting conviction of politician's husband for drunkenness and assaulting a police officer; this could affect voting decisions and so was, at least to some degree, a matter of public interest (para. 45)).

[22] (1992) 14 EHRR 445. See also *Incal v Turkey* (1998) 29 EHRR 449 (virulent remarks about the policy of the Turkish government that fell short of inciting violence); cf. *Zana v Turkey* (1997) 27 EHRR 667 (conviction held compatible by 12 to 8 where a former mayor (albeit ambiguously) expressed support for a terrorist organisation at a time when it was attacking civilians; this 'had to be regarded as likely to exacerbate an already explosive situation' (para. 60). See A.R. Mowbray [1999] PL 703.

'Very weighty reasons' must be advanced to justify interfering with freedom of expression exercised during proceedings of a local council or parliament.[23]

The ECtHR[24] has rejected an argument of a government that:

the wide limits of acceptable criticism in political discussion did not apply to the same extent in the discussion of other matters of public interest. The issues of public interest raised by the applicant's articles could not be included in the category of political discussion, which denoted direct or indirect participation by citizens in the decision-making process in a democratic society.

3. Both the recognition of the importance of freedom of expression as a value recognised by the common law and Art. 10 have been influential in shaping important aspects of defamation law in England and Wales. Landmark cases include *Derbyshire County Council v Times Newspapers*,[25] where the House of Lords held that a local authority cannot sue in libel in respect of its governing or administrative reputation; *Reynolds v Times Newspapers*[26] where the House expanded the scope of the defence of qualified privilege in respect of the publication of information on matters of public concern; and curbs on excessive damages awards in the contxt of the decision of the ECtHR in *Tolstoy Miloslavsky v United Kingdom*[27] that a jury award of £1.5m in respect of an allegation that Lord Aldington was a major war criminal was not proportionate.

4. Article 10 does not protect the intentional promotion of racist views, the support of Nazi ideology or Holocaust-denial.[28]

5. The interpretation of the words relating to the protection of confidences was discussed by the ECtHR (GC) in *Stoll v Switzerland*:[29]

58. Whereas the French wording of Article 10 § 2 of the Convention talks of measures necessary '*pour empêcher la divulgation d'informations confidentielles*', the English text refers to measures necessary 'for preventing the disclosure of information received in confidence'. The latter wording might suggest that the provision relates only to the person who has dealings in confidence with the author of a secret document and that, accordingly, it does not encompass third parties, including persons working in the media.

59. The Court does not subscribe to such an interpretation, which it considers unduly restrictive....

61. ...the Court considers it appropriate to adopt an interpretation of the phrase 'preventing the disclosure of information received in confidence' which encompasses confidential information disclosed either by a person subject to a duty of confidence or by a third party and, in particular, as in the present case, by a journalist.

---

[23] *Jerusalem v Austria*, Judgment of 27 February 2001, para. 40 (these were 'essential fora for public debate').

[24] In *Thorgeir Thorgeirson v Iceland* (1992) 14 EHRR 843, paras 61, 64 (this concerned allegations of police brutality by 'beasts in uniform'; conviction for criminal defamation violated Art. 10).

[25] [1993] AC 534.

[26] [2001] 2 AC 127. Considered further by the House in *Jameel v Wall Street Journal Europe SPRL* [2006] UKHL 44.

[27] (1995) 20 EHRR 442.

[28] *Jersild v Denmark* (1994) 19 EHRR 1 (racist comments by young people interviewed for TV not protected; conviction of the broadcaster contrary to Art. 10: he did not have a racist purpose although he did edit programme in such a way as to include the comments; he was seeking to expose, analyse and explain this group and this was a serious news programme); *Witsch v Germany* (Adm Dec 13 December 2005) (denial of Hitler's and the Nazis' responsibility in the extermination of the Jews; conviction for disparaging the dignity of the deceased compatible with Art. 10); cf. *Lehideux and Isorni v France* (1998) 30 EHRR 665 (conviction in respect of expression of support for Marshal Petain, head of the Vichy government during the Second World War, held by 15 to 6 to violate Art. 10; the applicants had expressly disapproved Nazi atrocities and persecution).

[29] Judgment of 10 December, 2007. See further p. 629.

6. Article 10 issues arise directly in the chapters contained in Part Four of this book and in the chapters on privacy in Part Three. They also appear frequently in cases and statutes in the context of public order and terrorism considered in the chapters in Part Two. The following case is a leading example of the articulation and application of these principles by the House of Lords.

- **R v Shayler** [2002] UKHL 11, [2003] 1 AC 247, House of Lords

S was a member of the security service from November 1991 to October 1996. At the outset of his service he signed a declaration pursuant to the Official Secrets Act 1989, acknow-ledging the confidential nature of documents and other information relating to security or intelligence that might come into his possession as a result of his position, and an acknow-ledgement that he was under a contractual obligation not to disclose, without authority, any information that came into his possession by virtue of his employment. On leaving the ser-vice he signed a further declaration acknowledging that the provisions of the Act continued to apply to any information, documents or other articles relating to security or intelligence which might have come into his possession as a result of his previous employment. In 1997 the defendant disclosed a number of documents relating to security or intelligence matters to a national newspaper. Shortly thereafter he left the country. In August 2000 he returned to the UK and was charged with disclosing documents or information without lawful author-ity, contrary to ss. 1 and 4 of the 1989 Act. In the course of a preparatory hearing, the trial judge ruled (1) that the defence of duress or necessity of circumstances was not open to the defendant, having by implication been excluded by the 1989 Act, nor (2) could he argue, at common law or as a result of the coming into force of the Human Rights Act 1998, that his disclosures were necessary in the public interest to avert damage to life or limb or serious damage to property. The Court of Appeal dismissed the defendant's appeal and ruled that the defence of duress or necessity of circumstances was available to a person who committed an otherwise criminal act to avoid an imminent danger to life or serious injury to himself or to individuals for whom he reasonably regarded himself as being responsible, but that the defence was not available to the defendant since there was no sufficient nexus between his disclosures and possible injury to members of the public, that having regard to national security the restrictions placed The House of Lords unanimously dismissed an appeal. It held, first, that the judge's power at a preparatory hearing was limited to questions of law 'relating to the case', and that limitation was to be strictly observed; that the facts of the defendant's case did not raise any questions relating to the defences of necessity or duress of circumstances, and that therefore neither the judge nor the Court of Appeal should have made any ruling on those defences; and that, accordingly, it was unnecessary to consider or express any view on them.

Lord Bingham of Cornhill:

[His Lordship summarised the background to the enactment of the 1989 Act, and set out its provisions]

CONSTRUCTION OF SECTION 1(2) AND 4(1) OF THE OSA 1989

20 It is in my opinion plain, giving sections 1(1)(a) and 4(1) and (3)(a) their natural and ordinary meaning and reading them in the context of the OSA 1989 as a whole, that a defendant prosecuted under these sections is not entitled to be acquitted if he shows that it was or that he believed that it was in the public or national interest to make the disclosure in question or if the jury conclude that it may have been or that the defendant may have believed it to be in the public or national interest to make the disclosure in question. The sections impose no obligation on the prosecution to prove that the disclosure was not in

the public interest and give the defendant no opportunity to show that the disclosure was in the public interest or that he thought it was. The sections leave no room for doubt, and if they did the 1988 White Paper quoted above, which is a legitimate aid to construction, makes the intention of Parliament clear beyond argument.

THE RIGHT TO FREE EXPRESSION

21 The fundamental right of free expression has been recognised at common law for very many years: see, among many other statements to similar effect, *Attorney General v Guardian Newspapers Ltd* [1987] 1 WLR 1248, 1269b, 1320g; *Attorney General v Guardian Newspapers Ltd (No 2)* [1990] 1 AC 109, 178e, 218d, 220c, 226a, 283e; *R v Secretary of State for the Home Department, Ex p Simms* [2000] 2 AC 115, 126e; *McCartan Turkington Breen v Times Newspapers Ltd* [2001] 2 AC 277, 290–291. The reasons why the right to free expression is regarded as fundamental are familiar, but merit brief restatement in the present context. Modern democratic government means government of the people by the people for the people. But there can be no government by the people if they are ignorant of the issues to be resolved, the arguments for and against different solutions and the facts underlying those arguments. The business of government is not an activity about which only those professionally engaged are entitled to receive information and express opinions. It is, or should be, a participatory process. But there can be no assurance that government is carried out for the people unless the facts are made known, the issues publicly ventilated. Sometimes, inevitably, those involved in the conduct of government, as in any other walk of life, are guilty of error, incompetence, misbehaviour, dereliction of duty, even dishonesty and malpractice. Those concerned may very strongly wish that the facts relating to such matters are not made public. Publicity may reflect discredit on them or their predecessors. It may embarrass the authorities. It may impede the process of administration. Experience however shows, in this country and elsewhere, that publicity is a powerful disinfectant. Where abuses are exposed, they can be remedied. Even where abuses have already been remedied, the public may be entitled to know that they occurred. The role of the press in exposing abuses and miscarriages of justice has been a potent and honourable one. But the press cannot expose that of which it is denied knowledge.

22 Despite the high value placed by the common law on freedom of expression, it was not until incorporation of the European Convention into our domestic law by the Human Rights Act 1998 that this fundamental right was underpinned by statute. Article 10(1) of the Convention, so far as relevant, provides:

'Everyone has the right to freedom of expression. This right shall include freedom to hold opinions and to receive and impart information and ideas without interference by public authority and regardless of frontiers.'

Section 12 of the 1998 Act reflects the central importance which attaches to the right to freedom of expression. The European Court of Human Rights for its part has not wavered in asserting the fundamental nature of this right. In paragraph 52 of its judgment in *Vogt v Germany* (1995) 21 EHRR 205 the court said:

'The court reiterates the basic principles laid down in its judgments concerning article 10:

(i) Freedom of expression constitutes one of the essential foundations of a democratic society and one of the basic conditions for its progress and each individual's self-fulfilment. Subject to article 10(2), it is applicable not only to "information" or "ideas" that are favourably received or regarded as inoffensive or as a matter of indifference, but also to those that offend, shock or disturb; such are the demands of that pluralism, tolerance and broadmindedness without which there is no "democratic society".'

It is unnecessary to multiply citations to the same effect. Thus for purposes of the present proceedings the starting point must be that the appellant is entitled if he wishes to disclose information and documents in his possession unless the law imposes a valid restraint upon his doing so.

ARTICLE 10(2)

23 Despite the high importance attached to it, the right to free expression was never regarded in domestic law as absolute. Publication could render a party liable to civil or criminal penalties or restraints on a

number of grounds which included, for instance, libel, breach of confidence, incitement to racial hatred, blasphemy, publication of pornography and, as noted above, disclosure of official secrets. The European Convention similarly recognises that the right is not absolute: article 10(2) qualifies the broad language of article 10(1) by providing, so far as relevant to this case:

> 'The exercise of these freedoms, since it carries with it duties and responsibilities, may be subject to such formalities, conditions, restrictions or penalties as are prescribed by law and are necessary in a democratic society, in the interests of national security, territorial integrity or public safety, for the prevention of disorder or crime…for the protection of the…rights of others, for preventing the disclosure of information received in confidence …'

It is plain from the language of article 10(2), and the European Court has repeatedly held, that any national restriction on freedom of expression can be consistent with article 10(2) only if it is prescribed by law, is directed to one or more of the objectives specified in the article and is shown by the state concerned to be necessary in a democratic society. 'Necessary' has been strongly interpreted: it is not synonymous with 'indispensable', neither has it the flexibility of such expressions as 'admissible', 'ordinary', 'useful', 'reasonable' or 'desirable': *Handyside v United Kingdom* (1976) 1 EHRR 737, 754, para 48. One must consider whether the interference complained of corresponded to a pressing social need, whether it was proportionate to the legitimate aim pursued and whether the reasons given by the national authority to justify it are relevant and sufficient under article 10(2): *The Sunday Times v United Kingdom* (1979) 2 EHRR 245, 277–278, para 62.

24 In the present case there can be no doubt but that the sections under which the appellant has been prosecuted, construed as I have construed them, restricted his prima facie right to free expression. There can equally be no doubt but that the restriction was directed to objectives specified in article 10(2) as quoted above. It was suggested in argument that the restriction was not prescribed by law because the procedure for obtaining authorisation was not precisely specified in the OSA 1989, but I cannot accept this. The restriction on disclosure is prescribed with complete clarity. A member or former member of any of the security or intelligence services wishing to obtain authority to disclose could be in no doubt but that he should seek authorisation from his superior or former superior in the relevant service or the head of that service, either of whom might no doubt refer the request to higher authority. It was common ground below, in my view, rightly, that the relevant restriction was prescribed by law. It is on the question of necessity, pressing social need and proportionality that the real issue between the parties arises.

25 There is much domestic authority pointing to the need for a security or intelligence service to be secure. The commodity in which such a service deals is secret and confidential information. If the service is not secure those working against the interests of the state, whether terrorists, other criminals or foreign agents, will be alerted, and able to take evasive action; its own agents may be unmasked; members of the service will feel unable to rely on each other; those upon whom the service relies as sources of information will feel unable to rely on their identity remaining secret; and foreign countries will decline to entrust their own secrets to an insecure recipient: see, for example, *Attorney General v Guardian Newspapers Ltd (No 2)* [1990] 1 AC 109, 118c, 213–214, 259a, 265f; *Attorney General v Blake* [2001] 1 AC 268, 287d–f. In the *Guardian Newspapers Ltd (No 2)* case, at p 269e–g, Lord Griffiths expressed the accepted rule very pithily:

> 'The Security and Intelligence Services are necessary for our national security. They are, and must remain, secret services if they are to operate efficiently. The only practical way to achieve this objective is a bright-line rule that forbids any member or ex-member of the service to publish any material relating to his service experience unless he has had the material cleared by his employers. There is, in my view, no room for an exception to this rule dealing with trivia that should not be regarded as confidential. What may appear to the writer to be trivial may in fact be the one missing piece in the jigsaw sought by some hostile intelligence agency.'

As already shown, this judicial approach is reflected in the rule laid down, after prolonged consideration and debate, by the legislature.

26 The need to preserve the secrecy of information relating to intelligence and military operations in order to counter terrorism, criminal activity, hostile activity and subversion has been recognised by the European Commission and the Court in relation to complaints made under article 10 and other articles under the Convention: see *Engel v The Netherlands (No 1)* (1976) 1 EHRR 647, paras 100–103; *Klass v Federal Republic of Germany* (1978) 2 EHRR 214, para 48; *Leander v Sweden* (1987) 9 EHRR 433, para 59; ... The thrust of these decisions and judgments has not been to discount or disparage the need for strict and enforceable rules but to insist on adequate safeguards to ensure that the restriction does not exceed what is necessary to achieve the end in question. The acid test is whether, in all the circumstances, the interference with the individual's Convention right prescribed by national law is greater than is required to meet the legitimate object which the state seeks to achieve. The OSA 1989, as it applies to the appellant, must be considered in that context.

27 The OSA 1989 imposes a ban on disclosure of information or documents relating to security or intelligence by a former member of the service. But it is not an absolute ban. It is a ban on disclosure without lawful authority. It is in effect a ban subject to two conditions. First of all, the former member may, under section 7(3)(a), make disclosure to a Crown servant for the purposes of his functions as such.

[His Lordship referred to the possibilities of disclosure to a staff counsellor; the Attorney-General, DPP or police; a minister, the Secretary to the Cabinet or the Joint Intelligence Committee; the staff of the Comptroller and Auditor General, the National Audit Office and the Parliamentary Commissioner for Administration; or (in general terms) the oversight commissioners.] ...

29 One would hope that, if disclosure were made to one or other of the persons listed above, effective action would be taken to ensure that abuses were remedied and offenders punished. But the possibility must exist that such action would not be taken when it should be taken or that, despite the taking of effective action to remedy past abuses and punish past delinquencies, there would remain facts which should in the public interest be revealed to a wider audience. This is where, under the OSA 1989 the second condition comes into play: the former member may seek official authorisation to make disclosure to a wider audience.

30 As already indicated, it is open to a former member of the service to seek authorisation from his former superior or the head of the service, who may no doubt seek authority from the secretary to the cabinet or a minister. Whoever is called upon to consider the grant of authorisation must consider with care the particular information or document which the former member seeks to disclose and weigh the merits of that request bearing in mind (and if necessary taking advice on) the object or objects which the statutory ban on disclosure seeks to achieve and the harm (if any) which would be done by the disclosure in question. If the information or document in question were liable to disclose the identity of agents or compromise the security of informers, one would not expect authorisation to be given. If, on the other hand, the document or information revealed matters which, however, scandalous or embarrassing, would not damage any security or intelligence interest or impede the effective discharge by the service of its very important public functions, another decision might be appropriate. Consideration of a request for authorisation should never be a routine or mechanical process: it should be undertaken bearing in mind the importance attached to the right of free expression and the need for any restriction to be necessary, responsive to a pressing social need and proportionate.

31 One would, again, hope that requests for authorisation to disclose would be granted where no adequate justification existed for denying it and that authorisation would be refused only where such justification existed. But the possibility would of course exist that authority might be refused where no adequate justification existed for refusal, or at any rate where the former member firmly believed that no adequate justification existed. In this situation the former member is entitled to seek judicial review of the decision to refuse, a course which the OSA 1989 does not seek to inhibit. In considering an application for

judicial review of a decision to refuse authorisation to disclose, the court must apply (albeit from a judicial standpoint, and on the evidence before it) the same tests as are described in the last paragraph. It also will bear in mind the importance attached to the Convention right of free expression. It also will bear in mind the need for any restriction to be necessary to achieve one or more of the ends specified in article 10(2), to be responsive to a pressing social need and to be no more restrictive than is necessary to achieve that end.

32 For the appellant it was argued that judicial review offered a person in his position no effective protection, since courts were reluctant to intervene in matters concerning national security and the threshold of showing a decision to be irrational was so high as to give the applicant little chance of crossing it. Reliance was placed on *Chahal v United Kingdom* (1996) 23 EHRR 413 and *Tinnelly & Sons Ltd v United Kingdom* (1998) 27 EHRR 249, in each of which the European Court was critical of the effectiveness of the judicial review carried out.

33 There are in my opinion two answers to this submission. First the court's willingness to intervene will very much depend on the nature of the material which it is sought to disclose. If the issue concerns the disclosure of documents bearing a high security classification and there is apparently credible unchallenged evidence that disclosure is liable to lead to the identification of agents or the compromise of informers, the court may very well be unwilling to intervene. If, at the other end of the spectrum, it appears that while disclosure of the material may cause embarrassment or arouse criticism, it will not damage any security or intelligence interest, the court's reaction is likely to be very different. Usually, a proposed disclosure will fall between these two extremes and the court must exercise its judgment, informed by article 10 considerations. The second answer is that in any application for judicial review alleging an alleged violation of a Convention right the court will now conduct a much more rigorous and intrusive review than was once thought to be permissible. The change was described by Lord Steyn in *R (Daly) v Secretary of State for the Home Department* [2001] 2 AC 532, 546–548...

'26....There is a material difference between the *Wednesbury* and *Smith* grounds of review and the approach of proportionality applicable in respect of review where Convention rights are at stake.'

This approach contrasts sharply with that adopted in the authorities on which the appellant based his submission. In *Chahal* , on applications for both habeas corpus and judicial review, there was no effective judicial inquiry into the legality of the applicant's detention, and this was of even greater importance where the applicant faced the risk of torture or inhuman or degrading treatment: 23 EHRR 413, paras 132, 150–151. In *Tinnelly* the issue of conclusive certificates had effectively prevented any judicial determination of the merits of the applicants' complaints: 27 EHRR 249, para 77.

34 The appellant contended that even if, theoretically, judicial review offered a means of challenging an allegedly wrongful refusal of authorisation to disclose, it was in practice an unavailable means since private lawyers were not among those to whom disclosure could lawfully be made under section 7(3)(a), and a former member of the service could not be expected to initiate proceedings for judicial review without the benefit of legal advice and assistance. I would for my part accept that the fair hearing guaranteed by article 6(1) of the Convention to everyone in the determination of their civil rights and obligations must ordinarily carry with it the right to seek legal advice and assistance from a lawyer outside the government service. But this is a matter to be resolved by seeking official authorisation under section 7(3)(b). The service would at that stage, depending on the nature of the material sought to be disclosed, be fully entitled to limit its authorisation to material in a redacted or anonymised or schematic form, to be specified by the service; but I cannot envisage circumstances in which it would be proper for the service to refuse its authorisation for any disclosure at all to a qualified lawyer from whom the former member wished to seek advice. If, at the hearing of an application for judicial review, it were necessary for the court to examine material said to be too sensitive to be disclosed to the former member's legal advisers, special arrangements could be made for the appointment of counsel to represent the applicant's interests as envisaged by the Court of Appeal in *Secretary of State for the Home Department v Rehman* [2003] 1 AC 153, 186–187, paras 31–32.

35 There is one further safeguard which deserves mention. By section 9(1) of the OSA 1989 the consent of the Attorney General is required before any prosecution is instituted for an offence under (among other sections) sections 1(1) and 4(1) and (3). The appellant submitted that this is not an effective safeguard since there are no criteria to govern the giving of consent. Successive Directors of Public Prosecutions, acting under the general superintendence of the Attorney General, have, however, published codes for the guidance of Crown prosecutors, and the practice of the Attorney General is to follow this guidance, although he may of course take a broader view of the public interest. The tests laid down comprise a merits or evidential test, requiring a realistic prospect of securing a conviction, and a public interest test. The Attorney General will not give his consent to prosecution unless he judges prosecution to be in the public interest. He is unlikely to consent if the disclosure alleged is trivial or the information disclosed stale and notorious or the facts are such as would not be thought by reasonable jurors or judges to merit the imposition of criminal sanctions. The consent of the Attorney General is required as a safeguard against ill-judged or ill-founded or improperly motivated or unnecessary prosecutions.

36 The special position of those employed in the security and intelligence services, and the special nature of the work they carry out, impose duties and responsibilities on them within the meaning of article 10(2): *Engel v The Netherlands (No 1)* 1 EHRR 647, para 100; *Hadjianastassiou v Greece* 16 EHRR 219, para 46. These justify what Lord Griffiths called a brightline rule against disclosure of information of documents relating to security or intelligence obtained in the course of their duties by members or former members of those services. (While Lord Griffiths was willing to accept the theoretical possibility of a public interest defence, he made no allowance for judicial review: *Attorney General v Guardian Newspapers Ltd (No 2)* [1990] 1 AC 109, 269g). If, within this limited category of case, a defendant is prosecuted for making an unauthorised disclosure it is necessary to relieve the prosecutor of the need to prove damage (beyond the damage inherent in disclosure by a former member of these services) and to deny the defendant a defence based on the public interest; otherwise the detailed facts concerning the disclosure and the arguments for and against making it would be canvassed before the court and the cure would be even worse than the disease. But it is plain that a sweeping, blanket ban, permitting of no exceptions, would be inconsistent with the general right guaranteed by article 10(1) and would not survive the rigorous and particular scrutiny required to give effect to article 10(2). The crux of this case is whether the safeguards built into the OSA 1989 are sufficient to ensure that unlawfulness and irregularity can be reported to those with the power and duty to take effective action, that the power to withhold authorisation to publish is not abused and that proper disclosures are not stifled. In my opinion the procedures discussed above, properly applied, provide sufficient and effective safeguards. It is, however, necessary that a member or former member of a relevant service should avail himself of the procedures available to him under the Act. A former member of a relevant service, prosecuted for making an unauthorised disclosure, cannot defend himself by contending that if he had made disclosure under section 7(3)(a) no notice or action would have been taken or that if he had sought authorisation under section 7(3)(b) it would have been refused. If a person who has given a binding undertaking of confidentiality seeks to be relieved, even in part, from that undertaking he must seek authorisation and, if so advised, challenge any refusal of authorisation. If that refusal is upheld by the courts, it must, however reluctantly, be accepted. I am satisfied that sections 1(1) and 4(1) and (3) of the OSA 1989 are compatible with article 10 of the Convention; no question of reading those sections conformably with the Convention or making a declaration of incompatibility therefore arises. On these crucial issues I am in agreement with both the judge and the Court of Appeal. They are issues on which the House can form its own opinion. But they are also issues on which Parliament has expressed a clear democratic judgment....

Lords Hope of Craighead and **Hutton** delivered concurring speeches; **Lords Hope, Hobhouse of Woodborough** and **Scott of Foscote** agreed with Lord Bingham. Lord Scott also agreed with Lord Hope and (subject to one point) Lord Hutton.

NOTES

1. Lord Hope was more sceptical as to the sufficiency of the safeguards in themselves: 'institutions tend to protect their own and to resist criticism from wherever it may come'; but the possibility of judicial review of a refusal of official authorisation, applying the, more intensive, proportionality approach in accordance with *Daly*, made the difference.[30]

2. The House had little difficulty in holding that a public interest defence could not be read into the Act. Lord Hope was clear that if the Act had been incompatible, a declaration of incompatibility would have to have been made.[31] In some cases, the courts have gone to extreme lengths to read in words to secure compatibility,[32] but the current trend is not to be unduly adventurous.[33] The decision of the House leaves a proportionality issue to be determined by a judge. The absence of a public interest defence means that the matters related to that issue never reach a jury (subject to the point that a jury ultimately has the power in practice to acquit for whatever reason it chooses).[34]

On the defence of duress of circumstances, Lord Bingham said[35] 'I should not for my part be taken to accept all that the Court of Appeal said on these difficult topics, but in my opinion it is unnecessary to explore them in this case.' Notwithstanding that, it is in practice still open for the defence to be run in prosecutions under the Act.[36]

3. The *Shayler* case proceeded to trial.[37] He defended himself. Some evidence was heard *in camera*. He admitted disclosing MI5 documents and information from phone taps to journalists and disclosing information in a *Mail on Sunday* article. These included agents' names and other sensitive information. He claimed he had acted honourably because of a matter he had seen. However, Moses J prevented him from going into detail, on the ground that his reasons for his actions were not relevant to the charges against him. The prosecution raised the point that he had received £40,000 from the *Mail on Sunday*. S asked the jury not to convict him, but they did. He was sentenced to six months' imprisonment, the judge saying that he was prepared to accept that he was motivated by a desire to expose what he thought was wrong, not money.

The Court of Appeal dismissed an appeal[38] put forward on the ground that the trial process had been unfair. S sought to challenge three rulings by Moses J. First, three members of the security service and one former member were allowed to give evidence from behind a (brown paper) screen and not to be named in public. The judge had held there was a real risk that disclosure of their names would give rise to a real risk to their safety, and that there was no real risk of prejudice to S, who knew them all. Second, S was required to give the court advance notice of any evidence he sought to introduce relating or purporting to relate to security and intelligence (but not the questions he proposed to ask) so that the judge could rule in chambers on relevance, and if relevant, consider any application for those matters to be heard *in camera*. The CA stated that it was difficult to envisage how the judge could have made a less restrictive ruling. Third, S was not permitted to ask certain questions in relation to credit of a witness because the judge found that they would not affect the witness's credibility in respect of the limited matters on which he was to testify. Furthermore, they were part of a design to go beyond the rulings at the preparatory hearing, as considered by the

---

[30] Paras [70]–[79].   [31] Para. [53].   [32] E.g. *R v A (No. 2)* [2002] 1 AC 45.

[33] See pp. 50–51.   [34] Cf. *R v Ponting*, below, p. 788.

[35] Para. [17]. See further D. Ormerod, *Smith and Hogan Criminal Law* (12th edn, 2008), pp. 342–345.

[36] See the prosecution of Gun, below p. 793. For comments on *Shayler*, see A.T.H. Smith [2002] CLJ 514.

[37] *The Guardian*, 2 and 5 November 2002; *The Observer*, 3 November 2002. For further background, see pp. 791–793.

[38] [2003] EWCA Crim 2218.

Court of Appeal and House of Lords. The court held that each of the judge's three rulings was correct and the cumulative effect of the rulings had not resulted in any unfairness to the defendant.

4. In *Stoll v Switzerland*,[39] a journalist was convicted of an offence under Swiss law for publishing extracts from a confidential document prepared by a senior Swiss diplomat for the purposes of difficult negotiations between, among others, the World Jewish Congress and Swiss banks concerning compensation due to Holocaust victims for unclaimed assets deposited in Swiss bank accounts. The ECtHR (GC), reversing a Chamber decision, held by 12 to 5 that this did not violate Art. 10. The relevant justification was that of preventing breaches of confidence, the conviction not being based the protection of national security or public safety. The Court held that it was not disproportionate and fell within the state's margin of appreciation. The articles were capable of contributing to the public debate on the issue of unclaimed assets; not all diplomatic confidences necessarily deserved protection; but the language used by the diplomat was 'bellicose'; the publication posed a risk to diplomatic relations in general and the negotiations in particular (although they were not shown to have been affected); the journalist could not claim in good faith to be unaware that disclosure to him of the document in question was punishable under the Criminal Code; the editing was selective, sensationalist, exaggerated and misleading; only a small fine had been imposed. It is likely that a different view would have been taken if the journalism had been more responsible.

---

[39] Judgment of 10 December 2007.

10

FREEDOM OF EXPRESSION: CENSORSHIP AND OBSCENITY

In the context of indecency and obscenity, prior restraint in the form of state censorship is now limited in England and Wales to videos, DVDs and certain computer games; the arrangements for the censorship of films are technically extra-statutory but do have a statutory underpinning in practice through the cinema licensing powers of local authorities. In the US, most state visual prior censorship laws and procedures have been held unconstitutional.[1]

1. THEATRE CENSORSHIP

- Theatres Act 1968

1. Abolition of censorship of the theatre

(1) The Theatres Act 1843 is hereby repealed; and none of the powers which were exercisable there under by the Lord Chamberlain of Her Majesty's Household shall be exercisable by or on behalf of Her Majesty by virtue of Her royal prerogative.

NOTE

1. The Theatres Act 1968 ended official censorship of plays. Originating in legislation of 1737 (provoked by Sir Robert Walpole's sensitivity to his caricaturisation in plays), and extended in 1843 for the preservation of 'good manners' and 'decorum', the power of the Lord Chamberlain as regards the licensing of plays was, even in the years immediately preceding the 1968 Act, certainly no dead letter. Political characterisation, let alone satire, was closely controlled by the Lord Chamberlain, thus imposing significant restrictions on dramatic treatment of political issues of the day. Equally, the Lord Chamberlain firmly acted as guardian of the theatre-going public's 'decency'. A particularly strict line was taken as regards any allusions to homosexuality, with little or no regard taken to considerations of dramatic or other merit.

Although unpopular with dramatists and directors, commercial theatre managers quite favoured the Lord Chamberlain's activities. It was unlikely that any prosecution (e.g. for obscenity) would be brought in respect of the performance of any play in respect of which he had granted his approval. Managers could therefore feel confident that they would only be involved in the presentation of 'safe' plays unlikely to cause

---

[1] *Kingsley International Pictures v Regents* 360 US 684 (1959) (film); *Southeastern Promotions Ltd v Conrad* 419 US 892 (1975) (theatre).

much controversy amongst audiences or the public at large.[2] Writers and directors took a less sanguine view of the restrictions imposed by this licensing control, and, following a campaign mounted by the state-subsidised Royal Shakespeare Company, the matter was considered by a Parliamentary Joint Committee which reported in 1967. The Committee's recommendation that theatre censorship be abolished was implemented by the 1968 Act.

The absence of 'official' censorship of the theatre does not, of course, mean that writers and directors may not encounter difficulties staging plays with controversial content. Commercial theatre managers may prefer to present pieces with more assured audience attraction, and even the subsidised theatre has from time to time been said to act with one eye on the attitude of its funding bodies.[3]

2. FILM CENSORSHIP[4]

The Licensing Act 2003 amalgamated six licensing regimes, including the licensing of film exhibitions under the Cinemas Act 1985, and replaced them with a single system of premises licences. For the exhibition of films mandatory conditions apply.

• Licensing Act 2003

20 Mandatory condition: exhibition of films

(1) Where a premises licence authorises the exhibition of films, the licence must include a condition requiring the admission of children to the exhibition of any film to be restricted in accordance with this section.

(2) Where the film classification body is specified in the licence, unless subsection (3)(b) applies, admission of children must be restricted in accordance with any recommendation made by that body.

(3) Where—

(a) the film classification body is not specified in the licence, or

(b) the relevant licensing authority has notified the holder of the licence that this subsection applies to the film in question,

admission of children must be restricted in accordance with any recommendation made by that licensing authority.

---

[2] Compare the establishment, by the film industry itself, of the British Board of Film Censors.

[3] For accounts of the Lord Chamberlain's exercise of his powers of censorship, see R. Findlater, *Banned! A Review of Theatrical Censorship in Britain* (1967); N. De Jongh, *Politics, prudery and perversions: the censoring of the English Stage 1901–1968* (2000); P. O'Higgins, *Censorship* (1972), pp. 95–99; G. Robertson, *Freedom, the Individual and the Law* (7th edn, 1993), pp. 238–241.

[4] See further on film censorship, N. March Hunnings, *Film Censors and the Law* (1967), pp. 29–148; Williams Committee on Obscenity and Film Censorship (Cmnd 7772, 1979), Appendix 2; J. Trevelyan, *What the Censor Saw* (1973) and 'Film Censorship and the Law' in R. Dhavan and C. Davies (eds), *Censorship and Obscenity* (1978), pp. 98–108; G. Phelps, *Film Censorship* (1975); B. Brown, *Screen*, Vol. 23 No. 5, p. 2; E. Wistrich, *I Don't Mind the Sex it's the Violence* (1972); G. Robertson, *Freedom, the Individual and the Law* (7th edn, 1993), pp. 258–272; James C. Robertson, *The British Board of Film Censors: Film Censorship in Britain 1896–1950*, and *The Hidden Cinema: British Film Censorship in Action 1913–1975* (2nd edn, 1993); A. Aldgate, *Censorship and the Permissive Society: British Cinema and Theatre 1955–1965* (1995); S. Brody, *Screen Violence and Film Censorship* (HMSO).

(4) In this section—

'children' means persons aged under 18; and

'film classification body' means the person or persons designated as the authority under section 4 of the Video Recordings Act 1984 (c 39) (authority to determine suitability of video works for classification).

NOTES

1. Whilst local authorities issue licenses to cinemas under the 2003 Act, and can decide which films are permitted to be shown, in practice films are in fact classified on their behalf by the British Board of Film Classification (BBFC). The film industry established the British Board of Film Censors (as its predecessor was known) in 1912 as a response to the assertion, under 1909 licensing legislation, of censorship powers by local authorities. The aim was to establish a body which would be independent of both central and local government and which might help to secure achievement of reasonably informed, and reasonably uniform, decision-making on this matter by councils across the country. Being a non-statutory body its powers (in relation to film) are only those of advice, but in the main, its objectives seem to have been achieved. Historically, councils have been willing to accept the classification decisions of the BBFC in most cases, and film makers have gained familiarity with the criteria adopted by the BBFC in deciding whether or not to grant a certificate and, if so, what viewing classification to impose. Inevitably, not all film makers (as compared with film distributors) have been happy with this system of 'control'. As a previous President of the BBFC, the Earl of Harewood, explained, 'one man's safeguards are another's shackles'. Controversy has arisen, over the years, in connection with numerous films. In some cases councils have chosen to ban a film from being shown in their areas even though it was passed by the BBFC—e.g. *Crash, Straw Dogs, Clockwork Orange, Life of Brian.* In other cases councils have chosen to allow films to be shown despite the fact that the BBFC felt unable to grant a certificate—e.g. *More about the Language of Love, Texas Chain Saw Massacre*[5] (both passed by the former Greater London Council). In truth, however, it appears that most councils have no wish to devote resources to the regular scrutiny of films and have been pleased to rely on the judgment of the BBFC.[6]

2. A virtue of the BBFC system is that decisions are taken by persons who have actually seen the film in question. Film examiners are drawn from outside the film industry, with a balance kept between men and women. They comprise persons with a broad range of ages and backgrounds (including from the ethnic minority communities: note that many films and videos are in foreign languages, designed for Hindi and Cantonese audiences). The examiners usually work in pairs but viewing by one examiner is used where the examination work is known not to be difficult. All proposals from examiners require the approval of a member of BBFC's senior staff (the director, the deputy director and senior examiners) to whom the President of the BBFC has delegated his authority. The BBFC views over 500 films annually. In 2007, 574 films were processed with cuts being made to five.[7]

By contrast to these arrangements, there have been occasions where a local council has banned the showing of a feature film, basing its decision upon press reports of the film's

---

[5] *The Texas Chain Saw Massacre* was subsequently classified by the BBFC in 1999.

[6] See D. Holbrook (1973) 123 NLJ 701 and correspondence at pp. 754, 775, 794, 833 and 915; and *Report of the Williams Committee on Obscenity and Film Censorship* (Cmnd 7772, 1979), p. 27.

[7] See www.bbfc.co.uk/statistics/index.php.

nature and content alone.[8] In 1988 concern was expressed in the press about the allegedly blasphemous content of a film, *The Last Temptation of Christ* (directed by Martin Scorsese). The Board received some 1,870 letters and petitions about the film even prior to its arrival in the UK. On viewing the film the BBFC came to the conclusion that it was a 'reinterpretation' of Christ's life and passion rather than a scurrilous attack on the Christian religion! An '18' certificate was granted. The BBFC took the view that the film did not contravene the offence of blasphemy. This was, however, not sufficient to prevent the film being banned by a number of local authorities.

The functions of the BBFC were significantly extended in 1985 by the Video Recordings Act 1984.[9] In this connection the BBFC takes decisions which themselves have legal effect under the Act. As regards films it continues to have no more than the power of recommendation to local authorities as to the exercise of their functions.

The Classification Guidelines[10] explain the background and role of the BBFC and the legal considerations to which it must have regard.[11] The Classification Principles and Guidelines are as follows:

Classification Principles

In classifying films, videos or digital media, the BBFC also gives consideration to the following basic principles

– adults should be free to choose what they see, providing that it remains within the law and is not potentially harmful to society

– works should be allowed to reach the widest audience that is appropriate for their theme and treatment

– the context in which something (e.g. sex or violence) is presented is central to the question of its acceptability

– the BBFC's Guidelines will be reviewed periodically. The Guidelines, and the Board's practice in applying them, have particular regard to any changes in public taste, attitudes and concerns; changes in the law or new evidence from research or expert sources.

The Guidelines

The classification categories are:

• U, Uc—suitable for all.

• PG—General viewing but some scenes may be unsuitable for younger children.

• 12A, 12, 15 and 18 which restrict viewing by age.

• R18 which is only available to adults in licenced outlets.[12]

Occasionally, a work lies on the margin between the two categories. In making a final judgement, the BBFC takes into account the intentions of the film-maker, the expectations of the public in general and the work's audience in particular, and any special merits of the work.

---

8 See, e.g., G. Phelps, *Sight and Sound*, Vol. 42 No. 3 p. 138, discussing press reports about, and local authority decisions in respect of *Last Tango in Paris*.

9 See further, below, p. 634, note 4.

10 The most recent guidelines were published in 2005 with consultation on amendments taking place in 2008.

11 Under the Video Recordings Act 1984, the Cinematography Films (Animals) Act 1937 (which makes it illegal to show any scene 'organised or directed' to involve actual cruelty to animals; this was applied in requiring a cut to the film *Before Night Falls* in June 2001), the Protection of Children Act 1978, the Obscene Publications Act 1959 and 'other unlawful material' (i.e. 'material which is itself unlawful, or has arisen from the commission of an unlawful act').

12 On the R18 category, see: C. Munro [2006] Crim LR 957.

Classification decisions may be stricter on video than on film. This is because of the increased possibility of under-age viewing recognised in the Video Recordings Act, and of works being replayed or viewed out of context. Accordingly, a work may receive a higher age classification on video, or require heavier cuts.

Classification decisions are most strict on trailers and advertisements. This is because difficult content, which may be mediated by the context of the original work, may have a much starker effect in the brief and unprepared context of the trailer/advertisement.

Classification decisions may be less strict where they are justified by context.

Anything not permitted in these Guidelines at a particular category (PG to 18) is unacceptable also at all preceding lower categories. Similarly, anything permitted at one level is acceptable at all higher levels.

The BBFC provides further guidance in each classification category as to what is acceptable in regard to various themes, namely: language; nudity; sex; violence; imitable techniques; horror and drugs. The Board gives 'consumer advice' about the content of classified works to the public. Films (or videos and DVDs) which are unacceptable for any category may be dealt with by making appropriate cuts or requiring warning captions. If this is unacceptable to the distributor then the film may be refused a classification. Of particular concern are scenes of:

graphic rape or torture; sadistic violence or terrorisation; illegal or instructive drug use; material likely to incite racial hatred or violence; portrayals of children in a sexualised or abusive content; sex accompanied by non-consensual pain, injury or humiliation; or other material likely to be found obscene by the courts.

An appeal lies to the Board or (in the case of videos) the Video Appeals Committee and in the case of films a submission can be made to the licensing authority.

3. If a film or video is considered to be obscene within the meaning of the Obscene Publications Acts, or is considered to offend against some other aspect of the criminal law, a certificate will be refused altogether. In 1989 the BBFC refused a certificate to an 18-minute erotic video, *Visions of Ecstasy,* on grounds of blasphemy. Its nudity and sexual imagery were well within the normal bounds of an '18' classification. However, the sexual imagery focused on the crucified figure of Christ, and featured overt expressions of sexuality on the part of a nun. Having taken legal advice on the issue of blasphemy the BBFC denied a certificate, and the decision was upheld by the Video Appeals Committee.

The BBFC has been willing in its annual reports, press releases and elsewhere, to explain its approach to certain issues which it has to tackle. One long-term theme is that there has been a dramatic decline in the number of films cut for cinema release, from 34 per cent of the total in 1974 to fewer than 1 per cent in 2007.[13] The annual reports detail how various films have been awarded a particular classification and how the BBFC has responded to complaints from the public.

4. *Videos.* The Video Recordings Act 1984 established 'censorship' controls over the distribution of video recordings. The need felt for some such control stemmed from concern over 'video-nasties'; and, in particular, newspaper assertions as to the large numbers of children who were viewing such videos.[14] The provisions of the 1984 Act, superseding an earlier 'voluntary' BBFC classification system, extend beyond those necessary simply to deal with the 'video-nasties' problem, and introduced for video a thorough-going statutory system of video classification and censorship modelled on that which has long applied to the cinema. The Act also applies to DVDs and computer games.

---

[13] www.bbfc.co.uk/statistics/index.php.   [14] See further, J. Petley, *Screen.,* Vol. 25, No. 2, p. 68.

The basic offences under the Act are those of (a) supplying, or offering to supply, a video recording of an unclassified work, (b) possessing such a recording for the purposes of supply, and (c) supplying a video recording in breach of its classification.[15] The Act provides quite complex definitions of terms used. 'Video recording' refers to the disc, tape or any other device capable of storing data electronically containing the 'video work': any 'series of visual images' that is 'produced electronically by the use of information contained on any disc and shown as a moving picture,[16] magnetic tape or any other device capable of storing data electronically'. 'Supply' need not be for reward, and includes sales, lettings on hire, exchanges and loans.[17] 'Classified' means that a 'classification certificate' has been issued by the BBFC. Where such a certificate is issued it must state (a) that the work is suitable for general viewing and unrestricted supply, or (b) that the work is suitable for viewing only by persons above an age specified in the certificate (not being more than 18) and that no recording containing the work is to be supplied to any person below that age, or (c) that in addition to the statement in (b) above, no recording containing the work is to be supplied other than in a licensed sex shop (the R18 category).[18] Some video works will be refused classification certificates altogether. In reaching its decisions the designated authority is required to have 'special regard to the likelihood of video works...being viewed in the home'.[19] The letter of designation to the BBFC specifically enjoins it 'to seek to avoid classifying works which are obscene within the meaning of the Obscene Publications Acts 1959 and 1964 or which infringe other provisions of the criminal law'.

The certification requirements do not, however, apply to 'exempted works' or to 'exempted supplies'. The former are works which, taken as a whole, are designed to 'inform, educate or instruct', are concerned with 'sport, religion or music' or are 'video games'. However, such works are not exempt if to any significant extent they depict 'human sexual activity'[20] or acts of force or restraint associated with such activity; mutilation or torture of, or other acts of gross violence towards, humans or animals; human genital organs or human urinary or excretory functions; or techniques likely to be useful in the commission of offences. Exemption is also forfeit if a work is likely to any significant extent to stimulate or encourage sexual activity, is likely to any extent to encourage gross violence to humans or animals, or depicts criminal activity which is likely to stimulate or encourage commission of offences.[21] 'Exempted supplies' include supplies other than for reward and not in the course or furtherance of business, and supplies to participants of recordings of events or occasions so long as not significantly depicting anything referred to in s. 2, i.e. the video-recording of a wedding ceremony but not the honeymoon. If dissatisfied with a decision of the BBFC in relation to a video recording an appeal may be taken to the Video Appeals Committee. Enforcement of the provisions of the 1984 Act became in 1988 a matter for local 'weights and measures' authorities.[22]

---

[15] Ss. 9–11.

[16] The brevity of the display of the images is irrelevant provided the sequence is long enough to show continuity of movement: *Meechie v Multi-Media Market (Canterbury) Ltd* (1995) 94 LGR 474.

[17] S. 1, as amended by the Criminal Justice and Public Order Act 1994, s. 89.

[18] S. 7; in *Interfact Ltd v Liverpool City Council* [2005] 1 WLR 3118, it was held that videos classed as R18 must be supplied on the relevant premises in a face to face transaction.

[19] S. 4(1)(a).

[20] Activity short of masturbation may qualify for this description: *Meechie v Multi-Media Marketing (Canterbury) Ltd* (1995) 94 LGR 474.

[21] S. 2. See also the Criminal Justice and Immigration Act 2008 and the offence of possession of extreme pornography, considered below.

[22] S. 16A as amended by the Criminal Justice Act 1988, s. 162 and the Criminal Justice and Public Order Act 1994, s. 91.

A general defence was added by the Video Recordings Act 1993: it is a defence to a charge of committing any offence under the 1984 Act 'to prove (a) that the commission of the offence was due to the act or default of a person other than the accused, and (b) that the accused took all reasonable precautions and exercised all due diligence to avoid the commission of the offence by any person under his control'.[23]

In the autumn of 1993 two young boys were convicted of the murder of two-year-old James Bulger. In passing sentence the trial judge, Morland J commented that there might have been some connection between the behaviour of the two boys and the fact that the father of one of them had over the previous year rented several hundred 'adult' videos, including one of particular notoriety.[24]

Subsequently, there was much press coverage of a report authored by Professor Elizabeth Newson, a professor of developmental psychology, in which, purporting to speak also for others in her profession, she wrote:

> Many of us hold our liberal freedom of expression dear, but begin to feel we were naive in our failure to predict the extent of damaging material and its all too free availability to children. It now seems that professionals in child health and psychology underestimated the degree of brutality and sustained sadism that film makers were capable of inventing and willing to portray…and we certainly underestimated how easy would be children's access to them.[25]

This apparent change of stance amongst child development professionals at one and the same time spurred on those who sought tighter controls over video content and availability, and also produced a critical response on the part of those who had studied the evidence as regards the particular effect of film on children and others. For example, Dr Guy Cumberbatch (an academic applied psychologist) was quoted as commenting that although research showed that violent children liked violent films there was no firm evidence to show that such films cause violent or criminal behaviour. Studies suggesting the contrary, mostly American, have been difficult to replicate this side of the Atlantic.[26]

In response a new s. 4A was inserted into the 1984 Act, which provides matters to which the BBFC is required to have 'special regard' in the exercise of its functions under the 1984 Act. Such special regard shall be had to:

> any harm that may be caused to potential viewers or, through their behaviour, to society by the manner in which the work deals with—(a) criminal behaviour, (b) illegal drugs, (c) violent behaviour or incidents, (d) horrific behaviour or incidents, or (e) human sexual activity.

For the purposes of this section, 'potential viewer' means 'any person (including a child or young person) who is likely to view the video work in question' if a certificate (or one of a particular description) were issued.

---

[23] S. 14A.   [24] *Child's Play 3*.

[25] *Sunday Times*, 3 April 1994. See E. Newson, *Video Violence and the Protection of Children*, Report of the Home Affairs Committee, 29 June 1994.

[26] For a critical response to the Newson Report, see M. Barker and J. Petley, *Ill Effects: The Media Violence Debate* (1997), discussed by L. Bibbings (1998) 3 Communications Law 103. Bibbings also reviews a series of other reports on media violence, noting the difficulties of defining and coding 'violence' and the continuing absence of cogent evidence that video violence causes crime. Further, see L. Kutner and C. Olsen, *Grand Theft Childhood: The Surprising Truth about Violent Video Games and What Parents Can Do* (2008); C. Anderson, D. Gentile and K. Buckley, *Violent Video Game Effects on Children and Adolescents: Theory, Research, and Public Policy* (2007); D. Trend, *The Myth of Media Violence: A Critical Introduction* (2006).

The 1994 Act also stiffened the penalties which may be imposed following conviction for offences under the 1984 Act. Thus, for example, in relation to the principal offence under s. 9 (supplying video recording of an unclassified work) trial may now be on indictment (formerly summary only); and in either case a prison term may be imposed (maximum two years and six months respectively).

The Video Appeals Committee has overturned decisions of the BBFC in a number of cases.[27]

In 1997, the BBFC unilaterally relaxed its guidelines, and classified a number of videos containing more explicit material than previously classified, including scenes of actual penetration and oral sex. The Home Secretary was concerned that this was inconsistent with the approach taken by the customs and police in seizing material under, respectively, the Customs Consolidation Act 1876 and the Obscene Publications Act 1959. He instructed the BBFC to rescind the policy change. Accordingly, in 1998, the BBFC refused to classify *Makin' Whoopee!* that had been given an interim classification certificate under the revised guidelines. However the publishers successfully appealed to the Video Appeal Committee, which took the view that it was not obscene. The Board gave it an R18 classification, but refused to regard the decision as a precedent. Further explicit videos were refused classification. Seven were the subject of successful appeals to the VAC. The BBFC's application for judicial review of the VAC's decision was dismissed by Hooper J in *R v Video Appeals Committee of the British Board of Film Classification, ex p British Board of Film Classification*.[28] It was found that the VAC had applied the s. 4A criteria and was entitled to conclude that the risk of the videos being viewed by and causing harm to children and young persons was, on the present evidence, insignificant, and so an R18 classification should be granted. The approach adopted by the BBFC was that where the risk of harm to children was unquantifiable (as here) certification should be refused until the risk was quantified and shown to be acceptable in the light of the other factors. This approach was itself reasonable, but the VAC was entitled not to adopt it. Where harm is thought to be certain to even a small number of children, what justifications are there for the classification of highly explicit videos? The BBFC decided not to appeal and reconsidered the R18 Guidelines in the light of the judgment.[29] New guidelines were published that spelled out clearly what was *not* acceptable as well as what was allowed.[30]

The VAC's decision led to the issue of a consultation paper by the Home Office,[31] which noted that 'there remains substantial public concern that such material may fall into the hands of children' and 'that the mechanistic and impersonal way sexual activity can be portrayed in the videos could cause harm to children if they view it'.[32] But would complete ban on the sale of such videos, even from restricted specialist outlets, be a proportionate response?

---

[27] E.g., in 1989 the BBFC refused a certificate to *International Guerrillas*, a video which appeared to depict the author, Salman Rushdie, as a drunken murderer of Muslims. The BBFC feared that the video might be blasphemous. The Appeals Committee rejected this view. A second refusal by the Board was based upon the view that the video involved a *criminal* libel of Rushdie. This decision was also overturned by the Appeals Committee, following a plea against such censorship from Rushdie himself.

[28] [2000] COD 239.

[29] BBFC News Release, 22 May 2000.

[30] BBFC News Release, 18 July 2000.

[31] *Home Office, Consultation Paper on the Regulation of R18 Videos*, July 2000.

[32] Para. 2.7.

3. BROADCASTING

In this section we shall be principally concerned with the following issues: (a) the independence of broadcasting authorities from governmental influence and control; (b) the political impartiality of the broadcasting media—issues of political 'neutrality' and political 'balance'; and (c) the regulation and enforcement of standards to be observed by broadcasters as regards matters of sex, violence, taste and decency.

The importance of these issues is easily demonstrated. In the modern world most people obtain the bulk of their information on matters of contemporary interest from the broadcasting media. A state which controls the broadcasters thereby possesses considerable power to manipulate opinion. There should, therefore, be a presumption in any Western-style democracy against governmental influence over broadcasters. Any influence or control should be restricted to wholly exceptional or emergency situations; and even then the fact of influence should, wherever possible, be declared to viewers and listeners.

As worrying as governmental influence over broadcasting is the possibility of limits being imposed on what is broadcast by those in control of the broadcasting stations. How independent, and how influential are the government-appointed members of the BBC Trust? Who owns the 'independent' television and radio channels? Might the identity of the corporate owner make certain issues taboo? Might ownership of a broadcasting station be regarded as a way of wielding corporate political influence? These questions have commonly been raised in Britain in relation to ownership of the press. They are coming to be asked in relation to television and radio. During the 1980s and 1990s the BBC, on several occasions, encountered the hostility of members of the Government and of the Conservative Party. In 2004, following a report by a BBC journalist that the Government was aware that the report into Iraq's weapons of mass destruction had been 'sexed up' both the Chairman and the Director General of the BBC resigned following criticism in the Hutton Report[33] that the BBC's editorial process was defective. The criticism of the BBC related to its ability to regulate itself and led to the establishment of the BBC Trust as being separate from the governors.

The past 20 years have seen considerable changes to the arrangements for the licencing of independent television and radio. Following on from the Broadcasting Act 1990, the most recent substantial amendments have come in the Communications Act 2003. If a licence application is made under the Act to Ofcom (the regulatory body) it may refuse it if the proposed service would be likely to involve contraventions of the standards for programmes and advertising. Provisions exist to prevent any individual or corporation achieving an excessive degree of media dominance. Also, the tradition in British broadcasting that no overt editorial stance shall be taken continues in force. Moreover, the legislation preserves, and elaborates upon, the traditional obligation, as a part of the requirement of station neutrality, to achieve 'political balance' in programmes.

As well as being of prime significance in the way in which it informs us, and moulds our ideas, the broadcasting medium is unique in the way in which it 'intrudes' into our homes, and is therefore subject to greater regulation than the press and other media. Individuals can quite easily choose to avoid reading books, or looking through magazines, or watching films or videos, if these will offend them. By contrast, there appears to be a public expectation that television and radio should, although 'invited' into the home, behave there as reasonable guests, not offending or outraging those who might be expected to be watching at the time in

---

[33] Lord Hutton, *Report of the Inquiry into the Circumstances Surrounding the Death of Dr David Kelly C.M.G.* (2004) HC 247.

question. Controversy here, inevitably, concerns the point at which the mark is overstepped. What one person may regard as an appropriately forceful presentation, in dramatic form or as a news or current affairs item, of an important issue of the day, will likely shock or affront another. Difficulty in drawing this line should not mean that such issues be avoided, or that they should be treated in a wholly anodyne way.[34] In the digital age, where it is possible at the push of a button for the viewer to access a menu and consider the nature and content of programmes or ensure that certain programmes or channels are PIN protected, is it acceptable to retain the current regulations or should the viewer be held more responsible for their own viewing?

- ## Communications Act 2003

198 Functions of OFCOM in relation to the BBC

(1) It shall be a function of OFCOM, to the extent that provision for them to do so is contained in—

 (a) the BBC Charter and Agreement, and

 (b) the provisions of this Act and of Part 5 of the 1996 Act,

to regulate the provision of the BBC's services and the carrying on by the BBC of other activities for purposes connected with the provision of those services.

(2) For the purposes of the carrying out of that function OFCOM—

 (a) are to have such powers and duties as may be conferred on them by or under the BBC Charter and Agreement; and

 (b) are entitled, to the extent that they are authorised to do so by the Secretary of State or under the terms of that Charter and Agreement, to act on his behalf in relation to that Charter and Agreement.

(3) The BBC must pay OFCOM such penalties in respect of contraventions by the BBC of provision made by or under—

 (a) this Part, or

 (b) the BBC Charter and Agreement,

as are imposed by OFCOM in exercise of powers conferred on them by that Charter and Agreement.

(4) The BBC are also to be liable to pay OFCOM such sums in respect of the carrying out by OFCOM of their functions in relation to the BBC as may be—

 (a) agreed from time to time between the BBC and OFCOM; or

 (b) (in default of agreement) fixed by the Secretary of State.

(5) The maximum penalty that may be imposed on the BBC on any occasion by OFCOM in exercise of a power conferred by virtue of the BBC Charter and Agreement is £250,000.

Programme and fairness standards for television and radio

319 OFCOM's standards code

(1) It shall be the duty of OFCOM to set, and from time to time to review and revise, such standards for the content of programmes to be included in television and radio services as appear to them best calculated to secure the standards objectives.

---

[34] See, generally, T. Gibbons, *Regulating the Media* (2nd edn, 1998); M. Feintuck and N. Varney, *Media Regulation. Public Interest and the Law* (2nd edn, 2006); G. Robertson and A. Nicol, *Media Law* (5th edn, 2007).

(2) The standards objectives are—

    (a) that persons under the age of eighteen are protected;

    (b) that material likely to encourage or to incite the commission of crime or to lead to disorder is not included in television and radio services;

    (c) that news included in television and radio services is presented with due impartiality and that the impartiality requirements of section 320 are complied with;

    (d) that news included in television and radio services is reported with due accuracy;

    (e) that the proper degree of responsibility is exercised with respect to the content of programmes which are religious programmes;

    (f) that generally accepted standards are applied to the contents of television and radio services so as to provide adequate protection for members of the public from the inclusion in such services of offensive and harmful material;

    (g) that advertising that contravenes the prohibition on political advertising set out in section 321(2) is not included in television or radio services;

    (h) that the inclusion of advertising which may be misleading, harmful or offensive in television and radio services is prevented;

    (i) that the international obligations of the United Kingdom with respect to advertising included in television and radio services are complied with;

    (j) that the unsuitable sponsorship of programmes included in television and radio services is prevented;

    (k) that there is no undue discrimination between advertisers who seek to have advertisements included in television and radio services; and

    (l) that there is no use of techniques which exploit the possibility of conveying a message to viewers or listeners, or of otherwise influencing their minds, without their being aware, or fully aware, of what has occurred.

(3) The standards set by OFCOM under this section must be contained in one or more codes.

(4) In setting or revising any standards under this section, OFCOM must have regard, in particular and to such extent as appears to them to be relevant to the securing of the standards objectives, to each of the following matters—

    (a) the degree of harm or offence likely to be caused by the inclusion of any particular sort of material in programmes generally, or in programmes of a particular description;

    (b) the likely size and composition of the potential audience for programmes included in television and radio services generally, or in television and radio services of a particular description;

    (c) the likely expectation of the audience as to the nature of a programme's content and the extent to which the nature of a programme's content can be brought to the attention of potential members of the audience;

    (d) the likelihood of persons who are unaware of the nature of a programme's content being unintentionally exposed, by their own actions, to that content;

    (e) the desirability of securing that the content of services identifies when there is a change affecting the nature of a service that is being watched or listened to and, in particular, a change that is relevant to the application of the standards set under this section; and

    (f) the desirability of maintaining the independence of editorial control over programme content.

(5) OFCOM must ensure that the standards from time to time in force under this section include—

   (a) minimum standards applicable to all programmes included in television and radio services; and

   (b) such other standards applicable to particular descriptions of programmes, or of television and radio services, as appear to them appropriate for securing the standards objectives.

(6) Standards set to secure the standards objective specified in subsection (2)(e) shall, in particular, contain provision designed to secure that religious programmes do not involve—

   (a) any improper exploitation of any susceptibilities of the audience for such a programme; or

   (b) any abusive treatment of the religious views and beliefs of those belonging to a particular religion or religious denomination.

...

320 Special impartiality requirements

(1) The requirements of this section are—

   (a) the exclusion, in the case of television and radio services (other than a restricted service within the meaning of section 245), from programmes included in any of those services of all expressions of the views or opinions of the person providing the service on any of the matters mentioned in subsection (2);

   (b) the preservation, in the case of every television programme service, teletext service, national radio service and national digital sound programme service, of due impartiality, on the part of the person providing the service, as respects all of those matters;

   (c) the prevention, in the case of every local radio service, local digital sound programme service or radio licensable content service, of the giving of undue prominence in the programmes included in the service to the views and opinions of particular persons or bodies on any of those matters.

(2) Those matters are—

   (a) matters of political or industrial controversy; and

   (b) matters relating to current public policy.

(3) Subsection (1)(a) does not require—

   (a) the exclusion from television programmes of views or opinions relating to the provision of programme services; or

   (b) the exclusion from radio programmes of views or opinions relating to the provision of programme services.

(4) For the purposes of this section—

   (a) the requirement specified in subsection (1)(b) is one that (subject to any rules under subsection (5)) may be satisfied by being satisfied in relation to a series of programmes taken as a whole;

   (b) the requirement specified in subsection (1)(c) is one that needs to be satisfied only in relation to all the programmes included in the service in question, taken as a whole.

(5) OFCOM's standards code shall contain provision setting out the rules to be observed in connection with the following matters—

   (a) the application of the requirement specified in subsection (1)(b);

   (b) the determination of what, in relation to that requirement, constitutes a series of programmes for the purposes of subsection (4)(a);

   (c) the application of the requirement in subsection (1)(c).

(6) Any provision made for the purposes of subsection (5)(a) must, in particular, take account of the need to ensure the preservation of impartiality in relation to the following matters (taking each matter separately)—

(a) matters of major political or industrial controversy, and

(b) major matters relating to current public policy,

as well as of the need to ensure that the requirement specified in subsection (1)(b) is satisfied generally in relation to a series of programmes taken as a whole.

…

321 Objectives for advertisements and sponsorship

(1) Standards set by OFCOM to secure the objectives mentioned in section 319(2)(a) and (g) to (j)—

(a) must include general provision governing standards and practice in advertising and in the sponsoring of programmes; and

(b) may include provision prohibiting advertisements and forms and methods of advertising or sponsorship (whether generally or in particular circumstances).

(2) For the purposes of section 319(2)(g) an advertisement contravenes the prohibition on political advertising if it is—

(a) an advertisement which is inserted by or on behalf of a body whose objects are wholly or mainly of a political nature;

(b) an advertisement which is directed towards a political end; or

(c) an advertisement which has a connection with an industrial dispute.

(3) For the purposes of this section objects of a political nature and political ends include each of the following—

(a) influencing the outcome of elections or referendums, whether in the United Kingdom or elsewhere;

(b) bringing about changes of the law in the whole or a part of the United Kingdom or elsewhere, or otherwise influencing the legislative process in any country or territory;

(c) influencing the policies or decisions of local, regional or national governments, whether in the United Kingdom or elsewhere;

(d) influencing the policies or decisions of persons on whom public functions are conferred by or under the law of the United Kingdom or of a country or territory outside the United Kingdom;

(e) influencing the policies or decisions of persons on whom functions are conferred by or under international agreements;

(f) influencing public opinion on a matter which, in the United Kingdom, is a matter of public controversy;

(g) promoting the interests of a party or other group of persons organised, in the United Kingdom or elsewhere, for political ends.

…

336 Government requirements for licensed services

(1) If it appears to the Secretary of State or any other Minister of the Crown to be appropriate to do so in connection with any of his functions, the Secretary of State or that Minister may at any time by notice require OFCOM to give a direction under subsection (2).

(2) A direction under this subsection is a direction to the holders of the Broadcasting Act licences specified in the notice under subsection (1) to include an announcement so specified in their licensed services.

(3) The direction may specify the times at which the announcement is to be broadcast or otherwise transmitted.

(4) Where the holder of a Broadcasting Act licence includes an announcement in his licensed service in pursuance of a direction under this section, he may announce that he is doing so in pursuance of such a direction.

(5) The Secretary of State may, at any time, by notice require OFCOM to direct the holders of the Broadcasting Act licences specified in the notice to refrain from including in their licensed services any matter, or description of matter, specified in the notice.

(6) Where—

    (a) OFCOM have given the holder of a Broadcasting Act licence a direction in accordance with a notice under subsection (5),

    (b) in consequence of the revocation by the Secretary of State of such a notice, OFCOM have revoked such a direction, or

    (c) such a notice has expired,

the holder of the licence in question may include in the licensed service an announcement of the giving or revocation of the direction or of the expiration of the notice, as the case may be.

(7) OFCOM must comply with every requirement contained in a notice under this section.

...

NOTES

1. The Broadcasting Act 1990 established the Independent Television Commission charged with licensing and regulating non-BBC television services. The BBC, as a body established under Royal Charter, operated under the terms of that Charter and also its Licence and Agreement from the Home Secretary.[35] In the Broadcasting Act 1996 the Broadcasting Standards Commission was established. This was tasked to consider standards and fairness in broadcasting. OFCOM replaces this somewhat confused and overlapping form of regulation. OFCOM'S general duties are contained in s. 3 of the 2003 Act. More specifically, OFCOM states that its specific duties fall into six categories:

- Ensuring the optimal use of the electro-magnetic spectrum.
- Ensuring that a wide range of electronic communications services—including high speed data services—is available throughout the UK.
- Ensuring a wide range of TV and radio services of high quality and wide appeal.
- Maintaining plurality in the provision of broadcasting.
- Applying adequate protection for audiences against offensive or harmful material.
- Applying adequate protection for audiences against unfairness or the infringement of privacy

---

[35] See Department for Culture, Media and Sport, *Broadcasting: Copy of Royal Charter for the continuance of the British Broadcasting Corporation* (Cmnd 6925, 2006); *An Agreement Between Her Majesty's Secretary of State for Culture, Media and Sport and the British Broadcasting Corporation* (Cmnd 6872, 2006).

Under s. 12(1) of the 2003 Act OFCOM has established a 'content board' of 12 members which covers matters principally concerning harm and offence, accuracy and impartiality, fairness and privacy. The majority of the members are part time and drawn from a diverse range of backgrounds.

2. OFCOM's regime covers both independent broadcasters and the BBC. The BBC still has to operate within the boundaries of the Charter and Agreement, but if it contravenes Pt 3 of the 2003 Act OFCOM may impose financial penalties. Does the dual form of regulation replicate the confusing standards that applied in independent broadcasting before OFCOM took an all-encompassing role in that field? Should the BBC be involved in self-regulation at all, or will there inevitably be a conflict of interests?[36]

3. The standards for television and radio broadcasts are established in s. 319 and the Broadcasting Code established by OFCOM.[37] The Code has detailed provisions relating to (a) the protection of under 18s; (b) harm and offence; (c) crime; (d) religion; (e) due impartiality and due accuracy; (f) elections and referendums; (g) fairness; (h) privacy; (i) sponsorship; (j) commercial references. All licensed broadcasters must observe all the terms and viewers or listeners may complain to OFCOM about potential breaches of the Code.[38] The majority of adverse findings relate to breaches of r. 1 which is perhaps a reflection of a liberal attitude by OFCOM in seeking to protect minors from harm rather than protecting adults from what might be termed 'bad taste'. This is further exemplified by OFCOM's decision to clear the BBC of infringing the Code (the code was then the BSC code) when over 16,000 people complained to the BBC and over 8,000 complained to OFCOM following the airing of *Jerry Springer—The Opera* which satirised Christianity. OFCOM stated:

The Code states that 'challenging and deliberately flouting the boundaries of taste in drama and comedy is a time-honoured tradition. Although these programmes have a special freedom, this does not give them unlimited licence to be cruel or to humiliate individuals or groups gratuitously'. Ofcom recognises that a great number of complainants felt that the Opera denigrated the Christian religion. Complainants clearly felt that the programme mocked their strongly held beliefs. However, in Ofcom's view, serious thought had been given to the material, its production and its transmission. The subject of the Opera was '*The Jerry Springer Show*' and the society it reflects. The show was created as a caricature of modern television. Importantly, in Ofcom's view the Opera did not gratuitously humiliate individuals or any groups and in particular the Christian community. Its target was television and fame.[39]

Recently there have been a number of findings relating to competitions.[40] Complaints upheld by OFCOM include a finding against the BBC in 2007 for a fictitious competition on *Blue Peter* which breached r. 1.26, which requires broadcasters to take due care over the physical and emotional welfare of people under 18.[41] In December 2007 OFCOM found that Channel Four had breached r. 10.10 when selecting competition entrants early, before premium rate entry lines had closed, for a quiz on *Richard and Judy*. A financial penalty of £1,000,000 was imposed for breaches over a six-year period.[42] The BBC was ordered to pay £45,000 following

---

[36] See, further, *The Review of the BBC's Royal Charter*, First Report of Session 2005–06, HL 50.

[37] See www.ofcom.org.uk/tv/ifi/codes/bcode/. The latest version of the Code came into effect in 2005.

[38] The BBC is not bound to observe (e), (f), (i) and (j) though its own guidelines cover much the same ground.

[39] OFCOM Broadcast Bulletin, Issue No. 34, May 2005, p. 15.

[40] See, e.g., OFCOM Broadcast Bulletin, Issue number 115, August 2008.

[41] OFCOM, Content Sanctions Committee Adjudications 09/07/2007: www.ofcom.org.uk/tv/obb/ocsc_adjud/.

[42] Ibid., 20 December 2007.

a breach of r. 2.11 when a fake winner of a competition was announced on *Comic Relief* in 2007. In the same year MTV was fined for breaching rr. 1 and 2 following extensive offensive language on the programme *Totally Boyband*.[43] In 2005 *Bloomberg TV* was found to have breached r. 3.3 on due impartiality when it provided extensive coverage of the launch of the Labour Party's business manifesto whilst giving no equivalent coverage to other parties during the election campaign.[44]

4. Following *Vgt Verein Gegeng Tierfabriken v Switzerland*[45] it was argued that the blanket ban on political advertising in s. 321 would amount to a breach of Art. 10, given that political speech is considered to be particularly worthy of protection as a form of expression.[46] The position under the 2003 Act is premised on the notion that such a ban provides 'appropriate weight to the legitimate objective of securing equality of opportunity for political expression'.[47] The House of Lords has recently confronted this issue: see *R (on the application of Animal Defenders International) v Secretary of State For Culture, Media and Sport* detailed below at p. 649.

5. Despite s. 321, party election broadcasts and party political broadcasts are permitted subject to the relevant parties satisfying the applicable criteria, such as qualification on the basis of contesting one-sixth or more of the seats up for election.[48] However, such broadcasts are still subject to the terms of the Broadcasting Code, an issue that was the subject of challenge in *R (on the application of Pro-Life Alliance) v BBC*.[49] The BBC and independent broadcasters refused to broadcast a party election broadcast by the Pro-Life Alliance on the ground that a video showing an abortion would cause offence and infringed the broadcasting guidelines[50] as to taste and decency. In considering the importance of political speech within a democracy the Court of Appeal held that only rarely would issues of taste and decency prevail over freedom of speech, especially during an election period. The BBC appealed to the House of Lords who allowed the appeal. Their Lordships found that the Court of Appeal decision effectively meant that the relevant guidelines should not apply to election broadcasts and this was clearly contrary to the intent of the legislation. Rather, the decision was not whether guidelines were applicable at all but whether they had been correctly applied to these facts, and a body of specialists (the broadcasting bodies) were better able to determine this.[51] Without doubt this decision will hold considerable weight but it remains possible that, given the value attached to political speech in Strasbourg, a legal challenge to s. 319 in the 2003 Act and its application to political speech might yet be made. Should the courts defer to broadcasting bodies in such issues? Whatever the decision of the regulator should the courts not still consider the issue of whether the type of speech overrides the determination as to offensiveness?

6. The formal power of 'veto' described above in s. 336 is very similar to previous powers, for example s. 10(3) of the Broadcasting Act 1990, but has rarely been used by government.[52] In the early days of broadcasting, in 1927, the BBC was directed not to broadcast matters of

---

43 Ibid., 4 June 2008.   44 Ibid., 29 November 2005.

45 App. No. 24699/94 (2002) 34 EHRR 4.   46 See the discussion by T. Lewis [2007] EHRLR 663.

47 Joint Committee on Human Rights, Draft Communications Bill, Nineteenth Report of Session 2001–2002, HC 149, para. 63.

48 Relevant criteria are contained in the OFCOM Rules: www.ofcom.org.uk/tv/ifi/guidance/ppbrules/.

49 [2003] 2 All ER 977.

50 At the relevant time these were the BBC Producers' Guidelines and the ITC Programme Code.

51 On this controversial case, see E. Barendt [2003] PL 580; I. Hare [2003] CLJ 525; J. Rowbottom (2003) 119 LQR 553.

52 Note also Communications Act 2003 s.133 which contains an emergency power for the Home Secretary to order a licensed service to restrict or cease broadcasting.

political, industrial or religious controversy. This directive only lasted until 1928. Later, in 1955, the BBC and the independent broadcasting authorities were ordered not to derogate from the primacy of Parliament as the proper forum for debating the affairs of the nation by broadcasts of their own programmes or discussions on the matter without 14 days of the Parliamentary debate. This embargo on discussion of issues of current concern also lasted for only a short period.

More recently this formal power has been used by government to seek to deprive terrorists of the 'oxygen of publicity'. In October, 1988, the Home Secretary ordered that the BBC and the independent companies refrain from broadcasting words spoken by representatives, or purported representatives, of certain specified organisations, or words spoken in support of, or which solicited or invited support for such an organisation. Words spoken by representatives were only proscribed when the representative was speaking in that capacity rather than in a personal capacity—a distinction requiring of broadcasters a careful exercise of judgment. When speaking as a representative of such an organisation the ban applied however innocent the actual content of the words. The ban was unsuccessfully challenged by the National Union of Journalists and others, but not the broadcasting organisations themselves, in judicial review proceedings in *R v Secretary of State for the Home Department, ex p Brind*.[53] Following the IRA declaration of a total cessation of violence, in September 1994, the ban was lifted.

7. The 1988 ban followed a considerable period of tension between broadcasters and government about the broadcasting of Irish affairs. As far back in the present troubles as 1972 controversy arose over a proposed BBC programme, *The Question of Ulster*, a programme in which both loyalist and republican proponents were to be given full opportunity to argue their cases. Following representations from the Home Secretary about the proposed programme, the Chairman and Director-General met the minister and told him that if the Government felt that the programme should not be shown the proper course was for the minister to ban the programme and for the BBC to broadcast the fact of the ban. The Home Secretary apparently made further representations about the programme but declined to exercise his powers to prevent it from occurring.

In 1985, the Home Secretary, Leon Brittan, wrote an open letter to the Chairman of the BBC contending that a proposed programme[54] in a series called *Real Lives* should not be broadcast. The programme was to feature interviews with both Martin McGuinness (IRA) and Gregory Campbell, a hardline loyalist. The Governors immediately took the highly unusual step of previewing the programme themselves, rather than referring the matter for the judgment of the Director-General. In this case the Director-General was, in fact, temporarily unavailable and the preview took place in his absence. Following their viewing of the film the Governors withdrew the programme from the schedules. The Home Secretary denied having brought improper pressure on the BBC, claiming that it was appropriate for a minister to let the Government's opinion on broadcasting by terrorists be known. He denied that the decision to ban the programme was anything other than the exercise of independent judgment by the Governors. Nevertheless, journalists at both the BBC and independent television staged a one-day strike a week after this action of the Governors, protesting at the failure of the Board to take a clear stance to protect news and current affairs journalism from government pressures. In due course the programme was shown, minor cuts having been made.[55] In 1988, Thames Television broadcast a *This Week* documentary, *Death on the Rock,* investigating the circumstances of the shooting of three, as it transpired unarmed,

---

[53] [1991] 2 WLR 588.   [54] *At the Edge of the Union.*
[55] See further, C. Horrie and S. Clarke, *Fuzzy Monsters: Fear and Loathing at the BBC* (1994), pp. 47–49.

members of the IRA in Gibraltar earlier in the year. Government explanations were that the killings were of members of an active service unit of the IRA intent on planting a bomb on the island, and that they were shot by members of the SAS acting in self-defence. The documentary, however, included evidence from a 'new' witness to the events who asserted that those killed had been shot without warning and with their hands in the air. The documentary rekindled debate about the existence of a 'shoot-to-kill' policy on the part of the security forces in dealing with terrorists. The documentary was strongly denounced by the Prime Minister, Mrs Thatcher; and similar material in a BBC programme shown in Northern Ireland met with expressions of disapproval from the Foreign Secretary. Sir Geoffrey Howe. The IBA (the forerunner of the ITC and OFCOM) supported the showing of the Thames documentary. Thames later set up an independent inquiry under Lord Windlesham. His report largely exonerated the documentary makers.[56]

In addition to these events in connection with Irish affairs a number of other recent examples of government seeking to interfere with broadcasting freedom (or of governmental annoyance at broadcasting bias!) may be noted. In 1986 a critical analysis of television news coverage was published by the Conservative Party. This followed strong criticism by Mr Tebbitt of the BBC's coverage of the US air raid, launched from UK bases, on Tripoli earlier in the year. In 1987, the BBC responded to Government concerns and banned the showing of a documentary, on the secret *Zircon* spy-satellite project, made by Duncan Campbell in his *Secret Society* series. The film was eventually shown, in slightly altered form, in 1988. Also not shown in this series was a documentary on the working of cabinet government. The film was re-made by Channel 4 and eventually broadcast in 1991.[57] Note also the decision of the IBA not to permit the broadcast of a programme in the *20/20 Vision* series in which a former employee of MI5, Cathy Massiter, had spoken of the very wide scope of that body's surveillance activities. The ban was eventually lifted following wide knowledge of the contents of the programme. Was this an example of undue deference to governmental desire for secrecy as regards the activities of the security services, or simply proper action on the part of a regulatory body in response to evidence of clear breach of the Official Secrets legislation? Over the years a number of *Panorama* programmes have been substantially revised following an elaborate 'referral up' process within the BBC.[58] The incident with perhaps the most far reaching effects was the clash between the Government and the BBC over the allegedly 'sexed-up' Iraq dossier, Government allegations of bias by the BBC, and the death of the government scientist Dr David Kelly, which ultimately led to the resignation of both the BBC Chairman and the Director-General.[59]

8. *The internet.*[60] The development of the internet has posed particular challenges with the rapid growth in the number of sites devoted to pornographic material, which are, in the

---

56 Windlesham Report, *Death on the Rock* (1989). See also R. Bolton, *Death on the Rock and Other Stories* (1990).

57 See further, P. Fiddich, 'Broadcasting: A Catalogue of Confrontation' in N. Buchan and T. Sumner (eds), *Glasnost in Britain: Against Censorship and in Defence of the Word* (1989).

58 E.g. in 1990 'Who Pays for the Party'—an investigation of Conservative Party finances; and an episode on the Iraqi Super-gun. Note also the controversy following the *Panorama* film, 'Maggie's Militant Tendency' (1984). See C. Horrie and S. Clarke, *Fuzzy Monsters: Fear and Loathing at the BBC* (1994), passim.

59 See Lord Hutton, *Report of the Inquiry into the Circumstances Surrounding the Death of Dr David Kelly C.M.G.* (2004) HC 247; K. Bloomfield, *The BBC at the Watershed: An Insider's Account from Hussey to the Hutton Enquiry* (2008); G. Smith and D. Sandelson [2004] Ent LR 137.

60 See G. Smith, *Internet Law and Regulation* (2007); C. Reed and J. Angel, *Computer Law: The Law and Regulation of Information Technology* (2007); Y. Akdeniz, 'Governance of Pornography and Child Pornography on the Global Internet: A Multi-Layered Approach' in L. Edwards and C. Waelde (eds), *Law and the Internet* (1997), Chap. 13; Y. Akdeniz, C. Walker and D. Wall (eds), *The Internet, Law and Society* (2000).

nature of things, easily accessible. In addition, OFCOM reports[61] that 99 per cent of young people (8–17 years old) have accessed the internet. Various proprietary rating and filtering systems have been developed to manage access to the internet. In 2008 the House of Commons Culture, Media and Sport Committee produced a report on harmful content on the internet.[62] It provided, *inter alia*, a summary of the current position of internet regulation and took into account the recommendations of the Byron Review on *Safer Children in a Digital World*.[63] It stated:

58. Certain bodies have been established by the Government to help manage the risks arising specifically from the Internet. The most all-embracing is the Home Office Taskforce on Child Protection on the Internet, formed in 2001 to bring together the Government, online technology providers, statutory and non-statutory bodies, law enforcement and child protection specialists.

60. Dr Byron's report recommended that the existing Task Force should be transformed into a new UK Council for Child Internet Safety, with a strengthened secretariat and responsibility for leading a strategy across Government.

67. …While there might be an expectation that most of the Council's effort would be directed towards child protection, we believe that there is a danger of overlooking possible harm to vulnerable adults, and we recommend that the Government should give this proper consideration when deciding the Council's terms of reference.

71. Businesses which provide Internet content, access and services, either from fixed terminals (such as PCs) or from mobile devices, have recognised the particular dangers posed by certain types of content on the Internet. In 1996, the Internet Watch Foundation was formed as a self-regulatory industry body, to minimise the availability of potentially illegal or otherwise harmful content on the Internet, and to take action to prevent exposure to illegal content, in particular by:

- operating a hotline enabling the public to report such instances;

- operating a notice and takedown service to alert hosting service providers of criminal content found on their servers; and

- alerting relevant law enforcement agencies to the content.

All major Internet service providers and search engines are members of the Foundation, as are all mobile network operators.

72. The Foundation's Board aims to minimise the availability of potentially illegal Internet content, specifically:

- child sexual abuse images hosted anywhere in the world;

- criminally obscene content hosted in the UK;

- content inciting racial hatred hosted in the UK.

For illegal content hosted in the UK, the Foundation may issue a 'take-down' notice to the content host. If the content host fails to comply, it becomes liable to prosecution. Mr Galvin, representing BT, told us that he could not think of a single example when an Internet service provider had refused to take down a site once it had been requested to do so. If the content is hosted outside the UK, the Foundation has no powers to require the site host to take down the material: it told us that 'we do not have any relationships with any other government or any other hotline in the world to put them on notice about these types of

---

[61] OFCOM, *Children, Young People & Online Content* (2007).

[62] House of Commons Committee on Culture, Media and Sport, *Harmful content on the Internet and in video games*, Tenth Report, Session 2007–08, HC 353-I.

[63] The Report of the Byron Review, *Safer Children in a Digital World* (2008). For discussion see, I. Simmons [2008] Ent LR 143.

websites'. It will, however, inform the relevant authorities and add the website to its database of addresses hosting illegal content.

73. The overwhelming majority of domestic consumers' Internet connections are operated by Internet service providers (ISPs) which block access to sites listed in this database. All major search engines block access to such sites. The Foundation claimed that it had achieved 'remarkable internationally recognised success' in that, since 2003, less than 1% of reports of online child sexual abuse content processed by the Foundation had been traced to content hosted in the UK, compared to 18% in 1997. However the Chief Executive of the Internet Watch Foundation did tell us that, with a degree of technical knowledge, it is possible to circumvent the blocks imposed.

79. It is already an offence to publish or distribute certain types of content on the Internet or any-where else: these include indecent images of children, material which is deemed obscene and likely to 'deprave or corrupt', words intended to stir up racial hatred, and statements likely to be understood as encouraging terrorism....In certain cases it is not merely publication which is illegal: it is an offence to possess indecent images of children, extreme pornography (but not other pornography, even though it may fail the 'publication' test under the Obscene Publications Act 1959), and any 'terrorist publication' if it can be demonstrated that it is possessed with a view to distribution or provision to others, including by electronic means.[64]

NOTE

1. The new UK Council for Child Internet Safety was launched in September 2008 and will bring together over 100 public and private organisations in an attempt to provide a workable code on internet safety. The UKCCIS will also seek to take down illegal sites and promote responsible advertising to children. Is it possible to provide a national solution to such a global phenomenon as the internet?

- **R (on the application of Animal Defenders International) v Secretary of State for Culture, Media and Sport** [2008] UKHL 15, [2008] 3 All ER 193, House of Lords

In 2005 Animal Defenders International (ADI)[65] launched a campaign entitled 'My Mate's a Primate' with the object of directing public attention towards the use of primates by humans and the threat presented by such use to the survival of primates. The campaign was to include newspaper advertising, direct mailshots, and also an advertisement on television. However, the Broadcast Advertising Clearance Centre (now known as Clearcast)[66] declined to clear the advert on the ground that its transmission would breach the prohibition on political adver-tising in s. 321(2) of the Communications Act 2003, the appellant being a body with mainly political objects as defined by the Act. ADI sought a declaration under s. 4 of the HRA that s. 321(2) was incompatible with Art. 10 of the ECHR. The Divisional Court refused to make such a declaration,[67] and the case was brought before the House of Lords.

Lord Bingham of Cornhill:

26. There is much common ground between the parties to this appeal. Thus it is accepted that section 319 and 321 of the 2003 Act constitute an interference with the appellant's exercise of its right to free

---

64 For further details about the relevant offences see section 4 below.
65 Because of its campaigning objectives it is not eligible for registration as a charity.
66 Clearcast is part of the Advertising Standards Authority which has a contract with OFCOM to regulate advertisements. Clearcast checks advertisements on behalf of TV broadcasters before they go on air.
67 [2006] EWHC 3069 (Admin).

expression, and article 10 of the Convention is engaged. It is accepted that this is a restriction prescribed by law and has the legitimate aim of protecting the rights of others, namely their democratic rights. The only issue is whether the restriction is necessary in a democratic society. And even here there is common ground. For a restriction to be necessary there must be a pressing social need for it, and it is for the member state which imposes the restriction to justify it. While the right to freedom of expression is not absolute, and no one has a right of access to the airwaves, the importance of free expression is such that the standard of justification required of member states is high and their margin of appreciation correspondingly small, particularly where political speech is in issue. The problem here is not one which can be resolved by exercise of the interpretative power given to the courts by section 3 of the 1998 Act. All this is agreed. Yet the importance of this case to the functioning of our democracy is in my view such as to call for the rehearsal of some very familiar but fundamental principles.

27. Freedom of thought and expression is an essential condition of an intellectually healthy society. The free communication of information, opinions and argument about the laws which a state should enact and the policies its government at all levels should pursue is an essential condition of truly democratic government. These are the values which article 10 exists to protect, and their importance gives it a central role in the Convention regime, protecting free speech in general and free political speech in particular.

28. The fundamental rationale of the democratic process is that if competing views, opinions and policies are publicly debated and exposed to public scrutiny the good will over time drive out the bad and the true prevail over the false. It must be assumed that, given time, the public will make a sound choice when, in the course of the democratic process, it has the right to choose. But it is highly desirable that the playing field of debate should be so far as practicable level. This is achieved where, in public discussion, differing views are expressed, contradicted, answered and debated. It is the duty of broadcasters to achieve this object in an impartial way by presenting balanced programmes in which all lawful views may be ventilated. It is not achieved if political parties can, in proportion to their resources, buy unlimited opportunities to advertise in the most effective media, so that elections become little more than an auction. Nor is it achieved if well-endowed interests which are not political parties are able to use the power of the purse to give enhanced prominence to views which may be true or false, attractive to progressive minds or unattractive, beneficial or injurious. The risk is that objects which are essentially political may come to be accepted by the public not because they are shown in public debate to be right but because, by dint of constant repetition, the public has been conditioned to accept them. The rights of others which a restriction on the exercise of the right to free expression may properly be designed to protect must, in my judgment, include a right to be protected against the potential mischief of partial political advertising.

30. The question necessarily arises why there is a pressing social need for a blanket prohibition of political advertising on television and radio when no such prohibition applies to the press, the cinema and all other media of communication. The answer is found in the greater immediacy and impact of television and radio advertising.

33. The weight to be accorded to the judgment of Parliament depends on the circumstances and the subject matter. In the present context it should in my opinion be given great weight, for three main reasons. First, it is reasonable to expect that our democratically-elected politicians will be peculiarly sensitive to the measures necessary to safeguard the integrity of our democracy. It cannot be supposed that others, including judges, will be more so. Secondly, Parliament has resolved, uniquely since the 1998 Act came into force in October 2000, that the prohibition of political advertising on television and radio may possibly, although improbably, infringe article 10 but has nonetheless resolved to proceed under section 19(1) (b) of the Act. It has done so, while properly recognising the interpretative supremacy of the European Court, because of the importance which it attaches to maintenance of this prohibition. The judgment of Parliament on such an issue should not be lightly overridden. Thirdly, legislation cannot be framed so as to address particular cases. It must lay down general rules: *James v United Kingdom* (1986) 8 EHRR 123,

para 68; *Mellacher v Austria* (1989) 12 EHRR 391, paras 52–53; *R (Pretty) v Director of Public Prosecutions* [2001] UKHL 61, [2002] 1 AC 800, para 29; *Wilson v First County Trust (No 2)* [2003] UKHL 40, [2004] 1 AC 816, paras 72–74; *R (Carson) v Secretary of State for Work and Pensions* [2005] UKHL 37, [2006] 1 AC 173, paras 41, 91. A general rule means that a line must be drawn, and it is for Parliament to decide where. The drawing of a line inevitably means that hard cases will arise falling on the wrong side of it, but that should not be held to invalidate the rule if, judged in the round, it is beneficial.

34. If, as in *VgT*, a body with aims similar to those of the applicant in that case or the appellant in this had grounds for wishing to counter the effect of commercial advertising bearing on an issue of public controversy, it would have strong grounds for seeking an opportunity to put its case in the ordinary course of broadcast programmes. The broadcaster, discharging its duty of impartiality, could not ignore such a request. But that is not this case. A question of compatibility might arise if a body whose objects were wholly or mainly of a political nature sought to broadcast an advertisement unrelated to its objects, or if an advertisement were rejected as of a political nature or directed towards political ends when it did not fall within section 321(3)(a), (b), (c), (d), (e) or (g) but only within section 321(3)(f). But the present is not such a case. The appellant's proposed advertisement was, as one would expect, consistent with its objects and, as the appellant's chief executive makes plain in her evidence, its object is to persuade Parliament to legislate. If such a limited challenge were to arise, there might well be scope for resort to section 3 of the 1998 Act, agreed to be inappropriate in the present case.

36. For these reasons, ... I conclude that the ban on political advertising in sections 319 and 321 is necessary in a democratic society and so compatible with the Convention. I would accordingly dismiss this appeal.

Baroness Hale of Richmond:

47. There was an elephant in the committee room, always there but never mentioned, when we heard this case. It was the dominance of advertising, not only in elections but also in the formation of political opinion, in the United States of America. Enormous sums are spent, and therefore have to be raised, at election times: it is estimated that the disputed 2000 elections for President and Congress cost as much as US$3 billion. Attempts to regulate campaign spending are struck down in the name of the First Amendment: 'Congress shall make no law ... abridging the freedom of speech, or of the press': see particularly *Buckley v Valco*, 424 US 1 (1976). *A fortiori* there is no limit to the amount that pressure groups can spend on getting their message across in the most powerful and pervasive media available.

48. In the United Kingdom, and elsewhere in Europe, we do not want our government or its policies to be decided by the highest spenders. Our democracy is based upon more than one person one vote. It is based on the view that each person has equal value. 'Within the sphere of democratic politics, we confront each other as moral equals' (Ackerman and Ayres, *Voting with Dollars*, 2003, p 12). We want everyone to be able to make up their own minds on the important issues of the day. For this we need the free exchange of information and ideas. We have to accept that some people have greater resources than others with which to put their views across. But we want to avoid the grosser distortions which unrestricted access to the broadcast media will bring.

49. So this case is not just about permissible restrictions on freedom of expression. It is about striking the right balance between the two most important components of a democracy: freedom of expression and voter equality. There are aspects of the ban on broadcasting political advertisements which no-one disputes: in particular, advertising by candidates for election, or by political parties, whether or not at election times. But this case is about advertising by a particular interest group which campaigns for changes in the law.

51. For all the reasons which my noble and learned friend, Lord Bingham of Cornhill, has so eloquently and comprehensively given, I agree that the ban as it operates in this case is not incompatible with the appellants' Convention rights. It is a balanced and proportionate response to the problem: they can seek to put their case across in any other way, but not the one which so greatly risks distorting the public

debate in favour of the rich. There has to be the same rule for the same kind of advertising, whatever the cause for which it campaigns and whatever the resources of the campaigners. We must not distinguish between causes of which we approve and causes of which we disapprove. Nor in practice can we distinguish between small organisations which have to fight for every penny and rich ones with access to massive sums. Capping or rationing will not work, for the reasons Lord Bingham gives.

Lords Scott of Foscote, **Carswell** and **Neuberger of Abbotsbury** concurred.

Appeal dismissed.

NOTES

1. When the Communications Bill had been introduced to Parliament, the Secretary of State was aware off the decision in *Vgt Verein Gegeng Tierfabriken v Switzerland* and felt unable to make a statement pursuant to s. 19(1)(a) of HRA 1998 that the provisions of the Bill were compatible with Convention rights. Despite a possible incompatibility the Government nevertheless wished to proceed with the measure.

2. Both the Joint Committee on the Draft Communications Bill[68] and the Joint Committee on Human Rights[69] urged caution in moving away from the ban on political advertising concerned that the democratic process might be annexed by the rich and powerful.[70]

3. Their Lordships were clearly of the view that Parliament was better placed to determine whether a complete ban on political advertising was necessary in a democratic society. Do you agree? Is there a place for advertisements with a political message that are aired outside of an election period? Is it fair to argue that such a ban is *necessary* in a democratic society?

4. OBSCENITY AND INDECENCY

(A) INTRODUCTION

The extent to which it is appropriate for the law to impose criminal penalties in relation to the publication or display of material which is obscene or indecent has been, and remains, a matter of acute theoretical and practical debate. In terms of theory, a helpful discussion may be found in Joel Bakan.[71] Bakan identifies three principal factions in this 'law and morality' debate: 'liberals', 'legal moralists' and 'feminists'. He writes, perhaps a little over-simply,

all appear to agree that, in certain circumstances, restrictions on pornography are justified, but they vehemently disagree as to why and in what circumstances such restrictions are justified. Liberals argue that restricting pornography means curtailing freedom of expression and the right to individual liberty, and that such restrictions are only justified where the exercise of these rights and freedoms can be shown to cause harm.... Legal moralists, on the other hand, argue that restrictions on pornography are necessary even where no harm to individuals can be shown. Pornography, they claim, is immoral, and the law must protect society from breaches of its moral standards. Feminists are not concerned with the moral or the immoral nature of pornography, but with the harm that pornography causes to ... women. In this sense the feminist position is consistent with liberal theory....

---

[68] HL 169–1, HC 876–1.   [69] Nineteenth Report of the Session 2001–2002, HL 149, HC 1102.
[70] [2008] UKHL 15, see Lord Bingham at paras 13–21.   [71] (1984) 17 Ottawa Law Review 1.

Note that for 'liberals' any restraints imposed (whether pre-publication censorship or post-publication sanctions) may infringe both their cherished 'freedom of expression' and also the more general notion of 'liberty of the individual'. This will be the case at any rate in circumstances where the obscene material can be regarded as an 'expressive' act.

As regards the liberal thesis much may depend on what is meant by 'harm to others': their accepted justification for constraints. Two particular arguments are commonly deployed in attempts to justify aspects of obscenity/indecency laws in terms of liberal principles. First, it is argued by some that pornographic material does indeed have an adverse and harmful effect on those who are its consumers. The truth or falsity of this assertion has long been controversial, and will probably remain so. At the time of the Williams Committee Report (1979) the prevailing view appeared to be that no causal link had been clearly demonstrated between pornography and such 'harm', either in terms of intrinsic 'corruption' of the mind of the individual consumer—arguably not harm in the liberal sense—or in terms of harm being caused by such persons to others. The difficult matter is the demonstration of causality. To some it is highly plausible that one who has exposed himself to, for example, violent and sadistic pornography may go on to commit sex offences (and, of course, from time to time it is discovered that such offenders have indeed collected such material). To others, in contrast, it may seem inconceivable that any person without a propensity to such criminal behaviour might be driven to commit such acts as a result of exposure to such material. A middle view, albeit in a context where middle views tend not to be voiced, might be to believe that for some people at least such exposure might just 'tip the scales'. A further complication, however, to note in this discussion of pornography and harm is the contrary view that for some persons who may have a propensity towards anti-social/criminal sexual behaviour the availability of pornography may constitute a 'safety-valve', offering catharsis to help them to refrain from such harmful behaviour.

Over the past decade those who assert a causal connection between pornography, violence and anti-social/criminal behaviour have become inclined to assert that studies are tending to support their contentions. Compare in this connection the approach to this issue of the (US) Federal Commission on Obscenity and Pornography (1970) and the (UK) Williams Committee (1979), with that of the (US) Meese Commission in 1986. However, many remain sceptical, arguing that research findings from US studies have been difficult to replicate, and may be flawed in terms of methodology.

It will be apparent that the range of possible connections between pornography and behaviour, and the difficulties of proof of causality, are considerable. This leads discussion on to the question: assuming that clear proof of a connection is not possible, what stance should the law take? Should it strive to offer protection to those who may be the victims of pornography on the basis that, even in the absence of a proven connection, a 'precautionary' approach is appropriate. Or should freedom of liberty/expression be regarded as inviolable in the absence of clear proof of harm?

Another 'harm' argument, and this time one commonly accepted by the liberal camp, involves the harm of causing offence by foisting obscene or indecent displays onto unwitting and undesiring individuals. It is one thing for images to be presented on the inside pages of a magazine which would only be opened by a person well aware of the likely contents; it is another, as one writer has put it, to utilise a 'billboard on Times Square to promulgate to the general populace the techniques and the pleasures of sodomy'. This notion of harm justifies controls on the basis of the nuisance caused by unsolicited experience of obscene and indecent material. As will be seen in the materials which follow it forms the basis of several pieces of legislation over the past two decades. It is not, however, a justification which is without some theoretical difficulty: at any rate in so far as we may be considering material which may be said to intend to communicate ideas or seek to promote some set of values. To proscribe involuntary exposure of others to such material is to accept that one person's liberty to express those ideals/values may be restrained because another person may thereby hear and see things which he or she does not wish to hear and see. The right to be an ostrich takes precedence over the liberty to bring before others one's ideas of right and wrong, of moral and immoral, or whatever. Perhaps most people would defend an individual's right of choice not to be unwittingly exposed to ideas which may be shocking and disturbing: and some have, in any event, argued that pornography does not express ideas and values, and so does not warrant protection on the grounds of freedom of expression—a protection to be afforded, in principle, to even the most offensive views and opinions. But this may be too easy an escape from the problem. Civil rights organisations have long wrestled with the tricky question of their attitude towards the pornographer. Some have taken up controversial stances, acknowledging that the issues are difficult ones which cannot be simply resolved. A spokesperson for the American Civil Liberties Union not so long ago made clear that whatever, ultimately, should be the law relating to pornography it was not right to seek to deny that pornography (and other lewd and indecent entertainment) presents and promotes to the world certain ideas, implicit within its explicitness, of the legitimacy of particular kinds of sexual behaviour.

A further notion of harm is that which has attracted the attention of feminist writers. This literature, which is itself quite diverse, has enhanced the debate by focusing on additional and rather different and subtle notions of harm which may be a consequence of pornography. In particular, feminists have argued that pornography has potential, by its demeaning and degrading images of women and in some instances in the hatred of women it seems to display, to provoke misogynist attitudes in men. In other words, over and above the fear of particular incidents of anti-social/criminal sexual conduct, exposure to pornography may also harm women by its influence on the way in which men perceive women. Additionally, feminists have argued strongly that it must be considered to be harmful to the female portion of the population that they have to live in a community which appears (because men make and enforce the laws) to tolerate a substantial and profitable industry sector which is involved in the production for men of material which, at best, does little to foster respect and mature relations between the sexes.

It is at this point that considerations of the gender equality under the law come into the picture. Feminists have argued that to debate the pornography issue in terms of protecting individual liberty and protecting freedom of expression is to debate in terms of constitutional libertarian principles devised essentially for men and by men. Once the debate is turned towards equal treatment under the law, and the promotion of fairness and equity within the state, different considerations may apply and different conclusions be drawn.[72]

In *Belfast City Council v Miss Behavin' Limited*[73] the House of Lords recognised that pornography does have some protection as a form of expression albeit at a rather low level. Lord Hoffmann stated that:

---

[72] In *R v Butler* (1992) 89 DLR 449, the Canadian Supreme Court considered the relationship between the Constitutional Guarantees of the Charter of Rights and the obscenity offences of the Canadian Criminal Code. the court referred expressly to the idea that the kinds of material covered by the offences under the Code were such as to undermine the ideas of equality and dignity of all human beings, and referred to the 'equality' guarantees of the Charter: 'There is a substantial body of opinion that holds that the portrayal of persons being subjected to degrading and dehumanising sexual treatment results in harm, particularly to women, and therefore to society as a whole.'

[73] [2007] UKHL 19.

If article 10 and article 1 of Protocol 1 are engaged at all, they operate at a very low level. The right to vend pornography is not the most important right of free expression in a democratic society.[74]

Baroness Hale added:

38. My Lords, there are far more important human rights in this world than the right to sell pornographic literature and images in the backstreets of Belfast City Centre. Pornography comes well below celebrity gossip in the hierarchy of speech which deserves the protection of the law. Far too often it entails the sexual exploitation and degradation of women for the titillation of men. But there is always room for debate about what constitutes pornography.

(B) OBSCENE PUBLICATIONS ACTS 1959 AND 1964

(I) THE OFFENCES

- **Obscene Publications Act 1959**

An Act to amend the law relating to the publication of obscene matter; to provide for the protection of literature; and to strengthen the law concerning pornography.

2. Prohibition of Publication of Obscene Matter

(1) Subject as hereinafter provided, any person who, whether for gain or not, publishes an obscene article [or who has an obscene article for publication for gain (whether gain to himself or gain to another)][75] shall be liable—

(a) on summary conviction to a fine not exceeding [the prescribed sum] or to imprisonment for a term not exceeding six months;

(b) on conviction on indictment to a fine or to imprisonment for a term not exceeding [five][76] years or both....

(3) A prosecution...for an offence against this section shall not be commenced more than two years after the commission of the offence.

[(3A)[77] Proceedings for an offence under this section shall not be instituted except by or with the consent of the Director of Public Prosecutions in any case where the article in question is a moving picture film of a width of not less than sixteen millimetres and the relevant publication or the only publication which followed or could reasonably have been expected to follow from the relevant publication took place or (as the case may be) was to take place in the course of a [film exhibition]; and in this subsection 'the relevant publication' means—

(a) in the case of any proceedings under this section for publishing an obscene article, the publication in respect of which the defendant would be charged if the proceedings were brought; and

(b) in the case of any proceedings under this section for having an obscene article for publication for gain, the publication which, if the proceedings were brought, the defendant would be alleged to have had in contemplation.]

---

74 Ibid., at para. 16.
75 Words in square brackets added by the Obscene Publications Act 1964, s. 1(1).
76 Substituted by Criminal Justice and Immigration Act 2008, s. 71.
77 Added by the Criminal Law Act 1977, s. 53.

(4) A person publishing an obscene article shall not be proceeded against for an offence at common law consisting of the publication of any matter contained or embodied in the article where it is of the essence of the offence that the matter is obscene.

[(4A)[78] Without prejudice to subsection (4) above, a person shall not be proceeded against for an offence at common law—

(a) in respect of [an exhibition of a film][79] or anything said or done in the course of [an exhibition of a film], where it is of the essence of the common law offence that the exhibition or, as the case may be, what was said or done was obscene, indecent, offensive, disgusting or injurious to morality; or

(b) in respect of an agreement to give [an exhibition of a film] or to cause anything to be said or done in the course of such an exhibition where the common law offence consists of conspiring to corrupt public morals or to do any act contrary to public morals or decency.]

...

NOTES

1. The Obscene Publications Act 1964, s. 1(2) provides that for the purpose of any proceedings for an offence under s. 2 of the 1959 Act 'a person shall be deemed to have an article for publication for gain if with a view to such publication he has the article in his ownership, possession or control'.

2. The Obscene Publications Act 1964, s. 1(5) provides that the term 'publication for gain' shall mean 'any publication with a view to gain, whether the gain is to accrue by way of consideration for the publication or in any other way'.

3. The Obscene Publications Acts 1959 and 1964 have superseded, though without actually abolishing, the common law offence of obscene libel.[80] The 1959 Act followed recommendations of a committee set up by the Society of Authors in response to a 'spate' of prosecutions of 'serious literature' during 1954, and the deliberations of a Parliamentary Select Committee[81]. The 1954 prosecutions revealed various unsatisfactory features of the common law offence.[82] The summing-up of Stable J in *R v Martin Secker Warburg*[83] was, however, much praised. The 1964 Act was passed to remedy certain flaws that had become apparent in the provisions of the 1959 Act.[84]

The 1959 Act was intended to provide greater safeguards for those who create or deal in works of 'art' or 'literature' whilst, at the same time, making better provision for the effective prosecution of those who create or deal in 'pornography' and for the seizure and forfeiture of such material. Neither aim appears to have been achieved. The protection afforded to literature depends more on levels of tolerance of jurors and magistrates than on the law itself, and pornography is such profitable business that the possibility of conviction, or forfeiture of material, provides no real deterrent. Moreover, the publicity which such proceedings bring may well provide a more than compensatory boost to future sales. The difficulties of enforcing

---

78 Ibid.   79 Substituted by the Licensing Act 2003, s. 198(1), Sch. 6, para. 28(1), (2).

80 Further on obscene libel, see: P. Kearns [2007] Crim LR 667.

81 1956–57 HC 245; 1957–58 HC 122 and 123.

82 See C.H. Rolph, *Books in the Dock* (1969), pp. 93–109; N. St John-Stevas [1954] Crim LR 817 and *Obscenity and the Law* (1956); series of unattributed articles in (1954) 118 JPN at 664, 680, 694. 709, 725, 812; G. Robertson, *Obscenity* (1979), Chap. 2.

83 [1954] 2 All ER 683, [1954] 1 WLR 1178.

84 See, e.g., *R v Clayton and Halsey* [1963] 1 QB 163, CCA and *Mella v Monahan* [1961] Crim LR 175, DC.

the obscenity laws prompted Sir Robert Mark, then Metropolitan Police Commissioner, to describe the task as 'a self-defeating attempt to eradicate the ineradicable'.[85] See also *R v Metropolitan Police Comr, ex p Blackburn (No. 3)*.[86] A further difficulty for the police was the vigilance necessary to ensure that their own officers did not succumb to offers of bribes held out by the pornographers.[87]

Inevitably there have been many proposals for reform of the law. Some have sought to provide a more workable legal formula for distinguishing what is permissible from what is not.[88] Others have favoured relaxation of the obscenity laws, though usually recognising the need to afford children some protection. A distinction has commonly been drawn between those who *foist* offensive displays on others and those who simply supply material to those who *actively seek* it.[89] A committee, chaired by Professor Bernard Williams, was appointed in 1977 to review, *inter alia*, 'the laws concerning obscenity, indecency and violence in publications, displays and entertainments in England and Wales, except in the field of broadcasting'. It reported in 1979.[90] It recommended that the existing variety of laws be scrapped and a fresh start made, avoiding the uncertainties resulting from couching criminal laws in terms like 'obscene', 'indecent', 'deprave' and 'corrupt'. In determining the scope of laws on these matters the committee considered that the following basic principles should govern. It was necessary to draw a clear distinction between material which should be 'prohibited', and thereby denied even to those who wish access to it; and material which should not be prohibited but merely 'restricted'—which should not be thrust, so as to cause offence, on to the ordinary public. Material should only be 'prohibited', and denied to those who wish to see it, where harm is likely to be caused by the material. The committee regarded the current state of scientific evidence as justifying only very limited prohibitions on adult access to material. The committee acknowledged, however, that the law should provide for broader categories of material to be kept from, more vulnerable, young persons. The committee also felt that a distinction should also be drawn between the printed word and other material. It recommended that the former should never be prohibited nor restricted. By its very nature it is not 'immediately offensive' in the way in which other material foisted on an unsuspecting public might be; and a specially protected status is justified for the written word because of its importance in conveying ideas. The many detailed recommendations of the Williams Committee, fleshing out these principles into more concrete proposals, have not, in terms, been implemented. Note, however, that certain of these ideas, but not the whole 'balanced package', have been implemented in the sex cinema/sex shop licensing legislation, in the R18 film and video classification system and the Video Recordings Act 1984, and in the Indecent Displays (Control) Act 1981.[91]

---

[85] Sir R. Mark, *Policing a Perplexed Society* (1977), p. 60.   [86] [1973] QB 241, CA.

[87] For accounts of such corruption and its 'rooting out' see B. Cox, J. Shirley and M. Short, *The Fall of Scotland Yard* (1977); Sir R. Mark, *In the Office of Constable* (1978), pp. 173–174, 263–269; *Report of the Williams Committee on Obscenity and Film Censorship* (Cmnd 7772, 1979), pp. 39–41.

[88] See, e.g., *Pornography: The Longford Report* (1972); *The Pollution of the Mind: New Proposals to Control Public Indecency and Obscenity* (Society of Conservative Lawyers, 1972); Obscene Publications Bill 1986.

[89] See, e.g., *The Obscenity Laws: Report of Arts Council Working Party* (1969); proposals of the Defence of Literature and the Arts Society (DLAS), reported at (1978) 128 NLJ 423. For appraisals of a variety of possible reforms see C. H. Rolph, *Books in the Dock* (1969), Chap. 6; G. Robertson, *Obscenity* (1979), Chap. 11.

[90] Cmnd 7772.

[91] See further, pp. 661, 663 and 715. For discussion of the Williams Report see C. Manchester. (1980) 31 NILQ 103 and (1980) 14 UWAL Rev 172; S. Coldham (1980) 43 MLR 306; A.W.B. Simpson, *Pornography and Politics—the Williams Report in Retrospect* (1983)—discussion by member of the committee: R. Dworkin (1981) 1 OJLS 177.

4. Research by Edwards[92] shows that it is not possible to assess the effectiveness of the obscenity laws by reliance on the official statistics. She argues that the ambiguity of the 'deprave and corrupt' test for obscenity results in practices which divert cases from jury trial. However, there were convictions in four of the five cases in the study that went to jury trial. Other defendants were acquitted by direction of the judge because of such matters are breaches of PACE.

5. The provisions in s. 2(4) of the 1959 Act were intended to prevent defendants being denied the various safeguards contained in the 1959 Act by being charged at common law with obscene libel. It has, however, been held that the subsection does not prevent charges of conspiracy to corrupt public morals or conspiracy to outrage public decency since in such cases the essence of the offence is not the *publication* of obscene matter but the *agreement* to act in a corrupting or outrageous manner. See *Shaw v DPP*;[93] and *Knuller (Publishing, Printing and Promotions Ltd) v DPP*[94] per Lord Reid: 'Technically the distinction…is correct but it appears to me to offend against the policy of the Act….'. Fears lest the bringing of such charges might circumvent the Obscene Publications Acts led to assurances to Parliament from the law officers that such charges would not be brought where to do so would deprive defendants of those Acts' safeguards.[95] Note, however, the prosecution brought, and the decision of the Court of Appeal in *R v Gibson*.[96] Two defendants were convicted of having outraged public decency contrary to common law. The charges followed the display at an art gallery run by one of the defendants of an item made by the other defendant. The offending item was a pair of earrings, each of which was made out of a freeze-dried foetus of three or four months' gestation. The gallery was in a parade of shops and was open to the public to enter to browse. On appeal it was argued that the charges brought were precluded by the terms of s. 2(4) above. The Court of Appeal began by confirming that there was an offence at common law of outraging public decency, adopting the words of Lord Reid in *Shaw*'s case: 'it is an indictable offence to say or do or exhibit anything in public which outrages public decency, whether or not it also tends to corrupt and deprave those who see or hear it'. The next issue was whether, as was required for s. 2(4) to apply, the obscenity of the earrings was the essence of the offence charged. This depended, the court held, on whether the word 'obscenity' was used in the subsection in its colloquial sense (which would cover an item's tendency to outrage public decency), or in its narrower sense, as defined in s. 1(1) of the Act, as depending solely on an item's tendency to deprave or corrupt. There being no suggestion that the display was likely to corrupt or deprave any member of the public, the court held that the essence of the offence was the likely outrage to decency caused by the display. Interpreting s. 2(4) the court held that there was no reason to depart from the Act's usual meaning of the term 'obscene'. Accordingly, the appellants' arguments failed. The court was unwilling to accept that this interpretation denied a defendant the 'artistic' merit safeguard intended by the enactment of the 1959 Act. It took the view that in the kind of case where a prosecution for outraging public decency might succeed it was 'unlikely that a defence of public good could possibly arise'.

Would the court have been able to have come to the same decision had the charge at common law been that of *corruption* of public morals? Note that the 'public good' defence proceeds on the basis that an admittedly obscene publication should not constitute the commission of a criminal offence because of its aesthetic value. In other words the defence does

[92] 'On the Contemporary Application of the Obscene Publications Act 1959' [1998] Crim LR 843.
[93] [1962] AC 220, HL at 268, 290, 291.   [94] [1973] AC 435, HL at 456.
[95] See 695 HC Deb, 3 June 1964, col. 1212; 698 HC Deb, 7 July 1964, cols 315–16.
[96] [1990] 2 QB 619.

not negative obscenity—it justifies obscenity. Does this not suggest that the view of the court in *Gibson*, that this defence would be inapplicable in the case of an item which outrages decency, is misguided?[97]

The court also ruled that it was not necessary for the prosecution to prove that the defendant intended to outrage public decency (or was reckless).

In *S and G v United Kingdom*[98] the European Commission of Human Rights held that complaints by the art gallery curator and the artist that their convictions were contrary to Art. 10 ECHR were inadmissible. The convictions had involved an interference with freedom of expression, but that interference was prescribed by law, the offence having been clear or 'accessible' at least since *Knuller*. It would have been open to the defendants to have submitted to the trial court that the sculpture was not an outrage to public decency given that the atmosphere of tolerance was in itself part of public decency in a plural society, and so freedom of expression was not wholly irrelevant. Furthermore, the restriction was a proportionate act taken for the protection of morals, within the wide margin of appreciation in such cases.

6. The time-limit on prosecutions contained in the 1959 Act, s. 2(3) protects those who 'publish' or 'have for publication' rather than secondary parties who aid and abet such 'publication', e.g. authors, cameramen, actors. Time runs from the 'publication' or 'having for publication' rather than from the, perhaps much earlier, date of the secondary party's contribution to that eventual 'having' or 'publication'.[99] The Court of Appeal suggested that a person will not be regarded as having aided or abetted publication if he 'disassociated' himself from such publication, but did not give guidance as to what conduct would amount to such a 'disassociation'.

7. Challenges to convictions under the Obscene Publications Acts have been rejected by the ECtHR. In *Handyside v United Kingdom*[100] the applicant was the publisher of the *Little Red Schoolbook*. The book, which was aimed at children, had chapters on education, learning, teachers, pupils and 'the system'. The chapters on pupils had subsections giving advice on sexual matters. H was convicted of having in his possession obscene articles for gain. The Court held by 13 to 1 that this could be justified as being for the protection of morals, the state in such cases having a wide margin of appreciation. There is no uniform European conception of morals. 'By reason of their direct and continuous contract with the vital force of their countries, State authorities are in principle in a better position than the international judge to give an opinion on the exact content of [the requirements of morals] as well as on the "necessity" of a "restriction" or "penalty" intended to meet them.'[101] Similarly, in *Hoare v United Kingdom*[102] the Commission declared inadmissible a complaint by a person convicted under s. 2 of the 1959 Act in respect of the distribution of hardcore videos to persons

---

97 See also, on *Gibson*, M. Childs [1991] PL 20 (and P. Kearns [2000] Crim LR 652 (criticising the absence of the opportunity to give evidence of artistic merit)). For full discussion of these conspiracy offences see D. Ormerod, *Smith and Hogan Criminal Law* (11th edn, 2005), pp. 390–393; Law Commission Report No. 76, *Conspiracy and Criminal Law Reform* (1976), pp. 74–80; G. Robertson, *Obscenity* (1979), pp. 210–236.

98 App. No. 17634/91.

99 See G. Robertson, *Obscenity* (1979), at pp. 74–76 quoting from transcript of the Court of Appeal judgment in *R v Barton* [1976] Crim LR 514.

100 (1976) 1 EHRR 737. See also *Müller v Switzerland* (1988) 13 EHRR 212 (confirming that indecent or obscene art is not excluded from the definition of 'expression' but upholding convictions in respect of paintings of, *inter alia*, sexual relations between men and animals, found by the Swiss courts to be obscene): cf. *Scherer v Switzerland* (1994) 18 EHRR 276 (Commission found conviction of sex-shop owner for showing pornographic films in his unmarked shop not 'necessary in a democratic society': case subsequently struck out on S's death).

101 Para. 48.   102 App. No. 31211/96 [1997] EHRLR 678.

who responded to advertisements in *The Sport* newspaper. The conviction was proportionate given the risk that the videos might fall into the hands of minors and that there was no claim to artistic merit.

(II) THE DEFINITION OF 'OBSCENE'

- ### Obscene Publications Act 1959

1. Test of obscenity

(1) For the purposes of this Act an article shall be deemed to be obscene if its effect or (where the article comprises two or more distinct items) the effect of any one of its items is, if taken as a whole, such as to tend to deprave and corrupt persons who are likely, having regard to all relevant circumstances, to read, see or hear the matter contained or embodied in it.

(2) In this Act 'article' means any description of article containing or embodying matter to be read or looked at or both, any sound record, and any film or other record of a picture or pictures…

2. Prohibition of publication of obscene matter…

(6) In any proceedings against a person under this section the question whether an article is obscene shall be determined without regard to any publication by another person unless it could reasonably have been expected that the publication by the other person would follow from publication by the person charged.

- ### Obscene Publications Act 1964

1. Obscene articles intended for publication for gain

(3) In proceedings brought against a person under the said section 2[103] for having an obscene article for publication for gain the following provisions shall apply in place of subsections (5) and (6) of that section, that is to say,—

   (*a*) [104]

   (*b*) the question whether the article is obscene shall be determined by reference to such publication for gain of the article as in the circumstances it may reasonably be inferred he had in contemplation and to any further publication that could reasonably be expected to follow from it, but not to any other publication.

NOTES

1. The Obscene Publications Act 1964, s. 2(1) extends the meaning of 'article' as defined in s. 1(2) of the 1959 Act. It provides:

The Obscene Publications Act 1959 (as amended by this Act), shall apply in relation to anything which is intended to be used, either alone or as one of a set. for the reproduction or manufacture therefrom of articles containing or embodying matter to be read, looked at or listened to, as if it were an article containing or embodying that matter so far as that matter is to be derived from it or from the set.

Whether or not such an article is obscene is to be determined in accordance with the Obscene Publications Act 1964, s. 2(2) which provides:

---

103 I.e. Obscene Publications Act 1959, s. 2.   104 Considered below.

For the purposes of the Obscene Publications Act 1959 (as so amended), an article shall be deemed to be had or kept for publication if it is had or kept for the reproduction or manufacture therefrom of articles for publication; and the question whether an article so had or kept is obscene shall—

(a) for the purposes of section 2 of the Act be determined in accordance with section 1(3)(b) above as if any reference to publication of them were a reference to publication of articles reproduced or manufactured from it; and

(b) for purposes of section 3 of the Act by determined on the assumption that articles reproduced or manufactured from it would be punished in any manner likely having regard to the circumstances in which it was found, but in no other manner.[105]

2. In *A-G's Reference (No. 5 of 1980)*[106] it was held that a video-cassette was an 'article' within s. 2(1) above in that it was a 'record of... pictures'; and that a cinema showing video films was 'publishing' such article because the cassettes were being 'played or projected'.[107]

3. In *DPP v Whyte*,[108] Lord Wilberforce, commenting on the statutory test of obscenity, said:

...the Act has adopted a relative conception of obscenity. An article cannot be considered obscene in itself: it can only be so in relation to its likely readers... in every case, the magistrates, or the jury are called upon to ascertain who are likely readers and then to consider whether the article is likely to deprave and corrupt them.

An example of the application of the test was given by Lord Pearson:[109]

The question whether an article is obscene depends not only on its inherent character but also on what is being or is to be done with it. Suppose that there is a serious book on *Psychopathia Sexualis* designed to be read only by medical men or scientists concerned with such matters, and that it is kept in the library of a hospital or university and so far as possible reserved for use by such medical men or scientists. Such a book should not be regarded as obscene for the purpose of the Act, because it is not likely to come (though possibly it might come) into the hands of anyone who might be corrupted by it.

Lord Simon commented:[110]

The intention of the Act was... to enable serious literary, artistic, scientific or scholarly work to draw on the amplitude of human experience without fear of allegation that it could conceivably have a harmful effect on persons other than those to whom it was in truth directed...

The defence raised in *Whyte*, which the magistrates had accepted, was that by virtue of a policy of excluding young persons from the defendant's bookshop, the likely purchasers of the pornographic books were males of middle age and upwards described by the magistrates as 'inadequate, pathetic, dirty-minded men... addicts to this type of material, whose morals were already in a state of depravity and corruption'. Since this likely audience was no longer open to immoral influence (being already corrupt and depraved) the articles could not be considered obscene within the meaning of the 1959 Act. The prosecutor appealed to the House of Lords. The majority held that the facts as found by the magistrates were sufficient to

---

105 For the Obscene Publications Act 1959, s. 3, see below, p. 667.
106 [1980] 3 All ER 816, CA (CD).   107 As required by s. 1(3). Below, p. 666.
108 [1972] AC 849, HL at 860.   109 Ibid., at 864.   110 Ibid., at 867.

constitute the offence charged. The minority (Lords Simon and Salmon) held that the magistrates' conclusions on the facts could not be interfered with, as it had not been shown that
they lacked any evidential basis. Their Lordships were generally agreed that the Act covered
more than cases of once and for all corruption. Lord Wilberforce explained:[111]

> …the Act's purpose is to prevent the depraving and corrupting of men's minds by certain types of writing:
> it could never have been intended to except from the legislative protection a large body of citizens merely
> because, in different degrees, they had previously been exposed, or exposed themselves, to the 'obscene'
> material. The Act is not merely concerned with the once and for all corruption of the wholly innocent;
> it equally protects the less innocent from further corruption, the addict from feeding or increasing his
> addiction.

Lord Simon said:[112]

> …a defence is available not merely that the likely expose is too aesthetic, too scientific or too scholarly to
> be likely of corruption by the particular matter in question, but also that he is too corrupt to be further cor-
> rupted by it. I would, however, express my concurrence with the view…that the language of the statute is
> apt to extend to the maintenance of a state of corruption which might otherwise be escaped, and…that
> a person can be recorrupted…

Lord Salmon commented:[113]

> …there was no finding that these dirty minded old men were other than depraved and corrupted long
> before they became customers of the respondents, nor that what they found there made them any worse
> than they already were or kept them in a state of depravity or corruption from which they might otherwise
> have escaped.

4. The courts have deprecated judicial attempts to explain to juries the meaning of the
terms 'corrupt and deprave'.[114] In general the matter should be left at large for the jury.[115]
However judges have, from time to time, stressed the seriousness of the terms. For example,
in *Knuller v DPP*[116] Lord Reid commented that one may 'lead persons morally astray without depraving and corrupting them'. On the other hand, in *DPP v Whyte*[117] the House of
Lords stressed that the formula covered moral or spiritual corruption and depravity not
manifesting itself in corrupt and depraved conduct. If an article produces in the minds of
its audience thoughts which a magistrate or jury, as the case may be, regards as having corrupted and depraved the audience's minds, the article is obscene.

How far, and in what ways, might it be possible to define more precisely the content of an
obscenity law? Consider the principle that justice requires that the criminal law should be
clear in its terms. An American judge once despaired of the search for a judicial yardstick to
delimit the extent to which obscenity laws might make inroads on freedom of expression:
'I know it when I see it.'[118]

---

[111] Ibid., at 863.   [112] Ibid., at 867.   [113] Ibid., at 876.

[114] See, e.g., Salmon LJ in *R v Calder and Boyars Ltd* [1969] 1 QB 151 at 168 referring to 'attempts to improve
upon or re-define' the statutory formula.

[115] See *R v O'Sullivan* (1994) Times, 3 May: judge's summing-up should inform juries of the words of 1959
Act, ss. 1(1) and 1(3) and 1964 Act, s. 1(3)(b), adding only a comment about the proportion of the audience which
need be shown to have been corrupted.

[116] [1973] AC 435, HL at 456.   [117] [1972] AC 849.

[118] Per Stewart J, *Jacobellis v Ohio* 378 US 184 (1964).

5. A consequence of defining obscenity in terms of tendency to deprave and corrupt is that the concept is not confined to sexual matters. In *Calder (John) (Publications) Ltd v Powell* Lord Parker CJ said:[119]

> In my judgment it is perfectly plain that depravity, and, indeed, obscenity (because obscenity is treated as a tendency to deprave) is quite apt to cover what was suggested by the prosecution in this case. This book—the less said about it the better—concerned the life, or imaginary life, of a junkie in New York, and the suggestion of the prosecution was that the book high-lighted the favourable effects of drug-taking and, so far from condemning it, advocated it, and that there was a real danger that those into whose hands the book came might be tempted at any rate to experiment with drugs and get the favourable sensations high-lighted by the book.
>
> In my judgment there is no reason whatever to confine obscenity and depravity to sex and there was ample evidence upon which the justices could hold that this book was obscene.

During 1984 a number of comics and pamphlets dealing with the taking of drugs were the subject of prosecutions at the Old Bailey. Note criticisms of the trials in the *New Statesman*.[120] What other matter might be regarded as having a tendency to deprave and corrupt? Violence? See *DPP v A and BC Chewing Gum Ltd*.[121]

6. Some guidance has been given by the courts as to what proportion of an article's audience a magistrate or jury need regard as being susceptible to an article's corrupting and depraving effect for the article to be obscene. In *R v Calder and Boyars Ltd*[122] Salmon LJ said at p. 168: 'the jury should have been directed to consider whether the effect of the book was to tend to deprave and corrupt a significant proportion of those persons likely to read it. What is a significant proportion is a matter entirely for the jury to decide.' Earlier he had said that the term 'persons' in s. 1 of the 1959 Act 'clearly . . . cannot mean all persons, nor can it mean any person, for there are individuals who may be corrupted by almost anything. On the other hand, it is difficult to construe "persons" as meaning the majority of persons or the average reader . . .'. Salmon LJ's formulae were approved by the House of Lords in *DPP v Whyte*,[123] Lord Cross explaining that 'a significant proportion of a class means a part which is not numerically negligible but which may be much less than half' and Lord Pearson stating that 'if a seller of pornographic books has a large number of customers who are not likely to be corrupted by such books, he does not thereby acquire a licence to expose for sale or sell such books to a small number of customers who are likely to be corrupted by them'. The concept of 'more than a negligible number' was approved in the Court of Appeal in *R v O'Sullivan*.[124] In *Perrin*[125] the Court of Appeal held that the prosecution could consider the likely audience for a web page in considering obscenity, and not merely those police officers who had in fact seen the material.

7. A defence sometimes raised is that an article does not deprave and corrupt its audience if it so revolts them that it averts them from the sort of conduct it depicts. In *R v Calder and Boyars Ltd*, Salmon LJ said:[126]

> The defence . . . was that the book . . . gave a graphic description of the depths of depravity and degradation in which life was lived in Brooklyn. This description was compassionate and condemnatory. The only effect that it would produce in any but a minute lunatic fringe of readers would be horror, revulsion and

---

[119] [1965] 1 QB 509, DC at 515.   [120] 8 June and 3 August 1984. See *R v Skirving* [1985] QB 819, CA.
[121] [1968] 1 QB 159, DC.   [122] [1969] 1 QB 151, CA (Cr D).
[123] [1972] AC 849.   [124] [1995] 1 Cr App R 455.   [125] [2002] EWCA Crim 747.
[126] [1969] 1 QB 151, CA (Cr D), at 168.

pity; it was admittedly and intentionally disgusting, shocking and outrageous; it made the reader share in the horror it described and thereby so disgusted, shocked and outraged him that, being aware of the truth, he would do what he could to eradicate those evils and the conditions of modern society which so callously allowed them to exist. In short, according to the defence, instead of tending to encourage any-one to homosexuality, drug-taking or senseless, brutal violence, it would have precisely the reverse effect. Unfortunately, whilst the judge told the jury in general terms that it was not enough for the Crown to prove merely that the book tended to horrify, shock, disgust or nauseate, he never put a word of the specific defence to the jury when he summed up on the issue of obscenity.

This is a serious defect in the summing-up.... With a book such as this, in which words appear on almost every page and many incidents are described in graphic detail which, in the ordinary, colloquial sense of the word, anyone would rightly describe as obscene, it is perhaps of particular importance to explain to the jury what the defendant alleges to be the true effect of those words and descriptions within their con-text in the book.

In *R v Anderson*,[127] Lord Widgery CJ said:

...the defence...said this material in the magazine [Oz No. 28 School Kids Issue] was not likely to deprave or corrupt; that it may shock is accepted, but it is not likely to cause people to act in a depraved or corrupted fashion. One of the arguments advanced in support of that line of defence was that many of the illustrations in the magazine were so grossly lewd and unpleasant that they would shock in the first instance and then would tend to repel. In other words, it was said that they had an aversive effect and that far from tempting those who had not experienced the acts to take part in them, they would put off those who might be tempted so to conduct themselves. The argument which Mr Mortimer [counsel for the defendant] put forward on this point is that the trial judge never really got over to the jury this argu-ment of aversion,...Strangely enough the same situation arose in [an] earlier decision in this court...*R v Calder and Boyars Ltd*...was in fact a then well-publicised criminal trial dealing with the book *Last Exit to Brooklyn* and Mr Mortimer appeared for the defence, and in this court Mr Mortimer argued, and this court held rightly argued, that the failure of the judge to put what one might call the aversion argument was fatal to the retention of the conviction.

The appellants' convictions under s. 2 were accordingly quashed.

8. Section 1(1) of the 1959 Act requires that an article be considered as a whole in estimat-ing its effect on its likely audience. This contrasts with the position prior to 1959 in trials for obscene libel when prosecutors might read 'purple passages' in isolation from their context to juries. Note the effect, however, of s. 1(1) of the 1959 Act on articles comprising more than one item. In *R v Anderson*[128] Lord Widgery CJ said:

...At the trial the prosecution accepted the proposition that in deciding whether the offences under the Act of 1959 had been made out, it was right for the jury to consider the magazine as a whole and not to look at individual items in isolation. That was a proposition accepted by the prosecution...largely in fairness to the defence, and, being accepted by both parties, it was a proposition which was accepted by the judge as well. It certainly did the defence no harm; it was much to their interests; but in the judgment of this court it was entirely wrong. It is in our view quite clear from section 1 that where you have an article such as this comprising a number of distinct items, the proper view of obscenity under section 1 is to apply the test to the individual items in question. It is equally clear that if, when so applied, the test shows one item to be obscene that is enough to make the whole article obscene.

---

[127] [1972] 1 QB 304 at 314, CA (Cr D).   [128] [1972] 1 QB 304 at 312 CA (Cr D).

> Now that may seem unfair at first reading, but it is the law in our judgment without any question. A novelist who writes a complete novel and who cannot cut out particular passages without destroying the theme of the novel is entitled to have his work judged as a whole, but a magazine publisher who has a far wider discretion as to what he will, and will not, insert by way of items is to be judged under the Act on what we call the 'item by item' basis. This was not done in this case. Our main concern in mentioning the point now is to ensure that it will be done in future....

It is for the judge to rule whether as a matter of law a work is capable of comprising more than one item, and a question for fact for the jury whether that is indeed the case; where this arises, the Crown should make clear what it contends to be the separate items.[129]

9. The courts have usually refused to permit expert evidence as to the effect that an article may have on its likely audience. The matter is one for the jury to assess without expert guidance.[130] In *R v Anderson* Lord Widgery CJ said:[131]

> ...a majority of the expert evidence called by the defence in this case...was...directed to showing that the article was not obscene. In other words, it was directed to showing that in the opinion of the witness it would not tend to deprave or corrupt. Now whether the article is obscene or not is a question exclusively in the hands of the jury, and it was decided in this court in *R v Calder and Boyars Ltd* [1969] 1 QB 151 that expert evidence should not be admitted on the issue of obscene or no. It is perfectly true that there was an earlier Divisional Court case in which a somewhat different view had been taken. It was *DPP v A and BC Chewing Gum Ltd* [1968] 1 QB 159. That case in our judgment should be regarded as highly exceptional and confined to its own circumstances, namely, a case where the alleged obscene matter was directed at very young children, and was of itself of a somewhat unusual kind. In the ordinary run of the mill cases in the future the issue 'obscene or no' must be tried by the jury without the assistance of expert evidence on that issue, and we draw attention to the failure to observe that rule in this case in order that that failure may not occur again.
>
> We are not oblivious of the fact that some people, perhaps many people, will think a jury, unassisted by experts, a very unsatisfactory tribunal to decide such a matter. Those who feel like that must campaign elsewhere for a change of the law. We can only deal with the law as it stands, and that is how it stands on this point.

In *DPP v Jordan* Viscount Dilhorne expressed some doubt about the correctness of the *Chewing Gum* case and felt the exception certainly should not be extended. Lord Wilberforce stated the alleged exception to the general rule and commented:[132]

> we are not obliged to validate, or otherwise this exception or to define its scope, because the evidence was not directed to showing that the class of likely readers consisted of, or as to a significant number included, sexual abnormals or deviants. The case was one of normal readers, and was to be judged by the jury in relation to them, and, since normal readers were in question here, [expert] evidence...was inadmissible at the stage when section 1 was being considered.

Note, however, the decision in *R v Skirving*.[133] The appellants, partners in a book distribution business, had been convicted of having an obscene article for publication for gain, contrary to s. 1(1) of the 1959 Act. The article in question was a pamphlet entitled 'Attention

---

129 *R v Goring (Jonathan)* [1999] Crim LR 670.
130 Cf. the use of expert testimony under s. 4 of the 1959 Act, see below.
131 [1972] 1 QB 304, CA (Cr D) at 313.   132 [1977] AC 699, HL at 718.
133 [1985] QB 819, CA (Cr D).

Coke Lovers—Freebasing, the Greatest Thing Since Sex', copies of which had been discovered by police following a search of their office premises. The pamphlet contained instructions ('recipes') as to how to take cocaine to maximum effect—in particular, how to smoke or 'freebase' the drug. The prosecution had, at the trial, obtained leave to adduce expert evidence from a professor of addiction behaviour as to the effects of taking cocaine. This had been permitted by the trial judge on the ground that the jury would need to consider the effects of 'freebasing', and that this was not within the knowledge or experience of the ordinary person. On appeal, the appellants argued that such evidence should not have been admitted. The Court of Appeal upheld the decision of the trial judge, holding that unlike the sexual obscenity cases (such as *Anderson* and *Jordan*) where the jury were in a reasonable position to assess from their own experience the likely effect of material, in this case the jury would have been 'in the dark' 'guessing and no more' at its likely effect. The Court of Appeal did emphasise, however, that the proper question for the jury was not whether the act of taking cocaine 'corrupted or depraved', but, rather, the linked but separate question whether the pamphlet itself could be said to have that effect. The court was content, however, that the trial judge had properly distinguished these questions in his summing-up.

(III) THE DEFINITION OF 'PUBLICATION'

- **Obscene Publications Act 1959**

1. Test of obscenity

(3) For the purposes of this Act a person publishes an article who—

   (*a*) distributes, circulates, sells, lets on hire, gives, or lends it, or who offers it for sale or for letting on hire; or

   (*b*) in the case of an article containing or embodying matter to be looked at or a record, shows, plays or projects it, [or, where the matter is data stored electronically, transmits that data].[134]

NOTES

1. In *R v Taylor (Alan)*[135] T had developed and printed photographic films depicting obscene acts. The Court of Appeal held that the sale of the prints to the owners of the developed film constituted a 'publication'. 'High Street' photographic developing-processing outlets have long exercised some caution in the material they are willing to return to customers. Periodically, press reports appear of difficulties experienced by would-be serious artists in securing the return, for self-portrait purposes, of 'snaps' they have taken of themselves. Camcorders have, no doubt, eased the difficulties of others with less legitimate purposes.

2. In *R v Fellows and Arnold*[136] the Court of Appeal (Criminal Division) held that the making available of a computer archive of obscene photographs constituted the 'publication' of the obscene articles by 'sharing or projecting' them. See further below[137] in respect of offences under the Protection of Children Act 1978. The transmission of data to a website in the US from which it is downloaded in the UK constitutes a publication in the UK.[138]

---

[134] Words added by Criminal Justice and Public Order Act 1994, Sch. 9, para. 3.
[135] (1994) Times, 4 February 1994, CA.   [136] [1997] 2 All ER 548.
[137] P. 711.   [138] *R v Waddon (Graham Lester Ian)* (unreported, 6 April 2000).

(IV) FORFEITURE OF OBSCENE ARTICLES

- **Obscene Publications Act 1959**

3. Powers of search and seizure

(1) If a justice of the peace is satisfied by information on oath that there is reasonable ground for suspecting that, in any premises […][139] or on any stall or vehicle in that area, being premises or a stall or vehicle specified in the information, obscene articles are, or are from time to time, kept for publication for gain, the justice may issue a warrant under his hand empowering any constable to enter (if need be by force) and search the premises, or to search the stall or vehicle,…and to seize and remove any articles found therein or thereon which the constable has reason to believe to be obscene articles and to be kept for publication for gain.

(2) A warrant issued under the foregoing subsection shall, if any obscene articles are seized under the warrant, also empower the seizure and removal of any documents found in the premises or, as the case may be, on the stall or vehicle which relate to a trade or business carried on at the premises or from the stall or vehicle.

(3) [Subject to subsection (3A) of this section][140] any articles seized under subsection (1) of this section shall be brought before a justice of the peace acting [in the local justice area in which the articles were seized, who][141] may thereupon issue a summons to the occupier of the premises or, as the case may be, the user of the stall or vehicle to appear on a day specified in the summons before a magistrates' court for that petty sessions area to show cause why the articles or any of them should not be forfeited; and if the court is satisfied, as respects any of the articles, that at the time when they were seized they were obscene articles kept for publication for gain, the court shall order those articles to be forfeited:

[Provided that if the person summoned does not appear, the court shall not make an order unless service of the summons is proved.

Provided also that this subsection does not apply in relation to any article seized under subsection (1) of this section which is returned to the occupier of the premises or, as the case may be, the user of the stall or vehicle in or on which it was found.][142]

- **Obscene Publications Act 1964**

1. Obscene articles intended for publication for gain

(4) Where articles are seized under section 3 of the Obscene Publications Act 1959…and a person is convicted under section 2 of that Act of having them for publication for gain, the court on his conviction shall order the forfeiture of those articles:…

- **Obscene Publications Act 1959**

3. Powers of search and seizure

[(3A)[143] Without prejudice to the duty of a court to make an order for the forfeiture of an article where section 1(4) of the Obscene Publications Act 1964 applies (orders made on conviction), in a case where by virtue of subsection (3A) of section 2 of this Act proceedings under the said section 2

---

139 Words omitted repealed by the Courts Act 2003, s. 109(1).
140 Inserted by the Criminal Law Act 1977, ss. 53(5).
141 Substituted by the Courts Act 2003, s. 109(1).
142 Added by the Criminal Law Act 1977, s. 53.
143 Section 3(3A) added by the Criminal Law Act 1977, s. 53.

for having an article for publication for gain could not be instituted except by or with the consent of the Director of Public Prosecutions, no order for the forfeiture of the article shall be made under this section unless the warrant under which the article was seized was issued on an information laid by or on behalf of the Director of Public Prosecutions.]

(4) In addition to the person summoned, any other person being the owner, author or maker of any of the articles brought before the court, or any other person through whose hands they had passed before being seized, shall be entitled to appear before the court on the day specified in the summons to show cause why they should not be forfeited.

(5) Where an order is made under this section for the forfeiture of any articles, any person who appeared, or was entitled to appear, to show cause against the making of the order may appeal to the Crown Court;…

(6) If as respects any articles brought before it the court does not order forfeiture, the court may if it thinks fit order the person on whose information the warrant for the seizure of the articles was issued to pay such costs as the court thinks reasonable to any person who has appeared before the court to show cause why those articles should not be forfeited; and costs ordered to be paid under this subsection shall be enforceable as a civil debt.

(7) For the purposes of this section the question whether an article is obscene shall be determined on the assumption that copies of it would be published in any manner likely having regard to the circumstances in which it was found, but in no other manner.

…

NOTES

1. The Criminal Justice Act 1967, s. 25 provides that a warrant under s. 3 may not be issued except on an information laid by or on behalf of the DPP or by a constable. This restriction followed the successful private forfeiture proceedings, in 1966, against *Last Exit to Brooklyn*. These proceedings forced the hand of the DPP to reverse his original decision not to prosecute the publishers under s. 2.[144]

2. The provision in s. 3(4) of the 1959 Act granting rights to appear to interested parties other than the occupier of the premises searched was regarded as an important new provision in the 1959 Act. The opportunity it provides to authors etc. to defend their work is somewhat diminished by the absence of any procedure for making such interested persons aware of the existence of the forfeiture proceedings. Much depends on press publicity of the seizure or the actions of the person from whom the articles were seized in contacting such other interested parties.

3. Prior to the 1959 Act a practice had developed whereby the police, having discovered articles which they and the DPP considered obscene, would persuade the occupier of the premises to sign a form disclaiming any interest in the articles. The police would then destroy the articles and no court proceedings would take place. This practice was disapproved by the 1957 Parliamentary Select Committee on Obscene Publications.[145] Section 3(3) of the 1959 Act (as amended) requires articles seized to be returned to the occupier or brought before the magistrates. See also the adverse comments of the Court of Appeal concerning the 'disclaimer' practice in *R v Metropolitan Police Comr, ex p Blackburn (No. 3)*.[146]

---

[144] See further *R v Calder and Boyars Ltd* [1969] 1 QB 151, CA (Cr D).
[145] 1957–58 HC 123–1.   [146] [1973] QB 241 at 252–254.

4. It not uncommonly appears that there are differences between the attitudes of magistrates and juries in their application of the test of obscenity. For example, comment was aroused when magistrates at Watford ordered forfeiture of an edition of the magazine *Men Only* at about the time that an Old Bailey jury acquitted the editors of *Nasty Tales* of the offence under s. 2.[147] Note also the jury acquittal of the publishers of *Inside Linda Lovelace* in 1976 and comment[148] and in the Williams Committee Report:[149]

...the view was expressed to us by representatives of the Metropolitan Police that the failure of that prosecution meant that the law was unlikely to be invoked again against the written word. Their view (which appeared from his summing up to have been shared by the trial judge) was that it was difficult to imagine what written material would be regarded as obscene if that was not.

5. In *Darbo v DPP*[150] D was convicted under Police Act 1964, s. 51(3) for having obstructed a police officer in the execution of his duty. The officer had been seeking to execute a warrant which purported to authorise the search for 'any other material of a sexually explicit nature...'. D's appeal succeeded. Under the 1959/1964 Acts it was not possible to equate the notions of 'obscene' and 'sexually explicit': and only searches for, and seizure of, material of the former kind could be authorised by a s. 3 warrant.

6. Section 3 was relied upon controversially by the police in 1998 in seizing a book of homoerotic photographs by the late Robert Mapplethorpe from the library of the University of Central England. The Vice Chancellor, Dr Peter Knight, indicated that any proceedings would be resisted and bought another copy from Waterstones to replace the one seized. Proceedings were subsequently dropped.

(V) DEFENCE OF 'PUBLIC GOOD'

- **Obscene Publications Act 1959**

4. Defence of Public Good[151]

(1) [Subject to subsection (1A) of this section] a person shall not be convicted of an offence against section two of this Act, and an order for forfeiture shall not be made under the foregoing section, if it is proved that publication of the article in question is justified as being for the public good on the ground that it is in the interests of science, literature, art or learning, or of other objects of general concern.

[(1A) Subsection (1) of this section shall not apply where the article in question is moving picture film or soundtrack, but—

(*a*) a person shall not be convicted of an offence against section 2 of this Act in relation to any such film or soundtrack, and

(*b*) an order for forfeiture of any such film or soundtrack shall not be made under section 3 of this Act,

if it is proved that publication of the film or soundtrack is justified as being for the public good on the ground that it is in the interests of drama, opera, ballet or any other part, or of literature or learning.][152]

---

147 See (1973) 127 JPN 82.   148 (1976) 126 NLJ 126.   149 At p. 35.
150 (1994) Times, 11 July.
151 Words in square brackets, s. 4(1A) and s. 4(3) added by the Criminal Law Act 1977, s. 53.
152 Added by the Criminal Law Act 1977, s. 53(6), (7).

(2) It is hereby declared that the opinion of experts as to the literary, artistic, scientific or other merits of an article may be admitted in any proceedings under this Act either to establish or to negative the said ground.

...

NOTES

1. Section 4 provides that the publication of an article which, taken as a whole, is regarded by a magistrate or a jury as having a tendency to corrupt and deprave its likely audience may nevertheless be found to be justified as being for the public good as furthering certain objects or ends. Expert evidence may be presented as to the merit (or, lack of merit) of the articles, although the ultimate question whether such merit justifies the adverse effect of the articles is one for the court or jury and not a matter for expert opinion. In *R v Calder and Boyars Ltd* Salmon LJ explained:[153]

...In the view of this court, the proper direction on a defence under section 4 in a case such as the present is that the jury must consider on the one hand the number of readers they believe would tend to be depraved and corrupted by the book, the strength of the tendency to deprave and corrupt, and the nature of the depravity or corruption; on the other hand, they should assess the strength of the literary, sociological or ethical merit which they consider the book to possess. They should then weigh up all these factors and decide whether on balance the publication is proved to be justified as being for the public good. A book may be worthless; a book may have slight but real merit; it may be a work of genius. Between those extremes the gradations are almost infinite. A book may tend to deprave and corrupt a significant but comparatively small number of its readers or a large number or indeed the majority of its readers. The tendency to deprave and corrupt may be strong or slight. The depravity and corruption may also take various forms. It may be to induce erotic desires of a heterosexual kind or to promote homosexuality or other sexual perversions or drug-taking or brutal violence. All these are matters for the jury to consider and weigh up; it is for them to decide in the light of the importance they attach to these factors whether or not the publication is for the public good. The jury must set the standards of what is acceptable, of what is for the public good in the age in which we live....[154]

2. In *DPP v Jordan* the defence sought to argue that the publication of the articles in question, which they admitted to be 'hard pornography', was justified in that the articles had 'some psychotherapeutic value for various categories of persons of heterosexual taste unable to achieve satisfactory heterosexual relationships, for persons of deviant sexuality, and for homosexuals and other perverts...providing...appropriate material to relieve their sexual tensions by way of sexual fantasy and masturbation'. Also 'that such release was beneficial to such persons and would act as a safety valve to save them from psychological disorders and...divert them from anti-social and possibly criminal activities directed at others'. The House of Lords rejected this argument. Lord Wilberforce said:[155]

...Whatever the exact meaning of the expressions used in section 4 may be, one thing is apparent. The section is dealing with a different range, or dimension, of considerations from that with which section 1 is concerned....It assumes that, apart from what section 4 itself may do, that issue would be resolved in

---

[153] [1969] 1 QB 151, CA (Cr D) at 171.

[154] See generally on the role of the expert witness in obscenity cases, F. Bates (1977–78) CLQ 250; C. Nowlin (2001) CLWR 94.

[155] [1977] AC 699 at 718, HL.

favour of 'deprave and corrupt' and having assumed that, it allows a contention to be made and evidence to be given that publication of the material is, on specified grounds, for the public good.

Each of its subsections provides guidance as to the conception of public good which is in mind. Subsection (1) provides a list which one may suspect (from the long title) started with 'literature' and was expanded to include science, art and learning and still further to include 'other objects of general concern'. The latter phrase is no doubt a mobile phrase; it may, and should, change in content as society changes. But... even if this is not strictly a case for applying a rule of eiusdem generis (the genus being one of intellectual or aesthetic values), the structure of the section makes it clear that the other objects, or, which is the same argument, the nature of the general concern, fall within the same area, and cannot fall in the totally different area of effect on sexual behaviour and attitudes, which is covered in section 1. In other words it introduces a new type of equation—possibly between incommensurables—between immediate and direct effect on people's conduct or character (section 1) and inherent impersonal values of a less transient character assumed, optimistically perhaps, to be of general concern (section 4).... The judgment to be reached under section 4(1), and the evidence to be given under section 4(2), must be in order to show that publication should be permitted in spite of obscenity—not to negative obscenity. Section 4 has been diverted from its proper purpose, and indeed abused, when it has been used to enable evidence to be given that pornographic material may be for the public good as being therapeutic to some of the public. I respectfully agree with the observations to this effect of Lord Denning MR and of Phillimore and Roskill LJJ in *R v Metropolitan Police Comr, ex p Blackburn (No 3)* [1973] QB 241 and I consider that such cases as *R v Gold* (unreported), 3 November, 1972, Central Criminal Court (see (1973] QB 241 and 250) took a wrong turning. Indeed, I have the impression that if those cases are right the more 'obscene' an article, the more likely it would be that the appellant's defence would apply to it. To produce such a result would in my opinion involve a total alteration in the Act....

3. In *A-G's Reference (No. 3 of 1977)* the respondents had been allowed to produce at their trial expert witnesses as to the merit of the magazines, which they had sold, in providing information to their readers about sexual matters. They had contended, successfully before the trial judge, that this sex-education role of the magazines brought them within the term 'learning' in s. 4(1). On appeal, Lord Widgery CJ, giving the judgment of the court:[156]

...it seems to us that the fundamental question is whether 'learning' in this context is a noun, in which case... it must mean the product of scholarship. The only possible meaning of 'learning' as a noun... would have been something whose inherent excellence is gained by the work of the scholar. I would reject at once the idea that 'learning' in this context is a verb.

Accordingly, since 'learning' could not be equated with 'teaching' or 'education' the trial judge had been wrong in allowing the expert testimony.

(VI) IGNORANCE AS TO NATURE OF ARTICLE

- **Obscene Publications Act 1959**

2. Prohibition of obscene matter

(5) A person shall not be convicted of an offence against this section if he proves that he had not examined the article in respect of which he is charged and had no reasonable cause to suspect that it was such that his publication of it would make him liable to be convicted of an offence against this section.

---

[156] [1978] 3 All ER 1166 at 1169, CA (Cr D).

- **Obscene Publications Act 1964**

1. Obscene articles intended for publication for gain

(3) In proceedings brought against a person under the said section 2[157] for having an obscene article for publication for gain the following provisions shall apply in place of subsections (5) and (6) of that section, that is to say—

    (*a*) he shall not be convicted of that offence if he proves that he had not examined the article and had no reasonable cause to suspect that it was such that his having it would make him liable to be convicted of an offence against that section; and

    (*b*) [considered above under (ii)]

(C) THE CRIMINAL JUSTICE AND IMMIGRATION ACT 2008

63 Possession of extreme pornographic images

(1) It is an offence for a person to be in possession of an extreme pornographic image.

(2) An 'extreme pornographic image' is an image which is both—

    (a) pornographic, and

    (b) an extreme image.

(3) An image is 'pornographic' if it is of such a nature that it must reasonably be assumed to have been produced solely or principally for the purpose of sexual arousal.

(4) Where (as found in the person's possession) an image forms part of a series of images, the question whether the image is of such a nature as is mentioned in subsection (3) is to be determined by reference to—

    (a) the image itself, and

    (b) (if the series of images is such as to be capable of providing a context for the image) the context in which it occurs in the series of images.

(5) So, for example, where—

    (a) an image forms an integral part of a narrative constituted by a series of images, and

    (b) having regard to those images as a whole, they are not of such a nature that they must reasonably be assumed to have been produced solely or principally for the purpose of sexual arousal,

the image may, by virtue of being part of that narrative, be found not to be pornographic, even though it might have been found to be pornographic if taken by itself.

(6) An 'extreme image' is an image which—

    (a) falls within subsection (7), and

    (b) is grossly offensive, disgusting or otherwise of an obscene character.

(7) An image falls within this subsection if it portrays, in an explicit and realistic way, any of the following—

    (a) an act which threatens a person's life,

    (b) an act which results, or is likely to result, in serious injury to a person's anus, breasts or genitals,

---

[157] I.e. Obscene Publications Act 1959, s. 2.

(c) an act which involves sexual interference with a human corpse, or

(d) a person performing an act of intercourse or oral sex with an animal (whether dead or alive),

and a reasonable person looking at the image would think that any such person or animal was real.

(8) In this section 'image' means—

(a) a moving or still image (produced by any means); or

(b) data (stored by any means) which is capable of conversion into an image within paragraph (a).

(9) In this section references to a part of the body include references to a part surgically constructed (in particular through gender reassignment surgery).

(10) Proceedings for an offence under this section may not be instituted—

(a) in England and Wales, except by or with the consent of the Director of Public Prosecutions;

...

65 Defences: general

(1) Where a person is charged with an offence under section 63, it is a defence for the person to prove any of the matters mentioned in subsection (2).

(2) The matters are—

(a) that the person had a legitimate reason for being in possession of the image concerned;

(b) that the person had not seen the image concerned and did not know, nor had any cause to suspect, it to be an extreme pornographic image;

(c) that the person—

(i) was sent the image concerned without any prior request having been made by or on behalf of the person, and

(ii) did not keep it for an unreasonable time.

...

NOTES

1. Material that can be said to be pornographic and extreme would be caught under the Obscene Publications Act if published. However, the difficulties posed by the internet mean that despite the fact that extreme pornography can be made available to a wide audience it is very difficult to hold those responsible to account, especially when operating from abroad. Therefore, this legislation seeks to place responsibility on the 'consumer'. The Act will not apply to materials that would not currently fall foul of the law, or which have been classified by the BBFC.

2. The impetus for the new legislation came partly as a result of the case of *Coutts*[158] in which a young woman was murdered and the perpetrator was found to have accessed extreme pornography both before and after the murder.

3. The consultation paper on the new offence reported that the number of prosecutions under the OPA had fallen from 309 in 1994 to 39 in 2003.[159] However, the number of prosecutions under the Protection of Children Act 1978 and s. 160 of the Criminal Justice Act 1988, which make it illegal to make, distribute and possess indecent photographs of children, has

---

[158] [2005] EWCA Crim 52.

[159] Home Office, *Consultation on the Possession of Extreme Pornographic Material* (2005), para. 15. See J. Rowbottom [2006] Crim LR 97.

risen from 93 in 1994 to 1,890 in 2003. The Paper argues that 'in part this reflects a higher priority being given to combating the increasing availability of indecent photographs of children through the Internet'.[160] However, such statistics perhaps further support the case for a thorough overhaul of the obscenity laws rather than the current piecemeal approach.

4. The legislation is directed at prosecuting adults for the possession of various types of pornography within the privacy of their own home—the first such criminalisation of possession of adult pornography in Europe.[161] In the absence of any identifiable harm the demands of proportionality may be difficult to meet. However, it has been noted that the European Court affords a wider margin of appreciation in relation to this type of expression.

(D) THEATRES ACT 1968

A play cannot come within the definition of 'article' for the purposes of the OPA but the Theatres Act 1968 prohibits the presentation of obscene performances of plays.[162] Section 2(1) states 'a performance of a play shall be deemed to be obscene if taken as a whole, its effect was such as to tend to deprave and corrupt persons who were likely, having regard to all the circumstances, to attend it'. The offence is committed if the play is performed in public or private (but not in a private dwelling on a domestic occasion) but in both circumstances the consent of the Attorney-General is required.

Section 2(4) states:

no person shall be proceeded against in respect of a performance of a play or anything said or done in the course of such a performance

  (a) for an offence at common law where it is of the essence of the offence that the performance or, as the case may be, what was said or done was obscene, indecent, offensive, disgusting or injurious to morality; and no person shall be proceeded against for an offence at common law of conspiring to corrupt public morals, or to do any act contrary to public morals or decency, in respect of an agreement to present or give a performance of a play, or to cause anything to be said or done in the course of such a performance.

This was tested recently in *R (on the application of Green) v City of Westminster Magistrates' Court*,[163] where the Bench Divisional Court held that no prosecution for blasphemous libel could be brought in respect of a theatre production of *Jerry Springer—the Opera*.

There is a public good defence whereby giving of the performance in question can be justified as being for the public good on the ground that it was in the interests of drama, opera, ballet or any other art, or of literature or learning. Expert evidence can be used to support such a case.

● **Public Order Act 1986**

20. Public performance of play
(1) If a public performance of a play is given which involves the use of threatening, abusive or insulting words or behaviour, any person who presents or directs the performance is guilty of an offence if—

  (a) he intends thereby to stir up racial hatred, or

---

[160] Ibid.   [161] See C. McGlynn and E. Rackley [2007] Crim LR 677.
[162] For the prosecution of indecent performances not coming within the terms of the 1968 Act see R.T.H. Stone (1977) 127 NLJ 452.
[163] [2007] EWHC 2785 (Admin).

(b) having regard to all the circumstances (and, in particular, taking the performance as a whole) racial hatred is likely to be stirred up thereby.

(2) If a person presenting or directing the performance is not shown to have intended to stir up racial hatred, it is a defence for him to prove—

(a) that he did not know and had no reason to suspect that the performance would involve the use of the offending words or behaviour, or

(b) that he did not know and had no reason to suspect that the offending words or behaviour were threatening, abusive or insulting, or

(c) that he did not know and had no reason to suspect that the circumstances in which the performance would be given would be such that racial hatred would be likely to be stirred up.

(3) This section does not apply to a performance given solely or primarily for one or more of the following purposes—

(a) rehearsal,

(b) making a recording of the performance, or

(c) enabling the performance to be [included in a programme service];[164]

but if it is proved that the performance was attended by persons other than those directly connected with the giving of the performance or the doing in relation to it of the things mentioned in paragraph (b) or (c), the performance shall, unless the contrary is shown, be taken not to have been given solely or primarily for the purposes mentioned above.

(4) For the purposes of this section—

(a) a person shall not be treated as presenting a performance of a play by reason only of his taking part in it as a performer,

(b) a person taking part as a performer in a performance directed by another shall be treated as a person who directed the performance if without reasonable excuse he performs otherwise than in accordance with that person's direction, and

(c) a person shall be taken to have directed a performance of a play given under his direction notwithstanding that he was not present during the performance;

and a person shall not be treated as aiding or abetting the commission of an offence under this section by reason only of his taking part in a performance as a performer.

...

(E) OFFENCES INVOLVING INDECENCY

● **Postal Services Act 2000**

85 Prohibition on sending certain articles by post

(3) A person commits an offence if he sends by post a postal packet which encloses—

(a) any indecent or obscene print, painting, photograph, lithograph, engraving, cinematograph film or other record of a picture or pictures, book, card or written communication, or

(b) any other indecent or obscene article (whether or not of a similar kind to those mentioned in paragraph (a)).

---

164 Substituted by the Broadcasting Act 1990, s. 164(1), (2)(b).

(4) A person commits an offence if he sends by post a postal packet which has on the packet, or on the cover of the packet, any words, marks or designs which are of an indecent or obscene character.

(5) A person who commits an offence under this section shall be liable—

(a) on summary conviction, to a fine not exceeding the statutory maximum,

(b) on conviction on indictment, to a fine or to imprisonment for a term not exceeding twelve months or to both

NOTE

1. The meaning of the words 'indecent or obscene' as used in the Post Office Act 1953 was considered in *R v Stanley*. Lord Parker CJ explained:[165]

…The words 'indecent or obscene' convey one idea, namely, offending against the recognised standards of propriety, indecent being at the lower end of the scale and obscene at the upper end of the scale…As it seems to this court, an indecent article is not necessarily obscene, whereas an obscene article almost certainly must be indecent.…

Lord Parker also quoted with approval the following passage from Lord Sands' judgment in *McGowan v Langmuir*:[166]

I do not think that the two words 'indecent' and 'obscene' are synonymous. The one may shade into the other, but there is a difference of meaning. It is easier to illustrate than define, and I illustrate thus. For a male bather to enter the water nude in the presence of ladies would be indecent, but it would not necessarily be obscene. But if he directed the attention of a lady to a certain member of his body his conduct would certainly be obscene.…

In *R v Anderson*[167] it was held to have been no misdirection on the charge under the Post Office Act 1953 for the trial judge to have directed the jury to consider whether the material was 'repulsive', 'filthy', 'loathsome' or 'lewd'.[168]

● **Customs Consolidation Act 1876**

42. Prohibitions and restrictions

The goods enumerated and described in the following table of prohibitions and restrictions inwards arc hereby prohibited to be imported or brought into the United Kingdom, save as thereby excepted…

Goods prohibited to be imported

Indecent or obscene prints, paintings, photographs, books, cards, lithographic and other engravings, or any other indecent or obscene articles.

● **Customs and Excise Management Act 1979**

49. Forfeiture of goods improperly imported

(1) Where—

(a) …

---

[165] [1965] 2 QB 327, CCA at 335.   [166] 1931 JC 10.   [167] [1972] 1 QB 304, CA (Cr D).
[168] See also *R v Kirk* [2006] EWCA Crim 725; N. Parpworth (2006) 170 JP 384.

(b) any goods are imported, landed or unloaded contrary to any prohibition or restriction for the time being in force with respect thereto under or by virtue of any enactment; or

(c) ...

those goods shall...be liable to forfeiture.

NOTES

1. The forfeiture of indecent material under the customs legislation set out above has been challenged as being in breach of EC obligations. In *Conegate Ltd v Customs and Excise Comrs*[169] the appellants had sought to import into the UK from West Germany a quantity of life-size rubber dolls of a sexual nature and other erotic articles. The items were forfeited by customs officers at Heathrow airport. The appellants contended that the prohibition imposed by s. 42 of the 1876 Act constituted a quantitative restriction on imports between EC states contrary to Art. 30 of the EC Treaty (now Art. 28 EC). Although there is a provision in Art. 36 (now Art. 30 EC) which permits restrictions where this is justified on grounds, *inter alia*, of public morality, the appellants argued that this could not protect the seizure because at least in so far as the materials were indecent rather than obscene such materials could be manufactured and sold perfectly legally within the UK (though certain restrictions might apply to the public display of the items, or to sending them through the post). In other words the restriction on importation was in reality an act of discrimination in favour of domestic producers of such items and against foreign competitors. The matter was referred to the Court of Justice of the European Communities. The ECJ upheld the contentions of the appellants, and when the case returned to the English courts the forfeiture order was quashed and the goods returned.

It remains the case that where an item is obscene within the meaning of the 1959 legislation its forfeiture may be justified under Art. 30 EC.[170] Customs forfeitures of 'obscene' material were upheld in *R v Bow St Metropolitan Stipendiary Magistrate, ex p Noncyp Ltd*[171] and in *R v Uxbridge Justices, ex p David Webb*.[172] Both these cases involved proceedings in respect of explicit homosexual material. In the former the court refused to admit evidence on the issue of 'public good', holding that there could be no lawful trade in obscene articles within the UK even in circumstances where a public good defence might succeed. It appears that it is necessary only to find that an article is itself obscene within the meaning of s. 1(1) of the 1959 Act, i.e. that its publication in the UK would be an offence. It is not necessary to show that a person in whose possession it is found on importation into the UK was at that time also committing an offence under the 1959 or 1964 Acts.[173]

2. The Customs and Excise Commissioners have noted that with paedophiles making increasing use of the internet, the quantity of obscene and indecent material detected

---

[169] [1987] QB 254.
[170] See also *R v Henn and Darby* [1981] AC 850, [1980] 2 All ER 166, ECJ and HL: affirming that for the purpose of Art. 36 (now Art. 30 EC) each Member State may determine the requirements of public morality in accordance with its own scale of values.
[171] [1990] 1 QB 123.   [172] [1994] CMLR 288, DC appeal dismissed, 26 January 1996, CA (CD).
[173] See *R v Uxbridge Justices, ex p Webb*, above; *Wright v Comrs of Customs and Excise* [1999] 1 Cr App R 69 (importation of obscene horror films for applicant's private collection liable to forfeiture; not necessary to consider the purpose for which the particular goods would be used, but there was sufficient to invoke the 'public morality' exception in the potential for distribution and the purpose of protecting the less innocent from further corruption).

at the physical frontier has fallen significantly, and that they believe this trend will continue; emphasis at the frontier has shifted further towards identifying active child molesters.[174]

- **Protection of Children Act 1978**[175]

1. Indecent photographs of children[176]

(1) [Subject to sections 1A and 1B,][177] it is an offence for a person—

   (a) to take, or permit to be taken [or to make], any indecent photograph [or pseudo photograph] of a child; or

   (b) to distribute or show such indecent photographs or [pseudo-photographs]; or

   (c) to have in his possession such indecent photographs or [pseudo-photographs], with a view to their being distributed or shown by himself or others; or

   (d) to publish or cause to be published any advertisement likely to be understood as conveying that the advertiser distributes or shows such indecent photographs or [pseudo-photographs], or intends to do so.

(2) For purposes of this Act, a person is to be regarded as distributing an indecent photograph or [pseudo-photograph] if he parts with possession of it to, or exposes or offers it for acquisition by, another person.

(3) Proceedings for an offence under this Act shall not be instituted except by or with the consent of the Director of Public Prosecutions.

(4) Where a person is charged with an offence under subsection (1)(b) or (c), it shall be a defence for him to prove—

   (a) that he had a legitimate reason for distributing or showing the photographs [or pseudo-photographs] or (as the case may be) having them in his possession; or

   (b) that he had not himself seen the photographs [or pseudo-photographs] and did not know, nor had any cause to suspect, them to be indecent…

2. Evidence… [178]

(3) In proceedings under this Act [relating to indecent photographs of children] a person is to be taken as having been a child at any material time if it appears from the evidence as a whole that he was then under the age of 16.

6. Punishments

(1) Offences under this Act shall be punishable either on conviction on indictment or on summary conviction.

(2) A person convicted on indictment of any offence under this Act shall be liable to imprisonment for a term of not more than [ten][179] years, or to a fine or to both.

---

[174] 91st Report for 1999–2000, pp. 15–16.

[175] See M.D.A. Freeman, *Current Law Statutes Annotated 1978* and, on the events leading to the passage of the Act, M.A. McCarthy and R.A. Moodie (1981) 34 Parliamentary Affairs 47. See generally S.S.M. Edwards, 'Prosecuting child pornography' (2000) 22 JSWL 1. On applying the Act to incidents of voyeurism see A. Gillespie [2008] Crim LR 370.

[176] Added by the Criminal Justice and Public Order Act 1994, s. 84, Sch. 11.

[177] Inserted by the Sexual Offences Act 2003, s. 139.

[178] Added by the Criminal Justice and Public Order Act 1994, s. 84, Sch. 11.

[179] Substituted by the Criminal Justice and Court Services Act 2000, s. 41(1).

(3) A person convicted summarily of any offence under this Act shall be liable—

    (a) to imprisonment for a term not exceeding 6 months; or

    (b) to a fine not exceeding the prescribed sum … or to both.

● Criminal Justice Act 1988

160. Summary offence of possession of indecent photograph of child

(1) It is an offence for a person to have any indecent photograph or pseudo-photograph of a child in his possession.

(2) Where a person is charged with an offence under subsection (1) above, it shall be a defence for him to prove—

    (*a*) that he had a legitimate reason for having the photograph or pseudo-photograph in his possession; or

    (*b*) that he had not himself seen the photograph or pseudo-photograph and did not know. nor had any cause to suspect, it to be indecent; or

    (*c*) that the photograph or pseudo-photograph was sent to him without any prior request made by him or on his behalf and that he did not keep it for an unreasonable time.

(3) A person shall be liable on summary conviction of an offence under this section to imprisonment for a term not exceeding six months or a fine not exceeding level 5 on the standard scale or both [currently, £5,000].

(4) Sections 1(3), 2(3), 3 and 7 of the Protection of Children Act 1978 shall have effect as if any reference in them to that Act included a reference to this section.

NOTES

1. As noted above, the number of prosecutions under the OPA has fallen from 309 in 1994 to 39 in 2003,[180] whilst the number of prosecutions under the Protection of Children Act 1978 and s. 160 of the Criminal Justice Act 1988, which make it illegal to make, distribute and possess indecent photographs of children, has risen from 93 in 1994 to 1,890 in 2003.[181]

2. Sections 4 and 5 of the 1978 Act provide powers to entry, search, seizure and forfeiture in terms substantially similar to the provisions of the Obscene Publications Act 1959, s. 3. The Sexual Offences Act 2003 raised the age of a 'child' for the purposes of the 1978 Act to 18. Further, the SOA 2003 also introduced a new s. 1A to the 1978 Act which excludes from the Act photographs in the possession of a husband, wife or partner in a family relationship where there is no evidence of distribution to a third party. A new s. 1B also provides a defence if the accused can establish that it was necessary for him to make the photograph or pseudo-photograph for the purposes of the prevention, detection or investigation of crime, or for the purposes of criminal proceedings.[182]

3. In *R v Graham-Kerr*[183] a naturist was convicted under s. 1(1) of the above Act of having taken photographs of a naked seven-year-old boy at a naturists-only session at a swimming pool. The prosecution at the trial adduced evidence of the purpose and motive for having taken the photos (i.e. sexual gratification) in order to seek to show that the pictures were

---

180 Home Office, *Consultation on the Possession of Extreme Pornographic Material* (2005), para. 15.

181 On sentencing issues see A. Gillespie [2003] Crim LR 81.

182 See A. Gillespie [2004] Crim LR 361.   183 [1988] 1 WLR 1098.

indecent. The Court of Appeal, allowing the appeal against conviction, held that the photos should be considered objectively, as to whether they infringed recognised standards of propriety, without consideration being given to the motivation of the person who had taken them. That person's state of mind would only be relevant where an issue arose as to whether pictures were taken intentionally or by accident.[184]

4. In *R v Fellows and Arnold*[185] the Court of Appeal (Criminal Division) held that, even prior to the amendments effected by the 1994 Act, the words of the statute covered the storage of a large archive of indecent photographs on a computer disk. The disk itself was not a 'photograph' as there was no 'picture or other image' on or in the disk. However, it was a 'copy of an indecent photograph', analogous to a piece of work with invisible ink, in that it contained data not visible to the eye which could be converted by appropriate technical means into a screen image and a print; the data itself 'represents the original photograph, in another form'.[186] The 1978 Act was to be interpreted as covering forms of photographs not in existence at the time the Act was passed. The court held, further, that the words 'with a view to them being distributed or shown by himself' extended to cover the situation where the defendant made available the archive to be downloaded by those to whom a password was given. If active conduct on the part of the defendant were required, the e-mail correspondence with and the giving of a password to others was sufficient. Moreover, the fact that the downloading of material involved a fresh reproduction of data did not mean that the defendant had not possessed photographs with a view to those same (copy) photographs being shown to others: 'the same data is transmitted to the recipient so that he shall see the same visual reproductions as is available to the sender whenever he has access to the archive himself'.[187]

A photograph or pseudo-photograph can be 'made' by downloading it and creating a file on a computer disk.[188] However, 'making' under s. 1(1)(a) of the 1978 Act requires an intentional act of creation; unknowingly storing images in a cache is not sufficient.[189] Furthermore, the 'possession' offence under s. 160 of the 1988 Act is not committed unless the defendant knows he has photographs in his possession. If the images have been deleted or can no longer be retrieved then they are not in 'possession'.[190] But voluntarily down loading an indecent image from an internet site on to a computer screen does amount to an act of making a photograph or pseudo-photograph; there is no need for an intention to store the images with a view to future retrieval.[191]

The offence under s. 1(1)(c) of the 1978 Act does not arise where photographs (here, a cine film) are only to be 'shown' to the defendant himself.[192]

Whether there is a 'legitimate reason' under s. 1(4)(a) of the 1978 Act or s. 160(2)(a) of the 1988 Act is a question of fact. The central issue where the defence is legitimate research is whether 'the defendant is essentially a person of unhealthy interests in possession of indecent photographs in the pretence of undertaking research, or by contrast a genuine researcher with no alternative but to have this sort of unpleasant material in his possession'.[193] For the

---

[184] See also *R v Smethurst* (2002) 1 Cr App R 6.

[185] [1997] 2 All ER 548. On the ruling at trial, see C. Manchester [1996] Crim LR 645.

[186] Per Evans LJ at 557.   [187] Ibid., at 558.

[188] *R v Bowden* [2000] 2 All ER 418, CA (Cr D) and *Atkins v DPP* [2000] 2 All ER 425, DC (rejecting the argument that 'make' only applied to pseudo-photographs); *R v Mould (David Frederick)* (6 November 2000, unreported).

[189] *Atkins v DPP*, above.   [190] *R v Porter* [2006] EWCA Crim 560.

[191] *R v Smith, R v Jayson* [2003] 1 Cr App R 212.

[192] *R v T (Child Pornography)* (1999) 163 JP 349.

[193] Per Simon Brown LJ in *Atkins v DPP*, above at 432–433.

defence under s. 1(4)(b) to be established, it is not enough that the defendant does not know there are indecent images of children in material where he does know there are indecent images.[194]

Section 2(3) makes it clear that it is a question of fact, based on inference, whether a person is a 'child' for these purposes; paediatric or expert evidence is not required.[195]

An item that is obviously comprised of parts of two different photographs cannot 'appear to be a photograph' for the purposes of s. 7(7) of the 1978 Act.[196]

5. The 1978 Act was invoked by the police in requiring the Saatchi Gallery in London to remove two photographs by the American photographer Tierney Gearon of his children (in various states of undress) from the *I Am A Camera* exhibition and the international fine art publisher Edward Booth-Clibborn to withdraw the book of the exhibition. The CPS subsequently ruled that there was no realistic prospect of any conviction and no charges were brought.[197] Would artistic expression amount to a 'legitimate reason' under s. 1(4)? Note that s. 1(4) does not apply to taking or making the photograph. It has been argued that this might render a conviction in some circumstances contrary to Art. 10 ECHR.[198] In *R v Smethhurst (John)*[199] the Court of Appeal held, however, that the offence did not contravene Arts 8 and 10 ECHR. The concept of 'indecent' was sufficiently certain, as assessed objectively by the jury; there was no need to imply a requirement that the photograph should be intended for an indecent purpose; and the offence was justified under Art. 10(2) as being for the protection of children.

- **Indecent Displays (Control) Act 1981**[200]

1. Indecent Displays

(1) If any indecent matter is publicly displayed the person making the display and any person causing or permitting the display to be made shall be guilty of an offence.

(2) Any matter which is displayed in or so as to be visible from any public place shall, for the purposes of this section, be deemed to be publicly displayed.

(3) In subsection (2) above, 'public place', in relation to the display of any matter, means any place to which the public have or are permitted to have access (whether on payment or otherwise) while that matter is displayed except—

(a) a place to which the public are permitted to have access only on payment which is or includes payment for that display; or

(b) a shop or any part of a shop to which the public can only gain access by passing beyond an adequate warning notice;

but the exclusions contained in paragraphs (a) and (b) above shall only apply where persons under the age of 18 years are not permitted to enter while the display in question is continuing.

(4) Nothing in this section applies in relation to any matter—

[(a) included by any person in a television broadcasting service or other television programme service (within the meaning of Part I of the Broadcasting Act 1990);][201]

---

[194] *R v Matrix (Billy)* [1997] Crim LR 901.   [195] *R v Land (Michael)* [1998] QB 65.

[196] *Goodland v DPP* [2000] 2 All ER 425 (heard with *Atkins v DPP*).

[197] *Index on Censorship*, 20 March 2001.

[198] A. Nicol, G. Millar and A. Sharland, *Media Law & Human Rights* (2001), pp. 119–120.

[199] [2001] EWCA Crim 722.

[200] See C. Manchester [1982] Stat LR 31; R. Stone (1981) 45 MLR 62; C. Munro (1981) 132 NLJ 629.

[201] As substituted by Broadcasting Act 1990, Sch. 20, para. 30.

(*b*) included in the display of an art gallery or museum and visible only from within the gallery or museum; or

(*c*) displayed by or with the authority of, and visible only from within a building occupied by, the Crown or any local authority; or

(*d*) included in a performance of a play (within the meaning of the Theatres Act 1968); or

[(*e*) included in a film exhibition as defined in the Cinemas Act 1985—

(i) given in a place which as regards that exhibition is required to be licensed under section 1 of that Act or by virtue only of sections 5, 7, or 8 of that Act, is not required to be so licensed; or

(ii) which is an exempted exhibition to which section 6 of that Act applies given by an exempted organisation as defined in subsection (6) of that section.][202]

(5) In this section 'matter' includes anything capable of being displayed, except that it does not include an actual human body or any part thereof; and in determining for the purpose of this section whether any displayed matter is indecent—

(*a*) there shall be disregarded any part of that matter which is not exposed to view; and

(*b*) account may be taken of the effect of juxtaposing one thing with another.

(6) A warning notice shall not be adequate for the purposes of this section unless it complies with the following requirements—

(*a*) The warning notice must contain the following words, and no others—

'WARNING

Persons passing beyond this notice will find material on display which they may consider indecent. No admittance to persons under 18 years of age.'

(*b*) The word 'WARNING' must appear as a heading.

(*c*) No pictures or other matter shall appear on the notice.

(*d*) The notice must be so situated that no one could reasonably gain access to the shop or part of the shop in question without being aware of the notice and it must be easily legible by any person gaining such access.

NOTES

1. Section 2(2) authorises constables to seize articles reasonably believed to be, or to contain, indecent matter and to have been used in the commission of an offence under the Act. Section 2(3) authorises justices of the peace to issue warrants authorising any constable to enter specified premises (if need be by force) and to seize any article reasonably believed to be or to contain, indecent matter and to have been used in the commission of an offence under the Act. The justice of the peace must be satisfied that there are reasonable grounds for suspecting commission of an offence under the Act.

2. Section 3 provides for the criminal liability of directors, managers, secretaries and other officers of corporate bodies which commit offences under the Act. The consent, connivance or neglect of the individual in question must be proved.

---

[202] As substituted by Cinemas Act 1985, Sch. 2, para. 13.

3. In *R v South Western Magistrates' Court, ex p Heslop*[203] the Divisional Court held that a stipendiary magistrate had been entitled to find, applying *R v Stanley*,[204] that a poster featuring a well-known model dressed only in underwear, to which offensive graffiti had been added, was not 'indecent'.

4. Section 46 of the Criminal Justice and Police Act 2001 created an offence of placing an advertisement relating to prostitution on or in the immediate vicinity of a public telephone. It may be extended, by order, to other public structures (s. 47).

---

[203] 18 May 1994, unreported.   [204] [1965] 1 All ER 1035.

11

CONTEMPT OF COURT

1. INTRODUCTION[1]

It is obvious that the administration of justice must be preserved free from improper interference and obstruction, and it is more or less inevitable that the courts will play a significant part in securing that end. There are a number of substantive criminal offences relating to the administration of justice, for example, perjury, subornation (i.e. inducing a witness to commit perjury), embracery (i.e. attempting to corrupt or improperly to influence a jury), perversion or obstruction of the course of public justice, and impeding the prosecution of a person who has committed an arrestable offence, contrary to s. 4(1) of the Criminal Law Act 1967. These offences have been considered by the Law Commission, who proposed the creation or retention of over 20 specific offences in order to bring more certainty into this area of the law.[2]

Superimposed upon these criminal offences is the power of the superior courts to punish contempts. The contempt power is of wide and uncertain scope, and in the UK is exercised according to a summary procedure unknown to any other branch of the law. Trial on indictment is a theoretical possibility, but proceedings are today invariably conducted summarily.[3] The summary procedure is of doubtful historical origin.[4] However, it is now too late to argue that the courts may not punish contempts summarily, given that many judges of high authority have acted on the then unchallenged assumption that they could.[5]

Classification of contempt is not easy. A basic distinction is drawn in England (although not in Scotland) between 'civil' and 'criminal' contempts. The former are cases of disobedience to an order of a court made in civil proceedings such as an injunction, the object of such contempt proceedings being essentially coercive (although occasionally punitive).[6] Other illustrations of civil contempts include breaches of undertakings given by litigants or their lawyers, illustrated graphically by the decision of the House of Lords in *M v Home*

---

[1] The main works cited in this chapter are: *Abraham:* H.J. Abraham and B.A. Perry, *Freedom and the Court* (7th edn, 1998); *Arlidge, Eady and Smith:* Sir David Eady and A.T.H. Smith, *Arlidge, Eady and Smith on Contempt* (3rd edn, 2005); *Borrie and Lowe:* N. Lowe and B. Sufrin, *Borrie and Lowe's Law of Contempt* (3rd edn, 1996); *Miller:* C.J. Miller, *Contempt of Court* (3rd edn, 2000); *Phillimore: Report of the Committee on Contempt of Court* (Cmnd 5794, 1974). In addition, see *Contempt of Court: A Discussion Paper* (Cmnd 7145, 1978); D. Feldman, *Civil Liberties and Human Rights in England and Wales* (2nd edn, 2002), Chap. 17; G. Robertson and A.G.L. Nicol, *Media Law* (5th edn, 2007), Chaps 7–9.

[2] See *Law Commission Report No. 96 on Offences Relating to Interference with the Course of Justice* (1979); R. Leng [1981] Crim LR 151.

[3] See *Arlidge, Eady and Smith*, p. 183.

[4] See *R v Almon* (1765) Wilm 243; Sir John Fox, *Contempt of Court* (1927); Frankfurter and Landis, 37 Harv LR 1010, 1046ff.

[5] See *James v Robinson* (1963) 109 CLR 593; Frankfurter J in *Green v United States* 356 US 165 at 189 (1958).

[6] See *Enfield London Borough Council v Mahoney* [1983] 2 All ER 901, CA.

Office[7] that Ministers of the Crown are amenable to this aspect of the contempt jurisdiction.[8] Criminal contempts are cases of interference with the administration of justice, and the aims of the proceedings are punitive and deterrent. There are some minor differences between the two forms. The most significant used to be that in civil contempt, committals could be *sine die*, until the contempt is purged: in criminal contempts, committals could only be for a fixed term.

Criminal contempts may be grouped under five headings:[9] (1) publications prejudicial to a fair criminal trial; (2) publications prejudicial to fair civil proceedings; (3) publications interfering with the course of justice as a continuing process; (4) contempt in the face of the court; and (5) acts which interfere with the course of justice. The materials given here concentrate on the first three aspects, as these tend to impinge most on freedom of expression, and the fourth, as this generates problems of natural justice and the right to a fair trial under Art. 6(1) ECHR. The general principles underlying the law of contempt are discussed in *A-G v Times Newspapers Ltd*[10] the first contempt case to reach the House of Lords.

The contempt power gives rise to concern on a number of points. Firstly, there is uncertainty as to its scope, which is undesirable given the heavy punishments that may be imposed. Secondly, it may inhibit unduly freedom of expression. Thirdly, the summary process may lack the qualities of procedural fairness that are essential for orthodox criminal proceedings. These considerations led the Phillimore Committee on Contempt of Court[11] to recommend that conduct *intended* to pervert the course of justice should be dealt with as a criminal offence unless there are compelling reasons requiring it to be dealt with as a matter of urgency by means of summary contempt procedures. Where there is no such intention, then the law of contempt should apply, but on a narrower basis than previously. Accordingly, strict liability should only attach to publications (and no other kinds of conduct) which create a risk of serious prejudice to the course of justice and which are addressed to the public at large during the currency of proceedings. The relevant time limits should be more narrowly drawn than the existing sub judice period. 'Scandalising the court' should no longer be punished as contempt, but as a criminal offence. Contempt in the face of the court should where appropriate be dealt with as a criminal offence, and where dealt with summarily there should be additional procedural safeguards for the defendant. The distinctions between 'civil' and 'criminal' contempt should be abolished. Many of these proposals were implemented in the Contempt of Court Act 1981,[12] although the Government took the view that on a number of points the Phillimore proposals for reducing the scope of contempt were too radical.[13] The 1981 Act has had some effect in narrowing and clarifying the law of contempt. However, recent decisions have shown that the common law of contempt, outside the 1981 Act, is by no means defunct. There have been important decisions dealing with publications *intended* to interfere with the administration of justice[14] and conduct which involves failure to respect the terms of an injunction directed to third parties.[15] The latter in particular has opened up what is in effect a new field of criminal contempt.

---

[7] [1994] 1 AC 377.

[8] See also *Harman v Secretary of State for the Home Department* [1983] 1 AC 280, HL; CPR 31.22; *Miller*, pp. 338–342. A civil contempt is not a criminal offence but does give rise to the privilege against self-incrimination: *Cobra Golf Ltd v Rata* [1997] 2 All ER 150. However, in *Lord Saville of Newdigate v Harnden* [2003] NICA 6, the Northern Ireland Court of Appeal held that contempts arising out of a journalist's refusal to reveal sources were criminal in nature.

[9] See *Borrie and Lowe*.   [10] [1974] AC 273. See below, p. 721.

[11] Cmnd 5794, 1974.   [12] See below, p. 687.   [13] Cmnd 7145.

[14] Pp. 718–720.   [15] Pp. 726–734.

Ultimately, in this context the law must draw an appropriate balance between the protection of free expression and ensuring fairness in the administration of justice. Both interests are reflected in explicit guarantees in the European Convention on Human Rights (Arts 10 and 6).[16] The first case before the European Court of Human Rights from the UK dealing with these issues, *Sunday Times v United Kingdom*[17] led to the Contempt of Court Act 1981[18] but whether English law has yet got the balance right remained controversial.

In the US, the contempt power has been much more narrowly defined by comparison with the British position. The Supreme Court has applied the Constitution's First Amendment guarantees of freedom of speech and of the press strictly against exercises of the contempt power. In *Bridges v California; Times-Mirror v California*[19] the Court held by 5 to 4 that utterances can only be punished as contempt where there is a clear and present danger to the orderly and fair administration of justice in relation to pending litigation: 'The substantive evil must be extremely serious and the degree of imminence extremely high before utterances can be punished.'[20] A 'reasonable tendency' is not sufficient. Subsequent cases have shown that the law of contempt is virtually a dead letter in protecting the trial process from prejudicial comment.[21] In addition, the constitutional right to jury trial in serious criminal cases (Fifth, Sixth and Fourteenth Amendments) has been held applicable to contempt cases.[22] In federal courts, the summary contempt power is limited by statute[23] to: '(1) Misbehaviour of any person in its presence or so near thereto as to obstruct the administration of justice; (2) Misbehaviour of any of its officers in their official transactions; (3) Disobedience or resistance to its lawful writ, process, order, rule, decree, or command.' The words 'so near thereto' have been held by the Supreme Court to bear a geographical rather than a causative meaning.[24] Some states have similar legislation narrowing the scope of the contempt power.

The *Sunday Times* case did not raise directly issues under Art. 6(1) ECHR. The relationship between Arts 6(1) and 10 was discussed by the European Court of Human Rights in *Worm v Austria*.[25] During the trial of a former minister for tax evasion W wrote an article asserting his guilt. The Court found that W's conviction for an offence of having exercised prohibited influence on criminal proceedings did not violate Art. 10. The Court stated:

50. Restrictions on freedom of expression permitted by the second paragraph of Article 10 'for maintaining the authority and impartiality of the judiciary' do not entitle States to restrict all forms of public discussion on matters pending before the courts.

There is general recognition of the fact that the courts cannot operate in a vacuum. Whilst the courts are the forum for the determination of a person's guilt or innocence on a criminal charge...this does not mean that there can be no prior or contemporaneous discussion of the subject matter of criminal trials elsewhere, be it in specialised journals, in the general press or amongst the public at large (see, *mutatis mutandis*, the *Sunday Times* (no. 1) p. 40 § 65]).

Provided that it does not overstep the bounds imposed in the interests of the proper administration of justice, reporting, including comment, on court proceedings contributes to their publicity and is thus perfectly consonant with the requirement under Article 6 § 1 of the Convention that hearings be public. Not only do the media have the task of imparting such information and ideas: the public also has a right to

---

[16] See above, pp. 29, 30.   [17] Above, p. 614.   [18] Below, p. 687.
[19] 314 US 252 (1941).   [20] Per Black J at 263.   [21] See below, pp. 714–715.
[22] *Bloom v Illinois* 391 US 194 (1968); *Miller*, pp. 136–138.
[23] 18 US Code, § 401, as derived originally from an Act of 1831.
[24] *Nye v United States* 313 US 33 (1941).
[25] (1997) 25 EHRR 454. See A. Mowbray, *Cases and Materials on the European Convention on Human Rights* (2nd edn), pp. 719–721.

receive them (ibid.). This is all the more so where a public figure is involved, such as, in the present case, a former member of the Government. Such persons inevitably and knowingly lay themselves open to close scrutiny by both journalists and the public at large (see, among other authorities, the *Lingens v Austria* judgment of 8 July 1986, Series A no. 103, p. 26, § 42). Accordingly, the limits of acceptable comment are wider as regards a politician as such than as regards a private individual (ibid.).

However, public figures are entitled to the enjoyment of the guarantees of a fair trial set out in Article 6, which in criminal proceedings include the right to an impartial tribunal, on the same basis as every other person. This must be borne in mind by journalists when commenting on pending criminal proceedings since the limits of permissible comment may not extend to statements which are likely to prejudice, whether intentionally or not, the chances of a person receiving a fair trial or to undermine the confidence of the public in the role of the courts in the administration of criminal justice.

Accordingly, there is no room for 'balancing'. This point was confirmed by the Privy Council in *Montgomery and Coulter v HM Advocate*.[26] Here the Privy Council upheld the decision of the High Court of Justiciary that to proceed to the trial of the applicants for murder notwithstanding considerable prejudicial publicity would not breach Art. 6(1). Lord Hope stated:

Reference was also made to Application No. 17265/90 *Baragiola v Switzerland* (1993) 75 D.R. 76. In that case the Commission observed, at p. 120, that, while particular importance should be attached to the freedom of the press because of the public's right to information, a fair balance must nevertheless be struck between that freedom and the right to a fair trial guaranteed by article 6 of the Convention and that a restrictive interpretation of article 6(1) would not correspond to the aim and purpose of that provision. As I understand these observations, however, they were intended to emphasise the point that primacy must be given to the right to a fair trial. Article 6, unlike articles 8 to 11 of the Convention, is not subject to any words of limitation. It does not require, nor indeed does it permit, a balance to be struck between the rights which it sets out and other considerations such as the public interest. In so far as the *Baragiola* case may be taken as suggesting that in the application of article 6(1) a balance must be struck between the right of an individual to a fair trial and the freedom of the press or the public's right to information, I would be inclined not to follow it on the ground that this suggestion is inconsistent with the wording of the Convention. The suggestion is not, so far as I am aware, supported by any other authority.

Even without balancing, however, the European Court of Human Rights has yet to find a breach of Art. 6(1) arising from prejudicial publicity.[27] The Court will take account of the role of the judge in giving directions to the jury in ensuring a fair trial.[28]

2. THE CONTEMPT OF COURT ACT 1981[29]

In this section we set out the provisions of the Contempt of Court Act 1981. This Act does not codify the whole of the law of contempt of court. It simply modifies certain aspects of the previously existing law. One significant feature that should be noted is that the first seven

---

[26] DRA Nos 1 and 2 of 2000 [2001] 2 WLR 779.

[27] See D.J. Harris, M. O'Boyle and C. Warbrick, *The European Convention on Human Rights* (1995), p. 216, noting that the Commission seemed to require proof of a prejudicial effect on a jury in fact rather than just an indication that it is likely.

[28] Cf. *Pullar v UK* (1996) 22 EHRR 391 (P's misgivings about the impartiality of a juror could not be objectively justified).

[29] The Act is considered in the following works: *Borrie and Lowe; Miller; Arlidge, Eady and Smith; Current Law Statutes Annotated 1981* (annotations by A.G.L. Nicol and (for Scotland) C.H.W. Gane): N. Lowe [1982] PL 20; C.J. Miller [1982] Crim LR 71; S.H. Bailey (1982) 45 MLR 301; P.J. Cooke [1983] V (1) Liverpool LR 35.

sections deal with what the Act terms the 'strict liability rule', as defined in s. 1. Accordingly, conduct *intended* to interfere with the course of justice will be regulated by (a) the common law of contempt except insofar as it is modified by the remaining provisions of the 1981 Act or (b) the substantive offences relating to the administration of justice.[30]

In the remaining sections of the chapter we consider in turn the main varieties of criminal contempt, and within each section the position at common law is set out first, followed by a summary of the position following the enactment of the Contempt of Court Act 1981.

- **Contempt of Court Act 1981**

Strict liability

1. The strict liability rule

In this Act 'the strict liability rule' means the rule of law whereby conduct may be treated as a contempt of court as tending to interfere with the course of justice in particular legal proceedings regardless of intent to do so.

2. Limitation of scope of strict liability

(1) The strict liability rule applies only in relation to publications, and for this purpose 'publication' includes any speech, writing, [programme included in a programme service][31] or other communication in whatever form, which is addressed to the public at large or any section of the public.

(2) The strict liability rule applies only to a publication which creates a substantial risk that the course of justice in the proceedings in question will be seriously impeded or prejudiced.

(3) The strict liability rule applies to a publication only if the proceedings in question are active within the meaning of this section at the time of the publication.

(4) Schedule 1 applies for determining the times at which proceedings are to be treated as active within the meaning of this section.

[(5) In this section 'programme service' has the same meaning as in the Broadcasting Act 1990.][32]

3. Defence of innocent publication or distribution

(1) A person is not guilty of contempt of court under the strict liability rule as the publisher of any matter to which that rule applies if at the time of publication (having taken all reasonable care) he does not know and has no reason to suspect that relevant proceedings are active.

(2) A person is not guilty of contempt of court under the strict liability rule as the distributor of a publication containing any such matter if at the time of distribution (having taken all reasonable care) he does not know that it contains such matter and has no reason to suspect that it is likely to do so.

(3) The burden of proof of any fact tending to establish a defence afforded by this section to any person lies upon that person....

4. Contemporary reports of proceedings

(1) Subject to this section a person is not guilty of contempt of court under the strict liability rule in respect of a fair and accurate report of legal proceedings held in public, published contemporaneously and in good faith.

---

[30] See above, p. 684.   [31] Substituted by the Broadcasting Act 1990, Sch. 20, para. 31.
[32] Added by the Broadcasting Act 1990, Sch. 20. See s. 201, as amended.

(2) In any such proceedings the court may, where it appears to be necessary for avoiding a substantial risk of prejudice to the administration of justice in those proceedings, or in any other proceedings pending or imminent, order that the publication of any report of the proceedings, or any part of the proceedings, be postponed for such period as the court thinks necessary for that purpose.

[(2A) Where in proceedings for any offence which is an administration of justice offence for the purposes of section 54 of the Criminal Procedure and Investigations Act 1996 (acquittal tainted by an administration of justice offence) it appears to the court that there is a possibility that (by virtue of that section) proceedings may be taken against a person for an offence of which he has been acquitted, subsection (2) of this section shall apply as if those proceedings were pending or imminent.][33]

(3) For the purposes of subsection (1) of this section [...][34] a report of proceedings shall be treated as published contemporaneously—

(a) in the case of a report of which publication is postponed pursuant to an order under subsection (2) of this section, if published as soon as practicable after that order expires;

[(b) in the case of a report of committal proceedings to which publication is permitted by virtue only of subsection (3) of section 8 of the Magistrates' Courts Act 1980, if published as soon as practicable after publication is so permitted.[35]]

5. Discussion of public affairs

A publication made as or as part of a discussion in good faith of public affairs or other matters of general public interest is not to be treated as a contempt of court under the strict liability rule if the risk of impediment or prejudice to particular legal proceedings is merely incidental to the discussion.

6. Savings

Nothing in the foregoing provisions of this Act—

(a) prejudices any defence available at common law to a charge of contempt of court under the strict liability rule;

(b) implies that any publication is punishable as contempt of court under that rule which would not be so punishable apart from those provisions;

(c) restricts liability for contempt of court in respect of conduct intended to impede or prejudice the administration of justice.

7. Consent required for institution of proceedings

Proceedings for a contempt of court under the strict liability rule (other than Scottish proceedings) shall not be instituted except by or with the consent of the Attorney-General or on the motion of a court having jurisdiction to deal with it.

Other aspects of law and procedure

8. Confidentiality of jury's deliberations

(1) Subject to subsection (2) below, it is a contempt of court to obtain, disclose or solicit any particulars of statements made, opinions expressed, arguments advanced or votes cast by members of a jury in the course of their deliberations in any legal proceedings.

(2) This section does not apply to any disclosure of any particulars—

(a) in the proceedings in question for the purpose of enabling the jury to arrive at their verdict, or in connection with the delivery of that verdict, or

---

33 Added by the Criminal Procedure and Investigations Act 1996, s. 57(3).
34 Words repealed by the Defamation Act 1996, Sch. 2.
35 To be replaced by the Criminal Justice Act 2003, s. 41, Sch. 3, Pt 2, para. 53 from a day to be appointed.

(b) in evidence in any subsequent proceedings for an offence alleged to have been committed in relation to the jury in the first mentioned proceedings, or to the publication of any particulars so disclosed.

(3) Proceedings for a contempt of court under this section (other than Scottish proceedings) shall not be instituted except by or with the consent of the Attorney-General or on the motion of a court having jurisdiction to deal with it.

9. Use of tape recorders

(1) Subject to subsection (4) below, it is a contempt of court—

(a) to use in court, or bring into court for use, any tape recorder or other instrument for recording sound, except with the leave of the court;

(b) to publish a recording of legal proceedings made by means of any such instrument, or any recording derived directly or indirectly from it, by playing it in the hearing of the public or any section of the public, or to dispose of it or any recording so derived. with a view to such publication;

(c) to use any such recording in contravention of any conditions of leave granted under paragraph (a).

(2) Leave under paragraph (a) of subsection (1) may be granted or refused at the discretion of the court, and if granted may be granted subject to such conditions as the court thinks proper with respect to the use of any recording made pursuant to the leave; and where leave has been granted the court may at the like discretion withdraw or amend it either generally or in relation to any particular part of the proceedings.

(3) Without prejudice to any other power to deal with an act of contempt under paragraph (a) of subsection (1). the court may order the instrument, or any recording made with it, or both, to be forfeited; and any object so forfeited shall (unless the court otherwise determines on application by a person appearing to be the owner) be sold or otherwise disposed of in such manner as the court may direct.

(4) This section does not apply to the making or use of sound recordings for purposes of official transcripts of proceedings.

10. Sources of information

No court may require a person to disclose, nor is any person guilty of contempt of court for refusing to disclose, the source of information contained in a publication for which he is responsible, unless it be established to the satisfaction of the court that disclosure is necessary in the interests of justice or national security or for the prevention of disorder or crime.

11. Publication of matters exempted from disclosure in court

In any case where a court (having power to do so) allows a name or other matter to be withheld from the public in proceedings before the court, the court may give such directions prohibiting the publication of that name or matter in connection with the proceedings as appear to the court to be necessary for the purpose for which it was so withheld.

12. Offences of contempt of magistrates' courts

(1) A magistrates' court has jurisdiction under this section to deal with any person who—

(a) wilfully insults the justice or justices, any witness before or officer of the court[36] or any solicitor or counsel having business in the court, during his or their sitting or attendance in court or in going to or returning from the court; or

(b) wilfully interrupts the proceedings of the court or otherwise misbehaves in court.

---

[36] The reference to any officer of the court includes a reference to any court security officer assigned to the court-house in which the court is sitting: Criminal Justice Act 1991, Sch. 11, para. 29. On court security officers, see the 1991 Act, ss. 76–79.

(2) In any such case the court may order any officer of the court, or any constable, to take the offender into custody and detain him until the rising of the court; and the court may, if it thinks fit, commit the offender to custody for a specified period not exceeding one month or impose on him a fine not exceeding [£2,500] or both....

[(2A) A fine imposed under subsection (2) above shall be deemed, for the purposes of any enactment, to be a sum adjudged to be paid by a conviction.][37] ...

(4) A magistrates' court may at any time revoke an order of committal made under subsection (2) and, if the offender is in custody, order his discharge...

Penalties for contempt and kindred offences

14. Proceedings in England and Wales

(1) In any case where a court has power to commit a person to prison for contempt of court and (apart from this provision) no limitation applies to the period of committal, the committal shall (without prejudice to the power of the court to order his earlier discharge) be for a fixed term, and that term shall not on any occasion exceed two years in the case of committal by a superior court, or one month in the case of committal by an inferior court.

(2) In any case where an inferior court has power to fine a person for contempt of court and (apart from this provision) no limit applies to the amount of the fine, the fine shall not on any occasion exceed [£2,500]....

[(2A) A fine imposed under subsection (2) above shall be deemed, for the purposes of any enactment, to be a sum adjudged to be paid by a conviction.][38] ...

(4) and (4A) [*Persons suffering from mental illness or severe mental impairment*]

[(4A) For the purposes of the preceding provisions of this section a county court shall be treated as a superior court and not as an inferior court.] ...

19. Interpretation

In this Act

'court' includes any tribunal or body exercising the judicial power of the State, and 'legal proceedings' shall be construed accordingly;

'publication' has the meaning assigned by subsection (1) of section 2, and 'publish' (except in section 9) shall be construed accordingly;...

'the strict liability rule' has the meaning assigned by section 1;

'superior court' means the Court of Appeal, the High Court, the Crown Court, the Courts-Martial Appeal Court, the Restrictive Practices Court, the Employment Appeal Tribunal and any other court exercising in relation to its proceedings powers equivalent to those of the High Court, and includes the House of Lords in the exercise of its appellate jurisdiction...[39]

---

37 Substituted by the Criminal Justice Act 1993, Sch. 3, para. 6(4).

38 Substituted by the Criminal Justice Act 1993, Sch. 3, para. 6(5).

39 A reference to the Supreme Court is to be added and the reference to the House of Lords repealed by the Constitutional Reform Act, Sch. 9, Pt 3, para. 35(1), (3).

SCHEDULE 1

TIMES WHEN PROCEEDINGS ARE ACTIVE FOR PURPOSES OF SECTION 2

Preliminary

1. In this Schedule 'criminal proceedings' means proceedings against a person in respect of an offence, not being appellate proceedings or proceedings commenced by motion for committal or attachment in England and Wales or Northern Ireland; and 'appellate proceedings' means proceedings on appeal from or for the review of the decision of a court in any proceedings.[40]

2. Criminal, appellate and other proceedings are active within the meaning of section 2 at the times respectively prescribed by the following paragraphs of this Schedule; and in relation to proceedings in which more than one of the steps described in any of those paragraphs is taken, the reference in that paragraph is a reference to the first of those steps.

Criminal proceedings

3. Subject to the following provisions of this Schedule, criminal proceedings are active from the relevant initial step specified in paragraph 4 [or 4A][41] until concluded as described in paragraph 5.

4. The initial steps of criminal proceedings are:—

   (a) arrest without warrant;

   (b) the issue, or in Scotland the grant, of a warrant for arrest;

   (c) the issue of a summons to appear, or in Scotland the grant of a warrant to cite;

   (d) the service of an indictment or other document specifying the charge;

   (e) except in Scotland, oral charge.

[(4A) Where as a result of an order under section 54 of the Criminal Procedure and Investigations Act 1996 (acquittal tainted by an administration of justice offence) proceedings are brought against a person for an offence of which he has previously been acquitted the initial step of the proceedings is a certification under subsection (2) of that section; and paragraph 4 has effect subject to this.][42]

5. Criminal proceedings are concluded

   (a) by acquittal or, as the case may be, by sentence;

   (b) by any other verdict, finding, order or decision which puts an end to the proceedings:

   (c) by discontinuance or by operation of law.

6. The reference in paragraph 5(a) to sentence includes any order or decision consequent on conviction or finding of guilt which disposes of the case, either absolutely or subject to future events, and a deferment of sentence under [section 1 of the Powers of Criminal Courts (Sentencing) Act 2000]....

7. Proceedings are discontinued within the meaning of paragraph 5(c)—

   (a) in England and Wales or Northern Ireland, if the charge or summons is withdrawn or a nolle prosequi entered;

   [(aa) in England and Wales, if they are discontinued by virtue of section 23 of the Prosecution of Offences Act 1985;][43] ...

   (b) in the case of proceedings in England and Wales or Northern Ireland commenced by arrest without warrant, if the person arrested is released, otherwise than on bail, without having been charged.

---

[40] The reference to an offence is to include a service offence within the meaning of the Armed Forces Act 2006, from a day to be appointed: 2006 Act, Sch. 16, para. 92, inserting para. 1A in the Schedule.

[41] Added by the Criminal Procedure and Investigations Act 1996, s. 57(4).

[42] Ibid.   [43] Added by the Prosecution of Offences Act 1985, Sch. 1, para. 4.

8. Criminal proceedings before a court-martial or standing civilian court are not concluded until the completion of any review of finding or sentence.

9. Criminal proceedings in England and Wales or Northern Ireland cease to be active if an order is made for the charge to lie on the file, but become active again if leave is later given for the proceedings to continue.

[9A. Where proceedings in England and Wales have been discontinued by virtue of section 23 of the Prosecution of Offences Act 1985, but notice is given by the accused under subsection (7) of that section to the effect that he wants the proceedings to continue, they become active again with the giving of that notice.][44]

10. Without prejudice to paragraph 5(*b*) above, criminal proceedings against a person cease to be active—

   (*a*) if the accused is found to be under a disability such as to render him unfit to be tried or unfit to plead...; or

   (*b*) if a hospital order is made in his case under [section 51(5) of the Mental Health Act 1983]...

   but become active again if they are later resumed.

11. Criminal proceedings against a person which become active on the issue or the grant of a warrant for his arrest cease to be active at the end of the period of twelve months beginning with the date of the warrant unless he has been arrested within that period, but become active again if he is subsequently arrested.

Other proceedings at first instance

12. Proceedings other than criminal proceedings and appellate proceedings are active from the time when arrangements for the hearing are made or, if no such arrangements are previously made, from the time the hearing begins, until the proceedings are disposed of or discontinued or withdrawn; and for the purposes of this paragraph any motion or application made in or for the purposes of any proceedings, and any pre-trial review in the county court, is to be treated as a distinct proceeding.

13. In England and Wales or Northern Ireland arrangements for the hearing of proceedings to which paragraph 12 applies are made within the meaning of that paragraph—

   (*a*) in the case of proceedings in the High Court for which provision is made by rules of court for setting down for trial, when the case is set down;

   (*b*) in the case of any proceedings, when a date for the trial or hearing is fixed....

Appellate proceedings

15. Appellate proceedings are active from the time when they are commenced—

   (*a*) by application for leave to appeal or apply for review, or by notice of such an application;

   (*b*) by notice of appeal or of application for review;

   (*c*) by other originating process,

   until disposed of or abandoned, discontinued or withdrawn.

16. Where, in appellate proceedings relating to criminal proceedings, the court—

   (*a*) remits the case to the court below; or

   (*b*) orders a new trial or a venire de novo....,

   any further or new proceedings which result shall be treated as active from the conclusion of the appellate proceedings.

----

44 Added by the Prosecution of Offences Act 1985, Sch. 1, para. 5.

NOTES

1. By mistake, two sub-ss. (4A) have been inserted in s. 14. The second (the one printed here) was introduced by the County Court (Penalties for Contempt) Act 1983 and was enacted to deal with the restriction on the powers of county courts to deal with civil contempts high-lighted by the decision of the House of Lords in *Peart v Stewart*.[45] The fines in ss. 12(2) and 14(2) were increased by the Criminal Justice Act 1991, Sch. 4. The limits to the penalties for contempt apply to civil as well as criminal contempts.[46] A judge may not impose on one occa-sion consecutive sentences which cumulatively exceed two years.[47] A person found guilty of criminal contempt is not 'convicted of an offence' and so may not be put on probation.[48]

2. The real impetus to reform seems to have been the decision of the European Court of Human Rights in the *Sunday Times* case[49] that the restriction placed upon freedom of speech by the injunction against the newspaper, upheld by the House of Lords in *A-G v Times Newspapers Ltd*[50] was contrary to Art. 10 of the European Convention on Human Rights. The Bill was introduced in the House of Lords by Lord Hailsham of St Marylebone LC.[51] He said that his 'poor little ewe lamb' of a Bill was intended to be a liberalising measure. The three main purposes of the first group of sections, dealing with the so-called rule of strict liability in criminal contempt, were: (a) implementation of the main recommendations of the Phillimore report, with 'minor deviations'; (b) harmonisation of the law of England and Wales with the European Court's judgment in the *Sunday Times* case; and (c) harmonisation of the laws of England, Scotland and Northern Ireland into a coherent set of rules. The other sections either sought to implement other recommendations of the Phillimore Committee or to deal with problems that had arisen since the Committee reported. The Act came into force on 27 August 1981. It has been a matter of debate whether the Act does enough to bring English law into conformity with the European Convention on Human Rights,[52] but there have not been major challenges under the Human Rights Act 1998.

3. PUBLICATIONS PREJUDICIAL TO A FAIR CRIMINAL TRIAL

The main area where uncertainties in the law of contempt cast a shadow over free expres-sion is that of publications which tend to prejudice the fair trial of either criminal or civil proceedings, or otherwise interfere with the course of justice. The important criticisms made to the Phillimore Committee were (a) 'the lack of clear definition of the kind of statement, criticism or comment which will be held to amount to contempt'[53] and (b) 'the uncertainty as to the time when the law of contempt applies'.[54] Where it is sought to hold persons liable under the 'strict liability rule'[55] the law on these points has been modified by ss. 2 and 3 of and Sch. 1 to the 1981 Act.[56] Prior to the 1981 Act it was more or less settled that the common law imposed strict liability for this form of contempt, subject to certain statutory defences.[57] Strict liability can now only be imposed by virtue of ss. 1–7 of the 1981 Act. Recent cases have

---

[45] [1983] 2 AC 109, HL.   [46] *Linnett v Coles* [1987] QB 555, CA.
[47] *Re R (a minor) (contempt: sentence)* [1994] 2 All ER 144; *Villiers v Villiers* [1994] 2 All ER 149, CA.
[48] *R v Palmer* [1992] 3 All ER 289, CA (Cr D).   [49] Above, p. 614.
[50] Below, p. 721.   [51] 415 HL Deb, 9 December 1980, cols 657–665.
[52] See below, p. 725, n. 4.   [53] Para. 83.   [54] Para. 84.
[55] Contempt of Court Act 1981, s. 1; above p. 687.
[56] Above, pp. 688–693 and below pp. 698–708 and 716–717.   [57] See below, pp. 717.

made it clear that publications (and indeed other conduct) *intended* to interfere with justice can still be dealt with under the common law of contempt. Here, the issues of what constitutes contempt, when the sub judice rule applies and the scope of liability are regulated by the common law and not the 1981 Act.[58]

The balance between freedom of expression and the right to a fair trial is different in the UK and the US, and there are important sectors of opinion in each country which express dissatisfaction with their country's own position.

(A) WHAT CONSTITUTES CONTEMPT?

(I) AT COMMON LAW

- **R v Evening Standard Co Ltd** [1954] 1 QB 578, [1954] 1 All ER 1026,
  [1954] 2 WLR 861, Queen's Bench Divisional Court

Mr Kemp was on trial for the murder of his wife, who had been dead for a considerable time before his arrest and whose body was discovered in a trunk which he had caused to be moved with his effects. Part of the case for the Crown was that the defendant had told many lies with regard to the disappearance of his wife. The *Evening Standard* carried a report that a witness had said that Kemp had asked her to marry him. In fact, this evidence had been given at the committal proceedings but ruled inadmissible at the trial, as it was highly prejudicial. The reporter at the trial was responsible for the error—he had attended the committal proceedings, and had left the trial during the discussion as to the admissibility of part of Miss Briggs' evidence, returning just after she had completed her evidence. In fact the jury found the defendant not guilty.

The Attorney-General applied for leave to issue a writ of attachment against the Evening Standard Co Ltd, the editor of the *Evening Standard* and the reporter. According to an affidavit filed by the editor the reporter had for 10 years been a trusted reporter on the staff of the newspaper and had previously reported many trials without any complaint as to the accuracy of his reports, and had proved himself a thoroughly competent and reliable reporter. He had thought the report perfectly accurate and genuine and he and the proprietors had published it in good faith.

Lord Goddard CJ delivered the judgment of the court (**Lord Goddard CJ**, **Hilbery** and **Hallett JJ**):....
This is surely a proper matter to bring before this court. It is just as well that the nature of the jurisdiction which this court exercises on these occasions with regard to reports of trials in newspapers should be understood. It is called contempt of court, and that is a convenient expression because it is akin to a contempt. But the essence of the jurisdiction is that reports, if they contain comments on cases before they are tried, or alleged histories of the prisoner who is on trial—such as in the case of the *Daily Mirror* (*R v Bolam. ex p Haigh* (1949) 93 Sol Jo 220), in which this court had to intervene about five years ago—and all misreports are matters which tend to interfere with the due course of justice. The foundation of the jurisdiction is that such reports are an interference with the due course of justice, and one of the earliest cases, if not the earliest, in which this jurisdiction was invoked was in 1742, in a case known as *The St. James Evening Post* ((1742) 2 Atk 469) before that great judge, Lord Hardwicke LC. In that case there was a motion to commit an editor for publishing a libel upon a litigant and it was objected that it was

---

[58] See below, pp. 695–698, 715–716, 718–720.

not a matter for the summary jurisdiction of the court because there was a remedy at law for libel. Lord Hardwicke pointed out that he was dealing with the matter of the publication of a libel upon a litigant in a case which had not then come to a conclusion or been heard. He started his judgment by saying (ibid.): 'Nothing is more incumbent upon courts of justice, than to preserve their proceedings from being misrepresented;—that is, of course, what has happened here—'nor is there any thing of more pernicious consequence, than to prejudice the minds of the public against persons concerned as parties in causes, before the cause is finally heard.' After rejecting the argument that he could not deal summarily with the case because there was a remedy at law, he considered the different sorts of contempt. The last one was (ibid. p. 471): 'There may be also a contempt of this court, in prejudicing mankind against persons before the cause is heard. There cannot be any thing of greater consequence, than to keep the streams of justice clear and pure, that parties may proceed with safety both to themselves and their characters.'...

We have said, perhaps more frequently in recent years, that the summary jurisdiction of this court should only be invoked and will only be exercised in cases of real and serious moment; and have deprecated in certain cases a motion to attach where there has not really been a serious interference with justice. This case might have been a disastrous interference with justice; but, as Lord Hewart CJ said in *R v Editor of the New Statesman, ex p DPP* (1928) 44 TLR 301 at 303 the gravity of the penalty or sanction which the court will impose must depend upon the circumstances of each particular case. If a comment is gratuitously published either in a newspaper or in any other form of public dissemination, this court would not hesitate to impose a severe penalty, and even, as in the recent case of the *Daily Mirror* (*R v Bolam, ex p Haigh* (1949) 93 Sol Jo 220) to inflict the penalty of imprisonment. In this case, however, I am glad to be able to come to the conclusion that there was here no intentional interference with the course of justice. I cannot believe that the reporter for a moment deliberately or intentionally sent out false information. He, as a responsible journalist, would know that doing so would land him in the gravest possible difficulty. Nor can one attach moral blame, if I may use that expression, to the editor, who had no reason to suppose that a reporter of the 'Standard' had sent him information in an inaccurate form. There are, therefore, mitigating circumstances, and one can only be thankful that the matter did not react unfavourably on the prisoner, though, as I have said whether it reacts favourably or unfavourably upon the prisoner is not the test.

Sir Hartley Shawcross said that, while his clients desired to abide by the well understood rule of journalism that the editor and proprietors of papers must in a case such as this take responsibility, he would suggest to the court that vicarious liability, as it is called, ought not in law to be visited upon them and that they ought not to be made vicariously liable for the mistake or misconduct of the reporter. I do not think that we can possibly agree with that submission, which seems contrary to what Lord Russell and Wright J said in *R v Payne* [1896] 1 QB 577 where they pointed out that the court would interfere where the publication was intended or calculated or likely to interfere with the course of justice. Wright J (ibid. p. 582) used the word 'likely,' Lord Russell (ibid. p. 580) used the word 'calculated'.

[The court held that all the defendants were guilty of contempt, but that no penalty should be imposed on the editor and reporter. The publishers were fined £1,000.]

NOTES

1. Note that the Divisional Court was not concerned with the actual effect upon proceedings, but the potential effect, particularly on a jury.[59] This and other cases show that the test at common law was whether a publication was 'calculated' or 'likely' to interfere with the course of justice or, in other words, whether it created a real risk that the fair and proper trial of pending proceedings might be prejudiced. This remains the test where contempt

---

[59] Cf. *A-G for New South Wales v John Fairfax & Sons Ltd* [1980] 1 NSWLR 362, 368 (NSWCA).

proceedings are taken in respect of conduct *intended* to interfere with the course of justice, with the possible qualification that the proceedings need not be pending or imminent.[60] The common law is also of relevance in as much as s. 6(b) of the Contempt of Court Act 1981 provides that nothing in ss. 1–5 implies that any publication is punishable as contempt of court under the strict liability rule which would not have been so punishable apart from those provisions: i.e. at common law.

2. The following are some examples of contempt in cases decided before the 1981 Act came into operation. Some involved prejudging the merits of cases at common law. In *R v Bolam, ex p Haigh*[61] B, the editor of the *Daily Mirror,* was imprisoned for three months, and the proprietors were fined £10,000 for describing Haigh as a 'vampire' and, after saying that he was charged with one murder, stating that he had committed others, giving the names of the victims.[62] In the 1920s, various newspapers conducted systematic 'criminal investigations' whose results were then published. This led to fines of £1,000 imposed on the *Evening Standard,* and of £300 on two other newspapers, with a warning that repetition of the offence would lead to imprisonment.[63]

In the *Sunday Times* case,[64] the House of Lords held that prejudgment of the merits amounted to a contempt of court. The facts concerned civil proceedings, but a distinction between civil and criminal proceedings was not drawn for this purpose. However, in subsequent cases the Divisional Court held that prejudgment only amounted to contempt where it created a real risk that the fair and proper trial of pending proceedings might be prejudiced.[65]

Other examples include comments on a defendant's character,[66] the revelation of guilty plea during a trial that had been kept from the jury[67] and the publication of a photograph of a person on the day he was due to take part in an identification parade.[68]

3. As discussed below[69] common law liability for contempt may arise from conduct (including publications) which, with the requisite intent, 'frustrates, thwarts or subverts the purpose of the court's order and thereby interferes with the due administration of justice in the particular action'; 'purpose' here means the purpose the court was intending to fulfil: *A-G v Times Newspapers Ltd.*[70] This principle applies where the order in question is directed at persons other than the respondent to the contempt proceedings (see further *A-G v Newspaper Publishing plc*[71] and *A-G v Times Newspapers Ltd*[72] concerning orders made in civil proceedings). In *A-G v Newspaper Publishing plc,*[73] the Court of Appeal (Criminal Division) at the end of the hearing of the appeals of four persons connected with Ordtech Ltd against convictions for conspiracy to export armaments to Iraq in breach of control orders, ordered that various documents previously the subject of PII claims but now disclosed for the purpose of the appeal only should be returned. Lord Taylor CJ also

---

[60] See below, pp. 716, 718–720.   [61] (1949) 93 Sol Jo 220.

[62] Cf. *R v Odham's Press Ltd, ex p A-G* [1957] 1 QB 73.

[63] *R v Evening Standard, ex p DPP* (1924) 40 TLR 833.   [64] Below p. 721.

[65] *Blackburn v BBC* (1976) Times, 15 December; *R v Bulgin, ex p BBC* (1977) Times, 14 July.

[66] *R v Thomson Newspapers, ex p A-G* [1968] 1 All ER 268; the defendant's appeal against conviction was, however, rejected: *R v Malik* [1968] 1 All ER 582n.

[67] *R v Border Television Ltd, ex p A-G; R v Newcastle Chronicle and Journal Ltd, ex p A-G* (1978) 68 Cr App R 375, DC.

[68] *R v Evening Standard Co Ltd, ex p A-G* (1976) Times, 3 November, DC.

[69] Pp. 718–720.

[70] [1992] 1 AC 191, 222–223, per Lord Oliver, cited by Lord Bingham CJ in *A-G v Newspaper Publishing plc* [1997] 3 All ER 159 at 168.

[71] [1988] Ch 333.   [72] [1992] 1 AC 191, below, p. 733.   [73] [1997] 3 All ER 159.

expressed the hope 'that we will not see any more of the documents appearing on television or in the newspapers'. Subsequently the *Independent* published a facsimile of part of one of these documents and some sentences from another, including words that had not been quoted in the judgment. The Court of Appeal (Criminal Division) held that these publications did not constitute contempt. For contempt the order in question had to be clear and infringement would have to have 'some significant adverse effect on the administration of justice' (although not necessarily that it had been 'wholly frustrated or rendered utterly futile').[74] 'Recognising that the restraints upon freedom of expression should be no wider than are truly necessary in a democratic society, we do not accept that conduct by a third party which is inconsistent with a court order in only trivial or technical way should expose a party to conviction for contempt.'[75] The breaches here were very minor: the publication of a few additional sentences and the reproduction of the form of documents did not amount to a significant interference with the administration of justice. Furthermore, mens rea was not established given that the respondents were genuinely uncertain as to the effect of the order.[76]

(II) UNDER THE 'STRICT LIABILITY RULE'

Section 2 of the Contempt of Court Act 1981[77] provides that there can only be liability for contempt under the strict liability rule where a 'publication' (see s. 2(1)) 'creates a substantial risk that the course of justice in the proceedings in question will be seriously impeded or prejudiced' (s. 2(2)). This is more stringent than the test at common law. This test was based on that recommended by the Phillimore Committee[78] but with the addition of the word 'substantial'. Note that strict liability is now confined to 'publications', as recommended by the Phillimore Committee[79] whose view was that strict liability should be confined to public conduct. To what extent does the new test constitute a real and not merely a 'semantic' or 'cosmetic' relaxation in the application of the law of contempt? See *Borrie and Lowe*.[80] Do you think that any of the cases where D was convicted at common law would have been decided differently had the new test been in operation? Section 2(2) has been applied in *A-G v English*[81] and *A-G v Times Newspapers*.[82] As to its application in respect of civil cases, see below.[83]

● **A-G v English** [1983] 1 AC 116, [1982] 2 All ER 903, [1982] 3 WLR 278, House of Lords

In October 1981 the *Daily Mail* published an article under the heading 'The vision of life that wins my vote' written by the journalist and broadcaster Malcolm Muggeridge in support of a parliamentary candidate, Mrs Marilyn Carr, who was seeking election as a pro-life candidate. The article was concerned with preserving the sanctity of human life. It also noted that Mrs Carr had been born without arms and continued: 'Today the chances of such a baby surviving would be very small indeed. Someone would surely recommend letting her die of starvation, or otherwise disposing of her.' The article was published on the third day of the trial of a consultant paediatrician, Dr Leonard Arthur, for the murder of John Pearson, a baby suffering from Down's syndrome. The trial judge, Farquharson J, referred the article to the Attorney-General, who applied to the Divisional Court for an order of committal against the editor of the *Daily Mail*, David English, and the newspaper's owners. He relied on

---

[74] [1997] 3 All ER 159, 168.   [75] Ibid.
[76] See further on mens rea, below, pp. 717–720.   [77] Above, p. 688.
[78] Cmnd 5794, 1974, pp. 44–49.   [79] Pp. 33–35.   [80] Pp. 113–115.
[81] [1983] 1 AC 116, HL.   [82] (1983) Times, 12 February, DC.   [83] Pp. 734–737.

the 'strict liability rule' contained in s. 1 of the Contempt of Court Act 1981. The defendant relied on s. 5 of the 1981 Act.[84] The Divisional Court held that the publication amounted to contempt. No penalty was imposed on the editor; he had been absent from the office at the relevant times and was not personally responsible for the publication. A 'nominal' fine of £500 was imposed on the owners. The defendants appealed to the House of Lords.

Lord Diplock:...There is, of course, no question that the article in the *Daily Mail* of which complaint is made by the Attorney-General was a 'publication' within the meaning of section 2(1). That being so, it appears to have been accepted in the Divisional Court by both parties that the onus of proving that the article satisfied the conditions stated in section 2(2) lay upon the Attorney-General and that, if he satisfied that onus, the onus lay upon the appellants to prove that it satisfied the conditions stated in section 5. For my part, I am unable to accept that this represents the effect of the relationship of section 5 to section 2(2). Section 5 does not take the form of a proviso or an exception to section 2(2). It stands on an equal footing with it. It does not set out exculpatory matter. Like section 2(2) it states what publications shall *not* amount to contempt of court despite their tendency to interfere with the course of justice in particular legal proceedings.

[L]ogically the first question always is: has the publication satisfied the criterion laid down by section 2(2) i.e. that it 'creates a substantial risk that the course of justice in the proceedings in question will be seriously impeded or prejudiced.'

My Lords, the first thing to be observed about this criterion is that the risk that has to be assessed is that which was created by the publication of the allegedly offending matter at the time when it was published. The public policy that underlies the strict liability rule in contempt of court is deterrence. Trial by newspaper or, as it should be more compendiously expressed today, trial by the media, is not to be permitted in this country. That the risk that was created by the publication when it was actually published does not ultimately affect the outcome of the proceedings is, as Lord Goddard CJ said in *R v Evening Standard Co Ltd* [1954] 1 QB 578, 582 'neither here nor there.' If there was a reasonable possibility that it might have done so if in the period subsequent to the publication the proceedings had not taken the course that in fact they did and Dr Arthur was acquitted, the offence was complete. The true course of justice must not at any stage be put at risk.

Next for consideration is the concatenation in the subsection of the adjective 'substantial' and the adverb 'seriously', the former to describe the degree of risk, the latter to describe the degree of impediment or prejudice to the course of justice. 'Substantial' is hardly the most apt word to apply to 'risk' which is a noumenon. In combination I take the two words to be intended to exclude a risk that is only remote. With regard to the adverb 'seriously' a perusal of the cases cited in *A-G v Times Newspapers Ltd* [1974] AC 273 discloses that the adjective 'serious' has from time to time been used as an alternative to 'real' to describe the degree of risk of interfering with the course of justice, but not the degree of interference itself. It is, however, an ordinary English word that is not intrinsically inapt when used to describe the extent of an impediment or prejudice to the cause of justice in particular legal proceedings, and I do not think that for the purposes of the instant appeal any attempt to paraphrase it is necessary or would be helpful. The subsection applies to all kinds of legal proceedings, not only criminal prosecutions before a jury. If, as in the instant case and probably in most other criminal trials upon indictment, it is the outcome of the trial or the need to discharge the jury without proceeding to a verdict that is put at risk, there can be no question that that which in the course of justice is put at risk is as serious as anything could be.

My Lords, that Mr Malcolm Muggeridge's article was capable of prejudicing the jury against Dr Arthur at the early stage of his trial when it was published, seems to me to be clear. It suggested that it was a common practice among paediatricians to do that which Dr Arthur was charged with having done, because they thought that it was justifiable in the interest of humanity even though it was against the law. At this

---

stage of the trial the jury did not know what Dr Arthur's defence was going to be; and whether at that time the risk of the jury's being influenced by their recollection of the article when they came eventually to consider their verdict appeared to be more than a remote one, was a matter which the judge before whom the trial was being conducted was in the best position to evaluate, even though this evaluation, although it should carry weight, would not be binding on the Divisional Court or on your Lordships. The judge thought at that stage of the trial that the risk was substantial, not remote. So, too, looking at the matter in retrospect, did the Divisional Court despite the fact that the risk had not turned into an actuality since Dr Arthur had by then been acquitted. For my part I am not prepared to dissent from this evaluation. I consider that the publication of the article on the third day of what was to prove a lengthy trial satisfied the criterion for which section 2(2) of the Act provides.

The article, however, fell also within the category dealt with in section 5. It was made, in undisputed good faith, as a discussion in itself of public affairs, viz, Mrs Carr's candidature as an independent pro-life candidate in the North West Croydon by-election for which the polling day was in one week's time. It was also part of a wider discussion on a matter of general public interest that had been proceeding intermittently over the last three months, upon the moral justification of mercy killing and in particular of allowing newly born hopeless handicapped babies to die. So it was for the Attorney-General to show that the risk of prejudice to the fair trial of Dr Arthur, which I agree was created by the publication of the article at the stage the trial had reached when it was published, was not 'merely incidental' to the discussion of the matter with which the article dealt.

My Lords, any article published at the time when Dr Arthur was being tried which asserted that it was a common practice among paediatricians to let severely physically or mentally handicapped new born babies die of starvation or otherwise dispose of them would (as, in common with the trial judge and the Divisional Court, I have already accepted) involve a substantial risk of prejudicing his fair trial. But an article supporting Mrs Carr's candidature in the by-election as a pro-life candidate that contained no such assertion would depict her as tilting at imaginary windmills. One of the main planks of the policy for which she sought the suffrage of the electors was that these things did happen and ought to be stopped.

I have drawn attention to the passages principally relied upon by the Divisional Court as causing a risk of prejudice that was not 'merely incidental to the discussion'. The court described them as 'unnecessary' to the discussion and as 'accusations'. The test, however, is not whether an article could have been written as effectively without these passages or whether some other phraseology might have been substituted for them that could have reduced the risk of prejudicing Dr Arthur's fair trial; it is whether the risk created by the words actually chosen by the author was 'merely incidental to the discussion', which I take to mean: no more than an incidental consequence of expounding its main theme. The Divisional Court also apparently regarded the passages complained of as disqualified from the immunity conferred by section 5 because they consisted of 'accusations' whereas the court considered, [1983] 1 AC p. 128e–f, that 'discussion' was confined to 'the airing of views and the propounding and debating of principles and arguments'. I cannot accept this limited meaning of 'discussion' in the section. As already pointed out, in the absence of any accusation, believed to be true by Mrs Carr and Mr Muggeridge, that it was a common practice among some doctors to do what they are accused of doing in the passages complained of, the article would lose all its point whether as support for Mrs Carr's parliamentary candidature or as a contribution to the wider controversy as to the justifiability of mercy killing. The article would be emasculated into a mere contribution to a purely hypothetical problem appropriate, it may be, for debate between academic successors of the mediaeval schoolmen, but remote from all public affairs and devoid of any general public interest to readers of the *Daily Mail*.

My Lords, the article that is the subject of the instant case appears to me to be in nearly all respects the antithesis of the article which this House (pace a majority of the judges of the European Court of Human Rights) held to be a contempt of court in *A-G v Times Newspapers Ltd* [1974] AC 273. There the whole subject of the article was the pending civil actions against Distillers Co. (Biochemicals) Ltd, arising out of their having placed upon the market the new drug thalidomide, and the whole purpose of it was to put pressure upon that company in the lawful conduct of their defence in those actions. In the instant case, in contrast, there is in the article no mention at all of Dr Arthur's trial. It may well be that many readers of the *Daily Mail* who saw the article and had read also the previous day's report of Dr Arthur's trial, and certainly if they were members of the jury at that trial, would think, 'that is the sort of thing that Dr Arthur is being tried for; it appears to be something that quite a lot of doctors do.' But the risk of their thinking that and allowing it to prejudice their minds in favour of finding him guilty on evidence that did not justify such a finding seems to me to be properly described in ordinary English language as 'merely incidental' to any meaningful discussion of Mrs Carr's election policy as a pro-life candidate in the by-election due to be held before Dr Arthur's trial was likely to be concluded, or to any meaningful discussion of the wider matters of general public interest involved in the current controversy as to the justification of mercy killing. To hold otherwise would have prevented Mrs Carr from putting forward and obtaining publicity for what was a main plank in her election programme and would have stifled all discussion in the press upon the wider controversy about mercy killing from the time that Dr Arthur was charged in the magistrates' court in February 1981 until the date of his acquittal at the beginning of November of that year; for those are the dates between which, under section 2(3) and Schedule 1, the legal proceedings against Dr Arthur would be 'active' and so attract the strict liability rule.

Such gagging of bona fide public discussion in the press of controversial matters of general public interest, merely because there are in existence contemporaneous legal proceedings in which some particular instance of those controversial matters may be in issue, is what section 5 of the Contempt of Court Act 1981 was in my view intended to prevent. I would allow this appeal.

Lords Elwyn-Jones, Keith, Scarman and **Brandon** agreed with Lord Diplock's speech.

Appeal allowed.

NOTES

1. The word 'noumenon' means an 'object of intellectual intuition devoid of all phenomenal attributes' (OED).

2. Are the interpretation and application of s. 2(2) satisfactory?[85] Consider (a) whether the word 'substantial' in s. 2(2) should have been accorded such a narrow interpretation by the House of Lords and (b) whether, even on that narrow approach, you would be satisfied the publication created the necessary risk. (See Zellick,[86] who argues that the decision on this point 'seriously misinterpreted the subsection and confirms the traditional breadth of the contempt law which Parliament had been at pains to curb'.)

3. *A-G v English* may be contrasted with the decisions of the Divisional Court in *A-G v Times Newspapers Ltd* (heard with four other cases).[87] The Attorney-General brought contempt proceedings under the strict liability rule against the publishers of five newspapers in respect of news stories and articles about Michael Fagan, an intruder into the Queen's bedroom. He had already been charged with offences arising out of three previous incidents: (1) a charge of burglary in respect of a previous entry into Buckingham Palace, during which he had drunk some wine; (2) a charge of taking a motor vehicle without the owner's consent; and (3) a charge of assaulting his stepson. Lord Lane CJ noted that under s. 2(2) a slight or trivial risk of serious prejudice was not enough nor was a substantial risk of slight prejudice. Five cases were heard together.

---

85 See G.J. Zellick [1982] PL 343; A. Ward (1983) 46 MLR 85; M. Redmond [1983] CLJ 9.
86 Op. cit., p. 344.   87 (1983) Times, 12 February, DC.

(a) The *Sun* was prosecuted in respect of assertions that Fagan had a long standing drug problem, was a glib liar and had stolen cigars from the Palace. Lord Lane 'accepted the view that jurors were to be credited with more independence of mind than was sometimes suggested'. The risk that the fair trial on the burglary charge would be prejudiced was 'too remote to qualify for the description of substantial'.

(b) The *Daily Star* had published allegations similar to the *Sun* and was accordingly acquitted in respect of those. In addition, it had asserted (i) that Fagan admitted to stealing the wine and (ii) that he intended to commit suicide, the inferential suggestion being that he was unbalanced. Assertion (i) amounted to contempt, but assertion (ii) did not: 'However independent minded a jury might be and however cynical about the accuracy of newspaper reporting nevertheless there would inevitably be a real risk, whether the judge gave a warning about disregarding extraneous facts or not, that the memory of [assertion (i)] would remain in the jurors' minds and would affect the outcome of their deliberations.' It was conceded that s. 5 provided no defence. Nevertheless, no penalty was imposed.

(c) Neither of the matters complained of against the *Sunday People* amounted to contempt: (i) allegations that Fagan had been addicted to drugs were similar to those made by the *Sun* and the *Daily Star;* (ii) reported comments, said to have emanated from a Palace spokesman, that some of Fagan's reported statements were 'quite absurd and fanciful suggestions' (thus implying that he was untruthful) were not likely to influence a juror.

(d) The *Mail on Sunday* had published an article by Lady Falkender which contained the clear suggestion of a possible homosexual liaison between Fagan and Commander Trestrail, who had recently resigned as Queen's Police Officer because of a homosexual relationship with a male prostitute. It also referred to Fagan as a 'rootless neurotic with no visible means of support'. The court held that this could not fail to have an effect on anyone considering Fagan's honesty. Although the burglary charge was not mentioned, everybody reading any newspaper would be well aware of it. 'Accordingly the article had the necessary ingredient under s. 2.' However, it fell within s. 5: 'the appalling state of the safeguards designed to protect Her Majesty together with the proclivities of her bodyguard were matters which were of the greatest public concern' and 'the article was part of the discussion about the Queen's safety'.

(e) The *Sunday Times* had alleged that Fagan was charged with stabbing his stepson in the neck with a screwdriver: it was now conceded that there was never any such allegation and that the only allegation was one of assault. This inaccuracy 'on its own did not cause the publication to amount to contempt. Where however the inaccuracy was of that extent and was given front-page prominence then the publisher put himself at risk'. A second article repeated the false suggestion that Fagan was charged with wounding and also stated that the whole affair arose out of a genuine misunderstanding that the boy had received his injuries not at Fagan's hands but in some earlier incident before Fagan arrived on the scene. These statements were held to be prejudicial to the trial of the assault charge. The second article also stated, falsely, that the charge of taking a motor vehicle had been dropped. This was held to be prejudicial to the prosecution in respect of this charge. Section 5 was not applicable. The alleged assault was no more than a domestic fracas that was irrelevant to the public discussion of the matter of the Queen's security. The articles nevertheless went into great detail about it and could not be described as 'merely incidental' to the expounding of the main theme. Ackner LJ agreed with Lord Lane CJ. Oliver LJ generally agreed, but doubted whether the *Mail on Sunday* article fell foul of s. 2, and held that the first *Sunday Times* article did so not because of any possible influence on jurors but because it caused Fagan, on legal advice, to elect for jury trial rather than summary trial: any extraneous factor which impeded or restricted the defendant's right of election was a serious prejudice. Cf. the placing of improper pressure on litigants in civil proceedings.[88] Oliver LJ's approach was followed in *A-G v Unger*[89] (no contempt on the facts).

Borrie and Lowe[90] note that: if s. 2(2) was thought to be restrictively interpreted in *A-G v English*, it must be considered to be generously interpreted in the *Fagan* cases.

The pattern of subsequent case law suggests that it has been increasingly difficult for the Attorney-General to secure convictions under the strict liability rule other than in very clear cut cases. Successful prosecutions include the following: *A-G v BBC*; *A-G v Hat Trick Productions Ltd:*[91] (presenter of *Have I Got News for You* referred to sons of Robert Maxwell as 'heartless scheming bastards' six months before their trial for conspiracy to defraud: programme repeated notwithstanding protest from their solicitor; respondents each fined £10,000); *A-G v Associated Newspapers Ltd*[92] (acknowledged breach by the *Evening Standard* of s. 4 order prohibiting publication of terrorist background of prisoners to be tried for offences arising out of a break-out from Whitemoor Prison led to permanent stay of proceedings; £40,000 fine imposed); *A-G v Morgan; AG v News Group Newspapers Ltd*[93] (publication in the *News of the World* of the results of journalist's investigations into conspiracy to distribute counterfeit money the day after the alleged conspirators were arrested, treating the alleged conspiracy as a fact and referring to the defendants' criminal records, led to stay of proceedings and was held to be a contempt; £50,000 fine imposed); *A-G v Birmingham Post and Mail Ltd*[94] (publication during murder trial suggesting that the murder was carried out by members of a notorious criminal gang connected with drug dealing and gangland activities led to retrial; £20,000 fine); *A-G v Mirror Group Newspapers Ltd* [2002] EWHC 907 (Admin) (MGN fined £75,000 for publishing claims that an alleged attack on a person by well-known Leeds United footballers was racially motivated; the trial was proceeding on a different basis and had to be abandoned; there was an unreserved apology); *A-G v Express Newspapers* [2004] EWHC 2859 (Admin) (£60,000 fine for publication by *Daily Star* of identification information; requests and advice from the police and the A-G had been 'overlooked').

A significant number of the reported cases have, however, been unsuccessful. The courts have examined in detail the nature and circumstances of the publication and its likely impact on jurors and parties and consequently on the course of proceedings. The grant before or at trial of a temporary or permanent stay of proceedings has not *automatically* been taken to prove the existence of a 'substantial risk of serious prejudice' under s. 2(2), although is a strong pointer in that direction.

In *A-G v Guardian Newspapers,*[95] the publication of the fact that one unidentified defendant out of six on trial in Manchester was awaiting trial in the Isle of Man on other charges was held not to give rise to any practical risk of engendering bias in a juror of ordinary good sense. In *A-G v Independent Television News Ltd*[96] TV news and newspapers (the *Daily Mail, Today, Daily Express* and *Northern Echo*) published the fact that Patrick Magee, who had been arrested for the murder of a special constable and the attempted murder of a police constable, was a convicted IRA terrorist who had escaped from jail in Belfast where he was serving a life sentence for the murder of an SAS officer. The court held that there was no contempt given the likely (and actual) lapse of time of over nine months before any trial, the ephemeral nature of a single news item on TV news, and the limited circulation of the first (and only offending) editions of the newspapers in question. In particular in the case of the *Northern*

---

88 Below, p. 726.   89 [1998] 1 Cr App R 308.   90 P. 150.
91 [1997] EMLR 76.   92 [1998] EMLR 711.   93 [1998] EMLR 294.
94 [1998] 4 All ER 49.   95 [1992] 3 All ER 38.   96 [1995] 2 All ER 370, DC.

Echo, where only 146 copies were distributed in London, at King's Cross Station, there was no risk. In *A-G v MGN Ltd,*[97] coverage (accurate and inaccurate) in the *Daily Mirror,* the *Daily Star,* the *Sun, Today* and the *Daily Mail* in April and May 1995 of aspects of an alleged assault by Geoffrey Knights on Martin Davies led to an indefinite stay of proceedings being ordered by Judge Sanders in October of that year. However, the Divisional Court held that this coverage did not constitute contempt in view of the earlier saturation media coverage of Knights and his 'erstwhile girl friend' Gillian Taylforth who had had 'a major role in a popular television programme'. The publicity had included frequent references to Knights' prison record for violence. See also *A-G v Unger*[98] (no contempt where newspaper story setting out evidence, but not any inadmissible evidence, was published many months before an possible trial); *A-G v Sunday Business Newspapers Ltd*[99] (no contempt by 'obscure weekly publication').

4. Varying views have been expressed on the relationship between the approaches that should be taken on: (a) proceedings for contempt; (b) applications for a stay of proceedings; and (c) appeals against conviction. Some have accepted that a publication may constitute a contempt without being sufficient to undermine the safety of a subsequent conviction. According to Simon Brown LJ in *A-G v Birmingham Post and Mail Ltd,*[100] this 'can only be because s. 2(2) postulates a lesser degree of prejudice than is required to make good an appeal against conviction' or a stay. Conversely, 'to create a seriously arguable ground of appeal is a sufficient basis for finding strict liability contempt'.

However, in *A-G v Guardian Newspapers Ltd,*[101] for Collins J and Sedley LJ the prejudice required by s. 2(2) is not in itself different; instead, the difference lies in the point that the risk ordinarily has to be gauged prospectively in a contempt case and retrospectively in a criminal appeal. Collins J agreed with Simon Brown LJ that creation of a seriously arguable ground of appeal was sufficient for contempt; for Sedley LJ, however, the issue turned on whether or not a ground of appeal was made out: 'any substantial risk...that a conviction has been contributed to by a prejudicial publication will ordinarily make it unsafe.' Collins J deferred to Sedley LJ's view that on the facts here no contempt was established. Collins J implicitly and Sedley LJ expressly adopted as a test (anticipating implementation of the Human Rights Act 1998) whether either prior restraint or subsequent punishment would be 'a proportionate response in a society which, as a democracy, values and protects freedom of the press'.

5. *The s. 5 defence.* In *A-G v TVS Television Ltd,*[102] TVS broadcast a programme, 'The New Rachman', on 29 January 1988, exposing certain landlords in Reading who were alleged to be obtaining money by deception from the DHSS, as part of a general discussion of the causes of a new wave of Rachmanism in Southern England. The trial of one of the landlords, which had commenced on 4 January, had to be aborted (at a cost of £215,000). TVS accepted that the broadcast was a publication which had created a substantial risk of serious prejudice, and the Attorney-General accepted that TVS had acted in good faith. The court held that the s. 5 defence was not available: the reference to the landlords was not 'merely incidental' to the matter of general public interest discussed in the programme: the thrust of the discussion was directed to the Reading landlords. TVS were fined £25,000.

To what extent is the defendant's intention relevant to the s. 5 limitation?[103] Is the test for 'good faith' objective or subjective?[104] Note that s. 5 was held to be applicable in the *Mail on*

---

97 [1997] 1 All ER 456.   98 [1998] 1 Cr App R 308.   99 Unreported, 20 January 1998.

100 [1998] 4 All ER 49, 57.   101 [1999] EMLR 904.   102 (1989) Times, 7 July, DC.

103 See M. Redmond [1983] CLJ 9, 11–12.   104 See N. Lowe (1981) 131 NLJ 1167, 1169.

Sunday case[105] notwithstanding that the article mentioned the accused.[106] In *A-G v TVS Television Ltd*[107] Lloyd LJ stated that in determining whether a risk was merely incidental:

> ...a better and surer test is simply to look at the subject matter of the discussion and see how closely it relates to the particular legal proceedings. The more closely it relates the easier it will be for the Attorney-General to show that the risk of prejudice is not merely incidental to the discussion. The application of the test is largely a matter of first impression.

In *A-G v Guardian Newspapers*, Mann LJ[108] agreed that the application of the test was largely one of impression. The Divisional Court held that the s. 5 defence was made out where in the course of an article criticising the alleged propensity of judges in major fraud trials to impose reporting restrictions, reference was made to a particular case where restrictions were imposed because a defendant was awaiting trial elsewhere. Brooke J stated[109] that the inclusion of examples was 'no more than an incidental consequence of expounding the main theme of the article'. On the burden of proof, Professor J.C. Smith,[110] pointed out that while s. 3(3)[111] states explicitly that the onus of proving the defence of innocent publication or distribution is on the defendant there is no such provision in s. 4 or 5. Nevertheless, in *A-G v TVS Television Ltd*,[112] the Attorney-General accepted that the burden of proving liability rested on him for the purposes of both ss. 2(2) and 5 of the 1981 Act. Professor Smith also considered whether an article written with reference to the issue of principle raised by the trial itself would amount to contempt:

> Arguably, proceedings are not 'impeded' or 'prejudiced' by a discussion in good faith of issues of principle, even if it is intended to influence the court to reach a 'correct' decision. Many commentaries on decisions of the Court of Appeal published in this *Review* have been written in the hope they might influence the House of Lords, either directly or through their adoption by counsel, to reach a particular decision and have not (so far) been treated as contemptuous. If, in the course of the published debate following the acquittal of Dr. Arthur, a similar charge had been brought against another doctor, would it have been necessary to suspend the debate? It is submitted that it would not.

Does s. 5 apply only in respect of incidental risks created by the continuation of an *existing* public debate or does it extend in addition to articles which *initiate* such a debate?[113]

(III) OTHER ASPECTS OF CONTEMPT

Protection of inferior courts and tribunals. Inferior courts generally only have power to punish contempts in the face of the court.[114] However, the Divisional Court fulfils a protective role over the proceedings of inferior courts and tribunals. Accordingly, it has been held that that court can punish publications likely to prejudice proceedings before consistory courts,[115] coroners courts,[116] courts martial[117] and county courts.[118] However, in

---

105 Above, n. 3.   106 Cf. *A-G v English*, above, p. 698.   107 (1989) Times, 7 July.

108 [1992] 3 All ER 38 (see above, p. 703), at 45.   109 Ibid., at 49.

110 [1982] Crim LR 744.   111 Above, p. 704.   112 (1989) Times, 7 July, DC.

113 See C.J. Miller [1982] Crim LR 71, 78–79.   114 See below, p. 745.

115 *R v Daily Herald, ex p Bishop of Norwich* [1932] 2 KB 402.

116 See *R v Clarke, ex p Crippen* (1910) 103 LT 636, 641, per Lord Coleridge CJ; *Peacock v London Weekend Television* (1985) 150 JP 71, CA.

117 See *R v Daily Mail, ex p Farnsworth* [1921] 2 KB 733.

118 See *R v Edwards, ex p Welsh Church Temporalities Comrs* (1933) 49 TLR 383 and *Manchester City Council v McCann* [1999] 2 QB 1214 (below, p. 750).

A-G v BBC[119] the House of Lords held that the contempt jurisdiction was not co-extensive with the High Court's general supervisory jurisdiction, but was only exercisable in relation to 'inferior courts'.[120] The House was unanimous in holding that this contempt power did not apply to local valuation courts. A mental health review tribunal[121] or an industrial tribunal is an 'inferior court' for these purposes,[122] but the Professional Conduct Committee of the General Medical Council is not.[123]

Powers to sit in camera. In general court proceedings must take place in public. This is a common law principle[124] and enshrined in Art. 6 ECHR. However, courts have inherent power to sit in private where that is necessary to serve the ends of justice, and there are also statutory exceptions. The principles were stated as follows by Lord Diplock in *A-G v Leveller Magazine Ltd.*[125]

The application of this principle of open justice has two aspects: as respects proceedings in the court itself it requires that they should be held in open court to which the press and public are admitted and that, in criminal cases at any rate, all evidence communicated to the court is communicated publicly. As respects the publication to a wider public of fair and accurate reports of proceedings that have taken place in court the principle requires that nothing should be done to discourage this.

However, since the purpose of the general rule is to serve the ends of justice it may be necessary to depart from it where the nature or circumstances of the particular proceedings are such that the application of the general rule in its entirety would frustrate or render impracticable the administration of justice or would damage some other public interest for whose protection Parliament has made some statutory derogation from the rule. Apart from statutory exceptions, however, where a court in the exercise of its inherent power to control the conduct of proceedings before it departs in any way from the general rule, the departure is justified to the extent and to no more than the extent that the court reasonably believes it to be necessary in order to serve the ends of justice.

This last stated point may in appropriate circumstances justify a decision to sit *in camera* or the imposition of restrictions on the reporting of certain matters.[126]

Where the prosecutor or defendant intends to apply for an order that all or part of a trial be held in camera for reasons of national security or the protection of the identity of a witness or any other person, notice must be served and a copy displayed within the court.[127]

---

119 [1981] AC 303.   120 See RSC Ord. 52, r. 1(2)(a)(iii).

121 *Pickering v Liverpool Daily Post and Echo Newspapers Ltd* [1991] 2 AC 370.

122 *Peach Grey & Co (a firm) v Sommers* [1995] 2 All ER 513.

123 *General Medical Council v BBC* [1998] 3 All ER 426.   124 *Scott v Scott* [1913] AC 417, HL.

125 [1979] AC 440 at 450. See also *R v Ealing Justices, ex p Weafer* (1982) 74 Cr App R 204, DC; *R v Reigate Justices, ex p Argus Newspapers and Larcombe* (1983) 147 JP 385, DC; *R v Chief Registrar of Friendly Societies, ex p New Cross Building Society* [1984] QB 227; *Polly Peck International plc v Nadir* (1991) Times, 11 November; *R (on the application of Mersey Care Trust) v Mental Health Review Tribunal* [2004] EWHC 1749 (Admin), [2005] 2 All ER 820 (tribunal required to reconsider decision to sit in private to review position of Ian Brady); *R (on the application of Malik) v Central Criminal Court* [2006] 4 All ER 1141 (bail applications should normally be in public). Proceedings under the Children Act are normally heard in private: *P-B (A Minor) (Child Cases: Hearings in Open Court* [1997] 1 All ER 58; *B v UK, P v UK* (2002) EHRR 529; *Norfolk CC v Webster* [2007] 2 FLR 415; but the position is different in Scotland. As to the position in family cases, see *Clibbery v Allan* [2002] Fam 261; the matter is under review: Ministry of Justice Consultation Paper CP10/07, *Confidence & Confidentiality: Openness in family courts—a new approach* and the response, *Family Justice in View* (December 2008) (proposing that the media should be allowed to attend court proceedings unless the court otherwise orders). See generally *Robertson and Nicol*, Chaps 8 and 9.

126 See below.

127 Crim PR, r. 16.10 (1), (2). This covers 'all or part of the trial process': *Ex p Guardian Newspapers Ltd* [1999] 1 All ER 65, CA (Cr D) (the court also gave guidance on the procedure to be followed).

In civil and arbitration cases, there are powers for the judge or arbitrator to sit 'in private' which means 'in secret'.[128]

A decision to sit *in camera* may be challenged (in the case of an inferior court or tribunal) on an application for judicial review or (in the case of a trial on indictment) an appeal to the Court of Appeal under the Criminal Justice Act 1988, s. 159. See, for example, *Re Crook*,[129] where the Court of Appeal gave guidance as to the circumstances in which applications in connection with trials on indictment could properly be heard in chambers. If the public are excluded from a hearing, the Press should be excluded as well.[130] The policy of a particular bench to withhold the names of justices during the hearing of cases and from both public and press afterwards was held to be unlawful (as contrary to the principles of open justice) in *R v Felixstowe Justices, ex p Leigh*.[131]

Powers to prohibit reporting; Contempt of Court Act 1981, s. 11. It has been established that a judge has jurisdiction to order that the name of a witness should not be disclosed in the proceedings if there is a danger that a lack of anonymity would deter such witnesses from coming forward. Disclosure may then amount to contempt. In *R v Socialist Worker Printers and Publishers Ltd, ex p A-G*,[132] prosecution witnesses at the trial of Janie Jones on charges (*inter alia*) of blackmail were referred to in court as 'Y' and 'Z' by direction of the judge. Their names were published in the *Socialist Worker*. There was no specific direction to the press not to publish the names. Nevertheless, the publishers and editor (Paul Foot) were each fined £250 for contempt. This was both 'an affront to the authority of the court' and 'an act calculated to interfere with the due course of justice'.[133]

The New Zealand Court of Appeal has similarly held that it is contempt to disobey directions not to reveal the identities of members of the NZ Security Intelligence Service who were prosecution witnesses in a well publicised trial.[134]

In *A-G v Leveller Magazine Ltd*,[135] three newspapers (*Leveller, Peace News* and *Journalists*) published the name of a witness in the committal proceedings which led to the 'ABC trial'.[136] He had been allowed to give evidence as 'Colonel B' for security reasons. They were convicted of contempt and fined, on the ground that flouting (or deliberate disregard) outside the court will be a contempt if it frustrates the court's ruling.[137] The House of Lords allowed the defendants' appeals on a variety of grounds.

(a) (Lord Diplock, Viscount Dilhorne and Lord Russell.[138]) In evidence at the committal proceedings 'Colonel B' gave the name and number of his unit and referred to the fact that his posting was recorded in a particular issue of 'Wire', the Royal Signals magazine, which was available to the general public. His identity could thus be deduced from evidence given in open court without objection from the prosecution. Accordingly, the disclosure could not interfere with the due administration of justice and could not amount to contempt. In the words of Lord Russell, 'the gaff was already blown'.[139] Viscount Dilhorne[140] and Lord Russell[141] gave this as the only reason for their decision.

---

128 CPR, rr. 39.2, 62.10; *R (on application of Pelling) v Bow County Court* [2001] UKHRR 165; *Department of Economics, Policy and Development of the City of Moscow v Bankers Trust Co* [2004] EWCA Civ 314, [2005] QB 207 (presumption in favour of secrecy for arbitration cases not incompatible with Art. 6 ECHR).

129 (1989) 93 Cr App R 17.   130 Ibid.

131 [1987] QB 582. See also *R v Malvern Justices, ex p Evans*, below, p. 710.

132 [1975] QB 637, DC.   133 Per Lord Widgery CJ at 151.

134 *A-G v Taylor* [1975] 2 NZLR 675; *A-G v Hancox* [1976] 1 NZLR 171; W.C. Hodge (1976) 7 NZ Universities LR 171.

135 [1979] 1 All ER 745, HL; R.T.H. Stone (1980) 96 LQR 22.   136 Below, p. 786.

137 [1978] 3 All ER 731 at 736, per Lord Widgery CJ.   138 Ibid., at 752, 753–4, 764.

139 Ibid., at 764.   140 Ibid., at 754.   141 Ibid., at 764.

(b) (Lord Edmund-Davies.[142]) The Attorney-General had sought the orders of committal on the basis that the defendants had ignored an explicit *direction* of the magistrates. It subsequently appeared from the affidavit of the court clerk that no such direction had been given. Lord Edmund-Davies stated that:[143]

> it was not open to the Divisional Court (and particularly after refusing to allow him to amend his grounds of application) to entertain an entirely different case on which to commit the appellants for criminal contempt....Persons charged with criminal misconduct are entitled to know with reasonable precision the basis of the charge.

(c) (Lord Scarman.[144]) The nature and object of the ruling was unclear on the facts, and so the defendants' conduct could not be said to be a deliberate frustration of the effort of the court to protect justice from interference. It was not clear that the justices understood that the national security risk was also a risk to the administration of justice; there was doubt as to whether the 'ruling' was a decision, an indication or only a request.

There was general agreement that the courts at common law had no power to make an order prohibiting publication of information by the media, disobedience to which was automatically contempt.[145] (This proposition has since been confirmed by the Privy Council in *Independent Publishing Co Ltd v Attorney General of Trinidad and Tobago*.[146]) There was also general agreement that anonymity orders or rulings could lawfully be made in appropriate cases.[147] Indeed, a risk to a witness's life may give rise to a Convention right to anonymity.[148] In what circumstances would publication of information constitute contempt on the basis that it defeated the intention of the order or ruling? On this, Lord Diplock said:[149]

> ...[W]here (1) the reason for a ruling which involves departing in some measure from the general principle of open justice within the courtroom is that the departure is necessary in the interests of the due administration of justice and (2) it would be apparent to anyone who was aware of the ruling that the result which the ruling is designed to achieve would be frustrated by a particular kind of act done outside the courtroom, the doing of such an act with knowledge of the ruling and of its purpose may constitute a contempt of court, not because it is a breach of the ruling but because it interferes with the due administration of justice....

---

[142] Ibid., at 757–759.   [143] Ibid., at 759.

[144] Ibid., at 767–768. Viscount Dilhorne (at 754–755) and Lord Russell (at 764) disagreed, regarding the purpose of the court as clear. Cf. Lord Diplock at 752, stating that no one ought to be exposed to penal sanctions for failing to draw an inference or recognise an implication about what it is permissible to publish, unless it is so obvious as to speak for itself. Similarly Lord Edmund-Davies at 759.

[145] Viscount Dilhorne at 754, Lord Edmund-Davies at 761 and Lord Scarman at 768. Lord Edmund-Davies at 751 left the point open.

[146] [2004] UKPC 26, [2005] 1 All ER 499. The Privy Council disagreed with the view of the New Zealand Court of Appeal on this point to the contrary in *A-G v Taylor* [1975] 2 NZLR 67.

[147] For Lord Diplock (at 750–751) this derived from the point that the court could otherwise have decided to sit in camera by virtue of s. 8(4) of the Official Secrets Act 1920 and s. 12(1) of the Administration of Justice Act 1960; anonymity involved less derogation from the general principle of open justice. See also Viscount Dilhorne at 755–756; Lord Edmund-Davies at 761. There was also general approval of the power to order anonymity of witnesses in blackmail cases: Lord Diplock at 751, Viscount Dilhorne at 756, Lord Scarman at 756. Lord Edmund-Davies though this would not necessarily be appropriate in all blackmail cases: pp. 759–760.

[148] See p. 499; *Re Officer L* [2007] UKHL 36, [2007] 1 WLR 2135; *Re Times Newspapers Ltd* [2008] EWCA Crim 2559 (anonymity granted to witnesses who were members of Special Forces, on the basis of a real and immediate risk to their lives if identified).

[149] Ibid., at 751.

There may be many cases in which the result intended to be achieved by a ruling by the court as to what is to be done in court is so obvious as to speak for itself; it calls for no explicit statement. Sending the jury out of court during a trial within a trial is an example of this; so may be the common ruling in prosecutions for blackmail that a victim called as a witness be referred to in court by a pseudonym....

The other members of the House did not appear to dissent from this view. However, there was a division between those judges who thought that the reason for the justices' ruling here on the facts had been clear,[150] and those who thought that it was not.[151] Accordingly, while there was agreement that an express warning against publication was not necessary in every case for a contempt conviction,[152] a form of explanation on warning might well have been necessary for a conviction here, on the approach of the majority.

The difficulties of the *Leveller* case are not solved by s. 11 of the Contempt of Court Act 1981.[153] Note that s. 11 does not *confer* any power to withhold information in court, does not indicate what consequences are to flow from a breach of a direction made under the section, and does not make it clear whether the deliberate publication of matter withheld in court may constitute contempt where there has not also been an express direction to the press to refrain from publication. It has, however, been held that an order cannot be made under s. 11 prohibiting the publication of a name in connection with proceedings unless the name has been withheld during the proceedings.[154] Anonymity orders have been made, for example, to protect witnesses in blackmail trials,[155] in connection with security matters,[156] in pornography trials[157] to prohibit the publication of the name and address of a person with a notifiable disease against whom an *ex parte* order was made under the Public Health (Control of Disease) Act 1984, s. 37, requiring his removal to hospital[158] and where there was a risk of psychological harm to an applicant for judicial review with advanced HIV disease should his identity be publicised.[159] Anonymity orders may also be justified where a witness is in fear for himself or his family.[160] An order can be made under s. 11 prohibiting the reporting of evidence inadvertently given in open court which should have been given *in camera*; alternatively the judge could make it plain that to publish the evidence would be a contempt as frustrating an order lawfully made by the court.[161] However, an order prohibiting the publication of matter that might reveal the matter covered by the *in camera* order was too wide. This would cover speculation (which did not make it plain that it was mere speculation) as to the evidence given *in camera*; publication of this would not be the publication of the name or matter withheld and the prohibition would not be necessary for the purpose of preventing the name or matter

---

[150] Viscount Dilhorne at 754–755; Lord Russell at 763. Their Lordships would have dismissed the appeals had it not been for ground (1) set out above.

[151] Lord Diplock at 751–752; Lord Edmund-Davies at 759; Lord Scarman at 767–768.

[152] See, e.g., Lord Edmund-Davies at 762.

[153] See above, p. 690.

[154] *R v Arundel Justices, ex p Westminster Press Ltd* [1985] 2 All ER 390, DC, following *dicta* in *R v Central Criminal Court, ex p Crook* (1984) Times, 8 November, DC; *R v Z* [2005] UKHL 22, [2005] 2 AC 467, per Lord Bingham at para. [2].

[155] *R v Socialist Worker*, above.   [156] *A-G v Leveller*, above.

[157] *R v Hove Justices, ex p Gibbons* (1981) Times, 19 June.

[158] *Birmingham Post and Mail Ltd v Birmingham City Council* (1993) Times, 25 November: the s. 11 order was, however, not to be continued once all reasonable opportunity to challenge the hospital order had passed.

[159] *Re D* (1997) 45 BMLR 191.

[160] *R v Watford Magistrates' Court, ex p Lenman* [1993] Crim LR 388, [1992] COD 474, DC; *R v Taylor (Gary)* (1994) Times, 17 August, CA(Cr D).

[161] *Re Times Newspapers Ltd* [2007] EWCA Crim 1925.

becoming known. However, it is likely that such speculation would constitute a contempt at common law.[162]

The growing use of powers to sit *in camera*[163] and to make orders under s. 11 was viewed with concern by the National Union of Journalists, the Association of British Editors and the Press Council. However, the tide was to an extent stemmed by two decisions of the Divisional Court. In *R v Malvern Justices, ex p Evans*,[164] the Divisional Court affirmed the jurisdiction of a magistrates' court to sit *in camera* if the administration of justice so required, but doubted that the court's discretion to do so had been properly exercised in the circumstances of the case. A woman pleaded guilty to driving with excess alcohol but sought to advance special reasons why she should not be disqualified which concerned embarrassing and intimate details of her personal life with her husband and her pending divorce proceedings. The justices acceded to her request that this be heard *in camera*. The case was only argued on the question of jurisdiction, but Watkins LJ also indicated that he regarded the justices' reason for sitting *in camera* as 'wholly unsustainable and out of accord with principle'.[165] Moreover, it was held in *R v Evesham Justices, ex p McDonagh*,[166] that a magistrates' court has no power to make a s. 11 order prohibiting publication of the defendant's address merely on the ground that he feared he would be subjected to severe harassment by his ex-wife if his address were made public.[167]

An application for a hearing to be held *in camera,* or for suppression of (for example) a name or address, should itself be heard *in camera*: the court can then determine whether there is any substance in the application without prejudicing the applicant: *R v Tower Bridge Magistrates' Court, ex p Osborne*.[168]

Finally, it should be noted that the House of Lords has held that the adoption of arrangements to maintain witness anonymity that on the facts prevented defence counsel from investigating the witnesses or pursuing in cross-examination any effective challenge to the decisive evidence they had given had rendered the trial unfair.[169] Power to make witness anonymity orders is now conferred by the Criminal Evidence (Witness Anonymity) Act 2008, which replaces the common law rules relating to the power of a court to make an order for securing that the identity of a witness in criminal proceedings is withheld from the defendant (or, on a defence application, from other defendants), but not the rules as to PII claims.

Statutory reporting restrictions. There are various statutory provisions which impose reporting restrictions disobedience to which constitutes a statutory offence.[170] See, for example, the Magistrates' Court Act 1980, s. 8C[171] (pre-trial hearings); ibid., s. 71 (family proceedings); the Criminal Justice Act 1987, ss. 11, 11A (applications to the Crown Court for dismissal of charges and preparatory hearings in serious fraud cases); Children and

---

[162] Ibid.   [163] See p. 706 above and p. 711 below.   [164] [1988] QB 540.

[165] Ibid., at 550.   [166] [1988] QB 553, DC.

[167] See also *R v Dover Justices, ex p Dover District Council* (1991) 156 JP 433 (justices could not prevent or restrict publicity of proceedings against a restaurant business alleging food hygiene offences on account of the very severe economic damage caused); *R v Westminster City Council, ex p Castelli* (1995) 30 BMLR 123 (no anonymity for HIV-positive applicant; ordinarily, a litigant's name will be published); *R v Legal Aid Board, ex p Kaim Todner* [1998] 3 All ER 541 (no special treatment for legal profession); *Aziz v Aziz* [2007] EWCA Civ 712 (no additional entitlement to anonymity just because the person in question is a head of state, here the Sultan of Brunei).

[168] (1987) 88 Cr App R 28, DC.   [169] *R v Davis* [2008] UKHL 36, [2008] 3 WLR 125.

[170] See, generally, *Borrie and Lowe,* pp. 281–333; G. Robertson and A. Nicol, *Media Law* (5th edn, 2007), Chap. 8; D. Brogarth and C. Walker (1988) 138 NLJ 909; *Reporting Restrictions in the Crown Court* (Guidelines endorsed by the Senior Presiding Judge, 30 August 2000); *Miller,* Chap. 10.

[171] Substituted by the Courts Act 2003, Sch. 3.

Young Persons Act 1933, ss. 39[172] (children or young persons involved in court proceedings) and 49[173] (youth court and other proceedings);[174] Judicial Proceedings (Regulation of Reports) Act 1926 (indecent matter); Sexual Offences (Amendment) Act 1992[175] (victims of sexual offences); the Youth Justice and Criminal Evidence Act 1999, ss. 44–52 (restrictions on reporting alleged offences involving persons under 18; power to restrict reporting of criminal proceedings involving persons under 18; power to restrict reporting about vulnerable adult witnesses);[176] Criminal Justice Act 2003, s. 82 (1), (3) (retrial following operation of new power to quash an acquittal under s. 76).[177] The position as to reporting proceedings properly held in private is governed by s. 12 of the Administration of Justice Act 1960.[178]

Powers to delay reporting; Contempt of Court Act 1981, s. 4. Distinct from the powers set out in the previous note are the powers of a court to *postpone* publication of certain matters. The position at common law was uncertain.[179] Apart from those authorities, it was accepted that a criminal court had power to hold a 'trial within a trial' in the absence of the jury (e.g. to determine whether evidence is legally admissible) and to withhold information from a jury (e.g. that the accused has pleaded guilty to some but not all the charges). The premature publication of these matters was regarded as an obvious contempt.[180]

The position is now regulated by s. 4 of the Contempt of Court Act 1981.[181] Section 4 was considered by the Court of Appeal in *R v Horsham Justices, ex p Farquharson,*[182] where a journalist and others sought judicial review to quash an order made by magistrates under s. 4(2). The court held that an order could validly be made under s. 4(2) restricting the reporting of 'old style' committal proceedings notwithstanding that the restrictions imposed by s. 3 of the Criminal Justice Act 1967 (subsequently the Magistrates' Courts Act 1980, s. 8) had been lifted under s. 3(2). The two sections were regarded as applying in different situations and for different purposes. However, the magistrates' order was quashed on the ground that it was too wide. Another point concerned the relationship between ss. 4(2) and 6(b). Counsel for the applicants argued that breach of a s. 4(2) order could only amount to contempt if it (a) constituted a breach of the 'strict liability rule' (s. 2(2)) and (b) that the conduct would

---

172 See *R v Tyne Tees Television* (1997) Times, 20 October, CA (Cr D) (fine of £10,000 for contempt of court for breach of s. 39 quashed; summary proceedings should have been taken under s. 39(2) where the maximum fine was £5,000); *R v Crown Court at Manchester, ex p H* [2000] 2 All ER 166 (decision to lift s. 39 order at the end of trial open to judicial review and held to be wrong as the judge had failed to take the possibility of a retrial properly into account); cf. *R v Central Criminal Court, ex p W, B and C* [2001] 1 Cr App R 7 (discretion to lift restrictions not confined to rare and exceptional circumstances, unlike the position in the youth court). Section 39 is to be amended by the Youth Justice and Criminal Evidence Act 1999, Sch. 2, para. 2, to apply only to civil proceedings.

173 Substituted by the Criminal Justice and Public Order Act 1994, s. 49 and to be amended by the Youth Justice and Criminal Evidence Act 1999, Sch. 2, para. 3.

174 See *McKerry v Teesdale and Wear Valley Justices* [2000] Crim LR 594 (partial lifting of reporting restrictions upheld although no place for a 'naming and shaming' approach; the power to lift restrictions as regards proceedings in the youth court should be exercised rarely).

175 As amended by the Youth Justice and Criminal Evidence Act 1999, Sch. 2, paras 6–14.

176 Not yet in force. See D. Birch and R. Leng, *Blackstone's Guide to the Youth Justice and Criminal Evidence Act 1999* (2000), Chap. 8.

177 See *Re D (acquitted person: retrial)* [2006] EWCA Crim 733, [2006] 1 WLR 1998.

178 See *Re F (a minor) (Publication of Information)* [1977] Fam 58; *Re L (a minor) (wardship: freedom of publication)* [1988] 1 All ER 418; *Pickering v Liverpool Daily Post and Echo Newspapers plc* [1991] 2 AC 370, HL; *A-G v Pelling* [2005] EWHC 515, [2006] 1 FLR 93 (see p. 734). and cf. p. 564 above.

179 See *R v Clement* (1821) 4 B & Ald 218; *R v Poulson* [1974] Crim LR 141; cf. *R v Kray* (1969) 53 Cr App R 412, CA (Cr D). See discussion in *Independent Publishing Co Ltd v A-G of Trinidad and Tobago* [2005] 1 All ER 499.

180 See above, p. 695.   181 Above, p. 688.   182 [1982] QB 762, CA.

have amounted to contempt at common law (s. 6(b)). Lord Denning MR[183] accepted this argument, but it was rejected by his brethren. Ackner LJ held that 'a new head of contempt of court has been created, separate and distinct from the strict liability rule.... If a journalist reports proceedings that are the subject matter of a postponement order under s. 4(2) then he is guilty of a contempt of court'.[184] Shaw LJ stated that 'a premature publication in contravention of an order of which the publisher is aware could not be said to be in good faith'[185] and would accordingly fall outside the protection of s. 4(1). Both the Divisional Court and the Court of Appeal were, however, agreed that the press are entitled under s. 4(1) to publish anything occurring in open court unless an order has been made under s. 4(2); accordingly an order is now necessary to prohibit reporting of a 'trial within a trial' or guilty pleas.[186] An order can only be made under s. 4(2) to postpone publication of reports of 'legal proceedings held in public'; this term means proceedings held in court at a hearing, and does not enable a court to ban the showing of a film of the defendant's arrest.[187] The power under s. 4(2) can only be used to restrain reports of the proceedings, not extraneous publications, it then being a question of fact whether such publications are discrete.[188]

In 1982 a Practice Direction was made by Lord Lane CJ in respect of orders under ss. 4(2) and 11:[189]

> It is necessary to keep a permanent record of such orders for later reference. For this purpose all orders made under section 4(2) must be formulated in precise terms, having regard to the decision of *R v Horsham Justices, ex p Farquharson* [1982] QB 762, and orders under both sections must be committed to writing either by the judge personally or by the clerk of the court under the judge's directions. An order must state (a) its precise scope, (b) the time at which it shall cease to have effect, if appropriate, and (c) the specific purpose of making the order.
>
> Courts will normally give notice to the press in some form that an order has been made under either section of the Act and court staff should be prepared to answer any inquiry about a specific case, but it is, and will remain, the responsibility of those reporting cases, and their editors, to ensure that no breach of any order occurs and the onus rests with them to make inquiry in any case of doubt.

In *R v Clerkenwell Metropolitan Stipendiary Magistrate, ex p Telegraph plc*,[190] the Divisional Court held that the court had a discretion to hear representations from the media, which should ordinarily be exercised when the media asked to be heard either on the making of an order or in regard to its continuance. (For subsequent proceedings, see *R v Clerkenwell Justices, ex p Trachtenberg*,[191] where the Divisional Court upheld the magistrate's decision to revoke a s. 4(2) order.)

Orders under s. 4 or 11 imposed by inferior courts or the Crown Court (other than in respect of a trial on indictment) may be challenged on an application for judicial review under the ultra vires doctrine. Orders in relation to a trial on indictment[192] can now be

---

[183] Ibid., at 790–795.   [184] Ibid., at 805.   [185] Ibid., at 798.

[186] Cf. above, p. 697: the *Border TV* case would now be decided differently.

[187] *R v Rhuddlan Justices, ex p HTV Ltd* [1986] Crim LR 329.

[188] *R v Guardian Newspapers Ltd* [2001] EWCA Crim 1351 (orders upheld after the halting of the first trial of Leeds United footballers (see p. 703) to prevent reporting of the reasons for discharge of the jury and any reference to a racial motive).

[189] *Practice Direction (Contempt: Reporting Restrictions)* [1982] 1 WLR 1475. See now the Consolidated Criminal Practice Direction, para. I.3.3.

[190] [1993] QB 462.   [191] [1993] COD 93.

[192] But not a refusal to make an order or a decision to discharge one previously made: *R v S* [1995] 2 Cr App R 347; cf. *Re Saunders* (1990) Times, 8 February (decision to refuse s. 4(2) order at preparatory hearing

challenged by a 'person aggrieved' by way of an appeal to the Court of Appeal,[193] under which the role of the court is to form its own view and not merely review the decision of the trial judge.[194] Applications for leave to appeal and appeals under s. 159 are determined on written submissions without a hearing.[195]

The Court of Appeal (Criminal Division) has taken a robust approach in setting aside or restricting s. 4(2) orders. In *R v Beck, ex p Daily Telegraph plc,*[196] the court set aside an order restricting reporting of the trial of three social workers on the first of three indictments alleging serious offences of sexual and physical abuse of children in the care of Leicestershire Social Services, until end of the trial, when the matter would be reconsidered. The court had to consider separately (a) whether there was a substantial risk of prejudice and (b) whether, if so, it was necessary to make an order. The latter step involving balancing the considerations that supported a fair trial against the requirement of open justice and a legitimate public interest and concern in the matters in question. Here, there was a substantial risk of prejudice if the first trial were reported, but in view of the widespread public concern over the circumstances that gave rise to the trial, no order should be made. In *R v Sherwood, ex p Telegraph plc,*[197] the Court of Appeal stated that a three-stage test should be applied: (1) would reporting give rise to a not insubstantial risk of prejudice to the administration of justice in the relevant proceedings; if not that would be an end of the matter; (2) if such a risk was perceived, would a s. 4(2) order eliminate it; if not there would clearly be no necessity to impose a ban and that was the end of the matter; if it would, the judge would still have to consider whether the risk could satisfactorily be overcome by less restrictive means; if it could, an order would not be necessary; (3) even if there was no other way of eliminating the risk it did not follow that an order had to be made; a value judgment might still have to be made between competing public interests. In *R v B,*[198] the Court of Appeal set aside an order postponing reporting of a sentencing hearing for a Muslim defendant who had pleaded guilty to conspiracy to murder, until after the trial of his co-defendants. While there would be extensive media coverage, there were two safeguards against a risk to a fair trial, the responsibility of the media and the integrity of the jury.

It has been proposed that there should be a unified statutory code governing the reporting of criminal cases.[199]

Quashing convictions, retrials and stays. Media coverage during a trial that creates a real risk of prejudice against the defendant may cause the conviction to be quashed as unsafe. In *R v McCann,*[200] convictions of the 'Winchester three' for conspiracy to murder Tom King,

---

under Part I of the Criminal Justice Act 1987 can be challenged on appeal under s. 9(11) of that Act, but only if erroneous in law).

193 Criminal Justice Act 1988, s. 159.

194 *Ex p Telegraph plc* [1993] 2 All ER 971, 977, CA (Cr D).

195 Crim PR 67, 2(6), (7): upheld as *intra vires* by the Divisional Court in *Ex p Guardian Newspapers* (1993) Times, 26 October and held not to be incompatible with Art. 6 ECHR, in *Re A* [2006] EWCA Crim 4, [2006] 2 All ER 1.

196 [1993] 2 All ER 177. See also *Re Central Television plc* [1991] 1 All ER 347; *Ex p Telegraph plc* [1993] 2 All ER 971; *MGN Pension Trustees Ltd v Bank of America National Trust and Savings Association* [1995] 2 All ER 355 (s. 4(2) order refused); *R v News Group Newspapers Ltd* (1999) Times, 21 May (s. 4(2) order set aside on appeal). On s. 4(2) orders and committal proceedings see *R v Beaconsfield Justices, ex p Westminster Press Ltd* (1994) 158 JP 1055, QBD.

197 (2001) Times, 12 June.   198 [2006] EWCA Crim 2692.

199 C. Walker, I. Cram and D. Brogarth, 'The Reporting of Crown Court Proceedings and the Contempt of Court Act 1981' (1992) 55 MLR 647. See also M.J. Beloff, 'Fair Trial—Free Press? Reporting Restrictions in Law and Practice' [1992] PL 92.

200 (1990) 92 Cr App R 239, CA (Cr D).

the Secretary of State for Northern Ireland, were quashed following extensive media coverage during the trial of the Government 's proposals to change the law on the right to silence.
This included interviews with Tom King and Lord Denning, expressing in strong terms the
view that in terrorist cases a failure to answer questions or to give evidence was tantamount
to guilt; two defendants had refused to answer questions and all had elected not to give evidence at trial. The Court of Appeal held that the jury should have been discharged. The risk
of prejudice could not be eliminated by the judge's direction.

In *R v Taylor and Taylor*[201] coverage had been sensational and inaccurate, with headlines
such as 'Love Crazy Mistress Butchered Rival Wife Court Told' (the court 'had been told no
such thing'[202]). Apart from the effect on the fairness of the trial, the court also declined to
order a retrial on the ground that a fair trial would not now be possible. The papers were sent
to the Attorney-General, but he decided that no further action should be taken. An application for judicial review of that decision was dismissed, *inter alia* on the ground that the
court had no jurisdiction to review the Attorney-General's decision because of his unique
constitutional position.[203] In subsequent cases, however, the courts have been more sceptical
of arguments that a fair trial or retrial will not be possible.[204]

Injunctions. In an appropriate case the High Court may grant an injunction to restrain
a publication that would be a contempt of court by prejudicing criminal proceedings. For
example, in *A-G v British Broadcasting Corpn*[205] Wilkie J granted an injunction (a) preventing the BBC reporting the contents of a document in which it was alleged by a Downing
Street official that Lord Levy has asked her 'to lie for him about the "Cash for Honours"
police investigation', and (b) ordering that the hearing be treated as if held in private, with
details of the reasons to be divulged only to named persons, such as the Director General of
the BBC, save with the permission of the court or the agreement of the Attorney-General.
Lord Levy was under arrest in connection with the investigation and it was claimed that
disclosure would breach the strict liability rule on the ground that it would deprive the
police of the ability to reveal the contents to suspects or witnesses at the time of their choos-
ing. Publication of the fact that the Attorney-General had obtained an injunction and the
identity of the sender and recipient of the document, and that it referred to Lord Levy, was
not prohibited, and received extensive publicity. Element (a) was subsequently discharged
when an application in the same terms against the *Guardian* was rejected on the grounds
that 20,000 to 30,000 copies were in distribution and could not be recalled. Element (b) was
maintained by Swift J, but this was reversed by the Court of Appeal on the ground that any
remaining impact on the investigation was speculative. (It is arguable that the significance
of the police concerns was in any event overstated.) On injunctions in the context of publications in respect of civil proceedings, see below.[206]

The position in the US. The strong line taken by the US Supreme Court against inhibitions on freedom of expression and freedom of the press[207] has meant that broadcasting and
press publication of prejudicial material have been a considerable problem. There has been
an extensive debate on whether the balance between the right of free expression and the right

---

[201] (1993) 98 Cr App R 361, CA (Cr D). See B. Naylor [1994] CLJ 492.

[202] Per McCowan LJ at 369.   [203] *R v Solicitor-General, ex p Taylor* (1995) Times, 14 August.

[204] *R v Stone* [2001] Crim LR 465; *Montgomery v HM Advocate* [2003] 1 AC 641, per Lord Hope at 673,
noting research in New Zealand that suggested that the impact of pre-trial publicity and prejudicial coverage
during trial was minimal; *R v Abu Hamza* [2006] EWCA Crim 2918 (no stay on proceedings). Cf. T.M. Honess
et al. [2002] Crim LR 719, arguing that emotive imagery presented in a story-like form is especially difficult
to set aside.

[205] [2007] EWCA Civ 280. See also *Coe v Central Television* (1993) Independent, 11 August.

[206] Pp. 721–734.   [207] See above, p. 686.

to a fair trial is correctly drawn.[208] The Supreme Court has had to quash convictions in some extreme *causes célèbres: Irwin v Dowd*;[209] *Estes v Texas*[210] (where the courtroom, according to the *New York Times*, 'was turned into a snake-pit by the multiplicity of cameras, wires, microphones and technicians milling about the chamber');[211] and *Sheppard v Maxwell*.[212] In the last case, Sheppard's conviction was quashed after he had been in prison for 10 years convicted of murder after a sensationalised 'circus-like' trial. He was acquitted following a re-trial. The disquiet engendered by such cases has led to the employment of a number of safety devices: use of the voir dire examination of jurors to determine whether they are capable of ignoring pre-trial publicity; sequestration of the jury during the trial; transferring a case to another county; and the exercise of control by judges and public authorities over police officers, lawyers and court officials to prevent the release of prejudicial information. In addition, there is the encouragement of self-regulation by the press—the voluntary observation of proper standards of press coverage. These devices are constitutional, but doubts are expressed as to their efficacy. Following *Sheppard v Maxwell*, with its emphasis on the defendant's right to a fair trial under the Sixth and Fourteenth Amendments, trial courts have imposed specific reporting restrictions ('gag orders') on the press in individual cases where prejudicial publicity is apprehended. In *Nebraska Press Association v Stuart*,[213] the Supreme Court held that a 'gag order' will normally be an unconstitutional restriction on press freedom.[214]

(B) WHEN DOES THE SUB JUDICE RULE APPLY?

(I) AT COMMON LAW

1. Commencement

There were uncertainties both as to the commencement and the conclusion of the period within which matters were sub judice so as to render comments or acts that were prejudicial, contempts. If proceedings were 'pending' they were clearly sub judice. Proceedings were held to be 'pending' where a defendant had been arrested by virtue of a warrant (*R v Clarke, ex p Crippen*),[215] and it was suggested obiter in the same case that they were 'pending' from the time the warrant was issued. The authorities conflicted on the question whether matters were sub judice when proceedings were merely 'imminent'. In *James v Robinson*,[216] the High Court of Australia held that, as a matter of law, contempt of court could not be committed before the proceedings in question began. The view that the law of contempt applied when proceedings were merely imminent was expressed in *R v Savundranayagan*,[217] but those were not contempt proceedings, and in *R v Beaverbrook Newspapers Ltd*.[218]

The Phillimore Committee concluded[219] that the application of the concept of 'imminence' presented too many problems, and that the right starting point in England and Wales was the moment when the suspected man was charged or a summons served.

---

[208] See, e.g., *Abraham*, pp. 174–183; Donnelly and Goldfarb (1961) 24 MLR 239.
[209] 366 US 717 (1961).   [210] 381 US 532 (1965).   [211] *Abraham*, p. 177.
[212] 384 US 333 (1966).   [213] 427 US 539 (1976).
[214] See A.M. Schatz (1975) 10 Harv Civ Rights–Civ Lib LR 608; Note (1977) 87 Yale LJ 342.
[215] (1910) 103 LT 636, DC.   [216] (1963) 109 CLR 593.   [217] [1968] 3 All ER 439n.
[218] [1962] NI 15, QBD (NI) (fines imposed for publishing details about a man under close police surveillance and two days later arrested for murder).
[219] Pp. 49–52.

2. Conclusion

Technically, the proceedings were not over until the trial had been completed and either the time for appealing had expired, or any appeals had finally been determined.[220] However, it was unlikely that any comment would be regarded as giving rise to any risk of prejudice to the fair conduct of proceedings. 'A judge is in a very different position to a juryman. Though in no sense superhuman, he has by his training no difficulty in putting out of his mind matters which are not evidence in the case.'[221] The Phillimore Committee recommended that the law of contempt should cease to apply at the conclusion of the trial or hearing at first instance unless: (a) sentence is postponed, in which case restrictions should continue until sentence is passed; or (b) no verdict is reached, in which case restrictions should continue unless and until it is clear that there will be no further trial; or (c) a new trial is ordered on appeal, in which case restrictions should again apply; or (d) there is an appeal from a magistrates' court to the Crown Court, in which case restrictions should apply from the moment the appeal is set down.[222]

(II) PUBLICATIONS INTENDED TO INTERFERE WITH JUSTICE

In *A-G v News Group Newspapers plc*,[223] the Divisional Court indicated[224] that where a publication was intended to interfere with justice and created a real risk of prejudice to proceedings, contempt proceedings could be taken notwithstanding that proceedings were neither pending nor imminent. On the facts, however, the proceedings were properly to be regarded as 'imminent'. However, in *A-G v Sport Newspapers Ltd*,[225] the Divisional Court was divided on the point, Bingham LJ following the *News Group* case (with some reluctance), but Hodgson J holding that proceedings had to be pending. The court was agreed that the requisite intention had not been proved.[226]

(III) UNDER THE 'STRICT LIABILITY RULE'

The time limits for the sub judice period in relation to the 'strict liability rule' are now to be found in s. 2(3), (4) of and Sch. 1 to the Contempt of Court Act 1981.[227] The Government took the view that the Phillimore proposal in relation to commencement went 'too far in allowing prejudicial publication before a formal charge is made, so endangering the trial of accused persons'.[228] Accordingly the provisions in Sch. 1, para. 4 were enacted. It should be noted that proceedings are not technically 'active' while a person is voluntarily 'helping police with their inquiries'. It may be difficult for outsiders to discover whether an arrest warrant has been issued or an arrest without warrant effected. Note the defence in s. 3 of the 1981 Act.[229] This defence was found to be established by the Divisional Court in *R v Duffy; A-G v News Group Newspapers Ltd*,[230] where the *News of the World* in November 1994 published a story alleging that D had committed drugs offences for which he had, unknown to the journalist, already been arrested. The court found the s. 3 defence made out. The journalist had discussed D and the proposed publication with senior officers involved in his case and the officers had failed to mention the arrest, thus leading the journalist to believe that proceedings were not active. The journalist was found to have taken all reasonable care. The rules for

---

[220] See *Delbert-Evans v Davies and Watson* [1945] 2 All ER 167, DC; *R v Duffy, ex p Nash* [1960] 2 QB 188, DC.
[221] Per Lord Parker CJ in *R v Duffy, ex p Nash* [1960] 2 QB 188 at 198.
[222] Para. 132.   [223] [1989] QB 110.   [224] Below, p. 718.   [225] [1992] 1 All ER 503.
[226] See below, p. 720.   [227] See above, pp. 688–693.   [228] Cmnd 7145, 1978, para. 14.
[229] Above, p. 688.   [230] Unreported, 9 February 1996.

the conclusion of the sub judice period are found in Sch. 1, paras 5–11. The provision in para. 11 was intended to cover the 'Lucan situation' i.e. where a suspect remains undiscovered or goes abroad and cannot be extradited. Appellate proceedings will be 'active' according to the provisions of Sch. 1, para. 15.[231] These are wider than those recommended by the Phillimore Committee.[232] It is submitted that this is unjustified given the limited effect comments are likely to have on appellate judges.[233]

(C) THE SCOPE OF LIABILITY: MENS REA

(I) AT COMMON LAW GENERALLY

A defendant was liable for contempt if he published matter in circumstances where such publication, objectively judged, created a real risk that the fair trial of proceedings might be prejudiced. An intention to prejudice proceedings was not apparently enough if there was in fact no risk of prejudice: *R v Ingrams, ex p Goldsmith*.[234] However authorities to the contrary collected in Borrie and Lowe[235] were not mentioned by the members of the court in Ingrams, and Eveleigh J was reported as saying that he did not think the article in question 'would—or had been intended to—prejudice the fair trial of the litigation' against *Private Eye*.

There appeared to be no requirement of mens rea beyond an intention to publish the matter in question and no defence of 'innocent dissemination' at common law.[236] However, s. 11 of the Administration of Justice Act 1960 provided defences in two situations where publication could be said to be 'innocent': (a) where the defendant 'did not know and had no reason to suspect that the proceedings were pending, or that such proceedings were imminent, as the case may be' (s. 11(1)); and (b) where the distributor of a publication 'did not know that it contained any [matter calculated to interfere with the course of justice in connection with any proceedings pending or imminent at the time of publication] and had no reason to suspect that it was likely to do so' (s. 11(2)). It was also argued that the person who supplied information to a newspaper should not be held liable unless he had mens rea.[237]

The Phillimore Committee recommended that the unintentional creation of a risk of prejudice should continue to be regarded as contempt:

> The risk of damage resulting from potentially prejudicial publications is such that we are sure that, broadly speaking, no change of principle is required. A liability which rested only on proof of intent or actual foresight would favour the reckless at the expense of the careful. Most publishing is a commercial enterprise undertaken for profit, and the power of the printed or broadcast word is such that the administration of justice would not be adequately protected without a rule which requires great care to be taken to ensure that offending material is not published.[238]

This recommendation was taken up: see section (iii)[239] on the strict liability rule.

---

[231] Above, p. 693.   [232] See above, p. 716.   [233] Cf. below, pp. 735–737.

[234] [1977] Crim LR 40, DC.   [235] Ibid., at 79–80.

[236] *R v Odhams Press Ltd* [1957] 1 QB 73, DC; *R v Griffiths, ex p A-G* [1957] 2 QB 192, DC

[237] See *Smith and Hogan* (6th edn, 1988), p. 776, criticising *R v Evening Standard Co Ltd* [1954] 1 QB 578; but cf. *Borrie and Lowe*, pp. 389–393.

[238] Para. 74.   [239] Below, p. 720.

(II) COMMON LAW LIABILITY FOR INTENDED CONTEMPT

This category is of significance where the circumstances fall outside the scope of the 'strict liability rule'. The leading cases are *A-G v Times Newspapers Ltd*[240] and *A-G v News Group Newspapers plc*.[241]

- **A-G v News Group Newspapers plc** [1989] QB 110, [1988] 2 All ER 906, [1988] 3 WLR 163, 132 Sol Jo 934, 87 Cr App R 323, Queen's Bench Divisional Court

The respondents, proprietors of the *Sun*, published articles entitled 'Rape Case Doc: Sun Acts', 'He's a real swine' and 'Beast must be named says MP', accusing a Dr B of raping an eight-year-old girl. The second article, 'Rape Case Doc' and 'Doc groped me, says girl', named the girl and accused him of the indecencies. NGN wrote to the girl's mother's solicitor offering to fund a private prosecution, as the police and the DPP had decided, in the absence of corroboration, not to prosecute Dr B. Nine months later, a private prosecution of the doctor resulted in his acquittal. The Attorney-General applied to the court for NGN to be fined for contempt of court at common law, proceedings not having been active for the purposes of the strict liability rule. NGN argued that at the time of publication proceedings were neither pending nor imminent.

Watkins LJ:...

No one could possibly resist the conclusion that in the circumstances I have assumed for the present purpose that the contents of the articles complained of here posed a real risk of prejudice to a fair trial of Dr B. Publication of them during pending proceedings could not, in my view, have failed to have had that effect, so grave are the allegations made against the doctor and so prominent, widespread and so savage, in headline at least, is the publicity given to them....

The ascertainment of the existence of intention is, of course, quite a different matter....

Mr Alexander [counsel for NGN] submits that it would be wrong to infer the required intent from the contents of the articles, for which proposition he relies on *R v Moloney* [1985] AC 905.

If, in so submitting, he intended us to conclude that the contents are all we have to consider, I cannot agree with him, nor do I accept that the contents of these articles are not alone capable of giving rise to the inference that the respondent intended to prejudice the fair trial of Dr. B, if and when that proceeding took place. I agree with Mr. Pannick, who appeared with Mr. Laws [counsel for the A-G], that we are not bound to accept the editor's assertion that he did not intend to interfere with the course of administration of justice. But the articles do not stand alone. The respondent's affidavits and financial support to the mother stand with them in forming the whole of the circumstances to be considered for the purpose of ascertaining by inference whether the intent required was present.

Mr. Laws submits that we should draw the inference that the respondent intended to prejudice the fair trial because (1) the contents of the articles strikingly showed that it took the view that Dr B. was guilty; in paragraph 11 of his affidavit, Mr Mackenzie states: 'I believe that what we were publishing was true;' (2) although the risk of being in contempt was never mentioned, so they say, in discussions between him and Mr Crone [NGN's deputy legal manager], Mr Crone thought there would be an answer to an allegation of being in contempt in regard to which he states in paragraph 10 of his affidavit that he dismissed this as a likely danger since the proceedings were not in an active period under Schedule 1 to the Act of 1981 and that any proceedings likely to ensue were a long way off; (3) Mr Mackenzie and Mr Crone thought proceedings were likely to ensue otherwise why go to the lengths they did to put the mother

---

[240] [1992] 1 AC 191 (below p. 733) in the section on publications prejudicial to civil proceedings.
[241] [1989] QB 110, DC (below).

in funds and, further, they could only have printed articles of such a kind if they were campaigning for a conviction, as they clearly were.

I regard that as a powerful and persuasive submission. I simply cannot accept that an experienced editor such as Mr. Mackenzie could have failed to have foreseen that the material which he published in the articles complained of and the steps he announced he was taking to assist the mother to prosecute would incur a real risk of prejudicing the fairness of a trial of Dr B. The inescapable inference is, in my judgment, that Mr Mackenzie became so convinced of Dr. B's guilt and incensed by that and the failure to prosecute him that he endeavoured to persuade readers of 'The Sun' to take a similar view. Some of those obviously could possibly have formed part of a jury to try the doctor. That is trial by newspaper, a form of activity which strikes directly at a jury's impartiality.

Furthermore, what conceivable reason could there be for publishing the article headed 'Doc groped me, says girl' unless it was intended to prejudice a fair trial by bringing to the notice of readers of 'The Sun,' including possibly potential jurors, extremely damaging matter affecting Dr. B. which would be inadmissible as evidence in his trial....

[His Lordship then held that recklessness was insufficient for mens rea for this form of contempt, expressing agreement with Lloyd LJ in *A-G v Newspaper Publishing plc* [1988] Ch 333, 381–383. He then proceeded to consider whether this head of contempt only applies where proceedings are pending or imminent and if so whether the proceedings here satisfied that test.]

The circumstances in which a criminal contempt at common law can be committed are not necessarily, in my judgment, confined to those in which proceedings are either pending or imminent, 'an imprecise word by which to mark out a period of time,' *per* Windeyer J in *James v Robinson* (1963) 109 CLR 593, 618. The common law surely does not tolerate conduct which involves the giving of encouragement and practical assistance to a person to bring about a private prosecution accompanied by an intention to interfere with the course of justice by publishing material about the person to be prosecuted which could only serve to and was so intended to prejudice the fair trial of that person. This is especially so where the publisher of them makes it plain that he believes the person referred to in the articles is guilty of serious crime, is deserving of punishment for that and that he has committed some other similar crime.

The common law is not a worn out jurisprudence rendered incapable of further development by the ever increasing incursion of Parliamentary legislation. It is a lively body of law capable of adaptation and expansion to meet fresh needs calling for the exertion of the discipline of law....

The need for a free press is axiomatic, but the press cannot be allowed to charge about like a wild unbridled horse. It has, to a necessary degree, in the public interest, to be curbed. The curb is in no circumstance more necessary than when the principle that every man accused of crime shall have a fair trial is at stake. It is a principle which, in my experience, newspaper proprietors and editors are usually as alert as anyone to avoid violating.

There may not have been in fact, as was suggested, another case quite like this, but the kind of threat which the articles complained of posed to the proper administration of justice is by no means novel, as reports of previous cases of criminal contempt committed by publishers of newspaper articles show.

The respondent here had very much in mind particular proceedings which it was determined, as far as it lay within its power and influence, to ensure took place. If it is necessary for the Attorney-General to establish that proceedings were imminent, he has, I think, done so. In my judgment, where a prosecution is virtually certain to be commenced and particularly where it is to be commenced in the near future, it is proper to describe such proceedings as imminent. Such was the case here.

Thus, for the reasons I have explained, I find that the Attorney-General justifiably complains of the conduct of the respondent whom I would hold is in contempt of court at common law and liable to be punished therefor.

Mann LJ agreed.

NOTE

1. The respondent was fined £75,000, with costs. The House of Lords refused leave to appeal.[242] In *A-G v Sport Newspapers*,[243] the Divisional Court dismissed the Attorney-General's application against the publishers and editors of the *Sport,* a tabloid newspaper that carried 'some general news stories, many of them with a sexual slant and generally written in a sensational style'.[244] The Attorney-General alleged that the deliberate publication of a wanted man's previous convictions, contrary to the wishes of the police expressed at a press conference, amounted to common law contempt. The court, however, held that it had not been proved beyond reasonable doubt that at the date of publication the editor had the specific intention to prejudice the fair conduct of proceedings, whose existence he regarded at that time as being speculative and remote. (An arrest warrant was issued two days after publication of the article; the wanted man, David Evans, was arrested three days later in France, extradited, and subsequently convicted of murder.)

(III) THE 'STRICT LIABILITY RULE'

By virtue of s. 1 of the Contempt of Court Act 1981[245] conduct may be treated as a contempt of court as tending to interfere with the course of justice 'regardless of intent to do so'. However, it will still be necessary to prove that the defendant intended to publish the material in question.[246] Moreover, the 1981 Act enacts a number of defences and limitations to liability under the 'strict liability rule' (but not other aspects of the law of contempt, e.g. scandalising the court).[247] These provisions follow the recommendations of the Phillimore Committee.[248] Section 3[249] corresponds to s. 11 of the Administration of Justice Act 1960 (which is now repealed). Section 4(1)[250] enacts what was probably a defence at common law;[251] s. 5[252] enacts a limitation to the scope of liability which is recognised in the Commonwealth[253] and might have been recognised in this country.[254] The leading case on s. 5 is *A-G v English.*[255]

4. PUBLICATIONS PREJUDICIAL TO CIVIL PROCEEDINGS

(A) AT COMMON LAW

As the jury is today rarely used in civil proceedings, so the risk of prejudice to the fairness of trials from the publication of information and comments concerning pending litigation is accordingly reduced. However, where there is trial by jury the law of contempt obviously applies in the same way as in criminal proceedings,[256] and the *Sunday Times* case (below) illustrated that the law protected litigants and witnesses from improper pressure, and indeed

---

[242] [1989] QB 135.   [243] [1992] 1 All ER 503. See A.T.H. Smith [1992] CLJ 203.

[244] Bingham LJ at 506.   [245] Above, p. 688.

[246] See *Borrie and Lowe,* pp. 92–94.   [247] Below pp. 737–744.

[248] Pp. 52–62.   [249] Above, p. 688.   [250] Above, p. 688.

[251] See *Borrie and Lowe,* pp. 267–275.   [252] Above, p. 689.

[253] *Re Truth and Sportsman Ltd, ex p Bread Manufacturers Ltd* (1937) 37 SRNSW 242.

[254] Cf. Lord Simon in *A-G v Times Newspapers Ltd* [1974] AC 273 at 321.

[255] Above, p. 698.   [256] See above, pp. 695–698.

protected the administration of justice from being devalued by the development of 'trial by newspaper'.

- **A-G v Times Newspapers Ltd** [1974] AC 273, [1973] 3 All ER 54, [1973] 3 WLR 298, House of Lords

In 1958, Distillers, a drug company, began to make and sell in the United Kingdom a sedative which contained the drug thalidomide. The product was prescribed for many pregnant women for whom it was said to be quite safe. Many of the mothers who had taken the drug gave birth to babies suffering from grave deformities. It was subsequently established that the deformities were caused by the action of thalidomide on the unborn child at certain stages of the pregnancy. As soon as that was realised Distillers withdrew the product in 1961. Between 1962 and 1968 some 70 actions for negligence were brought against Distillers on behalf of the deformed children. Early in 1968 a settlement was reached in those proceedings. Subsequently further writs were issued; by February 1969, 248 writs had been issued in proceedings which were not covered by the 1968 settlement. Negotiations took place with a view to a settlement and no further steps were taken in the proceedings in which writs had been issued to bring the actions to trial. Distillers made it a condition of any settlement that all claimants should accept it. The parties were, however, unable to come to agreement. In June 1972 Distillers made new proposals but they were not accepted; there were then some 389 claims outstanding. The editor of the *Sunday Times* took a keen interest in the matter. On 24 September 1972 the newspaper published a long and powerful article which criticised the law relating to the liability of drug companies and the methods of assessing damages. The sting of the article was however contained in a paragraph which stated that 'the thalidomide children shame Distillers' and urged Distillers to offer much more than they had done so far. The paragraph continued: '... the law is not always the same as justice. There are times when to insist on the letter of the law is as exposed to criticism as infringement of another's legal rights. The figure in the proposed settlement is £3.25 million, spread over 10 years. This does not shine as a beacon against pre-tax profits last year of £64.9 million and company assets worth £421 million. Without in any way surrendering on negligence, Distillers could and should think again.' Distillers brought the article to the attention of the Attorney-General maintaining that it was a contempt of court. The Attorney-General decided to take no action and Distillers let the matter drop. The editor of the *Sunday Times* was, however, minded to publish a further article of a different character. That article consisted in the main of detailed evidence and argument intended to show that Distillers had not exercised due care to see that thalidomide was safe for pregnant mothers before they put it on the market. The editor sent the article to the Attorney-General who commenced proceedings for an injunction against the respondents, the proprietors of the *Sunday Times,* restraining them from publishing that article. The Divisional Court ([1972] 3 All ER 1136) granted an injunction but the Court of Appeal ([1973] 1 All ER 815) allowed the respondents' appeal and discharged the injunction on the grounds, *inter alia,* that the article contained comments which the authors honestly believed to be true on matters of outstanding public interest and did not prejudice pending litigation since the litigation had been dormant for several years and no active steps had been taken or were likely to be taken to bring it before the courts. The Attorney-General appealed.

The House held unanimously (1) that the Attorney-General was a proper person to commence contempt proceedings, and (2) that an injunction should be granted to restrain publication of the second article. Lords Reid and Cross of Chelsea stated obiter that the first article did not amount to contempt. Lords Diplock and Simon of Glaisdale disagreed. They held that the first article improperly held Distillers up to public obloquy. Lord Simon would in addition have held that 'private pressure' to forgo legal rights was in general impermissible, and could only be justified within narrow limits as where there existed such a common interest that fair, reasonable and moderate personal representations could be appropriate. Lord Diplock took the view that 'private pressure' could not constitute contempt.

Lord Reid:... The law on this subject is and must be founded entirely on public policy. It is not there to protect the private rights of parties to a litigation or prosecution. It is there to prevent interference with the administration of justice and it should, in my judgment, be limited to what is reasonably necessary for that purpose. Public policy generally requires a balancing of interests which may conflict. Freedom of speech should not be limited to any greater extent than is necessary but it cannot be allowed where there would be real prejudice to the administration of justice....

We are particularly concerned here with 'abusing parties' and 'prejudicing mankind' against them. Of course parties must be protected from scurrilous abuse: otherwise many litigants would fear to bring their cases to court. But the argument of the Attorney-General goes far beyond that. His argument was based on a passage in the judgment of Buckley J in *Vine Products Ltd v Green* [1966] Ch 484 at 495–496:

'It is a contempt of this court for any newspaper to comment on pending legal proceedings in any way which is likely to prejudice the fair trial of the action. That may arise in various ways. It may be that the comment is one which is likely in some way or other to bring pressure to bear upon one or other of the parties to the action, so as to prevent that party from prosecuting or from defending the action, or encourage that party to submit to terms of compromise which he otherwise might not have been prepared to entertain, or influence him in some other way in his conduct in the action, which he ought to be free to prosecute or to defend, as he is advised, without being subject to such pressure.'

I think that this is much too widely stated. It is true that there is some authority for it but ... it does not seem to me to be in accord with sound public policy. Why would it be contrary to public policy to seek by fair comment to dissuade Shylock from proceeding with his action? Surely it could not be wrong for the officious bystander to draw his attention to the risk that, if he goes on, decent people will cease to trade with him. Or suppose that his best customer ceased to trade with him when he heard of his lawsuit. That could not be contempt of court. Would it become contempt if, when asked by Shylock why he was sending no more business his way, he told him the reason? Nothing would be more likely to influence Shylock to discontinue his action. It might become widely known that such pressure was being brought to bear. Would that make any difference? And though widely known must the local press keep silent about it? There must be some limitation of this general statement of the law.

And then suppose that there is in the press and elsewhere active discussion of some question of wide public interest, such as the propriety of local authorities or other landlords ejecting squatters from empty premises due for demolition. Then legal proceedings are begun against some squatters, it may be by some authority which had already been criticised in the press. The controversy could hardly be continued without likelihood that it might influence the authority in its conduct of the action. Must there then be silence until that case is decided? And there may be a series of actions by the same or different landlords. Surely public policy does not require that a system of stop and go shall apply to public discussion.

I think that there is a difference between direct interference with the fair trial of an action and words or conduct which may affect the mind of a litigant. Comment likely to affect the minds of witnesses and of the tribunal must be stopped for otherwise the trial may well be unfair. But the fact that a party refrains from seeking to enforce his full legal rights in no way prejudices a fair trial, whether the decision is or is not influenced by some third party. There are other weighty reasons for preventing improper influence being brought to bear on litigants, but they have little to do with interference with the fairness of a trial. There must be absolute prohibition of interference with a fair trial but beyond that there must be a balancing of relevant considerations....

So I would hold that as a general rule where the only matter to be considered is pressure put on a litigant, fair and temperate criticism is legitimate, but anything which goes beyond that may well involve contempt of court. But in a case involving witnesses, jury or magistrates, other considerations are involved: there even fair and temperate criticism might be likely to affect the minds of some of them so as to involve contempt. But it can be assumed that it would not affect the mind of a professional judge....

The crucial question on this point of the case is whether it can ever be permissible to urge a party to a litigation to forgo his legal rights in whole or in part. The Attorney-General argues that it cannot and I think that the Divisional Court has accepted that view. In my view it is permissible so long as it is done in a fair and temperate way and without any oblique motive. The *Sunday Times* article of 24 September 1972, affords a good illustration of the difference between the two views. It is plainly intended to bring pressure to bear on Distillers. It was likely to attract support from others and it did so. It was outspoken. It said: 'There are times when to insist on the letter of the law is as exposed to criticism as infringement of another's legal rights' and clearly implied that that was such a time. If the view maintained by the Attorney-General were right I could hardly imagine a clearer case of contempt of court. It could be no excuse that the passage which I quoted earlier was combined with a great deal of other totally unobjectionable material. And it could not be said that it created no serious risk of causing Distillers to do what they did not want to do. On the facts submitted to your Lordships in argument it seems to me to have played a large part in causing Distillers to offer far more money than they had in mind at that time. But I am quite unable to subscribe to the view that it ought never to have been published because it was in contempt of court. I see no offence against public policy and no pollution of the stream of justice by its publication.

Now I must turn to the material to which the injunction applied.... [I]t consists in the main of detailed evidence and argument intended to show that Distillers did not exercise due care to see that thalidomide was safe before they put it on the market.

If we regard this material solely from the point of view of its likely effect on Distillers I do not think that its publication in 1972 would have added much to the pressure on them created, or at least begun, by the earlier article of September 24....

But, to my mind, there is another consideration even more important than the effect of publication on the mind of the litigant. The controversy about the tragedy of the thalidomide children has ranged widely but as yet there seems to have been little, if any, detailed discussion of the issues which the court may have to determine if the outstanding claims are not settled. The question whether Distillers were negligent has been frequently referred to but, so far as I am aware, there has been no attempt to assess the evidence. If this material were released now, it appears to me to be almost inevitable that detailed answers would be published and there would be expressed various public prejudgments of this issue. That I would regard as very much against the public interest.

There has long been and there still is in this country a strong and generally held feeling that trial by newspaper is wrong and should be prevented. I find, for example, in the report in 1969 of Lord Salmon's committee dealing with the Law of Contempt in relation to Tribunals of Inquiry (Cmnd. 4078) a reference to the 'horror' in such a thing (p. 12, para. 29). What I think is regarded as most objectionable is that a newspaper or television programme should seek to persuade the public by discussing the issues and evidence in a case before the court, whether civil or criminal, that one side is right and the other wrong. If we were to ask the ordinary man or even a lawyer in his leisure moments why he has that feeling, I suspect that the first reply would be—'well, look at what happens in some other countries where that is permitted.' As in so many other matters, strong feelings are based on one's general experience rather than on specific reasons, and it often requires an effort to marshal one's reasons. But the public policy is generally the result of strong feelings, commonly held, rather than of cold argument....

There is ample authority for the proposition that issues must not be prejudged in a manner likely to affect the mind of those who may later be witnesses or jurors. But very little has been said about the wider proposition that trial by newspaper is intrinsically objectionable. That may be because if one can find more limited and familiar grounds adequate for the decision of a case it is rash to venture on uncharted seas.

I think that anything in the nature of prejudgment of a case or of specific issues in it is objectionable, not only because of its possible effect on that particular case but also because of its side effects which may be far reaching. Responsible 'mass media' will do their best to be fair, but there will also be ill-informed, slap-dash or prejudiced attempts to influence the public. If people are led to think that it is easy to find the truth, disrespect for the processes of the law could follow, and, if mass media are allowed to judge, unpopular people and unpopular causes will fare very badly. Most cases of prejudging of issues fall within the exist-ing authorities on contempt. I do not think that the freedom of the press would suffer, and I think that the law would be clearer and easier to apply in practice if it is made a general rule that it is not permissible to prejudge issues in pending cases....

There is no magic in the issue of a writ or in a charge being made against an accused person. Comment on a case which is imminent may be as objectionable as comment after it has begun. And a 'gagging' writ ought to have no effect.

But I must add to prevent misunderstanding that comment where a case is under appeal is a very differ-ent matter. For one thing it is scarcely possible to imagine a case where comment could influence judges in the Court of Appeal or noble and learned Lords in this House. And it would be wrong and contrary to existing practice to limit proper criticism of judgments already given but under appeal.

Now I must deal with the reasons which induced the Court of Appeal to discharge the injunction. It was said that the actions had been dormant or asleep for several years. Nothing appears to have been done in court, but active negotiations for a settlement were going on all the time. No one denies that it would be contempt of court to use improper pressure to induce a litigant to settle a case on terms to which he did not wish to agree. So if there is no undue procrastination in the negotiations for a settlement I do not see how in this context an action can be said to be dormant.

Then it was said that there is here a public interest which counter-balances the private interests of the litigants. But contempt of court has nothing to do with the private interests of the litigants. I have already indicated the way in which I think that a balance must be struck between the public interest in freedom of speech and the public interest in protecting the administration of justice from interference. I do not see why there should be any difference in principle between a case which is thought to have news value and one which is not. Protection of the administration of justice is equally important whether or not the case involves important general issues....

Lord Cross of Chelsea: ...I agree with my noble and learned friend [Lord Reid] that we should maintain the rule that any 'prejudging' of issues, whether of fact or of law, in pending proceedings—whether civil or criminal—is in principle an interference with the administration of justice although in any particular case the offence may be so trifling that to bring it to the notice of the court would be unjustifiable....

Appeal allowed.

NOTES

1. The injunction was discharged in 1976,[257] and the article subsequently appeared in the *Sunday Times*.[258]

2. The Phillimore Committee did not like the 'prejudgment' test propounded by the House of Lords, while recognising the force of the policy arguments against 'trial by newspaper' or 'trial by television':

---

[257] *The Times*, 24 June.

[258] See case notes by C.J. Miller (1974) 37 MLR 96; M. O'Boyle (1974) 25 NILQ 57; D.G.T. Williams [1973] CLJ 177; and see C.J. Miller [1975] Crim LR 132 and M. Rosen, *The Sunday Times Thalidomide Case* (1979).

111. The test of prejudgment might well make for greater certainty in one direction—provided a satisfactory definition of prejudgment could be found—but it is by no means clear that it is satisfactory in others, for instance, in the case of the 'gagging' writs.... It can be arbitrary in its application. For example, an opinion expressed on a legal issue in a learned journal would fall within the description of prejudgment given by Lord Cross of Chelsea. Again, there has been much discussion and expression of opinion in scientific journals as to the manner in which thalidomide operates to produce deformities. These, too, would fall within the test of prejudgment and would therefore be contempts. Furthermore, the scope and precise meaning of the words 'prejudge' or 'prejudgment' as used in the House of Lords are no easier to determine in practice than the phrase 'risk of prejudice'. At what point does legitimate discussion or expression of opinion cease to be legitimate and qualify as prejudgment? This may depend as much upon the quality and the authority of the party expressing the opinion as upon the nature of the opinion and the form of its expression.... Further, the expression of opinion and even its repetition can be so framed as to disclaim clearly any intention to offer a concluded judgment and yet be of highly persuasive and influential character. The simple test of prejudgment therefore seems to go too far in some respects and not far enough in others. We conclude that no satisfactory definition can be found which does not have direct reference to the mischief which the law of contempt is and always has been designed to suppress. That mischief is the risk of prejudice to the due administration of justice.

The Committee's preferred test for contempt under the strict liability rule formed the basis of what is now s. 2(2) of the Contempt of Court Act 1981.[259]

3. It was formerly thought that once a writ for libel was issued, subsequent repetition of the libel would amount to contempt of court. So, persons with little or no intention of pursuing proceedings issued so-called 'gagging' writs in order to stifle further comment. The best view, prior to the 1981 Act, was that the issue of a writ did not *automatically* render repetition of the alleged libel contempt, but that repetition might be contempt if there was a risk of prejudice to the pending proceedings. If a court was not convinced that the plaintiff genuinely intended to proceed, or if the repetition was well before the trial, then there was likely to be no risk of prejudice and so no contempt. Salmon LJ seemed to go further when he said (*obiter*) in *Thomson v Times Newspapers Ltd*[260] that it was a 'widely held fallacy that the issue of a writ automatically stifles further comment'. This was approved by Lord Denning MR in *Wallersteiner v Moir*.[261] Note also Lord Reid's remark in the *Sunday Times* case[262] that 'a gagging writ ought to have no effect'. There is now less scope for 'gagging writs' (or now, presumably, 'gagging claims') in view of the provisions of the Contempt of Court Act 1981 that: (a) delay commencement of the sub judice period in civil cases (Sch. 1); (b) strengthen the test for contempt (s. 2(2);[263] and (c) establish a public interest defence (s. 5).[264] However, it has been held that the rule in *Bonnard v Perryman* does not apply if there is an infringement of the strict liability rule.[265]

4. The decision of the European Court of Human Rights in the *Sunday Times* case is considered above.[266] The Contempt of Court Act 1981 was intended to fulfil the requirements of that decision. It has been a matter of debate whether this has been achieved.[267]

[259] See p. 688.   [260] [1969] 3 All ER 648 at 651, CA.   [261] [1974] 3 All ER 217 at 230, CA.

[262] Above, p. 724.   [263] See *A-G v News Group Newspapers Ltd* below, p. 735, n. 2.

[264] Above, p. 689.

[265] *A-G v News Group Newspapers Ltd*, p. 735, n. 2. See further on 'gagging writs': *Borrie and Lowe*, pp. 189–196; *Miller*, pp. 385–390.

[266] At p. 614.

[267] See N.V. Lowe in M.P. Furmston et al. (eds), *The Effect on English Domestic Law of Membership of the European Communities and of Ratification of the European Convention on Human Rights* (1983), Chap. 10.

5. *Borrie and Lowe*[268] argue that in *A-G v Times Newspapers*[269] Lords Reid, Cross and Morris took the view that fair and temperate criticism of a litigant, whether public or private, designed, for example, to encourage him to settle or not to insist on his strict legal rights, is not contempt.[270] For an example of illegitimate pressure, see *Dove Group plc and Jaguar Cars Ltd v Hynes,*[271] where H conducted a campaign of harassment against Dove Jaguars in respect of a Jaguar Sovereign car which was the subject of pending litigation between the parties in the county court. H's actions included driving the car around with a large cardboard box on the roof simulating a battery and making it clear that it was insufficiently powered, arranging for the car to be towed around the streets by shire horses having alerted the media beforehand, interfering with car salesmen and visiting Mr Dove's country home in his absence to Mrs Dove's alarm. H was fined. The Phillimore Committee[272] recommended that only conduct directed against a litigant which amounts to intimidation or unlawful threats should be capable of being treated as a contempt. The Green Paper[273] expressed the view that this would tip the balance too far against the interests of justice. The Law Commission[274] proposed an offence of making an unwarranted demand with menaces that a person should either not institute judicial proceedings, or should withdraw or should settle those proceedings. No action has been taken on these recommendations.

- **A-G v Punch Ltd** [2002] UKHL 50, [2003] 1 AC 1046, House of Lords

In 1997 the Attorney-General obtained interlocutory injunctions against David Shayler, a former MI5 officer, and Associated Newspapers, a newspaper publisher, restraining the publication of information relating to the security service pending the trial of an action for alleged breach of confidence by Shayler. The injunction restrained the newspaper from publishing information obtained from Shayler 'in the course of or as a result of his employment in and position as a member of the Security Service, whether in relation to the work of, or in support of, security and intelligence services or otherwise'. A proviso permitted the publication of information previously disclosed in a specific newspaper article and that to which the Attorney-General had given his written consent. The editor (James Steen) and publishers of *Punch* magazine, knowing the terms of the injunctions and without the Attorney-General's consent, published an article by Shayler entitled 'MI5 could have stopped the bomb going off' which included information restrained by the injunctions but which the editor did not believe was harmful to the national interest. The Attorney-General commenced proceedings for common law contempt against the editor and the publisher alleging that the publication interfered with the administration of justice. Some of the information disclosed in the article had not been previously published and was not in the public domain. The judge held that by publishing material specified in the injunctions, whether previously published or not, the purpose of the court in granting the interlocutory injunctions, which was to ensure that the specified information was not published before trial, had been frustrated and that the actus reus of contempt was proved. He further held that the editor knew of the injunctions, that he intended to act in breach of its terms, that such an intention equated with an intention to interfere with the administration of justice and that the mens rea of contempt was also established. The judge fined the editor £5,000 and the publisher £20,000. The editor appealed on the ground, *inter alia*, that the relevant purpose of the orders in question was to prevent publication of matter that was likely to damage the national security and that, since

---

[268] Pp. 204–210.   [269] Above.
[270] Cf. Hunt J in *Commercial Bank of Australia Ltd v Preston* [1981] 2 NSWLR 554, Sup Ct NSW.
[271] [1993] COD 174.   [272] Pp. 25–30.   [273] Cmnd 7145, pp. 15–17.
[274] Law Com No. 96, pp. 59–62.

no evidence had been adduced that he had intended to frustrate that purpose, the Attorney-General had failed to prove the requisite mens rea of contempt. The Court of Appeal allowed the appeal.

Lord Nicholls of Birkenhead:

1 My Lords, this appeal concerns the interaction of two principles of fundamental importance in this country: freedom of expression, and the rule of law....

2 Contempt of court is the established, if unfortunate, name given to the species of wrongful conduct which consists of interference with the administration of justice. It is an essential adjunct of the rule of law. Interference with the administration of justice can take many forms. In civil proceedings one obvious form is a wilful failure by a party to the proceedings to comply with a court order made against him. By such a breach a party may frustrate, to greater or lesser extent, the purpose the court sought to achieve in making the order against him. That is not the form of contempt in question in this case. In 1997 the court made an order against Mr Shayler, restraining him from disclosing information about the Security Service. But neither Punch Ltd nor Mr Steen was a party to those proceedings. No order was made against either of them.

3 The form of contempt asserted by the Attorney General in the present case is different, although closely related. Sometimes the purpose a court seeks to achieve in making an order against a party to proceedings may be deliberately impeded or prejudiced by the conduct of a third party. This may take more than one form. The third party may be assisting, that is, aiding and abetting, a breach of the order by the person against whom the order was made. Then he is an accessory to the breach of the order. That also is not the case presented by the Attorney General against Mr Steen, although the case could have been framed in this way. Punch Ltd and Mr Steen furthered Mr Shayler's breaches of the order made against him by publishing an article he wrote specially for them. However, the Attorney General has not advanced a case against Mr Steen or the company on this footing.

4 Aiding and abetting a breach of the order by the person specifically restrained by the order is not always an essential ingredient of 'third party' contempt. The purpose of a court in making an order may be deliberately frustrated by a third party even though he is acting independently of the party against whom the order was made. An interlocutory order for the non-disclosure of information is the paradigm example of the type of order where this principle is in point. The *Spycatcher* litigation is the best known recent instance of this. It is a contempt of court by a third party, with the intention of impeding or prejudicing the administration of justice by the court in an action between two other parties, himself to do the acts which the injunction restrains the defendant in that action from committing if the acts done have some significant and adverse affect on the administration of justice in that action: see Lord Brandon of Oakbrook in *Attorney General v Times Newspapers Ltd* [1992] 1 AC 191, 203d,206g-h, and, for the latter part, Lord Bingham of Cornhill CJ in *Attorney General v Newspaper Publishing plc* [1997] 1 WLR 926, 936. Lord Phillips MR [2001] QB 1028, 1055, para 87 neatly identified the rationale of this form of contempt:

'The contempt is committed not because the third party is in breach of the order—the order does not bind the third party. The contempt is committed because the purpose of the judge in making the order is intentionally frustrated with the consequence that the conduct of the trial is disrupted.'

5 I shall have to consider later what is meant by 'the purpose of the judge in making the order' and like expressions. In the Court of Appeal Lord Phillips MR's approach on this point resulted in his giving contempt of court in this context a narrower scope than Lord Brandon.

6 The Attorney General's claim in the present case is of this character. The Attorney General's case against Punch Ltd and Mr Steen is presented solely on the basis that they deliberately impeded or prejudiced the purpose the court sought to achieve in making its non-disclosure order against Mr Shayler....

26 On this appeal Mr Steen accepts that in publishing the offending article he committed the actus reus of contempt. The sole issue on this appeal is whether his intention in acting as he did constituted the intention requisite for contempt of court in this case.

FREEDOM OF EXPRESSION, NATIONAL SECURITY AND THE RULE OF LAW

27 This appeal concerns a restraint on the freedom of expression. Freedom of expression includes, importantly, the right to impart information without interference by public authority, to use the language of article 10(1) of the European Convention for the Protection of Human Rights. Restraints on the freedom of expression are acceptable only to the extent they are necessary and justified by compelling reasons. The need for the restraint must be convincingly established. Restraints on the freedom of the press call for particularly rigorous scrutiny.

28 This appeal also concerns protection of national security. National security is one of the reasons, set out in the familiar list in article 10(2) of the Convention, which may justify a restraint on freedom of expression. The interests of national security may furnish a compelling reason for preventing disclosure of information about the work of the Security Service.

29 But, let it also be said at once, the Security Service is not entitled to immunity from criticism. In principle the public has a right to know of incompetence in the Security Service as in any other government department. Here, as elsewhere where questions arise about the freedom of expression, the law has to strike a balance. On the one hand, there is the need to protect the nation's security. On the other hand, there is a need to ensure that the activities of the Security Service are not screened unnecessarily from the healthy light of publicity. In striking this balance the seriousness of the risk to national security and the foreseeable gravity of the consequences if disclosure occurs, and the seriousness of the alleged incompetence and errors sought to be disclosed, are among the matters to be taken into account.

30 The rule of law requires that the decision on where this balance lies in any case should be made by the court as an independent and impartial tribunal established by law. Clearly, if a decision on where the balance lies is to be effective, the court must be able to prevent the information being disclosed in the period which will necessarily elapse before the court is in a position to reach an informed decision after giving a fair hearing to both parties to the dispute. Once public disclosure occurs confidentiality is lost for ever. If disclosure were permitted to occur in advance of the trial serious and irreparable damage could be done to national security.

31 Thus, depending on all the circumstances of the case, a temporary injunction for a reasonable period pending the trial may be necessary for the protection of national security. Even a temporary restriction on the exercise of freedom of expression is not to be imposed lightly. News is a perishable commodity. Public and media interest in topical issues fades. But, when granted, such an injunction becomes an integral feature of the due administration of justice in the proceedings in which it was made.

32 Equally clearly, if a temporary injunction is to be effective the law must be able to prescribe appropriate penalties where a person deliberately sets the injunction at nought. Without sanctions an injunction would be a paper tiger. Sanctions are necessary to maintain the rule of law; in the language of the Convention, to maintain the authority of the judiciary. If the rule of law is to be meaningful, the decision of the court on how, and to what extent, the status quo should be maintained pending the trial must be respected. It must be respected by third parties as well as the parties to the proceedings.

THE TERMS OF HOOPER J'S ORDER

33 I come now to one of the difficulties in the present case. The Attorney General has stated that his purpose in seeking an interlocutory injunction against Mr Shayler was not to stifle criticism of the security service. His purpose was to protect national security. But whether disclosure of any particular information would pose a risk of damaging national security is a matter of dispute between the Attorney General and Mr Shayler, a dispute which can only be resolved at the trial of the action.

34 This situation gives rise to a practical difficulty in the formulation of an interlocutory injunction. It is a difficulty of a type familiar enough in the drafting of many forms of interlocutory injunctions. What is needed, so far as this can be achieved, is a form of words which is apt to keep confidential until the trial information whose disclosure arguably poses a risk of damaging national security but which is not

wider in its scope. In principle, an order having a wider scope is not sustainable as a necessary restriction. A restraint on the publication of manifestly innocuous material is, in principle, excessive. The order of Hooper J, for instance, is capable of catching information which is plainly not confidential. In the course of oral argument my noble and learned friend Lord Steyn instanced information about the quality of food served in the staff cafeteria of the Security Service.

35 Here arises the practical difficulty of devising a suitable form of words. An interlocutory injunction, like any other injunction, must be expressed in terms which are clear and certain. The injunction must define precisely what acts are prohibited. The court must ensure that the language of its order makes plain what is permitted and what is prohibited. This is a well established, soundly-based principle. A person should not be put at risk of being in contempt of court by an ambiguous prohibition, or a prohibition the scope of which is obviously open to dispute. An order expressed to restrain publication of 'confidential information' or 'information whose disclosure risks damaging national security' would be undesirable for this reason.

36 For the same reason an order restraining publication of material whose disclosure '*arguably* risks damaging national security', or words to the like effect, would not be satisfactory. Its ambit would not be sufficiently certain. An injunction against Mr Shayler drawn in such terms would clearly exclude from its scope some information whose disclosure would be harmless. But such a formula would still not produce a clear boundary line. Including the word 'arguably' in the injunction would not render clear a boundary which otherwise would lack certainty in its application. There may well be matters where it would not be readily obvious whether disclosure would or would not 'arguably' risk damaging national security. There may well be matters whose disclosure would attract diametrically opposite views, the Attorney General contending that disclosure would risk damaging national security and Mr Shayler contending that disclosure would not even arguably pose such a risk. An interlocutory order ought not to be drawn in terms where it is apparent that such a dispute may arise over its scope.

37 I shall return to this question, and its practical implications, at a later stage. For the moment it is sufficient to note that Hooper J's order, set out above, avoided this difficulty by being expressed in clear, if wide, terms. The scope of the order was clear.

THE PURPOSE OF HOOPER J'S ORDER

38 Before considering what was the 'purpose' of Hooper J's order it is necessary to be clear on what this expression, and cognate expressions, mean in this context.

39 On this two points seem to me clear. Fundamental to the concept of contempt in this context is the intentional impedance or prejudice of the purpose of the *court*. The underlying purpose of the Attorney General, as the plaintiff in the proceedings against Mr Shayler, in seeking the order against Mr Shayler is nothing to the point. Lord Oliver of Aylmerton adverted to this distinction in *Attorney General v Times Newspapers Ltd* [1992] 1 AC 191, 223:

'"Purpose", in this context, refers, of course, not to the litigant's purpose in obtaining the order or in fighting the action but to the purpose which, in seeking to administer justice between the parties in the particular litigation of which it had become seised, the court was intending to fulfil.'

40 The second point is that the purpose of the court in making an interlocutory order means no more than the effect its terms show it was intended to have between the parties to the action in which it was made. Normally there will be no difficulty in gleaning this purpose from a reading of the order. The purpose of the order and its terms are co-extensive. It is right this should be so. If third parties are bound to respect the purpose of an order made in an action between other persons, it is essential they should be able to perceive this purpose readily from reading the order.

41 In the Court of Appeal Lord Phillips MR expressed a different view. He said that the effect and primary purpose of the third party contempt jurisdiction are to render it a criminal offence for any third

party who is aware of the injunction to commit 'the *potential* wrong which the injunction is designed to prevent'. That, he said, is surely the most serious aspect of the contempt, and the fact that it will at the same time render the litigation pointless is a subsidiary consideration. He rejected the principle as summarised by Lord Brandon in the passage I have mentioned. A principle of this width, he said, would run foul of the established principle of English law that an injunction does not bind a third party: see [2001] QB 1028, 1054–1055, paras 84–87.

42 From a reading of his judgment as a whole it is clear that Lord Phillips MR was troubled by the width of the interlocutory order which led to these contempt proceedings. I share his concern. But I fear that this disquiet led Lord Phillips MR astray on the basic principles of this jurisdiction.

43 When proceedings come before a court the plaintiff typically asserts that he has a legal right which has been or is about to be infringed by the defendant. The claim having come before the court, it is then for the court, not the parties to the proceedings or third parties, to determine the way justice is best administered in the proceedings. It is for the court to decide whether the plaintiff's asserted right needs and should have any, and if so what, interim protection. If the court orders that pending the trial the defendant shall not do certain acts the court thereby determines the manner in which, in this respect, the proceedings shall be conducted. This is the court's determination on what interim protection is needed and is appropriate. Third parties are required to respect this determination, as expressed in the court's order. The reason why the court grants interim protection is to protect the plaintiff's asserted right. But the manner in which this protection is afforded depends upon the terms of the interlocutory injunction. The purpose the court seeks to achieve by granting the interlocutory injunction is that, pending a decision by the court on the claims in the proceedings, the restrained acts shall not be done. Third parties are in contempt of court if they wilfully interfere with the administration of justice by thwarting the achievement of *this* purpose in *those* proceedings.

44 This is so, even if in the particular case, the injunction is drawn in seemingly over-wide terms. The remedy of the third party whose conduct is affected by the order is to apply to the court for the order to be varied. Furthermore, there will be no contempt unless the act done has some significant and adverse effect on the administration of justice in the proceedings. This tempers the rigour of the principle.

45 Departure from this straightforward approach runs into serious practical difficulties. If, in this context, the purpose of the court in granting an interlocutory injunction means something other than the effect its terms show it was intended to have between the parties, how is a third party to know what it is? How is a third party to know what is the purpose, which he must respect, if it is something other than the purpose evident on the face of the order? Uncertainty is bound to follow, with consequential difficulties in proving that a third party knowingly impeded or prejudiced the purpose the court sought to achieve when granting the injunction. I see no justification or need to go down this route, which is not supported by authority.

46 This discussion does, of course, underline how important it is for courts to seek to ensure that injunctions are not drawn in wider terms than necessary. This is of particular importance when the terms of the injunction may, in practice, affect the conduct of third parties.

47 On this basis I turn to consider the purpose of Hooper J's order. In my view, not only was the scope of the order clear, so also was its purpose; clear, indeed, beyond a peradventure. Self-evidently, the purpose of the judge in making the order was to preserve the confidentiality of the information *specified in the order* pending the trial so as to enable the court at trial to adjudicate effectively on the disputed issues of confidentiality arising in the action. This is apparent from merely reading the order. The Attorney General's claim for a permanent injunction might be defeated in advance of the trial if, before the trial, Mr Shayler was at liberty to put this information into the public domain. In other words, but to the same effect, the purpose of the court in making the order was to ensure that the court's decision on the claims in the proceedings should not be pre-empted by Mr Shayler disclosing any of the information specified in the order before the trial.

48 This being the purpose of the injunction, the actus reus of contempt lies in thwarting this purpose by destruction of the confidentiality of the material which it was the purpose of the injunction to preserve.

49 As already stated, Mr Steen accepts that the publication of the offending magazine article constituted the actus reus of contempt. He is right to do so. He did an act which Hooper J's order prohibited Mr Shayler from doing. Publication of the information by 'Punch' was destructive in part of the purpose of Hooper J's order.

50 Although Mr Steen seems not to accept this, this is not a case where the conduct was inconsistent with the court's order in only a technical or trivial way. Disclosure of the three pieces of information mentioned above, not previously published, has had a significant and adverse effect on the trial of the action against Mr Shayler. Contrary to the court's object in granting the interlocutory injunction, the Attorney General's claim to keep these pieces of information confidential has now been thwarted in advance of the trial.

MENS REA: MR STEEN'S INTENTION

51 Before your Lordships' House the argument presented on behalf of Mr Steen was that it matters not whether the purpose of Hooper J's order was as set out above or as stated by Lord Phillips MR. Either way, the Attorney General failed to prove that Mr Steen possessed the necessary mens rea. Mr Steen's evidence was that he thought the purpose of the order was to prevent damage to national security, it was not his intention to damage national security in any way, and he did not consider he was doing so. Before Silber J the Attorney General did not seek to challenge Mr Steen's evidence that when he published the article he did not believe it contained any damaging disclosures. Accordingly, so the argument runs, the Attorney General did not establish that Mr Steen intended to thwart the court's purpose in making the interlocutory injunction.

52 I am not impressed by this argument. The facts speak for themselves. Mr Steen is an intelligent man and experienced journalist. He knew that the action against Mr Shayler raised confidentiality issues relating wholly or primarily to national security. He must, inevitably, have appreciated that by publishing the article he was doing precisely what the order was intended to prevent, namely, pre-empting the court's decision on these confidentiality issues. That is knowing interference with the administration of justice.

53 I do not see how on this issue, which is the relevant issue, the admitted or proved facts are susceptible of any other interpretation. The judge was entitled so to conclude, even though these conclusions were not put in so many words to Mr Steen in the course of his cross-examination. No credible alternative conclusion regarding Mr Steen's relevant beliefs or intentions has been advanced on his behalf. Mr Steen may have thought the order was intended to protect national security, and that publication would not damage national security. He may have had, as he says, no intention of damaging national security. Those beliefs and intentions are not inconsistent with an intention to take it upon himself to make a decision which, as he knew, the court had reserved to itself. I have to say, however, that even on the basis of his stated beliefs and intentions Mr Steen's conduct was surprisingly irresponsible. He frankly admitted, as is obvious, that he was not qualified to assess whether disclosure of any particular information would damage national security. Despite this he proceeded to publish information whose disclosure was, as he knew, asserted by the Attorney General to be damaging to national security.

INFORMATION IN THE PUBLIC DOMAIN

[Lord Nicholls proceeded to hold that disclosure of information which is already fully and clearly in the public domain would not normally constitute contempt of court in this kind of case as this would not have an adverse effect on the administration of justice in the action. The court's purpose in making its interlocutory order would, by then, already been defeated by the acts of others, whether they occurred before or after the court made its order (para [55]). His Lordship doubted, but left open, whether it would be necessary for the Attorney to prove that the defendant knew that the material in question was not in the public domain; on the facts the judge was entitled to draw the inference that when publishing the article Mr Steen was not acting in the mistaken belief that this information was already in the public domain (para [56]).]

57 In my view therefore this appeal succeeds. Silber J was right to hold that both the actus reus and mens rea were proved to the requisite high standard. I would set aside the order of the Court of Appeal and restore the order of the judge.

[Lord Nicholls (at paras [58]–[60] rejected criticism that the role of the Attorney under the proviso subjected the press to censorship by him, as it was always open to the press to apply to the court to vary its order so as to permit the disclosure of particular information. The proviso provided an additional 'simple, expeditious and inexpensive procedure which avoids the necessity of an application to the court whose outcome would not be in dispute'.]

THE WORDING OF THIS TYPE OF ORDER

61 The second matter I must mention, to which I have already alluded, concerns the difficulty of drafting an interlocutory order in terms which are sufficiently certain but go no wider than is necessary to restrain disclosure of information in respect of which the Attorney General has an arguable case for confidentiality. In the present case the wide terms of Hooper J's order did not operate in a disproportionately restrictive manner so far as Punch Ltd and Mr Steen were concerned. They knowingly published previously unpublished material whose disclosure was, as they knew, asserted by the Attorney General to be damaging to national security.

62 This may not always be so. In particular, an interlocutory injunction in the wide form used in the present case may well in practice have a significant 'chilling' effect on the press and the media generally, inhibiting discussion and criticism of the Security Service. Parts of the media may well be discouraged from publishing even manifestly innocuous material which falls within the literal scope of the order. A newspaper may be unwilling to approach the Attorney General, the plaintiff in the action in which the order was made. An application to the court for a variation of the order may involve delay and expense. Even less attractive is the prospect of proceeding to publish without further ado, at the risk of having to face contempt proceedings and penal sanctions. The ability to defend such proceedings, on the basis that disclosure of the material had no adverse effect on the administration of justice, will not usually afford much consolation to a journalist.

63 This is not a satisfactory state of affairs. It is to be hoped that it may be possible to devise an improved form of words for interlocutory injunctions of this type which will give the Attorney General the protection he seeks in sufficiently certain terms but without being as all embracing as the order in the present case. It is to be hoped that the drafting difficulties may be capable of being overcome, at least to some extent. This is a matter for consideration by the Attorney General in the first instance. It is also a matter judges will wish to have in mind in future when asked to make interlocutory orders in this type of case.

Lords Hoffmann and **Hope of Craighead** delivered concurring speeches, **Lord Hope** also agreeing with Lords Nicholls and Hoffmann; **Lord Steyn** agreed with Lord Nicholls; **Lord Walker of Gestingthorpe** agreed with all three speeches.

Appeal allowed

NOTES

1. Mr Shayler was subsequently convicted of offences under the Official Secrets Act 1989 and a permanent injunction granted against him in the civil proceedings.[275]

---

[275] See pp. 628, 792–793.

2. This decision is founded on the decision of the House of Lords in *Attorney General v Times Newspapers Ltd.*[276] In 1985, the Attorney-General obtained an interim injunction in Australia restraining Peter Wright from publishing *Spycatcher: The Candid Memoirs of an Intelligence Officer.* In June 1986, before the trial of the Australian proceedings, the *Guardian* and the *Observer* published articles outlining allegations contained in the Wright memoirs. The Attorney-General obtained interlocutory injunctions against the newspapers restraining them, with certain exceptions, from disclosing any information obtained by Wright in his capacity as a member of the security service (*A-G v Observer Newspapers Ltd and the Guardian*).[277] He intended to seek final injunctions, based on Mr Wright's breach of confidence. In April 1987, the *Independent,* the *London Evening Standard* and the *London Daily News,* who were not parties to the 1986 injunctions, published further material derived from Wright's memoirs. The Attorney-General brought proceedings for contempt of court. A preliminary issue of law was tried, namely whether a publication made in knowledge of an outstanding injunction against another party and which if made by that party would be in breach of the injunction, could constitute a criminal contempt of court on the ground that it interfered with the process of justice in relation to that injunction. Sir Nicolas Browne-Wilkinson V-C held that the law of contempt did not apply where the only act complained of was not a breach of the express terms of the order and the alleged contemnor was neither party nor privy to any breach of the order by others. The Attorney-General appealed. He conceded that the strict liability rule did not apply as proceedings were not active, but argued that the defendants could be liable for contempt at common law as their conduct was intended to impede or prejudice the administration of justice. On 15 July 1987, the Court of Appeal[278] held that the respondents' publications could amount to contempt of court, and remitted the case for trial. Meanwhile, on 12 July, the *Sunday Times,* having been advised by leading counsel that it would not constitute contempt, published extracts from *Spycatcher.* On 13 July, the Attorney-General commenced contempt proceedings against the publishers of the *Sunday Times* (Times Newspapers Ltd) and its editor, Andrew Neil.

Both sets of proceedings were heard by Morritt J. At this stage the Attorney-General pressed for substantive relief only against the *Independent* and the *Sunday Times.* Morritt J held[279] that the publishers and editors of these papers had been guilty of contempt by publishing extracts from or summaries of *Spycatcher.* The respective publishers were each fined £50,000. On appeal, the Court of Appeal[280] upheld the finding of contempt, but discharged the fines. Times Newspapers appealed to the House of Lords. The only matter at issue was whether the appellants had committed the actus reus of contempt. The House of Lords unanimously dismissed the appeal, firmly rejecting the argument that had been relied on by Sir Nicolas Browne-Wilkinson. Lord Oliver of Aylmerton stated[281] that

Once the conclusion is reached that the fact that the alleged contemnor is not party to or personally bound by the court's order then, given the intention on his part to interfere with or obstruct the course of justice, the sole remaining question is whether what he has done has that effect in the particular circumstances of the case.

---

[276] [1991] 2 All ER 398, [1992] 1 AC 191.   [277] [1986] NLJ Rep 799, CA.
[278] [1988] Ch 333.   [279] [1989] 1 FSR 457.
[280] *A-G v Newspaper Publishing plc* (1990) Times, 28 February.
[281] At pp. 418, 419.

This would turn on whether the publication

...frustrates, thwarts, or *subverts the purpose* of the court's order and thereby interferes with the due administration of justice in the particular action.'[282] 'Purpose,' in this context, refers, of course, not to the litigant's purpose in obtaining the order or in fighting the action but to the purpose which, in seeking to administer justice between the parties in the particular litigation of which it had become seized, the court was intending to fulfil.

Lord Jauncey said[283] that it 'can only be in a limited type of case that independent action by a third party will have the effect of interfering with the operation of an order to which he is not a party. Cases involving confidential information are obvious examples.' Others might include destruction of a valuable object or demolition of a listed building, but it would 'only be in exceptional circumstances that a third party would be free to achieve this result without also incurring liabilities other than for contempt of court'.

The same principles were subsequently held to apply in respect of orders made in criminal proceedings: *A-G v Newspaper Publishing plc*.[284]

3. A further example of intentional interference with the administration of justice in civil cases is *A-G v Pelling*,[285] where the Divisional Court held that the publication by P of a transcript of a judgment in a hearing concerning his children held in private constituted contempt. Protection of the interests of the children was an aspect of the administration of justice and the law was sufficiently certain.

4. Is there any room in the law on intentional contempt for any public interest defence analogous to s. 5 of the Contempt of Court Act 1981.[286] John Laws[287] argues that public interest considerations cannot affect the actus reus of intended contempt (if D intends to impede justice he can hardly argue that he was discussing *in good faith* matters of general public interest). They might, however, tend to negative the necessary intent. In *A-G v Times Newspapers Ltd*, Lord Jauncey did consider the public interest, and concluded 'that in these cases the public interest in having justice done unimpeded between parties must prevail over that interest in the freedom of the press'.

(B) UNDER THE STRICT LIABILITY RULE

The test for contempt under the 'strict liability rule' is to be found in s. 2(2) of the Contempt of Court Act 1981[288] and is the same as for criminal cases.[289] The time limits are enacted in Sch. 1, paras 12–14 and (for appellate proceedings) paras 15 and 16.[290] These largely follow the recommendations of the Phillimore Committee, which took the view that in the light of the length of civil as compared with criminal proceedings, the decrease in jury trials and the unlikelihood that judges will be improperly influenced, strict liability need not be imposed from the commencement of proceedings in civil cases. The defences under ss. 3, 4(1) and 5 of the 1981 Act are available.[291]

---

[282] Derived from the decision of the House of Lords in *A-G v Leveller Magazine Ltd* [1979] AC 440.
[283] At 427.   [284] [1997] 3 All ER 159, above, p. 697.
[285] [2006] 1 FLR 93.   [286] Above, p. 689.   [287] (1990) 43 CLP 99, 110–111.
[288] Above, p. 688.   [289] Above, pp. 698–705.   [290] Above, pp. 692–693.
[291] See above, pp. 688–689.

NOTES

1. How would the *Sunday Times* case be decided under the 1981 Act? Consider (a) the test for contempt; (b) the time-limits; (c) the defences. Note Lord Diplock's remarks in *A-G v English*[292] and *Re Lonrho plc.*[293]

2. The relationship between the rule in *Bonnard v Perryman*[294] and the law of contempt of court was considered by the Court of Appeal in *A-G v News Group Newspapers Ltd.*[295] In 1984, Ian Botham, the England Test cricketer, began libel proceedings in respect of an article in the *Mail on Sunday* alleging, *inter alia*, the misuse of drugs while on tour in New Zealand. The defendants intended to plead justification and the case was set down for trial no earlier than March 1987. Under the rule in *Bonnard v Perryman*, applicable under the law of defamation, the plaintiff would not be able to seek an interlocutory injunction restraining the defendants from repeating the allegations subsequently. On 6 April 1986, the *News of the World* repeated the allegations, and a further story, with further details, was intended for publication on 13 April. The Attorney-General sought an injunction restraining the defendants from publishing allegations covering substantially the same ground as the *Mail on Sunday* allegations of 1984. The Court of Appeal held that the rule in *Bonnard v Perryman* was decisive only in so far as the strict liability rule was not invoked. However, on the facts here, the proposed publication by the *News of the World* at this time would not involve a breach of the strict liability rule. There had to be a 'not insubstantial' risk of serious prejudice. While there was a reasonable chance that the *News of the World* story would have been read by at least one member of the jury that would hear the case, the trial would not take place for at least 10 months. 'Much water' would have 'flowed under the many bridges and that would blunt the impact of the publication; the drama of the trial would probably have the effect of excluding from recollection that which went before'.

Cf. *A-G v Associated Newspapers Group plc*[296] where proceedings for criminal contempt arising out of publicity surrounding a previous application by the plaintiff to a Mental Health Review Tribunal were dismissed, *inter alia*, on the ground that any risk of prejudice by any effect on the tribunal or expert witnesses was remote.

3. The application of the strict liability rule to appellate proceedings was considered by the Appellate Committee of the House of Lords in *Re Lonrho plc.*[297] Here, an appellate committee of the House of Lords was due on 10 April 1989 to hear an appeal by Lonrho against the refusal of the Secretary of State (1) to refer the acquisition of Harrods by the Al Fayed brothers to the Monopolies and Mergers Commission, and (2) to publish the report of inspectors who had investigated the acquisition. On 30 March, the *Observer*, a Lonrho subsidiary, published in a special edition extracts from and comments on the report, including an allegation that the Secretary of State had acted in bad faith. A differently constituted appellate committee held that this did not constitute contempt. It considered whether the publication of the special edition constituted contempt under the strict liability rule (a) by prejudging these issues; or (b) by pre-empting the outcome of the judicial review proceedings. On prejudgment, the Committee noted that the test for contempt under the strict liability rule (s. 2(2)) had to be

---

[292] Above, p. 698.   [293] Below, p. 736.
[294] Above, p. 537.   [295] [1987] QB 1.   [296] [1989] 1 All ER 604, DC.
[297] [1990] 2 AC 154. See also *R v Bow Street Magistrates' Court, ex p Mirror Group Newspapers Ltd* [1992] COD 15 (s. 4(2) order designed to prevent publicity that might prejudice the administration of justice in judicial review proceedings in the Divisional Court quashed).

applied without any preconception derived from *A-G v Times Newspapers Ltd*[298] as to what kind of publication is likely to impede or prejudice the course of justice:

7.3 ...Before proceedings have come to trial and before the facts have been found, it is easy to see how critical public discussion of the issues and criticism of the conduct of the parties, particularly if a party is held up to public obloquy, may impede or prejudice the course of the proceedings by influencing the conduct of witnesses or parties in relation to the proceedings. If the trial is to be by jury, the possibility of prejudice by advance publicity directed to an issue which the jury will have to decide is obvious. The possibility that a professional judge will be influenced by anything he has read about the issues in a case which he has to try is very much more remote. He will not consciously allow himself to take account of anything other than the evidence and argument presented to him in court.

7.4 After an action has been tried or an application for judicial review determined and when proceedings are pending on appeal from the decision of first instance or, as here, from the Court of Appeal to the House of Lords, the possibility that a publication which discusses the issues arising on the appeal or the merits of the decision appealed against or of the conduct of the parties in relation thereto will impede or prejudice the course of justice in those proceedings is very much narrower. In the ordinary case, as here, there will be no question of influencing witnesses. In general terms the possibility that the parties will be influenced is remote. When a case has proceeded so far it is unlikely, save in exceptional circumstances, that criticism would deter an appellant from pursuing his appeal or induce a respondent to forgo the judgment in his favour or to reach a compromise of the appeal. So far as the appellate tribunal is concerned, it is difficult to visualise circumstances in which any court in the United Kingdom exercising appellate jurisdiction would be in the least likely to be influenced by public discussion of the merits of a decision appealed against or of the parties' conduct in the proceedings. Discussion and criticism of decisions of first instance or of the Court of Appeal which are subject to pending appeals are a commonplace in legal journals, but on matters of more general public interest examples also readily spring to mind of criticism in the general press directed against, for example, criminal convictions, sentences imposed, damages awarded in libel actions and other court decisions which arouse public controversy. No case was drawn to our attention in which public discussion of the issues arising in, or criticism of the parties to, litigation already decided at first instance has been held to be a contempt on the ground that it was likely to impede or prejudice the course of justice in proceedings on appeal from that decision.

7.5 ...[W]e do not consider that the editorial comment in 'The Observer' special edition, however intemperate the language in which it was expressed may have been, created any risk that the Secretary of State, having succeeded in the Court of Appeal in both appeals, would be deterred from seeking to uphold those decisions in opposition to the appeals or deflected from the course he would otherwise have followed in relation to the appellate proceedings. Nor was the publication in this regard capable of exerting any influence on the decision of the Appellate Committee on either appeal.

As to the argument that the publication of the special edition 'pre-empted' the ruling of the House on the legality of the Secretary of State's decision to defer publication, the Committee commented:

8.4 ...We think that it would be a novel extension of the law of contempt to hold that direct action taken by a litigant to secure the substance of a remedy which he was seeking in judicial proceedings amounted to a contempt in relation to those proceedings and that the publication of extracts from the inspectors' report in 'The Observer' special edition did not create any risk that the course of justice in the appellate proceedings challenging the lawfulness of the Secretary of State's decision to deter publication would be impeded or prejudiced.

[298] Above, p. 721.

(In this case an injunction was obtained *after* publication; had one been obtained *before* publication, would the principle of *A-G v Times Newspapers Ltd*[299] have been applicable?)

4. In *A-G v Hislop*,[300] Ian Hislop and Pressdram Ltd, respectively editor and publisher of *Private Eye*, were fined £10,000 each in respect of two articles relating to Sonia Sutcliffe, the wife of Peter Sutcliffe, the so-called 'Yorkshire Ripper'. They were published in 1989, when the trial of a libel action by Mrs Sutcliffe against *Private Eye*, arising out of allegations that she had sold her story to the *Daily Mail* for £250,000, was about three months away. The articles alleged that Mrs Sutcliffe had provided a false alibi for her husband, knew about his activities before his arrest and was defrauding the DSS. Mrs Sutcliffe was successful in the first action, and a second libel action arising out of 1989 articles was settled in her favour. In the present proceedings, the Court of Appeal held that the articles constituted both common law contempt and contempt under the strict liability rule in that they constituted improper pressure on Mrs Sutcliffe to discontinue the first libel action; and contempt under the strict liability rule in that they created a substantial risk that a juror or jurors might be prejudiced against her. On the first point Parker LJ noted that the articles 'went far further than fair and temperate criticism. They were plain abuse'.[301] There was no defence under s. 5 of the 1981 Act: 'Mr Hislop's intention negatived the existence of good faith'.[302]

5. PUBLICATIONS INTERFERING WITH THE COURSE OF JUSTICE AS A CONTINUING PROCESS

(A) SCANDALISING THE COURT[303]

- **R v Gray** [1900] 2 QB 36, 69 LJQB 502, 82 LT 534, 64 JP 484,
  Queen's Bench Divisional Court

On 15 March 1900, one Wells was tried before Darling J at Birmingham Assizes for publishing certain obscene and filthy words, and for publishing an obscene libel. Before the trial commenced Darling J made some observations in court, pointing out that, whatever might be the rights of the case, it was inexpedient that the press should give anything like a full or detailed account of what passed at the trial, and that, although a newspaper had the right to publish accounts of proceedings in a law court, and for many purposes was protected for doing so, there was absolutely no protection to a newspaper for the publication of objectionable, obscene, and indecent matter, and any newspaper which did so might as easily be prosecuted as anybody else. He further said that, although he hoped and believed that his advice would be taken, if it was disregarded he should make it his business to see that the law was in that respect enforced.

---

299 Above, p. 733.   300 [1991] 1 QB 514.

301 At 527.   302 Per Nicholls LJ at 532.

303 On the historical background to this head of contempt, see D. Hay, 'Contempt by Scandalizing the Court: A Political History of the First Hundred Years' (1987) 25(3) OHLJ 431 and, for Australia, H. Burmester (1985) 15 Melb ULR 313. On the position more recently, see C. Walker, 'Scandalising in the Eighties' (1985) 101 LQR 359 and O. Litaba [2003] Deakin L Rev 6.

The following day, after the Wells trial was over, Gray wrote and published in the *Birmingham Daily Argus* an article which included the following passage (printed in 82 LT 534):

No newspaper can exist except upon its merits, a condition from which the Bench, happily for Mr Justice Darling, is exempt. There is not a journalist in Birmingham who has anything to learn from the impudent little man in horsehair, a microcosm of conceit and empty-headedness, who admonished the Press yesterday. It is not the credit of journalism, but of the English Bench, that is imperilled in a speech like Mr Justice Darling's. One is almost sorry that the Lord Chancellor had not another relative to provide for on that day that he selected a new judge from among the larrikins of the law. One of Mr Justice Darling's biographers states that 'an eccentric relative left him much money'. That misguided testator spoiled a successful bus conductor. Mr Justice Darling would do well to master the duties of his own profession before undertaking the regulation of another.

The Attorney-General brought the matter to the attention of the Queen's Bench Divisional Court on 27 March.

Lord Russell of Killowen CJ delivered the judgment of the court (**Lord Russell CJ, Grantham** and **Phillimore JJ**): ...

Any act done or writing published calculated to bring a Court or a judge of the Court into contempt, or to lower his authority, is a contempt of Court. That is one class of contempt. Further, any act done or writing published calculated to obstruct or interfere with the due course of justice or the lawful process of the Courts is a contempt of Court. The former class belongs to the category which Lord Hardwicke LJ characterised as 'scandalising a Court or a judge' (*Re Read and Huggonson* (1742) 2 Atk 291, 469). That description of that class of contempt is to be taken subject to one and an important qualification. Judges and Courts are alike open to criticism, and if reasonable argument or expostulation is offered against any judicial act as contrary to law or the public good, no Court could or would treat that as contempt of Court. The law ought not to be astute in such cases to criticise adversely what under such circumstances and with such an object is published; but it is to be remembered that in this matter the liberty of the press is no greater and no less than the liberty of every subject of the Queen. Now, as I have said, no one has suggested that this is not a contempt of Court, and nobody has suggested, or could suggest, that it falls within the right of public criticism in the sense I have described. It is not criticism: I repeat that it is personal scurrilous abuse of a judge as a judge. We have, therefore, to deal with it as a case of contempt, and we have to deal with it brevi manu. This is not a new-fangled jurisdiction; it is a jurisdiction as old as the common law itself, of which it forms part. ... It is a jurisdiction, however, to be exercised with scrupulous care, to be exercised only when the case is clear and beyond reasonable doubt; because, if it is not a case beyond reasonable doubt, the Courts will and ought to leave the Attorney-General to proceed by criminal information.

[The court fined Gray £100, with £25 costs.]

- **R v Metropolitan Police Commissioner, ex p Blackburn (No. 2)** [1968] 2 QB 150, [1968] 2 All ER 319, [1968] 2 WLR 1204, Court of Appeal

In January 1968 the Court of Appeal delivered judgment in an application by a private citizen, [Raymond Blackburn], for an order of mandamus against the Metropolitan Police Commissioner in connection with the non-enforcement of the Gaming Acts. In their judgments the court expressed opinions on the conduct of the police and on earlier decisions on the Acts in the Queen's Bench Divisional Court [see [1968] 2 QB 118]. After reports of the judgments had appeared in the Press, [Quintin Hogg], a Privy Councillor who was also a Member of Parliament and Queen's Counsel, wrote an article in the weekly newspaper *Punch* in a section entitled 'Political Parley' in which he vigorously criticised the Court of Appeal and its dicta, wrongly attributing to that court decisions of the Divisional Court.

The applicant applied to the same Court of Appeal for an order that the writer had been guilty of contempt of court in (a) that the article falsely stated that the Act was 'rendered virtually unworkable by the unrealistic, contradictory and, in the leading case, erroneous decisions of the courts, including the Court of Appeal' and ridiculed that court by suggesting that it should apologise for the expense and trouble to which it had put the police; (b) that without proper knowledge of the facts the writer sought to ridicule the court for its alleged 'blindness'; and (c) that the writer had stated that 'a prudent policeman may well turn a somewhat blind eye towards a law which does not make sense and which Parliament may be about to repeal,' thereby encouraging police officers to flout the court's decision and commit breaches of their duty to enforce the law. For the writer it was stated that no disrespect of the court was intended but that he was exercising his right to criticise on a matter which he believed to be of public importance.

Lord Denning MR:...

That article is certainly critical of this court. In so far as it referred to the Court of Appeal, it is admittedly erroneous. This court did not in the gaming cases give any decision which was erroneous, nor one which was overruled by the House of Lords. But is the article a contempt of court?

This is the first case, so far as I know, where this court has been called on to consider an allegation of contempt against itself. It is a jurisdiction which undoubtedly belongs to us but which we will most sparingly exercise: more particularly as we ourselves have an interest in the matter.

Let me say at once that we will never use this jurisdiction as a means to uphold our own dignity. That must rest on surer foundations. Nor will we use it to suppress those who speak against us. We do not fear criticism, nor do we resent it. For there is something far more important at stake. It is no less than freedom of speech itself.

It is the right of every man, in Parliament or out of it, in the Press or over the broadcast, to make fair comment, even outspoken comment, on matters of public interest. Those who comment can deal faithfully with all that is done in a court of justice. They can say that we are mistaken, and our decisions erroneous, whether they are subject to appeal or not. All we would ask is that those who criticise us will remember that, from the nature of our office, we cannot reply to their criticisms. We cannot enter into public controversy. Still less into political controversy. We must rely on our conduct itself to be its own vindication.

Exposed as we are to the winds of criticism, nothing which is said by this person or that, nothing which is written by this pen or that, will deter us from doing what we believe is right; nor, I would add, from saying what the occasion requires, provided that it is pertinent to the matter in hand. Silence is not an option when things are ill done.

So it comes to this: Mr Quintin Hogg has criticised the court, but in so doing he is exercising his undoubted right. The article contains an error, no doubt, but errors do not make it a contempt of court. We must uphold his right to the uttermost.

I hold this not to be a contempt of court, and would dismiss the application.

Salmon LJ: The authority and reputation of our courts are not so frail that their judgments need to be shielded from criticism, even from the criticism of Mr Quintin Hogg. Their judgments, which can, I think, safely be left to take care of themselves, are often of considerable public importance. It is the inalienable right of everyone to comment fairly upon any matter of public importance. This right is one of the pillars of individual liberty—freedom of speech, which our courts have always unfailingly upheld.

It follows that no criticism of a judgment, however vigorous, can amount to contempt of court, providing it keeps within the limits of reasonable courtesy and good faith. The criticism here complained of, however rumbustious, however wide of the mark, whether expressed in good taste or in bad taste, seems to me to be well within those limits....

No one could doubt Mr Hogg's good faith. I, of course, entirely accept that he had no intention of holding this court up to contempt; nor did he do so. Mr Blackburn complains that Mr Hogg has not apologised. There was no reason why he should apologise, for he owes no apology, save, perhaps, to the readers of *Punch* for some of the inaccuracies and inconsistencies which his article contains. I agree that this application should be dismissed.

Edmund Davies LJ delivered a concurring judgment.

Application dismissed.

NOTES

1. In *McLeod v St Aubyn*,[304] attacks upon the competence and partiality of St Aubyn, the Acting Chief Justice of St Vincent, appeared in the *Federalist* newspaper. McLeod gave a copy of the newspaper to a librarian. It was not alleged that he was the author of either the article or the letter in question, although he was the paper's agent and correspondent in St Vincent. Neither was he aware of the contents of the offending issue. The Privy Council held that McLeod was not guilty of contempt. 'A printer and publisher intends to publish, and so intending cannot plead as a justification that he did not know the contents. The appellant in this case never intended to publish'.[305] Lord Morris also stated:[306]

The power summarily to commit for contempt of Court is considered necessary for the proper administration of justice. It is not to be used for the vindication of the judge as a person. He must resort to action for libel or criminal information. Committal for contempt of Court is a weapon to be used sparingly, and always with reference to the interests of the administration of justice. Hence, when a trial has taken place and the case is over, the judge or the jury are given over to criticism.

It is a summary process, and should be used only from a sense of duty and under the pressure of public necessity, for there can be no landmarks pointing out the boundaries in all cases. Committals for contempt of Court by scandalising the Court itself have become obsolete in this country. Courts are satisfied to leave to public opinion attacks or comments derogatory or scandalous to them. But it must be considered that in small colonies, consisting principally of coloured populations, the enforcement in proper cases of committal for contempt of Court for attacks on the Court may be absolutely necessary to preserve in such a community the dignity of and respect for the Court.

2. The case of *R v Gray*,[307] decided the following year, showed that this aspect of contempt was not obsolete. Hughes[308] argued strongly that Lord Morris's view was to be preferred. According to Abel-Smith and Stevens:[309] 'within a decade [of *R v Gray*] the criticism of judicial behaviour which had been so outspoken was replaced in the press by almost unbroken sycophantic praise for the judges'.

---

[304] [1899] AC 549, PC.   [305] Per Lord Morris at 562.   [306] At 561.
[307] [1900] 2 QB 36, above p. 737. See also *R v New Statesman Editor, ex p DPP* (1928) 44 TLR 301, DC (allegation that Avory J had been prejudiced in his summing up in a libel action held to be contempt, but no penalty imposed in view of unqualified expressions of regret).
[308] A.E. Hughes (1900) 16 LQR 292.
[309] *Lawyers and the Courts* (1967), pp. 126–127.

3. In *Ambard v A-G for Trinidad and Tobago*,[310] a reasoned criticism of the sentences passed in two cases in a Port of Spain court was held by the Privy Council not to constitute contempt. There was no evidence to support the finding of the Supreme Court of Trinidad that the article was written 'with the direct object of bringing the administration of the criminal law in this Colony by the judges into disrepute and disregard'. Lord Atkin stated:[311]

> But whether the authority and position of an individual judge, or the due administration of justice, is concerned, no wrong is committed by any member of the public who exercises the ordinary right of criticising, in good faith, in private or public, the public act done in the seat of justice. The path of criticism is a public way: the wrong headed are permitted to err therein: provided that members of the public abstain from imputing improper motives to those taking part in the administration of justice, and are genuinely exercising a right of criticism, and not acting in malice or attempting to impair the administration of justice, they are immune. Justice is not a cloistered virtue: she must be allowed to suffer the scrutiny and respectful, even though outspoken, comments of ordinary men.

4. The last successful contempt proceedings of this nature in England were in the 1930s.[312] It is noteworthy that contempt proceedings were not instituted in respect of attacks on the National Industrial Relations Court which were at times virulent (see *Phillimore*).[313] In 1997, the Attorney-General commenced proceedings for scandalising the court against Geoffrey Scriven, a frustrated litigant who had made repeated allegations of corruption against judges involved in various pieces of litigation. The contempt proceedings were dropped on the basis of S's undertaking not to allege corruption and the like against judges. He continued to litigate and broke that undertaking, and the Attorney-General moved to commit him for contempt of breach of it. The Divisional Court was 'troubled' by the motion to commit given that the Attorney-General was not prepared to assert that S's underlying conduct constituted contempt. The court had granted a separate application by the Attorney-General to have S declared a vexatious litigant, and the Attorney-General accepted that that order proceeded 'sufficient protection in the public interest in relation to Mr Scrivin's litigious activities'. The court discharged the undertaking. There have, however, been examples in the Commonwealth.[314] However, in *R v Kopyto*,[315] following the dismissal of a civil action against the police, the plaintiff's lawyer, K, criticised the decision in a newspaper interview as a 'mockery of justice. It stinks to high hell... [the plaintiff and I are] wondering what is the point of appealing and continuing this charade of the Courts in this country which are warped in favour of protecting the police.' A majority of the Ontario Court of Appeal held that K's conviction for scandalising the court in respect of his expression of opinion was contrary to the guarantee of freedom of expression in s. 2(b) of the Canadian Charter of Rights and Freedoms. While the objective of protecting the administration of justice was of sufficient importance to warrant overriding a constitutionally protected right or freedom, the means chosen were not reasonable and demonstrably justified. In particular, the scandalising offence did not require the Crown to prove that the statements actually constituted

---

[310] [1936] AC 322, PC.   [311] At 335.

[312] *R v Wilkinson* (1930) Times, 16 July; *R v Colsey* (1931) Times, 9 May.

[313] Para. 160 and Chap. 11.

[314] See *R v Glanzer* (1963) 38 DLR (2d) 402; *Re Wiseman* [1969] NZLR 55; *Re Borowski* (1971) 19 DLR (3d) 537; *Re Ouellet* (1976) 67 DLR (3d) 73; and *Gallagher v Durack* (1983) 57 ALJR 191, HCA (see T. Caillard (1983) 14 Melb ULR 311); *Nationwide News Pty Ltd v Wills* (1992) 177 CLR 1, HCA; *A-G for State of Queensland v Colin Lovitt QC* [2003] QSC 279 (muttered statement to journalists that magistrate was a cretin, reckless as to whether it would be published); *Hoser and Kotabi Pty Ltd v The Queen* [2003] VSCA 194.

[315] (1987) DLR 213.

a serious danger to the administration of justice, merely that they were 'calculated' to have that effect. Of the three judges in the majority on this point two (Cory and Goodman JJA) thought that the offence could be redefined so as to meet constitutional standards (e.g. where statements cause a clear, significant and imminent or present danger to the fair and effective administration of justice); the third (Houlden JA) thought that it could not, stating that the Canadian judiciary and courts were strong enough to withstand criticism after a case has been decided no matter how outrageous or scurrilous.

5. *Mens rea.* It is not clear whether mens rea is required for liability for this form of contempt.[316] *R v New Statesman Editor, ex p DPP*[317] seems to indicate that it does not. This was followed in New Zealand in *Solicitor General v Radio Avon Ltd.*[318] In *Ahnee v DPP*[319] the Privy Council asserted without examining the authorities that mens rea was not a requirement:

> The publication was intentional. If the article was calculated to undermine the authority of the court, and if the defence of fair criticism in good faith was inapplicable, the offence was established. There is no additional element of mens rea.

Authorities to the contrary are *S v Van Niekerk*[320] and *Re Ouellet.*[321] In *S v Van Niekerk,*[322] the defendant, a senior lecturer in law, wrote in an article in the South African Law Journal[323] that a significant proportion of judges and advocates who responded to a questionnaire believed that justice as regards capital punishment was meted out to the different races on a deliberately differential basis. Claassen J held[324] that 'before a conviction can result the act complained of must not only be wilful and calculated to bring into contempt but must also be made with the intention of bringing the judges in their judicial capacity into contempt or of casting suspicion on the administration of justice'. As Van N did not have that intention he was not convicted.[325]

6. There is some Commonwealth authority in support of a defence of fair comment,[326] and of a defence that the statement was true and for the public benefit: *Nationwide News Pty Ltd v Wills*[327] per Brennan J. Arlidge, Eady and Smith[328] doubt that such a restrictive rule would accord with the requirements of Art. 10 ECHR.

7. This variety of the law of contempt is virtually a dead letter in the US. In *Bridges v California; Times-Mirror Co v California,*[329] in applying the 'clear and present danger' test,[330] Black J discounted 'disrespect for the judiciary' as a 'substantive evil' which could properly be averted by restricting freedom of expression: 'The assumption that respect for the judiciary can be won by shielding judges from published criticism wrongly appraises the character of American public opinion. For it is a prized American privilege to speak one's mind, although not always with perfect good taste, on all public institutions. And an enforced silence, however limited solely in the name of preserving the dignity of the bench, would

---

[316] See *Miller*, pp. 581–583; *Borrie and Lowe*, pp. 359–360; *Arlidge, Eady and Smith*, pp. 399–400.
[317] (1928) 44 TLR 301, above.   [318] [1978] 1 NZLR 225, NZCA.
[319] [1999] 2 AC 294 at 307.   [320] [1970] 3 SA 655 (T).
[321] (1976) 67 DLR (3d) 73, 91–92 (Qu Sup Ct).   [322] [1970] 3 SA 655.
[323] (1969) 86 SALJ 457 and (1970) 87 SALJ 60.   [324] At 657.
[325] See H.R. Hahlo (1971) 21 U of Toronto LJ 378 and J.R.L. Milton (1970) 87 SALJ 424.
[326] Per Griffith CJ in *R v Nicholls* (1911) 12 CLR 280 at 286; *A-G for New South Wales v Mundey* [1972] 2 NSWLR 887 at 910; *Solicitor-General v Radio Avon Ltd* [1978] 1 NZLR 225 at 231.
[327] (1992) 177 CLR 1 at 39, per Brennan J.   [328] Op. cit., p. 354.
[329] 314 US 252 (1941).   [330] See above, p. 686.

probably engender resentment, suspicion, and contempt much more than it would enhance respect.'[331]

Press allegations of judicial bias, directed to pending proceedings, have been held not to constitute a clear and present danger to the administration of justice.[332]

8. Does the law on scandalising the court comply with Art. 10 ECHR? Cf. *Barfod v Denmark*[333] where the court held that a conviction in the Greenland High Court for defaming two lay judges (imputing biased voting in a tax case in favour of their employer, the Greenland Local Government) did not violate Art. 10. The interference with freedom of expression was prescribed by law, and justifiable as necessary in a democratic society for the protection of the reputation of others and, indirectly, the maintenance of the authority of the judiciary. B was perfectly entitled to question the composition of the court, but not to allege actual bias without any supporting evidence. In *Ahnee v DPP*,[334] the Privy Council upheld A's conviction for scandalising the court in respect of a newspaper article alleging, incorrectly, that the Chief Justice of Mauritius had improperly fixed the date of the hearing of a defamation action brought by himself, and had chosen the judges and that the appointed judges would hear the case despite the fact they would be witnesses. The Supreme Court found the article imputed improper motives, and had been calculated to bring into contempt the administration of justice in Mauritius; that the journalist had failed to make reasonable enquiries; and that he had not acted in good faith but with the intention to mislead. The Privy Council found that the jurisdiction to punish for this form of contempt still existed in Mauritius and rejected the claim that the offence was inconsistent with the protection of freedom of expression guaranteed by s. 12 of the Constitution. This provided, *inter alia*, that nothing contained in or done under the authority of any law should be held to be inconsistent with that guarantee to the extent that the law in question made provision 'for the purpose...of maintaining the authority and independence of the courts' unless this was 'shown not to be reasonably justifiable in a democratic society'. The Privy Council noted that 'the need for the offence of scandalising the court on a small island is greater' than in the UK.[335] The judgment continued:

Moreover, it must be borne in mind that the offence is narrowly defined. It does not extend to comment on the conduct of a judge unrelated to his performance on the bench. It exists solely to protect the administration of justice rather than the feelings of judges. There must be a real risk of undermining public confidence in the administration of justice. The field of application of the offence is also narrowed by the need in a democratic society for public scrutiny of the conduct of judges, and for the right of citizens to comment on matters of public concern. There is available to a defendant a defence based on the 'right of criticising, in good faith, in private or public, the public act done in the seat of justice': see *R. v Gray* [1900] 2 Q.B. 36, 40; *Ambard v Attorney-General for Trinidad and Tobago* [1936] AC 322, 335 and *Badry v Director of Public Prosecutions* [1983] 2 AC 297. The classic illustration of such an offence is the imputation of improper motives to a judge. But, so far as *Ambard's* case [1936] AC 322 may suggest that such conduct must invariably be an offence their Lordships consider that such an absolute statement is not nowadays acceptable. For example, if a judge descends into the arena and embarks on extensive and plainly biased questioning of a defendant in a criminal trial, a criticism of bias may not be an offence. The exposure and

---

331 Pp. 270–271.   332 *Pennekamp v Florida* 328 US 331 (1946); *Re Turner* 174 NW (2d) 895 (1969).

333 (1989) 13 EHRR 493, ECtHR (Series A No. 149).

334 [1999] 2 AC 294. See also *Badry v DPP of Mauritius* [1983] 2 AC 297, PC (holding that this head of contempt applies only to 'courts of justice properly so called' and not a judge in his capacity as a Commissioner conducting a statutory inquiry).

335 At 306.

criticism of such judicial misconduct would be in the public interest. On this point their Lordships prefer the way of the Australian courts that such conduct is not necessarily an offence: *R v Nicholls* (1911) 12 CLR 280. Given the narrow scope of the offence of scandalising the court, their Lordships are satisfied that the constitutional criterion that it must be necessary in a democratic society is in principle made out. The contrary argument is rejected.'

9. *Reform.* The Phillimore Committee recommended that attacks on courts or judges should not be dealt with under the law of contempt, unless there is a risk of serious prejudice to particular proceedings in progress. However, there should be a substantive criminal offence consisting of the publication of matter imputing improper or corrupt judicial conduct with the intention of impairing confidence in the administration of justice. It should be triable only on indictment, and only with the leave of the Attorney-General or the Lord Advocate. The Law Commission[336] took the view that there would be difficulties in interpreting the 'intent' provision, and that it would be too wide to include imputations of 'improper' conduct. Accordingly they recommended that it should be an offence to publish or distribute false matter, with intent that it be taken as true and knowing it to be false or being reckless whether it is false, when it imputes corrupt judicial conduct to any judge, tribunal or member of a tribunal. A prosecution could only be brought with the consent of the Attorney-General but the offence would be triable either way.

(B) PUBLICATION OF JURY SECRETS[337]

This is now regulated by s. 8 of the Contempt of Court Act 1981.[338] The section as originally drafted incorporated the limitation that it was not to apply to publications which did not identify the proceedings, or the names of particular jurors, and which did not enable such matters to be identified. Moreover, the disclosure or the solicitation of the disclosure of particulars was only to be an offence when done in the contemplation that they would be published. Neither the Criminal Law Revision Committee,[339] the Phillimore Committee nor the Law Commission had recommended legislation. Interesting accounts by jurors of their jury service had indeed been published.[340] However, the publication in the *New Statesman* of an interview with a juror after the trial of Jeremy Thorpe and others led to contempt proceedings against the newspaper.[341] The juror was interviewed after the trial was over and no money was paid. It was conceded that the publication could not in any respect interfere with the administration of justice in the *Thorpe* case and that the juror's comments showed that the jury had approached its task in a sensible and reasonable manner, but it was contended that any disclosure of jury-room secrets would tend to imperil the finality of jury verdicts and affect adversely the attitude of future jurymen. The Divisional Court held that if a publication had that tendency it was capable of being a contempt, but did not accept that the disclosure of jury-room secrets would necessarily have that effect, and did not accept that the article in question constituted contempt. The court did not explain why it thought the article in question was not objectionable; it indicated that no exception could be taken to disclosures which did not indentify the persons concerned, but the *New Statesman* article could not of course be exonerated on that ground.

---

336 Report (No. 96) on *Offences Relating to Interference with the Course of Justice*, pp. 67–68.
337 See, generally, E. Campbell (1985) 11(4) Monash ULR 169; P. Robertshaw (1993) 14 J Media L&P 114.
338 Above, p. 689.
339 Tenth Report: Secrecy of the Jury Room (Cmnd 3750, 1968).
340 See, e.g., E. Devons (1965) 28 MLR 561.
341 *A-G v New Statesman* [1981] QB 1; M.J. Richardson [1980] 11 Liverpool LR 126.

It was argued by some that the exceptions built into the original clause were too narrow. However, Lord Hutchinson and Lord Wigoder persuaded the House of Lords at the last minute to remove the exceptions altogether on the ground that any approaches to jurors were undesirable, whether by 'respectable professors from Birmingham', 'Marxist professors from the English Faculty at Cambridge', by 'any scribbler or any journalist,' or by that 'most dangerous animal, the sociologist'.[342] Accordingly, it is now a contempt for any juror to disclose particulars of a case to anyone, even a spouse or a friend. The only safeguard is the requirement of the Attorney-General's consent to prosecution, and even this is not necessary where proceedings are instituted on the motion of a court. It is appropriate to rely upon that safeguard where the ambit of a law is uncertain and the considerations to be borne in mind when exercising the discretion to prosecute are particularly sensitive. It is clearly undesirable to have to rely upon that safeguard in relation to an offence that is drawn so widely that it catches many situations about which there is general agreement that they should not be regarded as criminal at all.

In *A-G v Associated Newspapers Ltd*,[343] the House of Lords held that the prohibition against 'disclosure' in s. 8 extended to the publication by a newspaper of the deliberations of jurors in the jury room, obtained from a source other than the jurors. The *Mail on Sunday* had published material from transcripts of interviews apparently conducted by independent 'researchers' with jurors at the 'Blue Arrow' fraud trial. The House rejected the argument that s. 8 should be construed narrowly to apply only to a revelation by a juror to another person; the section was not ambiguous and what the appellants had done amounted to 'disclosure' within the ordinary meaning of that word. The House upheld fines of £30,000 on the publishers, £20,000 on the editor, Stewart Steven, and £10,000 on the responsible journalist, Clive Wolman.

The Royal Commission on Criminal Justice[344] recommended[345] that s. 8 should be amended to enable research to be conducted into juries' reasons for their verdicts. Section 8 does not prevent a trial or appellate court from considering complaints by a juror of misconduct of a fellow juror: *R v Mirza*.[346] This does not extend to protect a disclosure to the defendant's mother.[347] There was here no defence to be implied by virtue of s. 3 of the Human Rights Act 1998 for a juror who disclosed jury deliberations rather than the court where he was motivated by a desire to expose a miscarriage of justice, and where he had (erroneously as it turned out) been instructed in a leaflet that he could not disclose to anyone.

6. CONTEMPT IN THE FACE OF THE COURT

It is obvious that the public interest in the due administration of justice requires that legal proceedings be free from disruption or direct interference. Some kinds of disruption are ordinary criminal offences, for example violent attacks on judges or jurors. All kinds of disruption will also amount to contempt in the face of the court, and may be dealt with summarily (e.g. *Balogh v Crown Court at St Albans*).[348] The law of contempt in this context does to an extent inhibit freedom of expression, such as the expression of the views of a disappointed litigant as to the defects of the English legal system in general, and the defects of the judge who has just tried his case in particular. Moreover, the disruption of legal

---

[342] 416 HL Deb, 20 January 1981, col. 371. 422 HL Deb, July 1981, cols 239–254.
[343] [1994] 2 AC 238.   [344] Cm 2263, 1993.   [345] P. 2.
[346] [2004] 1 AC 1118. See also *R v Smith; R v Mercieca* [2005] UKHL 12, [2005] 2 All ER 29.
[347] *A-G v Scotcher* [2004] UKHL 36, [2005] 3 All ER 1.   [348] [1975] QB 73, below, p. 746.

proceedings in order to gain publicity for a particular cause has been roundly condemned in the Court of Appeal.[349] However, the law here cannot convincingly be criticised on the basis of interference with free speech. Most of the criticism has centred on the summary nature of the procedure. The two main criticisms made to the Phillimore Committee were, 'first, that the judge appears to assume the role of prosecutor and judge in his own cause, especially where the missile or insult is directed against him personally; and secondly, that the contemnor usually has little or no opportunity to defend himself or make a plea in mitigation'.[350] The refusal of a witness to answer a question or produce a document may also constitute contempt in the face. This can pose particular problems for journalists, who may be required to divulge their sources of information. This is now regulated by s. 10 of the Contempt of Court Act 1981,[351] which was considered by the House of Lords in *X Ltd v Morgan-Grampian (Publishers) Ltd*.[352]

(A) THE SCOPE OF CONTEMPT IN THE FACE OF THE COURT

- **Balogh v St Albans Crown Court** [1975] QB 73, [1974] 3 All ER 283, [1974] 3 WLR 314, Court of Appeal

Balogh, a temporary clerk in a solicitor's office, while attending a criminal trial at a Crown Court, devised a plan to enliven the proceedings by releasing nitrous oxide ('laughing gas') down a ventilation duct on the roof into the trial court. He stole a cylinder of the gas from a hospital lorry and climbed up on to the roof at night to locate the particular inlet duct. The next morning he left the cylinder in his briefcase in the public gallery of the court next door (Court 1) from which there was access to the roof, intending to carry out his plan later in the day. Police, who had seen him on the roof, found his brief case, opened it, and later cautioned Balogh who at once admitted what he had done and planned to do. He was charged with theft of the cylinder. The police reported the matter to Melford Stevenson J, the senior judge, who was presiding in Court 1. Balogh was brought before the judge who said that his admitted conduct was a serious contempt of court and that he would consider the penalty overnight. Balogh was to be kept in custody.

The next morning Balogh told the judge that he did not feel competent to conduct his own case on contempt and that he understood that the only charge against him was theft. The judge said that he would not deal with that charge, but committed him to six months' imprisonment for contempt of court. Balogh then said: 'You are a humourless automaton. Why don't you self-destruct.' Subsequently, he wrote from prison to the Official Solicitor asking to be allowed to apologise in the hope that his contempt would be purged. Accordingly, he appealed to the Court of Appeal.

Lord Denning MR:...

THE JURISDICTION OF THE CROWN COURT

The Crown Court is a superior court of record: section 4(1) of the Courts Act 1971. In regard to any contempt of court, it has the like powers and authority as the High Court: section 4(8) [see now the Supreme Court Act 1981, s. 45(1)(4)]....

---

[349] *Morris v Crown Office* [1970] 2 QB 114, below p. 749.   [350] *Phillimore*, para. 29.
[351] Above, p. 690.   [352] [1991] 1 AC 1, below, p. 758.

[RSC Order 52, r. 5]...preserves the power of the High Court 'to make an order of committal of its own motion against a person guilty of contempt of court'....

In what circumstances can the High Court make an order 'of its own motion?' In the ordinary way the High Court does not act of its own motion. An application to commit for contempt is usually made by motion either by the Attorney-General or by the party aggrieved:...and such a motion can, in an urgent case be made ex parte: see *Warwick Corpn v Russell* [1964] 2 All ER 337, [1964] 1 WLR 613....All I find in the books is that the court can act upon its own motion when the contempt is committed 'in the face of the court'. Wilmot CJ in his celebrated opinion in *R v Almon* (1765) Wilm 243 at 254 said: 'It is a necessary incident to every court of justice to fine and imprison for a contempt to the court, acted in the face of it.' *Blackstone* in his *Commentaries,* 16th edn. (1825), Book IV, p. 286, said: 'If the contempt be committed in the face of the court, the offender may be instantly apprehended and imprisoned, at the discretion of the judges'. In *Oswald on Contempt,* 3rd edn. (1910), p. 23 it is said: 'Upon contempt in the face of the court an order for committal was made instanter' and not on motion. But I find nothing to tell us what is meant by 'committed in the face of the court'. It has never been defined. Its meaning is, I think, to be ascertained from the practice of the judges over the centuries. It was never confined to conduct which a judge saw with his own eyes. It covered all contempts for which a judge of his own motion could punish a man on the spot. So 'contempt in the face of the court' is the same thing as 'contempt which the court can punish of its own motion'. It really means 'contempt in the cognisance of the court'.

Gathering together the experience of the past, then, whatever expression is used, a judge of one of the superior courts or a judge of Assize could always punish summarily of his own motion for contempt of court whenever there was a gross interference with the course of justice in a case that was being tried, or about to be tried or just over—no matter whether the judge saw it with his own eyes or it was reported to him by the officers of the court, or by others—whenever it was urgent and imperative to act at once. This power has been inherited by the judges of the High Court and in turn by the judges of the Crown Court. To show the extent of it, I will give some instances:

(i) *In the sight of the court.* There are many cases where a man has been committed to prison at once for throwing a missile at the judge, be it a brickbat, an egg, or a tomato. Recently, too, when a group of students broke up the trial of a libel action Lawton J very properly sent them at once to prison: see *Morris v Crown Office* [1970] 2 QB 114. There is an older case, too, of great authority, where a witness refused to answer a proper question. The judge of Assize at York Castle at once sentenced him to prison for six months and imposed a fine of £500: see *Ex p Fernandez* (1861) 10 CBNS 3.

(ii) *Within the court room but not seen by the judge.* At the Old Bailey a man distributed leaflets in the public gallery inciting people to picket the place. A member of the public reported it to a police officer, who reported it to the judge. The offender denied it. Melford Stevenson J immediately heard the evidence on both sides. He convicted the offender and sentenced him to seven days' imprisonment. The man appealed to this court. His appeal was dismissed: *Lecointre v Court's Administrator of the Central Criminal Court* (1973) 8 February Bar Library Transcript No 57A (unreported).

(iii) *At some distance from the court.* At Bristol 22 men were being tried for an affray. The first witness for the prosecution was a school girl. After she had given her evidence, she went to a cafe for a meal. A man clenched his fist at her and threatened her. She told the police, who told the judge. Park J had the man arrested. He asked counsel to represent him. He broke off the trial. He heard evidence of the threat. He committed the man. He sentenced him to three months' imprisonment. The man appealed to this court. His appeal was dismissed: *Moore v Clerk of Assize, Bristol* [1972] 1 All ER 58. Another case was where a man was summoned to serve on a jury. His employer threatened to dismiss him if he obeyed the summons. Melford Stevenson J said it was a contempt of court which made him liable to immediate imprisonment: see 'The Rule of Law and Jury Service' (1966) 130 JP 622.

Those are modern instances. I have no doubt that there were many like instances in the past which were never reported, because there was until recently no right of appeal. They bear out the power which I have already stated—a power which has been inherited by the judges of the Crown Court.

This power of summary punishment is a great power, but it is a necessary power. It is given so as to maintain the dignity and authority of the court and to ensure a fair trial. It is to be exercised by the judge of his own motion only when it is urgent and imperative to act immediately—so as to maintain the authority of the court—to prevent disorder—to enable witnesses to be free from fear—and jurors from being improperly influenced—and the like. It is, of course, to be exercised with scrupulous care, and only when the case is clear and beyond reasonable doubt: see *R v Gray* [1900] 2 QB 36 at 41 by Lord Russell of Killowen CJ. But properly exercised it is a power of the utmost value and importance which should not be curtailed.

Over 100 years ago Erie CJ said that '... these powers,... as far as my experience goes, have always been exercised for the advancement of justice and the good of the public': see *Ex p Fernandez* (1861) 10 CBNS 3 at 38. I would say the same today. From time to time anxieties have been expressed lest these powers might be abused. But these have been set at rest by section 13 of the Administration of Justice Act 1960, which gives a right to appeal to a higher court.

As I have said, a judge should act of his own motion only when it is urgent and imperative to act immediately. In all other cases he should not take it upon himself to move. He should leave it to the Attorney-General or to the party aggrieved to make a motion in accordance with the rules in RSC Ord 52. The reason is that he should not appear to be both prosecutor and judge: for that is a role which does not become him well.

Returning to the present case, it seems to me that up to a point the judge was absolutely right to act of his own motion. The intention of Mr Balogh was to disrupt the proceedings in a trial then taking place. His conduct was reported to the senior judge then in the court building. It was very proper for him to take immediate action, and to have Mr Balogh brought before him. But once he was there, it was not a case for summary punishment. There was not sufficient urgency to warrant it. Nor was it imperative. He was already in custody on a charge of stealing. The judge would have done well to have remanded him in custody and invited counsel to represent him. If he had done so counsel would, I expect, have taken the point to which I now turn.

THE CONDUCT OF MR BALOGH

Contempt of court is a criminal offence which is governed by the principles applicable to criminal offences generally. In particular, by the difference between an attempt to commit an offence and an act preparatory to it.

[His Lordship held that B's conduct amounted at most to 'acts preparatory']...

So here Mr Balogh had the criminal intent to disrupt the court, but that is not enough. He was guilty of stealing the cylinder, but no more.

On this short ground we think the judge was in error. We have already allowed the appeal on this ground. But, even if there had not been this ground, I should have thought that the sentence of six months was excessive. Balogh spent 14 days in prison: and he has now apologised. That is enough to purge his contempt, if contempt it was...

Stephenson and **Lawton LJJ** delivered concurring judgments.

Appeal allowed.

NOTES

1. Lord Denning MR equates 'contempt in the face of the court' and the power to the High Court to 'make an order of committal on its own motion'. *Borrie and Lowe*[353] argue that the

---

[353] Pp. 12–15.

concept of 'contempt in the face' should be construed more narrowly, particularly in the context of the inherent powers of *inferior* courts to punish contempts, to cover misconduct in the court room and (perhaps) other misbehaviour that actually interrupts proceedings or where there is an admission by the defendant or all the witnesses are before the court. In *McKeown v R*[354] Laskin J (in a dissenting judgment) held that the concept of contempt in the face was confined to cases where 'all the circumstances are in the personal knowledge of the court'.[355]

2. In *Morris v Crown Office*,[356] a group of young Welsh students interrupted the proceedings in a libel action (*Broome v Cassell & Co*) being heard by Lawton J. They shouted slogans, scattered pamphlets and sang songs. The judge adjourned the hearing. When order was restored, the judge returned to court and sentenced three students to three months' imprisonment each for contempt. At the rising of the court, he dealt with 19 others. Eight apologised, and were fined £50 each and bound over to keep the peace. Eleven did not apologise, saying that they acted as a matter of principle on behalf of the Welsh language. They each received three-month sentences. The 11 students appealed to the Court of Appeal, arguing (*inter alia*) that the sentences were too severe. The Court of Appeal held that the sentences when passed were appropriate. However, as the students had spent a week in prison, and shown respect to the court, the prison sentences were remitted and the defendants bound over to be of good behaviour, to keep the peace, and to come up to judgment if called on to do so.[357] Apart from general disturbances to proceedings in court, contempts may be committed by parties,[358] advocates, witnesses (for example in refusing to answer proper questions) and jurors (by refusing to participate properly).

3. There were suggestions in *Balogh* that the court could only act of its motion where that was 'urgent and imperative to act immediately'[359] or 'if nothing else will do'.[360] Subsequent cases have held that this overstates the position and that the judge may be entitled to adjourn the matter; it may indeed by unfair to take action immediately: *Wilkinson v S*;[361] *Santiago v R*[362] There are indeed three possible procedures: (1) a truly, non-adversial, summary procedure where the judge inquires into the matter, identifies the grounds of complaint, selects the witnesses, and decides on guilt and sentence;[363] (2) a formal adversarial procedure before the same judge; or (3) referring the matter to the prosecuting authorities. It is for the judge to decide as a matter of discretion which to pursue.[364] The *Balogh* dicta are eminently justified in so far as they relate to procedure (1),[365] and indeed the adoption of this approach today is seldom if ever justified. Conversely, reference to the CPS may well be

---

[354] (1971) 16 DLR (3d) 390, 408.

[355] Contra, *Registrar. Court of Appeal v Collins* [1982] 1 NSWLR 682, NSWCA, but see *European Asian Bank AG v Wentworth* (1986) 5 NSWLR 445.

[356] [1970] 2 QB 114, CA. See also *R v Powell* (1993) 98 Cr App R 224 (conviction arising out of wolfwhistle at female juror upheld, but 14-day prison sentence quashed as excessive).

[357] On the problem of disruptive defendants see G. Zellick (1980) 43 MLR 121 and 284; *R v Logan* [1974] Crim LR 609; *R v Aquarius* (1974) 59 Cr App R 165.

[358] E.g. by threatening judge, jurors or witnesses, or (*Gough v McFadyen* 2008 SCCR 20) by appearing naked.

[359] Lord Denning MR at 80.   [360] Stephenson LJ at 90.

[361] [2003] EWCA Civ 95, [2003] 2 All ER 184 (depending on the circumstances detention until the next working day may be lawful).

[362] [2005] EWCA Crim 556.

[363] See *R v Griffin* (1989) 88 G App R 63, per Mustill LJ.

[364] *R v S* [2008] EWCA Crim 138.   [365] See *R v S*, per Thomas LJ at para. [20].

disproportionate if the matter can be dealt with fairly through the formal procedure.[366] On procedural aspects see further note 9 below.

4. In England, inferior courts have statutory power to punish certain kinds of conduct amounting to contempt in the face. For county courts see the County Courts Act 1984, ss. 14(1) (assault on officer of the court), 55(1) (refusals to produce documents, to be sworn or to give evidence), 118(1) (insults towards judge, juror, witness or officer of the court whether in court or in going to or returning from the court, and misbehaviour in court). For magistrates' courts see the Magistrates' Courts Act 1980, s. 97(4) (refusals to produce documents, to be sworn or to give evidence) and s. 12 of the Contempt of Court Act 1981.[367] Binding-over powers may be used, and offenders can be removed from the court. In Parliament, the main point of controversy on s. 12 was whether the power to deal with insults was necessary or even desirable. Where the object of the insult is the magistrate he will be 'the victim, the witness, the prosecution, the judge and the jury'.[368] This is already accepted to be the main cause of concern with the law of contempt in the face of the court, but one may perhaps have greater confidence in the objectivity of professional judges than of magistrates.[369] In 1981 a man was reported to have been imprisoned for one month for refusing to stand while certain charges against him were read out in court.[370] In *Re Hooker (Patricia) and the Contempt of Court Act 1981*,[371] the Divisional Court set aside a conviction under s. 12(1)(b) of the 1981 Act and a £500 fine in respect of the use of a tape recorder by H, a court reporter, without leave, contrary to s. 9(1)(a) of that Act.[372] In construing the words 'otherwise misbehaves' in s. 12(1)(b), regard had to be had to the fact that this was a criminal statute and that the other prohibitions in s. 12 were qualified by the word 'wilfully'. Accordingly, there had to be some other element of defiance, or at least conduct such that the court could not reasonably be expected to tolerate. Neither element was present here.

In *R v Tamworth Justices, ex p Walsh*,[373] the Divisional Court quashed the justices' order that a solicitor be detained in custody under s. 12(2) until the rising of the court following an insult to the clerk of the court (a reference to 'ridiculous listing' by the clerk). The court noted that the justices could have ordered the solicitor's removal from the court (should he have refused to withdraw the remark), reported him to the Law Society or adjourned the matter to another day. Instead, they 'had taken a sledgehammer to crack a nut'.

5. Threats to a witness outside the court have been held not to constitute 'insults' which can be dealt with under s. 12(1)(a): *R v Havant Justices, ex p Palmer*.[374] The statutory powers supersede any inherent power (*R v Lefroy*);[375] however, s. 118 of the County Courts Act 1984 extends more broadly than contempt in the face at common law (*Manchester City Council v McCann*)[376] and 'insults' includes 'threatens' (ibid.). Proceedings can be 'interrupted' under s. 12(1)(b) by acts done outside, as well as inside the court: *Bodden v Metropolitan Police Comr*[377] (use of loudhailer in the street outside court preventing witness being heard). The interruption is 'wilful' if the defendant commits the acts causing the interruption deliberately with the intention that they should interrupt proceedings or if, knowing that there was a risk of interruption, he nevertheless goes on deliberately to do those acts.[378] The power under s. 12(1) includes all incidental powers necessary to enable the court to exercise its jurisdiction in a judicial manner, such as power to direct an officer of

---

[366] *R v S* at para. 22.   [367] Above p. 690.
[368] Lord Gifford, 416 HL Deb, 20 January 1981, col. 385.   [369] But see further note 9 below.
[370] (1981) Times, 19 December.   [371] [1993] COD 190.   [372] See above, p. 690.
[373] (1994) Times, 3 March.   [374] (1985) 149 JP 609.   [375] (1873) 8 QB 134 at 138.
[376] [1999] QB 1214.   [377] [1990] 2 QB 397, CA.   [378] Ibid.

the court to bring a person reasonably believed to be responsible for a wilful interruption before the court.[379]

An appeal against conviction or sentence lies to the Crown Court.[380]

6. Section 41 of the Criminal Justice Act 1925 prohibits (in general) photography and sketching in court. Tape-recording in court is now regulated by s. 9 of the Contempt of Court Act 1981.[381]

7. The fact that many examples of contempt in the face of the court have their humorous side should not conceal the very real difficulties faced by judges in 'political' trials. These seem to be more endemic in the US than in Britain.[382]

8. An excellent illustration of the dangers inherent in use of the summary procedures in this context is *McKeown v R*,[383] where the Supreme Court of Canada managed to uphold a contempt conviction based on slender evidence, over strong dissents by Spence and Laskin JJ. See also *Maharaj v A-G for Trinidad and Tobago (No. 2)*,[384] where the Privy Council held that the failure of a judge to make plain the specific nature of the contempt with which M was being charged vitiated the judge's order committing M to the 'Royal Goal' [sic] for contempt in the face of the court. Subsequently the Privy Council held that M was entitled to claim damages for the imprisonment, under the Constitution of Trinidad and Tobago, on the ground that he had been deprived of his liberty otherwise than by due process of law (*Maharaj v A-G for Trinidad and Tobago (No. 2)*).[385]

9. Provision for legal aid is made by s. 29 of the Legal Aid Act 1988.[386] Recent cases have emphasised the need for natural justice and the requirements of Art. 6 ECHR, to be observed in summary contempt proceedings. The defendant must be given the chance to defend himself and, in appropriate cases, should be given the opportunity of being legally represented. There has been, and continues to be an unfortunate line of cases where decisions of judges (usually but not invariably at the circuit level) and magistrates are quashed because of procedural unfairness. Errors include: failure to formulate the nature of the alleged contempt with sufficient precision;[387] failure to allow legal representation, in particular before imposing a custodial sentence;[388] failure to allow sufficient time for consultation with a lawyer;[389] failing to

---

379 Ibid.

380 1981 Act, s. 12(5), as interpreted in *Haw and Tucker v City of Westminster Magistrates' Court* (2008) 172 JP 122.

381 Above, p. 690. See *Practice Direction* [1981] 3 All ER 848 (applicable to the Supreme Court and county courts), Home Office Circular No. 79/1981 (26 August 1981) (magistrates' courts), *Re Hooker*, above, and *R v Cullinane* [2007] EWCA Crim 2682 (sentence of four months imprisonment excessive and replaced by one for 26 days; there was no prejudice to a fair trial or recording of private conversations of those involved in the court process).

382 See, e.g., the *Transcript of the Contempt Citations, Sentences, and Responses of the Chicago Conspiracy 10* (1970). For entertainment, see R.E. Megarry, *A Second Miscellany-at-Law* (1973), pp. 70–83.

383 (1971) 16 DLR (3d) 390.   384 [1979] AC 385.

385 [1979] AC 385, PC. For a discussion of the problems arising out of alleged misconduct by lawyers in the face of the court, see P. Butt [1978] Crim LR 463.

386 See *R (on the application of Daltry) v Selby Magistrates' Court* (2000) Times, 1 December (clerk to justices wrong to advise that because no contempt had been found there was no need to grant legal aid to cover the legal representation at a s. 12 hearing that had actually been provided by D's own solicitor).

387 *R v Griffin* (1989) 88 Cr App R 63.

388 *R v K* (1983) 78 Cr App R 82; *R v Selby Justices, ex p Frame* [1992] QB 72; *Re Hooker* [1993] COD 190 (see note 4) (legal representation not permitted).

389 *R v Huggins* [2007] EWCA Civ 732 (judge acted unfairly in allowing only 10 minutes for H to speak to counsel, before sending him to prison for 28 days for an outburst in court). See D.C. Ormerod [2007] Crim LR 798.

allow the defendant to give an explanation for his conduct[390] or an apology;[391] dealing with a refusal to testify at an early stage in the trial when it was not possible to assess the effect of the refusal on its course, which would be relevant to sentence;[392] failing to take time for reflection, for example by adjourning the case overnight with the defendant in custody;[393] prejudgment;[394] and using the summary procedure when there was no urgency.[395] In a number of cases, appellate courts have given guidance on good practice to be followed.[396] It does not, however, follow that a failure to follow such guidelines will amount to breach of natural justice or Art. 6.

There are a number of areas of particular difficulty. First, is there a right to legal representation? There is no right to *funded* legal representation; the court must exercise a discretion. The same seems to be the case as regards representation itself. However, it has been stated that it should be the almost invariable practice that a person found with the prospect of imprisonment for contempt should be afforded legal representation where practicable.[397] However, in cases of sudden outbursts in court that interrupt proceedings it has been said that it may be necessary for the court to take swift punitive action without affording an opportunity of legal representation.[398] In the *Newbury* case 11 women created a disturbance in court which seriously disrupted the court's business and were removed to the cells. Three subsequently apologised and were released; eight refused and were committed for 14 days for contempt. They were not afforded access to legal advice. The Divisional Court, however, held that in the circumstances this was not a requirement of natural justice. It is submitted that it will rarely, if ever, be justified to proceed without affording an opportunity for legal representation, and that there was no justification here, given that order had been restored (as in the *Morris* case).[399] A clear distinction should be drawn between (a) the steps needed to restore order (restraining or detaining a person; removing him or her from court) and (b) the process of establishing that this behaviour constitutes contempt and determining sentence.

A second difficult question is when a case must be referred to a different judge to avoid an appearance of bias. It is not the case that the mere fact that the judge is a witness gives

---

[390] *R v K*, above (K was sentenced to three months' imprisonment for refusing to testify against a fellow prison inmate on trial for wounding him; K could have presented evidence of duress which might have constituted a valid defence). Cf. *R v Selby Justices, ex p Frame* [1992] QB 72 (no opportunity for F to deny or admit his disturbance of the court).

[391] *R v Moran* (1985) 81 Cr App R 51.

[392] *R v Phillips* (1983) 78 Cr App R 88 (P's evidence would have added little or nothing; sentence of 14 days detention replaced four months).

[393] *R v Huggins*, above.

[394] *R v Jales* [2007] EWCA Crim 393 (procedure adopted by judge 'grotesquely unfair;' he made it plain early in the contempt proceedings that he had effectively made up his mind that a member of public in court had then imparted information to a witness due to testify, and that there was contempt).

[395] *R v Schot (Bonnie Belinda); R v Barclay (Carole Andrea)* (1997) 161 JP 473 (jurors who refused to reach a verdict due to their 'conscious beliefs' should have been excused and not sent to prison for 30 days; judge should not have dealt with the matter as there was a real danger of bias); *R v Moore (Peter Oliver Stace)* (unreported, 12 September 2000); *R v Stafforce Personnel Ltd* (unreported, 24 November 2000) (finding of contempt in respect of dismissal of juror while on jury service quashed).

[396] E.g. *R v Moran* (1985) 81 G App Rep 51 (Lawton LJ); *R v Hill* [1986] Crim LR 457; *R v Schot, R v Bentley*, above; *R v Dodds* [2002] EWCA Crim 1328 (jurors).

[397] Hobhouse LJ in *R v Bromell* [1996] TLR 67. A number of findings of contempt have been quashed where this is not respected: see above.

[398] Per Stephenson LJ (*obiter*) in *Balogh v St Albans Crown Court* [1975] QB 73 (citing *Morris v Crown Office* as an example); per Watkins LJ (*obiter*) in *R v K* (1983) 78 Cr App R 82, 87; *R v Newbury Justices, ex p Du Pont* (1983) 148 JP 248; *R v Moran* (1985) 81 Cr App R 51, 53.

[399] See the comment in *Arlidge, Eady and Smith*, para. 10.59.

rise to such a risk.[400] However, there may well be real possibility of bias[401] where the facts to which the judge is a witness are equivocal or disputed, on where the conduct is directed at the judge personally. The latter point is illustrated by the decision of the Grand Chamber in *Kyprianou v Cyprus*[402] that the decision of an assye court to imprison an advocate for five days for contempt following exchanges in which he criticised the judges for their conduct of the case (e.g. by passing notes (termed 'love letters') between them) was in breach of Art. 6(1). Under the 'objective test' applied by the court, which related simply to the roles played by the judges,

> the confusion of roles between complainant, witness, prosecutor and judge could self-evidently prompt objectively justified fears as to the conformity of the proceedings with the principle that no one should be a judge in his or her own cause and, consequently, as to the impartiality of the bench.[403]

Misgivings about impartiality were also justified under the 'subjective test' applied by the court, which related to the personal conviction or interest of the judge(s) in the particular case. The judges had stated they had been 'deeply insult' 'as persons' by K's conduct; their emphatic language displayed a sense of indignation; they expressed early on in their discussion with K that they considered him guilty. Overall they were not 'sufficiently detached.'[404] The Court also found a violation of Art. 10, in that while there was some disrespect, the sentence of imprisonment was disproportionately severe and capable of having a chilling effect on the performance by lawyers of their duties as defence counsel.[405]

Since *Kyprianou* the High Court of Justiciary has rejected an argument that in every case in which imprisonment is a possibility, it should not be competent for the court to deal with it itself.[406] The court confirmed that where the conduct was directed at the administration of justice rather than the judge personally, *Kyprianou* did not require transfer.

10. Is it contempt of court for a member of the public to raise two fingers in the direction of a limousine carrying two High Court judges on their way to court? Should it make any difference that the member of the public believes the car to be that of the local mayor, whom he regards as responsible for the latest increase in rates? Cf. the case of Mr Bangs,[407] who spent two hours in a cell before being admonished by Lawson J.

11. *Mens rea.* It is clear that it must be shown that the accused intended to do the act in question. At common law it was uncertain whether it was necessary to prove in addition an intention to interfere with the course of justice.[408] It does seem that such an intention must be shown where it is sought to hold an advocate or witness in contempt for failure to attend court:[409] or interference with jurors is alleged: *R v Giscombe*.[410] It has also been argued that

---

400 See *Wilkinson v S* [2003] EWCA Civ 95, [2003] 2 All ER 184 (foul abusive and threatening language, and violence, by father in proceedings concerning his child; guilt was clear); *Santiago v R* [2005] EWCA Crim 556 (defendant tussled with dock officer and refused to return to court for sentence; there was no issue as to the essential facts).

401 The test established in *Porter v Magill* [2002] 2 AC 357.

402 [2005] ECHR 73797/01.   403 Para. 127.   404 Paras 130, 131.

405 Paras 176–183.

406 *Robertson v McFadyen; Gough v McFadyen* 2008 SCCR 20. This is consistent with Wilkinson and *Santiago*, above.

407 *Miller*, pp. 156–157, *The Times*, 24 May 1973, *Daily Telegraph*, 23 May 1973.

408 *A-G v Butterworth* [1963] 1 QB 696; Borrie and Lowe, pp. 64–65, 410–412.

409 *Weston v Central Criminal Court Courts' Administrator* [1976] QB 32, 43 (per Lord Denning MR); *Re Dr A S Rayan* (1983) 148 JP 569, DC.

410 (1985) 79 Cr App R 79, CA (Cr D).

the Contempt of Court Act 1981, by limiting the scope of strict liability in relation to conduct alleged to interfere with the course of justice in particular proceedings,[411] now imports a full mens rea requirement for contempt in the face of the court.[412] In principle, however, there should be a full mens rea requirement, although this might properly extend to include recklessness.[413] Cf. Arlidge, Eady and Smith,[414] suggesting that the same approach is likely to be adopted as in common law publication cases, where recklessness is insufficient for mens rea.

(B) PROTECTION OF JOURNALISTS' SOURCES[415]

- **Ashworth Hospital Authority v MGN Ltd** [2002] UKHL 29,
  [2002] 1 WLR 2033, House of Lords

Ian Brady, a convicted murderer detained in custody at a secure hospital managed by Ashworth, was on hunger strike and conducting a media campaign about his treatment. An article was published in the defendants' newspaper, the *Daily Mirror*, containing verbatim extracts from B's medical records. The information had been supplied to the *Mirror* by an intermediary, who had been paid for it, and it was probable that an employee at the hospital had supplied the intermediary with a printout from the hospital's computer database. The employee would in so doing have been in breach of his duty of confidentiality under his contract of employment. Ashworth, having attempted unsuccessfully to identify the informant, applied for orders against the defendants (i) requiring them to deliver up to it all medical records or copies or extracts therefrom in their possession, power, custody or control relating to the hospital's care or treatment of the patient, (ii) restraining them from publishing, distributing or otherwise disseminating information contained in those records and (iii) requiring them to explain how they had come to be in such possession or control and identifying any employee and others involved. The judge ordered the defendants to serve a witness statement on the authority explaining how they had come to be in possession or control of the records and identifying any employee and other persons involved. The Court of Appeal dismissed the defendants' appeal. The House of Lords dismissed a further appeal. It held that disclosure of the identity of an informant might be ordered against a person who, though not himself guilty of a civil or criminal wrong, was involved in wrongdoing by the informant; and that it was not necessary, for disclosure to be ordered, that the claimant intended to bring legal proceedings against the informant, provided that some other legitimate purpose in seeking disclosure was identified (here an intention to dismiss the employee). The following extract deals with the question whether disclosure of sources should be ordered.

---

[411] See ss. 1, 2: above p. 689.

[412] *Borrie and Lowe*, ibid.; cf. *Miller*, p. 197, suggesting that the 1981 Act affords at best a weak inference to this effect.

[413] See *Miller*, p. 199.

[414] Op. cit., pp. 765–766. Cf. D.C. Ormerod [2007] Crim LR 798, suggesting that it may be that 'all that is necessary is for D to have performed an intentional act with foresight of the consequences, and that that latter element can be established by inference from the surrounding circumstances'.

[415] See T.R.S. Allan, 'Disclosure of Journalists' Sources, Civil Disobedience and the Rule of Law' [1991] CLJ 131; S. Palmer, 'Protecting Journalists' Sources: Section 10, Contempt of Court Act 1981' [1992] PL 61; see also I. Cram (1992) 55 MLR 400 (case note on *X v Morgan-Grampian*) and S. Walker (1991) 14(2) UNSWLJ 302. For cases at common law in this area, which have now been superseded by s. 10, see pp. 307–308 of the 2nd edition of this book.

Lord Woolf CJ:...

THE SOURCE OF THE INFORMATION SENT TO THE 'DAILY MIRROR'

13 It was Mr Jones's evidence that he did not know the identity of the initial source of the information, but that he assumed it to be an employee of Ashworth. However, he accepted that he did know the identity of the intermediary who supplied the material to him. It is also accepted that knowledge of the intermediary would in all probability lead to the identity of the original source. Mr Jones had previously dealt with the intermediary on the understanding that he would be paid for stories supplied. On this occasion he paid £1,500.

14 It was found by the Court of Appeal and was not disputed on this appeal that it was the overwhelming likelihood that the source provided the intermediary with a printout from Ashworth's computer database which is used to record data about patients ('PACIS'). This meant the source was probably an employee of the authority.

15 Rougier J found that the extracts of the information published in the article were no more than a watered down version of material which Ian Brady had placed already in the public domain in furtherance of his campaign....

SECTION 10 AND ARTICLE 10 ISSUES

37 [His Lordship set out s. 10 of the 1981 Act and Art. 10 ECHR.]

38 Judicial opinion differs as to the extent that section 10 was passed in order that our domestic law might reflect article 10....However, whatever was the objective of those promoting section 10, there can be no doubt now that both section 10 and article 10 have a common purpose in seeking to enhance the freedom of the press by protecting journalistic sources. The approach of the European Court of Human Rights as to the role of article 10 in achieving this was clearly set out by the court in *Goodwin v United Kingdom* (1966) 22 EHRR 123, 143, para 39 in these terms:

'The court recalls that freedom of expression constitutes one of the essential foundations of a democratic society and that the safeguards to be afforded to the press are of particular importance. Protection of journalistic sources is one of the basic conditions for press freedom, as is reflected in the laws and the professional codes of conduct in a number of contracting states and is affirmed in several international instruments on journalistic freedoms. Without such protection, sources may be deterred from assisting the press in informing the public on matters of public interest. As a result the vital public watchdog role of the press may be undermined and the ability of the press to provide accurate and reliable information may be adversely affected. Having regard to the importance of the protection of journalistic sources for press freedom in a democratic society and the potentially chilling effect an order of source disclosure has on the exercise of that freedom, such a measure cannot be compatible with article 10 of the Convention unless it is justified by an overriding requirement in the public interest.'

The same approach can be applied equally to section 10 now that article 10 is part of our domestic law.

39 The decision in the *Goodwin* case followed on from the decision of their Lordships in *X Ltd v Morgan-Grampian (Publishers) Ltd* [1991] 1 AC 1. Lord Bridge of Harwich, with whom Lord Oliver of Aylmerton and Lord Lowry agreed, indicated how the approach to be adopted to section 10 involved very much the same balancing exercise as is involved in applying article 10. Lord Bridge expressed the position in these terms, at pp 43–44:

'But the question whether disclosure is necessary in the interests of justice gives rise to a more difficult problem of weighing one public interest against another. A question arising under this part of section 10 has not previously come before your Lordships' House for decision. In discussing the section generally Lord Diplock said in *Secretary of State for Defence v Guardian Newspapers Ltd* [1985] AC 339, 350: "The exceptions include no reference to 'the public interest' generally and I would add that in my view the expression 'justice', the interests of which are entitled to protection, is not used in a general sense as the antonym of 'injustice' but in the technical sense of the administration of justice in the course of legal proceedings in a court of law, or, by reason of the extended definition of 'court' in section 19 of the 1981 Act, before a tribunal or body exercising the judicial power of the state". I agree entirely with the first half of this dictum. To construe "justice" as the antonym of "injustice" in section 10 would be far too wide. But to confine it to "the technical sense of the administration of justice in the course of legal proceedings in a court of law" seems to me, with all respect due to any dictum of the late Lord Diplock, to be too narrow. It is, in my opinion, "in the interests of justice", in the sense in which this phrase is used in section 10, that persons should be enabled to exercise important legal rights and to protect themselves from serious legal wrongs whether or not resort to legal proceedings in a court of law will be necessary to attain these objectives. Thus, to take a very obvious example, if an employer of a large staff is suffering grave damage from the activities of an unidentified disloyal servant, it is undoubtedly in the interests of justice that he should be able to identify him in order to terminate his contract of employment, notwithstanding that no legal proceedings may be necessary to achieve that end. Construing the phrase "in the interests of justice" in this sense immediately emphasises the importance of the balancing exercise. It will not be sufficient, per se, for a party seeking disclosure of a source protected by section 10 to show merely that he will be unable without disclosure to exercise the legal right or avert the threatened legal wrong on which he bases his claim in order to establish the necessity of disclosure. The judge's task will always be to weigh in the scales the importance of enabling the ends of justice to be attained in the circumstances of the particular case on the one hand against the importance of protecting the source on the other hand. In this balancing exercise it is only if the judge is satisfied that disclosure in the interests of justice is of such preponderating importance as to override the statutory privilege against disclosure that the threshold of necessity will be reached.'

40 It will be seen immediately from this passage of the speech of Lord Bridge that Lord Bridge was adopting a broader approach to what is 'in the interests of justice' for the purposes of section 10 than the approach suggested by Lord Diplock in the earlier case of *Secretary of State for Defence v Guardian Newspapers Ltd* . Lord Oliver in the *Morgan-Grampian* case, at pp 53–54, also questioned Lord Diplock's construction which he regarded as imposing a limitation not easily defensible in logic....

ORDER FOR DISCLOSURE MADE IN THIS CASE

61 It is contended that the order for disclosure was not proportionate or necessary on the facts of this case. This argument is not based on technicalities and it raises considerations of considerable importance as to how section 10 and article 10 in practice protect journalist's sources. Any disclosure of a journalist's sources does have a chilling effect on the freedom of the press. The court when considering making an order for disclosure in exercise of the *Norwich Pharmacal* jurisdiction must have this well in mind. The position is analogous to the long recognised position of informers under the criminal law. In *D v National Society for the Prevention of Cruelty to Children* [1978] AC 171 their Lordships applied the approach of the courts to police informants to those who provided information to the NSPCC. Having referred, at p 218, to *Marks v Beyfus* (1890) 25 QBD 494 Lord Diplock explained the rationale of the rule as being plain: if the identity of informers were too readily liable to be disclosed in a court of law the sources of information would dry up and the police would be hindered in their duty of preventing and detecting crime. Ordering journalists to disclose their sources can have similar consequences. The fact is that information which should be placed in the public domain is frequently made available to the press by individuals who would lack the courage to provide the information if they thought there was a risk of their identity being disclosed. The fact that journalists' sources can be reasonably confident that their identity will not be disclosed makes a significant contribution to the ability of the press to perform their role in society of making information available to the public. It is for this reason that it is well established now that the courts will normally protect journalists' sources from identification. However, the protection is not unqualified. Both section 10 and article 10 recognise this. This leads to the difficult issue at the heart of this appeal, namely whether the disclosure ordered was necessary and not disproportionate. The requirements of necessity and proportionality are here separate concepts which substantially cover the same area. In his submissions

Mr Browne relied correctly on the decision of the European Court in *Goodwin v United Kingdom* 22 EHRR 123. I find no difficulty in accepting the approach that the European Court emphasised, in pp 143–144, para 40 of its judgment, that (i) 'As a matter of general principle, the 'necessity' for any restriction of freedom of expression must be convincingly established' and (ii) 'limitations on the confidentiality of journalistic sources call for the most careful scrutiny by the court'.

62 Furthermore, I would also adopt Mr Browne's contention that any restriction on the otherwise unqualified right to freedom of expression must meet two further requirements. First, the exercise of the jurisdiction because of article 10(2) should meet a 'pressing social need' and secondly the restriction should be proportionate to a legitimate aim which is being pursued.

63 In applying these tests to the facts of this case to which I have already referred (at pp 127–129, paras 16 to 18) it is also important to have in mind the evidence of Dr James Collins who is the responsible medical officer for Ian Brady. He explains why it is essential for the care and safety of individual patients and the safety of other patients and staff that relevant information is entered in the patients' notes and why, those entries having been made, their integrity and confidentiality should be preserved. He refers to the fact that psychiatry, more than any other branch of medicine, depends on a trusting relationship between therapists and patients. In addition he draws attention to the fact that the basis of virtually all assessment, diagnosis, treatment and analysis of risk is dependent on information provided by others. He explains that if the staff feel that if there is a possibility of what they report entering the public domain their reporting will be inhibited as they will think that this will place staff or patients at risk. In addition, Mr Brewster (information manager), in his statement, sets out the reasons why it is important that the authority should be able to identify the employee or employees who are responsible for the wrongful disclosure. These include preventing further disclosure and removing the cloud of suspicion that at present hangs generally over the authority's employees who have access to the records which were published. Medical records will always be confidential but this is particularly important in the case of the class of patients that the authority is responsible for caring for at Ashworth. This is confirmed by the approach of the European Court to medical records in relation to article 8. I refer to the judgment of that court in *Z v Finland* (1997) 25 EHRR 371, 405–406:

'94. In determining whether the impugned measures were 'necessary in a democratic society', the court will consider whether, in the light of the case as a whole, the reasons adduced to justify them were relevant and sufficient and whether the measures were proportionate to the legitimate aims pursued.

'95. In this connection, the court will take into account that the protection of personal data, not least medical data, is of fundamental importance to a person's enjoyment of his or her right to respect for private and family life as guaranteed by article 8 of the Convention. Respecting the confidentiality of health data is a vital principle in the legal systems of all the contracting parties to the Convention. It is crucial not only to respect the sense of privacy of a patient but also to preserve his or her confidence in the medical profession and in the health services in general. Without such protection, those in need of medical assistance may be deterred from revealing such information of a personal and intimate nature as may be necessary in order to receive appropriate treatment and, even, from seeking such assistance, thereby endangering their own health and, in the case of transmissible diseases, that of the community. The domestic law must therefore afford appropriate safeguards to prevent any such communication or disclosure of personal health data as may be inconsistent with the guarantees in article 8 of the Convention.'

Those paragraphs of the judgment were of course addressing the question of whether medical data should be disclosed in a different context from the present and it was not necessary for the court to balance the conflicting interests which are at play as is essential here. However, the court's judgment provides a useful guide as to the significance of the wrongdoing which occurred here....

66 ...The situation here is exceptional, as it was in *Financial Times Ltd v Interbrew SA* [2002] EWCA Civ 274 and as it has to be, if disclosure of sources is to be justified. The care of patients at Ashworth is fraught with difficulty and danger. The disclosure of the patients' records increases that difficulty and danger and

to deter the same or similar wrongdoing in the future it was essential that the source should be identified and punished. This was what made the orders to disclose necessary and proportionate and justified. The fact that Ian Brady had himself disclosed his medical history did not detract from the need to prevent staff from revealing medical records of patients. Ian Brady's conduct did not damage the integrity of Ashworth's patients' records. The source's disclosure was wholly inconsistent with the security of the records and the disclosure was made worse because it was purchased by a cash payment.

67 I would dismiss this appeal with costs. …

Lords Slynn of Hadley, Browne-Wilkinson, Nolan and **Hobhouse of Woodborough** agreed with Lord Woolf. **Lord Hobhouse** delivered a concurring opinion with which Lords Browne-Wilkinson and Nolan agreed.

Appeal dismissed.

NOTES

1. In the event, disclosure of the intermediary's identity (Robin Ackroyd) did not lead to disclosure of the original source. Some years later Ashworth brought similar proceedings against the intermediary, but failed, on the ground that with the elapse of time, the balance was to be drawn differently: *Mersey Care NHS Trust v Ackroyd (No. 2).*[416] The Court of Appeal held that the judge had been entitled to refuse to make the order, taking account of points that procedures at the hospital had been tightened up; the original source had not been paid, and so their motive had not been financial but to act in the public interest; Ian Brady was no longer concerned to protect his privacy rights; although A was mixed up in the wrong-doing so as to engage the *Norwich Pharmacal* principle, the disclosure of the notes was not in breach of a duty to B (who probably had authorised or encouraged the disclosure);[417] A was an investigative journalist concerned about the possibility of mistreatment of B and to expose wrongdoing at the hospital, if any was occurring.[418]

[85] In all the circumstances, the judge was in our opinion entitled to hold that it was not convincingly established that there was in 2006 a pressing social need that the source or sources should be identified. He was also entitled to hold that an order for disclosure would not be proportionate to the pursuit of the hospital's legitimate aim to seek redress against the source, given the vital public interest in the protection of a journalist's source.

2. In *X Ltd v Morgan-Grampian (Publishers) Ltd,*[419] a highly confidential draft business plan was stolen from the plaintiffs, two associated private companies. The following day, the third defendant, William Robin Goodwin, a trainee journalist employed by the first and second defendants, publishers of *The Engineer,* was telephoned by an unidentified source and given information which could be inferred to have been obtained from the stolen plan. He decided to write an article based on the information and contacted the plaintiffs to check certain facts. The plaintiffs immediately sought and obtained an ex parte injunction against the publishers restraining them from publishing information derived from the draft plan, on the ground that the information had been imparted to them in breach of confidence.

It being their intention to bring proceedings against the source for recovery of the plan, they applied for an order requiring the journalist and publishers to disclose the source,

---

[416] [2007] EWCA Civ 101, 94 BMLR 84.

[417] See Sir Anthony Clarke MR at para. [64]. There was still wrongdoing against the hospital: ibid.

[418] See para. [62].   [419] [1991] 1 AC 1.

and sought discovery of Mr Goodwin's notes of the telephone conversation as a means of discovering the source's identity. The publishers did not know the source's identity and had no means of coercing Mr Goodwin. Accordingly, the plaintiffs directed their attention on Mr Goodwin. Hoffmann J granted the orders sought.[420] On appeal, the Court of Appeal varied the order by giving him the option of disclosing the notes, or delivering them to court in a sealed envelope which would remain sealed until final determination of his appeal against the order. Mr Goodwin declined to comply. The Court of Appeal dismissed the defendants' appeal against the orders.[421] The defendants appealed to the House of Lords. The House of Lords held unanimously that the court had jurisdiction to make an order against the defendants requiring disclosure of the source's identity: the defendants were parties to the injunction proceedings for breach of confidence, and were in any event 'mixed up in the tortious acts' of the source.[422] The House also held that the claim was not barred by s. 10 of the 1981 Act.

On 10 April 1990, the High Court fined Goodwin £5,000 for contempt of court. The European Court of Human Rights[423] subsequently found (by 11 to 7) that both the order requiring Goodwin to reveal his source and the fine imposed for having to do so violated Art. 10 ECHR. It was undisputed that the measures interfered with Goodwin's rights to freedom of expression. The Court decided that, notwithstanding, that s. 10 conferred a discretion, the measures were 'prescribed by law': 'the interpretation of the relevant law made by the House of Lords in the applicant's case did not go beyond what could be reasonably foreseen in the circumstances.... Nor does [the Court] find any other indication that the law in question did not afford the applicant adequate protection against arbitrary interference.'[424] It was not disputed that the interference pursued a 'legitimate aim', the protection of the plaintiffs' rights. The Court did not reach a conclusion on the Government's claim that the measures were also taken for the prevention of crime. However, the Court found that the interference was not 'necessary in a democratic society'. The plaintiffs' interests were largely protected by the ex parte injunction against Goodwin and the publishers of *The Engineer*. This had been notified to all the national newspapers and relevant journals:

The Court cannot find that [the plaintiffs'] interests in eliminating, by proceedings against the source, the residual threat of damage through dissemination of the confidential information otherwise than by the press, in obtaining compensation and in unmasking a disloyal employee or collaborator were, even if considered cumulatively, sufficient to outweigh the vital public interest in the protection of the applicant journalist's source.

There was thus not 'a reasonable relationship of proportionality between the legitimate aim pursued by the disclosure order and the means deployed to achieve that aim'.[425] Seven judges dissented, noting that the majority had undertaken no detailed assessment of the plaintiffs' interests in securing the additional measures of protection sought and concluding that the conclusion of the House of Lords fell within the margin of appreciation allowed to national authorities.

UK courts subsequently discerned little if any difference in the principles stated by the House of Lords and by the ECtHR. In *Camelot Group plc v Centaur Communications Ltd*[426]

---

[420] [1990] 1 All ER 608.   [421] [1991] 1 AC 1.
[422] Cf. Lord Reid in *Norwich Pharmacal Co v Customs and Excise Comrs* [1974] AC 133, 175.
[423] *Goodwin v UK* (1996) 22 EHRR 123.
[424] Para. 33.   [425] Paras 45, 56.
[426] [1998] 1 All ER 251 at 257–260. See T.R.S. Allan [1998] CLJ 235.

Schiemann LJ said: 'The difference of opinion between the House of Lords and the Court of Human Rights seems to me in large measure to be attributable to [a] different view taken of the facts' (i.e. of the significance to the plaintiffs of the additional protection that might be secured through a disclosure order). In *Ashworth Hospital Authority v MGN Ltd*[427] Lord Phillips MR agreed with this point, but added that he was inclined to accept that ECtHR decisions 'demonstrate that the freedom of the press has in the past carried greater weight in Strasbourg than it has in the courts of this country'.[428] This judgment was endorsed by the House of Lords.[429]

3. As Lord Bridge pointed out in *X v Grampian*,[430] where disclosure is necessary in the interests of national security or the prevention of crime, the courts are unlikely to allow sources to be protected. Where one of the other interests specified in s. 10 is invoked, the picture is more mixed. In some of the reported cases the courts have found disclosure not to be necessary. For example, in *X v Y*,[431] Rose J refused to order the disclosure of the source of stories in a national newspaper identifying two doctors who were carrying on general practice despite having contracted AIDS. The stories were based on information obtained from hospital records by one or more employees of the plaintiff health authority, and passed to the newspaper for payment. The health authority argued that disclosure was necessary 'for the prevention of crime'; there was prima facie evidence of offences of corruption under the Public Bodies Corrupt Practices Act 1889 and the Prevention of Corruption Act 1906, and they wished to ensure that such disclosures in breach of confidence did not happen again. Rose J held that the evidence adduced fell short of establishing necessity; prevention of crime was not one of the health authority's tasks and it was not clear that criminal investigation was the intended or likely consequence of disclosure.

In *John v Express Newspapers plc*[432] the Court of Appeal declined to order disclosure of the source of a copy of draft legal advice prepared for Sir Elton John by junior counsel that came into the possession of a journalist; other means of identifying the source through inquiries in chambers had not been pursued.

By contrast, in *Re an Inquiry under the Company Securities (Insider Dealing) Act 1985*,[433] Jeremy Warner, a financial journalist, was required by inspectors appointed under the 1985 Act to investigate suspected leaks from government departments of price-sensitive information about take-over bids, to reveal the sources of information on which he had based articles in *The Times* and the *Independent*. The inspectors certified his refusal to answer questions to the High Court under s. 178 of the Financial Services Act 1986, the High Court having power to punish a person who refuses to answer questions, without reasonable excuse, as if he had been guilty of contempt. The House of Lords held that the test set out in s. 10 should be applied to determine whether Mr Warner had a 'reasonable excuse', but that disclosure would here be 'necessary ... for the prevention of ... crime'. The House rejected a narrow construction of this test that would have limited it to a situation where disclosure would lead to the prevention of a particular identifiable future crime or crimes; it was sufficient that it would lead to the prevention of leaks of information and criminal insider dealing generally.

---

[427] [2001] 1 All ER 991.   [428] Ibid., at 1012.

[429] [2007] EWCA Civ 101, at para. [69].   [430] [1991] 1 AC 1 at 43.

[431] [1998] 2 All ER 648. See also *Maxwell v Pressdram Ltd* [1987] 1 All ER 656 (disclosure of course of libellous *Private Eye* article not necessary as it related only to whether there was liability for aggravated and exemplary damages and the matter could be dealt with adequately by a strong direction to the jury); *Chief Constable of Leicestershire Constabulary v Garavelli* [1997] EMLR 543.

[432] [2000] 3 All ER 257. See also *Special Hospital Services Authority v Hyde* (1994) 20 BMLR 75; *Saunders v Punch Ltd* [1998] 1 WLR 986.

[433] [1988] AC 660.

Mr Warner persisted in his refusal, and was fined £20,000 (*Re an Inquiry under the Company Securities (Insider Dealing) Act 1985*).[434]

4. It has been argued[435] that the case law in this area has not yet adopted sufficiently demanding standards in applying Art. 10(2); ordering disclosure should be 'truly exceptional'.

5. Disobedience to an order made by a circuit judge under the Prevention of Terrorism (Temporary Provisions) Act 1989, Sch. 7, para. 3,[436] requiring the production of information is punishable as a contempt. Such proceedings should invariably be heard in the Divisional Court; that court has no jurisdiction in contempt proceedings to review the exercise of the circuit judge's discretion—the order must be obeyed until set aside. These propositions were established in *DPP v Channel 4 Television Co Ltd*,[437] where the Divisional Court fined Channel 4 and Box Productions £75,000 for refusing to divulge material collected in the preparation of a programme in the 'Dispatches' series which made allegations of widespread and systematic collusion between members of the RUC and loyalist terrorists. The companies feared that the disclosure of their source would imperil both his life and that of their researcher, and had promised the source anonymity. Woolf LJ stated[438] that the companies should not have given unqualified assurances in view of the terms of the 1989 Act and the fact than an inquiry into the allegations was inevitable. Accordingly, they were responsible for their own dilemma of being compelled for genuinely held moral considerations to disobey what they knew to be their legal duty, and had to accept the consequences. However, the court refused the Attorney-General's application for sequestration orders against the companies, accepting the reality that they would not now change their stance. Section 10 of the 1981 Act was not relied on by the companies 'since, presumably, it was accepted it provided no protection'.[439] According to Miller,[440] s. 10 was not pleaded as it was regarded as disapplied by the Prevention of Terrorism (Temporary Provision) Act 1989, Sch. 7, para. 5(5)(b). This case has been described as dealing 'a severe blow to investigative journalism'.[441]

7. INTERFERENCE WITH THE COURSE OF JUSTICE

This head of contempt covers a variety of matters including interference with witnesses,[442] jurors[443] and judges and court officers,[444] whether the interference takes place before, during or after the relevant proceedings. In *R v Runting*,[445] the Court of Appeal quashed a

---

[434] (1988) Times, 27 January. See also *John Reid Enterprises Ltd v Pell* [1999] EMLR 675; *Camelot Group plc v Centaur Communications Ltd* [1999] QB 124 (order granted for return of documents to plaintiff company to enable it to identify disloyal employee who had leaked draft accounts with information that was embarrassing to the company directors, but did not disclose iniquity); *Michael O'Mara Books Ltd v Express Newspapers* [1999] FSR 49 ((order granted for disclosure of course of copies of typescript of a book acquired in breach of copyright); *Interbrew SA v Financial Times* [2002] EWCA Civ 274 (order to deliver leaked, doctored copies of documents prepared for purpose of takeover).

[435] R. Costigan [2007] PL 464. See also J. Brabyn (2006) 69 MLR 895.

[436] See now the Terrorism Act 2000, Sch. 5 above, pp. 429–430.

[437] [1993] 2 All ER 517.   [438] Ibid., at 529.   [439] Woolf LJ at 530.

[440] C.J. Miller [1993] All ER Rev 95.   [441] R. Costigan (1992) 142 NLJ 1417, 1418.

[442] E.g. *A-G v Butterworth* [1962] 3 All ER 326; *Moore v Clerk of Assize, Bristol* [1972] 1 All ER 58 (above, p. 747); *R v Mulvaney* [1982] Crim LR 462, DC; *A-G v Jackson* [1994] COD 171, DC.

[443] *R v Martin* (1848) 5 Cox CC 356; *R v Owen* [1976] 3 All ER 239; *R v Goult* (1982) 76 Cr App R 140; *A-G v Judd* (1994) Times, 15 August.

[444] E.g. an assault on the Clerk of the Lists: *Re De Court* (1997) Times, 27 November.

[445] (1988) 89 Cr App R 243.

conviction for contempt of court of a *Sun* photographer who pursued a defendant outside court in an attempt to take a close-up picture. The photographer had not struck or physically jostled his quarry; there were no intentional acts of sufficient gravity to amount to the actus revs of contempt of court by way of an interference with the course of justice.

Intentional interferences are clearly contempts: it is unclear, however, how far mens rea is a requirement, both at common law and after the enactment of the 1981 Act.[446] The issue of mens rea was left open in *R v Runting*, above.

Other illustrations include bringing improper pressure to bear on parties (cf. *A-G v Times Newspapers*)[447] and interfering with a prisoner's right of access to the courts;[448] and inspecting documents on a court file if it was known that leave was required or to gain access to a court file by deception or subterfuge.[449]

Intimidation of persons assisting in the investigation of offences, jurors and potential witnesses or jurors is now a substantive offence. Similarly, it is an offence to harm or threaten to harm a person because they have been so involved. This is in addition to any offence at common law.[450]

8. JURISDICTION

The position as to the jurisdiction to deal with criminal contempts is complex.[451] In brief, the superior courts of record (e.g. House of Lords, Court of Appeal, High Court) have inherent power, acting on their own motion, to punish contempts committed both in the face and outside the court. Formal applications for committal, as by the Attorney-General[452] must be made to the Queen's Bench Divisional Court: (a) if the alleged contempt is committed in connection with criminal proceedings (except where the contempt is committed in the face of the court or consists of disobedience to a court order or breach of an undertaking);[453] (b) if the alleged contempt concerns proceedings in an inferior court;[454] or (c) if the contempt is committed otherwise than in connection with any proceedings.[455] However, the Court of Appeal may also exercise jurisdiction in relation to contempt of itself.[456] Criminal contempts committed in relation to civil proceedings may be dealt with by a High Court judge of the appropriate Division.[457] Inferior courts have inherent or statutory powers to deal with contempt in the face.[458] Applications for injunctions (e.g. by the Attorney-General: *A-G v Times*

---

[446] See *Borrie and Lowe*, pp. 410–412, 414–416; *A-G v Butterworth*, above.

[447] [1974] AC 273, HL, above, p. 721.

[448] *Raymond v Honey* [1983] 1 AC 1, HL.

[449] *Dobson v Hastings* [1992] Ch 394 (on the facts there was no contempt as a journalist had obtained access to a court file without deception or trickery, and the editor responsible for the subsequent publication of information acquired from the file had no intention to interfere with the course of justice). For consideration of whether the victimisation of anti-discrimination complainants may amount to contempt, see E. Ellis and C.J. Miller [1993] PL 80.

[450] Criminal Justice and Public Order Act 1994, s. 51: see *R v Patrascu* [2004] EWCA Crim 2417, [2004] 4 All ER 1066 Similar offences now apply in respect of civil proceedings: Criminal Justice and Police Act 2001, ss. 39–41.

[451] See *Borrie and Lowe*, Chap. 12.

[452] Cf. s. 7 of the Contempt of Court Act 1981, above, p. 689.

[453] Civil Procedure Rules, Sch. 1, RSC Ord. 52, r. 1(2)(a)(ii).

[454] Ibid., r. 1(2)(a)(iii); above p. 705.   [455] Ibid., r. 1(2)(b).

[456] Ibid.   [457] Ibid., r. 1(3).   [458] See above, pp. 750–751.

Newspapers)[459] should be made to the High Court.[460] Proceedings under the strict liability rule can only be brought by or with the consent of the Attorney-General or on the motion of a court with jurisdiction to deal with such a contempt.[461] This restriction does not, however, apply to proceedings for an injunction to restrain the likely commission of an offence under the Act: *Peacock v London Weekend Television*.[462]

Appeals are governed by s. 13 of the Administration of Justice Act 1960. In most cases they lie to the Court of Appeal (Civil Division) but appeals against decisions of the Crown Court lie to the Court of Appeal (Criminal Division)[463] and against the decisions of some inferior courts to the High Court. Appeals lie from the High Court or Court of Appeal to the House of Lords.

---

[459] Above, p. 721.

[460] On the role of the Attorney-General in contempt proceedings, see J.L.J. Edwards, *The Attorney-General, Politics and the Public Interest* (1984), pp. 161–176.

[461] 1981 Act, s. 7, above p. 689; *Taylor v Topping* (1990) Times, 15 February.

[462] (1985) 150 JP 71, CA.

[463] Supreme Court Act 1981, s. 53(2)(b); Criminal Justice Act 1988, s. 159.

12

GOVERNMENT SECRECY
AND NATIONAL SECURITY

1. INTRODUCTION[1]

The materials in this chapter illustrate a variety of legal and extra-legal inhibitions on freedom of expression and access to information which protect the interest of the state in keeping certain matters secret. At the heart of the legal restrictions are the Official Secrets Acts[2] which cover matters ranging from serious breaches of national security to the unauthorised disclosure of certain classes of official information. These have reinforced the tendency towards excessive secrecy which has been one of the hallmarks of the public service. There have for some years been moves towards more open government.[3] Government departments are prepared (and obliged) to release much more information than formerly. The Official Secrets Act 1989, which repealed the 'catch all' provisions of s. 2 of the Official Secrets Act 1911, narrowed the scope of criminal sanctions. The Freedom of Information Act 2000 fully came into force on 1 January 2005. This confers legal rights of access to official information. The courts have restricted the circumstances in which a public authority may decline to divulge information in the course of legal proceedings on the ground that it would be contrary to the public interest.[4] At the same time, the state has taken advantage of the developing law relating to the restraint by injunction of breaches of confidence.[5]

Extra-legal factors are equally significant in the maintenance of secrecy and security. The press have to an extent acceded to a system of self-censorship in defence and security matters ('D' (now 'DA') Notices).[6] There are extensive measures for maintaining the physical security of classified information. There are procedures for vetting applicants for positions in the Civil Service that have been aimed in particular at excluding persons with Communist associations or character defects from sensitive positions. Civil Servants responsible for unauthorised disclosures may be disciplined or dismissed.

The issue of government secrecy is one of a range of matters where the state may seek to justify interference with individual liberties by reference to national security. Other contexts dealt with elsewhere in this book[7] include decisions to deport individuals as conducive

---

[1] See, generally, D.G.T. Williams, *Not in the Public Interest* (Heineman, 1965), (1968) 3 Federal LR 20 and 'Official Secrecy and the Courts' in P. Glazebrook (ed.), *Reshaping the Criminal Law* (1978) (hereafter cited as *D.G.T. Williams* (1978)); G. Robertson and A. Nicol, *Media Law* (Penguin Books, 5th edn, 2007), Chap. 11; P. Birkinshaw, *Freedom of Information: The Law, the Practice and the Ideal* (3rd edn, 2001), *Government and Information* (Tottel, 3rd edn, 2005) and *Reforming the Secret State* (1990); L. Lustgarten and I. Leigh, *In from the Cold: National Security and Parliamentary Democracy* (OUP, Oxford, 1994); N. Whitty, T. Murphy and S. Livingstone, *Civil Liberties Law: The Human Rights Act Era* (Butterworths, London, 2001), Chap. 7.

[2] Below, pp. 768–794.   [3] Below, pp. 849–855.   [4] Below, p. 817.
[5] Below, pp. 803–822.   [6] Below, pp. 798–803.
[7] See pp. 411–412.

to the public good and to impose measures under terrorism legislation. Traditionally, the courts have adopted a deferential stance where the government seeks to justify a decision by reference to considerations of national security. However, there are indications that the judges may adopt a more assertive role.[8] Accordingly, the House of Lords in *Council of Civil Service Unions v Minister for the Civil Service*[9] held that the government would need to adduce evidence that a decision was in fact based on national security grounds if the adoption of an unfair procedure was to be justified.[10] However, that case also established that once such evidence was adduced, the decision in question was not justiciable and so was not open to challenge on *Wednesbury* grounds. The courts have insisted on a certain level of evidence beyond the government's *ipse dixit* on this question.[11] The position of non-justiciability is, however, difficult to defend given the flexibility of the *Wednesbury* doctrine[12] and the vagueness of 'national security' as a concept. An alternative and more defensible approach (although expressly rejected by Jowitt J in *R v Secretary of State for the Home Department, ex p Manelfi*)[13] would, even in a national security case, require the government to give reasons for a decision that interfered with fundamental rights subject to its duty in a proper case to make a claim of public interest immunity.

The apparent 'non justiciability' of national security matters has come under some pressure in more recent cases. It has been stated[14] that

38 ...it seems to me, first, to be plain that the law of England will not contemplate what may be called a merits review of any honest decision of government upon matters of national defence policy....[T]here is more than one reason for this. The first, and most obvious, is that the court is unequipped to judge such merits or demerits. The second touches more closely the relationship between the elected and unelected arms of government. The graver a matter of State and the more widespread its possible effects, the more respect will be given, within the framework of the constitution, to the democracy to decide its outcome. The defence of the realm, which is the Crown's first duty, is the paradigm of so grave a matter. Potentially such a thing touches the security of everyone; and everyone will look to the government they have elected for wise and effective decisions. Of course they may or may not be satisfied, and their satisfaction or otherwise will sound in the ballot-box. There is not, and cannot be, any expectation that the unelected judiciary play any role in such questions, remotely comparable to that of government. The position is not unlike that taken by their Lordships' House in relation to attempts to challenge government decisions of what is sometimes called 'macro-economic' policy: see for example *Ex p. Nottinghamshire CC* [1986]

---

[8] B. Dickson, 'Judicial review and National Security' in B. Hadfield (ed.), *Judicial Review: A Thematic Approach* (1995).

[9] [1985] AC 374.

[10] Per Lord Fraser at 402. See also Taylor J in *R v Secretary of State for the Home Department, ex p Ruddock* [1987] 1 WLR 482, below, p. 831; *R v Secretary of State for the Home Department, ex p Chahal* [1995] 1 All ER 658; *R v Director of GCHQ, ex p Hodges*, below, p. 830; *R v Secretary of State for Foreign and Commonwealth Affairs, ex p Manelfi* (unreported, 25 October 1996).

[11] *CCSU*: affidavit evidence that the Minister considered that prior consultation with GCHQ staff before decision to ban trade unions could have involved a risk of precipitating disruption; *Manelfi*: affidavit from Head of Security Division (R) at GCHQ that the nationality rule and waiver policy applied in recruitment were maintained to ensure loyalty, in the interest of national security.

[12] *R v Ministry of Defence, ex p Smith* [1996] QB 517.

[13] Unreported, 25 October 1996.

[14] Laws LJ in *R (on the application of Marchiori) v Environment Agency* [2002] EWCA Civ 3 (authorisation under Radioactive Substances Act 1993 for the discharge of nuclear waste at sites where Trident warheads were manufactured not open to challenge on the basis that the nuclear defence programme was a detriment; the EA was not obliged to consider the merits of the programme, and these were not justiciable; the HRA did not arise).

AC 240 and *Ex p. Hammersmith and Fulham LBC* [1991] 1 AC 521; and this approach is, I conceive, consistent with recent observations in the House of Lords in cases such as *Kebilene* [2000] 2 AC 326 and *R v A* [2001] 2 WLR 1546 as to the deference owed by the court to the democratic decision-maker.

39. I recognise that the notion of so grave a matter of State lacks sharp edges. But it is now a commonplace that the intensity of judicial review depends upon the context (see for example *Daly* [2001] 2 WLR 1622 per Lord Steyn at paragraph 28). One context will shade into another; there is for instance a distinction between a deportation decision affecting a specific individual (as in *Rehman*)[15] and a decision of defence policy (such as Trident), though both involve matters of national security.

40. Secondly, however, this primacy which the common law accords to elected government in matters of defence is by no means the whole story. Democracy itself requires that all public power be lawfully conferred and exercised, and of this the courts are the surety. No matter how grave the policy issues involved, the courts will be alert to see that no use of power exceeds its proper constitutional bounds. There is no conflict between this and the fact that upon questions of national defence, the courts will recognise that they are in no position to set limits upon the lawful exercise of discretionary power in the name of reasonableness. Judicial review remains available to cure the theoretical possibility of actual bad faith on the part of ministers making decisions of high policy. In the British State I assume that is overwhelmingly unlikely in practice. Closer to reality, perhaps, is the possibility that a statute might itself require the courts to review high policy decisions (or decisions involving judgment of deeply controversial social questions) upon which traditionally they would advisedly have had no voice. That I think was the position in Operation Dismantle.[16] In this jurisdiction such a state of affairs may most obviously arise in the execution of the judges' duty under the Human Rights Act 1998.

In *R (on the application of Gentle) v Prime Minister*[17] it was stated that issues relating to the conduct of international relations and military operations outside the UK are not justiciable.[18] This was supported by two further propositions: that 'constitutionally such matters lie within the exclusive prerogative of the executive' and 'that they are governed by international and not domestic law'. However it has also been said that the 'general trend of modern authority' lies in the direction of holding that all but the rarest cases are justiciable.[19] Accordingly, decisions of the Army Board that two soldiers who had been convicted of murder should be retained in employment;[20] of the Attorney-General to refuse to certify a scheduled offence in Northern Ireland[21] as suitable for trial with jury instead of trial by judge alone;[22] and of a minister to refuse to (confirm or) deny that the[23] applicant was an undercover agent for the government, have been held to raise justiciable issues, although

---

[15] See pp. 472–473 (*ed.*).

[16] *Ed.* I.e. *Operation Dismantle* [1985] 1 SCR 441, where the Supreme Court of Canada held that the compatibility with s. 7 of the Canadian Charter of Rights and Freedoms of a decision of the Canadian Government, taken by the Cabinet, to allow the US to test cruise missiles in Canada, was in principle reviewable, notwithstanding that it was concerned with national defence: Laws LJ held that this turned on the provisions of the Canadian Charter and was not applicable here.

[17] [2006] EWCA Civ 1689, [2007] QB 689. The court rejected claims that the UK was obliged by Art. 2 ECHR to set up an independent inquiry into all the circumstances surrounding the 2003 invasion of Iraq (in the course of which the claimant's sons were killed). This would include in particular the steps taken to obtain timely legal advice on the legality of the invasion. The House of Lords dismissed an appeal on the narrow ground that such an inquiry could not be required by Art. 2: [2008] UKHL 20.

[18] Sir Anthony Clarke MR at para. [26].

[19] Kerr LCJ in *Re Shuker's Application for Judicial Review* [2004] NIQB 20 at para. [13].

[20] *Re McBride's Application (No. 2)* [2003] NI 319.

[21] Terrorism Act 2000, Sch. 9.　　　[22] *Shuker.*

[23] *Re Scappaticci* [2003] NIQB 56. The issue was whether this was required by Art. 2 ECHR, and the court held that it was not; S subsequently vanished from public view: *The Guardian*, 5 April 2006.

all the applications were dismissed on their merits. The significance of these developments have, however, been reduced by the extent to which the courts continue to defer to ministers on the basis that they, unlike the courts, have access to full information.

Under the ECHR, certain rights are non-derogable while others can be infringed by reference to a range of considerations that include national security (Arts 6(1), 8, 9, 10, 11). National security has been advanced as a justification for such actions as barring access to the courts and the maintenance of arrangements for the secret surveillance of and the keeping of files on citizens. The European Court of Human Rights has taken a firmer line in the former than the latter. As to the former it held in *Chahal v United Kingdom*[24] that the exclusion of persons deported on grounds of national security from access to the courts violated Arts 5(4) and 13 ECHR. In *Tinnelly and McElduff v United Kingdom*[25] the Court held that the issue of certificates under s. 42 of the Fair Employment (Northern Ireland) Act 1976 that decisions not to award certain building contracts to the applicants were acts 'done for the purpose of safeguarding national security or of protecting public safety or public order' was a disproportionate restriction on their right of access to a court or tribunal, contrary to Art. 6(1). Such a certificate was conclusive evidence that the act was done for the stated purpose. The 1976 Act conferred rights to complain of unlawful religious or political discrimination, but did not apply in respect of acts done for any of the stated purposes. There was no provision for any independent scrutiny of the facts which led to the Secretary of State issuing the certificates. As in *Chahal v United Kingdom*,[26] the Court stated[27] that:

The right guaranteed to an applicant under Article 6§ 1 of the Convention to submit a dispute to a court or tribunal in order to have a determination of questions of both fact and law cannot be displaced by the *ipse dixit* of the executive.

The need to protect the security of the process of intelligence gathering and vetting of potential contractors that lay behind the decisions was not sufficient to justify a complete exclusion of access to a court or tribunal. Alternative models could be adopted whereby sensitive cases are heard by a special tribunal in the absence (in whole or in part) of the applicant and his advisers, with limitations on the disclosure of evidence and with a special advocate appointed by the Attorney-General to represent the applicant's interests, albeit without responsibility to him. Such a model has indeed been adopted in each of these situations,[28] and extended to others.[29] These arrangements would seem to help ensure compliance with Art. 6, but a supposedly adversarial arrangement from which one party is partially excluded is inevitably compromised although the gap may be reduced if the tribunal adopts an inquisitorial approach.[30]

By contrast the Court has tended to uphold arrangements for secret surveillance themselves.[31] Such arrangements do interfere with private life, home and correspondence (Art. 8) but the protection of national security is a legitimate aim and arrangements are justified if they are 'in accordance with the law' and 'necessary in a democratic society'. On the first of these points, the law must be accessible to the individual and its consequences for him

---

[24] Judgment of 15 November 1996 (1997) 23 EHRR 418.

[25] Judgment of 10 July 1998 (1998) 27 EHRR 249. See C. White [1999] PL 406. Followed in the context of a refusal to appoint the applicant to a junior civil service post in *Devlin v UK*, Judgment of 30 October 2001.

[26] Para. 131.   [27] Para. 77.

[28] Special Immigration Appeals Act 1997; Northern Ireland Act 1998, s. 90 and Fair Employment and Treatment (NI) Order 1998, SI 1998/3162 (NI 21).

[29] See above, pp. 475–485 (control orders).   [30] See C. White [1999] PL 406, 413.

[31] *Leander v Sweden*, Judgment of 25 Febuary 1997 (1987) 9 EHRR 433.

must also be foreseeable. However, the requirement of foreseeability in the national security context cannot mean that an individual should be able to foresee precisely what checks will be made on him. It is enough in the case of a system applicable to citizens generally that the law is:

> sufficiently clear in its terms to give them an adequate indication as to the circumstances in which and the conditions on which the public authorities are empowered to resort to this kind of secret and potentially dangerous interference with private life.

Where implementation of such a law consists of secret measures, the law must:

> indicate the scope of any discretion conferred on the competent authority with sufficient clarity, having regard to the legitimate aim of the measure in question, to give the individual adequate protection against arbitrary interference.[32]

As to 'necessity', the Court accepts that arrangements for security vetting are indeed necessary for the protection of national security and that:

> the margin of appreciation available to the respondent State in assessing the pressing social need in the present case, and in particular in choosing the means for achieving the legitimate aim of protecting national security, was a wide one.[33]

However, the Court must be satisfied that there exist adequate and effective guarantees against abuse.[34] In *Leander v Sweden,* the Court rejected challenges to security vetting arrangements in Sweden.[35]

2. THE OFFICIAL SECRETS ACTS

(A) THE OFFICIAL SECRETS ACTS 1911–1989

(I) OFFICIAL SECRETS ACT 1911[36]

1. Penalties for spying

(1) If any person for any purpose prejudicial to the safety or interests of the State—

   (a) approaches, [inspects, passes over] or is in the neighbourhood of, or enters any prohibited place within the meaning of this Act; or

---

[32] *Leander,* para. 51.   [33] Ibid., para. 59.

[34] Ibid., para. 60; *Klass v Germany,* Judgment of 6 September 1978 (1978) EHRR 214, paras 49–50.

[35] (1987) 9 EHRR 433. Cf. *Amann v Switzerland,* Judgment of 16 February 2000 (violation of Art. 8 in respect of telephone tapping and creation and storage of a card with information about A as Swiss law did not indicate with sufficient clarity the scope of the authorities' discretion); *Rotaru v Romania,* Judgment of 4 May 2000 (violation of Arts 8, 13 and 6(1) in respect of Romanian Intelligence Service's holding of information concerning his private life: insufficient clarity in authority's discretion; lack of safeguards against abuse); *Segerstedt-Wiberg v Sweden,* Judgment of 6 June 2006 (continued storage of attendance at a political meeting in Warsaw in 1967 not supported by relevant and sufficient reasons).

[36] The words in square brackets were added by the Official Secrets Act 1920.

(*b*) makes any sketch, plan, model, or note which is calculated to be or might be or is intended to be directly or indirectly useful to an enemy; or

(*c*) obtains, [collects, records, or publishes,] or communicates to any other person [any secret official code word, or pass word, or] any sketch, plan, model, article, or note, or other document or information which is calculated to be or might be or is intended to be directly or indirectly useful to an enemy;

he shall be guilty of felony....

(2) On a prosecution under this section, it shall not be necessary to show that the accused person was guilty of any particular act tending to show a purpose prejudicial to the safety or interests of the State, and, notwithstanding that no such act is proved against him, he may be convicted if, from the circumstances of the case, or his conduct, or his known character as proved, it appears that his purpose was a purpose prejudicial to the safety or interests of the State; and if any sketch, plan, model, article, note, document, or information relating to or used in any prohibited place within the meaning of this Act, or anything in such a place [or any secret official code word or pass word], is made, obtained, [collected, recorded, published], or communicated by any person other than a person acting under lawful authority, it shall be deemed to have been made, obtained, [collected, recorded, published] or communicated for a purpose prejudicial to the safety or interests of the State unless the contrary is proved....

3. Definition of prohibited place

For the purposes of this Act, the expression 'prohibited place' means—

[(*a*) Any work of defence, arsenal, naval or air force establishment or station, factory, dockyard, mine, minefield, camp, ship, or aircraft belonging to or occupied by or on behalf of His Majesty, or any telegraph, telephone, wireless or signal station, or office so belonging or occupied, and any place belonging to or occupied by or on behalf of His Majesty and used for the purpose of building, repairing, making, or storing any munitions of war, or any sketches, plans, models, or documents relating thereto, or for the purpose of getting any metals, oil, or minerals of use in time of war]; and

(*b*) any place not belonging to His Majesty where any [munitions of war], or any [sketches, models, plans] or documents relating thereto, are being made, repaired, [gotten] or stored under contract with, or with any person on behalf of, His Majesty, or otherwise on behalf of His Majesty; and

(*c*) any place belonging to [or used for the purposes of] His Majesty which is for the time being declared [by order of a Secretary of State] to be a prohibited place for the purposes of this section on the ground that information with respect thereto, or damage thereto, would be useful to an enemy; and

(*d*) any railway, road, way, or channel, or other means of communication by land or water (including any works or structures being part thereof or connected therewith), or any place used for gas, water, or electricity works or other works for purposes of a public character, or any place where any [munitions of war], or any [sketches, models, plans] or documents relating thereto, are being made, repaired, or stored otherwise than on behalf of His Majesty, which is for the time being declared [by order of a Secretary of State] to be a prohibited place for the purposes of this section, on the ground that information with respect thereto, or the destruction or obstruction thereof, or interference therewith, would be useful to an enemy....

7. Penalty for harbouring spies

If any person knowingly harbours any person whom he knows, or has reasonable grounds for supposing, to be a person who is about to commit or who has committed an offence under this Act, or knowingly permits to meet or assemble in any premises in his occupation or under his control any such persons, or if any person having harboured any such person, or permitted to meet or assemble in any premises in his occupation or under his control any such persons, [wilfully omits or refuses] to disclose to a superintendent of police any information which it is in his power to give in relation to any such person he shall be guilty of a misdemeanour....

8. Restriction on prosecution
A prosecution for an offence under this Act shall not be instituted except by or with the consent of the Attorney-General.

12. Interpretation
In this Act, unless the context otherwise requires,—

Any reference to a place belonging to His Majesty includes a place belonging to any department of the Government of the United Kingdom or of any British possessions, whether the place is or is not actually vested in His Majesty;...

Expressions referring to communicating...include any communicating...whether in whole or in part, and whether the sketch, plan, model, article, note, document, or information itself or the substance, effect, or description thereof only be communicated...expressions referring to obtaining or retaining any sketch, plan, model, article, note, or document, include the copying or causing to be copied the whole or any part of any sketch, plan, model, article, note, or document; and expressions referring to the communication of any sketch, plan, model, article, note or document include the transfer or transmission of the sketch, plan, model, article, note or document;

The expression 'document' includes part of a document;

The expression 'model' includes design, pattern, and specimen;

The expression 'sketch' includes any photograph or other mode of representing any place or thing;

[The expression 'munitions of war' includes the whole or any part of any ship, submarine, aircraft, tank or similar engine, arms and ammunition, torpedo, or mine, intended or adapted for use in war, and any other article, material or device, whether actual or proposed, intended for such use;]

The expression 'office under His Majesty' includes any office or employment in or under any department of the Government of the United Kingdom, or of any British possession;

The expression 'offence under this Act' includes any act, omission, or other thing which is punishable under this Act.

(II) OFFICIAL SECRETS ACT 1920

7. Attempts, incitements, etc.
Any person who attempts to commit any offence under the principal Act or this Act, or solicits or incites or endeavours to persuade another person to commit an offence, or aids or abets and does any act preparatory to the commission of an offence under the principal Act or this Act, shall be guilty of a felony or a misdemeanour or a summary offence according as the offence in question is a felony, a misdemeanour or a summary offence, and on conviction shall be liable to the same punishment, and to be proceeded against in the same manner, as if he had committed the offence.

(III) OFFICIAL SECRETS ACT 1989

1. Security and intelligence

(1) A person who is or has been—

(a) a member of the security and intelligence services; or

(b) a person notified that he is subject to the provisions of this subsection,

is guilty of an offence if without lawful authority he discloses any information, document or other article relating to security or intelligence which is or has been in his possession by virtue of his position as a member of any of those services or in the course of his work while the notification is or was in force.

(2) The reference in subsection (1) above to disclosing information relating to security or intelligence includes a reference to making any statement which purports to be a disclosure of such information or is intended to be taken by those to whom it is addressed as being such a disclosure.

(3) A person who is or has been a Crown servant or government contractor is guilty of an offence if without lawful authority he makes a damaging disclosure of any information, document or other article relating to security or intelligence which is or has been in his possession by virtue of his position as such but otherwise than as mentioned in subsection (1) above.

(4) For the purposes of subsection (3) above a disclosure is damaging if—

(a) it causes damage to the work of, or of any part of, the security and intelligence services; or

(b) it is of information or a document or other article which is such that its unauthorised disclosure would be likely to cause such damage or which falls within a class or description of information, documents or articles the unauthorised disclosure of which would be likely to have that effect.

(5) It is a defence for a person charged with an offence under this section to prove that at the time of the alleged offence he did not know, and had no reasonable cause to believe, that the information, document or article in question related to security or intelligence or, in the case of an offence under subsection (3), that the disclosure would be damaging within the meaning of that subsection.

(6) Notification that a person is subject to subsection (1) above shall be effected by a notice in writing served on him by a Minister of the Crown; and such a notice may be served if, in the Minister's opinion, the work undertaken by the person in question is or includes work connected with the security and intelligence services and its nature is such that the interests of national security require that he should be subject to the provisions of that subsection.

(7) Subject to subsection (8) below, a notification for the purposes of subsection (1) above shall be in force for the period of five years beginning with the day on which it is served but may be renewed by further notices under subsection (6) above for periods of five years at a time.

(8) A notification for the purposes of subsection (1) above may at any time be revoked by a further notice in writing served by the Minister on the person concerned; and the Minister shall serve such a further notice as soon as, in his opinion, the work undertaken by that person ceases to be such as is mentioned in subsection (6) above.

(9) In this section 'security or intelligence' means the work of, or in support of, the security and intelligence services or any part of them, and references to information relating to security or intelligence include references to information held or transmitted by those services or by persons in support of, or of any part of, them.

2. Defence

(1) A person who is or has been a Crown servant or government contractor is guilty of an offence if without lawful authority he makes a damaging disclosure of any information, document or other article relating to defence which is or has been in his possession by virtue of his position as such.

(2) For the purposes of subsection (1) above a disclosure is damaging if—

(a) it damages the capability of, or of any part of, the armed forces of the Crown to carry out their tasks or leads to loss of life or injury to members of those forces or serious damage to the equipment or installations of those forces; or

(b) otherwise than as mentioned in paragraph (a) above, it endangers the interests of the United Kingdom abroad, seriously obstructs the promotion or protection by the United Kingdom of those interests or endangers the safety of British citizens abroad; or

(c) it is of information or of a document or article which is such that its unauthorised disclosure would be likely to have any of those effects.

(3) It is a defence for a person charged with an offence under this section to prove that at the time of the alleged offence he did not know, and had no reasonable cause to believe, that the information, document or article in question related to defence or that its disclosure would be damaging within the meaning of subsection (1) above.

(4) In this section 'defence' means—

(a) the size, shape, organisation, logistics, order of battle, deployment, operations, state of readiness and training of the armed forces of the Crown;

(b) the weapons, stores or other equipment of those forces and the invention, development, production and operation of such equipment and research relating to it;

(c) defence policy and strategy and military planning and intelligence;

(d) plans and measures for the maintenance of essential supplies and services that are or would be needed in time of war.

3. International relations

(1) A person who is or has been a Crown servant or government contractor is guilty of an offence if without lawful authority he makes a damaging disclosure of—

(a) any information, document or other article relating to international relations; or

(b) any confidential information, document or other article which was obtained from a State other than the United Kingdom or an international organisation, being information or a document or article which is or has been in his possession by virtue of his position as a Crown servant or government contractor.

(2) For the purposes of subsection (1) above a disclosure is damaging if—

(a) it endangers the interests of the United Kingdom abroad, seriously obstructs the promotion or protection by the United Kingdom of those interests or endangers the safety of British citizens abroad; or

(b) it is of information or of a document or article which is such that its unauthorised disclosure would be likely to have any of those effects.

(3) In the case of information or a document or article within subsection (1)(b) above—

(a) the fact that it is confidential, or

(b) its nature or contents,

may be sufficient to establish for the purposes of subsection (2)(*b*) above that the information, document or article is such that its unauthorised disclosure would be likely to have any of the effects there mentioned.

(4) It is a defence for a person charged with an offence under this section to prove that at the time of the alleged offence he did not know, and had no reasonable cause to believe, that the information, document or article in question was such as is mentioned in subsection (1) above or that its disclosure would be damaging within the meaning of that subsection.

(5) In this section 'international relations' means the relations between States, between international organisations or between one or more States and one or more such organisations and includes any matter relating to a State other than the United Kingdom or to an international organisation which is capable of affecting the relations of the United Kingdom with another State or with an international organisation.

(6) For the purposes of this section any information, document or article obtained from a State or organisation is confidential at any time while the terms on which it was obtained require it to be held in confidence or while the circumstances in which it was obtained make it reasonable for the State or organisation to expect that it would be so held.

4. Crime and special investigation powers

(1) A person who is or has been a Crown servant or government contractor is guilty of an offence if without lawful authority he discloses any information, document or other article to which this section applies and which is or has been in his possession by virtue of his position as such.

(2) This section applies to any information, document or other article—

    (a) the disclosure of which—

        (i) results in the commission of an offence; or

        (ii) facilitates an escape from legal custody or the doing of any other act prejudicial to the safekeeping of persons in legal custody; or

        (iii) impedes the prevention or detection of offences or the apprehension or prosecution of suspected offenders; or

    (b) which is such that its unauthorised disclosure would be likely to have any of those effects.

(3) This section also applies to—

    (a) any information obtained by reason of the interception of any communication in obedience to a warrant issued under section 2 of the Interception of Communications Act 1985 [or under the authority of an interception warrant under section 5 of the Regulation of Investigatory Powers Act 2000],[37] any information relating to the obtaining of information by reason of any such interception and any document or other article which is or has been used or held for use in, or has been obtained by reason of, any such interception; and

    (b) any information obtained by reason of action authorised by a warrant issued under section 3 of the Security Services Act 1989 [or under section 5 of the Intelligence Services Act 1994 or by an authorisation given under section 7 of that Act][38] any information relating to the obtaining of information by reason of any such action and any document or other article which is or has been used or held for use in, or has been obtained by reason of, any such action.

---

[37] Inserted by the 2000 Act, Sch. 4, para. 5.
[38] Inserted by the Intelligence Services Act 1994, Sch. 4, para. 4.

(4) It is a defence for a person charged with an offence under this section in respect of a disclosure falling within subsection (2)(*a*) above to prove that at the time of the alleged offence he did not know, and had no reasonable cause to believe, that the disclosure would have any of the effects there mentioned.

(5) It is a defence for a person charged with an offence under this section in respect of any other disclosure to prove that at the time of the alleged offence he did not know, and had no reasonable cause to believe, that the information, document or article in question was information or a document or article to which this section applies.

(6) In this section 'legal custody' includes detention in pursuance of any enactment or any instrument made under an enactment.

5. Information resulting from unauthorised disclosures or entrusted in confidence

(1) Subsection (2) below applies where—

    (a) any information, document or other article protected against disclosure by the foregoing provisions of this Act has come into a person's possession as a result of having been—

        (i) disclosed (whether to him or another) by a Crown servant or government contractor without lawful authority; or

        (ii) entrusted to him by a Crown servant or government contractor on terms requiring it to be held in confidence or in circumstances in which the Crown servant or government contractor could reasonably expect that it would be so held; or

        (iii) disclosed (whether to him or another) without lawful authority by a person to whom it was entrusted as mentioned in sub-paragraph (ii) above; and

    (b) the disclosure without lawful authority of the information, document or article by the person into whose possession it has come is not an offence under any of those provisions.

(2) Subject to subsections (3) and (4) below, the person into whose possession the information, document or article has come is guilty of an offence if he discloses it without lawful authority knowing, or having reasonable cause to believe, that it is protected against disclosure by the foregoing provisions of this Act and that it has come into his possession as mentioned in subsection (1) above.

(3) In the case of information or a document or article protected against disclosure by sections 1 to 3 above, a person does not commit an offence under subsection (2) above unless—

    (a) the disclosure by him is damaging; and

    (b) he makes it knowing, or having reasonable cause to believe, that it would be damaging; and the question whether a disclosure is damaging shall be determined for the purposes of this subsection as it would be in relation to a disclosure of that information, document or article by a Crown servant in contravention of section 1(3), 2(1) or 3(1) above.

(4) A person does not commit an offence under subsection (2) above in respect of information or a document or other article which has come into his possession as a result of having been disclosed—

    (a) as mentioned in subsection (1)(a)(i) above by a government contractor; or

    (b) as mentioned in subsection (1)(a)(iii) above,

unless that disclosure was by a British citizen or took place in the United Kingdom, in any of the Channel Islands or in the Isle of Man or a colony.

(5) For the purposes of this section information or a document or article is protected against disclosure by the foregoing provisions of this Act if—

    (a) it relates to security or intelligence, defence or international relations within the meaning of section 1, 2 or 3 above or is such as is mentioned in section 3(1)(b) above; or

(b) it is information or a document or article to which section 4 above applies; and information or a document or article is protected against disclosure by sections 1 to 3 above if it falls within paragraph (a) above.

(6) A person is guilty of an offence if without lawful authority he discloses any information, document or other article which he knows, or has reasonable cause to believe, to have come into his possession as a result of a contravention of section 1 of the Official Secrets Act 1911.

6. Information entrusted in confidence to other States or international organisations

(1) This section applies where—

(a) any information, document or other article which—

(i) relates to security or intelligence, defence or international relations; and

(ii) has been communicated in confidence by or on behalf of the United Kingdom to another State or to an international organisation, has come into a person's possession as a result of having been disclosed (whether to him or another) without the authority of that State or organisation or, in the case of an organisation, of a member of it; and

(b) the disclosure without lawful authority of the information, document or article by the person into whose possession it has come is not an offence under any of the foregoing provisions of this Act.

(2) Subject to subsection (3) below, the person into whose possession the information, document or article has come is guilty of an offence if he makes a damaging disclosure of it knowing, or having reasonable cause to believe, that it is such as is mentioned in subsection (1) above, that it has come into his possession as there mentioned and that its disclosure would be damaging.

(3) A person does not commit an offence under subsection (2) above if the information, document or article is disclosed by him with lawful authority or has previously been made available to the public with the authority of the State or organisation concerned or, in the case of an organisation, of a member of it.

(4) For the purposes of this section 'security or intelligence', 'defence' and 'international relations' have the same meaning as in sections 1, 2 and 3 above and the question whether a disclosure is damaging shall be determined as it would be in relation to a disclosure of the information, document or article in question by a Crown servant in contravention of sections 1(3), 2(1) and 3(1) above.

(5) For the purposes of this section information or a document or article is communicated in confidence if it is communicated on terms requiring it to be held in confidence or in circumstances in which the person communicating it could reasonably expect that it would be so held.

7. Authorised disclosures

(1) For the purposes of this Act a disclosure by—

(a) a Crown servant; or

(b) a person, not being a Crown servant or government contractor, in whose case a notification for the purposes of section 1(1) above is in force,

is made with lawful authority if, and only if, it is made in accordance with his official duty.

(2) For the purposes of this Act a disclosure by a government contractor is made with lawful authority if, and only if, it is made—

(a) in accordance with an official authorisation; or

(b) for the purposes of the functions by virtue of which he is a government contractor and without contravening an official restriction.

(3) For the purposes of this Act a disclosure made by any other person is made with lawful authority if, and only if, it is made—

(a) to a Crown servant for the purposes of his functions as such; or

(b) in accordance with an official authorisation.

(4) It is a defence for a person charged with an offence under any of the foregoing provisions of this Act to prove that at the time of the alleged offence he believed that he had lawful authority to make the disclosure in question and had no reasonable cause to believe otherwise.

(5) In this section 'official authorisation' and 'official restriction' mean, subject to subsection

(6) below, an authorisation or restriction duly given or imposed by a Crown servant or government contractor or by or on behalf of a prescribed body or a body of a prescribed class.

(7) In relation to section 6 above 'official authorisation' includes an authorisation duly given by or on behalf of the State or organisation concerned or, in the case of an organisation, a member of it.

8. Safeguarding of information

(1) Where a Crown servant or government contractor, by virtue of his position as such, has in his possession or under his control any document or other article which it would be an offence under any of the foregoing provisions of this Act for him to disclose without lawful authority he is guilty of an offence if—

(a) being a Crown servant, he retains the document or article contrary to his official duty; or

(b) being a government contractor, he fails to comply with an official direction for the return or disposal of the document or article, or if he fails to take such care to prevent the unauthorised disclosure of the document or article as a person in his position may reasonably be expected to take.

(2) It is a defence for a Crown servant charged with an offence under subsection (1)(a) above to prove that at the time of the alleged offence he believed that he was acting in accordance with his official duty and had no reasonable cause to believe otherwise.

(3) In subsections (1) and (2) above references to a Crown servant include any person, not being a Crown servant or government contractor, in whose case a notification for the purposes of section 1(1) above is in force.

(4) Where a person has in his possession or under his control any document or other article which it would be an offence under section 5 above for him to disclose without lawful authority, he is guilty of an offence if—

(a) he fails to comply with an official direction for its return or disposal; or

(b) where he obtained it from a Crown servant or government contractor on terms requiring it to be held in confidence or in circumstances in which that servant or contractor could reasonably expect that it would be so held, he fails to take such care to prevent its unauthorised disclosure as a person in his position may reasonably be expected to take.

(5) Where a person has in his possession or under his control any document or other article which it would be an offence under section 6 above for him to disclose without lawful authority, he is guilty of an offence if he fails to comply with an official direction for its return or disposal.

(6) A person is guilty of an offence if he discloses any official information, document or other article which can be used for the purpose of obtaining access to any information, document or other article protected against disclosure by the foregoing provisions of this Act and the circumstances in which it is disclosed are such that it would be reasonable to expect that it might be used for that purpose without authority.

(7) For the purposes of subsection (6) above a person discloses information or a document or article which is official if—

    (a) he has or has had it in his possession by virtue of his position as a Crown servant or government contractor; or

    (b) he knows or has reasonable cause to believe that a Crown servant or government contractor has or has had it in his possession by virtue of his position as such.

(8) Subsection (5) of section 5 above applies for the purposes of subsection (6) above as it applies for the purposes of that section.

(9) In this section 'official direction' means a direction duly given by a Crown servant or government contractor or by or on behalf of a prescribed body or a body of a prescribed class.

9. Prosecutions

(1) Subject to subsection (2) below, no prosecutions for an offence under this Act shall be instituted in England and Wales or in Northern Ireland except by or with the consent of the Attorney General or, as the case may be, the Attorney General for Northern Ireland.

(2) Subsection (1) above does not apply to an offence in respect of any such information, document or article as is mentioned in section 4(2) above but no prosecution for such an offence shall be instituted in England and Wales or in Northern Ireland except by or with the consent of the Director of Public Prosecutions or, as the case may be, the Director of Public Prosecutions for Northern Ireland.

10. Penalties

(1) A person guilty of an offence under any provision of this Act other than section 8(1), (4) or (5) shall be liable—

    (a) on conviction on indictment, to imprisonment for a term not exceeding two years or a fine or both;

    (b) on summary conviction, to imprisonment for a term not exceeding six months or a fine not exceeding the statutory maximum or both.

(2) A person guilty of an offence under section 8(1), (4) or (5) above shall be liable on summary conviction to imprisonment for a term not exceeding three months or a fine not exceeding level 5 on the standard scale or both.

11. Arrest, search and trial

(3) Section 9(1) of the Official Secrets Act 1911 (search warrants) shall have effect as if references to offences under that Act included references to offences under any provision of this Act other than section 8(1), (4) or (5); and the following provisions of the Police and Criminal Evidence Act 1984, that is to say—

    (a) section 9(2) (which excludes items subject to legal privilege and certain other material from powers of search conferred by previous enactments); and

    (b) paragraph 3(b) of Schedule 1 (which prescribes access conditions for the special procedure laid down in that Schedule),

shall apply to section 9(1) of the said Act of 1911 as extended by this subsection as they apply to that section as originally enacted....

(4) Section 8(4) of the Official Secrets Act 1920 (exclusion of public from hearing on the grounds of national safety) shall have effect as if references to offences under that Act included references to offences under any provision of this Act other than section 8(1), (4) or (5).

(5) Proceedings for an offence under this Act may be taken in any place in the United Kingdom.

12. 'Crown servant' and 'government contractor'

(1) In this Act 'Crown servant' means—

   (a) a Minister of the Crown;...

   [(ab) The First Minister for Wales, a Welsh Minister appointed under section 48 of the Government of Wales Act 2006, the Counsel General to the Welsh Assembly Government or a Deputy Welsh Minister;][39] ...

   (c) any person employed in the civil service of the Crown, including Her Majesty's Diplomatic Service, Her Majesty's Overseas Civil Service, the civil service of Northern Ireland and the Northern Ireland Court Service;

   (d) any member of the naval, military or air forces of the Crown including any person employed by an association established for the purposes of [Part XI of the Reserve Forces Act 1996];[40]

   (e) any constable and any other person employed or appointed in or for the purposes of any police force[41] [(including the Police Service of Northern Ireland and the Police Service of Northern Ireland Reserve)][42] [or the Serious Organised Crime Agency];[43]

   (f) any person who is a member or employee of a prescribed body or a body of a prescribed class and either is prescribed for the purposes of this paragraph or belongs to a prescribed class of members or employees of any such body;

   (g) any person who is the holder of a prescribed office or who is an employee of such a holder and either is prescribed for the purposes of this paragraph or belongs to a prescribed class of such employees.[44]

(2) In this Act 'government contractor' means, subject to subsection (3) below, any person who is not a Crown servant but who provides, or is employed in the provision of, goods or services—

   (a) for the purposes of any Minister or person mentioned in paragraph (a) [,(ab)] or (b) of subsection (1) above, [of any office-holder in the Scottish Administration,][45] of any of the services, forces or bodies mentioned in that subsection or of the holder of any office prescribed under that subsection;

   [(aa) for the purpose of the National Assembly for Wales];[46] or

   (b) under an agreement or arrangement certified by the Secretary of State as being one to which the government of a State other than the United Kingdom or an international organisation is a

[39] Inserted by the Government of Wales Act 2006, Sch. 10, para. 34(a).

[40] Substituted by the Reserve Forces Act 1996, Sch. 10, para. 22.

[41] Inserted by the Police Act 1997, Sch. 9, para. 62.3.

[42] Inserted by the Police (Northern Ireland) Act 2000, Sch. 6, para. 9.

[43] Substituted by the Serious Organised Crime and Police Act 2005, Sch. 4, para. 58.

[44] A number of persons and bodies are prescribed under s. 12(1)(f) and (g) of the 1989 Act by the Official Secrets Act 1989 (Prescription) Order 1990, SI 1990/200, as amended. These include (under s. 12(1)(f)) employees and Board members of British Nuclear Fuels plc and Urenco Ltd, and members, officers and employees of the UK Atomic Energy Authority and the Nuclear Decommissioning Authority and (under s. 12(1)(g)), the Comptroller and Auditor General and the staff of the National Audit Office, officers of the Parliamentary Commissioner for Administration not otherwise Crown servants, and a private Secretary to the Sovereign. Other officials are taken to be 'Crown servants' by virtue of specific provisions: see e.g. Government of Wales Act 2006, s. 92 (the First Minister, Welsh Ministers and Deputy Ministers, the Counsel General), Sch. 8, para. 3(2) (the Auditor General for Wales); Public Services Ombudsman (Wales) Act 2000, Sch. 1, para. 2(3) (the Ombudsman).

[45] Inserted by the Scotland Act 1998, Sch. 8, para. 26(2), (3).

[46] Inserted by the Government of Wales Act 1998, Sch. 12, para. 30.

party or which is subordinate to, or made for the purposes of implementing, any such agreement or arrangement.

(3) Where an employee or class of employees of any body, or of any holder of an office, is prescribed by an order made for the purposes of subsection (1) above—

  (a) any employee of that body, or of the holder of that office, who is not prescribed or is not within the prescribed class; and

  (b) any person who does not provide, or is not employed in the provision of, goods or services for the purposes of the performance of those functions of the body or the holder of the office in connection with which the employee or prescribed class of employees is engaged,

shall not be a government contractor for the purposes of this Act....

[(4A) In this section the reference to a police force includes a reference to the Civil Nuclear Constabulary.][47] ...

13. Other interpretation provisions

(1) In this Act—

'disclose' and 'disclosure', in relation to a document or other article, include parting with possession of it;

'international organisation' means, subject to subsections (2) and (3) below, an organisation of which only States are members and includes a reference to any organ of such an organisation;

'prescribed' means prescribed by an order made by the Secretary of State;

'State' includes the government of a State and any organ of its government and references to a State other than the United Kingdom include references to any territory outside the United Kingdom.

(2) In section 12(2)(*b*) above the reference to an international organisation includes a reference to any such organisation whether or not one of which only States are members and includes a commercial organisation.

(3) In determining for the purposes of subsection (1) above whether only States are members of an organisation, any member which is itself an organisation of which only States are members, or which is an organ of such an organisation, shall be treated as a State....

15. Acts done abroad and extent

(1) Any act—

  (a) done by a British citizen or Crown servant; or

  (b) done by any person in any of the Channel Islands or the Isle of Man or any colony, shall, if it would be an offence by that person under any provision of this Act other than section 8(1), (4) or (5) when done by him in the United Kingdom, be an offence under that provision....

NOTES

1. The maximum penalty under s. 1 of the 1911 Act is 14 years' imprisonment, and for the other offences under the two Acts (other than ss. 4 and 5 of the 1920 Act) is two years' imprisonment. A search warrant may be granted by a justice of the peace under s. 9(1) of the 1911 Act if satisfied there is reasonable ground for suspecting that an offence under the Act has been or is about to be committed. A superintendent of police may confer such powers by

---

47 Inserted by the Energy Act 2004, Sch. 14, para. 6.

order if it appears to him that the case is one of great emergency and that in the interests of the state immediate action is necessary (s. 9(2)).

There are special provisions concerning atomic energy. Section 11 of the Atomic Energy Act 1946 makes it an offence to communicate to an unauthorised person information relating to atomic energy plant.[48] Section 13 makes it an offence for any person to disclose, without authority, any information obtained in the exercise of powers under the Act. Any place belonging to or used for the purposes of the Authority may be declared to be a prohibited place under the Official Secrets Act 1911, s. 3(c).[49] Similar provisions apply to the Civil Aviation Authority,[50] the holders of a nuclear site licence[51] and public telecommunications operators.[52] It is also an offence for a member of any Euratom institution or committee, an officer or servant of Euratom or a person who has dealings with Euratom to disclose classified information acquired from that source.[53] The current orders under s. 3(c) are The Official Secrets (Prohibited Places) Orders 1955 and 1994.[54] They cover the Capenhurst and Sellafield works of British Nuclear Fuels Ltd, and various establishments of the Atomic Energy Authority, including Dounreay, Windscale and Harwell.

2. It is an offence under section 1(1) of the 1920 Act (for example) to wear official (or similar) uniform, make a false statement, tamper with a passport, possess a forged official document, personat a Crown Officer, or use or possess an unauthorised or counterfeited die, seal or stamp[55] for the purpose of gaining admission to a prohibited place or for any other purpose prejudicial to the safety or interests of the State. Section 1(2) creates various offences, including retaining an official document for any purpose prejudicial to the safety or the interests of the state; communicating an official document or a secret official code word or password issued for the defendant's use alone; possessing another's document or word without lawful authority or excuse; or on obtaining possession of an official document failing to restore it to the authority that issued it, or the police. It is also an offence to obstruct, knowingly mislead or otherwise interfere with or impede any police officer, or any member of the forces on guard, patrol or similar duty, 'in the vicinity of a prohibited place'.[56]

3. The fact that a person has been in communication with a foreign agent constitutes evidence in proceedings against him under s. 1 of the 1911 Act that he has for a purpose prejudicial to the safety or the interests of the State, obtained or attempted to obtain information which may be useful to an enemy.[57] There is also a power whereby a Secretary of State may require the production of telegrams.[58] Persons who carry on the business of receiving postal packets for delivery or forwarding must be registered with the police.[59] A chief officer of police who has reasonable grounds for suspecting that a s. 1 offence has been committed may, with the permission of the Secretary of State, authorise a police officer not below the rank of inspector to require a person reasonably believed to be able to furnish information as to the offence or suspected offence, to do so. Permission is not needed if the chief officer has reasonable grounds to believe that the case is one of great emergency and that in the interests of the state immediate action is necessary.[60]

---

[48] See SR & O 1947/100.   [49] Atomic Energy Authority Act 1954, s. 6(3).
[50] Civil Aviation Act 1982, s.18.   [51] Nuclear Installations Act 1965, Sch. 1.
[52] Telecommunications Act 1984, Sch. 4, para. 12(2).
[53] European Communities Act 1972, s.11(2).   [54] SIs 1955/1497 and 1994/968.
[55] See *R v Sanchez and Garcia*, unreported, 5 July 1984.   [56] 1920 Act, s. 3.
[57] 1920 Act, s. 2.   [58] 1920 Act, s. 4.   [59] 1920 Act, s. 5.
[60] 1920 Act, s. 6.

4. If, in the course of any court proceedings under the Acts:

…application is made by the prosecution, on the ground that the publication of any evidence to be given or of any statement to be made in the course of the proceedings would be prejudicial to the national safety, that all or any portion of the public shall be excluded during any part of the hearing, the court may make an order to that effect, but the passing of sentence shall in any case take place in public[61]

5. The 1911 Official Secrets Bill[62] was presented by the Government as a measure which was aimed at spying and was essential on grounds of national security.[63] Section 2[64] was not mentioned. It passed all its Commons stages in less than an hour. The files show that the legislation had been desired for some time by governments, the Official Secrets Act 1889 having proved inadequate to prevent the leakage of official information by civil servants, and that it had been carefully prepared over a period of years.[65] The background to the 1989 Act is discussed below.[66]

6. *Aspects of interpretation.* The term 'enemy' includes a potential enemy, and so all the provisions of s. 1 are applicable in peace time.[67] The leading case on s. 1, *Chandler v DPP*, is given below.[68] Section 3 of the 1920 Act was used in a prosecution of four members of the Committee of 100, including Pat Arrowsmith, in 1964. They were fined £25 for inciting people to obstruct police officers at the USAF base at Ruislip in connection with a demonstration there.[69] Williams points out[70] that it was not necessary for the Official Secrets Acts to be invoked against the nuclear disarmers in the 1960s, in preference to prosecutions for the general public order offences.

In *Adler v George*,[71] A obstructed a member of the armed forces engaged in security duty while within the boundaries of Marham RAF station. His conviction under s. 3 of the 1920 Act was upheld by the Divisional Court, which held that the words 'in the vicinity of' had to be read as meaning 'in or in the vicinity of'.

Another alteration in the statutory language to the detriment of a defendant was made by the Court of Criminal Appeal in *R v Oakes*.[72] The court treated s. 7 of the 1920 Act as if it read 'aids or abets *or* does any act preparatory' so as to render liable a person who had done an 'act preparatory' without 'aiding or abetting'.

It seems to the court that it is quite clear in the present case what the intention was, and that there has been merely a faultiness of expression.[73]

O had also been convicted under s. 2 of the 1911 Act. In *R v Bingham*[74] the Court of Appeal (Criminal Division) held that an 'act preparatory' was 'an act done by the accused with the commission of an offence under the principal Act in mind', and that it was sufficient to show that the transmission of prejudicial information was 'possible' and not 'probable'.[75]

---

61 1920 Act, s. 8(4).

62 The origins of the Officials Secrets Acts are discussed in D.G.T. Williams, *Not in the Public Interest* (1965), Chap. 1; Report of the Franks Committee on Section 2 of the Official Secrets Act 1911 (Cmnd 5104), Chap. 4 and Appendix III; D. French, 'Spy Fever in Britain, 1900–1915' (1978) 21(2) *The Historical Journal*, 355; K G. Robertson, *Public Secrets* (1982), Chaps 4 and 5.

63 Franks Report, p. 24.   64 See below, p. 787.   65 Franks Report, p. 25.

66 Pp. 787–789.   67 *R v Parrott* (1913) 8 Cr App R 186, CCA.   68 P. 783.

69 D.G.T. Williams, *Not in the Public Interest* (1965), p. 109.   70 At p. 111.

71 [1964] 2 QB 7.   72 [1959] 2 QB 350.   73 Per Lord Parker CJ at 357.

74 [1973] QB 870.   75 Per Lord Widgery CJ at 875.

It is not obvious that something should be an offence which is even more remote from the substantive offence than an attempt to commit it.

7. *Powers of search.* The powers of search granted by s. 9 of the 1911 Act were relied upon by the police in the 'Zircon affair'.[76] In 1986 the BBC commissioned Duncan Campbell to make a series of programmes entitled *Secret Society*. One of these revealed the existence of a secret Ministry of Defence project, Project Zircon, to put a spy satellite in space. The programme also revealed its cost (c. £500m) and the fact that the existence and cost of the project had been concealed from Parliament, but not its technical details. On 15 January 1987, the programme was banned on national security grounds by Alasdair Milne, the BBC's Director General (having previously been cleared by Assistant Director General Alan Protheroe). An injunction was obtained against Duncan Campbell on 21 January, but not served in time to prevent the Zircon story being told in the *New Statesman* of 23 January 1987 ('Spy in the Sky'), published on 22 January. On the same day, the Attorney-General failed to obtain an injunction to prevent the programme being shown in the Palace of Westminster, Ian Kennedy J stating that it was for the House to regulate its own proceedings; but persuaded the Speaker, after a briefing 'on Privy Counsellor terms', to impose a ban on its being shown while the injunction against Campbell was in force (it was lifted on 25 February in the light of a detailed undertaking given by Campbell).

Over the weekend of 24–25 January, Special Branch police officers searched the offices of the *New Statesman;* on 25 January, officers searched Duncan Campbell's home, and on 31 January, the Glasgow offices of BBC Scotland. Substantial quantities of documents were removed, especially from the BBC. The London warrants were granted under the Police and Criminal Evidence Act 1984, s. 9 and Sch. 1 under the warrant procedure exceptionally available as an alternative to obtaining an order inter partes. The basis of the warrant in Glasgow was s. 9 of the 1911 Act, the PACE provisions not extending to Scotland.[77] It was claimed that the legal proceedings involved were instigated by the Attorney-General in England and the Lord Advocate in Scotland rather than Ministers.[78]

The Government's actions were widely criticised as an attempt to intimidate the press, particularly in view of the broad terms in which the search warrants were granted. The question why the authorities, who had known about the proposed programme since the middle of 1986, waited until early 1987 to take any action was never satisfactorily answered.

A majority of the Committee of Privileges subsequently concluded that the Speaker had acted 'wholly correctly in this matter', and stated that the private showing of the programme could not constitute a 'proceeding in Parliament' protected by Parliamentary privilege.[79]

Section 9(2) and Sch. 1, para. 3(b) of PACE now apply to warrants under s. 9(1) of the 1911 Act.[80]

---

[76] See, generally, the *New Statesman* for 23 and 30 January and 6 February 1987; P. Thornton, *The Civil Liberties of the Zircon Affair* (NCCL, 1987); P. Gill (1987) 9 Liverpool LR 189; debates on the Special Branch Raids, 109 HC Deb, 2 and 3 February 1987, cols 691–700, 815–858; K.D. Ewing and C.A. Gearty, *Freedom Under Thatcher* (1990), pp. 147–152.

[77] See G.J. Zellick (1987) 137 NLJ 160.

[78] See, e.g., 110 HC Deb, 19 February 1977, cols 796–798, written answer by Malcolm Rifkind MP, Secretary of State for Scotland.

[79] See *First Report from the Committee of Privileges 1986–87, Speaker's Order of 22 January 1987 on a Matter of National Security* (1986–87 HC 365); A.W. Bradley [1987] PL 1 and 488.

[80] Official Secrets Act 1989, s. 11(3). See above, pp. 173, 181–183.

(B) SECTION 1 OF THE OFFICIAL SECRETS ACT 1911: ESPIONAGE, SABOTAGE AND WHAT ELSE?

- **Chandler v Director of Public Prosecutions** [1964] AC 763, [1962] 3 All ER 142, [1962] 3 WLR 702, House of Lords

The appellants, five men and a woman, were members of the Committee of 100 who sought to further the aims of the Campaign for Nuclear Disarmament by non-violent demonstrations of civil disobedience. They took part in organising a demonstration held on 9 December 1961, at Wethersfield Airfield, which was a 'prohibited place' within section 3 of the Official Secrets Act 1911, and which was occupied at the material time by United States Air Force squadrons assigned to the Supreme Commander Allied Forces, Europe. The plan was that on 9 December 1961, some demonstrators would take up a position outside the entrances to the airfield and would remain there sitting for five hours, while others would enter the airfield and, by sitting in front of the aircraft, would prevent them from taking off. On that date, many demonstrators did travel to Wethersfield, but were prevented from entering the airfield. The admitted objects were to ground all aircraft, to immobilise the airfield and to reclaim the base for civilian purposes. The appellants were charged with conspiring together to incite diverse persons to commit, and with conspiring together and with others to commit, 'a breach of section 1 of the Official Secrets Act 1911, namely, for a purpose prejudicial to the safety or interests of the State to enter a Royal Air Force Station...at Wethersfield'. A prosecution witness, Air Commodore Magill, gave evidence that interference with the ability of aircraft to take off was prejudicial to the safety or interests of the State. The judge refused to allow counsel for the defence to cross-examine or call evidence as to the appellants' beliefs that their acts would benefit the State or to show that the appellants' purpose was not in fact prejudicial to the safety or interests of the State. The appellants were convicted and sentenced to terms of imprisonment (18 months each for the men and 12 for the woman).

They appealed on the grounds that the facts did not disclose a conspiracy to commit a breach of s. 1 of the Act of 1911, and that the judge was wrong in excluding cross-examination and evidence as to the facts on which the appellants' beliefs were based, and as to whether the appellants' purpose was in fact prejudicial to the state. Their appeals were dismissed by the Court of Criminal Appeal[81] and the House of Lords.

> **Lord Reid:** ...In cross-examination [of Air Commodore Magill] objection was taken to his being asked as to the armament of these squadrons. Counsel for the accused said that they sought to adduce evidence that their purpose was not prejudicial to the interests of the State, and that the basis of the defence was that these aircraft used nuclear bombs and that it was not in fact in the interests of the State to have aircraft so armed at that time there. So, he said, it would be beneficial to the State to immobilise these aircraft. Then counsel further submitted that he was entitled to adduce evidence to show that the accused believed, and reasonably believed, that it was not prejudicial but beneficial to the interests of the State to immobilise these aircraft: the jury were entitled to hold that no offence had been committed because the accused did not have a purpose prejudicial to the State, and it was for the jury to determine their purpose....[C]ounsel said that his evidence would deal with the effect of exploding a nuclear bomb and...reference was made to the possibility of accident or mistake, and other reasons against having nuclear bombs. He said that he wished to cross-examine as to the basic wrongness of the conception of

---

[81] [1964] AC 771.

a deterrent force and the likelihood of it attracting hostile attack. In reply the Attorney-General submitted that an objective test must determine whether the purpose of grounding aircraft was a prejudicial purpose, that the accuseds' beliefs were irrelevant and so was the reasonableness of their beliefs. Havers J then ruled that the defence were not entitled to call evidence to establish that it would be beneficial for this country to give up nuclear armament or that the accused honestly believed that it would be.... [Section 1 of the Official Secrets Act 1911] has a side note 'Penalties for spying', and it was argued that this limits its scope. In my view side notes cannot be used as an aid to construction. They are mere catchwords and I have never heard of it being supposed in recent times that an amendment to alter a side note could be proposed in either House of Parliament. Side notes in the original Bill are inserted by the draftsman. During the passage of the Bill through its various stages amendments to it or other reasons may make it desirable to alter a side note. In that event I have reason to believe that alteration is made by the appropriate officer of the House—no doubt in consultation with the draftsman. So side notes cannot be said to be enacted in the same sense as the long title or any part of the body of the Act. Moreover, it is impossible to suppose that the section does not apply to sabotage and what was intended to be done in this case was a kind of temporary sabotage.

The first word in the section that requires consideration is 'purpose'.... The accused both intended and desired that the base should be immobilised for a time, and I cannot construe purpose in any sense that does not include that state of mind. A person can have two different purposes in doing a particular thing and even if their reason or motive for doing what they did is called the purpose of influencing public opinion that cannot alter the fact that they had a purpose to immobilise the base. And the statute says 'for any purpose'. There is no question here of the interference with the aircraft being an unintended or undesired consequence of carrying out a legitimate purpose.

Next comes the question of what is meant by the safety or interests of the State. 'State' is not an easy word. It does not mean the Government or the Executive. And I do not think that it means, as counsel argued, the individuals who inhabit these islands. The statute cannot be referring to the interests of all those individuals because they may differ and the interests of the majority are not necessarily the same as the interests of the State.... Perhaps the country or the realm are as good synonyms as one can find and I would be prepared to accept the organised community as coming as near to a definition as one can get.

Who, then, is to determine what is and what is not prejudicial to the safety and interests of the State? The question more frequently arises as to what is or is not in the public interest. I do not subscribe to the view that the Government or a Minister must always or even as a general rule have the last word about that.

But here we are dealing with a very special matter—interfering with a prohibited place which Wethersfield was. The definition in section 3 shows that it must either be closely connected with the armed forces or be a place such that information regarding it or damage to it or interference with it would be useful to an enemy. It is in my opinion clear that the disposition and armament of the armed forces are and for centuries have been within the exclusive discretion of the Crown and that no one can seek a legal remedy on the ground that such discretion has been wrongly exercised. I need only refer to the numerous authorities gathered together in *China Navigation Co Ltd v A-G* [1932] 2 KB 197. Anyone is entitled, in or out of Parliament, to urge that policy regarding the armed forces should be changed; but until it is changed, on a change of Government or otherwise, no one is entitled to challenge it in court.

Even in recent times there have been occasions when quite large numbers of people have been bitterly opposed to the use made of the armed forces in peace or in war. The 1911 Act was passed at a time of grave misgiving about the German menace, and it would be surprising and hardly credible that the Parliament of that date intended that a person who deliberately interfered with vital dispositions of the armed forces should be entitled to submit to a jury that Government policy was wrong and that what he did was really in the best interests of the country, and then perhaps to escape conviction because a unanimous verdict on that question could not be obtained. Of course we are bound by the words which Parliament has used in the Act. If those words necessarily lead to that conclusion then it is no answer that it is inconceivable that Parliament can have so intended. The remedy is to amend the Act. But we must be clear that the words of the Act are not reasonably capable of any other interpretation.

I am prepared to start from the position that, when an Act requires certain things to be established against an accused person to constitute an offence, all of those things must be proved by evidence which the jury accepts, unless Parliament has otherwise provided. But normally such things are facts and where questions of opinion arise they are on limited technical matters on which expert evidence can be called. Here the question whether it is beneficial to use the armed forces in a particular way or prejudicial to interfere with that use would be a political question—a question of opinion on which anyone actively interested in politics, including jurymen, might consider his own opinion as good as that of anyone else. Our criminal system is not devised to deal with issues of that kind. The question therefore is whether this Act can reasonably be read in such a way as to avoid the raising of such issues.

The Act must be read as a whole and paragraphs (c) and (d) of section 3 appear to me to require such a construction. Places to which they refer become prohibited places if a Secretary of State declares that damage, obstruction or interference there 'would be useful to an enemy'. Plainly it is not open to an accused who has interfered with or damaged such a place to a material extent to dispute the declaration of the Secretary of State and it would be absurd if he were entitled to say or lead evidence to show that, although he had deliberately done something which would be useful to an enemy, yet his purpose was not prejudicial to the safety or interests of the State. So here at least the trial judge must be entitled to prevent the leading of evidence and to direct the jury that if they find that his purpose was to interfere to a material extent they must hold that his purpose was prejudicial. If that be so, then, in view of the matters which I have already dealt with, it appears to me that the same must necessarily apply to the present case.

I am therefore of opinion that the ruling of Havers J excluding evidence was right and that his direction to the jury was substantially correct.... I think it was proper to give to the jury a direction to the effect that if they were satisfied that the intention and desire of the accused was to procure the immobilisation of these aircraft in a way which they knew would or might substantially impair their operational effectiveness then the offence was proved and they should convict.

maintained by the Crown for the protection of the realm....

Viscount Radcliffe and **Lords Hodson, Devlin** and **Pearce** delivered concurring speeches.

Appeal dismissed.

NOTES

1. The decision in this case was severely criticised by Thompson.[82] He pointed out that Parliament had been assured by two Attorneys-General (Sir Gordon Hewart and Sir Hartley Shawcross) and Lord Maugham LC that s. 1 applied only to espionage, and that the expression 'for a purpose prejudicial to the safety or interests of the state' would be for the courts to construe and determine. Indeed the current form of s. 6 of the 1920 Act was adopted in order to limit its operation to cases of espionage, and linking it with s. 1 of the 1911 Act was thought to have that effect. While reference to proceedings in Parliament was not permissible as an aid to construction, 'it was indefensible on the part of the Attorney-General to press arguments upon the courts to give the section a wider meaning'.[83] Thompson also challenged the legal reasoning.[84]

---

[82] D. Thompson [1963] PL 201.   [83] Ibid., at 210–211.

[84] Cf. J.C. Smith and B. Hogan, *Criminal Law* (6th edn, 1988), pp. 839–841; G. Marshall in R.F. Bunn and W.G. Andrews (eds), *Politics and Civil Liberties in Europe* (1967), pp. 5–35.

2. Apart from *Chandler v DPP*, prosecutions under s. 1 have generally been confined to cases of espionage. It is certainly open to the Attorney-General to have regard to assurances given to Parliament in exercising the discretion whether to authorise a prosecution. However, the then Attorney-General, Sir Reginald Manningham-Buller said:

> In considering whether or not to prosecute, I must direct my mind to the language and spirit of the Acts and not to what my predecessors said about them many years ago in an entirely different context.[85]

Persons convicted for contravening or conspiring to contravene s. 1 since the war include Dr Fuchs, the members of the Portland 'spy ring', George Blake[86] and W.J.C. Vassall.[87] In 1978 proceedings were instituted under ss. 1 and 2 against John Berry, a former corporal in the Intelligence Corps, and two journalists, Duncan Campbell and Crispin Aubrey. B communicated information to the journalists concerning Britain's Signals Intelligence Organization. Mars-Jones J hinted that the use of charges under s. 1 was oppressive in a non-spying case. None of the defendants intended to use the information to assist an enemy. Counsel for the prosecution offered to prove that the defendants' conduct was prejudicial, notwithstanding that the burden of proof as to this matter technically lay on the defendants under s. 1(2). Mars-Jones J was unable to accept this arrangement in view of the clear words of s. 1(2). The Attorney-General decided to drop the s. 1 charges.[88] See further, below. Other matters of significance were (a) the proceedings for contempt of court brought in relation to the disclosure of the identity of one of the witnesses;[89] and (b) the revelation that the potential jurors had been vetted for their potential loyalty or disloyalty.[90]

More recent prosecutions under s. 1 have related to espionage. In 1982, Geoffrey Arthur Prime, who worked at Government Communications Headquarters (GCHQ) was sentenced to a total of 35 years' imprisonment for s. 1 offences for passing a vast quantity of information concerning his signals intelligence work to the Russian Intelligence Service.[91] Shortly afterwards, a Canadian economist, Professor Hugh Hambleton, admitted passing secret NATO documents to KGB agents and was sentenced to 10 years' imprisonment.[92] Lance-Corporal Philip Aldridge pleaded guilty to doing an act preparatory to the commission of an offence under s. 1 in abstracting a highly classified document with the intention of communicating it to the Russian Intelligence Service; he was sentenced to four years' imprisonment.[93] Michael Bettaney, an MI5 counter-espionage officer, was convicted of six charges under s. 1(1) of the 1911 Act and four under s. 7 of the 1920 Act, and was sentenced to a total of 23 years' imprisonment. He had communicated some secret information to the Russians and had collected much more for the purposes of becoming an agent for them.[94] Sentences of 10 years' imprisonment on two East Germans who settled in England with a view to espionage were upheld in *R v Schulze and Schulze*.[95] In 1993, Michael John Smith, who worked for two top defence

---

[85] 657 HC Deb, 5 April 1962, col. 611.

[86] Sentenced to 14 years' imprisonment on each of five separate counts the first three to run consecutively: (1961) 45 Cr App R 292.

[87] See the Report of the Radcliffe Tribunal of Inquiry (Cmnd 2009, 1963).

[88] *The Times*, 31 October 1978.   [89] See above, pp. 707–709.

[90] See H. Harman and J. Griffith, *Justice Deserted* (NCCL, 1979).

[91] *The Times*, 11, 12 November 1982; *The Sunday Times*, 14 November 1982; *R v Prime* (1983) 5 Cr App R (S) 127; Report of the Security Commission, May 1983 (Cmnd 8876); Statement by the Prime Minister, 42 HC Deb, 12 May 1983, cols 431–434, written answer.

[92] *The Times*, 30 November and 1, 2, 3, 7, 8 December 1982.

[93] *The Times*, 19 January 1983; Report of the Security Commission, March 1984 (Cmnd 9212, 1984).

[94] *The Sunday Times*, 25 March 1984; *The Times*, 9, 11, 17 April 1984.

[95] (1986) 8 Cr App R (S) 463.

research companies, was sentenced to 25 years' imprisonment for spying for the Russians, reduced to 20 years on appeal.[96] In 2002, Raphael Bravo was sentenced to 11 years' imprisonment for stealing secret documents from BAE, and seeking to sell them to an M15 officer posing as a Russian.[97] In 2003 Ian Parr, another BAE worker, was sentenced to 10 years' for seeking to sell information on military projects to Russia.[98] In 2008, Daniel James, an Iranian-born British citizen and Territorial Army corporal who had served as an interpreter in the armed forces in Afghanistan, was sentenced to 10 years' imprisonment for passing information to an enemy state (Iran).[99]

3. The failure of the authorities to prosecute individuals who have been identified as spies has attracted criticism. Material in the archive of Vasili Mitrokhin, a KGB officer who defected to the West in 1992, showed that Mrs Melita Norwood had revealed secrets between 1945 and 1949 while working for the British Non-Ferrous Metal Research Association; her security clearance was revoked in 1951 and suspicions about her were confirmed by the Mitrokhin archive. This did not, however, include original documents and was not itself of evidential value. The Intelligence and Security Committee[100] was critical of the 'serious failure' of the Security Service to consult the law officers in mid 1993 about a possible prosecution, the Service taking the view that police action was inappropriate given in particular Mrs Norwood's age and the passage of time since her espionage activities; by the time they were consulted, in March 1999, the law officers were of the view that it was now too late to institute proceedings. The ISC reaffirmed the point that prosecution decisions were for the law officers not the Security Service. The Government agreed.[101] Political criticism of the failure to prosecute agents of the Stasi, the East German intelligence organisation continued.[102]

(C) UNAUTHORISED DISCLOSURES: THE OFFICIAL SECRETS ACT 1989

(I) SECTION 2 OF THE OFFICIAL SECRETS ACT 1911

The Official Secrets Act 1989 replaced, at long last, s. 2 of the Official Secrets Act 1911. Section 2, as amended by the Official Secrets Act 1920, was the product of a highly convoluted piece of draftsmanship. However, its essence was simple and breathtakingly wide in its scope. Section 2(1) penalised the disclosure of official information by D to anyone 'other than a person to whom he is authorised to communicate it, or a person to whom it is in the interest of the State his duty to communicate it'. The categories of protected information in question included any information which was obtained in contravention of the Act or owing to D's position or former position as an office holder under the Crown or as a government contractor. Section 2(2) penalised the receipt of any information by D, knowing or having reasonable ground to believe that the information was communicated to him in contravention of the Act, unless he proved that the communication was contrary to his desire.

Many prosecutions concerned the improper disclosure of police information for the purposes of crime or to journalist or private detectives. However, there were a number of

---

96 *The Times*, 19 November 1993; Report of the Security Commission, July 1995 (Cm 2930).
97 *The Guardian*, 2 February 2002. 98 *The Times*, 5 April 2003.
99 *The Times*, 29 November 2008.
100 *The Mitrokhin Inquiry Report* (Cm 4764, 2000).
101 *Government Response* (Cm 4765, 2000).
102 *The Times*, 18 September 2000, referring to decoded Stasi files.

controversial prosecutions.[103] These included those of Jonathan Aitken and Brian Roberts (editor of the *Sunday Telegraph*);[104] John Berry, a former corporal in the Intelligence Corps; Duncan Campbell, a *New Statesman* journalist and Crispin Aubrey, a *Time Out* journalist;[105] Sarah Tisdall, a clerk in the Foreign Secretary's private office;[106] and Clive Ponting, an assistant secretary at the Ministry of Defence.[107]

The breadth of these provisions was widely regarded as unsatisfactory. The Franks Committee on s. 2 of the Official Secrets Act 1911[108] recommended the repeal of s. 2 and its replacement by narrower and more specific provisions. Various bills, both government and private member's, designed to secure reform, failed. Ultimately, the Government, following the White Paper, *Reform of Section 2 of the Official Secrets Act 1911*,[109] secured the passage of the Official Secrets Act 1989. The extent to which this would prove in practice to be a liberalising measure was, however, hotly debated.

(II) THE OFFICIAL SECRETS ACT 1989

The Official Secrets Act 1989[110] was based on the Government's White Paper, *Reform of Section 2 of the Official Secrets Act 1911*.[111]

By comparison with the 1911 Act, s.2, the 1989 Act narrows the scope of protection of official information by the criminal law to categories: (a) security and intelligence; (b) defence; (c) international relations; (d) information obtained in confidence from other states or international organisations; (e) information disclosure of which is likely to result in the commission of an offence or to impede the prevention or detection of offences; and (f) information obtained by special investigations authorised by warrant.[112] The categories reflect the post-Franks consensus that Cabinet documents and economic information should not automatically be protected. The unauthorised disclosure of information in these categories by a Crown servant or government contractor is an offence. Note that in categories (b) to (e), the disclosure must be 'damaging' in the ways specified in the sections. The tests for 'damage' are more precise but less strict than those envisaged by Franks, and there is no system of ministerial certification.[113] In category (a), the unauthorised disclosure or purported disclosure by a member of the security and intelligence services, and others notified that they are subject to this provision, of information obtained by virtue of their work, is an offence without any proof of damage; damage

---

[103] For further detail, see the previous edition of this book at pp. 827–832.

[104] Acquitted by the jury on charges related to the passing of a confidential assessment of the situation in Nigeria during the Biafran War by A to the *Sunday Telegraph*.

[105] Convicted under s. 2 in respect of B's communication of information to C and A about Britain's signals intelligence (SIGINT); charges were originally brought under s. 1. C and A were given conditional discharge and B a six-month suspended prison sentence.

[106] Convicted under s. 2 for leaking copies of two documents about the arrival of cruise missiles at Greenham Common; she had learned that the Secretary of State had proposed to delay the announcement until after their arrival, which she regarded as objectionable 'political subterfuge'; sentenced to six months' imprisonment. The sentence was widely criticised.

[107] Acquitted by the jury on charges relating to the passing of documents to Tom Dalyell MP concerning the sinking of the Argentinean warship, the General Belgrano. The judge directed that mens rea was not required, but the jury acquitted nevertheless.

[108] Cmnd 5104, 1972.   [109] Cm 408, 1988.

[110] See generally on the 1989 Act, J.A.G. Griffith (1989) 16 JLS 273; S. Palmer [1990] PL 243; Annotations by J. Mayhew and P. O'Higgins in *Current Law Statutes Annotated 1989*; P. Birkinshaw, *Reforming the Secret State* (1990), pp. 15–29; A. Bailin [2008] Crim LR 625. On the White Paper, see S. Palmer [1988] PL 523.

[111] Cm 408, 1988.   [112] 1989 Act, ss. 1–4.

[113] Except, in effect, under s. 1(4)(b): see P. Birkinshaw, *Reforming the Secret State* (1990), pp. 11, 20.

must, however, be proved where a disclosure of information relating to security and intelligence is otherwise made by a Crown servant or government contractor. Similarly, there is no requirement to prove damage in respect of category (f). Mere receipt of information is no longer an offence.

It is generally a defence for the accused to prove that he did not know that the information fell into the protected category in question, or that disclosure would be damaging in the relevant sense.[114] Under s. 5, it is for the prosecution to prove that the accused knew or had reasonable cause to believe that the information was protected against disclosure and that disclosure would be damaging.[115] There is no defence that disclosure was in the public interest or (except in the limited situation covered in s. 6(3)) that the information had previously been published. As to the first, the Government argued that such a defence would make the law less clear and was in any event inappropriate given that the criminal law would be confined to 'information which demonstrably requires its protection in the public interest'; as to the second, prior publication should at most be regarded as a factor in determining whether a disclosure would be damaging in a relevant way.[116]

The narrowing of the scope of the criminal law in the area can only be welcomed. There are, however, a number of criticisms that were forcefully articulated during the passage of the Bill but which left the Government unmoved. These include:

(a) the blanket prohibition of disclosure of information by members of the security and intelligence services irrespective of damage;

(b) the blanket prohibition of disclosure of information derived from e.g. authorised telephone tapping, also irrespective of damage;

(c) the absence of any public interest defence and any general defence of prior publication;

(d) the imposition of the burden of proof to establish certain defences on the accused, contrary to normal principle.

As to (a), the absolute prohibition would extend to prevent, for example, the exposure of unlawful behaviour and thus is to be contrasted with the law of confidence.[117] Amendments proposed to prevent the Secretary of State from unreasonably withholding consent to the disclosure of information (e.g. in memoirs) by a former member of the security and intelligence services, or to establish a Publications Review Board with power to authorise disclosure, were rejected. A mechanism for considering complaints was, however, established by the Security Service Act 1989,[118] although this fell short of providing independent scrutiny. The absence of a public interest defence is designed to discourage 'whistleblowers'. Again, a mechanism has been created whereby members and former members of the security and intelligence services may approach a 'staff counsellor' with any grievance about their work. The counsellor has unrestricted access to the Prime Minister, and access to all documents, to all levels of management and the Cabinet Secretary.[119] Public disclosure is not, however, to be available in the last resort where other avenues have been exhausted.

Prosecutions under the 1989 Act

These have been relatively rare. In 1991, Arthur Henry Price and Joseph Terrence Wilson pleaded guilty to making a damaging disclosure to a foreign power. W, a security guard at

---

[114] 1989 Act, ss. 1(5), 2(3), 3(4), 4(4), (5).   [115] S. 5(2), (3); cf. similar provisions in s. 6(2).
[116] White Paper, paras 58–64.   [117] Below, pp. 803–822.
[118] Below, p. 590.   [119] See 121 HC Deb, cols 508 (2 November 1987) and 796 (3 November 1987).

the VSEL shipyard in Barrow-in-Furness, stole an acoustic tile used on submarines from the yard. W and F (a mini-cab driver) subsequently offered to sell it to a man (Nick) believed to be a Russian for £3m. The man turned out to be a British security agent. W's counsel said that the exercise had been conceived and executed as a joke. 'My indications are that Nick's Russian accent was wholly unconvincing. He kept saying "Ja" as in German, and he couldn't pronounce "Moscow".' The Security Services had got in touch with W and P via an advert in the local press. W had subsequently seen police officers enter the phone booths they had just left and start dusting for fingerprints. Nevertheless, the matter was not treated as a joke by Brooke J, who sentenced each of them to 15 months' imprisonment. Charges of conspiracy to contravene the 1911 Act were changed to charges under the 1989 Act, with the authority of the Attorney-General.[120]

In 1998, Chief Petty Officer Steven Hayden was sent to prison for 12 months for an offence against s. 1(3) of the 1989 Act for leaking to the *Sun* (for £10,000) a report about an alleged Iraqi anthrax threat. Also in 1998, MoD police searched the home of journalist Tony Geraghty in relation to the publication of *The Irish War,* which gave details of army computer surveillance in Northern Ireland. He was charged under s. 5 of the 1989 Act but proceedings were subsequently dropped.[121] Nigel Wylde, a retired colonel who was formerly a bomb disposal officer in Northern Ireland, was charged with disclosing classified documents to Geraghty and was due to stand trial in November 2000, after the implementation of the Human Rights Act 2000. This too was dropped after the prosecution read a report from Duncan Campbell, due to be an expert witness for the defence, explaining why there was nothing in the book that the PIRA did not know or had not worked out for itself 20 years earlier.

Tomlinson[122]

Further difficulties for the intelligence services have been caused by disaffected former officers. Richard Tomlinson was dismissed by SIS in 1995 having not satisfactorily completed a probationary period. Like all intelligence officers he had signed a confidentiality undertaking. He commenced proceedings for unfair dismissal. SIS complained that he then breached the Official Secrets Act by retaining material and preparing material for a book on SIS, and disclosing information to *The Sunday Times.* In September 1996 the High Court granted final injunctions restraining him from further disclosing information obtained by him in the course of his employment with SIS, apart from his lawyers for the purpose of legal proceedings. Further court orders led to recovery of a copy of the book and computer disks disclosing contacts with a New York literary agent. The unfair dismissal proceedings were settled. T obtained some financial benefits (subsequently said to be a loan and a job outside SIS) undertook to deliver to SIS any material relating to his work in and the activities of SIS, assigned copyright to the Crown, acknowledged his obligations under the Official Secrets Act and undertook to observe confidentiality and contractual undertakings. However, in 1997, while in Australia he disclosed confidential information to publishers. This led to a conviction under the 1989 Act on 18 December 1997 for which he was sentenced to 12 months' imprisonment. After his release in May 1998 he went to France. He had continued to discuss publication of a book with publishers. On 2 August 1998 *The Sunday Times* published an article attributing to T statements that he had plans to reveal details of a MI6 plot to murder Col. Gaddafi and details of MI6 operations. T flew to

---

[120] See the *North Western Evening Mail,* 8–11 July 1991.

[121] HC Deb, 23 May 2000, col. 462w.

[122] *A-G for England and Wales v Tomlinson* [1999] 3 NZLR 722; *Guardian Unlimited,* 2 November 2000. See A. Reid and N. Ryder (2000) I & CTL 61.

New Zealand, where the Attorney General obtained an interim injunction in similar terms to the High Court orders. T left New Zealand without then defending the proceedings. Further disclosures followed in magazines in New Zealand and England. He also revealed the names of MI6 officers on his website in Switzerland. The Attorney-General obtained an interim injunction in Geneva to close it down but the information subsequently appeared on a US website. The New Zealand Court of Appeal held that T's application to extend time to defend the injunction proceedings be stayed until such time as he returned to New Zealand and submitted to the jurisdiction of the court and purged his contempt. In May 1999, John Wadham, his solicitor, stated that since being:

banned from going to the industrial tribunal…he feels he has been harassed by the authorities. He has had injunctions against him in every country he has visited, been ejected from Australia, the US and France, and has not been able to obtain a visa to settle anywhere to build a new life.[123]

Legal remedies can thus be used across the world against the disaffected, but publication on the internet is obviously difficult to control. In January 2001, T's book *The Big Breach* was published in Russia. The Court of Appeal ruled that once the book was in the public domain, extracts could be published in the press.[124] Copies of the book were imported into the UK.[125] The FCO did not seek an injunction to restrain publication of the book but action was taken to freeze profits from the memoirs.[126]

Shayler

Even more publicity has attended the activities of David Shayler.[127] Shayler joined MI5 in 1991. At different times he worked in branches that dealt with subversion (since disbanded), Irish terrorism and international terrorism. He became disillusioned with the Service, taking the view that it was in many respects overly bureaucratic, incompetent and poorly managed. He resigned in 1997, having already decided to take steps to publish his criticisms but without endangering MI5 operations. He made contact with the *Mail on Sunday*, which on Sunday 24 August 1997 published a story based on information provided by him. It included revelations that MI5 had placed a phone tap on Peter Mandelson, had maintained files on Mandelson and Jack Straw (now Home Secretary), had kept a *Guardian* journalist, Victoria Brittain, under surveillance for over a year and allegations of further MI5 'blunders'. He left for Amsterdam shortly before the story appeared. He was paid a total of £39,000. The legal moves that followed included the launch of a police investigation into breaches of the Official Secrets Act 1989, the obtaining of production orders under s. 93H of the Criminal Justice Act 1988 against the *Mail on Sunday*, the BBC and three banks requiring them to supply details of payments made to Shayler, and the grant by Keene J of a temporary injunction against the *Mail on Sunday*. The injunction restrained the *Mail on Sunday* from publishing further information Shayler had gained as a result of his employment with MI5 and Shayler himself from disclosing such information to anyone. On 4 September the injunction was continued, by consent, by Hooper J. Provision was made, however, for particular stories to be published if no objection was raised by the Home

---

123 *Guardian Unlimited Archive*, 13 May 1999.
124 *A-G v Times Newspapers* [2001] EWCA Civ 97.
125 *Guardian Unlimited Special Report*, 30 January 2001.
126 *Guardian Unlimited Special Report*, 3 February 2001.
127 The following summary is based on M. Hollingsworth and N. Fielding, *Defending the Realm: MI5 and the Shayler Affair* (1999).

Secretary.[128] Shayler's flat was searched under a warrant granted under s. 9(1) of the Official Secrets Act 1911. Shayler had transferred the money received to friends. These were arrested on money-laundering charges, which were subsequently dropped.

In November 1997, a further story was published, following an indication by the Home Secretary that the Government would not seek to restrain publication. This concerned allegations that MI5 had ignored warnings of a bomb at the Israeli Embassy in 1994. In 1998, steps were taken by the *Mail on Sunday* to hand over to the Treasury Solicitor 28 MI5 documents that had been passed to them by Shayler. These had been recognised as sensitive and stored securely in accordance with the terms of the 4 September injunction. A further development in 1998 was the publication by the BBC *Panorama* programme and the *Guardian* (following appearance of the story in the *New York Times*) of Shayler's allegations of MI6 involvement in a plot by dissidents to kill the Libyan leader, Colonel Gaddafi. (The Foreign Office denied that there was an official plot to kill Gaddafi.) Shayler subsequently sent a dossier concerning the allegations to the Home Secretary. In August, a warrant was issued for the arrest of Shayler for two offences under s. 1(1)(a) of the 1989 Act. He was now in France. The UK sought his extradition and he was arrested and held in custody, but the French court ultimately ruled that the case fell within the 'political offence' exception to extradition arrangements.

In August 2000, Shayler returned to the UK following negotiations between his lawyers and the Government . On 21 August he was charged with two s. 1 offences of disclosing information in the *Mail on Sunday* and passing documents to newspapers, which were obtained by virtue of being a member of the Security Service. A third charge, of passing on material obtained through telephone tapping contrary to s. 4 of the 1989 Act, was added when, on 21 September, he was committed for trial. No charges were laid in respect of the Gaddafi allegation. The Metropolitan Police Special Branch has conducted an investigation into the alleged MI6 involvement in the Gaddafi plot and sent a report to the CPS.[129]

The book by Hollingsworth and Fielding, which repeats Shayler's revelations, was published with some of the deletions suggested by the Secretary to the Defence, Press and Broadcasting Committee and following an assurance by the Attorney-General that an injunction would not be sought. *Punch* magazine and its editor, James Steen, were found guilty of contempt of court in publishing an article by Shayler, but this was set aside on appeal.[130] Production orders under PACE, obtained by the police against the *Guardian*, following publication of a letter by Shayler confirming his account of the alleged Gaddafi plot, and against the *Observer*, following an article by Martin Bright which stated that Shayler had revealed to them the name of two serving intelligence officers involved in the plot, were quashed by the Divisional Court on the ground that the access conditions were not fulfilled.[131]

The prosecution of Shayler (see p. 622) was a test case, in which the House of Lords upheld the compatibility of the 1989 Act with the Human Rights Act 1998. The Government position was that Shayler's disclosures had been damaging to national security. In the application for a temporary injunction, the Government alleged damage in four areas:

---

[128] The writ against the *Mail on Sunday* claiming damages for breach of confidence and demanding the return of documents was dropped in December 2000: *Guardian Unlimited Special Report*, 2 December 2000 (R. Norton-Taylor).

[129] *Guardian Unlimited Special Report*, 1 September 2000.   [130] See above, p. 726.

[131] *R v Central Criminal Court, ex p Rushbridger, Alton and Bright* [2001] 2 All ER 244.

(*a*) enabling targets of investigations to become aware of the particular surveillance used against them and therefore avoid them; (b) enabling targets to identify sources from which information has come into the possession of the Security Service, thereby jeopardising the usefulness of such sources; (c) jeopardising the confidence of the Service of those who assist it in operational matters; (d) a similar loss of confidence on the part of potential future informers.[132]

Katharine Gun[133]

Katharine Gun was a translator at GCHQ. She leaked a top secret e-mail to the *Observer*, claiming it was from US spies asking British officers to bug UN delegates before the Iraq war. They were from countries as yet undecided as to how they would vote on a relevant UN resolution. She was dismissed and charged under s. 1 of the 1989 Act. The disclosure caused serious diplomatic difficulties. She claimed that the disclosures exposed serious wrongdoing by the US and were 'necessary to prevent an illegal war' (invoking the defence recognised by the Court of Appeal in *Shayler*). At a plea and directions hearing, the prosecution offered no evidence on the ground that there was no longer sufficient evidence for a realistic prospect of conviction. There was speculation that there was concern in GCHQ about the unwelcome publicity and that there were concerns that she could not get a fair trial because of the refusal of the Attorney-General and GCHQ to disclose relevant evidence to the court. The defence sought disclosure of the Attorney-General's advice as to the legality of the Iraq war, which at that time the Government was refusing to publish. The Attorney-General, Lord Goldsmith QC, stated in the House of Lords that the case had been dropped on legal, not political grounds.[134] The decision had been taken by the CPS, on the advice of the prosecutor, and the concurrence of the DPP, after consulting him. 'The evidential difficulty related to the prosecution's inability, within the current statutory framework, to disprove the defence of necessity to be raised on the particular facts of this case.' This had 'nothing to do' with the A-G's advice on the Iraq war, and was a determination made in advance of the defence request for disclosure. The Government announced a review of the Act.

David Keogh and Leo O'Connor[135]

David Keogh, a Cabinet Office civil servant, and Leo O'Connor, an MP's researcher, were convicted of breaches of the 1989 Act. K had passed to O'C an account of a meeting in the Oval Office between Tony Blair and George Bush on Iraq. According to O'C, K believed the document exposed Mr Bush as a 'madman'. O'C passed it to the MP for whom he worked. The document was not published, being covered by a PII certificate; the contents were disclosed to the jury *in camera*. They argued that the disclosure was not damaging. K was sentenced to six months' imprisonment and O'C three months. The Court of Appeal had previously ruled[136] that the wording in ss. 2(3) and 3(4), which in their natural meaning imposed a legal burden on the defendant to establish the defences, should be 'read down' by virtue of s. 3 of the Human Rights Act 1998 as imposing only an evidential burden: i.e. the defence must adduce evidence raising the issue, but the court then assumes that the defence is satisfied unless the prosecution proves beyond reasonable doubt that it is not.[137]

---

132 M. Hollingsworth and N. Fielding, op. cit., pp. 176–177.

133 *The Guardian*, 28 November 2003, pp. 20–22, 25, 26 February 2004.

134 HL Deb, 26 February 2004, cols 338–351.   135 *The Guardian*, 10 May 2007.

136 [2007] EWCA Crim 528, [2007] 3 All ER 789.   137 Cf. Terrorism Act 2000, s. 118.

Derek Pasquill[138]

Derek Pasquill was a civil servant in the Foreign Office who leaked documents to the *Observer* and *New Statesman* about what Britain knew of America's policy of extraordinary rendition and guidance about which Muslim organisations ministers should embrace. Two years after his arrest, charges under s. 3 of the 1989 Act were dropped on the ground that there was no longer a realistic prospect of conviction. The prosecutor indicated that internal FCO papers revealed that the senior officials privately admitted that, far from harming British interests, the leaks had helped to provoke a constructive debate. (It would accordingly be difficult to establish these were damaging disclosures.) The papers had been written shortly after P's arrest but the police and prosecution lawyers had not been aware of them until the previous month, and the defence the previous day. The defence lawyers were (rightly) very critical of the conduct of the FCO in allowing the matter to proceed for two years before disclosing their views.

(III) CIVIL SERVANTS AND MINISTERS

Following the Ponting affair,[139] the Head of the Home Civil Service, Sir Robert Armstrong, issued Notes for Guidance on *The Duties and Responsibilities of Civil Servants in Relation to Ministers*.[140] The Armstrong Memorandum stated, *inter alia*, that the duty of the individual civil servant was first and foremost to the Minister at the head of his department and that there was an obligation to keep confidences. However, a civil servant should not be required to do anything unlawful. Issues of conscience should be raised within the department with, from 1987, the possibility of an appeal to the head of the Civil Service.[141] These arrangements were replaced by the Civil Service Code[142] with effect from 1 January 1996. The Code was revised on 13 May 1999 to take account of devolution, and a further revised version published on 6 June 2006.

Civil servants are encouraged to raise matters first with line management or their department's nominated officers appointed to advise staff on the Code. If they do not receive what they consider a reasonable response they may write to the Commissioners. The Commissioners will also consider taking a complaint direct. A civil servant can write directly to them or through the person within the department or agency who considered the matter internally; the latter may add comments but cannot amend the appeal itself. The Commissioners, assisted by their staff, will examine the papers and other evidence and may interview the civil servant in question and other people in the department or agency. If the Commissioners support the appeal they make recommendations to the department or agency; otherwise the civil servant 'should abide by [their] department's or agency's instructions on the matter'.[143] The Commissioners report annually to Parliament in general terms on the outcome of appeals.[144] From 2004, nominated officers, outside the line management chain, have been

[138] *The Guardian*, 10 January 2008; *The Observer*, 13 January 2008.

[139] Above, p. 788.

[140] Reproduced at 74 HC Deb, 26 February 1985, cols 128–130, written answer.

[141] 123 HC Deb, 2 December 1987, cols 572–575, written answer; Treasury and Civil Service Committee, 7th Report, *Civil Servants and Ministers: Duties and Responsibilities*, 1985–86 HC 92 I, II; G. Drewry [1986] PL 514.

[142] Based on a proposal from the Treasury and Civil Service Committee, 5th Report, 1994–95 HC 27-I. For further discussion, see N. Lewis and D. Longley, 'Ethics and the Public Service' [1994] PL 596.

[143] Procedure for appealing to the Civil Service Commissioners under the Civil Service Code (www. civilservicecommissioners.org/Publications/Procedure_for_Appealing).

[144] *Annual Reports of the Civil Service Comrs to Her Majesty the Queen*. By 2000, three appeals had been investigated and all were upheld, in whole or in part. Two concerned the deliberate misrepresentation by civil

appointed in departments to give impartial advice to colleagues about the Code. They have direct access to the Permanent Secretary. The Commissioners have taken steps to promote awareness of the Code.[145]

Civil servants, other than employees of the Security Service, SIS and GCHQ,[146] are also now protected by the Public Interest Disclosure Act 1998[147] which provides that dismissals as a result of 'protected disclosures' are unfair and confers a right not to suffer detriment on the ground of such a disclosure. Civil Servants are advised to use the procedure under the Civil Service Code to make protected disclosures.[148] An important limitation, however, is that 'a disclosure of information is not a qualifying disclosure if the person making the disclosure commits an offence by making it'.[149] This would include a breach of the Official Secrets Acts.

(IV) OTHER MEANS OF MAINTAINING SECURITY

The Franks Committee proposals were shaped by their view that s. 2 was properly described as 'a long stop or a safety net.... Section 2 is not the main protection: its function is to provide an extra margin of protection, in case other measures should fail'.[150] The 'other measures' are discussed in Chap. 5 of the Committee's report. They point out that a civil servant who is regarded as unreliable, or who tends to overstep the mark and talk too freely, may fail to obtain promotion or may be given less important and attractive jobs. Breach of the formal discipline code[151] may lead to penalties ranging from reprimand to dismissal.

Employment legislation has, however, applied subject to limitations and restrictions where national security is concerned. Action taken for the purpose of safeguarding national security may not form the basis of a complaint for unfair dismissal[152] or detriment in respect of trade union membership[153] by virtue of s. 10(1) of the Employment Tribunals Act 1996.[154] The Minister no longer has power to issue a conclusive certificate that specified action was taken for that purpose,[155] or, more generally, to issue a certificate excepting employment of a specified description from provisions of the Employment Rights Act 1996 on national

---

servants of statistics relating to a performance measure; the third, difficulties arising from the interpretation of statutory regulations. In 2002/3, in the case of three appeals by one officer alleging non-compliance with statutory requirements, there was an adequate response by the department and in one concerning the propriety of handling contracts appropriate measures had already been taken. There were no appeals in the period 2003/6 and two in 2006/7 (one found a breach in respect of a statement by a civil servant that could be taken as politically motivated; there was no breach in the other, an allegation that a senior civil servant tried to influence the release of information requested under the FOI, contracted consultants who were personal acquaintances and did not provide ministers with objective advice).

[145] CSC Annual Report 2004–05, pp. 25–26.

[146] Employment Rights Act 1996, s. 191, as amended by the 1998 Act, s. 10 and s. 193, as substituted by the Employment Relations Act 1999, Sch. 8, para. 1.

[147] Inserting Part IVA and s. 47B in the 1996 Act. See J. Bowers, J. Mitchell and J. Lewis, *Whistleblowing: The New Law* (1999) and Y. Cripps in J. Beatson and Y. Cripps (eds), *Freedom of Expression and Freedom of Information* (2000), Chap. 17.

[148] *Directory of Civil Service Guidance Vol. 2*, 'Whistleblowing', www.cabinet-office.gov.uk/propriety_and_ethics/civil_service/civil_service_guidance.aspx.

[149] 1996 Act, s. 43B(3), inserted by the 1998 Act, s. 1.

[150] Franks Committee, p. 30.   [151] See above.

[152] Employment Rights Act 1996, s. 111.

[153] Trade Union and Labour Relations (Consolidation) Act 1992, s. 146 or s. 145A (inducements relating to union membership or activities) or s. 145B (inducements relating to collective bargaining).

[154] As substituted by the Employment Relations Act 1999, Sch. 8, para. 3.

[155] Employment Tribunals Act 1996, s. 10(5), repealed by the 1999 Act, Sch. 8, para. 3.

security grounds.[156] Employment tribunal procedure regulations may provide for an employment tribunal to be specially composed where this is directed by a Minister or ordered by a president of Employment Tribunals or a regional chairman on the grounds that he considers it expedient in the interests of national security; a direction by a Minister must relate to 'particular Crown employment proceedings'. A Minister may also direct a tribunal to sit in private or exclude the applicant and/or his representatives from all or part of such proceedings, to conceal the identity of a particular witness and to keep secret all or part of its reasons. A tribunal can be enabled to do any of these of its own motion. Where a person has been excluded, regulations may provide for the appointment by the Attorney-General of a special advocate to represent his interests, about the publication and registration of reasons for its decision and permitting the person to make a statement to the tribunal. Proceedings are 'Crown employment proceedings' if the employment is Crown employment or is connected with the performance of functions on behalf of the Crown.[157] These arrangements replace one whereby a Minister could direct a case, on grounds of national security, to be heard by a president of the Employment Tribunals alone.

These provisions are an improvement on the pre-1999 Act arrangements. However, the Intelligence and Security Committee was strongly critical of the Government's introduction of these changes at the Report Stage of the Bill in the House of Lords without consultation with the Committee on the drafting. The Committee did not see any need for power to exclude from *all* (as opposed to part) of proceedings and was of the view that use of the powers of exclusion should be subject to examination by the Commissioners for the Security Service Act 1989 and the Intelligence Services Act 1994.[158]

The government's recruitment procedures are designed to ensure fitness for appointment. There are vetting procedures to check the suitability of those with access to particularly sensitive information.[159] Precautions are also taken to ensure the physical security of documents according to their classification. Following the report of the Security Commission on the Prime case[160] random searches have been made of staff leaving GCHQ premises, a practice also followed by the Security Service and SIS.[161]

(V)   CLASSIFICATION OF DOCUMENTS

In 1994, the Government revised its approach to the classification of documents, as explained by John Major in a written answer:[162]

The Prime Minister: In recent years, the nature of the threats of Government security has changed. While some of the traditional threats to national security may have somewhat reduced, others have not. The security of Government is also increasingly threatened by, for example, theft, copying and electronic surveillance, as well as by terrorism.

To ensure that one approach to security reflects current threats, the Government have recently completed a review of arrangements for the management of protective security in Departments and agencies.

---

[156] Employment Rights Act 1996, s. 193, replaced by differently worded provisions by the 1999 Act, Sch. 8, para. 1.

[157] Employment Tribunals Act 1996, s. 10(2)–(9), substituted by the 1999 Act, Sch. 8, para. 3. See Employment Tribunals Constitution and Rules of Procedure Regulations 2004, SI 2004/1861, regs. 10–12, Sch. 2.

[158] Annual Report 1998–99 (Cm 4532), paras 31–34.

[159] See below, pp. 822–831.   [160] Cmnd 8876, 1983: see above, p 786.

[161] Report of the Security Commission on Steven Hayden (2000), pp. 17–18. The Commission endorsed the agencies' view that more intrusive searching could not be justified.

[162] 240 HC Deb, 23 March 1994, cols 259–260.

This has recommended a new protective marking system for documents which will help identify more precisely those which need protecting, enabling them to be protected more effectively according to their value. The new system will also be more closely related to the code of practice on Government information announced in the Government's White Paper on openness [below, p. 849].

In addition, the review has concluded that existing security measures should be examined closely to ensure they are necessary in relation to today's threats; that commercially available security equipment should be more widely used; and that personnel vetting enquiries should be streamlined particularly in routine cases. Overall, the aim is to give departments and agencies, and management units within them, greater responsibility for assessing the nature of the risks they face and for making decisions, within the framework of common standards of protection, about the security measures they need to put in place. Substantial cost savings will result.

The first stage of the implementation of the proposals of this review will be the introduction of a new protective marking system with effect from 4 April 1994 alongside the code of practice on access to Government information. The new definitions, which will allow fewer Government documents to be classified, particularly at the higher levels, are set out. The other elements of the new approach to protective security will be put in place in due course.

THE FOUR CATEGORIES OF PROTECTIVE MARKING: DEFINITIONS

The markings to be allocated to any asset, including information, will be determined primarily by reference to the practical consequences that are likely to result from the compromise of that asset or information. The levels in the new protective marking system are defined as follows:

TOP SECRET: the compromise of this information or material would be likely: to threaten directly the internal stability of the United Kingdom or friendly countries; to lead directly to widespread loss of life; to cause exceptionally grave damage to the effectiveness or security of United Kingdom or allied forces or to the continuing effectiveness of extremely valuable security or intelligence operations; to cause exceptionally grave damage to relations with friendly governments; to cause severe long-term damage to the United Kingdom economy.

SECRET: the compromise of this information or material would be likely: to raise international tension; to damage seriously relations with friendly governments; to threaten life directly, or seriously prejudice public order, or individual security or liberty; to cause serious damage to the operational effectiveness or security of United Kingdom or allied forces or the continuing effectiveness of highly valuable security or intelligence operations; to cause substantial material damage to national finances or economic or commercial interests.

CONFIDENTIAL: the compromise of this information or material would be likely: materially to damage diplomatic relations (ie cause formal protest or other sanction); to prejudice individual security or liberty; to cause damage to the operational effectiveness or security of United Kingdom or allied forces or the effectiveness of valuable security or intelligence operations; to work substantially against national finances or economic and commercial interests; substantially to undermine the financial viability of major organisations; to impede the investigation or facilitate the commission of serious crime; to impede seriously the development or operation of major government policies; to shut down or otherwise substantially disrupt significant national operations.

RESTRICTED: the compromise of this information or material would be likely: to affect diplomatic relations adversely; to cause substantial distress to individuals; to make it more difficult to maintain the operational effectiveness or security of United Kingdom or allied forces; to cause financial loss or loss of earning potential to or facilitate improper gain or advantage for individuals or companies; to prejudice the investigation or facilitate the commission of crime; to breach proper undertakings to maintain the confidence of information provided by third parties; to impede the effective development or operation of government policies; to breach statutory restrictions on disclosure of information; to disadvantage government in commercial or policy negotiations with others; to undermine the proper management of the public sector and its operations.

3. DA NOTICES

(A) DEFENCE PRESS AND BROADCASTING ADVISORY COMMITTEE[163]

GENERAL INTRODUCTION TO DA-NOTICES

1. Public discussion of the United Kingdom's defence and counter-terrorist policy and overall strategy does not impose a threat to national security and is welcomed by Government. It is important however that such discussion should not disclose details which could damage national security. The DA Notice System is a means of providing advice and guidance to the media about defence and counter-terrorist information the publication of which would be damaging to national security. The system is voluntary, it has no legal authority and the final responsibility for deciding whether or not to publish rests solely with the editor or publisher concerned.

2. DA-Notices are issued by the Defence, Press and Broadcasting Advisory Committee (DPBAC), an advisory body composed of senior civil servants and editors from national and regional newspapers, periodicals, news agencies, television and radio. It operates on the shared belief that there is a continuing need for a system of guidance and advice such as the DA-Notice System, and that a voluntary, advisory basis is best for such a system.

3. When these notices were first published under their new title of Defence Advisory Notices in 1993, they reflected the changed circumstances following the break-up of the Soviet Union and the Warsaw Pact. The 2000 revision has allowed an overall reduction in the scope of the notices while retaining those parts that are appropriate for the current level of threat that involves grave danger to the State and/or individuals. Compliance with the DA-Notice system does not relieve the editor of responsibilities under the Official Secrets Act.

4. The Secretary DPBAC (the DA-Notice Secretary) is the servant of the Government and the Press and Broadcasting sides of the Committee. He is available at all times to Government departments and the media to give advice on the system and, after consultation with Government departments as appropriate, to help in assessing the relevance of a DA-Notice to particular circumstances. Within this system, all discussions with editors, publishers and programme makers are conducted in confidence…

HOW THE SYSTEM WORKS

PURPOSE

1. The Defence, Press and Broadcasting Advisory Committee oversees a voluntary code which operates between those Government departments which have responsibilities for national security and the media; using as its vehicle the DA-Notice system.

COMPOSITION

2. The Committee is chaired by the Permanent Under-Secretary of State for Defence.

3. Membership may be varied from time to time by agreement. At present there are four members representing Government departments, one each from the Home Office, the Ministry of Defence, and the Foreign and Commonwealth Office and the Cabinet Office.

4. At present there are thirteen members nominated by the media; three by the Newspaper Publishers Association, two by the Newspaper Society, two by the Periodical Publishers Association and one each

---

[163] www.dnotice.org.uk. Minutes of meetings of the Committee are published on this site.

by the Scottish Daily Newspaper Society, the Press Association, the BBC, ITN. ITV, and Sky TV. The Publishers Association was invited in 1993 and in 2000 to nominate a representative but declined.

5. The press and broadcasting members select one of their number as Chairman of their side and Vice Chairman of the Committee. He leads for their side at Committee meeting and provides a point of day-to-day contact for them and for the Secretary.

6. The Committee is served by a full-time Secretary and part-time Deputy Secretary who substitutes in the Secretary's absence on leave etc....

RESPONSIBILITY OF MEMBERSHIP

7. The Press and Broadcasting members respond to proposals from the government departments concerned and advise the Committee on those areas of information in which it may be reasonable to invite guidance reflecting the interests of national security. Official proposals may not be issued in DA-Notice form without the consent of the Press and Broadcasting members.

MEETINGS

8. The Committee normally has a Spring and an Autumn meeting each year. It reviews the Secretary's report of guidance sought and advice offered over the previous six months. It also reviews the content of the DA-Notices as necessary to ensure that amendments are made to meet the changing needs of national security....

DA-NOTICES

9. The DA-Notices are intended to provide to national and provincial newspaper editors, to periodicals editors, to radio and television organisations and to relevant book publishers, general guidance on those areas of national security which the Government considers it has a duty to protect. The Notices, together with a General Introduction, details of the Committee and how to contact the Secretary, are widely distributed to editors, producers and publishers and also to officials in Government departments, military commanders, chief constables and some institutions. The Notices have no legal standing and advice offered within their framework may be accepted or rejected partly or wholly.

10. Although the system is normally applied through the standing DA-Notices, should it be found necessary to issue a DA-Notice on a specific matter, the Government department concerned will agree a draft of the proposed Notice with the Secretary who, from his experience, can advise upon the form and content which are likely to make it acceptable to the press and broadcasting members. The Secretary will then seek the agreement of both sides of the DPBAC to the draft and, if it is obtained, issue the text as a DA-Notice...

SECRETARY DPBAC

11. The Secretary is normally a retired two-star officer from the Armed Forces, employed as a Civil Servant on the budget of the Ministry of Defence. He is the servant of the Government and Press and Broadcasting sides of the Committee, a fact which is recognised by the Vice Chairman being involved in the process of his selection. Similar arrangements apply for the Deputy Secretary who is also normally a retired service officer.

12. The Secretary (or Deputy Secretary) is available at all times to Government departments and the media to give advice on the system, taking into account the general guidance given to him by the Committee. DA-Notices are necessarily drafted in somewhat general terms and it is the application of a DA-Notice to a particular set of circumstances on which the Secretary is expected to give guidance, consulting as necessary with appropriate department officials. He is not invested with the authority to give rulings nor to advise on considerations other than national security.

13. If the Secretary agrees that a Government Department may quote the DA-Notices in release of information to the media, he should ensure that the Department makes it clear that it is doing so on his authority and therefore that of the Committee....

NOTES

1. The Report of the (Radcliffe) Committee of Privy Counsellors[164] concerned the revelation by Chapman Pincher in the *Daily Express* that private cables and telegrams were vetted by the security authorities. The Government claimed, and persisted in claiming notwithstanding the contrary view expressed by the Radcliffe Committee, that this contravened two D Notices.[165]

Chapman Pincher suggested that the minority of Government representatives on the Committee almost always got their way and that prior to 1967, journalists tended to rely heavily on the view of the Secretary as to whether a story was covered by a D Notice, confident that clearance by the Secretary would cover them in practice as regards possible prosecution under the Official Secrets Act (although it could not affect the legal position). According to Pincher, the affair, 'effectively destroyed the D-notice system', which he thereafter 'virtually ignored'.[166] This seems to stem from his loss of confidence in the changed role of the Secretary and the emphasis in the revised arrangements that clearance by the Secretary would not affect the position under the Official Secrets Act. In the Oral Evidence to the Franks Committee the Chairman of the Defence, Press and Broadcasting Committee, Sir James Dunnett, stated that it would be an 'extreme case' in which the DPP would want to prosecute an editor where clearance had been given, and that the Attorney-General in deciding to give his fiat under the Act would wish to know whether the editor had been in touch with the Secretary to the Committee.[167]

2. The D Notice system was again put under strain in 1987 over a proposed BBC radio series, *My Country Right or Wrong*, which was to examine issues raised by the *Spycatcher* litigation. On the eve of the first programme, Henry J granted an interlocutory injunction sought by the Attorney-General to prevent the broadcasting of any interviews with or information derived from members or past members of the security and intelligence services relating to any aspect of the work of the services, including their identity as members. The terms of the injunction were subsequently modified by agreement to permit fair and accurate reports of proceedings in Parliament and the courts.[168] The injunction was subsequently continued by Owen J.[169] The injunction was lifted in respect of one of the programmes in March 1988, and the others in May 1988, after the scripts had been vetted.[170] The programme's producer had previously obtained an indication from the Secretary to the D Notice Committee that he did not advise that the broadcast would be potentially prejudicial to national security.[171] The apparent contradiction was subsequently explained by the Secretary on the basis that his advice concerned the lack of a threat to national

[164] Cmnd 3309, 1967.

[165] See the White Paper (Cmnd 3312, 1967); P. Hedley and C. Aynsley, *The D Notice Affair* (1967); Chapman Pincher, *Inside Story* (1978); M. Creevy, 'A Critical review of the Wilson Government's Handling of the D-Notice Affair 1967' (1999) 14 Intelligence and National Security 209. As to the pre-1965 position, see D.G.T. Williams, *Not in the Public Interest* (1965), pp. 80–87. The system was reviewed by the Defence Committee, Third Report, 1979–80 HC 773, 640 i-v, *The D Notice System*. See also J. Jaconelli [1982] PL 37, noting a reduction in the number of notices from 12 to 8.

[166] Op. cit., p. 244.

[167] P. 57.

[168] See D. Oliver in D. Kingsford-Smith and D. Oliver (eds), *Economical with the Truth* (1990), p. 43.

[169] *A-G v BBC* (1987) Times, 18 December, applying the *American Cyanamid* principles (below, p. 814) and *A-G v Guardian Newspapers* [1987] 1 WLR 1248 (below, pp. 814–816).

[170] See P. Thornton, *Decade of Decline* (1989), pp. 9–11.

[171] The nearest the Secretary gets to giving a 'clearance': see D. Fairley (1990) 10 OJLS 430, 431, 435.

security whereas the Government's claim to an injunction was based on breach of confidence. It was, he said, 'a pity that the two issues have become entwined'.[172] Nevertheless, as Fairley comments,

> Given that the policy argument upon which the existence and scope of the alleged duty of confidentiality depended in *Spycatcher* was that of potential damage to national security, it is hard to see how there can be two separate issues....[173]

He argues that the real difference lay in the approach to the assessment of the implications for national security; the Secretary was concerned solely with prejudice arising from the *contents* of the particular document or broadcast, whereas the Government was asserting the broader basis for the duty of confidence also put forward in *A-G v Guardian Newspapers Ltd (No. 2)*[174] and *Lord Advocate v Scotsman Publications Ltd*,[175] namely that there would be long term damage to the Security Service as a result of media pressure on MI5 members for similar disclosures, and loss of confidence in MI5 on the part of other countries and potential informants. This broader basis was ultimately rejected by the House of Lords in the *Scotsman* case (where, again, the editor had obtained a 'no advice' response from the D Notice Secretary before publication). This does not, however, remove the difficulty: Fairley argues that a claim to confidentiality based on the *contents* of a document would be likely to succeed before the courts even if the Secretary had offered 'no advice'.[176]

Fairley's survey of newspaper and periodical editors showed that formal participation in the system was fairly widespread, but actual use infrequent: most of the respondents:

> felt that, in the light of recent Government behaviour, they would be more influenced by the advice of their lawyers than by that of the Secretary of the D Notice Committee.[177]

The effect of the Government's increasing use of the civil courts has been to 'marginalize the significance of the D Notice system and to destroy the atmosphere of mutual trust' between press and government on which voluntary prior restraint can be based. Nevertheless, evidence of a 'no advice' response by the Secretary still may be of relevance to a civil action, or to a prosecution under the Official Secrets Act 1989 (e.g. in respect of an argument that there was no reasonable cause to believe that damage would result from disclosure of information), or in respect of sentence.[178]

3. The system was again reviewed by the Committee in 1992, leading to a number of changes.[179] The aim of the review 'was to make the system more transparent and relevant in the light of international changes and the increased emphasis on openness in Government'.

---

172 *Guardian*, 10 December 1987.
173 (1990) 10 OJLS 430, 435.
174 Below, p. 806.
175 Below, p. 817.
176 (1990) 10 OJLS 430, 437.
177 Ibid., p. 438.
178 Ibid., pp. 439, 440.
179 See *The Defence Advisory Notices: A Review of the D Notice System* (Ministry of Defence Open Government Document No. 93/06). A survey in 2007 concluded that the system had remained relatively unchanged since 1993: P. Sadler, 'Still keeping secrets? The DA-Notice System post 9/11' (2007) Comms L 205.

The Notices were revised, reduced in number from 8 to 6 and renamed Defence Advisory Notices 'better to reflect the voluntary and advisory nature of the system'. They were revised again in 2000 and the number reduced to five. The introduction and procedure are set out above.[180] The content of the six DA Notices is now freely published. They cover: No. 1, Military Operations, Plans and Capabilities; No. 2, Nuclear and Non-Nuclear Weapons and Equipment; No. 3, Ciphers and Secure Communications; No. 4, Sensitive Installations and Home Addresses; and No. 5, United Kingdom Security and Intelligence Services and Special Forces. Each notice is accompanied by a stated 'rationale'. For example, DA Notice No. 5 states:

DA-NOTICE NO. 5: UNITED KINGDOM SECURITY AND INTELLIGENCE SERVICES AND SPECIAL FORCES

1. Information falling within the following categories is normally regarded as being highly classified. It is requested that such information, unless it has been the subject of an official announcement or has been widely disclosed or discussed, should not be published without first seeking advice:

(a) specific covert operations, sources and methods of the Security Service, SIS and CGHQ, and those involved with them, including the Special Forces, the application of those methods, including the interception of communications, and their targets; the same applies to those engaged on counter-terrorist operations;

(b) the identities, whereabouts and tasks of people who are or have been employed by these services or engaged on such work, including details of their families and home addresses, and any other information, including photographs, which could assist terrorist or other hostile organisations to identify a target;

(c) addresses and telephone numbers used by these services, except those now made public.

2. Rationale. Identified staff from the intelligence and security services, others engaged sensitive counter-terrorist operations, including the Special Forces, and those who are likely targets for attack are at real risk from terrorists. Security and intelligence operational contacts and techniques are easily compromised, and therefore need to be pursued in conditions of secrecy. Publicity about an operation which is in train finishes it. Publicity given even to an operation which has been completed, whether successfully or not, may well deny the opportunity for further exploitation of a capability, which may be unique against other hostile and illegal activity. The disclosure of identities can prejudice past present and future operations. Even inaccurate speculation about the source of information on a given issue can put intelligence operations (and, in the worst case, lives) at risk and/or lead to the loss of information which is important in the interests of national security. Material, which has been the subject of an official announcement is not covered by this notice.

Note that the revised DA Notice documentation states that the system provides advice as to whether a publication would *actually* involve 'grave damage to the State and/or individuals'. This is recognised by the Committee to be narrower than the test applicable under the Official Secrets Act 1989, and it decided that this should be brought to the attention of officials.[181]

4. Some journalists and writers have expressly disassociated themselves from the D Notice system. Bloch and Fitzgerald, authors of *British Intelligence and Covert Action* (1983), which named British officials it claimed were, or had been, involved in British

---

[180] P. 798.   [181] Record of meeting held 5 December 2000.

Intelligence, 'freely admit ignoring D Notice No. 6 (and several others besides). Neither ourselves nor our publishers are represented on the D Notice Committee, nor are we party to any other cosy agreement between Whitehall and the media'.[182] In response to this book preparatory work was apparently undertaken on a draft law to prohibit the naming in public of MI5 and MI6 officers and agents.[183] The Whitehall consensus on this book was that 'its publication was 'indefensible' as unlike most other studies of British intelligence, it covered events and personalities "so near to the present day", as one insider put it'.[184] The DA Notice 'request' that nothing shall be published without reference to the DPBAC Secretary which identifies officers can be contrasted with the US Intelligence Identities Protection Act 1982, which makes it an offence for persons with access to classified information intentionally to reveal the identities of covert agents working outside the USA for agencies such as the CIA, and for other persons to do so 'in the course of a pattern of activities intended to identify and expose covert agents... with reason to believe that such activities would impair or impede the foreign intelligence activities of the United States'.[185] $15,000/three years' imprisonment/both for 'outsiders'. The legislation is directed at those such as the former CIA agent, Philip Agee, who wished to expose and nullify covert political intervention in the affairs of other countries.[186] The Act was at the heart of a political controversy in the US around the alleged leak by the White House of the fact that Valerie Plame was a CIA agent. After a grand jury investigation, no indictment was preferred in respect of the leak, but Lewis Libby, Chief of Staff of Vice President Dick Cheney, was convicted on four counts of perjury, obstruction of justice and making false statements.[187]

5. In January 2008, the ISC reported, in the light of the reporting in the press of leaked and sensitive intelligence, including current operations, that the current system of handling security information through DA Notices and the agencies' relationship with the media more generally, was not working as effectively as it might and this was putting lives at risk. The government should engage with the media to develop a more effective system.[188]

4. BREACH OF CONFIDENCE

The use of the law of breach of confidence to protect official secrets was thrown into prominence in the *Spycatcher* litigation, in which the Attorney-General, in a number of jurisdictions throughout the world, sought to restrain the publication of the memoirs of Peter Wright, a former member of MI5. As the chronology set out below shows, the litigation was lengthy and complex, and saw the invocation of the law of contempt as well as the law of confidence against a variety of parties. So far as the UK and the law of breach of confidence was concerned, the matter culminated in the decision of the House of Lords in *A-G v Guardian Newspapers Ltd (No. 2)*.[189]

---

182 Letter to *The Times,* 25 April 1984.
183 P. Hennessy, *The Times,* 9 April 1984.
184 Ibid.   185 50 USC § 421–426.
186 The Act's constitutionality is considered by S.D. Charkes (1983) 83 Colum L Rev 727.
187 See generally Valerie Plame Wilson, *Fair Game: My life as a Spy, My Betrayal by the White House* (2007).
188 ISC Annual Report 2006–07 (Cm 7299, 2008), pp. 20–21.
189 Below, p. 806.

CHRONOLOGY OF THE *SPYCATCHER* LITIGATION

1985	A-G commences proceedings in NSW against Peter Wright and Heinemann Publishers Australia Pty Ltd seeking an injunction restraining publication of *Spycatcher* or, alternatively, an account of profits. Pending trial, undertakings restraining publication of the book or disclosure of information obtained by W as a MI5 officer were given by W, H, and Malcolm Turnbull, the solicitor acting for them.
22, 23 June 1986	The *Observer* and the *Guardian* publish articles reporting on the forthcoming hearing.
27 June 1986	*Ex parte* injunctions against the newspapers granted by Macpherson J.
11 July 1986	*Inter partes* injunctions against the newspapers granted by Millett J, restraining them from disclosing any information obtained by W as an MI5 officer or from attributing any information about MI5 to him, with certain exceptions: [1989] 2 FSR 3.
25 July 1986	The Court of Appeal upholds the injunctions, with slight modifications: *A-G v Observer Newspapers Ltd* (1986) Times, 26 July, [1986] NLJ Rep 799, [1989] 2 FSR 15.
17 November 1986	NSW trial begins before Powell J.
13 March 1987	A-G's action dismissed: (1987) 8 NSWLR 341. Undertakings continued pending appeal.
27 April 1987	Articles published by the *Independent*, the *Evening Standard* and the *London Daily News* based on the contents of the book.
3 May 1987	The *Washington Post* publishes extracts from the manuscript of *Spycatcher*.
7 May 1987	Proceedings for contempt commence against the newspapers in respect of the articles of 27 April.
14 May 1987	Viking Penguin Inc announces its intention to publish *Spycatcher* in the US.
2 June 1987	Sir Nicolas Browne-Wilkinson V-C holds on a preliminary point of law that contempt proceedings against the *Independent*, the *Evening Standard* and the *London Daily News* cannot succeed as they were not party to the Millett injunctions: *A-G v Newspaper Publishing plc* [1988] Ch 333.[190]
12 July 1987	The *Sunday Times*, having obtained a copy of the manuscript from Viking Penguin in the US, publishes extracts from *Spycatcher* in its second edition.
13 July 1987	A-G commences contempt proceedings against the *Sunday Times*.
15 July 1987	*Spycatcher* on sale in the US. (Reasons given 17 July.) Court of Appeal allows an appeal against the decision of the Vice-Chancellor, holding that the publication of the 27 April articles could constitute contempt: *A-G v Newspaper Publishing plc* [1988] Ch 333.
16 July 1987	A-G granted interlocutory injunction restraining the *Sunday Times* from publishing further extracts from *Spycatcher*.
22 July 1987	Sir Nicolas Browne-Wilkinson V-C discharges the Millett injunctions on the ground that the book was now 'freely available to all': *A-G v Guardian Newspapers Ltd* [1987] 3 All ER 316.

---

[190] Above, p. 733.

24 July 1987	Millett injunctions restored by the Court of Appeal: [1987] 3 All ER 316, in modified form, permitting the publication of a 'summary in very general terms' of W's allegations.
30 July 1987	(Reasons given 13 August) Appeal to the House of Lords dismissed by 3–2. Millett injunctions endorsed, and without the exceptions, *inter alia,* permitting the reporting of what had taken place in open court in the Australian proceedings: [1987] 3 All ER 316.
2 August 1987	*News on Sunday* publishes an article with quotations from the *Sunday Times* article of 12 July.
24 September 1987	New South Wales Court of Appeal dismisses A-G's appeal: *A-G for the United Kingdom v Heinemann Publishers Australia Pty Ltd* (1987) 75 ALR 353.
29 September 1987	Deane J in the High Court of Australia declines to grant temporary injunctions pending the hearing of an application by the A-G for leave to appeal to the HCA.
12, 13 October 1987	*Spycatcher* goes on sale in Ireland and Australia.
27 October 1987	A-G commences proceedings against the *Sunday Times* for breach of confidence.
21 December 1987	Scott J discharges the interlocutory injunctions against the *Observer* and the *Guardian,* holds that the *Sunday Times* is accountable for profits resulting from the first extract of the serialisation on 12 July, and refuses the A-G an injunction restraining future publication of information derived from W: *A-G v Guardian Newspapers Ltd (No. 2)* [1990] 1 AC 109, [1988] 3 All ER 545.
10 February 1988	Decision of Scott J upheld by Court of Appeal: *A-G v Guardian Newspapers Ltd (No. 2)* [1990] 1 AC 109, [1988] 3 All ER 545 at 594.
2 June 1988	High Court of Australia dismisses A-G's appeal: *A-G for the United Kingdom v Heinemann Publishers Australia Pty Ltd (No. 2)* (1988) 165 CLR 30, 78 ALR 449.
13 October 1988	Decision of Scott J and the Court of Appeal upheld by the House of Lords (4–1): [1990] 1 AC 109, [1988] 3 All ER 545 at 638 (below).
8 May 1989	The *Independent,* the *Sunday Times* and the *News on Sunday* each fined £50,000 for contempt by Morritt J; contempt proceedings against the *Evening Standard,* the *London Daily News* and the *Daily Telegraph* dismissed: *A-G v Newspaper Publishing plc:* [1989] FSR 457.
27 February 1990–11 April 1991	Decision of Morritt J upheld by the Court of Appeal: *A-G v Newspaper Publishing plc* (1990) Times, 28 February; and the House of Lords: *A-G v Times Newspapers Ltd.*[191]
26 November 1991	European Court of Human Rights gives judgment in *Observer and Guardian v UK* (Series A No. 216) and *Sunday Times v UK (No. 2)* (Series A No. 217).[192]

---

[191] Ibid.   [192] Below, p. 816.

- **A-G v Guardian Newspapers Ltd (No. 2)** [1990] 1 AC 109, [1988]
  3 All ER 545, House of Lords

The facts are set out in Lord Keith's speech. The House of Lords held:
  (1) (Lord Griffiths dissenting) that the publications by *The Observer* and *The Guardian* on
      22 and 23 June 1986 did not constitute an actionable breach of confidence, as they were
      not damaging to the public interest;
  (2) that the *Sunday Times'* publications on 12 July 1987 did constitute a breach of
      confidence, for which the Crown was entitled to an account of profits;
  (3) that no injunction should lie against (a) *The Observer* and *The Guardian* or (b) (Lord
      Griffiths dissenting) the *Sunday Times* to prevent any future serialisation of the book;
      neither would the newspaper be liable for any account of profits: the information was
      now in the public domain;
  (4) that the A-G was not entitled to any general injunction restraining future publica-
      tion of information derived from Mr Wright or other members or ex-members of the
      Security Service.

Lord Keith of Kinkel: My Lords, from 1955 to 1976 Peter Wright was employed in a senior capacity by the counter-espionage branch of the British Security Service known as MI5. In that capacity he acquired knowledge of a great many matters of prime importance to the security of the country. Following his retirement from the service he went to live in Australia and later formed the intention of writing and publishing a book of memoirs describing his experiences in the service. He wrote the book in association with a man named Paul Greengrass, and it was accepted for publication by Heinemann Publishers Pty. Ltd., the Australian subsidiary of a well known English publishing company. The Attorney-General in right of the Crown, learning of the intended publication of the book, instituted in 1985 proceedings in New South Wales against Mr. Wright and Heinemann Publishers claiming an injunction to restrain the publication in Australia or alternatively an account of profits. Pending trial, Mr. Wright, the publishers and their solicitors gave undertakings not to reveal the contents of the book. The Attorney-General's action failed before Powell J and again before the Court of Appeal of New South Wales. Special leave to appeal was granted by the High Court of Australia, but the respondents were released from their undertakings. So the book was published in Australia on 13 October 1987, under the title of *Spycatcher*. On 2 June 1988 the High Court dismissed the Attorney-General's appeal upon the sole ground that an Australian court should not accept jurisdiction to enforce an obligation of confidence owed to a foreign government so as to protect that government intelligence secrets and confidential political information. In the meantime *Spycatcher* had on 14 July 1987 been published in the United States of America by Viking Penguin Inc., a subsidiary of an English publishing company. Her Majesty's Government had been advised that, in view of the terms of the First Amendment to the United States Constitution, any attempt to restrain publication there would be certain to fail. Publication also took place in Canada, the Republic of Ireland, and a number of other countries. Her Majesty's Government decided that it was impracticable and undesirable to take any steps to prevent the importation into the United Kingdom of copies of the book, and a very substantial number of copies have in fact been imported. So the contents of the book have been disseminated world-wide and anyone in this country who is interested can obtain a copy without undue difficulty.

  ... The issues raised in the litigation are thus summarised in the judgment of Sir John Donaldson M.R. in the Court of Appeal, ante, pp. 180h–181c:

  '(1) Were the "Observer" and "The Guardian" in breach of their duty of confidentiality when, on 22 and 23 June 1986, they respectively published articles on the forthcoming hearing in Australia? If so, would they have been restrained from publishing if the Attorney-General had been able to seek the assistance of the court?... (2) Was "The Sunday Times" in breach of its duty of confidentiality when, on 12 July 1987 it published the first extract of an intended serialisation of *Spycatcher?*... (3) Is the Attorney-General now entitled to an injunction (a) in relation to the "Observer" and "The Guardian" and (b) in relation to "The Sunday Times" with special consideration to further serialisation?...(4) Is the Attorney-General entitled to an account of the profits accruing to "The Sunday Times" as a result of the serialisation of *Spycatcher?*... (5) Is the Attorney-General entitled to some general injunction restraining future publication of information derived from Mr. Wright or other members or ex-members of the Security Service?'

As regards issue (1) Scott J. and the majority of the Court of Appeal (Dillon and Bingham L.JJ.; Sir John Donaldson M.R. dissenting) held that the publication of the articles in question was not in breach of an obligation of confidence.

On issue (2) Scott J. and the majority of the Court of Appeal (Bingham L.J. dissenting) held that the publication of the first extract from *Spycatcher* was in breach of an obligation of confidence.

Upon issue (3) Scott J. and the Court of Appeal held that the Attorney-General was not entitled to an injunction against the 'Observer' and 'The Guardian' nor (Sir John Donaldson M.R. dissenting) against further serialisation of *Spycatcher* by 'The Sunday Times'.

As to issue (4) Scott J. and the majority of the Court of Appeal (Bingham L.J. dissenting) decided this in favour of the Attorney-General.

Issue (5) was decided against the Attorney-General both by Scott J. and by the Court of Appeal.

The Attorney-General now appeals to your Lordships' House upon all the issues on which he failed below. 'The Sunday Times' cross-appeals against the decision on account of profits.

The Crown's case upon all the issues which arise invokes the law about confidentiality. So it is convenient to start by considering the nature and scope of that law. The law has long recognised that an obligation of confidence can arise out of particular relationships. Examples are the relationships of doctor and patient, priest and penitent, solicitor and client, banker and customer. The obligation may be imposed by an express or implied term in a contract but it may also exist independently of any contract on the basis of an independent equitable principle of confidence: *Saltman Engineering Co Ltd v Campbell Engineering Co Ltd* (1963) 65 RPC 203. It is worthy of some examination whether or not detriment to the confider of confidential information is an essential ingredient of his cause of action in seeking to restrain by injunction a breach of confidence. Presumably that may be so as regards an action for damages in respect of a past breach of confidence. If the confider has suffered no detriment thereby he can hardly be in a position to recover compensatory damages. However, the true view may be that he would be entitled to nominal damages. Most of the cases have arisen in circumstances where there has been a threatened or actual breach of confidence by an employee or ex-employee of the plaintiff, or where information about the plaintiff's business affairs has been given in confidence to someone who has proceeded to exploit it for his own benefit: an example of the latter type of case is *Seager v Copydex Ltd* [1967] 1 WLR 923. In such cases the detriment to the confider is clear. In other cases there may be no financial detriment to the confider, since the breach of confidence involves no more than an invasion of personal privacy. Thus in *Duchess of Argyll v Duke of Argyll* [1967] Ch 302 an injunction was granted against the revelation of marital confidences. The right to personal privacy is clearly one which the law should in this field seek to protect. If a profit has been made through the revelation in breach of confidence of details of a person's private life it is appropriate that the profit should be accounted for to that person. Further, as a general rule, it is in the public interest that confidences should be respected, and the encouragement of such respect may in itself constitute a sufficient ground for recognising and enforcing the obligation of confidence even where the confider can point to no specific detriment to himself. Information about a person's private and personal affairs may be of a nature which shows him up in a favourable light and would by no means expose him to criticism. The anonymous donor of a very large sum to a very worthy cause has his own reasons for wishing to remain anonymous, which are unlikely to be discreditable. He should surely be in a position to restrain disclosure in breach of confidence of his identity in connection with the donation. So I would think it a sufficient detriment to the confider that information given in confidence is to be disclosed to persons whom he would prefer not to know of it, even though the disclosure would not be harmful to him in any positive way.

The position of the Crown, as representing the continuing government of the country may, however, be regarded as being special. In some instances disclosure of confidential information entrusted to a servant of the Crown may result in a financial loss to the public. In other instances such disclosure may tend to harm the public interest by impeding the efficient attainment of proper governmental ends, and the revelation of defence or intelligence secrets certainly falls into that category. The Crown, however, as representing the nation as a whole, has no private life or personal feelings capable of being hurt by the disclosure of confidential information. In so far as the Crown acts to prevent such disclosure or to seek redress for it on confidentiality grounds, it must necessarily, in my opinion, be in a position to show that the disclosure is likely to damage or has damaged the public interest. How far the Crown has to go in order to show this must depend on the circumstances of each case. In a question with a Crown servant himself, or others acting as his agents, the general public interest in the preservation of confidentiality, and in encouraging other Crown servants to preserve it, may suffice. But where the publication is proposed to be made by third parties unconnected with the particular confidant, the position may be different. The Crown's argument in the present case would go to the length that in all circumstances where the original disclosure has been made by a Crown servant in breach of his obligation of confidence any person to whose knowledge the information comes and who is aware of the breach comes under an equitable duty binding his conscience not to communicate the information to anyone else irrespective of the circumstances under which he acquired the knowledge. In my opinion that general proposition is untenable and impracticable, in addition to being unsupported by any authority. The general rule is that anyone is entitled to communicate anything he pleases to anyone else, by speech or in writing or in any other way. That rule is limited by the law of defamation and other restrictions similar to these mentioned in article 10 of the Convention for the Protection of Human Rights and Fundamental Freedoms (1953) (Cmd. 8969). All those restrictions are imposed in the light of considerations of public interest such as to countervail the public interest in freedom of expression. A communication about some aspect of government activity which does no harm to the interests of the nation cannot, even where the original disclosure has been made in breach of confidence, be restrained on the ground of a nebulous equitable duty of conscience serving no useful practical purpose.

There arc two important cases in which the special position of a government in relation to the preservation of confidence has been considered. The first of them is *A-G v Jonathan Cape Ltd* [1976] QB 752. That was an action for injunctions to restrain publication of the political diaries of the late Richard Crossman. which contained details of Cabinet discussions held some ten years previously, and also of advice given to Ministers by civil servants. Lord Widgery CJ. said, at pp. 770–771:

'In these actions we are concerned with the publication of diaries at a time when 11 years have expired since the first recorded events. The Attorney-General must show (a) that such publication would be a breach of confidence; (b) that the public interest requires that the publication be restrained, and (c) that there are no other facets of the public interest contradictory of and more compelling than that relied upon. Moreover, the court, when asked to restrain such a publication, must closely examine the extent to which relief is necessary to ensure that restrictions are not imposed beyond the strict requirement of public need.'

Lord Widgery went on to say that while the expression of individual opinions by Cabinet Ministers in the course of Cabinet discussions were matters of confidence, the publication of which could be restrained by the court when clearly necessary in the public interest, there must be a limit in time after which the confidential character of the information would lapse. Having read the whole of volume one of the diaries he did not consider that publication of anything in them, ten years after the event, would inhibit full discussion in the Cabinet at the present time or thereafter, or damage the doctrine of joint Cabinet responsibility. He also dismissed the argument that publication of advice given by senior civil servants would be likely to inhibit the frankness of advice given by such civil servants in the future. So in the result Lord Widgery's decision turned on his view that it had not been shown that publication of the diaries would do any harm to the public interest.

The second case is *Commonwealth of Australia v John Fairfax & Sons Ltd* (1980) 147 CLR 39. That was a decision of Mason J. in the High Court of Australia, dealing with an application by the Commonwealth for an interlocutory injunction to restrain publication of a book containing the texts of government documents concerned with its relations with other countries, in particular the government of Indonesia in connection with the 'East Timor Crisis'. The documents appeared to have been leaked by a civil servant. Restraint of publication was claimed on the ground of breach of confidence and also on that of infringement of copyright. Mason J. granted an injunction on the latter ground but not on the former. Having mentioned, at p. 51, an argument for the Commonwealth that the government was entitled to protect information which was not public property, even if no public interest is served by maintaining confidentiality, he continued, at pp. 51–52:

> 'However, the plaintiff must show, not only that the information is confidential in quality and that it was imparted so as to import an obligation of confidence, but also that there will be "an unauthorised use of that information to the detriment of the party communicating it" (*Coco v A N Clark (Engineers) Ltd* [1969] RPC 41, 47). The question then, when the executive government seeks the protection given by equity, is: What detriment does it need to show?
>
> ... [I]t can scarcely be a relevant detriment to the government that publication of material concerning its actions will merely expose it to public discussion and criticism. It is unacceptable in our democratic society that there should be a restraint on the publication of information relating to government when the only vice of that information is that it enables the public to discuss, review and criticise government action.
>
> Accordingly, the court will determine the government's claim to confidentiality by reference to the public interest. Unless disclosure is likely to injure the public interest, it will not be protected.
>
> The court will not prevent the publication of information which merely throws light on the past workings of government, even if it be not public property, so long as it does not prejudice the community in other respects. Then disclosure will itself serve the public interest in keeping the community informed and in promoting discussion of public affairs. If, however, it appears that disclosure will be inimical to the public interest because national security, relations with foreign countries or the ordinary business of government will be prejudiced, disclosure will be restrained. There will be cases in which the conflicting considerations will be finely balanced, where it is difficult to decide whether the public's interest in knowing and in expressing its opinion, outweighs the need to protect confidentiality.'

I find myself in broad agreement with this statement by Mason J. In particular I agree that a government is not in a position to win the assistance of the court in restraining the publication of information imparted in confidence by it or its predecessors unless it can show that publication would be harmful to the public interest.

In relation to Mr. Wright, there can be no doubt whatever that had he sought to bring about the first publication of his book in this country, the Crown would have been entitled to an injunction restraining him. The work of a member of MI5 and the information which he acquires in the course of that work must necessarily be secret and confidential and be kept secret and confidential by him. There is no room for discrimination between secrets of greater or lesser importance, nor any room for close examination of the precise manner in which revelation of any particular matter may prejudice the national interest. Any attempt to do so would lead to further damage. All this has been accepted from beginning to end by each of the judges in this country who has had occasion to consider the case and also by counsel for the respondents. It is common ground that neither the defence of prior publication nor the so called 'iniquity' defence would have availed Mr. Wright had he sought to publish his book in England. The sporadic and low key prior publication of certain specific allegations of wrongdoing could not conceivably weigh in favour of allowing publication of this whole book of detailed memoirs describing the operations of the Security Service over a lengthy period and naming and describing many members of it not previously known to be such. The damage to the public interest involved in a publication of that character, in which the allegations in question occupy a fairly small space, vastly outweighs all other considerations. The question whether Mr. Wright or those acting for him would be at liberty to publish *Spycatcher* in

England under existing circumstances does not arise for immediate consideration. These circumstances include the world-wide dissemination of the contents of the book which has been brought about by Mr. Wright's wrongdoing. In my opinion general publication in this country would not bring about any significant damage to the public interest beyond what has already been done. All such secrets as the book may contain have been revealed to any intelligence services whose interests are opposed to those of the United Kingdom. Any damage to the confidence reposed in the British Security and Intelligence Services by those of friendly countries brought about by Mr. Wright's actions would not be materially increased by publication here. It is, however, urged on behalf of the Crown that such publication might prompt Mr. Wright into making further disclosures, would expose existing and past members of the British Security and Intelligence Services to harassment by the media and might result in their disclosing other secret material with a view, perhaps, to refuting Mr. Wright's account and would damage the mor-ale of such members by the spectacle of Mr. Wright having got away with his treachery. While giving due weight to the evidence of Sir Robert Armstrong on these matters, I have not been persuaded that the effect of publication in England would be to bring about greater damage in the respects founded upon than has already been caused by the widespread publication elsewhere in the world. In the result, the case for an injunction now against publication by or on behalf of Mr. Wright would in my opinion rest upon the principle that he should not be permitted to take advantage of his own wrongdoing.

The newspapers which are the respondents in this appeal were not responsible for the world-wide dissemination of the contents of *Spycatcher* which has taken place. It is a general rule of law that a third party who comes into possession of confidential information which he knows to be such, may come under a duty not to pass it on to anyone else. Thus in *Duchess of Argyll v Duke of Argyll* [1967] Ch 302 the newspaper to which the Duke had communicated the information about the Duchess was restrained by injunction from publishing it. However, in that case there was no doubt but that the publication would cause detriment to the Duchess in the sense I have considered above. In the present case the third parties are 'The Guardian' and the 'Observer' on the one hand and 'The Sunday Times' on the other hand. The first two of these newspapers wish to report and comment upon the substance of the allegations made in *Spycatcher*. They say that they have no intention of serialising it. By virtue of section 6 of the Copyright Act 1956 they might, without infringing copyright, quote passages from the book for purposes of 'criticism or review'. 'The Sunday Times' for their part, wish to complete their serialisation of *Spycatcher*. The ques-tion is whether the Crown is entitled to an injunction restraining the three newspapers from doing what they wish to do. This is the third of the issues identified by Sir John Donaldson MR in the court below. For the reasons which I have indicated in dealing with the position of Mr. Wright, I am of the opinion that the reports and comments proposed by 'The Guardian' and the 'Observer' would not be harmful to the public interest, nor would the continued serialisation by 'The Sunday Times'. I would therefore refuse an injunction against any of the newspapers. I would stress that I do not base this upon any balancing of public interests nor upon any considerations of freedom of the press, nor upon any possible defences of prior publication or just cause or excuse, but simply upon the view that all possible damage to the interest of the Crown has already been done by the publication of *Spycatcher* abroad and the ready availability of copies in this country.

It is possible, I think, to envisage cases where, even in the light of widespread publication abroad of certain information, a person whom that information concerned might be entitled to restrain publication by a third party in this country. For example, if in the *Argyll* case the Duke had secured the revelation of the marital secrets in an American newspaper, the Duchess could reasonably claim that publication of the same material in England would bring it to the attention of people who would otherwise be unlikely to learn of it and who were more closely interested in her activities than American readers. The publica-tion in England would be more harmful to her than publication in America. Similar considerations would apply to, say, a publication in America by the medical adviser to an English pop group about diseases for which he had treated them. But it cannot reasonably be held in the present case that publication in England now of the contents of *Spycatcher* would do any more harm to the public interest than has already been done.

In relation to future serialisation by 'The Sunday Times' the Master of the Rolls took the view that this newspaper stood in the shoes of Mr. Wright by virtue of the licence which it has been granted by the publishers. The cost of this licence was £150,000 of which £25,000 was to be paid at once and the balance after the serialisation. So Mr. Wright and his publishers will benefit from future instalments of it. The Master of the Rolls considered that there was a strong public interest in preventing Mr. Wright and his publishers from profiting from their wrongdoing. There can be no doubt that the prospect of Mr. Wright receiving further sums of money from 'The Sunday Times' as a reward for his treachery is a revolting one. But a natural desire to deprive Mr. Wright of profit does not appear to me to constitute a legally valid ground for enjoining the newspaper from a publication which would not in itself damage the interests of the Crown. Indeed, it appears that Mr. Wright would have no legally enforceable claim against 'The Sunday Times' for payment, upon the principle of ex turpi causa non oritur actio. Whether 'The Sunday Times' is bound to account for the profits of serialisation I shall consider later.

The next issue for examination is conveniently the one as to whether 'The Sunday Times' was in breach of an obligation of confidentiality when it published the first serialised extract from *Spycatcher* on 12 July 1987. I have no hesitation in holding that it was. Those responsible for the publication well knew that the material was confidential in character and had not as a whole been previously published anywhere. Justification for the publication is sought to be found in the circumstance that publication in the United States of America was known to be imminent. That will not hold water for a moment. It was Mr. Wright and those acting for him who were about to bring about the American publication in breach of confidence. The fact that a primary confidant, having communicated the confidential information to a third party in breach of obligation, is about to reveal it similarly to someone else, does not entitle that third party to do the same. The third party to whom the information has been wrongfully revealed himself comes under a duty of confidence to the original confider. The fact that his informant is about to commit further breaches of his obligation cannot conceivably relieve the third party of his own. If it were otherwise an agreement between two confidants each to publish the confidential information would relieve each of them of his obligation, which would be absurd and deprive the law about confidentiality of all content. The purpose of 'The Sunday Times' was of course to steal a march on the American publication so as to be the first to reveal, for its own profit, the confidential material. The evidence of Mr. Neil, editor of 'The Sunday Times', makes it clear that his intention was to publish his instalment of *Spycatcher* at least a full week before the American publication and this was in the event reduced to two days only because circumstances caused that publication to be brought forward a week. There can be no question but that the Crown, had it learned of the intended publication in 'The Sunday Times', would have been entitled to an injunction to restrain it. Mr. Neil employed peculiarly sneaky methods to avoid this. Neither the defence of prior publication nor that of just cause or excuse would in my opinion have been available to 'The Sunday Times'. As regards the former, the circumstance that certain allegations had been previously made and published was not capable of justifying publication in the newspaper of lengthy extracts from *Spycatcher* which went into details about the working of the Security Service. As to just cause or excuse it is not sufficient to set up the defence merely to show that allegations of wrongdoing have been made. There must be at least a prima facie case that the allegations have substance. The mere fact that it was Mr. Wright, a former member of MI5 who, with the assistance of a collaborator, had made the allegations, was not in itself enough to establish such a prima facie case. In any event the publication went far beyond the mere reporting of allegations, in so far as it set out substantial parts of the text of *Spycatcher*. For example, the alleged plot to assassinate Colonel Nasser occupies but one page of a book, in paperback of 387 pages, and the alleged plot to destabilise Mr Wilson's government about five pages. In this connection it is to be noted that counsel for 'The Sunday Times' accepted that neither of the two defences would have availed Mr. Wright had he sought to publish the text of *Spycatcher* in England. There is no reason of logic or principle why 'The Sunday Times' should have been in any better position acting as it was under his licence.

[His Lordship held that the Crown was entitled to an account of profits from the *Sunday Times* in respect of the publication on 12 July 1987, and the *Sunday Times* was not entitled to deduct the fees paid to W's publishers for the licence], since neither Mr. Wright nor his publishers were or would in the future be in a position to maintain an action in England for recovery of such payments. Nor would the courts of this country enforce a claim by them to the copyright in a work the publication of which they had brought about contrary to the public interest: cf. *Glyn v Weston Feature Film Co* [1916] 1 Ch 261, 269. Mr. Wright is powerless to prevent anyone who chooses to do so from publishing *Spycatcher* in whole or in part in this country, or to obtain any other remedy against them. There remains of course, the question whether the Crown might successfully maintain a claim that it is in equity the owner of the copyright in the book. Such a claim has not yet been advanced, but might well succeed if it were to be.

In relation to future serialisation of further parts of the book, however, it must be kept in mind that the proposed subject matter of it has now become generally available and that 'The Sunday Times' is not responsible for this having happened. In the circumstances 'The Sunday Times' will not be committing any wrong against the Crown by publishing that subject matter and should not therefore be liable to account for any resultant profits. It is in no different position from anyone else who now might choose to publish the book by serialisation or otherwise.

[His Lordship then held that on balance the prospects were that the Crown would not have been able to obtain a permanent injunction to prevent publication of their articles on 22 and 23 June 1986. The information about the allegations described in the two articles must have been obtained from someone in the office of the publishers or in that of their solicitors although they had given undertakings to the New South Wales court, pending trial of the action there, not to disclose any information gained by Mr. Wright in the course of his service with MI5. The newspapers must have known of the undertakings that had been given. Some of the allegations, albeit of minor significance, had never previously been published at all. Others had been made publicly, but not attributed to Mr Wright. One had been made publicly by Mr Wright. No injunction would have been granted in respect of this last allegation; it was highly doubtful that the publication of the attribution could reasonably be regarded as damaging to the public interest of the United Kingdom in the direct sense that the information might be of value to unfriendly foreign intelligence services, or as calculated to damage that interest indirectly in any of the ways spoken of in evidence by Sir Robert Armstrong.]

The final issue is whether the Crown is entitled to a general injunction against all three newspapers restraining them from publishing any information concerned with the Spycatcher allegations obtained by any member or former member of the Security Service which they know or have reasonable grounds for believing to have come from any such member or former member, including Mr. Wright, and also from attributing any such information in any publication to any member or former member of the Security Service. The object of an injunction on these lines is to set up a second line of defence, so to speak, for the confidentiality of the operations of the Security Service. The first and most important line of defence is obviously to take steps to secure that members and ex-members of the service do not speak about their experiences to the press or anyone else to whom they are not authorised to speak. Obviously the Director-General of the Service is in a position to impose a degree of discipline upon the existing members of the service so as to prevent unauthorised disclosures, and it is reasonable to suppose that in any event the vast majority of these members are conscientious and would never consider making such disclosures. In so far as unconscientious ex-members are concerned, in particular Mr. Wright, the position under existing circumstances is more difficult, although measures may now be introduced which are apt to discourage breaches of confidence by such people. There are a number of problems involved in the general width of the injunction sought. Injunctions are normally aimed at the prevention of some specific wrong, not at the prevention of wrongdoing in general. It would hardly be appropriate to subject a person to an injunction on the ground that he is the sort of person who is likely to commit some kind of wrong, or that he has an interest in doing so. Then the injunction sought would not leave room for the possibility that a defence might be available in a particular case. If Mr. Wright were to publish a second book in America or Australia or both and it were to become readily available in this country, as has happened in regard to his first book, newspapers which published its contents would have as good a defence as the respondents in the present case. It would not be satisfactory to have the availability of any defence tested on contempt proceedings. In my opinion an injunction on the lines sought should not be granted.

A few concluding reflections may be appropriate. In the first place I regard this case as having established that members and former members of the Security Service do have a lifelong obligation of confidence owed to the Crown. Those who breach it, such as Mr. Wright, are guilty of treachery just as heinous as that of some of the spies he excoriates in his book. The case has also served a useful purpose in bringing to light the problems which arise when the obligation of confidence is breached by publication abroad. The judgment of the High Court of Australia reveals that even the most sensitive defence secrets of this country may not expect protection in the courts even of friendly foreign countries, although a less extreme view was taken by Sir Robin Cooke P. in the New Zealand Court of Appeal (A-G v Wellington Newspapers Ltd (No 2) [1988] 1 NZLR 180)....

Lords Brightman, Goff and **Jauncey of Tullichettle** delivered generally concurring speeches. **Lord Griffiths** dissented in part.

Appeal and cross-appeal dismissed.

NOTES

1. The important question of the circumstances in which the duty of confidence owed by an officer of the security and intelligence services might be overridden was addressed more explicitly by Scott J at first instance, who stated that this:

would not extend to information of which it could be said that, notwithstanding the needs of national security, the public interest required disclosure. Nor, in my opinion, would the duty extend to information which was trivial or useless or which had already been disclosed under the authority of the government.

For example, the duty of confidence could not be used to prevent the press from informing the public of the allegation of a plot to assassinate President Nasser, and the press were entitled to report the fact that allegations of an MI5 plot to destabilise the Wilson Government had been repeated by an insider:

The press has a legitimate role in disclosing scandals by government. An open democratic society requires that that be so. If an allegation be made by an insider that, if true, would be a scandalous abuse by officers of the Crown of their powers and functions, and the allegation comes to the attention of the press, the duty of confidence cannot, in my opinion, be used to prevent the press from repeating the allegation.... Nor is it, in my opinion, necessarily an answer to say that the allegation should not have been made public but should have been reported to some proper investigating authority. In relation to some, perhaps many, allegations made by insiders, that may be the only proper course open to the press. But the importance to the public of this country of the allegation that members of MI5 endeavoured to undermine and destroy public confidence in a democratically elected government makes the public the proper recipient of the information.[193]

---

[193] [1988] 3 All ER 545 at 585, 588–589.

In the House of Lords, Lord Griffiths denied the existence of an exception for trivia. He was, however, prepared to countenance a public interest defence, while finding it very difficult to envisage the circumstances where the facts would justify it:

> But, theoretically, if a member of the service discovered that some iniquitous course of action was being pursued that was clearly detrimental to our national interest, and he was unable to persuade any senior member of his service or any member of the establishment, or the police, to do anything about it, then he should be relieved of his duty of confidence so that he could alert his fellow citizens to the impending danger.[194]

However, no such considerations arose in *Spycatcher*. Lord Goff's position was similar.[195] Lord Keith was more concerned with the point that the public interest defence would not in any event have been open to Mr Wright on the facts.

2. Opinions were expressed on a number of other points that did not directly arise for consideration.

(a) Would Peter Wright or his publishers be restrained now from publishing *Spycatcher* in the UK? Lord Griffiths and Lord Jauncey of Tullichettle were clear that he would, on the ground that his duty of confidence persisted;[196] Lord Goff was very doubtful;[197] Lord Keith and Lord Brightman left the point open, but indicated that such an injunction would be based on the principle that he should not be permitted to take advantage of his own wrongdoing, and not on the basis of breach of confidence.[198]

(b) The position as to copyright. The House was clear that neither Wright nor his publishers had any copyright in *Spycatcher* that was enforceable in the UK[199] and, indeed, it was suggested that copyright might well be vested in the Crown.[200] See Cripps,[201] noting that the Government had based its claim for an account of profits on breach of confidence and not on a constructive trust imposed on any copyright which Wright or his publishers might hold. In a future case, the law of copyright might prove more fruitful, especially as there is no 'public domain' defence.[202]

3. The question for the House of Lords at the 'interlocutory stage' was whether the Millett interlocutory injunctions should be continued or discharged. The general approach to be adopted when considering whether an interlocutory injunction should be granted was laid down by the House of Lords in *American Cyanamid Co v Ethicon Ltd*,[203] and requires the judge to consider: (1) whether the plaintiff applicant for the injunction has an arguable case in law; (2) if so, whether damages would be an adequate or appropriate remedy should an interlocutory injunction be refused and the plaintiff ultimately succeed at trial; and (3) if not,

---

[194] [1988] 3 All ER 545, 650.   [195] [1988] 3 All ER 545, 660–661.

[196] [1990] 1 AC 109, 271, 293.   [197] [1990] 1 AC 109, 284–289.

[198] [1990] 1 AC 109, 259, 265–266.

[199] See Lord Keith at 262–263, Lord Brightman at 267, Lord Griffiths at 275–276 and Lord Jauncey at 294.

[200] See Lord Keith at 263, Lord Brightman at 266, Lord Griffiths at 276 and Lord Goff at 288.

[201] Y. Cripps [1989] PL 13.

[202] Ibid., pp. 14–15, 19–20. The various stages of the *Spycatcher* litigation are considered by D.G.T. Williams [1988] CLJ 2, 329, [1989] CLJ 1 and (1989) 12 Dalhousie LJ 209; Y. Cripps [1989] PL 13 (on breaches of copyright and confidence) and E. Barendt [1989] PL 204 (on freedom of speech); S. Lee (1987) 103 LQR 506 (on the interlocutory stage); M. Turnbull and M. Howard (1989) 19 UWALR 117, (1989) 105 LQR 382 (on the Australian decisions); P. Birks (1989) 105 LQR 501; J. Michael (1989) 52 MLR 389; Lord Oliver of Aylmerton (1989) 23 Israel LR 409; G. Jones (1989) 42 CLP 49; D. Kingsford-Smith and D. Oliver (eds), *Economical with the Truth* (1990), chapters by D. Pannick and R. Austin; K.D. Ewing and C.D. Gearty, *Freedom under Thatcher* (1990), pp. 152–169. See also M. Turnbull, *The Spycatcher Trial* (1988).

[203] [1975] AC 396.

where the balance of convenience lay. Sir Nicolas Browne-Wilkinson V-C held that since the Millett injunctions had been granted in 1986 there had been a material change in the circumstances, given the publicity given to the Australian trial, the widespread publication of *Spycatcher* material in the foreign press and the publication of *Spycatcher* itself in the US. The Government had taken the view that proceedings in the US to restrain publication would be doomed to failure, in the light of the 1st Amendment guarantees of freedom of speech. It also decided not to seek to prevent importation of *Spycatcher*, which could accordingly be obtained in the UK by mail order or simply brought back by travellers (it was apparently a best seller on the bookstall at JF Kennedy Airport). The Vice-Chancellor (*A-G v Guardian Newspapers Ltd*)[204] concluded, with reluctance, that the A-G had an arguable case for permanent injunctions; it was clear that damages would not be an appropriate remedy. However, the balance of convenience was against continuing the injunctions: the public interest in terms of deterring the publication of memoirs by members of the Security Service was small compared with the public interest in freedom of the press: 'One of the safeguards of our country and our system is to have a press that can search matters out, disclose them, and give rise to informed public discussion.... [O]ne should not restrain publication in the press unless it is unavoidable.'[205] Moreover, 'If the courts were to make orders manifestly incapable of achieving their avowed purpose, such as to prevent the dissemination of information which is already disseminated, the law would to my mind indeed be an ass'.[206]

The Court of Appeal allowed an appeal by the A-G, and a further appeal by the newspapers was dismissed by the House of Lords (*A-G v Guardian Newspapers Ltd*)[207] by 3–2, Lords Brandon, Templeman and Ackner, Lords Bridge and Oliver dissenting. The decision was announced on 30 July with reasons given later. Their Lordships were agreed that the injunctions had originally properly been granted and that the compromise solution adopted by the Court of Appeal, permitting publication of 'a summary in very general terms' of the *Spycatcher* allegations, was unworkable. The majority were agreed that the A-G still had an arguable case for permanent injunctions. Lord Brandon argued that discharge of the injunctions now would cause permanent and irrevocable damage to the A-G's case for permanent injunctions; their continuance would merely postpone reporting by the newspapers, should *they* ultimately prevail at trial. The potential injustice to the A-G of the first course of action outweighed the potential injustice to the newspapers of the second. The approaches of Lord Templeman and Lord Ackner were more robust. Lord Templeman condemned Peter Wright's 'treachery' and held that there were good reasons for continuing the injunctions: the mass circulation of extracts from *Spycatcher* in the UK would expose members of the Security Service to the harassment of accusations to which they could not respond; discharge of the injunctions would create an 'immutable precedent' for 'any disgruntled public servant or holder of secret or confidential information relating to the Security Service' to 'achieve mass circulation in this country of damaging truths and falsehoods by the device of prior publication anywhere else abroad'; the newspaper reports were contrary to the object and purpose of the Millett injunctions, had originated with Wright and his publishers abroad, and were intended to bring pressure on the English courts to allow *Spycatcher* to be published here. Moreover, these reasons would make the interference with freedom of expression 'necessary in a democratic society in the interests of national security' and thus justified in terms of Art. 10 of the European Convention on Human Rights. Finally, the injunctions should be modified so as to prevent reporting of extracts from *Spycatcher* read in open court in Australia. Lord Ackner's speech was on similar lines, although he was even more critical

---

204 [1987] 3 All ER 316.   205 [1987] 3 All ER 316 at 331.
206 Ibid., at 332.   207 [1987] 3 All ER 316.

of the conduct of the press, in particular in their response to the decision to continue the injunction that was announced on 30 July:

> It has required no imagination to anticipate the resentment which the newspaper, and, indeed, the entire media, would feel and vociferously express if we ultimately imposed a restraint on publication, albeit a temporary restraint. Moreover, it is a fact of life, however regrettable, that there are elements in the press as a whole which lack not only responsibility but integrity…It would have been absurd and naive of your Lordships not to have appreciated that every attempt would inevitably have been made to frustrate your Lordship's orders. The "antic disposition" of the press and the media following the announcement of the orders establishes this fully.[208]

The modification to the injunctions was necessary to close a 'loophole' that might have been used by such elements to nullify the temporary damage limitation operation determined essential by the majority.

The speeches of the minority provided a stark contrast. Given the publication of *Spycatcher* in the US, an injunction would, in the view of Lord Bridge, now be 'futile'. Any remaining national security interest which the Millett injunctions were capable of protecting was of insufficient weight 'to justify the massive encroachment on freedom of speech' which their continuance would necessarily involve. He continued:[209]

> …I can see nothing whatever, either in law or on the merits, to be said for the maintenance of a total ban on discussion in the press of this country of matters of undoubted public interest and concern which the rest of the world now knows all about and can discuss freely. Still less can I approve your Lordships' decision to throw in for good measure a restriction on reporting court proceedings in Australia which the Attorney General had never even asked for.
>
> Freedom of speech is always the first casualty under a totalitarian regime. Such a regime cannot afford to allow the free circulation of information and ideas among its citizens. Censorship is the indispensable tool to regulate what the public may and what they may not know. The present attempt to insulate the public in this country from information which is freely available elsewhere is a significant step down that very dangerous road. The maintenance of the ban, as more and more copies of the book *Spycatcher* enter this country and circulate here, will seem more and more ridiculous. If the government are determined to fight to maintain the ban to the end, they will face inevitable condemnation and humiliation by the European Court of Human Rights in Strasbourg. Long before that they will have been condemned at the bar of public opinion in the free world.

Lord Oliver endorsed the approach that had been taken by the Vice-Chancellor. Continuance of the injunctions 'on which I may call the Admiral Byng principle, 'pour encourager les autres' would involve misuse of the injunctive remedy, as would be its use to punish Mr Wright. (Lord Goff expressly agreed with this view in *A-G v Guardian Newspapers Ltd (No. 2)*).[210] The newspapers were not responsible for the publication of *Spycatcher* in the US. He did not think the Attorney-General would have an arguable case for a permanent injunction at trial. In the event, of course, permanent injunctions were refused.

4. In *Observer and Guardian v United Kingdom*,[211] and *Sunday Times v United Kingdom*,[212] the grant of the interlocutory injunctions was considered by the European Court of Human

---

[208] Ibid., at 365. [209] Ibid., at 346–347. [210] [1990] 1 AC 109, 288.
[211] Judgment of 26 November 1991. Series A No. 216.
[212] Judgment of 26 November 1991, Series A No. 217.

Rights. The court concluded by 14 to 10 that the injunctions up until the publication of *Spycatcher* in the US in July 1987 did not violate Art. 10 ECHR, but concluded unanimously that the continuation of the injunctions thereafter was such a violation.[213]

5. It was clear in the outcome of the *Spycatcher* litigation that the law of confidence, like the criminal law, will be ineffective in reaching persons outside the jurisdiction. Lord Oliver, for one, argued that 'in the end, the preservation of security secrets has to depend on the imposition on members of the Security Services of extremely tight *contractual* obligations which can be enforced interlocutorily without the assumption of any burden beyond the proof of the contract'[214] (cf. the position in the US).[215] Section 1 of the Official Secrets Act 1989[216] now imposes a 'lifelong duty of confidence' on members of the Security Services.

6. *A-G v Guardian Newspapers Ltd (No. 2)* was applied by the House of Lords in *Lord Advocate v Scotsman Publications Ltd*.[217] Here Anthony Cavendish, an MI6 officer from 1948 to 1953, wrote memoirs but was refused authorisation to publish. He gave copies to private individuals, one of which reached the *Scotsman*, which published an article including some material from it. The House of Lords upheld the refusal of the lower courts in Scotland to grant an interim interdict restraining the *Scotsman* and any person having notice of the interdict from publishing (with certain exceptions) any information obtained by C in the course of his employment in MI6. During argument before the Second Division, the Crown had conceded that the book contained no information the disclosure of which was capable of damaging national security.

7. *Cabinet documents.* The foundation for the use of the law of confidence by the Crown was provided by the decision of Lord Widgery CJ in *A-G v Jonathan Cape Ltd*[218] (the Crossman Diaries case), discussed by Lord Keith.[219]

8. Cabinet documents may also be protected from disclosure in litigation by a claim that disclosure would be contrary to the public interest.[220] Note that in relation to both claims of public interest immunity and government applications to restrain threatened breaches of confidence the courts must balance competing interests. In the former, the public interest in the proper administration of justice is balanced against the public interest in keeping certain matters confidential. In the latter the public interest in confidentiality is balanced against other public interests, such as the freedom of speech.

9. The conventions as to the publication of ministerial memoirs were considered by the *Committee of Privy Counsellors on Ministerial Memoirs*.[221] The committee endorsed the view taken by the Cabinet in 1946 that it was necessary

to keep secret information of two kinds, disclosure of which would be detrimental to the public interest:

(*a*) In the international sphere, information whose disclosure would be injurious to us in our relations with other nations, including information which would be of value to a potential enemy.

---

213 See J. McDermott (1992) J Media L & P 137 and S. Colver, ibid., p. 142.

214 (1989) 23 Israel LR at 424.   215 Below, p. 820.   216 Above, p. 771.

217 1988 SLT 490, [1990] 1 AC 812. See N. Walker [1990] PL 354.

218 [1976] QB 752.

219 Above, p. 808. On this case see Hugo Young. *The Crossman Affair* (1976); R. K. Middlemass (1976) 47 PQ 39; M.W. Bryan (1976) 92 LQR 180; D.G.T. Williams [1976] CLJ 1; D.L. Ellis, 'Collective Ministerial Responsibility and Collective Solidarity' [1980] PL 367.

220 See below, p. 854.

221 Chairman, Lord Radcliffe (Cmnd 6386, 1976).

(b) In the domestic sphere, information the publication of which would be destructive of the confidential relationships on which our system of government is based and which may subsist between Minister and Minister, Ministers and their advisers, and between either and outside bodies or private persons.[222]

The committee suggested further 'working rules' as to the reticence due from an ex-Minister:

(a) In dealing with the experience that he has acquired by virtue of his official position, he should not reveal the opinions or attitudes of colleagues as to the Government business with which they have been concerned. That belongs to their stewardship, not to his. He may, on the other hand, describe and account for his own.

(b) He should not reveal the advice given to him by individuals whose duty it has been to tender him their advice or opinions in confidence. If he wishes to mention the burden or weight of such advice, it must be done without attributing individual attitudes to identifiable persons. Again, he will need to exercise a continuing discretion in any references that he makes to communications received by him in confidence from outside members of the public.

(c) He should not make public assessments or criticisms, favourable or unfavourable, of those who have served under him or those whose competence or suitability for particular posts he has had to measure as part of his official duties.[223]

As to enforcement, the committee did not regard the legal principles expounded by Lord Widgery CJ in the Crossman Diaries case as providing 'a system which can protect and enforce those rules of reticence that we regard as called for when ex-Ministers compose their memoirs....' According to his Lordship, each case would have to be decided on its own facts—there were 'no fixed principles of legal enforceability'.[224] The committee did not regard a judge as 'so equipped as to make him the best arbitrator of the issues involved. The relevant considerations are political and administrative....' Moreover, the legal principles did not protect confidences of or about civil servants. Neither did legislation offer the right solution. The 'burden of compliance' should be 'left to rest on the free acceptance of an obligation of honour'.[225] Whenever a former Minister intends to publish information derived from his ministerial experience he should submit the full text in advance to the Secretary of the Cabinet. If clearance is refused in relation to information concerning national security or international affairs, the Minister may appeal to the Prime Minister, whose decision is final. If clearance is refused in relation to other information it is for the Minister to decide whether to publish; moreover, the information may be published after 15 years in any event, except that beyond that point he should not reveal the advice tendered by individuals who are still members of the public service nor make public assessment or criticisms of them. The Government accepted these recommendations[226] and they remain operative.[227] However, not all ministers have observed them.[228] 'Everything which the Government failed

[222] P. 7. [223] Pp. 20–21. [224] P. 24. [225] P. 26.
[226] 903 HC Deb, 22 January 1976, cols 521–523.
[227] Ministerial Code (Cabinet Office, July 2007), para. 8.10; www.cabinet-office.gov.uk/propriety_and_ethics/ministers/ministerial_code.aspx; Directory of Civil Service Guidance, vol. 2, 'Ministerial Memoirs.' From 2001 the Code was extended to make it clear that while in office, ministers may not enter into any agreement to publish their memoirs on leaving their ministerial position.
[228] See B. Castle, The Castle Diaries (1980); H. Jenkins, The Culture Gap (1979).

to have decided in its favour in the *Crossman Diaries* case was duly enshrined in [these] constitutional conventions.'[229]

The position as to civil servants is set out in similar but not identical terms.[230] No civil servant can publish memoirs while still in the Service; former civil servants must provide a copy of the text in good time before publication to the head of their former department. They must abide by the decision of the head of that Service in respect of state secrets, or information whose disclosure would be prejudicial to the UK's international relations, but also in respect of matters of trust and confidentiality falling within the 15 years recommended by Radcliffe. The wording of the Diplomatic Service Regulations was different, and did not extend to matters of trust and confidentiality.

Controversy over the publication of memoirs by ministers, civil servants and diplomats led to the announcement of policy changes by the Cabinet Office and the Foreign Secretary in the middle of a general consideration of these matters by the House of Commons Public Administration Select Committee. Particularly irritating for ministers were the 'racy' memoirs of Sir Christopher Meyer, former Ambassador to Washington, which contained unflattering assessments of ministers and reported private conversations.[231] The rules for diplomats were extended to prohibit them from 'writing anything that would damage the confidential relationship between ministers, or between ministers and officials'.[232] There was an explicit bar on memoirs by serving officials. All contracts of employment and letters on retirement or resignation would draw attention to the rules and staff would be required to sign an undertaking that they had read, understood and agreed to be bound by the rules. A Cabinet Office memorandum to PASC[233] proposed similar reminders for civil servants. The requirements as to undertakings would apply to staff in sensitive areas. Furthermore, in such letters of undertaking they would be asked to assign copyright to the government of future works (this would deprive them of the profits of any work based on official information and experience). The PASC Report[234] broadly endorsed the changes. It stressed the importance of confidentiality and trust between ministers and civil servants. As long as the latter are not publicly accountable for their actions, and do not publish accounts of their experiences, it would not be right for former ministers or special advisers to criticise named civil servants who have no right of reply; public servants should keep to the bargain.[235] The basic principles governing publication should be stated in the same terms for ministers, civil servants and special advisers, although there would be differences in what it was appropriate for each group to publish. The recent changes had, however, been introduced in an incoherent and haphazard way. In turn, the Government accepted PASC's detailed recommendations.[236] The Directory of Civil Service Guidance would be updated.

---

[229] G. Robertson, *Freedom, the Individual and the Law* (7th edn, 1993), p. 194. See further R. Brazier, *Constitutional Practice* (3rd edn, 1999), pp. 127–129.

[230] Directory of Civil Service Guidance 2000: *Memoirs and Books: Publication by Civil Servants*; www.cabinet-office.gov.uk/propriety_and_ethics/civil_service/civil_service_guidance.aspx. The criteria for approval of publications by former members of the security and intelligence services were set out by Douglas Hurd MP, Foreign Secretary, at 241 HC Deb 20 April 1994, cols 539–540, written answer. Authorisation for disclosure within 30 years would be 'especially rare and exceptional'.

[231] *DC Confidential* (Weidenfeld and Nicholson, 2005).

[232] Jack Straw MP, HC Deb, 8 March 2006, cols 61–62 WS.

[233] PASC Report Vol. II, p. 108.

[234] *Whitehall Confidential? The Publication of Political Memoirs* (5th Report 2005–06 HC 689).

[235] The Committee gave Sir Christopher Meyer a very hard time when he gave oral evidence.

[236] PASC 4th Special Report 2007–08 HC 91. The Government did, however, reject a recommendation that there should be a right to appeal to an Advisory Committee on Memoirs, comprising Privy Counsellors or other senior figures.

10. An injunction will only rarely be granted by a civil court to restrain a threatened breach of the criminal law, such as a breach of the Official Secrets Acts.[237] In the *Gouriet* case[238] Lord Wilberforce stated that it is:

an exceptional power confined, in practice, to cases where an offence is frequently repeated in disregard of a, usually, inadequate penalty—see *A-G v Harris* [1961] 1 QB 74; or to cases of emergency—see *A-G v Chaudry* [1971] 1 WLR 1614.

Threatened breaches of the Official Secrets Acts might well count as an 'emergency' for these purposes, at least where 'grave and irreparable' harm[239] would be caused. Cf. *Commonwealth of Australia v John Fairfax & Sons Ltd.*[240] Here, the federal government discovered that long extracts from unpublished government documents were to be printed in two newspapers and a book. The documents related to various defence and foreign affairs issues, but did not contain technical information of military significance. Many of them were classified. The Government sought an interim injunction on three grounds: (a) the threatened breach of s. 79 of the Crimes Act 1914 (Cth), which is similar in terms to the Official Secrets Act 1911, s. 2(1)(a) and (b); (b) breach of confidence; and (c) breach of copyright. Mason J acceded to the application on ground (c) alone. On ground (a) his Lordship stated:[241]

It may be that in some circumstances a statutory provision which prohibits and penalizes the disclosure of confidential government information or official secrets will be enforceable by injunction. This is more likely to be the case when it appears that the statute, in addition to creating a criminal offence, is designed to provide a civil remedy to protect the government's right to confidential information. I do not think that s. 79 is such a provision. It appears in the *Crimes Act* and its provisions are appropriate to the creation of a criminal offence and to that alone. The penalties which it imposes are substantial. There is nothing to indicate that it was intended in any way to supplement the rights of the Commonwealth to relief by way of injunction to restrain disclosure of confidential information or infringement of copyright. There is no suggested inadequacy in these two remedies which would lead me to conclude that it is inappropriate to regard s. 79 as a foundation for injunctive relief.

Do you think these observations would be applicable to a threatened breach of the Official Secrets Acts? Are they unduly restrictive? This case was referred to by Lord Keith on the breach of confidence point.[242] On the copyright point, note that actual Crown documents were involved, and not merely a work written by a former Crown servant.

An attempt by the Court of Appeal to extend this jurisdiction to freeze the proceeds of a spy's autobiography was rejected by the House of Lords.[243]

11. In the US there is a heavy presumption against any prior restraint on the freedom of the press guaranteed by the First Amendment. In *New York Times v United States*[244] the Supreme Court rejected by 6 to 3 the Government 's application for an injunction to prevent publication of the 'Pentagon Papers', a series of secret Government documents dealing with the origins of the US involvement in Vietnam. Black and Douglas JJ held that the First

---

[237] See *Gouriet v Union of Post Office Workers* [1978] AC 435: D.G.T. Williams [1977] Crim LR 703; D. Feldman (1979) 42 MLR 369: J.M. Evans, *de Smith's Judicial Review of Administrative Action* (4th edn, 1980), pp. 455–457.

[238] *Gouriet v Union of Post Office Workers* [1978] AC 435 at 481.

[239] See *de Smith*, p. 456.   [240] (1980) 55 ALJR 45, 147 CLR 39, HCA.

[241] 147 CLR at 50.   [242] Above, p. 809.

[243] *A-G v Blake* [2000] 4 All ER 385, below.   [244] 403 US 713 (1971).

Amendment prevented any judicial restraint on speech and press. Brennan, Stewart and White JJ held, in varying degrees, that the Government had failed to show that publication *would* (not could) cause direct, immediate and irreparable harm to the nation. Marshall J held that an injunction could not be issued in the absence of the specific statutory authority of Congressional legislation. Burger CJ and Harlan and Blackmun JJ held that the courts should not refuse to enforce the executive branch's claim, provided that a Cabinet-level officer personally so decided.[245] It was left unclear whether the strict tests propounded by Brennan, Stewart and White would be applicable where there was a specific statutory provision.

In 1979 a US district judge granted an injunction to restrain publication of materials on the hydrogen bomb: these had been specifically defined as 'restricted data' in the Atomic Energy Authority Act 1954, and the Act had also empowered the courts to issue injunctions against the publication of such material.[246]

Then in 1980 the Supreme Court held that an agreement requiring CIA employees not to publish any information about the agency without specific prior approval was a judicially enforceable contract applicable to both classified and non-classified information. Moreover, CIA employees were in a fiduciary position. An ex-employee of the CIA published without permission a highly critical account (*Decent Interval*) of the CIA's evacuation of South Vietnam after the fall of Saigon. The Supreme Court imposed a constructive trust on all profits from the sales in favour of the CIA and permanently enjoined the author from publishing future writings concerning the CIA or intelligence activities without submitting them to the CIA for prepublication review. This was notwithstanding the concession that the book contained no information that the CIA could have suppressed under the secrecy agreement.[247]

A similar outcome to that reached in *Snepp* was achieved by the House of Lords in *A-G v Blake (Jonathan Cape Ltd, third party)*.[248] George Blake was a member of SIS from 1944 to 1961. He had signed an Official Secrets Act declaration by which he agreed not to divulge any official information gained as a result of his employment either in the press or in book form. In 1951 he became an agent for the Soviet Union. In 1961 he was convicted under s. 1 of the Official Secrets Act 1911.[249] In 1966 he escaped to Moscow. In 1989 he wrote his autobiography (*No Other Choice*) and agreed to its publication by JC. No injunction to restrain publication was sought as the information was no longer confidential. However, his actions were in breach of contract. JC agreed to pay £150,000 as advance against the royalties. The House of Lords held by 4 to 1[250] that the Attorney-General was entitled, exceptionally, to restitutionary damages for the breach of contract.[251] The trial judge and the Court of Appeal[252] had rejected the Attorney's original case based on a breach of fiduciary duty (B was no longer an employee of the Crown) or breach of confidence (the information was no longer

---

[245] See N. Sheehan et al., *The Pentagon Papers* (1971); L. Henkin (1971) 120 U Pa L Rev 271; Nimmer (1974) 26 Stan L Rev 311; M. Supperstone, *Brownlie's Law of Public Order and National Security* (2nd edn, 1981), pp. 271–274; C.R. Sunstein 74 Calif LR 889 (1986).

[246] 42 USC §. 2014(y)–2162, 2274, 2280: *United States v Progressive Inc* 467 F Supp 990 (1979) (the litigation was dropped after similar materials were published elsewhere).

[247] *Snepp v United States* 444 US 507 (1980) (see Comment (1979) 14 Harv Civ Rights–Civ Lib L Rev 665; Comment (1980) 32 Stan L Rev 409; D.F. Orentlicher (1981) 81 Colum LR 662; C.R. Sunstein 74 Calif LR 889, 912–921 (1986)).

[248] [2000] 4 All ER 385.   [249] Above, p. 786.

[250] Lords Nicholls, Goff, Browne-Wilkinson and Steyn, Lord Hobhouse dissenting.

[251] A declaration that the Attorney-General was entitled to be paid a sum equal to whatever amount was due and owing to B from JC Ltd under the 1989 publishing agreement.

[252] [1997] Ch 84, [1998] Ch 439.

confidential). The Court of Appeal had upheld an alternative, public law, basis of claim flowing from the Attorney-General's capacity as guardian of the public interest, and granted an injunction freezing (but not confiscating) payments resulting from exploitation of *No Other Choice*. This basis was unanimously disapproved by the House of Lords on the ground that the court had no common law power to make what was in substance, albeit not in form, a confiscation order. 'There is no common law power to take or confiscate property without compensation.'[253]

It has been argued that there was no principled basis for the decision of the House, it being new law made to fit Blake's case.[254] The ECtHR subsequently held[255] that the proceedings against B had not been pursued with the diligence required by Art. 6(1) ECHR, and so had not been determined in a reasonable time. It awarded €5,000, with €2,000 costs and expenses.

12. From 1996, members of the UK Special Forces such as the SAS have been required to enter contracts preventing the publication of memoirs or other information about the work of the forces that have not been cleared by the Ministry of Defence. These obligations have been held to be contractually enforceable, there being no duress (military orders) or undue influence.[256]

5. SECURITY VETTING

Processes by which individuals are 'vetted' by the state to ensure that they are not employed in situations that might compromise security have existed in one form or another for many years. From, at the latest, 1937, a relatively obscure branch (later C Division) of the Security Service conducted checks of the names of new civil servants against MI5 files. Analogous organisations in the US and Canada in addition, in a proportion of cases, took positive steps to investigate the backgrounds of individuals.[257] As matters turned out, the record of MI5 was mixed. On the one hand there was little if any evidence of penetration by enemy agents during the war; on the other hand a number of persons with known Communist backgrounds succeeded in joining the Security Service or the Secret Intelligence Service and subsequently operated successfully as agents for the USSR. After the war vetting procedures in the UK were applied more rigorously and arrangements for positive vetting were introduced.

(A) THE 'PURGE' PROCEDURE

In 1945, the defection of Igor Gouzenko stimulated a chain of events which led to the unravelling of major spy rings in Canada, the US and Britain. This included the arrest and conviction in 1946 of Dr Alan Nunn May, a nuclear scientist who had spied for Russia

---

[253] Per Lord Nicholls at 402, citing *A-G v De Keyser's Royal Hotel Ltd* [1920] AC 508 and *Burmah Oil Co v Lord Advocate* [1965] AC 75.

[254] S. Hedley (2000) 4 Web JCLI, noting that while Blake's treachery was very serious it was not so clear that the breach of his contractual undertaking was. See also D. Fox [2001] CLJ 333, noting the deterrent effect of the award; C. Munro [2006] PL 58.

[255] *Blake v UK*, Judgment of 26 September 2006.

[256] '*R*' *v Attorney-General of England and Wales* [2003] UKPC 22 (Lord Scott dissenting on the ground of undue influence). See also *Ministry of Defence v Griffin* [2008] UKHC 1542 (QB), where Eady J continued an interlocutory injunction restraining disclosures by former member of UKSF claimed to be in breach of confidentiality agreement and equitable duty of confidence.

[257] See L. Hannant, 'Inter-war security screening in Britain, the United States and Canada' (1991) 6(4) Intelligence and National Security 711.

while working in Canada. A number of civil servants, suspected of communist or fascist sympathies, were transferred to non-sensitive posts.[258] 'MI5 feared its covert purge might be "blown" as the number of transferees grew.' Accordingly, in 1948 the prime Minister, Mr Attlee, made a public statement to the effect that:

the only prudent course to adopt is to ensure that no one who is known to be a member of the Communist Party, or to be associated with it in such a way as to raise legitimate doubts about his or her reliability, is employed in connection with work, the nature of which is vital to the security of the state.[259]

The same rule was to govern persons known to be actively associated with Fascist organisations. These were included to give the appearance of impartiality: Communists were considered the real threat. 'The security authorities were overjoyed when they eventually found a fascist in one of the service departments.'[260] The procedure was revised in 1957, 1962 and 1985. Where the Minister ruled that there was a prima facie case, but the allegation was not accepted by the public servants, the matter would be referred to the 'Three Advisers' who would hear representations from the individual without disclosing the sources of evidence. The Three Advisers would report to the Minster but the final decision lay with him. If he upheld the ruling the public servant would be transferred to non-secret work or dismissed. The procedure applied also to certain cases of employment outside the public service, including employees of firms engaged in classified government contracts.[261] By November 1954, 124 civil servants had been removed from their posts for security reasons. Between 20 and 30 were dismissed; almost as many resigned; the remainder were transferred.[262] There were no cases under the purge procedure after 1969; this case was not, in the end, referred to the Three Advisers.[263] The procedure declined in importance with the introduction of positive vetting and can now be regarded as having lapsed.[264]

(B) POSITIVE VETTING

'By today's standards, the purge procedure was rudimentary, almost naive.'[265] The US authorities regarded it as 'feeble'.[266] The arrest and conviction of Klaus Fuchs in 1950, a nuclear scientist who had leaked atomic secrets to the Russians, led to the introduction of 'positive vetting'. Instead of simply ensuring that the Security Service had no adverse record of a candidate, a conscious effort should be made to confirm his reliability. The introduction of positive vetting was announced in a press statement released on 8 January 1952. The arrangements have been revised on a number of occasions, the latest being in 1994, as explained in the following extract from *Hansard*.

----

258 See P. Hennessy and G. Brownfeld, 'Britain's Cold War Security Purge: The Origins of Positive Vetting' (1982) 25(4) Historical Journal 965–973; R.J. Aldrich, *The Hidden Hand* (2001), pp. 117–121.

259 448 HC Deb, 15 March 1948, cols 1703–1704.

260 P. Hennessy and G. Brownfeld, op. cit., p. 968.

261 Statement of the procedure to be followed when the reliability of a public servant is thought to be in doubt on security grounds (Cabinet Office). See D.G.T. Williams, *Not in the Public Interest* (1965), pp. 170–185; D.C. Jackson, (1957) 20 MLR 346, [1963] PL 51; I. Linn, *Application Refused* (1990): NCCL Trade Union Liaison Committee, *The Purging of the Civil Service* (1985).

262 D.G.T. Williams, op. cit., p. 171.

263 Information supplied by the Cabinet Office. The Three Advisers last sat in 1967.

264 Information supplied by the Security Vetting Appeals Panel.

265 P. Hennessy and G. Brownfeld, op. cit., p. 967.

266 Ibid., p. 969.

- **Vol. 251 HC Deb, cols 764–766,** written answer, 15 December 1994

The Prime Minister: [...To] ensure that security measures and procedures reflect current threats, the Government have recently completed a fundamental review of their arrangements for the management of protective security in Departments and agencies. In the area of personnel security, the review concluded that the vetting process served a worthwhile purpose, not only in disclosing circumstances which might lead to breaches of security but as a deterrent to those who might otherwise seek to undermine that security. The review recommended, however, that there should be a streamlining of the procedures that made up the vetting process. That work has now been completed.

The new framework should ensure that personnel security objectives are properly defined and that responsibility for achieving them is clearly established. There will be a greater emphasis on ensuring that personnel security resources are targeted on, and proportionate to, the threat and add necessarily and cost-effectively to the protection of government assets. Between 1 January and 31 March 1995, the existing arrangements will be replaced by a new personnel security regime which will consist of two levels of vetting, a security check and developed vetting. A security check will be similar to the current PV(S)—positive vetting (secret)—clearance, but will in addition include a check on the financial status of the individual. Developed vetting will replace the present PV(TS)—positive vetting (top secret)—and EPV–extended positive vetting—levels of vetting. The current system of counter terrorist checks will remain unchanged, but will be subject to review.

As at present, all candidates for security vetting will be asked to complete a security questionnaire which will explain the purpose of the procedure and invite them to provide the personal details required for the necessary checks to be carried out. Vetting will then be carried out on the basis of the statement of policy set out below.

STATEMENT OF HM GOVERNMENT'S VETTING POLICY

In the interests of national security, safeguarding the Parliamentary democracy and maintaining the proper security of the Government's essential activities, it is the policy of HMG that no one should be employed in connection with work the nature of which is vital to the interests of the state who:

is, or has been involved in, or associated with any of the following activities:

— espionage,

— terrorism,

— sabotage,

— actions intended to overthrow or undermine Parliamentary democracy by political, industrial or violent means; or

is, or has recently been:

— a member of any organisation which has advocated such activities; or

— associated with any organisation, or any of its members in such a way as to raise reasonable doubts about his or [sc. her] reliability; or

is susceptible to pressure or improper influence, for example because of current or past conduct: or

has shown dishonesty or lack of integrity which throws doubt upon their reliability; or

has demonstrated behaviour, or is subject to circumstances which may otherwise indicate unreliability.

In accordance with the above policy, Government departments and agencies will carry out a Security Check (SC) on all individuals who require long term, frequent and uncontrolled access to SECRET information or assets. A Security Check may also be applied to staff who are in a position directly or indirectly to bring about the same degree of damage as such individuals or who need access to protectively marked material originating from other countries or international organisations. In some circumstances, where it would not be possible for an individual to make reasonable progress in their career without clearance to SECRET level, it may be applied to candidates for employment whose duties do not, initially, involve such regular access.

An SC clearance will normally consist of:

a check against the National Collection of Criminal Records and relevant departmental and police records;

in accordance with the Security Service Act 1989, where it is necessary to protect national security, or to safeguard the economic well-being of the United Kingdom from threats posed by persons outside the British Islands, a check against Security Service records; and credit reference checks and where appropriate, a review of personal finances.

In some circumstances further enquiries, including an interview with the subject, may be carried out.

Individuals employed on government work who have long term, frequent and uncontrolled access to TOPSECRET information or assets, will be submitted to the level of vetting clearance known as Developed Vetting (DV). This level of clearance may also be applied to people who are in a position directly or indirectly to cause the same degree of damage as such individuals and in order to satisfy the requirements for access to protectively marked material originating from other countries and international organisations. In addition to a Security Check, a DV will involve:

an interview with the person being vetted; and references from people who are familiar with the person's character in both the home and work environment. These may be followed up by interviews. Enquiries will not necessarily be confined to past and present employers and nominated character referees.

It is also the Government's policy that departments and agencies will carry out Counter Terrorist Checks (CTC) in the interest of national security before anyone can be:

authorised to take up posts which involve proximity to public figures at particular risk of attack by terrorist organisations, or which give access to information or material assessed to be of value to terrorists;

granted unescorted access to certain military, civil and industrial establishments assessed to be at particular risk of attack by a terrorist organisation.

The purpose of such checks is to prevent those who may have connections with terrorist organisations, or who may be vulnerable to pressure from such organisations, from gaining access to certain posts, and in some circumstances, premises, where there is a risk that they could exploit that position to further the aims of a terrorist organisation. A CTC will include a check against Security Service records. Criminal record information may also be taken into account.

Departments and agencies generally assure themselves, through the verification of identity, and written references from previous employers, that potential recruits are reliable and trustworthy. Such Basic Checks (BC) are already standard procedure for many departments and agencies. Where access needs to be granted to Government information or assets at CONFIDENTIAL level, departments, agencies and contractors engaged on government work are required to complete such checks. In some cases, at the CONFIDENTIAL level, where relevant, the Basic Check may be augmented with some of the checks normally carried out for security clearances.

TERMS OF REFERENCE FOR THE SECURITY VETTING APPEALS PANEL (UPDATED OCTOBER 2000)

1. The current policy on security vetting as announced in the Prime Minister's statement to the House of Commons on 15 December 1994, [see above]...

2. Where an employee of a department, agency or other organisation specified in the Annex is aggrieved by the withdrawal or refusal of security clearance, and has exhausted appropriate internal appeal mechanisms, they may appeal to the Security Vetting Appeals Panel. The Panel will:

   i. Examine whether the appeal falls within the remit of the Panel; if so, it will:

   ii. examine the procedure by which the vetting authority obtained and assessed the information underpinning the adverse vetting decision;

   iii. examine the merits of the vetting decision, taking into account the interests of national security and the rights of the individual;

   iv. produce a report of their recommendations for the Head of Department or equivalent; and

   v. produce a report for the complainant. As far as is possible, this should duplicate that sent to the Head of Department or equivalent.

Details of the Security Vetting Appeals Panel's operations are shown at Annex.

SECURITY VETTING APPEALS PANEL

BACKGROUND

1. All departments and agencies should have in place an internal appeals process to consider challenges by individuals to security vetting decisions. The process should include an ultimate right of appeal to the Head of Department or equivalent. The appeals process should be available to all staff employed by the department or agency, or by its contractors, who are subject to vetting (but not to candidates for employment).

2. An independent Security Vetting Appeals Panel has been established to provide a final means of challenging a decision to refuse or withdraw security clearance. It is available to hear appeals from individuals in departments and other organisations, or those employed by contractors of those departments and organisations, who have exhausted the internal appeals process and who remain dissatisfied with the outcome.

ORGANISATIONS COVERED BY THE SECURITY VETTING APPEALS PANEL

3. All staff of the following organisations (excluding members of the Security and Intelligence Agencies, who are subject to different arrangements), who have been refused security clearance or have had it withdrawn, and who have exhausted the internal procedures for challenging the decision, have the right to appeal to the Security Vetting Appeals Panel:

The Civil Service

The Diplomatic Service

The Armed Forces

Other organisations and their subsidiaries which are listed in the Arrangements under section 2(3) of the Security Service Act 1989. These include:

   the Police Forces;

   the UKAEA;

   the Civil Aviation Authority;

   the Post Office;

   British Telecommunications plc;

   The Bank of England; and

   Contractors of the above organisations.

Separate independent avenues of appeal against adverse vetting decisions are available to directly employed staff on the Security and Intelligence Agencies (and to those of their contractors) through the Security Service or Intelligence Services Tribunals as appropriate.

ACCESS TO THE SECURITY VETTING APPEALS PANEL

4. Security Division of the Cabinet Office provides the Secretariat for the Security Vetting Appeals Panel and handles the mechanics of the appeals process. The Panel will be convened to hear cases as they arise.

5. Departments and other organisations are responsible for drawing the attention of staff to the existence of the Panel when individuals are informed of the arrangements for the internal appeals process. It is the responsibility of Security Division to explain the Panel's procedures to these individuals. They should be told to write to The Secretary, Security Vetting Appeals Panel, Room 209, 4 Central Buildings, Matthew Parker Street, London SW1H 9NL.

HOW THE PANEL WILL OPERATE

6. An appellant will be allowed to put their case to the Panel in person, accompanied, if they so wish, by a 'friend'. As the issues to be considered by the Panel are not matters of law, formal legal representation is not permitted. The role of the 'friend' is confined to helping the appellant to present their case. A member of the Panel will not hear a case where there is a possible conflict of interest.

7. The defending department or organisation can also present their case in person to the Panel. Appellants should be provided, as far as possible and in advance of the hearing, with the reasons for the decision to refuse or withdraw security clearance, unless considerations of security or confidentiality prohibit this. When it is not possible to provide the appellant with the full reasons, the defending department or organisation should nevertheless submit them to the Panel in the normal way.

8. The Panel will follow an informal procedure. The hearing will be confidential to the parties concerned. A party to an appeal may submit information or make representations to the panel in the absence of the other party.

9. The department or organisation must disclose or give to the Panel such documents or information as they may require to carry out their functions.

10. The Panel is required to carry out their functions in such a way as to ensure that no document or information given to them by any person is disclosed, without the originator's consent, to any other person.

11. The Panel will produce a report of their findings. The report will include their recommendations, if any. Subject to the need to withhold any information in accordance with paragraph 10, the report will be published in full to both the appellant and the Head of the defending department or organisation.

RECOMMENDATIONS OPEN TO THE SECURITY VETTING APPEALS PANEL

12. The Panel will make recommendations to the Head of the department or organisation in the light of its findings. It can recommend:

— that the decision to refuse or withdraw security clearance should stand; or

— that security clearance should be granted or restored.

The Panel may also comment on the adequacy of the internal appeals process and make recommendations.

13. The department or organisation will inform the Panel's Secretary of the subsequent action taken.

14. The Panel will consider the merits of an appeal against a decision to refuse or withdraw security clearance. It will not become involved in examining any subsequent action which may be taken by the department or organisation over the continued employment of the appellant and will not therefore be

concerned wit questions of compensation. No department or organisation can be required to retain an individual in whom they have lost confidence. However, it would be open to an individual who feels that they have been unfairly dismissed as a result of a decision to refuse or withdraw security clearance, to use existing procedures for challenging the decision.

15. More generally, any person who believes that the Security Service has disclosed information about them for use in determining whether they should be employed, or continue to be employed, by any person or in any office or capacity, may complain to the Security Service Tribunal asking them to investigate the complaint. Further information is available from The Security Service Tribunal, PO Box 18, London SE1 0TZ.

NOTES

1. The Security Commission reported on the operation of procedures in the case of three persons convicted under the Official Secrets Acts who had received PV clearance:[267] Lord Bridge reported on the PV clearance of Commander Trestrail, who resigned as Queen's Police Officer following the revelation of his homosexuality.[268] The 1994 guidelines replaced guidelines published in 1990.[269] While the procedures have been streamlined, the policy is generally similar, except that it applies to people whose work is vital to the 'interests' rather than the 'security' of the state; there is a general reference to susceptibility to pressure or improper influence (not just pressure from a subversive organisation, a foreign intelligence service or a hostile power); character defects that expose the person to blackmail or other influence by a subversive organisation or foreign intelligence service are no longer expressly mentioned as indications of unreliability (but presumably still are). There seems to be an intention to apply a higher degree of scrutiny (including financial checks) to a narrower range of personnel.[270]

2. In 1950 it was contemplated that PV would be applied to about 1,000 posts.[271] By 1982 the number of posts covered had risen to 68,000.[272] The Security Commission noted that the procedure was expensive and time-consuming, and recommended that the number of PV posts should be reviewed. In particular PV should no longer be an automatic requirement for officials of Under-Secretary rank and above and officials in the private offices of ministers. It remains a requirement for all members of the Diplomatic Service and the police special branches. It is also used in the UK Atomic Energy Authority and in firms which have contracts involving access to classified material. Following the review, some 2,000 posts were removed from the PV category.[273] Records of the number of posts subject to security vetting are, however, not kept centrally (information from the Cabinet Office). The number of clearances given to 'secret' and 'top secret' is now reported by the Defence Vetting Agency (see below), but not refusals. In 1999/2000, 926 people were refused a CTC

---

[267] Geoffrey Arthur Prime, Report of May 1983 (Cmnd 8876), Philip Leslie Aldridge, Report of March 1984 (Cmnd 9212) and Steven John Hayden, Report of February 2000 (Cm 4578). For earlier reports, see the Radcliffe *Committee on Security Procedures in the Public Service* (Cmnd 1681, 1961) and the *Statement on the Recommendations of the Security Commission* (Cmnd 8540, 1982).

[268] 1982–83 HC 59. See generally M. Hollingsworth and R. Norton-Taylor, *Blacklist: The Inside Story of Political Vetting* (1988); S. Fredman and G.S. Morris, *The State as Employer* (1989), pp. 232–236; I. Linn, *Application Refused: Employment Vetting by the State* (1990).

[269] 177 HC Deb, 24 July 1990, cols 159–161, written answer.

[270] See *Independent*, 16 December 1994.

[271] P. Hennessy and I. Brownfeld, op. cit., p. 969.

[272] Cmnd 8540, p. 5.   [273] I. Linn, op. cit., p. 21.

or had such a clearance withdrawn.[274] The DVA carries out some 150,000 vetting checks and investigations each year.[275]

PV clearance does not apply to political ministers, although on appointment they are given specific instructions upon security problems and procedures. It does, however, apply to special advisers to ministers where they have regular access to highly classified information.

On 1 April 1997, various service units were combined to form the Defence Vetting Agency. It conducts vetting for the armed forces, MoD and defence industries and may undertake such work for other government departments.[276] It is an Executive Agency of the MoD.

3. The details of the processes are being revised following a Cabinet Office Review of Personnel security in 2004.[277] The Basic Check (BC) and Enhanced Basic Check (EBC) have been renamed the Baseline Personnel Security Standard (BPSS) and Enhanced Baseline Standard (EBS); they are 'not formal security clearances, but are a package of pre-employment checks that represent good recruitment and employment practice. A BPSS or EBS aims to provide an appropriate level of assurance as to the trustworthiness, integrity, and probable reliability of prospective employees.' They apply to all successful applicants for employment in the public sector and armed forces and all private sector employees working on government contracts (e.g. contractors and consultants), who require access to, or knowledge of, government assets protectively marked up to and including confidential. They are normally conducted by the recruitment authorities or companies themselves to the agreed standard.[278]

4. *Criteria for clearance.* These are summarised in the 1994 statement. The policy on homosexuality was reviewed in 1991:[279]

Because homosexual acts, even between consenting adults, remain criminal offences in a number of overseas countries, evidence of homosexuality, even if acknowledged, has been treated under this policy as a bar to clearance at PV(TS)—positive vetting (top secret)—or enhanced positive vetting (EPV) level in overseas posts and therefore as a bar to recruitment to certain areas of employment, including the diplomatic service. In the light of changing social attitudes towards homosexuality in this country and abroad, and the correspondingly greater willingness on the part of homosexuals to be open about their sexuality, their lifestyle and their relationships, the Government have reviewed this policy and concluded that in future there should be no posts involving access to highly classified information for which homosexuality represents an automatic bar to security clearance, except in the special case of the armed forces where homosexual acts remain offences under the service disciplinary Acts.

The susceptibility of the subject to blackmail or pressure by a foreign intelligence service will continue to be a factor in the vetting of all candidates for posts involving access to highly classified information. An individual assessment is made in each case, taking account of the evidence which emerges in the course of the vetting process and the level of security clearance required.

5. *Appeals.* An independent Security Vetting Appeals Panel was established on 1 July 1997 'to hear appeals against refusal or withdrawal of clearance at SC or DV levels and to

[274] HC Deb, 25 January 2001, col. 693W.   [275] DVA Corporate Plan 2008–2013.

[276] HC Deb, 20 March 1997, col. 857, written answer; *Defence Vetting Agency Framework Document*, April 1997. The latest Framework Document was published in 2006: see www.mod.uk/DefenceInternet/AboutDefence/WhatWeDo/SecurityandIntelligence/DVA/.

[277] See Cabinet Office, HMG Baseline Personnel Security Standard, A Good Practice Guide to the Pre-Employment Screening of Government Staff and Contractors (2006) and CPNI, A Good Practice Guide on Pre-Employment Screening (2nd edn, 2008).

[278] DVA website.   [279] 195 HC Deb, 23 July 1991, col. 474, written answer.

advise the head of the organisation concerned. The Panel is available to all those, other candidates for recruitment, in the public and private sectors and in the armed forces who are subject to security vetting at these levels, have exhausted existing appeals mechanisms within their own organisations and remain dissatisfied with the results.' Staff of the security and intelligence agencies are to have recourse to the appropriate Service Tribunal (now the Tribunal under RIPA). The Panel replaced the Three Advisers. It is chaired by Dame Janet Smith, and includes a High Court judge and other panel members with a background at a senior level in the Civil Service, the armed forces, the trades unions and industry, and related experience in security matters.[280] It heard two appeals in 1998 and two in 1999, and since then has heard 32 cases. It has 'stressed the need for as much openness as possible about the reasons for any doubts, giving the appellant opportunity to comment. Where decisions involve sensitive information, real efforts must be made to obtain the authority of the source to disclose or to agree a disclosable edited version.'[281] Formal legal representation is not permitted 'as the issues to be considered by the panel are not matters of law'.[282] However, appellants are often accompanied by solicitors or barristers who can help them present their case.[283] The special advocate procedure has been extended to the Panel.[284]

6. *Judicial review.* The limitations of judicial review as a mechanism for protecting the interests of those refused PV clearance were shown in *R v Director of Government Communications Headquarters, ex p Hodges*.[285] H, who had been employed at GCHQ since he was 16, informed his employers, when he was 21, that he had concluded that he was homosexual. Although he was entirely open about this, and had a current steady relationship, his PV clearance was removed as it was thought he might be subject to blackmail because of his lifestyle. The Divisional Court rejected his application for judicial review holding (a) that, in the light of the decision of the House of Lords in *Council of Civil Service Unions v Minister for the Civil Service*,[286] the court was not entitled even to consider whether the decision was *Wednesbury* unreasonable; and (b) that the procedure adopted was procedurally fair, notwithstanding that notes of an interview with his employers were not revealed. (H had been given a résumé of the facts, and had indeed been interviewed on a number of occasions.) In case he was wrong on point (a), Glidewell LJ also indicated that on the facts the Director's decision was not *Wednesbury* unreasonable.

7. In his report on the *Trestrail* case[287] Lord Bridge concluded that the PV procedures were not and could not be infallible; here, they were carried out efficiently and thoroughly. Where the subject was determined to conceal disqualifying factors this would present the PV investigator with an almost impossible task. They might be discovered by a 'system of random and covert surveillance of the subject's private activities'. However, this would '(a) add enormously to the cost of PV; (b) not necessarily be successful—this would depend on the length of the surveillance and the frequency of the subject's irregular behaviour; and (c) be strongly resented by most public servants as an unjustifiable invasion of their privacy'.[288] On the other hand, in the *Hayden* case the Security Commission was critical of a decision to overrule the recommendation of an investigator that Hayden's clearance be withdrawn. He was known to be in debt and a clear security risk. The Commission approved changes in vetting practice that the MoD had already implemented.

[280] HC Deb, 19 June 1997, col. 243, written answer: 23 April 1998, col. 676, written answer.
[281] Letter from the Secretary to the Panel, 13 October 2000.   [282] Ibid.
[283] Letter from the Secretary to the Panel, 24 April 2008.   [284] Ibid.
[285] (1988) Times, 26 July.   [286] [1985] AC 374.
[287] 1982–83 HC 59.   [288] Ibid., pp. 21–22.

8. In *TD, DE and MF v United Kingdom*[289] the European Commission considered complaints that the applicants had been refused posts following adverse reports from security vetting. Complaints to the Security Service Tribunal were not upheld. The applicants alleged that information as to their private lives was kept on secret files by MI5 and/or police special branches and/or the PNC and/or GCHQ and that this infringed Art. 8(1) ECHR. The Government submitted that TD and MF's job applications were not in fact referred to the Security Service or other agency as their long residence abroad rendered it impossible to carry out a satisfactory security clearance. The Commission concluded that they had failed to establish that there was a reasonable likelihood that the Security Service or other agency had compiled or retained information about their private life. The third case was adjourned for further examination of the facts, but was subsequently declared inadmissible on the ground that the legislative regime of the Security Service Act 1989 complied with Art. 8.[290]

6. THE SECURITY AND INTELLIGENCE SERVICES

There is now a vast literature on the activities of the security and intelligence services, ranging from official histories and other works of historical scholarship,[291] through books by knowledgeable observers apparently based on inside information[292] to journalistic pot-boilers. It has only been where the authors have themselves been members or former members of the relevant services that the Government has taken serious steps to prevent publication, ultimately with comparatively little success.[293] With the growth in the amount of information about the services that has been made public has come increased concern at the constitutional position of the services, and at the illegality or impropriety of some of their activities. Examples of the latter include Peter Wright's claims that he and others 'bugged and burgled our way across London at the State's behest, while pompous, bowler-hatted civil servants in Whitehall pretended to look the other way';[294] his claims of an MI5 plot to destabilise the Wilson Government;[295] and the revelations of Cathy Massiter.[296] The last of these led to an application for judicial review by three prominent CND members challenging *inter alia* the legality of the tapping of one of the three's telephone: *R v Secretary of State for the Home Department, ex p Ruddock.*[297] The challenge ultimately failed, but was nevertheless embarrassing for the Government . Moreover, in autumn 1988, the European Commission on Human Rights declared admissible a case brought by two former NCCL officers, Patricia

---

[289] App. Nos 18600/91, 18601/92 and 18602/91, 12 October 1992.

[290] *Esbester v UK* (App. No. 18601/91, 2 April 1993), below p. 845.

[291] E.g. C. Andrew, *Secret Service* (1985); F.H. Hinsley and C.A.G. Simkins, *British Intelligence in the Second World War* (1990); I. Leigh and L. Lustgarten, *In from the Cold* (1994); J. Curry, *The Security Service 1908–1945* (1999). Professor Andrew is writing an official history for publication in 2009.

[292] E.g. books by Nigel West (the pseudonym of Rupert Allason) including *MI5: British Security Service Operations 1909–45* (1981); *A Matter of Trust: MI5 1945–72* (1982); *MI6: British Secret Intelligence Service Operations 1909–45*; *Molehunt* (1986); *GCHQ: The Secret Wireless War 1909–86*; *The Friends: Britain's Post-War Secret Intelligence Operations* (1988); M. Smith, *New Cloak. Old Dagger* (1996).

[293] See above, pp. 803–822.   [294] *Spycatcher* (1987), p. 54.

[295] Ibid., pp. 362–372; D. Leigh, *The Wilson Plot* (1988). According to *MI5 The Security Service* (3rd edn. 1998), p. 39. 'Wright himself finally admitted in an interview with BBC's *Panorama* programme in 1988 that his account had been unreliable.'

[296] That MI5 tapped telephones of trade unionists involved in strike action; had persistently disregarded the rules as to telephone tapping; and maintained files on NCCL officers.

[297] [1987] 2 All ER 518 (see I. Leigh [1987] PL 12).

Hewitt and Harriet Harman, complaining of their classification as 'subversive' by MI5, which had placed them under surveillance.[298] One of their grounds of challenge was the absence of any effective remedy for complainants. In May 1989, the Commission found that there had been breaches of Arts 8 and 13 ECHR.[299] In response the Government secured the passage of the Security Service Act 1989. This places the Security Service (MI5) on a statutory footing, but does little to answer the many concerns that have been expressed.

The Security Service (MI5) operates at home and in the colonies, and has traditionally been concerned with counter-espionage. The Secret Intelligence Service (MI6), which mainly operates abroad, in co-operation with the Foreign Office, collects intelligence by covert means. Government Communications Headquarters (GCHQ) intercepts and analyses signals intelligence, including the communications of foreign countries, friendly and otherwise, companies and private individuals. SIS and GCHQ have now also been placed on a statutory basis by the Intelligence Services Act 1994. The work of the Security Service was summarised in a glossy booklet issued by HMSO: *MI5, The Security Service*.[300] In 1997/98, direct expenditure on the Service's case areas was apportioned as follows: terrorism related to Northern Ireland, 25 per cent; international terrorism, 15.5 per cent; espionage, 12 per cent; protective security, 7.5 per cent; serious crime, 2.5 per cent and proliferation (countering the threat posed by the spread of weapons of mass destruction), 2.0 per cent.[301] The main changes in recent years are, first, that there are currently no investigations in the area of subversion. Since the late 1980s the threat from subversive (Communist, Trotskyists and Fascist) groups 'has declined and is now insignificant'. In 1997/8 only 0.3 per cent of the Service's resources were devolved to 'the remnants of this work, predominantly to pay the pensions of retied agents'.[302] Secondly, the Security Service Act 1996 added supporting law enforcement agencies in work on serious crime to its statutory functions.[303] In October 1992, it took over from Special Branch lead responsibility for the intelligence effort against Irish republican terrorism on the British mainland.[304] By 2008, there had been further changes in the balance, with the allocation of resources by core business being counter-terrorism and protective security, 91 per cent; counter espionage, 3.5 per cent; counter-proliferation (of weapons of mass destruction), 3 per cent; external assistance, 2 per cent; emerging and other threats (from 'indigenous extremism'), 0.5 per cent.[305] The level of resources dedicated to the fight against terrorism has grown in recent years because of the increased threat of international terrorism; 15 per cent of resources still go to Northern Ireland work. Resources for all three agencies were significantly increased in 2006, although work on serious crime was suspended in the same year.

- ## Security Service Act 1989

1. The Security Service

(1) There shall continue to be a Security Service (in this Act referred to as 'the Service') under the authority of the Secretary of State.

(2) The function of the Service shall be the protection of national security and, in particular, its protection against threats from espionage, terrorism and sabotage, from the activities of agents of foreign powers and from actions intended to overthrow or undermine parliamentary democracy by political, industrial or violent means.

---

[298] *H and H v UK*, App. No. 12175/86.　　　[299] *Hewitt and Harman v UK* (1989) 14 EHRR 657.
[300] 1993; 3rd edn, 1998. Now a glossy website: www.mi5.gov.uk.
[301] *MI5. The Security Service* (3rd edn, 1998), pp. 6–7.　　　[302] Ibid., pp. 18–19.
[303] See below, p. 833.　　　[304] Ibid., p. 14.
[305] www.mi5.gov.uk/output/Page68.html.

(3) It shall also be the function of the Service to safeguard the economic well-being of the United Kingdom against threats posed by the actions or intentions of persons outside the British Islands.

[(4) It shall also be the function of the Service to act in support of the activities of police forces, [the Serious Organised Crime Agency] and other law enforcement agencies in the prevention and detection of serious crime.][306]

[(5) Section 81(5) of the Regulation of Investigatory Powers Act 2000 (meaning of 'prevention' and 'detection'), so far as it relates to serious crime, shall apply for the purposes of this Act as it applies for the purposes of the provisions of that Act not contained in Chapter 1 of Part 1.][307]

2. The Director-General

(1) The operations of the Service shall continue to be under the control of a Director-General appointed by the Secretary of State.

(2) The Director-General shall be responsible for the efficiency of the Service and it shall be his duty to ensure—

(a) that there are arrangements for securing that no information is obtained by the Service except so far as necessary for the proper discharge of its functions or disclosed by it except so far as necessary for that purpose or for the purpose of [the prevention or detection of][308] serious crime [or for the purpose of any criminal proceedings;[309] and

(b) that the Service does not take any action to further the interests of any political party; [and

(c) that there are arrangements, agreed with [the Director General of the Serious Organised Crime Agency][310] for co-ordinating the activities of the Service in pursuance of section 1(4) of this Act with the activities of police forces [the Serious Organised Crime Agency] and other law enforcement agencies.][311]

(3) The arrangements mentioned in subsection (2)(a) above shall be such as to ensure that information in the possession of the Service is not disclosed for use in determining whether a person should be employed, or continue to be employed, by any person, or in any office or capacity, except in accordance with provisions in that behalf approved by the Secretary of State.

[(3A) Without prejudice to the generality of subsection (2)(a) above, the disclosure of information shall be regarded as necessary for the proper discharge of the functions of the Security Service if it consists of—

(a) the disclosure of records subject to and in accordance with the Public Records Act 1958; or

(b) the disclosure, subject to and in accordance with arrangements approved by the Secretary of State, of information to the Comptroller and Auditor General for the purposes of his functions.][312]

(4) The Director-General shall make an annual report on the work of the Service to the Prime Minister and the Secretary of State and may at any time report to either of them on any matter relating to its work....

---

306 Inserted by the Security Service Act 1996, s. 1(1) and amended by the Serious Organised Crime and Police Act 2005, Sch. 4, paras 55, 56.

307 Inserted by the Regulation of Investigatory Powers Act 2000, Sch. 4, para. 4(1).

308 Inserted by ibid., Sch. 4, para. 4(2).

309 Inserted by the Intelligence Services Act 1994, Sch. 4, para. 1(1).

310 Substituted by the 2005 Act, Sch. 4, paras 55, 57(a).

311 Inserted by the Security Service Act 1996, s. 1(2) and amended by the 2005 Act, Sch. 4, paras 55, 57(b).

312 Inserted by ibid., para. 1(2).

- ## Intelligence Services Act 1994

The Secret Intelligence Service

1. The Secret Intelligence Service

(1) There shall continue to be a Secret Intelligence Service (in this Act referred to as 'the Intelligence Service') under the authority of the Secretary of State; and, subject to subsection (2) below, its functions shall be—

(a) to obtain and provide information relating to the actions or intentions of persons outside the British Islands; and

(b) to perform other tasks relating to the actions or intentions of such persons.

(2) The functions of the Intelligence Service shall be exercisable only—

(a) in the interests of national security, with particular reference to the defence and foreign policies of Her Majesty's Government in the United Kingdom; or

(b) in the interests of the economic well-being of the United Kingdom; or

(c) in support of the prevention or detection of serious crime.

2. The Chief of the Intelligence Service

(1) The operations of the Intelligence Service shall continue to be under the control of a Chief of that Service appointed by the Secretary of State.

(2) The Chief of the Intelligence Service shall be responsible for the efficiency of that Service and it shall be his duty to ensure—

(a) that there are arrangements for securing that no information is obtained by the Intelligence Service except so far as necessary for the proper discharge of its functions and that no information is disclosed by it except so far as necessary—

(i) for that purpose;

(ii) in the interests of national security;

(iii) for the purpose of the prevention or detection of serious crime; or

(iv) for the purpose of any criminal proceedings; and

(b) that the Intelligence Service does not take any action to further the interests of any United Kingdom political party.

[Sub-ss. (3) and (4) follow the terms of s. 2(3A) and (4) of the Security Service Act 1989 (above, p. 833.]

GCHQ

3. The Government Communications Headquarters

(1) There shall continue to be a Government Communications Headquarters under the authority of the Secretary of State; and, subject to subsection (2) below, its functions shall be—

(a) to monitor or interfere with electromagnetic, acoustic and other emissions and any equipment producing such emissions and to obtain and provide information derived from or related to such emissions or equipment and from encrypted material; and

(b) to provide advice and assistance about—

(i) languages, including terminology used for technical matters, and

(ii) cryptography and other matters relating to the protection of information and other material, to the armed forces of the Crown, to Her Majesty's Government in the United Kingdom or to a Northern Ireland Department or to any other organisation which is determined for the purposes of this section in such manner as may be specified by the Prime Minister.

(2) The functions referred to in subsection (1)(*a*) above shall be exercisable only—

    (a) in the interests of national security, with particular reference to the defence and foreign policies of Her Majesty's Government in the United Kingdom; or

    (b) in the interests of the economic well-being of the United Kingdom in relation to the actions or intentions of persons outside the British Islands; or

    (c) in support of the prevention or detection of serious crime.

(3) In this Act the expression 'GCHQ' refers to the Government Communications Headquarters and to any unit or part of a unit of the armed forces of the Crown which is for the time being required by the Secretary of State to assist the Government Communications Headquarters in carrying out its functions.

4. The Director of GCHQ

(1) The operations of GCHQ shall continue to be under the control of a Director appointed by the Secretary of State.

(2) The Director shall be responsible for the efficiency of GCHQ and it shall be his duty to ensure—

    (a) that there are arrangements for securing that no information is obtained by GCHQ except so far as necessary for the proper discharge of its functions and that no information is disclosed by it except so far as necessary for that purpose or for the purpose of any criminal proceedings; and

    (b) that GCHQ does not take any action to further the interests of any United Kingdom political party.

[Sub-ss. (3) and (4) follow the terms of s. 2(3A) and (4) of the Security Service Act 1989 (above, p. 833.)]

Authorisation of certain actions

5. Warrants: general

(1) No entry on or interference with property or with wireless telegraphy shall be unlawful if it is authorised by a warrant issued by the Secretary of State under this section.

(2) The Secretary of State may, on an application made by the Security Service, the Intelligence Service or GCHQ, issue a warrant under this section authorising the taking, subject to subsection (3) below, of such action as is specified in the warrant in respect of any property so specified or in respect of wireless telegraphy so specified if the Secretary of State—

    (a) thinks it necessary for the action to be taken [for the purpose of][313] in assisting, as the case may be,—

        (i) the Security Service in carrying out any of its functions under the 1989 Act; or

        (ii) the Intelligence Service in carrying out any of its functions under section 1 above; or

        (iii) GCHQ in carrying out any function which falls within section 3(1)(a) above; and

    (b) is satisfied that the taking of the action is proportionate to what the action seeks to achieve;][314] and

    (c) is satisfied that satisfactory arrangements are in force under section 2(2)(a) of the 1989 Act (duties of the Director-General of the Security Service), section 2(2)(a) above or section 4(2)(a) above with respect to the disclosure of information obtained by virtue of this section and that any information obtained under the warrant will be subject to those arrangements.

---

313 Substituted by the 2000 Act, s. 74.   314 Substituted by the 2000 Act, s. 74.

[(2A) The matters to be taken into account in considering whether the requirements of subsection (2) (*a*) and (*b*) are satisfied in the case of any warrant shall include whether what it is thought necessary to achieve by the conduct authorised by the warrant could reasonably be achieved by other means.][315]

[(3) A warrant issued on the application of the Intelligence Service or GCHQ for the purposes of the exercise of their functions by virtue of section 1(2)(*c*) or 3(2)(*c*) above may not relate to property in the British Islands.

(3A) A warrant issued on the application of the Security Service for the purposes of the exercise of their function under section 1(4) of the Security Service Act 1989 may not relate to property in the British Islands unless it authorises the taking of action in relation to conduct within subsection (3B) below.

(3B) Conduct is within this subsection if it constitutes (or, if it took place in the United Kingdom, would constitute) one or more offences, and either—

(a) it involves the use of violence, results in substantial financial gain or is conduct by a large number of persons in pursuit of a common purpose; or

(b) the offence or one of the offences is an offence for which a person who has attained the age of twenty-one and has no previous convictions could reasonably be expected to be sentenced to imprisonment for a term of three years or more.][316]

(4) Subject to subsection (5) below, the Security Service may make an application under section (2) above for a warrant to be issued authorising that Service (or a person acting on its behalf) to take such action as is specified in the warrant on behalf of the Intelligence Service or GCHQ and, where such a warrant is issued, the functions of the Security Service shall include the carrying out of the action so specified, whether or not it would otherwise be within its functions.

(5) The Security Service may not make an application for a warrant by virtue of subsection (4) above except where the action proposed to be authorised by the warrant—

(a) is action in respect of which the Intelligence Service or, as the case may be, GCHQ could make such an application; and

(b) is to be taken otherwise than in support of the prevention or detection of serious crime.

6. Warrants: procedure and duration, etc.

(1) A warrant shall not be issued except—

(a) under the hand of the Secretary of State…[or

(b) in an urgent case where the Secretary of State has expressly authorised its issue and a statement of that fact is endorsed on it, under the hand of a senior official […];[317] …

[or

(d) in an urgent case where the Secretary of State has expressly authorised the issue of warrants in accordance with this paragraph by specified senior officials and a statement of that fact is endorsed on the warrant, under the hand of any of the specified officials].

[(1A) But a warrant issued in accordance with subsection (1)(d) may authorise the taking of action only if the action is an action in relation to property which, immediately before the issue of the warrant, would, if done outside the British Islands, have been authorised by virtue of an authorisation under section 7 that was in force at that time.

---

315 Inserted by the 2000 Act, s. 74.   316 Inserted by the Security Services Act 1996, s. 2.
317 The words 'of his department' were repealed by the Regulation of Investigatory Powers Act 2000, Sch. 5.

(1B) A senior official who issues a warrant in accordance with subsection (1)(d) must inform the Secretary of State about the issue of the warrant as soon as practicable after issuing it.][318]

(2) A warrant shall, unless renewed under subsection (3) below, cease to have effect—

(a) if the warrant was under the hand of the Secretary of State…at the end of the period of six months beginning with the day on which it was issued; and

(b) in any other case, at the end of the period ending with the [fifth][319] working day following that day.

(3) If at any time before the day on which a warrant would cease to have effect the Secretary of State considers it necessary for the warrant to continue to have effect for the purpose for which it was issued, he may by an instrument under his hand renew it for a period of six months beginning with that day.

(4) The Secretary of State shall cancel a warrant if he is satisfied that the action authorised by it is no longer necessary.

(5) In the preceding provisions of this section 'warrant' means a warrant under section 5 above.

(6) As regards the Security Service, this section and section 5 above have effect in place of section 3 (property warrants) of the 1989 Act, and accordingly—

(a) a warrant issued under that section of the 1989 Act and current when this section and section 5 above come into force shall be treated as a warrant under section 5 above, but without any change in the date on which the warrant was in fact issued or last renewed; and

(b) section 3 of the 1989 Act shall cease to have effect.

7. Authorisation of acts outside the British Islands

(1) If, apart from this section, a person would be liable in the United Kingdom for any act done outside the British Islands, he shall not be so liable if the act is one which is authorised to be done by virtue of an authorisation given by the Secretary of State under this section.

(2) In subsection (1) above 'liable in the United Kingdom' means liable under the criminal or civil law of any part of the United Kingdom.

(3) The Secretary of State shall not give an authorisation under this section unless he is satisfied—

(a) that any acts which may be done in reliance on the authorisation or, as the case may be, the operation in the course of which the acts may be done will be necessary for the proper discharge of a function of the Intelligence Service [or GCHQ]; and

(b) that there are satisfactory arrangements in force to secure—

(i) that nothing will be done in reliance on the authorisation beyond what is necessary for the proper discharge of a function of the Intelligence Service [or GCHQ];[320] and

(ii) that, in so far as any acts may be done in reliance on the authorisation, their nature and likely consequences will be reasonable, having regard to the purposes for which they are carried out; and

(c) that there are satisfactory arrangements in force under section 2(2)(a) [or 4(2)(a)] above with respect to the disclosure of information obtained by virtue of this section and that any information obtained by virtue of anything done in reliance on the authorisation will be subject to those arrangements.

---

318 Inserted by the Terrorism Act 2006, s. 31(1)–(3).
319 Substituted for 'second' by the Terrorism Act 2006, s. 31(1), (4).
320 Inserted by the Anti-terrorism, Crime and Security Act 2001, s. 116(1)(a).

(4) Without prejudice to the generality of the power of the Secretary of State to give an authorisation under this section, such an authorisation—

    (a) may relate to a particular act or acts, to acts of a description specified in the authorisation or to acts undertaken in the course of an operation so specified;

    (b) may be limited to a particular person or persons of a description so specified; and

    (c) may be subject to conditions so specified.

(5) An authorisation shall not be given under this section except—

    (a) under the hand of the Secretary of State; or

    (b) in an urgent case where the Secretary of State has expressly authorised it to be given and a statement of that fact is endorsed on it, under the hand of a senior official [...].[321]

(6) An authorisation shall, unless renewed under subsection (7) below, cease to have effect—

    (a) if the authorisation was given under the hand of the Secretary of State, at the end of the period of six months beginning with the day on which it was given;

    (b) in any other case, at the end of the period ending with the [fifth] working day following the day on which it was given.

(7) If at any time before the day on which an authorisation would cease to have effect the Secretary of State considers it necessary for the authorisation to continue to have effect for the purpose for which it was given, he may by an instrument under his hand renew it for a period of six months beginning with that day.

(8) The Secretary of State shall cancel an authorisation if he is satisfied that any act authorised by it is no longer necessary.

[(10) Where—

    (a) a person is authorised by virtue of this section to do an act outside the British Islands in relation to property,

    (b) the act is one which, in relation to property within the British Islands, is capable of being authorised by a warrant under section 5,

    (c) a person authorised by virtue of this section to do that act outside the British Islands, does the act in relation to that property while it is within the British Islands, and

    (d) the act is done in circumstances falling within subsection (11) or (12),

this section shall have effect as if the act were done outside the British Islands in relation to that property.

(11) An act is done in circumstances falling within this subsection if it is done in relation to the property at a time when it is believed to be outside the British Islands.

(12) An act is done in circumstances falling within this subsection if it—

    (a) is done in relation to property which was mistakenly believed to be outside the British Islands either when the authorisation under this section was given or at a subsequent time or which has been brought within the British Islands since the giving of the authorisation; but

    (b) is done before the end of the fifth working day after the day on which the presence of the property in the British Islands first becomes known.

---

[321] Repealed by the Regulation of Investigatory Powers Act 2000, Sch. 5.

(13) In subsection (12) the reference to the day on which the presence of the property in the British Islands first becomes known is a reference to the day on which it first appears to a member of the Intelligence Service or of GCHQ, after the relevant time—

(a) that the belief that the property was outside the British Islands was mistaken; or

(b) that the property is within those Islands.

(14) In subsection (13) 'the relevant time' means, as the case may be—

(a) the time of the mistaken belief mentioned in subsection (12)(a); or

(b) the time at which the property was, or was most recently, brought within the British Islands.][322]

The Intelligence and Security Committee

10. The Intelligence and Security Committee

(1) There shall be a Committee, to be known as the Intelligence and Security Committee and in this section referred to as 'the Committee', to examine the expenditure, administration and policy of—

(a) the Security Service;

(b) the Intelligence Service; and

(c) GCHQ.

(2) The Committee shall consist of nine members—

(a) who shall be drawn both from the members of the House of Commons and from the members of the House of Lords; and

(b) none of whom shall be a Minister of the Crown.

(3) The members of the Committee shall be appointed by the Prime Minister after consultation with the Leader of the Opposition, within the meaning of the Ministerial and other Salaries Act 1975; and one of those members shall be so appointed as Chairman of the Committee.

(4) Schedule 3 to this Act shall have effect with respect to the tenure of office of members of, the procedure of and other matters relating to, the Committee; and in that Schedule 'the Committee' has the same meaning as in this section.

(5) The Committee shall make an annual report on the discharge of their functions to the Prime Minister and may at any time report to him on any matter relating to the discharge of those functions.

(6) The Prime Minister shall lay before each House of Parliament a copy of each annual report made by the Committee under subsection (5) above together with a statement as to whether any matter has been excluded from that copy in pursuance of subsection (7) below.

(7) If it appears to the Prime Minister, after consultation with the Committee, that the publication of any matter in a report would be prejudicial to the continued discharge of the functions of either of the Services or, as the case may be, GCHQ, the Prime Minister may exclude that matter from the copy of the report as laid before each House of Parliament....

12. Short title, commencement and extent

....

(4) Her Majesty may by Order in Council direct that any of the provisions of this Act specified in the Order shall extend, with such exceptions, adaptations and modifications as appear to Her to be necessary or expedient, to the Isle of Man, any of the Channel Islands or any colony.[323]

---

[322] Inserted by the Terrorism Act 2006, s. 31(1), (6).

[323] See the Intelligence Services Act 1994 (Channel Islands) Order 1994, SI 1994/2955; the Intelligence Services Act 1994 (Dependent Territories) Order 1995, SI 1995/752, as amended by SI 1996/2896.

● Regulation of Investigatory Powers Act 2000

59. Intelligence Services Commissioner

(1) The Prime Minister shall appoint a Commissioner to be known as the Intelligence Services Commissioner.

(2) Subject to subsection (4), the Intelligence Services Commissioner shall keep under review, so far as they are not required to be kept under review by the Interception of Communications Commissioner—

    (a) the exercise by the Secretary of State of his powers under sections 5 to 7 of the Intelligence Services Act 1994 (warrants for interference with wireless telegraphy, entry and interference with property etc.);

    (b) the exercise and performance by the Secretary of State, in connection with or in relation to—

        (i) the activities of the intelligence services, and

        (ii) the activities in places other than Northern Ireland of the officials of the Ministry of Defence and of members of Her Majesty's forces,

    of the powers and duties conferred or imposed on him by Parts II and III of this Act;

    (c) the exercise and performance by members of the intelligence services of the powers and duties conferred or imposed on them by or under Parts II and III of this Act;

    (d) the exercise and performance in places other than Northern Ireland, by officials of the Ministry of Defence and by members of Her Majesty's forces, of the powers and duties conferred or imposed on such officials or members of Her Majesty's forces by or under Parts II and III; and

    (e) the adequacy of the arrangements by virtue of which the duty imposed by section 55 is sought to be discharged—

        (i) in relation to the members of the intelligence services; and

        (ii) in connection with any of their activities in places other than Northern Ireland, in relation to officials of the Ministry of Defence and members of Her Majesty's forces.

(3) The Intelligence Services Commissioner shall give the Tribunal all such assistance (including his opinion as to any issue falling to be determined by the Tribunal) as the Tribunal may require—

    (a) in connection with the investigation of any matter by the Tribunal; or

    (b) otherwise for the purposes of the Tribunal's consideration or determination of any matter.

(4) It shall not be the function of the Intelligence Services Commissioner to keep under review the exercise of any power of the Secretary of State to make, amend or revoke any subordinate legislation....

NOTES

1. Provision for the making of complaints is made by Pt 4 of the Regulation of Investigatory Powers Act 2000. This establishes a Tribunal (known as the Investigatory Powers Tribunal) with jurisdiction over a range of matters, including proceedings against the intelligence services,[324] and provides for the appointment of an Intelligence Services Commissioner. He reviews the use of intrusive surveillance and property warrants, directed surveillance and the use of covert human intelligence sources. These replace separate Tribunals and

---

[324] See p. 590. In *A v B* [2008] EWHC 1512 (Admin), Collins J held that the Tribunal did not have exclusive jurisdiction to consider a challenge to the Security Services' refusal to authorise the publication of the memoirs of a former members.

Commissioners for the Security Service and for SIS and GCHQ.[325] Every member of an intelligence service, official of the department of the Secretary of State and every member of HM Forces must disclose to the Commissioner all documents and information he may require for his functions. The Commissioner must make an annual report to Parliament, to be laid before Parliament.

2. The Security Service Act 1996 extended the role of the Security Service to include that of acting in support of the activities of the police and other law enforcement agencies in the prevention and detection of serious crime. This was criticised by O'Higgins[326] who argued that they contravene the ECHR; reverse the fundamental constitutional principle established by *Entick v Carrington*[327] (by providing for executive warrants outside the national security context); are open to abuse, given the absence of a definition of 'serious crime,' with, for example, words limiting its scope to 'organised crime' as apparently intended by the Government ; and will lead to difficulties given the very different legislative regimes governing the Security Service and the police. The MI5 website notes that 'Work in this area was suspended in April 2006, following the launch of the Serious Organised Crime Agency and the need to redeploy Service resources in order to combat the increased threat to the UK from international terrorism.'[328]

3. In his tenth and final report as Security Service Commissioner[329] Stuart-Smith LJ reported that as of 31 December 1999 the Tribunal had considered 338 complaints. In 42 cases the complainants were the subject of a Security Service personal file and in 85 cases he or she had corresponded with the Service or had been the subject of a vetting disclosure. In no case had the tribunal made a determination in favour of the complainant. He had considered as Commissioner 141 property complaints over the ten years. A warrant had been issued in one case only. Aside from complaint cases, the Commissioner had discovered a small number of warrants authorised by a Secretary of State under the urgency procedure to be issued to an official of another department; s. 6(1)(b) of the 1994 Act, as originally drafted, contemplated such warrants being issued under the hand of a senior official 'of his department'. The Commissioner's view was that this meant that, although properly targeted, they were 'technically flawed' and he advised that they be reissued.[330] The Commissioner also discovered other errors.[331] He has concluded that it would not be in the public interest to publish statistics of warrants.[332] In interpreting s. 1(2) of the Act he noted that the term 'national security' was not defined in the Act, and was not limited to the matters listed 'in particular' in that subsection:[333]

> The concept of national security...is wider than this and is not easily defined; indeed it is probably undesirable that I attempt an all embracing definition. In my opinion it includes the defence of the realm and the government's defence and foreign policies involving the protection of vital national interests

---

[325] The two offices were held by Stuart Smith LJ from their inception, and he was succeeded by Simon Brown LJ.

[326] P. O'Higgins, *Current Law Statutes Annotated 1996*. See also P. Duffy and M. Hunt (1997) EHRLR 11.

[327] Above, p. 88.　　　[328] www.mi5.gov.uk/output/Page52.html.

[329] Report for 1999 (Cm 4779), para. 37.　　　[330] Ibid., paras 25–28.

[331] Ibid., para. 43: (1) an operational team deployed outside the target location specified in the property warrant: 'an unauthorised intrusion had clearly occurred'; (2) operation continued after warrant was cancelled where paperwork was delayed: 'all product received in this unwarranted period has been destroyed.' See also Cm 4365, paras 14–18.

[332] 1990 Report, paras 12 and 14: 1999 Report, para. 18; IS Commissioner 2006 Report (2007–08 HC 253), para. 32.

[333] Ibid., para. 10.

in this country and abroad. In this regard I would draw a distinction between national interests and the interests, which are not necessarily the same, of the government of the day. What is a vital national interest is a question of fact and degree, more easily recognised when being considered than defined in advance.

In his 1992 Report, Stuart-Smith LJ noted that, while being unable to be categorical, it was his opinion that unauthorised operations were not undertaken. His reasons were:[334]

First, I believe that very tight control over such operations as are conducted is exercised by those in managerial positions in the Service. Secondly, technical operations of this kind are complex and expensive in money and human resources; it is unlikely that such resources would be squandered on unauthorised as opposed to authorised operations. Thirdly, such is the complexity of most technical operations that it would not be feasible to conceal from the management and colleagues the number of people, use of equipment and time which would need to be deployed on such unauthorised activity. Fourthly, if the target is a legitimate one within the functions of the Service, there should be no difficulty in obtaining a warrant: the Service can have no interest or reason to conduct unauthorised operations which, if discovered, would give rise to possible legal action and certain scandal.

He was also of the view that the internal application procedure worked effectively, involving a number of checks at senior level, both within the Service and in the Warrantry Department, before submission to the Home Secretary or the Secretary of State for Northern Ireland.[335] His working methods over the years included the examination of security files relating to warrants, the examination of the product of operations and interviews with officers of the Service. Reports as Commissioner under the 1994 Act similarly revealed no case where a complaint was upheld.[336]

Subsequent reports of the Intelligence Services Commissioner[337] reveal a similar pattern. 'Errors' noted have included taking emergency action outside the terms of a property warrant;[338] retrieving rubbish from a bin on the forecourt of commercial premises without a property warrant or the informed consent of a senior company official;[339] the absence of valid a authorisation or warrant in respect of surveillance and interference with property;[340] and an unauthorised and unintended interference with property.[341] The one complaint upheld so far by the Investigatory Powers Tribunal[342] did not relate to the agencies reviewed by the Commissioner.[343]

---

[334] Cm 2174, para. 8: reaffirmed Cm 4002, para. 27; cf. IS Commissioner 2003 Report (2003–04 HC), para. 29: 'In the difficult and dangerous world in which we live there are more than enough legitimate targets for the various intelligence agencies to focus upon and therefore little if any temptation for them to seek to engage upon inappropriate operations.'

[335] Report for 1999 (Cm 4779), paras 7–13.   [336] Cm 3288, 3677, 3975, 4361.

[337] The first was Simon Brown LJ, subsequently Lord Brown of Eaton-under-Heywood. He was succeeded by Sir Peter Gibson from 1 April 2006. The report from 2001 can be found at www.intelligence.gov.uk/accountability/commissioners_and_tribunal/reports.aspx.

[338] 2001 Report (2001–02 HC 1244), para. 35: 'I am convinced that minimum action was taken and that, while unauthorised, it was both necessary and proportionate'. (The action was presumably unlawful: Ed.)

[339] 2002 Report (2002–03 HC 1048), para. 37: 'It is difficult to imagine a more technical and less serious breach'; no destruction order made.

[340] 2004 Report, 2004–05 HC 548, para. 45. Internal procedures were tightened up.

[341] Ibid. A property warrant was subsequently obtained. See also the 2005/06 Report (2006–07 HC 314), para. 39: 12 surveillance and warrants errors, 'in good faith'.

[342] See p. 590.

[343] 2005/06 Report, para. 38.

4. The reception of the Security Service Act 1989 and the Intelligence Services Act 1994 has generally been critical.[344] Among the criticisms of the 1989 Act made by Leigh and Lustgarten,[345] were:

(a) The broad definition of 'subversion' reflected in s. 1(2): 'Actions intended to overthrow or undermine parliamentary democracy by political, industrial or violent means.' This was based on, but even broader than a definition given by Lord Harris when a Home Office Minister in a House of Lords debate:

activities which threaten the safety or wellbeing of the state, and are intended to undermine or overthrow parliamentary democracy by political, industrial or violent means.[346]

Leigh and Lustgarten argue that this is unacceptably broad given the inherent rightwing bias of security agencies.[347] While 'subversion' does not at present account for any of the Service's work[348] the involvement of the Service and Special Branch in the past in the surveillance of such bodies as the NCCL[349] and in covert operations against the NUM in the miners' strike[350] is not reassuring.[351]

(b) Lack of clarity in the arrangements for ministerial responsibility and control.[352] The Act failed to acknowledge the central place of the Prime Minister in the security and intelligence scheme, and left unclear the extent to which the Director-General may be given direct orders and the extent to which, conversely, ministers should be consulted by the Director-General. See now note 9, below.

(c) Absence of any form of parliamentary oversight, or even a non-parliamentary oversight committee comprising privy councillors.[353] See now note 12, below.

(d) The broad legal powers conferred by s. 3 (see now ss. 5, 6 of the 1994 Act).[354] Warrants are issued by the Secretary of State rather than a judicial officer; unlike under PACE there are no privileged or exempted categories of information;[355] and there are no requirements as to the degree of detail required in warrant applications.

The section amounts to statutory authorisation of ministerial general warrants for reasons of state necessity of the kind which the common law disapproved in the celebrated case of *Entick v Carrington.*[356]

---

[344] On the 1989 Act, see I. Leigh and L. Lustgarten (1989) 52 MLR 801; P. Birkinshaw, *Reforming the Secret State* (1990), pp. 34–43. On the 1994 Act, see J. Wadham (1994) 57 MLR 916; M. Supperstone [1994] PL 329.

[345] (1989) 52 MLR 801.

[346] 357 HL Deb, 26 February 1975, col. 947; endorsed by the Home Secretary, Merlin Rees, 947 HC Deb, 6 April 1978, col. 618: see R J. Spjut (1979) 6 BJLS 254.

[347] See (1989) 52 MLR 801, 805–809.

[348] Above, p. 832.   [349] Above, pp. 831–832.

[350] See S. Milne, *The Enemy Within: MI5, Maxwell and the Scargill Affair* (1994).

[351] See also the accounts, from an earlier era, of the surveillance of the Communist Party of Great Britain, the National Unemployed Workers Movement and the NCCL: R. Thurlow, *The Secret State* (1994), Chap. 5 ('Reds in the Bed'); 'British Fascism and State Surveillance 1934–45 (1988) 3 Intelligence and National Security 77; and '"A Very Clever Capitalist Class". British Communism and State Surveillance 1939–45' (1997) 12 Intelligence and National Security; I.J. Morgan, *Conflict and Order* (1987), Chap. 8 ('The Police and the Unemployed Marchers. 1918-1939'). A range of files of historical interest have now been placed in the public domain: see www.mi5.gov.uk.

[352] (1989) 52 MLR 801 at 810–814.   [353] Ibid., pp. 814–822.

[354] Ibid., pp. 822–828.   [355] See above, pp. 172–192.

[356] Above, p. 88.

It is also uncertain whether the royal prerogative may continue as a source of legal power for the Service (cf. *R v Secretary of State for the Home Department, ex p Northumbria Police Authority*).[357]

(e) The inadequacy of the complaints mechanism.[358] Particular difficulties include how a person will know whether he has been 'bugged, burgled or investigated' (Service personnel who feel they have been asked to behave improperly in this way are *not* permitted to complain to the Tribunal or Commissioner); the complainant will not be given reasons for the Tribunal's decision; judicial review is excluded.

A further general cause for concern is these arrangements provide insufficient basis for satisfaction that appropriate systems are in place for the co-ordinated circulation and evaluation of intelligence in an effective and timely manner. Details of this work do not normally come into the public domain; an exception is provided by the Report of the Scott Inquiry[359] which revealed an 'appalling chronicle of intelligence failure'.[360]

5. One of the areas of concern has been the process by which the Service creates and maintains files on individuals. The current position[361] is that files can only be opened for the purposes of the Service's statutory functions. They are kept under continual review and are formally checked every year to ensure they remain up to date and relevant. Sixty-two per cent of the current file stock relates to individuals, who at some time since 1909 have been the subject of enquiry or investigation. Ten per cent of these are open for active investigation; the rest are closed and scheduled for destruction or have been converted to microfilm. Staff cannot make enquiries about the subjects of these files. They may access microfilmed files only with specific authority where necessary in the course of their work or for a specific research purpose. Records must be kept of enquiries made about a complainant, or if any disclosure made for vetting purposes, since December 1989, so that they can be provided to the Tribunal. There are also arrangements for the transfer of records of historical interest to the Public Record Office. Between 1909 and the early 1970s, over 175,000 files were destroyed as they became obsolete following a major contraction in the Service; from the early 1990s, a further 200,000 files have been destroyed. An individual may have a right under the Data Protection Act 1998 to discover whether personal data is held about him or her. The Service considers on a case-by-case basis whether exemption from the DPA is required and justified.[362] Where the Secretary of State certifies that the national security exemption applicable, this provides conclusive proof that this is required. An appeal lies to the Information Tribunal (National Security Appeals Panel).[363]

6. In *R v Security Service Tribunal, ex p Hewitt*,[364] Kennedy J refused to hold that the retention of records by the Service necessarily meant that there was no 'discontinuance' of 'inquiries', giving the tribunal jurisdiction under the 1989 Act, Sch. 1, para. 9, to deal with the question whether files on the applicants were still open and in the possession of the Service. His Lordship refused leave to apply for judicial review, having accepted 'for today's purposes' that it is arguable that in certain circumstances the court could entertain such

---

[357] [1988] 1 All ER 556.   [358] (1989) 52 MLR 801, 828–835.

[359] *Export of Defence Equipment and Dual-Use Goods to Iraq and Related Prosecutions* (1995–96 HC 115). See R. Austin (ed.), *Iraqgate: The Constitutional Implications of the Matrix-Churchill Affair* (1996); A. Tomkins, *The Constitution After Scott* (1998) [1996] PL Autumn issue.

[360] Tomkins, op. cit., p. 130.   [361] See www.mi5.gov.uk.

[362] Cf. *Baker v Secretary of State for the Home Department* (2001) *Telegraph*, 9 October, Information Tribunal (blanket exemption certificate for the Security Service held unlawful).

[363] See *Your right under the Data Protection Act 1998. Subject access requests to the security and intelligence agencies*: www.mi5.gov.uk/files/pdf/DPA_leaflet.pdf.

[364] Unreported, 14 February 1992.

an application notwithstanding s. 5(4) of the 1989 Act (which provided that decisions of the Tribunal and Commissioner '(including decisions as to their jurisdictions) shall not be subject to appeal or liable to be questioned in any court').

In *R v Security Service Tribunal, ex p Clarke*,[365] the Court of Appeal rejected C's application for leave to move for judicial review of the Tribunal's decision to reject a complaint by her that the Service had infringed 'every single one of her human rights'. The court held that s. 5(4) was an 'insuperable bar' and there was no requirement for the Tribunal to give reasons, except in accordance with the Act. At first instance, Sullivan J had held that even if s. 5(4) did not apply in a case of fraud or bad faith, there was no evidence of that whatsoever. The equivalent of s. 5(4) is s. 67(8) of the Regulation of Investigatory Powers Act 2000.[366]

7. In three cases, the European Commission of Human Rights has rejected as inadmissible complaints of breaches of Arts 8 and 13 ECHR holding that the structure of the 1989 Act was sufficiently certain for interference with private life arising from surveillance to be 'in accordance with the law' and necessary in a democratic society in the interests of national security under Art. 8 ECHR.[367] It took a similar view in respect of the regime established by the Interception of Communications Act 1985.[368]

8. Given the absence, prior to the 1989 Act, of any specific legal powers, the Security Service has in practice operated in conjunction with the Special Branches attached to each police force. According to the *Guidelines on Special Branch Work in Great Britain*:[369]

> Special Branches…acquire and develop intelligence to help protect the public from national security threats, especially terrorism and other extremist activity.

They are part of local police forces under the direction of the chief officer, but their primary function is covert intelligence work in relation to national security and 'they should not be diverted from this unless absolutely necessary'. National strategy is developed by the Association of Chief Police Officers Forum on Terrorism and Allied Matters (ACPO/TAM) and there is a National Co-ordinator of Special Branch appointed by ACPO. There are also National Co-ordinators for Ports Policing and Counter Terrorism Investigation (the latter being the head of the Metropolitan Police Anti-Terrorist Branch). In London, Special Branch and the Anti-Terrorist Branch were merged in a new Counter Terrorism Command (S015) in 2006.[370]

9. The Intelligence Services Act 1994 put the Secret Intelligence Service (sometimes known as MI6) and GCHQ on the same statutory footing as the Security Service. Points (4) and (5) made by Leigh and Lustgarten in relation to the 1989 Act (see note 4) remain relevant here. However, there has been some clarification of the arrangements for ministerial responsibility,[371] and some provision for external oversight (see n.11). The Prime Minister is

---

365 Unreported, 20 May 1998.   366 Above, p. 590.

367 See *Esbester v UK* (App. No. 18601/91, 2 April 1993), *Redgrave v UK* (App. No. 20271/92. 1 September 1993); and *Hewitt and Harman v UK* (App. No. 20317/92, 1 September 1993) (a further application), discussed by Stuart-Smith LJ in his 1993 Report (Cm 2523).

368 *Christie v UK* App. No. 21482/93, 27 June 1994.

369 Home Office, Scottish Executive Northern Ireland Office, March 2004. On the historical background see R. Allason, *The Branch: A History of the Metropolitan Police Special Branch 1883–1983* (1983); and B. Porter, *The Origins of the Vigilant State* (1987).

370 www.met.police.uk/so/counter_terrorism.htm.

371 See the booklet on the *Central Intelligence Machinery* published by HMSO in 1993 replaced by a document on *National Intelligence Machinery* in 2000, the most recent edition of which was published in November 2006: see www.intelligence.gov.uk.

responsible for intelligence and security matters overall, supported by the Cabinet Secretary, and the Head of Security, Intelligence and Resilience who acts as Security Adviser to the PM.[372] The Home Secretary is responsible for the Security Service, the Foreign Secretary for SIS and GCHQ and the Secretary of State for Defence for the Defence Intelligence Staff. There is a Ministerial Committee on the Intelligence Services (CSI),[373] assisted by the Permanent Secretaries' Committee on the Intelligence Service (PSIS). The Joint Intelligence Committee (JIC), based in the Cabinet Office, sets the UK's national intelligence requirements and produces a weekly survey on intelligence. It includes senior officials and the heads of the three services. Its chairman, the Head of Intelligence Assessment, has direct access to the Prime Minister. The Joint Terrorism Analysis Centre (JTAC) was established in 2003 as a mechanism for analysing all-source intelligence on the activities, intentions and capabilities of international terrorists. The Head of JTAC is accountable to the DG of the Security Service.

The existence of GCHQ was formally acknowledged by the Prime Minister after the Prime affair.[374] The decision to ban trade unionism at GCHQ led to litigation that was ultimately unsuccessful[375] and the dismissal of some employees.[376] The ban was lifted by the Labour Government in 1997.

Section 7 of the 1994 Act is the 'statutory equivalent of James Bond's "licence to kill"'.[377]

10. It was formerly government policy to prevent access to industrial (now employment) tribunals by members of the intelligence services. This was changed in 1996 so that cases were reviewed on a case-by-case basis to see whether national security considerations could be met by measures short of a certificate under (ultimately) s. 193 of the Employment Rights Act 1996 (as originally enacted) excluding the individual from bringing tribunal proceedings. This power has now been repealed.[378] Members of the intelligence services are, however, expressly excluded from bringing proceedings under Part IVA and s. 47B of the 1996 Act (whistleblowing) and from rights under ss. 10–13 of the 1999 Act in respect of the right to be accompanied at disciplinary or grievance hearings.[379]

11. The nationality rules for employment by the intelligence services have been relaxed. An applicant or employee must (as before) be a British citizen and hold no other citizenship and at least one parent must be British or have substantial ties with the UK.[380]

12. The Intelligence Services Act 1994 also introduced an element of independent oversight (the Intelligence and Security Committee). The Government did not accept a proposal by the Home Affairs Select Committee that it should provide oversight, and

---

[372] For two years, the positions of security adviser to the PM and Chair of the JIC were combined in the Office of Permanent Secretary, Intelligence, Security and Resilience (held by Sir Richard Mottram) but this was criticised as creating a conflict of interests and the post separated in 2007 see 'Security Structures in the Cabinet Office' New Release CAB/067–07, 25 July 2007.

[373] This met in December 2003 for the first time since 1995, a step welcomed by the ISC (Annual Report, 2003–04), p. 31.

[374] See above, p. 786.

[375] *Council of Civil Service Unions v Minister for the Civil Service* [1985] AC 374.

[376] See S. Fredman and G.S. Morris, *The State as Employer* (1989), pp. 98–102; K.D. Ewing and C. Gearty, *Freedom under Thatcher* (1990), pp. 130–136: H. Canning and R. Norton-Taylor, *A Conflict of Loyalties: GCHQ 1984–1991* (1991).

[377] J. Wadham (1994) 57 MLR 916, 922, noting that 'the Minister has stated that: 'It is inconceivable that, *in ordinary circumstances*, ... the Secretary of State ... would authorise the use of lethal force' (emphasis supplied). HC Standing Committee E, col. 34, 3 March 1994.

[378] See above, pp. 795–796.

[379] 1996 Act, s. 193, substituted by the Employment Relations Act 1999, Sch. 8, para. 1; 1999 Act, s. 15.

[380] HC Deb, 5 February 1998, col. 753, written answer.

declined to respond in detail to the Committee's view that the Service in any event fell within its jurisdiction as an associated body of the Home Office.[381] Detailed provision for the Committee is made by Sch. 3. A member of the Committee holds office for the duration of the Parliament in which he is appointed, but must vacate office if he ceases to be an MP or member of the House of Lords or becomes a Minister, may be replaced by the Prime Minister or may resign. If the Committee seeks information from any of the heads of the intelligence services, he must either disclose it in accordance with arrangements approved by the Secretary of State, or inform the Committee that it cannot be disclosed (i) because it is sensitive information which in his opinion should not be made available, or (ii) because the Secretary of State has determined that it should not be disclosed. The Secretary of State may override the head of service's view under (i) if he 'considers it desirable in the public interest'.[382] He may not make a determination under (ii) 'on the grounds of national security alone', and, subject to that, 'he shall not make such a determination unless the information appears to him to be of such a nature that, if he were requested to produce it before a Departmental Select Committee of the House of Commons, he would think it proper not to do so' (para. 3(4)). Disclosures under para. 3 are to be regarded as disclosures necessary for the proper discharge of the functions of the respective services, for the purposes of the 1989 and 1994 Acts.[383] 'Sensitive information' is defined as:[384]

(a) information which might lead to the identification of, or provide details of, sources of information, other assistance or operational methods available to the Security Service, the Intelligence Service or GCHQ;

(b) information about particular operations which have been, are being or are proposed to be undertaken in pursuance of any of the functions of those bodies; and

(c) information provided by, or by an agency of, the Government of a territory outside the United Kingdom where that Government does not consent to the disclosure of the information.

It will be noted that while the Committee is comprised of Members of Parliament, it is appointed by and responsible to the Prime Minister, although its reports are to be laid before Parliament in the same way as those of the Tribunals and Commissioners under the 1989 and 1994 Acts. The members are to be notified under s. 1(1)(b) of the Official Secrets Act 1989.[385] It is not clear why the Committee's access to information should be more restricted than the Commissioners.[386] The current chairman is Margaret Beckett MP. Her predecessors were Tom King MP, Ann Taylor MP, and Paul Murphy MP.

These arrangements may be compared with those in other jurisdictions. In Canada, the domestic Security Service was put on a statutory basis by the Canadian Security Intelligence Service Act 1984, with oversight provided by an Inspector-General and a Security Intelligence Review Committee comprising Privy Councillors who arc not members of the Senate or the House of Commons. The Australian Security Intelligence Organisation Act 1956 (Cth) put ASIO on a statutory basis. In 1986, two oversight mechanisms were established. The Inspector-General of Intelligence and Security's remit includes inquiry

---

[381] See the 1st Report of the HAC. 1992–93 HC 265, *Accountability of the Security Service,* and Government Reply (Cm 2197, 1993).

[382] Para. 3(3).   [383] Para. 3(5).   [384] Para. 4.

[385] Above, p. 771. See J. Wadham (1994) 57 MLR 926–927.

[386] See J. Wadham, op. cit., at p. 926. Thus far it has refused access on one matter: ISC Annual Report, 2006–07, p. 36.

into ASIO's compliance with the law, ministerial directions and human rights, and the propriety of their activities. The Parliamentary. Joint Committee on ASIO comprises seven members, with a majority of government members, and a majority from the House of Representatives, appointed after consultation with the leaders of each political party represented in Parliament. The latter development was controversial, but the Committee's powers are circumscribed.[387]

It is difficult to judge the effectiveness of this Committee given that it operates within the 'ring of secrecy' and its published reports are edited. It has been criticised for its limited comments on the Scott Inquiry's report on intelligence deficiencies.[388] However, it has been energetic, has addressed a wide range of topics and has included Parliamentarians of recognised independence of mind. It has appointed an Investigator to assist with its work. The Director General of the Security Service has indicated that on occasions, he felt able to go further than the law required in terms of providing information to the Committee.[389] Not all of its recommendations have been palatable to the Government. For example, it reported[390] that it was not satisfied with the Government's response to its Report on *Iraqi Weapons of Mass Destruction* in 2003.[391]

The Home Affairs Committee[392] has described the ISC as a 'great step forward over previous arrangements in providing democratic accountability'. Its reports 'have shed light on areas of Security Service activity which hitherto had lain in darkness'. However, it should be replaced by a special Parliamentary select committee. While the differences between these two models were small, a change would address 'the absence of openness and of an overt independence in the present system'. The Government 'was not convinced that there is a strong case for change in the fundamental structure of these arrangements now', notwithstanding that some of its members took the other view when in opposition.[393] Substantial reforms were, however, proposed subsequently in the White Paper, *The Governance of Britain—Constitutional Renewal*.[394] In advance of legislation, the appointment procedure would be amended to enable the full participation of Parliament, with a process similar to that for Joint Select Committee; public briefings would be arranged where possible; the post of investigator should be revived; debates in the House would be opened by the Chair of the Committee or the senior Lords Committee member.

13. The Intelligence and Security Committee must be distinguished from the Security Commission, a body that advises the Prime Minister, normally on breaches of security.[395]

---

[387] See H.P. Lee (1989) 38 ICLQ 890; Lustgarten and Leigh, op. cit., pp. 455–458; H. Barnett. 'Legislation-based National Security Services: Australia' (1994) 9 Intelligence and National Security 287. On Canada's arrangements, see Lustgarten and Leigh, op. cit., pp. 458–466; A. Goldsmith [1985] PL 39; J.LI.J. Edwards (1985) 5 OJLS 143; M. Rankin (1986) 36 UTLJ 249; S. Farson [1992] PL 377 and (2000) 15(2) Intelligence and National Security 225.

[388] A. Tomkins, *The Constitution After Scott* (1998), pp. 159–162.

[389] Cited by Date Campell-Savours MP (a Committee member), HC Deb, 29 March 2001, col. 1154.

[390] Annual Report, 2003–04 (Cm 6240, 2004), p. 25.

[391] Cm 5972, 2003; Government Response, Cm 6118, 2004. For criticisms of the UK's involvement in rendition, see Cm 7171, 2007, and Government Responses, Cm 7172, 2007.

[392] Third Report, 1998–99 HC 291, *Accountability of the Security Service*.

[393] Government Reply (Cm 4588, 2000).

[394] Cm 7342, 2008, paras 235–244.

[395] See I. Leigh and L. Lustgarten, 'The Security Commission: Constitutional Achievement or Curiosity?' [1991] PL 215 and Lustgarten and Leigh, op. cit., pp. 476–491. It last reported in 2004 on the events concerning the obtaining by a *Mirror* reporter of a job as a footman at Buckingham Palace (Cm 6177, 2004).

7. ACCESS TO INFORMATION

There has for many years been pressure for the creation of a general public right of access to official information.[396] There has been a steady increase in the number of specific rights of access created by legislation.[397] In 1994, the Conservative Government introduced a new *Code of Practice on Access to Government Information*.[398] Subject to an extensive list of exemptions, this committed departments and public bodies under the jurisdiction of the Parliamentary Commissioner for Administration to publish the facts and analysis behind the major policy proposals and decisions; to publish explanatory material on departments' dealings with the public; to give reasons for administrative decisions to those affected; to publish comparable information on the running of public services; and to release, in response to specific requests, information relating to policies, acts and decisions and other matters related to their areas of responsibility. There was no commitment that pre-existing documents, as distinct from information, would be released.

Many overseas jurisdictions enacted freedom of information laws, including the US, Sweden, Norway, Denmark, New Zealand, Australia and Canada. The UK has now followed suit, with the Freedom of Information Act 2000, which fully came into force from 1 January 2005.[399] This gives a general right of access to information held by public authorities, subject to many detailed exceptions. The key elements are these. Any person making a request in writing for information to a public authority[400] is entitled (a) to be informed in writing by the authority whether it holds information of the description specified in the request (the 'duty to confirm or deny'); and (b) if that is the case, to have that information communicated to him.[401] A very large number of bodies are covered, including local and central government, schools, universities, the police, the NHS and many other agencies boards and committees. The BBC is covered, 'in respect of information held for purposes other than those of journalism, art or literature.'[402] Where a public authority is listed only in relation to information of a specified description, nothing in Pts 1–5 of the Act applies to any other information held

---

[396] See, generally, P. Birkinshaw, *Freedom of Information* (3rd edn, 2001) and *Government and Information* (2nd edn, 2001); D. Vincent, *The Culture of Secrecy: Britain, 1832–1998* (1998); A. McDonald and G. Terrill, *Open Government* (1998); J. Beatson and Y. Cripps (eds), *Freedom of Expression and Freedom of Information* (2000), Pt II.

[397] E.g. the Local Government (Access to Information) Act 1985; Access to Personal Files Act 1987; Access to Medical Reports Act 1988; Environment and Safety Information Act 1990; Access to Health Records Act 1990. See now the Data Protection Act 1998.

[398] Following the White Paper, *Open Government* (Cm 2990, 1993). See HC Research Paper 97/69.

[399] See the White Paper, *Your Right to Know* (Cm 3818, 1997); Public Administration Committee Report on *Your Right to Know* (1997–98 HC 398) and *Government Response* (1997–98 HC 1020); *Freedom of Information Consultation on Draft Legislation* (Cm 4355, 1999); Report of Select Committee on Draft FOI Bill, 27 July 1999; O. Gay, HC Research Paper 00/09; J. Macdonald et al., *Law of Freedom of Information* (2003); P. Coppell, *Information Rights* (2nd edn, 2007); J. Wadham et al., *Blackstone's Guide to the Freedom of Information Act 2000* (3rd edn, 2007).

[400] I.e. any body, person or office-holder listed in Sch. 1 or designated by order of the Secretary of State under s. 5, or publicly-owned company as defined by s. 6. To be added, a body or office must be established by the royal prerogative or legislation or by a minister or government department or Welsh ministers, the First Minister, or the Counsel General for Wales, appointments to it made by the Crown or a minister etc: s. 4.

[401] Sections 1(1)(a) and (b), 8.

[402] Sch. 1, Pt VI. See *BBC v Sugar* [2007] EWHC 905 (Admin), [2007] 4 All ER 518. (Information Commissioner entitled to hold that report on news coverage of the Middle East (following allegations of bias) was held for the purposes of journalism; the application of this expression was a matter of judgment for the Commissioner and not of jurisdictional fact; it was to be interpreted broadly rather than narrowly, and could extend beyond

by the authority.[403] These duties do not apply if (a) there is an absolute exemption, or[404] (b) in all the circumstances of the case the public interest in excluding the duty to confirm or deny or maintaining the exemption (as the case may be) outweighs the public interest in disclosure.[405] A fee is normally chargeable, there are time limits for responses, and there is an exemption or a right to charge a higher fee where the cost of compliance exceeds a specified limit.[406] There is no obligation to comply with a vexatious request, or, unless a reasonable interval has elapsed from compliance with the previous request, a repeated request.[407] There is a duty to provide advice and assistance to persons who propose to make, or have made, requests for information, so far as is reasonable.[408] Reasons must be given for the refusal of a request.[409]

(A) EXEMPTIONS

Part II sets out a long list of cases where information is exempt from disclosure and (except in the case of s. 21) the duty to confirm or deny does not apply.

These are:

s. 21 information reasonably accessible to applicant by other means;

s.22 information intended for future publication where it is reasonable that it should be withheld until then;

s. 23 information supplied by, or relating to bodies dealing with security matters;[410]

s. 24 Other information where exemption is required for the purpose of safeguarding national security;[411]

s. 26 (defence) where disclosure would, or would be likely to, prejudice (a) the defence of the British Islands or of any colony or (b) the capability, effectiveness or security of the armed forces;

s. 27 (international relations) where disclosure would, or would be likely to prejudice relations between the UK and any other state, or any international organisation or court, the interests of the UK abroad, or the promotion or protection by the UK of those interests, or if it is confidential information obtained from another State etc.;

s. 28 (relations within the UK) where disclosure would, or would be likely to prejudice relations between any UK administration (i.e. the UK Government, the Scottish

---

the collection and communication of news to include matters of assessment, quality control or management processes.) The Court of Appeal dismissed an appeal: [2008] All ER (D) 185 (Jan).

[403] Section 7(1). This is not confined to 'information' but extends to 'requests for information': *BBC v Sugar*, above, at para. [34].

[404] This applies only to ss. 21, 23, 32, 34, 36 (as regards information held by the House of Commons or House of Lords, 40 (mostly), 41 and 44: s. 2(3).

[405] Section 2(1), (2). In applying this test it is not necessary for the decision-maker to identify a specific public interest beyond the general public interest in the disclosure of information held by public authorities implicit in s. 1 and explicit in s. 19(3): *Office of Government Commerce v Information Comr* [2008] EWHC 774 (Admin), paras [68]–[71].

[406] Sections 9, 10, 12, 13. See the Freedom of Information and Data Protection (Appropriate Limit and Fees) Regulations 2004, SI 2004/3244.

[407] S. 14.   [408] S. 16.   [409] S. 17.

[410] The bodies are listed and include the Security Services, SIS, GCHQ, special forces, the various security tribunals, the Security Vetting Appeals Panel and the Serious and Organised Crime Agency.

[411] S. 24. A ministerial certificate that information was supplied etc. or that exemption is or was required as specified in s. 23 or 24 is conclusive evidence of that fact. The power can only be exercised by a Cabinet Minister or the Attorney-General: s. 25(a).

Administration, the Executive Committee of the Northern Ireland Assembly or the Welsh Assembly Government);

s. 29 (the economy) where disclosure would, or would be likely to prejudice the economic interests of the UK or any part of it or the financial interest of any UK administration;

s. 30 investigations and proceedings conducted by public authorities;

s. 31 (law enforcement) information not exempt by virtue of s. 30, if its disclosure under the Act would, or would be likely to, prejudice the prevention or detection of crime, the apprehension or prosecution of offenders, the administration of justice, tax assessment or collection, the operation of immigration controls, the maintenance of security and good order in prisons, the exercise of a range of related functions by a public authority, or any civil proceedings brought by a public authority for such purposes;

s. 32 (court records) various court records and documents and documents concerning an inquiry or arbitration;

s. 33 (audit functions) where disclosure would, or would be likely to prejudice the exercise by a public authority of audit functions in respect of other public authorities;

s. 34 (parliamentary privilege) where exemption is required to avoid an infringement of the privileges of either House;

s. 35 (formulation of government policy etc.) where information relates to the formation or development of government policy (including the policy of the Executive Committee of the NI Assembly and of the Welsh Assembly Government); ministerial communications, including Cabinet and Cabinet Committee proceedings; Law Officers' advice; the operation of any ministerial private office;[412]

s. 36 (prejudice to the effective conduct of public affairs) information held by a public authority if, in the reasonable opinion of a qualified person,[413] disclosure would or would be likely to prejudice the maintenance of collective ministerial responsibility, or the work of the Executive Committee of the Northern Ireland Assembly or the Cabinet of the Welsh Assembly Government; or to inhibit the free and frank provision of advice, or the free and frank exchange of views for the purposes of deliberation; or would otherwise prejudice, or would be likely otherwise to prejudice, the effective conduct of public affairs;

s. 37 (communications with Her Majesty etc. and honours) where information relates to communications with the Queen, other members of the Royal Family or the Royal Household or the conferment of any honour or dignity;

s. 38 (health and safety) where disclosures would, or would be likely to, endanger the physical or mental health or the safety of any individual;

s. 39 (environmental information) where the public authority holding the information is obliged by environment information regulations to make it available to the public in accordance with the regulations, or would be so obliged but for any exemption contained in the regulations;

---

[412] S. 35 does not create any presumption of a public interest in non-disclosure in respect of situations falling within it; it is for the decision-maker to identify whether there is such a public interest and, if there is, to balance it against the public interest in disclosure: *Office of Government Commerce v Information Comr* [2008] EWHC 774 (Admin), paras [72]–[79].

[413] Specified in s. 36(5) (e.g. any minister of the Crown in respect of a government department in the charge of a minister; the case of bodies such as local authorities, a minister or (if authorised by a minister) the authority).

s. 40 (personal information) information constituting personal data of which the applicant is the data subject or, otherwise, (broadly) where either disclosure to a member of the public would contravene data protection principles or the information is exempt from the data subject's right of access under the Data Protection Act 1998, by virtue of Pt 4 of that Act;[414]

s. 41 (information provided in confidence) where disclosure would be an actionable breach of confidence;

s. 42 information protected by legal professional privilege;

s. 43 (commercial interests) information which constitutes a trade secret or whose disclosure would, or would be likely to, prejudice the commercial interests of any person (including the public authority holding it);

s. 44 (prohibitions on disclosure) where disclosure (otherwise under the Act) by the public authority holding it is prohibited by or under any enactment,[415] is incompatible with any Community obligation, or would constitute or be punishable as a contempt of court.

(B) OTHER MATTERS

The Secretary of State may issue a code of practice in connection with the discharge of an authority's functions under Pt 1. The Lord Chancellor may issue a code of practice as to the keeping, management and destruction of records. Each public authority must maintain a publication scheme, and publish information in accordance with it. The Information Commissioner appointed under s. 18 must promote good practice,[416] and may give a 'practice recommendation' where it appears to him that it does not conform to the codes of practice.

(I) ENFORCEMENT

The enforcement process established by the Act provides for applications by a complainant to the Information Commissioner for a decision whether, in any specified respect, a request for information made by the complainant to a public authority has been dealt with in accordance with the requirements of Part I. The Commissioner must make a decision unless it appears to him that the complainant has not exhausted any complaints procedure provided in conformity with the Code of Practice under s. 45, that there has been undue delay in making the application, or that the application is frivolous or vexatious or has been withdrawn or abandoned. The Commissioner must either: (a) notify the complainant that he has not made any decision as a result of the application, and why; or (b) serve a 'decision notice' on the complainant and the public authority. If he finds that the authority has failed to communicate information, or to provide confirmation or denial, where required by s. 1(1), or has failed to comply with any of the requirements of ss. 11–17, the decision notice must specify the steps to be taken and the period within which they must be taken. The Commissioner may obtain information about a public authority's practice by serving an 'information notice'. If he is satisfied that a public authority has failed to comply with

---

[414] Accordingly, access to personal data is governed by the 1998 Act.

[415] See *Secretary of State for the Home Department v British Union for the Abolition of Vivisection* [2008] EWHC 892 (QB) (disclosure of information requested in respect of licence applications under the Animals (Scientific Procedures) Act 1986 held to be prohibited by s. 24 of the 1986 Act which made it an offence for an official to disclose information which he knew or had reasonable grounds for believing to have been given in confidence. The Secretary of State has a general power to repeal or amend such an enactment for the purpose of removing or relaxing the prohibition: s. 75).

[416] Ss. 19, 20, 46, 47, 48.

any of the requirements of Part I he may serve an 'enforcement notice' requiring specified steps to be taken.[417] Accordingly, the Commissioner may take a different view from that of the authority on matters such as the balance of public interests. However, a decision or enforcement notice served on a government department, the Welsh Assembly Government or a public authority designated by an order made by the Secretary of State, and which relates to a failure: (a) to comply with s. 1(1)(a) in respect of information which falls within any provision of Part II stating that the duty to confirm or deny does not arise; or (b) to comply with s. 1(1)(b) in respect of exempt information, ceases to have effect if a ministerial certificate is given to the Commissioner within 20 days. This certificate must be signed by a Cabinet Minister, the Attorney-General, the First Minister for Wales or the First Minister and deputy First Minister in Northern Ireland acting jointly, and must state that he has on reasonable grounds formed the opinion that there was no failure under s. 1(1)(b).[418] Non-compliance with a decision notice requiring steps to be taken, an information notice or an enforcement notice may be certified by the Commissioner to the High Court for the court to deal with as if there had been a contempt of court.[419] The Commissioner may obtain a warrant from a Circuit judge authorising entry and inspection.[420] The Act confers no right of action in civil proceedings.[421]

The complainant or the public authority may appeal to the Information Tribunal[422] against a decision notice; an authority may appeal against an information or enforcement notice. The permitted grounds of appeal are that the notice is not in accordance with the law or (to the extent that the notice involved an exercise of discretion by the Commissioner that he ought to have exercised his discretion differently. A further appeal on a point of law lies to the High Court.[423] The Commissioner or any applicant affected may appeal to the Tribunal against a national security certificate.[424] A decision that a body is not a public authority for the purposes of the Act is only challengeable by judicial review and cannot be the subject of an appeal to the Tribunal.[425] The Tribunal has no power to compel disclosure of information not in the possession of the public authority, or which has not been requested by the complainant.[426]

(II) HISTORICAL RECORDS

A record becomes a 'historical record' at the end of a period of 30 years beginning with the calendar year following that in which it was created; all the records in one file are treated as having been created when the latest record was created. Information in a historical record cannot be exempt information by virtue of ss. 28, 30(1), 32, 33, 35, 36, 37(1)(a), 42 or 43. A 60-year period is specified in relation to s. 37(1)(b)(honours), and 100 years in relation to s. 31 (law enforcement). Information in a historical record cannot be exempt information by virtue of s. 21 or 22.[427]

---

[417] Ss. 50–52.   [418] S. 53.   [419] S. 54.   [420] S. 55, Sch. 3.

[421] S. 56.   [422] Formerly the Data Protection Tribunal. See Sch. 4.

[423] Ss. 57–59. Appeals are dealt with in accordance with procedures in the Data Protection Act 1998, Sch. 6, as amended by the 2000 Act, Sch 4, s. 61.

[424] S. 60. See ss. 23(2), 24(3).

[425] *BBC v Sugar* [2007] EWHC 905 (Admin), [2007] 4 All ER 518 (here, there is no 'decision notice'). The CA dismissed an appeal: [2008] All ER (D) 185 (Jan).

[426] *Office of Government Commerce v Information Comr* [2008] EWHC 774 (Admin), paras [104]–[109]. This does not prevent the Tribunal ordering disclosure of the gist or a summary of requested information under s. 50(4) ibid., para. [110].

[427] Ss. 62, 63, 64.

Where a PRO receives a request for information which relates to information which is, or if it existed would be, contained in a public record which has been transferred to it, and either the duty to confirm or deny is excluded (but not absolutely) or the information is exempt information (but not absolutely), the PRO must copy the request to the 'responsible authority' that transferred the record.[428] Unless that authority has designated information in a record as 'open information for the purposes of this section' the PRO must consult the authority before determining whether: (a) it falls within any provision of Part II relating to the duty to confirm or deny; or (b) is exempt information. Any question as to the application of s. 2(1)(b) or (2)(b) (where there is no absolute exemption) is to be determined by the responsible authority after consulting the Lord Chancellor.[429]

The new statutory regime replaces the regime of access to and closure of records in the Public Record Office which largely depended on the discretion of the Lord Chancellor. Records were not normally available for public inspection for 30 years; longer periods were prescribed for certain categories.[430]

(III) CRITICISMS

The FOI Bill was regarded as a disappointment by comparison with the White Paper and even the Code.[431] Concerns that remain with the provisions ultimately enacted include the fact that a Minister may have the last word on the public interest;[432] the number of exemptions that are class based, and the use of 'prejudice' rather than 'substantial harm' as a test where harm has to be established; and the existence of broadly drafted exemptions in such areas as the formulation of government policy and prejudice to the effective conduct of public affairs.[433]

There are many specific statutory provisions preventing the disclosure without lawful authority of information acquired from citizens.[434]

Government information may be protected from disclosure by a claim of public interest immunity.[435] In *Balfour v Foreign and Commonwealth Office*[436] the Court of Appeal held that while the court must always be vigilant to ensure that a claim of public interest immunity is raised only in appropriate circumstances and with appropriate particularity, once a Minister certifies that disclosure of documents poses a risk to national security, the court should not exercise its right to inspect those documents. The PII claims in the course of the prosecution of Matrix Churchill executives for deception in obtaining licences to export machine tool to Iraq, for use in armaments manufacture were particularly controversial.[437] The Labour Government has affirmed the approach of its predecessor that PII will not be asserted by the Government unless the relevant Minister believes that disclosure of a document or piece of 'information will cause real damage to the public interest. The test will

---

[428] S. 15.   [429] S. 66.

[430] See White Paper on *Open Government* (Cm 2290, 1993), Chap. 9.

[431] See O. Gay, HC Research Paper 99/61, pp. 38–40; CFI Press Release, 24 May 1999.

[432] S. 53.   [433] Ss. 35, 36.

[434] See Y. Cripps [1983] PL 600, 628–631, and the lists of statutes set out in Birkinshaw, *Government and Information* (1990), pp. 345–348. Annex B to the White Paper on *Open Government* lists over 200 provisions concerning disclosure of official information, most protecting third-party information.

[435] See P.P. Craig, *Administrative Law* (5th edn, 2003), Chap. 25; Simon Brown LJ [1994] PL 579; and A. Tomkins, *The Constitution after Scott* (1998), Chap. 5.

[436] [1994] 1 WLR 681.

[437] See G. Ganz (1993) 56 MLR 564, (1995) 58 MLR 417; T.R.S. Allan [1993] Crim LR 660; I. Leigh [1993] PL 630; and A. Tomkins, ibid., p. 650.

be applied rigorously. Where public interest immunity applies, Ministers will nevertheless make voluntary disclosure if they consider that the interests of justice outweigh the public interest in withholding the document or information in question. In all cases, a Minister's claim for public interest immunity is subject to the court's power to order disclosure. The approach will be followed in both criminal and civil cases.'[438]

It is argued that the 'right to know' cannot be an integral part of freedom of expression, on the ground that the freedom would then be claimed 'where there is no willing speaker'.[439] There are other views on this point.[440] Article 10(1) ECHR does not confer a general right to freedom of information against state bodies.[441] However, a right of access to such information as is necessary for enjoyment of the rights conferred by Art. 8 ECHR is implicit in that article.[442]

---

[438] HC Deb, 11 July 1997, cols 616–617, written answer by the Attorney-General, referring to a paper placed in the Libraries of the House on 18 December 1996.

[439] E. Barendt, *Freedom of Speech* (2nd edn), pp. 26–27.

[440] For a different view, see P. Bayne, 'Freedom of Information and Political Free Speech' in T. Campbell and W. Sadurski (eds), *Freedom of Communication*, Chap. 10 and the discussion by Sir Anthony Mason in J. Beatson and Y. Cripps (eds), *Freedom of Expression and Freedom of Information* (2000), Chap. 13.

[441] *Leander v Sweden* (1987) 9 EHRR 433; *Guerra v Italy* (1998) 26 EHRR 357, para. 53.

[442] *Guerra v Italy; McGinley and Egan v UK* (1998) 27 EHRR 1.

PART FIVE: Discrimination

13

ECHR PROTECTION FROM DISCRIMINATION: ARTICLE 14

1. INTRODUCTION

- **Article 14, European Convention**

The enjoyment of the rights and freedoms set forth in this Convention shall be secured without discrimination on any ground such as sex, race, colour, language, religion, political or other opinion, national or social origin, association with a national minority, property, birth or other status

- **Protocol 12 to the Convention**

The member States of the Council of Europe signatory hereto,

- Having regard to the fundamental principle according to which all persons are equal before the law and are entitled to the equal protection of the law;

- Being resolved to take further steps to promote the equality of all persons through the collective enforcement of a general prohibition of discrimination by means of the Convention for the Protection of Human Rights and Fundamental Freedoms signed at Rome on 4 November 1950 (hereinafter referred to as "the Convention");

- Reaffirming that the principle of non-discrimination does not prevent States Parties from taking measures in order to promote full and effective equality, provided that there is an objective and reasonable justification for those measures,

Have agreed as follows:

Article 1—General prohibition of discrimination

1 The enjoyment of any right set forth by law shall be secured without discrimination on any ground such as sex, race, colour, language, religion, political or other opinion, national or social origin, association with a national minority, property, birth or other status.

2 No one shall be discriminated against by any public authority on any ground such as those mentioned in paragraph 1…

NOTES

1. Article 14 provides only 'parasitic' protection against discrimination, requiring to be read in conjunction with one or more rights protected by the Convention or a Protocol thereto. By contrast Protocol 12, which entered into force on 1 April 2005, includes a free-standing prohibition on discrimination. The Explanatory Report to Protocol 12 states that 'The meaning of the term "discrimination" in Article 1 is intended to be identical to that in Article 14 of the Convention', but the 'general non-discrimination clause...extends beyond the "enjoyment of the rights and freedoms set forth in [the] Convention"' to cover, in particular, cases where a person is discriminated against:

i.   in the enjoyment of any right specifically granted to an individual under national law;

ii. in the enjoyment of a right which may be inferred from a clear obligation of a public authority under national law, that is, where a public authority is under an obligation under national law to behave in a particular manner;

iii. by a public authority in the exercise of discretionary power (for example, granting certain subsidies);

iv. by any other act or omission by a public authority (for example, the behaviour of law enforcement officers when controlling a riot).[1]

2. The UK Government has accepted that the Convention should contain a free-standing prohibition on discrimination, but has refused to sign the Protocol because its wording is regarded as too wide. Concern has been expressed, in particular, that the words 'rights set forth by law' might extend to rights included in international conventions to which the UK is not a party. Further, and in an objection which is odd on its face given the strict limits on positive action in domestic law (see pp. 940–50), on the basis that 'it does not make provision for positive measures'.[2] Not only has the European Court taken a permissive approach to positive action under Art. 14 (see further below), but the third recital of the preamble to Protocol 12 makes clear that 'measures [taken] in the measure provided that there is an objective and reasonable justification for them'. Further, according to the Explanatory Report: 'The fact that there are certain groups or categories of persons who are disadvantaged, or the existence of de facto inequalities, may constitute justifications for adopting measures providing for specific advantages in order to promote equality, provided that the proportionality principle is respected.'[3]

Protocol 12 has been ratified by 16 member states of the Council of Europe by December 2008 and signed by a further 21, but countries including Denmark, France, Sweden and the UK had neither signed nor ratified and the European Court has yet to reach any decisions on it.

2. APPLICATION OF ART. 14

● **Abdulaziz v United Kingdom** (1985) 7 EHRR 471

The case involved a challenge by women resident in the UK to immigration rules by which their husbands and fiancés were restricted from joining them in circumstances such that fiancées and wives of resident men would have been entitled to enter the UK. They challenged UK immigration rules under Arts 8 and 14.

---

[1] Paras 18 and 21–22.

[2] 617 HL Debs, 11 October 2000, col. WA37, response from Lord Bassam, Parliamentary Under-Secretary of State for the Home Office, to Lord Lester. Lord Bassam also made the surprising observation that Protocol 12 'does not follow the case law of the European Court of Human Rights in allowing objective and reasonably justified distinctions'. The availability of justification under Art. 14 has, however, been read into the provision rather than being evident on its face.

[3] Para. 16.

JUDGMENT

68 ... In the present case, the applicants have not shown that there were obstacles to establishing family life in their own or their husbands' home countries or that there were special reasons why that could not be expected of them...

69. There was accordingly no 'lack of respect' for family life and, hence, no breach of Article 8 taken alone.

70. The applicants claimed that, as a result of unjustified differences of treatment in securing the right to respect for their family life, based on sex, race and also—in the case of Mrs Balkandali—birth, they had been victims of a violation of Article 14 of the Convention, taken together with Article 8...

71. According to the Court's established case-law, Article 14 complements the other substantive provisions of the Convention and the Protocols. It has no independent existence since it has effect solely in relation to 'the enjoyment of the rights and freedoms' safeguarded by those provisions. Although the application of Article 14 does not necessarily presuppose a breach of those provisions—and to this extent it is autonomous—, there can be no room for its application unless the facts at issue fall within the ambit of one or more of the latter... The Court has found Article 8 to be applicable.... Although the United Kingdom was not obliged to accept Mr Abdulaziz, Mr Cabales and Mr Balkandali for settlement and the Court therefore did not find a violation of Article 8 taken alone... the facts at issue nevertheless fall within the ambit of that Article...

Article 14 also is therefore applicable...

NOTE

1. Article 14 adds value to the other Convention rights because it may be breached even where the right in conjunction with which it is read in a particular case is not.[4] The classic illustration is *Abdulaziz*. Other examples of cases in which breaches of Art. 14, but not of the substantive Convention right, have been found include *Sahin v Germany*,[5] which concerned discrimination against unmarried fathers in terms of access to children and *Gaygasuz v Austria*,[6] which concerned discrimination on grounds of nationality in access to a state benefit.[7] In *Reynolds v Secretary of State for Work and Pensions* Laws LJ, in the Court of Appeal,[8] summed up the effect of the jurisprudence as follows:

[34] ...one might readily construct an example where (say) free speech in some particular area is proscribed by the state in various instances. Grounds to justify the prohibition are then put forward by the state under art 10, para 2. In the example, let it be said that in each given instance taken alone the proscription is well justified under para 2 on the grounds put forward. However the grounds of justification thus advanced are more, or less, intrusive or onerous between instances and the difference is attributable to a prohibited discriminatory ground. In that case the fact of such differential justifications between classes (or persons) will offend art 14 unless the state can justify the difference or differences.

---

[4] This was recognised by the ECtHR in the first Art. 14 case: *Case 'Relating To Certain Aspects Of The Laws On The Use Of Languages In Education In Belgium' v Belgium (No. 2)* 1 EHRR 252, para. 9.

[5] (2003) 36 EHRR 765.

[6] (1997) 23 EHRR 364. Breach of Art. 1 Protocol 1 was not argued in *Gaygasuz* but, had it been, would inevitably have failed in light of the jurisprudence on Art. 1 Protocol 1 at the time.

[7] In *Fretté v France* (2004) 38 EHRR 21, *Petrovic v Austria* (1998) 33 EHRR 307 and *Van Der Mussele v Belgium* (1983) 6 EHRR 163 the Court accepted that treatment not breaching the relevant substantive provision fell within Art. 14, though it went on in each case to rule that the differential treatment was justifiable.

[8] [2003] 3 All ER 577.

[35] ...in connection with art 6 a complaint under art 14 may arise where it is said that upon any of these variables ['fairness, publicity, delay, independence, impartiality'] the state has applied a different standard to one class of persons compared to another, and done so on a prohibited discriminatory ground. A crude instance of arts 6/14 discrimination would thus arise if a legal system adopted a different rule for the admission of confession evidence for members of one class of society (or for members of a particular racial group) compared with the rule adopted for another. In the courts of ancient Athens the evidence of a slave was inadmissible *unless* he had been tortured.

[37] [citing Gaygusuz]...although the conditions of entitlement to a state benefit under a domestic legal scheme (and an applicant's failure to fulfil them)—as opposed to any conditions under which such a benefit might be *withdrawn*—could not in principle give rise to a claim under art 1P taken on its own, yet they could yield a good claim under art 14 taken with art 1P...

3. THE PROTECTED GROUNDS

● R (Clift) v Secretary of State for the Home Department [2007] 1 AC 484

Baroness Hale

51 ...Article 14 of the European Convention on Human Rights adds 'association with a national minority' to [the list of grounds protected by Art. 26 of the ICCPR]. The list is clearly non-exhaustive so that analogous grounds may be recognised as social conditions change. The most obvious example is sexual orientation.

52 ...The French text is even more open-ended from the English referring to 'toute autre situation' rather than 'other status'. So, was article 14 intended to be a general prohibition of discrimination in relation to the enjoyment of the Convention rights unless it could objectively be justified, with the specific grounds listed as a warning that discrimination on such grounds would be particularly difficult to justify? Or were the grounds and the reference to 'other status' intended to limit the kinds of classification which might be covered by the article?

53 The classic accounts of article 14 repeated time and time again in the Strasbourg case law do not specifically address this question...

56 Although the issue is not always addressed, when it is addressed it is clear from the Strasbourg case law that not every basis of distinction between different sorts of people is included in the list of prohibited grounds and residual category of 'other status'...

58 In the vast majority of Strasbourg cases where violations of article 14 have been found, the real basis for the distinction was clearly one of the proscribed grounds or something very close: race, sex, religion, marital or birth status, national origin, foreign residence, language, or sexual orientation. Unusually, in *Pine Valley Developments Ltd v Ireland* (1991) 14 EHRR 319, the court found a violation of article 14 without reference to a prohibited ground, but the point was not argued because the government was denying that the legislation drew the distinction complained of at all.

59 More instructive are the cases in which the basis of the discrimination has been held to fall outside the proscribed grounds. One example is different laws in different jurisdictional regions within the territory of a member state. Thus, it was not a difference in treatment on grounds of personal status for people in Scotland to be subject to the poll tax before people in England (*P v United Kingdom* (Application No 13473/87) (unreported) 11 July 1988) or for juvenile offenders in Scotland not to be entitled to the remission granted to juvenile offenders in England and Wales: *Nelson v United Kingdom* (1986) 49 DR 170.

60 Another example, pertinent to this case, is differences in the treatment of different criminal offences. In *Gerger v Turkey* (Application No 24919/94) (unreported) 8 July 1999, the court deduced from the fact

that people convicted of terrorist offences would be treated less favourably with regard to automatic parole 'that the distinction is made not between different groups of people, but between different types of offence, according to the legislature's view of their gravity': para 69. In *Budak v Turkey* (Application No 57345/00) (unreported) 7 September 2004, the court repeated the 'personal characteristic' test from *Kjeldsen* and held that a distinction in procedure and sentences for offences tried before the state security court from those tried before other courts was made, again, not between different groups of people but between different types of offence.

61 All of this is entirely consistent with the view taken by this House in *R (S) v Chief Constable of South Yorkshire Police* [2004] 1 WLR 2196. At para 48, Lord Steyn cited *Kjeldsen* and continued:

'the proscribed grounds in article 14 cannot be unlimited, otherwise the wording of article 14 referring to 'other status' beyond the well-established proscribed grounds, including things such as sex, race or colour, would be unnecessary. It would then preclude discrimination on any ground. That is plainly not the meaning of article 14.'

In that case it was held that the possession of fingerprints and DNA samples by the police was simply a matter of historical fact rather than the personal status or characteristics of the people who had supplied them.

62 In this case, it is plain, and now accepted by the Secretary of State, that a different parole regime for foreigners who are liable to deportation from that applicable to citizens or others with the right to remain here, falls within the grounds proscribed by article 14 and thus (subject to the ambit issue) requires object-ive justification. The same would surely apply to a difference in treatment based on race, sex or the colour of one's hair. But a difference in treatment based on the seriousness of the offence would fall outside those grounds. The real reason for the distinction is not a personal characteristic of the offender but what the offender has done.

NOTES

1. The decision in *R (S)*, referred to by Baroness Hale, was appealed to the European Court of Human Rights and fast-tracked direct to the Grand Chamber. In December 2008 that Court ruled that the retention of DNA samples from people not convicted of criminal offences breached Art. 8. It declined to consider the Art. 14 complaint.[9]

2. Protocol 12 was mentioned above. The Protocol was criticised by some because it did not expand the list of explicitly protected grounds, in particular to include sexual orientation, disability and age. The Explanatory Report to the Protocol defends the failure to add to the list of grounds expressly protected by Art. 14 as follows:

This solution was considered preferable over others, such as expressly including certain additional non-discrimination grounds (for example, physical or mental disability, sexual orientation or age), not because of a lack of awareness that such grounds have become particularly important in today's societies as com-pared with the time of drafting of Article 14 of the Convention, but because such an inclusion was consid-ered unnecessary from a legal point of view since the list of non-discrimination grounds is not exhaustive, and because inclusion of any particular additional ground might give rise to unwarranted *a contrario* inter-pretations as regards discrimination based on grounds not so included. It is recalled that the European Court of Human Rights has already applied Article 14 in relation to discrimination grounds not explicitly mentioned in that provision [citing, in particular, the decision in *Salgueiro da Silva Mouta v Portugal* on sexual orientation[10]].

---

[9] *S and Marper v UK*, Judgment of 4 December 2008 (Nos 30562/04 and 30566/04). Note, on protected grounds, the decision of the European Court in *Carson v UK*, Judgment of 4 November 2008 (No. 42184/05).
[10] [2001] 31 EHRR 47.

It is certainly clear from the *Clift* extract that the grounds protected by Art. 14 (and hence by Protocol 12) go well beyond those listed therein.

4. ESTABLISHING 'DISCRIMINATION'

(A) COMPARATOR-DRIVEN APPROACH

- **Lindsay v United Kingdom, App. No. 11089/84** (1987) 9 EHRR CD555

The applicants, who were married, challenged the fact that married couples were subject to less favourable tax rules than unmarried cohabiting couples. Having accepted that the complaint fell within the scope of Art. 1 Protocol 1 the Commission continued:

The applicants in the present case seek to compare themselves, a married couple, with a man and woman who receive the same income, but who live together without being married. The Commission is of the opinion that these are not analogous situations. Though in some fields, the *de facto* relationship of cohabitees is now recognised, there still exist differences between married and unmarried couples, in particular, differences in legal status and legal effects. Marriage continues to be characterised by a corpus of rights and obligations which differentiate it markedly from the situation of a man and woman who cohabit. The Commission accordingly concludes that the situation of the applicants is not comparable to that of an unmarried couple and that part of the application therefore does not enclose any appearance of a violation of Prot. No. 1 Art. 1 read in conjunction with Art. 14 of the Convention. It follows that this part of the application is manifestly ill-founded within the meaning of Art. 27(2) of the Convention.[11]

- **Paulik v Slovakia** (2008) 46 EHRR 10

The applicant challenged the fact that, whereas national law did not allow him to challenge paternity once it had been established by a court,[12] a mother could request that the state challenge paternity on her behalf as could a man whose paternity had been presumed rather than established by a court. The Government argued that the applicant could not be considered to be in an analogous situation for the purposes of Art. 14 of the Convention to those men whose paternity had not been conclusively established by final judicial decision. The Court disagreed.

JUDGMENT

54. The Court accepts that there may be differences between, on the one hand, the applicant and, on the other hand, the putative fathers and the mothers in situations where paternity is legally presumed but has not been judicially determined. However, the fact that there are some differences between two or more individuals does not preclude them from being in sufficiently comparable positions and from having sufficiently comparable interests. The Court finds that with regard to their interest in contesting a status relating to paternity, the applicant and the other parties in question were in an analogous situation for the purposes of art 14 of the Convention.

---

[11] See also *Van der Musselle v Belgium* (1983) 6 EHRR 163, upon which the Commission relied, *Stubbings v UK* (1996) 23 EHRR 213 (though see now on the question of substance *A v Hoare* [2008] UKHL 6, [2008] 2 WLR 311), and the subsequent decision of the Commission in *Shackell v UK* 27 April 2000, Application No. 45851/99.

[12] By means of a legal presumption arising from his relationship with the child's mother, in circumstances such that at the time when paternity was legally established no DNA testing had been undergone. This was later done and it was at this stage that he wished to challenge paternity but was prevented from so doing.

● **Burden v United Kingdom** (2008) 47 EHRR 38

The applicants were sisters who had always lived together and who owned significant property both jointly and individually. The estate of each was worth in excess of the threshold at which inheritance tax became payable at the relevant time. Inheritance tax does not apply as between married or civil partners who leave property to each other. The sisters complained that they had been discriminated against because inheritance tax did apply between them. The Government argued that the applicants could not claim to be in an analogous situation to a couple created by marriage or civil partnership while the applicants argued that they were, and that 'the very reason that [they] were not subject by law to the same corpus of legal rights and obligations as other couples was that they were prevented, on grounds of consanguinity, from entering into a civil partnership' and it was 'circular' for the Government to hold this against them.

JUDGMENT

62. The Grand Chamber commences by remarking that the relationship between siblings is qualitatively of a different nature to that between married couples and homosexual civil partners under the United Kingdom's Civil Partnership Act. The very essence of the connection between siblings is consanguinity, whereas one of the defining characteristics of a marriage or Civil Partnership Act union is that it is forbidden to close family members…The fact that the applicants have chosen to live together all their adult lives, as do many married and Civil Partnership Act couples, does not alter this essential difference between the two types of relationship…

65. As with marriage, the Grand Chamber considers that the legal consequences of civil partnership under the 2004 Act, which couples expressly and deliberately decide to incur, set these types of relationship apart from other forms of co-habitation. Rather than the length or the supportive nature of the relationship, what is determinative is the existence of a public undertaking, carrying with it a body of rights and obligations of a contractual nature. Just as there can be no analogy between married and Civil Partnership Act couples, on one hand, and heterosexual or homosexual couples who choose to live together but not to become husband and wife or civil partners, on the other hand (see *Shackell*), the absence of such a legally binding agreement between the applicants renders their relationship of co-habitation, despite its long duration, fundamentally different to that of a married or civil partnership couple. This view is unaffected by the fact that, as noted in paragraph 26 above, Member States have adopted a variety of different rules of succession as between survivors of a marriage, civil partnership and those in a close family relationship and have similarly adopted different policies as regards the grant of inheritance tax exemptions to the various categories of survivor; States, in principle, remaining free to devise different rules in the field of taxation policy.

66. In conclusion, therefore, the Grand Chamber considers that the applicants, as co-habiting sisters, cannot be compared for the purposes of Article 14 to a married or Civil Partnership Act couple. It follows that there has been no discrimination and, therefore, no violation of Article 14 taken in conjunction with Article 1 of Protocol No.1.

CONCURRING OPINION OF JUDGE DAVID THÓR BJÖRGVINSSON[13]

When Article 14 is applied, in essence two questions must be answered: first, whether there is a difference in treatment of persons in relevantly similar or analogous situations; secondly, if this is the case, whether the difference in treatment is justified…

---

13 Judge Bratza also preferred to deal with justification rather than focusing on comparators. This had been the approach of the Chamber also ((2007) 44 EHRR 51).

The reasoning of the majority, as presented in paragraphs 62–65 of the judgment, is in my view flawed by the fact that it is based on comparison of factors of a different nature and which are not comparable from a logical point of view. It is to a large extent based on reference to the specific legal framework which is applicable to married couples and civil partnership couples but which does not, under the present legislation, apply to the applicants as cohabiting sisters…

I believe that in these circumstances any comparison of the relationship between the applicants, on the one hand, and the relationship between married couples and civil partnership couples, on the other, should be made without specific reference to the different legal framework applicable, and should focus only on the substantive or material differences in the nature of the relationship as such. Despite important differences, mainly as concerns the sexual nature of the relationship between married couples and civil partner couples, when it comes to the decision to live together, closeness of the personal attachment and for most practical purposes of daily life and financial matters, the relationship between the applicants in this case has, in general and for the alleged purposes of the relevant inheritance tax exemptions in particular, more in common with the relationship between married or civil partnership couples, than there are differences between them. Despite this fact, the law prohibits them from entering into an agreement similar to marriage or civil partnership and thus take advantage of the applicable rules, including the inheritance tax rules. That being so, I am not convinced that the relationship between the applicants as cohabiting sisters cannot be compared with married or civil partner couples for the purposes of Article 14 of the Convention. On the contrary there is in this case a difference in treatment of persons in situations which are, as a matter of fact, to a large extent similar and analogous…

NOTES

1. In most cases the person seeking to rely on Art. 14 will have to establish that he or she has been treated less favourably than another person in the same material circumstances was or would have been. This approach has the virtue of simplicity in many cases in pinpointing the reason for the differential treatment complained of. Thus in *Fredin v Sweden* (1991) 13 EHRR 784, in which the applicants challenged the revocation of a licence as discrimination against them as independent operators of a gravel exploitation business in their region, the claim failed because they failed to provide evidence that they were similarly situated to any companies whose licences were not revoked. In other words, the differential treatment complained of by the applicants may have been attributable to factors other than the fact that they were independent contractors.[14] But comparators have come to play a different and, arguably, illegitimate role in the jurisprudence of the European Commission/Court and, latterly, the domestic courts.

2. This use of the comparator in *Lindsey* is problematic because it allows the precise ground of discrimination that is the basis of the challenge to block the discrimination claim, without any (explicit) requirement that the differential treatment be justified (see section 6 below). In a number of the cases in which the comparator test has been thus applied the European Court has suggested that any differential treatment was justified in any event.[15] But the technique puts the judicial 'horse before the cart' and results in only the most cursory consideration, if any, of the question of justification. It appeared to have fallen into disfavour in

---

[14] For a full discussion of this see A. McColgan, 'Cracking the Comparator Problem, 'Equal' Treatment and the Role of Comparisons' [2006] EHRLR 650.

[15] See, e.g., *Stubbings v UK*, n. 11 above.

recent years in a number of cases culminating in *Paulik v Slovakia*, above.[16] In *DH v Czech Republic*[17] the Court adopted a fluid approach to Art. 14, as it had done in *Thlimmenos v Greece*.[18] Both of those cases are considered below. But subsequently, in *Burden v United Kingdom*, above, the Grand Chamber used a formalistic, comparator-based approach to deny the applicants' claim. The majority and concurring opinions from that case illustrate neatly the formal and substantive approaches to the discrimination question.

3. Judge Thór Björgvinsson went on in *Burden* to conclude that the differential treatment complained of in this case was justified by the legitimate aims pursued by the protection afforded to marriage and civil partnership (the promotion of stable committed partnerships, whether heterosexual or homosexual) and the fact that all distinctions between taxpayers resulted in 'marginal situations and individual cases of apparent hardship or injustice', it being: 'primarily for the State to decide how best to strike the balance between raising revenue and pursuing social objectives'[19] and

each and every step taken [to extend the legal implications of marriage beyond its traditional scope], positive as it may seem to be from the point of view of equal rights, potentially has important and far reaching consequences for the social structure of society, as well as legal consequences, *i.e.* for the social security and tax system in the respective countries. It is precisely for this reason that it is not the role of this Court to take the initiative in this matter and impose upon the Member States a duty further to extend the applicability of these rules with no clear view of the consequences that it may have in the different Member States. In my view it must fall within the margin of appreciation of the respondent State to decide when and to what extent this will be done.

4. The justification of discrimination is further considered below. It should be noted here, however, that a strict comparator-based approach such as that evidenced in a number of the decisions discussed above is not of its nature applicable where *indirect* discrimination is at issue.[20] The jurisprudence of the European Court of Human Rights in this area was, until recently, noticeably absent,[21] and it is still in an early stage of development. Having said this, it is clear, as a result of the decision of the Grand Chamber in *DH v Czech Republic*,[22] that indirect discrimination can violate Art. 14. What is perhaps less clear is whether the discrimination there complained of was best characterised as direct or indirect at all, and whether that decision is better viewed as indicating a shift towards a less formalistic approach to discrimination, than adopting a rigid dual approach to 'direct' and 'indirect' discrimination.

---

[16] See, e.g., *Sidabras v Lithuania* (2006) 42 EHRR 6.

[17] (2008) 47 EHRR 3.

[18] (2001) 31 EHRR 15.

[19] The judge adopting the reasoning of the Chamber cited at para. 47 of the Grand Chamber's decision.

[20] *Direct* discrimination is generally characterised as comprising less favourable treatment on a protected ground, *indirect* discrimination as apparently neutral treatment whose *effect*, rather than *form* or *aim*, is to disadvantage persons of particular groups defined by reference to a protected ground, and which is not justified.

[21] In the *Belgian Linguistics* case the Court suggested that Art. 14 was concerned with the 'aim *and effects* of the measure under consideration' (emphasis added), though that decision was concerned with differential treatment, rather than disparate impact. In *Abdulaziz v UK* (1985) 7 EHRR 471, discussed above (section 2), the Court signally failed to apply the correct approach to indirect discrimination, accepting that a measure was justified on the bare ground that its racially discriminatory impact was not intended.

[22] N. 17 above.

(B) A NEW APPROACH TO DISCRIMINATION?

- **Thlimmenos v Greece** (2001) 31 EHRR 411

The applicant was convicted of a felony on the basis that, as a Jehovah's Witness, he was a conscientious objector and had refused to wear his military uniform during a period of national service. Some five years later he was refused access to the chartered accountancy profession because he had been convicted of a felony.

JUDGMENT

33. The court notes that the applicant did not complain about his initial conviction for insubordination. The applicant complained that the law excluding persons convicted of a felony from appointment to a chartered accountant's post did not distinguish between persons convicted as a result of their religious beliefs and persons convicted on other grounds. The applicant invoked art 14 of the convention taken in conjunction with art 9 . . .

41. The court notes that the applicant was not appointed a chartered accountant as a result of his past conviction for insubordination consisting in his refusal to wear the military uniform. He was thus treated differently from the other persons who had applied for that post on the ground of his status as a convicted person. The court considers that such difference of treatment does not generally come within the scope of art 14 in so far as it relates to access to a particular profession, the right to freedom of profession not being guaranteed by the convention.

42. However, the applicant does not complain of the distinction that the rules governing access to the profession make between convicted persons and others. His complaint rather concerns the fact that in the application of the relevant law no distinction is made between persons convicted of offences committed exclusively because of their religious beliefs and persons convicted of other offences. In this context the court notes that the applicant is a member of the Jehovah's Witnesses, a religious group committed to pacifism, and that there is nothing in the file to disprove the applicant's claim that he refused to wear the military uniform only because he considered that his religion prevented him from doing so. In essence, the applicant's argument amounts to saying that he is discriminated against in the exercise of his freedom of religion, as guaranteed by art 9 of the convention, in that he was treated like any other person convicted of a felony although his own conviction resulted from the very exercise of this freedom. Seen in this perspective, the court accepts that the 'set of facts' complained of by the applicant—his being treated as a person convicted of a felony for the purposes of an appointment to a chartered accountant's post despite the fact that the offence for which he had been convicted was prompted by his religious beliefs— 'falls within the ambit of a convention provision', namely art 9 . . .

44. The court has so far considered that the right under art 14 not to be discriminated against in the enjoyment of the rights guaranteed under the convention is violated when states treat differently persons in analogous situations without providing an objective and reasonable justification . . . However, the court considers that this is not the only facet of the prohibition of discrimination in art 14. The right not to be discriminated against in the enjoyment of the rights guaranteed under the convention is also violated when states without an objective and reasonable justification fail to treat differently persons whose situations are significantly different . . .

NOTE

1. The seeds of what might be called a 'substantive' approach were sewn in the *Thlimmenos* case. The ECJ, which found that Art. 14 had been violated, did not use the term 'indirect discrimination', and it is arguable that the approach there adopted is more radical in its impact than the orthodox approach to indirect discrimination. Under the latter, where it

is established that a policy or practice etc.[23] has a disproportionately negative impact on a group defined by reference to a protected ground, that policy or practice etc. can continue to be applied if it is objectively justified[24] across the board, and despite its negative impact on the particular claimant. So, for example, if required working hours disadvantage religious Jews who cannot, consistent with working these hours, be at home in time for Sabbath on a Friday night in winter, the question on an indirect discrimination analysis is whether those hours are justified notwithstanding the fact that they serve to disadvantage religious Jewish people. If the general impact on religious Jews is slight (because few are to be found in the industry or area), or if the economic imperative for inflexible working hours in the particular industry, occupation or workplace is strong, the policy may be justified notwithstanding its devastating impact on a particular observant Jew (the claimant) who is effectively excluded from the particular work by it.

It is possible that a court might take the view that the policy should allow a degree of flexibility where it would otherwise serve to exclude workers because of their individual circumstances. But, at least in jurisdictions in which a strict symmetrical approach to discrimination is adopted (i.e., White as well as Black, men as well as women, irreligious as well as religious protected from discrimination) the employer will not be able to create an exception for religious Jews alone (or, indeed, where non-believers as well as believers are protected by law) for those whose religious beliefs prevent compliance with normal working hours.[25] So the employer will be able to maintain a blanket hours requirement unless proportionality required, on the facts, the operation of a broad and flexible exception policy that did not directly discriminate between Jew and non-Jew, religious and irreligious etc.

Under the *Thlimmenos* approach, while the first question is probably the same as that applicable in a classic indirect discrimination case—whether applying the same rule to everyone disadvantages someone for reasons associated with a protected ground—it appears that the second is different. Instead of asking whether the particular rule is nevertheless justified and, if it is not, modifying it (the modification not making explicit reference to any protected ground), it appears that the court asks whether failure to apply a different rule to persons defined by reference to a protected ground was justified. The implication, then, may be that positive action may have to be targeted at a group defined by reference to a protected ground.

5. PROVING DISCRIMINATION

● **Nachova v Bulgaria** (2006) 42 EHRR 43

Military personnel had shot some Roma deserters after tracking them to a family home, from which they (unarmed) tried to escape, the weapon used having been a kalashnikov discharged while the deserters had been running away and (according to one eyewitness) the shooting having been accompanied by racist abuse. The Grand Chamber overturned a Chamber decision that Arts 2 and 14 had been breached, the Chamber's decision on Art. 14 having been based on the Government's failure to rebut a presumption of discrimination which in the Chamber's view arose from the failure of the state to investigate the possibility that the killings were racist despite the eyewitness evidence and the excessive force employed

---

[23] See Chap. 14.

[24] The exact test for justification turns on the legislative framework, see further Chap. 14.

[25] The UK generally takes a symmetrical approach to discrimination and is very restrictive when it comes to positive action (see further Chap. 14). The ECtHR takes a more flexible approach (see section 6 below).

against the deceased. According to the Grand Chamber, which acknowledged the concern expressed by the European Commission against racism and intolerance at the Council of Europe (ECRI) about racially-motivated police violence against Roma in a number of countries including Bulgaria and reports by Human Rights Project and Amnesty International of 'numerous incidents of alleged racial violence against Roma in Bulgaria, including by law enforcement agents':

JUDGMENT

148. The applicants have referred to several separate facts and they maintain that sufficient inferences of a racist act can be drawn from them.

149. First, the applicants considered revealing the fact that Major G had discharged bursts of automatic fire in a populated area, in disregard of the public's safety. Considering that there was no rational explanation for such behaviour, the applicants were of the view that racist hatred on the part of Major G was the only plausible explanation and that he would not have acted in that manner in a non-Roma neighbourhood.

150. The court notes, however, that the use of firearms in the circumstances at issue was regrettably not prohibited under the relevant domestic regulations, a flagrant deficiency which it has earlier condemned...The military police officers carried their automatic rifles 'in accordance with the rules' and were instructed to use all necessary means to effect the arrest...The possibility that Major G was simply adhering strictly to the regulations and would have acted as he did in any similar context, regardless of the ethnicity of the fugitives, cannot therefore be excluded. While the relevant regulations were fundamentally flawed and fell well short of the convention requirements on the protection of the right to life, there is nothing to suggest that Major G would not have used his weapon in a non-Roma neighbourhood...

152. The applicants also stated that the military police officers' attitude had been strongly influenced by their knowledge of the victims' Roma origin. However, it is not possible to speculate on whether or not Mr Angelov's and Mr Petkov's Roma origin had any bearing on the officers' perception of them. Furthermore, there is evidence that some of the officers knew one or both of the victims personally...

153. The applicants referred to the statement given by Mr MM, a neighbour of one of the victims, who reported that Major G had shouted at him 'You damn Gipsies' immediately after the shooting. While such evidence of a racial slur being uttered in connection with a violent act should have led the authorities in this case to verify Mr MM's statement, that statement is of itself an insufficient basis for concluding that the respondent state is liable for a racist killing.

154. Lastly, the applicants relied on information about numerous incidents involving the use of force against Roma by Bulgarian law enforcement officers that had not resulted in the conviction of those responsible.

155. It is true that a number of organisations, including intergovernmental bodies, have expressed concern about the occurrence of such incidents...However, the court cannot lose sight of the fact that its sole concern is to ascertain whether in the case at hand the killing of Mr Angelov and Mr Petkov was motivated by racism.

156. In its judgment the Chamber decided to shift the burden of proof to the respondent government on account of the authorities' failure to carry out an effective investigation into the alleged racist motive for the killing. The inability of the government to satisfy the Chamber that the events complained of were not shaped by racism resulted in its finding a substantive violation of art 14 of the convention, taken together with art 2.

157. The Grand Chamber reiterates that in certain circumstances, where the events lie wholly, or in large part, within the exclusive knowledge of the authorities, as in the case of death of a person within their control in custody, the burden of proof may be regarded as resting on the authorities to provide a satisfactory and convincing explanation of, in particular, the causes of the detained person's death.

The Grand Chamber cannot exclude the possibility that in certain cases of alleged discrimination it may require the respondent government to disprove an arguable allegation of discrimination and—if they fail to do so—find a violation of art 14 of the convention on that basis. However, where it is alleged—as here—that a violent act was motivated by racial prejudice, such an approach would amount to requiring the respondent government to prove the absence of a particular subjective attitude on the part of the person concerned. While in the legal systems of many countries proof of the discriminatory effect of a policy or decision will dispense with the need to prove intent in respect of alleged discrimination in employment or the provision of services, that approach is difficult to transpose to a case where it is alleged that an act of violence was racially motivated. The Grand Chamber, departing from the Chamber's approach, does not consider that the alleged failure of the authorities to carry out an effective investigation into the alleged racist motive for the killing should shift the burden of proof to the respondent government with regard to the alleged violation of art 14 in conjunction with the substantive aspect of art 2 of the convention...

- **DH v Czech Republic** (2008) 47 EHRR 3, Grand Chamber

A claim was brought under Art. 14 with Art. 1 of Protocol 2 to the Convention (which protects the right to education) on behalf of a number of Roma children who had been allocated to 'special schools' after psychological testing and with their parents' consent. The schools, which were intended for children with mental disabilities who were unable to attend ordinary primary schools followed a radically less advanced curriculum than ordinary schools.

The Czech Republic's own 1999 report under the Framework Convention for the Protection of National Minorities acknowledged that 'Romany children with average or above-average intellect are often placed in such schools on the basis of results of psychological tests', that the tests 'are conceived for the majority population and do not take Romany specifics into consideration' and that 'In some special schools Romany pupils made up between 80% and 90% of the total number of pupils'. Prior to 1989 most Roma children were educated in such schools. At the material time, 56 per cent of children in special schools in the Ostrava (from which the applicants in the instant case came) were Roma, whereas Roma children comprised only 2.26 per cent of all primary school children in the town. Across the Czech Republic, over half of Roma children were in special schools whose pupils were in some cases 70 per cent Roma.

The Court noted that Roma, despite a presence in Europe of some six or seven centuries,

are not recognised by the majority society as a fully-fledged European people and they have suffered throughout their history from rejection and persecution [which] culminated in their attempted extermination by the Nazis, who considered them an inferior race. As a result of centuries of rejection many Roma communities today live in very difficult conditions, often on the fringe of society in the countries where they have settled, and their participation in public life is extremely limited.

It reviewed the jurisprudence on indirect and race discrimination arising under EC law, the ICCPR, CERD, the Convention on the Rights of the Child, UNESCO's Convention against Discrimination in Education of 14 December 1960 and Declaration on Race and Racial Prejudice of 27 November 1978, as well as reports of the European Monitoring Centre on Racism and Xenophobia (now the European Union Agency for Fundamental Rights) on education in the Czech Republic and the decisions of the House of Lords in *European Roma Rights Centre v Immigration Officer at Prague Airport* and the US Supreme Court in

Griggs v Duke Power Co, in which that Court recognised indirect discrimination for the first time.[26]

JUDGMENT

175. The court has established in its case law that discrimination means treating differently, without an objective and reasonable justification, persons in relevantly similar situations…However, art 14 does not prohibit a member state from treating groups differently in order to correct 'factual inequalities' between them; indeed in certain circumstances a failure to attempt to correct inequality through different treatment may in itself give rise to a breach of the article…[27] The court has also accepted that a general policy or measure that has disproportionately prejudicial effects on a particular group may be considered discriminatory notwithstanding that it is not specifically aimed at that group [28]…and that discrimination potentially contrary to the convention may result from a de facto situation [29]…

176. Discrimination on account of, inter alia, a person's ethnic origin is a form of racial discrimination. Racial discrimination is a particularly invidious kind of discrimination and, in view of its perilous consequences, requires from the authorities special vigilance and a vigorous reaction. It is for this reason that the authorities must use all available means to combat racism, thereby reinforcing democracy's vision of a society in which diversity is not perceived as a threat but as a source of enrichment…The court has also held that no difference in treatment which is based exclusively or to a decisive extent on a person's ethnic origin is capable of being objectively justified in a contemporary democratic society built on the principles of pluralism and respect for different cultures…

177. As to the burden of proof in this sphere, the court has established that once the applicant has shown a difference in treatment, it is for the government to show that it was justified…

178. As regards the question of what constitutes prima facie evidence capable of shifting the burden of proof on to the respondent state…proof may follow from the coexistence of sufficiently strong, clear and concordant inferences or of similar unrebutted presumptions of fact. Moreover, the level of persuasion necessary for reaching a particular conclusion and, in this connection, the distribution of the burden of proof are intrinsically linked to the specificity of the facts, the nature of the allegation made and the convention right at stake.

179. The court has also recognised that convention proceedings do not in all cases lend themselves to a rigorous application of the principle *affirmanti incumbit probatio* (he who alleges something must prove that allegation…In certain circumstances, where the events in issue lie wholly, or in large part, within the exclusive knowledge of the authorities, the burden of proof may be regarded as resting on the authorities to provide a satisfactory and convincing explanation…

180. As to whether statistics can constitute evidence, the court has in the past stated that statistics could not in themselves disclose a practice which could be classified as discriminatory *(Jordan v UK)*[30] However, in more recent cases on the question of discrimination, in which the applicants alleged a difference in the effect of a general measure or de facto situation…[31], the court relied extensively on statistics produced by the parties to establish a difference in treatment between two groups (men and women) in similar situations…

181. Lastly, as noted in previous cases, the vulnerable position of Roma/gipsies means that special consideration should be given to their needs and their different lifestyle both in the relevant regulatory framework and in reaching decisions in particular cases…

---

[26] *European Roma Rights Centre v Immigration Officer* at Prague Airport [2005] 2 AC 1; *Griggs v Duke Power Co* 401 US 424 (1971).

[27] Citing *Belgian Linguistics*, n. 4 above, para. 10; *Thlimmenos v Greece* (2001) 31 EHRR 411, para. 44; and *Stec v UK* (2006) 48 EHRR 47, para. 51.

[28] Citing *Jordan v UK* (2003) 37 EHRR 2.

[29] *Zarb Adami v Malta* (2006) 20 BHRC 703, para. 76.   [30] N. 27 above.

[31] Citing *Hoogendijk v Netherlands* (App. No. 58461/00) (admissibility decision, 6 January 2005); and *Zarb Adami v Malta*, n. 29 above, paras 77–78.

2. APPLICATION OF THE AFOREMENTIONED PRINCIPLES TO THE INSTANT CASE

182. The court notes that as a result of their turbulent history and constant uprooting the Roma have become a specific type of disadvantaged and vulnerable minority.... As the court has noted in previous cases, they therefore require special protection...As is attested by the activities of numerous European and international organisations and the recommendations of the Council of Europe bodies...this protection also extends to the sphere of education. The present case therefore warrants particular attention, especially as when the applications were lodged with the court the applicants were minor children for whom the right to education was of paramount importance.

183. The applicants' allegation in the present case is not that they were in a different situation from non-Roma children that called for different treatment or that the respondent state had failed to take affirmative action to correct factual inequalities or differences between them...In their submission, all that has to be established is that, without objective and reasonable justification, they were treated less favourably than non-Roma children in a comparable situation and that this amounted in their case to indirect discrimination.

184. The court has already accepted in previous cases that a difference in treatment may take the form of disproportionately prejudicial effects of a general policy or measure which, though couched in neutral terms, discriminates against a group...In accordance with, for instance, Council Directives 97/80/EC and 2000/43/EC (see paras 82 and 84 above) and the definition provided by ECRI (see para 60 above), such a situation may amount to 'indirect discrimination', which does not necessarily require a discriminatory intent.

(a) Whether a presumption of indirect discrimination arises in the instant case

185. It was common ground that the impugned difference in treatment did not result from the wording of the statutory provisions on placements in special schools in force at the material time. Accordingly, the issue in the instant case is whether the manner in which the legislation was applied in practice resulted in a disproportionate number of Roma children—including the applicants—being placed in special schools without justification, and whether such children were thereby placed at a significant disadvantage.

186. As mentioned above, the court has noted in previous cases that applicants may have difficulty in proving discriminatory treatment...In order to guarantee those concerned the effective protection of their rights, less strict evidential rules should apply in cases of alleged indirect discrimination.

187. On this point, the court observes that Council Directives 97/80/EC of 15 December 1997 and 2000/43/EC stipulate that persons who consider themselves wronged because the principle of equal treatment has not been applied to them may establish, before a domestic authority, by any means, including on the basis of statistical evidence, facts from which it may be presumed that there has been discrimination...The recent case law of the Court of Justice of the European Communities...shows that it permits claimants to rely on statistical evidence and the national courts to take such evidence into account where it is valid and significant.

The Grand Chamber further notes the information furnished by the third-party interveners that the courts of many countries and the supervisory bodies of the United Nations treaties habitually accept statistics as evidence of indirect discrimination in order to facilitate the victims' task of adducing prima facie evidence...

188. In these circumstances, the court considers that when it comes to assessing the impact of a measure or practice on an individual or group, statistics which appear on critical examination to be reliable and significant will be sufficient to constitute the prima facie evidence the applicant is required to produce. This does not, however, mean that indirect discrimination cannot be proved without statistical evidence.

189. Where an applicant alleging indirect discrimination thus establishes a rebuttable presumption that the effect of a measure or practice is discriminatory, the burden then shifts to the respondent state,

which must show that the difference in treatment is not discriminatory…Regard being had in particular to the specificity of the facts and the nature of the allegations made in this type of case, it would be extremely difficult in practice for applicants to prove indirect discrimination without such a shift in the burden of proof…

191. …In view of their comment that no official information on the ethnic origin of the pupils exists, the court accepts that the statistics submitted by the applicants may not be entirely reliable. It nevertheless considers that these figures reveal a dominant trend that has been confirmed both by the respondent state and the independent supervisory bodies which have looked into the question…

193. In the court's view, the latter figures, which do not relate solely to the Ostrava region and therefore provide a more general picture, show that, even if the exact percentage of Roma children in special schools at the material time remains difficult to establish, their number was disproportionately high. Moreover, Roma pupils formed a majority of the pupils in special schools. Despite being couched in neutral terms, the relevant statutory provisions therefore had considerably more impact in practice on Roma children than on non-Roma children and resulted in statistically disproportionate numbers of placements of the former in special schools.

194. Where it has been shown that legislation produces such a discriminatory effect, the Grand Chamber considers that, as with cases concerning employment or the provision of services, it is not necessary in cases in the educational sphere…to prove any discriminatory intent on the part of the relevant authorities…

195. In these circumstances, the evidence submitted by the applicants can be regarded as sufficiently reliable and significant to give rise to a strong presumption of indirect discrimination. The burden of proof must therefore shift to the government, which must show that the difference in the impact of the legislation was the result of objective factors unrelated to ethnic origin.

NOTES

1. Proof of discrimination varies according to the nature of the wrong alleged. A similar approach to that in *Nachova* had been taken in *Jordan v United Kingdom* in which the Court rejected an Art. 14 claim brought on behalf of a young Catholic man shot dead by the security forces in Northern Ireland.[32] His family claimed that he had been killed contrary to Art. 2 and that the disproportionate killing by the security forces in Northern Ireland of young Catholic/nationalist men[33] amounted to discrimination on grounds of national origin or association with a national minority contrary to Art. 14 taken with Art. 2 of the Convention. The Court did not find a breach of Art. 2 arising from the killing itself, noting that there was insufficient evidence before it to make that finding.[34] It accepted that 'Where a general policy or measure has disproportionately prejudicial effects on a particular group, it is not excluded that this may be considered as discriminatory notwithstanding that it is not specifically aimed or directed at that group.'[35] But the Court went on to deny that 'statistics can in themselves disclose a practice which could be classified as discriminatory within the meaning of Article 14. There is no evidence before the Court which would entitle it to conclude that any of those killings, save the four which resulted in convictions, involved the unlawful or excessive use of force by members of the security forces'.

---

[32] N. 28 above.

[33] Between 1969 and March 1994, the overwhelming majority of the 357 people killed by the security forces were young Catholic or nationalist men. Only 31 prosecutions had followed from which had resulted only four convictions at the date of the application.

[34] It did however find a breach of Art. 2 because of the state's failure adequately to investigate the death.

[35] Para. 154.

The Grand Chamber in *Nachova* ruled that there was a procedural breach of Arts 2 and 14 taken together because the state had failed to investigate a possible causal link between alleged racist attitudes and the killing of the two men, this because 'any evidence of racist verbal abuse being uttered by law enforcement agents in connection with an operation involving the use of force against persons from an ethnic or other minority...must be verified and—if confirmed—a thorough examination of all the facts should be undertaken in order to uncover any possible racist motives'.[36] Its refusal to shift the burden of proof to the state, however, meant that the substantive Art. 14/Art. 2 claim failed. Subsequently, however, in *DH v Czech Republic*, the Grand Chamber did agree to shift the burden in a case which it regarded as concerning indirect race discrimination, rather than allegations of deliberately racist behaviour.

2. The decision in *DH* is to be welcomed, not only for its embrace of indirect discrimination but also because of its more flexible approach to proof. Having said this, the Court did not there find that the Czech Republic had been guilty of *direct* race discrimination in its treatment of Roma children, and did not overrule the more restrictive approach it took in *Nachova*, in which racist motivation was at issue.[37] Such cases are likely to remain difficult indeed to establish.

6. JUSTIFYING DIFFERENTIAL TREATMENT

● **Belgian Linguistic Case (No. 2) (1968) 1 EHRR 252**

The case which involved a challenge to differential funding of French and Flemish schools in a Flemish area of Belgium.

JUDGMENT

10. In spite of the very general wording of the French version ('*sans distinction aucune*'), Article 14 does not forbid every difference in treatment in the exercise of the rights and freedoms recognised. This version must be read in the light of the more restrictive text of the English version ('without discrimination').

In addition, and in particular, one would reach absurd results were one to give Article 14 an interpretation as wide as that which the French version seems to imply. One would, in effect, be led to judge as contrary to the Convention every one of the many legal or administrative provisions which do not secure to everyone complete equality of treatment in the enjoyment of the rights and freedoms recognised. The competent national authorities are frequently confronted with situations and problems which, on account of differences inherent therein, call for different legal solutions; moreover, certain legal inequalities tend only to correct factual inequalities. The extensive interpretation mentioned above cannot consequently be accepted.

It is important, then, to look for the criteria which enable a determination to be made as to whether or not a given difference in treatment, concerning of course the exercise of one of the rights and freedoms set forth, contravenes Article 14. On this question the Court, following the principles which may be extracted from the legal practice of a large number of democratic States, holds that the principle of equality of treatment is violated if the distinction has no objective and reasonable justification. The existence

---

[36] Para. 164.

[37] In the *EB v France* case, discussed below, the Grand Chamber held against the state its failure to provide statistical information on the frequency of reliance on the absence of a male or female referent according to the sexual orientation of prospective adopters (para. 74) accepting that it burden of proof of disproving discrimination on the facts.

of such a justification must be assessed in relation to the aim and effects of the measure under consideration, regard being had to the principles which normally prevail in democratic societies. A difference of treatment in the exercise of a right laid down in the Convention must not only pursue a legitimate aim: Article 14 is likewise violated when it is clearly established that there is no reasonable relationship of proportionality between the means employed and the aim sought to be realised.

In attempting to find out in a given case, whether or not there has been an arbitrary distinction, the Court cannot disregard those legal and factual features which characterise the life of the society in the State which, as a Contracting Party, has to answer for the measure in dispute. In so doing it cannot assume the rôle of the competent national authorities, for it would thereby lose sight of the subsidiary nature of the international machinery of collective enforcement established by the Convention. The national authorities remain free to choose the measures which they consider appropriate in those matters which are governed by the Convention. Review by the Court concerns only the conformity of these measures with the requirements of the Convention.

- **DH v Czech Republic** (2008) 47 EHRR 3, Grand Chamber

196 The Court reiterates that a difference in treatment is discriminatory if 'it has no objective and reasonable justification', that is, if it does not pursue a 'legitimate aim' or if there is not a 'reasonable relationship of proportionality' between the means employed and the aim sought to be realised. Where the difference in treatment is based on race, colour or ethnic origin, the notion of objective and reasonable justification must be interpreted as strictly as possible.

197 In the instant case, the Government sought to explain the difference in treatment between Roma children and non-Roma children by the need to adapt the education system to the capacity of children with special needs. In the Government's submission, the applicants were placed in special schools on account of their specific educational needs, essentially as a result of their low intellectual capacity measured with the aid of psychological tests in educational psychology centres. After the centres had made their recommendations regarding the type of school in which the applicants should be placed, the final decision had lain with the applicants' parents and they had consented to the placements. The argument that the applicants were placed in special schools on account of their ethnic origin was therefore unsustainable.

For their part, the applicants strenuously contested the suggestion that the disproportionately high number of Roma children in special schools could be explained by the results of the intellectual capacity tests or be justified by parental consent.

198 The Court accepts that the Government's decision to retain the special-school system was motivated by the desire to find a solution for children with special educational needs. However, it shares the disquiet of the other Council of Europe institutions who have expressed concerns about the more basic curriculum followed in these schools and, in particular, the segregation the system causes.

199 The Grand Chamber observes, further, that the tests used to assess the children's learning abilities or difficulties have given rise to controversy and continue to be the subject of scientific debate and research. While accepting that it is not its role to judge the validity of such tests, various factors in the instant case nevertheless lead the Grand Chamber to conclude that the results of the tests carried out at the material time were not capable of constituting objective and reasonable justification for the purposes of Art.14 of the Convention.

200 In the first place, it was common ground that all the children who were examined sat the same tests, irrespective of their ethnic origin. The Czech authorities themselves acknowledged in 1999 that, 'Romany children with average or above-average intellect' were often placed in such schools on the basis of the results of psychological tests and that the tests were conceived for the majority population and did

not take Roma specifics into consideration. As a result, they had revised the tests and methods used with a view to ensuring that they 'were not misused to the detriment of Roma children'.

In addition, various independent bodies have expressed doubts over the adequacy of the tests. Thus, the Advisory Committee on the Framework Convention for the Protection of National Minorities observed that children who were not mentally handicapped were frequently placed in these schools, '[owing] to real or perceived language and cultural differences between Roma and the majority'. It also stressed the need for the tests to be, 'consistent, objective and comprehensive'. ECRI noted that the channelling of Roma children to special schools for the mentally retarded was reportedly often 'quasi-automatic' and needed to be examined to ensure that any testing used was 'fair' and that the true abilities of each child were 'properly evaluated'. The Council of Europe Commissioner for Human Rights noted that Roma children were frequently placed in classes for children with special needs, 'without an adequate psychological or pedagogical assessment, the real criteria clearly being their ethnic origin'.

Lastly, in the submission of some of the third-party interveners, placements following the results of the psychological tests reflected the racial prejudices of the society concerned.

201 The Court considers that, at the very least, there is a danger that the tests were biased and that the results were not analysed in the light of the particularities and special characteristics of the Roma children who sat them. In these circumstances, the tests in question cannot serve as justification for the impugned difference in treatment.

202 As regards parental consent, the Court notes the Government's submission that this was the decisive factor without which the applicants would not have been placed in special schools. In view of the fact that a difference in treatment has been established in the instant case, it follows that any such consent would signify an acceptance of the difference in treatment, even if discriminatory, in other words a waiver of the right not to be discriminated against. However, under the Court's case law, the waiver of a right guaranteed by the Convention—in so far as such a waiver is permissible—must be established in an unequivocal manner, and be given in full knowledge of the facts, that is to say on the basis of informed consent and without constraint.

203 In the circumstances of the present case, the Court is not satisfied that the parents of the Roma children, who were members of a disadvantaged community and often poorly educated, were capable of weighing up all the aspects of the situation and the consequences of giving their consent. The Government themselves admitted that consent in this instance had been given by means of a signature on a pre-completed form that contained no information on the available alternatives or the differences between the special-school curriculum and the curriculum followed in other schools. Nor do the domestic authorities appear to have taken any additional measures to ensure that the Roma parents received all the information they needed to make an informed decision or were aware of the consequences that giving their consent would have for their children's futures. It also appears indisputable that the Roma parents were faced with a dilemma: a choice between ordinary schools that were ill-equipped to cater for their children's social and cultural differences and in which their children risked isolation and ostracism and special schools where the majority of the pupils were Roma.

204 In view of the fundamental importance of the prohibition of racial discrimination, the Grand Chamber considers that, even assuming the conditions referred to at [192] above were satisfied, no waiver of the right not to be subjected to racial discrimination can be accepted, as it would be counter to an important public interest.

NOTES

1. The *Belgian Linguistic* case made it clear from the earliest Art. 14 case law that differential treatment on a protected ground did not inevitably breach Art. 14. The threshold of justification in *Belgian Linguistics* and in a number of cases which followed it was not high, emphasis

being placed by the Court on the 'margin of appreciation' accorded to the state 'in assessing whether and to what extent differences in otherwise similar situations justify a different treatment in law'.[38] Over time, however, a variegated approach has emerged. Although the jurisprudence of the European Court does not create a formal tiered approach (such as applies in the US: discrimination on grounds of race and illegitimacy is subject to 'strict scrutiny' and almost impossible to justify, discrimination on all other grounds except sex is subject only to 'rational review' and is rarely found unlawful, while discrimination on grounds of sex attracts 'intermediate scrutiny'),[39] a de facto hierarchy has emerged with some grounds differential treatment in connection with which is justified in line with the test set out in *Belgian Linguistics*, others in respect of which 'very weighty reasons' are required by way of justification. This approach has not been fully reasoned to date by the European Court but it is clear that discrimination on grounds such as race/ethnicity, sex, sexual orientation and religion[40] is more difficult to justify than discrimination, for example, between trade unions or (as regards applicable time limits) victims of intentional and unintentional torts.[41] The strict approach to justification is evident in the *DH* case, extracted above.

2. It is perhaps difficult to envisage a case in which race discrimination (as distinct from positive action designed to counter disadvantage associated with race/ethnicity)[42] will ever be regarded as justified. Indeed, in the *DH* case the Grand Chamber stated that 'no difference in treatment which is based exclusively or to a decisive extent on a person's ethnic origin is capable of being objectively justified in a contemporary democratic society built on the principles of pluralism and respect for different cultures ...'[43] citing its previous decision in *Timishev v Russia*[44] which concerned the imposition of travel restrictions on Russian nationals of Chechen origin.

3. This is not to say that differential treatment on a 'suspect' ground will always breach Art. 14 (or, indeed, that differential treatment on a non-suspect ground is effectively immune from challenge). In *Petrovic v Austria*[45] discrimination between fathers and mothers as regards access to paid parental leave was found to be within the state's margin of appreciation in circumstances such that the legislative provision had subsequently been equalised and there was no common standard across the EU in this area, Austria being, if anything, rather in the vanguard of the move towards equalisation. The absence of a general European acceptance of gay adoption also resulted in the decision in *Fretté v France*,[46] in which, after a string of cases in which the Court had found discrimination on grounds of sexual orientation to breach Arts 8 and/or 14, the Court ruled against an applicant refused permission to adopt because of his sexual orientation. Having accepted that the refusal pursued a 'legitimate aim', that protecting 'the health and rights of children who

---

[38] See *National Union of Belgian Police v Belgium* (1975) 1 EHRR 578 and *Swedish Engine Drivers' Union v Sweden* (1976) 1 EHRR 617, which concerned alleged discrimination between trade unions. See also *Rasmussen v Denmark* (1984) 7 EHRR 371: sex discrimination in relation to the establishment of paternity (putative fathers could only contest within the first year after birth whereas mothers could contest paternity at any time).

[39] See, generally, Suzanne Goldberg, 'Equality without Tiers' (2003–4) 77 Southern California Law Review 481.

[40] *DH v Czech Republic*, n. 17 above; *Abdulaziz*, n. 21 above; *Salgueiro da Silva Mouta v Portugal*, n. 10 above; and *Hoffmann v Germany* (App. No. 34045/96) [2001] ECHR 34045/96, respectively. Also illegitimacy (*Inze v Austria* (1987) 10 EHRR 394), nationality (*Gaygusuz v Austria*, n. 6 above, and unmarried parental status (*Elsholz v Germany* [2000] ECHR 25735/94, [2000] 2 FLR 486).

[41] *Stubbings*, n. 11 above.   [42] See para. 175 of *DH v Czech Republic*, n. 17 above.

[43] Para. 176.   [44] (2007) 44 EHRR 37.

[45] (1998) 33 EHRR 307.   [46] (2002) 38 EHRR 438.

could be involved in an adoption procedure' the Court stated that, in assessing whether the differential treatment was justified, one of the factors relevant to the state's 'margin of appreciation in assessing whether and to what extent differences in otherwise similar situations justify a different treatment in law...may be the existence or non-existence of common ground between the laws of the Contracting States'.[47] By January 2008, the sands had shifted to the extent that, in *EB v France*,[48] the Grand Chamber of the Court ruled that France had breached Art. 14 by refusing to allow a lesbian woman to adopt, the refusal being based on the authorities' concern over the lack of a 'male referent' in the household (the applicant lived with another women) and the fact that the applicant's partner was not to be involved in the adoption.

The Court in *EB* referred to the wide margin of appreciation it had provided to the state in *Frett v France* and accepted that it was legitimate to have concerns over the attitude of a prospective adopter's partner. But it found, contrary to the French courts, that the applicant's sexual orientation had been a determining factor in the refusal of authorisation. Accepting that the authorities' concern over the lack of a male referent in the applicant's household did 'not necessarily raise a problem in itself';[49] the Court however took the view that, because the impact of any requirement for such a referent ran 'the risk of rendering ineffective the right of single persons to apply for authorisation [and it]...might therefore have led to an arbitrary refusal and have served as a pretext for rejecting the applicant's application on grounds of her homosexuality', the burden of proof was on the state to prove that this factor was not used disproportionately against gay/lesbian adopters, and that the state's failure to produce statistics had the effect that the burden was not discharged.[50]

80. ...these two main grounds [concerns over the partner's attitude and the lack of a male referent in the household] form part of an overall assessment of the applicant's situation. For this reason, the Court considers that they should not be considered alternatively, but concurrently. Consequently, the illegitimacy of one of the grounds has the effect of contaminating the entire decision...

89 ...The Court considers that the reference to the applicant's homosexuality was, if not explicit, at least implicit. The influence of the applicant's avowed homosexuality on the assessment of her application has been established and, having regard to the foregoing, was a decisive factor leading to the decision to refuse her authorisation to adopt...

91. The Court reiterates that, for the purposes of Article 14, a difference in treatment is discriminatory if it has no objective and reasonable justification, which means that it does not pursue a 'legitimate aim' or that there is no 'reasonable proportionality between the means employed and the aim sought to be realised'...Where sexual orientation is in issue, there is a need for particularly convincing and weighty reasons to justify a difference in treatment regarding rights falling within Article 8...

92. In that connection the Court observes that the Convention is a living instrument, to be interpreted in the light of present-day conditions...

93. In the Court's opinion, if the reasons advanced for such a difference in treatment were based solely on considerations regarding the applicant's sexual orientation this would amount to discrimination under the Convention...

94. The Court points out that French law allows single persons to adopt a child...thereby opening up the possibility of adoption by a single homosexual, which is not disputed. Against the background of the domestic legal provisions, it considers that the reasons put forward by the Government cannot be regarded as particularly convincing and weighty such as to justify refusing to grant the applicant authorisation.

---

[47] Paras 40–41.
[48] App. No. 43546/02, 22 January 2008, [2008] 1 FLR 850; (2008) 47 EHRR 21.
[49] Para. 73. [50] Para. 74.

95. The Court notes, lastly, that the relevant provisions of the Civil Code are silent as to the necessity of a referent of the other sex, which would not, in any event, be dependent on the sexual orientation of the adoptive single parent. In this case, moreover, the applicant presented, in the terms of the judgment of the *Conseil d'Etat*, 'undoubted personal qualities and an aptitude for bringing up children', which were assuredly in the child's best interests, a key notion in the relevant international instruments...

96. Having regard to the foregoing, the Court cannot but observe that, in rejecting the applicant's application for authorisation to adopt, the domestic authorities made a distinction based on considerations regarding her sexual orientation, a distinction which is not acceptable under the Convention...

97. Consequently, having regard to its finding under paragraph 80 above, the Court considers that the decision in question is incompatible with the provisions of Article 14 taken in conjunction with Article 8.

The Court suggested that there were a number of differences between this case and *Fretté*, stating that the domestic authorities 'did not—expressly at least—refer to E.B.'s "choice of lifestyle"'; that they 'mentioned the applicant's qualities and her child-raising and emotional capacities, unlike in *Fretté* where the applicant was deemed to have had difficulties in envisaging the practical consequences of the upheaval occasioned by the arrival of a child' and that they 'had regard to the attitude of E.B.s partner... which was a factor that had not featured in the application lodged by Mr Fretté'. Given, however, the finding in *Fretté* that ' "choice of lifestyle"... implicitly yet undeniably made his homosexuality the decisive factor', and that the attitude of the applicant's partner in the instant case was regarded as a factor which could have weighed against her, it is difficult to escape the conclusion that all that differentiated the cases in truth was the passage of a short period of time and its impact (albeit in *EB*'s case not explicitly dealt with) on the appropriate 'margin of appreciation'.

4. Just as discrimination on a suspect ground may be justified, so discrimination on a non-suspect ground may breach Art. 14. In *Sidabras v Lithuania*,[51] for example, the European Court ruled that a ban on former KGB operatives which related to some private sector, as well as public sector, jobs breached Art. 14 read with Art. 8, and in *Chassagnou v France*[52] a legislative distinction on grounds of size of property holding was regarded as unjustified.[53] In *Sidabras* the Court took the view that the purported justification for the ban—an absence of loyalty to the (newly constituted) state—was not an 'an inherent condition of employment' in the private sector.[54] And in *Chassagnou* the imposition on small landowners of an obligation to permit hunting on their land despite any ethical objections to the practice breached Art. 14 because the state failed to provide any 'convincing explanation how the general interest could be served by the obligation for small landowners only to transfer their hunting rights'.

5. Specific issues of justification arise where differential treatment is intended to ameliorate existing disadvantage. In *Gudmundsson v Iceland* the Commission rejected an Art. 14 claim against Iceland's progressive income tax structure on the basis that unequal cases could and should be treated unequally in proportion to their inequality,[55] and ruled that such a system 'is not discriminatory, provided the progressive measure is proportional and consequently results in a fairer distribution of income than would be the case without it'. The subsequent decision in *Thlimmenos* suggests that positive action could actually be *required* under Art. 14

---

[51] N. 16 above.   [52] (1999) 29 EHRR 615.
[53] In *Gillow v UK* (1986) 11 EHRR 335 the Court rejected a challenge to preferential treatment based on a residency requirement on the basis that the requirement was justified.
[54] Para. 57.   [55] App. No. 511/59 (1960) *Yearbook* III 394.

(the Court ruling that equality may require different treatment of differently situated persons). In the *DH* case Judge Cabral Barreto, who dissented from the Chamber decision,[56] stated that 'pupils who, for various reasons—whether cultural, linguistic or other—find it difficult to pursue a normal school education should be entitled to expect the State to take positive measures to compensate for their handicap and to afford them a means of resuming the normal curriculum' (emphasis added). The Grand Chamber also asserted in that case that 'art 14 does not prohibit a member state from treating groups differently in order to correct "factual inequalities" between them; indeed in certain circumstances a failure to attempt to correct inequality through different treatment may in itself give rise to a breach of the article'.[57]

The approach taken by the European Court of Human Rights to positive discrimination is to be welcomed, and casts into doubt one of the UK's proffered justifications for its refusal to sign up to Protocol 12 (see section 1 above). But the decision of the Grand Chamber in *Stec v United Kingdom,* discussed below, suggests that too quick a reliance on arguments about the amelioration of disadvantage can result in the acceptance of measures whose impact is actually to exacerbate, rather than reduce, existing inequalities.[58]

7. EXCUSING SEX DISCRIMINATION?

- **Abdulaziz v United Kingdom** (1985) 7 EHRR 471

72. For the purposes of Article 14, a difference of treatment is discriminatory if it 'has no objective and reasonable justification', that is, if it does not pursue a 'legitimate aim' or if there is not a 'reasonable relationship of proportionality between the means employed and the aim sought to be realised'.

The Contracting States enjoy a certain margin of appreciation in assessing whether and to what extent differences in otherwise similar situations justify a different treatment in law ... but it is for the Court to give the final ruling in this respect.

73. In the particular circumstances of the case, the Court considers that it must examine in turn the three grounds on which it was alleged that a discriminatory difference of treatment was based.

B. ALLEGED DISCRIMINATION ON THE GROUND OF SEX ...

75. According to the Government, the difference of treatment complained of had the aim of limiting 'primary immigration' ... and was justified by the need to protect the domestic labour market at a time of high unemployment. They placed strong reliance on the margin of appreciation enjoyed by the Contracting States in this area and laid particular stress on what they described as a statistical fact: men were more likely to seek work than women, with the result that male immigrants would have a greater impact than female immigrants on the said market. Furthermore, the reduction, attributed by the Government to the 1980 Rules, of approximately 5,700 per annum in the number of husbands accepted for settlement in the United Kingdom ... was claimed to be significant. This was said to be so especially when the reduction was viewed in relation to its cumulative effect over the years and to the total number of acceptances for settlement.

This view was contested by the applicants. For them, the Government's plea ignored the modern role of women and the fact that men may be self-employed and also, as was exemplified by the case of

---

[56] (2006) 43 EHRR 41.

[57] Para. 175, extracted above, citing *Belgian Linguistics*, n. 4 above, para. 10; *Thlimmenos v Greece*, n. 18 above, para. 44; and *Stec v UK* (2006) 43 EHRR 47, para. 51.

[58] Ibid.

Mr Balkandali...create rather than seek jobs. Furthermore, the Government's figure of 5,700 was said to be insignificant and, for a number of reasons, in any event unreliable...

76. The Government further contended that the measures in question were justified by the need to maintain effective immigration control, which benefited settled immigrants as well as the indigenous population. Immigration caused strains on society; the Government's aim was to advance public tranquillity, and a firm and fair control secured good relations between the different communities living in the United Kingdom.

To this, the applicants replied that the racial prejudice of the United Kingdom population could not be advanced as a justification for the measures...

78. The Court accepts that the 1980 Rules had the aim of protecting the domestic labour market. The fact that, as was suggested by the applicants, this aim might have been further advanced by the abolition of the 'United Kingdom ancestry' and the 'working holiday' rules...in no way alters this finding...

Whilst the aforesaid aim was without doubt legitimate, this does not in itself establish the legitimacy of the difference made in the 1980 Rules as to the possibility for male and female immigrants settled in the United Kingdom to obtain permission for, on the one hand, their non-national wives or fiancées and, on the other hand, their non-national husbands or fiancés to enter or remain in the country.

Although the Contracting States enjoy a certain 'margin of appreciation' in assessing whether and to what extent differences in otherwise similar situations justify a different treatment, the scope of this margin will vary according to the circumstances, the subject-matter and its background...

As to the present matter, it can be said that the advancement of the equality of the sexes is today a major goal in the member States of the Council of Europe. This means that very weighty reasons would have to be advanced before a difference of treatment on the ground of sex could be regarded as compatible with the Convention.

79. In the Court's opinion, the Government's arguments summarised in para. 75 above are not convincing.

It may be correct that on average there is a greater percentage of men of working age than of women of working age who are 'economically active' (for Great Britain 90% of the men and 63% of the women) and that comparable figures hold good for immigrants (according to the statistics, 86% for men and 41% for women for immigrants from the Indian sub-continent and 90% for men and 70% for women for immigrants from the West Indies and Guyana)...

Nevertheless, this does not show that similar differences in fact exist—or would but for the effect of the 1980 Rules have existed—as regards the respective impact on the United Kingdom labour market of immigrant wives and of immigrant husbands. In this connection, other factors must also be taken into account. Being 'economically active' does not always mean that one is seeking to be employed by someone else. Moreover, although a greater number of men than of women may be inclined to seek employment, immigrant husbands were already by far outnumbered, before the introduction of the 1980 Rules, by immigrant wives...many of whom were also 'economically active'. Whilst a considerable proportion of those wives, in so far as they were 'economically active', were engaged in part-time work, the impact on the domestic labour market of women immigrants as compared with men ought not to be underestimated.

In any event, the Court is not convinced that the difference that may nevertheless exist between the respective impact of men and of women on the domestic labour market is sufficiently important to justify the difference of treatment, complained of by the applicants, as to the possibility for a person settled in the United Kingdom to be joined by, as the case may be, his wife or her husband.

80. In this context the Government stressed the importance of the effect on the immigration of husbands of the restrictions contained in the 1980 Rules, which had led, according to their estimate, to an annual reduction of 5,700 (rather than 2,000, as mentioned in the Commission's report) in the number of husbands accepted for settlement.

Without expressing a conclusion on the correctness of the figure of 5,700, the Court notes that in point of time the claimed reduction coincided with a significant increase in unemployment in the United Kingdom and that the Government accepted that some part of the reduction was due to economic conditions rather than to the 1980 Rules themselves...

In any event, for the reasons stated in para. 79 above, the reduction achieved does not justify the difference in treatment between men and women.

81. The Court accepts that the 1980 Rules also had, as the Government stated, the aim of advancing public tranquillity. However, it is not persuaded that this aim was served by the distinction drawn in those rules between husbands and wives.

82. There remains a more general argument advanced by the Government, namely that the United Kingdom was not in violation of Article 14 by reason of the fact that it acted more generously in some respects—that is, as regards the admission of non-national wives and fiancées of men settled in the country—than the Convention required.

The Court cannot accept this argument. It would point out that Article 14 is concerned with the avoidance of discrimination in the enjoyment of the Convention rights in so far as the requirements of the Convention as to those rights can be complied with in different ways. The notion of discrimination within the meaning of Article 14 includes in general cases where a person or group is treated, without proper justification, less favourably than another, even though the more favourable treatment is not called for by the Convention.

83. The Court thus concludes that the applicants have been victims of discrimination on the ground of sex, in violation of Article 14 taken together with Article 8.

- **Stec v United Kingdom** (2006) 43 EHRR 47

The challenge in *Stec* was to differential ages at which men and women ceased to be entitled to reduced earnings allowance (REA) which was designed to supplement the income of those whose earning power had been reduced by virtue of industrial injuries. Entitlement to the benefit ceased at state pensionable age which was at the relevant time 65 for men, 60 for women. Ms Stec started to receive the benefit in 1990 but ceased to be entitled to it in 1993 when she became 60. She complained that, had she been a man, she would have been entitled to go on receiving REA until she reached 65. The European Court noted the fact that the differential state retirement ages had been introduced in 1940 'in response to a campaign by unmarried women, many of whom spent much of their lives caring for dependent relatives, and also as part of a package to enable married couples, where the wife was usually younger than the husband and financially dependent on him, to receive a pension at the couples' rate when the husband reached 65', and that the decision to phase out discriminatory retirement ages was implemented gradually so as to give 'women affected by the change and their employers... ample time to adjust their expectations and arrange their financial affairs accordingly'.

JUDGMENT

51. Article 14 does not prohibit a member state from treating groups differently in order to correct 'factual inequalities' between them; indeed in certain circumstances a failure to attempt to correct inequality through different treatment may in itself give rise to a breach of the article. A difference of treatment is, however, discriminatory if it has no objective and reasonable justification; in other words, if it does not pursue a legitimate aim or if there is not a reasonable relationship of proportionality between the means employed and the aim sought to be realised. The contracting state enjoys a margin of appreciation in assessing whether and to what extent differences in otherwise similar situations justify a different treatment.

52. The scope of this margin will vary according to the circumstances, the subject matter and the background. As a general rule, very weighty reasons would have to be put forward before the court could regard a difference in treatment based exclusively on the ground of sex as compatible with the convention. On the other hand, a wide margin is usually allowed to the state under the convention when it comes to general measures of economic or social strategy. Because of their direct knowledge of their society and its needs, the national authorities are in principle better placed than the international judge to appreciate what is in the public interest on social or economic grounds, and the court will generally respect the legislature's policy choice unless it is 'manifestly without reasonable foundation'…

54. The court recalls that REA is an earnings-related benefit designed to compensate employees or former employees for an impairment of earning capacity due to an accident at work or work-related illness. In or around 1986 it was decided, as a matter of policy, that REA should no longer be paid to claimants who had reached an age at which, even if they had not suffered injury or disease, they would no longer be in paid employment… The applicants concede that it was reasonable to aim to stop paying REA to workers after the age when they would, in any event, have retired, and the court agrees, since the benefit in question is designed to replace or supplement earnings, and is therefore closely connected to employment and working life.

55. The applicants do not accept, however, that in order to achieve this aim it was necessary to adopt as the upper limit the age at which a man or woman becomes entitled to the state retirement pension, since state pensionable age is at present different for men and women. They suggest that a single cut-off age and/or overlapping benefit regulations could have been used instead.

56. The court observes, though, that a single cut-off age would not have achieved the same level of consistency with the state pension scheme, which is based upon a notional 'end of working life' at 60 for women and 65 for men. The benefits to which the applicants refer as having the same starting age for men and women—winter fuel payment, prescription charges and bus passes…are not inextricably linked to the concept of paid employment or 'working life' in the way that REA is. Overlapping benefit regulations, to ensure that any REA received was deducted from the state retirement pension would, moreover, have maintained the impugned difference of treatment, since women would still have become entitled to their pensions and liable to start receiving reduced-rate REA five years before men.

57. The government, for their part, have explained that the use of the state pension age as the cut-off point for REA made the scheme easy to understand and administer… The court considers that such questions of administrative economy and coherence are generally matters falling within the margin of appreciation referred to in para 52, above.

58. Moreover it finds it significant that, in the present applicants' case, the ECJ found [in *Hepple v Adjudication Officer* Case C-196/98 [2000] ECR I-3701], that since REA was intended to compensate people of working age for loss of earning capacity due to an accident at work or occupational disease, it was necessary, in order to preserve coherence with the old-age pension scheme, to link the age-limits…While it is true that art 7(1)(a) of the Directive provides an express exception to the general prohibition on discrimination in social security…the ECJ was called upon, in deciding whether the case fell within the art 7 exception, to make a judgment as to whether the discrimination in the REA scheme arising from the link to differential pensionable age was objectively necessary in order to ensure consistency with the pension scheme. In reaching a conclusion on this issue which, while not determinative of the issue under art 14 of the convention, is none the less of central importance, particular regard should be had to the strong persuasive value of the ECJ's finding on this point.

59. The court considers, therefore, for the above reasons, that both the policy decision to stop paying REA to persons who would otherwise have retired from paid employment, and the decision to achieve this aim by linking the cut-off age for REA to the notional 'end of working life', or state pensionable age, pursued a legitimate aim and were reasonably and objectively justified.

60. It remains to be examined whether or not the underlying difference in treatment between men and women in the State pension scheme was acceptable under art 14.

61. Differential pensionable ages were first introduced for men and women in the United Kingdom in 1940, well before the Convention had come into existence, although the disparity persists to the present day. It would appear that the difference in treatment was adopted in order to mitigate financial inequality and hardship arising out of the woman's traditional unpaid role of caring for the family in the home rather than earning money in the workplace. At their origin, therefore, the differential pensionable ages were intended to correct 'factual inequalities' between men and women and appear therefore to have been objectively justified under art 14.

62. It follows that the difference in pensionable ages continued to be justified until such time that social conditions had changed so that women were no longer substantially prejudiced because of a shorter working life. This change, must, by its very nature, have been gradual, and it would be difficult or impossible to pinpoint any particular moment when the unfairness to men caused by differential pensionable ages began to outweigh the need to correct the disadvantaged position of women. Certain indications are available to the Court. Thus, in the 1993 White Paper, the Government asserted that the number of women in paid employment had increased significantly, so that whereas in 1967 only 37% of employees were women, the proportion had increased to 50% in 1992. In addition, various reforms to the way in which pension entitlement was assessed had been introduced in 1977 and 1978, to the benefit of women who spent long periods out of paid employment. As of 1986, it was unlawful for an employer to have different retirement ages for men and women.

63. According to the information before the Court, the Government made a first, concrete, move towards establishing the same pensionable age for both sexes with the publication of the Green Paper in December 1991. It would, no doubt, be possible to argue that this step could, or should, have been made earlier. However, as the Court has observed, the development of parity in the working lives of men and women has been a gradual process, and one which the national authorities are better placed to assess. Moreover, it is significant that many of the other Contracting States still maintain a difference in the ages at which men and women become eligible for the State retirement pension. Within the European Union, this position is recognised by the exception contained in the Directive.

64. In the light of the original justification for the measure as correcting financial inequality between the sexes, the slowly evolving nature of the change in women's working lives, and in the absence of a common standard amongst the Contracting States, the Court finds that the United Kingdom cannot be criticised for not having started earlier on the road towards a single pensionable age.

65. Having once begun the move towards equality, moreover, the Court does not consider it unreasonable of the Government to carry out a thorough process of consultation and review, nor can Parliament be condemned for deciding in 1995 to introduce the reform slowly and in stages. Given the extremely far-reaching and serious implications, for women and for the economy in general, these are matters which clearly fall within the State's margin of appreciation.

66. In conclusion, the court finds that the difference in state pensionable age between men and women in the United Kingdom was originally intended to correct the disadvantaged economic position of women. It continued to be reasonably and objectively justified on this ground until such time that social and economic changes removed the need for special treatment for women. The respondent state's decisions as to the precise timing and means of putting right the inequality were not so manifestly unreasonable as to exceed the wide margin of appreciation allowed it in such a field... Similarly, the decision to link eligibility for REA to the pension system was reasonably and objectively justified, given that this benefit is intended to compensate for reduced earning capacity during a person's working life. There has not, therefore, been a violation of art 14 taken in conjunction with art 1 of the first protocol in this case...

NOTE

1. Is the decision in *Stec* justifiable? Can it be characterised as an example of positive discrimination? Is it consistent with the approach of the European Court in *Abdulaziz*?

14

STATUTORY DISCRIMINATION
PROVISIONS

1. INTRODUCTION

(A) PRELIMINARIES

The main focus of this chapter is on the domestic statutory provisions which prohibit discrimination on grounds (broadly) of race, sex, disability, sexual orientation, religion and belief and age. Much of the case law which has developed under these provisions relates to employment. However significant this area of application, it is not our central concern here.[1] Many employment-related cases will be mentioned in our discussion of core issues such as the meaning of discrimination, this because such cases comprise the vast bulk of decisions under the various discrimination provisions, but our primary focus is on the application of the discrimination provisions to public authorities *qua* public authorities, and in relation to other aspects of public life.[2] Also mentioned will be a number of provisions that deal with issues such as incitement to racial and religious hatred and enhanced sentencing in cases of racially aggravated crime and, from time to time, Art. 14 of the European Convention on Human Rights, which is the subject of Chap. 13.

There are a large number of primary and secondary legislative provisions that deal with discrimination on the grounds mentioned above. In June 2008 the Government announced its intention to move forward with a single Equality Act which will amalgamate all these provisions into a single statute and which will make some amendments of more or less significance. Some proposed amendments will be mentioned where relevant, but nothing is certain at the time of writing.

Prior to any single equality legislation the domestic statutory provisions consist of the following (in chronological order):

- the Equal Pay Act 1970 (EqPA),
- the Sex Discrimination Act 1975 (SDA),
- the Race Relations Act 1976 (RRA),
- the Disability Discrimination Act 1995 (DDA),

---

[1] For full discussion see, e.g., A. McColgan, *Discrimination Law: Text, Cases and Materials* (Hart Publishing, Oxford, 2nd edn, 2005), K. Monaghan, *Equality Law* (OUP, Oxford, 2007), and H. Collins, K.D. Ewing and A. McColgan, *Labour Law: Text and Materials* (Hart Publishing, Oxford, 2nd edn, 2005), Chap. 3.

[2] Because the statutory provisions dealing with 'office holders' is equated to the employment provisions it will be omitted, as will the DDA's prohibitions on discrimination in relation to members of public authorities (ss. 15A–15C DDA).

- the Employment Equality (Religion or Belief) Regulations 2003 (RB Regs),
- the Employment Equality (Sexual Orientation) Regulations 2003 (SO Regs),
- the Equality Act 2006 (EA 2006),
- the Employment Equality (Age) Regulations 2006 (Age Regs), and
- the Equality Act (Sexual Orientation) Regulations 2007 (EA Regs).

Between them these provisions regulate discrimination on grounds of race (including 'colour, race nationality or ethnic or national origins'; sex (including pregnancy and gender reassignment), status as a married person or a person in a civil partnership (but not a single person); disability, sexual orientation, religion and belief (including the absence of any religious belief) and age. The precise protection provided varies according to the ground with race ('colour' and nationality excluded) at the top of the hierarchy and married/civil partner status at the bottom (current protection extending only to the employment sphere). The detail will change with the likely implementation of a single Equality Act, which is expected to bring age more broadly into line with the other grounds and to bring nationality and 'colour' into line with the other 'racial' grounds.

Enforcement is by way of individual application to the county court (other than in the context of employment or disability discrimination in schools); to the employment tribunal (in the case of employment-related disputes); to SENDIST or its Welsh equivalent in the case of disability discrimination in schools; or to the High Court in an application for judicial review (see further section 2(B) below). The Equality and Human Rights Commission also has significant enforcement powers, as did its predecessor ('legacy') commissions. Those powers are found in the Equality Act 2006, which establishes the Commission, and include powers to enforce a number of the anti-discrimination provisions on the Commission's own initiative, to intervene in litigation, to take proceedings in judicial review where it has sufficient interest and to support litigation by others.[3] The EHRC also has powers to enforce the specific equality duties,[4] powers of formal investigation and power to issue non-discrimination notices, enforceable through the courts.[5] In practice these powers, materially similar to those enjoyed by the legacy commissions, are almost never used in practice because of the procedural hurdles imposed on the predecessor commissions by a largely hostile judiciary.[6] Considerations of space preclude discussion of the role of the EHRC. It is useful to note, however, that the codes of practice to which reference is made throughout this chapter have statutory force by virtue of the Acts under which the legacy commissions and the EHRC itself were created. This does not mean that they are authoritative statements of the law or that they impose any legal obligations in themselves. However, courts and tribunal are bound to take into account any part of such codes that might be relevant to a question arising before them.[7]

(B) MATERIAL SCOPE OF THE ANTI-DISCRIMINATION PROVISIONS

At present the RRA, SDA and DDA prohibit discrimination in employment, education, housing, the provision of goods, services and facilities and by public authorities, and impose

---

[3] See, generally, EA 2006, ss. 25 and 28–30.   [4] EA 2006, ss. 31–32.

[5] EA 2006, ss. 22–24.

[6] See A. McColgan, *Discrimination Law: Text, Cases and Materials*, n. 1 above, Chap. 5 and the EA 2006, Pt 1.

[7] EA 2006, s. 15.

positive obligations on such authorities to promote equality of opportunity on grounds of race, sex and disability respectively. The SDA also prohibits employment-related discrimination against married persons and discrimination in connection with gender reassignment, while the EqPA deals with sex discrimination in the contractual terms of employment (such discrimination being excluded from the provisions of the SDA). The DDA, unlike the other provisions, is asymmetric, its protections only applying to those 'disabled' for the purposes of the Act (though see the discussion of *Coleman v Attridge Law* at section 11(B) below).[8] The SO Regs and the RB Regs regulate discrimination on grounds of sexual orientation and religion and belief in the context (only) of employment and third-level education, the EA 2006 and EA Regs applying to discrimination by public authorities and in relation to advertising, education, the provision of goods and services and housing.

(C) INFLUENCE OF EU LAW

The current statutory scheme is complex and inconsistent between the vaious grounds, significantly as a result of legislative history rather than principle. Until relatively recently (2003)[9] EU law had limited influence except in relation to sex. The SDA preceded the Equal Treatment Directive (Directive 76/207/EEC) but has been amended over time to give effect to the obligations imposed on the UK by that Directive and more recently by Directives 2003/73/EC (amending the Equal Treatment Directive) and 2004/113/EC on gender equality in goods and services. The RRA, although preceded (unlike the SDA) by the Race Relations Acts of 1965 and 1968, was modelled in significant part on the SDA and has benefitted over the years by being interpreted consistent with the SDA. The SDA in turn was interpreted in line with EU requirements, although the RRA itself had no EU 'underpinning' until 2003 with the coming into force of the Race Directive (Directive 2000/34/EC) which, in a single leap, overtook EU legislative prohibitions on sex discrimination.[10] Even prior to this, the RRA had been amended by the Race Relations (Amendment) Act 2000, in the wake of the Stephen Lawrence murder and Macpherson report on 'institutional discrimination',[11] and by July 2001 imposed negative and positive legal obligations on public authorities that were not imposed by the SDA and DDA until 2006 and 2005 respectively.[12]

EU law is of central importance to domestic discrimination law, in particular as it applies to employment. At present, EU law prohibits discrimination related to sexual orientation, religion or belief, age and disability only in the areas of employment (broadly defined) and third-level education. But the prohibitions on sex and race discrimination imposed by EU law go well beyond these spheres, applying also in the case of sex to the provision of goods and services, the disposal of premises and matters of social security generally and, in the case of race, to the provision of goods and services, housing, education and to health care, any other form of social protection and any form of social advantage.[13] Discrimination in

---

8   Also note that the Act's victimisation provisions apply regardless of disability.

9   This being the date of implementation of Council Directives 2000/34/EC (race equality) and 222/78/EC (employment equality).

10   The Race Directive, unlike EU gender equality provisions, applies, *inter alia*, to education and advertisements.

11   See www.archive.official-documents.co.uk/document/cm42/4262/4262.htm (accessed 4 August 2008). For further discussion see, e.g., A. McColgan, n. 1 above, Chap. 7, K. Monaghan n. 1 above, 6.01–6.04.

12   This with the amendment of the SDA and DDA by the Equality Act 2006 and the Disability Discrimination Act 2005 respectively.

13   Art. 3 Directive 2000/78/EC.

relation to gender-reassignment is regulated because of the ECJ's decision in Case 13/94, *P v S & Cornwall County Council*[14] that such discrimination fell within the Equal Treatment Directive. The SDA was amended to apply this protection only in relation to employment (this being within the material scope of the Directive), but further amendments were made in 2006 with the implementation of Council Directive 2002/73, which prohibited sex discrimination in access to goods and services.

The exact meaning of terms like 'social advantage' is unclear and has given rise to some litigation concerning whether a particular act of discrimination which falls within the RRA is or is not also covered by the Directive.[15] The significance of the question is to whether the challenge will benefit from, for example, the new definitions of indirect discrimination and harassment set out in the RRA but applicable only to that discrimination covered also by the Directive, or to the applicable burden of proof (see further section 9(B) below). Whatever the eventual settlement of these questions, both the RRA and the SDA are characterised at present by complex structures that apply different provisions to discrimination depending, in the case of the RRA, largely on whether it is discrimination on grounds of racial or ethnic or national origin, on the one hand (to which the Race Directive applies) or discrimination on grounds of colour or nationality (to which it does not). The faultline in the SDA is between employment/occupation (broadly defined), vocational training and goods and services not including advertisements (to which Directives 1976/117/EEC as amended and 2002/73/EC apply), on the one hand, and education, discrimination by public authorities and the remaining material scope of the SDA, on the other.[16] The DDA's distinction is between discrimination in the context of employment/occupation (broadly defined), vocational training and higher education (to which Council Directive 2000/78/EC applies), on the one hand, and the remaining material scope of the Act, on the other.

In July 2008 the European Commission proposed a directive implementing the principle of equal treatment between persons irrespective of religion or belief, disability, age or sexual orientation which, if adopted in its current form, would extend the prohibition on these forms of discrimination to cover education; social protection, including social security and health care; social advantages and publicly accessible goods and services. At the time of writing, domestic law extends beyond EU requirements in the case of disability, sexual orientation and religion or belief.[17] No such extension has occurred in relation to age, though the Government announced in June 2008 that this would result from the (planned) new single Equality Act.

The current legislative arrangements are extremely complex and are liable to imminent change. Every attempt will be made in this chapter to discuss the issues at the level of principle but reference to multiple legislative provisions is inevitable if the law is to be stated with any accuracy. It should be noted at the outset, for the avoidance of doubt, that the statutory regimes prohibit *only* those acts of discrimination that fall within their material scope (that

---

[14] [1996] ECR I–2143.

[15] See *R (Primrose) v Secretary of State for Justice* [2008] All ER (D) 156 (Jul.), *R (Couronne) v Crawley Borough Council* [2007] EWCA Civ 1086, [2007] All ER (D) 50 (Nov.).

[16] See ss. 1(3) SDA and 1(1B) RRA.

[17] These provisions, the EA 2006 (Pt 2) which governs discrimination on grounds of religion and belief, and the EA Regs, which govern sexual orientation discrimination, are unusual in that they apply EU standards of proof and something like EU definitions of indirect discrimination despite the lack of EU underpinning, while the SDA, RRA and DDA apply EU standards only where required by EU law. The reason is perhaps that existing provisions were amended by statutory instrument under the European Communities Act 1972, which permits amendment of primary legislation by secondary legislation only reasonably broadly to secure compliance with relevant EU law. But it has always been a matter of political decision to utilise the 1972 Act rather than to proceed by way of primary legislation, the latter course having been adopted where regarded as beneficial (as in the case of the DDA 2005 and the RR(A)A 2000).

scope differing between the regimes) and do not prohibit all discrimination on the relevant grounds.[18]

2. LIABILITY AND DUTIES OF PUBLIC AUTHORITIES *QUA* PUBLIC AUTHORITIES

(A) LIABILITY FOR DISCRIMINATION

The RRA was the first Act expressly to prohibit discrimination by public authorities, this because of concern about institutionalised racism in the wake of the murder of Stephen Lawrence and the resulting Macpherson inquiry. It now provides as follows:

- **Race Relations Act 1976**

19B. Discrimination by public authorities

(1) It is unlawful for a public authority in carrying out any functions of the authority to do any act which constitutes discrimination

(1A) It is unlawful for a public authority to subject a person to harassment in the course of carrying out any functions of the authority which consist of the provision of—

   (a) any form of social security;

   (b) healthcare;

   (c) any other form of social protection; or

   (d) any form of social advantage,

which does not fall within section 20.

(2) In this section 'public authority'—

   (a) includes any person certain of whose functions are functions of a public nature: but

   (b) does not include any person mentioned in subsection (3).

(3) The persons mentioned in this subsection are—

   (a) either House of Parliament;

   (b) person exercising functions in connection with proceedings in Parliament;

   (c) the Security Service;

   (d) the Secret Intelligence Service;

   (e) the Government Communications Headquarters; and

   (f) any unit or part of a unit of any of the naval, military or air forces of the Crown which is for the time being required by the Secretary of State to assist the Government Communications Headquarters in carrying out its functions.

(4) In relation to a particular act, a person is not a public authority by virtue only of subsection (2)(a) if the nature of the act is private.

(5) This section is subject to sections 19C to 19F.

---

[18] On this see *Amin v Entry Clearance Officer, Bombay* [1983] 2 AC 818, *De Souza v Automobile Association* [1986] ICR 514.

(6) Nothing in this section makes unlawful any act of discrimination or harassment which—

    (a) is made unlawful by virtue of any other provision of this Act; or

    (b) would be so made but for any provision made by or under this Act.

19C. Exceptions or further exceptions from section 19B for judicial and legislative acts etc

(1) Section 19B does not apply to—

    (a) any judicial act (whether done by a court, tribunal or other person); or

    (b) any act done on the instructions, or on behalf, of a person acting in a judicial capacity.

(2) Section 19B does not apply to any act of, or relating to, making, confirming or approving any enactment or Order in Council or any instrument made by a Minister of the Crown under an enactment.

(3) Section 19B does not apply to any act of, or relating to, making or approving arrangements, or imposing requirements or conditions, of a kind excepted by section 41.

(4) Section 19B does not apply to any act of, or relating to, imposing a requirement, or giving an express authorisation, of a kind mentioned in section 19D(3) in relation to the carrying out of immigration functions.

19D. Exception from section 19B for certain acts in immigration and nationality cases

(1) Section 19B does not make it unlawful for a relevant person to discriminate against another person on grounds of nationality or ethnic or national origins in carrying out immigration functions.

(2) For the purposes of subsection (1), 'relevant person' means—

    (a) a Minister of the Crown acting personally; or

    (b) any other person acting in accordance with a relevant authorisation.

(3) In subsection (2), 'relevant authorisation' means a requirement imposed or express authorisation given—

    (a) with respect to a particular case or class of case, by a Minister of the Crown acting personally;

    (b) with respect to a particular class of case—

        (i) by any of the enactments mentioned in subsection (5); or

        (ii) by any instrument made under or by virtue of any of those enactments.

(3) For the purposes of subsection (1), 'immigration functions' means functions exercisable by virtue of any of the enactments mentioned in subsection (5).

(4) Those enactments are—

    (a) the Immigration Acts (within the meaning of section 44 of the Asylum and Immigration (Treatment of Claimants, etc) Act 2004) excluding sections 28A to 28K of the Immigration Act 1971 so far as they relate to offences under Part III of that Act) and excluding section 14 of the Asylum and Immigration (Treatment of Claimants, etc) Act 2004;

    (b) the Special Immigration Appeals Commission Act 1997 (c 68);

    (c) provision made under section 2(2) of the European Communities Act 1972 (c 68) which relates to immigration or asylum; and

    (d) any provision of Community law which relates to immigration or asylum

19F. Exceptions from section 19B for decisions not to prosecute etc

Section 19B does not apply to—

    (a) a decision not to institute criminal proceedings and, where such a decision has been made, any act done for the purpose of enabling the decision whether to institute criminal proceedings to be made;

(b) where criminal proceedings are not continued as a result of a decision not to continue them, the decision and, where such a decision has been made—

    (i) any act done for the purpose of enabling the decision whether to continue the proceedings to be made; and

    (ii) any act done for the purpose of securing that the proceedings are not continued.

NOTES

1. Even before the amendment of the RRA to include s. 19B, the Act had contained a provision (now s. 19A) prohibiting discrimination by planning authorities. Section 19A has no equivalents in the other discrimination legislation and had generated little case law, though in *Davis v Bath and North East Somerset District Council*[19] a county court awarded £750,000 plus costs to a claimant whose applications for planning permission had been repeatedly obstructed by the council's staff.

2. The *European Roma Rights* case,[20] considered below, is one in which discrimination was found to have occurred contrary to s. 19B in connection with immigration. In that case, which concerned discrimination against Roma (a group defined by ethnicity), the relevant minister had in fact issued the Race Relations (Immigration and Asylum) (No. 2) Authorisation 2001, under s. 19D(2)(b), which provided that immigration officers could subject persons of Roma origin 'to a more rigorous examination than other persons in the same circumstances' and 'by reason of [their] ethnic or national origin...decline to give or refuse the person leave to enter before he arrives in the United Kingdom'. The state did not, however, seek to rely on the authorisation, which was revoked in 2002, and which was said never to have been adopted or made use of in connection with the scheme under challenge, whose legality therefore fell to be assessed under s. 19B RRA.

3. The SDA and DDA have more recently been amended to provide in generally similar terms to s. 19B (ss. 21A and 21B respectively), save that no specific provision is made in relation to immigration functions and, in the case of the SDA, a table of exceptions is set out in the relevant provision (s. 21A(9) SDA) which covers a wide range of functions, to the extent that there is no incompatibility with EU law, including those relating to the making of or compliance with legislation, judicial functions, the 'provision of a service for one sex only where only persons of that sex require the service [or]...where a joint service would or might be less effective', and '[a]ction taken for the purpose of assisting one sex to overcome—(a) a disadvantage (as compared with the other sex), or (b) the effects of discrimination.' Regulation 8 of the EA Regs imposes a broadly similar prohibition on discrimination on grounds of sexual orientation as does s. 52 EA 2006 in relation to religion or belief, the particular exceptions to that prohibition including, *inter alia*, decisions made in the immigration context on the basis that a person's exclusion from the UK 'is conducive to the public good' (s. 52(4)(f), (g)), and:

Section 52 EA 2006

    (k) action in relation to-

        (i) the curriculum of an educational institution,

        (ii) admission to an educational institution which has a religious ethos,

---

[19] Bristol CC, Claim No. 9324149, discussed by K. Monaghan, n. 1 above, p. 511 fn. 67.

[20] *European Roma Rights Centre v Immigration Officer at Prague Airport* [2005] 2 WLR 1.

> (iii) acts of worship or other religious observance organised by or on behalf of an educational institution (whether or not forming part of the curriculum),
>
> (iv) the governing body of an educational institution which has a religious ethos,
>
> (v) transport to or from an educational institution, or
>
> (vi) the establishment, alteration or closure of educational institutions…
>
> (l) the exercise of the power under section 2 of the Local Government Act 2000 (c 22) (promotion of well-being), or

We shall see, below, that wide exceptions are provided in relation to the EA 2006 Act's prohibitions on discrimination on grounds of religion or belief in the context of schools.

4. As originally enacted and interpreted by the courts, the RRA and SDA only applied to discrimination by public authorities to a limited extent. Public authorities have always been subject to sections of the anti-discrimination legislation covering particular areas of activity, such as their employment of staff, provision of education and public housing (see generally below). But 'the services of…any local or other public authority' (see discussion of s. 20 RRA and its equivalents below) were covered by the anti-discrimination provisions, prior to relatively recent amendment, only in relation to 'acts which are similar to acts that could be done by private persons'.[21] This did not include many acts of the police, the prison service, the immigration authorities, and tax inspectors, etc., in the exercise of their functions,[22] and resulted in a very significant gap in the scope of coverage of the anti-discrimination provisions which generated a great deal of concern in the aftermath of the Stephen Lawrence murder and the resulting exposure of endemic racism in the police service. The inclusion of s. 19B RRA directly resulted from this and the prohibition of other forms of discrimination by public authorities followed in due course.

5. Section 19B(6) RRA makes it clear that the provision is a 'last resort' where the discrimination at issue does not fall within any other section of the Act. The same is true of the SDA and DDA[23] but the EA 2006 and the EA Regs provide that discrimination by public authorities in relation to goods and services should be challenged as discrimination by the public authority *qua* public authority, but that otherwise it should be challenged under any other applicable provision of the Act or Regs (e.g., where it relates to housing, education, etc.)[24]

6. Claims of discrimination contrary to s. 19B RRA and its equivalent provisions may be brought before a county court in accordance with the arrangements for other non-employment claims under the various provisions.[25] They may also, however, be brought by way of judicial review and it is in this context that the prohibitions on discrimination by public authorities has really started to 'bite'. One example of this is the decision of the House of Lords in the *Roma Rights* case, considered above and below, in which an application for judicial review of the practices of British immigration officers at Prague airport resulted in a declaration that 'United Kingdom Immigration Officers operating under the authority of the Home Secretary at Prague airport discriminated against Roma who were seeking to travel from that airport to the United Kingdom by treating them less favourably on racial grounds than they treated others who were seeking to travel from that airport to the

---

[21] *Amin v Entry Clearance Officer, Bombay* [1983] 2 AC 818.

[22] See, generally, A. McColgan, *Discrimination Law: Text, Cases and Materials*, n. 1 above, Chap. 4.

[23] Ss. 21A SDA, paras 15 and 16, and 21B(7), respectively.

[24] Ss. 48(4) and 52(4)(m) EA 2006 and reg. 4(3) and Sch. 1, Pt 2, para. 7 EA Regs.

[25] E.g. s. 57 RRA as amended by the RR(A)A 2000.

United Kingdom...' More recently, the landmark decision in *R (on the application of Elias) v Secretary of State for Defence*,[26] which 'kick started' s. 71 RRA litigation (see further below), also resulted in a declaration that the scheme there at issue, compensation payments for civilians interned by the Japanese during the second world war, discriminated on grounds of national origin contrary to s. 19B RRA. Judicial review applications do not generally permit a claim for compensation (except where the HRA is relied upon), but may be used for the purposes of clarifying difficult legal questions while a compensation claim in the county court is initiated and then stayed pending the outcome of the judicial review.[27] A number of other s. 19 challenges have been unsuccessful because, for example, a defence was successfully pleaded (*R (Mohammed) v Secretary of State for Defence*)[28] or a discrimination claim defeated on comparator or other grounds (*R (Al Rawi) v Secretary of State for Foreign and Commonwealth Affairs, R (E) v Governing Body of the Jews Free School* and *Couronnes v Crawley Borough Council*,[29] all of which are discussed below). The growing pace of litigation under this provision and s. 71 RRA indicates a very exciting bringing together of public law and anti-discrimination norms previously given scant effect in this context.[30]

7. Should the state be permitted to discriminate on grounds other than nationality in its immigration function? In particular, what are the possible justifications for taking into account (a) ethnicity, (b) religious affiliation?

(B) DUTIES OF PUBLIC AUTHORITIES

- **Race Relations Act 1976**

71. Specified authorities: general statutory duty

(1) Every body or other person specified in Schedule 1A or of a description falling within that Schedule shall, in carrying out its functions, have due regard to the need—

   (a) to eliminate unlawful racial discrimination; and

   (b) to promote equality of opportunity and good relations between persons of different racial groups.

(2) The Minister may by order impose, on such persons falling within Schedule 1A as he considers appropriate, such duties as he considers appropriate for the purpose of ensuring the better performance by those persons of their duties under subsection (1).

(3) An order under subsection (2)—

   (a) may be made in relation to a particular person falling within Schedule 1A, any description of persons falling within that Schedule or every person falling within that Schedule;

   (b) may make different provision for different purposes.

(4) Before making an order under subsection (2), the Minister shall consult the Commission.

---

[26] [2005] EWHC (Admin), [2005] IRLR 788 (first instance) and [2006] EWCA Civ 1293, [2006] 1 WLR 3213 (CA).

[27] This technique was adopted in *Elias*—see the decision of the Court of Appeal, n. 26 above, paras 218 ff, though the claim was dismissed on the facts of that particular case.

[28] [2007] All ER (D) 09 (CA), considered below, in which s. 41 was relied on in a case which the courts accepted involved discrimination on grounds of nationality alone.

[29] [2006] EWCA Civ 1279, [2007] 2 WLR 1219 (CA); [2008] EWHC 1535 and 1536 (Admin), [2008] All ER (D) 54 (Jul) and [2007] EWCA Civ 1086, [2007] All ER (D) 50 (Nov.), respectively.

[30] See A. McColgan, 'Discrimination Law and the Human Rights Act 1998' in T. Campbell, K.D. Ewing and A. Tomkins (eds), *Sceptical Approaches to Human Rights* (OUP, Oxford, 2001).

(5) The Minister may by order amend Schedule 1 A; but no such order may extend the application of this section unless the Minister considers that the-extension relates to a person who exercises functions of a public nature.

(6) An order under subsection (2) or (5) may contain such incidental, supplementary or consequential provision as the Minister considers appropriate (including provision amending or repealing provision made by or under this Act or any other enactment).

(7) This section is subject to section 71A and 71B and is without prejudice to the obligation of any person to comply with any other provision of this Act.

71 A. General statutory duty: special cases

(1) In relation to the carrying out of immigration and nationality functions, section 71(1)(b) has effect with the omission of the words 'equality of opportunity and

(1A) In subsection (1) 'immigration and nationality functions' means functions exercisable by virtue of—

   (a) the Immigration Acts (within the meaning of section 158 of the Nationality, Immigration and Asylum Act 2002) excluding sections 28A to 28K of the Immigration Act 1971 so far as they relate to offences under Part III of that Act;

   (b) the British Nationality Act 1981;

   (c) the British Nationality (Falkland Islands) Act 1983 (c 6);

   (d) the British Nationality (Hong Kong) Act 1990 (c 34);

   (e) the Hong Kong (War Wives and Widows) Act 1996 (c 41);

   (f) the British Nationality (Hong Kong) Act 1997 (c 20);

   (g) the Special Immigration Appeals Commission Act 1997 (c 68);

   (h) provision made under section 2(2) of the European Communities Act 1972 (c 68) which relates to the subject matter of an enactment within any of paragraphs (a) to (g); or

   (i) any provision of Community law which relates to the subject matter of an enactment within any of those paragraphs.

(2) Where an entry in Schedule 1A is limited to a person in a particular capacity, section 71(1) does not apply to that person in any other capacity.

(3) Where an entry in Schedule 1A is limited to particular functions of a person, section 71(1) does not apply to that person in relation to any other functions.

NOTES

1. The list of public authorities to which the RRA applies is very lengthy, additions having been made by Order over the years to the 60 originally covered. They include Ministers of the Crown and government departments, the armed forces, health authorities, local authorities, planning committees, probation committees, police authorities and magistrates' committees. The other statutory regimes do not list the bodies to which the general duties apply.[31]

2. The SDA and DDA now include provisions similar to s. 71 RRA (ss. 76A SDA and 49A DDA respectively). The main differences between the Acts concern the matters to which the public authority is to have regard. In the case of the SDA this consists of 'the need—(a) to eliminate unlawful discrimination and harassment, and (b) to promote equality of

---

[31] Ss. 21B DD, 21A SDA, 52 EA 2006 and reg. 9 EA Regs.

opportunity between men and women'. The DDA requires that due regard be had to '(a) the need to eliminate discrimination that is unlawful under this Act; (b) the need to eliminate harassment of disabled persons that is related to their disabilities; (c) the need to promote equality of opportunity between disabled persons and other persons; (d) the need to take steps to take account of disabled persons' disabilities, even where that involves treating disabled persons more favourably than other persons; (e) the need to promote positive attitudes towards disabled persons; and (f) the need to encourage participation by disabled persons in public life.'[32]

Another significant difference between the RRA and the DDA and SDA in this context is that neither the DDA nor the SDA list the public authorities to which the general duties apply, the SDA providing instead that a 'public authority' 'includes any person who has functions of a public nature' (subject to exceptions covering similar bodies to those to which s. 19B RRA does not apply), and the DDA (s. 49B(1)a)) that 'public authority' 'includes any person certain of whose functions are functions of a public nature' subject to a similar set of exceptions. Further (s. 49B(2) DDA) 'In relation to a particular act, a person is not a public authority by virtue only of subsection (1)(a) if the nature of the act is private.' Finally, the specific duties imposed by order differ between the various Acts. It should be noted that, in the case of the SDA and DDA, as in that of the RRA, these specific duties apply only to listed public authorities.[33] There is little purpose in discussing the detail of the special duties as these are likely to alter if and when the single Equality Act, expected to be published within months, eventually becomes law. Suffice it to say here that the special duties are generally process-driven, concerned with the drawing up and publication of racial, sex and disability equality schemes which set out how public authorities will 'mainstream' the general duties into their practices.

3. The CRE (now absorbed into the EHRC) has drawn up a Code of Practice on the Duty to Promote Race Equality.[34] The Code, and its accompanying non-statutory guidance, has proved very influential in the judicial interpretation of s. 71.[35] The Code provides as follows (Chap. 3):

HOW TO MEET THE GENERAL DUTY

3.11 Public authorities should consider the following four steps to meet the general duty.

a. Identify which of their functions and policies are relevant to the duty, or, in other words, affect most people.

b. Put the functions and policies in order of priority, based on how relevant they are to race equality.

c. Assess whether the way these 'relevant' functions and policies are being carried out meets the three parts of the duty.

d. Consider whether any changes need to be made to meet the duty, and make the changes.

---

[32] The consultation document on a single Equality Act (*A Framework for Fairness*) proposed that the separate duties applicable to race, sex and disability be replaced with a single duty applicable to all protected grounds.

[33] See the Sex Discrimination Act 1975 (Public Authorities) (Statutory Duties) Order 2006, SI 2006/2930 and the Disability Discrimination (Public Authorities) (Statutory Duties) Regulations 2005, SI 2005/2966.

[34] 'Statutory Code of Practice on the Duty to Promote Race Equality' (and the Scottish Code), also the 'Gender Equality Duty—Code of Practice for England and Wales' and, Scottish Code, and 'The Duty to Promote Disability Equality: Statutory Code of Practice: England and Wales', and Scottish Code, all available from the EHRC website (www.equalityhumanrights.com/en/foradvisers/codesofpractice/pages/codesofpractice.aspx, accessed 7 August 2008).

[35] See for example the decision in *Kaur & Shah v London Borough of Ealing* [2008] EWHC 2062 (Admin), [2008] All ER (D) 08 (Oct.). 'The Duty to Promote Race Equality—A Guide for Public Authorities' is available from the EHRC's website (www.equalityhumanrights.com).

IDENTIFYING RELEVANT FUNCTIONS

3.12 To identify relevant functions, a public authority will find it useful, first, to make a list of all its functions, including employment. It should then assess how relevant each function is to each part of the general duty. As shown in paragraph 3.4, some functions may, by their nature, have little or no relevance.

3.13 A public authority should consider setting priorities, and giving priority to those functions that are most relevant to race equality.

ASSESSING IMPACT AND CONSIDERING CHANGE

3.14 To assess the impact its functions and policies have on race equality, the authority may find it useful to draw up a clear statement of the aims of each function or policy. It should then consider whether it has information about how different racial groups are affected by the function or policy, as employees or users (or possible users) of services. The authority should also consider whether its functions and policies are promoting good race relations. The authority could get this information from various sources; for example previous research, records of complaints, surveys, or local meetings. These methods should help public authorities to assess which of their services are used by which racial groups, or what people think of their services, and whether they are being provided fairly to people from different racial groups. This kind of evidence should help public authorities to decide what they might need to do to meet all three parts of the general duty.

3.15 Public authorities may also need to consider adapting their existing information systems, so that they can provide information about different racial groups and show what progress the authority is making on race equality.

3.16 To assess the effects of a policy, or the way a function is being carried out, public authorities could ask themselves the following questions.

a. Could the policy or the way the function is carried out have an adverse impact on equality of opportunity for some racial groups? In other words, does it put some racial groups at a disadvantage?

b. Could the policy or the way the function is carried out have an adverse impact on relations between different racial groups?

c. Is the adverse impact, if any, unavoidable? Could it be considered to be unlawful racial discrimination? Can it be justified by the aims and importance of the policy or function? Are there other ways in which the authority's aims can be achieved without causing an adverse impact on some racial groups?

d. Could the adverse impact be reduced by taking particular measures?

e. Is further research or consultation necessary? Would this research be proportionate to the importance of the policy or function? Is it likely to lead to a different outcome?

3.17 If the assessment suggests that the policy, or the way the function is carried out, should be modified, the authority should do this to meet the general duty.

4. In *R (Baker) v Secretary of State for Communities & Local Government* Dyson LJ stated that 'due regard' is 'the regard that is appropriate in all the circumstances. These include on the one hand the importance of the areas of life of the members of the disadvantaged racial group that are affected by the inequality of opportunity and the extent of the inequality; and on the other hand, such countervailing factors as are relevant to the function which the decision-maker is performing.'[36]

The case law which has emerged under s. 71 RRA (the longest in position) demonstrates that the general duty is a powerful tool in the struggle against discrimination. It has

---

[36] [2008] EWCA Civ 141, [2008] All ER (D) 412 (Feb.), para. 31.

become clear through a succession of cases that public authorities may not reach decisions which have any potentially significant disparate impact by race, gender or disability status without undertaking rigorous equality impact assessment of such decisions and, where significant disparate impact is shown to be likely, without adequately considering how such impact may be avoided or reduced. Such impact assessment must not be *ex post facto* justification of decisions already reached, or even reached contingent on the results of a subsequent impact assessment, but must be *ex ante*, rigorous and recorded. Thus in *R (E) v Governing Body of the Jews Free School* Munby J declared that 'The object of section 71 ... is to ensure that the potential racial impact of a decision is *always* taken into account by public authorities as a mandatory relevant consideration.'[37] In *R (Elias) v Secretary of State for Defence* the Administrative Court ruled, and the Court of Appeal agreed, that the defendant had failed to comply with the s. 71 duty because it had failed to assess the question of racial impact at the stage of formulating policy, and had not therefore considered the extent of any adverse impact or ways of eliminating or minimising such impact at a formative stage. Counsel for the Secretary of State argued that there had, by the time of the court hearing, been a careful consideration of the racial impact of the policy and that it was not therefore necessary for the court to consider any earlier breach. Elias J disagreed:

the purpose of this section is to ensure that the body subject to the duty pays due regard at the time the policy is being considered—that is, when the relevant function is being exercised—and not when it has become the subject of challenge. Moreover...there will be in many cases a tendency, perhaps subconscious, to make the assessment whether discrimination might arise with an eye on the outcome of the litigation. That will not produce the same unbiased analysis as might occur if consideration is given to the section 71 factors at the proper time.[38]

The Court of Appeal took a similar approach in the *Elias* case, Arden LJ stating that:

It is the clear purpose of section 71 to require public bodies to whom that provision applies to give advance consideration to issues of race discrimination before making any policy decision that may be affected by them. This is a salutary requirement, and this provision must be seen as an integral and important part of the mechanisms for ensuring the fulfilment of the aims of anti-discrimination legislation. It is not possible to take the view that the Secretary of State's non-compliance with that provision was not a very important matter. In the context of the wider objectives of anti-discrimination legislation, section 71 has a significant role to play.[39]

And in *R (BAPIO Action Ltd and Yousaf) v Secretary of State for the Home Department and Secretary of State for Health* Sedley LJ emphasised the requirement for 'compliance with s. 71, not as rearguard action following a concluded decision but as an essential preliminary to any such decision. Inattention to it is both unlawful and bad government.'[40] See also *Kaur & Shah v Ealing*, discussed further below (section 8(C)) in which Moses LJ, sitting in the Administrative Court, ruled that the s. 71 RRA duty to impact assess policy had to be fulfilled in advance of its adoption (as opposed to making a decision which was stated to be 'contingent' on an assessment to be carried out subsequently).[41]

37 N. 28 above, para. 206.   38 N. 25 above, para. 99.
39 N. 25 above, para 274.   40 [2007] EWCA Civ 1139, paras 2–3.
41 *Kaur & Shah v London Borough of Ealing*, n. 35 above.

5. In the *BAPIO* case, at first instance, Stanley Burnton J ruled that 'An important reason why the laws of discrimination have moved from derision to acceptance to respect over the last three decades has been the recognition of the importance not only of respecting rights *but also of doing so visibly and clearly by recording the fact*' (emphasis added).[42] But recording that the impact of a policy or decision has been assessed in advance is insufficient, Dyson LJ demanding in *R (Baker) v Secretary of State for Communities & Local Government* that 'the substance of the decision and its reasoning' be considered by the court.[43] In *R (Chavda) v Harrow LBC*,[44] one of the early cases brought under s. 49A DDA, the court ruled that a process in which an equalities impact assessment identified 'risk of impact', but where there was no evidence that the decision makers were made fully aware of the legal obligations imposed by s. 49A DDA, was insufficient to comply with that provision. The claimants were in receipt of community care services from the defendant local authority which, due to budgetary pressure, proposed to limit the provision of such services only to those persons who were assessed as having a 'critical' level of need. An equalities impact assessment was carried out which pointed to 'a potential conflict with the DDA [because a] . . . change in criteria could be seen as limiting access for some people to services'. The authority's decision to press ahead with the restriction of community care services was found by the Administrative Court to be in breach of s. 49A DDA:

36. ...The disability equality duty ('DED') is mentioned in none of the documents produced by the Defendant. That absence is striking given the requirements of the DED [disability equality duty] for a pro-active approach. There was no effort proactively to seek the views of the disabled or to refer to the duty in the planning stages of the consultation. There was no mention of the DED either at the Cabinet meeting on 15 March or at the portfolio holder meeting on 22 March. The Defendant did conduct an 'equality impact assessment' before 25 July and referred to it in the report to the meeting. That assessment addressed different groups of service users and found that there was a risk of impact and that it should be monitored in future but it did not address the DED. The Claimants say that Section 49A required the assessment to have explicit regard to promotion of equality of disabled people. The report did not mention what measures could be taken to avoid disadvantage to the disabled. The DED was mentioned on 25 July in an oral question but the answer simply referred back to the equality impact assessment already carried out...

37. The Claimants also rely upon *Eisai v National Institute of Clinical Excellence* [2007] EWHC 1941 (Admin) Dobbs J observed in relation to duties under Section 49 'I take the view that the approach of the Appeal Panel was flawed, in that no proper consideration was given to NICE's duties as a public authority to promote equal opportunities and to have due regard to the need to eliminate discrimination. It was unreasonable and unlawful to overlook that responsibility'. Mr Cragg [for the claimant] submits that that approach is consistent with that set out Arden LJ in *Secretary of State for Defence v Elias*...

40. The effect of the decision was to deprive those in substantial as opposed to critical need, many of whom are disabled, of a service of which they were, by definition, in need. In its extensive process of consultation the Council had regard to the position of disabled users in the ways I have mentioned. I recognise that in the indirect respects which Mr McCarthy [for the respondents] identifies the importance of these matters may have been drawn to the attention of the decision-takers on or before 25 July. I recognise that the general duty on the Council under Section 49A is only to have 'due regard' to the listed considerations (but as I have mentioned the Code states that this requires more than simply giving

---

[42] [2007] EWHC 199, para. 69. See also *R (Chavda) v Harrow LBC* [2007] EWHC 3064, para. 40; *R (Watkins-Singh) v Governing Body of Aberdare Girls' High School* [2008] EWHC 1865 (Admin), [2008] 3 FLR 203, para. 121.

[43] N. 35 above, para. 37.

[44] [2007] EWHC 3064 (Admin), 100 BMLR 27, [2007] All ER (D) 337 (Dec).

consideration to the issue of disability). These are important duties nonetheless including the need to promote equality of opportunity and to take account of disabilities even where that involves treating the disabled more favourably than others. There is no evidence that this legal duty and its implications were drawn to the attention of the decision-takers who should have been informed not just of the disabled as an issue but of the particular obligations which the law imposes. It was not enough to refer obliquely in the attached summary to' potential conflict with the DDA'- this would not give a busy councillor any idea of the serious duties imposed upon the Council by the Act. The Council could not weigh matters properly in the balance without being aware of what its duties were. I recognise that the authorities relied upon by Mr Cragg are all distinguishable on their facts and some relate to different statutes. This is however a discrimination statute like any other and the considerations identified by Arden LJ in *Elias* seem to me to be important and relevant. It is important that Councillors should be aware of the special duties the Council owes to the disabled before they take decisions. It is not enough to accept that the Council has a good disability record and assume that somehow the message would have got across. An important reason why the laws of discrimination have moved from derision to acceptance to respect over the last three decades has been the recognition of the importance not only of respecting rights but also of doing so visibly and clearly by recording the fact. These considerations lead me to conclude that if the relevance of the important duties imposed by the Act had been adequately drawn to the attention of the decision-makers there would have been a written record of it....

6. Most of the cases here discussed deal with s. 71 RRA, the race and gender duties being of much more recent vintage. How do you think the gender duty should affect the policy making of (a) NHS Trusts, (b) public authorities in the exercise of their criminal justice functions?[45]

7. We shall see, below (section 11(c)) that a failure to comply with the positive obligations imposed by s. 71 RRA and its equivalent can assist a finding that any disparately impacting policy etc. is unjustified and therefore itself unlawful.

3. EDUCATION

Section 22 SDA

(1) It is unlawful, in relation to an educational establishment falling within column 1 of the following table, for a person indicated in relation to the establishment in column 2 (the 'responsible body') to discriminate against a woman—

   (a) in the terms on which it offers to admit her to the establishment as a pupil, or

   (b) by refusing or deliberately omitting to accept an application for her admission to the establishment as a pupil, or

   (c) where she is a pupil of the establishment—

     (i) in the way it affords her access to any benefits, facilities or services, or by refusing or deliberately omitting to afford her access to them, or

     (ii) by excluding her from the establishment or subjecting her to any other detriment.

TABLE...

---

[45] Note the gender duty codes of practice, n. 34 above. Note also the exceptions to the prohibition on sex discrimination discussed at section 8 below, in particular, ss. 35 and 46 SDA.

(2) It is unlawful for the governing body of an institution of further or higher education to discriminate against a woman in the arrangements it makes for the purpose of selecting people for admission to the institution.

(3) It is unlawful for the governing body of an institution of further or higher education to subject a woman to harassment if that woman is a student at the institution or has applied for admission to the institution...

NOTES

1. Discrimination in education is regulated on grounds of sex, race, religion or belief, sexual orientation and religion, and in third-level education also on grounds of age.

2. Section 17 RRA is materially similar to s. 22 SDA. The educational establishments covered by ss. 17 RRA and 22 SDA include all those maintained by local education authorities in England and Wales or by education authorities in Scotland, independent schools, Scottish grant-aided schools, universities and bodies providing further and higher education. It should be noted that the prohibition on harassment in s. 22(2) SDA, which applies only in relation to third-level education, has more general application under the RRA (s. 17(2)). It is worth noting that, even where harassment is expressly regulated in the educational context, educational providers will not generally be vicariously liable for harassment of pupils by other pupils (see *Pearce*, section 9 below), but only for their own failures to protect if those failures are themselves discriminatory.

3. Section 28A DDA is similar to s. 22 SDA but it only covers schools, institutions of further and higher education being dealt with separately by s. 28R. Section 28A DDA applies also to discrimination 'in the arrangements [a school] makes for determining admission to the school as a pupil' while the Act also regulates discrimination by local education authorities,[46] and imposes specific obligations on schools and education authorities to draw up accessibility plans and strategies.[47] These relate to physical access and are imposed because the duties of reasonable accommodation imposed upon schools (see further section 12(B) below) do not include duties to make alterations to premises. Where disability is at issue the provisions of the Special Education Needs and Disability Act 2001 (SENDA), which seeks to 'mainstream' pupils with special educational needs (SEN) into ordinary schools where possible, must also be taken into account. That Act is outside the scope of this book except in as much as it amended the DDA to apply to the educational context. The Employment Equality Directive not extending to first- and second-level education, the DDA does not in this context expressly prohibit 'harassment' (but does in the third-level context). Section 28R DDA, which covers third-level education, is in similar terms to s. 22 SDA, referring to 'student services' rather than 'benefits, facilities or services' and, in addition, prohibiting discrimination (s. 28R(3A) DDA) '(a)...in the arrangements [made] for the purpose of determining upon whom to confer a qualification; (b) in the terms on which it is prepared to confer a qualification on [a disabled person]; (c) by refusing or deliberately omitting to grant any application by [a disabled person] for a qualification; or (d) by withdrawing a qualification from [a disabled person] or varying the terms on which [a disabled person] holds it'.[48]

4. Local education authorities are liable under ss. 17 RRA, 22 SDA and 28A and Sch. 4 DDA for discrimination by maintained schools in relation to the authority's functions (the

---

[46] S. 28F DDA.   [47] Ss. 28D and 28E DDA.
[48] Note that education authorities are regulated by s. 28U DDA where they provide third-level education.

governing bodies of the schools being similarly responsible for discrimination in their own functions). Such authorities are also prohibited from discriminating in relation to any of their statutory functions by ss. 18, 23 and 28F of the RRA, SDA and DDA respectively.[49] Discrimination which arises *between* rather than *within* institutions (such as where, for example, pupils at a boys' school are treated more favourably than those at a girls' school) falls under s. 18 RRA and its equivalent provisions. Thus, for example, while *Mandla v Dowell Lee*[50] was brought under s. 17 RRA, the challenge in *EOC v Birmingham City Council*[51] was brought under s. 23 SDA. Sections 18A, 18B and 18D RRA regulate discrimination and harassment by Further Education and Higher Education Funding Councils, Scottish Further and Higher Education Funding Councils and the Teacher Training Agency in carrying out their respective functions while ss. 23A, 23B and 23D SDA apply similarly (but without express reference to harassment) in relation to sex discrimination.

5. The SO Regs, RB Regs and Age Regs prohibit discrimination, in broadly similar terms to s. 22 SDA, but only by third-level education providers.[52] Section 49 of the EA 2006 and reg. 7 of the EA Regs provide in very similar terms to s. 22 SDA in relation to schools, but do not cover harassment. There are no provisions equivalent to ss. 18A, 18B and 18D RRA or 23A, 23B and 23D SDA (see preceding paragraph) in the DDA or the provisions regulating discrimination on grounds of sexual orientation, religion or belief. Any gaps which would otherwise apply are filled, however, by the prohibition by the Act and the Regs of discrimination by public authorities (see section 2 above).

6. There have been relatively few reported decisions on the education-related provisions of the statutory discrimination provisions, this no doubt due in part to difficulties of funding litigation outside the employment tribunals (where the normal costs rules do not apply).[53] Of some importance, however, have been a number of decisions relating to the '11 plus' exam by which students in various parts of the UK are streamed into grammar and non-grammar schools at the age of 11. *R v Birmingham City Council, ex p EOC* concerned the setting of different pass marks for girls and boys by the Council to accommodate the fact that it had available more boys' than girls' grammar school places.[54] In the 1980s the practice in Northern Ireland was to set different pass marks for boys and girls to ensure that equal numbers of the sexes passed (this because boys tend to lag behind girls educationally at 11 but catch up significantly in later years). Northern Ireland's High Court, in an unreported case, allowed a claim for judicial review by Northern Ireland's EOC and declared the practice contrary to Northern Ireland's equivalent of s. 23 SDA.[55] '11 plus' papers then had to be marked and places awarded irrespective of the sex of the pupils. *Mandla v Dowell Lee*, discussed below, illustrates that the imposition of uniform requirements as a precondition for entry into a school may discriminate contrary to s. 17 RRA and its equivalents.[56] That case, discussed below, was regarded by some as threatened by the decision of the House of Lords in *R (Begum) v Head Teacher and Governors of Denbeigh*

---

49 In addition see the positive duties imposed by ss. 25 and 25A SDA.
50 [1983] 2 AC 548.   51 [1989] AC 1155.
52 Reg. 20 SO Regs and RB Regs and reg. 23 Age Regs.
53 Note that enforcement proceedings in relation to discrimination against school pupils must be taken in the Special Educational Needs and Disability Tribunal (in Wales the Special Educational Needs Tribunal), but the FE and HE provisions are enforceable (like the education provisions of the DA and RRA) only in the county courts (or, in the case of an application for judicial review, the High Court).
54 N. 51 above.
55 The case is discussed in the subsequent decision in *Re Equal Opportunities Commission for Northern Ireland's Application* [1989] IRLR 64.
56 N. 50 above.

High School,[57] in which an unsuccessful challenge brought under Art. 9 of the European Convention and the HRA to a school's uniform policy was defeated. As Silber J recently pointed out in *R (Watkins-Singh) v Governing Body of Aberdare Girls' High School,* that and other recent uniform challenges had 'been founded largely, if not solely, on the provisions of the [HRA] but in this case the claim is based mainly on the totally different provisions of the [RRA]...and [EA 2006]'.[58] There the court accepted that the refusal to permit an observant Sikh pupil to wear the Kara (a steel bangle worn by Sikhs as a visible sign of their identity and faith) breached ss. 49 EA and 17 RRA.

7. Exceptions are provided by the SDA (ss. 26–28) in relation to single-sex schools, schools transitioning from single-sex to co-educational and physical education courses. There are, unsurprisingly, no equivalent provisions in the RRA (which, further, expressly defines segregation as a form of race discrimination).[59] That Act does not, however, apply (s. 36) to discrimination on grounds of colour or nationality in the provision of education or training for persons not ordinarily resident in Great Britain 'where it appears to [the provider] that the persons in question do not intend to remain in Great Britain after their period of education or training there'. Further, the RRA provides (s. 35) that 'Nothing in Parts II to IV shall render unlawful any act done in affording persons of a particular racial group access to facilities or services to meet the special needs of persons of that group in regard to their education, training or welfare, or any ancillary benefits.' That provision is of wide importance outside the education field as well as within it and is discussed at section 8(C) below. The DDA does not provide for specific exceptions but, except in the context of third-level education, allows the justification of all discrimination (see further section 12(D) below). Neither the SO Regs nor the EA Regs provide any exceptions to the prohibition on sexual orientation in education, while the Age Regs allow a general justification defence even to direct discrimination. Of great significance are the broad exceptions provided by the EA 2006 (s. 49 is set out for ease of reference together with the exceptions thereto).

(A) EDUCATION AND RELIGIOUS DISCRIMINATION

Section 49 EA 2006: Educational establishments

(1) It is unlawful for the responsible body of an educational establishment listed in the Table to discriminate against a person—

(a) in the terms on which it offers to admit him as a pupil,

(b) by refusing to accept an application to admit him as a pupil, or

(c) where he is a pupil of the establishment—

(i) in the way in which it affords him access to any benefit, facility or service,

(ii) by refusing him access to a benefit, facility or service,

(iii) by excluding him from the establishment, or

(iv) by subjecting him to any other detriment...

---

[57] [2007] 1 AC 100.   [58] N. 42 above, para. 2.

[59] Section 1(2). This provision was narrowly construed in *Furniture, Timber and Allied Trades Union v Modgill; Pel Ltd v Modgill* [1980] IRLR 142 so as not to cover *de facto* segregation which an employer had permitted to occur, eventually employing only Asians in a factory workshop as a result of 'word of mouth' recruitment. The CRE's 1980 Annual Report discusses *Qadus v Henry Robinson (Ironfounders) Ltd,* an industrial tribunal decision that the defendant had infringed s. 1(1)(a) by having separate toilets for Asian and White employees.

Section 45 EA 2006: Section 49: exceptions

(1) Section 49(1)(a), (b) and (c)(i) and (ii) shall not apply in relation to—

(a) a school designated under section 69(3) of the School Standards and Framework Act 1998 (c 31) (foundation or voluntary school with religious character),

(b) a school listed in the register of independent schools for England or for Wales if the school's entry in the register records that the school has a religious ethos,

(c) a school transferred to an education authority under section 16 of the Education (Scotland) Act 1980 (transfer of certain schools to education authorities) which is conducted in the interest of a church or denominational body,

(d) a school provided by an education authority under section 17(2) of that Act (denominational schools),

(e) a grant-aided school (within the meaning of that Act) which is conducted in the interest of a church or denominational body, or

(f) a school registered in the register of independent schools for Scotland if the school-

(i) admits only pupils who belong, or whose parents belong, to one or more particular denominations, or

(ii) is conducted in the interest of a church or denominational body.

(2) Section 49(1)(c)(i), (ii) or (iv) shall not apply in relation to anything done in connection with—

(a) the content of the curriculum, or

(b) acts of worship or other religious observance organised by or on behalf of an educational establishment (whether or not forming part of the curriculum)...

51 Local education authorities and education authorities

(1) It is unlawful for a local education authority (in England and Wales) or an education authority (in Scotland) in the exercise of their functions to discriminate against a person.

(2) In its application to local education authorities the prohibition in subsection (1) shall not apply to-

(a) the exercise of an authority's functions under section 14 of the Education Act 1996 (c 56) (provision of schools),

(b) the exercise of an authority's functions in relation to transport,

(c) the exercise of an authority's functions under section 13 of that Act (general responsibility for education) in so far as they relate to a matter specified in paragraph (a) or (b) above, or

(d) the exercise of functions as the responsible body for an establishment listed in the Table in section 49...[60]

NOTES

1. These provisions serve to preserve religious schools whether in the state or independent sector by providing that discrimination on grounds of religion in admission decisions of such schools, and that authorities' support of such schools, do not contravene the EA 2006. Note, however, that s. 50 EA 2006 does not permit the exclusion or subjection to other detriment, on religious grounds, of students by religious schools (which are, however, permitted to police the boundaries of admission and access to 'benefits, facilities and services' on religious grounds).

[60] S. 51(3) EA 2006 makes similar provision in relation to Scotland.

2. Particularly contentious (especially to those concerned with gay rights issues) is s. 50(2) EA 2006 which applies to *all* schools, and which exempts from the prohibition on discrimination on grounds of religion or belief *'anything* done in connection with (a) the content of the curriculum, or (b) acts of worship or other religious observance…'. While this exemption does not apply to discrimination on grounds of sexual orientation, it is not always easy to define the boundary between discrimination on grounds of religion and belief, on the one hand, and discrimination on grounds of sexual orientation, on the other.[61] Exposure of a class to tub-thumping evangelical rhetoric on the abominable nature of gay sex[62] could involve, and/or result in, both discrimination on grounds of belief against those who adopt other views (in which case it would be protected by s. 50(2) EA 2006) and also on grounds of sexual orientation against those who are or are perceived to be gay (in which case it would have no defence under the EA Regs). It may however prove difficult to ensure that s. 50(2), in particular, does not undermine the rights provided by the (subordinate) EA Regs 2006.

3. List the circumstances in which schools may differentiate on the grounds of (a) sex, (b) race, (c) religion and (d) sexual orientation.

4. GOODS, FACILITIES AND SERVICES

Section 29 SDA

(1) It is unlawful for any person concerned with the provision (for payment or not) of goods, facilities or services to the public or a section of the public to discriminate against a woman who seeks to obtain or use those goods facilities or services—

    (a) by refusing or deliberately omitting to provide her with any of them, or

    (b) by refusing or deliberately omitting to provide her with goods, facilities or services of the like quality, in the like manner and on the like terms as are normal in his case in relation to male members of the public or (where she belongs to a section of the public) to male members of that section.

(2) The following are examples of the facilities and services mentioned in subsection (1)—

    (a) access to and use of any place which members of the public or a section of the public are permitted to enter;

    (b) accommodation in a hotel, boarding house or other similar establishment;

    (c) facilities by way of banking or insurance or for grants, loans, credit or finance;

    (d) facilities for education;

    (e) facilities for entertainment, recreation or refreshment;

---

[61] See also the race/religion boundary discussed at section 10(G) below. The limited scope of s. 50 EA (that is, its application *only* to discrimination on grounds of *religion*, was remarked upon by Munby J in *R (E) v JFS*, n. 29 above, para. 137, 'All [the provision] does is to immunise a school such as JFS from liability for religious discrimination under the Equality Act 2006; it does not immunise such a school from any liability for racial discrimination it may have under the [RRA]. In other words, while religious belief may be an answer to a claim based on alleged religious discrimination contrary to the 2006 Act, precisely the same religious belief will not necessarily be an answer to a claim on the same facts based on alleged racial discrimination contrary to the 1976 Act…'

[62] See, e.g., the recent comments by Iris Robinson MA, chair of the Northern Ireland Parliament's Health Committee (and wife of the Northern Ireland First Minister). Having suggested in a talk show interview that homosexuality was a mental health condition which could be 'cured' by counselling, Ms Robinson subsequently retracted this suggestion and clarified her view (*Belfast Telegraph*, 1 July 2008) that 'homosexuality, like all sin, is an abomination'.

(f) facilities for transport or travel;

(g) services of any profession or trade, or any local or other public authority.

(2A) It is unlawful in connection with the provision of goods, facilities or services to the public or a section of the public (except in so far as they relate to an excluded matter) for any person to subject to harassment—

(3) For the avoidance of doubt it is hereby declared that where a particular skill is commonly exercised in a different way for men and for women it does not contravene subsection (1) for a person who does not normally exercise it for women to insist on exercising it for a woman only in accordance with his normal practice or, if he reasonably considers it impracticable to do that in her case, to refuse or deliberately omit to exercise it.

(a) a woman who seeks to obtain or use those goods, facilities or services, or

(b) a woman to whom he provides those goods, facilities or services.

NOTES

1. The 'excluded matters' under the SDA are (s. 35ZA SDA) '(a) education (including vocational training); (b) the content of media and advertisements; (c) the provision of goods, facilities or services (not normally provided on a commercial basis) at a place (permanently or for the time being) occupied or used for the purposes of an organised religion'. These are not regarded as falling within the scope of Council Directive 2004/114/EC.

2. Section 20 RRA is materially identical to s. 29 SDA save that it does not contain any equivalent of s. 29(3) SDA and has broader application in relation to harassment (there being no equivalent of s. 29(2A)'s 'excluded matters'). Regulation 4 of the EA Regs is materially similar to s. 29(1) and (2) SDA but does not contain any equivalent of s. 29(2A) or (3) SDA and further, does not contain any reference to 'facilities for education' (s. 29(2)(d) SDA). It does, however, provide that:

Reg 4 EA Regs

(3) Paragraph (1) does not apply—

(a) in relation to the provision of goods, facilities or services by a person exercising a public function, or

(b) to discrimination in relation to the provision of goods, facilities or services, where such discrimination—

(i) is unlawful by virtue of another provision of these regulations or by virtue of a provision of the Employment Equality (Sexual Orientation) Regulations 2003 ('the 2003 Regulations'), or

(ii) would be unlawful by virtue of another provision of these Regulations or of the 2003 Regulations but for an express exception.

Section 46 EA 2006 makes virtually identical provision to reg. 4 EA Regs in relation to religion or belief, providing in addition that:

Section 45 EA 2006

(3) Where a skill is commonly exercised in different ways in relation to or for the purposes of different religions or beliefs, a person who normally exercises it in relation to or for the purpose of a religion or belief does not contravene subsection (1) by-

(a) insisting on exercising the skill in the way in which he exercises it in relation to or for the purposes of that religion or belief, or

(b) if he reasonably considers it impracticable to exercise the skill in that way in relation to or for the purposes of another religion or belief, refusing to exercise it in relation to or for the purposes of that other religion or belief.

3. Section 19 DDA is materially similar to s. 29 SDA except that the prohibition on discrimination consisting in a failure 'to provide [a woman] with goods, facilities or services of the like quality, in the like manner and on the like terms as are normal in his case in relation to' men (s. 29(1)(b) SDA) is replaced by a prohibition (s. 19(c)–(d) DDA) on discrimination 'in the standard of service which he provides to the disabled person or the manner in which he provides it to him; or in the terms on which he provides a service to the disabled person'. In addition, the list of facilities and services includes (s. 19(3) DDA) '(b) access to and use of means of communication; (c) access to and use of information services [and] (g) facilities provided by employment agencies or under section 2 of the Employment and Training Act 1973' but does not contain (s. 29(2)(d) and (f) SDA) 'facilities for education... transport or travel'. Section 19(4A) goes on to provide that s. 19 DDA 'does not apply to anything that is governed by Regulation (EC) No. 1107/2006 of the European Parliament and of the Council of 5 July 2006 concerning the rights of disabled persons and persons with reduced mobility when travelling by air',[63] and s. 19(5A) that it does not apply to discrimination falling within Pt 4 of the Act (which regulates discrimination in education). Discrimination which falls within the scope of the employment or education provisions of the SDA or RRA cannot be challenged under their goods and services provisions.[64]

4. Section 29 SDA was applied by the Court of Appeal in *Gill v El Vino Co Ltd* to cover a wine bar's refusal to serve women unless they were seated and, in *Quinn v Williams Furniture Ltd*, to a shop's refusal to extend credit facilities to a woman unless her husband stood as a guarantor.[65] The House of Lords in *James v Eastleigh* applied the provision to discriminatory charges for access to a public swimming pool[66] while s. 20 RRA has been applied by the Court of Appeal to race discrimination in access to prison work, in affording tax relief and in the issue of marriage licences.[67] In *R v Commission for Racial Equality, ex p Cottrell & Rothon* the High Court accepted that the provision applied to race discrimination by estate agents.[68]

5. 'Hotel' in the phrase 'hotel, boarding house or other similar establishment' can be taken to have the meaning that it has in the Hotel Proprietors Act 1956, s. 1(3): 'An establishment held out by the proprietor as offering food, drink and if so required sleeping accommodation, without special contract, to any traveller presenting himself who appears able and willing to pay a reasonable sum for the services and facilities provided and who is in a fit state to be received.' This definition is also that of an inn at common law. An innkeeper is obliged at common law to receive all comers without discrimination, one of the very rare early examples of the regulation of discrimination by the common law.[69] In *Constantine v*

---

[63] This Regulation provides certain limited rights to disabled air passengers.

[64] Ss. 23(1) RRA, 35(3) SDA.   [65] Respectively [1983] QB 425 and [1981] ICR 328.

[66] [1990] 2 AC 751.

[67] Respectively *Alexander v The Home Office* [1988] IRLR 190; *Savjani v Inland Revenue Comrs* [1981] QB 458; *Tejani v The Superintendent Registrar for the District of Peterborough* [1986] IRLR 502.

[68] [1980] IRLR 279.

[69] See, generally, A. McColgan, 'Discrimination Law and the Human Rights Act 1998', n. 30 above, but note the more recent developments in, e.g., *Gurung v Ministry of Defence* [2002] EWHC 2463 (Admin), [2003] 06 LS Gaz R 25, (2002) Times, 28 December [2002] All ER (D) 409 (Nov.).

Imperial Hotels Ltd[70] judgment was awarded against an innkeeper for refusing to accommodate a well-known Black cricketer during the Second World War for fear of upsetting members of the US armed forces. The case would now fall within s. 20 RRA and the claimant would have to bring proceedings under the Act and not at common law.[71] The examples listed in s. 20(2) are not exhaustive[72] and it could be that as far as accommodation is concerned there is some overlap between ss. 20 and 21, below. In that case, the generality of the wording of s. 20 ('facilities for . . .') might in a few cases make it more useful than the more precise wording of s. 21. In the *Hackney* case, for example,[73] an enforcement notice was issued in respect of both ss. 20 and 21. The 'small premises' exceptions discussed below (section 5) apply to both ss. 20 and 21 RRA and their equivalents.

6. Note the application of s. 29 SDA and its equivalents only to goods, facilities or services which are available 'to the public or a section of the public'. This has the effect that private associations are exempted from the regulation of discrimination in relation to their provisions of goods, services and facilities to their members (*Race Relations Board v Charter*, *Dockers' Labour Club and Institute Ltd v Race Relations Board*, in which the House of Lords ruled that the RRA 1968 Act's equivalent of s. 29 SDA did not apply to discrimination in access to a Conservative club and by a working men's club to a member of an associated club).[74] See however the discussion of discrimination by private clubs at section 6 below).

7. The application of the goods, facilities and services provisions to the public sector was severely curtailed by the decision of the House of Lords in *Amin v Entry Clearance Officer, Bombay*,[75] which restricted their application to those activities of the Crown that resembled those carried out by private actors. The impact of these decisions has been done away with in practice by the implementation of s. 19B RRA and its equivalents (see section 2(A) above), which render unlawful discrimination on grounds of race, sex, disability, sexual orientation and religion and belief by public authorities.

8. The prohibition on disability discrimination here, as elsewhere, includes an obligation to make reasonable adjustment (see section 12(B) below). And, whereas the duty of reasonable adjustment comes into operation in the employment context only in relation to individual disabled people who are disadvantaged by an employer's or prospective employer's practices, etc., the duty is of broader application in the context of goods and services. As the DRC's Code of Practice 'Rights of Access: services to the public, public authority functions, private clubs and premises' points out (section 4.14):[76]

6.16 Service providers should not wait until a disabled person wants to use a service which they provide before they give consideration to their duty to make reasonable adjustments. They should be thinking now about the accessibility of their services to disabled people. Service providers should be planning continually for the reasonable adjustments they need to make, whether or not they already have disabled customers. They should anticipate the requirements of disabled people and the adjustments that may have to be made for them. In many cases, it is appropriate to ask customers to identify whether they have any particular requirements and, if so, what adjustments may need to be made. Failure to anticipate the need for an adjustment may render it too late to comply with the duty to make the adjustment. Furthermore, it may not of itself provide a defence to a claim that it was reasonable to have provided one . . .

---

70 [1944] 1 KB 693.   71 This because of the Act's restriction on proceedings (see section 9 (B)).
72 See Lord Simon in *Applin v Race Relations Board* [1975] AC 259, 291, HL.
73 See section 5, n. 94 below.   74 Respectively [1973] AC 868 and [1976] AC 285.
75 [1983] 2 AC 818.   76 Available from the EHRC website as at n. 34 above.

9. It is important to note that it is the *provision* of services to the disabled, rather than the nature of the services provided, which is covered by s. 19 DDA. The DRC's Code of Practice states that:

10.39 …a service provider does not have to comply with a duty to make reasonable adjustments in a way which would so alter the nature of its business that the service provider would effectively be providing a completely different kind of service.

– A restaurant refuses to deliver a meal to the home of a disabled person with severe agoraphobia (a fear of public or open spaces) on the grounds that this would result in the provision of a different kind of service. This is unlikely to be against the law. However, if the restaurant already provides a home delivery service, it is likely to be discriminatory to refuse to serve the disabled person in this way.

– A night club with low level lighting is not required to adjust the lighting to accommodate customers who are partially sighted if this would fundamentally change the atmosphere or ambience of the club.

– A hair and beauty salon provides appointments to clients at its premises in a town centre. A disabled person with a respiratory impairment is unable to travel into town because this exacerbates her disability. She asks the salon to provide her with an appointment at home. The salon refuses as it does not provide a home appointment service to any of its clients. This is likely to be within the law.

10.40 However, there might be an alternative reasonable adjustment which would ensure the accessibility of the services. If this can be provided without fundamentally altering the nature of the services or business, it would be a reasonable step for the service provider to have to take.

10. Section 19(4A) DDA was mentioned above (section 4, Note 3). Section 19 DDA also has to be read with s. 21ZA DDA, and the Regulations made thereunder, which first exclude and then selectively reapply s. 19 to cases 'where the service is a transport service and, as provider of that service, the provider of services discriminates against a disabled person (a) in not providing, or in providing, him with a vehicle; or (b) in not providing, or in providing, him with services when he is travelling in a vehicle provided in the course of the transport service.' (In the DDA as it was originally enacted transport was dealt with largely by the imposition of accessibility standards rather than individual rights but the balance has shifted over time.) Section 21ZA DDA having excluded the application of s. 19 DDA from such services, the Disability Discrimination (Transport Vehicles) Regulations 2005[77] provide that the exclusion does *not* apply (and so s. 19 DDA *does* apply) to passenger vehicles having no more than eight passenger seats or having more than eight passenger seats but weighing no more than five metric tons, to goods vehicles weighing no more than 3.75 metric tons, to private hire vehicles, public service vehicles, rail vehicles, taxis, recovery service vehicles, and 'vehicles deployed on a system using a mode of guided transport' (reg. 3). In addition, whereas s. 21ZA DDA provides that, for the purposes of the duty of reasonable adjustment it is never reasonable for a provider of services, as a provider of a transport service 'to have to take steps which would involve the alteration or removal of a physical feature of a vehicle used in providing the service' or 'affect whether vehicles are provided in the course of the service or what vehicles are so provided, or … where a vehicle is provided in the course of the service, affect what happens in the vehicle while someone is travelling in it', the 2005 Regs selectively disapply the exclusion (and so reapply to some extent the duty to make adjustments) to all the vehicles above listed (reg. 4).[78]

---

[77] SI 2005/3190.

[78] See 'Provision and use of transport vehicles: Statutory Code of Practice, Supplement to Part 3 Code of Practice', available from the EHRC website as at n. 34 above.

The provisions discussed in the preceding paragraph significantly reduce the previous sphere of disapplication of s. 19 DDA in relation to the provision of transport services. Even prior to the passage of the 2005 Regs the DDA had begun to have some individual 'bite' in the transport context. Section 19 DDA had always applied to 'all the infrastructure related to the means of transport which do not themselves involve the use of the mode of transport itself... a caf on a railway platform... Transport infrastructure such as bus or tram stops, stations and termini... airport facilities. Timetables, ticketing arrangements, booking facilities and waiting areas.'[79] In *Ross v Ryanair*,[80] Judge Crawford Lindsay QC ruled that Ryanair had discriminated against a passenger contrary to s. 19 DDA when it charged him £18 each way for the use of a wheelchair at Stansted Airport, and the claimant awarded £1,336 including £1,000 for injury to feelings. Part V DDA also provides a statutory basis for the imposition of specific obligations on transport providers. These obligations for the most part relate to accessibility standards, and have been imposed in relation to public service vehicles and rail vehicles, though are yet to be appointed as they apply to taxis. Taxis and private hire vehicles are, however, regulated as regards the carriage of guide and hearing dogs and by s. 19 DDA as set out above.[81]

11. The goods, facilities and services provisions of the SDA and RRA do not apply to goods, facilities or services outside Britain or to 'facilities by way of banking or insurance or for grants, loans, credit or finance, where the facilities are for a purpose to be carried out, or in connection with risks wholly or mainly arising, outside Great Britain' except where the goods, facilities or services are on 'any ship registered at a port of registry in Great Britain, any aircraft or hovercraft registered in the United Kingdom and operated by a person who has his principal place of business, or is ordinarily resident, in Great Britain' or 'any ship, aircraft or hovercraft belonging to or possessed by Her Majesty in right of the Government of the United Kingdom' or, in the case of facilities for travel outside Britain, the refusal or omission occurs in Britain or on such a ship, aircraft or hovercraft.[82] The DDA applies for the most part to the UK rather than Great Britain,[83] and s. 19 applies only to those 'concerned with the provision, in the United Kingdom, of services to the public or to a section of the public'.[84] The EA 2006 and EA Regs apply only to Great Britain.[85]

12. The RRA provides an exception (s. 23(2)) to the prohibition on discrimination and harassment in relation to goods and services and, in addition, premises, in relation to 'anything done by a person as a participant in arrangements under which he (for reward or not) takes into his home, and treats as if they were members of his family, children, elderly persons, or persons requiring a special degree of care and attention'. This exception is reflected in s. 62 EA 2006 and reg. 6(1) of the EA Regs. It does not extend (*Conwell v Newham London Borough Council*)[86] to discrimination by a local authority (through a social services manager it employed) in refusing to allow a Black child in its care to go on holiday with a White family because the manager thought he should mix instead with Black people. The EAT there ruled that s. 20 RRA applied to the authority when it was looking after children as defined an that the exception provided by s. 23(2) RRA did not apply to the relationship between a local

---

79 C. Palmer et al., *Discrimination Law Handbook* (Legal Action Group, 2002), p. 901.

80 January 2004, Central London County Court, unreported.

81 Sections 37 and 37A DDA and the Disability Discrimination Act 1995 (Private Hire Vehicles) (Carriage of Guide Dogs etc) (England and Wales) Regulations 2003, SI 2003/3122.

82 Ss. 36 SDA, 27 RRA.

83 Unlike the other discrimination provisions the Act applies to Northern Ireland as well as Great Britain.

84 S. 19(2)(b) DDA.   85 S. 80 EA 2006, reg. 34 EA Regs.

86 [2000] 1 All ER 696.

authority and a child who was being looked after by that authority, since a local authority did not have a family, did not treat children as if they were members of its family, and did not have a 'home' within the meaning of s. 23(2). Section 23(2) RRA has no equivalent in the DDA or the SDA, but the DDA provides for the justification of discrimination in the goods and services context (see section 12(C) below) and the SDA's 'small premises' exception (s. 32) applies to the prohibition on discrimination in relation to both goods and services as well as premises (see section 5 below) and goes beyond s. 32(2) RRA.

13. Also worthy of note is s. 59 EA 2006 which provides that the Act's prohibition on discrimination in relation to goods and services shall not apply to 'educational institution[s] established or conducted for the purpose of providing education relating to, or within the framework of, a specified religion or belief' which 'restrict the provision of goods, facilities or services' or 'the use or disposal of premises' (a) 'by reason of or on the grounds of the purpose of the institution', or (b) 'in order to avoid causing offence, on grounds of the religion or belief to which the institution relates, to persons connected with the institution'. The exception does not apply to the educational functions of such schools (see section 3 above).

14. Section 44 SDA permits competitive 'sport[s], game[s] or other activit[ies] of a competitive nature to discriminate as regards participation as a competitor against women (or men)' where 'the physical strength, stamina or physique of the average woman puts her at a disadvantage to the average man'. The exception is complete only to the extent that the SDA exceeds EU law, otherwise applying 'if the discrimination is necessary to secure (a) fair competition, or (b) the safety of competitors, at such events'. Section 39 RRA also provides an exception from the Act's prohibitions which applies to selection to represent 'a country, place or area, or any related association', where that selection is based on 'nationality or place of birth or the length of time for which he has been resident in a particular area or place'. These exceptions are said to be of general application but are most likely to apply in the context of ss. 20 RRA and 29 SDA (also possibly in relation to ss. 19B and 71 RRA, 21A and 76A SDA, discussed above).

15. The SDA provides a number of exceptions to the prohibition on discrimination in relation to goods and services. These are found in s. 34 SDA, which allows the restriction by sex of membership of 'voluntary bodies' ('bod[ies] the activities of which are carried on otherwise than for profit, and [were] which was not set up by any enactment') and, where membership is so restricted, the provision of benefits, facilities or services to members of any such body even where that provision would otherwise fall within s. 29 because membership is open to the public or to a section thereof. Where the discrimination at issue falls within EU law, s. 34(5) provides that the exception applies only to the extent that the discrimination '(a) a proportionate means of achieving a legitimate aim, or (b) for the purpose of preventing or compensating for a disadvantage linked to sex'. This restriction was put in place in order to bring the provision into compliance with Council Directive 2004/113/EC. Amendments have also been made to s. 35 SDA which now provides as follows (note that s. 30 SDA regulates discrimination in relation to premises):

Section 35 SDA: Further exceptions from ss 29(1) and 30

(1) A person who provides at any place facilities or services restricted to men does not for that reason contravene section 29(1) if any of the conditions in subsections (1A) to (1C) is satisfied.

(1A) The condition is that the place is, or is part of—

   (a) a hospital, or

   (b) any other establishment for persons requiring special care, supervision or attention.

(1B) The condition is that the place is (permanently or for the time being) occupied or used for the purposes of an organised religion, and the facilities or services are restricted to men so as to comply with the doctrines of that religion or avoid offending the religious susceptibilities of a significant number of its followers.

(1C) The condition is that the facilities or services are provided for, or are likely to be used by, two or more persons at the same time, and—

   (a) the facilities or services are such, or those persons are such, that male users are likely to suffer serious embarrassment at the presence of a woman, or

   (b) the facilities or services are such that a user is likely to be in a state of undress and a male user might reasonably object to the presence of a female user.

(2) A person who provides facilities or services restricted to men does not for that reason contravene section 29(1) if the services or facilities are such that physical contact between the user and any other person is likely, and that other person might reasonably object if the user were a woman.

(2A) In their application to discrimination falling within section 2A, subsections (1A), (1C) and (2) shall apply to the extent that any such discrimination is a proportionate means of achieving a legitimate aim . . .

In addition, s. 46 SDA provides a general exception applicable in connection with 'communal accommodation', where 'the accommodation is managed in a way which, given the exigencies of the situation, comes as near as may be to fair and equitable treatment of men and women'.

16. The SDA also contains a partial exception to the prohibition on discrimination in relation to insurance, providing that:

Section 45 SDA

(1) Nothing in Parts II to IV shall render unlawful the treatment of a person in relation to an annuity, life assurance policy, accident insurance policy, or similar matter involving the assessment of risk, where the treatment—

   (a) was effected by reference to actuarial or other data from a source on which it was reasonable to rely, and

   (b) was reasonable having regard to the data and any other relevant factors.

(2) In the case of discrimination under section 29, 30 or 31, subsection (1) applies only in so far as that section relates to—

   (a) an excluded matter;[87] or

   (b) differences in premiums and benefits applicable to a person under a contract of insurance or related financial services entered into before the appropriate date.

(3) Despite subsection (2), the treatment is not unlawful under section 29(1) if—

   (a) in the case of discrimination under a contract entered into on or after the appropriate date which relates to differences in premiums and benefits, each of the following conditions is satisfied—

      (i) the use of sex as a factor in the assessment of risk is based on relevant and accurate actuarial and statistical data;

      (ii) the data referred to in subparagraph (i) are compiled, published (whether in full or in summary form) and regularly updated in accordance with guidance issued by the Treasury;

---

87 See section 4, Note 1 above.

    (iii) the differences in treatment are proportionate having regard to the data mentioned in sub-paragraph (i);

    (iv) the differences do not result from costs related to pregnancy or to the fact that a woman has given birth at any time in the period of 26 weeks ending on the day the treatment occurs or begins; or

  (b) insurance or related financial services are provided only to members of one sex in relation to risks which only affect that sex.

(4) Subsection (3)(a) applies to discrimination under section 2A as if, in subsection (1) of that section, after 'other persons' there were inserted 'of B's sex'.

(5) For the purposes of this section, 'the appropriate date' means the date on which the Sex Discrimination (Amendment of Legislation) Regulations 2008 came into force [6 April 2008].

This provision, which in its original form permitted sex discrimination in relation to annuities, life assurance policies, accident insurance policies or similar matters concerning the assessment of risk where the discrimination resulted from reasonable reliance upon actuarial or other statistical evidence, has been amended in order to bring it into conformity with EU requirements. Prior to the adoption of Council Directive 2004/113/EC (gender equality in goods and services) the European Commission had proposed a complete prohibition on sex discrimination in relation to insurance. Its 'Explanatory Memorandum accompanying the Proposal for a Council Directive implementing the principle of equal treatment between women and men in the access to and supply of goods and services' stated that:

equal treatment for women and men is a fundamental right and the Commission believes that the freedom to set tariffs must be subject to that right. The separation of men and women into different pools leads to an unjustified difference of treatment and a resulting disadvantage for one sex or the other. The practice must be judged to be discriminatory and the legislator should therefore take action to prohibit it.

But the Commission accepted that a transitional period was necessary in order to permit 'individual insurance companies to move to sex-neutral pricing in the face of competition from other companies, as the members of the sex which benefits from the change will tend to move disproportionately to that company, while those who are disadvantaged will tend to leave it, thus leaving the company with a portfolio of risks which it is not able to cover without a general increase in premiums'. And the Directive as it was eventually adopted permitted discrimination in this context provided as follows:

- **Council Directive 2004/113/EC**

Article 5
Actuarial factors
1. Member States shall ensure that in all new contracts concluded after 21 December 2007 at the latest, the use of sex as a factor in the calculation of premiums and benefits for the purposes of insurance and related financial services shall not result in differences in individuals' premiums and benefits.

2. Notwithstanding paragraph 1, Member States may decide before 21 December 2007 to permit proportionate differences in individuals' premiums and benefits where the use of sex is a determining factor in the assessment of risk based on relevant and accurate actuarial and statistical data. The Member States concerned shall inform the Commission and ensure that accurate data relevant to

the use of sex as a determining actuarial factor are compiled, published and regularly updated. These Member States shall review their decision five years after 21 December 2007, taking into account the Commission report referred to in Article 16, and shall forward the results of this review to the Commission.

3. In any event, costs related to pregnancy and maternity shall not result in differences in individuals' premiums and benefits.

Member States may defer implementation of the measures necessary to comply with this paragraph until two years after 21 December 2007 at the latest. In that case the Member States concerned shall immediately inform the Commission.

17. The EA Regs also provide partial exceptions in relation to insurance, and also an exception relating to the donation of blood:

27 Insurance

Nothing in these Regulations shall make it unlawful for a person ('A') to treat a person less favourably than A treats or would treat others on grounds of sexual orientation in relation to an annuity, or life insurance policy, or similar matter involving the assessment of risk, where the treatment—

(a) is effected by reference to actuarial or other data from a source on which it is reasonable to rely, and

(b) is reasonable having regard to that data, and any other relevant factors.

28 Blood donation

(1) This regulation applies to any person operating a service for the collection and distribution of human blood for the purposes of medical services ('a blood service').

(2) Subject to paragraph (3), it is unlawful for a person operating a blood service to discriminate against a person on grounds of sexual orientation in the way it affords him access to any facility for the donation of his blood.

(3) Nothing in this regulation shall make it unlawful for a person operating a blood service to refuse to accept a donation of a person's blood where that refusal is determined by an assessment of risk to the public based on-

(a) clinical, epidemiological and other data which was obtained from a source on which it was reasonable to rely, and

(b) the refusal is reasonable having regard to that data, and any other relevant factors.

NOTES

1. What in your view is the purpose of regs 27 and 28 EA Regs? Are they justifiable? What dangers arise in connection with them?

2. Insurance falls within the DDA's goods, services and facilities provisions, the DDA permitting discrimination in this context where it is justifiable: see section 12(C) below.

5. HOUSING/PREMISES

Section 21 RRA

(1) It is unlawful for a person, in relation to premises in Great Britain of which he has power to dispose, to discriminate against another—

(a) in the terms on which he offers him those premises; or

   (b) by refusing his application for those premises; or

   (c) in his treatment of him in relation to any list of persons in need of premises of that description.

(2) It is unlawful for a person, in relation to premises managed by him, to discriminate against a person occupying the premises—

   (a) in the way he affords him access to any benefits or facilities, or by refusing or deliberately omitting to afford him access to them; or

   (b) by evicting him, or subjecting him to any other detriment.

(2A) It is unlawful for a person, in relation to such premises as are referred to in subsection (1) or (2), to subject to harassment a person who applies for or, as the case may be, occupies such premises.

(3) Subsection (1) does not apply to discrimination, on grounds other than those of race or ethnic or national origins, by a person who owns an estate or interest in the premises and wholly occupies them unless he uses the services of an estate agent for the purposes of the disposal of the premises, or publishes or causes to be published an advertisement in connection with the disposal.

Section 22 RRA

(1) Sections 20(1) and 21 do not apply to discrimination on grounds other than those of race or ethnic or national origins in either the provision by a person of accommodation in any premises, or the disposal of premises by him, if—

   (a) that person or a near relative of his ('the relevant occupier') resides, and intends to continue to reside, on the premises; and

   (b) there is on the premises, in addition to the accommodation occupied by the relevant occupier, accommodation (not being storage accommodation or means of access) shared by the relevant occupier with other persons residing on the premises who are not members of his household; and

   (c) the premises are small premises.

(2) Premises shall be treated for the purposes of this section as small premises if—

   (a) in the case of premises comprising residential accommodation for one or more households (under separate letting or similar agreements) in addition to the accommodation occupied by the relevant occupier, there is not normally residential accommodation for more than two such households and only the relevant occupier and any member of his household reside in the accommodation occupied by him;

   (b) in the case of premises not falling within paragraph (a), there is not normally residential accommodation on the premises for more than six persons in addition to the relevant occupier and any members of his household.

NOTES

1. The SDA, DDA, EA 2006 and EA Regs also regulate discrimination in connection with housing and premises. Section 30 SDA is in similar terms to s. 21 RRA save that it contains no equivalent of s. 21(3) RRA and the express prohibition on harassment applies only in relation to matters falling within EU law. Section 22 DDA, which does not expressly prohibit harassment, is otherwise broadly in similar terms[88] as is s. 47 EA 2006 and reg. 5 EA

---

[88] Note also s. 22A DDA which deals with consent to disposals in the context of commonholds and ss. 24A and 49G which deal with let premises.

Regs. All of the provisions contain small premises exceptions,[89] none of which are qualified, as is s. 22 RRA in its non-application to discrimination on grounds regulated by EU law. This is unsurprising in all but the case of the SDA, there being at present no relevant EU law in the case of disability, religion or belief or sexual orientation. Council Directive 2004/113/EC, however, although it does not in terms (unlike the Race Directive) include 'housing' within 'goods and services', does appear to envisage some application in this context: recital 16 provides that 'differences in treatment may be accepted only if they are justified by a legitimate aim. A legitimate aim may, for example, be the protection of victims of sex-related violence (in cases such as the establishment of single-sex shelters), reasons of privacy and decency (in cases such as the provision of accommodation by a person in a part of that person's home)...'.

2. 'Premises' includes 'land of any description' regardless of the use (residential, business, recreational, etc.) to which it is put.[90] Section 21 RRA and its equivalents do nor, however, cover the hire of hotel rooms and the like, or of premises (for example for the purposes of having a party in a pub), discrimination in connection with which is covered by the goods and services provisions considered at section 4 above. A 'power of disposal' includes the power to grant a right to occupy the premises[91] and 'disposal' includes the sale of a fee simple, the assignment or granting of a lease or tenancy, and the granting of a licence to occupy premises. Public housing authorities have the 'power to dispose' of housing within their control and an estate agent or letting agent will be subject to s. 21 RRA and its equivalents (as well as s. 20) if, as is sometimes the case, given a 'power to dispose'.

3. Section 24 RRA provides that it is unlawful (subject, in the case of discrimination on grounds of colour or nationality, to the small premises defence) for a landlord or other whose consent is required to the disposal of a tenancy to discriminate by refusing that consent or to subject a person seeking such consent to harassment. Section 31 SDA is in similar terms. So, too, are ss. 22(4) DDA, 47(3) EA 2006 and reg. 5(3) EA Regs which do not, however, expressly prohibit harassment.[92]

4. Note, in relation to the exception provided by s. 21(4) RRA and its equivalents, that a 'for sale' or 'vacancies' notice on the premises is an advertisement, so the exception is a very narrow one.

5. Relatively few cases have been litigated under the premises sections of the anti-discrimination legislation. The CRE carried out a number of formal investigations into race discrimination by local authorities in the provision of housing, and its predecessor body the Race Relations Board (RRB) similarly made some findings in relation to discrimination in this area. Local authority waiting list rules were the subject of several investigations by the RRB, which declared unlawful Wolverhampton Corporation's 'housing waiting list rule which, broadly speaking, treated people on the waiting list who were born outside the country less favourably than others by applying to them a longer qualifying waiting period'.[93] The rule was replaced by one which applied a residence (as opposed to a place of birth) test, a longer qualifying waiting period being applied to persons who had lived in the UK for less than 10 years, this rule itself being dropped after the RRB began an investigation of it.[94] In 1984 the CRE found that the London Borough of Hackney had been guilty of 'direct discrimination against Black applicants and tenants who had

---

[89] Ss. 32 SDA, 23 DDA and 48 EA 2006 and reg. 6 EA Regs.
[90] S. 78(1) RRA.   [91] S. 78(1) RRA.
[92] See also s. 19 Landlord and Tenant Act 1927 and *Schlegel v Corcoran* [1942] IR 19, 76 ILT 46.
[93] RRB Report 1970–71, p. 11.   [94] RRB Report 1970–71, p. 10.

been allocated housing from the waiting list ... in that Whites had received better-quality allocations of housing than Blacks'.[95]

> Although there were almost as many black applicants on the council waiting list as whites (45 per cent. compared with 49 per cent.), among white applicants 16 per cent. were allocated houses, 19 per cent. maisonettes and 65 per cent. flats, whereas 4 per cent. of blacks received houses, 11 per cent. maisonettes and 85 per cent. flats. Whites were more likely to be allocated new property than blacks (25 per cent., compared with 4 per cent.) moreover, a higher proportion of white tenants were awarded ground or first floor accommodation.[96]

The CRE's 1978 Annual Report also records that the London Borough of Islington complied with CRE pressure to change a rule whereby dependants were recognised for the purpose of its waiting list only if they were resident in the UK. The formal investigation at issue in *Hillingdon London Borough Council v Commission for Racial Equality* was the provision of housing by a public authority (the allegation under investigation being that the Council discriminated against non-White asylum seekers),[97] and another formal investigation of race discrimination in the private sector revealed that discrimination was practised by about 20 per cent of the accommodation agencies investigated.[98]

6. The CRE has issued statutory codes of practice on rented and non-rented (owner-occupied) housing (1991 and 1992 respectively).[99] Among the examples of potentially unlawful practices detailed therein are the imposition by a local authority of a lengthy residence qualification for accommodation with which persons of one racial group are less able to comply than others, the operation of a rule prioritising the offspring of current tenants for rehousing, and reliance on word-of-mouth recommendations from existing tenants, where this serves to advantage one or more racial groups over others. For the legal effect of such codes see text to n. 7 above.

7. What in your view are the main difficulties likely to face disabled people in relation to housing? Does s. 22 DDA address these adequately? (Note the duty of reasonable accommodation and the definition of discrimination in this context: ss. 24–27 DDA, discussed in brief at section 12(B) below).[100]

6. PRIVATE CLUBS

> 25 Discrimination: associations not within s 11
>
> (1) This section applies to any association of persons (however described, whether corporate or unincorporate, and whether or not its activities are carried on for profit) if—
>
> (a) it has twenty-five or more members; and
>
> (b) admission to membership is regulated by its constitution and is so conducted that the members do not constitute a section of the public within the meaning of section 20(1) ...

---

[95] C. Bourn and J. Whitmore, *Anti-discrimination Law in Britain* (Sweet & Maxwell, London, 3rd edn, 1996), para. 7.48. See also M. Bryan, 'Discrimination in the Public Provision of Housing: the Commission for Racial Equality Report on Housing in Hackney' [1984] Public Law 194.

[96] Bryan, ibid., p.196.   [97] [1982] AC 779.

[98] *Sorry Its Gone*, F Invest Rep 1990.

[99] These are available at the Commission website as at n. 34 above.

[100] See also the DDA Code of Practice: Rights of Access: services to the public, public authority functions, private clubs and premises, available at the Commission website as at n. 34 above.

(2) It is unlawful for an association to which this section applies, in the case of a person who is not a member of the association, to discriminate against him—

  (a) in the terms on which it is prepared to admit him to membership; or

  (b) by refusing or deliberately omitting to accept his application for membership.

(3) It is unlawful for an association to which this section applies, in the case of a person who is a member or associate of the association, to discriminate against him—

  (a) in the way it affords him access to any benefits, facilities or services, or by refusing or deliberately omitting to afford him access to them; or

  (b) in the case of a member, by depriving him of membership, or varying the terms on which he is a member; or

  (c) in the case of an associate, by depriving him of his rights as an associate, or varying those rights; or

  (d) In either case, by subjecting him to any other detriment…

26 Exception from s 25 for certain associations

(1) An association to which section 25 applies is within this subsection if the main object of the association is to enable the benefits of membership (whatever they may be) to be enjoyed by persons of a particular racial group defined otherwise than by reference to colour; and in determining whether that is the main object of an association regard shall be had to the essential character of the association and to all relevant circumstances including, in particular, the extent to which the affairs of the association are so conducted that the persons primarily enjoying the benefits of membership are of the racial group in question.

(2) In the case of an association within subsection (1), nothing in section 25 shall render unlawful any act not involving discrimination on the ground of colour.

NOTES

1. Section 25 has its origin in the restrictive approach taken by the House of Lords in the *Charter* and *Dockers' Labour Club* cases to the prohibition by the predecessor of s. 20 RRA of discrimination in relation to the provision of goods, services or facilities (see section 4 above).[101] Trade unions and similar organisations are separately regulated under the employment-related provisions of the anti-discrimination legislation.[102] It is interesting to note that s. 25 does not explicitly regulate harassment.

2. The SDA alone does not at present contain any provision similar to s. 25 RRA. Section 21F DDA is materially identical to s. 25 RRA save that it makes explicit provision in relation to discrimination against members' guests. Regulation 16 EA Regs is also materially identical to s. 25 RRA, reg. 17 providing the following exception:

17 Exceptions from regulation 16 for certain associations

(1) Regulation 16 does not apply to any association if the main object of the association is to enable the benefits of membership (whatever they may be) to be enjoyed by persons of a particular sexual orientation.

----

101 Respectively *Race Relations Board v Charter* [1973] AC 868, *Dockers' Labour Club and Institute Ltd v Race Relations Board* [1976] AC 285.

102 Sections 11, 12, 13 and regs 15, 15 and 18 of the RRA, SDA, DDA, SO Regs, RB Regs and Age Regs, respectively.

(2) In determining whether that is the main object of an association regard shall be had to the essential character of the association and to all relevant circumstances including, in particular, the extent to which the affairs of the association are so conducted that the persons primarily enjoying the benefits of membership are of the sexual orientation in question.

3. The provision made by the EA 2006 is different. That Act does not in terms prohibit discrimination by private members' organisations, though such discrimination would fall within s. 46 EA 2006 in so far as it relates to goods, services etc. provided to the public or a sector thereof. Sections 57, however, provide as follows in an attempt to hold the line between equality and religious freedom:

57 Organisations relating to religion or belief

(1) This section applies to an organisation the purpose of which is—

   (a) to practice a religion or belief,

   (b) to advance a religion or belief,

   (c) to teach the practice or principles of a religion or belief,

   (d) to enable persons of a religion or belief to receive any benefit, or to engage in any activity, within the framework of that religion or belief, or

   (e) to improve relations, or maintain good relations, between persons of different religions or beliefs.

(2) But this section does not apply to an organisation whose sole or main purpose is commercial.

(3) Nothing in this Part shall make it unlawful for an organisation to which this section applies or anyone acting on behalf of or under the auspices of an organisation to which this section applies—

   (a) to restrict membership of the organisation,

   (b) to restrict participation in activities undertaken by the organisation or on its behalf or under its auspices,

   (c) to restrict the provision of goods, facilities or services in the course of activities undertaken by the organisation or on its behalf or under its auspices, or

   (d) to restrict the use or disposal of premises owned or controlled by the organisation.

(4) Nothing in this Part shall make it unlawful for a minister—

   (a) to restrict participation in activities carried on in the performance of his functions in connection with or in respect of an organisation to which this section relates, or

   (b) to restrict the provision of goods, facilities or services in the course of activities carried on in the performance of his functions in connection with or in respect of an organisation to which this section relates.

(5) But subsections (3) and (4) permit a restriction only if imposed—

   (a) by reason of or on the grounds of the purpose of the organisation, or

   (b) in order to avoid causing offence, on grounds of the religion or belief to which the organisation relates, to persons of that religion or belief.

(6) In subsection (4) the reference to a minister is a reference to a minister of religion, or other person, who—

   (a) performs functions in connection with a religion or belief to which an organisation, to which this section applies, relates, and

   (b) holds an office or appointment in, or is accredited, approved or recognised for purposes of, an organisation to which this section applies.

4. Very controversial among religious groups (and welcomed by many others) has been the fact that the SO Regs do not allow religious organisations to discriminate in their provision of goods and services. Regulation 14 RB Regs having made provision for religious organisations, not being commercial or educational, to discriminate on grounds of sexual orientation in materially identical terms to s. 57(1)–(6) EA 2006 as it permits discrimination by such organisations on grounds of religion or belief, the provision continues:

Reg 14 RB Regs

(7) For the purposes of paragraph (3)(d), 'disposal' shall not include disposal of an interest in premises by way of sale where the interest being disposed of is the entirety of the organisation's interest in the premises, or the entirety of the interest in respect of which the organisation has power of disposal.

(8) This regulation does not apply where an organisation of the kind referred to in paragraph (1) or any person acting on its behalf or under its auspices—

(a) makes provision of a kind referred to in regulation 4 [provision of goods, facilities or services to (a section of) the public], or

(b) exercises a function of a kind referred to in regulation 8 [public functions],

on behalf of a public authority under the terms of a contract for provision of that kind between that authority and an organisation referred to in paragraph (1) or, if different, the person making that provision.

The significance of this is that it applies the Regulations' prohibition on sexual orientation discrimination in its full force to religious bodies providing, *inter alia*, adoption and fostering services. The impact of this prohibition was recognised in Regulation 15 which provided a period of grace for such organisations fully to comply with the Regs. That period of grace expired on 31 December 2008.

5. The application of s. 25 RRA was considered in *Triesman v Ali* in which the Court of Appeal dealt with alleged discrimination by the Labour Party in the selection of candidates for election to positions as Labour councillors.[103] Having ruled that such selection did not fall within the employment-related provisions of the RRA the court went on to express doubt as to whether s. 20 RRA applied (this because, per Peter Gibson LJ for the court, the party was 'a society with a serious purpose limited to... persons accepting and conforming to the constitution, programme, principles and policy of the Labour Party and no other party, [with] admission... subject to the procedure allowing objections to be made by the constituency Labour Party and to the general secretary's veto'), the court was prepared to accept 'on the limited evidence before us... that s. 25 is capable of application to the Labour Party'. Given the conclusion, however tentative, of the Court of Appeal in *Triesman* as to the (non)application of s. 20 RRA it is perhaps ironic that the SDA, which contains no equivalent of s. 25 RRA, and which accordingly does not prohibit discrimination by private associations,[104] does include ss. 33 and 42A which permit political parties to make special provision for women (or men) in their constitution, organisation or administration, and to regulate the selection of electoral candidates by sex 'for the purpose of reducing inequality in the numbers of men and women elected, as candidates of the party, to be members of the body concerned'.

---

103 [2002] IRLR 489. See more recently *Watt v Ashan* [2007] UKHL 51, [2008] 1 AC 696.

104 Except in relation to, e.g., employment or the provision of goods or services etc. to (a section of) the public.

6. There are attempts almost annually by MPs to regulate sex discrimination by private clubs. None has thus far succeeded but the Government did suggest in the consultation paper *A Framework for Fairness* that steps would be taken to bring the SDA into line with the other statutory regimes.[105]

7. Should private organisations be restricted from discriminating in relation to membership? What are the benefits of imposing such restrictions? What are the costs? How might the latter be minimised if, for example, the legislation on private clubs was extended to prohibit sex discrimination?

7. OTHER MISCELLANEOUS STATUTORY PROHIBITIONS ON DISCRIMINATION

Section 29 RRA: Discriminatory advertisements

(1) It is unlawful to publish or to cause to be published an advertisement which indicates, or might reasonably be understood as indicating, an intention by a person to do an act of discrimination, whether the doing of that act by him would be lawful or, by virtue of Part II or III, unlawful.

(2) Subsection (1) does not apply to an advertisement—

   (a) if the intended act would be lawful by virtue of any of sections 5, 6, 7(3) and (4), 10(3), 26, 34(2) (b), 35 to 39 and 41; or

   (b) if the advertisement relates to the services of an employment agency (within the meaning of section 14(1)) and the intended act only concerns employment which the employer could by virtue of section 5, 6 or 7(3) or (4) lawfully refuse to offer to persons against whom the advertisement indicates an intention to discriminate.

(3) Subsection (1) does not apply to an advertisement which indicates that persons of any class defined otherwise than by reference to colour, race or ethnic or national origins are required for employment outside Great Britain.

(4) The publisher of an advertisement made unlawful by subsection (1) shall not be subject to any liability under that subsection in respect of the publication of the advertisement if he proves—

   (a) that the advertisement was published in reliance on a statement made to him by the person who caused it to be published to the effect that, by reason of the operation of subsection (2) or (3), the publication would not be unlawful; and

   (b) that it was reasonable for him to rely on the statement.

(5) A person who knowingly or recklessly makes a statement such as is mentioned in subsection (4)(a) which in a material respect is false or misleading commits an offence, and shall be liable on summary conviction to a fine not exceeding [level 5 on the standard scale].

Section 30 RRA: Instructions to discriminate
It is unlawful for the person—

   (a) who has authority over another person; or

   (b) in accordance with whose wishes that other person is accustomed to act,

---

[105] Available free by post from Communities and Local Government Publications, PO Box 236, Wetherby, LS23 7NB. See also, more recently, *Framework for a Fairer Future* (published July 2008), available from the Women and Equality Unit website at www.equalities.gov.uk.

to instruct him to do any act which is unlawful by virtue of Part II or III, [section 76ZA or, where it renders an act unlawful on grounds of race or ethnic or national origins, section 76,] or procure or attempt to procure the doing by him of any such act…

Section 31 RRA: Pressure to discriminate

(1) It is unlawful to induce, or attempt to induce, a person to do any act which contravenes Part II or III.

(2) An attempted inducement is not prevented from falling within subsection (1) because it is not made directly to the person in question, if it is made in such a way that he is likely to hear of it…

Section 33 RRA: Aiding unlawful acts

(1) A person who knowingly aids another person to do an act made unlawful by this Act shall be treated for the purposes of this Act as himself doing an unlawful act of the like description.

(2) For the purposes of subsection (1) an employee or agent for whose act the employer or principal is liable under section 32 (or would be so liable but for section 32(3)) shall be deemed to aid the doing of the act by the employer or principal.

(3) A person does not under this section knowingly aid another to do an unlawful act if—

   (a) he acts in reliance on a statement made to him by that other person that, by reason of any provision of this Act, the act which he aids would not be unlawful; and

   (b) it is reasonable for him to rely on the statement.

(4) A person who knowingly or recklessly makes a statement such as is mentioned in subsection (3)(a) which in a material respect is false or misleading commits an offence, and shall be liable on summary conviction to a fine not exceeding [level 5 on the standard scale].

NOTES

1. Section 28 SDA is similar to s. 28 RRA, though sub-ss. (2) and (3) provide respectively that 'Subsection (1) does not apply to an advertisement if the intended act would not in fact be unlawful' and 'For the purposes of subsection (1), use of a job description with a sexual connotation (such as "waiter", "salesgirl", "postman" or "stewardess") shall be taken to indicate an intention to discriminate, unless the advertisement contains an indication to the contrary'. Section 54 EA 2006 is in similar terms to s. 29 RRA as is reg. 10 EA Regs. Sections 16B and 28UC DDA, which apply only in relation to Pts II and IV respectively (that is, to employment/occupation (broadly defined) and to third-level education, but not otherwise), prohibit the publication of advertisements that suggest an intention to discriminate by less favourable treatment or a reluctance to make a reasonable adjustment. Proceedings in respect of these provisions may be brought only by the EHRC[106] (formerly by the equality commissions) and are vanishingly rare.

2. Sections 39–40 and 42 SDA are materially identical to ss. 30–31 and 33 RRA. Sections 16C and 28UB DDA are similar to ss. 30 and 31 RRA (again only in relation to employment/occupation (broadly defined) and to third-level education), while s. 57 is in similar terms to s. 33 RRA and applies across the DDA except in relation to primary and secondary education. The EE 2006 and EA Regs provide only the equivalents of s. 33 RRA, and are couched in similar terms.[107]

---

[106] This by virtue of s. 29(6) RRA and equivalent provisions.

[107] Respectively ss. 74 and 73 EA 2006 and regs 30 and 29 EA Regs. The SO, RB and Age Regs provide similarly (respectively regs 22 and 23, 22 and 23 and 25 and 26), only the Age Regs making explicit provision in relation to instructions to discriminate (reg. 5), presumably because the Age Regs (see section 10(F) below) apply

3. Sections 30 and 31 RRA and their equivalents have generated virtually no litigation, this for the most part probably because they relied on the relevant equality commission (now the EHRC) for their enforcement. The meaning of 'knowingly aids' was considered in *Anyanwu v South Bank Student Union* in which the House of Lords, overturning the decisions of the lower courts, rejected the argument that the provision applied only to 'secondary actors'.[108] The case was brought by Black students employed by the university's student union of their university who, when they were expelled from the university, were dismissed by the student union because they were now barred from university premises. The House of Lords held that they were entitled to pursue the university as an 'aider' notwithstanding its pivotal role in their complaint.

8. GENERAL EXCEPTIONS

(A) STATUTORY AUTHORITY

Section 41 RRA: Acts done under statutory authority etc

(1) Nothing in Parts II to IV shall render unlawful any act of discrimination done—

    (a) in pursuance of any enactment or Order in Council; or

    (b) in pursuance of any instrument made under any enactment by a Minister of the Crown; or

    (c) in order to comply with any condition or requirement imposed by a Minister of the Crown (whether before or after the passing of this Act) by virtue of any enactment.

References in this section to an enactment, Order in Council or instrument include an enactment, Order in Council or instrument passed or made after the passing of this Act.

(1A) Subsection (1) does not apply to an act which is unlawful, on grounds of race or ethnic or national origins, by virtue of a provision referred to in section 1(1B).

(2) Nothing in Parts II to IV shall render unlawful any act whereby a person discriminates against another on the basis of that other's nationality or place of ordinary residence or the length of time for which he has been present or resident in or outside the United Kingdom or an area within the United Kingdom, if that Act is done—

    (a) in pursuance of any enactment or Order in Council; or

    (b) in pursuance of any instrument made under any enactment by a Minister of the Crown; or

    (c) in order to comply with any requirement imposed by a Minister of the Crown (whether before or after the passing of this Act) by virtue of any enactment; or

    (d) in pursuance of any arrangements made (whether before or after the passing of this Act) by or with the approval of, or for the time being approved by, a Minister of the Crown; or

    (e) in order to comply with any condition imposed (whether before or after the passing of this Act) by a Minister of the Crown.

Section 51 SDA: Acts done for purposes of protection of women

(3) In this section 'existing statutory provision' means (subject to subsection (4)) any provision of—

    (a) an Act passed before this Act, or

only to discriminate on grounds of the age of the person complaining, whereas the approach in *Weathersfield Ltd t/a Van & Truck Rentals v Sargent* [1999] ICR 425 (CA) (see section 11(B) above) will allow challenges to instructions and pressure to discriminate, albeit possible only from the person instructed or pressurised.

[108] [2001] 1 ICR 391.

(b) an instrument approved or made by or under such an Act (including one approved or made after the passing of this Act).

(4) Where an Act passed after this Act re-enacts (with or without modification) a provision of an Act passed before this Act, that provision as re-enacted shall be treated for the purposes of subsection (3) as if it continued to be contained in an Act passed before this Act.

Section 51A SDA

Acts done under statutory authority to be exempt from certain provisions of Part III

(1) Nothing in—

(za) sections 21A to 27, 32 and 33,

(a) the relevant provisions of Part III, or

(b) Part IV so far as it has effect in relation to those provisions,

shall render unlawful any act done by a person if it was necessary for that person to do it in order to comply with a requirement of an existing statutory provision within the meaning of section 51.

(2) In subsection (1) 'the relevant provisions of Part III' means the provisions of that Part (except sections 21A to 27, 32 and 33) in so far as they relate to an excluded matter.

Section 59 DDA

(1) Nothing in this Act makes unlawful any act done—

(a) in pursuance of any enactment; or

(b) in pursuance of any instrument made under any enactment by—

(i) a Minister of the Crown,

(ii) a member of the Scottish Executive, …

(iii) the National Assembly for Wales constituted by the Government of Wales Act 1998, or

(iv) the Welsh Ministers, the First Minister for Wales or the Counsel General to the Welsh Assembly Government; or

(c) to comply with any condition or requirement—

(i) imposed by a Minister of the Crown (whether before or after the passing of this Act) by virtue of any enactment,

(ii) imposed by a member of the Scottish Executive (whether before or after the coming into force of this sub-paragraph) by virtue of any enactment, …

(iii) imposed by the National Assembly for Wales constituted by the Government of Wales Act 1998 (whether before or after the coming into force of this sub-paragraph) by virtue of any enactment, or

(iv) imposed by the Welsh Ministers, the First Minister for Wales or the Counsel General to the Welsh Assembly Government.

(2) In subsection (1) 'enactment' includes one passed or made after the date on which this Act is passed and 'instrument' includes one made after that date.

NOTES

1. Section 6 EA 2006 is in broadly similar terms to s. 59 DDA except that it refers (s. 6(1)) to 'anything which is necessary or in so far as it is necessary, for the purpose of complying with' primary or secondary legislation, ministerial conditions etc. None of the Regulations contain any equivalent of these provisions, their status as secondary legislation meaning that they will be overridden in any event by incompatible primary legislation or by secondary legislation enacted subsequent to the Regulations.

2. The provisions set out above clearly create a hierarchy within the anti-discrimination Acts. The RRA, which was amended by the inclusion of s. 41(1A) to comply with the Race Directive, simply does not apply the exception to discrimination based on race, ethnicity or national origin (as distinct from colour or nationality) falling within the Directive except (s. 41(2) RRA) in so far as it concerns indirect discrimination based on residence require-ments. Section 51A SDA also disapplies the exemption where the discrimination at issue falls within EU law. It appears to be narrower in any event than the RRA as it applies to colour and nationality, in that the SDA exempts only acts 'necessary' for compliance with primary legis-lation pre-dating the SDA (including a provision pre-dating the SDA but re-enacted with or without modification after its adoption) or with an instrument approved or made there-under, whereas the RRA applies to acts done 'in pursuance of' a wider category of legislation or 'arrangements', or 'in order to comply with' Ministerial conditions or requirements. We shall see, below, that the term 'in pursuance of' has been narrowly construed but the general point remains. Broader again are the exceptions provided by s. 59 DDA and s. 6 EA 2006, which provisions have limited or no EU underpinning.[109]

3. Section 41 RRA was restrictively interpreted by the House of Lords in *Hampson v Department of Education and Science*[110] to apply only to those acts 'done in necessary per-formance of an express obligation in the instrument', and not to the exercise of discretion. In that case, further considered below, the Secretary of State made the Education (Teachers) Regulations 1982 under the Education Act 1980. The regulations provided that a person could not be employed as a teacher unless 'qualified' by reference to an 'approved' course, such a course being one which the Secretary of State had accepted as being 'comparable' to a domestic course. The claimant had completed a two-year teacher training qualification, had taught for a number of years, and had then completed a one-year additional course. The Secretary of State, in his discretion, took the view that a course had to consist of three consecutive years' study in order to be 'comparable' to the domestic three-year course, and sought to rely on s. 41 RRA. Lord Lowry, for the House, ruled that s. 41 did not apply. He accepted that it was possible to interpret s. 41 narrowly, so as to protect only those acts made necessary by the statutory provision, or widely, to include also the exercise of discretion con-ferred by the instrument. But he took the view, as Balcombe LJ (dissenting) had done below, that, s. 41 introducing wide exceptions to the Act's 'general purpose of outlawing discrimin-ation', a narrow approach was appropriate. Lord Lowry quoted Balcombe J's view that a wide construction of s. 41 would have the effect that 'The most important weapons contained in Pts II and III of the Act would be irretrievably blunted and, indeed, would not make sense' and continued

My Lords, the alleged act of discrimination…was to decide the appellant's application by reference to a test of acceptability of her teacher training course (in statutory language, 'a requirement') which indir-ectly discriminated against her within the meaning of s. 1(1)(b)(i) and (iii) of the 1976 Act. That require-ment was no doubt applied 'in pursuance of the 1982 regulations according to the wide construction, as defined by Balcombe LJ, but it was not so applied according to the narrow construction, under which the

---

[109] Presumably on the basis that Council Directive 2000/78/EC applies only to employment and third-level education, though it is not clear why some limitation is not necessary at least in these contexts.
[110] [1991] 1 AC 171.

requirement must be found in the regulations as, for example, is true of the courses described in para. 2(a)(i) of Sch. 5… Therefore the requirement of a course consisting of three consecutive years' training, assuming that it was discriminatory and also not justifiable under s. 1 (1)(b)(ii), was not protected by s. 41(1)(b).

There is a sound argument, based on public policy, for drawing the line in this way. I refer to the need and the opportunity for parliamentary scrutiny. Balcombe LJ put the matter aptly[111]:…

'If an enactment, Order in Council or statutory instrument imposes requirements compliance with which may lead to racial discrimination, those requirements can be debated in Parliament and their justification considered there. Similarly, if a minister of the Crown imposes a condition or requirement compliance with which could lead to racial discrimination (see s. 41(1)(c) of the 1976 Act) he can be made answerable in Parliament for his action. If what is done is not *necessary* to comply with a statutory requirement, then there can be no valid reason why it should not have to be justified before an industrial tribunal…'

What I would venture to describe as the fallacy of [the Court of Appeal's] approach can be recognised when one reflects that almost every discretionary decision, such as that which is involved in the appointment, promotion and dismissal of individuals in, say, local government, the police, the national health service and the public sector or the teaching profession, is taken against a statutory background which imposes a duty on someone, just as the 1982 regulations imposed a duty on the Secretary of State. It seems to me that to apply the reasoning of the majority here to the decisions I have mentioned would give them the protection of s. 41 and thereby achieve results which no member of the Court of Appeal would be likely to have thought acceptable.

4. The *Hampson* decision remained the only authority on s. 41 RRA until relatively recently when, with the increased use of the statutory equality provisions against public sector actors in reliance on s. 19B and its equivalents (see, for example, *R (Mohammed) v Secretary of State for Defence* on the interpretation of s. 41(2)(d) RRA[112] (but cf. the comments of the Court of Appeal in *R (Al Rawi) v Secretary of State for Foreign and Commonwealth Affairs*[113] and *Couronne v Crawley Borough Council*[114] on the correct approach to an habitual residence test under s. 41(2)).

(B) NATIONAL SECURITY

Section 42 RRA: Acts safeguarding national security
Nothing in Parts II to IV shall render unlawful an act done for the purpose of safeguarding national security if the doing of the act was justified by that purpose.

Section 52 SDA: Acts safeguarding national security
(1) Nothing in Parts II to IV shall render unlawful an act done for the purpose of safeguarding national security.

(2) A certificate purporting to be signed by or on behalf of a Minister of the Crown and certifying that an act specified in the certificate was done for the purpose of safeguarding national security shall be conclusive evidence that it was done for that purpose.[115]

(3) A document purporting to be a certificate such as is mentioned in subsection (2) shall be received in evidence and, unless the contrary is proved, shall be deemed to be such a certificate.

---

111 [1989] ICR 179, 188.
112 [2007] EWCA Civ 1023, (2007) Times, 9 May [2007] All ER (D) 09 (May).
113 N. 29 above, para. 82.   114 [2007] EWCA Civ 1086, [2007] All ER (D) 50 (Nov.).
115 Note that this provision and s. 52(3) were repealed, in relation to allegations of broadly employment-related discrimination by SI 1988/249.

NOTES

1. The DDA (s. 59) is materially identical to s. 42 RRA in so far as it regulates discrimination in the context, broadly defined, but materially similar to the SDA as it regulates discrimination outside that sphere. In other words, national security operates as an absolute defence under the SDA and under the non-employment-related provisions of the DDA[116] but as a qualified defence (subject to justification) under the RRA and the employment-related provisions of the DDA. Further, and except so far as the SDA regulates discrimination in the context of employment, provision is made for conclusive certification by a Minister. This provision was repealed in the context of employment after the decision of the ECJ in *Johnston v RUC* that it was inconsistent with EU law which at the time governed (broadly) only sex discrimination in the employment context.[117] Its continued inclusion in the SDA is of questionable compatibility with Council Directive 2004/113/EC and the operation of national security as an absolute defence in the SDA and the DDA as it applies to third-level education appears inconsistent with the Equal Treatment Directive as amended[118] and the Employment Equality Directive respectively. The EA 2006 (s. 63) and SO, RB and Age Regs (regs 24, 24 and 28 respectively) are materially identical to s. 42 RRA.

2. Recent amendments have been made to most of the statutory regimes to permit claimants to be excluded from proceedings where national security is argued. Thus, for example:

Section 67A RRA: National security: procedure

(1) Rules may make provision for enabling a court in which relevant proceedings have been brought, where it considers it expedient in the interests of national security—

(a) to exclude from all or part of the proceedings—

(i) the claimant;

(ii) the claimant's representatives; or

(iii) the assessors (if any) appointed by virtue of section 67(4);

(b) to permit a claimant or representative who has been excluded to make a statement to the court before the commencement of the proceedings, or the part of the proceedings, from which he is excluded;

(c) to take steps to keep secret all or part of the reasons for its decision in the proceedings.

(2) The Attorney General or, in Scotland, the Advocate General for Scotland, may appoint a person to represent the interests of a claimant in, or in any part of, any proceedings from which the claimant or his representatives are excluded by virtue of subsection (1).

(3) A person appointed under subsection (2)—

(a) if appointed for the purposes of proceedings in England and Wales, must have a general qualification (within the meaning of section 71 of the Courts and Legal Services Act 1990); and [be a person who, for the purposes of the Legal Services Act 2007, is an authorised person in relation to an activity which constitutes the exercise of a right of audience or the conduct of litigation (within the meaning of that Act), and

(b) if appointed for the purposes of proceedings in Scotland, must be—

(i) an advocate; or

(ii) qualified to practice as a solicitor in Scotland.

---

[116] For the application of an analogous defence in the employment context see *B v BAA plc* [2005] IRLR 927.
[117] Case C-222/84 [1986] ECR 01651.
[118] That is, Council Directive 76/117/EEC as amended most recently by Council Directive 2002/73/EC.

(4) A person appointed under subsection (2) shall not be responsible to the person whose interests he is appointed to represent… [emphasis added]

NOTES

1. Section 66B SDA is in similar terms as is s. 71 EA 2006, s. 59A DDA and reg. 25 EA Regs.[119] No rules have yet been brought into force.

2. What should be the effect, in a discrimination claim to which the reverse burden of proof applies, of a national security claim?[120]

(C) TARGETED SERVICES

Section 35 RRA

Nothing in Parts II to IV shall render unlawful any act done in affording persons of a particular racial group access to facilities or services to meet the special needs of persons of that group in regard to their education, training or welfare, or any ancillary benefits.

NOTES

1. Section 61 EA 2006 and reg. 13 of the EA Regs are materially identical, neither the SDA nor the DDA containing similar provisions (but see section 8(D) below and note that the DDA's provisions do not prohibit discrimination in favour of disabled people).

2. Section 35 RRA is dealt with here as a general exception because that is how it is positioned in the Act. It is, however, better understood (in the words of Moses LJ in *Kaur & Shah v Ealing*)[121] 'not [as] an exception to the 1976 Act. It does not derogate from it in any way.' That case, the first to be decided under s. 35 RRA or its equivalent provisions,[122] concerned a decision by the respondent council to divert domestic violence it had previously provided to Southall Black Sisters, a 'grassroots' organisation providing domestic violence and other services exclusively, but not entirely, to women of South Asian origin, to a single provider, borough-wide provider of domestic services which would be required to deliver services to all women regardless of ethnicity. The Administrative Court accepted that Ealing had failed to comply with its s. 71 RRA duty (see section 2(B) above), and ruled that the council had misconstrued the relationship between targeted provision (here for Black women by Black women) and race equality. The council had argued that s. 35 had to

---

[119] The Employment Tribunals (Constitution and Rules of Procedure) Regulations 2004, SI 2004/1861 allow similarly and the other legislation would apply to the third-level cases under the SO, RB and Age Regs: see Sch. 2: the Employment Tribunals (National Security) Rules of Procedure.

[120] Note *B v BAA plc* [2005] IRLR 927, *Barracks v Coles* [2006] EWCA Civ 1041, [2007] IRLR 73.

[121] *Kaur & Shah v London Borough of Ealing*, n. 35 above.

[122] Though there has been dicta in other cases about it, notably in the *E v JFS* case (n. 29 above) at paras 175–176 in which, in the context of education, Munby J expressed the view that 'the reference to 'special needs…in regard to…education' is, for example, to educational establishments providing a specifically religious training for priests, rabbis, imams and similar people, not to ordinary schools, even if they are faith schools'. Given the lack of argument on the point and what he recognised was its 'potentially…very wide significance' he 'prefer[red] not to come to any final conclusion on this particular point'.

be narrowly construed as an exception to the general prohibition on race discrimination. The court disagreed, Moses LJ ruling that s. 35 RRA was 'an important recognition of the principle that not only must like cases be treated alike but that unlike cases must be treated differently'. He went on to state that there was 'no dichotomy between social equality and cohesion and the provision of services to a minority', Ealing having been driven in part by the Government's 'social cohesion' agenda. 'Ealing's mistake was to believe that the provision of services from such a source would preclude social cohesion. It now appreciates that it was in error and that in some circumstances the law and the code can only be met by the provision of specialist services…Specialist services to a racial minority from a specialist source are anti-discriminatory and further the objectives of racial equality and social cohesion.' This case is of particular significance given the recent rush on the part of many local authorities to abandon targeted services in favour of a 'one size fits' all policy which may be inconsistent with equality considerations.[123]

(D) CHARITIES

Section 43 SDA: Charities

(1) Nothing in Parts II to IV shall—

  (a) be construed as affecting a provision to which this subsection applies, or

  (b) render unlawful an act which is done in order to give effect to such a provision.

(2) Subsection (1) applies to a provision for conferring benefits on persons of one sex only (disregarding any benefits to persons of the opposite sex which are exceptional or are relatively insignificant), being a provision which is contained in a charitable instrument.

(2A) But subsection (1) does not apply to discrimination under section 1 or 2A in its application to sections 29 to 31 unless the conferral of benefits is—

  (a) a proportionate means of achieving a legitimate aim, or

  (b) for the purpose of preventing or compensating for a disadvantage linked to sex…

In the application of this section to England and Wales, 'charitable purposes' means purposes which are exclusively charitable according to the law of England and Wales.

Section 58 EA 2006: Charities relating to religion or belief

(1) Nothing in this Part [regulation of discrimination on grounds of religion or belief outside the employment sphere] shall make it unlawful for a person to provide benefits only to persons of a particular religion or belief, if—

  (a) he acts in pursuance of a charitable instrument, and

  (b) the restriction of benefits to persons of that religion or belief is imposed by reason of or on the grounds of the provisions of the charitable instrument.

---

[123] See Commission on Integration & Cohesion, *Our Shared Future*, available at www.integrationand cohesion.org.uk (accessed 7 August 2008), but note the rather more nuanced Department for Communities and Local Government, 'Cohesion Guidance for Funders 2008: Consultation' and the Compact, 'Code of Good Practice: BME Voluntary & Community Organisations' (www.thecompact.org.uk). Note also the concerns expressed by the House of Commons Home Affairs Committee in its Sixth Report of 2007–08 ('Domestic Violence, Forced Marriage and "Honour"-Based Violence'), in particular at paras 395–396); see also the letter from Iain Wright MP, Parliamentary Under-Secretary of State for the Department for Communities and Local Government, to the Committee at Appendix 67 to that Report.

(2) Nothing in this Part shall make it unlawful for the Charity Commission or the holder of the Office of the Scottish Charity Regulator to exercise a function in relation to a charity in a manner which appears to the Commission or to the holder to be expedient in the interests of the charity, having regard to the provisions of the charitable instrument...

NOTE

1. Section 34(2) RRA is in similar terms where the charitable instrument 'provides for conferring benefits on persons of a class defined otherwise than by reference to colour', s. 34(1) providing that a charitable instrument 'which provides for conferring benefits on persons of a class defined by reference to colour shall have effect for all purposes as if it provided for conferring the like benefits on persons of the class which results if the restriction by reference to colour is disregarded'. In place of s. 39(2A) SDA (which modifies the impact of s. 43(1) in relation to the provision of goods, facilities, services and premises), s. 34(3A) RRA disapplies the exemption entirely in relation to discrimination on grounds of race or ethnic or national origins in the context of employment, narrowly defined.[124] Regulation 8 of the SO Regs is in materially identical terms to s. 58 EA 2006. Section 60 EA 2006 also provides that charities may require (prospective) members 'to make a statement which asserts or implies membership or acceptance of a religion or belief' as long as this requirement has been continuously imposed since before 18 May 2005.

9. VICARIOUS LIABILITY, ENFORCEMENT AND REMEDIES

(A) VICARIOUS LIABILITY

Section 32 RRA: Liability of employers and principals

(1) Anything done by a person in the course of his employment shall be treated for the purposes of this Act (except as regards offences thereunder) as done by his employer as well as by him, whether or not it was done with the employer's knowledge or approval.

(2) Anything done by a person as agent for another person with the authority (whether express or implied, and whether precedent or subsequent) of that other person shall be treated for the purposes of this Act (except as regards offences thereunder) as done by that other person as well as by him.

(3) In proceedings brought under this Act against any person in respect of an act alleged to have been done by an employee of his it shall be a defence for that person to prove that he took such steps as were reasonably practicable to prevent the employee from doing that act, or from doing in the course of his employment acts of that description.

NOTES

1. Section 32 RRA and its equivalents are of great significance, however, in allowing employers to be held liable for the actions of their employees (whether those actions are directed towards other employees or towards customers, clients, etc.). It is sufficient for present

---

[124] The DDA makes specific provision for charities in s. 18C which deals with employment.

purposes to state that s. 32(1) has been interpreted very generously since the decision of the Court of Appeal in *Jones v Tower Boot Co Ltd*,[125] in which that court rejected the previous restriction of liability to cases in which an employee performed an unauthorised act, albeit in an unauthorised way.[126] (In the *Jones* case the EAT's application of that test had resulted in the employer escaping liability for the actions of staff who had, *inter alia*, verbally racially abused, whipped and branded a 16-year-old colleague.) Waite LJ, delivering the judgment of the court, cited the words of Lord Templeman in *Savjani v IRC*, where his Lordship stated that the RRA 'was brought in to remedy very great evil. It is expressed in very wide terms, and I should be very slow to find that the effect of something which is humiliatingly discriminatory in racial matters falls outside the ambit of the Act.'[127] The court ruled that s. 32(1) was to be interpreted without reference to common law strictures but 'in the sense in which every layman would understand them'. The major limitation of the statutory approach to vicarious liability is that it does not impose liability on a school, for example for the actions of its students (see *Pearce v Governing Body of Mayfield School*, in which the House of Lords ruled that a school would not be responsible under statutory discrimination provisions for the actions of pupils (or, by analogy, third parties) unless the *school* discriminated *itself* on the relevant grounds in the manner in which it dealt with the actions complained of).[128]

2. Note that while police officers are not employees, and so would not usually attract vicarious liability, all the discrimination provisions arrange for them to be treated as if they were employees for the purpose of attaching vicarious liability for their actions to the relevant chief constable.[129]

3. Where discriminatory acts are undertaken by an agent rather than by an employee, is there any defence to liability?[130]

(B) ENFORCEMENT AND REMEDIES

Section 62 SDA: Restriction of proceedings for breach of Act

(1) Except as provided by this Act no proceedings, whether civil or criminal, shall lie against any person in respect of an act by reason that the act is unlawful by virtue of a provision of this Act.

(2) Subsection (1) does not preclude the making of an order of certiorari, mandamus or prohibition . . .

66 Claims under Part III

(1) A claim by any person ('the claimant') that another person ('the respondent')—

   (a) has committed an act of discrimination or harassment against the claimant which is unlawful by virtue of Part III, other than section 35A or 35B, or

   (b) is by virtue of section 41 or 42 to be treated as having committed such an act of discrimination or harassment against the claimant,

   may be made the subject of civil proceedings in like manner as any other claim in tort or (in Scotland) in reparation for breach of statutory duty.

---

[125] [1997] 2 All ER 407.

[126] The decision in *Jones* pushed statutory vicarious liability beyond the common law variety but the latter has subsequently caught up: see *Lister v Helsey Hall Ltd* [2002] 1 AC 215, HL.

[127] [1981] QB 458, 466–467.

[128] [2003] ICR 937.

[129] Ss. 76A, 76B RRA, 25 SDA, 64A DDA, 75 EA 2006, regs 11 RB and SO Regs, 13 Age Regs and 31 EA Regs respectively.

[130] See *Lana v Positive Training in Housing (London) Ltd* [2001] IRLR 501.

(2) Proceedings under subsection (1)—

  (a) shall be brought in England and Wales only in a county court, and

  (b) shall be brought in Scotland only in a sheriff court

  but all such remedies shall be obtainable in such proceedings as, apart from this subsection and section 62(1), would be obtainable in the High Court or the Court of Session, as the case may be.

(3) As respects an unlawful act of discrimination falling within section 1(1)(b)...no award of damages shall be made if the respondent proves that the requirement or condition in question was not applied with the intention of treating the claimant unfavourably on the ground of his sex...

(3A) Subsection (3) does not affect the award of damages in respect of an unlawful act of discrimination falling within section 1(2)(b).

(4) For the avoidance of doubt it is hereby declared that damages in respect of an unlawful act of discrimination or harassment may include compensation for injury to feelings whether or not they include compensation under any other head...

(5) Civil proceedings in respect of a claim by any person that he has been discriminated against, or subjected to harassment, in contravention of section 22 or 23 by a body to which section 25(1) applies shall not be instituted unless the claimant has given notice of the claim to the Secretary of State and either the Secretary of State has by notice informed the claimant that the Secretary of State does not require further time to consider the matter, or the period of two months has elapsed since the claimant gave notice to the Secretary of State; but nothing in this sub-section applies to a counterclaim.

(6) For the purposes of proceedings under subsection (1)—

  (a) section 63(1) (assessors) of the County Courts Act 1984 shall apply with the omission of the words 'on the application of any party', and

  (b) the remuneration of assessors appointed under the said section 63(1) shall be at such rate as may be determined by the Lord Chancellor with the approval of the Minister for the Civil Service...

(8) A county court or sheriff court shall have jurisdiction to entertain proceedings under subsection (1) with respect to an act done on a ship, aircraft or hovercraft outside its district, including such an act done outside Great Britain.

66A Burden of proof: county and sheriff courts

(1) This section applies to any claim brought under section 66(1) in a county court in England and Wales or a sheriff court in Scotland.

(2) Where, on the hearing of the claim, the claimant proves facts from which the court could, apart from this section, conclude in the absence of an adequate explanation that the respondent—

  (a) has committed an act of discrimination or harassment against the claimant which is unlawful by virtue of—

    (i) section 29, 30 or 31, or

    (ii) any other provision of Part 3 so far as it applies to vocational training, or

  (b) is by virtue of section 41 or 42 to be treated as having committed such an act of discrimination or harassment against the claimant,

  the court shall uphold the claim unless the respondent proves that he did not commit, or, as the case may be, is not to be treated as having committed, that act.

NOTES

1. Section 53 RRA is in materially identical terms to s. 62 SDA while s. 65 EA 2006 and reg. 19 EA Regs, which are otherwise materially similar, expressly exclude immigration proceedings from the restriction and the DDA's restrictions on proceedings are scattered throughout the Act (being specific to each part thereof).[131]

2. Section 57 RRA is materially similar to s. 66 SDA except that there is no provision equivalent to sub-s. (3A) and s. 57 contains restrictions on the availability of injunctions in criminal cases which are found in ss. 21A SDA, 21B DDA, 52 EA 2006 and reg. 22 EA Regs. The burden of proof is as in s. 66A(2) SDA where the claim arises on grounds of of race or ethnic or national origins and otherwise falls within EU law (but not otherwise). The same is true under the DDA.[132] Further, s. 57A RRA imposes restrictions on the bringing of proceedings under s. 57A in the immigration context if the issue could have been raised, or was defeated on RRA grounds, in immigration proceedings. Section 67 EA 2006 makes similar provision as does reg. 21 EA Regs. Sections 66 and 68 EA 2006 and regs 20 and 22 EA Regs have materially similar effect to ss. 66 and 66A SDA, the burden of proof being as set out in s. 66A(2) and the position as regards compensation being as at s. 66(3) SDA.

3. Claims generally have to be brought within six months (ss. 76 SDA, 68 RRA, s. 69 EA 2006, reg. 23 EA Regs).[133] There are in some cases questionnaires available to assist discrimination claimants, and specific rules apply in relation to time-limits in particular circumstances. Considerations of space preclude detailed discussion here. Nor will the quantum of damages available be discussed except to note the availability of compensation for injury to feelings.[134]

4. Note that litigation outside the employment context is relatively unusual, given that the normal rules as to costs apply and the law is complex and, to some extent, uncertain. Despite the shift in the burden of proof which applies in many cases, discrimination remains very difficult to prove.[135]

10. PROTECTED GROUNDS

(A) 'SEX'

The SDA regulates discrimination on grounds of sex (whether against men or women) and discrimination (in the employment field alone) against married persons. The Act was amended in 1999 and 2005 to provide protection from discrimination 'on the ground that [the person] intends to undergo, is undergoing or has undergone gender reassignment' and in 2005 and 2008 to provide explicit protection from discrimination in relation to pregnancy and (in the employment context) maternity or (in relation to goods and services) having given birth in the previous six months. Attempts to have 'sex' interpreted so as to provide protection in relation to discrimination connected with sexual orientation were unsuccessful,[136]

---

[131] See, e.g., s. 31AE, Sch. 3, Pt 2, para. 5, Pt 3, para. 9.

[132] Ss. 17A, 28V, 31ADA DDA.

[133] Also DDA Sch. 3, Pt 2, para. 6, Pt 3, para. 10, Pt 4, para. 13, Pt 5, para. 17.

[134] See, generally, A. McColgan, n. 1 above, Chap. 5 and K. Monaghan, n. 1 above, Chap. 14.

[135] For what the shift means in practice (and the remaining difficulties of proof) see, e.g., *Madarassy v Nomura International plc* [2007] EWCA Civ 33, [2007] IRLR 246.

[136] See most recently *Pearce v Mayfield School, MacDonald v Ministry of Defence*, n. 128 above.

though this is no longer of much practical significance given the implementation of the SO Regs and the EA Regs.

(B) 'RACE'

Section 3 RRA

(1) In this Act, unless the context otherwise requires—

'racial grounds' means any of the following grounds, namely colour, race, nationality or ethnic or national origins;

'racial group' means a group of persons defined by reference to colour, race, nationality or ethnic or national origins, and references to a person's racial group refer to any racial group into which he falls.

(2) The fact that a racial group comprises two or more distinct racial groups does not prevent it from constituting a particular racial group for the purposes of this Act.

NOTES

1. The Race Equality Directive, which has resulted in significant amendments to the RRA, applies to discrimination on grounds of 'racial or ethnic origin' and explicitly does not apply to discrimination in grounds of nationality. The RRA was amended only in so far as it applied to discrimination on grounds of 'race' and 'ethnic or national origin', leaving intact the Act's original (and less protective) provisions in relation to ' discrimination on grounds of 'colour' and 'nationality'. But the consultation paper *A Framework for Fairness*, published in July 2007, declared the Government's intention to 'level up' across the various sub-categories of 'race'.[137]

2. 'Ethnic origins' was interpreted by the House of Lords in *Mandla v Dowell Lee* so as to extend the protection of the Act to discrimination on grounds of religion where, as in the case of Judaism and Sikhism, religious and (historical) national identities are closely linked. This case was very important prior to the implementation of religious discrimination law, and will continue to have some application for as long as race discrimination is subject to more extensive protection than religious discrimination. For this reason it is set out here:

● **Mandla v Dowell Lee** [1983] 2 AC 548

A Sikh boy was refused admission to a private school because he wore a turban. The House of Lords had to decide whether, as a Sikh, the claimant was a member of a 'racial group' for the purposes of the RRA. The court accepted that Sikhs were 'racially' indistinguishable from others from the Punjabi area of India, with whom they shared a common language and where the religion had been founded some 500 years previously.

Lord Fraser:

[A]n ethnic group in the sense of the [RRA]...must...regard itself, and be regarded by others, as a distinct community by virtue of certain characteristics. Some of these characteristics are essential others are not essential but one or more of them will commonly be found and will help to distinguish the group from the surrounding community. The conditions which appear to me to be essential are these: (1) a long shared

---

[137] See n. 105 above. For the effect of the lacuna see *Okunu v G4S Security Services (UK) Ltd* [2008] ICR 598.

history, of which the group is conscious as distinguishing it from other groups, and the memory of which it keeps alive (2) a cultural tradition of its own, including family and social customs and manners, often but not necessarily associated with religious observance. In addition to those two essential characteristics the following characteristics are, in my opinion, relevant: (3) either a common geographical origin, or descent from a small number of common ancestors (4) a common language, not necessarily peculiar to the group (5) a common literature peculiar to the group (6) a common religion different from that of neighbouring groups or from the general community surrounding it (7) being a minority or being an oppressed or a dominant group within a larger community, for example a conquered people (say, the inhabitants of England shortly after the Norman conquest) and their conquerors might both be ethnic groups.

A group defined by reference to enough of these characteristics would be capable of including converts, for example, persons who marry into the group, and of excluding apostates. Provided a person who joins the group feels himself or herself to be a member of it, and is accepted by other members, then he is, for the purpose of the [RRA], a member. That appears to be consistent with the words at the end of sub-s (1) of s 3: 'references to a person's racial group refer to any racial group into which he falls.' In my opinion, it is possible for a person to fall into a particular racial group either by birth or by adherence, and it makes no difference, so far as the [RRA] is concerned, by which route he finds his way into the group...

The result is, in my opinion, that Sikhs are a group defined by a reference to ethnic origins for the purpose of the [RRA], although they are not biologically distinguishable from the other peoples living in the Punjab.

Lord Templeman:

[Having pointed out that the RRA did not prohibit discrimination on grounds of religion] a group of persons defined by reference to ethnic origins must possess some of the characteristics of a race, namely group descent, a group of geographical origin and a group history. The evidence shows that the Sikhs satisfy these tests. They are more than a religious sect, they are almost a race and almost a nation. As a race, the Sikhs share a common colour, and a common physique based on common ancestors from that part of the Punjab which is centred on Amritsar. They fail to qualify as a separate race because in racial origin prior to the inception of Sikhism they cannot be distinguished from other inhabitants of the Punjab. As a nation the Sikhs defeated the Moghuls, and established a kingdom in the Punjab which they lost as a result of the first and second Sikh wars they fail to qualify as a separate nation or as a separate nationality because their kingdom never achieved a sufficient degree of recognition or permanence. The Sikhs qualify as a group defined by ethnic origins because they constitute a separate and distinct community derived from the racial characteristics I have mentioned. They also justify the conditions enumerated by my noble and learned friend Lord Fraser. The Sikh community has accepted converts who do not comply with those conditions. Some persons who have the same ethnic origins as the Sikhs have ceased to be members of the Sikh community. But the Sikhs remain a group of persons forming a community recognisable by ethnic origins within the meaning of the [RRA].

(C) RELIGION/BELIEF

Section 44 RRA: Religion and belief

In this Part—

  (a) 'religion' means any religion,

  (b) 'belief' means any religious or philosophical belief,

  (c) a reference to religion includes a reference to lack of religion, and

  (d) a reference to belief includes a reference to lack of belief.

NOTES

1. The decision in *Mandla*, although it de-coupled ethnicity to some extent from notions of biological 'race' and brought gypsies and Irish travellers within the protection of the RRA,[138] proved insufficiently wide to extend that protection to religious discrimination suffered by Rastafarians (this on account of a relatively short 'shared history')[139] or, in many cases, Muslims.

- **B. Hepple QC and T. Choudhury,** *Tackling Religious Discrimination; Practical Implications for Policy-Makers and Legislators*[140]

Actions taken by an employer causing detriment to Muslims as a class, such as refusal to allow time off work for religious holidays, might be held to constitute indirect racial discrimination against those from an ethnic or national background that it predominantly Muslim. This does not help Muslims who come from a country where Muslims are in a minority. The limitation of using indirect race discrimination to tackle religious discrimination is highlighted in the decision of the tribunal in *Safouane & Bouterfas (1996)*. In that case two Muslim complainants were dismissed for doing prayers during their breaks. The tribunal held that the acts did not constitute indirect race discrimination because the applicants belonged to the same North African ethnic Arab minority as the respondents and they had a good record for employing staff from a diversity of backgrounds…

2. The EA 2006 and the RB Regs (reg. 2) now protect against discrimination in the terms set out in s. 44 above. According to the explanatory notes to the Act, which amended the definition in the Regulations explicitly to include the absence of religion or belief:

170. Section 44 defines what is meant by 'religion or belief' for the purposes of this Act. Section 44(a) defines 'religion' as 'any religion', a broad definition in line with the freedom of religion guaranteed by Article 9 of the ECHR. It includes those religions widely recognised in this country such as Christianity, Islam, Hinduism, Judaism, Buddhism, Sikhism, Rastafarianism, Baha'is, Zoroastrians and Jains. Equally, denominations or sects within a religion can be considered as a religion or religious belief, such as Catholics or Protestants within Christianity. The main limitation on what constitutes a 'religion' for the purposes of Article 9 of the ECHR is that it must have a clear structure and belief system.

The more detailed explanatory notes to the SO Regs and RB Regs published by the DTI in 2003 further provide as follows.

- **DTI, Explanatory Notes for the Employment Equality (Sexual Orientation) Regulations and the Employment Equality (Religion and Belief) Regulations**

12. The reference to 'similar philosophical belief' does not include any philosophical or political belief unless it is similar to a religious belief. This does not mean that a belief must include a faith in God/Gods or worship of a God/Gods to be 'similar' to a religious belief. It means that the belief in question should be a profound belief affecting a person's way of life, or perception of the world. Effectively, that belief

---

[138] The EAT had previously accepted in *Seide v Gillette* [1980] IRLR 427 that discrimination in connection with Judaism fell within the RRA (see further the discussion of the *R (E) v JFS* case at section 10(G) below).

[139] *Dawkins v Department of the Environment* [1993] ICR 517.

[140] Home Office, London, 2001, Home Office Research Study 221, p. 12, footnotes omitted.

should occupy a place in the person's life parallel to that filled by the God/Gods of those holding a particular religious belief. As with a religious belief, a similar philosophical belief must attain a certain level of cogency, seriousness, cohesion and importance, be worthy of respect in a democratic society, and not incompatible with human dignity... Examples of beliefs which generally meet this description are atheism and humanism; examples of beliefs which generally do not are support for a political party, support for a football team.

14. References to 'religious belief' and 'similar philosophical belief' include references to a person's belief structure involving the absence of particular beliefs, because these are two sides of the same coin. This is in line with Article 9 ECHR... For example, if a Christian employer refuses an individual a job, because he is not a Christian, regardless of whether he is Muslim, Hindu, atheist (etc), that would be direct discrimination on grounds of the individual's religious belief, which can be described as 'non-Christian'. It is not necessary to identify the individual as an atheist or a Hindu for the purposes of the Regulations in such circumstances if he can be identified as a 'non-Christian'. The same is true of persons who might describe themselves as 'unconcerned' by religious beliefs, or 'unsure' of them.

15. The definition of 'religion or belief' does not include the 'manifestation' of, or conduct based on or expressing a religion or belief (see also the distinction made in Article 9 ECHR). For example, a person may wear certain clothing, or pray at certain times in accordance with the tenets of her religion, or she may express views, and say or do other things reflecting her beliefs. In such a case it would not in itself constitute direct discrimination on grounds of religion or belief under the Regulations... if a person suffers a disadvantage because she has said or done something in this way. It would only be direct discrimination if a person with different beliefs (or no beliefs) was treated more favourably in similar circumstances. However, if an employer does set down requirements about (for example) clothing or breaks for prayers, these may constitute indirect discrimination... under the Regulations unless they are justified...

(D) 'DISABILITY'

Section 1 DDA: Meaning of 'disability' and 'disabled person'

(1) Subject to the provisions of Schedule 1, a person has a disability for the purposes of this Act... if he has a physical or mental impairment which has a substantial and long-term adverse effect on his ability to carry out normal day-to-day activities.

(2) In this Act... 'disabled person' means a person who has a disability.

Section 2 DDA: Past disabilities

(1) The provisions of this Part and Parts II to 4 and 5A... apply in relation to a person who has had a disability as they apply in relation to a person who has that disability.

(2) Those provisions are subject to the modifications made by Schedule 2...

Schedule 1
Long-term effects

2(1) The effect of an impairment is a long-term effect if—

   (a) it has lasted at least 12 months;

   (b) the period for which it lasts is likely to be at least 12 months; or

   (c) it is likely to last for the rest of the life of the person affected.

(2) Where an impairment ceases to have a substantial adverse effect on a person's ability to carry out normal day-to-day activities, it is to be treated as continuing to have that effect if that effect is likely to recur.

(3) For the purposes of sub-paragraph (2), the likelihood of an effect recurring shall be disregarded in prescribed circumstances.

Severe disfigurement

3(1) An impairment which consists of a severe disfigurement is to be treated as having a substantial adverse effect on the ability of the person concerned to carry out normal day-to-day activities.

Normal day-to-day activities

4(1) An impairment is to be taken to affect the ability of the person concerned to carry out normal day-to-day activities only if it affects one of the following—

(a) mobility;

(b) manual dexterity;

(c) physical co-ordination;

(d) continence;

(e) ability to lift, carry or otherwise move everyday objects;

(f) speech, hearing or eyesight;

(g) memory or ability to concentrate, learn or understand; or

(h) perception of the risk of physical danger.

(2) Regulations may prescribe—

(a) circumstances in which an impairment which does not have an effect falling within sub-paragraph (1) is to be taken to affect the ability of the person concerned to carry out normal day-to-day activities;

(b) circumstances in which an impairment which has an effect falling within sub-paragraph (1) is to be taken not to affect the ability of the person concerned to carry out normal day-to-day activities.

Effect of medical treatment

6(1) An impairment which would be likely to have a substantial adverse effect on the ability of the person concerned to carry out normal day-to-day activities, but for the fact that measures are being taken to treat or correct it, is to be treated as having that effect.

(2) In sub-paragraph (1) 'measures' includes, in particular, medical treatment and the use of a prosthesis or other aid.

(3) Sub-paragraph (1) does not apply—

(a) in relation to the impairment of a person's sight, to the extent that the impairment is, in his case, correctable by spectacles or contact lenses or in such other ways as may be prescribed; or

(b) in relation to such other impairments as may be prescribed, in such circumstances as may be prescribed.

6A(1) Subject to sub-paragraph (2), a person who has cancer, HIV infection or multiple sclerosis is to be deemed to have a disability, and hence to be a disabled person.

Progressive conditions

8(1) Where—

(a) a person has a progressive condition (such as cancer, multiple sclerosis or muscular dystrophy or [HIV infection]),

(b) as a result of that condition, he has an impairment which has (or had) an effect on his ability to carry out normal day-to-day activities, but

(c) that-effect is not (or was not) a substantial adverse effect,

he shall be taken to have an impairment which has such a substantial adverse effect if the condition is likely to result in his having such an impairment.

- **Disability Discrimination (Meaning of Disability) Regulations 1996, SI 1996/1455**[141]

Addictions

3(1) Subject to paragraph (2) below, addiction to alcohol, nicotine or any other substance is to be treated as not amounting to an impairment for the purposes of the Act.

(2) Paragraph (1) above does not apply to addiction which was originally the result of administration of medically prescribed drugs or other medical treatment.

Other conditions not to be treated as impairments

4(1) For the purposes of the Act the following conditions are to be treated as not amounting to impairments:—

(a) a tendency to set fires,

(b) a tendency to steal,

(c) a tendency to physical or sexual abuse of other persons,

(d) exhibitionism, and

(e) voyeurism.

(2) Subject to paragraph (3) below for the purposes of the Act the condition known as seasonal allergic rhinitis shall be treated as not amounting to an impairment.

(3) Paragraph (2) above shall not prevent that condition from being taken into account for the purposes of the Act where it aggravates the effect of another condition.

Tattoos and piercings

5 For the purposes of paragraph 3 of Schedule 1 to the Act a severe disfigurement is not to be treated as having a substantial adverse effect on the ability of the person concerned to carry out normal day-to-day activities if it consists of—

(a) a tattoo (which has not been removed), or

(b) a piercing of the body for decorative or other non-medical purposes, including any object attached through the piercing for such purposes.

Babies and Young Children

6 For the purposes of the Act where a child under six years of age has an impairment which does not have an effect falling within paragraph 4(1) of Schedule 1 to the Act that impairment is to be taken to have a substantial and long-term adverse effect on the ability of that child to carry out normal day-to-day activities where it would normally have a substantial and long-term adverse effect on the ability of a person aged 6 years or over to carry out normal day-to-day activities.[142]

---

[141] Made under Sch.1 DDA.

[142] The Secretary of State is also provided with power by s. 3 DDA to issue guidance on the meaning of disability. That guidance is currently available at http://83.137.212.42/SiteArchive/drc_gb/docs/DefnOfDisability.doc, accessed 4 August 2008.

NOTES

1. The DDA's prohibitions on discrimination apply only in relation to those it defines as 'disabled' (though see discussion of *Coleman v Attridge Law* at section 11(B) below).[143] The Act defines 'disability' in medical and functional terms rather than, as many disability activists would prefer, in *social* terms (that is, recognising that the built environment and societal attitudes disable the physically or mentally impaired more than the fact of those impairments).

2. The Act does not at present protect against discrimination on grounds of perceived disability (where, for example, someone is dismissed because he is wrongly believed to be suffering from HIV). This may, however, change as a result of the decision of the ECJ in Case 303/06, *Coleman v Attridge Law*, below.

3. In *A Framework for Fairness*[144] the Government proposed repeal of the list of capacities in Sch. 1, para. 4 DDA.

(E) SEXUAL ORIENTATION

Section 35 EA 2006

'sexual orientation' means an individual's sexual orientation towards—

   (a) persons of the same sex as him or her,

   (b) persons of the opposite sex, or

   (c) both.

NOTE

1. Regulation 2 of the SO Regs is in identical terms. The definition of the term 'sexual orientation', unusual in such anti-discrimination provisions, is the result of anxiety on the part of the Government that the Regulations could otherwise protect 'those who have unlawful sex, in particular paedophiles'. The DTI's consultation document *Towards Equality and Diversity* stated that concern about this had been 'voiced by some during negotiations on the text of the [Equality] Directive' which, despite these apparent concerns, contains no definition of 'sexual orientation'.[145] The definition adopted by the SO Regs and the EA may appear uncontroversial but the criticism which may be made of it concerns its tendency to 'pin down' the question of sexual orientation which is in the view of many not necessarily capable of rigid classification. It is unlikely that this conceptual objection could give rise to any legal challenge to the approach adopted by the UK however.

(F) AGE

The Age Regs do not define 'age', regulating discrimination 'on grounds of [a person's] age' and the application of 'a provision, criterion or practice which…puts or would put persons of the same age group as [a claimant] at a particular disadvantage'. There is no upper or lower age limit for the protection of the Age Regs.

---

143 Subject to what is said about that case, the only current exception relates to victimisation.

144 N. 105 above.

145 Para. 12.6. The document is available at www.dti.gov.uk/er/equality/consult.pdf.

(G) OVERLAPPING GROUNDS

- **R (E) v Governing Body of the Jews Free School** [2008] EWHC 1535, 1536 (Admin)

This case involved a challenge by an Orthodox Jewish school to admit a prospective pupil whose mother, who was of Italian ethnicity, had converted to Judaism. The prospective pupil was an observant Jew and was recognised as such by Reform synagogues, but not by the school. The school admitted only Orthodox Jews, though it did not require that they be religiously obser-vant. A history of the school published in 1998 recorded that: 'There is no requirement that the Jewish mother must be a practising Jewess or member of an orthodox synagogue. Anomalies abound. The accepted "Jewish" mother whose child is eligible to go to JFS might now be a mem-ber of the Reform synagogue or of no synagogue, be an agnostic or an atheist—that would not debar her child from entrance. An observant mother, who regularly attends synagogue and keeps a kosher home cannot enter her child at JFS if she, the mother, is Jewish by conversion under Reform or Liberal auspices.'[146] The school's admissions policy had the effect, as its web-site recorded, that, while '[m]any [of its intake] come from families who are totally committed to Judaism and Israel; others are unaware of Jewish belief and practice'.

The claim of discrimination contrary to s. 17 RRA failed because the High Court ruled that the refusal of admission had been based on the boy's religion and not on his race.

Munby J:

14. ...in Orthodox Judaism Jewish status is...'solely and irreducibly a religious issue'...'attendance at the services of a synagogue has no bearing on a person's Jewish status as a matter of Jewish religious law. Being Jewish is a matter of Jewish status, under Jewish religious law'...'Jewish status in Orthodox Judaism is thus different from the notion of belonging to a faith in proselytizing religions such as Christianity and Islam.' (Judaism is not a proselytizing religion, though anyone can convert to Judaism.)

15. Within Orthodox Judaism the criterion of Jewish identity, accepted for millennia within Jewish Orthodoxy, is that the person concerned is either (a) born to a Jewish mother or (b) has undergone a valid Orthodox conversion to Judaism....

19. An article by the Chief Rabbi in the Jewish Chronicle dated 8 July 2005 is illuminating in explaining the Orthodox Jewish approach to conversion...

> * If a convert, by his or her behaviour, demonstrates a genuine commitment to Jewish law and practice at the time of conversion, it remains valid even if he or she later abandons it. A lapsed convert is a lapsed Jew, not a lapsed gentile. If, however, there was no significant religious observance at the time, the conversion is void. Acceptance of the commands is constitutive of conversion. Without it, conversion cannot be said to have taken place.
>
>   * Converting to Judaism is a serious undertaking, because Judaism is not a mere creed. It involves a dis-tinctive, detailed way of life. When people ask me why conversion to Judaism takes so long, I ask them to consider other cases of changed identity. How long does it take for a Briton to become an Italian, not just legally but linguistically, culturally, behaviourally? It takes time...'

---

[146] Dr Gerry Black, 'JFS—A history of the Jews' Free School, London since 1732'. The decision records that one of the other prospective pupils whose application was rejected had been born to a mother who converted in Israel and was married by an Orthodox Rabbi in an Orthodox synagogue, but whose son was subsequently refused ritual circumcision by the London Beth Din (Jewish court) because his father, the man whom the con-verted mother had married, was a cohen (a member of a Jewish tribe by descent) who were prohibited by Jewish law from marrying converts. The very basis upon which the Beth Din rejected her conversion was that she had contracted a forbidden marriage so soon after it, such that her conversion was not accepted as having manifested full commitment to the tenets of the orthodox faith. She (the mother) herself taught at JFS but her daughter's application to JFS was rejected on the basis that she (the daughter) was not a Jew.

20. All the evidence I have seen is to the effect that all Jewish denominations treat being Jewish as a matter of status, not a matter of creed or religious observance...

146. In *Mandla* at page 561 Lord Fraser of Tullybelton had treated it as obvious that the 1976 Act applied to Jews and indeed his factors (1) and (2) are plainly apposite to embrace Jews. The point came up for direct decision in *Seide v Gillette Industries Ltd* [1980] IRLR 427...

147. In that case the complainant had been the victim of offensive remarks of anti-Semitic nature by a fellow employee. The question was whether, if there was discrimination at all...it was discrimination within the ambit of the 1976 Act. At paras [22]–[23] Mr Justice Slynn P said this:

> '...The point was quite rightly raised as to whether what had happened here was on the ground of Mr Seide's religion. If it was, then it appeared to be outside the provisions of the Race Relations Act. On the other hand, if it was on the ground of his race or ethnic origin then it would be within the ambit of the Act. Both sides accept and the Tribunal accepted that 'Jewish' could mean that one was a member of a race or a particular ethnic origin as well as being a member of a particular religious faith. The Tribunal, on that basis, found that what happened here was not because Mr Seide was of the Jewish faith but because he was a member of the Jewish race or of Jewish ethnic origin.
>
> It seems to us that their approach to this question was the right approach, as agreed by the parties, and that they were perfectly entitled to find on the facts of this case that Mr Garcia's remarks were on the basis of Mr Seide's race or ethnic origin.'

148. That decision is important, as it seems to me, for two quite separate reasons. In the first place, it is clear authority, if indeed authority were required for such an obvious proposition, that Jews are an ethnic group. Secondly, however, there is the clear recognition that anti-Semitic behaviour may be based on the victim's Jewish ethnic origin—in which case the 1976 Act applies—but may, on the other hand, be based simply on the victim's Jewish religion or faith—in which case the 1976 Act does not apply. And whether in any particular case it is one or the other is a matter of fact, to be determined on the facts of the particular case...

151. There is no room for doubt or dispute about the relevant policy and how it operates. So there is no room for argument about the 'reason why' M was treated as he was: it was because, in the view of the OCR,[147] and therefore of JFS, he is not Jewish, not being of Jewish matrilineal descent...

152. The only question, therefore, is whether...the criterion of being Jewish by virtue of Jewish matrilineal descent [is] one of ethnic origin?

154. Ms Rose asserts baldly [for the claimant] that it is 'evident' that ethnic origin is the 'reason why' children like M are less favourably treated than applicants recognised by the OCR as being Jewish; M, she says, is being less favourably treated than a child whose mother was born Jewish 'because of who he is and where he comes from, and not because of what he believes or practices.' He is, she says, being treated in the way he is entirely because of his mother's ethnicity. I do not agree.

155. Looking to the United States of America, Ms Rose seeks to draw an analogy with a faith group which recognises 'white members only': see *Bob Jones University v United States* (1983) 461 US 574. (Mr Wolfe [intervening] draws a similar analogy when referring to the South African Afrikaanse Protestante Kerk, which also allows only white members.) She submits that such a group could not avoid liability under the 1976 Act merely by asserting that its stance was based upon sincere religious belief. I entirely agree, even assuming (what I would not be prepared to accept) that such a group is entitled to be treated as a religion at all; I have in mind, for example, the principle stated by the Strasbourg court that the Convention recognises only religions which 'are worthy of respect in a 'democratic society' and are not incompatible with human dignity.'

156. But Ms Rose seeks to take the argument further, for she submits that the situation in the present case is even starker: it is not that JFS recognises only those who are of matrilineal Jewish descent as Jewish; it is that it recognises all those who are of matrilineal Jewish descent as Jewish irrespective of belief or

---

147 Office of the Chief Rabbi of the United Hebrew Congregation of the Commonwealth, which (broadly) represents Orthodox Judaism.

practice and excludes many other who are Jewish by belief and practice on grounds only of descent. So, she suggests, the proper analogy is with a religious group which embraces all white people as its members, whether or not they share its beliefs.

157. The short answer to this is provided by Mr Singh [intervening]. Being white is only and necessarily a matter of race. Being Jewish can be a matter of race, but it can also be purely a matter of religion. Someone can be Jewish as a matter of religion (for example, by conversion) but not racial origin. Someone can be Jewish as a matter of race but, unless they convert in a way recognised by the OCR, not Jewish as a matter of religion…a person can convert to Judaism and, once converted, is Jewish and, if a woman, will pass her Jewish status to her children. But no-one can change his or her colour.

158. However the importance of this part of Ms Rose's argument is that it brings into sharp focus that the central plank in E's case is the assumption—the assertion—that membership of a religious group based upon descent amounts to membership by reason of ethnic origins….

160. The…equiperation of descent and ethnic origin…involves a simple error of logic as well as an error of law. Because the concept of ethnic origin as explained by Lord Fraser of Tullybelton in *Mandla* embraces within it, as one of a number of factors, the concept of descent, it does not follow either as a matter of logic or as a matter of law that the concept of descent simpliciter necessarily has anything to do with ethnicity. Depending on the context it may do, but equally it may not. So merely to point to the fact that the rule applied by the OCR, and thus by JFS, is based on descent in the matrilineal line, does not, of itself, take Ms Rose anywhere…

162. Mr Singh helpfully distinguishes—and submits that it is important to distinguish—between:

i) Jewish ethnic origins—meaning those who are part of the Jewish ethnic group for the purposes of the 1976 Act in accordance with the approach taken in *Mandla*;
ii) Jewish descent—meaning those who have a Jewish parent; and
iii) Jewish status—meaning those who are recognised by Jewish law as being Jewish.

As he correctly submits, the fact that someone is of a particular 'descent' or has a particular 'status' at birth does not mean that that is their 'ethnic origin.' And he submits, correctly in my judgment, that there is discrimination 'on racial grounds' only if it based on someone's Jewish ethnic origins and not if it occurs on grounds of Jewish status or Jewish descent.

163. Mr Singh puts the point very neatly when he submits that the significance of 'descent' is that discrimination on grounds of descent from a person of a particular race or ethnic origin is obviously 'on racial grounds', and is thus racial discrimination, but discrimination on grounds only of descent from a person of a particular religious status is not racial discrimination if religious status means something different—as he says it does—from race or ethnic origins.

164. He illustrates the point by reference to Islam, founding his observation on the well-recognised fact that Muslims are not, within the meaning of the 1976 Act, a racial or ethnic group. So, as he points out, discrimination on the ground that an individual is a Muslim is not discrimination on racial grounds. Nor, and this is the important point, is discrimination on grounds that the individual, though not himself a Muslim, is descended from a Muslim. It is discrimination on grounds of religion, or descent from a religious status, and is not, in itself, racial discrimination. And it makes no difference that, as the Secretary of State understands it, a child born of a Muslim father is, as a matter of Muslim religious law, a Muslim. That, as Mr Singh says, is a matter of descent and status but not a matter of ethnic origins. So what, he asks rhetorically, is the difference between that and the present case?..

167. At the end of the day Ms Rose seeks to rely upon what she says is the combination of ethnicity and matrilineal descent. Putting it rather differently, she submits that 'Jewish descent' and 'Jewish ethnicity' are coterminous, because to be Jewish by descent you must be descended from a Jewish woman who was Jewish either by descent or by conversion and who was therefore necessarily, for the reasons given in *Mandla*, a member of the ethnic group. But the argument breaks down because, however the point is put,

in the final analysis it is based on a principle of Jewish religious law which identifies and defines a Jewish status which is neither founded on nor creative of any distinctively Jewish ethnicity.

168. The simple fact, in my judgment, is that JFS's admissions policy is, as the Schools Adjudicator correctly found, based on religious and not on racial (ethnic) grounds, reflecting, as it does, a religious and not an ethnic view as to who, in the eyes of the OCR and JFS, is or is not a Jew. Such an analysis, as both Mr Oldham and Mr Lewis point out [for the respondents], fits comfortably within the distinction drawn in *Seide* between actions by or in relation to Jews based on religious grounds and actions by or in relation to Jews based on racial (ethnic) grounds. As Mr Oldham succinctly observes, the cause of a non-Orthodox applicant failing to meet JFS's admission requirements can only be described as a religious cause...

169. As Mr Singh points out, the correctness or otherwise of Ms Rose's analysis can be tested by reference to a number of hypothetical cases. He examines three:

i) Hypothetical 1: A has three Jewish grandparents who identified themselves as Jewish as a matter of ethnicity/culture. His maternal grandmother was not Jewish. For the purposes of the 1976 Act, A would be regarded as Jewish as a matter of descent and ethnic origins, but he would not be admitted to JFS, even if his mother has converted, unless her conversion is recognised as valid by the OCR.

ii) Hypothetical 2: B's mother converted to Judaism before he was born. The conversion was recognised as valid by the OCR. Some years later, and before B was born, she ceased any Jewish practices and no longer identified herself as Jewish as a matter of culture/ethnicity. B's father is not Jewish. B would be recognised as Jewish by the OCR and JFS but he would not be Jewish as a matter of blood/descent, having no biological ancestors who are Jewish. And if he did not identify himself as Jewish as a matter of culture/history/language he would also not be Jewish as a matter of ethnic origin.

iii) Hypothetical 3: C's maternal grandmother was Jewish (either by descent or conversion) but not any of his other grandparents. C would be regarded as Jewish by the OCR and JFS...

170. What these hypotheticals demonstrate, according to Mr Singh, is that the ethnic origin of each of A, B and C (in terms of their identification with or participation in Jewish culture etc) is entirely irrelevant to JFS's admission arrangements. Those arrangements operate, as a matter of objective fact, he says, on religious and not on racial (ethnic) grounds. As he correctly observes, A would not come within JFS's admissions policy despite, as he puts it, being Jewish as a matter of descent/ethnic origin. B, on the other hand, would be admitted, despite, as Mr Singh puts it, not being Jewish as a matter of descent/ethnic origin. C would also be admitted even though, he suggests, A could be said to be more 'Jewish' as a matter of descent. Thus JFS, he says, will give preference in admissions to a child who is less racially/ethnically Jewish, or not racially/ethnically Jewish at all, over one who is Jewish as a matter of race (ethnicity), if that child is, in the eyes of the OCR and JFS, Jewish as a matter of religion. And this is borne out, he says, by the fact that it is immaterial whether the child's mother is Jewish as a matter of racial or ethnic origin; the only matter considered by the OCR and JFS is whether she is Jewish as a matter of religion.

171. The fact that, as he would submit, religion is the true focus here, is illustrated, Mr Singh says, by the very fact that at the heart of all the three cases I am considering is a dispute—a quintessentially religious dispute—about the validity of the conversion of the applicant child's mother. As Mr Singh rightly says, a dispute about what constitutes a valid conversion is simply not a matter which engages the 1976 Act at all; it is a question of religious doctrine on which the secular courts should be wary to tread. I entirely agree.

172. Ms Rose seeks to escape the implications of Mr Singh's hypotheticals by challenging his analysis. She says that A is only ¾ Jewish and not, if I can put it like this, Jewish as to the relevant ¼—his maternal grandmother. She says that B is indeed Jewish because his mother, at the moment of conversion, and by accepting membership of and by being accepted as a member of the Jewish community, became Jewish by ethnicity and culture. It seems to me, with all respect, that Ms Rose's ripostes merely go to demonstrate the essential correctness of Mr Singh's argument, for what, in the final analysis, she relies upon—has to rely upon—is a principle of Jewish religious law.

NOTE

1. Munby J noted that, if the case succeeded, it would threaten the ability of orthodox Jewish (but not other) religious schools to restrict their intake by reference to religion, citing the argument made by counsel for the school that the alternative suggestion, that the school adopt an entrance policy built on observance was 'built upon a central misconception, namely that religion, on his view, is confined to those who believe in a deity or are observant, whereas Orthodox Judaism... happens to be characterised by the belief, not that observance is a necessary part of membership, but that membership is defined by a status—acquired either by conversion or automatically through the matrilineal line—that cannot be lost'.[148] He took into account the Art. 9 jurisprudence on the state's duty of neutrality between religious groups[149] and his own role as a secular, rather than a religious, adjudicator.[150] The decision is under appeal but, given the difficulties which would be raised for Jewish (but not other religious) schools, it is unlikely to be reversed. Conceptually it is perhaps very difficult to untangle the discrimination at issue in *JFS* from race discrimination. On the other hand, as recognised by Munby J in the case, an concept of 'religion' which is based on behaviour, as distinct from status, is culturally Christian rather than neutral. It is tempting to suggest that one solution might be the prohibition of religious belief/status as a selection criteria for all schools, coupled with a change of policy to ensure that all schools are genuinely non-discriminatory as between pupils of particular religions and those with no religious belief. This may, however, be easier to propose than to achieve.

11. 'DISCRIMINATION': THE GENERAL PART

(A) PRELIMINARIES

One of the very fundamental issues that arises in connection with the statutory discrimination provisions concerns the meaning of 'discrimination'. This is not entirely consistent across the various statutory regimes which do, however, exhibit a significant degree of overlap distinguishing (except in the case of the DDA) between 'direct' and 'indirect' discrimination and (except in the case of the Age Regs) providing no general justification defence in relation to direct discrimination. The possibility of justification is, by contrast, an inevitable ingredient of indirect discrimination (see further section 11(D)). The approach of the DDA is significantly different from the other provisions and is dealt with in some detail below (section 12(C)) after consideration of the more general pattern. It should be noted here that all the statutory regimes prohibit 'victimisation' which is defined as occurring where less favourable treatment is accorded to someone because they have, or are suspected to have, taken steps in connecton with a complaint of discrimination under the relevant legislation (including, *inter alia*, assisting someone else with a claim). Victimisation complaints are common in the employment context but given the focus of this book the topic will not be considered further here.[151]

---

[148] Para. 92.
[149] See, e.g., *Moscow Branch of the Salvation Army v Russia* (2006) 44 EHRR 912, para. 58.
[150] Para. 107.   [151] For detailed analysis see A. McColgan, n. 1, Chap. 2 above.

(B) 'DIRECT' DISCRIMINATION

THE DEFINITIONS

Section 1 RRA

S.1 A person discriminates against another in any circumstances relevant for the purposes of any provision of this Act if—

(a) *on racial grounds* he treats that other less favourably than he treats or would treat other persons [emphasis added]...

Section 3 RRA

(4) A comparison of the case of a person of a particular racial group with that of a person not of that group under section 1(1) [or (1A)] must be such that the relevant circumstances in the one case are the same, or not materially different, in the other.

Section 1 SDA

S.1 A person discriminates against a woman in any circumstances relevant for the purposes of any provision of this Act if—

(a) on the grounds of her sex he treats her less favourably than he treats or would treat a man...

Section 5 SDA

(3) Each of the following comparisons, that is—

(a) a comparison of the cases of persons of different sex under section 1(1) or (2)...

must be such that the relevant circumstances in the one case are the same, or not materially different, in the other.

Section 3A DDA

(5) A person directly discriminates against a disabled person if, on the ground of the disabled person's disability, he treats the disabled person less favourably than he treats or would treat a person not having that particular disability whose relevant circumstances, including his abilities, are the same as, or not materially different from, those of the disabled person.

Section 45 EA 2006

(1) A person ('A') discriminates against another ('B') for the purposes of this Part if on grounds of the religion or belief of B or of any other person except A (whether or not it is also A's religion or belief) A treats B less favourably than he treats or would treat others (in cases where there is no material difference in the relevant circumstances).

(2) In subsection (1) a reference to a person's religion or belief includes a reference to a religion or belief to which he is thought to belong or subscribe.

Reg 3 RB Regs

(1) For the purposes of these Regulations, a person ('A') discriminates against another person ('B') if -

(a) on the grounds of the religion or belief of B or of any other person except A (whether or not it is also A's religion or belief) A treats B less favourably than he treats or would treat other persons...

(3) A comparison of B's case with that of another person under paragraph (1) must be such that the relevant circumstances in the one case are the same, or not materially different, in the other.

Reg 3 SO Regs

(1) For the purposes of these Regulations, a person ('A') discriminates against another person ('B') if—

(a) on grounds of sexual orientation, A treats B less favourably than he treats or would treat other persons...

(2) A comparison of B's case with that of another person under paragraph (1) must be such that the relevant circumstances in the one case are the same, or not materially different, in the other.

Reg 3 EA Regs

(1) For the purposes of these Regulations, a person ('A') discriminates against another ('B') if, on grounds of the sexual orientation of B or any other person except A, A treats B less favourably than he treats or would treat others (in cases where there is no material difference in the relevant circumstances).

(2) In paragraph (1) a reference to a person's sexual orientation includes a reference to a sexual orientation which he is thought to have...

(4) For the purposes of paragraphs (1) and (3), the fact that one of the persons (whether or not B) is a civil partner while the other is married shall not be treated as a material difference in the relevant circumstances.

Regulation 3, Age Regs

(1) For the purposes of these Regulations, a person ('A') discriminates against another person ('B') if -

(a) on grounds of B's age, A treats B less favourably than he treats or would treat other persons...

and A cannot show the treatment or, as the case may be, provision, criterion or practice to be a proportionate means of achieving a legitimate aim.

(2) A comparison of B's case with that of another person under paragraph (1) must be such that the relevant circumstances in the one case are the same, or not materially different, in the other.

NOTES

1. It is evident that definitions of direct discrimination differ across the protected grounds. Not only do some (the DDA, EA 2006 and EA Regs) incorporate the explicit need for comparison within the definition of direct discrimination itself,[152] the other provisions making reference to this in another subsection or section of the Act,[153] there are differences across the legislative provisions as to whether the prohibition on discrimination extends to *perceived* as well as actual status. That this is included is made clear in the EA 2006 and EA Regs. We shall see below that it is also implicitly included within the RRA, SO Regs and RB Regs but not within the SDA, DDA or Age Regs.

2. A secondary distinction arises in the context of sexual orientation between the SO regs and the EA Regs: only the latter makes it clear that discrimination on the grounds of the discriminator's *own* sexual orientation is not covered by the Regs (unless it also amounts to discrimination on the grounds of another's sexual orientation). It is unclear why a different definition of sexual orientation discrimination was adopted in the two sets of Regulations. It would not be unusual for the Government to adopt a narrower approach to discrimination not falling within EU law (as is the case of discrimination contrary to the EA Regs), but this does not appear to be the case here.

---

[152] The comparator question is further considered in text at n. 178 below.

[153] Or other sub provision of the Regulations.

3. The prohibition on discrimination 'on racial grounds' and 'on grounds of sexual orientation' (RRA and SO Regs) applies to discrimination connected to the race or sexual orientation of a person other than the victim. The cases below arose in the employment context but the principle they establish is of general application. In *Zarczynska v Levy* the EAT accepted that the claimant, who worked in a bar, was discriminated against contrary to the RRA when she was dismissed because of her refusal to comply with an order not to serve Black customers.[154] Kilner Brown J relied on Lord Denning in the Court of Appeal in the earlier case of *Race Relations Board v Applin*,[155] in which his Lordship had expressed the view that a refusal to allow entry to White women because they were accompanied by Black men would amount to race discrimination, and in *Nothman v London Borough of Barnet*,[156] in which the Master of the Rolls stated that 'Whenever the strict interpretation of a statute gives rise to an absurd and unjust situation, the judges can and should use their good sense to remedy it—by reading words in, if necessary—so as to do what parliament would have done had they had the situation in mind.' Taking into account the fact that Lord Denning had in *Nothman* characterised Kilner Brown J's approach as 'strict constructionist...the voice of those who go by the letter...of those who adopt the strict literal and grammatical construction of the words, heedless of the consequences' the same judge, having concluded that 'if Parliament had had pre-knowledge of this unfortunate lady's predicament they would have made clear that the great civilised principle upon which the Act was based was one which over-rode all apparent limitations expressed in other sections which had the effect of denying justice to someone who was victimised' was 'prepared to be a contemporary pragmatist and assume most respectfully that the Court of Appeal would find in favour of this lady's argument if we were to reject it' and to uphold her claim accordingly. A similar approach was applied by the EAT in *Showboat Entertainment Centre v Owen*,[157] in which a man was dismissed as manager of an amusement centre because he refused to follow an instruction to exclude young Black men from the centre, and in *Weathersfield v Sargent* by the Court of Appeal in which a White woman claimed race discrimination because she had been ordered unlawfully to discriminate against potential customers on racial grounds.

- **Weathersfield Ltd t/a Van & Truck Rentals v Sargent** [1999] ICR 425

Pill LJ (with whom **Swinton-Thomas** and **Beldam LJJ** agreed):
In Showboat Entertainment Centre Ltd v Owens...Browne-Wilkinson J, as he then was, stated that 'the words 'on racial grounds' are perfectly capable in their ordinary sense of covering any reason or action based on race, whether it be the race of the person affected by the action or others.' He added: 'We therefore see nothing in the wording of the Act which makes it clear that the words 'on racial grounds' cover only the race of the complainant...We find it impossible to believe that Parliament intended that a person dismissed for refusing to obey an unlawful discriminatory instruction should be without a remedy. It places an employee in an impossible position if he has to choose between being party to an illegality and losing his job. It seems to us that Parliament must have intended such an employee to be protected so far as possible from the consequences of doing his lawful duty by refusing to obey such an instruction...We therefore conclude that s.1(1)(a) covers all cases of discrimination on racial grounds whether the racial characteristics in question are those of the person treated less favourably or of some other person. The only question in this case is whether the unfavourable treatment afforded to the claimant was caused by racial considerations.' Browne-Wilkinson J also held that: 'The correct comparison in

---

[154] [1979] ICR 184.   [155] [1973] QB 815.   [156] [1977] IRLR 489.   [157] [1984] ICR 65.

this case would be between the applicant and another manager who did not choose to obey the unlawful racial instructions.'

16 …I respectfully agree with the reasoning in *Showboat* [1984] IRLR 7. In the context of the 1976 Act unfavourable treatment of an employee, if it requires the employee to carry out a racially discriminatory trading policy in circumstances such as the present, is treatment on racial grounds. That conclusion does involve giving a broad meaning to the expression racial grounds but it is one which in my view is justified and appropriate….

22. In the present case, the industrial tribunal were amply justified in holding that there was a constructive dismissal. In the first days of her employment, the employers had put Mrs Sargent in an outrageous and embarrassing position. It was understandable that she did not want immediately to confront the employers with her reason for leaving. In the event, and having taken advice, she did so within a matter of days. No other reason why she may have left the employment became apparent in the evidence.

4. The cases considered immediately above concern what might be called *associative* discrimination, and it is clear from them that discrimination based on the race or sexual orientation of the victim's sexual partner or child would breach the relevant prohibitions. Given the approach to interpretation adopted by the courts in *Zarczynska Showboat* and *Weathersfield*,[158] the terms 'on racial grounds' and 'on grounds of sexual orientation' clearly capture such discrimination even where it is not explicitly regulated. By contrast, however, the statutory approach to sex, disability and age discrimination (set out above) is considerably narrower. The SDA, DDA and Age Regs all require that the treatment complained of is causally related to the complainant's *own* status.

The relevant European directives, however, prohibit discrimination 'based on racial or ethnic origin' or 'on any of the [relevant] grounds'. This lack of fit caused an employment tribunal to refer to the ECJ the question whether Council Directive 2000/78/EC required protection to be provided to a woman discriminated against because of her son's disability (EAT accepting on appeal from the tribunal judgment that, if necessary, 'the DDA is capable of interpretation, consistent with an interpretation of the Directive favourable to the claimant, so as to include associative discrimination without distorting the words of the statute and consistent with the domestic Courts' responsibility to arrive at a construction which ensures that the Directive is fully effective').[159] In July 2008 the ECJ accepted the invitation of Advocate-General Miguel Poiares Maduro to find that the discrimination alleged by Ms Coleman fell within the Directive.

The Advocate-General had placed emphasis on the fact that the Directive, adopted under Art. 13 TEC, 'is an expression of the commitment of the Community legal order to the principle of equal treatment and non-discrimination', and that it had to be interpreted in light of the ECJ's jurisprudence on equal treatment and non-discrimination which made it clear that 'Equality is not merely a political ideal and aspiration but one of the fundamental principles of Community law' underpinned by the values of 'human dignity and personal autonomy'.[160] He took the view that these values were inconsistent with the taking into account of 'suspect characteristics' (ethnicity, sex, sexual orientation, disability, religion or belief or age) 'in any assessment as to whether it is right or not to treat someone less favourably',[161] and that 'One way of undermining the dignity and autonomy of people who belong to a certain group is to target not them, but third persons who are closely associated with them and do not themselves belong to the group', such that 'A robust conception of equality entails that these

---

[158]   And underpinned by the comments of Lord Templeman in *Savjani*—see n. 66 above.
[159]   [2007] ICR 654.   [160]   Para. 8.   [161]   Para. 10.

subtler forms of discrimination should also be caught by anti-discrimination legislation, as they, too, affect the persons belonging to suspect classifications.'[162]

22. As stated, the effect of the Directive is that it is impermissible for an employer to rely on religion, age, disability and sexual orientation in order to treat some employees less well than others. To do so would amount to subjecting these individuals to unjust treatment and failing to respect their dignity and autonomy. This fact does not change in cases where the employee who is the object of discrimination is not disabled herself. The ground which serves as the basis of the discrimination she suffers continues to be disability. The Directive operates at the level of grounds of discrimination. The wrong that it was intended to remedy is the use of certain characteristics as grounds to treat some employees less well than others; what it does is to remove religion, age, disability and sexual orientation completely from the range of grounds an employer may legitimately use to treat some people less well. Put differently, the Directive does not allow the hostility an employer may have against people belonging to the enumerated suspect classifications to function as the basis for any kind of less favourable treatment in the context of employment and occupation. As I have explained, this hostility may be expressed in an overt manner by targeting individuals who themselves have certain characteristics, or in a more subtle and covert manner by targeting those who are associated with the individuals having the characteristics. In the former case, we think that such conduct is wrong and must be prohibited; the latter is exactly the same in every material aspect. In both cases, it is the hostility of the employer towards elderly, disabled or homosexual people or people of a certain religious persuasion that leads him to treat some employees less well.

23. Therefore, if someone is the object of discrimination because of any one of the characteristics listed in Article 1 then she can avail herself of the protection of the Directive even if she does not posses one of them herself. It is not necessary for someone who is the object of discrimination to have been mistreated on account of 'her disability'. It is enough if she was mistreated on account of 'disability'. Thus, one can be a victim of unlawful discrimination on the ground of disability under the Directive without being disabled oneself; what is important is that that disability—in this case the disability of Ms Coleman's son—was used as a reason to treat her less well. The Directive does not come into play only when the claimant is disabled herself but every time there is an instance of less favourable treatment because of disability. Therefore, if Ms Coleman can prove that she was treated less favourably because of her son's disability she should be able to rely on the Directive.

It is fairly clear from this opinion that the Advocate-General would also interpret the Directive to regulate discrimination on the grounds of *perceived* disability (see in particular para. 23). The ECJ in its judgment adopted a similarly broad approach:

- **Case 303/06, Coleman v Attridge Law** [2008] IRLR 722

43 ...the fact that Directive 2000/78 includes provisions designed to accommodate specifically the needs of disabled people does not lead to the conclusion that the principle of equal treatment enshrined in that directive must be interpreted strictly, that is, as prohibiting only direct discrimination on grounds of disability and relating exclusively to disabled people. Furthermore, recital 6 in the preamble to the directive, concerning the Community Charter of the Fundamental Social Rights of Workers, refers both to the general combating of every form of discrimination and to the need to take appropriate action for the social and economic integration of disabled people...

47 So far as the objectives of Directive 2000/78 are concerned, as is apparent from paragraphs 34 and 38 of the present judgment, the directive seeks to lay down, as regards employment and occupation,

---

[162] Para. 12.

a general framework for combating discrimination on one of the grounds referred to in Article 1—including, in particular, disability—with a view to putting into effect in the Member States the principle of equal treatment. It follows from recital 37 in the preamble to the directive that it also has the objective of creating within the Community a level playing field as regards equality in employment and occupation.

48 As Ms Coleman, the Lithuanian and Swedish Governments and the Commission maintain, those objectives, and the effectiveness of Directive 2000/78, would be undermined if an employee in the claimant's situation cannot rely on the prohibition of direct discrimination laid down by Article 2(2)(a) of that directive where it has been established that he has been treated less favourably than another employee is, has been or would be treated in a comparable situation, on the grounds of his child's disability, and this is the case even though that employee is not himself disabled...

50 Although, in a situation such as that in the present case, the person who is subject to direct discrimination on grounds of disability is not herself disabled, the fact remains that it is the disability which, according to Ms Coleman, is the ground for the less favourable treatment which she claims to have suffered. As is apparent from paragraph 38 of this judgment, Directive 2000/78, which seeks to combat all forms of discrimination on grounds of disability in the field of employment and occupation, applies not to a particular category of person but by reference to the grounds mentioned in Article 1.

51 Where it is established that an employee in a situation such as that in the present case suffers direct discrimination on grounds of disability, an interpretation of Directive 2000/78 limiting its application only to people who are themselves disabled is liable to deprive that directive of an important element of its effectiveness and to reduce the protection which it is intended to guarantee.

NOTES

1. Council Directive 2000/78, whose interpretation was at issue in *Coleman*, applies only in relation to employment and third-level education. It is likely, however, that any amendment resulting from the *Coleman* will have more general application across the DDA, particularly in view of the publication in July 2008 of the European Commission's proposal for a directive on implementing the principle of equal treatment between persons irrespective of religion or belief, disability, age or sexual orientation.[163]

2. What in your view are the more general implications of the *Coleman* decision across the discrimination regimes?

(I) INTENTION, MOTIVATION AND DISCRIMINATION

● **James v Eastleigh Borough Council** [1990] 2 AC 751, House of Lords

The claimant, a man aged 61, complained that he had been discriminated against on grounds of sex when he was charged admission to a local authority swimming pool whereas his wife, who was the same age, was not. The council had a policy of providing free swimming for those who had reached state pensionable age, which at the relevant time was 60 for women, 65 for men. The defendant council argued (and the Court of Appeal had accepted) that, since its aim in applying its charging policy was to aid the needy, rather than give preference to one sex over the other, any discrimination was indirect and so capable of justification. The House of Lords overruled the Court of Appeal.

---

[163]   COM(2008)426 of 2 July 2008.

Lord Goff:

As a matter of impression, it seems to me that, without doing any violence to the words used in [s. 1(1)(a)]...it can properly be said that, by applying to the plaintiff a gender-based criterion, unfavourable to men...[the respondents] did on the ground of sex treat him less favourably than it treated women of the same age, and in particular his wife. In other words, I do not read the words 'on the ground of sex' as necessarily referring only to the reason why the defendant acted as he did, but as embracing cases in which a gender-based criterion is the basis on which the complainant has been selected for the relevant treatment. Of course, there may be cases where the defendant's reason for his action may bring the case within the subsection, as when the defendant is motivated by an animus against persons of the complainant's sex, or otherwise selects the complainant for the relevant treatment because of his or her sex. But it does not follow that the words 'on the ground of sex' refer only to cases where the defendant's reason for his action is the sex of the complainant and, in my opinion, the application by the defendant to the complainant of a gender-based criterion which favours the opposite sex is just as much a case of unfavourable treatment on the ground of sex. Such a conclusion seems to me to be consistent with the policy of the Act, which is the active promotion of equal treatment of men and women. Indeed, the present case is no different from one in which the defendant adopts a criterion which favours widows as against widowers, on the basis that the former are likely to be less well off, or indeed, as my noble and learned friend Lord Bridge has pointed out, a criterion which favours women between the ages of 60 and 65, as against men between the same ages, on the same basis. It is plain to me that, in those cases, a man in either category who was so treated could properly say that he was treated less favourably on the ground of sex, and that the fact that the defendant had so treated him for a benign motive (to help women in the same category, because they are likely to be less well off) was irrelevant...

I am reluctant to have to conclude that those who are concerned with the day-to-day administration of legislation such as the [SDA], who are mainly those who sit on industrial tribunals, should have to grapple with such elusive concepts as [intention, motive, reason and purpose]. However, taking the case of direct discrimination under s 1(1)(a) of the Act, I incline to the opinion that, if it were necessary to identify the requisite intention of the defendant, that intention is simply an intention to perform the relevant act of less favourable treatment. Whether or not the treatment is less favourable in the relevant sense, i e on the ground of sex, may derive either from the application of a gender-based criterion to the complainant, or from selection by the defendant of the complainant because of his or her sex but, in either event, it is not saved from constituting unlawful discrimination by the fact that the defendant acted from a benign motive. However, in the majority of cases, I doubt if it is necessary to focus on the intention or motive of the defendant in this way. This is because, as I see it, cases of direct discrimination under s 1(1)(a) can be considered by asking the simple question: would the complainant have received the same treatment from the defendant but for his or her sex? This simple test possesses the double virtue that, on the one hand, it embraces both the case where the treatment derives from the application of a gender-based criterion, and the case where it derives from the selection of the complainant because of his or her sex and on the other hand it avoids, in most cases at least, complicated questions relating to concepts such as intention, motive, reason or purpose, and the danger of confusion arising from the misuse of those elusive terms. I have to stress, however, that the 'but for' test is not appropriate for cases of indirect discrimination under s 1(1)(b), because there may be indirect discrimination against persons of one sex under that subsection, although a (proportionately smaller) group of persons of the opposite sex is adversely affected in the same way.

NOTES

1. A considerably less benign aspect of *James v Eastleigh* concerns its embrace of a *symmetrical* approach to equality/discrimination. Lord Griffiths, who dissented in *James*, did so on the basis that the council was 'following the very widespread and, in my view, wholly admirable practice of treating old age pensioners with generosity'[164] and that, while 'adopting pensionable age as the criterion to judge whether a person is living on a pension is to adopt a broad brush approach...given that it is the intention to give the concession to those who are living on a pension and thus of reduced means, it appears to me to be the only practical criterion to adopt. It would be quite impossible to interrogate every person as to whether they were or were not living on a pension or to apply some other form of means test before admitting them to the swimming pool.'[165] As Lord Lowry saw, the 'but for' test has the effect that discrimination (in the sense of less favourable treatment of persons of a group characterised by sexual or racial, etc, *advantage*, in order to ameliorate the disadvantage experienced by others, is contrary to the domestic statutory provisions. (The main exception to this is the DDA whose protections apply only to the 'disabled', with the effect that discrimination against persons not having disabilities is not prohibited by the Act.[166]) Thus 'positive discrimination' is lawful only where it is covered by a particular justification or exception.[167] Leaving aside those which relate to employment and training, the most important of these is s. 35 SDA and its equivalents which are discussed at section 8(C) above.

2. Leaving aside questions of positive discrimination, the decision in *James* followed a number of early SDA cases in which respondents had attempted to argue that treatment which, although less favourable in respect of one group than another, was not *aimed at* the disadvantaged group in the sense of being motivated by malice against them, did not amount to unlawful discrimination. This argument failed before the House of Lords in *R v Birmingham City Council, ex p Equal Opportunities Commission*,[168] which involved a challenge to the respondent's practice of fixing the '11 plus' mark higher for girls than for boys, because it had fewer grammar school places available for girls. The House of Lords, having first dismissed the argument that the EOC had to prove that grammar school education was better than the alternative (this because deprivation of choice amounted to less favourable treatment) went on to declare (per Lord Goff) that:

> The intention or motive of the defendant to discriminate, though it may be relevant so far as remedies are concerned...is not a necessary condition to liability...if [it were] it would be a good defence for an employer to show that he discriminated against women not because he intended to do so but (for example) because of customer preference, or to save money, or even to avoid controversy.

- **European Roma Rights Centre v Immigration Officer at Prague Airport**
  [2005] 2 WLR 1

A challenge was brought by way of a claim under ss. 1(1)(a) and 19B RRA to the practice of British immigration officials based at Prague airport by which Roma were 400 times more likely than others to be refused entry. The Court of Appeal ruled that differential treatment of Roma and non-Roma seeking to enter the UK from Prague did not amount to direct discrimination under the RRA because the policy 'was manifestly not to refuse Roma as Roma; rather it was to refuse prospective asylum seekers, or those who could not satisfy the immigration office to the requisite standard that they would not claim asylum on arrival',[169] and

---

[164] Para. 16.   [165] Para. 18.

[166] Except in the case of victimisation, see DDA, s. 55. The prohibitions on discrimination in relation to gender reassignment and against married persons are similarly asymmetric—see ss. 2A and 3 SDA.

[167] See further A. McColgan, *Discrimination: Text, Cases and Materials* n. 1 above, Chap. 3.

[168] N. 51 above.

[169] [2004] QB 811 per Simon Brown LJ, with whom Mantell LJ agreed, Laws LJ dissenting on this issue.

the application of greater scepticism to Roma than non-Roma applicants for entry to the UK was justified by the greater statistical likelihood of Roma making claims for asylum in the UK. The House of Lords disagreed:

Baroness Hale [with whom their Lordships agreed]:
The Roma were being treated more sceptically than the non-Roma. There was a good reason for this. How did the immigration officers know to treat them more sceptically? Because they were Roma. That is acting on racial grounds. If a person acts on racial grounds, the reason why he does so is irrelevant. The law reports are full of examples of obviously discriminatory treatment which was in no way motivated by racism or sexism and often brought about by pressures beyond the discriminators' control: the council which sacked a black road sweeper to whom the union objected in order to avoid industrial action...the council which for historical reasons provided fewer selective school places for girls than for boys [citing ex p EOC]. But it goes further than this. The person may be acting on belief or assumptions about members of the sex or racial group involved which are often true and which if true would provide a good reason for the less favourable treatment in question. But 'what may be true of a group may not be true of a signifi-cant number of individuals within that group'.[170] The object of the legislation is to ensure that each person is treated as an individual and not assumed to be like other members of the group. As Laws LJ observed dissenting, below:

'The mistake that might arise in relation to stereotyping would be a supposition that the stereotype is only vicious if it is *untrue*. But that cannot be right. If it were, it would imply that direct discrimination can be justified...'

As we have seen, the legislation draws a clear distinction between direct and indirect discrimination and makes no reference at all to justification in relation to direct discrimination. Nor, strictly, does it allow indir-ect discrimination to be justified. It accepts that a requirement or condition may be justified *independently* of its discriminatory effect.

3. The decisions of the lower courts in *Roma Rights* illustrate the dangers inherent in extend-ing the scope of radical legislation such as the equality enactments (the *Roma* case arose under s. 19B RRA, which was inserted into the legislation by the Race Relations (Amendment) Act 2000 to regulate discrimination by public authorities). This is not to say that such extension is not to be welcomed in as much as it prohibits discrimination in previously unregulated contexts. But it does impose a strain on radical legislative approaches which have gained judicial acceptance in some contexts (such as employment) when judges unfamiliar with those original contexts are confronted with what appear to them to be unpalatable results in fresh contexts. Thus in the *Roma* case it was Laws LJ who, well versed as he was in employ-ment discrimination cases, insisted that less favourable treatment of Roma amounted to direct race discrimination however sound customs officials' grounds for suspecting that would-be Roma travellers to the UK were more likely than their non-Roma compatriots to claim asylum on arrival. Had the UK Government wished to avoid a finding of race discrim-ination in that case, it could have made use of the exception in the Act which permitted the authorisation of discrimination on grounds of nationality in the immigration context. Simon Brown and Mantell LJJ, by contrast, adopted a 'common sense' approach which resulted in the trashing of 15 years' jurisprudence on the meaning of direct discrimination.[171]

---

170 Citing Hartmann J in *Equal Opportunities Commission v Director of Education* [2001] 2 HKLRD 690, High Court of Hong Kong.
171 A further illustration of the tension between breadth and depth of regulation by a single instrument is to be found in the *Malcolm* case discussed at section 12(A) below.

4. The decision of the House of Lords in the *Roma Rights* case restored the equilibrium for the moment, but the pressure on the RRA has not disappeared. In *R (Gillan) v Comr of Police for the Metropolis*,[172] a decision on the scope of police powers under the Terrorism Act 2002, Lords Hope, Scott and Brown took the opportunity (albeit *obiter*) to make clear their views that racial profiling by the police would not (necessarily) amount to discrimination for the purposes of the RRA. The case arose out of a challenge by two (White) claimants who objected to having been detained for search purposes under an authorisation granted under s. 44 of the 2000 Act, which permitted the police to stop and search without reasonable suspicion. The claimants had been en route to a demonstration outside an arms fair.

The House of Lords dismissed the arguments put for the claimants that their detentions had breached various provisions of the European Convention and, accordingly, the Human Rights Act. Those conclusions are open to criticism. Of more concern in the present context, however, is the attitude of Lords Hope and Brown to the RRA.[173] The former paid lip service to the propositions that 'if a person discriminates on racial grounds the reason why he does so is irrelevant' and that '[d]iscrimination on racial grounds is unlawful whether or not, in any given case, the assumptions on which it was based turn out to be justified',[174] and stated that 'the mere fact that the person appears to be of Asian origin is not a legitimate reason' for a police officer to utilise the power to stop and search. But he went on to state that racial identification may be one reason for an officer to select a person for scrutiny, so long as it was not the only one (in other words, while it would be unlawful to target only Asians, it would appear in his view to be lawful to target Asians with rucksacks, or Asians with beards, and if so perhaps even male Asians). Lord Brown characterised as 'inevitable... that so long as the principal terrorist risk against which use of the section 44 power has been authorised is that from al Qaeda, a disproportionate number of those stopped and searched will be of Asian appearance (particularly if they happen to be carrying rucksacks or wearing apparently bulky clothing capable of containing terrorist-related items)'.[175] He stated that '[e]thnic origin accordingly can and properly should be taken into account in deciding whether and whom to stop and search provided always that the power is used sensitively and the selection is made for reasons connected with the perceived terrorist threat and not on grounds of racial discrimination'[176] and took the opportunity to imply his disagreement with the approach adopted by the House of Lords in *Roma Rights* (in which, incidentally, the House had overturned his decision in the Court of Appeal). Having acknowledged the difficulties of distinguishing between, on the one hand, the 'greater scepticism logically felt by immigration officers towards Roma than non-Roma applicants (held in the *Roma Rights* case to have been unlawfully discriminatory)' and, on the other 'the greater preparedness which police officers understandably have to stop and search those of Asian appearance... given the perceived source of the main terrorist threat today'[177] he went on to say that:

90. The only basis I can see for a distinction (and I do not pretend to find it entirely satisfactory) is if one assumes that in the *Roma Rights* case the immigration officers had not sufficiently had regard to each Roma applicant as an individual, rather merely than as a stereotypical member of the group (see para 74 of Lady Hale's speech). It would, of course, have been wrong for immigration officers to

---

[172] [2006] 2 AC 307.

[173] Lord Scott took the view that any race discrimination would be justified under ss. 41(1)(a) and 42 RRA. As Moeckli points out in relation to s. 42 (national security), 'the objective of the Terrorism Act 2000 is to give the police special powers to target terrorists, not a particular racial group; nor is it obvious that discrimination against persons of Asian appearance is inherently necessary for the purpose of safeguarding national security'.

[174] Para. 44.   [175] Para. 80.   [176] Para. 81.   [177] Para. 89.

have treated every Roma applicant identically irrespective of how his answers to questions put to him affected the interviewing officer's view as to the genuineness of his particular application. But that surely, so far from according with common sense, would have been not merely wrong but also silly. Nevertheless the House appears to have concluded that this was indeed the immigration officers' approach and on that basis struck down the scheme.

- **Daniel Moeckli, 'Stop and Search Under the Terrorism Act 2000:**
  A Comment on R (Gillan) v Comr of Police for the Metropolis'
  (2007) 70 Modern Law Review 659

Since 11 September 2001, authorisations for blanket stop and searches have been used extensively and in almost every police authority area in Great Britain, including on a rolling basis in the London metropolitan area. As a consequence, tens of thousands of people have been stopped and searched under the Terrorism Act 2000: the number of searches has constantly risen from 8,550 in the year 2001–02 to 32,086 in 2004–05.

The available evidence suggests that the increase in the use of these powers has disproportionately affected ethnic minorities. Between 2001–02 and 2002–03, for example, the number of persons of Asian ethnicity subjected to s. 44 searches rose by 302 per cent as compared to a rise of 118 per cent for white people. By 2003–04, Asian people were about 2.9 times more likely, and black people about 3.3 times more likely, to be stopped and searched under the Terrorism Act 2000 than white people. In the first two months after the London bombings of July 2005, the number of Asian and black people stopped in the London metropolitan area under s. 44 increased twelvefold on the same period in 2004; for white people the increase was fivefold.

Various statements by Government officials suggest that this disparate use of stop and search powers under the Terrorism Act 2000 is not simply the result of decisions taken by officers in the field but part of a concerted effort to focus law enforcement resources on certain ethnic groups. For instance, the then Home Office Minister, Hazel Blears, made clear that the nature of the terrorist threat 'inevitably means that some of our counter-terrorist powers will be disproportionately experienced by people in the Muslim community'. Similarly, the Chief Constable of the British Transport Police has stated: 'We should not waste time searching old white ladies. It is going to be disproportionate. It is going to be young men, not exclusively, but it may be disproportionate when it comes to ethnic groups.' ...

JUSTIFICATIONS FOR ETHNIC PROFILING

In Lord Hope's view, the key to deciding whether ethnic profiling in the anti-terrorism context amounts to discrimination or not lies in the test set out by the House of Lords in the *Roma Rights* case... The central reason why the Prague operation was found to be discriminatory, both Lord Hope and Lord Brown concluded in *Gillan*, was that Roma passengers were not treated as individuals but assumed to be like all other members of their ethnic group: that 'all Roma were being treated in the same way simply because they were Roma.' Applied to the anti-terrorism context this means, according to Lord Hope, that persons cannot be stopped and searched *merely* because they appear to be of Asian origin but that there must be 'other, further, good reasons for doing so.' While Asian appearance 'may attract the constable's attention in the first place', this must be followed by a 'further selection process' based on criteria such as age, behaviour and general appearance, 'even if in the end it is based more on a hunch than on something that can be precisely articulated or identified.' Similarly, Lord Brown concluded that it is 'unacceptable to profile someone *solely* by reference to his ethnicity', but that the police can rely on ethnic origin as long as they 'have regard to other factors too.'

THE PROBLEMS WITH ETHNIC PROFILING

There are two problems with this 'further factors' test. The first problem is that it fails to provide clear guidance as to what is discriminatory and what is not. The fact that Lords Hope and Brown stressed that the police may not target people *solely* because of their ethnic appearance seems to suggest that profiling would automatically be permissible if it is based on at least one further element in addition to race or ethnicity. As a consequence, it would be lawful for the police to stop and search, say, all Asian *males*. Or the use of the plural in 'further factors' could mean that at least two additional indicators are required for a permissible profile, for example all Asian males (gender) between 18 and 40 (age). Instead of the mere number of factors, the test suggested by Lords Hope and Brown could also be interpreted as referring to the importance attached to, respectively, ethnicity and additional factors. But what degree of importance attached to ethnicity would make a profile discriminatory? According to Lord Brown, a profile may 'sometimes' still be permissible even if ethnic origin is a 'highly material part' of it. But what exactly does this mean and how can one measure the importance attached to the respective elements?

The second, more fundamental, problem is that it is doubtful that the 'further factors' test really provides the relevant criteria to determine whether a stop and search violates the non-discrimination norms at issue or not. As far as the Race Relations Act 1976 is concerned, the singling out of persons for stop and search based on their ethnic appearance may amount to direct discrimination, defined by the Act as less favourable treatment on racial or ethnic grounds. As the Court of Appeal correctly observed in *Owen & Briggs v James*, nothing in the language of the Act suggests that there can be no discrimination unless the racial factor was the *sole* reason for the less favourable treatment. Put otherwise, the existence of other factors than race or ethnic origin does not necessarily make the differential treatment lawful. Instead, it is sufficient that race or ethnicity was an *important* factor. It would, indeed, seem strange if the targeting of persons of Asian appearance by the police became permissible simply because the further element of, for example, gender was added to the profile. As a result, as far as ethnic appearance is used to 'attract the constable's attention in the first place' or where it plays a 'highly material part' in the selection process—the terms used by Lords Hope and Brown—the relevant stop and searches will be incompatible with the Race Relations Act 1976...[178]

5. Moeckli goes on to point out, in a discussion as to the application in this context of Art. 14 ECHR, that 'profiles based on ethnicity are . . . under-inclusive in that they may lead police officers to miss a range of potential terrorists who do not fit the profile', as well as being (obviously) over-inclusive in tarring some or all of those apparently of particular ethnicities with the same brush and, further, that they 'can shift the attention of police officers away from more pertinent indicators such as behavioural or psychological characteristics'. Thus, for example, 'In the late 1990s, the [US] Customs Service stopped using a profile that was based, among other factors, on ethnicity and gender in deciding whom to search for drugs. Instead, the customs agents were instructed to rely on observational techniques, behavioural analysis and intelligence. This policy change resulted in a rise in the proportion of searches leading to the discovery of drugs of more than 300 per cent'. Such lack of fit between discriminatory treatment and legitimate aim is likely to have the effect that a discrimination challenge ought to succeed on the grounds of (dis)proportionality.

6. Should the police be allowed engage in ethnic profiling? What difficulties might such profiling give rise to (a) in practice and (b) as a matter of principle? If we are to avoid ethnic profiling happening in practice, how might this best be achieved?

---

[178] Footnotes omitted.

(II) COMPARATORS

- **Shamoon v Chief Constable of the Royal Ulster Constabulary (Northern Ireland)** [2003] ICR 337, House of Lords

The claimant, a chief inspector, alleged sex discrimination because an appraisal function was removed from her in the wake of complaints made against her in connection with appraisals. She compared her treatment with that of two male chief inspectors against whom no complaints had been made, and who had retained their appraisal functions. Her claim was upheld by a tribunal but dismissed by Northern Ireland's Court of Appeal because her comparators were not similarly situated.[179] The House of Lords rejected her appeal, accepting that the unsuitability of her chosen *actual* comparators would not have prevented a claim by reference to *hypothetical* comparators, but ruling that there was simply no evidence from which the tribunal could have found that she had been treated less favourably than such hypothetical comparators would have been. More importantly, their Lordships made the following remarks about comparators in discrimination cases:

Lord Nicholls [with whom **Lord Rodger** agreed on this point]:

4 …where the act complained of consists of dismissal from employment, the statutory definition calls for a comparison between the way the employer treated the claimant woman (dismissal) and the way he treated or would have treated a man. It stands to reason that in making this comparison, with a view to deciding whether a woman who was dismissed received less favourable treatment than a man, it is necessary to compare like with like. The situations being compared must be such that, gender apart, the situation of the man and the woman are in all material respects the same.…

7 …In deciding a discrimination claim, one of the matters employment tribunals have to consider is whether the statutory definition of discrimination has been satisfied. When the claim is based on direct discrimination or victimisation, in practice tribunals in their decisions normally consider, first, whether the claimant received less favourable treatment than the appropriate comparator (the 'less favourable treatment' issue) and then, secondly, whether the less favourable treatment was on the relevant proscribed ground (the 'reason why' issue). Tribunals proceed to consider the reason-why issue only if the less favourable treatment issue is resolved in favour of the claimant. Thus the less favourable treatment issue is treated as a threshold which the claimant must cross before the tribunal is called upon to decide why the claimant was afforded the treatment of which she is complaining.

8 No doubt there are cases where it is convenient and helpful to adopt this two-step approach to what is essentially a single question: did the claimant, on the proscribed ground, receive less favourable treatment than others? But, especially where the identity of the relevant comparator is a matter of dispute, this sequential analysis may give rise to needless problems. Sometimes the less favourable treatment issue cannot be resolved without, at the same time, deciding the reason-why issue. The two issues are intertwined.

9 The present case is a good example. The relevant provisions in the Sex Discrimination (Northern Ireland)… Chief Inspector Shamoon claimed she was treated less favourably than two male chief inspectors. Unlike her, they retained their counselling responsibilities. Is this comparing like with like? Prima facie it is not. She had been the subject of complaints and of representations by Police Federation representatives, the male chief inspectors had not. This might be the reason why she was treated as she was. This might explain why she was relieved of her responsibilities and they were not. But whether this

---

179 A complaint under the Sex Discrimination (Northern Ireland) Order 1976, which is materially identical to the SDA—see in particular s. 5(3) SDA above.

factual difference between their positions was in truth a material difference is an issue which cannot be resolved without determining why she was treated as she was. It might be that the reason why she was relieved of her counselling responsibilities had nothing to do with the complaints and representations. If that were so, then a comparison between her and the two male chief inspectors may well be comparing like with like, because in that event the difference between her and her two male colleagues would be an immaterial difference.

10 I must take this a step further. As I have said, prima facie the comparison with the two male chief inspectors is not apt. So be it. Let it be assumed that, this being so, the most sensible course in practice is to proceed on the footing that the appropriate comparator is a hypothetical comparator: a male chief inspector regarding whose conduct similar complaints and representations had been made. On this footing, the less favourable treatment issue is this: was Chief Inspector Shamoon treated less favourably than such a male chief inspector would have been treated? But here also the question is incapable of being answered without deciding why Chief Inspector Shamoon was treated as she was. It is impossible to decide whether Chief Inspector Shamoon was treated less favourably than a hypothetical male chief inspector without identifying the ground on which she was treated as she was. Was it grounds of sex? If yes, then she was treated less favourably than a male chief inspector in her position would have been treated. If not, not. Thus, on this footing also, the less-favourable-treatment issue is incapable of being decided without deciding the reason-why issue. And the decision on the reason-why issue will also provide the answer to the less-favourable-treatment issue.

11 This analysis seems to me to point to the conclusion that employment tribunals may sometimes be able to avoid arid and confusing disputes about the identification of the appropriate comparator by concentrating primarily on why the claimant was treated as she was. Was it on the proscribed ground which is the foundation of the application? That will call for an examination of all the facts of the case. Or was it for some other reason? If the latter, the application fails. If the former, there will be usually be no difficulty in deciding whether the treatment, afforded to the claimant on the proscribed ground, was less favourable than was or would have been afforded to others.

12 The most convenient and appropriate way to tackle the issues arising on any discrimination application must always depend upon the nature of the issues and all the circumstances of the case. There will be cases where it is convenient to decide the less-favourable-treatment issue first. But, for the reason set out above, when formulating their decisions employment tribunals may find it helpful to consider whether they should postpone determining the less-favourable-treatment issue until after they have decided why the treatment was afforded to the claimant. Adopting this course would have simplified the issues, and assisted in their resolution, in the present case…

Lord Scott:

107 There has been, in my respectful opinion, some confusion about the part to be played by comparators in the reaching of a conclusion as to whether a case of Article 3(1) discrimination—or for that matter a case of discrimination under s.1(1) of the Sex Discrimination Act 1975, or under s.1(1) of the Race Relations Act 1976, or under the comparable provision in any other anti-discrimination legislation—has been made out. Comparators come into play in two distinct and separate respects.

108 First, the statutory definition of what constitutes discrimination involves a comparison: '… treats that other less favourably than he treats or would treat other persons'. The comparison is between the treatment of the victim on the one hand and of a comparator on the other hand. The comparator may be actual ('treats') or may be hypothetical ('or would treat') but 'must be such that the relevant circumstances in the one case are the same, or not materially different, in the other'… If there is any material difference between the circumstances of the victim and the circumstances of the comparator, the statutory definition is not being applied. It is possible that, in a particular case, an actual comparator capable of constituting the statutory comparator can be found. But in most cases a suitable actual comparator will not be available and a hypothetical comparator will have to constitute the statutory comparator…

109 But, secondly, comparators have a quite separate evidential role to play. [S.5(3) SDA] has nothing to do with this role. It is neither prescribing nor limiting the evidential comparators that may be adduced by either party. The victim who complains of discrimination must satisfy the fact-finding tribunal that, on a balance of probabilities, he or she has suffered discrimination falling within the statutory definition. This may be done by placing before the tribunal evidential material from which an inference can be drawn that the victim was treated less favourably than he or she would have been treated if he or she had not been a member of the protected class. Comparators, which for this purpose are bound to be actual comparators, may of course constitute such evidential material. But they are no more than tools which may or may not justify an inference of discrimination on the relevant prohibited ground, eg sex. The usefulness of the tool will, in any particular case, depend upon the extent to which the circumstances relating to the comparator are the same as the circumstances relating to the victim. The more significant the difference or differences, the less cogent will be the case for drawing the requisite inference. But the fact that a particular chosen comparator cannot, because of material differences, qualify as the statutory comparator, eg under [s. 5(3)], by no means disqualifies it from an evidential role. It may, in conjunction with other material, justify the tribunal in drawing the inference that the victim was treated less favourably than she would have been treated if she had been the Article 7 comparator.

110 In summary, the comparator required for the purpose of the statutory definition of discrimination must be a comparator in the same position in all material respects as the victim save only that he, or she, is not a member of the protected class. But the comparators that can be of evidential value, sometimes determinative of the case, are not so circumscribed. Their evidential value will, however, be variable and will inevitably be weakened by material differences between the circumstances relating to them and the circumstances of the victim…

NOTES

1. The significance of the *Shamoon* decision is that it calls into question an over-emphasis on comparators as the first step in a discrimination claim. Direct discrimination always involves some kind of comparison (this because it concerns *less favourable* treatment. And it is clear from the definitions of direct discrimination extracted at section 11(B) above that each either includes, or is accompanied by, an express reference to comparators along the lines (broadly) of that provision.[180] But it is important to bear in mind that the discrimination provisions permit comparison with a *hypothetical* comparator,[181] and it is by no means necessary (though, as Lord Scott pointed out, it may be very useful) to point to an actual identifiable comparator who has been treated more favourably.

2. The express comparator requirement has proved particularly problematic in relation to pregnancy cases brought under the SDA, in which tribunals experienced real conceptual difficulties in determining who the appropriate male comparator was for a pregnant woman. These particular issues have been resolved now by firm ECJ case law establishing that no comparator is necessary in the case of pregnancy-related discrimination, which has eventually resulted in specific statutory provision being made in the SDA to deal with pregnancy cases (see now ss. 3A and 3B). More recently it has surfaced in a number of claims brought under s. 19B RRA. One example is *R (Al Rawi) v Secretary of State for Foreign and Commonwealth Affairs*[182] in which the claimants, formerly British residents (but not nationals) who were imprisoned by the US authorities in Gantanamo Bay, sought to challenge

---

[180] See also s. 5(3) SDA, reg. 3(2) of each the SORs and the RBRs.
[181] With the exception of the Equal Pay Act 1970.   [182] N. 29 above.

the UK Government's failure to make a formal request to the American authorities for the release of the detainee claimants, claiming, *inter alia*, that this amounted to less favourable treatment of them than of UK nationals interned in Guantanamo. The High Court ruled, and the Court of Appeal agreed, that a person who was not a British national was not entitled, as a matter of legal fact, to the protection of a state-to-state claim made by the Foreign Secretary. This being the case, the claimants were in materially different situations than were UK nationals for the purpose of the exercise of the right of diplomatic protection by means of state-to-state claims and their differential treatment by the state did not amount to discrimination for the purposes of the RRA (or Art. 14 of the Convention). According to Laws LJ (for the court):

74. ...Mr Greenwood...correctly submits [for the respondent] that 'the appropriate characteristics of the comparator for the purposes of s.3(4) of the RRA cannot be identified without considering the reason why the detainee appellants were treated as they were' ['Lord Steyn's question'[183]]...

75. How in this case is 'Lord Steyn's question'—why were the detainee claimants treated as they were—to be answered? As in Roma Rights, it may be said there are two possible answers: (1) because they were not British nationals—as the appellants say; (2) because they were not persons whom the United Kingdom was by the rules of international law entitled to protect by means of a State to State claim—as the respondents say. Each answer is in a sense true. By what principle do we decide between them?

76. Mr Rabinder Singh's response has an attractive simplicity. He says we should simply apply the reasoning in Roma Rights, as of course we are bound to do if it is not distinguishable. He submits that just as in that case the officer treated the Roma less favourably (because Roma are more likely to wish to seek asylum and so put forward a false claim to enter the United Kingdom), so here the first respondent treated non-nationals less favourably because, on his view of the law, they were not candidates for State to State claims. In each case the engine of the decision was the 'impugned characteristic', namely race—being Roma, or being a non-(British) national.

77. But in our judgment the analogy is false, and for a reason closely touching the policy of the legislation. We have seen that as a rule the 'impugned characteristic' cannot be allowed to distinguish between putative victims of discrimination and their comparators. Why? Because if it did, that would license the very vice which the absolute statutory prohibition of direct discrimination is intended to suppress: racial stereotyping. To treat the impugned characteristic—race—as the actual factor said to distinguish the putative victim from the comparator is naked discrimination in the simplest case. In the more likely case, it is to assume or assert that persons possessing that characteristic are thereby differently inclined from the comparator: inclined to behave in some different and (to the alleged discriminator) undesirable way. That is, exactly, racial stereotyping.

78. But nothing of the kind applies in this case. A person who is not a British national is not entitled to the protection of a State to State claim made by the first respondent. That is not an attribute of the non-British national. It is not a function of how he is likely to behave. It is (subject of course to the wholly separate issues addressed by submission (iv) above) simply a legal fact. There is no question of the non-British national being, by virtue of that characteristic, more likely to do or not do this, that, or anything. Contrast the Roma who, by virtue of being Roma, was or was believed to be more likely to make a false asylum claim. The national and the non-national are in truth in materially different cases one from the other for the purpose of the exercise of the right of diplomatic protection by means

---

[183] From *Nagarajan v London Regional Transport* [2000] 1 AC 501, 521–522, approved by Baroness Hale in *Roma Rights*, para. 82.

of State to State claims. On the learning such a difference ought only to be disregarded if it assumes or implies a process of racial stereotyping. But it does not. The difference is therefore a proper and legitimate basis of distinction for the purposes of the RRA. The non-nationals have been treated differently from the nationals not because of their race (nationality) but because one group is entitled to diplomatic protection and the other is not. Their respective relevant circumstances are not the same. On the contrary they are materially different (s.3(4)). Accordingly there is no violation of s.1(1)(a) read with s.19B(1).

3. How does the domestic approach to comparators compare with that of the European Court of Human Rights (see Chap. 13)?

(C) HARASSMENT/SEXUAL HARASSMENT

(I) EUROPEAN UNDERPINNING

Article 2.3 of the Race Directive

3. Harassment shall be deemed to be discrimination within the meaning of paragraph 1, when an unwanted conduct related to racial or ethnic origin takes place with the purpose or effect of violating the dignity of a person and of creating an intimidating, hostile, degrading, humiliating or offensive environment. In this context, the concept of harassment may be defined in accordance with the national laws and practice of the Member States.

Article 2.2 Equal Treatment Directive as amended

2. For the purposes of this Directive, the following definitions shall apply...

   - harassment: where an unwanted conduct related to the sex of a person occurs with the purpose or effect of violating the dignity of a person, and of creating an intimidating, hostile, degrading, humiliating or offensive environment,

   - sexual harassment: where any form of unwanted verbal, non-verbal or physical conduct of a sexual nature occurs, with the purpose or effect of violating the dignity of a person, in particular when creating an intimidating, hostile, degrading, humiliating or offensive environment.

3. Harassment and sexual harassment within the meaning of this Directive shall be deemed to be discrimination on the grounds of sex and therefore prohibited.

A person's rejection of, or submission to, such conduct may not be used as a basis for a decision affecting that person.

NOTE

1. Article 2.3 of the Employment Equality Directive is in materially identical terms to Art. 2.3 of the Race Directive. The definition of sexual harassment is more complex (see Art. 22 of the Equal Treatment Directive) for reasons considered below.[184]

---

[184] See also D. Schiek, L. Waddington and M. Bell (eds), *Non-Discrimination Law* (Hart Publishing, Oxford, 2007), Chap. 4 ('Harassment').

(II) DOMESTIC REGULATION OF HARASSMENT

Section 4A SDA

(1) For the purposes of this Act, a person subjects a woman to harassment if—

    (a) he engages in unwanted conduct that is related to her sex or that of another person and has the purpose or effect—

        (i) of violating her dignity, or

        (ii) of creating an intimidating, hostile, degrading, humiliating or offensive environment for her,

    (b) he engages in any form of unwanted verbal, non-verbal or physical conduct of a sexual nature that has the purpose or effect—

        (i) of violating her dignity, or

        (ii) of creating an intimidating, hostile, degrading, humiliating or offensive environment for her, or

    (c) on the ground of her rejection of or submission to unwanted conduct of a kind mentioned in paragraph (a) or (b), he treats her less favourably than he would treat her had she not rejected, or submitted to, the conduct.

(2) Conduct shall be regarded as having the effect mentioned in sub-paragraph (i) or (ii) of subsection (1) (a) or (b) only if, having regard to all the circumstances, including in particular the perception of the woman, it should reasonably be considered as having that effect.

(3) For the purposes of this Act, a person ('A') subjects another person ('B') to harassment if—

    (a) A, on the ground that B intends to undergo, is undergoing or has undergone gender reassignment, engages in unwanted conduct that has the purpose or effect—

        (i) of violating B's dignity, or

        (ii) of creating an intimidating, hostile, degrading, humiliating or offensive environment for B, or

    (b) A, on the ground of B's rejection of or submission to unwanted conduct of a kind mentioned in paragraph (a), treats B less favourably than A would treat B had B not rejected, or submitted to, the conduct.

(4) Conduct shall be regarded as having the effect mentioned in sub-paragraph (i) or (ii) of subsection (3)(a) only if, having regard to all the circumstances, including in particular the perception of B, it should reasonably be considered as having that effect.

(5) Subsection (1) is to be read as applying equally to the harassment of men, and for that purpose shall have effect with such modifications as are requisite.

(6) For the purposes of subsections (1) and (3), a provision of Part 2 or 3 framed with reference to harassment of women shall be treated as applying equally to the harassment of men, and for that purpose will have effect with such modifications as are requisite.

Section 3A RRA

(1) A person subjects another to harassment in any circumstances relevant for the purposes of any provision referred to in section 1(1B) where, on grounds of race or ethnic or national origins, he engages in unwanted conduct which has the purpose or effect of [emphasis added] —

    (a) violating that other person's dignity, or

    (b) creating an intimidating, hostile, degrading, humiliating or offensive environment for him.

(2) Conduct shall be regarded as having the effect specified in paragraph (a) or (b) of subsection (1) only if, having regard to all the circumstances, including in particular the perception of that other person, it should reasonably be considered as having that effect.

Section 3B DDA

(1) For the purposes of this Part, a person subjects a disabled person to harassment where, for a reason which relates to the disabled person's disability, he engages in unwanted conduct which has the purpose or effect of [emphasis added]—

  (a) violating the disabled person's dignity, or

  (b) creating an intimidating, hostile, degrading, humiliating or offensive environment for him.

(2) Conduct shall be regarded as having the effect referred to in paragraph (a) or (b) of subsection (1) only if, having regard to all the circumstances, including in particular the perception of the disabled person, it should reasonably be considered as having that effect.

NOTES

1. The relevant provisions of the SO, RB and Age Regs are materially identical to s. 3A RRA.[185] Note that EU law, but not domestic law, expressly deems harassment to be a form of discrimination.

2. The prohibition of harassment outside the employment/third-level education contexts applies only in the case of race and sex, and then only to the extent required by EU law. Briefly, the SDA's explicit prohibitions on harassment apply in relation to the provision of goods and services, the disposal of premises and matters of social security generally, as well as in the contexts of employment and third-level education, while the RRA's explicit prohibitions apply to harassment on grounds of race, ethnic or national origin (but not colour or nationality) in relation to the provision of goods and services, the disposal of premises and, in addition, to education generally and to the functions of public authorities so far as they relate to any form of social security, health care, any other form of social protection and any form of social advantage, as well as employment. The DDA's explicit regulation of harassment applies only in relation to employment and higher education, while the SO Regs, RB Regs and Age Regs all regulate harassment but apply only to employment (broadly defined) and third-level education. Neither EA 2006 nor the EA Regs prohibit harassment as such, this in each case because of concern over the freedom of speech implications of such regulation.

3. The SDA's approach to the meaning of harassment is more extensive than that of the RRA or DDA in that it regulates:

  • 'harassment': (s. 4A(1)(a)) 'unwanted conduct . . . related to . . . sex',

  • 'sexual harassment': (s.4A(1)(b)) 'unwanted verbal, non-verbal or physical conduct of a sexual nature', and

  • 'quid pro quo harassment': (4A(1)(c)) detriment related to the rejection of or submission to harassment unwanted conduct of harassment or sexual harassment.[186]

This breadth of approach is reflective simply of the fact that 'sex' refers to conduct as well as status, and some harassment takes the form of behaviour which is sexualised not merely in

---

[185] Regs 5, 5, and 6, respectively.

[186] Interestingly the prohibition on this form of harassment applies also in relation to harassment connected with gender-reassignment (s. 4A(3)(b) SDA) but not in relation to the other grounds.

the sense that it is directed at a woman *because she is a woman*, but rather in the sense that it is *about sex*. This would be the case where, for example, a nurse sexually assaulted a patient in his or her care for the purposes of the nurse's sexual gratification.

4. The SDA had, after its amendment in 2005 explicitly to regulate harassment and sexual harassment,[187] used the same 'on grounds of' formulation as that adopted by the RRA and other legislation.[188] In *Equal Opportunities Commission v Secretary of State for Trade and Industry* the EOC successfully challenged this approach. The EOC argued that the domestic approach was inadequate to give effect to the Directive's prohibition of 'unwanted conduct related to the sex of a person [which] occurs with the purpose or effect of violating the dignity of a person, and of creating an intimidating, hostile, degrading, humiliating or offensive environment' (emphasis added), this because the use of the term 'on the ground of' imported the concept of causation into the Act, requiring an investigation of the reason for the conduct complained of, whereas the Directive, by referring to conduct 'related to' the sex of a person, defined harassment by association with sex. The EOC also argued that, whereas under s. 4A(1) SDA in its original form, the unwanted conduct had to be by reason of, or on the ground of, *the claimant's* sex, the definition of harassment in the Directive extended to a case where a female claimant is harassed by conduct which is directed at a man or another woman. The High Court accepted the EOC's arguments on both these grounds of challenge, resulting in the eventual amendment of the SDA to the version extracted above, but did not accept the EOC's challenge to the 'objective' test now set out by s. 4A(4) SDA above.

- **Equal Opportunities Commission v Secretary of State for Trade and Industry** [2007] EWHC 483 (Admin), [2007] IRLR 327

Burton J:

10 …The difference in practice between direct discrimination on grounds of sex and harassment related to sex is illustrated by Miss Rose by reference to examples drawn from a number of cases, all of them of course decided by reference to direct discrimination under s.1, Porcelli v Strathclyde Regional Council [1986] IRLR 134, Brumfitt v Ministry of Defence [2005] IRLR 4, Kettle Produce Ltd v Ward (EAT unreported 8 November 2006 EATS/0016/06) and B v A (EAT unreported 9 January 2007 EAT/0450/06). If, she submits, conduct cannot be shown to have been discriminatory, in that the reason for the conduct cannot be shown to have been on grounds of sex, it should still be capable of being shown, if it is otherwise unwanted conduct with the relevant purpose or effect, to have been harassment, if it related to sex.

11 Thus the training officer in *Brumfitt* was found, by dint of the generally unpleasant nature of his language and the fact that the audience was of mixed sexes, not to have discriminated against the claimant on grounds of sex. Given that the tribunal decided that the claimant had been exposed to language which was 'offensive and humiliating to her as a woman', it appears likely that she would have succeeded in a claim in respect of unwanted conduct related to her sex. Similarly, by reference to the facts of *B v A*, a claimant, who was unfairly treated on the grounds of jealousy because of her conduct with another man, may not be entitled to claim discrimination on grounds of sex, but would appear likely to be able to succeed in a claim for harassment by reference to unwanted conduct related to her sex. Again, by analogy from the facts in *Kettle*, a manager barging into the ladies toilet, when he would be likely to have similarly

---

[187] This by virtue of the Employment Equality (Sex Discrimination) Regulations 2005, SI 2005/2467 which amended the SDA in an attempt to comply with the Equal Treatment Directive as amended.

[188] Further, its approach was even narrower than that of the RRA, extracted above, in that the harassment/ sexual harassment had to be on the grounds of the complainant's *own* sex.

barged into a men's toilet, may not render his employer liable for discrimination on grounds of sex, but such conduct would be likely to be conduct related to sex…

13 None of these examples of unwanted conduct could (though Miss Rose submits they plainly should) come within the definition of s.4A, so firmly rooted as it is in causation, particularly given the identical wording in s.1, so often defined and constrained by the courts. It would be no answer even to seek to construe the words on the grounds of her sex widely, so as to assimilate it to the statutorily wider defin-ition to be found in s.3A of the Disability Discrimination Act, where it is discrimination if a person treats another less favourably 'for a reason which relates to the disabled person's disability': albeit wider, this is still causation-based, as would be expected of a complaint of discrimination, as opposed to the basis for the distinct complaint of harassment…

20 Miss Rose relies on the fact that the wording in s.1(1) is, subject to the comma, identical and has been so carefully addressed and construed, but must now, if Mr Pannick is right, be construed, albeit it identical, as meaning something different in s.4A. In any event, she submits, it is impossible to construe 'on the ground of her sex he engages in unwanted conduct' other than by reference to causation. Whether it is that a person has engaged on the ground of a complainant's sex in certain conduct, or whether he engaged in certain conduct on the ground of the complainant's sex, on either basis it is plain that the Court must address 'the reason why'…

63 I am satisfied that:

* (i) Section 4A(i)(a) should be recast so as to eliminate the issue of causation…

5. No amendments have been made to the other statutory prohibitions on harassment (that is, those contained in the RRA, DDA, SO, RB and Age Regs). In *English v Thomas Sanderson Blinds Ltd* the EAT ruled that the SO Regs failed to implement EC law because they regulated harassment 'on the grounds of' sexual orientation rather than harassment 'related to' sexual orientation.[189]

6. Notwithstanding the absence of explicit regulation of harassment in areas falling out-side the scope of EU discrimination law, such harassment will be unlawful if it amounts to discrimination on the relevant ground in a context regulated by domestic statutory provisions. We considered, above, the difficulties experienced by the English courts in selecting the appropriate comparator (real or hypothetical) in discrimination cases. These difficulties featured actuely in the response to harassment claims prior to the explicit regu-lation of such behaviour by the anti-discrimination provisions. In *Strathclyde Regional Council v Porcelli* the Court of Session took a fairly robust approach to the argument put for the employer that sexual harassment consisting of a sexual assault was no less favour-able than other forms of hostile treatment which might have been accorded to a man who was equally disliked by the perpetrators (the argument was that the harassment was moti-vated by individual dislike of the victim rather than, for example, a desire to maintain a male workplace).[190] The Court of Sessions took the view that, even where harassment 'had no sex related motive or objective', the *nature* of the treatment may amount to discrimin-ation. In the words of Lord President Emslie, a campaign of including deliberate staring, the making of 'suggestive remarks' and comments on the claimant's physical appearance and physical touching 'was plainly adopted against Mrs Porcelli because she was a woman. *It was a particular kind of weapon, based upon the sex of the victim, which… would not have been used against an equally disliked man*' (emphasis added). And in the memorable phrase of Lord Grieve if any of 'the weapons used against the complainer… could be identified as… "a sexual sword", and it was clear that the wound it inflicted was more than a mere

---

[189] [2008] IRLR 342.   [190] [1986] ICR 564.

scratch, the conclusion must be that the sword had been unsheathed and used because the victim was a woman'.

The Court of Sessions in *Porcelli* did not define sexual harassment as sex discrimination *per se*, but went some way towards allowing harassment to be dealt with as discrimination.[191] In *Pearce v Governing Body of Mayfield School*, however, the House of Lords cast doubt on the *Porcelli* decision. The case was brought by a lesbian school teacher who had been taunted as a 'lesbian', 'dyke', 'lesbian shit', 'lemon', 'lezzie' and 'lez'. Her claim that such taunting should be regarded as amounting to sex discrimination within *Porcelli* was rejected by the EAT, the Court of Appeal and the House of Lords:

- **Pearce v The Governing Body of Mayfield Secondary School**
  [2003] ICR 937, House of Lords

Lord Nicholls:

Sexual harassment is only prohibited by the [SDA] if the claimant can show she was harassed because she was a woman. Section 1(1)(a) requires the employment tribunal to compare the way the alleged discriminator treats the woman with the way he treats or would treat a man. In any case where discrimination is established, this exercise must involve comparing two forms of treatment which are different, whether in kind or in degree. It also involves the tribunal in evaluating the differences and deciding which form of treatment is less favourable.

The suggestion in some cases that if the form of the harassment is sexual or gender-specific, such as verbal abuse in explicitly sexual terms, that of itself constitutes less favourable treatment on the ground of sex, could not be reconciled with the language or the scheme of the statute. The fact that harassment is gender-specific in form cannot be regarded as of itself establishing conclusively that the reason for the harassment is gender-based, 'on the ground of her sex'. It will be evidence, whose weight will depend on the circumstances, that the reason for the harassment was the sex of the victim, although in some circumstances, the inference may readily be drawn that the reason for the harassment was gender-based, as where a male employee subjects a female colleague to persistent, unwanted sexual overtures. In such a case, the male employee's treatment of the woman is compared with his treatment of men, even though the comparison may be self-evident. However, the observation of Lord Brand in *Strathclyde Regional Council v Porcelli* that if a form of unfavourable treatment is meted out to a woman to which a man would not have been vulnerable, she has been discriminated against, and the observation of Lord Grieve in the same case that treatment meted out to a woman on the ground of her sex would fall to be regarded as less favourable treatment simply because it was sexually oriented, could not be approved insofar as they were suggesting that it was not relevant whether the claimant was treated less favourably than a man where the harassment is sexually oriented...

In the case of Ms Pearce, the natural inference to be drawn from the homophobic terms of abuse was that the reason for this treatment was her sexual orientation, even though the form which the abuse took was specific to her gender. The issue under s. 1(1)(a) cannot turn on a minute examination of the precise terms of the abuse. Ms Pearce had not put forward any evidence that a male homosexual teacher would have been treated differently. Therefore, she did not establish that the harassment was on the ground of her sex.

Lord Hope delivered a speech in similar terms to Lord Nicholls, Lord Rodger taking the more radical step of disapproving of the approach taken by Lord Emslie in the *Porcelli* case as a 'widening' of the concept of sexual harassment from the 'classic cases' in which conduct has a sexual motivation to cases 'where the motivation of the harasser was not sexual', and stating

---

[191] Though see *Stewart v Cleveland Guest (Engineering) Ltd* [1996] ICR 535 and *Smith v Gardner Merchant Ltd* [1999] ICR 134 for the limitations of the *Porcelli* approach.

that the decision though 'influential...is not satisfactory'. Lord Rodger's views did not command majority support, but the decision in *Porcelli* is fairly shaky authority for any claim that treatment which is not motivated by sexual orientation or religion/belief can amount to discrimination for the purposes of the EA Regs or EA 2006 respectively. Further, given the narrow approach to disability-related discrimination adopted by the House of Lords in *Malcolm* (section 12(A) below), similar difficulties are likely to arise in connection with disability.

7. The question of whether treatment specific to a group defined by reference to a protected ground is inevitably 'less favourable' has arisen outside the harassment context. In *R v Birmingham City Council, ex p Equal Opportunities Commission* the House of Lords rejected an argument based on the comparability of grammar and comprehensive schooling to the effect that, while the disputed treatment varied by sex, it was not 'less favourable' to the girls affected by it than it was or would have been to boys.[192] By contrast, it is characteristic of sex discrimination challenges to clothing and appearance rules that this argument has succeeded.[193]

(D) INDIRECT DISCRIMINATION

(I) ROOTS

- **Griggs v Duke Power Co 401 US 424 (1971)**

The African American applicants claimed that the employer's requirement, in respect of particular jobs, of a high school diploma or success in an IQ test, discriminated against them on grounds of race contrary to Title VII of the Civil Rights Act 1964. A disproportionate number of African American workers were excluded from these jobs by the requirement. The lower courts had found that the employer's previous practice of race discrimination had ended, and that there was no evidence that the requirements had been adopted in order to discriminate on racial grounds. The Supreme Court found in favour of the applicants.

Chief Justice Burger [for the Court]:
The objective of Congress in the enactment of Title VII is plain from the language of the statute. It was to achieve equality of employment opportunities and remove barriers that have operated in the past to favor an identifiable group of white employees over other employees. Under the Act, practices, procedures, or tests neutral on their face, and even neutral in terms of intent, cannot be maintained if they operate to 'freeze' the status quo of prior discriminatory employment practices...

...the Act does not command that any person be hired simply because he was formerly the subject of discrimination, or because he is a member of a minority group. Discriminatory preference for any group, minority or majority, is precisely and only what Congress has proscribed. What is required by Congress is the removal of artificial, arbitrary, and unnecessary barriers to employment when the barriers operate invidiously to discriminate on the basis of racial or other impermissible classification.

Congress has now provided that tests or criteria for employment or promotion may not provide equality of opportunity merely in the sense of the fabled offer of milk to the stork and the fox. On the contrary, Congress has now required that the posture and condition of the job-seeker be taken into account.

---

[192] N. 51 above.
[193] Space forbids consideration of the cases here but see A. McColgan, n. 1 above, Chap. 6 and, in particular, *Schmidt v Austicks Bookshops* [1978] ICR 85, *Smith v Safeway plc* [1995] ICR 868 and *Department for Work and Pensions v Thompson* [2004] IRLR 248.

It has—to resort again to the fable—provided that the vessel in which the milk is proffered be one all seekers can use. The Act proscribes not only overt discrimination but also practices that are fair in form, but discriminatory in operation. The touchstone is business necessity. If an employment practice which operates to exclude Negroes cannot be shown to be related to job performance, the practice is prohibited.

NOTE

1. This was the case in which the US Supreme Court first recognised 'disparate impact' discrimination, the concept which was to be reflected in 'indirect discrimination' in the UK and eventually EU law. 'Indirect discrimination' is concerned with the application of facially neutral rules, practices etc. which serve *in practice* to disadvantage groups of people defined by reference to a protected characteristic such as race, religion or belief, etc. This type of discrimination has undergone significant change in recent years as a result of EU developments that have simplified the test to be applied in the majority of cases. The original definition of indirect discrimination utilised by the SDA and RRA is considered below (the DDA does not employ the concept at all). It now applies, however, only to that sex and race discrimination that falls within the SDA and RRA respectively but outside the scope of EC law.[194] For this reason the main focus of this chapter will be on the new definitions of indirect discrimination.

(II) DOMESTIC REGULATION OF INDIRECT DISCRIMINATION

Section 1 RRA

(1) A person discriminates against another in any circumstances relevant for the purposes of any provision of this Act if...

    (b) he applies to that other a requirement or condition which he applies or would apply equally to persons not of the same racial group as that other but—

        (i) which is such that the proportion of persons of the same racial group as that other who can comply with it is considerably smaller than the proportion of persons not of that racial group who can comply with it; and

        (ii) which he cannot show to be justifiable irrespective of the colour, race, nationality or ethnic or national origins of the person to whom it is applied; and

        (iii) which is to the detriment of that other because he cannot comply with it.

(1A) A person also discriminates against another if, in any circumstances relevant for the purposes of any provision referred to in subsection (1B), he applies to that other a provision, criterion or practice which he applies or would apply equally to persons not of the same race or ethnic or national origins as that other, but—

    (a) which puts or would put persons of the same race or ethnic or national origins as that other at a particular disadvantage when compared with other persons,

    (b) which puts that other at that disadvantage, and

    (c) which he cannot show to be a proportionate means of achieving a legitimate aim.

---

[194] See ss. 1(1B) RRA and 1(3) SDA.

(1B) The provisions mentioned in subsection (1A) are—

    (a) Part II;

    (b) sections 17 to 18D;

    (c) section 19B, so far as relating to -

        (i) any form of social security;

        (ii) health care;

        (iii) any other form of social protection; and

        (iv) any form of social advantage;

  which does not fall within section 20;

    (d) sections 20 to 24;

    (e) sections 26A and 26B;

    (f) sections 76 and 76ZA; and

    (g) Part IV, in its application to the provisions referred to in paragraphs (a) to (f).

(1C) Where, by virtue of subsection (1A), a person discriminates against another, subsection (1)(b) does not apply to him.

Section 45 EA 2006

(3) A person ('A') discriminates against another ('B') for the purposes of this Part if A applies to B a provision, criterion or practice—

    (a) which he applies or would apply equally to persons not of B's religion or belief,

    (b) which puts persons of B's religion or belief at a disadvantage compared to some or all others (where there is no material difference in the relevant circumstances),

    (c) which puts B at a disadvantage compared to some or all persons who are not of his religion or belief (where there is no material difference in the relevant circumstances), and

    (d) which A cannot reasonably justify by reference to matters other than B's religion or belief.

NOTES

1. The RRA contains different definitions of indirect discrimination because that in s. 1(1A), which reflects EU law, has been applied to the RRA only in so far as that Act corresponds to the scope of the Race Directive, the original definition of indirect discrimination (s. 1(1)(b)) being left in place in relation to race discrimination (largely that related to colour or nationality), which is not regulated by EU law. The SDA similarly contains two different definitions of indirect discrimination, which are materially identical to those set out in s. 1(1)(b) and (1A) RRA, and which apply to discrimination falling within and outwith EU law.[195] These definitions. The scope of EU law is narrower as it applies to sex than race discrimination; s. 1(3) SDA applies the new definition of indirect discrimination only to those provisions of the Act that regulate employment (broadly defined) or the provision of goods, facilities, services and premises, but excludes (s. 35ZA) 'the content of media and advertisements' and 'the provision of goods, facilities or services (not normally provided on a commercial basis) at a place (permanently or for the time being) occupied or used for the purposes of an organised religion'.

---

[195] S. 1(1)(b) and (2) SDA.

2. Regulation 3(1)(b) of each the SO Regs, the RB Regs and the Age Regs are materially identical to s. 1(1A) RRA.[196] A slightly different formulation is adopted by s. 45 of the EA 2006, to which reg. 3(3) of the EA Regs is materially identical, which makes explicit references to the situation of comparators and defines justification in broadly similar terms to the original definitions set out in s. 1(1)(b) RRA and its SDA equivalent.[197]

3. The original definitions of indirect discrimination created enormous difficulties for applicants. The term 'requirement or condition' was very narrowly interpreted by the Court of Appeal in *Perera v The Civil Service Commission* and *Jones v University of Manchester* to apply only to criteria functioning as absolute bars, and was replaced with the deliberately broad 'provision, criterion or practice'.[198] The new definitions of indirect discrimination also replace the demand that this requirement or condition be 'such that the proportion of persons' of the claimant's group who can comply with it 'is considerably smaller than the proportion of persons not of that...group who can comply with it', which tended to result in protracted litigation about statistical proof,[199] with one that the provision, criterion or practice 'puts' or (other than in the case of the EA 2006 and EA Regs) 'would put', persons of the claimant's group 'at a particular disadvantage when compared with other persons' or (in the case of the EA 2006 and EA Regs) 'at a disadvantage compared to some or all others'. The original requirement that the claimant in an indirect discrimination claim suffers detriment *because of his or her inability to comply* with the impugned requirement or condition has been replaced by a requirement that the claimant is 'put at' the relevant disadvantage by the provision, criterion or practice, thus eliminating space for argument about whether the claimant might have been expected to compromise his or her beliefs etc. in order to comply with the disputed requirement or condition.[200] Finally, the test for justification has been amended other than in the case of the EA 2006 and EA Regs (see further n. 4). The new approach appears to have done away with the technical difficulties associated with the previous definitions (see, for example, the decisions in *Elias* and *R (E) v Jews Free School*).[201]

(III) JUSTIFYING INDIRECT DISCRIMINATION

- **Hampson v Department of Education and Science**
  [1989] ICR 179, Court of Appeal

The case concerned a challenge brought by the claimant, a Hong Kong Chinese teacher who had completed three (non-consecutive) years of training in accordance with Hong Kong requirements, to a decision by the Secretary of State for Employment that her training was not 'comparable' to a UK qualification (which involved a three-year course). She argued that the three consecutive years rule imposed by the Secretary of State indirectly discriminated against her as a Hong Kong Chinese person. The EAT and the Court of Appeal ruled against

---

[196] Save that the justification defence for age discrimination is also applicable to direct discrimination.

[197] S. 45(4) EA 2006 and reg. 3(4) EA Regs further provide in terms that 'the fact that one of the persons (whether or not B) is a civil partner while the other is married shall not be treated as a material difference in the relevant circumstances'.

[198] [1983] ICR 428 and [1993] ICR 474 respectively; see discussion in A. McColgan, n. 1 above, Chap. 2.

[199] See, e.g., *Kidd v DRG* [1985] ICR 405, *Jones v University of Manchester* [1993] ICR 474, *Allonby v Accrington & Rossendale College* [2001] ICR 1189, *Rutherford v Towncircle Ltd* ([2002] ICR 123 and *Rutherford v Town Circle (No. 2)* [2006] UKHL 19, [2006] ICR 785.

[200] See *Clymo v Wandsworth London Borough Council* [1989] ICR 250, discussed by Jeremy Lewis at (1989) 18 Industrial Law Journal 244, though cf. on this issue *Price v Civil Service Commission* [1978] ICR 27, *Mandla v Dowell Lee*, n. 50 above.

[201] At nn. 26 (Admin Court) and 29 above, paras 53 and 178–181, respectively.

her on the ground that the Secretary of State's act was protected under s. 41 RRA (this aspect of the decision is discussed further at section 8(A) above). But in his dissent in the Court of Appeal Balcombe LJ set out the test for justification of indirect discrimination which was subsequently adopted by the House of Lords in *Webb v EMO* as generally applicable to indirect discrimination.[202]

Balcombe LJ:

In *Ojutiku v Manpower Services* [1982] ICR 661 this court was concerned with the meaning of 'justifiable' where it appears in s 1(1)(b)(ii) of the [RRA] and of course that decision is binding on us insofar as it decides that meaning. However, I regret that I do not find, in two of the judgments in Ojutiku, any clear decision as to that meaning. The first judgment was that of Lord Justice Eveleigh. He dealt with the question in the following passage…

'… I myself would not accept that it is essential, or at least that it is always essential, for the employer to prove that the requirement is necessary for the good of his business. It may well be that in a particular case that is the argument which is advanced by the employer; it does not follow that that is what the statute demands. I am very hesitant to suggest another expression for that which is used in the statute, for fear that it will be picked up and quoted in other cases and built upon thereafter, with the result that at the end of the day there is a danger of us all departing far from the meaning of the word in the statute. For myself, it would be enough simply to ask myself: is it justifiable? But if I have to give some explanation of my understanding of that word, I would turn to a dictionary definition which says to adduce adequate grounds for; and it seems to me that if a person produces reasons for doing something, which would be acceptable to right-thinking people as sound and tolerable reasons for so doing, then he has justified his conduct.'

With all due respect to [Eveleigh LJ, and to Kerr LJ who concurred on similar grounds]…I derive little help from [their] judgments. 'Justifiable' and 'justify' are words which connote a value judgment, as is evident from the dictionary definition cited by Lord Justice Eveleigh: 'to produce adequate grounds for', but neither Lord Justice indicates what test should be applied. Lord Justice Kerr says it applies a lower standard than 'necessary', but does not indicate how much lower. It was, however, accepted by Mr Carlisle, and rightly so, that whatever test is to be applied it is an objective one: it is not sufficient for the employer to establish that he considered his reasons adequate.

However, I do derive considerable assistance from the judgment of Lord Justice Stephenson. At p 423 he referred to:

'…the comments, which I regard as sound, made by Lord McDonald, giving the judgment of [EAT] given by Phillips J in *Steel v Union of Post Office Workers* [[1978] ICR 181]…What Phillips J there said is valuable as rejecting justification by convenience and requiring the party applying the discriminatory condition to prove it to be justifiable in all the circumstances on balancing its discriminatory effect against the discriminator's need for it. But that need is what is reasonably needed by the party who applies the condition…'

In my judgment 'justifiable' requires an objective balance between the discriminatory effect of the condition and the reasonable needs of the party who applies the condition. This construction is supported by the recent decision of the House of Lords in *Rainey v Greater Glasgow Health Board*…[in which the House of Lords applied] the decision of the European Court in *Bilka-Kaufhaus GmbH v Weber von Hartz*…to the effect that, in order to justify indirect sex discrimination] the employer had to show a real need on the part of the undertaking, objectively justified, although that need was not confined to economic grounds; it might, for instance, include administrative efficiency in a concern not engaged in commerce or business. Clearly it may, as in the present case, be possible to justify by reference to grounds other than economic or administrative efficiency…

---

202 [1993] ICR 175.

I can find no significant difference between the test adopted by Lord Justice Stephenson in *Ojutiku* and that adopted by the House of Lords in *Rainey*. Since neither Lords Justices Eveleigh nor Kerr in *Ojutiku* indicated what they considered the test to be—although Lord Justice Kerr said what it was not—I am content to adopt Lord Justice Stephenson's test as I have expressed it above, which I consider to be consistent with *Rainey*. It is obviously desirable that the tests of justifiability applied in all these closely related fields [i.e., under the SDA, the RRA and the EqPA] should be consistent with each other.

NOTES

1. It is central to the concept of indirect discrimination that it is capable of justification. How radical the impact of a prohibition on indirect discrimination is turns on the approach taken to the justification test. The starting point is the decision of the Court of Appeal in *Hampson*, above. The *Hampson* test for justification claims to incorporate the ECJ's approach to the justification of indirect sex discrimination into UK law. *Hampson* was a race discrimination case but, as Balcombe LJ pointed out in that case, s. 1(1)(b)(ii) SDA 'is identical, *mutatis mutandis*, to section 1(1)(b)(ii) [RRA]'. Accordingly, he applied the same approach to justification under the RRA as he would have applied under the SDA. This approach, in Balcombe LJ's view, was consistent with that adopted by the ECJ in *Bilka-Kaufhaus*.

- **Case 170/84 Bilka-Kaufhaus GmbH v Weber von Hartz**
  [1986] ECR 1607, European Court of Justice

The applicant alleged a breach of Art. 141 (then Art. 119) on the grounds that, as a part-time worker, she had been refused pension payments under a contractual scheme wholly funded by her employer and supplementary to the German state pension. One issue which arose for consideration was whether such pension payments were 'pay' within Art. 141. This aspect of the decision is further considered below. Here we are concerned with the question whether, consistent with Art. 141, part-timers could be paid less than full-timers where this practice impacted disadvantageously upon women.

Judgment

Mrs Weber…asserted that the requirement of a minimum period of full-time employment for the payment of an occupational pension placed women workers at a disadvantage, since they were more likely than their male colleagues to take part-time work so as to be able to care for their family and children.

Bilka on the other hand, argued that…there were objectively justified economic grounds for its decision to exclude part-time employees from the occupational pension scheme. It emphasized in that regard that in comparison with the employment of part-time workers the employment of full-time workers entails lower ancillary costs and permits the use of staff throughout opening hours. Relying on statistics concerning the group to which it belongs, Bilka stated that up to 1980 81.3% of all occupational pensions were paid to women, although only 72% of employees were women. Those figures, it said, showed that the scheme in question does not entail discrimination on the basis of sex…

if…it should be found that a much lower proportion of women than of men work full time, the exclusion of part-time workers from the occupational pension scheme would be contrary to Article [141] of the Treaty where, taking into account the difficulties encountered by women workers in working full-time that measure could not be explained by factors which exclude any discrimination on grounds of sex.

However, if the undertaking is able to show that its pay practice may be explained by objectively justified factors unrelated to any discrimination on grounds of sex there is no breach of article [141]…

It is for the national court, which has sole jurisdiction to make findings of fact, to determine whether and to what extent the grounds put forward by an employer to explain the adoption of a pay practice which applies independently of a worker's sex but in fact affects more women than men may be regarded as objectively justified economic grounds. If the national court finds that the measures chosen by Bilka correspond to a real need on the part of the undertaking, are appropriate with a view to achieving the objectives pursued and are necessary to that end, the fact that the measures affect a far greater number of women than men is not sufficient to show that they constitute an infringement of article [141].

2. The ECJ subsequently developed the test for justification through the decisions in cases including Case 171/88, *Rinner-Kühn v FWW Spezial-Gebaudereinigung GmbH* and Case 109/88, *Handels-og Kontorfunktionaererernes Forbund I Danmark v Dansk Arbejdsgiverforenin g (acting for Danfoss).*[203] In *Rinner-Kühn* the Court ruled that 'generalizations about certain categories of workers [there the assertion that (predominantly female) workers working less than 10 hours a week, for whom the state did not reimburse sick pay, were not as integrated in, or as dependent on, the undertaking employing them as other workers] do not enable criteria which are both objective and unrelated to any discrimination on grounds of sex to be identified'. In *Danfoss* it ruled that disparately impacting pay practices could be justified only to the extent that the factors rewarded were 'of importance for the performance of specific tasks entrusted to the employee'.

3. The *Bilka Kaufhaus, Rinner-Kühn* and *Danfoss* cases concerned discrimination by employers. In cases where the discrimination is practised by the state against categories of persons (such as part-time workers), 'somewhat broader considerations apply' and the ECJ accepted in *Rinner-Kühn* that such discrimination may be justifiable where they 'meet a necessary aim of [a Member State's] social policy and that they are suitable and requisite for attaining that aim'. The test is still a proportionality one, but it appears easier to satisfy. More recently, however, in Case 226/98, *Jørgensen v Foreningen af Speciallæger, Sygesikringens Forhandlingsudvalg,* the ECJ ruled that 'budgetary considerations cannot in themselves justify discrimination on grounds of sex'.[204] This approach, the ECJ explains, is necessary to avoid the varying application of the principle of equal treatment with the public finances of individual Member States. This approach was applied again in Case 77/02, *Steinicke v Bundesanstalt für Arbeit*[205] and in *Kutz-Bauer* in which the ECJ ruled that a scheme which encouraged part-time work by those not yet entitled to a state pension (which was provided to the majority of women at 60, and the majority of men at 65) breached the Equal Treatment Directive.

- **Case 187/00, Kutz-Bauer v Freie und Hansestadt Hamburg**
  [2003] ECR I–02741

Judgment

The German Government submits that one of the aims pursued by a scheme such as the one at issue in the main proceedings is to combat unemployment by offering the maximum incentives for workers who are not yet eligible to retire to do so and thus making posts available. To allow a worker who has already acquired entitlement to a retirement pension at the full rate to benefit from the scheme of part-time work for older employees implies, first, that a post which the scheme intends to allocate to an unemployed person would continue to be occupied and, second, that the social security scheme would bear the additional costs, which would divert certain resources from other objectives.

---

203 Respectively [1989] ECR 2743 and [1989] ECR 3199.
204 [2000] ECR I-02447.   205 [2003] ECR I-09027.

As regards the argument which the German Government derives from the encouragement of recruitment, it is for the Member States to choose the measures capable of achieving the aims which they pursue in employment matters. The Court has recognised that the Member States have a broad margin of discretion in exercising that power...

Furthermore, as the Court stated at paragraph 71 of its judgment in *Seymour-Smith and Perez*, it cannot be disputed that the encouragement of recruitment constitutes a legitimate aim of social policy [but]...mere generalisations concerning the capacity of a specific measure to encourage recruitment are not enough to show that the aim of the disputed provisions is unrelated to any discrimination based on sex or to provide evidence on the basis of which it could reasonably be considered that the means chosen are or could be suitable for achieving that aim.

As regards the German Government's argument concerning the additional burden associated with allowing female workers to take advantage of the scheme at issue in the main proceedings even where they have acquired entitlement to a retirement pension at the full rate, the Court observes that although budgetary considerations may underlie a Member State's choice of social policy and influence the nature or scope of the social protection measures which it wishes to adopt, they do not in themselves constitute an aim pursued by that policy and cannot therefore justify discrimination against one of the sexes...

Nor can the City of Hamburg, whether as a public authority or as an employer, justify discrimination arising from a scheme of part-time work for older employees solely because avoidance of such discrimination would involve increased costs...

It is therefore for the City of Hamburg to prove to the national court that the difference in treatment arising from the scheme of part-time work for older employees at issue in the main proceedings is justified by objective reasons unrelated to any discrimination on grounds of sex.

4. It is questionable whether the rubric adopted by s. 1(1A)(c) RRA and its equivalents is adequate to transpose the European definition of justification which is couched in terms of 'appropriate and necessary' means of achieving 'legitimate aims'. A further potential problem lies in the fact that, under the definition adopted in these domestic provisions, there is no requirement to establish justification *irrespective* of the race, etc., of the person to whom the provision, criterion or practice applied. It remains to be seen whether this is the case in practice, though the benefit of the amended test is that it may leave room for the justification of indirectly discriminatory practices that are intended to ameliorate, rather than designed (wittingly or otherwise) to perpetuate, the disadvantage experienced by certain groups defined by race, sex, religion or belief or sexual orientation.[206] Having said this, any court is obliged to interpret the statutory test in conformity with EC law set out above. And in *Elias* the Administrative Court ruled that 'the *Bilka-Kaufhaus* test was "reflected in the language of section 1A of the [RRA]"' and that 'There should be no difference in the application of the two tests'.[207]

5. The test established by the ECJ in *Bilka-Kaufhaus* (and, by implication, the subsequent developments thereto) is applicable to the SDA and the RRA and also, by implication, applicable to the SO Regs, the RB Regs and the Age Regs, given their EU provenance, and arguably also to the EA 2006 and the EA Regs.[208] There remains a certain tension between the balancing approach established in *Hampson* and subsequently approved by the House of Lords in *Webb*, and the more demanding approach of the ECJ. A fairly rigorous approach appears to have been taken in recent years, however, to the justification of discrimination. In *Elias* the High Court ruled that justification put forward by the Secretary of State had to be 'carefully

---

[206] Note that direct as well as indirect age discrimination is capable of justification.
[207] Paras 58–59.   [208] Given their similarity.

scrutinise[d]', in particular because 'the extent of the discrimination on grounds of national origin is very marked indeed'.[209] 'The criteria chosen were very closely linked to national origins. Using these criteria was by no means the only way in which the Minister could achieve his legitimate objective...It follows that in my judgment the scheme as adopted is unlawful.'[210]

In the *JFS* case, Munby J accepted that indirect race discriminatory could be justified only by '"severe" or "intense" scrutiny and "very weighty reasons"; that the burden of justification fell on the school; that the measure in question must be shown to correspond to a real need; that the means adopted must be "appropriate" and "necessary" to achieving that objective'; that '[t]here must be a "real match" between the end and the means'; and that 'what has to be justified in a case such as this is the discrimination, not just the underlying policy objective...it is not just the desire to keep a "culturally Jewish" school which must ultimately be justified—that is merely the legitimate aim—what has also to be justified are the discriminatory means adopted of seeking to achieve this objective'.[211] He went on, however, to find that the burden of justification was made out in this case: faith-based admission criteria complied with governmental policy regarding diversity and choice, and their prohibition was a matter for Parliament. They were, moreover, consistent with Art. 2 of Protocol 1, and faith-based admission criteria based on 'membership' of a faith rather than religious 'practice' were explicitly permitted by the School Admissions Code. The prohibition of such criteria would (para. 190) prejudice religions, such as Judaism, which define membership exclusively of 'educat[ing] those who, in the eyes of the OCR, are Jewish, irrespective of their religious beliefs, practices or observances, in a school whose culture and ethos is that of Orthodox Judaism'.[212] This was not contradicted by the fact that the school did admit some non-orthodox Jews, while giving clear preference to Orthodox Jews, and it amounted to:

194 ...an entirely legitimate aim meeting a real need. If, as Mr Singh has correctly argued, it is legitimate for a Muslim school to give preference to those who are born Muslim, or for a Catholic school to give preference to those who have been baptised, even if they have fallen away from the faith, with the aim of educating them in an appropriate religious ethos—perhaps with the view of bringing them back within the fold—then why should it not be equally legitimate for a school like JFS to give preference to those whom it treats as Jews even if they have fallen away from or have never known the faith? There is, in my judgment, no material difference at all; certainly it can make no difference that in the one case 'membership' of the religion depends upon the father's status, in another upon a religious rite conducted in infancy and in the third upon the mother's status.

199. The only remaining question is whether the policy, given that it pursues a legitimate aim, can be justified as a proportionate and necessary means to that end. Ms Rose submits not, asserting that JFS's admissions policy does not properly balance the impact of the policy on those like M adversely affected by it and the needs of the school. The Schools Adjudicator did not agree, Nor do I.

200. Two quite separate considerations drive me to this conclusion. In the first place, the kind of admissions policy in question here is not, properly analysed, materially different from that which gives preference in admission to a Muslim school to those who were born Muslim or preference in admission

---

[209] N. 26 above, para. 84.

[210] N. 26 above, paras 89–90. See also the decision of the Court of Appeal in the case, n. 26 above, paras 158–162.

[211] N. 29 above, paras 184–185 citing, *inter alia*, Arden LJ in *Elias*, n. 26 above, paras 270–271; *R (Carson) v Secretary of State for Work and Pensions* [2006] 1 AC 173, paras 57–58 and *Allonby v Accrington and Rossendale College* [2001] ICR 1189, para. 28.

[212] Ibid., para. 192.

to a Catholic school to those who have been baptised. But no-one suggests that such policies, whatever their differential impact on different applicants, are other than a proportionate and lawful means of achieving a legitimate end. Why, Mr Oldham asks rhetorically, should it be any different in the case of Orthodox Jews? And to this pointed question there has, as he says, been no effective answer—hardly surprisingly, he adds, because any such difference in the treatment of the two cases would plainly be discriminatory against Jews. I agree. Indeed, the point goes even wider that the two examples I have given for, as Mr Oldham submits, if E's case on this point is successful then it will probably render unlawful the admission arrangements in a very large number of faith schools of many different faiths and denominations.

201. The other point is that made both by the Schools Adjudicator and by Mr Oldham. Adopting some alternative admissions policy based on such factors as adherence or commitment to Judaism (even assuming that such a concept has any meaning for this purpose in Jewish religious law) would not be a means of achieving JFS's aims and objectives; on the contrary it would produce a different school ethos. If JFS's existing aims and objectives are legitimate, as they are, then a policy of giving preference to children who are Jewish applying Orthodox Jewish principles is, they say, necessary and proportionate—indeed, as it seems to me, essential—to achieve those aims. Mr Oldham puts the point very clearly. JFS exists as a school for Orthodox Jews. If it is to remain a school for Orthodox Jews it must retain its existing admissions policy; if it does not, it will cease to be a school for Orthodox Jews. Precisely. To this argument there is, and can be, no satisfactory answer.

6. Should, in your view, it be possible to justify a disparately impacting practice or policy etc. which has been adopted in breach of s. 71 RRA or its equivalent (i.e., in particular, in the absence of a proper equality impact assessment)?[213]

12. DISABILITY DISCRIMINATION: UNIQUE PROVISIONS

(A) DISABILITY-RELATED DISCRIMINATION

(I) BACKGROUND

Section 20 DDA

(1) For the purposes of section 19, a provider of services discriminates against a disabled person if—

    (a) for a reason which relates to the disabled person's disability, he treats him less favourably than he treats or would treat others to whom that reason does not or would not apply; and

    (b) he cannot show that the treatment in question is justified...

NOTES

1. The comparator-related difficulties posed by s. 5(3) SDA and its equivalents did not, until very recently, apply to the concept of 'disability-related' discrimination which is prohibited, subject to justification, by the DDA. Direct discrimination is defined, for the purposes of the

[213] See the decision of the Admin Court in *Elias*, n. 26 above, paras 55–56 and that of the CA, n. 26 above, paras 128–133 and 176.

DDA, as at section 11(B) above and is subject to no justification defence. It is expressly regulated only in the context of employment and third-level education. But the Act also regulates the apparently wider form of discrimination set out above.

2. Section 20 applies to discrimination in access to goods, facilities and services but it is reflected by ss. 3A(1) (employment), 21D (public authorities), 21G (private clubs), 24 (premises) 28B and 28S (education) and 31AB (general qualifications bodies). In each case disability-related discrimination is capable of justification. But, whereas in the case of employment and education the test for justification is a general one (see section 12(C) below), in other contexts detailed specific justifications are provided. It is this difference of approach which resulted in the recent downfall of the approach set out in *Clark v Novacold*, immediately below.

3. 'Disability-related discrimination' as defined in s. 20(1) above *includes* direct discrimination, in which case it is not (in the case of employment and third-level education) capable of justification. But, at least prior to the decision of the House of Lords in *Malcolm* (below), it was not understood to be *limited to* direct discrimination.[214] (Note that the concept of direct discrimination had not yet been introduced into the DDA at the time of the judgment and that when Mummery LJ refers to 'discrimination' he means what we refer to as 'disability-related discrimination'.) The classic approach to 'disability-related discrimination' is set out in the following case:

- **Clark v TDG Ltd (t/a Novacold)** [1999] ICR 951, Court of Appeal

The applicant was dismissed because he had been absent from work because of a back injury. His DDA claim was rejected by a tribunal which ruled that his treatment had to be compared with that of someone (real or hypothetical) who was absent from work other than for a disability-related reason. Mr Clark's appeal to the EAT was dismissed but the Court of Appeal allowed his appeal.

Mummery LJ [for the Court]:

THE 1995 ACT: GENERAL

The provisions of the [DDA] relating to employment are contained in Part II. Although their general aims are clear and commendable, the language in which the detailed implementation of them is expressed is not easy to interpret or to apply to particular cases.

30 Contrary to what might be reasonably assumed, the exercise of interpretation is not facilitated by familiarity with the pre-existing legislation prohibiting discrimination in the field of employment (and elsewhere) on the grounds of sex...and race...Indeed, it may be positively misleading to approach the [DDA] with assumptions and concepts familiar from experience of the workings of the [SDA] and the [RRA]...

33 In Part II of the [DDA], 'discrimination' is defined as less favourable treatment which is not shown to be justified; if the less favourable treatment of a disabled person is shown to be justified it is not 'discrimination' within the meaning of the Act. This is to be contrasted with the [SDA] and the [RRA] under which a person directly 'discriminates' against another if, on the specified ground of sex or race, he treats that other less favourably than he treats or would treat other persons. Justification does not enter into it. Such treatment can never be shown to be justified...

---

[214] Indeed, if it had been no limited there would have been no need to introduce a prohibition on (non-justifiable) 'direct discrimination' in amending the DDA to implement Council Directive 2000/78/EC. The obvious course of action would simply have been to remove the justification defence in the employment context.

59 In the historical context of discrimination legislation, it is natural to do what the industrial and the appeal tribunal (though 'without great confidence') did, namely to interpret the expression 'that reason' so as to achieve a situation in which a comparison is made of the case of the disabled person with that of an able-bodied person and the comparison is such that the relevant circumstances in the one case are the same, or not materially different, in the other case. This might be reasonably considered to be the obvious way of determining whether a disabled person has been treated less favourably than a person who is not disabled.

60 But, as already indicated, the [DDA] adopts a significantly different approach to the protection of disabled persons against less favourable treatment in employment. The definition of discrimination in the [DDA] does not contain an express provision requiring a comparison of the cases of different persons in the same, or not materially different, circumstances. The statutory focus is narrower: it is on the 'reason' for the treatment of the disabled employee and the comparison to be made is with the treatment of 'others to whom that reason does not or would not apply'. The 'others' with whom comparison is to be made are not specifically required to be in the same, or not materially different, circumstances: they only have to be persons 'to whom that reason does not or would not apply'…

62 The result of this approach is that the reason would not apply to others even if their circumstances are different from those of the disabled person. The persons who are performing the main functions of their jobs are 'others' to whom the reason for dismissal of the disabled person (ie inability to perform those functions) would not apply.

63 In the context of the special sense in which 'discrimination' is defined in s.5 of the [DDA] it is more probable that Parliament meant 'that reason' to refer only to the facts constituting the reason for the treatment, and not to include within that reason the added requirement of a causal link with disability: that is more properly regarded as the cause of the reason for the treatment than as in itself a reason for the treatment. This interpretation avoids the difficulties which would be encountered in many cases in seeking to identify what the appeal tribunal referred to as 'the characteristics of the hypothetical comparator'. It would avoid the kind of problems which the English (and Scottish) courts and the tribunals encountered in their futile attempts to find and identify the characteristics of a hypo-thetical non-pregnant male comparator for a pregnant woman in sex discrimination cases before the decision of the European Court of Justice in *Webb v EMO Air Cargo (UK) Ltd*… This interpretation is also consistent with the emphasis on whether the less favourable treatment of the disabled person is shown to be justified. That defence is not available in cases of direct discrimination under the other discrimination Acts.

64 It is also more consistent with the scheme of the [DDA] as a whole. As Roch LJ pointed out in the course of argument, the language of s.5(1) is replicated in other Parts of the Act relating to the definition of discrimination in other areas: goods, facilities and services in s.20(1); and premises in s.24(1). Although neither side sought to place before the court any *Pepper v Hart* [1993] IRLR 33 material on s.5, such material appears to be available on the provisions relating to access to services. The interpretation of the provisions in s.20(1) is relevant to the interpretation of s.5, as they are in the same terms.

65 On the second reading of the Bill for this Act the Minister for Social Security and Disabled People stated:

'The Bill is drafted in such a way that indirect as well as direct discrimination can be dealt with…A situation where dogs are not admitted to a cafe, with the effect that blind people would be unable to enter it, would be a prima facie case of indirect discrimination against blind people and would be unlawful' (253 HC Official Report (6th series) col. 150, 24 January 1995)…

67 …if Novacold are correct in their interpretation of s.5(1), it would follow that s.20(1), which is in the same terms, would have to bear a meaning inconsistent with the specific statement of the Minister on the intended effect of those provisions.

68 Consider his example. If no dogs are admitted to a cafe, the reason for denying access to refreshment in it by a blind person with his guide dog would be the fact that no dogs are admitted. That reason 'relates to' his disability. His guide dog is with him because of his disability.

69 On the Novacold interpretation of the comparison to be made, the blind person with his guide dog would *not* be treated less favourably than the relevant comparator, ie 'others', to whom that reason would not apply, would be sighted persons who had their dogs with them. There could not therefore be any, let alone prima facie, discrimination. But the Minister specifically stated that this would be a prima facie case of disability discrimination, ie less favourable treatment, unless justified. It could only be a case of less favourable treatment and therefore a prima facie case of discrimination, if the comparators are 'others' *without dogs*: 'that reason' for refusing access to refreshment in the cafe would not apply to 'others' without dogs…

90 …Treatment is less favourable if the reason for it does not or would not apply to others.

91 In deciding whether that reason does not or would not apply to others, it is not appropriate to make a comparison of the cases in the same way as in the [SDA] and the [RRA]. It is simply a case of identifying others to whom the reason for the treatment does not or would not apply. The test of less favourable treatment is based on the reason for the treatment of the disabled person and not on the fact of his disability. It does not turn on a like-for-like comparison of the treatment of the disabled person and of others in similar circumstances…

(II) RECENT DEVELOPMENTS

- **Mayor and Burgesses of the London Borough of Lewisham v Malcolm** [2008] UKHL 43, [2008] 3 WLR 194, House of Lords

The defendant, who suffered from schizophrenia, was served with an eviction notice by the council because he had, in breach of his tenancy agreement, sub-let the flat during a period in which his condition was uncontrolled by medication. The sub-letting had the effect that the defendant lost his secured tenancy status and his right to buy, which right he had been actively pursuing.

The defendant claimed that any breach of the terms of the tenancy had been caused by his disability with the effect that 'the reason why the claimant is seeking possession is because of the…disability', and that the court was precluded by the DDA from making any order for possession against him. This argument failed in the High Court but succeeded before the Court of Appeal, which accepted that the notice to quit and possession action constituted unlawful discrimination contrary to the DDA, because there was 'an appropriate relationship' between the reason for the authority's actions and the defendant's illness; his treatment had been less favourable than that of others to whom that reason did not apply; and (by a majority) that the fact that the authority did not know of the disability did not preclude a finding of discrimination.

The House of Lords allowed the authority's appeal (Baroness Hale dissenting), ruling that the correct comparator for the purposes of s. 24(1)(a) was a secure tenant of the authority with no mental illness who had sub-let his property, rather than a secure tenant of the authority who had not. According to their Lordships, it was insufficient for the defendant to show an objective connection between his schizophrenia and his sub-letting. He needed to show, in addition, that his disability had played a motivating part in the authority's actions. Even had the claimant known of his condition and known that there might be a link between his schizophrenia and his behaviour in putting his secure tenancy at risk by sub-letting, there was no evidence that those matters had played any part in the authority's decision to take action to recover possession of the flat and so there had been no 'less favourable' treatment of the defendant.

Lord Bingham:

9. It seems to me…that the task of the court is to ascertain the real reason for the treatment, the reason which operates on the mind of the alleged discriminator. This may not be the reason given, and may not be the only reason, but the test is an objective one. Here, it seems to me inescapable that Lewisham, as a social landlord with a limited stock of housing and a heavy demand from those on its waiting list, acted as it did because it was not prepared to allow tenancies to continue where the tenant was not living in the premises demised. That, I think, was the real reason for the treatment, a reason in no way inconsistent with that which the parties agreed. Lewisham could have been the subject of reasonable criticism, and might even have been judicially reviewed, had it acted otherwise than it did in any ordinary case.

(4) DID THAT REASON RELATE TO MR MALCOLM'S DISABILITY?

10. As well explained by Lindsay J in *H J Heinz Co Ltd v Kenrick* [2000] ICR 491, para 27, and *Rowden v Dutton Gregory* [2002] ICR 971, para 5, with reference to section 5 of the Act (which uses similar language) it seems clear that the draftsman of section 24(1)(a) deliberately eschewed the conventional language of causation in favour of the broader and less precise expression 'relates to'. In this context I take the expression to denote some connection, not necessarily close, between the reason and the disability. Judged by this yardstick, most of the decided cases and frequently-discussed examples fall into place…the dismissal of the absent claimant in *Clark v Novacold* [1999] ICR 951, the refusal of entry to a blind person with a dog or the refusal of service to a customer with eating difficulties (hypothetical examples considered in that case and elsewhere), or the dismissal for slowness of a one-legged postman (a hypothetical example discussed by Lindsay J in *Heinz v Kenrick*, above), would all, in my opinion, disclose a connection between the reason for dismissal and the disability in question. But in borderline cases it will be hard to decide whether there is or is not an adequate connection.

11. I would accept that, but for his mental illness, Mr Malcolm would probably not have behaved so irresponsibly as to sublet his flat and moved elsewhere. He had, after all, worked in Lewisham's housing department for a time, and must have been well aware of the ground rules. But Lewisham's reason for seeking possession—that Mr Malcolm had sublet the flat and gone to live elsewhere—was a pure housing management decision which had nothing whatever to do with his mental disability. With some hesitation I would resolve this issue against Mr Malcolm.

(5) WITH THE TREATMENT OF WHAT COMPARATORS SHOULD THE TREATMENT OF MR MALCOLM BE COMPARED?…

13. The problem of identifying the correct comparator is one which Mummery LJ examined with care and in detail in *Clark v Novacold*. The problem can be re-stated on the facts of the present case, assuming (contrary to the conclusion I have expressed in answer to question (4) above) that Lewisham's treatment of Mr Malcolm was for a reason which related to Mr Malcolm's disability. Are 'the others' with whose treatment the treatment of Mr Malcolm is to be compared (a) persons without a mental disability who have sublet a Lewisham flat and gone to live elsewhere, or (b) tenants of Lewisham flats who have not sublet or gone to live elsewhere, or (c) some other comparator group, and if so what?

14. As I understand the judgment in *Clark v Novacold*, the correct comparison is said to be with group (b). But that, I think, is difficult to accept for the reason succinctly given by Toulson LJ:[215]

'the complainant is logically bound to be able to satisfy the requirement of showing that his treatment is less favourable than would be accorded to others to whom the reason for his treatment did not apply. For without the reason there would not be the treatment.'

---

215 In the Court of Appeal in the instant case: [2008] 2 WLR 369, para. 55.

The truth of that observation is vividly illustrated by the present case: if a tenant had not sublet and gone to live elsewhere Lewisham would not, in the absence of other grounds, have contemplated seeking possession (or, probably, been entitled to do so), and thus no question of discrimination could ever have arisen.

15. A more natural comparison, as it seems to me, is with group (a). On this analysis the comparison would fall to be made on the bases rejected in *Clark v Novacold*: with a person who had a dog but no disability or a diner who was a very untidy eater but had no disability-related reason for eating in that way. This, as I have said, seems to me a much more natural comparison, in no way inconsistent with the statutory language. In this case it would defeat Mr Malcolm's complaint of discrimination, since it is clear that Lewisham would have claimed possession against any non-disabled tenant who had sublet and gone to live elsewhere. The same result would be likely to follow in many cases, with the consequence that the reach of the statute would be reduced. That would make it attractive, if possible, to identify an intermediate comparator group (c) which would avoid absurdity and give fair effect to the statute. But I do not think that any such intermediate comparator group has been suggested, and none is identified by the statutory language. I find it hard to accept that *Novacold* was rightly decided. I am in any event satisfied that a different principle must be applied in the present context.

16. I would accordingly, not without misgiving, hold the correct comparison in this case (on the assumption indicated) to be with persons without a mental disability who have sublet a Lewisham flat and gone to live elsewhere. Mr Malcolm has not been treated less favourably than such persons. He has been treated in exactly the same way.

(6) IS IT RELEVANT WHETHER LEWISHAM KNEW OF MR MALCOLM'S DISABILITY?

17. It has been held that the alleged discriminator's knowledge of a complainant's disability is irrelevant (*London Borough of Hammersmith and Fulham v Farnsworth* [2000] IRLR 691, para 36), although some doubt about this conclusion has been expressed by the Employment Appeal Tribunal[216] and the Court of Appeal.[217]

18. Section 25(1) provides that a claim based on unlawful discrimination on grounds of disability may be made the subject of civil proceedings in the same way as any other claim in tort, damages being recoverable (section 25(2)) for injury to feelings in addition to other relevant heads of damage. This points, in my opinion, towards a requirement of knowledge. Otherwise, an actionable tort would arise on the following facts. A telephones restaurant B to book a table. He asks if he may bring a dog. B says that dogs are not allowed in its restaurant. A does not say, and B does not know, that A is blind. It seems to me contrary to principle to hold that on such facts B has committed an actionable tort sounding in damages. Like Toulson LJ in the Court of Appeal, para 161,

> 'I do not believe that Parliament would have intended to make a person liable in tort for disability discrimination if that person had no awareness or grounds for awareness at the relevant time that the complainant was suffering from a disability or that his disability might have any connection with the matters giving rise to the treatment said to constitute unlawful discrimination.'

Baroness Hale (dissenting)

70. Are the 'others', with whose treatment the treatment of the disabled person is to be compared, people to whom 'the reason which relates to his disability' does not apply, in other words, non-disabled people in the same situation as the disabled person? Or are they people to whom 'that reason' does not apply, in other words, people who have not supplied the employer, the provider or the landlord with the

---

216 Citing *Heinz v Kenrick* [2000] ICR 491, paras 44–48.
217 Citing *Manchester City Council v Romano (Disability Rights Commission intervening)* [2005] 1 WLR 2775, paras 121–123.

same reason for acting as they did? In our case, is the Council's treatment of Mr Malcolm to be compared with how they would treat a non-disabled person who had sub-let? Or is it to be compared with how they would treat some-one, whether or not disabled, who had not sub-let at all?

71. The leading case on this issue in the employment context is *Clark v Novacold Ltd* [1999] ICR 951. As Mummery LJ observed, at p 962, 'Linguistically section 5(1)(a) is ambiguous. The expression 'that reason' is, as a matter of ordinary language, capable of bearing either of the suggested meanings'. The Court of Appeal decided that it meant the latter. Prima facie, this may appear surprising. It does not fit with our normal assumptions about discrimination. In effect, as Toulson LJ pointed out in the Court of Appeal, it reduces the comparison test to one which will always be met. My noble and learned friend, Lord Neuberger of Abbotsbury, has rehearsed all the inconveniences of such an approach in this particular context.

72. On closer examination, however, the decision in *Clark v Novacold* makes sense. There is also good reason to conclude that it reflects the actual intention of Parliament. The object of the earlier race and sex discrimination legislation was to secure that like cases were treated alike regardless of race or sex. The treatment given to a woman was to be compared with the treatment given to a man whose circumstances were alike in every material respect except their sex. The treatment given to a black person was to be compared with the treatment given to a white person whose circumstances were alike in every material respect except their race. The DDA undoubtedly intended that a disabled person should be treated in the same way as a non-disabled person whose circumstances were alike in every other material respect. The formulation readily covers direct discrimination of that sort. If the employer, provider or landlord refuses a job, a haircut or a flat to a disabled person who is just as capable as anyone else of doing the job, sitting in the barber's chair, or paying the rent and observing the covenants in the tenancy agreement, simply because he is disabled, then 'that reason' is the disability itself and would not apply to other people.

73. But this might not be enough. The race and sex legislation recognise both direct discrimination of that sort, when race or sex or disability is the reason why the landlord behaves as he does, and indirect discrimination, where the landlord imposes some requirement which is ostensibly neutral but has a disproportionate effect on one sex, or one race, and which cannot be justified. The DDA undoubtedly aimed to cover this sort of discrimination too. An obvious example is a ban on dogs in restaurants, which has a disproportionate effect upon blind people who rely upon guide dogs to get about. The White Paper, *Ending discrimination against disabled people*, 1995, Cm 2729, which preceded the 1995 Act, made it clear in para 4.5 that the intention was to cover such cases.

74. One way of dealing with this would have been to provide for both direct and indirect discrimination in the same way that the race and sex discrimination legislation does. But this was not done. One reason may be that it would not have gone far enough. Restaurant owners may have very good reasons for a general rule banning dogs in their establishments. This would not have helped the blind person who had a very good reason for wanting them to make an exception in his case. The race and sex legislation could simply require that race and sex be ignored when employers and service providers made their decisions. The premise was the race and sex were irrelevant (save in some very narrowly defined circumstances). No special consideration was needed (save in some very narrowly defined circumstances) for a particular sex or a particular race. But if the object of the disability discrimination legislation is to 'level the playing field', to enable disabled people to do things that they otherwise would not be able to do, then simply ignoring their disability and asking that they be treated in exactly the same way as non-disabled people will not do. A reasonable adjustment has to be made for the special difficulties which their disabilities present.

75. The question in essence is whether the definition of discrimination in sections 5(1), 20(1) and 24(1) was intended to require employers and suppliers or goods, facilities, services and accommodation to be kinder to disabled people than they would be to others. It could be said that any duty to make reasonable adjustments to cater for the special needs of disabled people is covered, in the employment field by

section 6, and in the goods, facilities and services field by section 21. Section 21(1), for example, is apt to cover the guide dog example: it would require the restaurant owner to make an exception for the blind person with a guide dog, without requiring the restaurant owner to let everyone take dogs into his restaurant. Thus, it could be said, sections 5(1), 20(1) and 24(1) were designed only to ensure that disabled people were treated in the same way as non-disabled people in the same situation.

76. One problem with this construction in our context is that there is (or rather was at the material time) no express duty on landlords and others with the power to dispose of premises to make any adjustments to cater for disabled people. To take the narrower construction of section 24(1)(a) would mean that only direct discrimination against disabled people, or against people with a particular disability, would clearly be covered. Indirect discrimination might be included in the concept of treating someone 'less favourably' but it would not be clear how far that went. There would be no duty to give special consideration to the needs of disabled people.

77. The more serious problem with this construction is that Parliament could have chosen a form of words which made it entirely plain that it intended the comparison to be made with people who did not have the disability in question but Parliament deliberately chose a different formulation...

80. [Consideration of the Parliamentary debates]...confirms that the construction chosen by the Court of Appeal in *Clark v Novacold Ltd* was indeed the construction which Parliament intended. There is nothing to suggest that, when Parliament changed all three provisions at the same time, so that they had all the same wording, it was intended that they should have different meanings. The fact that they were all changed at the same time (and that one of them had previously been different from the other two) suggests that they were all intended to have the same meaning. The history also explains why there are three different provisions defining discrimination in exactly the same way. It may well be that Parliament had not understood that the narrow scope for justification in relation to services and premises would give rise to the problems we face in this case. But in the light of the Parliamentary history, I do not think that it is possible, either to hold that *Clark v Novacold Ltd* was wrongly decided or to distinguish it on the ground that the same words mean something different in the context of employment. They must mean the same throughout, however inconvenient the result may now appear to be.

81. In reaching this conclusion I believe that I am faithfully following the intention of Parliament. I am sorry to be disagreeing with your Lordships, but even more sorry that the settled understanding of employment lawyers and tribunals is to be disturbed as a result of your Lordships' disapproval of *Clark v Novacold*. That decision has stood unchallenged for nine years and has not, so far as we are aware, caused difficulty in practice. Furthermore, Parliament has since legislated on the basis that it is correct. The definition of discrimination for employment purposes is now contained in section 3A of the DDA (inserted by the 2003 Amendment Regulations). Section 3A(1) is in the same terms as the old section 5(1). A new section 3A(5) provides:

> 'A person directly discriminates against a disabled person if, on the ground of the disabled person's disability, he treats the disabled person less favourably than he treats or would treat a person not having that particular disability whose relevant circumstances, including his abilities, are the same as, or not materially different from, those of the disabled person.'

Direct discrimination of this sort cannot be justified. If the old section 5(1) (now section 3A(1)) had had the narrow scope which your Lordships' interpretation would give it, it is difficult to see why Parliament needed to introduce section 3A(5). It could simply have repealed the justification provision in section 5(1)(b).

'A REASON RELATED TO HIS DISABILITY'

82. I appreciate that, as Lord Neuberger explains, on your Lordships' interpretation of the comparison required by section 24(1), the closeness of the connection between the person's disability and the reason for the landlord's treatment of him becomes less critical. On my interpretation of the comparison,

it becomes more important. ... How close, therefore, does the connection have to be between the reason for the landlord's behaviour and the complainant's disability?

83. The focus is on the reason why the landlord acted as he did. In a direct discrimination case, the reason may be the disability itself. In other cases, the reason may not be the disability, but the disability may have been the cause of the reason. But that is not necessarily enough. The connection between the disability and the reason must not be too remote. It is not easy to lay down a simple test by which the judge that remoteness. The number of links in the chain may be a pointer.

84. Another pointer, it seems to me, is whether or not the landlord knew or ought to have known of the disability and of its connection with the reason for the landlord's decision. Again, in a direct discrimination case, this is obvious. The landlord has failed to let the flat to the disabled person because of the disability. The example given in Standing Committee E was a landlord who refused to let a flat to a disabled woman who was perfectly capable of looking after herself because he feared that in due course she might become a burden (*Official Report, Standing Committee E, Disability Discrimination Bill*, 28 February 1995, col 453).

85. In an indirect discrimination case, it may be less obvious. The landlord may not know that a particular policy has a disproportionate effect upon disabled people. When he decides on the policy, he is not treating any particular disabled person less favourably for a reason relating to his disability. But if he is told of the effect of that policy, and still applies it to the particular disabled person, then his reason may now be related to the disability in a way which it was not before. Thus, if the landlord has a 'no animals' policy, it may not have occurred to him that this will have a disproportionate effect on blind people with guide dogs. If he is simply asked whether a prospective tenant may keep a dog, his refusal has nothing to do with the disability. It has to do with his policy and the reasons for the policy. But if he is told that the prospective tenant is blind, the position alters. He has to think about it. His reason for acting may still be the policy and the reasons for the policy. This was, for example, the position in *Williams v Richmond Court (Swansea) Ltd* [2006] EWCA Civ 1719, where the landlord refused to allow a stair-lift to be installed for the benefit of (and at the expense of) a disabled tenant. There were several reasons why the claim had to fail, but among them was the fact that the landlord's reasons for not wanting a stair-lift had nothing to do with the disability.

86. I agree with Lord Bingham that to establish liability for the statutory tort of discrimination against a disabled person, it is necessary to show that the alleged discriminator either knew or ought to have known of the disability (not, of course, that in law it amounted to disability within the meaning of the Act). This not only accords with principle. It also accords with the language of the Act in two ways. First, the alleged discriminator is liable if he cannot show that the treatment in question is justified: section 24(1)(b). Justification depends upon his having formed an opinion that one of the specified justifications exists: section 24(2). He could not do that without knowing of the disability. Secondly, although the DDA does not adopt the language of the sex and race discrimination legislation, which talks of less favourable treatment 'on grounds of' race or sex, it does require a relationship between the treatment and the disability. This suggests that the person doing the treating must have at least the means of knowing about that relationship...

NOTES

1. Baroness Hale went on to decide that, neither the council's decision to serve the notice to quit nor the bringing of the possession proceedings were 'for a reason related to' Mr Malcolm's disability. Neither the fact of his illness nor the potential link between it and his behaviour appeared to have been 'present to their minds' when the decision to issue the notice was taken and, although the council did know of Mr Malcolm's illness at the time it brought possession proceedings, the judge had in her view been entitled to find as she did that (para. 93) 'the reason for the treatment, that is the subletting, was not causally related to the illness' but was a rational decision to 'enable him to service the mortgage and get some return on the

property while he was out of work'. Had Baroness Hale concluded otherwise, however, she would have ruled that 'comparison has to be made with people who had not sublet' and that Mr Malcolm had been treated less favourably than such comparators:

This does place a huge focus on the reason for the treatment and the closeness of the connection between that reason and the treatment. But it appears that that was the result which Parliament intended.[218]

2. Which approach do you prefer? Do you agree with Lord Scott that if a blind man who relies upon a guide dog refused entry to a restaurant which does not accept dogs 'The reason for the treatment would not have related to the blindness; it would have related to the dog'?[219]

3. The significance of the *Malcolm* decision cannot be over-stated. The approach of the House of Lords there overturns a decade of case law on the scope of 'disability-related discrimination', and cuts a swathe through the various codes of practice on disability discrimination. The concept would appear now to apply only to cases where less favourable treatment occurs because of generalised or stereotypical assumptions about disability or its effects, such as where (to use the examples of *direct* disability discrimination provided by the DRC's Code of Practice) a blind woman is not shortlisted for a job involving computers because the employer wrongly assumes that blind people cannot use them; a severely disfigured man is denied a job as a shop assistant because the employer is concerned that other employees would be uncomfortable working alongside him; or a job description that anyone with a history of mental illness would not be suitable for the post.

4. The underlying reason for the decision of the majority in *Malcolm* was the narrowness of the statutory justifications for disability-related discrimination in the context of premises.[220] Whereas, in the employment context (in which the vast bulk of litigation arises), disability-related discrimination 'is justified ... if, but only if, the reason for it is both material to the circumstances of the particular case and substantial' (s. 3A(3) DDA), a test which is notoriously easy to satisfy,[221] such discrimination is justified in the context of premises (also the provision of goods and services) only if it falls within one of a closed list of reasons (see section 12(C) below). It may well be the case that there was an oversight on the part of the legislature and that the application of the broad approach in the context of premises, without amendment of the justification defence, would lead to injustice. But it is a matter of real concern that the House of Lords, instead of following the *Clark v Novacold* approach and inviting Parliament to amend the relevant statutory justification defence, took a sledgehammer to the legislative prohibition of a form of discrimination which had been deliberately crafted in wide terms and which had operated without apparent injustice for a decade. The only saving grace is that failure to comply with the duties of reasonable adjustment themselves give rise to acts of unlawful discrimination irrespective of any disability-related discrimination. The duties of reasonable adjustment are considered immediately below.

5. In November 2008 the consultation paper *Improving Protection From Disability*.[222]

---

218 Para. 96. Note that in some contexts (leaving aside employment, ss. 28B, 28S, 31AD) the DDA makes a lack of knowledge expressly relevant to the duty to adjust.

219 Para. 35.

220 See, e.g, the speech of Lord Neuberger at para. 140.

221 See *Post Office v Jones* [2001] ICR 805, CA, discussed at p. 988 below.

222 Available from www.officefordisability.gov.uk/docs/indirect-discrimination.pdf, accessed 17 December 2008, proposed that indirect disability discrimination be regulated, this in response to the *Malcolm* decision.

(B) THE DDA'S DUTIES TO MAKE REASONABLE ADJUSTMENTS

20 Meaning of 'discrimination'

(2) For the purposes of section 19 [provision of goods and services], a provider of services...discriminates against a disabled person if—

   (a) he fails to comply with a section 21 duty imposed on him in relation to the disabled person; and

   (b) he cannot show that his failure to comply with that duty is justified...

21D Meaning of 'discrimination' in section 21B

(2) For the purposes of section 21B(1) [discrimination by public authorities], a public authority...discriminates against a disabled person if—

   (a) it fails to comply with a duty imposed on it by section 21E in circumstances in which the effect of that failure is to make it—

   (i) impossible or unreasonably difficult for the disabled person to receive any benefit that is or may be conferred, or

   (ii) unreasonably adverse for the disabled person to experience being subjected to any detriment to which a person is or may be subjected,

   by the carrying-out of a function by the authority; and

   (b) it cannot show that its failure to comply with that duty is justified under subsection (3), (5) or (7)(c)...

28B Meaning of 'discrimination'

(2) For the purposes of section 28A [primary and secondary education], a responsible body...discriminates against a disabled person if—

   (a) it fails, to his detriment, to comply with section 28C; and

   (b) it cannot show that its failure to comply is justified.

(3) In relation to a failure to take a particular step, a responsible body does not discriminate against a person if it shows—

   (a) that, at the time in question, it did not know and could not reasonably have been expected to know, that he was disabled; and

   (b) that its failure to take the step was attributable to that lack of knowledge.

(4) The taking of a particular step by a responsible body in relation to a person does not amount to less favourable treatment if it shows that at the time in question it did not know, and could not reasonably have been expected to know, that he was disabled.

(5) Subsections (6) to (8) apply in determining whether, for the purposes of this section—

   (a) less favourable treatment of a person, or

   (b) failure to comply with section 28C,

   is justified.

28S Meaning of 'discrimination'

(2) For the purposes of this Chapter [third level education], a responsible body...discriminates against a disabled person if it fails to comply with a duty imposed on it by section 28T or 28UA(5) in relation to the disabled person.

(3) In relation to a failure to take a particular step, a responsible body does not discriminate against a person if it shows—

(a) that, at the time in question, it did not know and could not reasonably have been expected to know, that he was disabled; and

(b) that its failure to take the step was attributable to that lack of knowledge.[223]

NOTES

1. The DDA does not expressly prohibit indirect discrimination. Its perceived failure to regulate this type of discrimination formed one of the most significant grounds for criticism of the Act, though until the decision of the House of Lords in *Malcolm* the breadth of 'disability-related discrimination', coupled with the duties of reasonable adjustment it imposes, went a long way towards regulating what would otherwise be dealt with as indirect discrimination. In the aftermath of *Malcolm*'s gutting of the concept of disability-related discrimination the duties of reasonable adjustment have to carry the burden alone.

2. Sections 3A and 31AB DDA (which deal, respectively, with discrimination by employers and general qualifying bodies) are in similar terms to s. 28S DDA in that a failure to make a reasonable adjustment cannot be justified. Sections 21G, 24 and 28B (which apply respectively to discrimination in relation to private members' clubs and in relation to premises and primary and secondary education) all allow the justification of failures to make reasonable adjustment.[224] The question of justification, which applies also to disability-related discrimination, is considered at section 12 (G) below.

3. The nature of the duties to make reasonable adjustment varies across the scope of the DDA. They are too lengthy to set out here. Briefly, duties are imposed in the context of the supply of services (s. 21 DDA) where 'a practice, policy or procedure' or 'a physical feature (for example, one arising from the design or construction of a building or the approach or access to premises)' 'makes it impossible or unreasonably difficult for disabled persons to make use of a service'. The supplier of services must 'take such steps as it is reasonable, in all the circumstances of the case, for him to have to take in order to', in the first case, 'change that practice, policy or procedure so that it no longer has that effect' or in the second '(a) remove the feature; (b) alter it so that it no longer has that effect; (c) provide a reasonable means of avoiding the feature; or (d) provide a reasonable alternative method of making the service in question available to disabled persons'.[225] Further (s. 21(4) DDA) where an auxiliary aid or service, such as the provision of an interpreter, would '(a) enable disabled persons to make use of a service which a provider of services provides, or is prepared to provide, to members of the public, or (b) facilitate the use by disabled persons of such a service, it is the duty of the provider of that service to take such steps as it is reasonable, in all the circumstances of the case, for him to have to take in order to provide that auxiliary aid or service.' It should be noted (s. 20(6) DDA), that 'Nothing in this section requires a provider of services to take any steps which would fundamentally alter the nature of the service in question or the nature of his trade, profession or business.'

A duty is imposed upon public authorities (s. 21E) where 'a practice, policy or procedure' of the authority or 'a physical feature' 'makes it (a) impossible or unreasonably difficult

---

[223] S. 28B(3) is in similar terms.

[224] For provisions relating to private members clubs see also the Disability Discrimination (Private Clubs etc) Regulations 2005, SI 2005/3258.

[225] See ss. 3A(2), 4A and 18B DDA on the duty of reasonable adjustment in the employment sphere.

for disabled persons to receive any benefit that is or may be conferred, or (b) unreasonably adverse for disabled persons to experience being subjected to any detriment to which a person is or may be subjected, by the carrying-out of a function by the authority'. The duty in either case is similar to that on suppliers of services.

The duties which apply in relation to the disposal etc. of premises are complex and apply predominantly in relation to let premises, ss. 24C and 24D imposing duties on controllers of let premises to provide auxiliary aids or services and to change practices etc. that severely disadvantage disabled tenants and s. 24J applying in relation to prospective tenants.[226]

Duties are imposed on schools in cases in which (s. 28C) pupils or prospective pupils would otherwise be 'placed at a substantial disadvantage in comparison with persons who are not disabled', but schools are not obliged to 'remove or alter a physical feature' or to 'provide auxiliary aids or services'. And providers of third-level education are placed under duties of reasonable adjustment (s. 28T(1)) in relation to any 'provision, criterion or practice' or 'competence standard' applied by them or on their behalf 'place disabled persons at a substantial disadvantage in comparison with persons who are not disabled'.[227] See also the Disability Discrimination (Private Clubs etc) Regulations 2005 on the duties applicable to private clubs.[228]

(c) JUSTIFICATION UNDER THE DDA

20 Meaning of 'discrimination'

(3) For the purposes of this section, treatment is justified only if—

    (a) in the opinion of the provider of services, one or more of the conditions mentioned in subsection (4) are satisfied; and

    (b) it is reasonable, in all the circumstances of the case, for him to hold that opinion.

(4) The conditions are that—

    (a) in any case, the treatment is necessary in order not to endanger the health or safety of any person (which may include that of the disabled person);

    (b) in any case, the disabled person is incapable of entering into an enforceable agreement, or of giving an informed consent, and for that reason the treatment is reasonable in that case;

    (c) in a case falling within section 19(1)(a), the treatment is necessary because the provider of services would otherwise be unable to provide the service to members of the public;

    (d) in a case falling within section 19(1)(c) or (d), the treatment is necessary in order for the provider of services to be able to provide the service to the disabled person or to other members of the public;

    (e) in a case falling within section 19(1)(d), the difference in the terms on which the service is provided to the disabled person and those on which it is provided to other members of the public reflects the greater cost to the provider of services in providing the service to the disabled person.

---

[226] See the DRC's Code of Practice 'Rights of Access: services to the public, public authority functions, private clubs and premises', available from the EHRC website, n. 34 above.

[227] See also ss. 31AD (qualifications bodies), and 21H (private clubs).

[228] SI 2005/3258.

(5) Any increase in the cost of providing a service to a disabled person which results from compliance by a provider of services with a section 21 duty shall be disregarded for the purposes of subsection (4)(e)...[229]

28B DDA [schools]

(6) Less favourable treatment of a person is justified if it is the result of a permitted form of selection.

(7) Otherwise, less favourable treatment, or a failure to comply with section 28C, is justified only if the reason for it is both material to the circumstances of the particular case and substantial.

(8) If, in a case falling within subsection (1)—

(a) the responsible body is under a duty imposed by section 28C in relation to the disabled person, but

(b) it fails without justification to comply with that duty,

its treatment of that person cannot be justified under subsection (7) unless that treatment would have been justified even if it had complied with that duty.

28S DDA [third level education providers]

(5) Treatment, other than the application of a competence standard, is (subject to subsections (7) to (9)), justified for the purposes of subsection (1)(b) if, but only if, the reason for it is both material to the circumstances of the particular case and substantial.[230]

(6) The application by a responsible body of a competence standard to a disabled person is (subject to subsections (8) and (9)) justified for the purposes of subsection (1)(b) if, but only if, the body can show that—

(a) the standard is, or would be, applied equally to persons who do not have his particular disability, and

(b) its application is a proportionate means of achieving a legitimate aim.

(7) If in a case falling within subsection (1), other than a case where the treatment is the application of a competence standard, a responsible body is under a duty under section 28T or 28UA(5) in relation to the disabled person, but fails to comply with that duty, its treatment of that person cannot be justified under subsection (5) unless that treatment would have been justified even if it had complied with that duty.

(9) Treatment of a disabled person by a responsible body cannot be justified under subsection (5), (6) or (8) if it amounts to direct discrimination falling within subsection (10).

NOTES

1. Section 21D DDA is in similar terms to s. 20 as regards justification save that it provides a special justification in relation to 'treatment, or non-compliance with the duty [of reasonable adjustment, which], is necessary for the protection of rights and freedoms of other persons' or 'if the acts of the public authority which give rise to the treatment or failure

---

229 See s. 21ZA for special provisions applicable to transport services. See also the Disability Discrimination (Service Providers and Public Authorities Carrying Out Functions) Regulations 2005, SI 2005/2901 and the Disability Discrimination (Premises) Regulations 2006, SI 2006/887.

230 A 'competence standard' is (s. 28S DDA), 'an academic, medical or other standard applied by or on behalf of a responsible body for the purpose of determining whether or not a person has a particular level of competence or ability'.

are a proportionate means of achieving a legitimate aim'.[231] Section 21G, which applies to discrimination by private clubs, provides similar conditions of justification to s. 20 as does s. 24 (premises) while s. 31AB (general qualifications bodies) is in similar terms to ss. 28B and 28G.

2. A 'permitted form of selection' is, in relation to England and Wales, selection permitted under the School Standards and Framework Act 1998, s. 99(2) or (4), in the case of grammar schools, in the case of maintained schools 'any of its selective admission arrangements' and in the case of independent schools, 'any arrangements which make provision for any or all of its pupils to be selected by reference to general or special ability or aptitude, with a view to admitting only pupils of high ability or aptitude' (s. 28Q DDA).

3. The 'material and substantial' test for justification is the subject of appellate authority in the employment context. *Jones v Post Office* involved a claimant who had been removed from driving duties after he became insulin dependent as a result of diabetes. A tribunal took the view that the discrimination, which was conceded by the employer, was unjustified, this on the grounds that a correct appraisal of the claimant's medical condition would have led the Post Office to conclude that he was fit to continue driving duties. EAT overruled on the grounds that the employers were entitled to prefer their medical evidence to that put forward by the claimant. The employee's appeal was dismissed, the Court of Appeal ruling that the tribunal was not entitled to find against the employer on the justification issue on the basis that the medical evidence relied upon was incorrect.[232] The court ruled that s. 5(3) DDA, which is materially identical to ss. 28B(7) and 28S(5) above, confined tribunals to investigating facts and assessing the employer's decision by determining whether there was evidence on the basis of which a decision could properly be taken. So, for example, if the employer had not carried out any risk assessment, or had made a decision other than on the basis of appropriate medical evidence, or had acted irrationally, the tribunal could find the treatment unjustified. But (per Pill LJ) 'a properly conducted risk assessment provides a reason which is on its face both material and substantial, and is not irrational, the tribunal cannot substitute its own appraisal' and could not 'conclude that the reason is not material or substantial because the suitably qualified and competently expressed medical opinion, on the basis of which the employer's decision was made, was thought by them to be inferior to a different medical opinion expressed to them'. This approach has been much criticised,[233] but remains good law. It is important to note, however (a) that an educator cannot justify less favourable treatment unless, in a case in which a duty to adjust applied, the less favourable treatment would have been justified even if the educator had complied with the duty;[234] and (b) that a failure to make reasonable adjustments cannot be justified by reference to factors which had already been taken into account in deciding whether an adjustment was reasonable.[235]

13. MISCELLANEOUS CRIMINAL PROVISIONS

There are a number of criminal law provisions that are relevant to discrimination. They will only be listed and very briefly discussed here due to constraints of space. Briefly, they consist of:

---

[231] S. 21D(4)(d) and (5).   [232] [2001] IRLR 384.

[233] See, e.g., J. Davies, 'A Cuckoo in the Nest? A "Range of Reasonable Responses", Justification and the Disability Discrimination Act 1995' (2003) 32 Industrial Law Journal 164, 178–181.

[234] See, e.g., *Paul v National Probation Service* [2004] IRLR 190.

[235] *Collins v Royal National Theatre Board Ltd* [2004] IRLR 395.

- The Public Order Act 1986,[236] which criminalises the use of 'threatening, abusive or insulting words or behaviour', the display, publication or distribution of 'written material which is threatening, abusive or insulting', the public performance of a play which involves the use of threatening, abusive or insulting words or behaviour, the distribution, showing or playing of a recording of visual images or sounds that are threatening, abusive or insulting, and the broadcasting of programmes involving threatening, abusive or insulting visual images or sounds, in each case where the activity is intended or likely to stir up racial hatred.[237] The Act also criminalises the possession of written material which is threatening, abusive or insulting, or a recording of visual images or sounds which are threatening, abusive or insulting, where possession is with a view to its display, distribution etc. and with the requisite intent or likelihood regarding the stirring up of racial hatred.[238] Prosecutions may only be brought 'by or with the consent of' the Attorney-General. The Act was amended by the Racial and Religious Hatred Act 2006 to make similar provision in relation to the stirring up of religious hatred, an amendment that proved extremely controversial on free speech grounds. And in 2008 the provisions were extended by the Criminal Justice and Immigration Act 2008 to sexual orientation.[239] Sections 29J and 29JA provide, respectively, that:

  - 'Nothing in this Part shall be read or given effect in a way which prohibits or restricts discussion, criticism or expressions of antipathy, dislike, ridicule, insult or abuse of particular religions or the beliefs or practices of their adherents, or of any other belief system or the beliefs or practices of its adherents, or proselytising or urging adherents of a different religion or belief system to cease practising their religion or belief system' and

  - 'In this Part, for the avoidance of doubt, the discussion or criticism of sexual conduct or practices or the urging of persons to refrain from or modify such conduct or practices shall not be taken of itself to be threatening or intended to stir up hatred.'

- The Football (Offences) Act 1991 makes it an offence (s. 3) 'to engage or take part in chanting of an indecent or racialist nature at a designated football match', 'of a racialist nature' being defined to mean 'consisting of or including matter which is threatening, abusive or insulting to a person by reason of his colour, race, nationality (including citizenship) or ethnic or national origins'. This offence is punishable by a fine.

- The Crime and Disorder Act 1998 provides for greater penalties for offences which are racially or religiously aggravated, that is (s. 28), are motivated by, or involve the demonstration at the time or immediately before or after the offence, by the offender, of, 'hostility based on the victim's membership (or presumed membership) of a racial or religious group. The offences to which racial and religious aggravation apply are assaults (s. 29), criminal damage (s. 30), public order offences (s. 31) and harassment (s. 32). In addition, the Criminal Justice Act 2003 provides (ss. 145 and 146) for racial or religious

---

[236] For a history of the racial hatred provisions, on the earlier law and incitement to racial hatred generally, see G. Bindman (1982) 132 NLJ 299: id., in S. Coliver (ed.), *Striking a Balance: Hate Speech, Freedom of Expression and Non-discrimination* (1992), Chap. 28; R. Cotterrell [1982] PL 278; A. Dickey [1968] Crim LR 489; Gordon, *Incitement to Racial Hatred* (Runnymede Trust, 1982); Khan (1978) 122 Sol Jo 256; P. Leopold [1977] PL 389; D.G.T. Williams [1966] Crim LR 320; *Review of the Public Order Act 1936 and Related Legislation* (Cmnd 7891), pp. 29–31. On the 1986 Act, see W.J. Wolffe [1987] PL 85.

[237] Ss. 18–22. 'Racial hatred' is defined by s. 17 of the Act.

[238] S. 23.

[239] Ss. 28A and 28AB defining the terms 'religious hatred' and 'hatred on grounds of sexual orientation' respectively and ss. 28B–G establishing the material scope of the offences.

aggravation to increase sentences for offences other than those covered the 1998 Act, and for increased sentences for offences motivated by, or involving the demonstration at the time or immediately before or after the offence, by the offender, of, hostility based on the victim's actual or presumed sexual orientation or disability.

- **Liberty's Second Reading Briefing on the Criminal Justice and Immigration Bill in the House of Lords,** January 2008

36. The new offence of Hatred on the Grounds of Sexual Orientation…was introduced during committee stage on the bill in the House of Commons. During Second Reading debate on the Bill in the House of Commons on 8 October the Lord Chancellor Jack Straw said, *'We will propose a further step to strengthen the protection afforded to homosexual people. It is a measure of how far we have come as a society in the last 10 years that we are all now appalled by hatred and invective directed against gay people, and it is now time for the law to recognise the feeling of the public. In Committee, we will table an amendment to extend the offence of incitement to racial hatred to cover hatred against persons on the basis of their sexuality.'*

37. The offence is the third criminal offence of incitement to hatred. The offence of inciting or stirring up racial hatred has been progressively expanded since first introduced in1965… In 2006 the Racial and Religious Hatred Act amended the POA so that incitement to religious hatred was also a criminal offence. It is worth noting that incitement to commit any act that is in itself a criminal offence has been an offence at common law for two hundred years. The reason why incitement to hatred needs to be catered for through the creation of specific offences is that it is not a crime to hate someone.

38. In 2006 Liberty opposed the extension of race incitement to include religion. We stated that the main justification put forward for extension, that certain groups such as Muslims were not covered by race hate incitement, did not necessitate extension. We argued that speech used by the BNP, for example, used religion as a proxy for race. As a consequence we saw no reason why religiously expressed but racially motivated speech would not be covered by the existing offence. Liberty has also opposed the offence of 'encouragement of terrorism' created in the Terrorism Act 2006. We stated that it was overbroad in that it made a crime of careless speech, that it was unnecessary, that it would have little impact, and that it would be divisive through being seen as an attack on Muslim communities.

39. Liberty has also commented on the likely efficacy of speech offences. We have expressed concerns that, rather than reduce the incidence of hate speech, the offence of incitement to racial and religious hatred might be used for publicity purposes. We drew attention to comments on the BNP website relating to the trial of two members of the BNP for incitement to racial hatred that *'The party will be able to reap the maximum benefits from the huge publicity that the trial will attract'.*

40. Prosecutions for speech offences based on incitement are rare. During debate in the House of Lords on the Racial and Religious Hatred Bill the Home Office Minister Lord Bassam stated that between 1987 & 2005 there were just 76 prosecutions—about 4 a year. Since the offence of Encouragement of Terrorism came into force there has been a single prosecution. Offences involving speech are far more frequently based around other offences under the POA. In particular under s.5 POA a person is guilty of an offence if he uses threatening, abusive or insulting words or behaviour, or disorderly behaviour.

41. Arguably the greater impact from the creation of new speech offences derives from a 'chilling effect'. People are aware that certain types of speech are criminalised and refrain from expressing opinions as a consequence. This was a particular concern raised by Liberty over the offence 'encouragement of terrorism'. We said the opinions expressed by young British Muslims, angry over British foreign policy and believing that the West was at war with Islam, could easily fall into the broad definition of the offence.

42. Liberty's approach to the proposed creation of any new offence is to turn to the proportionality model contained in the human rights framework. If the right to free expression is to be limited we ask whether there the restriction serves a legitimate purpose. If it does serve such a purpose is the restriction necessary? We appreciate that Stonewall, who have lobbied the government to introduce the offence, believe new protections are necessary. However we are also concerned that piecemeal creation of speech offences can prove counterproductive in that they could be interpreted as creating a hierarchy of protections. Those groups not the subject of new hate incitement offences could feel that they are deemed less worthy of 'protection'. The Government has, for example, stated that it does not feel it necessary to introduce similar offences relating to transgendered people or the disabled. We are not sure what the rationale is for introducing one incitement offence but not another.

43. We are also concerned that the hate incitement offences have a disproportionate impact upon other minority groups. As stated earlier the offence of encouragement of terrorism is likely to affect the angry young Muslim rather than, for example Cherie Blair (who once stated that she could appreciate why young Palestinians became suicide bombers). Similarly, there may well be pressure to target the offence of incitement to homophobic at black 'dancehall' artists who have sometimes been criticised for the content of their lyrics

44. Incitement to hatred criminalises an incitement to do something that is not itself criminal. We are concerned that once the new offence is in place there it will be logically difficult to resist further extensions to cover other forms of hate incitement. Liberty believes that that rather than adopt a piecemeal approach, with new offences introduced as a consequence of who is lobbing hardest for them, there should a review of the efficacy and impact of the offences in existence. This would allow an opportunity to consider how effective the existing criminal law is, and whether extensions can be justified.

45. Free expression is not an absolute. Appropriate limitations are of course legitimate in a democratic society. We are not calling for the repeal of any existing law. All we propose is that an overarching review of speech offences is now appropriate. We have often criticised the government's tendency to over legislate and create new offences when unnecessary. Since 1997 over 3000 new offences have been added to the statute book. The expression of a view or opinion, however unpleasant, does not necessarily justify the creation of yet further criminal law.

NOTE

1. Do you agree? Is there any difference between the offences discussed in the Liberty note and the use of racist or other motivation as an aggravating feature for sentencing purposes? Should sexual violence against women be classified as a 'hate crime'?

INDEX

Abuse of rights
  prohibition against 30
Access
  entry powers of police, and 173
Access to information
  national information
    criticisms 854–55
    enforcement 852–53
    exemptions 850–52
    generally 849–50
    historical records 853–54
Accountability
  police
    auditing 97–100
    generally 88–90
    internal monitoring
      107–14
    judicial scrutiny 100–06
Admissibility
  confessions
    agent provocateurs 271–74
    common law 257
    entrapment 271–74
    mentally handicapped
      persons 255–56
    PACE s.78, 257–58
    physical evidence 257
    police deception 269–74
    statutory provisions
      254–55
    vulnerable suspects
      262–63
Advertisements
  discrimination 918
  freedom of expression
    generally 642
    political advertising
      645–47
Affray
  public order offences 331,
    336–37
Age discrimination
  protection against 937
Agent provocateurs
  admissibility of
    confessions 271–74
Animal rights extremism
  public order 367–68
Anti-social behaviour orders
  public order 368–70
Anti-terrorism
  Anti-Terrorism, Crime and
    Security Act 2001

deportation 472–74
derogation from Convention
  obligations 455–56,
  471–72
discrimination 465–68
facilitation of human rights
  breaches abroad 474–75
information derived from
  torture 474
proportionality 459–65
public emergency 457–59
scope of powers 455
Counter-terrorism Bill
  2007–08, 492–94
  introduction 407–08
political terrorism
  counter-terrorism
    strategy 410–11
  detention without
    trial 411–12
  meaning 408
  Northern Ireland 410
Prevention of Terrorism Act
  2005
  control orders 475–78,
    481–85
  deprivation of
    liberty 478–80
  obligations imposed on con-
    trolled persons 480–81
Terrorism Act 2000
  collection of informa-
    tion 448–49, 450–52
  counter-terrorist
    powers 431–48
  directing terrorist organisa-
    tions 448, 450
  historical origins 414–15
  inciting terrorism over-
    seas 449, 452–53
  introduction 413–14
  penalties 450
  police powers 453–55
  possession for terrorist pur-
    poses 448, 450–52
  proscribed
    organisations 417–26
  statistics and
    monitoring 416
  terrorism, meaning
    of 416–17
  terrorist bombing 449–50
  terrorist financing 450

terrorist
  investigations 426–31
Terrorism Act 2006
  dissemination of terrorist
    publications 486–87,
    489–90
  encouragement of terror-
    ism 486, 488–89
  preparation for terror-
    ism 487–88, 491
  streamlining
    legislation 485–86
  use of force 494–502
Appeals
  contempt of court 693–94
Arrest
  arrest outwith police
    station 198–99
  breach of the peace 395
  disposition after , 208
  entry, search and seizure
    powers of police
    after arrest 178–79
    effecting 177–78
  explaining grounds
    for 205–08
  further offences 200
  government recommendations
    in 2004, 201
  information given on 198
  official secrets 777
  search on 200–01, 208–09
  statistics 209
  validity 202–05
  voluntary attendance at police
    station 198
  without warrant
    counter-terrorism
      powers 431–32, 434–37
    generally 197–98
Art
  data protection 608
Assault
  police officers, on
    meaning 119–20
    scope of offence 127
Assembly, freedom of
  breach of the peace 380–81
  ECHR provisions 30
  public meetings and
    processions 322–25
  public order offences
    clothing 288–89

Assembly, freedom of (*cont.*)
ECHR 287
policing events 287–88
quasi-military
organisations 290–91
scope of protection 86
Association, freedom of
breach of the peace 380–81
ECHR provisions 30
public meetings and
processions 322–25
scope of protection 86
Attempts
official secrets 770
Audits
police accountability 97–100

Banning orders
public meetings and
processions
power to ban 314–18
trespass 312–13, 319–20
Binding over
public order 397–401
Blocking
data protection 607–08
Body samples
detention by police 238–39
Border controls
counter-terrorism powers 434
Breach of confidence
national security
introduction 803
Spycatcher litigation
804–22
privacy, protection of
compensation 561–63
generally 539–41
obligation of
confidence 542–61
quality of
confidence 541–42
Breach of contract
privacy, protection of 568
Breach of copyright
privacy, protection of 538–39
Breach of the peace
arrest for 395
freedom of assembly 380–81
freedom of expression
380–81
power to prevent future
breaches 376–95
Broadcasting
freedom of expression
advertising 642
child internet safety
649–52

generally 638–39
impartiality 641–42
internet
broadcasting 647–49
licences services 642–43
OFCOM, function of 639
OFCOM standards
code 639–41, 643–45
political advertising 645–47
sponsorship 642
Business premises
searches
privacy, right to 504–07

Cautions
detention by police 245–46
CCTV surveillance
privacy, right to 507–10
Charities
discrimination 926–27
Chief Constable of Police
role of 93–4
Chief of Intelligence Services
role of 834
Children
freedom of expression
indecency 678–79
internet safety 649–52
Civil liberties
human rights, development
of 3–5
introduction 1
liberty and right, distinction
between 9–10
meaning 1–3
protection of
Human Rights Act 1998,
16–65
pre-Human Rights
Act 11–16
UK Bill of Rights 65–98
Civil servants
national security
unauthorised
disclosures 794–95
Co-accused
admissibility of
confessions 255–62
Codes of practice
police powers
admissibility of
confessions 262
generally 154
detention 225
Cohabitation
homosexual couples
discrimination 43–51
Common law

admissibility of
confessions 257
contempt of court
mens rea 717
publication
prejudicial to civil
proceedings 720–34
publication prejudicial to
criminal trial 695–98
sub judice rule 715–16
public meetings and
processions 320–22
Comparators
discrimination 955–59
Compatibility
deference to Parliament 56–8
determination of 36
effect of declarations 63–5
homosexuality 43–51
incompatibility, declarations
of 37
margin of appreciation 57–8
parliamentary statements
of 27, 41–42
prison cell searches 59–63
self-incrimination 51–56
Compensation
data protection 607
Complaints
police officers, against 108–13
security and intelligence
services 840, 844
Confessions
admissibility
agent provocateurs 271–74
common law 257
entrapment 271–74
mentally handicapped
persons 255–56
PACE s.78, 257–58
physical evidence 257
police deception 269–74
statutory
provisions 254–55
vulnerable
suspects 262–63
breach of code of practice 262
co-accused 255, 262
exclusion of
grounds for 258–61
oppression 258–61
principles 256–57
unfair or illegal
evidence 263–68
unreliability 261–62
interpretation 256
Confidentiality
jury deliberations 689–90

Contempt of court
common law
mens rea 717
publication
prejudicial to civil
proceedings 720–34
publication prejudicial to
criminal trial 695–98
sub judice rule 715–16
contempt in face of court
introduction 745–46
journalistic sources,
protection of 754–61
scope of 746–54
Contempt of Court Act 1981
appellate
proceedings 693–94
confidentiality of jury's
deliberations 689–90
criminal
proceedings 692–93
information sources 690
introduction 687–88
magistrates' courts 690–91
penalties 691
publication of
matters exempted from
disclosure 690
strict liability 688–89
tape recorders, use of 690
interference with course of
justice 761–62
introduction 684–87
jurisdiction 762–63
mens rea
common law 717
intended contempt 718–20
strict liability rule 720
publications interfering with
course of justice
jury secrets 744–45
scandalising the
court 737–44
publications prejudicial to civil
proceedings
common law 720–34
strict liability rule
734–37
publications prejudicial to
criminal trial
common law 695–98
introduction 694–95
prohibition, powers
of 707–10
protection of inferior
courts 705–06
quashing
convictions 713–14

reporting restriction,
statutory 710–13
sitting in camera 706–07
strict liability rule 698–05
US position 714–15
strict liability
Contempt of Court
Act 688–89
mens rea 720
publication
prejudicial to civil
proceedings 734–37
publication prejudicial to
criminal trial 698–705
sub judice rule 716–17
sub judice rule
common law 715–16
publications intended to
interfere with justice 716
strict liability rule 716–17
Control orders
prevention of terrorism
generally 475–78, 481–85
obligations imposed
480–81
Convention rights
abuse of rights 30
assembly and association,
freedom of 30
compatibility, statements of 27
Crown right to
intervene 20–21
death penalties 31
derogations 25–6
discrimination
application of 857–59
establishing
discrimination 861–66
excusing sex
discrimination 878–82
introduction 856–57
justification of differential
treatment 872–78
proof of
discrimination 866–72
protected grounds 859–61
text of provision 30
education, right to 31
elections, right to free 31
expression, freedom of
ECHR provisions 25, 30
interference by public
authority 617–22
introduction 612–14
official secrets 622–29
prescribed by law 614–17
fair trial, right to 29
family life 29

forced labour, prohibition
of 28
incompatibility 20
liberty, right to 28
life, right to 27
marriage 30
political activity of aliens 30
privacy 29
property, protection of 31
public authorities
acts of 21
judicial acts 23–4
judicial remedies 23
proceedings involving
21–2
punishment without law
29
religious beliefs 25, 29–30
remedial action 24
remedial orders 31–2
reservations 26–7
restriction of 31
safeguarding existing human
rights 24
security, right to 28
slavery, prohibition of 28
thought, conscience and
religion, freedom of 25, 29–30
torture, prohibition of 27
Counter-terrorism
see also **Anti-terrorism**
2007–08 Bill 492–94
political terrorism 410–11
Terrorism Act 2000 powers
arrest without war-
rant 431–32, 434–37
authorisations 432–33
detention 434–40
duration of
authorisation 434
exercise of power 433
offences 434
parking 434
port and border
controls 434
search of persons 432
search of premises 432
stop and search
powers 440–48
terrorist, meaning of
431
travel controls 440
Covert surveillance
Police Act 1997, 578–80
Regulation of Investigatory
Powers Act 2000
acquisition of data 586–87
disclosure of data 586–87

Covert surveillance (*cont.*)
    exclusion of matters from
        legal proceedings 586
    Interception of
        Communications
        Commissioner 590–91
    interception, meaning
        of 582
    lawful interception without
        warrant 582–83
    metering 589–90
    notices requiring
        disclosure 596–98
    notices requiring disclosure,
        effect of 598–600
    policing
        techniques 591–96
    power to provide for lawful
        interception 583
    unlawful
        interception 580–82
    warrants for interception
        583–86, 588–89
Criminal proceedings
    contempt of court
        generally 692–93
    publication prejudicial
        to 695–98
Crown
    intervention in Convention
        rights 20–21
Crown servants
    official secrets 778
Custody officers
    detention by police
        duties after charge 214–15
        generally 210–13, 226
        responsibilities re detained
            persons 215–16
Custody records
    detention by police 225
Custody visitors
    role of 113–14

DA notices
    national security 798–803
Damages
    breach of human rights,
        and 39–40
    public order 364
    tortious actions against
        police 101–04
Data protection
    art 608
    blocking 607–08
    compensation 607
    destruction 607–08
    erasure 607–08

generally 609–11
interpretation 602–04
journalism 608
literature 608
personal data
    access to 604–06
    sensitive personal data 604
prevention of processing
    likely to cause damage or
        distress 606
principles 604, 609
rectification 607–08
special purposes 604
Death penalty
    ECHR provisions 31
Defamation
    privacy, protection of 536–38
Defence Press and Broadcasting
    Advisory Committee
    national security 798–803
Demonstrations and riots
    public order
        changing face of
            protest 282–83
        miner's strike 280–82
        Red Lion Square 279
Deportation
    anti-terrorism
        provisions 472–74
Deprivation of liberty
    prevention of
        terrorism 478–80
Derogations
    anti-terrorism provisions
        455–56, 471–72
    Human Rights Act provi-
        sions 25, 26
Destruction of data
    data protection 607–08
Detention by police
    after charge 223–24
    code of practice 225
    continued detention,
        authorisation of 219–21
    custody officers
        duties after charge 214–15
        generally 210–13, 226
        responsibilities re detained
            persons 215–16
    custody records 225
    DPP
        consultation with 213–14
        guidance by 213
    extensions 225
    limitations on 209–10
    questioning and treatment of
        detained persons
        body samples 238–39

caution 245–46
fingerprinting 237–38
identification 229–30
information to be provided
    on 233–34
interrogation
    process 239–43
intimate searches 230–31,
    234
legal advice, access
    to 232–33, 235–37
National DNA
    Database 239
photographing 237–38
right to have someone
    informed 231–32,
    234–35
right to silence 243–53
searches , 228–29, 234
self-incrimination
    246–47
special warning 253–54
review of 216–18
statistics 227–28
time limits without
    charge 218–19, 224
warrants for further
    detention 221–23
Detention without trial
    counter-terrorism 434–40
    political terrorism 411–12
Direct discrimination
    associative
        discrimination 945–47
    comparators 955–59
    definitions 943–45
    disabled persons 947–48
    gypsies 950–53
    sex discrimination 948–50
    stop and search 953–54
Director General
    security and intelligence
        services 833
Director of Public Prosecutions
    detention by police
        consultation 213–14
        guidance 213
Disability discrimination
    direct discrimination
        947–48
    justification 986–88
    protected grounds 934–37
    reasonable
        adjustments 984–86
    recent developments 977–83
    scope of 974–77
Disciplinary procedures
    police 107

Discrimination
advertisements 918
anti-terrorism
provisions 465–68
Article 14
application of 857–59
establishing
discrimination 861–66
excusing sex
discrimination 878–82
introduction 856–57
justification of differential
treatment 872–78
proof of
discrimination 866–72
protected grounds 859–61
charities 926–27
cohabitation
homosexual couples 43–51
criminal provisions
football 989
hatred on grounds of sexual
orientation 990
incitement to
hatred 990–91
public order 989
racially aggravated
offences 989
religiously aggravated
offences 989
direct discrimination
associative
discrimination 945–47
comparators 955–59
definitions 943–45
disabled persons 947–48
gypsies 950–53
sex discrimination 948–50
stop and search 953–54
disability discrimination
direct
discrimination 947–48
justification 986–88
reasonable
adjustments 984–86
recent developments 977–83
scope of 974–77
ECHR provisions 30
enforcement 928–30
goods, facilities and
services 902–11
harassment
domestic
legislation 960–62
EC law 959
sex discrimination,
and 962–64
sexual harassment 964–65

indirect discrimination
domestic
regulation 966–68
justification for 968–74
roots 965–66
instructions to
discriminate 918–19
national security 923–25
pressure to discriminate 919
private clubs 914–18
protected grounds
age 937
disability 934–37
overlapping
grounds 937–42
race 931–32
religion 932–34
sex 930–31
sexual orientation 937
public authorities 887–97,
919
statutory authority 920–23
statutory provisions
aiding unlawful acts 919
EC law, influence
of 885–87
education 897–902,
919–20
housing/premises 911–14
introduction 883–84
scope 884–85
targeted services 925–26
vicarious liability 927–28
Disguises, removal of
stop and search
powers 160–61
Dispersal powers
public orders 395–97
DNA
detention by police
body samples 238–39
National DNA
Database 239
Drugs
stop and search powers 163

Education, right to
discrimination 897–902,
919–20
ECHR provisions 31
Educational establishments
public meetings and
processions 307–09
Elections
ECHR provisions 31
public meetings and
processions 305
Emergency powers

Anti-Terrorism, Crime and
Security Act 2001
deportation 472–74
derogation from Convention
obligations 455–56,
471–72
discrimination 465–68
facilitation of human rights
breaches abroad 474–75
information derived from
torture 474
proportionality 459–65
public emergency 457–59
scope of powers 455
Counter-terrorism Bill
2007–08, 492–94
introduction 407–08
political terrorism
counter-terrorism
strategy 410–11
detention without
trial 411–12
meaning 408
Northern Ireland 410
Prevention of Terrorism Act
2005
control orders 475–78,
481–85
deprivation of
liberty 478–80
obligations imposed on controlled persons 480–81
Terrorism Act 2000
collection of informa-
tion 448–49, 450–52
counter-terrorist
powers 431–48
directing terrorist organisations 448, 450
historical origins 414–15
inciting terrorism over-
seas 449, 452–53
introduction 413–14
penalties 450
police powers 453–55
possession for terrorist
purposes 448, 450–52
proscribed
organisations 417–26
statistics and
monitoring 416
terrorism, meaning
of 416–17
terrorist bombing 449–50
terrorist financing 450
terrorist
investigations 426–31
Terrorism Act 2006

Emergency powers (*cont.*)
   dissemination of terrorist
     publications 486–87,
     489–90
   encouragement of terror-
     ism 486, 488–89
   preparation for terror-
     ism 487–88, 491
   streamlining
     legislation 485–86
   use of force 494–502
Enforcement
   access to information 852–53
   discrimination 928–30
Entrapment
   admissibility of
     confessions 271–74
Entry, search and seizure
   access 173
   arrest
     after 178–79
     effecting 177–78
   common law
     background 183–84
   consensual searches 195–97
   entry 192–95
   evidence, power to
     obtain 185–87
   excluded material 174
   human rights issues 184–85
   journalistic material 174
   Justice of the Peace,
     authorisation by 172–73
   legal privilege 173
   personal records 174
   premises, meaning 181
   retention 180
   search warrants 175–77,
     188–91
   seizure 179–80, 187–88,
     191–92
   special procedures
     material covered 174–75
     scope of 181–83
Erasure of data
   data protection 607–08
Ethnicity
   stop and search powers
     169–70
**European Convention on Human
   Rights**
   see **Convention rights**
Expression, freedom of
   breach of the peace 380–81
   broadcasting
     advertising 642
     child internet
      safety 649–52

     generally 638–39
     impartiality 641–42
     internet
      broadcasting 647–49
      licences services 642–43
     OFCOM, function of 639
     OFCOM standards
      code 639–41, 643–45
     political
      advertising 645–47
     sponsorship 642
   ECHR protection
     interference by public
      authority 617–22
     introduction 612–14
     official secrets 622–29
     prescribed by law 614–17
   ECHR provisions 30
   film censorship
     classification
      guidelines 633–34
     mandatory
      conditions 631–33
     obscene material 634
     videos 634–37
   Human Rights Act
     provisions 25, 41
   indecency
     children, protection
      of 678–79
     forfeiture of goods 676–78
     indecent displays 681–83
     prohibition from
      importing 676
     sending articles by
      post 675–76
   obscenity and indecency
     forfeiture of
      material 667–69
     ignorance as to nature of
      article 671–72
     introduction 652–55
     obscene
      publications 655–60
     obscene, meaning
      of 660–66
     public good, defence
      of 669–71
     publication, meaning of 666
     extreme pornographic
      images, possession
      of 672–74
     theatres 674–75
   theatre censorship 630–32

Fair trial, right to
   ECHR provisions 29
Family life, right to

   ECHR provisions 29
Film censorship
   freedom of expression
     classification
      guidelines 633–34
     mandatory
      conditions 631–33
     obscene material 634
     videos 634–37
Fingerprinting
   detention by police 237–38
Football
   discrimination offences 989
Force, use of
   anti-terrorism
     provisions 494–502
   police powers, and
     arrests, and 151–53
     reasonable force 153–54
Forced labour, prohibition of
   ECHR provisions 28
Forfeiture
   freedom of expression
     indecency 676–78
     obscene
      publications 667–69

**Government Communications
   Headquarters (GCHQ)**
   role of 834–35
Government secrecy
   see **National security**
Gypsies
   discrimination 950–53

Harassment
   domestic legislation 960–62
   EC law 959
   public order
     animal rights
      extremism 367–68
     civil remedy 358
     common law
      offences 359–60
     course of conduct 362–63
     damages 364
     defences 364
     injunctions 364–66
     offences 331–32, 342–55,
      358, 360–62
     prohibition of 357–58
     putting people in fear of
      violence 358–59, 363
     sentencing 366–67
   sex discrimination,
     and 962–64
   sexual harassment 964–65
Harbouring spies

national security 769–70
Hatred
  incitement to 990–91
  sexual orientation 990
HM Inspectorate of
  Constabulary
  role of 95
Highways, use of
  public meetings and
    processions
    obstruction 294–99
  private nuisance 293
  public nuisance 292–93
  trespass 292
Historic buildings
  public meetings and
    processions 305–06
Homosexuality
  discrimination
    cohabitation 43–51
    hatred on grounds of 990
Hospital patients
  privacy, protection of 524–28
Housing
  discrimination 911–14
Human rights
  historical development 3–9
  Parliamentary Joint
    Committee 42–3
  protection of
    Human Rights Act 1998,
      16–65
    pre-Human Rights
      Act 11–16
    UK Bill of Rights 65–98
    Universal Declaration 5–8
Human Rights Act 1998
  see also **Convention rights**
  common law, and 36–7
  compatibility of legislation
    deference to
      Parliament 56–8
    determination of 36
    effect of declarations 63–5
    homosexuality 43–51
    incompatibility,
      declarations of 37
    margin of
      appreciation 57–8
    parliamentary state-
      ments 27, 41–2
    prison cell searches 59–63
    self-incrimination 51–6
  Convention rights 33–4
  damages 39–40
  expression, freedom of 30, 41
  judicial independence,
    and 17–19

legislative process 16–7
  notes on 67–8
  private persons, acts of 38–9
  public authorities, acts
    of 21–24, 37–8
  religion, freedom of 25, 41
  remedial actions 24, 40–41
  retrospective effect 42
  scheme of 33
  Strasbourg jurisprudence,
    reliance on 34–6
  text of 19–32
  victims, claims by 39

Identification
  detention by police 229–30
Immunity
  proscribed organisations 420
Impartiality
  freedom of
    expression 641–42
Imports
  indecent or obscene material
    freedom of expression 676
Incitement
  official secrets 770
  terrorism 449, 452–53
Incompatibility, declarations of
  see also **Compatibility**
  deference to Parliament 56–8
  effect of 63–5
  generally 37
  homosexuality 43–51
  Human Rights Act provisions
    20
  margin of appreciation 57–8
  prison cell searches 59–63
  self-incrimination 51–6
Indecency
  see also **Obscene publications**
  freedom of expression
    children, protection
      of 678–79
    extreme pornographic
      images, possession
      of 672–74
    forfeiture 667–69, 676–78
    ignorance as to nature of
      article 671–72
    indecent displays 681–83
    introduction 652–55
    public good, defence
      of 669–71
    sending articles by
      post 675–76
    theatres 674–75
Independence
  police 96–7

Indirect discrimination
  domestic regulation 966–68
  justification for 968–74
  roots 965–66
Information
  access to
    national security 849–55
  provision of
    arrest, on 198
    contempt of court 690,
      754–61
    detention by police 233–34
Inhuman or degrading treatment
  scope of protection 81–3
Injunctions
  public order 364–66
Intelligence and Security
  Committee
  role of 839, 846–48
Intelligence Services
  Commissioner
  role of 840
Intention
  public order offences 332
Interception of communications
  Interception of
    Communications
    Commissioner 590–91
  lawful interception without
    warrant 582–83
  meaning of 582
  metering 589–90
  policing techniques 591–96
  power to provide for lawful
    interception 583
  privacy, right to 519–22
  unlawful interception 580–82
  warrants for 583–86, 588–89
Interference with course of
  justice
  contempt of court 761–62
  publications
    jury secrets 744–45
    scandalising the
      court 737–44
Internet
  freedom of expression
    child protection 649–52
    generally 647–49
Interrogation process
  generally 239–42
  recording interviews 242
  use of 242–43
Intimate searches
  detention by police 230–31, 234
Ireland
  proscribed
    organisations 423–24

Journalism
data protection 608
entry, search and seizure
powers 174
sources
contempt in face of
court 754–61
Judicial scrutiny
police accountability
civil action
statistics 104–05
criminal
prosecutions 105–06
judicial review
applications 106
tort, actions in 100–04
Jurisdiction
contempt of court 762–63
Jury deliberations
confidentiality 689–90
Justices of the Peace
entry, search and seizure
authorisation of 172–73

Legal advice
detention by police 232–33,
235–37
Legal privilege
entry, search and seizure 173
Liberties
meaning 9–10
Liberty, right to
deprivation of liberty
prevention of
terrorism 478–80
ECHR provisions 28
scope of protection 84–5
Life, right to
ECHR provisions 27
scope of protection 69–81
Literature
data protection 608

Magistrates' courts
contempt of court 690–91
Malice
tortious actions against
police 100
Marriage, right to
ECHR provisions 30
Media regulation
privacy, protection of
OFCOM 574–76
Press Complaints
Commission 570–74
Mens rea
contempt of court
common law 717

intended contempt 718–20
strict liability rule 720
Mentally handicapped persons
admissibility of
confessions 255–56
Ministers
national security
unauthorised
disclosures 794–95
Minors
privacy, protection of 563–68

National Front
public meetings and
processions 306–07
National security
access to information
criticisms 854–55
enforcement 852–53
exemptions 850–52
generally 849–50
historical records 853–54
breach of confidence
introduction 803
Spycatcher
litigation 804–22
DA notices
Defence Press and
Broadcasting Advisory
Committee 798–803
discrimination 923–25
espionage 783–87
introduction 763–68
official secrets
arrests 777
attempts 770
authorised
disclosures 775–76
crime and special investigation powers 773–74
Crown servant, meaning
of 778
defences 772
government con tractor,
meaning of 778–79
harbouring spies 769–70
incitement 770
information entrusted
in confidence to other
States 775
information resulting
from unauthorised
disclosures 774–75
international
relations 772–73
interpretation 781–82
penalties 777
prohibited places 769

prosecutions 777
restriction on
prosecution 770
safeguarding
information 776–77
searches 777, 782
security and intelligence
services 771
spying 768–69, 779–81
security and intelligence
services
authorisation of acts outside
British Isles 837–39
Chief of Intelligence
Services 834
complaints 840, 844
criticisms 843
Director-General 833
employment issues 846
generally 831–33
Government
Communications
Headquarters 834–35
Intelligence and Security
Committee 839, 846–48
Intelligence Services
Commissioner 840
maintenance of
files 844–45
reports 841–43
Secret Intelligence
Service 834
special branches 845–46
warrant
authorisation 835–37
unauthorised disclosures
civil servants 794–95
documents, classification
of 796–97
Gun 793
Keogh and O'Connor 793
Pasquill 794
maintaining
security 795–96
ministers 794–95
Official Secrets Act 1911,
787–88
Official Secrets Act 1989,
788–94
Shayler 791–93
Tomlinson 790–91
vetting
positive vetting 823–31
purge procedure 822–23
Negligence
police 101
Newspapers
photographs

privacy, right to 510–19
Northern Ireland
political terrorism 410
Nuisance
privacy, protection of 535–36
public meetings and
processions
private nuisance 293
public nuisance 292–93

Obscene publications
see also **Indecency**
freedom of expression
film censorship 634
forfeiture of
material 667–69
ignorance as to nature of
article 671–72
introduction 652–55
obscene
publications 655–60
obscene, meaning
of 660–66
public good, defence
of 669–71
publication, meaning of 666
extreme pornographic
images, possession
of 672–74
theatres 674–75
Obstruction
highways, of
public meetings and
processions 294–99
police, of
generally 127
intention 131–34
refusing to answer
questions 128–31
OFCOM
freedom of expression
function of 639
standards code 639–41,
643–45
privacy 574–76
Offences
counter-terrorism powers 434
discrimination
football 989
hatred on grounds of sexual
orientation 990
incitement to
hatred 990–91
public order 989
racially aggravated
offences 989
religiously aggravated
offences 989

police, against
assault 119–20, 127
generally 119–27
obstruction 127–34
proscribed organisations
generally 424–26
membership 421
support 421
uniform 421–22
public order
abolition of offences 333
affray 331, 336–37
harassment, alarm or
distress 331–32, 342–55
intention 332
provocation of violence, fear
of 331, 337–42
racially aggravated
disorder 355–57
riot 330, 334–35
violent disorder 330, 336
Official secrets
freedom of
expression 622–29
national security
arrests 777
attempts 770
authorised
disclosures 775–76
crime and special investigation powers 773–74
Crown servant, meaning
of 778
defences 772
government contractor,
meaning of 778–79
harbouring spies 769–70
incitement 770
information entrusted
in confidence to other
States 775
information resulting
from unauthorised
disclosures 774–75
international
relations 772–73
interpretation 781–82
penalties 777
prohibited places 769
prosecutions 777
restriction on
prosecution 770
safeguarding
information 776–77
searches 777, 782
security and intelligence
services 771
spying 768–69, 779–81

Oppression
exclusion of confessions from
evidence 258–61

Paparazzi photographs
privacy, right to 510–19
Parking
counter-terrorism powers 434
Parliament
public meetings and
processions 301–04
Penalties
contempt of court 691
official secrets 777
public meetings and
processions 314
terrorism 450
Personal data
see also **Data protection**
access to 604–06
entry, search and seizure 174
privacy
data protection 602–11
generally 600–02
sensitive, protection of 604
Photographs
detention by police 237–38
Police
see also **Police powers; Policing**
accountability
auditing 97–100
generally 88–90
internal monitoring
107–14
judicial scrutiny 100–06
assault on
meaning 119–20
scope of offence 127
complaints 108–13
conclusions 114–15
custody visitors 113–14
deception
admissibility of
confessions 269–74
disciplinary procedures
107
execution of duty, meaning
of 120–27
introduction 87
judicial scrutiny
civil action
statistics 104–05
criminal
prosecutions 105–06
judicial review
applications 106
tort, actions in 100–04
obstruction of police officer

Police (*cont.*)
generally 127
intention 131–34
refusing to answer
questions 128–31
offences against
assault 119–20, 127
generally 119–27
obstruction 127–34
structure
Chief Constable 93–4
HM Inspectorate of
Constabulary 95
independence 96–7
police authorities 91–3
Secretary of State 94
Police powers
arrest
arrest outwith police
station 198–99
disposition after , 208
explaining grounds
for 205–08
further offences 200
government recommenda-
tions in 2004, 201
information given on 198
search on 200–01, 208–09
statistics 209
validity 202–05
voluntary attendance at
police station 198
without warrant 197–98
codes of practice 154
confessions
admissibility 254–55
breach of code of
practice 262
common law
admissibility 257
entrapment 269–74
exclusion of unfair
evidence 256–57, 263–68
interpretation 256
mentally handicapped
persons 255–56
oppression 258–61
PACE 257–58
physical evidence 257
unreliability 261–62
use by/against
co-accused 255, 262
vulnerable
suspects 262–63
detention
after charge 223–24
code of practice 225
continued detention,
authorisation of 219–21

custody officers, duties after
charge 214–15
custody officers,
generally 210–13, 226
custody officers,
responsibilities re detained
persons 215–16
custody records 225
DPP, consultation
with 213–14
DPP, guidance by 213
extensions 225
limitations on 209–10
review of 216–18
statistics 227–28
time limits without
charge 218–19, 224
warrants for further
detention 221–23
entry, search and seizure
access 173
arrest, after 178–79
arrest, effecting 177–78
common law
background 183–84
consensual
searches 195–97
entry 192–95
evidence, power to
obtain 185–87
excluded material 174
human rights
issues 184–85
journalistic material 174
Justice of the Peace,
authorisation by 172–73
legal privilege 173
personal records 174
premises, meaning 181
retention 180
search warrants 175–77,
188–91
seizure 179–80, 187–88,
191–92
special procedure
material 174–75
special procedures 181–83
historical background
115–19
questioning and treatment of
detained persons
body samples 238–39
caution 245–46
fingerprinting 237–38
identification 229–30
information to be provided
on 233–34
interrogation
process 239–43

intimate searches 230–31,
234
legal advice, access
to 232–33, 235–37
National DNA
Database 239
photographing 237–38
right to have someone
informed 231–32,
234–35
right to silence 243–53
searches , 228–29, 234
self-incrimination 246–47
special warning 253–54
reasonable suspicion
Castorina, application
of 141–43
concept 134–41
definability 149
operational
questions 143–49
stereotypes 149–50
restriction to serious
offences 150
stop and search
anticipation of
violence 159–60
disguises, removal
of 160–61
drugs 163
effectiveness 170–70
ethnicity, and 169–70
general power 154–57
intelligence
gathering 167–69
public perceptions 167
reasonable
suspicion 163–64
recoding and
monitoring 164–67
records, duty to
keep 157–58
road checks 158–59,
171–72
scope of 161–62
statistics 169
terrorism 453–55
use of force
arrests, and 151–53
reasonable force 153–54
Policing
see also **Police; Police powers**
consumerist policing 97–100
managerial policing 97–100
public order
equipment 283–85
evidence gathering 286–87
militarisation 285–86
mutual assistance 285

training 285–86
Political activity of aliens
ECHR provisions 30
Political advertising
freedom of expression
645–47
Political terrorism
see also **Anti-terrorism**
counter-terrorism
strategy 410–11
detention without
trial 411–12
meaning 408
Northern Ireland 410
Pornography
freedom of
expression 672–74
Port controls
counter-terrorism powers 434
Postal services
indecent or obscene material
freedom of
expression 675–76
Press Complaints Commission
privacy
media regulation 570–74
Prevention of Terrorism
see also **Anti-terrorism**
control orders 475–78,
481–85
controlled persons, obligations
imposed on 480–81
deprivation of liberty 478–80
Prisoners
privacy, protection of
strip searching 528–33
Prisons
cell searches
incompatibility, declar-
ations of 59–63
Privacy, protection of
see also **Data protection**
ECHR provisions 29
general right of privacy
hospital patients,
interviewing and
photographing 524–28
strip searching of
prisoners 528–33
human rights
CCTV surveillance 507–10
interception of
communications 519–22
paparazzi
photographs 510–19
scope of 503–04
search of business
premises 504–07

indirect remedies
breach of
confidence 539–63
breach of contract 568
breach of
copyright 538–39
defamation 536–38
minors, jurisdiction to
protect 563–68
nuisance 535–36
trespass 533–35
voyeurism 569
introduction 523–24
media regulation
OFCOM 574–76
Press Complaints
Commission 570–74
personal data, storage of
data protection 602–11
generally 600–02
surveillance
covert surveillance 578–600
generally 576–77
overt video
surveillance 577–78
Private clubs
discrimination 914–18
Property, protection of
ECHR provisions 31
Proportionality
anti-terrorism
provisions 459–65
Proscribed organisations
de-proscription 419–20
human rights 420
immunity 420
Irish terrorism 423–24
judicial review 424
offences
generally 424–26
membership 421
support 421
uniform 421–22
proscription 417–19, 422
Provocation of violence
public order offences 331,
337–42
Public authorities
discrimination 887–97, 919
freedom of expression 617–22
Human Rights Act provisions
acts of 21
judicial acts 23–24
judicial remedies 23
proceedings
involving 21–22
Public good
obscene publications 669–71

Public meetings and processions
see also **Public order**
assembly and association, right
of 322–25
ban, power to
banning orders 314–18
delegation of 314
general power 311
trespassory assemblies
312–13, 319–20
common law 320–22
control, power to 309–26
advance notice 309–10,
318–19
conditions, imposition
of 310–12, 318
delegation of 314
highways, use of
obstruction 294–99
private nuisance 293
public nuisance 292–93
trespass 292
introduction 291
location
highways, use of 292–99
open spaces 299–301
parliament, proximity
to 301–04
publicly owned
premises 305–09
nuisance
private 293
public 292–93
open spaces 299–301
parliament, proximity
to 301–04
penalties 314
publicly owned premises
educational
establishments 307–09
elections 305
historic buildings 305–06
National Front 306–07
raves 328
trespass
banning orders 312–13,
319–20
designated sites 328
highways, use of 292
powers to direct trespassers
to leave land 326–28
Public order
see also **Public meetings and
processions**
anti-social behaviour
orders 368–70
binding over 397–401
breach of the peace

Public order (*cont.*)
  arrest for 395
  freedom of
    assembly 380–81
  freedom of
    expression 380–81
  power to prevent future
    breaches 376–95
  criminal procedure 333
  demonstrations and riots
    changing face of
      protest 282–83
    miner's strike 280–82
    Red Lion Square 279
  discrimination offences 989
  dispersal powers 395–97
  disruption of lawful activities
    aggravated trespass 371–76
    breaking up public
      meetings 370–71
  entry powers to preserve
    peace 401–06
  freedom of association
    clothing 288–89
    ECHR 287
    policing events 287–88
    quasi-military
      organisations 290–91
  harassment
    animal rights
      extremism 367–68
    civil remedy 358
    common law
      offences 359–60
    course of conduct 362–63
    damages 364
    defences 364
    injunctions 364–66
    offence 358, 360–62
    prohibition of 357–58
    putting people in fear of
      violence 358–59, 363
    sentencing 366–67
  introduction 275–77
  legislation 277–78
  offences
    abolition of offences 333
    affray 331, 336–37
    harassment, alarm or
      distress 331–32, 342–55
    intention 332
    provocation of violence, fear
      of 331, 337–42
    racially aggravated
      disorder 355–57
    riot 330, 334–35
    violent disorder 330, 336
  police, role of 279

  policing
    equipment 283–85
    evidence gathering 286–87
    militarisation 285–86
    mutual assistance 285
    training 285–86
  preventative powers
    binding over 397–401
    breach of the peace 376–97
    entry powers to preserve
      peace 401–06
  Red Lion Square Disorders 278
Publications
  disclosure, matters exempted
    from , 690
  interfering with course of
    justice
      jury secrets 744–45
      scandalising the
        court 737–44
  prejudicial to civil proceedings
    common law 720–34
    strict liability rule 734–37
  prejudicial to criminal trial
    common law 695–98
    introduction 694–95
    prohibition, powers
      of 707–10
    protection of inferior
      courts 705–06
    quashing
      convictions 713–14
    reporting restriction,
      statutory 710–13
    sitting in camera 706–07
    strict liability rule 698–05
    US position 714–15
  terrorist publications,
    dissemination of 486–87,
    489–90
Punishment without law
  ECHR provisions 29

Quasi-military organisations
  public order 290–91

Race
  discrimination
    protected grounds 931–32
    racially aggravated
      offences 989
  stop and search powers 169–70
Raves
  public meetings and
    processions 328
Reasonable adjustments
  disability
    discrimination 984–86

Reasonable suspicion
  Castorina, application
    of 141–43
  concept 134–41
  definability 149
  operational questions 143–49
  stereotypes 149–50
  stop and search
    powers 163–64
Regulation of Investigatory
Powers Act 2000
  acquisition of data 586–87
  disclosure of data 586–87
  exclusion of matters from legal
    proceedings 586
  Interception of
    Communications
    Commissioner 590–91
  interception, meaning of 582
  lawful interception without
    warrant 582–83
  metering 589–90
  notices requiring
    disclosure 596–98
  notices requiring disclosure,
    effect of 598–600
  policing techniques 591–96
  power to provide for lawful
    interception 583
  unlawful interception 580–82
  warrants for intercep-
    tion 583–86, 588–89
Reliability
  exclusion of confessions from
    evidence 261–62
Religion
  discrimination
    protected grounds 932–34
    religiously aggravated
      offences 989
  freedom of
    ECHR provisions 29–30
    Human Rights Act
      provisions 25, 41
Remedial actions
  Human Rights Act provi-
    sions 24, 40–41
Remedial orders
  Human Rights Act
    provisions 31–2
Reporting restrictions
  prejudice to criminal
    trials 710–13
Reservations
  Human Rights Act
    provisions 26–7
Right
  meaning 9–10

Riots, demonstrations and
  public order
    changing face of
      protest 282–83
    miner's strike 280–82
    offences 330, 334–35
    Red Lion Square 279
Roadside checks
  stop and search
    powers 158–59, 171–72

Search warrants
  entry, search and seizure
    execution 176–77, 189–91
    safeguards 175–76,
      188–89
Searches
  see also **Entry, search and**
    seizure
  arrest, on 200–01, 208–09
  business premises
    privacy, right to 504–07
  consensual searches 195–97
  counter-terrorism powers
    persons 432
    premises 432
    stop and search
      powers 440–48
  detention by police
    generally 228–29, 234
    intimate searches 230–31,
      234
  official secrets 777, 782
Secret Intelligence Service
  role of 834
Secretary of State
  police struxture, role in 94
Security and intelligence services
  authorisation of acts outside
    British Isles 837–39
  Chief of Intelligence
    Services 834
  complaints 840–44
  criticisms 843
  Director-General 833
  employment issues 846
  generally 831–33
  Government Communications
    Headquarters 834–35
  Intelligence and Security
    Committee 839, 846–48
  Intelligence Services
    Commissioner 840
  maintenance of files 844–45
  reports 841–43
  Secret Intelligence Service 834
  special branches 845–46
  warrant authorisation 835–37

Security, right to
  ECHR provisions 28
Seizure
  see **Entry, search and seizure**
Self-incrimination
  incompatibility, declarations
    of 51–6
  questioning by police 246–47
Sex discrimination
  direct discrimination 948–50
  harassment 962–64
  protected grounds 930–31
Sexual harassment
  generally 964–65
Sexual orientation
  discrimination
    cohabitation 43–51
    hatred on grounds of 990
    protected grounds 937
Silence, right to
  questioning by police
    caution 245–46
    compulsory questions 253
    generally 243–45
    inferences drawn
      from 246–43
    special warning 253–54
Slavery, prohibition of
  ECHR provisions 28
Special branch
  role of 845–46
Spying
  harbouring spies 769–70
  official secrets 768–69,
    779–81
Statistics
  arrest, on 209
  detention by police 227–28
  stop and search powers 169
  terrorism 416
Stop and search
  anticipation of
    violence 159–60
  counter-terrorism
    powers 440–48
  discrimination 953–54
  disguises, removal of 160–61
  drugs 163
  effectiveness 170–70
  ethnicity, and 169–70
  general power 154–57
  intelligence gathering 167–69
  public perceptions 167
  reasonable suspicion 163–64
  recoding and
    monitoring 164–67
  records, duty to keep 157–58
  road checks 158–59, 171–72

  scope of 161–62
  statistics 169
Strict liability
  contempt of court
    mens rea 720
    publication prejudicial to
      civil proceedings 734–37
    publication prejudicial to
      criminal trial 698–705
    statutory provisions
      688–89
    sub judice rule 716–17
Sub judice rule
  contempt of court
    common law 715–16
    generally 716–17
    publications intended to
      interfere with justice
      716
Surveillance
  privacy, protection of
    covert surveillance 578–600
    generally 576–77
    overt video
      surveillance 577–78

Tape-recorders, use of
  contempt of court 690
Terrorism Act 2000
  see also **Anti-terrorism;**
    Terrorism Act 2006
  collection of informa-
    tion 448–49, 450–52
  counter-terrorist powers
    arrest without
      warrant 431–32, 434–37
    authorisations 432–33
    detention 434–40
    duration of
      authorisation 434
    exercise of power 433
    offences 434
    parking 434
    port and border
      controls 434
    search of persons 432
    search of premises 432
    stop and search
      powers 440–48
    terrorist, meaning of 431
    travel controls 440
  directing terrorist
    organisations 448, 450
  historical origins 414–15
  inciting terrorism
    overseas 449, 452–53
  introduction 413–14
  penalties 450

Terrorism Act 2000 (*cont.*)
police powers 453–55
possession for terrorist purposes 448, 450–52
proscribed
organisations 417–26
de-proscription 419–20
human rights 420
immunity 420
Irish terrorism 423–24
judicial review 424
offences 421–26
proscription 417–19, 422
statistics and monitoring 416
terrorism, meaning of
416–17
terrorist bombing 449–50
terrorist financing 450
terrorist investigations
disclosure 427–28
generally 429–31
information about acts of
terrorism 426–27
meaning 426
terrorist property 428–29
Terrorism Act 2006
see also **Anti-terrorism;**
Terrorism Act 2000
dissemination of terrorist
publications 486–87, 489–90
encouragement of
terrorism 486, 488–89
preparation for
terrorism 487–88, 491
streamlining
legislation 485–86
Terrorist bombing
counter-terrorism
measures 449–50
Terrorist financing

counter-terrorism
measures 450
Terrorist investigations
disclosure 427–28
generally 429–31
information about acts of
terrorism 426–27
meaning 426
terrorist property 428–29
Theatres
freedom of expression
censorship 630–32
obscenity and
indecency 674–75
Thought, conscience and
religion, freedom of
ECHR provisions 29–30
Human Rights Act
provisions 25
Time limits
detention by police 218–24
Torture, prohibition of
ECHR provisions 27
Travel controls
counter-terrorism powers
440
Trespass
aggravated trespass 371–76
privacy, protection of 533–35
public meetings and
processions
banning orders 312–13,
319–20
designated sites 328
highways, use of 292
powers to direct trespassers
to leave land 326–28

Unreliability
exclusion of confessions from
evidence 261–62

Use of force
anti-terrorism
provisions 494–502
police powers, and
arrests, and 151–53
reasonable force 153–54

Vetting
national security
positive vetting 823–31
purge procedure
822–23
Vicarious liability
discrimination 927–28
Videos
film censorship
freedom of
expression 634–37
Violence, anticipation of
stop and search
powers 159–60
Violent disorder
public order offences 330,
336
Voluntary attendance at police
station
arrest powers, and 198
Voyeurism
privacy, protection of 569
Vulnerable suspects
admissibility of
confessions 262–63

Warrants
see also **Search warrants**
arrest without 197–98
further detention by police
extension of 223
requirements 221–22
security and intelligence
services 835–37